RRB ALP

Basic Science &
Mechanical / Automobile Engineering

for

Indian Railways (RRB)

ASSISTANT LOCO PILOT

Recruitment Examination 2024-2025

(Stage II)

Title : RRB -ALP : Basic Science & Mechanical / Automobile Engineering (Assistant Loco Pilot Stage II)

Language : English

Editor's Name : GKP Editorial Team

Typeset & Published by :

Career Launcher Infrastructure (P) Ltd.
A-45, Mohan Cooperative Industrial Area, Near Mohan Estate Metro Station, New Delhi - 110044

Marketed by :

G.K. Publications (P) Ltd.
Plot No. 63, Sector-27A, Near Sector - 28 Metro Station, Faridabad, Haryana-121003

ISBN : **978-93-56813-74-8**

Printer's Details : Printed in India, New Delhi.

For product information :
Visit ***www.gkpublications.com*** or email to ***gkp@gkpublications.com***

CONTENTS

Basic Science

Mechanical/Automobile

Basic Science

CHAPTER

Engineering Drawing

ENGINEERING DRAWING

Engineering drawing is a graphical representation of an object or a system that is created by engineers to communicate design and technical information. It serves as a precise and detailed visual reference that provides information about the size, shape, dimensions, and other geometric characteristics of a component, structure, or machine.

Engineering drawings are typically created using computer-aided design (CAD) software or drawn manually using traditional drafting techniques. They include various types of views, such as orthographic views (top, front, side), isometric views, sectional views, and auxiliary views. These views allow engineers, designers, and manufacturers to understand the object or system from different angles and perspectives.

The information conveyed in an engineering drawing includes dimensions, tolerances, materials, surface finishes, assembly instructions, and other specifications necessary for manufacturing, construction, or fabrication. Drawings also include symbols, notations, and annotations to indicate important features, such as holes, threads, welds, and part numbers.

Engineering drawings follow internationally recognized standards and conventions, such as those established by the American National Standards Institute (ANSI) or the International Organization for Standardization (ISO). These standards ensure consistency, clarity, and accuracy in communicating design intent across different industries and countries.

Overall, engineering drawings play a vital role in the design and production process, facilitating clear communication between engineers, manufacturers, and other stakeholders involved in the realization of a product or system.

Engineering drawings common features:

Engineering drawings typically include several common features to convey information accurately and consistently. Here are some of the common features found in engineering drawings:

1. Title Block: The title block is located in the lower right-hand corner of the drawing and contains important information about the drawing, such as the title, drawing number, revision status, scale, date, and the name of the drafter or designer.
2. Views: Engineering drawings feature different views of the object or system being represented. The most common views are orthographic views (top, front, side) that provide a 2D representation of the object from different perspectives. Other views, such as isometric views or sectional views, may also be included to provide additional clarity.
3. Dimensions: Dimensions are numerical values that specify the size, shape, and location of features on the object or system. Linear dimensions indicate lengths, while angular dimensions specify angles. Dimensions are typically shown with lines, arrows, and text indicating the measurement.
4. Geometric Tolerances: Geometric tolerances define the allowable variations in size, form, orientation, and location of features. These tolerances ensure that the manufactured component meets the design requirements. Geometric tolerances are represented using symbols and are usually accompanied by specific values or limits.
5. Sectional Views: Sectional views are used to reveal the internal structure or hidden details of an object. These views are obtained by cutting a part of the object and showing the internal features beyond the cutting plane. Sectional views are helpful for understanding the inner workings or complex arrangements within an object.
6. Symbols and Notations: Engineering drawings utilize a variety of symbols and notations to represent specific features or characteristics. For example, symbols can indicate surface finishes, welding, fasteners, electrical connections, or specific types of components. Notations may provide additional information or instructions related to the design or manufacturing process.
7. Assembly Information: In drawings for assemblies, there is often information regarding the relationship between different components, including how they fit together and how they are fastened or joined. This information helps in the assembly and manufacturing process.

8. Bill of Materials (BOM): A Bill of Materials lists all the components and parts required for manufacturing or assembling the object. It provides a comprehensive inventory of the materials needed, including part numbers, quantities, and sometimes additional specifications.

These are just a few common features found in engineering drawings. Depending on the specific application and industry, additional features and information may be included to ensure clear communication and accurate manufacturing or construction.

Examples of engineering drawings:

1. Mechanical Drawing: This type of drawing represents mechanical components and assemblies. It may include detailed views, dimensions, and annotations. For example, a mechanical drawing can show the exploded view of a gearbox, with all the individual parts labeled and dimensioned.
2. Electrical Schematic: An electrical schematic is a diagram that represents the electrical connections and components in a system. It uses standardized symbols to illustrate circuits and their interconnections. For instance, an electrical schematic can depict the wiring and connections of a control panel for a motor.
3. Civil Engineering Plan: A civil engineering plan is used in civil engineering projects, such as road construction or building design. It shows the layout, dimensions, and details of various elements like roads, buildings, drainage systems, and utilities. An example could be a site plan for a housing development, illustrating lot boundaries, roads, and utility connections.
4. Architectural Floor Plan: An architectural floor plan is a drawing that represents the layout of a building at the ground level. It typically shows the walls, doors, windows, and major fixtures within a building. For instance, an architectural floor plan could show the layout of rooms, corridors, and common areas in a house or office building.
5. Structural Drawing: A structural drawing provides details about the structural components of a building or infrastructure project. It includes information about beams, columns, foundations, and other load-bearing elements. For example, a structural drawing can illustrate the reinforcement details for a concrete beam.
6. Piping and Instrumentation Diagram (P&ID): A P&ID is a schematic representation of a process system, indicating the piping, instruments, valves, and equipment used in the system. It is commonly used in industries such as chemical plants or oil refineries. A P&ID could show the flow of fluids, the location of pumps and valves, and the instrumentation used for process control.

These are just a few examples of engineering drawings, and there are many other types depending on the specific field and purpose. Engineering drawings serve as communication tools, providing precise information to engineers, technicians, and manufacturers for the design, construction, and operation of various systems and structures.

Types of drawing

There are several types of drawings, each serving a different purpose and catering to various fields. Here are some common types of drawings:

1. Engineering Drawing: Engineering drawings are used to communicate technical details and specifications for the design, construction, and operation of various engineering systems. They can include mechanical drawings, electrical schematics, civil engineering plans, structural drawings, and more.
2. Architectural Drawing: Architectural drawings are created by architects to represent the design and construction of buildings and structures. They include floor plans, elevations, sections, and details that show the layout, dimensions, and materials used in architectural projects.
3. Technical Drawing: Technical drawings are detailed and precise drawings that provide specific instructions for the manufacturing, assembly, or installation of a product or system. They often include dimensions, annotations, and symbols to convey information clearly to technicians and manufacturers.
4. Perspective Drawing: Perspective drawings are used to represent three-dimensional objects or scenes on a two-dimensional surface, creating an illusion of depth and space. They are commonly used in architectural design, art, and illustration to provide a realistic representation of objects or spaces.
5. Isometric Drawing: Isometric drawings are a type of technical drawing that represents three-dimensional objects using a 30-degree angle. They show the object's height, width, and depth without distortion, making them useful for conveying the shape and layout of objects in engineering and design.
6. Exploded View Drawing: An exploded view drawing shows the individual components of an assembly separated and positioned in a way that illustrates how they fit together. It is commonly used in engineering and manufacturing to demonstrate the assembly process and to aid in understanding the relationship between different parts.
7. Conceptual Drawing: Conceptual drawings are often freehand sketches or illustrations used in the early stages of the design process to explore and communicate ideas. They are less detailed and more focused on conveying the overall concept or artistic vision.
8. Topographical Drawing: Topographical drawings, also known as contour maps, depict the elevation and features of a specific area of land. They are used in various fields, including civil engineering, urban planning, and environmental studies.

These are just a few examples of the types of drawings that exist. Different industries and disciplines may have their own specific types of drawings based on their requirements and purposes.

Types of Drawings

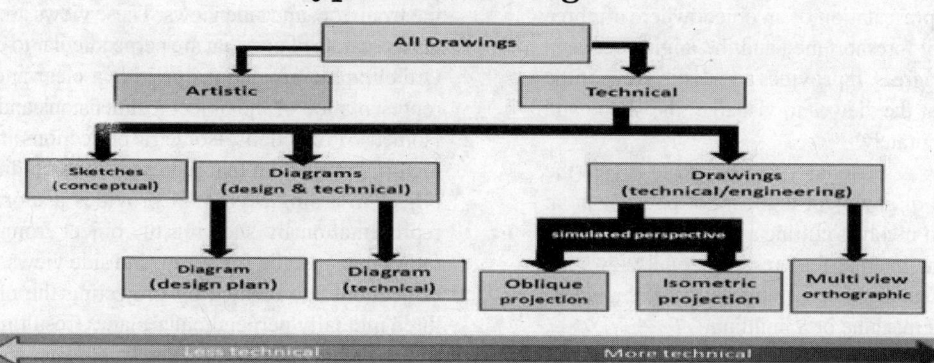

Dimensioning in engineering drawing:

Dimensioning in engineering drawing refers to the process of adding precise measurements, symbols, and notes to convey the size, location, and tolerances of features on a drawing. It is a crucial aspect of technical communication in engineering, as it provides clear instructions to manufacturers, fabricators, assemblers, and inspectors for the production and quality control of a design. Here are some key considerations for dimensioning in engineering drawing:

1. Types of Dimensions:
   - Linear Dimensions: Represent the length, width, and height of features using numerical values.
   - Angular Dimensions: Specify angles between lines, surfaces, or features.
   - Radial Dimensions: Indicate the radius or diameter of arcs, circles, or rounded features.
2. Placement of Dimensions:
   - Dimensions should be placed outside the outline of the object or feature, avoiding overcrowding or overlapping.
   - Use extension lines with arrowheads to indicate precisely where the dimensions apply.
   - Group related dimensions together and align them for clarity and ease of reading.
3. Dimensioning Techniques:
   - Aligned Dimensions: Dimensions are placed parallel to the feature being measured.
   - Baseline Dimensions: Dimensions are referenced from a common baseline or datum line.
   - Chain Dimensions: Dimensions are shown in a continuous chain, reducing the number of dimension lines.
   - Ordinate Dimensions: Dimensions are measured from a common reference point or coordinate system.
4. Dimensioning Standards:
   - Follow relevant standards such as ASME Y14.5 or ISO 129-1 to ensure consistency and compatibility with other drawings.
   - Use appropriate dimensioning symbols, line types, and text styles as per the chosen standards.
5. Tolerancing:
   - Specify tolerances to indicate allowable variations in dimensions.
   - Use appropriate tolerance notations, such as "+" or "-" signs, limit dimensions, or geometric tolerancing symbols.
   - Clearly communicate tolerance requirements for critical dimensions to ensure proper functionality and fit.
6. Units of Measurement:
   - Clearly specify the units of measurement (e.g., millimeters, inches) for each dimension.
   - Ensure consistency throughout the drawing, using a single unit system.
7. Clear Communication:
   - Dimensioning should be clear, concise, and unambiguous, leaving no room for misinterpretation.
   - Use clear and readable text, appropriate font sizes, and proper line weights.
8. Critical Dimensions:
   - Focus on dimensioning features that are critical to the design's functionality, form, or fit.
   - Clearly indicate which dimensions are critical by providing specific notes or callouts.

Dimensioning in engineering drawing plays a vital role in accurately conveying design intent, ensuring proper manufacturing, assembly, and inspection of components and products. By providing precise and clear dimensioning information, engineering drawings facilitate effective communication and collaboration between design teams and various stakeholders involved in the production process.

Views of engineering drawing:

Engineering drawings are essential tools used in various fields of engineering to communicate and document design information. Here are some common views used in engineering drawing:

1. Orthographic projection view: This is the most common method used to represent three-dimensional objects on a two-dimensional plane. Orthographic projection involves creating multiple views of an object from different directions, typically front, top, and right-side views. These views provide a comprehensive representation of the object's shape and dimensions.

2. Isometric View: Isometric projection is a three-dimensional representation of an object where all three axes are equally foreshortened and the angles between them are 120 degrees. It provides a realistic view of the object, allowing the viewer to visualize the shape and proportions accurately.
3. Sectional View: A sectional view is used to reveal the internal details of an object that cannot be seen in an external view. It involves cutting a portion of the object and showing the internal features. Sectional views are commonly used to illustrate complex structures, such as the interior of a machine or a building.
4. Exploded View: An exploded view is a pictorial representation that shows how various components of an object fit together and interact. The individual parts are separated and spaced apart to provide a clear understanding of their relationship and assembly sequence.
5. Auxiliary View: An auxiliary view is used to show features of an object that are not parallel to the principal views. It is created by projecting the object onto a plane that is perpendicular to the feature of interest. Auxiliary views are particularly useful when detailing inclined or oblique surfaces.
6. Detail View: A detail view is an enlarged portion of a larger drawing, providing a close-up view of a specific area or feature. It allows for a more detailed examination of intricate parts or areas that require additional attention.
7. Perspective View: Perspective views are used to represent objects as they appear in three-dimensional space. They provide a more realistic and natural representation by incorporating vanishing points and foreshortening. Perspective views are often used in architectural and industrial design presentations.
8. Cross-sectional views: Cross-sectional views are a type of view used in engineering drawings to show the internal features and structures of an object. They are created by cutting or slicing through an object and then revealing the resulting section. Cross-sectional views are particularly useful for illustrating the interior details, hidden components, and complex geometries of objects.

These different views help engineers, designers, and manufacturers communicate design intent, dimensions, and construction details accurately. They play a crucial role in ensuring that a product or structure is properly understood and manufactured according to specifications.

Projections of engineering drawing:

Projections in engineering drawing are graphical representations of objects in different views to accurately communicate their shape, size, and features. There are several types of projections commonly used, including orthographic projections, isometric projections, and perspective projections. Here's a brief overview of each:

1. Orthographic Projections: Orthographic projections are the most common type of projection used in engineering drawing. They show the object as a series of two-dimensional views from different directions, typically the front, top, and side views. These views are projected onto separate planes that are perpendicular to each other. Orthographic projections provide a clear and accurate representation of the object's dimensions and features.
2. Isometric Projections: Isometric projections are a type of pictorial projection that represents a three-dimensional object in a single view. It provides a more realistic representation by showing the object from an angle, rather than just the front, top, and side views. Isometric projections are created by projecting the object onto three mutually perpendicular planes, resulting in equal foreshortening along each axis. This creates an illusion of depth and helps visualize the object in three dimensions.
3. Perspective Projections: Perspective projections create a realistic representation of an object by simulating how it appears to the human eye. In perspective projections, the object is shown as it would be seen from a specific viewpoint. Unlike orthographic and isometric projections, perspective projections use vanishing points and converging lines to create depth and a sense of scale. Perspective projections are often used in architectural drawings or when a more lifelike representation is desired.
4. Oblique Projections: Oblique projections are another type of axonometric projection that shows an object with one face parallel to the picture plane and the other faces at an angle. In oblique projections, the receding lines are parallel, and the depth of the object is typically represented at a 45-degree angle. Oblique projections are often used when a quick and simple representation of an object is needed.
5. Auxiliary projections: Auxiliary projection, also known as auxiliary view, is a technique used in engineering drawing to show an object in a new view that is not one of the standard orthographic views (front, top, side). It is used to represent features of an object that are not easily visible or accurately shown in the standard views.

In engineering drawing, projections are typically created using drafting techniques or computer-aided design (CAD) software. They are essential for accurately communicating design intent, dimensions, and details of an object to manufacturers, fabricators, and other stakeholders involved in the production process.

Isometric projection:

Isometric projection is a type of graphical representation that depicts three-dimensional objects in a two-dimensional space. It is commonly used in engineering and technical drawings to provide a clear and accurate representation of objects from multiple angles.

In isometric projection, two isometric axes are held at an angle of 30 with the horizontal plane. While the third axis forms an angle of 90 with the horizontal plane. And all three principal axes of the object are equally foreshortened at a 120-degree angle, resulting in a three-dimensional appearance.

ISOMETRIC PROJECTION

Here are some key features and characteristics of isometric projection:

1. Equal foreshortening: In isometric projection, all three dimensions (length, width, and height) of an object are equally reduced or foreshortened. This means that the angles between any two axes are 120 degrees.
2. Fixed angles: Isometric projection maintains fixed angles between lines parallel to each of the three axes. Horizontal lines are inclined at **30 degrees** to the horizontal axis, while vertical lines remain parallel to the vertical axis.
3. Orthogonal lines: In isometric projection, lines parallel to the three principal axes (x, y, and z) are always mutually perpendicular.
4. No vanishing points: Unlike perspective projections, which have vanishing points and convey depth perception, isometric projection does not represent depth or distance and all dimensions appear uniformly scaled.
5. Easy measurement: Isometric drawings allow for accurate measurements along each axis, making it easier to determine the size and positioning of objects.

Isometric projection is widely used in various fields, including mechanical engineering, architecture, industrial design, and manufacturing, to represent objects and assemblies in a clear and understandable manner. It helps convey the spatial relationships and proportions of objects without the need for complex perspective calculations.

Orthographic projection:

Orthographic projection is a technique used in engineering and technical drawing to represent a three-dimensional object in two dimensions. It provides multiple views of an object from different angles to convey its shape, size, and details accurately. Here are the main types of orthographic projections:

1. Front View: The front view, also known as the elevation view or the front orthographic projection, shows the object as if it is viewed directly from the front. It provides a flat representation of the object's front face, displaying its width and height.
2. Top View: The top view, also called the plan view or the overhead orthographic projection, shows the object as if it is viewed directly from above. It provides a flat representation of the object's top face, displaying its length and width.
3. Side View: The side view, also known as the profile view or the side orthographic projection, shows the object as if it is viewed directly from one of its sides. It provides a flat representation of the object's side face, displaying its length and height.

ORTHOGRAPHIC PROJECTIONS

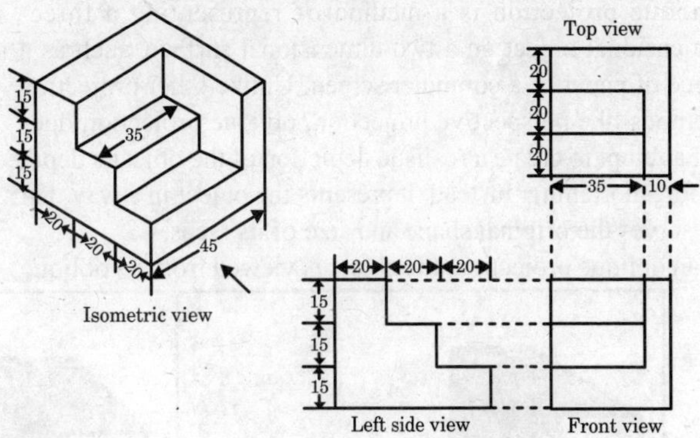

These three views (front, top, and side) are the fundamental projections used in orthographic drawings. By combining these views, a complete understanding of the object's shape and dimensions can be achieved. These views are typically placed orthogonally (at right angles) to each other, with each view representing a different perspective.

In addition to these primary views, orthographic projections may include other views to provide further details or specific information about the object. These can include sectional views, auxiliary views, or detail views, which show specific parts or aspects of the object in more detail.

Orthographic projections are an essential tool in engineering and technical drawing, allowing designers, engineers, and manufacturers to accurately represent and communicate the shape, size, and geometry of objects. They provide a clear and standardized representation of objects, aiding in the design, analysis, and fabrication processes.

Perspective projection:

In perspective projection the **center of projection** is at finite distance from **projection plane**. This projection produces realistic views but does not preserve relative proportions of an object dimensions. Projections of distant object are smaller than projections of objects of same size that are closer to projection plane.

The distance and angles are not preserved and parallel lines do not remain parallel. Instead, they all converge at a single point called **center of projection** or **projection reference point**. There are 3 types of perspective projections which are shown in the following chart.

- **One point** perspective projection is simple to draw.
- **Two point** perspective projection gives better impression of depth.
- **Three point** perspective projection is most difficult to draw.

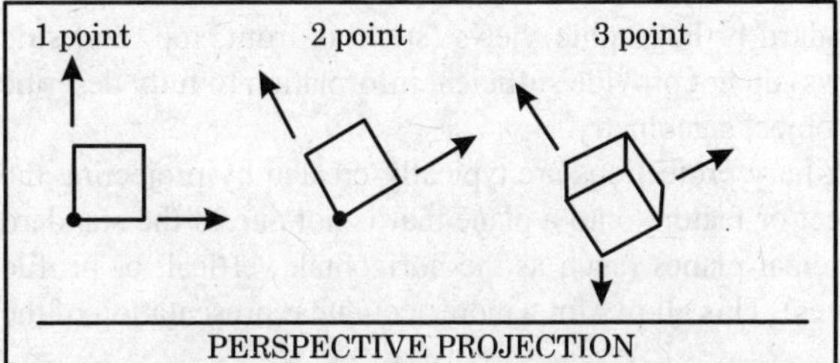

PERSPECTIVE PROJECTION

Oblique Projections:

Oblique projection is a method of representing a three-dimensional object on a two-dimensional surface, such as a piece of paper or a computer screen. Unlike other projection methods like perspective projection, oblique projection does not attempt to create a realistic depiction of the object's depth or foreshortening. Instead, it presents the object in a way that preserves the original shape and size of its faces.

In an oblique projection, the object is viewed from an oblique angle relative to the projection plane. Typically, one of the object's primary faces, called the "frontal face" or "principal face," is parallel to the projection plane. The other faces of the object are then projected onto the plane using parallel lines.

One distinguishing feature of oblique projection is the inclusion of a receding axis or receding lines. These lines are parallel to each other and are drawn at an angle from the frontal face, representing the object's depth. The angle at which the receding lines are drawn determines the type of oblique projection.

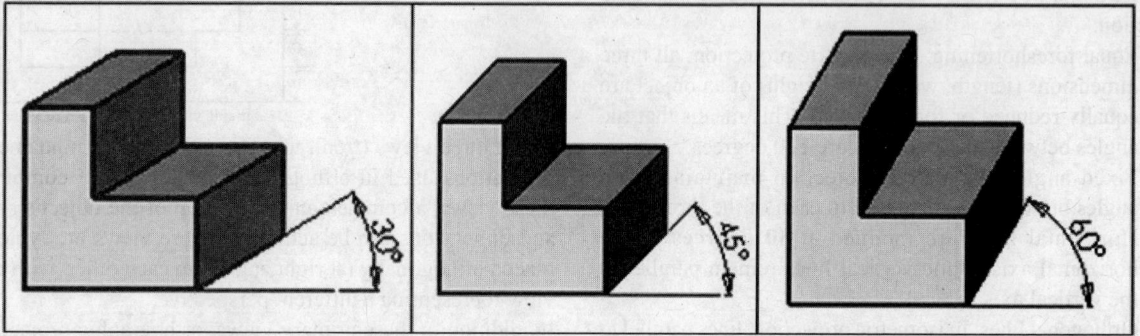

There are different types of oblique projections, but the two most common ones are:

1. **Cavalier Oblique Projection:** In a cavalier oblique projection, the receding lines are drawn at a 45-degree angle relative to the frontal face. This means that the depth of the object is represented at its full scale. However, this type of projection does not provide a realistic sense of depth.
2. **Cabinet Oblique Projection:** In a cabinet oblique projection, the receding lines are drawn at a lesser angle, usually 30 degrees, relative to the frontal face. This reduces the scale of the depth, making the object appear somewhat compressed or foreshortened along the depth axis. Cabinet oblique projection provides a more aesthetically pleasing representation while still maintaining a clear view of the object's faces.

Oblique projection is commonly used in technical drawings, architecture, engineering, and computer graphics when a simplified representation of an object is sufficient and maintaining accurate proportions is important. It is relatively easy to construct and can be a useful tool for conveying the basic form and dimensions of an object.

Auxiliary projections

Auxiliary projections, also known as auxiliary views or secondary views, are graphical techniques used in technical drawing to represent the true shape and size of an object or a specific feature of an object. They are employed when the standard orthographic views (such as front, top, and side views) do not provide sufficient information to fully describe the object's geometry.

Auxiliary projections are typically created by projecting the object or feature onto a plane that is not one of the standard principal planes (such as the horizontal, vertical, or profile planes). This allows for a more accurate representation of the object's true shape, eliminating the distortions that can occur in the standard orthographic views.

In this case, the drawing is prepared by placing the plane parallel to the inclined surface. Such a plane is called **Auxiliary Plane.** The drawing made on this plane is called **Auxiliary View.**

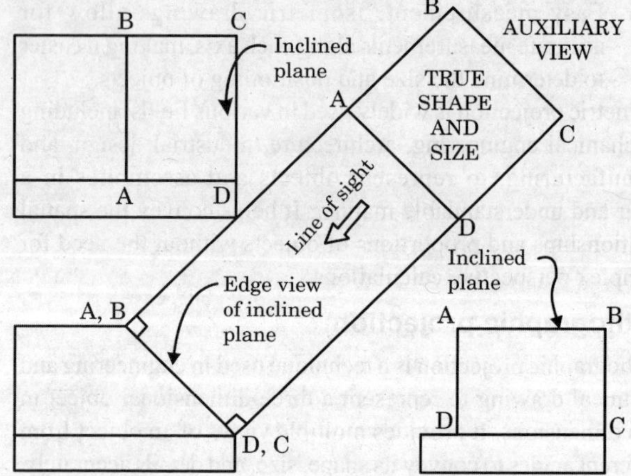

The process of creating an auxiliary projection involves the following steps:

1. Determine the plane of projection: Select a plane that will provide the most useful and informative view of the object or feature. This plane should be oriented in a way that showcases the desired details.
2. Establish reference lines: Draw reference lines between the object or feature and the plane of projection. These lines indicate the direction of the projection.
3. Project the points: Transfer the points from the object or feature along the reference lines onto the plane of projection. This is done by drawing perpendicular lines from the object to the reference lines and extending them until they intersect the projection plane.

4. Complete the projection: Connect the projected points on the projection plane to form the desired auxiliary view. This view can be used in conjunction with the other orthographic views to provide a comprehensive representation of the object.

Auxiliary projections are particularly useful when representing complex features, such as inclined surfaces, oblique planes, or irregular shapes that cannot be easily captured in the standard orthographic views. They provide additional clarity and help communicate the object's geometry more accurately, aiding in manufacturing, construction, and other technical processes.

Drawing instruments/tools:

Drawing instruments refer to tools and materials used for creating artwork, sketches, technical drawings, or illustrations. They can vary depending on the artist's preference, style, and the specific purpose of the drawing. Here are some commonly used drawing instruments:

1. Pencils: Pencils are versatile drawing tools and come in different grades, ranging from hard (H) to soft (B). They allow for precise lines and shading techniques.
2. Pens: Pens provide a consistent and permanent line. They come in various types, such as ballpoint, rollerball, gel, or fountain pens. Each type offers different line widths and ink characteristics.
3. Charcoal: Charcoal is a soft and dark drawing medium that produces rich, dramatic lines. It comes in various forms, including vine charcoal, compressed charcoal, and charcoal pencils.
4. Graphite Sticks: Graphite sticks are solid chunks of graphite that can be used for expressive and large-scale drawings. They allow for bold, dark lines and can be blended or smudged for shading.
5. Ink: Inks, available in bottles or cartridges, are used with dip pens or fountain pens. They offer a range of colors and can create fine lines or bold strokes.
6. Pastels: Pastels are sticks of pigment mixed with a binder. They come in soft pastels (chalk-like) and oil pastels (waxy). Pastels are known for their vibrant colors and are commonly used for drawing and painting.
7. Markers: Markers are popular for their bright and vivid colors. They come in various types, such as alcohol-based markers, water-based markers, or brush markers. Markers are often used for illustrations and graphic design.
8. Brushes: Brushes are used with various drawing mediums, including watercolors, inks, or acrylics. They come in different shapes, sizes, and bristle types, allowing for a wide range of brush strokes and textures.
9. Rulers and Compasses: These tools help artists and designers create precise lines, circles, angles, and geometric shapes. They are essential for technical drawings and architectural illustrations.
10. Erasers: Erasers are used to correct or remove unwanted lines, smudges, or marks from the drawing surface. Different types of erasers, such as kneaded erasers or vinyl erasers, are suitable for different drawing mediums.
11. Blending Tools: Blending tools, such as tortillons, blending stumps, or smudge sticks, are used to smudge or blend pencil, charcoal, or pastel lines to create smooth transitions and gradients.

These are just a few examples of drawing instruments. Artists often combine multiple tools and techniques to achieve their desired effects and styles. The choice of drawing instruments depends on personal preference, the intended artwork, and the artist's skill level.

LINE:

Lines in engineering drawing are fundamental graphical elements used to represent various features, dimensions, and relationships between objects or components. They play a crucial role in communicating information and conveying the design intent in a clear and standardized manner. Lines in engineering drawing can be categorized into different types, each serving a specific purpose.

Types of Lines:

Following are the different **types of lines** used in engineering drawing:

Type A -Continuous Thick (Visible Outline of Parts):

Outline of Parts type lines represent the visible edges of the objects, hence should be outstanding in appearance and therefore, are drawn as bold i.e., thick continuous lines.

Type B- Continuous Thin (Dimension, Projection, Leader, Hatching Lines):

Dimension, Projection, Leader, Hatching type lines must be drawn thin and continuous. The extension lines for dimensioning should run from the outlines without leaving a gap and extend beyond the dimension lines. This type is also used to draw outlines of adjacent and revolved sections.

Type C- Continuous Thin Freehand (Limits or Boundaries of Partial or Interrupted Views):

Limits or Boundaries of Partial or Interrupted Views type lines are drawn as continuous, thin, wavy, freehand lines to represent limits or boundaries of partial or interrupted views.

Type D- Break Lines- (Zig-Zag):

Break Lines type lines are ruled, short, zig-zag thin lines drawn to represent the breaks.

Type E-Hidden Lined (Dashes Thick):

Hidden Lined (Thick) type lines consist of thick short dashes, closely and evenly spaced. These lines are drawn to represent hidden or invisible edges of the objects.

Type F-Hidden Lines (Dashes Thin):

Hidden Lines (Thin) type lines consist of thin short dashes, closely and evenly spaced. These lines are drawn to represent hidden or invisible edges of the objects. Although THICK lines of Type-E are recommended for representing the hidden edges, THIN lines of Type-F are preferred.

Type G-Centre lines, Lines of Symmetry, Trajectories, and Pitch Circles (Chain Thin):

Centre lines, Lines of Symmetry, Trajectories, and Pitch Circles type of lines are long, thin, chain lines with alternately long and short dashes of proportion ranging from 6:1 to 4:1 and evenly spaced. The proportion once selected should be maintained throughout the drawing. The center lines are extended by a short distance beyond the outline. These lines are also drawn to represent the lines of symmetry, trajectories, pitch circles, etc.

Type H- Cutting Plane Lines (Cutting Plane):

Cutting Plane Lines are long lines, thickened ar ends and thin elsewhere, with alternately long and short dashes of proportion ranging from 4:1 to 6:1 and evenly spaced. The corners where the section plane charges the direction are made thick for a short length.

Type J-(Lines to indicate Surfaces which require Additional Treatment):

These are long thick lines with alternatively long and short dashes of proportion ranging from 6:1 to 4:1 and evenly spaced. These lines are drawn to indicate surfaces, to receive additional treatment like anodizing, plating, etc.

Type K-(Chain Thin)

Lines to indicate Outlines of Adjacent parts, Extreme positions of Movable Parts, Centroidal lines, Parts situated in front of the Cutting Planes, Initial outlines prior to forming. These are thin lines with a long and two short dashes alternately and evenly placed in the proportion ranging from 6:1 to 4:1. These lines are used to represent the outlines of adjacent parts, extreme positions of movable parts in the assembly drawings, parts situated in front of the cutting planes, initial outlines prior to forming, centroidal lines etc.

Type	Line	Description	Application
A		Continuous THICK	Visible outlines, Visible edges.
B		Continuous THIN	Dimension lines, Projection lines, Leader lines, Imaginary lines of intersections, Outlines of revolved sections.
C		Continuous THIN Freehand	Boundaries of Limits of Partial or Interrupted views.
D		Continuous THIN Zig-Zag	Long break lines
E		Dashed THICK	Hidden outlines, Hidden edges.
F		Dashed THIN	
G		Chain THIN	Centre lines, Lines of Symmetry, Trajectories.
H		Chain THIN and THICK at ends & Changes of Direction	Cutting Planes
J		Chain THICK	Indication of lines or surfaces to which special treatment required.
K		Chain THIN Double Dash	Outlines of adjacent parts, Alternate and Extreme positions of movable parts, Centroidal lines, Initial outlines, Prior to forming.

1. Visible Lines: These lines are solid, continuous lines that represent the visible edges or outlines of objects in the drawing.
2. Hidden Lines: Hidden lines are used to represent features that are not visible from the current viewing angle. They are often depicted as short dashes or evenly spaced dots.
3. Centerlines: Centerlines are used to indicate the center of a cylindrical or symmetrical object. They consist of long and short dashes alternately repeated.
4. Extension Lines: Extension lines are thin lines that extend from the object's outline and have arrowheads at the end. They indicate the boundaries or endpoints for dimensioning.
5. Dimension Lines: Dimension lines are used to specify the size, length, and location of features in the drawing. They are thin, continuous lines with arrowheads at each end and measurements placed in between.
6. Section Lines: Section lines are used in sectional views to indicate the material or internal features of an object. They are evenly spaced, thin lines that are usually inclined at a 45-degree angle.
7. Break Lines: Break lines are used to shorten long objects or to indicate that a section of an object is not shown in the drawing. They consist of a series of zigzag lines with two short parallel lines at the beginning and end.
8. Phantom Lines: Phantom lines are used to represent alternate positions, repeated detail, or temporary structures. They are composed of long dashes alternately interrupted by pairs of short dashes.
9. Construction Lines: Construction lines are lightly drawn lines used as guides to help in the construction or layout of the drawing. They are usually drawn using a dashed or dotted line style.
10. Leader Lines: Leader lines are used to connect notes, labels, or dimensions to specific features in the drawing. They are straight lines with an arrow or dot at one end and a text or symbol at the other end.

Scales in engineering drawing:

In engineering drawing, scales are used to represent the size of objects and the distances between them accurately. They are essential tools for communicating dimensions and proportions in technical drawings. Here are some common types of scales used in engineering drawings:

1. **Architect's Scale:** This type of scale is commonly used in architectural drawings. It typically consists of three scales: 1:1, 1:50, and 1:100. The 1:1 scale represents the actual size of the object, while the other scales represent a reduced size of the object.
2. **Engineer's Scale**: Engineer's scales are used in civil and mechanical engineering drawings. They are typically triangular in shape and have multiple scales on each edge. The most common engineer's scale is the 1:10 scale, which allows for larger objects to be drawn while still fitting on standard-sized paper.
3. **Metric Scale**: Metric scales are used in engineering drawings that adhere to the metric system. They are typically labeled with metric units such as millimeters (mm) or centimeters (cm) and represent the actual size of the object.
4. **Inch Scale**: Inch scales are used in engineering drawings that follow the imperial system. They are labeled with inches (in) and fractions of an inch (e.g., 1/2 inch, 1/4 inch) and represent the actual size of the object.

When using scales in engineering drawings, it's important to ensure that all objects are drawn to the correct proportion and that the dimensions are accurately conveyed.

Drawing standards:

Drawing standards in engineering refer to a set of guidelines and conventions that define how technical drawings should be created, interpreted, and communicated within the engineering field. These standards ensure consistency, clarity, and accuracy in engineering drawings, allowing engineers, designers, manufacturers, and other stakeholders to understand and work with the drawings effectively. Here are some key aspects of drawing standards in engineering:

1. Dimensioning and Tolerancing: Drawing standards specify the methods and conventions for dimensioning and tolerancing, including the placement, style, and format of dimensions, tolerances, and geometric symbols. This ensures that the dimensions and tolerances are clearly defined and can be interpreted correctly.
2. Line Types and Weights: Drawing standards define the different line types and weights used in technical drawings. For example, different line types may be used to represent visible edges, hidden lines, centerlines, and section lines. Consistent line weights help in differentiating between different features and provide visual clarity.
3. Title Blocks and Borders: Engineering drawings typically include a title block and border, which contain important information such as the drawing title, scale, author, revision history, and company details. Drawing standards provide guidelines for the placement and format of these elements, ensuring that the necessary information is included and easily accessible.
4. Symbols and Notations: Various symbols and notations are used in engineering drawings to represent features, materials, surface finishes, welding specifications, and other important information. Drawing standards specify the appropriate symbols and notations to be used, ensuring consistency and proper communication of technical details.
5. Drawing Views and Projections: Drawing standards define the types of views and projections that should be used to represent objects in different orientations. This includes orthographic projections (e.g., front view, top view, side view) and isometric or perspective views when necessary. The standards provide guidelines for the arrangement and alignment of views to accurately represent the object's shape and dimensions.
6. File Formats and Data Exchange: With the advancement of computer-aided design (CAD) software, drawing

standards also encompass guidelines for file formats, layering, naming conventions, and data exchange protocols. These standards facilitate the exchange of drawings and data between different software platforms and ensure compatibility and consistency in digital workflows.

Common drawing standards used in engineering include ASME Y14.5 for dimensioning and tolerancing, ISO 128 for general principles of presentation, and ANSI/ASME Y14.100 for engineering drawing practices. However, specific industries or organizations may have their own additional standards or variations to meet their unique requirements.

Adhering to drawing standards is crucial in engineering as it enables clear communication, promotes interoperability, and ensures that drawings are easily understood and accurately interpreted by all stakeholders involved in the design, manufacturing, and inspection processes.

Drawing sheet:

In engineering, drawing sheets are used to create detailed technical drawings and plans for various purposes, such as architectural design, mechanical engineering, civil engineering, and more. These drawings serve as a visual representation of the design and provide important information for the construction or manufacturing process. Here are some key aspects of drawing sheets in engineering:

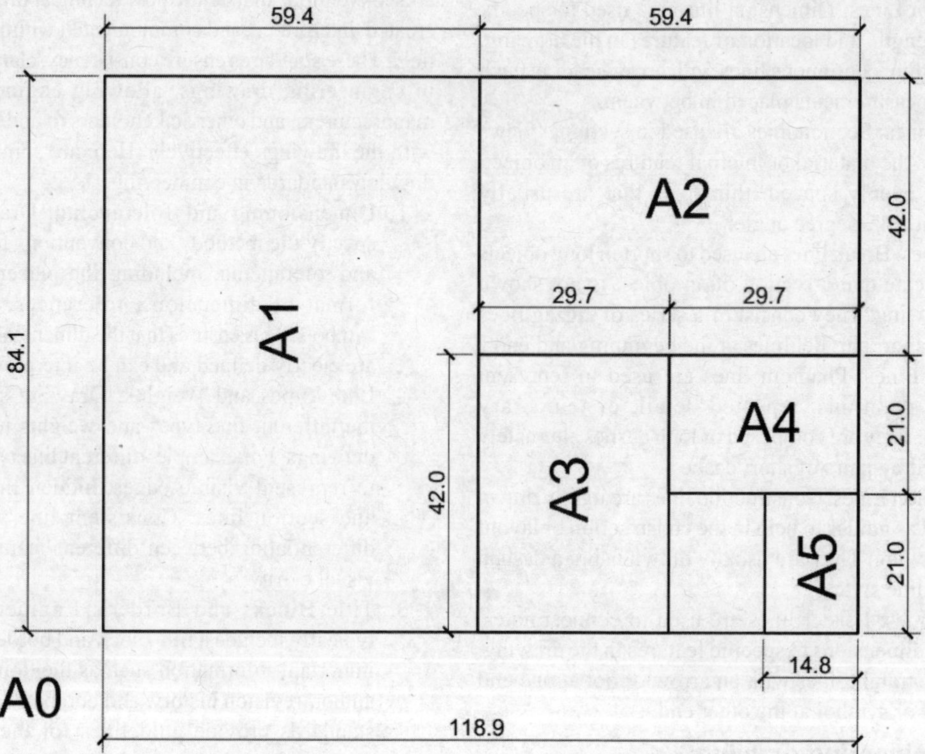

1. Paper Size: Drawing sheets typically follow standard paper sizes, such as ISO sizes (A0, A1, A2, A3, A4, etc.) or ANSI sizes (ANSI A, ANSI B, ANSI C, etc.). The choice of paper size depends on the scale and complexity of the drawing.

The most common ISO sizes for engineering drawings are:

- A0: 841 mm × 1189 mm (33.1 in × 46.8 in)
- A1: 594 mm × 841 mm (23.4 in × 33.1 in)
- A2: 420 mm × 594 mm (16.5 in × 23.4 in)
- A3: 297 mm × 420 mm (11.7 in × 16.5 in)
- A4: 210 mm × 297 mm (8.3 in × 11.7 in)

ANSI sizes for engineering drawings are:

- ANSI A: 216 mm × 279 mm (8.5 in × 11 in)
- ANSI B: 279 mm × 432 mm (11 in × 17 in)
- ANSI C: 432 mm × 559 mm (17 in × 22 in)
- ANSI D: 559 mm × 864 mm (22 in × 34 in)
- ANSI E: 864 mm × 1118 mm (34 in × 44 in)

2. Title Block: The title block is an area located at the bottom or right-hand side of the drawing sheet. It contains essential information about the drawing, including the title, drawing number, revision history, scale, date, and the name of the drafter.
3. Border and Frame: The drawing sheet is usually surrounded by a border or frame, which provides a clear boundary for the drawing. The border may include reference information, such as project name, company logo, and other relevant details.
4. Drawing Views: The main portion of the drawing sheet is dedicated to drawing views, which represent different aspects or sections of the design. These views can include orthographic projections (front, top, side views), isometric views, exploded views, and cross-sections.
5. Dimensions and Annotations: Dimensions and annotations are essential elements of engineering drawings. They provide precise measurements,

tolerances, and additional information about features, materials, and assembly instructions. Dimensions are typically shown using lines, arrows, and numerical values, while annotations include notes, symbols, and labels.

6. Scales: Drawings often require scaling to accurately represent the design within the available drawing space. Scales can be expressed as a ratio (e.g., 1:50) or represented graphically using a scale bar. The scale allows measurements on the drawing to be converted into real-world dimensions.
7. Layers and Line Types: Engineering drawings often utilize layers and different line types to distinguish various components or features. Different colors or line weights may be used to differentiate between object lines, hidden lines, centerlines, dimensions, and annotations.
8. Drawing Standards: Engineering drawings should adhere to specific standards, which vary depending on the industry and country. Common standards include ISO (International Organization for Standardization) and ASME (American Society of Mechanical Engineers) standards, among others.

It's important to note that with the advancement of computer-aided design (CAD) software, traditional drawing sheets are increasingly being replaced by digital formats. CAD software allows for easier editing, storage, and sharing of drawings, and provides additional tools for 3D modeling, simulations, and rendering.

Technical Lettering:

Technical lettering in engineering drawing refers to the process of creating clear and consistent letterforms on drawings to convey information effectively. It involves using specific guidelines and techniques to ensure legibility, uniformity, and accuracy in the lettering.

Here are some key aspects of technical lettering in engineering drawing:

1. Lettering Style: In technical drawing, a standardized lettering style is often used to maintain consistency and clarity. The most commonly used style is the Gothic style, which features block letters with uniform stroke widths.

   Lettering and numbering should be in a perfect manner style. The upper, lower case letters and numbers are neatly drawn in the below figure:

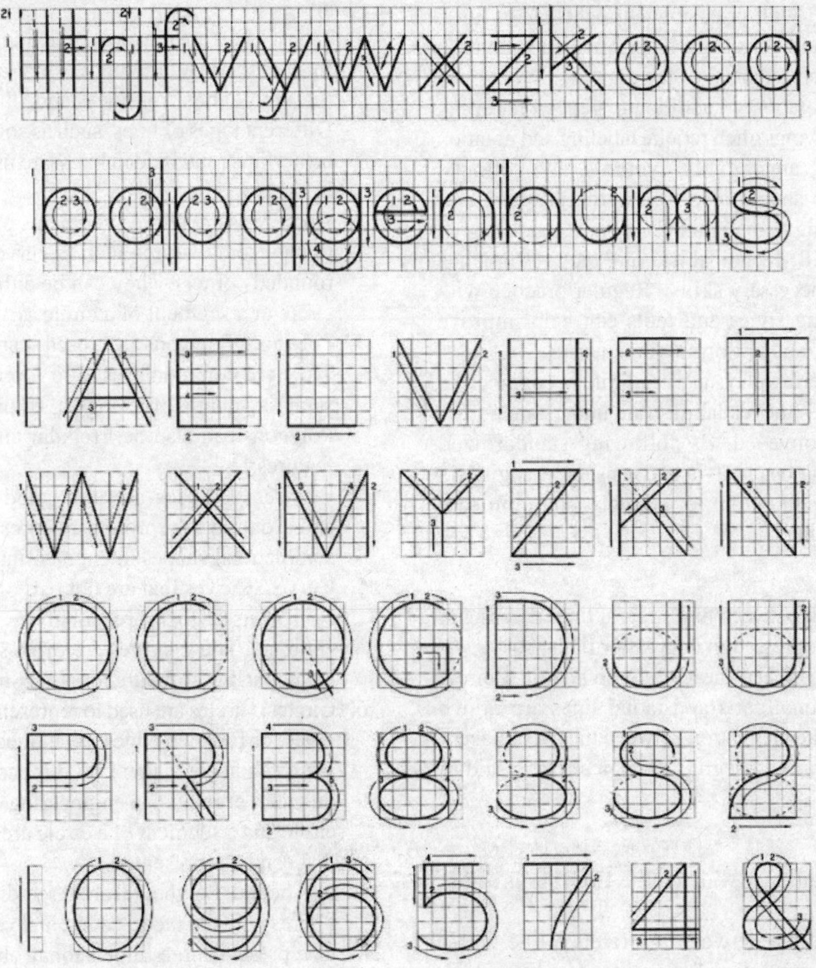

2. Lettering Tools: Technical lettering can be done using various tools, including mechanical pencils, technical pens, or lettering stencils. The choice of tool depends on personal preference and the level of precision required.
3. Lettering Height: The height of the letters is typically determined based on the scale of the drawing. It is essential to select a lettering size that ensures readability while also fitting within the available space.
4. Stroke Width: Consistent stroke widths are crucial for legible technical lettering. The strokes should be even and uniform throughout each letter. This can be achieved by maintaining a consistent pressure while lettering or using pens with fixed stroke widths.
5. Spacing: Proper spacing between letters, words, and lines is essential for readability. Adequate spacing ensures that the text does not appear cluttered or crowded. Generally, the spacing between letters is approximately equal to the width of the letter "I."
6. Alignment: The letters should be aligned vertically and horizontally. Horizontal alignment ensures that the baseline of each letter is consistent, while vertical alignment ensures that the letters are positioned correctly in relation to each other.
7. Neatness and Precision: Technical lettering should be done neatly and with precision. Straight, clean lines, sharp corners, and consistent letterforms contribute to the overall professionalism of the drawing.
8. Labeling and Notation: In addition to general lettering, engineering drawings often require labeling and notation for dimensions, annotations, symbols, and callouts. These elements should also follow the principles of technical lettering to maintain clarity and consistency.
9. Practice and Skill: Technical lettering requires practice to develop the necessary skills. Regular practice with different lettering styles and tools can help improve speed, accuracy, and uniformity in lettering.

Overall, technical lettering plays a crucial role in engineering drawings as it enhances the readability and understandability of the information conveyed. By following standardized guidelines and focusing on clarity and consistency, engineers can ensure that their drawings effectively communicate important details to others.

Angles:

Angle is the inclination between two straight lines meeting at a point. The angle is expressed in degrees or radians.

Concept of a degree: When the circumference of a circle is divided into 360 equal parts and radial lines are drawn through these points, the inclination between the two adjacent radia lines is defined as one degree. Thus, a circle is said to contain 360°.

Types of angles:

- **Acute angle:** If an angle which is **less than 90°** is called an acute angle.
- **Right angle:** Angle between a reference line and a perpendicular line is called right angle. A right angle is an **inclination between two perpendicular lines**.
- **Obtuse angle:** This refer to an angle between 90° and 180°
- **Straight angle:** This refers to an angle of 180°. This is also called as the angle of a straight line.
- Reflex angle: It is the angle which is more than 180° (two right angles).
- **Adjacent angles:** These are the **angles lying on either side of a line**.
- **Complementary angles:** The complementary angles are those when two angles together make 90°.
- **Supplementary angle:** The supplementary angles are those when two anglles together make 180°.

Geometric figures in engineering drawing:

In engineering drawing, geometric figures refer to precise mathematical entities that have well-defined properties, dimensions, and relationships. These figures are typically represented using specific geometric constructions, equations, or formulas. Geometric figures in engineering drawing include points, lines, curves, circle, arcs, polygons, and other shapes that can be precisely defined. They serve as the building blocks for creating accurate and detailed representations of objects in technical drawings.

Here are some common geometric figures used in engineering drawings:

1. Lines: Lines are the most fundamental geometric figures in engineering drawings. They are used to represent the boundaries, outlines, and dimensions of objects. Different types of lines, such as solid lines, dashed lines, centerlines, and hidden lines, are used to convey specific information.
2. Arcs: Arcs are curved segments of circles and are used to represent features such as curved surfaces, fillets, or rounded corners. They can be either part of a complete circle or a segment of a circle.
3. Polygons: Polygons are closed shapes with straight sides. They are commonly used to represent regular shapes, such as squares, rectangles, triangles, and hexagons. Polygons can also be irregular and represent complex features.
4. Ellipses: Ellipses are elongated or flattened circles and are used to represent features like holes, bores, or symmetrical shapes in engineering drawings.
5. Curves: Curves that are not part of a circle or an ellipse can be used to represent more complex shapes or contours. These curves are often sketched manually or created using software tools for smooth representation.
6. Circles: Circles are used to represent cylindrical features, holes, or rounded edges in engineering drawings. They are often accompanied by dimensions indicating their diameter or radius. In engineering drawing, a sector of a circle and a segment of a circle are two common shapes that can be represented.
7. Polyhedral: Polyhedral are three-dimensional geometric figures with flat faces, edges, and vertices. They are used to represent three-dimensional objects in engineering drawings. Common examples include cubes, pyramids, prisms, and cylinders.

8. Splines: Splines are smooth curves that are often used to represent complex or irregular shapes. They can be used to define contours or irregular profiles.
9. Solids: Solids, such as cubes, cylinders, and spheres, are used to represent three-dimensional objects in engineering drawings. They can represent components or provide a visual representation of the design.
10. Geometric Tolerances: Geometric tolerances, such as concentricity, parallelism, and perpendicularity, are used to specify the acceptable variation in dimensions and orientations of features. These geometric symbols are used alongside the geometric shapes to define the tolerance requirements.
11. Geometric Constructions: Geometric constructions are special figures created using specific rules or methods. These constructions may involve intersecting lines, perpendicular bisectors, parallel lines, or any other geometric relationships.

These geometric figures, along with appropriate annotations, dimensions, and symbols, help communicate the design intent, shapes, and sizes of objects in engineering drawings.

GEOMETRIC SHAPES

In engineering drawing, the term "shape" is used to describe the overall form or external appearance of an object. It focuses on the visual characteristics and outlines of an object rather than its precise mathematical properties. Shapes are commonly described using common geometric terms like squares, rectangles, triangles, or other irregular forms. They are often used to convey the general form or outline of an object in a drawing, providing a visual representation that aids in understanding without requiring precise measurements or calculations. Geometric shapes play a crucial role in engineering drawing as they form the basis for representing various components and features. Here are some common geometric shapes used in engineering drawing:

Types of Geometric Shapes

Quadrilaterals and their properties

Quadrilateral is a plane figure bounded by four sides and four angles. Sum of the four angles in a quadrilateral is of interior angles is equal to 360°. The side joining opposite corners is called diagonal. To construct a quadrilateral out of four sides, four angles and two diagonals a minimum of five dimensions are required of which two must be sides. Quadrlilaterals are also referred as Trapezoid.

Types of quadrilaterals: Square, Rectangle, Rhombus, Rhomboid/ Paralllelogram, Trapezoid, Trapezium

Square:

- In a square all the **four sides are equal**, and **its four angles are right angles.**
- The **two diagonals are equal and perpendicular** to each other.
- To construct a square, we need to know (a) length of the side or (b) length of the diagonal.

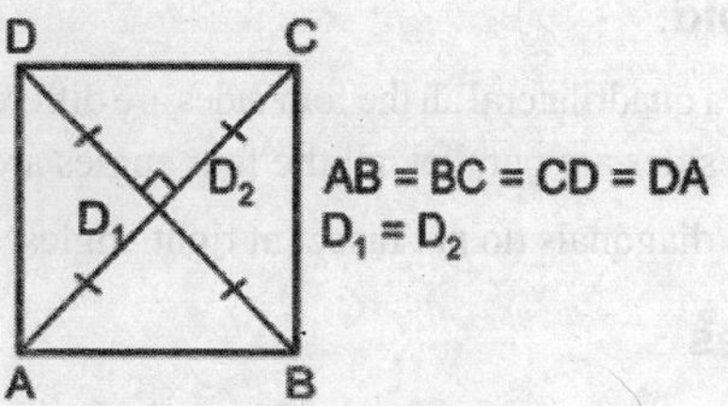

Rectangle:

- In a rectangle, opposite sides are equal and parallel, and all four angles are right angles.
- Diagonals AC and BD are equal, bisect but not at right angles.
- To construct a rectangle, we need to know the length (a) two adjacent sides or (b) diagonal and one side.

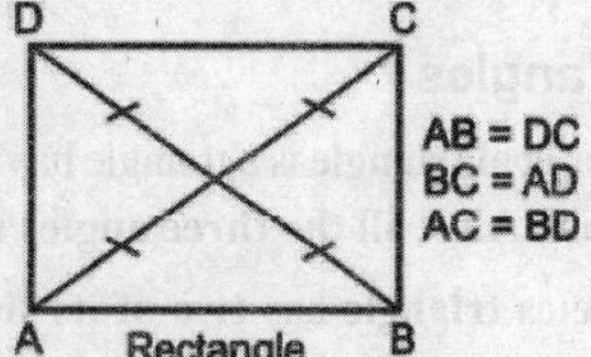

Rhombus:

- In rhombus all the **four sides are equal** but **only the opposite angles are equal.**
- **Diagonals AC and BD are not equal but bisecting at right angles.**
- To construct a rhombus, we need to know (a) two diagonals (b) one diagonal and an opposite angle or (c) one side and its adjacent angle.

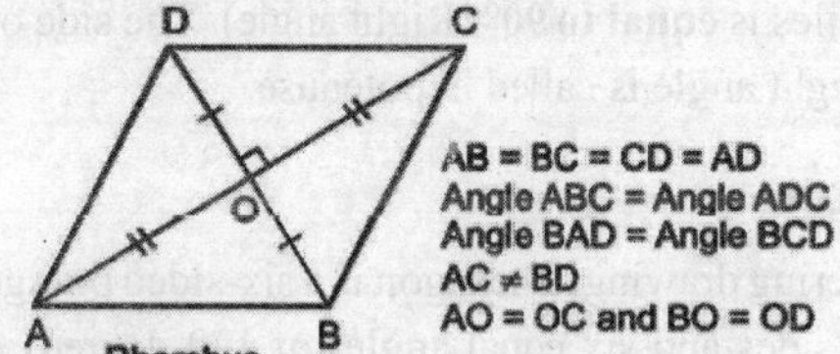

Rhomboid/Parallelogram:

- In a parallelogram **opposite sides are equal and parallel. Opposite angles are also equal.**
- **Diagonals are not equal but bisect each other.**
- Parallelogram is also known as rhomboid.
- To construct a parallelogram, we need (a) two adjacent sides and an angle between them or (b) one side, diagonal, and an angle between them or (c) two adjacent sides and perpendicular distance between the opposite sides.

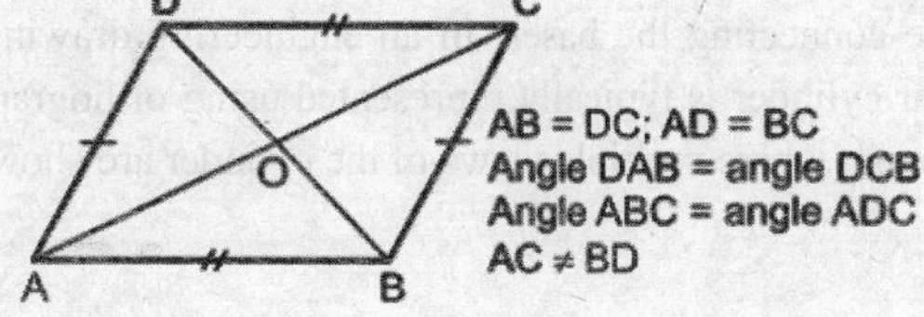

Trapezoid:

- It is a quadrilateral all the four sides are different and only two sides are parallel, all the four angles are different.
- The diagonals do not bisect at right angles.

Triangles

Triangle is a closed plane figure having three sides and three angles. The sum of the three angles always equals to 180°. The sum of any two sides is more than the third side. To define a triangle, we need to have a mmimum of three measurements as follows:

- 3 sides
- 2 sides and one angle
- 2 angles and one side

Types of tri'angles

- **An equilateral triangle** is a triangle having all the **three sides equal. Also, all the three angles are equal (60°)**
- **An isosceles triangle** has **two of its sides equal.** The angles opposite to the two equal sides are also equal.
- **A scalene triangle** has all the three sides unequal in lengths. All the three angles are also unequal.
- **An acute-angled triangle** is one in which **all the three angles are less than 90°.**
- **An obtuse-angled triangle** has **one of the angles as more than 90°.**
- **A right-angled triangle** is the one in wihich one of the angiles is **equal to 90°** (Right angle). The side opposite to right angle is called hypotenuse.

Hexagon:

In engineering drawing, a hexagon is a six-sided polygon with six equal sides and six equal angles of 120 degrees each. It is a commonly used shape in engineering and is often used to represent bolts, nuts, or other fasteners. When drawing a hexagon in engineering, we can use various methods depending on the requirements and the tools available.

Circular Cylinder & Cone

In engineering drawing, a circular cylinder and a cone are two common geometric shapes that are often represented. Here's a brief explanation of how they are typically depicted in engineering drawings:

Circular Cylinder: A circular cylinder is a three-dimensional shape with two parallel circular bases and a curved lateral surface connecting the bases. In an engineering drawing, a circular cylinder is typically represented using orthographic projection, where multiple views of the cylinder are shown.

To depict a circular cylinder, at least two orthographic views are commonly used: the front view and the top view. The front view shows the cylinder as a rectangle with circular arcs at the top and bottom, representing the bases. The top view displays the circular bases as complete circles, while the sides of the cylinder are not visible in this view.

Cone: A cone is a three-dimensional shape with a circular base and a curved lateral surface tapering to a point called the apex. Similar to a circular cylinder, a cone is represented using orthographic projection in engineering drawings.

To depict a cone, again, at least two orthographic views are generally used: the front view and the top view. The front view shows the cone as a triangle with a circular arc at the bottom, representing the base. The top view displays the circular base as a complete circle, while the tapering sides of the cone are not visible in this view.

In addition to the front and top views, engineering drawings may also include other views such as the side view or isometric view to provide a more comprehensive representation of the cylinder or cone.

Sphere:

In engineering drawing, a sphere is a three-dimensional shape that is often represented using orthographic projection. A sphere is a perfectly round geometrical object with all points on its surface equidistant from its center.

When depicting a sphere in an engineering drawing, multiple views are typically used to provide a comprehensive representation. The most common views used are the front view and the top view, similar to other geometric shapes.

The front view of a sphere shows a circle, representing the cross-section of the sphere. The circle should be drawn in a way that it appears tangent to the edges of the drawing frame. The top view displays a complete circle, representing the full extent of the spherical shape.

To provide a more accurate representation of the sphere, other views can be included, such as the side view or isometric view. The side view will show a semicircle, while the isometric view will display the sphere as an ellipse.

It's important to note that in engineering drawings, the diameter of the sphere is typically indicated for dimensional purposes. This information can be added to the drawing through dimensioning techniques, such as placing a linear dimension between two points on the sphere's circle.

As always, it is crucial to consult and adhere to applicable standards and guidelines when creating engineering drawings to ensure accurate and standardized representation of a sphere or any other geometric shape.

Symbolic representation in engineering drawing:

Symbolic representation in engineering drawing refers to the use of standardized symbols to represent different elements, features, and characteristics of a design or a component in a technical drawing. These symbols are typically used to convey information about dimensions, materials, surface finishes, tolerances, and other specifications related to the design.

Here are some commonly used symbolic representations in engineering drawing:

1. Geometric Symbols: These symbols represent basic geometric shapes such as lines, circles, arcs, and polygons. They are used to define the outline and shape of a component.
2. Dimensioning Symbols: These symbols indicate the size and location of features on a drawing. They include arrows, extension lines, dimension lines, and tolerance symbols.
3. Surface Finish Symbols: These symbols represent the desired surface texture or finish of a component. They provide information about parameters such as roughness, waviness, and lay.
4. Material Symbols: These symbols indicate the type of material to be used for a specific component. Common material symbols include letters or abbreviations representing different materials like steel, aluminum, plastic, or wood.
5. Welding Symbols: These symbols are used to represent different types of welds and welding operations. They provide information about the specific welding process, joint configuration, and additional requirements.
6. Electrical Symbols: In electrical engineering drawings, various symbols represent different electrical components such as resistors, capacitors, switches, and transformers. These symbols help in understanding the electrical connections and circuits.
7. Piping and Instrumentation Symbols: These symbols are used in piping and instrumentation diagrams (P&IDs) to represent different components and instruments in industrial processes, such as valves, pumps, tanks, and sensors.
8. Assembly Symbols: These symbols depict how multiple components fit together to form an assembly. They include exploded views, section views, and detail views to show the relationship and arrangement of parts.

It is important to note that there are several standardized symbol libraries, such as ANSI (American National Standards Institute) and ISO (International Organization for Standardization), which provide guidelines for symbolic representation in engineering drawings. These standards ensure clear and consistent communication of design intent across different engineering disciplines and industries.

Objective Type Questions

1. Which of the following is NOT a common feature found in engineering drawings?
   (a) Dimension lines (b) Section lines
   (c) Centerlines (d) Title blocks
2. Which feature is used to represent the contour of a cylindrical object on an engineering drawing?
   (a) Section lines (b) Hidden lines
   (c) Dimension lines (d) Centerlines
3. What is the purpose of a title block in an engineering drawing?
   (a) To provide information about the part being represented
   (b) To indicate the scale of the drawing
   (c) To show the overall dimensions of the part
   (d) To specify the material used for the part
4. Which type of line is used to represent hidden features in an engineering drawing?
   (a) Solid line (b) Dashed line
   (c) Dotted line (d) Centerline
5. What do dimension lines in an engineering drawing indicate?
   (a) The overall size of the part
   (b) The location of hidden features
   (c) The shape of the part
   (d) The material used for the part
6. Which feature is used to represent the symmetry of a part in an engineering drawing?
   (a) Dimension lines (b) Section lines
   (c) Hidden lines (d) Centerlines
7. What information is typically included in a revision block on an engineering drawing?
   (a) The title of the drawing
   (b) The name of the drafter
   (c) The date of the revision
   (d) The overall dimensions of the part
8. Which feature is used to represent a break in a long object on an engineering drawing?
   (a) Hidden lines (b) Dimension lines
   (c) Centerlines (d) Break lines
9. What does a section line indicate in an engineering drawing?
   (a) The location of hidden features
   (b) The material used for the part
   (c) The overall size of the part
   (d) The shape of the part in a specific section
10. Which feature is used to represent the center of a hole or a circle on an engineering drawing?
    (a) Hidden lines (b) Dimension lines
    (c) Centerlines (d) Break lines
11. Which type of drawing focuses on depicting the external appearance of an object or structure?
    (a) Isometric drawing
    (b) Perspective drawing
    (c) Orthographic drawing
    (d) Technical drawing
12. Which type of drawing represents a three-dimensional object on a two-dimensional surface using parallel lines that converge at a vanishing point?
    (a) Isometric drawing
    (b) Perspective drawing
    (c) Orthographic drawing
    (d) Technical drawing
13. Which type of drawing is commonly used in engineering and architecture to represent a three-dimensional object using three mutually perpendicular planes?
    (a) Isometric drawing
    (b) Perspective drawing
    (c) Orthographic drawing
    (d) Technical drawing
14. Which type of drawing shows the object as it appears when viewed from the top, front, and right side?
    (a) Isometric drawing
    (b) Perspective drawing
    (c) Orthographic drawing
    (d) Technical drawing
15. Which type of drawing is used to represent the exact dimensions, specifications, and construction details of an object?
    (a) Isometric drawing
    (b) Perspective drawing
    (c) Orthographic drawing
    (d) Technical drawing
16. Which type of drawing uses geometric shapes, lines, and patterns to create an abstract or non-representational artwork?
    (a) Sketching
    (b) Technical drawing
    (c) Perspective drawing
    (d) Graphic design

17. Which type of drawing involves creating a preliminary, rough representation of an object or idea?
(a) Sketching (b) Technical drawing
(c) Perspective drawing (d) Graphic design

18. Which type of drawing is often used in comic books and animations to tell a story or convey a sequence of events?
(a) Sketching (b) Technical drawing
(c) Storyboarding (d) Graphic design

19. Which type of drawing is used to create detailed, realistic representations of human figures or portraits?
(a) Sketching (b) Technical drawing
(c) Illustration (d) Graphic design

20. Which type of drawing focuses on capturing the essence or basic shapes of an object rather than its details?
(a) Sketching (b) Technical drawing
(c) Illustration (d) Graphic design

21. What is the purpose of dimensioning in engineering drawing?
(a) To make the drawing look visually appealing
(b) To provide instructions for manufacturing and inspection
(c) To indicate the scale of the drawing
(d) To showcase the artistic skills of the drafter

22. Which of the following is NOT a commonly used type of dimension line?
(a) Continuous thin line (b) Chain line
(c) Dotted line (d) Phantom line

23. What is the purpose of extension lines in dimensioning?
(a) To connect the dimension line with the object being dimensioned
(b) To indicate the centerline of a cylindrical feature
(c) To show hidden features in the object
(d) To mark the limits of the drawing sheet

24. Which of the following dimensioning systems allows for the most precise measurements?
(a) Decimal-inch system
(b) Fractional-inch system
(c) Metric system
(d) Engineering scale system

25. What is a tolerance in dimensioning?
(a) The allowable variation in the size of a feature
(b) The number of decimal places used in a dimension
(c) The distance between extension lines and dimension lines
(d) The thickness of the dimension lines

26. Which of the following is true about baseline dimensioning?
(a) It uses a common baseline for all dimensions in a group
(b) It places dimensions randomly throughout the drawing
(c) It is used only for circular features
(d) It is not a recognized dimensioning method

27. What is the purpose of a leader line in dimensioning?
(a) To indicate the overall size of the drawing
(b) To connect extension lines to dimension lines
(c) To highlight important dimensions
(d) To separate different sections of the drawing

28. What is the purpose of a centerline in dimensioning?
(a) To indicate symmetry in the object
(b) To represent hidden features in the object
(c) To provide a reference for measuring dimensions
(d) To mark the center of the drawing sheet

29. Which of the following is an example of a direct dimensioning method?
(a) Coordinate dimensioning
(b) Chain dimensioning
(c) Ordinate dimensioning
(d) Baseline dimensioning

30. When should a limit dimension be used?
(a) When the exact size is critical for functionality
(b) When the dimension is large and difficult to measure precisely
(c) When the drawing needs additional decorative elements
(d) When the dimension exceeds the size of the drawing sheet

31. Which of the following is NOT a commonly used view in engineering drawing?
(a) Isometric view (b) Front view
(c) Side view (d) Top view

32. What is the purpose of an auxiliary view in engineering drawing?
(a) To represent an object in a three-dimensional perspective
(b) To show hidden features that cannot be seen in the primary views
(c) To provide additional dimensions for complex features
(d) To indicate the scale of the drawing

33. Which view is typically used to depict the true shape and size of circular features?
(a) Front view (b) Side view
(c) Isometric view (d) Auxiliary view

34. What is the purpose of section views in engineering drawing?
(a) To represent an object in a three-dimensional perspective
(b) To show hidden features that cannot be seen in the primary views
(c) To provide additional dimensions for complex features
(d) To display internal details of an object

35. Which view is typically used to provide an overall representation of an object?
(a) Front view (b) Side view
(c) Isometric view (d) Top view

36. Which of the following views is typically used to show the depth of an object?
(a) Front view (b) Side view
(c) Isometric view (d) Top view

37. Which view is used to represent the topmost surface of an object?
(a) Front view (b) Side view
(c) Isometric view (d) Top view

38. What is the purpose of an isometric view in engineering drawing?
(a) To show hidden features that cannot be seen in other views
(b) To provide an overall representation of the object
(c) To depict the true shape and size of circular features
(d) To represent an object in a three-dimensional perspective

39. Which view is typically used to represent the front face of an object?
(a) Front view (b) Side view
(c) Isometric view (d) Auxiliary view

40. When is a detailed view used in engineering drawing?
(a) To represent an object in a three-dimensional perspective
(b) To show hidden features that cannot be seen in the primary views
(c) To provide an enlarged view of a specific area
(d) To indicate the scale of the drawing

41. In engineering drawing, a projection is a technique used to:
(a) Create 3D models
(b) Convert 2D views into 3D views
(c) Represent objects on a 2D surface
(d) Visualize engineering concepts

42. Which of the following is NOT a type of projection commonly used in engineering drawing?
(a) Isometric projection
(b) Orthographic projection
(c) Perspective projection
(d) Oblique projection

43. In orthographic projection, the object is represented using:
(a) One view (b) Two views
(c) Three views (d) Four views

44. Isometric projection is a type of projection that:
(a) Shows the object as it appears to the human eye
(b) Represents the object using only vertical and horizontal lines
(c) Uses three angles of 30° with respect to each other
(d) Represents the object in a distorted manner

45. The purpose of using auxiliary views in engineering drawing is to:
(a) Show hidden details that cannot be seen in the standard views
(b) Represent the object from different angles
(c) Highlight specific features of the object
(d) Create a 3D model of the object

46. In engineering drawing, the term "projection plane" refers to:
(a) The surface on which the projection is made
(b) The position from which the object is viewed
(c) The distance between the object and the viewer
(d) The line connecting the object to the viewer

47. Which of the following projections shows the true shape and size of the object's features?
(a) Front view (b) Side view
(c) Top view (d) Isometric view

48. The term "multiview projection" refers to:
(a) A technique that combines multiple projections of an object
(b) A projection that shows multiple objects simultaneously
(c) A projection technique used for complex objects only
(d) A projection that requires special equipment

49. A section view is used in engineering drawing to:
(a) Show the object in its entirety
(b) Highlight specific features of the object
(c) Represent the object in a 3D format
(d) Create a mirror image of the object

50. Which of the following projections provides the most realistic representation of an object?
(a) Isometric projection
(b) Orthographic projection
(c) Perspective projection
(d) Oblique projection

51. Which drawing instrument is commonly used to measure angles?
(a) Compass (b) Protractor
(c) T-square (d) French curve

52. Which drawing instrument is used to create circles and arcs?
(a) Compass (b) Protractor
(c) T-square (d) French curve

53. Which drawing instrument is primarily used for parallel line construction?
(a) Compass (b) Protractor
(c) T-square (d) French curve

54. Which drawing instrument is utilized to draw irregular curves?
(a) Compass (b) Protractor
(c) T-square (d) French curve

55. Which drawing instrument is employed to create straight horizontal and vertical lines?
(a) Compass (b) Protractor
(c) T-square (d) French curve

56. Which drawing instrument is commonly used to measure angles?
(a) Compass (b) Protractor
(c) T-square (d) French curve

57. Which drawing instrument is used to create circles and arcs?
(a) Compass (b) Protractor
(c) T-square (d) French curve

58. Which drawing instrument is primarily used for parallel line construction?
(a) Compass (b) Protractor
(c) T-square (d) French curve

59. Which drawing instrument is utilized to draw irregular curves?
(a) Compass (b) Protractor
(c) T-square (d) French curve

60. Which drawing instrument is employed to create straight horizontal and vertical lines?
(a) Compass (b) Protractor
(c) T-square (d) French curve

61. Which drawing instrument is used to create shading and blending in pencil drawings?
(a) Eraser (b) Smudge stick
(c) Ruler (d) Drawing compass

62. Which drawing instrument is used to remove graphite or charcoal marks from the drawing surface?
(a) Pencil sharpener (b) Eraser
(c) T-square (d) Compass

63. Which drawing instrument is used to measure and transfer proportions accurately?
(a) Compass (b) Ruler
(c) Divider (d) French curve

64. Which drawing instrument is used to create precise geometric shapes such as squares and rectangles?
(a) Protractor (b) T-square
(c) French curve (d) Compass

65. Which drawing instrument is used to create smooth and flowing curves?
(a) Compass (b) Protractor
(c) French curve (d) Smudge stick

66. What type of line is typically used to represent visible edges or outlines of an object in an engineering drawing?
(a) Hidden line (b) Centerline
(c) Object line (d) Extension line

67. Which type of line is used to represent edges or features that cannot be seen in the current view but are necessary for the complete understanding of the object?
(a) Hidden line (b) Centerline
(c) Phantom line (d) Section line

68. What type of line is used to indicate the axis of symmetry or centerline of a symmetrical object?
(a) Hidden line (b) Centerline
(c) Object line (d) Extension line

69. Which type of line is used to indicate the dimension of a feature or the distance between two points?
(a) Hidden line (b) Centerline
(c) Object line (d) Extension line

70. What type of line is used to represent alternate positions of a moving part in an assembly drawing?
(a) Hidden line (b) Centerline
(c) Phantom line (d) Section line

71. Which type of line is used to indicate the imaginary line along which a section view is cut?
(a) Hidden line (b) Break line
(c) Cutting plane line (d) Section line

72. What type of line is used to indicate a change in the surface contour or shape of an object in an engineering drawing?
(a) Hidden line (b) Centerline
(c) Break line (d) Section line

73. Which type of line is used to represent an imaginary line indicating the path of a cutting plane in a sectional view?
(a) Hidden line (b) Centerline
(c) Phantom line (d) Section line

74. What type of line is used to indicate the limit or boundary of a part or object in an engineering drawing?
(a) Hidden line (b) Dimension line
(c) Object line (d) Leader line

75. Which type of line is used to show the path of motion or movement in a mechanical drawing?
(a) Hidden line (b) Centerline
(c) Leader line (d) Dimension line

76. Which scale is commonly used to represent large objects or structures, such as buildings or bridges?
(a) Architectural scale (b) Engineering scale
(c) Metric scale (d) Isometric scale

77. Which scale is typically used in mechanical engineering drawings to represent precise measurements and dimensions?
(a) Architectural scale (b) Engineering scale
(c) Metric scale (d) Isometric scale

78. Which scale is commonly used in international standards and represents measurements in millimeters?
(a) Architectural scale (b) Engineering scale
(c) Metric scale (d) Isometric scale

79. Which scale is used to represent three-dimensional objects and shows all three principal axes in equal measure?
(a) Architectural scale (b) Engineering scale
(c) Metric scale (d) Isometric scale

80. Which scale is used to represent objects or structures in terms of their actual size?
(a) Architectural scale (b) Engineering scale
(c) Metric scale (d) Full-scale

81. Which scale would be appropriate for representing a building floor plan where 1 inch on the drawing represents 10 feet in real life?
(a) 1:10 (b) 1:20
(c) 1/8" = 1' (d) 1/4" = 1'

82. Which scale would be suitable for representing a small mechanical component where 1 cm on the drawing represents 2 mm in real life?
(a) 1:10 (b) 1:20
(c) 1:50 (d) 1:100

83. Which scale is commonly used in civil engineering drawings to represent large areas, such as maps or site plans?
(a) Architectural scale (b) Engineering scale
(c) Metric scale (d) Topographic scale

84. Which scale is used to represent objects or structures at a reduced size, where the ratio is less than 1?
(a) Enlarged scale (b) Reduced scale
(c) Fractional scale (d) Representative scale

85. Which scale is typically used in architectural drawings to represent the overall layout of a building or a floor plan?
(a) Architectural scale (b) Engineering scale
(c) Metric scale (d) Plotting scale

86. Which scale would be appropriate for representing a large machine or equipment in a technical drawing?
(a) 1:10 (b) 1:50
(c) 1:100 (d) 1:500

87. Which scale is commonly used in electrical engineering drawings to represent wiring diagrams or circuit layouts?
(a) Architectural scale (b) Engineering scale
(c) Metric scale (d) Electrical scale

88. Which scale would be suitable for representing a detailed part or component in an engineering drawing?
(a) 1:2 (b) 1:5
(c) 1:10 (d) 1:20

89. Which scale would be appropriate for representing a site plan where 1 inch on the drawing represents 50 feet in real life?
(a) 1:50 (b) 1:100
(c) 1:200 (d) 1:500

90. Which scale is commonly used in mechanical engineering drawings to represent assembly drawings or exploded views?
(a) Architectural scale (b) Engineering scale
(c) Metric scale (d) Assembly scale

91. Which scale is typically used in surveying and mapping to represent large areas, such as cities or regions?
(a) Architectural scale (b) Engineering scale
(c) Metric scale (d) Cartographic scale

92. Which scale would be suitable for representing a small electronic component with intricate details in an engineering drawing?
(a) 1:1000 (b) 1:2000
(c) 1:5000 (d) 1:10000

93. Which organization is responsible for developing and maintaining international drawing standards?
(a) ISO (International Organization for Standardization)
(b) ANSI (American National Standards Institute)
(c) ASME (American Society of Mechanical Engineers)
(d) DIN (Deutsches Institut für Normung)

94. Which type of line weight is typically used for object lines in engineering drawings?
(a) Thin line weight (b) Medium line weight
(c) Thick line weight (d) Variable line weight

95. Which unit of measurement is commonly used for dimensions in engineering drawings?
(a) Inches (b) Feet
(c) Millimeters (d) Meters

96. What does the abbreviation "GD&T" stand for in the context of engineering drawings?
(a) General Dimensioning and Text
(b) Geometric Design and Testing
(c) Geometric Dimensioning and Tolerancing
(d) Global Drafting Techniques

97. Which type of projection is commonly used in engineering drawings to represent three-dimensional objects on a two-dimensional plane?
(a) Orthographic projection
(b) Isometric projection
(c) Perspective projection
(d) Oblique projection

98. Which line type is used to indicate the dimension lines in engineering drawings?
(a) Hidden line (b) Centerline
(c) Extension line (d) Dimension line

99. Which standard format is commonly used for engineering drawings in the United States?
(a) ANSI A (8.5" x 11")
(b) ANSI B (11" x 17")
(c) ANSI C (17" x 22")
(d) ANSI D (22" x 34")

100. Which symbol is typically used to indicate a surface finish requirement on an engineering drawing?
(a) Diameter symbol (⌀)
(b) Concentricity symbol (⊗)
(c) Perpendicularity symbol (⊥)
(d) Roughness symbol (▽)

101. Which type of line is used to represent hidden or invisible edges in engineering drawings?
(a) Phantom line (b) Construction line
(c) Centerline (d) Section line

102. Which drawing view is typically used to represent an object as it would be seen by looking directly at one of its sides?
(a) Isometric view (b) Auxiliary view
(c) Section view (d) Front view

103. What is the standard size of an A4 drawing sheet?
(a) 210 mm × 297 mm (b) 297 mm × 420 mm
(c) 420 mm × 594 mm (d) 594 mm × 841 mm

104. Which type of drawing sheet is commonly used for architectural plans?
(a) A0 (b) A1
(c) A2 (d) A3

105. Which of the following is NOT a type of drawing sheet orientation?
(a) Landscape (b) Portrait
(c) Square (d) None of the above

106. What is the purpose of a title block on a drawing sheet?
(a) To indicate the type of drawing
(b) To provide information about the scale used
(c) To display the name of the drafter
(d) All of the above

107. Which type of line is typically used to indicate the visible edges of an object in a drawing?
(a) Solid line (b) Dashed line
(c) Dotted line (d) Wavy line

108. What is the purpose of drawing border lines on a drawing sheet?
(a) To frame the drawing
(b) To provide a clean edge
(c) To establish the drawing's boundary
(d) All of the above

109. Which of the following is NOT a common drawing sheet material?
(a) Paper (b) Vellum
(c) Tracing cloth (d) Aluminum

110. What does the term "scale" refer to in relation to a drawing sheet?
(a) The size of the drawing relative to the actual object
(b) The type of pencil used for drawing
(c) The thickness of the drawing sheet
(d) The color palette used in the drawing

111. Which type of drawing sheet is the largest in size?
(a) A0 (b) A1
(c) A2 (d) A3

112. Which of the following is a common unit of measurement used on drawing sheets?
(a) Meters (b) Centimeters
(c) Inches (d) All of the above

113. In engineering drawing, technical lettering is primarily used for:

(a) Adding decorative elements to the drawing
(b) Enhancing the aesthetics of the drawing
(c) Communicating important information clearly
(d) Providing a signature of the drafter

114. Which of the following is a commonly used lettering style in engineering drawing?

(a) Roman (b) Gothic
(c) Italic (d) Cursive

115. In engineering drawing, which type of lettering is typically used for dimensions, notes, and labels?

(a) Uppercase lettering (b) Lowercase lettering
(c) Capitalized lettering (d) Script lettering

116. The recommended letter height for uppercase letters in engineering drawing is generally:

(a) 1/8 inch (b) 1/4 inch
(c) 1/2 inch (d) 1 inch

117. Which of the following statements about technical lettering in engineering drawing is true?

(a) Lettering should always be done by hand.
(b) Mechanical or digital lettering is recommended for accuracy.
(c) Engineering drawing software automatically generates technical lettering.
(d) Technical lettering is not necessary in engineering drawing.

118. In engineering drawing, what is the purpose of using guidelines for technical lettering?

(a) To ensure consistent letter height
(b) To maintain uniform spacing between letters
(c) To align the baseline of the letters
(d) All of the above

119. Which of the following tools is commonly used for technical lettering in engineering drawing?

(a) Technical pens (b) Pencil
(c) Highlighters (d) Fountain pens

120. When creating uppercase letters in engineering drawing, the correct order of strokes is typically:

(a) Vertical strokes, horizontal strokes, and diagonal strokes
(b) Horizontal strokes, vertical strokes, and diagonal strokes
(c) Diagonal strokes, vertical strokes, and horizontal strokes
(d) Horizontal strokes, diagonal strokes, and vertical strokes

121. Which of the following fonts is commonly used for technical lettering in engineering drawings?

(a) Arial (b) Times New Roman
(c) Helvetica (d) Comic Sans

122. The recommended height for uppercase letters in technical lettering is typically:

(a) 4 mm (b) 6 mm
(c) 8 mm (d) 10 mm

123. Which of the following is the correct order for drawing a lowercase letter "a" in technical lettering?

(a) Vertical line, horizontal line, curved line
(b) Curved line, horizontal line, vertical line
(c) Horizontal line, vertical line, curved line
(d) Curved line, vertical line, horizontal line

124. In technical lettering, the space between characters is typically:

(a) Equal to the width of a character
(b) Half the width of a character
(c) One-third the width of a character
(d) Double the width of a character

125. When labeling dimensions in engineering drawings, which of the following should be used for fractions?

(a) Decimal format
(b) Decimal format with a slash (/) symbol
(c) Decimal format with parentheses ()
(d) Stacked fractions

126. Which of the following is the recommended method for emphasizing text in technical lettering?

(a) Underlining
(b) Italicizing
(c) Using a heavier stroke
(d) Capitalizing the letters

127. True or False: In technical lettering, the letters should be drawn with a consistent stroke width throughout the text.

(a) True (b) False

128. Which of the following is the correct order for drawing a number "9" in technical lettering?

(a) Curved line, vertical line, curved line
(b) Vertical line, curved line, horizontal line
(c) Horizontal line, vertical line, curved line
(d) Curved line, horizontal line, vertical line

129. Which of the following is NOT a characteristic of good technical lettering in engineering drawings?

(a) Legibility (b) Consistency
(c) Artistic flair (d) Uniformity

130. Which of the following is the recommended method for correcting errors in technical lettering?
(a) Erasing and redrawing the entire letter
(b) Using correction fluid
(c) Crossing out the error and writing the correct letter above or beside it
(d) Ignoring the error and moving on

131. Which geometric figure is commonly used to represent a hole in engineering drawings?
(a) Circle (b) Square
(c) Triangle (d) Rectangle

132. What is the name of the geometric figure used to represent a bolt or screw head in engineering drawings?
(a) Circle (b) Square
(c) Triangle (d) Hexagon

133. In engineering design, a cross-sectional view of a cylindrical object would appear as a:
(a) Circle (b) Square
(c) Triangle (d) Rectangle

134. Which geometric figure is commonly used to represent a gear in engineering drawings?
(a) Circle (b) Square
(c) Triangle (d) Hexagon

135. In engineering drawings, what geometric figure is used to represent a fillet or rounded corner?
(a) Circle (b) Square
(c) Triangle (d) Arc

136. A dimension line in an engineering drawing is typically represented by a:
(a) Straight line (b) Curved line
(c) Dotted line (d) Zigzag line

137. What geometric figure is used to represent an electrical connector or terminal in engineering drawings?
(a) Circle (b) Square
(c) Triangle (d) Rectangle

138. In engineering drawings, what geometric figure is commonly used to represent a chamfer or beveled edge?
(a) Circle (b) Square
(c) Triangle (d) Line segment

139. What is the name of the geometric figure used to represent a weld in engineering drawings?
(a) Circle (b) Square
(c) Triangle (d) Weld symbol

140. In engineering drawings, a hidden line is typically represented by a:
(a) Solid line (b) Dashed line
(c) Dotted line (d) Zigzag line

141. What is the definition of a circle?
(a) A polygon with six sides
(b) A closed curve with no straight sides
(c) A quadrilateral with opposite sides parallel
(d) A three-dimensional object with flat faces

142. What is the formula to calculate the circumference of a circle?
(a) $C = 2\pi r$ (b) $C = \pi d$
(c) $C = \pi r^2$ (d) $C = 4\pi r$

143. Which of the following is an example of a regular polygon?
(a) Rectangle (b) Triangle
(c) Pentagon (d) Trapezoid

144. What is the name of a three-dimensional shape with six rectangular faces?
(a) Cylinder (b) Pyramid
(c) Cube (d) Cone

145. Which of the following statements is true about an isosceles triangle?
(a) It has three equal sides
(b) It has three right angles
(c) It has two equal sides
(d) It has no equal sides

146. What is the formula to calculate the area of a rectangle?
(a) $A = \pi r^2$ (b) $A = l \times w$
(c) $A = 2\pi r$ (d) $A = bh$

147. Which of the following is a characteristic of a parallelogram?
(a) All sides are equal
(b) All angles are right angles
(c) Opposite sides are parallel and equal in length
(d) It has a curved shape

148. What is the name of a three-dimensional shape with a circular base and a curved surface that tapers to a point?
(a) Cylinder (b) Cone
(c) Sphere (d) Pyramid

149. Which of the following statements is true about a trapezoid?
(a) It has two pairs of parallel sides
(b) It has four equal sides
(c) It has three right angles
(d) It has no equal sides

150. What is the formula to calculate the volume of a sphere?
(a) $V = \pi r^2$ (b) $V = 2\pi r$
(c) $V = 4/3\pi r^3$ (d) $V = l \times w \times h$

151. In engineering drawing, what does a filled triangle symbol represent?
(a) Datum feature (b) Surface roughness
(c) Perpendicularity (d) Concentricity

152. What does a circle with two parallel lines passing through its center signify in engineering drawing?
(a) Position (b) True profile
(c) Concentricity (d) Circular runout

153. What does an 'R' with a circle around it stand for in engineering drawing?
(a) Radius (b) Roughness
(c) Runout (d) Right-hand thread

154. In engineering drawing, what does a perpendicular line with two small outward arrows at its end depict?
(a) Angularity (b) Perpendicularity
(c) Symmetry (d) Parallelism

155. What is the purpose of a diamond symbol in engineering drawing?
(a) Maximum material condition
(b) Center of gravity
(c) Dimension origin
(d) Flatness

156. What does a square symbol with an 'A' inside signify in engineering drawing?
(a) Area (b) Angularity
(c) Surface finish (d) Chamfer

157. In engineering drawing, what does an 'M' with a circle around it denote?
(a) Material thickness
(b) Surface roughness
(c) Maximum material condition
(d) Minimum material condition

158. What does a straight line with one long arrow and one short arrow signify in engineering drawing?
(a) Symmetry (b) Profile of a surface
(c) Position (d) Parallelism

159. What does a series of evenly spaced short lines on an engineering drawing denote?
(a) Surface roughness (b) Counterbore
(c) Tolerance zone (d) Symmetry

160. In engineering drawing, what does an 'X' symbol inside a circle represent?
(a) Center of gravity (b) Counterbore
(c) Spotface (d) Hole callout

Answers

1. (d)	**2.** (d)	**3.** (a)	**4.** (b)	**5.** (a)	**6.** (d)	**7.** (c)	**8.** (d)	**9.** (d)	**10.** (c)
11. (d)	**12.** (b)	**13.** (a)	**14.** (c)	**15.** (d)	**16.** (d)	**17.** (a)	**18.** (c)	**19.** (c)	**20.** (a)
21. (b)	**22.** (b)	**23.** (a)	**24.** (c)	**25.** (a)	**26.** (a)	**27.** (b)	**28.** (a)	**29.** (c)	**30.** (a)
31. (a)	**32.** (b)	**33.** (d)	**34.** (d)	**35.** (a)	**36.** (b)	**37.** (d)	**38.** (d)	**39.** (a)	**40.** (c)
41. (c)	**42.** (d)	**43.** (c)	**44.** (c)	**45.** (a)	**46.** (a)	**47.** (a)	**48.** (a)	**49.** (b)	**50.** (c)
51. (b)	**52.** (a)	**53.** (c)	**54.** (d)	**55.** (c)	**56.** (b)	**57.** (a)	**58.** (c)	**59.** (d)	**60.** (c)
61. (b)	**62.** (b)	**63.** (c)	**64.** (b)	**65.** (c)	**66.** (c)	**67.** (a)	**68.** (b)	**69.** (d)	**70.** (c)
71. (c)	**72.** (c)	**73.** (d)	**74.** (c)	**75.** (c)	**76.** (a)	**77.** (b)	**78.** (c)	**79.** (d)	**80.** (d)
81. (c)	**82.** (d)	**83.** (d)	**84.** (b)	**85.** (a)	**86.** (b)	**87.** (d)	**88.** (c)	**89.** (a)	**90.** (d)
91. (d)	**92.** (a)	**93.** (a)	**94.** (b)	**95.** (c)	**96.** (c)	**97.** (a)	**98.** (d)	**99.** (b)	**100.** (d)
101. (a)	**102.** (d)	**103.** (a)	**104.** (b)	**105.** (c)	**106.** (d)	**107.** (a)	**108.** (d)	**109.** (d)	**110.** (a)
111. (a)	**112.** (d)	**113.** (c)	**114.** (b)	**115.** (a)	**116.** (b)	**117.** (b)	**118.** (d)	**119.** (a)	**120.** (b)
121. (c)	**122.** (b)	**123.** (b)	**124.** (a)	**125.** (d)	**126.** (c)	**127.** (true)	**128.** (a)	**129.** (c)	**130.** (c)
131. (a)	**132.** (d)	**133.** (a)	**134.** (a)	**135.** (d)	**136.** (c)	**137.** (a)	**138.** (d)	**139.** (d)	**140.** (b)
141. (b)	**142.** (b)	**143.** (c)	**144.** (c)	**145.** (c)	**146.** (b)	**147.** (c)	**148.** (b)	**149.** (a)	**150.** (c)
151. (a)	**152.** (c)	**153.** (a)	**154.** (b)	**155.** (c)	**156.** (d)	**157.** (c)	**158.** (b)	**159.** (a)	**160.** (c)

Explanations

1. Title blocks are actually a common feature found in engineering drawings and are typically located in the lower right corner of the drawing. They contain information such as the title of the drawing, the name of the company or organization, the drawing number, the scale of the drawing, and other relevant details.
2. Centerlines are used to represent the contour of a cylindrical object on an engineering drawing. They indicate the center axis of the cylindrical feature and are typically drawn as long, dashed lines.
3. To provide information about the part being represented. The purpose of a title block in an engineering drawing is to provide essential information about the part or assembly being represented in the drawing. This information may include the part name, the drawing title, the drawing number, the date of creation, the scale of the drawing, and other pertinent details.
4. Dashed lines are commonly used to represent hidden features in an engineering drawing. These hidden features are typically those that cannot be seen in the current view but exist in the part or assembly.
5. The overall size of the part. Dimension lines in an engineering drawing indicate the overall size of the part. They are used to specify the lengths, widths, diameters, and other measurements of the features represented in the drawing.
6. Centerlines are used to represent the symmetry of a part in an engineering drawing. They are drawn as long, dashed lines and indicate the center axis or symmetry line of a feature or part.
7. A revision block on an engineering drawing typically includes information about the revisions made to the drawing. This information often includes the revision number, the date of the revision, the name or initials of the person who made the revision, and a brief description of the changes made.
8. Break lines are used to represent a break in a long object on an engineering drawing. They indicate that a portion of the object has been intentionally omitted for the purpose of clarity and to save space on the drawing.
9. A section line in an engineering drawing is used to indicate a specific section plane through the part or assembly. It represents the shape of the part when cut along that section plane.
10. Centerlines are used to represent the center of a hole or a circle on an engineering drawing. They indicate the exact center position of the feature and are typically drawn as long, dashed lines.
11. Technical drawing is a type of drawing that focuses on accurately representing the external appearance of an object or structure, usually with precise measurements and annotations.
12. Perspective drawing is a technique used to represent a three-dimensional object on a two-dimensional surface by creating the illusion of depth and space through the use of converging parallel lines that meet at a vanishing point.
13. Isometric drawing is commonly used in engineering and architecture to represent a three-dimensional object using three mutually perpendicular planes. The object is displayed without perspective and with all lines parallel to the three principal axes of the object.
14. Orthographic drawing, also known as multiview projection, shows the object as it appears when viewed from the top, front, and right side. It represents the object in two dimensions and provides multiple views to accurately depict its shape and features.
15. Technical drawing is used to represent the exact dimensions, specifications, and construction details of an object. It provides comprehensive and precise information for manufacturing, construction, or other technical purposes.
16. Graphic design uses geometric shapes, lines, and patterns to create visually appealing and communicative designs. While graphic design may incorporate elements of drawing, it is a broader field that encompasses various visual communication techniques, including digital media, typography, and layout design.
17. Sketching involves creating a preliminary, rough representation of an object or idea. It is often done quickly and freely to capture initial concepts, explore different possibilities, or communicate basic visualizations.
18. Storyboarding is a type of drawing used in comic books, animations, and filmmaking to visually plan and sequence a story or a series of events. It involves creating a series of rough sketches or panels that depict key moments and actions to guide the overall narrative.
19. Illustration is a type of drawing that is used to create detailed, realistic representations of human figures, portraits, or other subjects. It often focuses on capturing the likeness and characteristics of the subject matter, and it can be used in various contexts, including books, magazines, advertisements, and digital media.
20. Sketching often emphasizes capturing the essence or basic shapes of an object rather than its intricate details. It is a freehand technique that allows for a more spontaneous and expressive approach to drawing, often used for quick studies, brainstorming, or creating loose visual representations.
21. To provide instructions for manufacturing and inspection. Dimensioning in engineering drawing is essential to communicate the size, shape, and other geometric characteristics of the object being represented. It provides precise measurements and tolerances necessary for manufacturing and inspection processes.

22. Chain lines are not typically used for dimensioning purposes. Continuous thin lines, dotted lines, and phantom lines are commonly used to indicate dimensions, extension lines, and hidden features, respectively.

23. To connect the dimension line with the object being dimensioned. Extension lines are drawn from the object's edges to the dimension lines, indicating which part of the object is being measured.

24. The metric system is widely used in engineering and provides a decimal-based measurement system, allowing for more precise and consistent measurements compared to the fractional-inch and decimal-inch systems.

25. The allowable variation in the size of a feature. Tolerance specifies the acceptable range of variation in the dimensions of a part. It ensures that the manufactured part falls within the acceptable limits for functionality and fit.

26. It uses a common baseline for all dimensions in a group. Baseline dimensioning is a method where a single baseline is established, and all dimensions are measured from that line. It is commonly used for organizing dimensions in a group or when multiple features share a common measurement reference.

27. To connect extension lines to dimension lines. A leader line is a thin line with an arrowhead at one end. It is used to connect the extension lines to the dimension lines and point to the specific location on the object where the measurement applies.

28. To indicate symmetry in the object. A centerline is a thin, long-dashed line used to represent the axis of symmetry in an object. It helps to locate and dimension features symmetrically and accurately.

29. Ordinate dimensioning is a direct dimensioning method where each feature is dimensioned from a common baseline or origin. It involves using X and Y coordinates to specify the location of features, simplifying the dimensioning process.

30. When the exact size is critical for functionality. A limit dimension specifies the upper and lower acceptable limits for a feature's size. It is used when precise sizing is crucial to ensure the functionality, interchangeability, or fit of the part.

31. While isometric views are used to represent objects in a three-dimensional perspective, they are not typically used as the primary views in engineering drawings. Front view, side view, and top view are commonly used orthographic views.

32. To show hidden features that cannot be seen in the primary views. An auxiliary view is used to display a particular part or feature of an object that is not visible or fully understandable in the primary views. It provides a more detailed and accurate representation of the hidden features.

33. An auxiliary view is commonly used to show the true shape and size of inclined or oblique surfaces, as well as circular features such as holes, arcs, or cylinders. It provides a view perpendicular to the inclined or oblique surface, resulting in an accurate representation of the feature.

34. To display internal details of an object. Section views are used to reveal the internal structure, hidden parts, or complex features of an object. By cutting or slicing the object, the internal details become visible, aiding in understanding its construction and functionality.

35. The front view provides the principal view of an object and represents its external shape and features. It is usually the most descriptive and detailed view and serves as the starting point for creating other views.

36. The side view, also known as the profile view, provides a representation of an object from the side, showing its depth or thickness. It helps in understanding the overall shape and proportions of the object.

37. The top view, also known as the plan view, provides a representation of the object as seen from above. It shows the shape and arrangement of the object's top surface and is particularly useful for understanding the layout or arrangement of components.

38. To represent an object in a three-dimensional perspective. An isometric view is a pictorial representation that shows an object in a three-dimensional form. It provides a realistic view of the object by showing all three dimensions—length, width, and height—at the same time.

39. The front view is a two-dimensional representation that shows the object as viewed from the front or primary viewing direction. It provides a detailed representation of the object's external features, such as its contours, holes, or cutouts.

40. To provide an enlarged view of a specific area. A detailed view is used to magnify and show specific regions or features of an object that require more detailed representation. It allows for a closer examination of intricate areas without having to enlarge the entire drawing.

41. Projections in engineering drawing are used to represent three-dimensional objects on a two-dimensional surface, such as a piece of paper or a computer screen. It allows engineers to visualize and communicate the shape, size, and features of objects accurately.

42. Oblique projection is a type of projection commonly used in engineering drawing. It involves projecting the object onto the drawing plane at an oblique angle, typically 45 degrees. Orthographic projection, isometric projection, and perspective projection are other commonly used types.

43. Orthographic projection represents the object using three mutually perpendicular views: front view, top view, and side view. Each view shows the object from a different direction, providing a comprehensive representation of its shape and features.

44. Isometric projection is a type of projection that uses three angles of 30° with respect to each other. It provides a three-dimensional representation of an object with equal foreshortening along each of the three axes. This projection is commonly used to create technical illustrations.

45. Auxiliary views are additional views used in engineering drawing to show hidden details that cannot be adequately represented in the standard views (front, top, and side views). They provide a more detailed representation of specific features or surfaces of the object.

46. The projection plane in engineering drawing refers to the surface on which the projection is made, typically a flat surface such as a sheet of paper or a computer screen. It is where the views of the object are projected and drawn.

47. The front view in orthographic projection shows the true shape and size of the object's features that are parallel to the projection plane. It provides a two-dimensional representation of the object as it would appear when viewed directly from the front.

48. Multiview projection is a technique in engineering drawing that involves combining multiple projections of an object, such as front, top, and side views, to provide a comprehensive representation of its shape and features from different perspectives.

49. A section view in engineering drawing is used to highlight specific features of an object that are not easily visible in the standard views. It involves cutting a portion of the object and showing the internal details or hidden surfaces, providing a clearer understanding of its construction.

50. Perspective projection provides the most realistic representation of an object as it appears to the human eye.

51. A protractor is a drawing instrument specifically designed to measure angles. It typically consists of a semicircular or circular tool with degree markings. By aligning the protractor with the lines or edges on a drawing, you can accurately measure and draw angles.

52. A compass is a drawing instrument that consists of two adjustable arms joined at a pivot point. One arm holds a pencil or pen, while the other arm has a pointed end. By adjusting the arms, you can create circles or arcs of various sizes by rotating the compass around the pivot point while keeping the pointed end fixed.

53. A T-square is a drawing instrument with a long, straightedge and a perpendicular crosspiece. It is used to draw straight horizontal and vertical lines. By aligning the T-square's straightedge with the drawing surface's edge, you can create parallel lines by sliding the T-square along the edge while drawing.

54. A French curve is a flexible, curved tool made of plastic or metal. It is used to draw smooth and irregular curves in freehand drawing. The French curve comes in various shapes, allowing artists and designers to create a wide range of curved lines by tracing along its edges.

55. As mentioned earlier, a T-square is the drawing instrument used to draw straight horizontal and vertical lines. Its straightedge is aligned with the drawing surface's edge to ensure precise and straight lines are drawn at right angles.

56. A protractor is a drawing instrument specifically designed to measure angles. It typically consists of a semicircular or circular tool with degree markings. By aligning the protractor with the lines or edges on a drawing, you can accurately measure and draw angles.

57. A compass is a drawing instrument that consists of two adjustable arms joined at a pivot point. One arm holds a pencil or pen, while the other arm has a pointed end. By adjusting the arms, you can create circles or arcs of various sizes by rotating the compass around the pivot point while keeping the pointed end fixed.

58. A T-square is a drawing instrument with a long, straightedge and a perpendicular crosspiece. It is used to draw straight horizontal and vertical lines. By aligning the T-square's straightedge with the drawing surface's edge, you can create parallel lines by sliding the T-square along the edge while drawing.

59. A French curve is a flexible, curved tool made of plastic or metal. It is used to draw smooth and irregular curves in freehand drawing. The French curve comes in various shapes, allowing artists and designers to create a wide range of curved lines by tracing along its edges.

60. As mentioned earlier, a T-square is the drawing instrument used to draw straight horizontal and vertical lines. Its straightedge is aligned with the drawing surface's edge to ensure precise and straight lines are drawn at right angles.

61. A smudge stick, also known as a blending stump or tortillon, is a cylindrical tool made of tightly rolled paper or soft fabric. It is used to create shading and blending effects in pencil drawings. By gently rubbing the smudge stick over graphite or charcoal, artists can achieve smooth transitions and gradients.

62. An eraser is a drawing instrument used to remove unwanted graphite or charcoal marks from the drawing surface. It is available in various types, including kneaded erasers, vinyl erasers, and electric erasers. Erasers allow artists to correct mistakes or lighten areas of their drawings.

63. A divider is a drawing instrument with two pointed legs joined by a pivot. It is used to measure and transfer proportions accurately in drawings. By adjusting the distance between the legs and then transferring that measurement elsewhere on the drawing, artists can ensure consistent proportions.

64. A T-square is a drawing instrument consisting of a long, straightedge with a perpendicular crosspiece. It is primarily used to draw straight horizontal and vertical lines, but it can also be used to create precise geometric shapes such as squares and rectangles by aligning the T-square's straightedge with the drawing surface's edges.

65. As mentioned earlier, a French curve is a flexible, curved tool used to draw smooth and irregular curves. It is particularly useful for creating flowing curves in freehand drawing or when precision is required for repetitive curves.

66. Object lines are thick, continuous lines used to represent visible edges or outlines of an object in an engineering drawing. They define the shape and form of the object being represented.

67. Hidden lines are used to represent edges or features that are not visible in the current view but are necessary for a complete understanding of the object. They are typically drawn using a series of short dashes.

68. Centerlines are thin, alternating long and short dashes used to indicate the axis of symmetry or centerline of a symmetrical object. They are used to show the location of holes, slots, or other features that are symmetrical about a centerline.

69. Extension lines are thin lines used to indicate the dimension of a feature or the distance between two points. They extend from the object line to the dimension line and are typically terminated with an arrowhead.

70. Phantom lines are used to represent alternate positions of a moving part in an assembly drawing. They are drawn using long dashes alternating with pairs of short dashes and are used to indicate the possible positions of a component when it is in different operating modes or configurations.

71. Cutting plane lines are used to indicate the imaginary line along which a section view is cut. They are typically represented as a series of short dashes and two long dashes.

72. Break lines are used to indicate a change in the surface contour or shape of an object in an engineering drawing. They consist of a series of zigzag lines and are used to shorten the length of a long continuous line without changing its basic meaning.

73. Section lines are used to represent an imaginary line indicating the path of a cutting plane in a sectional view. They consist of evenly spaced thin lines and are used to distinguish the material that has been cut by the cutting plane.

74. Object lines are used to indicate the limit or boundary of a part or object in an engineering drawing. They are thick, continuous lines that define the shape and form of the object being represented.

75. Leader lines are used to show the path of motion or movement in a mechanical drawing. They consist of a thin solid line with an arrowhead and are typically used to connect notes, dimensions, or other annotations to specific features on the drawing.

76. Architectural scales are commonly used to represent large objects or structures, such as buildings or bridges. They typically use ratios like 1:50 or 1:100, where one unit on the drawing represents 50 or 100 units in real life.

77. Engineering scales are typically used in mechanical engineering drawings to represent precise measurements and dimensions. They use ratios such as 1:10 or 1:20, where one unit on the drawing represents 10 or 20 units in real life.

78. Metric scales are commonly used in international standards and represent measurements in millimeters. They use ratios such as 1:100 or 1:1000, where one unit on the drawing represents 100 or 1000 units in real life.

79. Isometric scales are used to represent three-dimensional objects and show all three principal axes in equal measure. They are often used in technical illustrations or drawings where a 3D representation is required.

80. Full-scale is used to represent objects or structures in terms of their actual size. It means that one unit on the drawing represents one unit in real life, without any scaling factor.

81. In the given scenario, the scale 1/8" = 1' would be appropriate. This means that one-eighth of an inch on the drawing represents one foot in real life.

82. In the given scenario, the scale 1:100 would be suitable. This means that one unit on the drawing represents 100 units in real life, so 1 cm on the drawing would represent 2 mm

83. Topographic scales are commonly used in civil engineering drawings to represent large areas, such as maps or site plans. They typically use ratios like 1:10,000 or 1:50,000, where one unit on the drawing represents 10,000 or 50,000 units in real life.

84. Reduced scale is used to represent objects or structures at a reduced size, where the ratio is less than 1. It means that the drawing is smaller than the actual size, and the dimensions are proportionally reduced.

85. Architectural scales are typically used in architectural drawings to represent the overall layout of a building or a floor plan. They use ratios such as 1/8" = 1' or 1/4" = 1', where one unit on the drawing represents a specific length in real life.

86. In the given scenario, the scale 1:50 would be appropriate for representing a large machine or equipment. This means that one unit on the drawing represents 50 units in real life, allowing for a detailed representation.

87. Electrical scales are commonly used in electrical engineering drawings to represent wiring diagrams or circuit layouts. They are specialized scales that allow for accurate representation of electrical components and connections.

88. In the given scenario, the scale 1:10 would be suitable for representing a detailed part or component. This means that one unit on the drawing represents 10 units in real life, allowing for a larger and more detailed representation.

89. In the given scenario, the scale 1:50 would be appropriate for representing a site plan. This means that one unit on the drawing represents 50 units in real life, allowing for a comprehensive representation of the site and its features.

90. Assembly scales are commonly used in mechanical engineering drawings to represent assembly drawings or exploded views. These scales are specific to the assembly or exploded view and may vary based on the level of detail required.

91. Cartographic scales are typically used in surveying and mapping to represent large areas, such as cities or regions. These scales are designed to accurately represent geographical features and distances.

92. In the given scenario, the scale 1:1000 would be suitable for representing a small electronic component with intricate details. This means that one unit on the drawing represents 1000 units in real life, allowing for a highly detailed and accurate representation.

93. ISO is responsible for developing and maintaining international drawing standards, such as ISO 128 for technical drawings.

94. Object lines in engineering drawings are typically represented using a medium line weight, which ensures clear visibility without excessive boldness.

95. Millimeters are commonly used as the unit of measurement for dimensions in engineering drawings, especially in international standards.

96. GD&T (Geometric Dimensioning and Tolerancing) is a system used to specify and control the geometric features of a part in engineering drawings.

97. Orthographic projection is commonly used in engineering drawings to represent three-dimensional objects accurately. It uses multiple views (top, front, side) to show different aspects of the object.

98. Dimension lines are used to indicate the measurements or dimensions in engineering drawings. They are usually represented using a thin, continuous line.

99. ANSI B (11" x 17") is a commonly used standard format for engineering drawings in the United States, especially for smaller-sized drawings.

100. The roughness symbol (∇) is used to indicate surface finish requirements on an engineering drawing, providing information about the desired texture or smoothness of a surface.

101. Phantom lines are used to represent hidden or invisible edges, such as edges obscured by other objects or features, in engineering drawings.

102. The front view is typically used to represent an object as it would be seen by looking directly at one of its sides in engineering drawings. It provides the most detailed and accurate representation of the object's shape and features from a specific orientation.

103. The standard size of an A4 drawing sheet is 210 mm × 297 mm. A4 is a widely used size for drawings, documents, and printouts.

104. The type of drawing sheet commonly used for architectural plans is A1. A1 sheets are larger than A4 and provide ample space for detailed architectural drawings.

105. The type of drawing sheet orientation that is NOT commonly used is Square. Drawing sheets are typically oriented in either landscape (wider than tall) or portrait (taller than wide) format.

106. The purpose of a title block on a drawing sheet is the title block contains important information about the drawing, such as the type of drawing, scale used, drafter's name, date, etc.

107. The type of line typically used to indicate the visible edges of an object in a drawing is Solid line. Solid lines are used to represent visible lines, while dashed or dotted lines are used for hidden or construction lines.

108. The purpose of drawing border lines on a drawing sheet is All the given options. Drawing border lines frame the drawing, provide a clean edge, and establish the drawing's boundary.

109. The material that is NOT a common drawing sheet material is Aluminum. Drawing sheets are commonly made of paper, vellum (a translucent material), or tracing cloth.

110. The term "scale" refers to the size of the drawing relative to the actual object. Scale indicates the ratio between the dimensions of the drawing and the actual object it represents.

111. The largest size of drawing sheet is A0. A0 sheets are the largest in the A-series of drawing sheet sizes, with dimensions of 841 mm × 1189 mm.

112. The common units of measurement used on drawing sheets are all the given options. Only depending on the region and industry, measurements can be expressed in meters, centimeters, or inches on drawing sheets.

113. Technical lettering in engineering drawing is used to convey essential details, such as labels, dimensions, notes, and other textual information, in a clear and legible manner.

114. Gothic lettering is widely used in engineering drawing due to its clear, uniform strokes and easy readability.

115. Uppercase letters are commonly used for dimensions, notes, and labels in engineering drawing because they provide clarity and distinction in the text.

116. In engineering drawing, the recommended letter height for uppercase letters is often around 1/4 inch (6.35 mm). This size ensures legibility without compromising the available drawing space.

117. Mechanical or digital lettering is recommended for accuracy. While hand-lettering is still common, mechanical or digital lettering methods are often recommended in engineering drawing to ensure precise and consistent letterforms

118. Guidelines are used in technical lettering to ensure consistent letter height, maintain uniform spacing between letters, and align the baseline of the letters. This helps in creating neat and well-organized lettering.

119. Technical pens, known for their consistent ink flow and fine lines, are commonly used for technical lettering in engineering drawing. They allow for precise and controlled strokes.

120. The correct answer is (b) Horizontal strokes, vertical strokes, and diagonal strokes. When creating uppercase letters, it is generally recommended to start with horizontal strokes, followed by vertical strokes, and then diagonal strokes. This stroke order helps maintain consistent letterforms and uniformity.

121. Helvetica is a widely used font for technical lettering in engineering drawings due to its simplicity, legibility, and uniform stroke width.

122. The 6 mm height ensures that the letters are clear and readable while allowing sufficient space for annotations and dimensions.

123. The correct answer is (b) Curved line, horizontal line, vertical line. This sequence accurately represents the shape of the letter "a" in most technical lettering styles.

124. The correct answer is (a) Equal to the width of a character. This spacing ensures proper readability and consistency throughout the text.

125. Stacked fractions are easier to read and interpret compared to other formats such as decimal format with a slash or parentheses.

126. Applying a slightly heavier stroke to certain letters or words helps to make them stand out without compromising overall legibility.

127. The statement is true. In technical lettering, maintaining a consistent stroke width throughout the text is crucial for uniformity and professional appearance.

128. The correct order for drawing a number '9' Curved line, vertical line, curved line. This sequence accurately represents the shape of the number "9" in most technical lettering styles.

129. Technical lettering focuses on clarity, legibility, and precision rather than artistic embellishments.

130. The correct answer is (c) Crossing out the error and writing the correct letter above or beside it. This approach ensures that the correct information is clearly conveyed and avoids confusion caused by erasures or correction fluid.

131. In engineering drawings, a hole is typically represented by a circle with specific dimensions indicating its diameter.

132. Bolt or screw heads are often represented by hexagons in engineering drawings, as they are typically designed to be tightened or loosened using a hexagonal wrench or socket.

133. When looking at a cylindrical object from a cross-sectional view, such as cutting it in half, the resulting shape is a circle.

134. Gears are typically represented by circles in engineering drawings, with additional details such as teeth and dimensions to indicate their specific design.

135. A fillet or rounded corner is represented by an arc in engineering drawings. The arc connects the straight lines of the intersecting surfaces, creating a smooth transition.

136. Dimension lines in engineering drawings are commonly represented by dotted lines. They indicate the distance or size of an object or feature.

137. Electrical connectors or terminals are often represented by circles in engineering drawings. The specific details and symbols within the circle indicate the type and characteristics of the connector.

138. A chamfer or beveled edge is represented by a line segment in engineering drawings. The line is typically drawn at an angle to indicate the specific bevel.

139. A weld is represented by a specific symbol in engineering drawings, typically consisting of a triangle or other shapes with specific details indicating the type and characteristics of the weld.

140. Hidden lines, which represent features that are not visible from a particular view, are typically represented by dashed lines in engineering drawings. The dashed lines help differentiate them from visible lines.

141. A closed curve with no straight sides. A circle is a geometric shape that consists of all points in a plane that are equidistant from a fixed center point. It is a curved shape with no straight sides.

142. The circumference of a circle is calculated by multiplying the diameter (d) of the circle by π (pi). So, $C = \pi d$.

143. A regular polygon is a polygon with equal-length sides and equal internal angles. A pentagon is a polygon with five sides, and if it is regular, then all five sides and angles are equal.

144. A cube is a three-dimensional shape with six rectangular faces, all of which are congruent squares.

145. An isosceles triangle is a triangle with at least two sides of equal length. The angles opposite the equal sides are also equal.

146. The area of a rectangle is calculated by multiplying the length (l) of one side by the width (w) of the rectangle $A = l \times w$.

147. Opposite sides are parallel and equal in length. A parallelogram is a four-sided polygons in which opposite sides are parallel and equal in length.

148. A cone is a three-dimensional shape with a circular base and a curved surface that tapers to a point called the apex.

149. It has two pairs of parallel sides. A trapezoid is a quadrilateral with at least one pair of parallel sides.

150. The volume of a sphere is calculated by multiplying 4/3π (pi) by the cube of the radius (r). The correct answer is (c) $V = 4/3\pi r^3$.

151. A filled triangle symbol is used to represent a datum feature. Datum features are reference surfaces or points used in the GD&T (Geometric Dimensioning and Tolerancing) system to establish a datum reference frame for dimensional control.

152. The circle with two parallel lines passing through its center represents concentricity. Concentricity is a GD&T tolerance that ensures the axis of a cylindrical feature is centered and aligned with a datum axis.

153. An 'R' with a circle around it represents the radius of a curved feature on the drawing. It indicates the dimension of the circular arc.

154. A perpendicular line with two small outward arrows at its end represents perpendicularity. It shows that the referenced surface or line is perpendicular to the datum reference.

155. A diamond symbol indicates the dimension origin point on the drawing, from which other measurements are taken. It is usually used as a reference point for locating other features.

156. A square symbol with an 'A' inside represents a chamfer. It indicates that the specified edges or corners should be beveled or rounded.

157. An 'M' with a circle around it represents the maximum material condition. It is used in GD&T to indicate that the referenced feature has the maximum amount of material within its tolerance zone.

158. A straight line with one long arrow and one short arrow indicates the profile of a surface. It represents the allowable variations in the shape of the surface within specified tolerances.

159. A series of evenly spaced short lines, often referred to as "finish marks," represents surface roughness. They provide information about the surface texture and the manufacturing process required for the specific part.

160. An 'X' symbol inside a circle indicates a spotface. A spotface is a flat, machined surface around a hole to provide a consistent seating area for fasteners.

Please note that engineering drawing practices may vary slightly depending on the standards and conventions followed in different countries and industries. The explanations provided above are based on general practices.

CHAPTER 2

Units and Measurements

PHYSICAL QUANTITIES

All the quantities in terms of which laws of physics can be expressed, described and can be measured directly or indirectly, caused physical quantities.

Physical quantities are classified as follows :

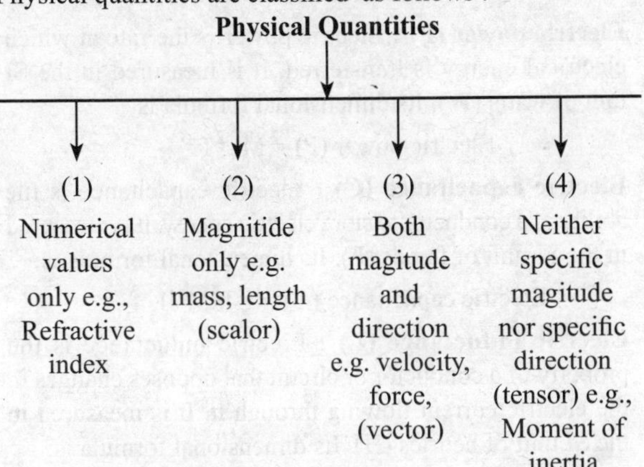

Its mainly two types.

Fundamental Quantity

Types of physical quantities :

Some fundamental quantities are given below.

S. No.	Quantity	SI Unit	Symbol
(i)	Length	metre	m
(ii)	Mass	kilogram	kg
(iii)	Time	second	s
(iv)	Electric current	ampere	A
(v)	Thermodynamic temperature	kelvin	K
(vi)	amount of substance	mole	mol
(vii)	Luminous intensity	candela	cd

Two supplementary units namely plane angle and solid angle are also defined. Their units are radian (rad) and steradian (st) respectively.

- To measure a physical quantity we need some standard, called units.
- Magnitude of physical quantity = Numerical value × System of units in which physical quantity is to be measured. (nu).

Derived unit : The physical quantities where unit can be derived from fundamental unit is called derived unit and quantities is said to be derived physical quantities e.g., force, young's modulum etc.

Dimensional equation and Dimensional formulae

Dimensional equations:

When a dimensional formula is equated to its physical quantity then the equation is called dimensional equation.

A dimensional equation is an equation that shows the relationship between the dimensions of physical quantities. It is a way of expressing the units of a physical quantity in terms of the fundamental units of measurement.

For example, the dimensional equation for velocity is:

$$[v] = [L]\,[T]^{-1}$$

This means that velocity is measured in units of length (L) divided by units of time (T). In other words, velocity has the dimensions of length per time.

Dimensional equation of force:

The dimensional equation of force can be derived from the formula for force,

which is F = m*a. In this formula, F is the force, m is the mass, and a is the acceleration.

The dimension of mass is M, the dimension of length is L, and the dimension of time is T. Therefore, the dimension of m is M, the dimension of a is T^{-2}, and the dimension of F is MLT^{-2}. So the dimensional equation of force is $M^1\,L^1\,T^{-2}$.

Dimensional equation of energy :

By, E = W = force* displacement.

The dimensional equation of energy (E) is $[M^1\,L^1T^{-2}]\,[L^1] = M^1\,L^2\,T^{-2}$. This means that energy is a quantity that has the dimensions of mass, length, and time, and that it is measured in units of Joules (J). One Joule is equal to one kilogram-meter squared per second squared ($kg\text{-}m^2/s^2$). The kinetic energy of an object is given by the formula KE = 1/2 mv^2, where KE is the kinetic energy, m is the mass of the object, and v is the velocity of the object. The dimension of kinetic energy is $M^1\,L^2\,T^{-2}$.

Dimensions in heat quantities :

Dimensions in heat quantities can be expressed in terms of the fundamental dimensions of mass, length, and time, denoted by M, L, and T, respectively. Here are some common heat quantities and their dimensional formulas:

1. **Heat (Q) :** Heat is a form of energy that is transferred between objects due to a temperature difference. Its dimensional formula is :

   Heat (Q) = MLT^{-2}

2. **Specific heat capacity (c) :** Specific heat capacity is the amount of heat energy required to raise the temperature of one unit mass of a substance by one degree Celsius or Kelvin. Its dimensional formula is :

   Specific heat capacity (c) = $ML^{-2}T^{-2}K^{-1}$

3. **Latent heat of fusion (L_f) :** Latent heat of fusion is the amount of heat energy required to change one gram of a solid substance to its liquid state at its melting point. Its dimensional formula is:

   Latent heat of fusion (L_f) = $ML^{-2}T^{-1}K^{-1}$

4. **Latent heat of vaporization (L_v) :** Latent heat of vaporization is the amount of heat energy required to change one gram of a liquid substance to its vapor state at its boiling point. Its dimensional formula is :

   Latent heat of vaporization (L_v) = $ML^{-2}T^{-1}K^{-1}$

5. **Thermal conductivity (k) :** Thermal conductivity is the ability of a material to conduct heat. It is defined as the amount of heat energy flowing through a unit area of a material per unit time per unit temperature gradient. Its dimensional formula is :

   Thermal conductivity (k) = $ML^{-2}T^{-3}K^{-1}$

6. **Heat transfer coefficient (h) :** Heat transfer coefficient is a measure of the efficiency of heat transfer between a fluid and a solid surface. Its dimensional formula is:

   Heat transfer coefficient (h) = $ML^{-2}T^{-3}K^{-1}$

7. **Heat flux (q) :** Heat flux is the rate of heat transfer per unit area. Its dimensional formula is:

   Heat flux (q) = $ML^{-2}T^{-3}K^{-1}$

Dimensions in electricity quantities:

Dimensions in electricity quantities can be expressed in terms of the fundamental dimensions of mass, length, and time, denoted by M, L, and T, respectively. Here are some common electrical quantities and their dimensional formulas:

1. **Electric charge (Q) :** Electric charge is a fundamental property of matter that determines its electromagnetic interactions. It is measured in the SI unit of coulombs (C). Its dimensional formula is:

   Electric charge (Q) = IT

   Where I represents electric current and T represents time.

2. **Electric current (I) :** Electric current is the flow of electric charge through a conductor. It is measured in the SI unit of amperes (A). Its dimensional formula is :

   Electric current (I) = CT^{-1}

3. **Electric potential (V) :** Electric potential is the electrical energy per unit charge. It is measured in the SI unit of volts (V). Its dimensional formula is:

   Electric potential (V) = $ML^{2}I^{-1}T^{-3}$

4. **Electric field (E) :** Electric field is the force per unit charge experienced by a small charged particle in the vicinity of other charged particles or electric fields. It is measured in the SI unit of volts per meter (V/m). Its dimensional formula is:

   Electric field (E) = $ML^{-2}I^{-3}T^{-1}$

5. **Electric resistance (R) :** Electric resistance is the opposition to the flow of electric current in a conductor. It is measured in the SI unit of ohms (Ω). Its dimensional formula is:

   Electric resistance (R) = $ML^{2}I^{-2}T^{-3}$

6. **Electric power (P) :** Electric power is the rate at which electrical energy is transferred. It is measured in the SI unit of watts (W). Its dimensional formula is:

   Electric power (P) = $ML^{2}T^{-3}$

7. **Electric capacitance (C) :** Electric capacitance is the ability of a conductor to store electric energy. It is measured in the SI unit of farads (F). Its dimensional formula is:

   Electric capacitance (C) = $I^{2}T^{4}M^{-1}L^{-2}$

8. **Electric inductance (L) :** Electric inductance is the property of a conductor or circuit that opposes changes in the electric current flowing through it. It is measured in the SI unit of henries (H). Its dimensional formula is:

   Electric inductance (L) = $ML^{2}I^{-2}T^{-2}$

Dimensions of magnetic quantities:

Dimensions in magnetic quantities can be expressed in terms of the fundamental dimensions of mass, length, and time, denoted by M, L, and T, respectively. Here are some common magnetic quantities and their dimensional formulas:

1. **Magnetic field (B) :** The magnetic field is a vector quantity that describes the force exerted on a moving charged particle. Its SI unit is the tesla (T). The dimensional formula for the magnetic field is:

   Magnetic field (B) = $MLT^{-1}C^{-1}$

2. **Magnetic flux (Φ) :** Magnetic flux is the amount of magnetic field passing through a surface. Its SI unit is the weber (Wb). The dimensional formula for magnetic flux is:

   Magnetic flux (Φ) = $MLT^{-1}C^{-1}L^{2}$

3. **Magnetomotive force (MMF) :** Magnetomotive force is a measure of the ability of a source to produce a magnetic field. Its SI unit is the ampere-turn (AT). The dimensional formula for magnetomotive force is:

   Magnetomotive force (MMF) = IT

4. **Magnetic permeability (μ):** Magnetic permeability is a measure of the ability of a material to be magnetized. Its SI unit is the henry per meter (H/m). The dimensional formula for magnetic permeability is :

$$\text{Magnetic permeability } (\mu) = MLT^{-2}I^{-1}$$

5. **Magnetic reluctance (R_m) :** Magnetic reluctance is a measure of the opposition to magnetic field lines passing through a material. Its SI unit is the ampere-turn per weber (AT/Wb). The dimensional formula for magnetic reluctance is:

$$\text{Magnetic reluctance } (R\_m) = T^2I$$

6. **Magnetic induction (B) :** Magnetic induction is the total magnetic field, including both the external magnetic field and the field produced by magnetization of the material. Its SI unit is the tesla (T). The dimensional formula for magnetic induction is:

$$\text{Magnetic induction } (B) = MLT^{-1}C^{-1}$$

7. **Magnetization (M) :** Magnetization is a measure of the alignment of magnetic moments within a material. Its SI unit is the ampere per meter (A/m). The dimensional formula for magnetization is:

$$\text{Magnetization } (M) = ITL^{-3}$$

8. **Magnetic susceptibility (χ_m):** Magnetic susceptibility is a measure of the ease with which a material can be magnetized. It is a dimensionless quantity. The dimensional formula for magnetic susceptibility is:

$$\text{Magnetic susceptibility } (\chi\_m) = L^3$$

Dimensionless quantity:

A dimensionless quantity is a quantity to which no physical dimension is assigned. Dimensionless quantities are widely used in many fields, such as mathematics, physics, chemistry, engineering, and economics.

Examples of dimensionless quantities include :

- The ratio of two lengths. For example, the aspect ratio of a rectangle is the ratio of its length to its width.
- The ratio of two areas. For example, the coverage ratio of a paint is the ratio of the area it covers to the area of the surface it is applied to.
- The ratio of two volumes. For example, the volume fraction of a solution is the ratio of the volume of one component of the solution to the total volume of the solution.

Dimensionless quantities can also be ratios of physical quantities that have different dimensions. For example, the Reynolds number is the ratio of the inertial forces to the viscous forces in a fluid. It is a dimensionless quantity that is used to characterize the flow of fluids.

Dimensionless quantities are useful because they are independent of the system of units that is used. This means that they can be compared directly, even if the measurements were made in different units. For example, the aspect ratio of a rectangle is the same, regardless of whether it is measured in meters, centimeters, or inches.

Another advantage of dimensionless quantities is that they can be used to simplify complex equations. For example, the Navier-Stokes equations, which describe the motion of fluids, can be simplified by introducing dimensionless variables. This can make it easier to solve the equations and to understand the behavior of fluids.

Overall, dimensionless quantities are a powerful tool that can be used to solve problems in a wide variety of fields.

Here are some additional examples of dimensionless quantities:

- The angle between two lines.
- The frequency of a wave.
- The efficiency of a machine.
- The probability of an event occurring.
- The correlation coefficient between two variables.

Dimensionless quantity:

A dimensionless quantity is a quantity to which no physical dimension is assigned. Dimensionless quantities can be ratios of two physical quantities that have different dimensions. For example, the Reynolds number is the ratio of the inertial forces to the viscous forces in a fluid. It is a dimensionless quantity that is used to characterize the flow of fluids.

Dimensionless quantities are often used to measure the efficiency of a process or the similarity between two objects. For example, the Froude number is a dimensionless quantity that is used to measure the hydrodynamic similarity of two objects.

Dimensionless quantities are also often used to define physical constants. For example, the fine-structure constant is a dimensionless quantity that is defined as the ratio of two fundamental physical constants: the electric charge and the Planck constant.

Dimensionless quantities are a powerful tool that can be used to solve problems in a wide variety of fields. They are often used to simplify complex equations and to make it easier to compare different systems.

Here are some examples of dimensionless quantities :

- The aspect ratio of a rectangle.
- The coverage ratio of paint.
- The volume fraction of a solution.
- The Reynolds number.
- The Froude number.
- The fine-structure constant.
- The angle between two lines.
- The frequency of a wave.
- The efficiency of a machine.
- The probability of an event occurring.
- The correlation coefficient between two variables.

Principle of homogeneity :

The principle of homogeneity states that the dimensions of all the terms in an equation must be the same. This principle is used to check the validity of physical equations and to convert units.

For example, in the equation F = ma, where F is force, m is mass, and a is acceleration, the dimension of all the terms must be the same. The dimension of force is MLT^{-2}, the dimension of mass is M, and the dimension of acceleration is LT^{-2}. Therefore, the equation F = ma is dimensionally correct.

The principle of homogeneity can also be used to convert units. For example, if we want to convert the velocity of an object from meters per second to kilometers per hour, we can use the following equation:

v = frac{d}/{t}

Where, v is the velocity, d is the distance traveled, and t is the time.

The dimension of velocity is LT^{-1}, the dimension of distance is L, and the dimension of time is T.

Therefore, the equation v = d/t, is a dimensionally correct.

The principle of homogeneity is a fundamental principle of physics. It is used to ensure that the laws of physics are consistent and to make it easier to solve problems.

Application of dimensional analysis:

Dimensional analysis is a powerful technique in physics that is used to derive relationships between physical quantities and to check the consistency of dimensional equations. It is based on the principle that physical quantities with the same dimensions can be added, subtracted, or multiplied.

Here are some of the applications of dimensional analysis :

- Deriving relationships between physical quantities. For example, dimensional analysis can be used to derive the relationship between the acceleration of a falling object and its mass and time of flight.
- Checking the consistency of dimensional equations. For example, dimensional analysis can be used to check whether the units of an equation are consistent. This is important because an equation with inconsistent units is meaningless.
- Converting units. For example, dimensional analysis can be used to convert units from one system to another. This is useful for solving problems in physics and engineering.
- Estimating values of physical quantities. For example, dimensional analysis can be used to estimate the value of a physical quantity that is difficult to measure directly.
- Understanding the nature of physical quantities. For example, dimensional analysis can be used to understand the relationship between the dimensions of a physical quantity and its physical properties.

Dimensional analysis is a valuable tool for physicists and engineers. It is a simple technique that can be used to solve a wide variety of problems.

Limitation of dimensional analysis:

Dimensional analysis is a powerful tool for understanding the relationships between physical quantities. However, it is important to be aware of its limitations.

1. **Cannot determine dimensionless constants :** Dimensional analysis is unable to determine the numerical values of dimensionless constants in an equation. For example, it can be used to determine that the period of oscillation of a pendulum is proportional to the square root of its length, but it cannot determine the exact value of the constant of proportionality.
2. **Cannot be used to derive relations with more than one term on one side :** Dimensional analysis is only able to derive relations between quantities that have the same dimensions. For example, it can be used to determine that the velocity of an object is proportional to the distance it travels divided by the time it takes to travel that distance, but it cannot be used to derive a relation between the velocity of an object, the force acting on it, and its mass.
3. **Cannot be used to derive relations with trigonometric functions, exponential functions, or logarithmic functions :** Dimensional analysis is only able to derive relations between quantities that can be expressed as products of powers of fundamental dimensions. For example, it can be used to determine that the kinetic energy of an object is proportional to its mass times its velocity squared, but it cannot be used to derive a relation between the kinetic energy of an object, its mass, and its velocity that includes a trigonometric function, exponential function, or logarithmic function.
4. **Cannot determine the vector vs scalar nature of a quantity :** Dimensional analysis can only determine the dimensions of a quantity, not whether it is a scalar or a vector. For example, it can determine that the velocity of an object has dimensions of length divided by time, but it cannot determine whether the velocity of an object is a scalar or a vector.
5. **Cannot determine the specific form of a relation :** Dimensional analysis can only determine the general form of a relation between quantities, not the specific form of the relation. For example, it can determine that the period of oscillation of a pendulum is proportional to the square root of its length, but it cannot determine the exact form of the proportionality constant.

Dimensions of a physical quantity are the powers to which the fundamental quantities must be raised to represent the given physical quantity.

For example,

$$\text{Density} = \frac{\text{mass}}{\text{volume}} = \frac{[M]}{[L^3]} = [ML^{-3}]$$

MEASUREMENT

(i) Least count of vernier callipers

= [value of 1 part of main scale (s)] – [value of 1 part of vernier scale (v)]

$\Rightarrow$ least count of vernier callipers = 1 MSD – 1 VSD

where MSD = Main Scale Division

VSD = Vernier Scale Division

(ii) Least count

$$= \frac{\text{Value of 1 part on main scale}(s)}{\text{Number of parts on vernier scale } (n)}$$

$$1 \text{ VSD} = \frac{9}{10} \text{ MSD} = 0.9 \text{ mm}$$

$$\text{VC} = 1 \text{ MSD} - 1 \text{ VSD}$$
$$= 1 \text{ mm} - 0.9 \text{ mm}$$
$$= 0.1 \text{ mm}$$
$$= 0.01 \text{ cm}$$

(iii) Least count of screw gauge

$$= \frac{\text{Pitch } (p)}{\text{No. of division on circular path } (n)}$$

If pitch is 1 mm and there are 100 divisions on circular scale then

$$\text{LC} = \frac{1\text{mm}}{100} = 0.01 \text{ mm} = 0.001 \text{ cm} = 1 \mu\text{m}.$$

- Smaller the least count, higher is the accuracy of measurement.
- Larger the number of significant figures after the decimal in a measurement, higher is the accuracy of measurement.
- Significant figures retained after mathematical operations (like addition, subtraction, multiplication and division) should be equal to the minimum, significant figures involved in any physical quantity in the given operation.

Measurement of large distance :

Large distances, such as the distances between planets, stars, and galaxies, are measured using a variety of methods, including :

- **Parallax method :** This method uses the apparent shift in the position of an object when viewed from two different locations. The parallax angle is the angle between the two lines of sight to the object. The parallax angle is inversely proportional to the distance to the object, so the larger the parallax angle, the closer the object. The parallax method is used to measure the distances to nearby stars.
- **Triangulation :** This method uses the angles between three known points to determine the distance to a fourth point. Triangulation is used to measure the distances to distant stars and galaxies.
- **Standard candles :** These are objects with known brightness, such as certain types of stars. By comparing the brightness of a standard candle to its apparent brightness, astronomers can determine its distance.
- **Redshift :** This is the shift in the wavelength of light from an object due to the object's motion away from the observer. The greater the redshift, the faster the object is moving away and the further away it is. Redshift is used to measure the distances to distant galaxies.

The units used to measure large distances include:

- **Astronomical unit (AU) :** The average distance between the Earth and the Sun (about 93 million miles).
- **Light-year :** The distance that light travels in one year (about 6 trillion miles).
- **Parsec (pc) :** A unit of distance used to measure distances to astronomical objects outside the solar system. One parsec is about 3.26 light-years.

Accuracy, precision, and errors in measurement :

Accuracy, precision, and errors in measurement are three important concepts in science and engineering. They are all related to the quality of a measurement.

Accuracy is how close a measured value is to the true value of the quantity being measured. It is a measure of how systematic the errors are in a measurement.

Precision is how close repeated measurements of the same quantity are to each other. It is a measure of how random the errors are in a measurement.

Errors in measurement are the differences between the measured value and the true value of the quantity being measured. They can be caused by a variety of factors, such as the limitations of the measuring instrument, environmental conditions, and human error.

Combination of errors :

The combination of errors in measurement is a fundamental aspect of scientific experimentation. It is important to understand how errors are combined in order to make accurate and reliable measurements.

There are two main types of errors in measurement: random errors and systematic errors. Random errors are caused by factors that are beyond the control of the experimenter, such as variations in the environment or fluctuations in the instrument. Systematic errors are caused by factors that are within the control of the experimenter, such as improper calibration of the instrument or a mistake in the experimental procedure.

The combination of errors in measurement depends on the type of operation being performed. For example, the combination of errors in addition and subtraction is different from the combination of errors in multiplication and division.

Here are the rules for combining errors in measurement :

- For addition and subtraction, the absolute errors are added.
- For multiplication and division, the relative errors are added.
- For a quantity raised to a power, the relative error is multiplied by the power.

For example, if you measure the length of a box to be 10.0 cm with an error of 0.1 cm, and you measure the width of the box to be 5.0 cm with an error of 0.05 cm, then the area of the box is 50.0 cm^2 with an error of 0.3 cm^2.

The combination of errors in measurement is an important part of data analysis. By understanding how errors are combined, you can make more accurate and reliable conclusions about your data.

Here are some additional tips for combining errors in measurement :

- Always use the same units of measurement when combining errors.
- Be aware of the magnitude of the errors when combining them.
- When possible, use a more precise instrument to reduce the error.

Significant figures:

Significant figures are the digits in a number that are relevant to its accuracy. They are important in scientific measurements because they allow scientists to express the precision of their results.

The number of significant figures in a number depends on the following rules :

- All non-zero digits are significant.
- Zeros between non-zero digits are significant.
- Zeros to the right of the decimal point and to the left of the first non-zero digit are significant if they are written behind a decimal point.
- Zeros to the left of the decimal point and to the right of the last non-zero digit are not significant.

For example, the number 0.00123 has four significant figures: 0, 0, 1, and 2. The number 1200 has four significant figures : 1, 2, 0, and 0. The number 0.00012 has two significant figures: 1 and 2.

Significant figures are important when adding, subtracting, multiplying, and dividing numbers. When performing these operations, the number of significant figures in the result is equal to the smallest number of significant figures in any of the numbers being added, subtracted, multiplied, or divided.

For example, when adding the numbers 1.23 and 0.0012, the result is 1.2312. This number has four significant figures because 0.0012 has only four significant figures.

When multiplying the numbers 2.34 and 1.2, the result is 2.808. This number has three significant figures because 1.2 has only three significant figures.

When dividing the number 12.34 by the number 0.0012, the result is 10290. This number has four significant figures because 0.0012 has only four significant figures.

Significant figures are an important part of scientific measurement and should be used carefully when reporting results.

Rounding off rules of rounding off uncertain digits:

When rounding off numbers, it is important to follow a consistent set of rules to ensure accuracy and consistency. The following are the rules for rounding off uncertain digits:

Rule 1 : If the uncertain digit is less than 5, do not change the preceding digit. For example, 2.34 rounded off to two decimal places is 2.34.

Rule 2 : If the uncertain digit is 5 or greater, add 1 to the preceding digit. For example, 2.35 rounded off to two decimal places is 2.35, and 3.75 rounded off to two decimal places is 3.80.

Rule 3 : If the uncertain digit is 5 and the preceding digit is even, do not change the preceding digit. For example, 2.45 rounded off to two decimal places is 2.45.

Rule 4 : If the uncertain digit is 5 and the preceding digit is odd, add 1 to the preceding digit. For example, 3.45 rounded off to two decimal places is 3.45, and 5.45 rounded off to two decimal places is 5.50.

These rules are essential for maintaining precision and accuracy in calculations and measurements. By following these rules, you can ensure that your results are consistent and reliable.

Errors in Measurement

(i) Let the measured values of a physical quantity be $a_1, a_2, \ldots, a_n$. The arithmetic mean of the values is

$$a_{\text{mean}} = \frac{a_1 + a_2 + \ldots + a_n}{n}$$

(ii) Mean absolute error

$$\Delta a_{\text{mean}} = \frac{|\Delta a_1| + |\Delta a_2| + \ldots + |\Delta a_n|}{n}$$

(iii) Fractional or relative error $= \dfrac{\Delta a_{\text{mean}}}{a_{\text{mean}}}$

(iv) Percentage error $= \dfrac{\Delta a_{\text{mean}}}{a_{\text{mean}}} \times 100$

Errors in some or difference

$$\Delta x = \pm(\Delta a + \Delta b)$$

Errors in product

$$\frac{\Delta x}{x} = \pm\left(\frac{\Delta a}{a} + \frac{\Delta b}{b}\right)$$

Errors in division

$$\frac{\Delta x}{x} = \pm\left(\frac{\Delta a}{a} + \frac{\Delta b}{b}\right)$$

Errors in quantity raised to some power

$$\frac{\Delta x}{x} = \pm\left(n\frac{\Delta a}{a} + m\frac{\Delta b}{b}\right) \text{ where, } x = \frac{a^n}{b^m}$$

Erros's can be classified as follow :

Errors

Based on cause of error	Based on magnitude of error
(1) Systematic error (where causy one known) to us	(1) Absolute error
	(2) Mean absolute error
	(3) Relative error
(2) Random error where causes one not know flous.	(4) Puntage error

So it can be minimixed by taking lange number of obsurvation and taking arithmatic mean of all the observations.

UNITS

A unit of measurement is a definite magnitude of a quantity, defined and adopted by convention or by law that is used as a standard for measurement of the same kind of quantity. Any other quantity of that kind can be expressed as a multiple of the unit of measurement. Units are used to make it possible to compare quantities that are of different magnitudes.

Some important properties of units are:

- **Units must be consistent :** This means that the same unit must be used to measure the same quantity throughout a calculation. For example, if you are measuring the length of a table in meters, you cannot suddenly switch to using centimeters in the middle of the calculation.
- **Units must be accurately defined :** This means that the definition of a unit must be clear and unambiguous. For example, the definition of a meter is "the distance traveled by light in a vacuum in 1/299,792,458 of a second."
- **Units must be reproducible :** This means that the same unit can be reproduced anywhere in the world with the same accuracy. For example, a meter is defined in terms of the speed of light, which is a universal constant.
- **Units must be universally recognized :** This means that the same unit must be accepted and used by scientists and engineers around the world. For example, the SI system of units is the most widely used system of units in the world.

Types of Units :

There are many types of units, including :

- **Base units :** Base units are the fundamental units of a system of units. They are not defined in terms of any other units. For example, the meter, kilogram, second, ampere, Kelvin, candela, and mole are the seven base units of the International System of Units (SI).
- **Derived units :** Derived units are units that are defined in terms of base units. For example, the unit of velocity is meters per second (m/s), which is derived from the base units of meters (m) and seconds (s).
- **SI prefixes :** SI prefixes are used to represent multiples and submultiples of base units. For example, the prefix kilo- (k) represents 1,000, so one kilometer (km) is equal to 1,000 meters (m).
- **Non-SI units :** Non-SI units are units that are not part of the SI system. Some examples of non-SI units include the inch, pound, and degree Fahrenheit.
- **Natural units :** Natural units are units that are based on fundamental constants of nature. For example, the unit of time in natural units is the Planck time, which is the time it takes for light to travel one Planck length.

Units of Some Physical Quantities in Different Systems

	Physical quantity	System		
		CGS	**MKS**	**FPS**
Fundamental	Length Mass Time	cm g s	m kg s	ft lb s
Derived	Four power impulse	N J/S N-s		

Some Practical Units are

(i) 1 fermi = 1 fm = 10^{-15} m

(ii) 1 X-ray unit = 1 XU = 10^{-13} m

(iii) 1 angstrom = 1Å = 10^{-10} m

(iv) 1 micron = 1 μm = 10^{-6} m

(v) 1 astronomical unit = 1 AU = 1.49×10^{11} m

[Average distance between sun and earth *i.e.*, radius of earth's orbit]

(vi) 1 light year = 1 ly = 9.46×10^{15} m

[distance that light travels in 1 year in vacuum]

(vii) 1 parsec = 1 pc = 3.08×10^{16} m = 3.26 light year

[The distance at which a star subtends an angle of parallex of 1 sec at an arc of 1 AU]

Objective Type Questions

1. An experiment measures quantities a, b and c and x is calculated from the formula

$X = \frac{ab^2}{c^3}$

If the percentage error in a, b and c are ± 1% ± 3% and ± 2% respectively. The percentage error in X will be

(a) ± 13% (b) ± 7%
(c) ± 4% (d) ± 1%

2. If radius of the sphere is (5.3 ± 0.1) cm. Then percentage error in its volume will be

(a) $3 + 6.01 \times \frac{100}{5.3}$ (b) $\frac{1}{3} \times 0.01 \times \frac{100}{5.3}$
(c) $\left(\frac{3 \times 0.1}{5.3}\right) \times 100$ (d) $\frac{0.1}{5.3} \times 100$

3. If voltage $V = (100 \pm 5)$ volt and current $I = (10 \pm 0.2)$ A, the percentage error in resistance R is

(a) 5.2% (b) 25%
(c) 7% (d) 10%

4. The values of two resistors are $R_1 = (6 \pm 0.3)$ kΩ and $R_2 = (10 \pm 0.2)$ kΩ. The percentage error in the equivalent resistance when they are connected in parallel is

(a) 5.125% (b) 2%
(c) 10.125% (d) 7%

5. The frequency of vibration of string is given by

$\nu = \frac{p}{2l}\left[\frac{F}{m}\right]^{1/2}$

Here p is number of segments in the string and l is the length. The dimensional formula for m will be

(a) $[M^0LT^{-1}]$ (b) $[ML^0T^{-1}]$
(c) $[ML^{-1}T^0]$ (d) $[M^0L^0T^0]$

6. The dimensions of $\frac{a}{b}$ in the equation $P = \frac{a - t^2}{bx}$, where P is pressure, x is distance and t is time are

(a) $[M^2LT^{-3}]$ (b) $[MT^{-2}]$
(c) $[LT^{-3}]$ (d) $[ML^3T^{-1}]$

7. $[ML^2T^{-3}I^{-1}A^{-1}]$ is the dimension of

(a) electric field (b) capacity
(c) potential (d) permittivity

8. A gas bubble formed from an explosion under water oscillates with a period T proportional to $p^a d^b E^c$, where p is pressure, d is the density of water and E is the total energy of explosion. The value of a, b, c are

(a) $a = 1, b = 1, c = 2$
(b) $a = 1, b = 2, c = 1$
(c) $a = \frac{5}{6}, b = \frac{1}{2}, c = \frac{1}{3}$
(d) $a = -\frac{5}{6}, b = \frac{1}{2}, c = \frac{1}{3}$

9. The physical quantities not having same dimensions are

(a) Torque and work
(b) Momentum and Planck's constant
(c) Stress and Young's modulus
(d) Speed and $(\mu_0\varepsilon_0)^{-1/2}$

10. Dimensions of $\frac{1}{\mu_0\varepsilon_0}$, where symbols have their usual meaning are:

(a) $[L^{-1}T]$ (b) $[L^2T^2]$
(c) $[L^2T^{-2}]$ (d) $[LT^{-1}]$

11. Which one of the following represents the correct dimensions of the coefficient of viscosity?

(a) $[ML^{-1}T^{-2}]$ (b) $[MLT^{-1}]$
(c) $[ML^{-1}T^{-1}]$ (d) $[ML^{-2}T^{-2}]$

12. Identify the pair whose dimensions are equal

(a) Torque and work (b) Stress and energy
(c) Torce and stress (d) force and work

13. Which of the following units denotes the dimensions $[ML^2/Q^2]$, where Q denotes the electric charge?

(a) Wb/m^2 (b) henry (H)
(c) H/m^2 (d) Weber (Wb)

14. Out of the following pairs which one does not have identical dimensions?

(a) Angular momentum and Plank's constant
(b) Impulse and momentum
(c) Moment of inertia and moment of a force
(d) Work and torque

15. A body of mass $m' = 3.513$ kg is moving along the x-axis with a speed of 5.00 ms^{-1}. The magnitude of its momentum is recorded as:

(a) 17.6 kg ms^{-1} (b) 17.565 kg ms^{-1}
(c) 17.56 kg ms^{-1} (d) 17.57 kg ms^{-1}

16. Two full turns of the circular scale of a screw gauge cover a distance of 1 mm on its main scale. The total number of divisions on the circular scale is 50. Further, it is found that screw gauge has zero error of – 0.03 mm. While measuring the diameter of a thin wire, a student notes the main scale reading of 3 mm and the number of circular scale divisions in line with main scale as 35. The diameter of wire is:

(a) 3.32 mm (b) 3.73 mm
(c) 3.67 mm (d) 3.38 mm

17. In an experiment the angles are required to be measured using an insrtument 29 divisions of the main scale exactly coincide with the 30 divisions of the vernier scale. If the smallest divisions of the main scale is hay-a-degree (= 0.5°) then the least count of the instrument is

(a) hay minute (b) one degree
(c) hay degree (d) one minute

18. The respective number of significant figures for the numbers 23.023; 0.0003 and 2.1×10^{-3} are:
(a) 4, 4, 2 (b) 5, 1, 2
(c) 5, 1, 5 (d) 5, 5, 2

19. A screw gauge gives the following reading when used to measure the diameter of a wire.
Main scale reading: 0 mm
Circular scale reading : 52 divisions
Given that 1 mm on main scale corresponds to 100 divisions of the circular scale. The diameter of wire from the above data is:
(a) 0.005 cm (b) 0.52 cm
(c) 0.052 cm (d) 0.026 cm

20. The dimensions of magnetic field in M, L, T and C(coulomb) is given by:
(a) $MLT^{-1}C^{-1}$ (b) $MT^{2}C^{-2}$
(c) $MT^{-1}C^{-1}$ (d) $MT^{-2}C^{-1}$

21. In the formula $X = 3YZ^2$, X and Z have dimensions of capacitance and magnetic induction respectively. What are the dimensions of Y in MKSQ system?
(a) $[M^{-3}L^{-1}T^{3}Q^{4}]$ (b) $[M^{-3}L^{-2}T^{4}Q^{4}]$
(c) $[M^{-2}L^{-2}T^{4}Q^{4}]$ (d) $[M^{-3}L^{-2}T^{4}Q^{1}]$

22. The dimensions of $\left(\frac{1}{2}\right)\varepsilon_0 E^2$ is:
(ε_0 – permittivity of free space, E – electric field)
(a) $[MLT^{-1}]$ (b) $[ML^{2}T^{-2}]$
(c) $[ML^{-1}T^{-2}]$ (d) $[ML^{2}T^{-1}]$

23. A cube has a side of length 1.2×10^{-2} m. Calculate its volume.
(a) 1.7×10^{-6} m^3 (b) 1.73×10^{-6} m^3
(c) 1.70×10^{-6} m^3 (d) 1.732×10^{-6} m^3

24. Let $[\varepsilon_0]$ denote of the permittivity of the vacuum, and $[\mu_0]$ denote the permeability of the vacuum. If M = mass, L = length, T = time and I = electric current, then the dimensional formulae of ε_0 and μ_0 are:
(a) $[\varepsilon_0] = [M^{-1}L^{-3}T^{2}I]$ (b) $[\varepsilon_0] = [M^{-1}L^{-3}T^{4}I^{2}]$
(c) $[\mu_0] = [MLT^{-2}I^{-2}]$ (d) $[\mu_0] = [ML^{2}T^{-1}I]$

25. The pair of physical quantities that have the same dimensions is:
(a) Reynolds number and coefficient of friction
(b) Curie and frequency of a light wave
(c) Latent heat and gravitational potential
(d) Planck's constant and torque

26. The dimensions of length are expressed as $G^x c^y h^z$. where G, c and h are the universal gravitational constant, speed of light and Planck's constant respectively, then:
(a) $x = (1/2), y = (1/2)$ (b) $x = (1/2), z = (1/2)$
(c) $y = (-3/2), z = (1/2)$ (d) $y = (1/2), z = (3/2)$

27. The SI unit of inductance, the henry can be written as:
(a) weber/ampere (b) volt-sec/amp
(c) joule/(ampere)^2 (d) ohm-second

Directions (Q. 28 to 30) : Consider C as velocity of light, the constant of gravitation G and Plank's constant h, be chosen as fundamental unit. Answer the following:

28. Find the value of a gram in new unit of mass, length and time.
(a) 1.8355×10^5 (b) 1.5×10^5
(c) 18.35×10^5 (d) 15×10^5

29. Find the value of a centimeter in the above units.
(a) 743×10^{42} (b) 7.43×10^{42}
(c) 74.3×10^{42} (d) 743.25×10^{42}

30. Find the value of a second in the above unit.
(a) 24.76×10^{32} (b) 2.476×10^{32}
(c) 2.476×10^{32} (d) 24×10^{32}

Directions (Q.31 to 33) : The van-der Waals equation is

$$\left(P + \frac{a}{V^2}\right)(V - b) = RT,$$

where P is pressure, V is molar volume and T is the temperature of the given sample of gas. R is called molar gas constant, a and b are called vander Waal constants.

31. The dimensional formula for b is same as that for
(a) P (b) V
(c) PV^2 (d) RT

32. The dimensional formula for a is same as that for
(a) V^2 (b) P
(c) PV^2 (d) RT

33. Which of the following does not possess the same dimensional formula as that for RT?
(a) PV (b) Pb
(c) a/V^2 (d) ab/V^2

Directions (Q. 34 to 36) : In the study of physics, we often have to measure the physical quantities. The numerical value of a measured quantity can only be approximate as it depends upon the least count of the measuring instrument used. The number of significant figures in any measurement indicates the degree of precision of that measurement. The importance of significant figures lies in calculation. A mathematical calculation cannot increase the precision of a physical measurement. Therefore, the number of significant figures in the sum or product of a group of numbers cannot be greater than the number that has the least of significant figures. A chain cannot be stronger than its weakest link.

34. A bee of mass 0.000087 kg sits on a flower of mass 0.0123 kg. What is the total mass supported by the stem of the flower upto appropriate significant figures?
(a) 0.012387 kg (b) 0.01239 kg
(c) 0.0124 kg (d) 0.012 kg

35. The radius of a uniform wire is $r = 0.021$ cm. The value π is given to be 3.142. What is the area of cross-section of the wire upto appropriate significant figures?

(a) 0.0014 cm^2 (b) 0.00139 cm^2

(c) 0.001386 cm^2 (d) 0.0013856 cm^2

36. A man runs 100.5 m in 10.3 s. His average speed upto appropriate significant figures is

(a) 9.76 ms^{-1} (b) 9.757 ms^{-1}

(c) 9.7573 ms^{-1} (d) 9.8 ms^{-1}

37. In SI units, the dimensions of $\sqrt{\frac{\epsilon_0}{\mu_0}}$ is

(a) $AT^{-3}ML^{3/2}$ (b) $A^{-1}TML^3$

(c) $AT^2M^{-1}L^{-1}$ (d) $A^2T^3M^{-1}L^{-2}$

38. Let $[\varepsilon_0]$ denote the dimensional formula of the permittivity of vacuum. If M = mass, L = Length, T = Time and A = electric current, then

(a) $[\varepsilon_0] = [M^{-1}L^{-3}T^2A]$

(b) $[\varepsilon_0] = [M^{-1}L^{-3}T^4A^2]$

(c) $[\varepsilon_0] = [M^{-2}L^2T^{-1}A^{-2}]$

(b) $[\varepsilon_0] = [M^{-1}L^2T^{-1}A^2]$

39. Which of the following sets have different dimensions?

(a) Pressure, Young's modulus, Stress

(b) Emf, Potential difference, Electric potential

(c) Heat, Work done, Energy

(d) Dipole moment, Electric flux, Electrict field

40. In the relation,

$$p = \frac{\alpha}{\beta} e^{-\frac{\alpha Z}{k\theta}}$$

p is pressure, Z is distance, k is Boltzmann's constant and θ is the temperature. The dimensional formula of β will be

(a) $[M^0L^2T^0]$ (b) $[ML^2T]$

(c) $[ML^0T^{-1}]$ (d) $[M^0L^2T^{-1}]$

Directions (Q. 41 to 42) : In electromagnetic theory, the electric and magnetic phenomena are related to each other. Therefore, the dimensions of electric and magnetic quantities must also be related to each other. In the question below, [E] and [B] stand for dimensions of electric and magnatic fields respectively, while $[\varepsilon_0]$ and $[\mu_0]$ stand for dimensions of the permittivity and permeability of free space respectively. [L] and [T] are dimensions of length and time respectively. All the quantities are given in SI units.

41. The relation between [E] and [B] is

(a) [E] = [B] [L] [T] (b) [E] = [B] $[L]^{-1}$ [T]

(c) [E] = [B] [L] $[T]^{-1}$ (d) [E] = [B] $[L]^{-1}$ $[T]^{-1}$

42. The relation between $[\varepsilon_0]$ and $[\mu_0]$ is

(a) $[\mu_0] = [\varepsilon_0]\,[L]^2\,[T]^{-2}$

(b) $[\mu_0] = [\varepsilon_0]\,[L]^{-2}\,[T]^2$

(c) $[\mu_0] = [\varepsilon_0]^{-1}\,[L]^2\,[T]^{-2}$

(d) $[\mu_0] = [\varepsilon_0]^{-1}\,[L]^{-2}\,[T]^2$

Directions (Q. 43 to 44) : If the measurement errors in all the independent quantities are known, then it is possible to determine the error in any dependent quantity. This is done by the use of series expansion and truncating the expansion at the first power of the error. For example, consider the relation $z = x/y$. If the errors in x, y and z are Δx, Δy and Δz, respectively, then

$$z \pm \Delta z = \frac{x \pm \Delta x}{y \pm \Delta y} = \frac{x}{y}\left(1 \pm \frac{\Delta x}{x}\right)\left(1 \pm \frac{\Delta y}{y}\right)^{-1}$$

The series expansion for $\left(1 \pm \frac{\Delta y}{y}\right)^{-1}$, to first power in $\Delta y/y$, is $1 \mp (\Delta y/y)$. The relative errors in independent variables are always added. So the error in z will be $\Delta z = z\left(\frac{\Delta x}{x} + \frac{\Delta y}{y}\right)$.

The above derivation makes the assumption that $\Delta x/x \ll 1$, $\Delta y/y \ll 1$. Therefore, the higher powers of these quantities are neglected.

43. Consider the ratio $r = \frac{(1-a)}{(1+a)}$ to be determined by measuring a dimensionless quantity a. If the error in the measurement of a is Δa ($\Delta a/a \ll 1$), then what is the error Δr in determining r?

(a) $\frac{\Delta a}{(1+a)^2}$ (b) $\frac{2\Delta a}{(1+a)^2}$

(c) $\frac{\Delta a}{(1-a^2)}$ (d) $\frac{2a\Delta a}{(1-a^2)}$

44. In an experiment the initial number of radioactive nuclei is 3000. It is found that 1000 ± 40 nuclei decayed in the first 1.0 s. For $|x| \ll 1$, $\ln(1 + x) = x$ up to first power in x. The error $\Delta\lambda$, in the determination of the decay constant λ, in s^{-1}, is

(a) 0.04 (b) 0.03

(c) 0.02 (d) 0.01

45. The density of a material in the shape of a cube is determined by measuring three sides of the cube and its mass. If the relative errors in mesuring in mass and length are respectively 1.5% and 1% the maximum error in determining the density is:

(a) 4.5% (b) 6%

(c) 2.5% (d) 3.5%

46. A person measures the depth of a well by measuring the time interval between dropping a stone and receiving the sound of impact with the bottom of the well. The error in his measurement of time is $\delta T = 0.01$s and he measures the depth of the well to be $L = 20$ m. Take the acceleration due to gravity $g = 10$ ms^{-2} and the velocity of sound is 300 ms^{-1}. Then the fractional error in the measurement, $\frac{\delta L}{L}$, is closest to

(a) 1% (b) 5%
(c) 3% (d) 0.2%

47. A Screw gauge with a pitch of 0.5 mm and a circular scale with 50 divisions is used to measure the thickness of a thin sheet of aluminium. Before starting the measurement, it is found that when the two jaws of the screw gauge are brought in contact, the 45th division coincides with the main scale line and that the zero of the main scale is barely visible. What is the thickness of the sheet, if the main scale reading is 0.5 mm and the 25th division coincides with the main scale line?

(a) 0.75 mm (b) 0.80 mm
(c) 0.70 mm (d) 0.50 mm

48. There are two vernier calipers both of which have 1 cm divided into 10 equal divisions on the main scale. The vernier scale of one of the calipers (C_1) has 10 equal divisions that correspond to 9 main scale divisions.

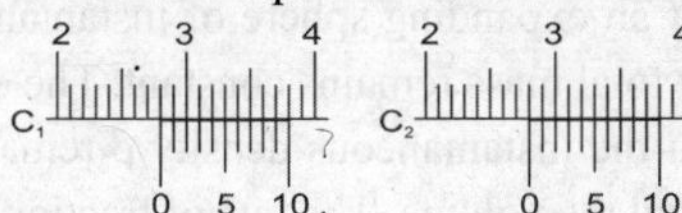

The vernier scale of the other caliper (C_2) has 10 equal divisions that correspond to 11 main scale divisions. The reading of the two calipers are shown in the figure. The measured values (in cm) by calipers C_1 and C_2 respectively, are

(a) 2.87 and 2.87 (b) 2.87 and 2.83
(c) 2.85 and 2.82 (d) 2.87 and 2.86

49. The period of oscillation of a simple pendulum is $T = 2\pi\sqrt{\frac{L}{g}}$. Measured value of L is 20.0 cm known to 1 mm accuracy and time for 100 oscillations of the pendulum is found to be 90 s using a wrist watch of 1s resolution. The accuracy in the determination of g is

(a) 3% (b) 2%
(c) 1% (d) 5%

50. The current voltage relation of diode is given by $I = (e^{1000V/T} - 1)$mA, where the applied voltage V is in volt and the temperature T is in kelvin. If a student makes an error measuring $\pm$ 0.01 V while measuring the current of 5 mA at 300 K, what will be the error in the value of current in mA?

(a) 0.2 mA (b) 0.02 mA
(c) 0.5 mA (d) 0.05 mA

51. A student measured the length of a rod and wrote it as 3.50 cm. Which instrument did he use to measure it?

(a) A meter scale
(b) A vernier caliper where 10 divisions in vernier scale matches with 9 divisions in main scale and main scale has 10 divisions in 1 cm
(c) A screw gauge having 100 divisions in the circular scale and pitch as 1 mm and pitch as 1 mm
(d) A screw gauge having 50 divisions in the circular scale

52. The diameter of a cylinder is measured using a vernier calipers with no zero error. It is found that the zero of the vernier scale lies between 5.10 cm and 5.15 cm of the main scale. The vernier scale has 50 division equivalent to 2.45 cm. The 24th division of the vernier scale exactly coincides with one of the main scale divisions. The diameter of the cylinder is

(a) 5.112 cm (b) 5.124 cm
(c) 5.136 cm (d) 5.148 cm

53. In the determination of Young's modulus $\left(Y = \frac{4MLg}{\pi l d^2}\right)$ by using Searle's method, a wire of length $L = 2$ m and diameter $d = 0.5$ mm is used. For a load $M = 2.5$ kg, an extension $l = 0.25$ mm in the length of the wire is observed. Quantities d and l are measured using a screw gauge and a micrometer, respectively. They have the same pitch of 0.5 mm. The number of divisions on their circular scale is 100. The contributions to the maximum probable error of the Y measurement is

(a) due to the errors in the measurements of d and l are the same
(b) due to the error in the measurement of d is twice that due to the error in the measurement of l
(c) due to the error in the measurement of l is twice that due to the error in the measurement of d
(d) due to the error in the measurement of d is four times that due to the error in the measurement of l

54. The density of a solid ball is to be determined in an experiment. The diameter of the ball is measured with a screw gauge, whose pitch is 0.5 mm and there are 50 divisions on the circular scale. The reading on the main scale is 2.5 mm and that on the circular scale is 20 divisions. If the measured mass of the ball has a relative error of 2%, the relative percentage error in the density is

(a) 0.9% (b) 2.4%
(c) 3.1% (d) 4.2%

55. A vernier calipers has 1 mm marks on the main scale. It has 20 equal divisions on the vernier scale which match with 16 main scale divisions. For this vernier calipers, the least count is

(a) 0.02 mm (b) 0.05 mm
(c) 0.1 mm (d) 0.2 mm

56. Students I, II and III perform an experiment for measuring the acceleration due to gravity (g) using a simple pendulum. They use different lengths of the pendulum and/or record time for different number of oscillations. The observations are shown in the table.

Least count for length = 0.1 cm, Least count for time = 0.1s.

Student	Length of the pendulum (cm)	Number of oscillations (n)	Total time for (n) oscillations (s)	Time period (s)
I	64.0	8	128.0	16.0
II	64.0	4	64.0	16.0
III	20.0	4	36.0	9.0

If E_{I}, E_{II} and E_{III} are the percentage errors in g, i.e. $\left(\frac{\Delta g}{g} \times 100\right)$ for students I, II and III, respectively.

(a) $E_I = 0$
(b) E_I is minimum
(c) $E_I = E_{II}$
(d) E_{II} is maximum

57. In the experiment to determine the speed of sound using a resonance column

(a) prongs of the tuning fork are kept in a vertical plane
(b) prongs of the tuning fork are kept in a horizontal plane
(c) in one of the two resonances observed, the length of the resonating air column is close to the wavelength of sound in air
(d) in one of the two resonances observed, the length of the resonating air column is close to half of the wavelength of sound in air

58. A student performs an experiment to determine the Young's modulus of a wire, exactly 2 m long, by Searle's method. In a particular reading, the student measures the extension in the length of the wire to be 0.8 mm with an uncertainty of ± 0.05 mm at a load of exactly 1.0 kg. The student also measures the diameter of the wire to be 0.4 mm with an uncertainty of ± 0.01 mm. Take g = 9.8 m/s^2 (exact? The Young's moduls obtained from the reading is close to

(a) $(2.0 \pm 0.3)\ 10^{11}$ N/m^2
(b) $(2.0 \pm 0.2) \times 10^{11}$ N/m^2
(c) $(2.0 \pm 0.1) \times 10^{11}$ N/m^2
(d) $(2.0 \pm 0.05) \times 10^{11}$ N/m^2

59. The circular scale of a screw gauge has 50 divisions and pitch of 0.5 mm. Find the diameter of sphere. Main scale reading is 2.

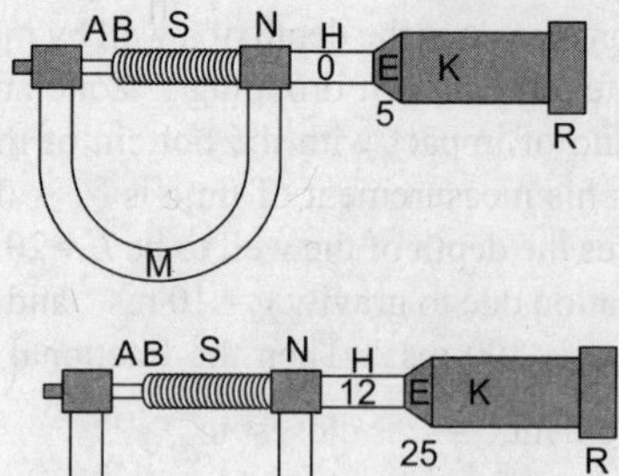

(a) 1.2 mm (b) 1.25 mm
(c) 2.20 mm (d) 2.25 mm

60. A wire has a mass (0.3 ± 0.003) g, radius (0.5 ± 0.005) mm and length (6 ± 0.06) cm. The maximum percentage error in the measurement of its density is

(a) 1 (b) 2
(c) 3 (d) 4

61. The density of a material in SI units is 128 kg m^{-3}. In certain units in which the unit of length in 25 cm and the unit of mass is 50 g, the numerical value of density of the material is :

(a) 40 (b) 16
(c) 640 (d) 410

62. Consider an expanding sphere of instantaneous radius R whose total mass remains constant. The expansion is such that the instantaneous density ρ remains uniform throughout the volume. The rate of fractional change in density $\left(\frac{1}{p}\frac{d\rho}{dt}\right)$ is constant. The velocity v of any point of the surface of the expanding sphere is proportional to

(a) R (b) $\frac{1}{R}$
(c) R^3 (d) $R^{\frac{2}{3}}$

63. Three vectors **P**/**Q** and **R** are shown in the figure. Let S be any point on the vector **R**. The distance between the points P and S is b [**R**]. The general relation among vectors **P**, **Q** and **S** is

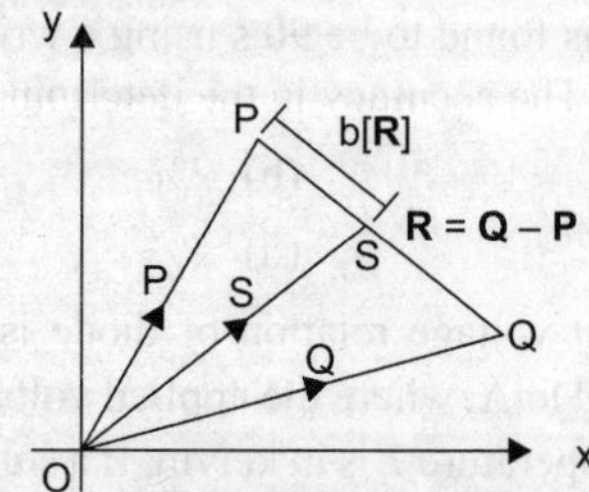

(a) $\mathbf{S} = (1 - b^2)\mathbf{P} + b\mathbf{Q}$
(b) $\mathbf{S} = (b - 1)\mathbf{P} + b\mathbf{Q}$
(c) $\mathbf{S} = (1 - b)\mathbf{P} + b\mathbf{Q}$
(d) $\mathbf{S} = (1 - b)\mathbf{P} + b^2\mathbf{Q}$

Directions (Q. 64 to 65) : A dense collection of equal number of electrons and positive ions is called neutral plasma. Certain solids containing fixed positive ions surrounded by free electrons can be treated as neutral plasma. Let N be the number density of free electrons, each of mass m. When the electrons are subjected to an electric field, they are displaced relatively away from the heavy positive ions. If the electric field becomes zero, the electrons begin to oscillate about the positive ions with a natural angular frequency ω_p, which is called the plasma frequency.

To sustain the oscillations, a time varying electric field needs to be applied that has an angular frequency ω, where a part of the energy is absorbed and a part of it is reflected. As ω approaches ω_p, all the free electrons are set to resonance together and all the energy is reflected. This is the explanation of high reflectivity of metals.

64. Taking the electronic charge as e and the permittivity as ε_0, use dimensional analysis to determine the correct expression for ω_p.

(a) $\sqrt{\dfrac{Ne}{m\varepsilon_0}}$

(b) $\sqrt{\dfrac{m\varepsilon_0}{Ne}}$

(c) $\sqrt{\dfrac{Ne^2}{m\varepsilon_0}}$

(d) $\sqrt{\dfrac{m\varepsilon_0}{Ne^2}}$

65. Estimate the wavelength at which plasma reflection will occur for a metal having the density of electrons $N \approx 4 \times 10^{27}$ m^{-3}. Take $\varepsilon_0 \approx 10^{-11}$ and $m \approx 10^{-30}$, where these quantities are in proper SI units.

(a) 800 nm

(b) 600 nm

(c) 300 nm

(d) 200 nm

Directions (Q. 66 to 68) : Phase space diagrams are useful tools in analysing all kinds of dynamical problems. They are especially useful in studying the changes in motion as initial position and momentum are changed. Here we consider some simple dynamical systems in one dimension. For such systems, phase space is a plane in which position is plotted along horizontal axis and momentum is plotted along vertical axis. The phase space diagram is $x(t)$ *vs* $p(t)$ curve in this plane. The arrow on the curve indicated the time flow. For example, the phase space diagram for a particle moving with constant velocity is a straight line as shown in the figure. We use the sign convention in which position or momentum upwards (or to right) is positive and downwards (or to left) in negative.

66. The phase space diagram for a ball thrown vertically up from ground is

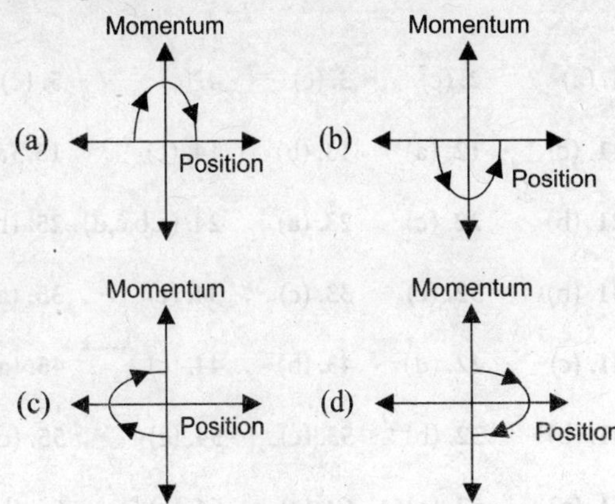

67. The phase space diagram for simple harmonic motion is a circle centered at the origin. In the figure, the two circles represent the same oscillator but for different initial conditions, and E_1 and E_2 are the total mechanical energies respectively. Then,

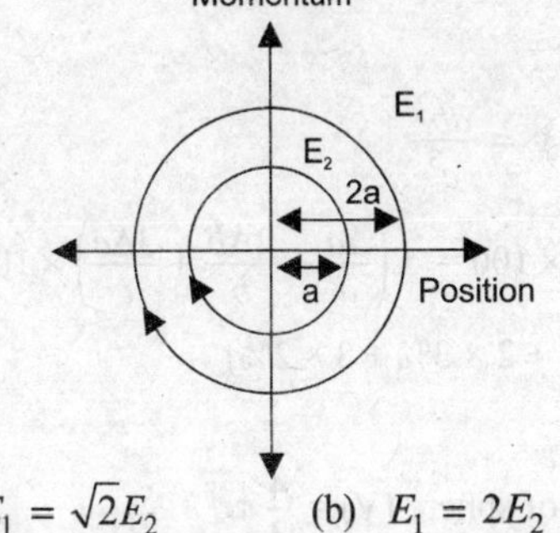

(a) $E_1 = \sqrt{2}E_2$ (b) $E_1 = 2E_2$

(c) $E_1 = 4E_2$ (d) $E_1 = 16E_2$

68. Consider the spring mass system, with the mass submerged in water, as shown in the figure. The phase space diagram for one cycle of this system is

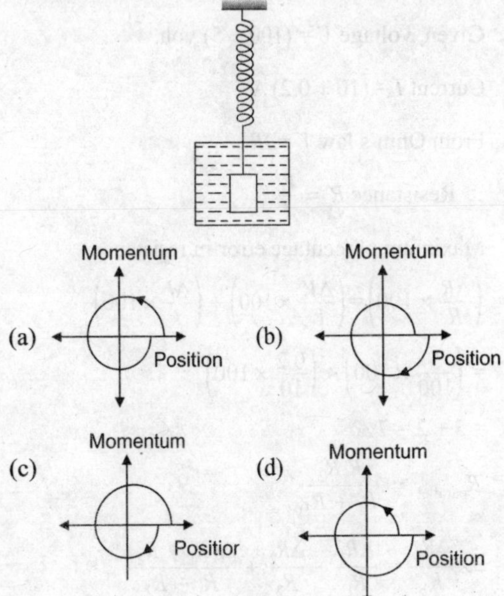

Answers

1. (a)	**2.** (c)	**3.** (c)	**4.** (c)	**5.** (c)	**6.** (b)	**7.** (c)	**8.** (d)	**9.** (b)	**10.** (c)
11. (c)	**12.** (a)	**13.** (b)	**14.** (c)	**15.** (a)	**16.** (d)	**17.** (d)	**18.** (b)	**19.** (c)	**20.** (c)
21. (b)	**22.** (c)	**23. (a)**	**24.** (a,b,c,d)	**25.** (b,c)	**26.** (a,b,c)	**27.** (b,c)	**28.** (a)	**29.** (b)	**30.** (c)
31. (b)	**32. (c)**	**33. (c)**	**34. (c)**	**35. (a)**	**36. (a)**	**37.** (d)	**38.** (b)	**39.** (d)	**40.** (a)
41. (c)	**42.** (d)	**43.** (b)	**44.** (c)	**45.** (a)	**46.** (a)	**47.** (b)	**48.** (b)	**49.** (a)	**50. (a)**
51. (b)	**52.** (b)	**53. (c)**	**54.** (c)	**55.** (d)	**56.** (b)	**57.** (a)	**58.** (b)	**59.** (a)	**60.** (d)
61. (a)	**62. (a)**	**63.** (c)	**64.** (c)	**65.** (b)	**66.** (d)	**67.** (c)	**68.** (d)		

Explanations

1. Given, $X = \dfrac{ab^2}{c^3}$

$$\therefore \frac{\Delta X}{X} \times 100 = \pm\left(\frac{\Delta a}{a} + \frac{2\Delta b}{b} + \frac{3\Delta c}{c}\right) \times 100$$

$= \pm (1\% + 2 \times 3\% + 3 \times 2\%)$

$= \pm 13\%$

2. Volume of sphere (V) $= \dfrac{4}{3}\pi r^3$

Percentage error in volume $= \dfrac{3 \times \Delta r}{r} \times 100$

$= \left(\dfrac{3 \times 0.1}{5.3}\right) \times 100$

3. Given, voltage $V = (100 \pm 5)$ volt,

Current $I = (10 \pm 0.2)$ A

From Ohm's law $V = IR$

$\therefore$ Resistance $R = \dfrac{V}{I}$

Maximum percentage error in resistance

$$\left(\frac{\Delta R}{R} \times 100\right) = \left(\frac{\Delta V}{V} \times 100\right) + \left(\frac{\Delta I}{I} \times 100\right)$$

$$= \left(\frac{5}{100} \times 100\right) + \left(\frac{0.2}{10} \times 100\right)$$

$= 5 + 2 = 7\%$

4. $R_{\text{parallel}} = \dfrac{R_1 R_2}{R_1 + R_2}$

$$\Rightarrow \frac{\Delta R_p}{R_p} = \frac{\Delta R_1}{R_1} + \frac{\Delta R_2}{R_2} + \frac{\Delta (R_1 + R_2)}{R_1 + R_2}$$

$$\Rightarrow \frac{\Delta R_p}{R_p} = \frac{0.3}{6} + \frac{0.2}{10} + \frac{0.3 + 0.2}{10 + 6}$$

$$\therefore \frac{\Delta R_p}{R_p} \times 100 = 10.125\%$$

5. Given $v = \dfrac{p}{2l}\left[\dfrac{F}{m}\right]^{1/2}$

Squaring the equation on either side, we have

$$v^2 = \frac{p^2}{4l^2}\left[\frac{F}{m}\right]$$

$$\Rightarrow m = \frac{p^2 F}{4l^2 v^2}$$

or $[m] = \dfrac{[MLT^{-2}]}{[L^2][T^{-1}]^2} = [ML^{-1}T^0]$

6. Given, $p = \dfrac{a - t^2}{bx}$ or $pbx = a - t^2$

By the law of homogenity of dimensions
Dimensions of a = dimensions of $t^2 = [T^2]$

Dimensions of b = dimensions of $\dfrac{t^2}{px}$

$= [M^{-1}T^4]$

So, dimensions of $\dfrac{a}{b}$ is $[ML^{-2}]$

7. $[ML^2T^{-3}A^{-1}]$ are the dimensions of potential

Because, potential $= \dfrac{\text{energy}}{\text{charge}}$

$$= \frac{[ML^2T^{-2}]}{[AT]} = [ML^2T^{-3}A^{-1}]$$

8. Given $T \alpha p^a d^b E^c$

We have $[M^0L^0T] = k\,[ML^{-1}T^{-2}]^a\,[ML^{-3}]^b\,[ML^2T^{-2}]^c$

where k is a constant.

Comparing dimensions of similar terms, we have

$[M^0L^0T] = k\,[M^{a+b+c}L^{-a-3b+2c}T^{-2a-2c}]$

Comparing powers of M, we have

$0 = a + b + c$ ....(i)

Comparing powers of L, we have

$0 = -a - 3b + 2c$ ....(ii)

Comparing powers of T, we have

$1 = -2a - 2c$ .....(iii)

Solving Eqs. (i), (ii) and (iii), we have

$a = -\frac{5}{6}, b = \frac{1}{2}, c = \frac{1}{3}$

9. [Momentum] = $[MLT^{-1}]$

Planck's constant = $[ML^2T^{-1}]$

Not same

Rest all are same.

10. $c^2 = \frac{1}{\mu_0\varepsilon_0}$ [where c is the speed of light]

Dimensions of $\frac{1}{\mu_0\varepsilon_0}$ is (velocity)^2

i.e., $[LT^{-1}]^2 = [L^2T^{-2}]$

11. The correct dimensions of viscosity is $[ML^{-1}T^{-1}]$

12. Out of the following pair, torque and work have same dimensions.

13. Dimensions of inductance, *i.e.*, henry are $[ML^2/Q^2]$.

14. Moment of inertia and moment of a force do not have same dimensions.

15. Magnitude of momentum

$P = mV = 3.513 \times 5.00 \approx 17.6$

Because in both the parameters least significant figure are 3.

16. Diameter of wire

= (main scale reading) + (circular scale reading) × (least count) + zero error

$= 3 + 35 \times \left(\frac{0.5}{50}\right) + 0.03 = 3.38$ mm

17. 30 VSD = 29 MSD

$1\text{ VSD} = \frac{29}{30}\text{MSD}$

$1\text{MSD} - 1\text{ VSD} = 1 - \frac{29}{30} = \frac{1}{30}\text{MSD}$

Least count $= \frac{1}{30} \times 0.5$

$= \frac{1}{60}$ degree or one minute

18. Number of significant figures in 23.023 are 5. Number of significant figures in 0.0003 are 1. Number of significant figures in 2.1×10^{-3} are 2.

19. Least count of screw gauge $= \frac{1}{100}$ mm = 0.01 mm

diameter of the wire = Divisions on circular scale × Least count + main scale reading

$= 52 \times 0.01 + 0$

= 0.52 mm = 0.052 cm

20. Magnetic field (B) $= \frac{F}{qv} = \frac{[MLT^{-2}]}{[C][LT^{-1}]}$

$= [MC^{-1}T^{-1}]$

21. The quantity $Y = \frac{X}{3Z^2}$

Thus, $[Y] = \frac{[M^{-1}L^{-2}T^2Q^2]}{[MT^{-1}Q^{-1}]^2}$

$[Y] = [M^3L^{-2}T^4Q^4]$

22. This physical quantity is energy per unit volume. Thus, its dimensions are

$\frac{ML^2T^{-2}}{L^3} = [ML^{-1}T^{-2}]$

23. volume (V) $= (1.2 \times 10^{-2})^3 = 1.728 \times 10^{-6}$ m^3 but since side length is having only two significant figure. Hence, volume will also contain two significant figures.

Thus, $V = 1.7 \times 10^{-6}$ m^3

24. $|\varepsilon_0| = \frac{[IT]^2}{[MLT^{-2}][L^2]}$

$[\varepsilon_0] = [M^{-1}L^{-3}T^4I^2]$

$\frac{1}{\sqrt{\mu_0\varepsilon_0}} = c$

$[\mu_0] = \frac{1}{\varepsilon_0 c^2}$

$\therefore$ Dimensions of $[\mu_0] = [MLT^{-2}I^{-2}]$

Thus, (b) and (c) are correct choices.

25. Reynolds number $= \frac{\text{Inertial force}}{\text{Viscous force}}$ = Dimensionless

Curie = No. of atoms/time = $|T^{-1}|$

Frequency = $|T^{-1}|$

Latent heat $= \frac{\text{Energy}}{\text{Mass}}$

Gravitational potential $= \frac{\textit{Energy}}{\textit{Mass}}$

Thus, only (a), (b), (c) are correct.

26. $[M^0L^1T^0] = [G]^x\,[c]^y\,[h]^z$

$[M^0L^1T^0] = [M^{-1}L^3T^{-2}]^x\,[LT^{-1}]^y\,[ML^2T^{-1}]^z$

Thus, $z - x = 0$

$3x + y + 2z = 1$

$-2x - y - z = 0$

Solving, we get $\begin{Bmatrix} x = 1/2 \\ y = -3/2 \\ z = 1/2 \end{Bmatrix}$

27. (a), (b), (c) and (d) all are correct

$$\phi = L.I \quad \Rightarrow [L] = \frac{\text{weber}}{\text{ampere}}$$

$$e = L\frac{dI}{dt} \quad \Rightarrow [L] = \left(\frac{\text{volt - second}}{\text{ampere}}\right)$$

$$U = \frac{1}{2}LI^2 \Rightarrow [L] = \frac{\text{joule}}{\text{ampere}^2}$$

$$e = L^2\frac{\Delta t}{t} \Rightarrow [L] = \left(\frac{e}{\Delta i}\right).(\Delta t)$$

= (Resistance) × (Time) = (ohm × second)

28. 1.8355×10^5

29. 7.43×10^{42}

30. 2.476×10^{32}

31. Principle of homogenity to identify the answer

32. as $\rho = \frac{a}{V^2} = a = \rho V^2$

33. From homogenity principle

$a = ML^5T^{-2} \cdot b = L^3$

$$\therefore \frac{a}{v^2} = \frac{ML^5T^{-2}}{L^6} \neq ML^{-2}T^{-2}$$

34. Total mass = 0.000087 + 0.0123 = 0.012387 kg. The mass of the bee is accurate upto sixth decimal place in kg, whereas the mass of the flower is accurate only upto the fourth decimal place. Hence the sum must be rounded off to the fourth decimal place. Therefore the correct choice is (c).

35. $A = \pi r^2 = 3.142 \times (0.021)^2 = 0.00138562 \text{ cm}^2$. Now, there are only two significant figures in 0.021 cm. Hence the result must be rounded off to two significant figure as $A = 0.0014 \text{ cm}^2$, which is choice (a).

36. Average speed = $\frac{100.5 \text{ m}}{10.3 \text{ s}} = 9.7573 \text{ ms}^{-1}$

The distance has four significant figures but the time has only three. Hence, the result must be rounded off to three significant figure to 9.76 ms^{-1}. Thus the correct choice is (a).

37. $\vec{P_1}\sqrt{\frac{\epsilon_0}{\mu}} = \frac{1}{z}$ = Impedence

$A^2T^3M^{-1}L^{-2}$

38. By Coulomb's law, we have

$$F = \frac{1}{4\pi\varepsilon_0}\frac{q_1q_2}{R^2}$$

$$\varepsilon_0 = \frac{q_1q_2}{4\pi FR^2}$$

On putting the units, we have

$$\varepsilon_0 = N - m^2 = \frac{[AT]^2}{[MLT^{-2}][L^2]} = [M^{-1}L^{-3}T^4A^2]$$

39. Dipole moment = (charge) × (distance)

Electric flux = (electric field) × (area)

Hence, the correct option is (d).

40. $\left[\frac{\alpha Z}{k\theta}\right] = [M^0L^0T^0]$

$$[\alpha] = \left[\frac{k\theta}{Z}\right]$$

Now

$$[P] = \left[\frac{\alpha}{\beta}\right]$$

$$[\beta] = \left[\frac{\alpha}{P}\right] = \left[\frac{k\theta}{Zp}\right]$$

As Dimensions of $k\,\theta$ represents energy. Hence,

$$[\beta] = \left[\frac{ML^2T^{-2}}{LML^{-1}T^{-2}}\right] = [M^0L^2T^0]$$

41. As $\frac{E}{B} = v$

So $\frac{E}{B} = \left[L^1T^{-1}\right]$

$[E] = [B]\,[L]\,[T]^{-1}$

42. $C = \frac{1}{\sqrt{\mu_0\varepsilon_0}} \Rightarrow C^2 = \frac{1}{\mu_0\varepsilon_0}$

$$L^2T^{-2} = \frac{1}{\mu_0\varepsilon_0}$$

$[\mu_0] = [\varepsilon_0]^{-1}\,[L]^{-2}\,[T]^2$

43. $r = \frac{(1-a)}{(1+a)}$

$\ln r = \ln(1-a) - \ln(1+a)$

So $\frac{\Delta r}{r} = \frac{\Delta a}{1-a} + \frac{\Delta a}{1+a}$

$$\frac{\Delta r}{r} = \frac{2\Delta a}{1-a^2}$$

$$(1+a)\,\frac{\Delta r}{(1-a)} = \frac{2(\Delta a)}{(1-a^2)}$$

So $\Delta r = \frac{2\Delta a}{(1+a)^2}$

44. Let number of nuclei decayed be N.

As we know that

$N = N_0(1 - e^{-\lambda t})$

$\lambda t = \ln\left(\frac{N_0}{N_0 - N}\right)$

$\lambda t = \ln N_0 - \ln(N_0 - N)$

$(\Delta\lambda)t = \frac{dN}{(N_0 - N)}$

$(\Delta\lambda) = \frac{40}{(3000 - 1000)} = 0.02\ s^{-1}$

45. Percentage error in m an $\frac{\Delta m}{m} \times 100 = 1.5$

Percentage error in length $\frac{\Delta\ell}{\ell} \times 100 = 1$

density is given by $d = \frac{m}{\ell^3}$

Now $\Rightarrow \frac{\Delta d}{d} \times 100 = \frac{\Delta m}{m} \times 100 + \frac{3\Delta\ell}{\ell} \times 100$

$= 1.5 + 3 = 4.5\%$

46. Distance moved by the stone

$L = \frac{1}{2}gt^2 = \frac{1}{2} \times 10 \times t^2$

$t_1 = \sqrt{\frac{L}{5}}$

∴ Time interval between dropping a stone and splash here is.

$dt = \frac{1}{\sqrt{5}}\frac{1}{2}L^{-1/2}dL + \left(\frac{1}{300}dL\right)$

$dt = \frac{1}{2\sqrt{5}}\frac{1}{\sqrt{20}}dL + \frac{dL}{300} = 0.01$

$dL\left(\frac{1}{20} + \frac{1}{300}\right) = 0.01$

$dL\left[\frac{15}{300}\right] = 0.01,\ dL = \frac{3}{16}$

$\frac{dL}{L} \times 100 = \frac{3}{16} \times \frac{1}{20} \times 100 = \frac{15}{16} \simeq 1\%$

47. As Least count of the instrument

$= \frac{\text{Pitch}}{\text{Number of Divisions on circular scale}} = \frac{0.5\text{mm}}{50}$

∴ LC = 0.01

Negative zero error = –5× LC = –0.005 mm

Measured value = main scale reading (M.S.R) + screw gauge reading – zero error

= 0.5 mm + {25 × 0.01 – (–0.05)} mm = 0.8 mm

48. For vernier C_1

10 VSD = 9 MSD = 9 mm

1 VSD = 0.9 mm

⇒ LC = 1 MSD – 1 VSD = 1mm – 0.9 mm = 0.1 mm

Reading of C_1 = MSR + (VSR) (LC)

= 28 mm + (7) (0.1)

Reading of C_1 = 28.7 mm = 2.87 cm

For vernier C_2 : the vernier C_2 is abnormal

So, we have to find the reading from basics.

The point where both of the marks are matching:

Distance measured from main scale = distance measured from vernier scale

28 mm + (1 mm) (8) = (28 mm + x) + (1.1 mm) (7)

on, Solving we get, x = 0.3 mm

Hence reading of C_2 = 28 mm + 0.3 mm = 2.83 cm

49. Time period is given by, $T = \frac{t}{n}$

As we know, $T = 2\pi\sqrt{\frac{L}{g}}$, $T^2 = 4\pi^2\frac{L}{g}$

$\Rightarrow g = \frac{(4\pi^2)L}{T^2} = \frac{(4\pi^2)(L)}{\left(\frac{t}{n}\right)^2} = (4\pi^2 n^2)\frac{L}{t^2}$

Percentage error in the value of 'g' will be

$\frac{\Delta g}{g} \times 100 = \left(\frac{\Delta L}{L}\right) \times 100 + 2\left(\frac{\Delta t}{t}\right) \times 100$

$= \frac{0.1}{20} \times 100 + 2 \times \left(\frac{1}{90}\right) \times 100$

$= 2.72\%$

∴ The nearest answer is 3%

50. Here Given that, $I = (e^{1000V/T} - 1)$ mA, $dV = \pm 0.01$V

$T = 300$ K

So, $I = e^{1000V/T} - 1$

$I + 1 = e^{1000V/T}$

Taking log on both sides, we get

$\log(I + 1) = \frac{1000V}{T}$

On differentiating, $\frac{dI}{I+1} = \frac{1000}{T}dV$

$dI = \frac{1000}{T} \times (I + 1)dV$

$\Rightarrow \quad dI = \frac{1000}{300} \times (5 + 1) \times 0.01 = 0.2$ mA

So, error in the value of current is 0.2 mA.

51. If student measures 3.50 cm, it means that there is an uncertainly of the order 0.01 cm.

For vernier scale with 1 MSD = $\frac{1}{10}$ cm

and 9 MSD = 10 VSD

LC of vernier caliper is given by = 1MSD – 1VSD

$= \frac{1}{10}\left(1-\frac{9}{10}\right) = \frac{1}{100}$ cm = 0.01 cm

52. Here 1 MSD = 5.15 cm – 5.10 cm = 0.05 cm

So 1 VSD = $\frac{2.45}{50}$ cm = 0.049 cm

$\therefore$ LC = 1 MSD – 1 VSD = 0.01 cm

Hence, diameter of cylinder = (Main scale reading) + (Vernier scale reading) (LC)

= 5.10 + (24) (0.001) = 5.124 cm

53. Here $\Delta d = \Delta l = \frac{0.5}{100}$ mm = 0.005 mm

As we know that young's modulus is given by

$$Y = \frac{MLg}{\pi l d^2} \Rightarrow \left(\frac{\Delta Y}{Y}\right)_{max} = \left(\frac{\Delta l}{l}\right) + 2\left(\frac{\Delta d}{d}\right)$$

Hence percentage error in length

$$\left(\frac{\Delta l}{l}\right) = \frac{0.5/100}{0.25} = 0.02 \text{ and } \frac{2\Delta d}{d} = \frac{(2)(0.5/100)}{0.5} = 0.02$$

or $\frac{\Delta l}{l} = 2\frac{\Delta d}{d}$

54. Here L.C of screw gauge = $\frac{0.5}{50}$ = 0.01 mm = Δr

Diameter, r = 2.5 mm + 20 × $\frac{0.5}{50}$ = 2.70 mm

$$\frac{\Delta r}{r} = \frac{0.01}{2.70} \text{ or } \frac{\Delta r}{r} \times 100 = \frac{1}{2.7}$$

Now, density, $d = \frac{m}{V} = \frac{m}{\frac{4}{3}\pi\left(\frac{r}{2}\right)^3}$

Here, r is the diameter.

Percentage error in diameter will be

$$\frac{\Delta d}{d} \times 100 = \left\{\frac{\Delta m}{m} + 3\left(\frac{\Delta r}{r}\right)\right\} \times 100$$

$$= \frac{\Delta m}{m} \times 100 + 3 \times \left(\frac{\Delta r}{r}\right) \times 100$$

$$= 2\% + 3 \times \frac{1}{2.7} = 3.11\%$$

55. LC of vernier calipers

LC = 1 MSD – 1 VSD

$$= \frac{\text{Smallest division on main scale}}{\text{Number of divisions on vernier scale}}$$

20 divisions of vernier scale = 16 divisions of main scale

$\therefore$ 1 VSD = $\frac{16}{20}$ mm = 0.8 mm

Hence, LC = 1MSD – 1VSD = 1 mm – 0.8 mm = 0.2 mm

56. $T = 2\pi\sqrt{\frac{l}{g}}$ or $\frac{t}{n} = 2\pi\sqrt{\frac{l}{g}}$

$$\therefore\ g = \frac{(4\pi^2)(n^2)l}{t^2}$$

% error in $g = \frac{\Delta g}{g} \times 100 = \left(\frac{\Delta l}{l} + \frac{2\Delta t}{t}\right) \times 100$

$$E_I = \left(\frac{0.1}{64} + \frac{2 \times 0.1}{128}\right) \times 100 = 0.3125\%$$

$$E_{II} = \left(\frac{0.1}{64} + \frac{2 \times 0.1}{64}\right) \times 100 = 0.46875\%$$

$$E_{III} = \left(\frac{0.1}{20} + \frac{2 \times 0.1}{36}\right) \times 100 = 1.055\%$$

Hence E_I is minimum.

57. Length of air column in resonance is odd integer multiple of $\lambda/4$.

58. Young's modulus of elasticity $Y = \frac{FL}{Al} = \frac{4FL}{\pi d^2 l}$

$$= \frac{(4)(1.0 \times 9.8)(2)}{\pi(0.4 \times 10^{-3})^2(0.8 \times 10^{-3})}$$

$= 2.0 \times 10^{11}$ N/m^2

Further $\frac{\Delta Y}{Y} = 2\left(\frac{\Delta d}{d}\right) + \left(\frac{\Delta l}{l}\right)$

So $\therefore\ \Delta Y = \left\{2\left(\frac{\Delta d}{d}\right) + \left(\frac{\Delta l}{l}\right)\right\} Y$

$$= \left\{2 \times \frac{0.01}{0.4} + \frac{0.05}{0.8}\right\} \times 2.0 \times 10^{11}$$

$= 0.225 \times 10^{11}$ N/m^2 = 0.2×10^{11} N/m^2

On rounding off

or $(Y \pm \Delta Y) = (2 \pm 0.2) \times 10^{11}$ N/m^2

59. As Least count (LC)

$$= \frac{\text{Pitch}}{\text{Number of divisions on circular scale}}$$

$$= \frac{0.5}{50} = 0.01 \text{ mm}$$

Now, diameter of ball

= (2 × 0.5 mm) + (25 – 5) (0.01)

= 1.2 mm

60. As Density, $\rho = \frac{m}{\pi r^2 L}$

So percentage error in density.

$$\therefore\ \frac{\Delta\rho}{\rho} \times 100 = \left(\frac{\Delta m}{m} + 2\frac{\Delta r}{r} + \frac{\Delta L}{L}\right) \times 100$$

On putting the values, we get the maximum percentage error in density = 4%

Hence, the correct option is (d).

61. Given density = 128 Kgm^{-3}

$$= 128(20 \times 50g)\left(\frac{1}{4 \times 25}\right)^3 = \frac{128 \times 20}{4^3}(50\,g)\left(\frac{1}{25\,\text{cm}}\right)^3$$

$$= 40(50\,g)\left(\frac{1}{25\,\text{cm}}\right)^3$$

62. Mass $m = \frac{4\pi R^3}{3} \times \rho$

On taking log both sides, we have

$$\text{In}(m) = \text{In}\left(\frac{4\pi}{3}\right) + \text{In}(\rho) + 3\text{In}(R)$$

On differentiating with respect to time, we get

$$0 = 0 + \frac{1 d\rho}{\rho\, dt} + \frac{3}{R}\frac{dR}{dt}$$

$$\Rightarrow \left(\frac{dR}{dt}\right) = -R \times \frac{1}{\rho}\left(\frac{d\rho}{dt}\right)$$

$$\because \frac{dR}{dt} = v$$

$$\therefore v = -R \propto \frac{1}{\rho}\left(\frac{d\rho}{dt}\right)$$

$$\therefore v \propto R$$

63. $\mathbf{S} = \mathbf{P} + b\mathbf{R} = \mathbf{P} + b(\mathbf{Q} - \mathbf{P}) = \mathbf{P}(1 - b) + b\mathbf{Q}$

64. N = Number of electrons per unit volume

$\therefore$ $[N] = [L^{-3}]$, $[e] = [q] = [It] = [AT]$

$[\varepsilon_0] = [M^{-1}L^{-3}T^4A^2]$

Putting the dimensions, we can see that

$$\left[\sqrt{\frac{Ne^2}{m\varepsilon_0}}\right] = [T^{-1}]$$

Angular frequency has also the dimension $[T^{-1}]$

65. As we know $\omega = \frac{2\pi}{T} = 2\pi f = \omega = 2\pi f = \frac{2\pi c}{\lambda}$

$$\therefore \lambda = \frac{2\pi c}{\omega} = \frac{2\pi c}{\sqrt{\frac{Ne^2}{m\varepsilon_0}}}$$

On putting the values, we get $\lambda \simeq 600$ nm.

66. Momentum is first positive but decreasing. Displacement (or say position) is initially zero. It will first increase. At highest point, momentum is zero and displacement is maximum. After that momentum is downwards (negative) and increasing but displacement is decreasing. Only (d) option satisfies these conditions.

67. $E = \frac{1}{2} m\omega^2 A^2$ or $E \alpha A^2$,

$$\frac{E_2}{E_1} = \left(\frac{A_2}{A_1}\right)^2 = \left(\frac{a}{2a}\right)^2 \text{ or } E_1 = 4E_2$$

68. In all the given four figure, at mean position, the position coordinate is zero.

At the same time, mass is starting from the extreme position in all four cases. In Fig. (c) and (d), extreme position is more than the initial extreme position. But due to viscosity opposite should be the case.

Hence, the answer should be either option (a) or option (b).

Correct answer is (b), because mass starts from positive extreme position (from uppermost position). Then, it will move downwards or momentum should be negative.

3

CHAPTER

Mass, Weight and Density

MASS

Mass is a fundamental property of matter that measures the quantity of matter contained within objects and it represents the inherent resistance of an object to changes in its state of motion and is often considered a measure of the amount of substance present. Mass is an intrinsic property and remains constant regardless of an object's location or the presence of gravity. It also represents the quantity of matter an object possesses and remains constant regardless of its location. The SI unit for mass is the kilogram (kg).

Mass can be measured using various units, including grams (g), metric tons (t), and ounces (oz). The conversion between units is as follows: 1 kg = 1000 g, 1 kg = 0.001 (t), 1 kg ≈ 35.27 (oz)

In simpler terms mass can be thought of as the "stuff" or material that makes up an object. It is the measure of how much matter an object contains. The greater the mass of an object, the more matter it possesses.

According to the law of conservation of mass, mass cannot be created or destroyed but can only be converted from one form to another. In any physical or chemical process, the total mass of the system remains constant.

Property of Mass:

Mass is a fundamental property of matter with several key characteristics:

1. Inertia: Mass is closely related to an object's inertia, which is the tendency of an object to resist changes in its state of motion. Objects with greater mass have greater inertia, meaning they require more force to accelerate or decelerate. This property is described by Newton's first law of motion, often referred to as the law of inertia.
2. Scalar Quantity: Mass is a scalar quantity, meaning it is described only by its magnitude and does not have a specific direction. The mass of an object is always positive and cannot be negative.
3. Additive Mass: When multiple objects are combined, the total mass is equal to the sum of the individual masses. For example, if two objects have masses m_1 and m_2, respectively, the total mass when they are combined is $m_1 + m_2$.
4. Conservation: According to the law of conservation of mass, mass is conserved in any isolated system. This means that in a closed system, the total mass before and after any physical or chemical process remains the same. Mass cannot be created or destroyed, only rearranged or converted into different forms.
5. Universal Gravitational Interaction: Mass interacts with other masses through gravitational forces. Every object with mass exerts a gravitational pull on other objects, and this force is proportional to the product of their masses and inversely proportional to the square of the distance between them. The universal law of gravitation, formulated by Sir Isaac Newton, describes this interaction.
6. Measurement: Mass is typically measured using the International System of Units (SI), specifically in kilograms (kg) or its multiples such as grams (g) or metric tons (t). Mass can also be measured using other units like ounces (oz) or pounds (lb) in non-SI systems.
7. Independence from Location: Mass is an intrinsic property of matter that remains constant regardless of an object's location or the presence of gravity. It is the same on Earth, in space, or on any other planet. Mass is different from weight, which is the force of gravity acting on an object and can vary with the strength of gravity.

Application of Mass:

Mass plays a crucial role in various scientific disciplines and has numerous practical applications. Here are a few examples and applications of mass:

1. Newton's Second Law of Motion: Mass is a key component of Newton's second law, which states that the acceleration of an object is directly proportional to the net force applied to it and inversely proportional to its mass. This law is fundamental in understanding and predicting the motion of objects under the influence of forces.
2. Engineering and Construction: Mass is a critical factor in designing structures, vehicles, and machines. Engineers must consider the mass of materials and components to ensure structural integrity, stability, and performance.

For example, when designing bridges or buildings, engineers need to calculate the mass of the structure to determine the appropriate materials and support systems.

3. Aerospace and Aviation: In the aerospace industry, mass plays a vital role in spacecraft and aircraft design. Engineers need to carefully calculate and distribute the mass of various components to ensure proper balance, stability, and fuel efficiency. Determining the mass of payloads, fuel, and equipment is crucial for successful missions.
4. Medicine and Pharmacology: Mass is essential in pharmaceutical research and dosage calculations. The mass of active ingredients in medications must be accurately measured and controlled to ensure the desired therapeutic effects and minimize potential side effects. Pharmacists and medical professionals rely on precise mass measurements to determine appropriate drug dosages for patients.
5. Environmental Sciences: Mass measurements are crucial in environmental sciences to assess pollution levels and monitor environmental impacts. For example, scientists measure the mass of pollutants in air, water, and soil samples to determine contamination levels and develop mitigation strategies. Mass measurements of greenhouse gases also help in understanding climate change.
6. Astrophysics and Cosmology: Mass plays a central role in astrophysics and cosmology, helping scientists understand the formation and evolution of celestial objects. The mass of stars, planets, galaxies, and black holes is measured and used to study gravitational interactions, stellar evolution, and the large-scale structure of the universe.

WEIGHT

Weight is a concept in physics that refers to the force exerted on an object due to gravity. It is a measure of how heavy an object is and is often represented by the symbol "W" or "Fg" (force of gravity). Weight is distinct from mass, although the two terms are often used interchangeably in everyday language.

1. Definition of Weight: Weight is defined as the force experienced by an object due to the gravitational attraction between the object and the Earth (or any other celestial body). It is a vector quantity, meaning it has both magnitude and direction. The magnitude of the weight is equal to the force of gravity acting on the object, while the direction is towards the center of the Earth.
2. Relationship between Weight and Mass: Mass and weight are related but different physical quantities. Mass refers to the amount of matter present in an object and is a scalar quantity. It remains constant regardless of the location of the object. Weight, on the other hand, depends on the gravitational field strength and varies with the location of the object.

   The relationship between weight and mass is given by Newton's second law of motion:

   $$F = m \times a$$

   where F is the force, m is the mass of the object, and a is the acceleration. In the case of weight, the force is the weight (W), mass (m) is the mass of the object, and the acceleration (a) is the acceleration due to gravity (g). Therefore, we have:

   $$W = m \times g$$

   Where, g is the acceleration due to gravity. On Earth's surface, the standard value for g is approximately 9.8 m/s^2. This equation shows that weight is directly proportional to the mass of an object. Consequently, if the mass increases, the weight also increases proportionally.
3. Units of Weight: The SI unit for weight is the Newton (N), named after Sir Isaac Newton. One Newton is defined as the force required to accelerate a one-kilogram mass by one meter per second squared. In everyday usage, weight is often expressed in pounds (lb) or kilograms (kg). For example, a person weighing 150 pounds has a weight of approximately 680 Newton's.
4. Weight and Gravitational Field Strength: Weight depends on the strength of the gravitational field acting on the object. The gravitational field strength varies depending on the distance from the center of the massive body. On Earth, the gravitational field strength is approximately constant near its surface but decreases with increasing distance from the surface (such as at higher altitudes or in outer space).

   As a result, an object will weigh less when moved to a location where the gravitational field strength is weaker. For example, an object on the Moon would weigh approximately one-sixth of its weight on Earth due to the Moon's weaker gravity.
5. Weightlessness: In situations where an object or a person experiences negligible gravitational forces, such as during free fall or in orbit around a planet, the sensation of weightlessness occurs. Weightlessness does not mean the absence of mass but rather the absence of a sensation of weight. Astronauts in space experience weightlessness because they are in a state of continuous free fall around the Earth.

The property of weight:

The property of weight refers to the measure of the gravitational force exerted on an object due to its mass. Weight is a vector quantity, which means it has both magnitude and direction. Weight is often confused with mass, but they are different concepts. Mass is a measure of the amount of matter in an object and is a scalar quantity, whereas weight depends on both the mass of an object and the acceleration due to gravity. The weight of an object can vary depending on the gravitational field strength, whereas its mass remains constant.

Applications of Weight:

The concept of weight has numerous practical applications across various fields. Here are some common applications of weight:

1. Engineering and Construction: Weight plays a crucial role in designing structures and determining load capacities. Engineers consider the weight of materials, equipment, and occupants to ensure the stability and integrity of buildings, bridges, and other structures.
2. Transportation and Logistics: Weight is essential in determining the maximum load capacity of vehicles such as trucks, airplanes, and ships. It is used to calculate payload capacity, fuel efficiency, and distribution of weight for safe transportation.
3. Product Design and Manufacturing: Weight is a critical factor in designing and manufacturing products, especially those involving safety, ergonomics, or portability. For example, the weight of a car affects its performance and fuel efficiency, while the weight of a handheld device influences its user-friendliness.
4. Health and Medicine: Weight is an essential measurement in the field of medicine. It is used to monitor patient health, calculate medication dosages, assess nutritional requirements, and diagnose conditions such as obesity. Body mass index (BMI), a weight-to-height ratio, is widely used to evaluate the overall health and risk factors associated with weight.
5. Agriculture and Food Industry: Weight is critical in agricultural practices, including the weighing of crops, livestock, and machinery. In the food industry, weight is used to measure ingredients, portion sizes, and packaging quantities to ensure consistency and quality control.
6. Astronomy and Space Exploration: Understanding the concept of weight is crucial in studying celestial bodies. Weight plays a role in calculating gravitational forces between objects, determining the trajectories of spacecraft, and analyzing the effects of gravity on astronauts during space missions.

DENSITY

Density is a physical property that measures how much mass is contained within a given volume. It is a fundamental property of matter and is often used to characterize and compare different substances.

Density can vary widely depending on the material or substance being considered. For example, substances like lead and gold are dense, meaning they have a high mass in a given volume. On the other hand, substances like air or helium are less dense, as they have a low mass in a given volume.

Density is often used to identify and classify materials. For instance, it can help differentiate between solids, liquids, and gases, as they have different densities due to the arrangement and spacing of their particles. Density can also be used to determine the purity or composition of a substance, as different materials typically have different densities.

One practical application of density is buoyancy. In fluids, an object will float or sink depending on its density relative to the density of the fluid. If the object is less dense than the fluid, it will float; if it is denser, it will sink. This principle is why objects made of wood or foam float on water, while metals sink.

The relationship between weight and density can be understood by considering the formula:

Weight = Mass × Acceleration due to gravity

Density is calculated by dividing the mass of an object or substance by its volume. The formula for density is:

Density = Mass / Volume

The standard SI unit for density is kilograms per cubic meter (kg/m^3), but other units such as grams per cubic centimeter (g/cm^3) or pounds per cubic inch (lb/in^3) are also commonly used.

From these formulas, we can see that weight depends on both mass and the acceleration due to gravity, while density depends on mass and volume.

The property of density:

Density is a fundamental property of matter that describes how much mass is contained within a given volume. It is commonly denoted by the symbol "ρ" (rho) and is calculated by dividing the mass of an object or substance by its volume. Density is a useful property because it helps us compare and classify different materials based on how closely their atoms or molecules are packed together. Materials with higher density have more mass in a given volume and are generally considered denser than materials with lower density.

Different states of matter have different average densities. Generally, solids are denser than liquids, and liquids are denser than gases. For example, water is denser in its liquid state compared to its solid (ice) or gaseous (water vapor) states.

Density is affected by temperature and pressure. As temperature increases, most substances expand and become less dense, while cooling them down usually increases their density. Similarly, increasing pressure can compress materials and increase their density, while decreasing pressure can cause them to expand and decrease in density.

Applications of density:

Density has numerous applications across various fields. Here are some common applications of density:

1. Identification of substances: Density is often used as a characteristic property to identify and classify substances. By measuring the density of an unknown material and comparing it to known densities of different substances, scientists can determine the composition and purity of the material.
2. Material selection: Density plays a crucial role in material selection for different applications. For example, in construction, the density of materials like concrete, wood, and steel is considered to ensure structural integrity and load-bearing capacity.

3. Buoyancy and flotation: Density is essential in understanding buoyancy and flotation. Objects with a lower density than the fluid they are immersed in will float, while those with a higher density will sink. This principle is utilized in designing ships, submarines, and flotation devices like life jackets and buoys.
4. Fluid mechanics: Density is a key parameter in fluid mechanics, where it affects fluid flow, pressure, and viscosity. It is used in calculations related to fluid dynamics, including the design of pipelines, pumps, and hydraulic systems.
5. Pharmaceutical industry: Density is crucial in the pharmaceutical industry for drug formulation and dosage calculations. It helps determine the concentration of active ingredients in a medication and ensures accurate dosing.
6. Environmental monitoring: Density measurements are employed in environmental monitoring to assess water quality. Changes in water density can indicate variations in temperature, salinity, or pollutant levels, providing valuable information for ecological studies.
7. Geology and mineralogy: Density is used to identify and classify minerals and rocks in geology. It helps determine the composition and type of geological formations, aiding in mineral exploration and resource evaluation.
8. Food and beverage industry: Density measurements are used in quality control and process monitoring within the food and beverage industry. It helps assess the concentration of ingredients, monitor fermentation processes, and ensure product consistency.

Types of density:

Density is a physical property that measures the amount of mass per unit volume of a substance. There are several types of density that are commonly referred to:

1. Energy density: Energy density refers to the amount of energy stored in a given volume or mass of a substance. It is commonly used in fields such as physics, engineering, and materials science. The unit for energy density depends on the context and can be expressed in joules per cubic meter (J/m^3), watt-hours per kilogram (Wh/kg), or other appropriate units.
2. Charge density: Charge density is a measure of the electric charge per unit volume of a material or a system. It is commonly used in physics and electrical engineering to describe the distribution of electric charge. The unit for charge density is coulombs per cubic meter (C/m^3).
3. Linear density: Linear density refers to the mass per unit length of a one-dimensional object, such as a string, wire, or thread. It is calculated by dividing the mass of the object by its length. The unit for linear density depends on the system of measurement used, such as kilograms per meter (kg/m) or grams per centimeter (g/cm)..
4. Mass density: Mass density, as mentioned earlier, is the most common type of density and is applicable to fluids as well. It represents the mass per unit volume of the fluid. The mass density of a fluid determines its inertia and is often used to characterize the fluid's behavior. The standard unit for mass density of fluids is kilograms per cubic meter (kg/m^3) in the SI system.
5. Fluid density: Fluid density specifically refers to the mass density of a fluid, such as a liquid or a gas. It represents how much mass is contained within a given volume of the fluid. Fluid density is an important property in fluid mechanics and is often used in calculations involving fluid flow, buoyancy, and pressure.
6. Weight density: Weight density, also known as gravitational density, is the force per unit volume exerted by a substance due to gravity. It is calculated by multiplying the mass density by the acceleration due to gravity (g). The units of weight density depend on the units used for mass density and acceleration due to gravity. For example, if mass density is given in kg/m^3 and g is approximately 9.8 m/s^2, then the weight density would be expressed in newton's per cubic meter (N/m^3).
7. Relative density: Relative density, also called specific gravity, compares the density of a substance to the density of a reference substance, usually water. It is a dimensionless quantity and is calculated by dividing the density of the substance by the density of the reference substance. Since water is commonly used as the reference substance, the relative density of water is typically 1. Relative density is often used to determine the purity or composition of a substance by comparing it to a known standard.
8. Volumetric density: Volumetric density, also known as volume density, is the reciprocal of the specific volume of a fluid. It represents the volume occupied by a unit mass of the fluid. Volumetric density is the inverse of mass density and is often used in thermodynamics and fluid mechanics. The unit for volumetric density is cubic meters per kilogram (m^3/kg).
9. Number density: Number density, as mentioned earlier, is a measure of the number of particles per unit volume. In the context of fluids, number density refers to the concentration of particles, such as molecules or ions, in the fluid. It is particularly relevant in studies involving gases or solutions. The unit for number density is particles per cubic meter (particles/m^3).
10. Partial density: Partial density refers to the density of a specific component or species within a mixture or solution. It represents the mass per unit volume of that particular component. Partial density is commonly used in chemical engineering and environmental science to analyze the composition and properties of mixtures. The unit for partial density is typically the same as mass density (kg/m^3).

Measurement of density

The density at any point of a homogeneou object equals its total mass divided by its total volume. The mass is normally measured with an appropriate scale or balance; the volume may be measured directly from the geometry of the object) or by the displarement of a fluid. Hydrostatic weighing, for instance uses, the displaoement of water due to a submerged object to determine the density of the object.

If the body is not homogeneous, then the density is a function of the position. In that case the density around any given location is determined by calculating the density of a small volume around that location. In the limit of an infinitesimal vohlme the density of an inhomogeneous object at a point becomes: $\rho(r)=dm/dV$, where dV is an elementary volume at position r. The mass of the body then can be expressed as

$$m = \int_V \rho(r)\, dV.$$

The density of granular material can be ambiguous depending on exactly how its volume is defined, and this may cause confusion in measurement. A common example is sand: if it is gently poured into a container, the density, will be low; if the same sand is then compacted it will occupy less volume and consequently exhibit a greater density. This is because sand, like all powders and granular solids, contains a lot of air space in between individual grains. The density of the material including the air spaces is the bulk density which differs significantly from the density of an individual grain of sand with no air in.eluded.

Specific gravity for measure the density:

Specific gravity is a relative measure of density that compares the density of a substance to the density of water at a specified temperature and pressure. It is a dimensionless quantity and is often used in industries such as mining and metallurgy to determine the concentration of minerals in ores or the purity of metals.

Mathematically, the specific gravity of a substance is measure by dividing its density by the density of the reference substance. Since water is commonly used as the reference substance, the specific gravity of a material is often a comparison of its density to that of water.

The formula for specific gravity (SG) is:

S.G = density of substance / density of water

Since water has a density of 1 gram per cubic centimeter (g/cm^3) or 1000 kilograms per cubic meter (kg/m^3), the specific gravity of a substance is numerically equivalent to its density in relation to water.

For example, if the specific gravity of a substance is 2, it means that the substance is twice as dense as water. If the specific gravity is less than 1, it means the substance is less dense than water.

Changes of density

In general, density can be changed by changing either the pressure or the temperature. Increasing the pressure always increases the density of a materal. Increasing the temperature generally decreases the density but there are notable exception to this generalization. For example, the density of water increases between its melting point at 0 °C and 4 °C; similar behavior is observed in silicon at low temperatures.

The effect of pressure and temperature on the densities of liquids and solids is small. The compressibility for a typical liquid or solid is 10^{-6} bar^{-1} (1 bar = 0.1 MPa) and a typical thermal expansivity is 10^{-5} K^{-1}. This roughly translates into needing around ten thousand times atmospheric pressure to reduce the volume of a substance by one percent. Although the pressures needed may be around a thousand times smaller for sandy soil and some clays.) A one percent expansion of volume typically requires a tempernture increase on the order of thousands of degrees Celsius.

In contrast, the density of gases is strongly affected by pressure. The density of an ideal gas is

$$\rho = \frac{MP}{RT},$$

where M is the molar mass, P is the pressure R is the universal gas constant, and T is the absolute temperature. This means that the density of an ideal gas can be doubled by doubling the pressure, or by halving the absolute temperature.

Density of solutions

The density of a solution is the sum of mass (massic) concentrations of the components of that solution. Mass (massic) concentration of a given component ρ_i in a solution can be called partial density of that component.

$$\rho = \sum_i \rho_i$$

Expressed as a function of the densities of pure components of the mixture and their volume participation it read:

$$\rho = \sum_i \rho_o i \frac{V_o i}{V}$$

Densities of Various Materials

Material	ρ in kg/m^3	Notes
Interstellar medium	$10^{-25} - 10^{-15}$	Assuming 90% H, 10% He; variable T
Earth's atmosphere	1.2	At sea level
Aerogel	1 – 2	
Styrofoam	30 – 120[6]	
Cork	220 – 260[6]	
Potassium	860[]	At STP
Sodium	970	At STP
Ice	916.7	
Water (fresh)	1000	At STP
Water (salt)	1030	
Plastics	850 – 1400	For polypropylene and PETE/PVC
Magnesium	1740	At STP
Gold	19320	At STP
Plutonium	19840	At STP
Platinum	21450	At STP
Iridium	22420	At STP
Osmium	22570	At STP
The core of the Sun	~150000	
White dwarf star	1×10^{9}[9]	
Atomic nuclei	2.3×10^{17} [10]	Does not depend strongly on size of nucleus
Neutron star	$8.4 \times 10^{16} - 1 \times 10^{18}$	
Black hole	4×10^{17}	Mean density inside the Schwarzschild radius of an Earth-mass black hole (theoretical)

Beryllium	1850	At STP
Glycerol[7] [8]	1261	
Silicon	2330	At STP
Aluminium	2700	At STP
Titanium	4540	At STP
Selenium	4800	At STP
The Earth	5515.3	Mean density
Vanadium	6100	At STP
Antimony	6690	At STP
Zinc	7000	At STP
Chromium	7200	At STP
Manganese	7210 - 7440	At STP
Tin	7310	At STP
Iron	7870	At STP
Niobium	8570	At STP
Cadmium	8650	At STP
Cobalt	8900	At STP
Nickel	8900	At STP
Copper	8920 – 8960	Near room temperature
Bismuth	9750	At STP
Molybdenum	10220	At STP
Silver	10500	At STP
Lead	11340	Near room temperature
Thorium	11700	At STP
Rhodium	12410	At STP
The Inner Core of the Earth	~13000	As listed in Earth
Mercury	13546	At STP
Tantalum	16600	At STP
Uranium	18800	At STP
Tungsten	19300	At STP

Objective Type Questions

1. Which of the following best defines mass?
(a) The force exerted on an object
(b) The amount of matter in an object
(c) The volume occupied by an object
(d) The speed at which an object moves
2. What is the SI unit of mass?
(a) Kilogram (kg) (b) Meter (m)
(c) Second (s) (d) Newton (N)
3. Which of the following statements is true about mass?
(a) It depends on the gravitational field.
(b) It changes with temperature.
(c) It is a vector quantity.
(d) It is conserved in all physical processes.
4. Which property of mass determines the amount of gravitational force between two objects?
(a) Inertia (b) Weight
(c) Volume (d) Density
5. Which of the following is an example of an extensive property of mass?
(a) Density (b) Weight
(c) Volume (d) Inertia
6. Which principle states that the acceleration of an object is directly proportional to the force acting on it and inversely proportional to its mass?
(a) Newton's first law (b) Newton's second law
(c) Newton's third law (d) Archimedes' principle
7. The inertia of an object is directly related to its:
(a) Acceleration (b) Mass
(c) Weight (d) Volume
8. Which property of mass determines how difficult it is to change the state of motion of an object?
(a) Inertia (b) Weight
(c) Volume (d) Density
9. Which of the following statements is true about the gravitational force acting on an object?
(a) It depends on the mass of the object.
(b) It depends on the shape of the object.
(c) It depends on the volume of the object.
(d) It depends on the density of the object.
10. Which of the following is an application of mass spectrometry?
(a) Determining the volume of an object
(b) Measuring the mass of celestial bodies
(c) Calculating the density of a liquid
(d) Studying the properties of electromagnetic waves
11. Which property of mass is used in the equation $E = mc^2$?
(a) Density (b) Weight
(c) Inertia (d) Energy equivalence
12. Which of the following devices measures the mass of an object?
(a) Thermometer (b) Barometer
(c) Spectrometer (d) Balance
13. Which property of mass is used to determine the purity of a substance?
(a) Inertia (b) Weight
(c) Density (d) Melting point
14. Which of the following statements is true about the relationship between mass and acceleration?
(a) Greater mass always leads to greater acceleration.
(b) Greater mass always leads to smaller acceleration.
(c) Mass and acceleration are unrelated.
(d) The relationship between mass and acceleration depends on the force applied.
15. Which property of mass determines the amount of matter contained within a given volume?
(a) Inertia (b) Weight
(c) Density (d) Kinetic energy
16. Which of the following is an application of mass balance?
(a) Measuring the speed of an object
(b) Determining the volume of a gas
(c) Measuring the force exerted by an object
(d) Quantifying the mass of a substance
17. Which property of mass plays a crucial role in the formation of stars and galaxies?
(a) Inertia (b) Weight
(c) Volume (d) Gravitational attraction
18. Which of the following is an example of a macroscopic application of mass?
(a) Atomic mass spectroscopy
(b) Gravitational wave detection
(c) Particle accelerator experiments
(d) Measurement of drug doses
19. Which property of mass determines the gravitational potential energy of an object?
(a) Inertia (b) Weight
(c) Volume (d) Height
20. Which of the following is an example of an application of mass in engineering?
(a) Determining the color of an object
(b) Designing structures to withstand forces
(c) Measuring the acidity of a solution
(d) Studying the behavior of subatomic particles

21. What is weight?
(a) The amount of matter in an object
(b) The force of gravity acting on an object
(c) The measure of an object's size
(d) The density of an object

22. Which of the following is not a property of weight?
(a) Weight is a vector quantity.
(b) Weight depends on the mass of an object.
(c) Weight is measured in kilograms.
(d) Weight can change with location.

23. When you travel to the Moon, your weight will:
(a) Increase (b) Decrease
(c) Remain the same (d) Become zero

24. The weight of an object can be determined by:
(a) Measuring its mass
(b) Measuring its volume
(c) Using a spring scale
(d) Counting the number of atoms in the object

25. Which of the following statements about weight is true?
(a) Weight and mass are the same thing.
(b) Weight is a scalar quantity.
(c) Weight can be negative.
(d) Weight depends on the shape of an object.

26. Which of the following objects will have the greatest weight on Earth?
(a) A 1 kg iron ball
(b) A 1 kg feather
(c) A 1 kg piece of wood
(d) They will all have the same weight.

27. The weight of an object is least on which of the following planets?
(a) Earth (b) Mars
(c) Jupiter (d) Venus

28. Which of the following factors does not affect the weight of an object?
(a) Mass of the object
(b) Distance from the center of the Earth
(c) Altitude above sea level
(d) Temperature of the object

29. The weight of an object on the Moon is approximately:
(a) One-sixth of its weight on Earth
(b) One-fourth of its weight on Earth
(c) Half of its weight on Earth
(d) The same as its weight on Earth

30. Which property allows weight to be measured using a balance scale?
(a) Inertia (b) Density
(c) Volume (d) Mass

31. The weight of an object in free fall is:
(a) Zero (b) Constant
(c) Increasing (d) Decreasing

32. Which of the following is an application of weight measurement?
(a) Determining the volume of an object
(b) Calculating the density of a substance
(c) Balancing chemical equations
(d) Measuring the force exerted by an object

33. The weight of an object is directly proportional to its:
(a) Density (b) Volume
(c) Mass (d) Temperature

34. Which of the following materials would have the greatest weight for the same volume?
(a) Wood (b) Plastic
(c) Steel (d) Aluminum

35. Which instrument is commonly used to measure weight?
(a) Barometer (b) Thermometer
(c) Hydrometer (d) Spring scale

36. Which property of weight allows objects to sink or float in a fluid?
(a) Buoyancy (b) Elasticity
(c) Viscosity (d) Cohesion

37. Weight is a measure of an object's:
(a) Speed (b) Size
(c) Force (d) Temperature

38. The weight of an object can be calculated using the formula:
(a) Weight = Mass × Volume
(b) Weight = Mass ÷ Volume
(c) Weight = Mass × Acceleration
(d) Weight = Mass × Gravity

39. Which of the following is not an example of weight conversion?
(a) Pounds to kilograms (b) Ounces to grams
(c) Newtons to pounds (d) Inches to meters

40. The weight of an object on the surface of the Earth is approximately:
(a) 9.8 N/kg (b) 1 N
(c) 9.8 kg (d) 1 kg

41. Which of the following statements about weight and mass is correct?
(a) Weight and mass are the same thing.
(b) Weight is a measure of the amount of matter in an object.
(c) Mass is a measure of the force of gravity acting on an object.
(d) Weight and mass have different units of measurement.

42. Which of the following is not a unit of weight?
(a) Newton (N) (b) Kilogram (kg)
(c) Pound (lb) (d) Gram (g)

43. Weightlessness occurs when:
(a) An object is in free fall
(b) An object is at rest on a surface
(c) The weight of an object is zero
(d) An object is in equilibrium

44. Which of the following is an example of weight being balanced by another force?
(a) A book resting on a table
(b) A car accelerating on a road
(c) A balloon floating in the air
(d) A person standing on the ground

45. The weight of an object is greatest at:
(a) The North Pole (b) The Equator
(c) Sea level (d) High altitudes

46. Which of the following is not a property of weight?
(a) Weight is a vector quantity.
(b) Weight depends on the location.
(c) Weight is independent of the mass of an object.
(d) Weight can be measured using a spring scale.

47. Weight plays a significant role in which of the following sports?
(a) Basketball (b) Gymnastics
(c) Swimming (d) Chess

48. Which property allows weight to be used in determining the stability of an object?
(a) Inertia (b) Elasticity
(c) Friction (d) Momentum

49. Which of the following industries relies heavily on weight measurement?
(a) Automotive (b) Information technology
(c) Fashion (d) Entertainment

50. Which property of weight allows it to be used in determining the mass of an object?
(a) Inertia (b) Buoyancy
(c) Gravitational force (d) Surface area

51. What is the definition of density?
(a) The amount of matter in an object
(b) The mass of an object divided by its volume
(c) The weight of an object divided by its volume
(d) The size of an object divided by its weight

52. Which of the following units is used to measure density?
(a) Newton (b) Joule
(c) Pascal (d) Kilogram per cubic meter

53. Which of the following substances has the highest density?
(a) Air (b) Water
(c) Gold (d) Aluminum

54. Which property does not affect the density of an object?
(a) Temperature (b) Pressure
(c) Shape (d) Mass

55. Which of the following substances has the lowest density?
(a) Lead (b) Iron
(c) Styrofoam (d) Copper

56. What happens to the density of a substance as its temperature increases?
(a) Density increases
(b) Density decreases
(c) Density remains constant
(d) Density depends on the substance

57. Which property allows objects with greater density to float on objects with lower density?
(a) Buoyancy (b) Gravity
(c) Viscosity (d) Inertia

58. Which instrument is used to measure the density of a liquid?
(a) Barometer (b) Hydrometer
(c) Thermometer (d) Manometer

59. Which property of density enables the layering of different liquids?
(a) Viscosity (b) Surface tension
(c) Refractive index (d) Relative density

60. Which property of density is used in medical imaging techniques like X-rays?
(a) Absorption (b) Reflection
(c) Refraction (d) Dispersion

61. Which property of density is used to separate substances in centrifugation?
(a) Viscosity (b) Solubility
(c) Buoyancy (d) Magnetic susceptibility

62. Which property of density is utilized in flotation devices?
(a) Viscosity (b) Compressibility
(c) Buoyancy (d) Refraction

63. Which factor has the most significant influence on the density of an object?
(a) Volume (b) Mass
(c) Temperature (d) Pressure

64. What is the density of an object that has a mass of 500 grams and a volume of 100 cubic centimeters?
(a) 5 g/cm^3 (b) 50 g/cm^3
(c) 100 g/cm^3 (d) 500 g/cm^3

65. Which property of density is used in the production of alloys?
(a) Reactivity (b) Ductility
(c) Malleability (d) Solubility

66. Which property of density is important in the design of skyscrapers and bridges?
(a) Elasticity (b) Tensile strength
(c) Hardness (d) Brittleness

67. Which property of density is responsible for the greenhouse effect?
(a) Absorption (b) Reflection
(c) Refraction (d) Scattering

68. Which property of density is used in the production of batteries?
(a) Conductivity (b) Elasticity
(c) Hardness (d) Solubility

69. Which property of density is used in geology to identify and classify minerals?
(a) Color (b) Hardness
(c) Luster (d) Specific gravity

70. Which property of density is used in the determination of alcohol content in beverages?
(a) Refractive index (b) Viscosity
(c) Density (d) Surface tension

71. Which property of density is utilized in the operation of hot air balloons?
(a) Viscosity (b) Buoyancy
(c) Surface tension (d) Refractive index

72. Which property of density is used in the flotation process to extract minerals from ore?
(a) Magnetic susceptibility
(b) Conductivity
(c) Surface tension
(d) Frothability

73. Which property of density is important in the selection of materials for shipbuilding?
(a) Ductility (b) Elasticity
(c) Compressibility (d) Buoyancy

74. Which property of density is used in the measurement of blood sugar levels?
(a) Conductivity (b) Refractive index
(c) Viscosity (d) Optical density

75. Which property of density is used in the production of plastics and polymers?
(a) Elasticity (b) Solubility
(c) Viscosity (d) Melt flow index

76. Which property of density is used in the determination of the purity of precious metals?
(a) Hardness (b) Conductivity
(c) Reactivity (d) Luster

77. Which property of density is used in the design of building insulation materials?
(a) Thermal conductivity
(b) Viscosity
(c) Surface tension
(d) Elasticity

78. Which property of density is utilized in the operation of air conditioning and refrigeration systems?
(a) Surface tension (b) Viscosity
(c) Latent heat (d) Thermal expansion

79. Which property of density is used in the analysis of petroleum products?
(a) Viscosity (b) Flash point
(c) Pour point (d) API gravity

80. Which property of density is important in the design of lightweight construction materials?
(a) Hardness
(b) Brittleness
(c) Compressive strength
(d) Specific strength

81. Which property of density is used in the determination of air pollution levels?
(a) Reflectivity (b) Transparency
(c) Absorption (d) Scattering

82. Which property of density is important in the field of aerodynamics?
(a) Surface tension (b) Viscosity
(c) Drag coefficient (d) Elastic modulus

83. Which property of density is used in the determination of groundwater levels?
(a) Permeability (b) Porosity
(c) Capillarity (d) Specific yield

84. Which property of density is utilized in the design of soundproofing materials?
(a) Elasticity
(b) Conductivity
(c) Absorption coefficient
(d) Malleability

85. Which property of density is used in the analysis of soil composition?
(a) pH level
(b) Particle size distribution
(c) Organic matter content
(d) Bulk density

86. Which property of density is important in the selection of materials for radiation shielding?
(a) Absorption coefficient
(b) Transparency
(c) Conductivity
(d) Damping coefficient

87. Which property of density is used in the measurement of fluid flow rates?
(a) Viscosity (b) Pressure
(c) Surface tension (d) Flow velocity

88. Which property of density is important in the design of vehicle safety features?
(a) Friction coefficient (b) Impact resistance
(c) Surface tension (d) Yield strength

89. Which property of density is utilized in the analysis of air quality?
(a) Reflectivity (b) Transparency
(c) Absorption (d) Scattering

90. Which property of density is important in the design of filtration systems?
(a) Porosity (b) Surface tension
(c) Permeability (d) Optical density

91. Which property of density is used in the measurement of soil moisture content?
(a) Conductivity (b) Capillarity
(c) Permeability (d) Water holding capacity

92. Which property of density is utilized in the design of optics and lenses?
(a) Refractive index (b) Elasticity
(c) Viscosity (d) Surface tension

93. Which property of density is used in the determination of water purity?
(a) pH level (b) Electrical conductivity
(c) Turbidity (d) Hardness

94. Which property of density is important in the design of packaging materials?
(a) Biodegradability (b) Elastic modulus
(c) Flexibility (d) Specific volume

95. Which property of density is utilized in the analysis of air humidity?
(a) Viscosity (b) Dew point
(c) Vapor pressure (d) Relative humidity

96. Which property of density is used in the determination of soil compaction?
(a) Permeability (b) Particle size distribution
(c) Bulk density (d) Organic matter content

97. Which property of density is important in the design of heat exchangers?
(a) Thermal conductivity
(b) Thermal expansion
(c) Specific heat capacity
(d) Thermal diffusivity

98. Which property of density is utilized in the determination of the concentration of solutions?
(a) pH level (b) Molarity
(c) Viscosity (d) Freezing point depression

99. Which property of density is important in the selection of materials for aerospace applications?
(a) Ductility (b) Thermal expansion
(c) Specific strength (d) Reflectivity

100. Which property of density is used in the determination of the sugar content in fruits and beverages?
(a) Refractive index (b) Viscosity
(c) Solubility (d) Optical density

Answers

1. (b) **2.** (a) **3.** (d) **4.** (b) **5.** (c) **6.** (b) **7.** (b) **8.** (a) **9.** (a) **10.** (b)
11. (c) **12.** (d) **13.** (c) **14.** (b) **15.** (c) **16.** (d) **17.** (d) **18.** (d) **19.** (b) **20.** (b)
21. (b) **22.** (c) **23.** (b) **24.** (c) **25.** (c) **26.** (d) **27.** (b) **28.** (d) **29.** (a) **30.** (d)
31. (a) **32.** (d) **33.** (c) **34.** (c) **35.** (d) **36.** (a) **37.** (c) **38.** (d) **39.** (d) **40.** (a)
41. (d) **42.** (b) **43.** (a) **44.** (a) **45.** (a) **46.** (c) **47.** (c) **48.** (a) **49.** (a) **50.** (a)
51. (b) **52.** (d) **53.** (c) **54.** (c) **55.** (c) **56.** (b) **57.** (a) **58.** (b) **59.** (d) **60.** (a)
61. (c) **62.** (c) **63.** (b) **64.** (a) **65.** (c) **66.** (a) **67.** (a) **68.** (a) **69.** (d) **70.** (c)
71. (b) **72.** (d) **73.** (d) **74.** (d) **75.** (d) **76.** (b) **77.** (a) **78.** (c) **79.** (d) **80.** (d)
81. (c) **82.** (c) **83.** (d) **84.** (c) **85.** (d) **86.** (a) **87.** (a) **88.** (b) **89.** (c) **90.** (a)
91. (d) **92.** (a) **93.** (b) **94.** (d) **95.** (d) **96.** (c) **97.** (a) **98.** (b) **99.** (c) **100.** (a)

Explanations

1. The amount of matter in an object. Mass is a fundamental property of matter that represents the quantity of matter in an object.
2. The kilogram is the base unit of mass in the International System of Units (SI).
3. Mass is a conserved quantity, meaning it remains constant regardless of changes in gravitational field or temperature. It is conserved in all physical processes.
4. Weight is the force experienced by an object due to the gravitational attraction of another object and is directly proportional to mass.
5. Extensive properties depend on the amount of substance present, and volume is an example of such a property.
6. Newton's second law of motion states that the acceleration of an object is directly proportional to the net force acting on it and inversely proportional to its mass.
7. Inertia is the resistance of an object to changes in its motion and is directly related to the mass of the object.
8. Inertia is the property of mass that determines how difficult it is to change the state of motion of an object.
9. The gravitational force acting on an object is directly proportional to its mass. It depends on the mass of the object.
10. Mass spectrometry is a technique used to measure the masses and relative abundances of atoms and molecules, and it has applications in various fields, including astronomy. So, it measuring the mass of celestial bodies.
11. The equation $E = mc^2$, derived by Einstein, relates energy (E) to the mass (m) of an object and the speed of light (c). It highlights the equivalence of mass and energy.
12. A balance is a device used to measure the mass of an object by comparing it with known masses.
13. The density of a substance can be used to determine its purity since impurities can affect the density.
14. According to Newton's second law of motion, for a given force, the acceleration is inversely proportional to the mass. Therefore, greater mass results in smaller acceleration and smaller acceleration.
15. Density is the ratio of mass to volume and provides information about the amount of matter contained within a given volume.
16. The mass of a substance. A mass balance is a device used to measure the mass of an object or substance accurately.
17. The mass of celestial bodies, such as stars and galaxies, determines the strength of their gravitational attraction, which plays a crucial role in their formation and behavior.
18. While the other options involve studying or measuring properties at the atomic or subatomic level, the measurementof drug doses involves the macroscopic application of mass.
19. The gravitational potential energy of an object is determined by its weight, which is directly related to its mass.
20. Designing structures to withstand forces. In engineering, knowledge of mass is essential for designing structures that can withstand the forces acting on them, ensuring their stability and safety.
21. Weight is the force of gravity acting on an object, so the correct answer is (b).
22. Weight is actually measured in newtons, not kilograms. So, the correct answer is (c).
23. Your weight will decrease on the Moon because the Moon has less gravitational force than Earth. So, the correct answer is (b).
24. The weight of an object can be determined by using a spring scale, which measures the force of gravity acting on the object. So, the correct answer is (c).
25. Weight and mass are not the same thing. Weight is a vector quantity, and it can never be negative. So, the correct answer is (c).
26. The weight of an object depends on its mass and the force of gravity. Since all the objects have the same mass (1 kg) and are on Earth, they will all have the same weight. So, the correct answer is (d).
27. The weight of an object is least on Mars because Mars has less gravitational force compared to Earth. So, the correct answer is (b).
28. The temperature of an object does not affect its weight. Weight depends on the mass of the object and the distance from the center of the Earth. So, the correct answer is (d).
29. The weight of an object on the Moon is approximately one-sixth of its weight on Earth because the Moon has approximately one-sixth of the gravitational force of Earth. So, the correct answer is (a).
30. Weight cannot be directly measured using a balance scale. Instead, a balance scale measures mass, which is indirectly related to weight. So, the correct answer is (d).
31. In free fall, the weight of an object is zero because there is no support force acting on it. So, the correct answer is (a).
32. Measuring the force exerted by an object is an application of weight measurement. So, the correct answer is (d).

33. The weight of an object is directly proportional to its mass. So, the correct answer is (c).

34. The weight of an object depends on its mass, not its volume. Therefore, the material with the highest density would have the greatest weight for the same volume. In this case, steel typically has a higher density than wood, plastic, and aluminum. So, the correct answer is (c).

35. A spring scale is commonly used to measure weight. So, the correct answer is (d).

36. Buoyancy, which is the upward force exerted on an object submerged in a fluid, determines whether an object will sink or float. So, the correct answer is (a).

37. Weight is a measure of the force of gravity acting on an object. So, the correct answer is (c).

38. The weight of an object can be calculated using the formula Weight = Mass × Gravity, where gravity is the acceleration due to gravity. So, the correct answer is (d).

39. Converting inches to meters is a conversion of length, not weight. So, the correct answer is (d).

40. The weight of an object on the surface of the Earth is approximately 9.8 N/kg, which is the acceleration due to gravity. So, the correct answer is (a).

41. Weight and mass are not the same thing. Mass is a measure of the amount of matter in an object, while weight is the force of gravity acting on an object. They have different units of measurement as well. So, the correct answer is (d).

42. Kilogram (kg) is not a unit of weight; it is a unit of mass. So, the correct answer is (b).

43. Weightlessness occurs when an object is in free fall and there is no support force acting on it. So, the correct answer is (a).

44. A book resting on a table is an example of weight being balanced by the support force exerted by the table. So, the correct answer is (a).

45. The weight of an object is greatest at the poles because the Earth's gravitational force is slightly stronger there due to the shape of the Earth. So, the correct answer is (a).

46. Weight is dependent on the mass of an object, so weight is not independent of mass. So, the correct answer is (c).

47. Weight plays a significant role in swimming because buoyancy and the weight of the swimmer affect their ability to float and move through the water. So, the correct answer is (c).

48. Inertia, which is the resistance of an object to changes in its motion, is related to weight and can be used to determine the stability of an object. So, the correct answer is (a).

49. The automotive industry relies heavily on weight measurement for purposes such as determining fuel efficiency, load capacity, and vehicle safety. So, the correct answer is (a).

50. Inertia, which is the resistance of an object to changes in its motion, is related to mass and can be used to determine the mass of an object indirectly. So, the correct answer is (a).

51. Density is the measure of how much mass is contained in a given volume. So, the mass of an object divided by its volume.

52. Density is typically measured in kilograms per cubic meter (kg/m^3) in the International System of Units (SI).

53. Gold has a higher density than air, water, and aluminum. Its high atomic mass and compact structure contribute to its high density.

54. The shape of an object does not affect its density. Density depends on the mass and volume of the object.

55. Styrofoam is a lightweight material with low density, whereas lead, iron, and copper have higher densities.

56. As temperature increases, most substances expand and become less dense.

57. Objects with greater density than the surrounding fluid will sink, while objects with lower density will float due to the upward buoyant force.

58. A hydrometer is a device that measures the density or specific gravity of a liquid. It typically consists of a weighted glass tube.

59. The relative density of liquids determines the order in which they will layer when different liquids are carefully poured into a container.

60. X-rays are absorbed by different tissues in the body based on their density, allowing for the creation of images.

61. Centrifugation uses the differences in densities of substances to separate them based on their buoyant forces in a rotating container.

62. Flotation devices like life jackets work by providing enough buoyant force to keep a person afloat due to the density difference between their body and water.

63. The mass of an object has the greatest influence on its density, as density is calculated by dividing mass by volume.

64. Density is calculated by dividing the mass (500 g) by the volume (100 cm^3), resulting in 5 g/cm^3.

65. Malleability, the ability of a substance to be hammered into thin sheets, is important in the production of alloys with desired densities and properties.

66. Elasticity, the ability of a material to regain its shape after being deformed, is crucial in ensuring the stability and safety of structures under varying loads.

67. Greenhouse gases like carbon dioxide absorb and re-emit infrared radiation, contributing to the greenhouse effect and the warming of the Earth's atmosphere.

68. The density of conductive materials, such as metals, is important in the production of batteries to ensure efficient flow of electrical charges.

69. Specific gravity, a measure of the density of a substance relative to the density of water, is often used to identify and classify minerals.

70. The density of a beverage is used to determine its alcohol content. Alcohol has a lower density than water, so the density measurement can indicate the alcohol concentration.

71. Hot air balloons work based on the principle of buoyancy, where the hot air inside the balloon is less dense than the surrounding air, causing it to rise.

72. Froth flotation relies on the property of density to separate minerals from ore. The minerals attach to bubbles with lower density and rise to the surface.

73. The buoyancy of materials is crucial in shipbuilding to ensure that a ship can float and carry its intended load without sinking.

74. Optical density, also known as absorbance, is used in measuring blood sugar levels through spectrophotometry, where the density of glucose affects the absorption of light.

75. Melt flow index is a measure of the flowability of plastics and polymers and is influenced by their density, molecular weight, and processing conditions.

76. The electrical conductivity of precious metals is used to determine their purity, as impurities can affect their conductivity and, thus, their density.

77. The thermal conductivity of insulation materials affects their ability to resist heat transfer, which is crucial for maintaining energy efficiency in buildings.

78. Latent heat, the heat absorbed or released during phase changes, is utilized in air conditioning and refrigeration systems to cool or heat air or fluids.

79. API gravity is a measure of the density of petroleum products relative to the density of water. It helps classify and compare different petroleum fractions.

80. Specific strength, the strength of a material relative to its density, is important in designing lightweight construction materials that can maintain structural integrity.

81. The absorption of light by air pollutants is used to determine their concentrations and measure air pollution levels in the atmosphere.

82. The drag coefficient, which is influenced by the shape and density of an object, is crucial in understanding and optimizing aerodynamic performance.

83. Specific yield is the ratio of the volume of water that drains from an aquifer to the decrease in its water level, which is used to estimate groundwater levels.

84. The absorption coefficient of materials affects their ability to absorb sound energy, making it an important property in soundproofing applications.

85. Bulk density, the mass of soil per unit volume, is used in analyzing soil composition, assessing soil health, and determining its suitability for various applications.

86. The absorption coefficient of materials determines their ability to attenuate or absorb radiation, making it crucial for radiation shielding applications.

87. Viscosity, a measure of a fluid's resistance to flow, is used in determining fluid flow rates and designing systems such as pumps and pipelines.

88. The impact resistance of materials is crucial in designing vehicle safety features, such as bumpers and crumple zones, to protect occupants in collisions.

89. The absorption of light by air pollutants is used to analyze air quality and determine the presence and concentration of specific pollutants.

90. The porosity of filtration materials affects their ability to allow fluid flow while retaining particles of certain sizes, making it important in filtration system design.

91. Water holding capacity is the ability of a soil to retain water and is influenced by its density and porosity, making it a measure of soil moisture content.

92. The refractive index, a measure of how light is bent when passing through a medium, is crucial in designing optics and lenses with specific properties.

93. The electrical conductivity of water is influenced by dissolved ions and impurities, making it a measure of water purity and its mineral content.

94. Specific volume, the reciprocal of density, is used in the design of packaging materials to optimize space utilization and reduce transportation costs.

95. Relative humidity is a measure of the amount of water vapor present in the air compared to the maximum amount it can hold at a given temperature, influencing density.

96. Bulk density, the mass of soil per unit volume, is used in determining soil compaction levels and assessing the suitability of soil for plant growth.

97. The thermal conductivity of materials affects their ability to transfer heat and is crucial in the design of efficient heat exchangers for various applications.

98. Molarity is a measure of the concentration of a solution, expressed as the number of moles of solute per liter of solution, which is influenced by density.

99. Specific strength, the strength of a material relative to its density, is crucial in aerospace applications where weight reduction and structural integrity are important.

100. The refractive index of liquids is influenced by their density and is used to measure the sugar content in fruits and beverages, such as refractometers.

CHAPTER 4

Speed and Velocity

KINEMATICS

It deals with the motion of particles and rigid bodies without accounting for the forces responsible for their motion.

Motion: When the body changes position *w.r.t.* observer, the body is said to be in motion. If the body doesn't change position then it is said to be at rest *w.r.t.* observer.

Rectilinear Motion: If the body is, however, of a small size such that its motion can be described by a point mass moving along a straight line, such a motion is called rectilinear motion or motion in one dimension.

Distance and Displacement: Distance is the actual length covered along the path, while displacement is the difference between the final and initial positions of the particle. The position of a particle is given by a position vector drawn from the origin to the particle.

The figure illustrates the difference between distance and displacement. The curve length AB is called the distance; the vector $r_{AB} = r_B - r_A$ is called the displacement.

(a) Distance is a scalar; displacement is vector.

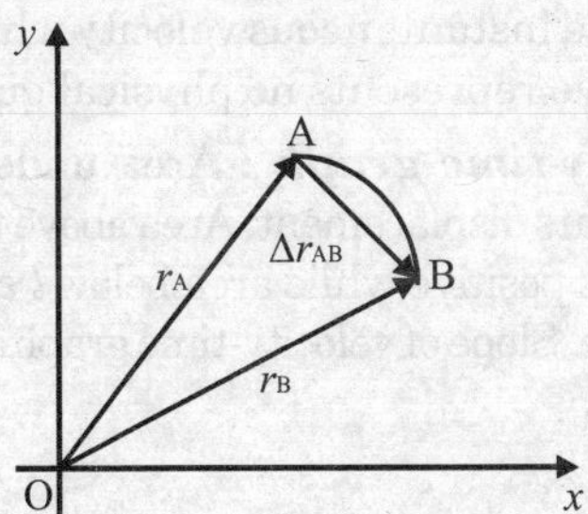

(b) The magnitude of displacement is always less than or equal to distance.

(c) For a moving body, displacement can be zero but distance cannot be zero.

Average Speed and Average Velocity

The average speed in a time interval is defined as the total distance travelled by the particle divided by the time interval.

$$\text{Average speed} = \frac{\text{Total distance travelled}}{\text{Total time taken}}$$

The average velocity is defined as

$$V_{av} = \frac{\text{displacement}}{\text{time elapsed}}$$

$$\text{or} \quad v = \frac{r_B - r_A}{t_B - t_A} = \frac{\Delta r_{AB}}{\Delta t}$$

(a) Average speed is a scalar quantity; average velocity is a vector quantity. Both are expressed in ms^{-1} or kmh^{-1}.

(b) Average velocity can be zero but average speed cannot be zero.

(c) The magnitude of average velocity is always less than or equal to the average speed.

$$|V_{av}| \leq v \text{ or } \left|\frac{\text{displacement}}{\text{time elapsed}}\right| \leq \frac{\text{distance}}{\text{time elapsed}}$$

thus $|\text{displacement}| \leq \text{distance}$

(d) Average speed does not mean the magnitude of the average velocity vector.

(e) Consider a body moving on the straight line having the initial position *A* at time t_i at a distance x_i from the origin. It travels a distance x_1 to reach B and thereafter travels a distance x_2 from B to C reaching at time t_f. C is the final position is at a distance x_f from the origin. The average speed will be equal to ratio of total distance covered to the total time.

$$\therefore \quad \text{Average speed} = \frac{x_1 + x_2}{t_f - t_i}$$

$$\text{Average velocity} = \frac{x_f - x_i}{t_f - t_i}$$

Instantaneous Speed and Instantaneous Velocity

The instantaneous speed and velocity are the respective average speed and velocity for the infinitesimally small time interval (*i.e.* $\Delta t \to 0$). Thus

$$\text{Instantaneous speed } v = \lim_{\Delta t \to 0} \frac{\Delta r}{\Delta t} = \frac{dr}{dt}$$

$$\text{Instantaneous velocity } v = \lim_{\Delta t \to 0} \frac{\Delta r}{\Delta t} = \frac{dr}{dt}$$

(a) The instantaneous velocity direction is always tangential to the path followed by the particle.

(b) The instantaneous speed is equal to the magnitude of the instantaneous velocity.

(c) A particle may have constant speed but variable velocity.

(d) For a particle moving with constant velocity, its average velocity and instantaneous velocity are always equal.

Average Acceleration and Instantaneous Acceleration: The acceleration is defined as the time rate of change of velocity. The average acceleration is defined as

$$a_{av} = \frac{v_2 - v_1}{t_2 - t_1} = \frac{\Delta v}{\Delta t}$$

The instantaneous acceleration is defined as

$$a = \lim_{\Delta t \to 0} \frac{\Delta v}{\Delta t} = \frac{dv}{dt}$$

(a) Acceleration is a vector quantity with S.I. units ms^{-2}.

(b) The direction of average acceleration vector is the direction of the change in velocity vector.

(c) There is no definite relation between the direction of velocity vector and the direction of acceleration vector.

(d) If the magnitude of velocity is constant and only its direction changes with time, then acceleration is perpendicular to the velocity vector.

(e) If a body is moving on a straight line with uniform acceleration, for such a body, average acceleration and instantaneous acceleration will be the same.

Types of Motion:

Motion can be broadly classified into three types

(a) **Uniform Motion :** The acceleration is zero. So the velocity remains constant.

displacement = velocity*time

(b) **Uniformly Accelerated Motion :** The acceleration of the body remains constant. The motion is described by sets of equation called as Equation of Motion.

Equation of Motion

$$v = u + at$$

$$s = ut + \frac{1}{2}at^2$$

$$v^2 = u^2 + 2as$$

Also, we have an equation for distance travelled in n^{th} second given by

$$x_n = u + \frac{a}{2}(2n-1)$$

Sign Convention: We need to use sign convention while using Equation of motion. Generally, upward direction is taken as positive and downward direction is taken as negative. While direction along right is taken as positive and direction along left is taken as negative.

Non-Uniformly Accelerated Motion : The acceleration of the body is variable with time and position.

Differentiation and Integration is used to solve such questions. We apply the following equations.

$$\frac{dv}{dt} = a \quad \text{...}(i)$$

$$\frac{dx}{dt} = v \quad \text{...}(ii)$$

Graphs:

(a) ***Position-time graph*** : The slope of $x - t$ curve gives the instantaneous velocity while area under the curve represents no physical quantity.

(b) ***Velocity-time graph*** : Area under $v - t$ curve represents displacement. Area above the time axis is taken as positive while area below t axis is taken as negative. Slope of velocity-time graph is accelertaion.

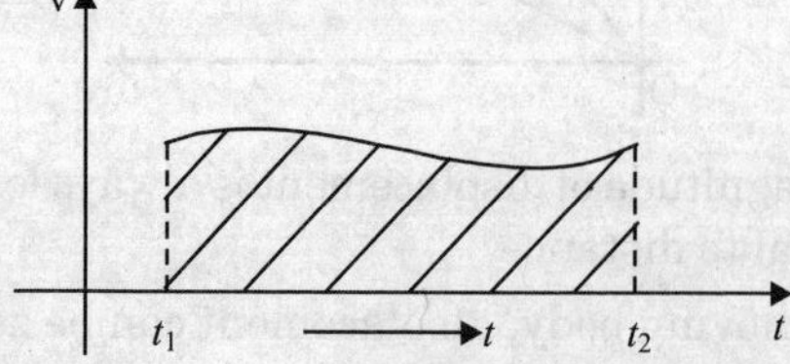

Total distance travelled is given by sum of magnitude of areas calculated in different time intervals.

(c) *Acceleration time graph* : Slope at any point gives no physical quantity.

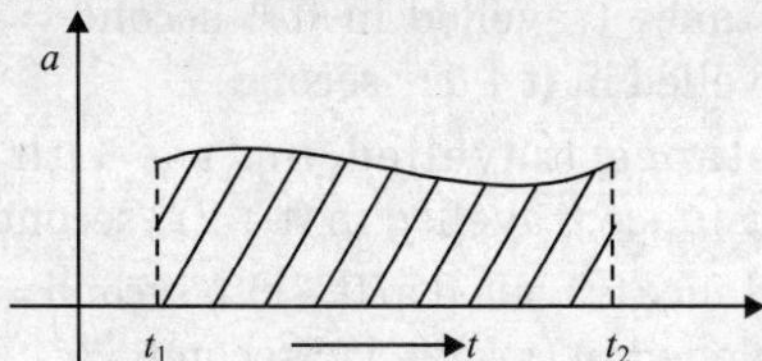

Area under the curve is equal to the change in velocity in time interval under consideration. Area above the time axis is taken as positive while area below t axis is taken as negative.

Important Points

1. If a body covers s_1 distance with speed v_1, s_2 with speed v_2, then its average speed is

$$V_{av} = \frac{s_1 + s_2}{\frac{s_1}{v_1} + \frac{s_2}{v_2}} = \frac{\sum s}{\sum \frac{s}{v}}$$

2. If a body coves first half distance with speed v_1 and next half with speed v_2, then Average speed

$$= \frac{2v_1v_2}{v_1 + v_2} \text{ (Harmonic mean)}$$

3. If a body travels with uniform speed v_1 time v_1 and with uniform speed v_2 for time t_2, then average speed

$$= \frac{v_1t_1 + v_2 + t_2}{t_1 + t_2} = \frac{\sum vt}{\sum t}.$$

If $t_1 = t_2 = \frac{T}{2}$ then $v_{av} = \frac{v_1 + v_2}{2}$

[T = time of journey] (Arithmetic mean)

4. If body covers first one third with speed v_1, next one third with speed v_2 and remaining one third with speed

v_3 then $v_{av} = \dfrac{3v_1v_2v_3}{v_1v_2 + v_2 + v_3 + v_3 + v_1}$

5. If a body moves from one point (A) to another point (B) with speed v_1 and returns back (from B to A) with speed v2 then average velocity is 0 but

average speed $= \dfrac{2v_1v_2}{v_1 + v_2}$

6. Slope of the chord joining two points on the displacement-time graph gives there average velocity during the time interval between those points.

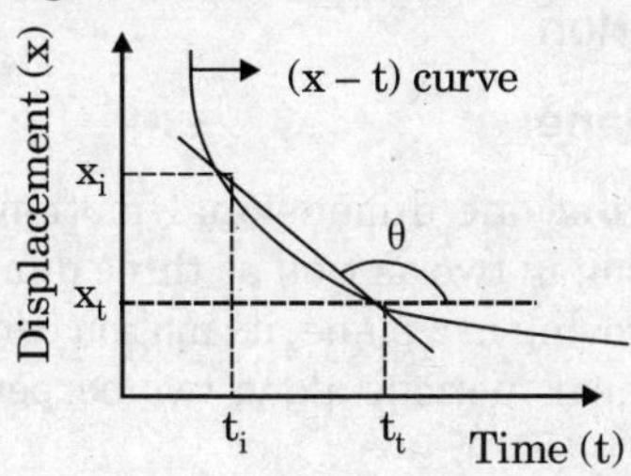

$$\tan\theta = \frac{x_f - x_i}{t_f - t_i} = V_{av}$$

7. Slope of the chord joining two points on the velocity-time graph gives the average acceleration during the time between those points.

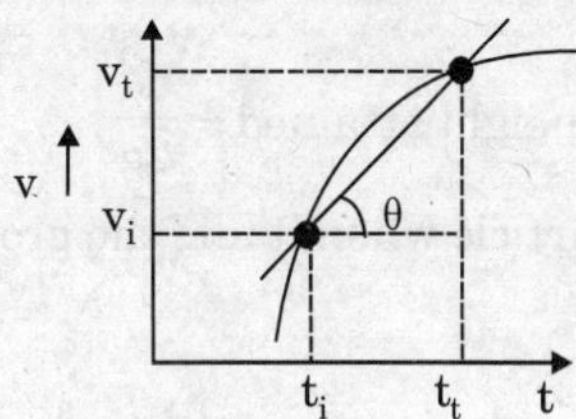

$$\tan\theta = \frac{x_f - x_i}{t_f - t_i} = V_{av}$$

= Average acceleration in time interval $t_f - t_i$.

8. The displacement-time graph cannot sharp turns because it gives two different velocities at that point.

9. The displacement-time graph cannot be symmetric about the time-axis because at an instant a particle cannot have two displacements, but the graph may be symmetric about the displacement-axis.

10. The distance-time graph is always an increasing curve for a moving body.

11. The displacement-time graph does not show the trajectory of the particle.

12. If a particle is moving with uniform acceleration and have velocity V_A at A and V_B at B, then velocity of particle midway on line AB is $V = \sqrt{\frac{V_A^2 + V_B^2}{2}}$.

13. If a body starts rest with acceleration α and then retards to rest with retardation β, such that total time of journey is T, then

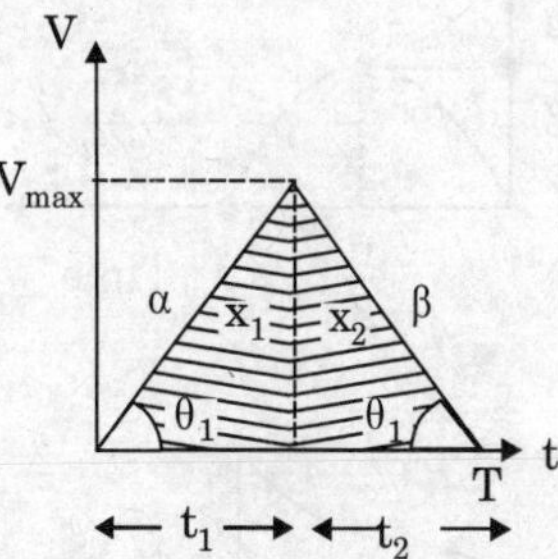

(a) Maximum velocity during the trip

$$v_{max} = \left(\frac{\alpha\beta}{\alpha + \beta}\right).T$$

(b) Length of the journey $L = \frac{1}{2}\left(\frac{\alpha\beta}{\alpha + \beta}\right)T^2$

(c) Average velocity of the trip

$$= \frac{v_{max}}{2} = \frac{\alpha\beta T}{2(\alpha + \beta)} \ \&$$

(d) $\dfrac{x_1}{x_2} = \dfrac{\beta}{\alpha} = \dfrac{t_1}{t_2}$.

14. A particle is projected from ground with velocity u in vertically upward direction then

(a) Time of ascent = Time of descent

$$= \frac{\text{Time of flight}}{2} = \frac{T}{2} = \frac{u}{g}$$

(b) Maximum height attained $= \dfrac{u^2}{2g}$

(c) Speed of particle when it hits the ground = u

(d) Graphs

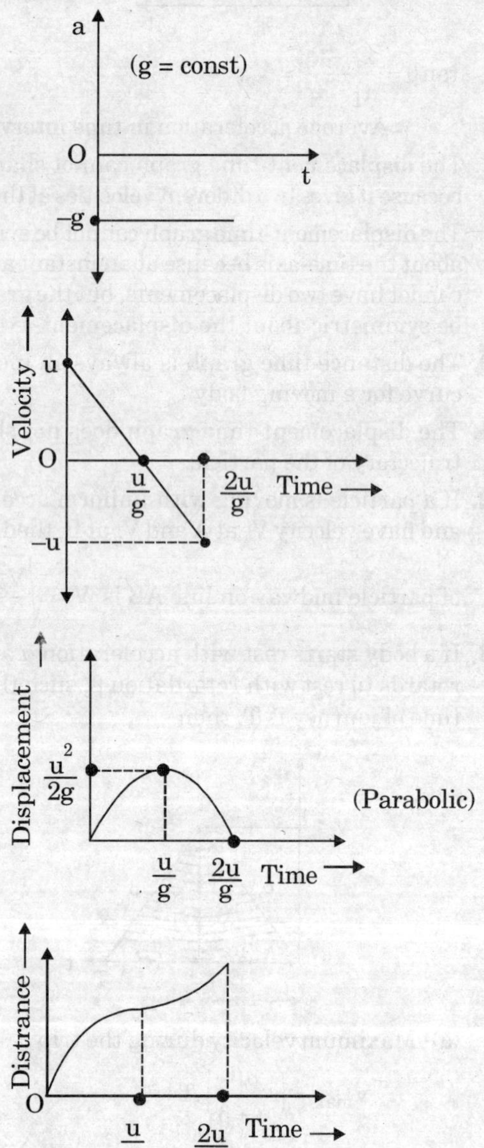

(e) Displacement of particle in complete journey = zero ⇒ average velocity $v_{av} = 0$

(f) Distance covered by particle journey $= \dfrac{u^2}{g}$

⇒ Average speed in complete journey $= \dfrac{u}{g}$

15. A body is thrown upward such that it takes t seconds to reach its highest point.

(a) Distance travelled in $(t)^{th}$ second = distance travelled in $(t + 1)^{th}$ second.

(b) Distance travelled in (t – 1)th second = distance travelled in $(t + 2)^{th}$ second.

(c) Distance travelled in (t – r)th second = distance travelled in $(t + r + 1)^{th}$ second.

16. From the top of a tower a body is projected upward with a certain speed, 2nd body is thrown downward with same speed and 3rd is let to fall freely from same point then

$$t_3 = \sqrt{t_1 t_2}$$

where, t_1 = Time of flight of body projected upward

t_2 = Time of flight of body thrown downward

t_3 = Time of flight of body dropped.

17. If u and v are velocity of particle at $t = t_1$ and $t = t_2$, which is moving with uniform acceleration, then average velocity of particle during time interval

$(t_2 - t_1)$ is $V_{av} = \dfrac{u + v}{2}$.

18. For a body starting from rest and moving with uniform acceleration, the ratio of distances covered in 1s, 2s, 3s, etc. is $1^2 : 2^2 : 3^2$ etc., 1 : 4 : 9 etc

19. A body starting from rest and moving with uniform acceleration has distances covered by it in 1st, 2nd and 3rd seconds in the ratio 1 : 3 : 5 etc. i.e., odd numbers only.

20. A body moving with a velocity v is stopped by application of brakes after covering a distance s. If the same body moves with a velocity nv, it stops after covering a distance n^2s by the application of same brake force.

21. In the absence of air resistance, the velocity of projection is equal to the velocity with which the body strikes the ground.

22. In case of air resistance, the time of ascent is less than time of descent for a body projected vertically upward.

23. For a body projected vertically upwards, the magnitude of velocity at any given point on the path is same whether the body is moving in upwards or downward direction.

Projectile Motion

Motion In a Plane:

The kinematics of one dimensional motion can be applied for motion in two as well as three dimensions. If a particle is moving in a plane, its motion can be split into two rectilinear motions along two perpendicular directions which are called the rectangular components for the displacement, velocity and acceleration for the two dimensional motion.

If a particle is moving along the path *AB* in *XY* plane, then at any time *t*, it reaches point *P(x,y)* where its radius vector **r** makes an angle ϕ with *x*-axis.

Then its component are $x = r\cos\phi$, $y = r\sin\phi$, $r = \sqrt{x^2 + y^2}$ and $\tan\phi = \frac{y}{x}$.

If the velocity vector **v** at *P* makes an angle θ with the *x*-direction, its rectangular component will be given by $v_x = v\cos\theta$, $v_y = v\sin\theta$, $v = \sqrt{v_x^2 + v_y^2}$ and $\tan\theta = \frac{v_y}{v_x}$.

Similarly the acceleration a at any time can be split up into components $\mathbf{a}_x$ and $\mathbf{a}_y$ along respective *x* and *y* directions.

In vectorial notation, the two dimensional motion can be described as per the following relations :

$$\mathbf{r} = x\mathbf{i} + y\mathbf{j}, \quad \mathbf{v} = v_x\mathbf{i} + v_y\mathbf{j}, \quad \mathbf{a} = a_x\,\mathbf{i} + a_y\,\mathbf{j}$$

Projectile Motion: When a body is projected at an angle in uniform force field(like uniform gravitational field), with the direction of force. The path followed by the body is known as projectile path.

If a particle is projected at origin *O* with velocity *u*, (called as velocity of projection) at angle θ (called as angle of projection)to the horizontal, its horizontal component $u\cos\theta$ remains constant whereas its vertical component $u\sin\theta$ changes continuously because of acceleration due to gravity which acts in the downward direction.

The vertical velocity decreases due to retardation *g* and becomes zero at the highest point at height *H*.

The vertical speed then increases when the body moves downwards until it reaches the *x*-axis covering a distance *R* in the horizontal direction which is called the horizontal range.

If v_x and v_y are the horizontal and the vertical components of velocity *u* after time *t*, then $v_x = u\cos\theta$, $v_y = u\sin\theta - gt$. If α is the angle subtended by *v* with horizontal,

$$\tan\alpha = \frac{v_y}{v_x} = \frac{u\sin\theta - gt}{u\cos\theta}$$

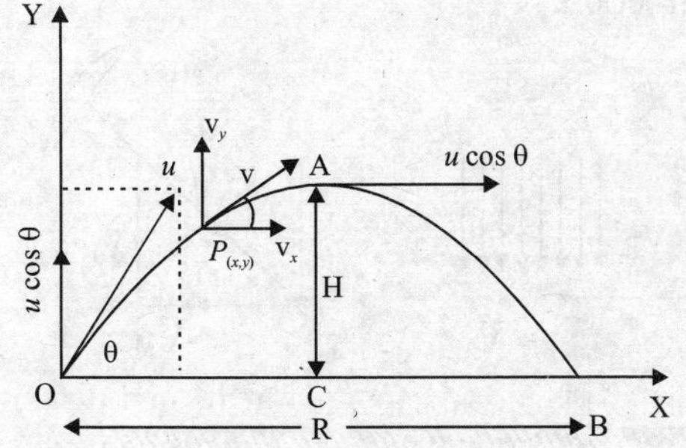

Maximum Height

If *H* is maximum height of the projectile, its velocity in the vertical direction is zero at this height.

$$H = \frac{u^2\sin^2\theta}{2g}$$

Time of Flight

If *T* is time of flight from *O* to *B*, for which vertical displacement $y = 0$, then

$$T = \frac{2u\sin\theta}{g}$$

Time to reach maximum height $= \frac{T}{2} = \frac{u\sin\theta}{g}$. It is called as time of ascent. The time taken to reach ground from maximum height is called as time of descent . Time of ascent is equal to time of descent

Range

$$R = \frac{u^2\sin 2\theta}{g}$$

The range *R* of a particle is maximum when $\sin 2\theta = 1$ or $2\theta = \frac{\pi}{2}$ or $\theta = \frac{\pi}{4} = 45°$.

Maximum value of horizontal range $= \frac{u^2}{g}$

There are two angles of projection *i.e.,* θ or $\frac{\pi}{2} - \theta$ for which the horizontal range of a particle is equal provided the initial velocity u is same in each case. This is called as *complemetry angle of projection*

Projectile thrown Horizontally from height : If a body is thrown horizontally from a height *h* with an initial speed *u*, its horizontal velocity remains unchanged whereas its vertical component increases due to acceleration of gravity in the downward direction. If a particle is projected from a height *h* with horizontal velocity *u*, its velocity *v* at any point *B* after time *t* has component $v_x = v\cos\theta = u$ and $v_y = v\sin\theta = gt$ where θ is the angle made by instantaneous velocity *w.r.t.* horizontal direction given then $\tan\theta = \frac{gt}{u}$.

$$v = \sqrt{u^2 + g^2t^2}$$

Horizontal distance travelled by the particle, $x = ut$

Vertical distance travelled by the particle, $y = \frac{1}{2}gt^2$

Equation of trajectory $y = \left(\frac{g}{2u^2}\right)x^2$

The resultant path or trajectory of the particle is a parabola. If T is the time taken by the particle to reach the ground from height h, then $h = \frac{1}{2}gT^2$ or $T = \sqrt{\frac{2h}{g}}$. The horizontal distance OC, covered to reach the ground, is called the horizontal range, R.

$$R = uT = u\sqrt{\frac{2h}{g}}$$

Projection on an Inclined Plane

Consider a particle projected with the velocity u at an angle θ to the horizontal on a plane inclined at angle β to the horizontal. The particle strikes the plane at point $P(x,y)$ having range $R = OP$ on the plane. The initial velocity of projection will have two components

(a) $u\cos(\alpha - \beta)$ along the plane

(b) $u\sin(\alpha - \beta)$ perpendicular to the plane.

Similarly, the acceleration $g \sin\beta$ is acceleration along the negative x axis and $g \cos\beta$ as acceleration perpendicular to theplane in negative y axis. Let t be the time taken by the particle to reach from O so that the P. Displacement perpendicular to OP is equal to zero.

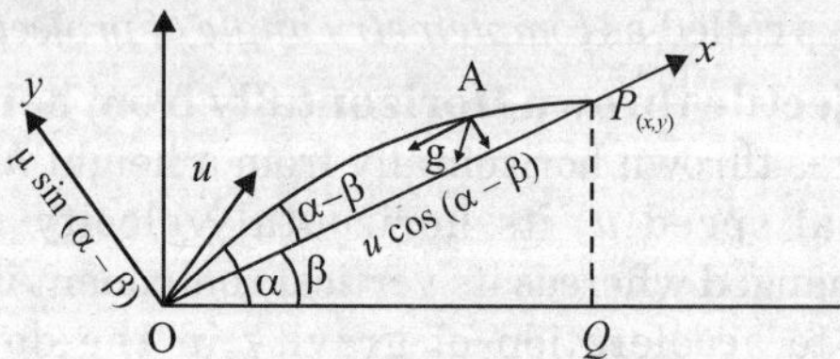

Time of Flight $= t = \frac{2u\sin(\alpha-\beta)}{g\cos\beta}$

$$\text{Range} = \frac{OQ}{\cos\beta} = \frac{2u^2\sin(\alpha-\beta)\cos\alpha}{g\cos^2\beta}$$

If it is down the incline plane just replace the negative sign everywhere with positive sign.

Relative Motion in One Dimension

1. If two bodies A and B are moving in straight line same direction with velocity V_A and V_B, then relative velocity of A with respect to B is $V_{AB} = V_A - V_B$. Similarly $V_{BA} = V_B - V_A$.

A V_A B V_B

2. If two bodies A and B are moving in straight line in opposite direction then

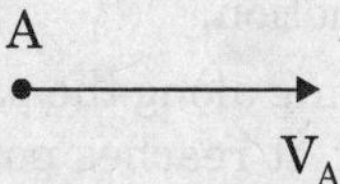

$V_{AB} = V_A + V_B$ (towards B)

$V_{BA} = V_B + V_A$ (towards A)

$V_{AB} = -V_{BA}$

Same concept is used for acceleration also.

3. If two cars A and B are moving in same direction with velocity V_A and V_B ($V_A > V_B$) when A is behind B at a distance d, driver in car A applies brake which causes retardation a in car A, then minimum value of d to avoid collision is

$$\frac{(V_A = -V_B)^2}{2a} \text{ i.e, } d > \frac{(V_A - V_B)^2}{2a}$$

4. A particle is dropped and another particle is thrown downward with initial velocity u, then
   (a) Relative acceleration is always zero
   (b) Relative velocity is always u.
   (c) Time at which their separation is x is $\frac{x}{u}$.

5. Two bodies are thrown upwards with same initial velocity with time gap τ. They will meet after a time t from projection of first body.

$$t = \frac{\tau}{2} + \frac{u}{g}$$

Relative Motion in Two Dimensions

Relative velocity :

Velocity of object A w.r.t object B is

$$\vec{V}_{AB} = \vec{V}_A - \vec{V}_B, \vec{V}_{BA} = \vec{V}_B - \vec{V}_A$$

1. **Direction of Umbrella** : A person moving one straight road has to hold his umbrella opposite to direction of relative velocity of rain. The angle θ is given by $\tan\theta = \frac{v_M}{v_R}$ with vertical in forward direction.

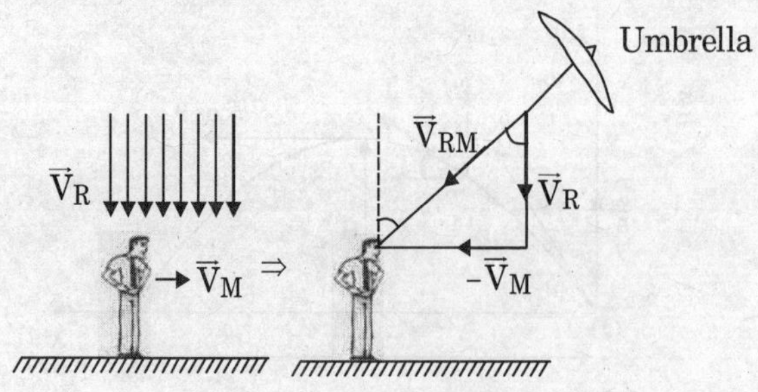

2. Closest approach : Two objects A and B having velocities $\vec{v}_A$ and $\vec{v}_B$ at separation x are shown in figure

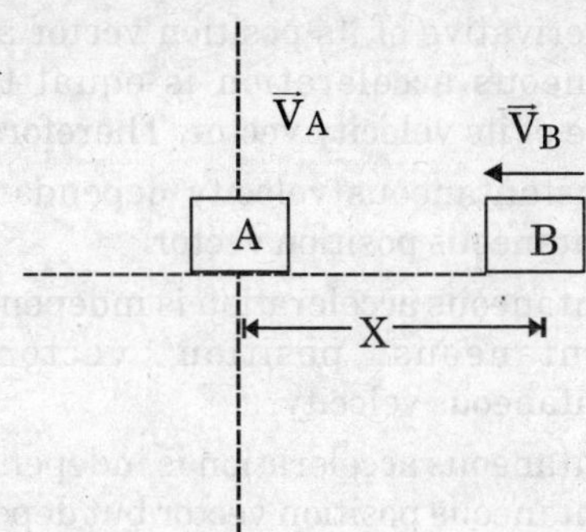

The relative velocity of A with respect to B is given by

$-\vec{V}_B$

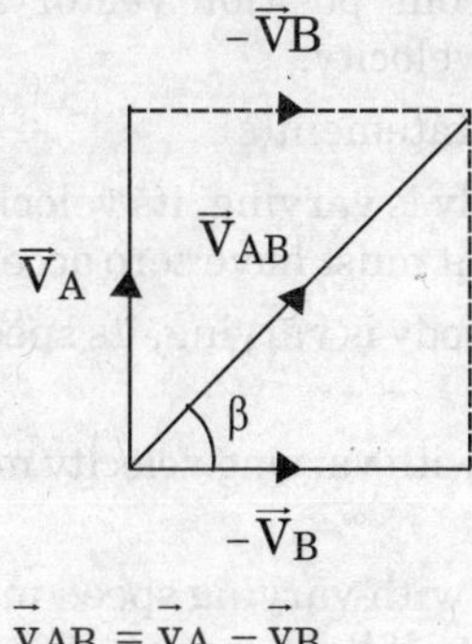

$-\vec{V}_B$

$$\vec{v}_{AB} = \vec{v}_A - \vec{v}_B$$

$$\tan\beta = \frac{v_A}{v_B}$$

The above situation is similar to figure given below y is the distance of closest approach.

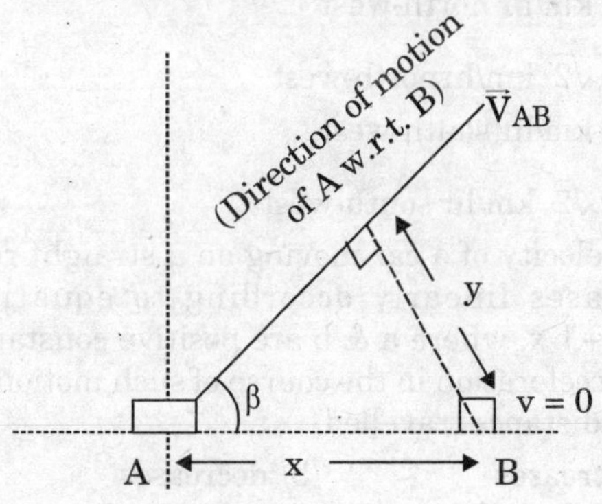

$$\text{Now, } \sin\beta = \frac{y}{x}$$

$$\Rightarrow y = x\sin\beta$$

$$y = \frac{x\tan\beta}{\sqrt{1+\tan^2\beta}} = \frac{xV_A}{\sqrt{V_B^2 + V_A^2}}$$

3. Crossing a river :

v = velocity of the man in still water

(also called velocity of swimmer wrt river = v_{SR})

θ = angle of which man swims w.r.t. normal to bank such that

$vx = -v\sin\theta,\ v_y = v\cos\theta.$

$v_R = U$

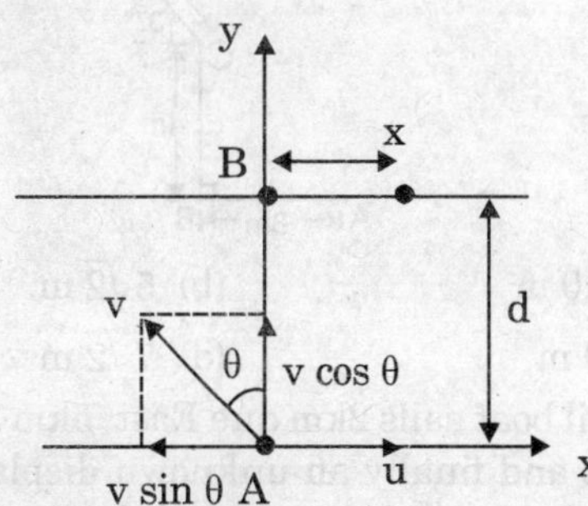

Velocity along the river

$$v'_x = u - v\sin\theta$$

Distance drifted along the river = $D = tv'_x$

$$x = \frac{d}{v\cos\theta}(u - v\sin\theta)$$

Case I :

The minimum time to cross the river is given by

$$\tau_{min} = \frac{d}{v} \text{ (when } \cos\theta = 1, \theta = 0°, u \perp v)$$

Distance drifted is given by

$$D = \frac{d}{v} \times u$$

Case II :

To cross the river straight

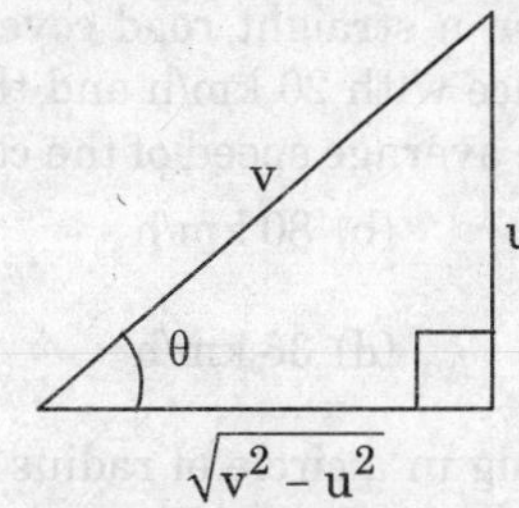

$$\text{drift } x = 0 \Rightarrow u - v\sin\theta = 0$$

$$\sin\theta = \frac{u}{v} \Rightarrow (v > u)$$

Time to cross the river straight across is given by

$$t = \frac{d}{v\cos\theta} = \frac{d}{\sqrt{v^2 - u^2}}$$

Objective Type Questions

1. A particle moves along a path ABCD as shown in the figure. Then the magnitude of net displacement of the particle from position A to D is :

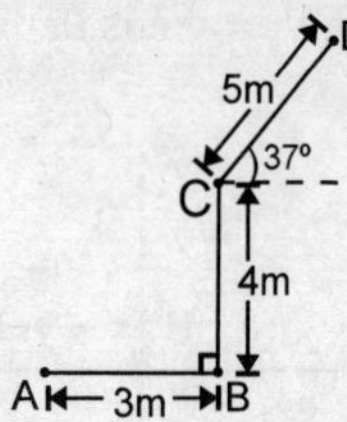

(a) 10 m (b) $5\sqrt{2}$ m

(c) 9 m (d) $7\sqrt{2}$ m

2. A sail boat sails 2km due East, 5km 37° South of East and finally an unknown displacement . If the final displacement of the boat from the starting point is 6km due East, the third displacement is

(a) 3 km (b) 4 km

(c) 5 km (d) 2 km

3. A body goes 10 km north and 20 km east. What will be the displacement from initial point ?

(a) 22.36 km (b) 2 km

(c) 5 km (d) 30 km

4. A particle starts from rest with uniform acceleration a. Its velocity after 'n' second is 'v'. The displacement of the body in the last two second is

(a) $\frac{2v(n-1)}{n}$ (b) $\frac{v(n-1)}{n}$

(c) $\frac{v(n+1)}{n}$ (d) $\frac{2v(2n+1)}{n}$

5. One car moving on a straight road covers one third of the distance with 20 km/h and the rest with 60 km/h. The average speed of the car is

(a) 40 km/h (b) 80 km/h

(c) $46\frac{2}{3}$ km/h (d) 36 km/h

6. A particle is moving in a circle of radius r with speed v as shown in the figure. The magnitude of change in velocity in moving from P to Q is:

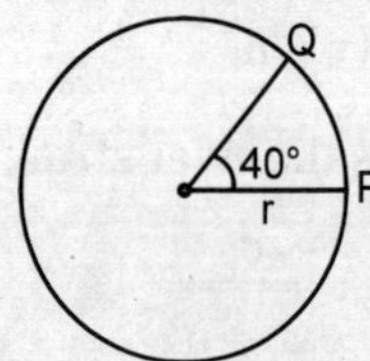

(a) 2 v cos 40° (b) 2 v sin 20°

(c) 2 v cos 20° (d) none of these

7. The instantaneous velocity of a particle is equal to time derivative of its position vector and the instantaneous acceleration is equal to time derivative of its velocity vector. Therefore:

(a) the instantaneous velocity depends on the instantaneous position vector

(b) instantaneous acceleration is independent of instantaneous position vector and instantaneous velocity

(c) instantaneous acceleration is independent of instantaneous position vector but depends on the instantaneous velocity

(d) instantaneous acceleration depends both on the instantaneous position vector and the instantaneous velocity.

8. Mark the correct statement(s).

(a) If speed of a body is varying, its velocity must be varying and it must have zero acceleration

(b) If velocity of a body is varying, its speed must be varying

(c) A body moving with varying velocity may have constant speed

(d) A body moving with varying speed may have constant velocity if its direction of motion remains constant.

9. A truck travelling due north at 50 km/hr turns west and travels at the same speed. What is the change in velocity.

(a) 50 km/hr north-west

(b) $50\sqrt{2}$ km/hrnorth-west

(c) 50 km/hr south-west

(d) $50\sqrt{2}$ km/hr south-west

10. The velocity of a car moving on a straight road increases linearly according to equation, v = a + bx, where a & b are positive constants. The acceleration in the course of such motion: (x is the distance travelled)

(a) increases (b) decreases

(c) stay constant (d) becomes zero

11. The speed v of a car moving on a straight road changes according to equation, $v^2 = a + bx$, where a & b are positive constants. Then the magnitude of acceleration in the course of such motion: (x is the distance travelled)

(a) increases

(b) decreases

(c) stay constant

(d) first decreases and then increases

12. Sign of acceleration tells us : (for rectilinear motion)
(a) whether the particle's speed is increasing or decreasing
(b) about change in speed depending on the choice of the positive direction of the velocity
(c) both of the above (a) & (B)
(d) none of the above (a) & (B)

13. The position vector of a particle is given as $\vec{r} = (t^2 - 4t + 6)\hat{i} + (t^2)\hat{j}$. The time after which the velocity vector and acceleration vector becomes perpendicular to each other is equal to
(a) 1sec (b) 2 sec
(c) 1.5 sec (d) not possible

14. A particle of mass m moves along a curve $y = x^2$. When particle has x – co-ordinate as 1/2m and x-component of velocity as 4m/s then.
(a) the magnitude of velocity at that instant is 4 m/s
(b) the magnitude of velocity at that instant is $2\sqrt{2}$ m/s
(c) the magnitude of velocity at that instant is $4\sqrt{2}$ m/s
(d) the magnitude of velocity at that instant is 2 m/s

15. The position of a particle moving rectilinearly is given by $x = t^3 - 3t^2 - 10$. Find the distance travelled by the particle in the first 4 seconds starting from t = 0.
(a) 24 units (b) 12 units
(c) 48 units (d) 6 units

16. Following statements are given for the motion of a particle along the straight line. Choose correct statement out of these :
(a) Magnitude of the average velocity is equal to the average speed.
(b) Distance travelled by the particle is always greater than magnitude of the displacement.
(c) A particle having negative acceleration may speed up.
(d) A particle having its velocity equal to zero at any instant of the motion, then its acceleration is also zero at that instant.

17. Each of the four particles move along an x axis. Their coordinates (in metres) as function of time (in seconds) are given by
Particle 1 : $x(t) = 3.5 - 2.7t^3$
Particle 2 : $x(t) = 3.5 + 2.7t^3$
Particle 3 : $x(t) = 3.5 + 2.7t^2$
Particle 4 : $x(t) = 3.5 - 3.4t - 2.7t^2$
which of these particles is speeding up for t > 0?
(a) All four (b) only 1
(c) only 1, 2 and 3. (d) only 2, 3 and 4.

18. For a particle moving along a straight line, the displacement x depends on time t as $x = \alpha t^3 + \beta t^2 + \gamma t + \delta$. The ratio of its initial acceleration to its initial velocity depends:
(a) only on α & β (b) only on β & γ
(c) only on α & γ (d) only on α

19. A man moves on his motorbike with 54 km/h and then takes a u turn (180°) and continues to move with same speed. The time of u turn is 10 s. Find the average acceleration during u turn.
(a) 0 (b) 3 ms^{-2}
(c) $1.5\sqrt{2}$ ms^{-2} (d) none of these

20. A particle moves in x-y plane according to equations, $x = 4t^2 + 5t + 16$ & $y = 5t$. The acceleration of the particle will be:
(a) 8 m/sec^2 (b) 13 m/sec^2
(c) 14 m/sec^2 (d) none of these

21. If $v = x^2 - 5x + 4$, find the acceleration of the particle when velocity of the particle is zero.
(a) 0 (b) 2
(c) 3 (d) none of these

22. The displacement of a body from a reference point is given by, $\sqrt{x} = 2t - 3$, where 'x' is in metres and t in seconds. This shows that the body:
(a) rest at t = 3/2 (b) is accelerated
(c) is decelerated (d) is in uniform motion

23. A car of mass *m*, travelling at speed *v*, stops in time *t* when maximum braking force is applied. Assuming the braking force is same for both cases, what time would be required to stop a car of mass 2*m* travelling at speed *v*?
(a) $\frac{1}{2}t$ (b) *t*
(c) $\sqrt{2}\,t$ (d) 2 *t*

24. A particle is moving eastward with a velocity of 5m/s. In 10 seconds the velocity changes to 5m/s northwards. The average acceleration $(\Delta\vec{v}/\Delta t)$ in this time is
(a) zero
(b) $1/\sqrt{2}$ m/s^2 towards north-west
(c) $1/\sqrt{2}$ m/s^2 towards north-east
(d) $1/\sqrt{2}$ m/s^2 towards north

25. A particle P is moving with a constant speed of 6m/s in a direction $2\hat{i}-\hat{j}-2\hat{k}$. When t = 0, P is at a point whose position vector is $3\hat{i}+4\hat{j}-7\hat{k}$. Find the position vector of the particle P after 4 seconds.

(a) $\vec{r}=19\hat{i}-4\hat{j}-23\hat{k}$ (b) $\vec{r}=19\hat{i}-4\hat{j}-23\hat{k}$

(c) $\vec{r}=19\hat{i}-4\hat{j}-23\hat{k}$ (d) $\vec{r}=19\hat{i}-4\hat{j}-23\hat{k}$

26. The velocity of a particle moving along a straight line is given by the equation $v = t^2 - 2t - 3$ where 't' is time. The minimum velocity of the particle is (Assume all are in S.I. unit)

(a) 4 m/s (b) – 1 m/s

(c) zero (d) – 4 m/s

27. A body travelling with uniform acceleration crosses two points A and B with velocities 20 m s^{-1} and 30 m s^{-1} respectively. The speed of the body at the mid-point of A and B is

(a) 24 m s^{-1} (b) 25 m s^{-1}

(c) 25.5 m s^{-1} (d) $10\sqrt{6}$ m s^{-1}

28. The velocity - time graph of a particle is as shown in figure

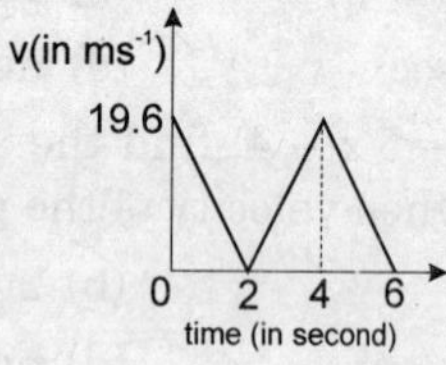

(a) It moves with a constant acceleration throughout

(b) It moves with an acceleration of constant magnitude but changing direction at the end of every two second

(c) The displacement of the particle is zero

(d) The velocity becomes zero at t = 4 second

29. A car starts from rest and moves with constant acceleration. The ratio of the distance covered in the nth second to that covered in n seconds is:

(a) $\frac{2}{n^2}-\frac{1}{n}$ (b) $\frac{2}{n^2}+\frac{1}{n}$

(c) $\frac{2}{n}-\frac{1}{n^2}$ (d) $\frac{2}{n}+\frac{1}{n^2}$

30. A particle is moving with initial velocity $\vec{u}=\hat{i}-\hat{j}+\hat{k}$. What should be its acceleration so that it can remain moving in the same straight line ?

(a) $\vec{a}=2\hat{i}-2\hat{j}+2\hat{k}$ (b) $\vec{a}=-2\hat{i}+2\hat{j}-2\hat{k}$

(c) $\vec{a}=3\hat{i}+3\hat{j}+-3\hat{k}$ (d) $\vec{a}=1\hat{i}-1\hat{j}$

31. A train is moving at speed of 40 km/h.As soon as another train going in the opposite direction passes by the window, the passenger of the first train started his stopwatch and noted that other train passedthe window in 3 s. Find the speed of the train going in the opposite direction if its length is 75 m.

(a) 25km/h (b) 50km/h

(c) 75km/h (d) 40km/h

Direction (Q. 32 to 35) : Following are three functions which relates the parameters of motion.

$$S(t)=ut+\frac{1}{2}at^2 \quad v(s)=\sqrt{u^2+2as} \quad v(t)=u+at$$

Where ; S, u, t, a, v are respectively the displacement (dependent variable), initial velocity (constant), time taken (independent variable), acceleration (constant) and final velocity (dependent variable) of the particle after time t.

32. Find displacement of a particle after 10 seconds starting from rest with an uniform acceleration of $2m/s^2$.

(a) 10 m (b) 100 m

(c) 50 m (d) 200 m

33. Find the velocity of the particle after 100 m –

(a) 10 m/s (b) 20 m/s

(c) 30 m/s (d) 0 m/s

34. Find the velocity of the particle after 10 seconds if its acceleration is zero in interval (0 to 10 s) –

(a) 10 m/s (b) 20 m/s

(c) 30 m/s (d) 0 m/s

35. Find the displacement of the particle when its velocity becomes 10 m/s if acceleration is 5 m/s^2 all through–

(a) 50 m (b) 200 m

(c) 10 m (d) 100 m

36. A body thrown vertically up from the ground passes the height 10.2 m twice at an interval of 10 sec. What was its initial velocity. [$g = 10\ m/s^2$]

(a) 52 m/s (b) 26 m/s

(c) 35 m/s (d) none of these

37. A balloon is ascending vertically with an acceleration of 0.4 m/s^{-2}. Two stones are dropped from it at an interval of 2 sec. Find the distance between them 1.5 sec. after the second stone is released. ($g = 10\ m/sec^2$)

(a) 26 m (b) 52m

(c) 78m (d) 13 m

38. Two bodies are thrown vertically upward, with the same initial velocity of 98 m/s, but the second one is thrown 4 sec. after the first is thrown. At what time after the first particle is thrown will both of them meet ? [g = 9.8 m/s2]

(a) 8 s (b) 10 s
(c) 6 s (d) 12 s

39. A particle moves rectilinearly with a constant acceleration 1 m/s^2. Its speed after 10 seconds is 5 m/s. The distance covered by the particle in this duration is (Initial & final velocities are in opposite direction)

(a) 20 m (b) 25 m
(c) 30 m (d) 50 m

40. A particle is moving along a straight line with constant acceleration. At the end of tenth second its velocity becomes 20 m/s and in tenth second it travels a distance of 10 m. Then the acceleration of the particle will be-

(a) 10 m/s^2 (b) 20 m/s^2
(c) $\frac{1}{5}$ m/s^2 (d) 3.8 m/s^2

41. A balloon is moving along with constant upward acceleration of 1 m/s^2. A stone is thrown from the balloon downwards with speed 10 m/s with respect to the balloon. At the time of projection balloon is at height 120 m from the ground and is moving with speed 20 m/s. The time required to fall on the ground by the stone after the projection will be -

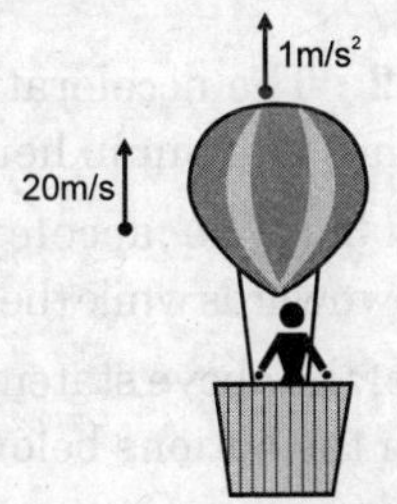

(a) 4 sec. (b) 5 sec.
(c) 6 sec. (d) None of these

42. A particle is moving along x axis with constant acceleration. At t = 0 sec. the particle is at x = 3 m and v = + 4 m/s. The maximum value of x coordinate of the particle is observed 2 sec. later. Starting fromt = 0 sec after what time particle reaches its initial position again

(a) 4 sec.
(b) 6 sec.
(c) 8 sec.
(d) 12 sec.

43. From the top of a tower a stone is dropped. If it covers 24.5 m in the last second of its motion, find the height of the tower.

(a) 40.1 m. (b) 42.1 m.
(c) 46.1 m. (d) 44.1 m.

44. A particle is thrown upwards from ground. It experiences a constant air resistance force which can produce a retardation of 2 m/s^2 . The ratio of time of ascent to the time of descent is : [g = 10 m/s^2]

(a) 1 : 1 (b) $\sqrt{\frac{2}{3}}$
(c) $\frac{2}{3}$ (d) $\sqrt{\frac{3}{2}}$

45. A stone is dropped from the top of a tower. When it has fallen by 5m from the top, another stone is dropped from a point 25m below the top. If both stones reach the ground at the same moment, then height of the tower from ground is : (take g = 10m/s^2)

(a) 45 m (b) 50m
(c) 60m (d) 65m

46. A ball is thrown vertically upwards in air. If the air resistance cannot be neglected (assume it to be directly proportional to velocity), then the acceleration of the ball at the highest point will be:

(a) 0 (b) g
(c) > g (d) < g

47. If a body starts with initial velocity 'u' with a constant acceleration 'a' then find out the increase in velocity after 't' seconds :

(a) u–at (b) u
(c) u + at (d) at

48. A stone thrown upwards, has its equation of motion s = 490 t - 4.9 t^2 where 's' in metres and t in seconds respectively. What is the maximum height reached by it ?

(a) 12000 m (b) 12250 m
(c)11000 m (d) 11250 m

49. The displacement of a body at any time t after starting is given by s = 15t – 0.4t^2. The velocity of the body will be 7 ms^{-1} after time :

(a) 20 s (b) 15 s
(c) 10 s (d) 5 s

50. The displacement of a body at any time t after starting is given by s = 10t – $\frac{1}{2}$ (0.2)t^2. The velocity of the body is zero after :

(a) 50 s (b) 100 s
(c) 80 s (d) 40 s

51. A particle is moving in a straight line with initial velocity u and uniform acceleration f. If the sum of the distances travelled in t^{th} and $(t + 1)^{th}$ seconds is 100 cm, then its velocity after t seconds, in cm s, is

(a) 20 (b) 30

(c) 50 (d) 80

52. The displacement of a body is given to be proportional to the cube of time elapsed. Acceleration of the body is proportional to:

(a) t^4 (b) t^3

(c) t^2 (d) t

53. The velocity of a particle moving on the x-axis is given by $v = x^2 + x$ where v is in m/s and x is in m. Find its acceleration in m/s^2 when passing through the point x = 2 m

(a) 0 (b) 5

(c) 11 (d) 30

54. Two particles, one with constant velocity 50m/s and the other with uniform acceleration $10m/s^2$, start moving simultaneously from the same position in the same direction. They will be at a distance of 125m from each other after

(a) 5 sec. (b) $5(1 + \sqrt{2})$ sec.

(c) Both A and B (d) None of these

55. A body moving with constant acceleration travels 200 cm in the first two seconds and 220 cm in the next four seconds. What will be the velocity at the end of 7 second from start?

(a) 12 cm s^{-1} (b) 8 cm s^{-1}

(c) 11 cm s^{-1} (d) 10 cm s^{-1}

56. A parachutist drops freely from an aeroplane for 10 s before the parachute opens out. Then he descends with a net retardation of 2.5 ms^{-2}. If he bails out of the plane at a height of 2495 m and g = 10 ms^{-2}, his velocity on reaching the ground will be :

(a) 2.5 ms^{-1} (b) 7.5 ms^{-1}

(c) 5 ms^{-1} (d) 10 ms^{-1}

57. A ball is thrown vertically upwards from the ground. It crosses a point at the height of 25 m twice at an interval of 4 secs. The ball was thrown with the velocity of

(a) 20 m/sec. (b) 25 m/sec.

(c) 30 m/sec. (d) 35 m/sec.

58. The distance travelled by a freely falling body is proportional to

(a) the mass of the body

(b) the square of the acceleration due to gravity

(c) the square of the time of fall

(d) the time of fall

59. A body is projected vertically downwards from A, the top of the tower reaches the ground in t_1 seconds. If it is projected upwards with same velocity it reaches the ground in t_2 seconds. At what time it will reach the ground if it is dropped from A.

(a) $\sqrt{t_1/t_2}$ (b) $\sqrt{t_2/t_1}$

(c) $\sqrt{t_1 t_2}$ (d) $t_1 t_2$

60. A stone is dropped from the top of building and at the same time a second stone is thrown vertically upward from the bottom of the building with a speed of 20 ms^{-1}. They pass each other 3 seconds later. Find the height of the building.

(a) 20 m (b) 25 m

(c) 30 m (d) 60 m

61. A stone is dropped from the top of a tall tower and after one second another stone is dropped from a balcony 20 m below the top. If both the stones reach the ground at the same instant, calculate the height of the tower.

(a) 30.25 m (b) 31.25 m

(c) 32.25 m (d) 36.25 m

62. A person throws a ball vertically up in air.The ball rises to maximum height and then falls back down such that the person catches it. Neglect the friction due to air. While the ball was in air, three statements are given below. ($g = 9.8\ m/s^2$)

Statement 1 : Just after the ball leaves the persons hand, the direction of its acceleration is upwards.

Statement 2 : The acceleration of ball is zero when it reaches maximum height.

Statement 3 : The acceleration of ball is $g = 9.8\ m/s^2$ downwards while the ball is falling down.

Then which of the above statement or statements are correct in the options below.

(a) Statement 1 only

(b) Statement 2 only

(c) Statement 3 only

(d) Both statement 2 and statement 3

63. For the graph shown in the fig. the distance covered by the body in the first 12 seconds is :

(a) 360 m

(b) 240 m

(c) 285 m

(d) none of these

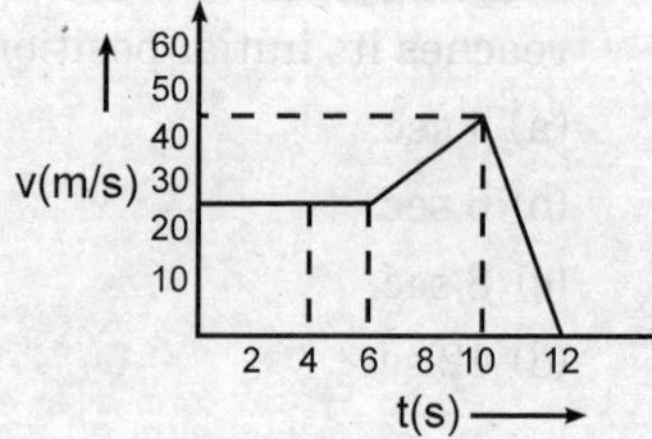

64. The acceleration time graph of a particle moving along a straight line is as shown in the figure. At what time the particle acquires its velocity equal to initial velocity?

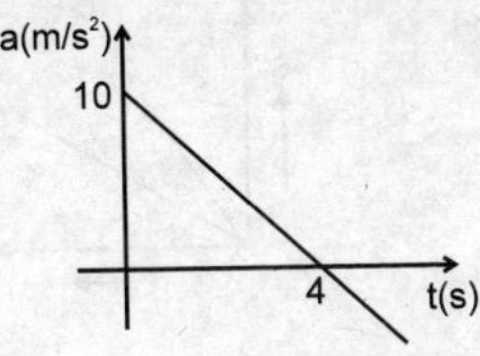

(a) 12 sec (b) 5 sec
(c) 8 sec (d) none of these

65. On a displacement/time graph, two straight lines make angles at 30° & 60° with the time axis. The ratio of the velocities represented by them is:

(a) 1 : 2 (b) 1 : 3
(c) 2 : 1 (d) 3 : 1

66. Figure shows the velocity time graph of a particle moving along straight line (v is m/s and t is in seconds). Its average velocity in 20 seconds will be:

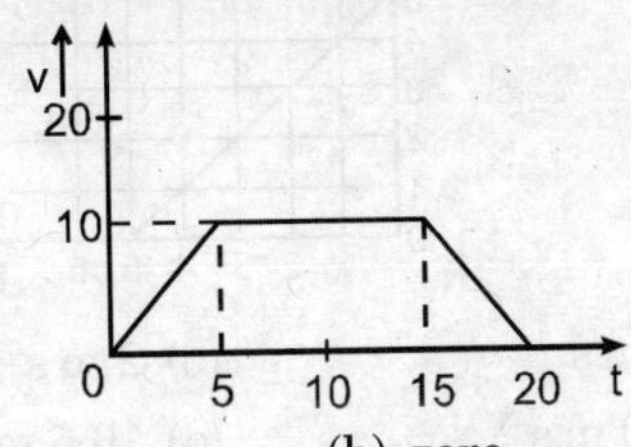

(a) 10 m/s (b) zero
(c) 3.75 m/s (d) 7.5 m/s

67. The velocity time graph of a linear motion is shown in the figure. The distance from the starting point after 8 seconds will be:

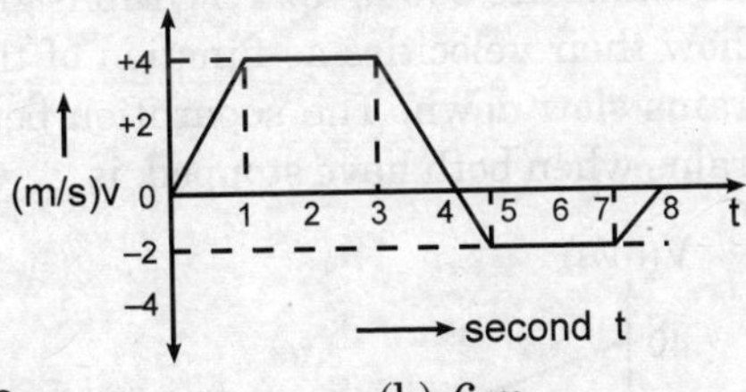

(a) 18 m (b) 6 m
(c) 8 m (d) none of these

68. A lift starts from rest. Its acceleration is plotted against time in the following graph. When it comes to rest its height above its starting point is:

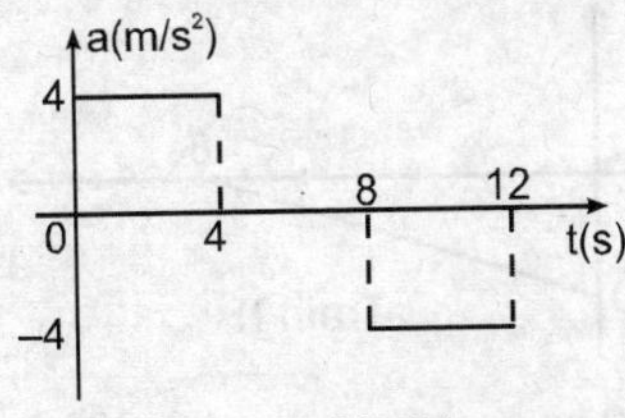

(a) 20 m (b) 64 m
(c) 32 m (d) 128 m

69. A particle can travel from point A to B from two different paths 1 and 2, as shown, in same interval of time. Then which of the following is incorrect?

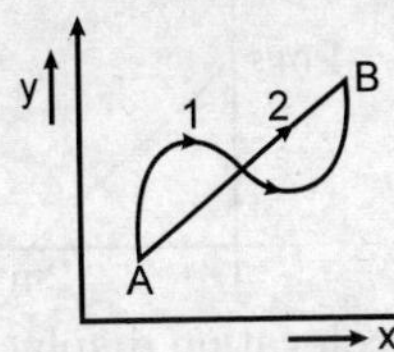

(a) Average velocity along the two paths must be equal
(b) The particle may travel along both the paths unaccelerated
(c) The direction of instantaneous velocity along the path 1 & 2 can be same for a maximum of two point on the paths.
(d) The average and instantaneous velocity along path 1 can have same direction.

70. Initially car A is 10.5 m ahead of car B. Both start moving at time t = 0 in the same direction along a straight line. The velocity time graph of two cars is shown in figure. The time when the car B will catch the car A, will be

(a) t = 21 sec
(b) t = $2\sqrt{5}$ sec
(c) t = 20 sec.
(d) None of these

71. For which of the following graphs the average velocity of a particle moving along a straight line for time interval (0, t) must be negative

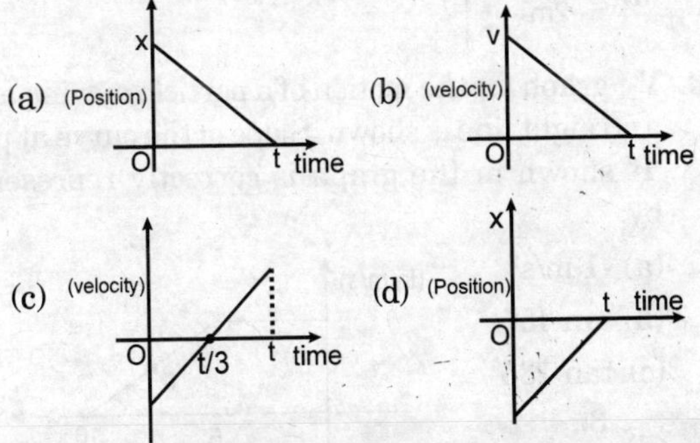

72. A person starts from origin and for his linear motion velocity is given as shown in figure. Find maximum displacement of the person.

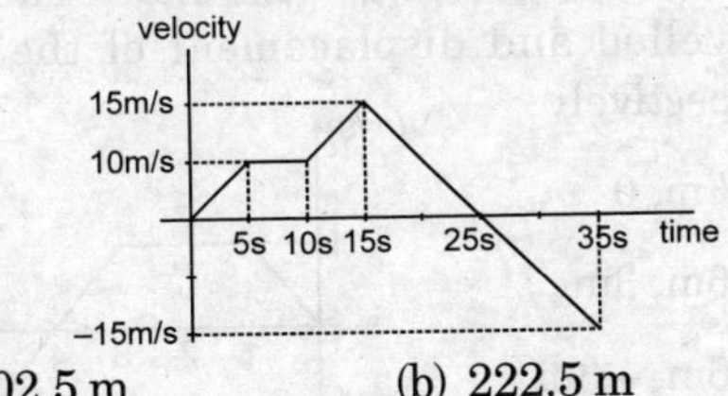

(a) 202.5 m (b) 222.5 m
(c) 232.5 m (d) 212.5 m

73. The velocity displacement graph of a particle moving along a straight line is shown in figure.

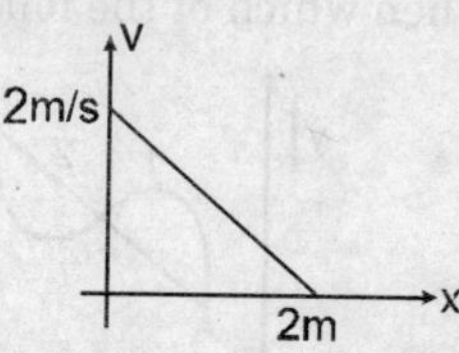

Then the acceleration displacement graph is.

(a)

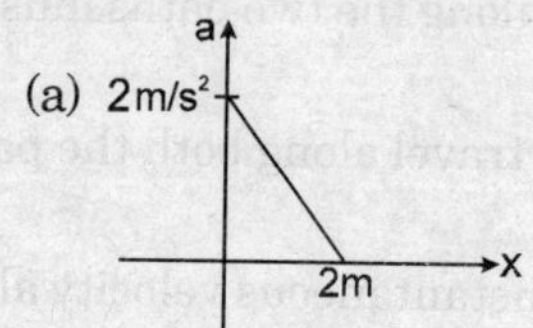

(b)

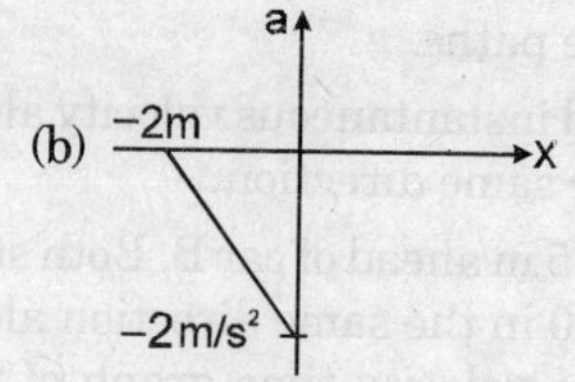

(c)

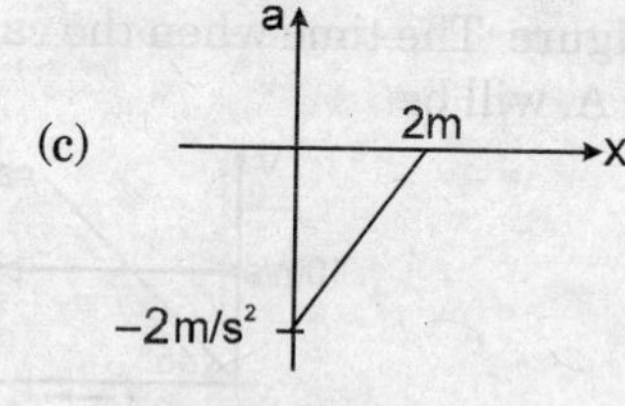

(d)

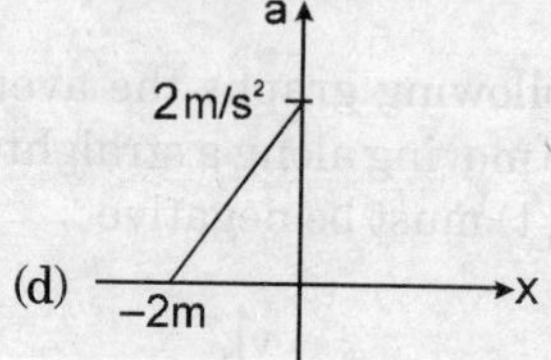

74. V-t graph for the motion of a particle moving along a straight line is shown. Slope of the curve at point 'P' shown in the graph is correctly represented by:

(a) -1 m/s^2

(b) tan 45°

(c) tan 135°

(d) $\frac{3\pi}{4}$

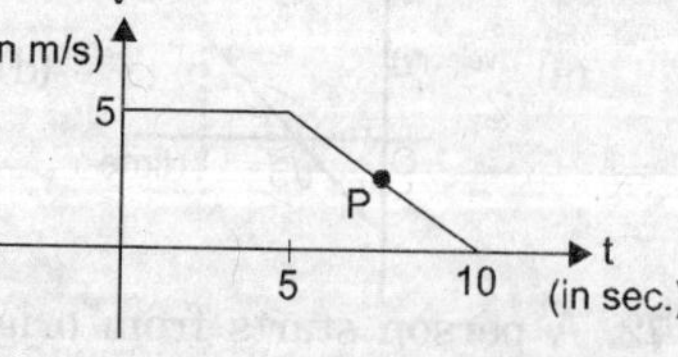

75. The velocity time graph of a body travelling along a straight line is given below. The distance travelled and displacement of the body are respectively

(a) 6m, 0

(b) 6m, 3m

(c) 6m, – 3m

(d) 0, 0

76. The displacement time graphs of two bodies A and B are shown in figure. The ratio of velocity of A, v_A to velocity of B, v_B is :

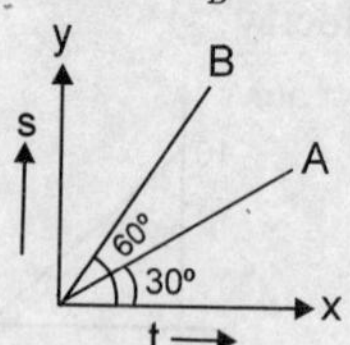

(a) $\frac{1}{\sqrt{3}}$ (b) $\sqrt{3}$

(c) $\frac{1}{3}$ (d) 3

77. Starting from rest at t = 0, a car moves in a straight line with an acceleration given by the accompanying graph. The speed of the car at t = 3 s is :

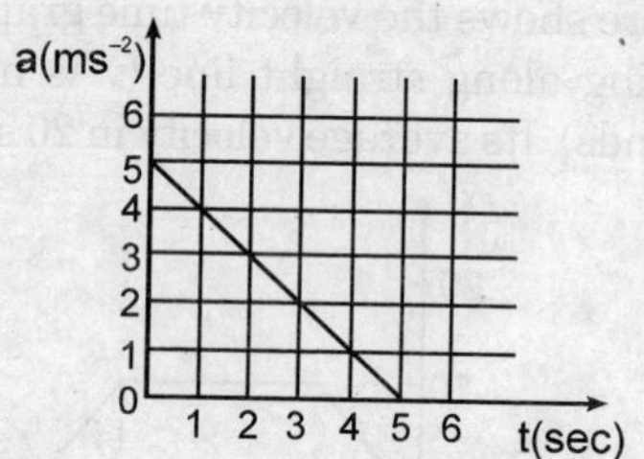

(a) 1 m s^{-1} (b) 2 m s^{-1}

(c) 6.0 m s^{-1} (d) 10.5 m s^{-1}

78. Two trains, which are moving along different tracks in opposite directions, are put on the same track due to a mistake. Their drivers, on noticing the mistake, start slowing down the trains when the trains are 300 m apart. Graphs given below show their velocities as function of time as the trains slow down. The separation between the trains when both have stopped, is :

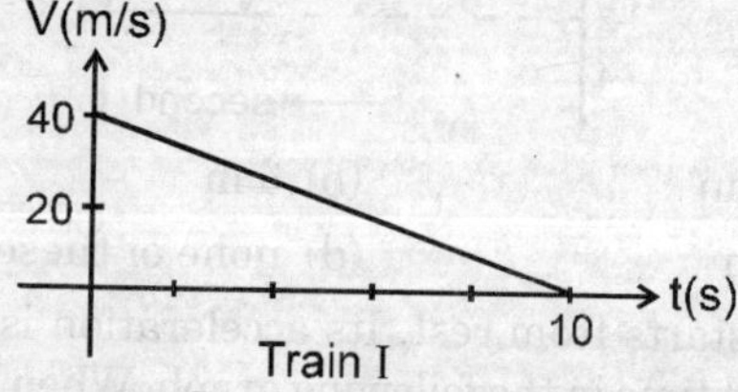

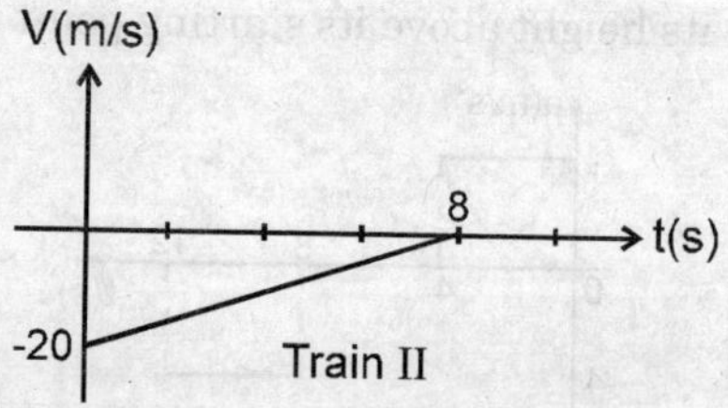

(a) 120 m (b) 280 m

(c) 60 m (d) 20 m.

79. Position (Km) - Time (min.) graph is shown for two cars 'A' and 'B'. Both collide at time t = 150 minute. Then the distance of position 'R' of accident from the starting point 'Q' of car A will be. (Initial distance between the two cars is 500 km) (Position in the graph shows the distance of the two cars from the point 'Q') -

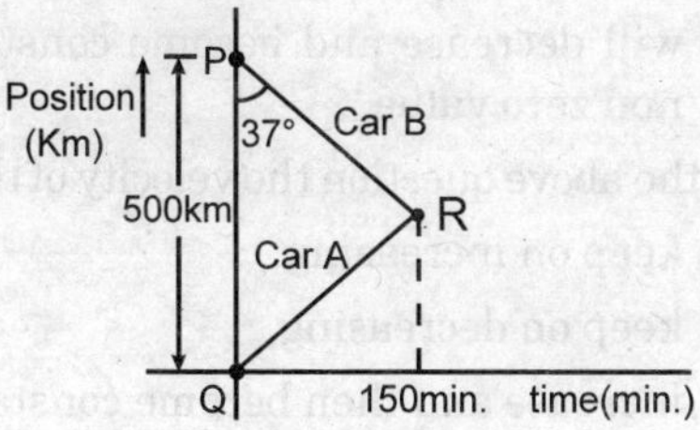

(a) 200 km (b) 300 km
(c) 250 km (d) 400 km

80. The velocity time graph of a particle moving in a straight line starting from a point P is shown in figure.

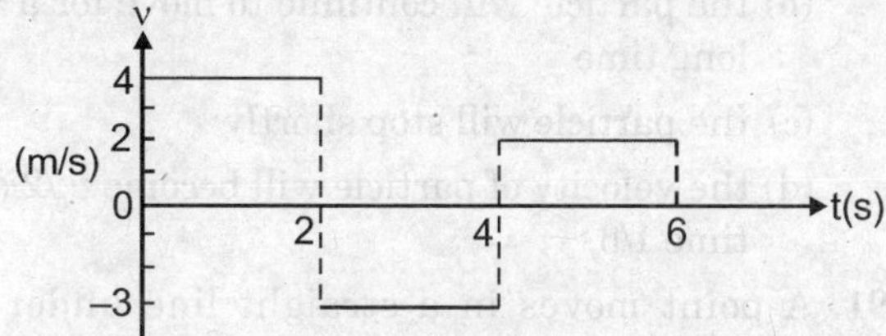

The distance of particle from P at the end of 6 seconds is :

(a) 6 m (b) 8 m
(c) 12 m (d) 18 m

81. The graph shown in the figure shows the velocity v versus time t of a body. Which of the graphs shown in figure represents the corresponding acceleration versus time graphs?

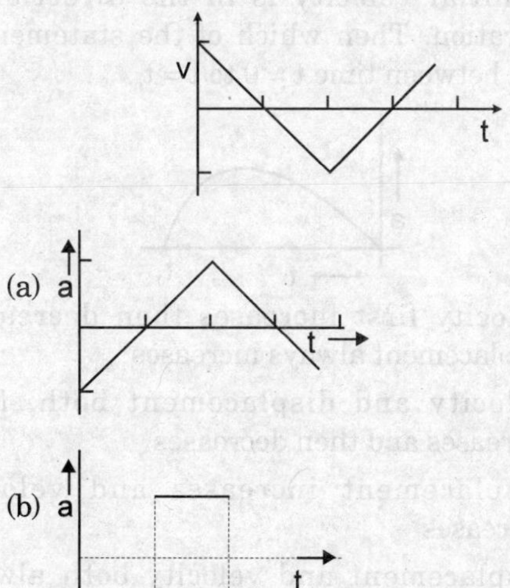

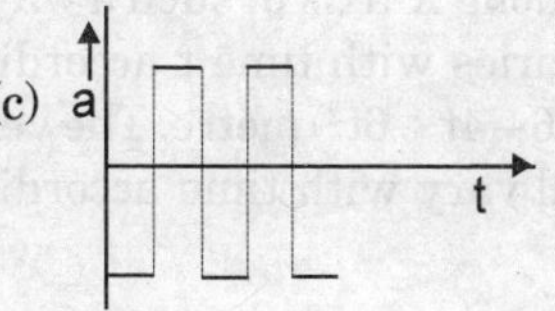

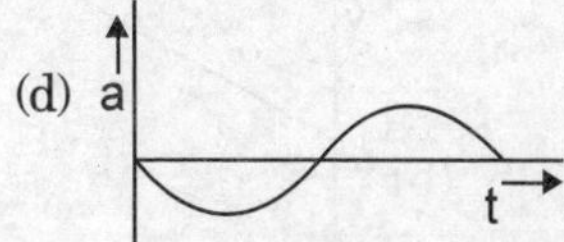

82. The diagram shows the velocity time graph for a particle moving in a straight line. The sum of the magnitudes of two shaded areas represents :

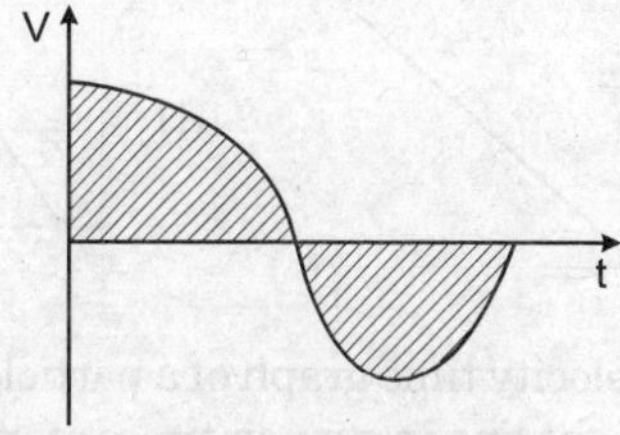

(a) displacement of the particle
(b) average velocity of the particle
(c) distance moved by the particle
(d) average speed of the particle.

83. The acceleration–time graph of a particle moving on a straight line is as shown in figure. The velocity of the particle at time t = 0 is 2m/s. The velocity after 2 seconds will be

(a) 6 m/s
(b) 4 m/s
(c) 2 m/s
(d) 8 m/s

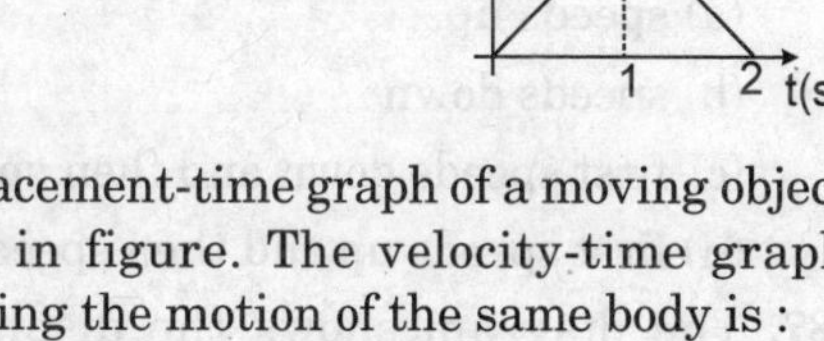

84. The displacement-time graph of a moving object is shown in figure. The velocity-time graph representing the motion of the same body is :

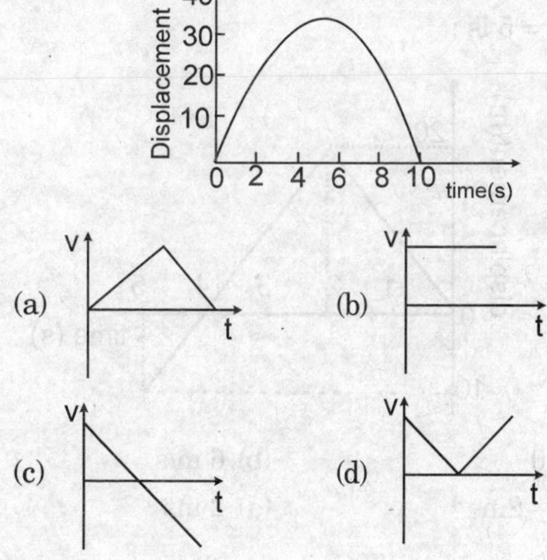

85. A particle moves along X-axis in such a way that its x-coordinate varies with time t according to the equation : $x = (6 - 4t + 6t^2)$ metre. The velocity of the particle will vary with time according to the graph

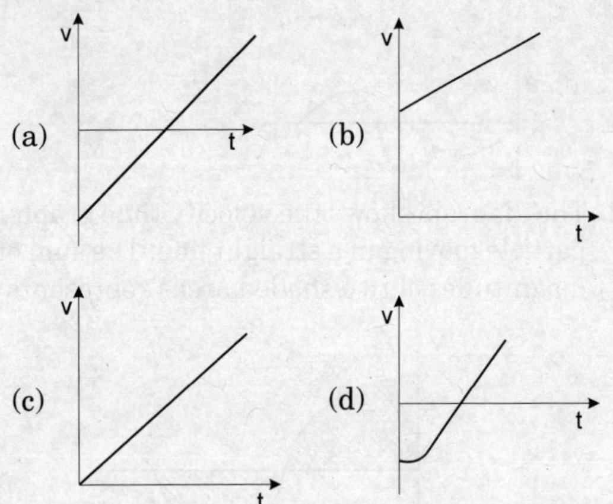

86. The velocity time graph of a particle moving along a straight line in a given time interval is as shown in figure. Then the particle (with increase in time starting from t = 0 sec.)

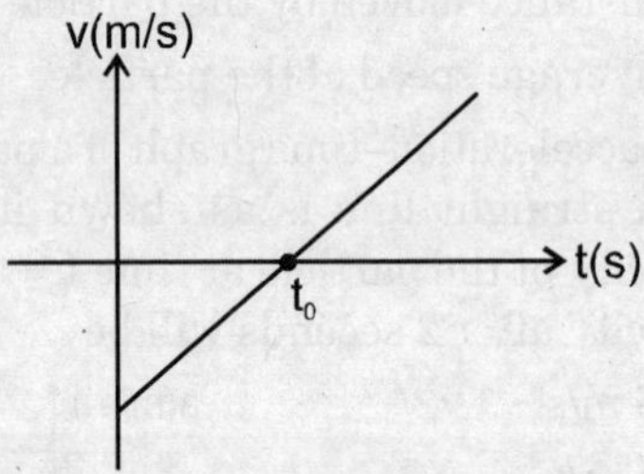

(a) speeds up

(b) speeds down

(c) first speeds down and then speeds up

(d) first speeds up and then speeds down

87. The diagram shows the displacement-time graph for a particle moving in a straight line. The average velocity for the interval from t = 0 to t = 5 is :

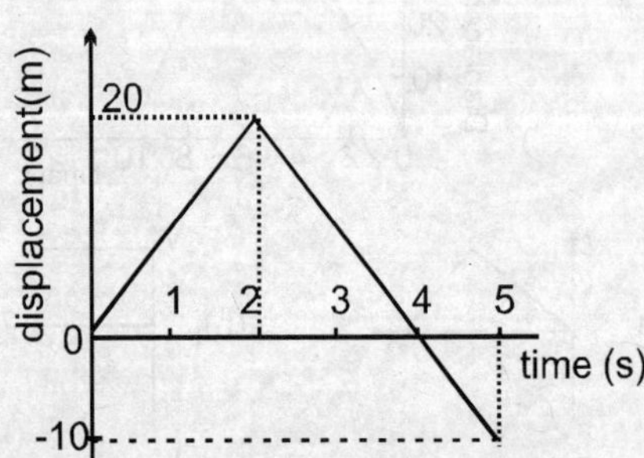

(a) 0 (b) 6 m/s^{-1}

(c) – $2ms^{-1}$ (d) 2 ms^{-1}

88. A particle initially at rest is subjected to two forces; one is constant, the other is a retarding force proportional to the particle velocity. In the subsequent motion of the particle, the acceleration:

(a) will increase then decrease

(b) will decrease than increase

(c) will decrease to zero

(d) will decrease and become constant at some non zero value.

89. In the above question the velocity of the block will:

(a) keep on increasing

(b) keep on decreasing

(c) increase and then become constant

(d) increase and then decrease

90. A particle moves with an initial velocity v_0 and retardation βv, where v is its velocity at any time t (β is a positive constant).

(a) the particle will cover a total distance of $2v_0/\beta$

(b) the particle will continue to move for a very long time

(c) the particle will stop shortly

(d) the velocity of particle will become $v_0/2$ after time $1/\beta$.

91. A point moves in a straight line under the retardation a v^2, where 'a' is a positive constant and v is speed. If the initial velocity is u, the distance covered in 't' seconds is :

(a) a u t (b) $\frac{1}{a}\log(a\,u\,t)$

(c) $\frac{1}{a}\log(1 + a\,u\,t)$ (d) a log (a u t)

92. A particle is moving in a straight line whose acceleration versus time graph is given. Assume that initial velocity is in the direction of acceleration. Then which of the statement is correct between time t = 0 to t = t_0.

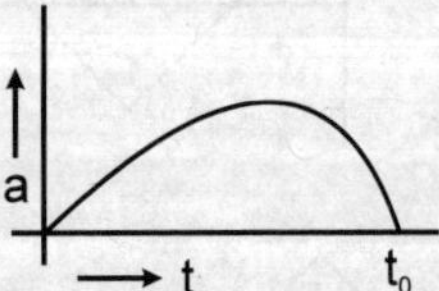

(a) Velocity first increases then decreases, displacement always increases

(b) Velocity and displacement both, first increases and then decreases

(c) Displacement increases and velocity decreases

(d) Displacement and velocity both always increases

93. A point moves in a straight line under the retardation kv^2. If the initial velocity is u, the distance covered in t seconds is:

(a) kut (b) $(1/k)\log_e(1+kut)$

(c) $(1/k)\log_e kut$ (d) $k\log_e kut$

94. A particle is moving rectilinearly so that its acceleration is given as $a = 3t^2+1$ m/s². Its initial velocity is zero.

(a) The velocity of the particle at t=1 sec will be 2m/s.

(b) The displacement of the particle in 1 sec will be 2m.

(c) The particle will NOT continue to move in positive direction.

(d) The particle will come back to its starting point after some time.

For Q. No. 95 to 97 :

If a man has a velocity varying with time given as $v = 3t^2$, then :

95. Find out the velocity of the man after 3 sec.

(a) 18 m/s (b) 9 m/s

(c) 27 m/s (d) 36 m/s

96. Find out his displacement after 2 seconds of his start :

(a) 10 m (b) 6 m

(c) 12 m (d) 8 m

97. Find out his acceleration after 3 seconds:

(a) 9 m/s² (b) 18 m/s²

(c) 12 m/s² (d) 6 m/s²

98. An aeroplane is flying in a horizontal direction with a velocity of 600 km/hour and at a height of 1960 m. When it is vertically below the point A on the ground a body is dropped from it. The body strikes the ground at point B. Calculate the distance AB.

(a) 3233 m (b) 3033 m

(c) 3433 m (d) 3333 m

99. Acceleration of a particle under projectile motion at the highest point of its trajectory is :

(a) g

(b) zero

(c) less than g

(d) dependent upon projection velocity

100. An object is thrown from a point 'A' horizontally from a tower and hits the ground 3s later at B. The line from 'A' to 'B' makes an angle of 30° with the horizontal. The initial velocity of the object is : (take g = 10 m/s²)

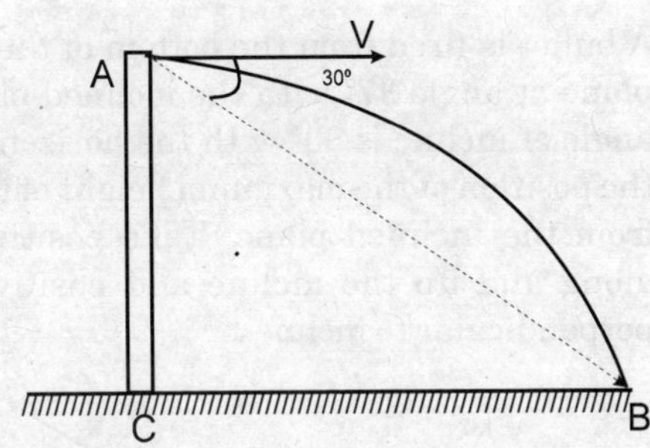

(a) $15\sqrt{3}$ m/s (b) 15 m/s

(c) $10\sqrt{3}$ m/s (d) $25/\sqrt{3}$ m/s

101. A partical A is projected with speed V_A from a point making an angle 60° with the horizontal. At the same instant, a second particle B is thrown vertically upwards from a point directly below the maximum height point of parabolic path of A, with velocity V_B. If the two particles collide then the ratio of V_A/V_B should be ;

(a) 1 (b) $2/\sqrt{3}$

(c) $\sqrt{3}/2$ (d) $\sqrt{3}$

102. A particle is projected at an angle of 60° from a horizontal plane. Then the path of projectile cannot appear a straight line to an observer:

(a) moving with constant acceleration in horizontal direction

(b) moving with constant velocity in horizontal direction

(c) moving downwards with constant acceleration 'g'

(d) none of these.

103. A particle is projected from a horizontal floor with speed 10 m/s at an angle 30° with the floor and striking the floor after sometime. State which is correct.

(a) Velocity of particle will be perpendicular to initial direction two seconds after projection.

(b) Minimum speed of particle will be 5 m/sec.

(c) Displacement of particle after half second will be 35/4 m.

(d) None of these

104. A particle is projected up the incline such that its component of velocity along the incline is 10 m/s. Time of flight is 2 sec and maximum height above the incline is 5 m. Then velocity of projection will be:

(a) 10 m/s (b) $10\sqrt{2}$ m/s

(c) $5\sqrt{5}$ m/s (d) none

105. A bullet is fired from the bottom of the inclined plane at angle 37° with the inclined plane. The angle of incline is 30° with the horizontal. Find the position of the maximum height of the bullet from the inclined plane. Take positive x-axis along and up the incline and positive y-axis perpendicular to incline.

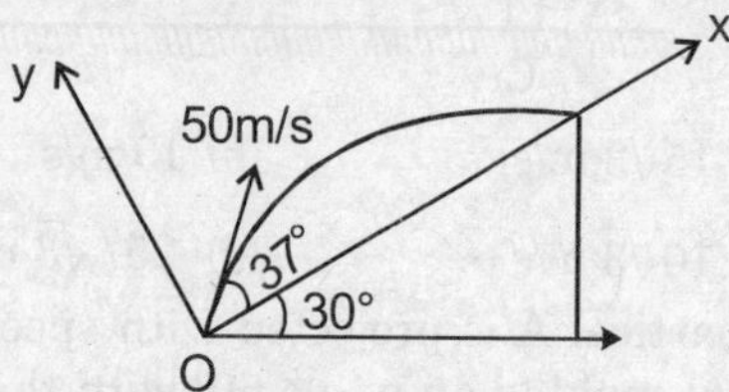

(a) $80\sqrt{3}$, $30\sqrt{3}$) (b) $80\sqrt{3}-30$, $30\sqrt{3}$)

(c) $80\sqrt{3}+30$, $30\sqrt{3}$) (d) none

106. Velocity of a stone projected, 2 second before it reaches the maximum height, makes angle 53° with the horizontal then the velocity at highest point will be

(a) 20 m/s (b) 15 m/s

(c) 25 m/s (d) 80/3 m/s

107. A pebble is thrown horizontally from the top of a 20 m high tower with an initial velocity of 10 m/s. The air drag is negligible. The speed of the pebble when it is at the same distance from top as well as base of the tower (g = 10 m/s²)

(a) $10\sqrt{2}$ m/s (b) $10\sqrt{3}$ m/s

(c) 20 m/s (d) 25 m/s

108. A particle is projected from the inclined plane at angle 37° with the inclined plane in upward direction with speed 10 m/s. The angle of inclined plane with horizontal is 53°. Then the maximum height attained by the particle from the incline plane will be -

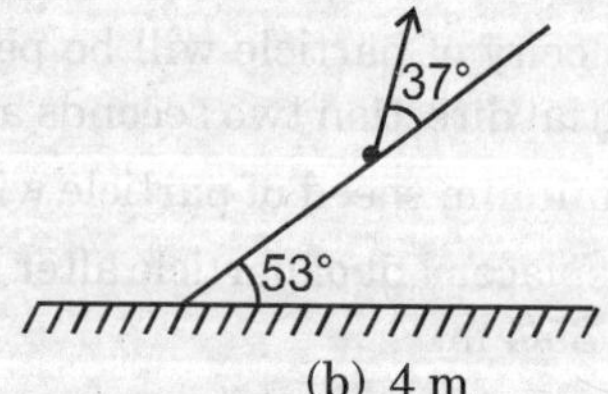

(a) 3m (b) 4 m

(c) 5 m (d) zero

109. A stone projected at angle 53° attains maximum height 25 m during its motion in air. Then its distance from the point of projection where it will fall is -

(a) 75 m (b) $\frac{400}{3}$ m

(c) 50 m (d) 60 m

110. A stone projected at angle 'θ' with horizontal from the roof of a tall building falls on the ground after three second. Two second after the projection it was again at the level of projection. Then the height of the building is-

(a) 5 m (b) 25 m

(c) 20 m (d) 15 m

111. A very broad elevator is going up vertically with a constant acceleration 1 ms^{-2}. At the instant when the velocity of the lift is 2 m/s, a stone is projected from the floor of the lift with a speed of 20 m/s relative to the floor at an elevation 30°. Find the time taken by the stone to return to the floor.

(a) 5/11 sec (b) 4/11 sec

(c) 3/11 sec (d) 2/11 sec

112. In the previous question find the range of the stone over the floor of the lift.

(a) $\frac{2}{11}$ m (b) $\frac{2\sqrt{3}}{11}$ m

(c) $\frac{2\sqrt{2}}{11}$ m (d) None of these

113. Ram can throw a ball on a horizontal surface upto a maximum distance of 50 m. The maximum height upto which he can throw the ball is

(a) 50 m (b) 25 m

(c) 12.5 m (d) 100 m

114. A ball is projected with velocity u at right angle to the slope down the incline which is inclined at an angle α with the horizontal. The distance 'x' along the inclined plane that it will travel before again striking the slope is -

(a) $\frac{2u^2}{g}\cos\alpha$ (b) $\frac{2u^2}{g}\tan\alpha$

(c) $\frac{2u^2 \tan\alpha}{g \cos\alpha}$ (d) $\frac{2u^2 \tan\alpha}{g \sin\alpha}$

115. Two bodies are thrown with the same speed at angles α and 90–α to the horizontal. Ratio of maximum heights reached by the bodies is -

(a) tan α (b) tan² α

(c) cot² α (d) cot α

116. For two projection angles θ_1 and θ_2 (at the same speed), the range of a projectile is the same and time of flights are t_1 and t_2. If the range isR then the product t_1 t_2 is proportional to :

(a) R (b) R²

(c) 1/R (d) $1/R_2$

117. The velocity at the maximum height of a projectile is half of its initial velocity u. Its range on the horizontal plane is:

(a) $\frac{2u^2}{3g}$ (b) $\frac{\sqrt{3}\,u^2}{2g}$

(c) $\frac{u^2}{3g}$ (d) $\frac{u^2}{2g}$

118. A cricket ball is hit for a six leaving the bat at an angle of 45° to the horizontal with kinetic energy k. At the top of trajectory the kinetic energy of the ball is :

(a) zero (b) k

(c) $\frac{k}{\sqrt{2}}$ (d) $\frac{k}{2}$

119. The trajectory of a projectile fired horizontally with velocity v is a parabola given by :

(a) $y = \frac{g}{2v^2}x^2$ (b) $y = -\frac{g}{2v^2}x^2$

(c) $x = \frac{g}{2v^2}y^2$ (d) $x = -\frac{g}{2v^2}y^2$

120. A body is projected with a speed u at an angle to the horizontal to have maximum range. At the highest point the velocity is:

(a) zero (b) $u\sqrt{2}$

(c) u (d) $\frac{u}{\sqrt{2}}$

121. Two particles are projected from the same point with the same speed at different angles θ_1 & θ_2 to the horizontal. They have the same range. Their times of flight are t_1 & t_2 respectively.

(a) $\theta_1 = 90 - \theta_2$ (b) $\frac{t_1}{\sin\theta_1} = \frac{t_2}{\sin\theta_2}$

(c) $\frac{t_1}{t_2} = \tan\theta_1$ (d) $\frac{t_1}{t_2} = \tan\theta_2$

122. Two balls are thrown from an inclined plane at angle of projection α with the plane one up the incline plane and other down the incline as shown in the figure. If R_1 & R_2 be their respective ranges, then which of the following is incorrect:

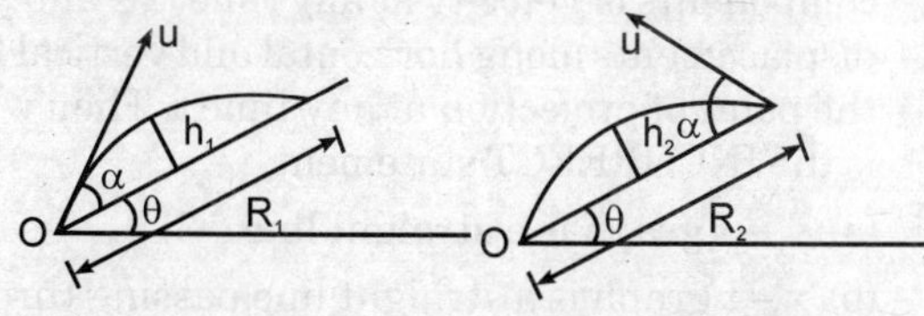

(a) $h_1 = h_2$ (b) $R_2 - R_1 = T_1^2$

(c) $R_2 - R_1 = g\sin\theta\, T_2^2$ (d) $R_2 - R_1 = g\sin\theta\, T_1^2$

[here T_1 & T_2 are times of flight in the two cases respectively]

123. A ball rolls off the top of a stair way with a horizontal velocity u m/s. If the steps are h metre high and b metres wide, the ball will hit the edge of the nth step if:

(a) $n = 2hu/gb^2$ (b) $n = 2hu^2/gb^2$

(c) $n = 2hu^2/gb$ (d) $n = hu^2/gb^2$

124. A particle has a range R on the horizontal plane. If h and h′ are the greatest heights in the two possible paths for this range and a given speed, then :

(a) $R = 4\sqrt{(h\,h')}$ (b) $R = \frac{4h}{h'}$

(c) $R = 4hh'$ (d) $R = \sqrt{h\,h'}$

125. A body is projected at time (t = 0) from a certain point on a planet's surface with a certain velocity at a certain angle with the planet's surface (assumed horizontal). The horizontal and vertical displacements x & y (in metre) respectively vary with time t in second as, $x = 10\sqrt{3}\,t$ & $y = 10t - t^2$. Then the max. height attained by the body is

(a) 200 m (b) 100 m

(c) 50 m (d) 25 m

126. A shell fired from a heavy gun at sea level rises to a maximum height of 5 km when fired at a ship 20 km away. The muzzle velocity (velocity relative to gun) should be:

(a) 7 m/sec (b) 14 m/s

(c) 28 m/sec (d) $200\sqrt{5}$ m/s

127. A particle is thrown from a platform with velocity v at an angle of 60° with the horizontal. The range obtained is R. If the platform moves horizontally in the direction of target with velocity v/2, the range will increase to :

(a) 3R/2 (b) 5R/2

(c) 2 R (d) 3 R

128. A ball is thrown upward at an angle of 30° with the horizontal and lands on the top edge of a building that is 20 m away. The top edge is 5m above the throwing point. The initial speed of the ball in metre/second is (take g = 10 m/s²) :

(a) 10 m/s (b) 20 m/s

(c) 25 m/s (d) 30 m/s

129. A ball is thrown from bottom of an incline plane at an angle α from the inclined surface up the plane. Another ball is thrown from a point on the inclined plane with same speed and at same angle α from the inclined surface down the plane. If in the two cases, maximum height attained by the balls with respect to the inclined surface during projectile motion are h_1 and h_2 then :

(a) $h_1 > h_2$ (b) $h_1 < h_2$

(c) $h_1 = h_2$ (d) All of these

130. A particle is projected with a velocity $10\sqrt{2}$ m/s making an angle 45° with the horizontal. Neglect the effect of air friction. Then after 1 seconds of projection. Take g=10 m/s^2

(a) the height of the particle above the point of projection is 5 m.

(b) the height of the particle above the point of projection is 10 m.

(c) the horizontal distance of the particle from the point of projection is 5 m.

(d) the horizontal distance of the particle from the point of projection is 15 m.

131. An aircraft moving with a speed of 1000 km/h is at a height of 6000 m, just overhead of an anti-aircraft gun. If the muzzle velocity of the gun is 540 m/s, the firing angle θ for the bullet to hit the aircraft should be

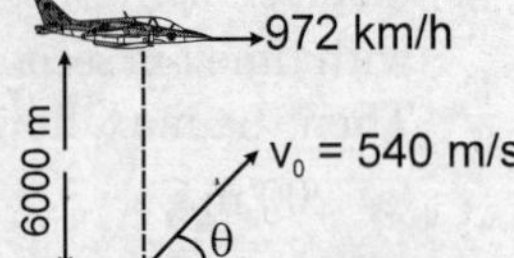

(a) 73^0

(b) 30^0

(c) 60^0

(d) 45^0

132. The vertical height of the projectile at time t is given by y = 4t – t^2 and the horizontal distance covered is given by x = 3t. What is the angle of projection with the horizontal?

(a) $\tan^{-1} 3/5$ (b) $\tan^{-1} 4/5$

(c) $\tan^{-1} 4/3$ (d) $\tan^{-1} 3/4$

133. A body is projected horizontally from the top of a tower with initial velocity 18 ms^{-1}. It hits the ground at angle 45°. What is the vertical component of velocity when it strikes the ground?

(a) $18\sqrt{2}$ ms^{-1} (b) 18 ms^{-1}

(c) $9\sqrt{2}$ ms^{-1} (d) 9 ms^{-1}

134. The equation of motion of a projectile is y = 12 x – 3/4 x^2. Given that g = 10 ms^{-2}. What is the range of the projectile?

(a) 36 m (b) 30.6 m

(c) 16 m (d) 12.4 m

135. An athlete runs with a speed 12 ms^{-1}. Determine the longest jump he can undertake.

(a) 14.4 (b) 12 m

(c) 12.1 m (d) 16.2 m

136. The maximum height attained by a projectile and its horizontal range are equal to each other if the projectile is projected at an angle θ given by

(a) θ = $\tan^{-1}$ (2) (b) θ = $\tan^{-1}$ (3)

(c) θ = $\tan^{-1}$ (4) (d) θ = $\tan^{-1}$ (5)

137. A bomb is dropped from an aeroplane when it is at a height h directly above the target. If the aeroplane is moving horizontally with a speed v, the distance by which the bomb will miss the target is given by

(a) $2v\sqrt{\frac{h}{g}}$ (b) $v\sqrt{\frac{h}{g}}$

(c) $v\sqrt{\frac{2h}{g}}$ (d) $v\sqrt{\frac{h}{2g}}$

138. A body is projected with kinetic energy k at angle ϕ with the vertical. Neglecting friction, its potential energy at the highest point will be

(a) k $\cos^2 \phi$ (b) k $\sin^2 \phi$

(c) k (d) zero

139. Distance between a frog and an insect on a horizontal plane is 10 m. Frog can jump with a maximum speed of $\sqrt{10}$ m/s. g =10 m/s^2. Minimum number of jumps required by the frog to catch the insect is:

(a) 5 (b) 10

(c) 100 (d) 50

140. A stone is projected from level ground such that its horizontal and vertical components of initial velocity are u_x = 10 m/s and u_y = 20 m/s respectively. Then the angle between velocity vector of stone one second before and one second after it attains maximum height is :

(a) 30° (b) 45°

(c) 60° (d) 90°

141. A stone is projected from point A with speed u making an angle 60° with horizontal as shown. The fixed inclined surface makes an angle 30° with horizontal. The stone lands at B after time t. Then the distance AB is equal to.

(a) $\frac{ut}{\sqrt{3}}$

(b) $\frac{\sqrt{3}ut}{2}$

(c) $\sqrt{3}ut$

(d) 2 ut

142. A stone is projected from level ground at time t=0. Let v_x and v_y are the horizontal and vertical components of velocity at any time t ; x and y are displacements along horizontal and vertical from the point of projection at any time t. Then which is the INCORRECT statement

(a) v_y – t graph is a straight line

(b) x – t graph is a straight line passing through origin

(c) y – t graph is a straight line passing through origin

(d) v_x – t graph is a straight line

143. A boat is rowed across a river at the rate of 4.5 km/hr. The river flows at the rate of 6 km/hr. The velocity of boat in m/s is:

(a) 3.1 (b) 2.1
(c) 2.9 (d) 5

144. A boat which can move with a speed of 5 m/s relative to water crosses a river of width 480 m flowing with a constant speed of 4 m/s. Find the time taken by the boat to cross the river along the path which is shortest.

(a) 160s (b) 80s
(c) 100s (d) 40s

145. Find also the length of shortest path in the previous question

(a) 160m (b) 400m
(c) 240m (d) 480m

146. The driver in a running car is at ________with respect to the person in the back seat of the car but is in ________with respect to a pedestrian on the road. Fill in the blanks

(a) rest, rest (b) motion, motion
(c) motion, rest (d) rest, motion

147. Man A is sitting in a car moving with a speed of 54 km/hr observes a man B in front of the car crossing perpendicularly a road of width 15 m in three seconds. Then the velocity of man B (in m/s) will be:

(a) $5\sqrt{10}$ towards the car at some angle
(b) $5\sqrt{10}$ away from the car at some angle
(c) 5 perpendicular to the road
(d) 15 along the road

148. A boat is moving towards east with velocity 4 m/s with respect to still water and river is flowing towards north with velocity 2 m/s and the wind is blowing towards north with velocity 6 m/s. The direction of the flag blown over by the wind hoisted on the boat is:

(a) north-west (b) south-east
(c) $\tan^{-1}\frac{1}{2}$ with east (d) north

149. A train is standing on a platform , a man inside a compartment of a train drops a stone . At the same instant train starts to move with constant acceleration . The path of the particle as seen by the person who drops the stone is :

(a) parabola
(b) straight line for sometime & parabola for the remaining time
(c) straight line
(d) variable path that cannot be defined

150. A man wearing a hat of extended length 12 cm is running in rain falling vertically downwards with speed 10 m/s. The maximum speed with which man can run, so that rain drops do not fall on his face (the length of his face below the extended part of the hat is 16 cm) will be :

(a) 7.5 m/s (b) 13.33 m/s
(c) 10 m/s (d) zero

151. A man holding a flag is running in North-East direction with speed 10 m/s. Wind is blowing in east direction with speed $5\sqrt{2}$ m/s. Find the direction in which flag will flutter.

(a) south (b) east
(c) north (d) west

152. A coin is released inside a lift at a height of 2 m from the floor of the lift. The height of the lift is 10 m. The lift is moving with an acceleration of 9 m/s^2 downwards. The time after which the coin will strike with the lift is : (g = 10 m/s^2)

(a) 4 s (b) 2 s
(c) $\frac{4}{\sqrt{21}}$ s (d) $\frac{2}{\sqrt{11}}$ s

153. A man in a balloon, throws a stone downwards with a speed of 5 m/s with respect to balloon. The balloon is moving upwards with a constant acceleration of 5 m/s^2. Then velocity of the stone relative to the man after 2 second is :

(a) 10 m/s (b) 30 m/s
(c) 15 m/s (d) 35 m/s

154. A boat is rowing in a river at the rate of 4.8 km/hr with respect to river. The river flows at the rate of 6 km/hr. The speed of boat in m/s can be :

(a) 3.1 (b) 2.1
(c) 4.5 (d) 5

155. P is a point moving with constant speed 10 m/s such that its velocity vector always maintains an angle 60° with line OP as shown in figure (O is a fixed point in space). The initial distance between O and P is 100 m. After what time shall P reach O.

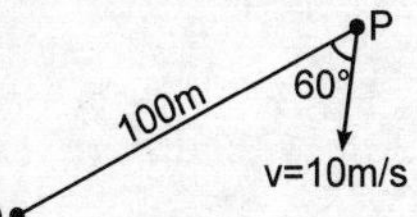

(a) 10 sec.
(b) 15 sec.
(c) 20 sec.
(d) $20\sqrt{3}$ sec

156. A man is sitting inside a moving train and observes the objects outside of the train. Then choose the single correct choice from the following statements -

(a) all stationary objects outside the train will move with same velocity in opposite direction of the train with respect to the man.

(b) stationary objects near the train will move with greater velocity & object far from train will move with lesser velocity with respect to the man.

(c) large objects like moon or mountains will move with same velocity as that of the train.

(d) all of these.

157. When two bodies move uniformly towards each other, the distance between them diminishes by 16 m every 10 s. If bodies move with velocities of the same magnitude and in the same direction as before the distance between then will decrease 3 m every 5 s. The velocity of each body is

(a) v_1 = 1 m/s and v_2 =0 .5 m/s.

(b) v_1 = 0.1 m/s and v_2 =0 .5 m/s.

(c) v_1 = 1.1 m/s and v_2 =1 .5 m/s.

(d) v_1 = 1.1 m/sand v_2 =0 .5 m/s.

158. Two particles are moving along a straight line as shown . The velocity of approach between A and B is

V_A (A) V_B (B)

(a) $V_A + V_B$ (b) $|V_A - V_B|$

(c) $V_A - V_B$ (d) $V_B - V_A$

159. A truck is moving with a velocity of 5 m/s. A man at the rear end of the truck throws a ball with a velocity 10 m/s at an angle of 60° with horizontal with respect to the truck and in the opposite direction to the direction of truck. Then the path (w.r.t. ground) of the particle is:

(a) a parabola

(b) linear motion in horizontal motion

(c) vertical linear motion

(d) none of these.

160. A train is standing on a platform , a man inside a compartment of a train drops a stone . At the same instant train starts to move with constant acceleration . The path of the particle as seen by the person who drops the stone is :

(a) parabola

(b) straight line for sometime & parabola for the remaining time

(c) straight line

(d) variable path that cannot be defined

161. A jet airplane travelling from east to west at a speed of 500 km h^{-1} ejected out gases of combustion at a speed of 1500 km h^{-1} with respect to the jet plane. What is the elocity of the gases with respect to an observer on the ground ?

(a) 1000 km h^{-1} in the direction west to east

(b) 1000 km h^{-1} in the direction east to west

(c) 2000 km h^{-1} in the direction west to east

(d) 2000 km h^{-1} in the direction east to west

162. Rain is falling vertically with a velocity of 3 kmh^{-1}. A man walks in the rain with a velocity of 4 kmh^{-1}. The rain drops will fall on the man with a velocity of

(a) 5 kmh^{-1} (b) 4 kmh^{-1}

(c) 3 kmh^{-1} (d) 1 kmh^{-1}

163. To a man running on level horizontal ground at a speed of 5 m/sec, rain drops appear to be falling at an angle of 45° from the vertical. If the rain drops are actually falling vertically downwards, then find the velocity of rain drops relative to ground?

(a) 4 m/s (b) 3 m/s

(c) 6m/s (d) 5m/s

164. A man who can swim at the rate of 2 km/hr (in still river) crosses a river to a point exactly opposite on the other bank by swimming in a direction of 120° to the flow of the water in the river. The velocity of the water current in km/hr is

(a) 1

(b) 2

(c) 1/2.

(d) 3/2

Answers

1. (d)	2. (a)	3. (a)	4. (a)	5. (d)	6. (b)	7. (b)	8. (c)	9. (d)	10. (a)
11. (c)	12. (b)	13. (a)	14. (c)	15. (a)	16. (c)	17. (a)	18. (b)	19. (b)	20. (a)
21. (a)	22. (b)	23. (d)	24. (b)	25. (d)	26. (c)	27. (c)	28. (b)	29. (c)	30. (a)
31. (b)	32. (b)	33. (b)	34. (d)	35. (c)	36. (a)	37. (b)	38. (d)	39. (b)	40. (b)
41. (c)	42. (a)	43. (d)	44. (b)	45. (a)	46. (b)	47. (d)	48. (d)	49. (c)	50. (a)
51. (c)	52. (d)	53. (d)	54. (c)	55. (d)	56. (c)	57. (c)	58. (c)	59. (c)	60. (c)
61. (b)	62. (c)	63. (c)	64. (c)	65. (b)	66. (d)	67. (b)	68. (d)	69. (b)	70. (a)
71. (a)	72. (d)	73. (c)	74. (a)	75. (a)	76. (c)	77. (d)	78. (d)	79. (b)	80. (a)
81. (b)	82. (c)	83. (a)	84. (c)	85. (a)	86. (d)	87. (c)	88. (c)	89. (c)	90. (b)
91. (c)	92. (d)	93. (b)	94. (a)	95. (c)	96. (d)	97. (b)	98. (d)	99. (a)	100. (a)
101. (b)	102. (d)	103. (d)	104. (b)	105. (b)	106. (b)	107. (b)	108. (a)	109. (a)	110. (d)
111. (d)	112. (b)	113. (b)	114. (c)	115. (b)	116. (a)	117. (b)	118. (d)	119. (b)	120. (d)
121. (a)	122. (b)	123. (b)	124. (a)	125. (d)	126. (b)	127. (c)	128. (b)	129. (c)	130. (a)
131. (c)	132. (c)	133. (b)	134. (c)	135. (a)	136. (c)	137. (c)	138. (a)	139. (b)	140. (d)
141. (a)	142. (c)	143. (b)	144. (a)	145. (d)	146. (d)	147. (b)	148. (a)	149. (c)	150. (a)
151. (a)	152. (b)	153. (d)	154. (b)	155. (c)	156 (a)	157. (d)	158. (d)	159. (c)	160. (c)
161. (a)	162. (a)	163. (d)	164. (a)						

Explanations

1. As can be seen from the figure

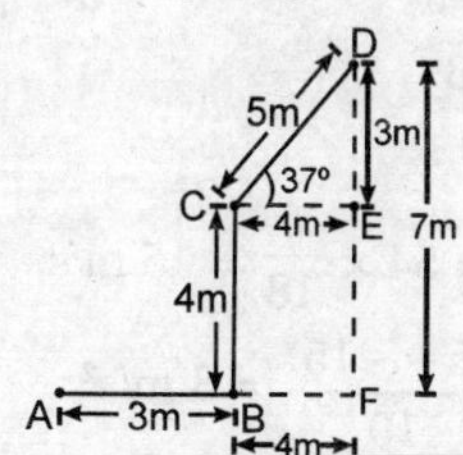

the displacement is $\sqrt{(AF)^2 + (FD)^2} = 7\sqrt{2}$ m

2. $\vec{d}_i = 2\hat{i}$

$\vec{d}_2 = 2\hat{i}$

$\vec{d}_2 = 5\cos 37\hat{i} - 5\sin 37\hat{j}$

$\vec{d}_3 = ?$

$\vec{d} = 6\hat{i}$

$\vec{d} = \vec{d}_1 + \vec{d}_2 + \vec{d}_3$

$\vec{d}_3 = 6\hat{i} - 2\hat{i} - 4\hat{i} + 3\hat{j} = 3\hat{j}$

3. $\vec{d} = \vec{d}_1 + \vec{d}_2$ where $\vec{d}_1 = 10\hat{j}$ and $\vec{d}_2 = 20\hat{i}$

$\vec{d} = 10\hat{j} + 20\hat{i}$

$|\vec{d}| = \sqrt{500} = 22.36$ km.

4. $S_2 = S_n - S_{n-2}$.

$$S_2 = \frac{1}{2}an^2 - \frac{1}{2}a(n-2)^2 \quad ....(1)$$

$$\text{and } v = an = a = \frac{v}{n} \quad ....(2)$$

5. $$v_{an} = \frac{\text{displacement}}{\text{time}} = \frac{x}{\frac{x}{3(20)} + \frac{2x}{3(60)}} = 36$$

6. $\vec{v}_i = v\hat{j}$

$\vec{v}_f = -v\sin\hat{i} + v\cos\theta\hat{j}$

$|\Delta\vec{V}| = |\vec{v}_F - \vec{v}_I| = |-(v + v\sin\theta)\hat{i} + v\cos\theta\,\hat{j}|$

$\Delta\vec{v} = \sqrt{(v + v\sin\theta)^2 + (v\cos\theta)^2} = 2v\sin 20°$

8. For example uniform circular motion.

9. $V_1 = 50\hat{j}$

$V_2 = -50\hat{i}$

$\Delta V = -50\hat{i} - 50\hat{j}$

10. $V = a + bx$

(V increases as x increases)

$$\frac{dV}{dt} = b\frac{dx}{dt} = bV$$

hence acceleration increases as V increases with x.

11. $v^2 = a + bx$

v increases as x increases

$$a = v\frac{dv}{dx} = \frac{1}{2}\frac{d}{dx}(v^2) = \frac{b}{2}$$

hence acceleration is constant.

12. About change in speed depending on the choice of the positive direction of the velocity

13. $\vec{r} = (t^2 - 4t + 6)\hat{i} + t^2\hat{j}$;

$$\vec{v} = \frac{d\vec{r}}{dt} = (2t - 4)\hat{i} + 2t\hat{j},$$

$$\vec{a} = \frac{d\vec{v}}{dt} = 2\hat{i} + 2\hat{j}$$

if $\vec{a}$ and $\vec{v}$ are perpendicular

$\vec{a}\cdot\vec{v} = 0$

$(2\hat{i} + 2\hat{j}).((2t - 4)\hat{i} + 2t\hat{j}) = 0$

$8t - 8 = 0$, $t = 1$ sec.

14. On the curve

$y = x^2$ at $x = 1/2$

$y = \frac{1}{4}$

Hence the coordinate $\left(\frac{1}{2}, \frac{1}{4}\right)$

Differentiating : $y = x^2$

$v_y = 2xv_x$

$v_y = 2\left(\frac{1}{2}\right)(4) = 4$ m/s

Which satisfies the line

$4x - 4y - 1 = 0$(tangent to the curve)

& magnitude of velocity :

$$|\vec{v}| = \sqrt{v_x^2 + v_y^2} = 4\sqrt{2} \text{ m/s}$$

15.

X_2

–14 (t = 2 sec.) –10 (t = 0 sec.) 0 6 (t = 4 sec.)

X_1

$x = t^3 - 3t^2 - 10$

$$v = \frac{dx}{dt} = 3t^2 - 6t$$

v = 0; gives t = 0

and t = 2 sec.

Velocity will become zero at t = 2 sec., so particle will change direction after t = 2 sec.

At t = 0

$x_{(0\,sec)} = -10$

At t = 2 sec.

$x_{(2\,sec)} = 2^3 - 3(2)^2 - 10$

$= 8 - 12 - 10 = -14$

At t = 4 sec.

$x_{(4\,sec)} = 4^3 - 3(4)^2 - 10 = 64 - 48 - 10 = 6$

Distance travelled $= x_1 + x_2$

$= |-14-(-10)| + |6-(-14)|$

$= 4 + 20 = 24$

16. If the velocity is in the direction of acceleration it will speed up.

17. At t = 0

$\frac{dx}{dt} = 0$ for particles 1,2 and 3 and $\left|\frac{d^2x}{dt^2}\right| > 0$ for $t > 0$

and= – 3.4 m/s for particle 4 and $\frac{d^2x}{dt^2}$ is negative for t > 0

Therefore for t > 0 ; $\left|\frac{dx}{dt}\right|$ is increasing in all.

18. $v_p = \left.\frac{dx}{dt}\right|_{t=0} = \gamma$ and $a_i = \left.\frac{d^2x}{dt^2}\right|_{t=0} = 2\beta$

$$\Rightarrow \frac{a_i}{v_i} = \frac{2\beta}{\gamma}$$

19. $54 \text{ km/h} = 54 \times \frac{5}{18} = 15$ m/s

$$\langle a \rangle = \frac{15-(-15)}{10} = 3 \text{ m/s}^2.$$

20. $a_x = \frac{d^2x}{dt^2} = 8\text{m/s}^2$

$a_y = \frac{d^2x}{dt^2} = 0$

21. $v = 0 \Rightarrow x^2 - 5x + 4 = 0$

x = 1m & 4m

$$\frac{dv}{dt} = (2x - 5)\,v = (2x - 5)\,(x^2 - 5x + 4)$$

at x = 1 m and 4m ; $\frac{dv}{dt} = 0$

22. $\sqrt{x} = (2t - 3)$

$x = (2t - 3)^2$

$\frac{dx}{dt} = 2(2t - 3)(2) = 4(2t - 3)$

$V = 4(2t - 3) = 0$

rest at t = 2/3

a = 8 m/s.

23. Let the acceleration of first car be a, then acceleration of second car is $\frac{a}{2}$.

For first car $\Rightarrow O = v - at$

or $t = \frac{v}{a}$

for second car $\Rightarrow O = v - \frac{a}{2}t'$ or $t' = \frac{2v}{a} = 2t$

24. $\vec{a}_{av} = \frac{\Delta\vec{v}}{\Delta t} = \frac{5\hat{j} - 5\hat{i}}{10} = \frac{1}{2}\hat{j} - \frac{1}{2}\hat{i}$

So $\frac{1}{\sqrt{2}} m/s^2$ is 2nd Quadrant

25. $\vec{V} = 6\frac{2\hat{i} - \hat{j} - 2\hat{k}}{3}$

$\vec{r} = \vec{r}_0 + \vec{v}t = 3\hat{i} + 4\hat{j} - 7\hat{k} + 4 \times 2(2\hat{i} - \hat{j} - 2\hat{k})$

$\Rightarrow \vec{r} = 19\hat{i} - 4\hat{j} - 23\hat{k}$

26. V_{min} when acceleration is zero

$\frac{dv}{dt} = 0 = 2t - 2 \Rightarrow t = 1 sec$

$\Rightarrow V_{min} = 1^2 - 2 \times 1 - 3 = 0$

27.

20m/s 30m/s

A C B

x x

$a = \frac{V_B^2 - V_A^2}{2 \times 2x} = \frac{900 - 400}{4x} = \frac{125}{x}$

$\therefore V_C = \sqrt{V_B^2 + 2ax}$

$= \sqrt{400 + 2 \times \frac{125}{x} \times x} = \sqrt{650} = 25.5$ m/s.

28. Magnitude of slope is same but sign is opposite.

29. $\frac{S_{nth}}{S_n} = \frac{\frac{a}{2}(2n - 1)}{\frac{a}{2}n^2} = \frac{2}{n} - \frac{1}{n^2}$

30. To move in a straight line

$\vec{a} \,||\, \vec{u}$

31. time $= \frac{75/1000}{40 + v} = \frac{3}{3600} = v = 50 km/h$.

32. $S = \frac{1}{2} \times 2 \times 10^2 = 100m$

33. $v = \sqrt{u^2 + 2as}$

$= \sqrt{0^2 + 2 \times 2 \times 100} = 2 \times 10 = 20$ m/sec.

34. Since acceleration is zero, and final velocity is dependent variable on a and u

So, v = 0 m/sec.

35. $V^2 = u^2 + 2as$

$(10)^2 = 0 + 2 \times 5 \times S$

$\Rightarrow S = 10$ m.

36. $10.2 = vt - \frac{1}{2}gt^2$

$gt^2 - 2vt + 20.4 = 0$

The difference of root is 10s

$\Rightarrow \frac{\sqrt{0^2 - 4 \times 10.2 \times 5}}{5} = 10$

$\Rightarrow v = 52$ m/s.

37. At position A balloon drops first particle

So, $u_A = 0$, $a_A = -g$, t = 3.5 sec.

$S_A = \left(\frac{1}{2}gt^2\right)$ ....(i)

Balloon is going upward from A to B in 2 sec.so distance travelled by balloon in 2 second.

$\left(S_B = \frac{1}{2}a_B t^2\right)$ ....(ii)

$a_B = 0.4 m/s^2$, t = 2 sec.

$S_1 = BC = (SB + SA)$ ....(iii)

Distance travell by second stone which is droped from balloon at B

$u_2 = u_B = a_B t = 0.4 \times 2 = 0.8$ m/s t = 1.5 sec.

B

S_B

A

S_A

C

$\left(S_2 = u_2 t - \frac{1}{2}gt^2\right)$ ....(iv)

Distance between two stone

$\Delta S = S_1 - S_2$.

38. if they meet position is same

$$x_1 = 98t - \frac{1}{2}(9.8)t^2$$

$$x_2 = 98(t-4) - \frac{1}{2}(9.8)(t-4)^2$$

$\Rightarrow x_1 = x_2 \Rightarrow t = 12s.$

39.

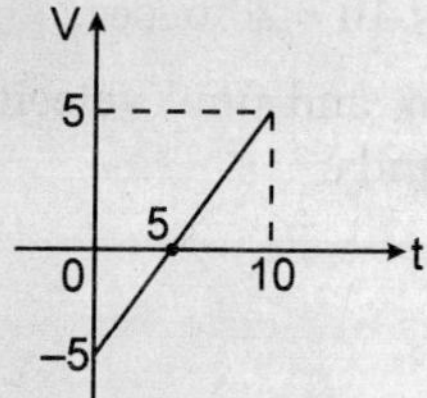

From the graph distance $= 2\left(\frac{1}{2}\times 5\times 5\right) = 25$ m

40. $v = u + at \Rightarrow 20 = u + a \times 10$ ....(1)

$s_n = u + \frac{a}{2}(2n - 1)$

$\Rightarrow 10 = u + \frac{a}{2}(2 \times 10 - 1)$ ....(2)

On solving (1) and (2) we get

$a = 20$ m/s^2

41. $V_{SB} = 10(\text{down})$

$V_B = 20(\text{up})$

$\vec{V}_S = \vec{V}_{SB} + \vec{V}_B = -10\hat{j} + 20\hat{j} = 10\hat{j}$

$120 = 10t = \frac{1}{2}\times 10t^2 \Rightarrow t = 6 \text{ or } -4$

42. At maximum displacement velocity is zero.

$0 = 4 + a(2) \Rightarrow = -2$ m/s^2

For displacement to be zero

$0 = 4(t) - \frac{1}{2}(2)t^2 \Rightarrow t = 4s.$

43. $t = \sqrt{\frac{2h}{g}}$

$S_{n_{th}} = 0 + \frac{g}{2}\left(2\sqrt{\frac{2h}{g}} - 1\right) = 24.5$

$\Rightarrow h = 44.1$ M

44. Let a be the retardation produced by resistive force, t_a and t_d be the time ascent and descent respectively.

If the particle rises upto a height h

then $h = \frac{1}{2}(g + a)t_a^2$ and $h = \frac{1}{2}(g - a)t_d^2$

$\therefore \frac{t_a}{t_d} = \sqrt{\frac{g-a}{g+a}} = \sqrt{\frac{10-2}{10+2}} = \sqrt{\frac{2}{3}}$

45. el. of Ist stone when passing at A →

$V^2 = 0 + 2.10.5$

$V = 10$ m/s

$S_1 - S_2 = 20$ m.

$\Rightarrow \left(10.t + \frac{1}{2}10.t^2\right) - \left(\frac{1}{2}.10.t^2\right) = 20$

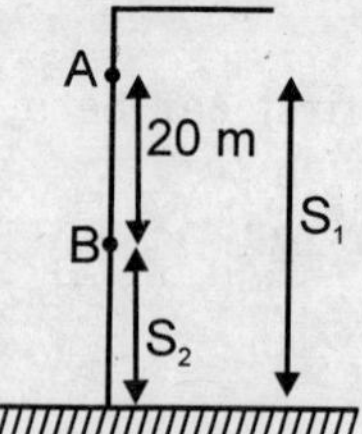

$t = 2s$

$S_2 = \frac{1}{2}.10.4 = 20$ m

Ht = 25 + 20 = 45 m.

46. At the highest point v = 0, so acceleration due to air to air resistance is zero.

47. $v = u + at$

$v - u = at$

48. $\frac{ds}{dt} = 490 - 9.8t = 0$

$\Rightarrow t = \frac{490}{9.8} = 50$

Maximum height reached $= 490 \times 50 - 4.9 \times 50^2$

$= 12250$ m.

49. Velocity of the body at any time t

$v = \frac{ds}{dt} = 15 - 0.8t$

when v = 7

$\Rightarrow 15 - 0.8t = 7$

$\Rightarrow t = \frac{15-7}{0.8} = 10$

50. Velocity of the body at any time t is

$v = \frac{ds}{dt} = 10 - 0.2t$

when v = 0

$t = \frac{10}{0.2} = 50$ s.

51. Sum of distance travelled in tth & (t + 1)th Seconds = 100 cm

$\Rightarrow u + \frac{a}{2}(2t - 1) + u + \frac{a}{2}(2(t+1) - 1) = 100$

$\Rightarrow 2u + 2ft = 100$

$\Rightarrow u + ft = 100/2$

$\Rightarrow v = 50$ cm/s.

52. $x \propto t^3 \Rightarrow x = ct^3$ (say)

Then, $\frac{dx}{dt} = 3ct^2$

and, $\frac{d^2x}{dt^2} = a = 6ct$

$\therefore$ $a \propto t$.

53. $V = x^2 + x$

$\Rightarrow \frac{dv}{dt} = 2x\frac{dx}{dt} + \frac{dx}{dt}$

$\Rightarrow a = (2x + 1)V = (2x + 1)(x^2 + x)$

$\therefore$ When x = 2m

$a = (2 \times 2 + 1)(2^2 + 2) = 5 \times 6 = 30\ m/s^2$.

54. Displacement of particle 1 after time t,

$x_1 = 50\ t$

Displacement of particle 2 after time t,

$x_2 = \frac{1}{2} \times 10 \times t^2 = 5t^2$

According to question,

$5t^2 - 50t = 125$ or $50t - 50t^2 = 125$

$\Rightarrow t^2 - 10t - 25 = 0$ or $t^2 - 10t + 25 = 0$

$\Rightarrow t = 5(1 + \sqrt{2})$s or $t^2 = 5$ sec.

55. According to question,

Displacement in 2 s = 200 cm

Displacement in 6 s = 200 + 220 = 420 cm

$\therefore\ 2u + \frac{1}{2} \times a \times 2^2 = 200$

$\Rightarrow 2u + 2a = 200$

$\Rightarrow u + a = 100$ ....(i)

$6u + \frac{1}{2} \times a \times 6^2 = 420$

$\Rightarrow 6u + 18a = 420$

$\Rightarrow u + 3a = 70$ ....(ii)

Solving equation, (i) & (ii)

$u = 115$ cm/s, $a = -15\ cm/s^2$

$\therefore\ v = u + at = 115 - 15 \times 7 = 115 - 105 = 10$ cm/s.

56. At B parachute opens out & he falls with a retardation of $2.5\ m/s^2$.

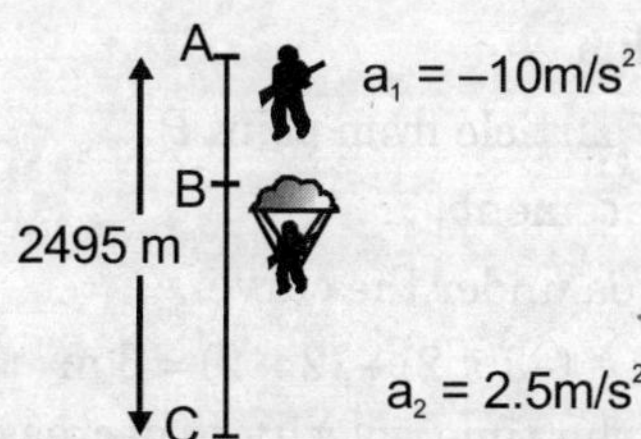

$\therefore\ AB = \frac{1}{2} \times 10 \times 10^2 = 500$ m

$\therefore$ BC = AC – AB = 2495 – 500 = 1995 m.

Velocity at B,

$V_B = gt = 10 \times 10 = 100$ m/s $\downarrow$

Velocity at C,

$V_C = \sqrt{V_B^2 + 2ay} = \sqrt{100^2 + 2 \times 2.5 \times (-1995)}$

$= \sqrt{25} = 5$ m/s $\downarrow$

57. Let initial velocity of the ball = u

$\therefore\ 25 = ut - \frac{1}{2}gt^2 = ut - 5t^2$

$\Rightarrow 5t^2 - ut + 25 = 0$

If t_1 and t_2 are the two solutions,

Then, $t_2 - t_1 = \sqrt{(t_2 + t_1)^2 - 4t_1t_2}$

58. Distance travelled by a freely falling body

$y = v\frac{1}{2}gt^2$

$\therefore\ y \propto t^2$.

59. For downward motion,

$h = ut_1 + \frac{1}{2}gt_1^2$ ....(i)

For upward motion,

$h = -ut_2 + \frac{1}{2}gt_2^2$ ....(ii)

From (1) & (2)

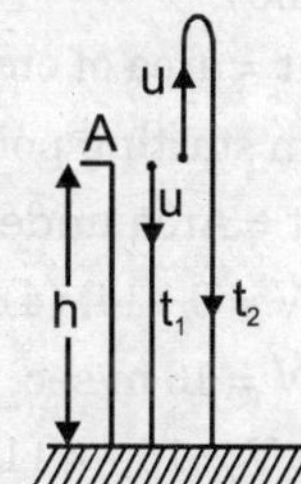

$ut_1 + \frac{1}{2}gt_1^2 = -ut_2 + \frac{1}{2}gt_2^2$

$\Rightarrow u(t_1 + t_2) = \frac{1}{2}g(t_2^2 - t_1^2)$

$\therefore\ h = \frac{g}{2}(t_1 - t_1)t_1 + \frac{g}{2}gt_1^2 = \frac{gt_2t_1}{2}$

$\therefore$ Reguired time $t = \sqrt{\frac{2h}{g}} = \sqrt{t_1t_2}$.

60.

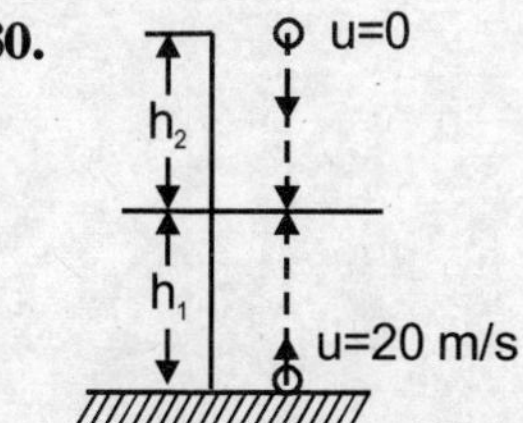

Height of the building

$H = h_1 + h_2 = \frac{1}{2}gt^2 + ut - \frac{1}{2}gt^2 = ut = 60$ m.

61. According to the question :

$$\sqrt{\frac{2h}{g}} - \sqrt{\frac{2(h-20)}{g}} = 1$$

$$\Rightarrow \frac{2h}{g} + \frac{2(h-20)}{g} = 2\sqrt{\frac{4(h-20)}{g^2}}$$

$$\Rightarrow \frac{4h}{g} - \frac{40}{g} - 1 = \frac{4}{g}\sqrt{h(h-20)}$$

Solving we get, $h = \frac{125}{4} = 31.25$ m.

62. The acceleration of ball during its flight is $g = 9.8 m/s^2$ downwards.

63. Distance = sum of modulus of displacement

Displacement = Area under v-t graph

64. $\frac{dv}{dt} = a = -2.5t + 1$

$$\int_U^U dV = \int_0^t (-2.5t + 10)\, dt$$

$$0 = -2.5\frac{t^2}{2} + 10t \Rightarrow t = 8s$$

65. Slope of displacement time graph is velocity

66. $V_{av} = \frac{\text{Displacement}}{\text{time}}$

Displacement = area of curve

67. Distance from starting point is

displacement = Area under v-t graph

68. At t = 4 sec, V = 0 + (4) (4) = 16 m/sec.

At t = 8 sec, V = 16 m/sec.

At t = 12 sec, V = 16 – 4 (12 – 8) = 0

For 0 to 4 sec $s_1 = ½ at^2 = ½ (4) (4)^2 = 32$ m

For 4 to 8 sec $s_2 = 16 (8 – 4) = 64$ m

For 8 to 12 sec $s_3 = 16 (4) – ½ (4) (4)^2 = 32$ m

So $s_1 + s_2 + s_3 = 32 + 64 + 32 = 128$ m

69. Along a curved path direction will continuously change. So velocity cannot be same.

70. $x_A = x_B$

$$10.5 + 10t = \frac{1}{2}at^2$$

$a = \tan 45° = 1$

$t^2 – 20t – 21 = 0$

$$t = \frac{20 \pm \sqrt{400 + 84}}{2}$$

t = 21 sec.

71. In (A) $x_f – x_2$

$0 – x = – x = –$ ve

So average velocity is – ve.

72. Maximum displacement is a 25 sec. displacement = 25 + 50 + 62.5 + 75 = 212.5 m.

73.

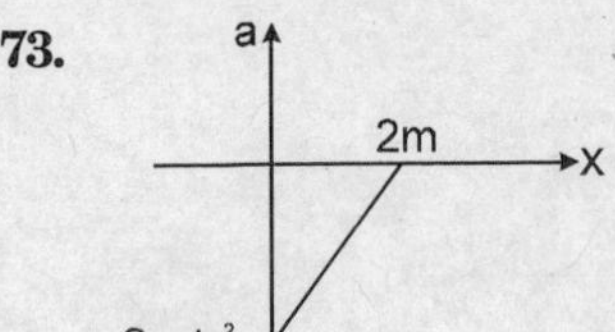

From the graph, we can write

$v = – x + 2$

$$a = \frac{dv}{dt} = -\frac{dx}{dt}$$

$= – v = – (– x + 2) = x – 2$

74. Slope of V-t graph = acceleration.

$$= -\frac{5}{10-5} = -1 \text{ m/s}^2.$$

75. Area under velocity-time graph

76. For A, $\frac{ds}{dt} = V_A = \frac{1}{\sqrt{3}}$

For B, $\frac{ds}{dt} = V_B = \sqrt{3}$

$$\frac{V_A}{V_B} = \frac{1}{3}$$

77. $V_{t=3} – V_{t=0}$ = area under a – t curve

$\therefore V_{t=3} = 10.5$ m/s

78. Area under velocity-time graph

79.

x
37°
53°
y

$$\tan 53° = \frac{x}{150} \text{ km/min}$$

$\Rightarrow x = 200$ km

$\Rightarrow y = 300$ km

80. Distance of particle from point P

= | displacement |

= Net Area under the curve

= (4 × 2) + (–3 × 2) + (2 × 2) = 6 m

81. For half of the time velocity is decreasing at a constant rate or $\frac{dv}{dt}$ is –ve, so acceleration will be –ve & similarly for the rest half acceleration will be +ve.

82. Sum of magnitude of displacement is distance

83. Area under a – t graph = Δv = 4 m/s

$\Delta v = v_f - v_i = 4$

$\Rightarrow v_f = 4 + v_i = 4 + 2 = 6$ m/s

84. velocity is slope of k – t graph and acceleration is slope of v – t graph.

85. $\frac{dx}{dt} = -4 + 12t$ straight line with –ve intercept.

86. From t = 0 sec. to t = t_0 second, the speed decreases and after t = t_0 second the speed increases. Hence particle first decelerates and then accelerates

87. Displacement from t = 0 to t = 5 second is = – 10 m

$\therefore$ Average velocity = $\frac{\text{Total displacement}}{\text{Total time}}$

$= -\frac{10}{5} = -2$ m/s

88. As velocity increases variable force will become equal to constant force. And thus net force will become zero.

89. So initially.

$a = F_c = F_v (F_c > F_v)$

So velocity will increase

after some time

$F_c = F_v = 0$

So velocity will become constant

90. (i) $V\frac{dv}{dx} = -\beta V$

(ii) $a = -\beta V$

$dv = -\beta dx \frac{dv}{dt} = -\beta V$

$\int_{v_0}^{0} dv = \beta \int_0^x dx$

$\int_{v_0}^{v} \frac{dv}{v} = -\beta \int_0^t dt$

$-v_0 = -\beta x$

$\ell n\left(\frac{V}{V_0}\right) = -\beta t$

$x = \frac{v_0}{\beta}$ $V = V_0 e^{-\beta t}$

$V = \frac{V_0}{e^{\beta t}}$

at $t \to \infty$ V = 0.

$\therefore$ A & B are correct answer

91. The retardation is given by

$\frac{dv}{dt} = -av^2$

Integrating between proper limits

$\Rightarrow -\int_u^v \frac{dv}{v^2} = \int_0^t a\, dt$ or

$\frac{1}{v} = at + \frac{1}{u}$

$\Rightarrow \frac{dt}{dx} = at + \frac{1}{u} \Rightarrow dx = \frac{u\, dt}{1+aut}$

Integrating between proper limits

$\Rightarrow \int_0^s dx = \int_0^t \frac{u\, dt}{1+aut}$

$\Rightarrow S = \frac{1}{a} \lambda n\,(1 + aut)$

92. It is clear from the figure that acceleration does not change sign, i.e., does not change in direction. Only the magnitude of acceleration first increases and then decreases.

$\therefore$ Velocity keeps on increasing.

Hence displacement also keeps on increasing.

93. The retardation is given by $\frac{dv}{dt} = -av^2$

Integrating between proper limits

$\Rightarrow -\int_u^v \frac{dv}{v^2} = \int_0^t a\, dt$ or $\frac{1}{v} = at + \frac{1}{u}$

$\Rightarrow \frac{dt}{dx} = at + \frac{1}{u} \Rightarrow dx = \frac{u\, dt}{1+aut}$

$\int_0^s dx = \int_0^t \frac{u\, dt}{1+aut} \Rightarrow S = \frac{1}{a} \lambda n\,(1 + aut)$

94. $a = 3t^2 + 1$

$\frac{dv}{dt} = 3t^2 + 1 \Rightarrow \int_0^v dv = \int_0^1 (3t^2+1)dt$

$v = \left(t^3 + t\right)_0^1 = 2$ m/s. $\Rightarrow v = t^3 + t$

$\therefore \int_0^s ds = \int_0^1 (t^3 + t)dt \Rightarrow S = \frac{1}{4} + \frac{1}{2} = 0.75$

95. $v = 3t^2$

v = 3(3)2 = 2.7 m/s

96. $\int_0^s dS = \int_0^2 3t^2 dt$

$S = \left[t^3\right]_0^2 = 8$

97. $f = 6t$

$f = 6 \times 3 = 18\ m/s^2$

99. Time of flight = $\sqrt{\frac{2H}{g}} = 20$ s

$\therefore AB = U_xT = 3333.3$ m = 3.333 km.

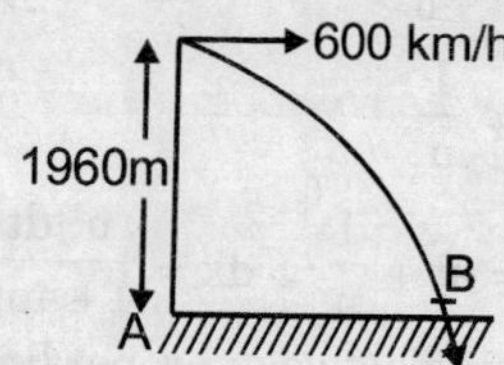

99. Gravitational acceleration is constant near the surface of the earthGravitational acceleration is constant near the surface of the earth

100. $AC = \frac{1}{2}\ gt^2 = 45$ m

$BC = 45\sqrt{3}$ m = u.t

$u = \frac{45}{\sqrt{3}} = 15\sqrt{3}$ m/s.

101. $\frac{(V_A \sin\theta)^2}{2g} = \frac{V_B{}^2}{2g}$

$\Rightarrow \frac{V_A}{V_B} = \frac{1}{\sin\theta} = \frac{2}{\sqrt{3}}$

104.

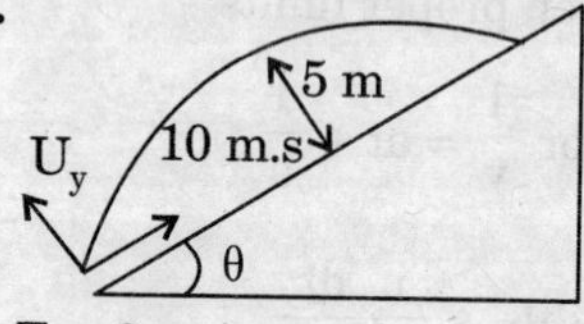

$T_f = 2$ sec

$a_x = -g \sin\theta,\ a_y = -g\cos\theta$

$T_f = \frac{2U_y}{ay} = 2$ .....(1)

$H = \frac{U_y{}^2}{2ay} = 5$ ...(2)

105.

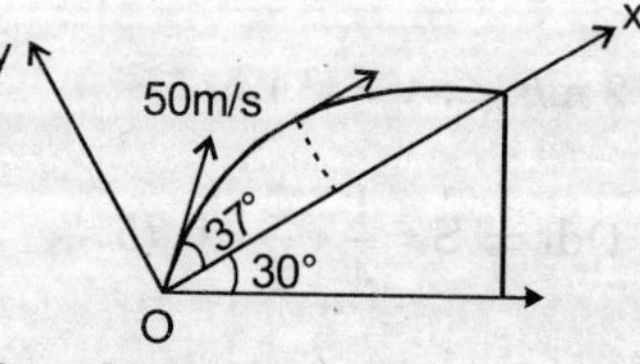

By taking axis system as shown in figure

At highest point $V_y = 0$

$V_y^2 = U_y^2 + 2a_y y$

$0 = (30)^2 - 2g\cos 30° y$

$y = 30\sqrt{3}$ ....(1)

Again for x coordinate

$V_y = U_y + a_y t$

$0 = 30 - g\cos 30° \times t$

$t = 2\sqrt{3}$

$x = U_x t + \frac{1}{2} a_x t^2$

$x = 40 \times \frac{1}{2} g \sin 30° \times (2\sqrt{3})^2$

$x = 80\sqrt{3} - 30$

106.

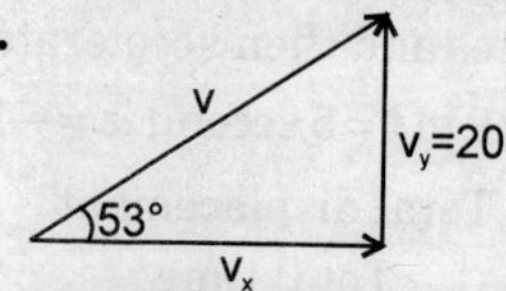

Two second before maximum height

$v_y = g \times 2 = 20$ cm/s

$\tan 53° = \frac{20}{V_x}\ v_x = 15$ m/s

107.

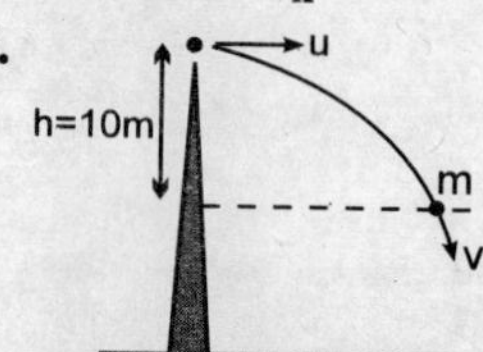

The pebble is at same distance from top and base of the tower after it falls down by a distance h = 10 m.

Applying conservation of energy.

$\frac{1}{2}\ mv^2 = \frac{1}{2}\ mu^2 + mgh$

or $v^2 = u^2 + 2gh = 100 + 2 \times 10 \times 10 = 300$

$\therefore v = 10\sqrt{3}$ m/s.

108. Maximum height from inclined plane is

$H = \frac{u_\perp^2}{2a_\perp} = \frac{(10\sin 37°)^2}{2g\cos 53°} = 3$ m

109. $H = \frac{U_y{}^2}{2g}, R = \frac{2U_xU_y}{g}$ and

$\frac{U_y}{U_x} = \tan 53°$

$\frac{H}{R} = \frac{U_y^2/2g}{2U_xU_y/g}$

$= \frac{U_y}{4U_x} = \frac{\tan 53°}{4}$

$\Rightarrow R = 75$ m

110.

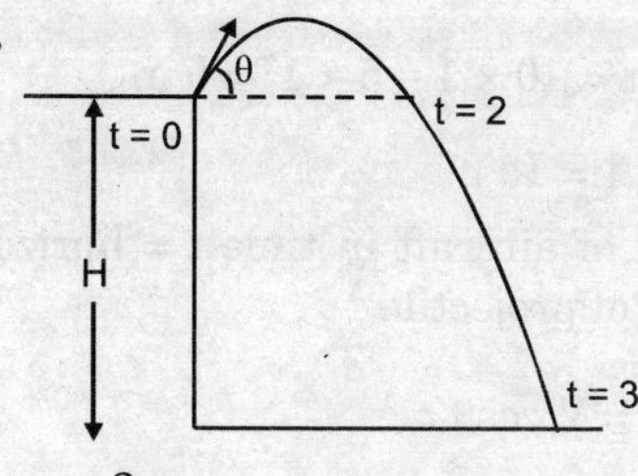

$2 = \frac{2u_y}{g} \Rightarrow u_y = 10$ m/s

Now, $H = -u_y t + \frac{1}{2}gt^2 = -30 + 45 = 15$ m.

111. Initial velocity of stone w.r.t. lift = $20 \sin 30^\circ \hat{j} + 20 \cos 30^\circ \hat{i} = (10\sqrt{3}\,\hat{i} + 10\hat{j})$ m/s

Initial velocity of stone w.r.t. ground

$= \left(10\sqrt{3}\,\hat{i} + 10\hat{j}\right)$ m/s

The initial position of stone & lift are same and when they again meet their final positions will also be same. So both will have same displacement in vertical direction in same time

Displacement of lift $= 2(t) + \frac{1}{2} \times 1 \times t^2 = 2t + \frac{t^2}{2}$

Displacement of stone $= 12(t) - \frac{1}{2} \times 10 \times t^2$

$= 12t - 5t^2$

so $2t + \frac{t^2}{2} = 12t - 5t^2$

$\frac{11t^2}{2} = 10t \Rightarrow t = \frac{20}{11}$ sec.

113. $R_{max} = \frac{u^2}{g} = 50 \Rightarrow u^2 = 500$

Maximum height he can throw is

$H_{max.} = \frac{u^2}{2g} = \frac{500}{20} = 25$ m

114. Equation for motion perpendicular to the incline

$\Rightarrow u.t - \frac{1}{2} g \cos\alpha.\, t^2 \Rightarrow t = \frac{2u}{g\cos\alpha}$

Along incline $x = 0 + \frac{1}{2} \times (g \sin\alpha)\left(\frac{2u}{g\cos\alpha}\right)^2$

115. $\frac{H_1}{H_2} = \frac{\frac{V_0^2 \sin^2\alpha}{2g}}{\frac{V_0^2 \sin^2(90-\alpha)}{2g}} = \tan^2\alpha$

116. $t_1 = \frac{2u\sin\theta}{g}$

$t_2 = \frac{2u\sin(90-\theta)}{g} = \frac{2u\cos\theta}{g}$

$t_1 t_2 = \frac{4u^2 \sin\theta\cos\theta}{g^2} = \frac{2}{g}R$

$t_1 t_2 \propto R$

117. At maximum height $v = u\cos\theta$

$\frac{u}{2} = v \Rightarrow \cos\theta = \frac{1}{2} \Rightarrow \theta = 60^\circ$

$R = \frac{u^2 \sin 2\theta}{g} = \frac{u^2 \sin(120^\circ)}{g} = \frac{u^2 \cos 30^\circ}{g} = \frac{\sqrt{3}u^2}{2g}$

118. At the top of trajectory,

$K' = \frac{1}{2}m(u\cos\theta)^2 = \frac{1}{2}mu^2.\cos^2 45^\circ = \frac{k}{2}$.

119.

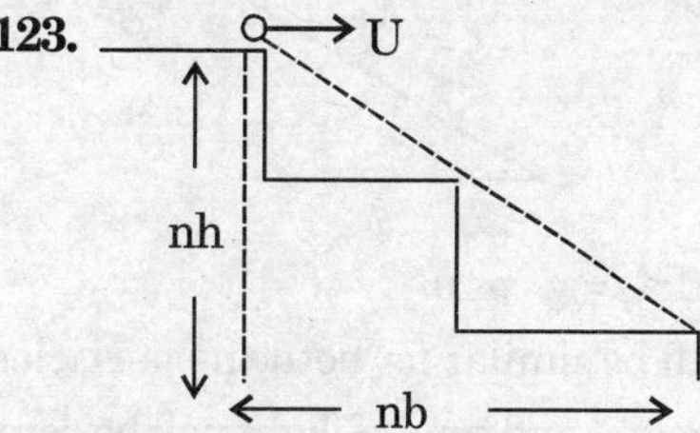

$x = vt$

$y = -\frac{1}{2}gt^2 = -\frac{1}{2}g.\frac{x^2}{v^2}$

$\therefore\ y = \frac{-g}{2v^2}x^2$.

120. For maximum range, $\theta = 45^\circ$

At the highest point, $v = u\cos\theta = \frac{u}{\sqrt{2}}$

121. $R = \frac{u^2 \sin 2\theta}{g}$ is same for angles θ & $90^\circ - \theta$.

$t_1 = \frac{2u\sin\theta_1}{g} = \frac{2u\sin(90^\circ - \theta_2)}{g}$

$t_2 = \frac{2u\sin\theta_2}{g} = 2u \sin\frac{(90^\circ - \theta_1)}{g}$

122. $R_1 = \frac{24^2 \sin\alpha\cos(\alpha+\theta)}{g\cos^2\theta}$

$R_2 = \frac{24^2 \sin\alpha\cos(\alpha-\theta)}{g\cos^2\theta}$

$R_1 - R_2 = g\sin\theta\, T_2^{\,2}$

$R_1 - R_2 = g\sin\theta\, T_1^{\,2}$

123.

$R = nb$

$H = nh$

$$t = \sqrt{\frac{2H}{g}},\ R = Ut$$

$$\Rightarrow (nb)^2 = U^2 \frac{2}{g}(nh)$$

124. $h = \dfrac{u^2 \sin^2 \theta_1}{2g}\ h' = \dfrac{u^2 \sin^2(90° - \theta_1)}{g}$;

$$R = \frac{u^2 \sin 2\theta_1}{g} \Rightarrow R = 4\sqrt{hh'}$$

125. $x = u_x t$ and $y = y = U_x t - \frac{1}{2}a_y t^2$

$\Rightarrow U_x = 10\sqrt{3}$ m/s

$U_y = 10$ m/s

$a_y = 2$ m/s

$$H = \frac{Uy^2}{2a_y} = \frac{(10)^2}{2 \times 2} = 25\text{m.}$$

126. R = 20 km, H = 5 km

127. $R = U_x T_f = (v \cos 60)\, T_f$.

$$R' = \left(v \cos 60 + \frac{v}{2}\right) T_f$$

$$\Rightarrow \frac{R}{R'} = \frac{1}{2} \Rightarrow R' = 2R$$

128.

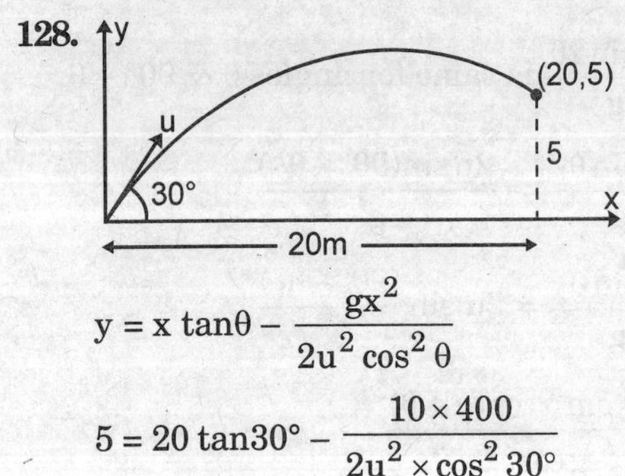

$$y = x \tan\theta - \frac{gx^2}{2u^2 \cos^2 \theta}$$

$$5 = 20 \tan 30° - \frac{10 \times 400}{2u^2 \times \cos^2 30°}$$

$\Rightarrow u \cong 20$ m/s

129. For both the particles

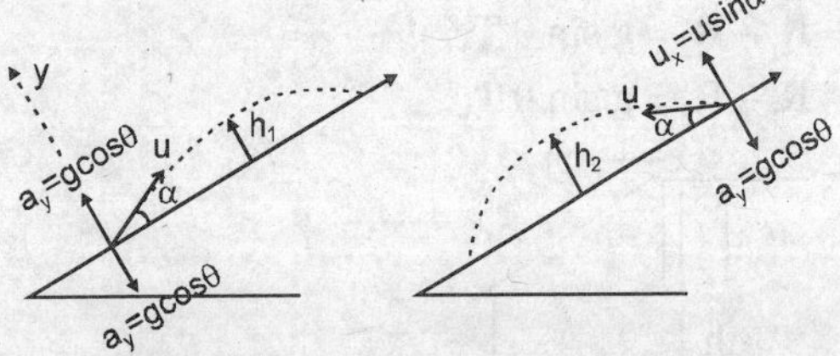

$u_y = u\sin\theta$ and $a_y = g\cos\theta$

So y motion will be similar for both the particles.

$\Rightarrow$ Maximum height and time of flight will be same for the both. $\Rightarrow h_1 = h_2$

130. $y = u_x t - \frac{1}{2}.gt^2 = 10 \times 1 - 5 \times 1^2 = 5$ m

$x = u_x t = 10 \times 1 = 10$ m

131. Displacement of aircraft in time t = horizontal displacement of projectile

$$\Rightarrow 972 \times \frac{5}{18} t = V_0 \cos\theta . t$$

$$\Rightarrow \cos\theta = \frac{54 \times 5}{540} = \frac{1}{2}$$

$\Rightarrow \theta = 60°$.

132.

u, 4y, θ, u_x

$y = 4t - t^2$, $x = 3t$

$$Vy = \frac{dy}{dt} = 4 - 2t,\ Vx = \frac{dy}{dt} = 3$$

$$\Rightarrow uy = vy|_{t=0} = 4,\ u_x = v_x|_{t=0}$$

The angle of projection :

$$\tan\theta = \frac{4y}{4x} = \frac{4}{3} \Rightarrow \theta = \tan^{-1}\left(\frac{4}{3}\right)$$ **Ans.**

133. $an45° = \dfrac{v_y}{v_x}$

$\Rightarrow v_y = v_x = 18$m/s Ans.

18m/s, V_x, 45°, V_y, V

134. $y = 12 \times \left(-\frac{3}{4}\right) x^2 = 12 \times \left(1 - \frac{x}{16}\right)$

$\Rightarrow$ Range = **16 m Ans.**

135. u = 12 m/s for longest jump; the range should be max.

i.e. $R_{max} = \dfrac{u^2}{g} = 14.4$ m

136. H = R

$$\frac{U_y^2}{2g} = \frac{2U_x U_y}{g}$$

$$\frac{U_y}{U_x} = 4\tan\theta$$

137. $R = U_x T_f = v\sqrt{\dfrac{2h}{g}}$

138. ϕ is with vertical $\Rightarrow H = \frac{U_y^2}{2g} = \frac{(U\cos\phi)^2}{2g}$

$U = mgH = mg\frac{(U\cos\theta)}{2g}$

$K = \frac{1}{2}nU^2$

139. Maximum distance covered in one jump

$= \frac{u^2}{g} = 1\text{ m}$

So minimum no. of jumps = 10

140. $T_F = \frac{2U_y}{g} = \frac{2\times 20}{10} = 4\text{ sec}$

$V_y = U_y - gt = 20 - 10\times 1 = 10\text{ m/s}$

$\Rightarrow \tan\theta_1 = \frac{10}{10} = 1 \Rightarrow \theta_1 = 45°$

also $\tan\theta_2 = 1 \Rightarrow \theta_2 = 45°$

$\Rightarrow$ angle is $\theta_1 + \theta_2 = 90°$

141. The horizontal displacement in time t is

$AC = u\cos 60°\, t = \frac{ut}{2}$

$\therefore$ Range on inclined plane $= \frac{AC}{\cos 30} = \frac{ut}{\sqrt{3}}$

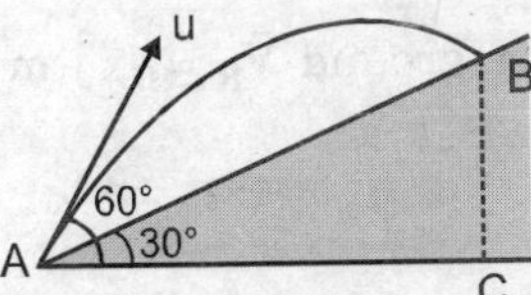

143. V_{boat}, river = 4.5 km/m

V_{rim}, ground = 6 km/hr.

V_{boat}, ground = $(6\hat{i}+4.5\hat{j})$ km/m

$= (6\hat{i}+4.5\hat{j})\times\frac{5}{18}$ m

V_{boat}, ground $= \sqrt{6^2+4.5^2}\times\frac{5}{18}$

$= 1.5\times 5\times\frac{5}{18} = \frac{37.5}{18} = 2.1$ m/sec.

147. $\vec{V}_{BA}$ (5m/s), $\vec{V}_B$, $\vec{V}_A$ (15m/s)

Velocity of A and velocity of B relative to A are as shown.

$\therefore\ \vec{V}_B = \vec{V}_{BA} + \vec{V}_A \Rightarrow V_0 = \sqrt{5^2+15^2} = 5\sqrt{12}$

and direction of $\vec{V}_B$ is away from $\vec{V}_A$.

148. Vboat, river = $4\hat{i}$

Vriver, ground = $2\hat{i}$

Vwind, ground = $6\hat{j}$

$\vec{V}$ wind, boat = $\vec{V}_{wg} + \vec{V}gr + \vec{V}_{rb} = 6\hat{j} - 2\hat{j} - 4\hat{i}$

$= -4\hat{i} + 4\hat{j}$

So flag blown in north west.

149. Relative to the person in the train, acceleration of the stone is 'g' downward, a (acceleration of train) backwards.

According to him : $x = \frac{1}{2}at^2, Y = \frac{1}{2}gt^2$

$\Rightarrow \frac{X}{Y} = \frac{a}{g} \Rightarrow Y = \frac{g}{a}x \Rightarrow$ straight line.

150. $V_{R/G(x)} = 0$, $V_{R/G(y)} = 10$ m/s

Let, velocity of man = v

$\tan\theta = \frac{16}{12} = \frac{4}{3}$

then, $v_{R/man} = v$ (opposite to man)

For the required condition :

$\tan\theta = \frac{V_{R/M(y)}}{V_{R/M(x)}} = \frac{10}{v} = \frac{4}{3}$

$\Rightarrow V = \frac{10\times 3}{4} = 7.5$ **Ans.**

151. From given data

$\vec{V}_M = 5\sqrt{2}\,\hat{i} + 5\sqrt{2}\,\hat{j}$

velocity of man

Velocity of wind

$\vec{V}_W = 5\sqrt{2}\,\hat{i}$

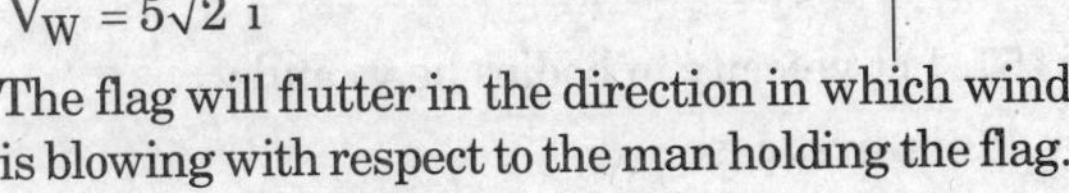

The flag will flutter in the direction in which wind is blowing with respect to the man holding the flag.

$\Rightarrow \vec{V}_{WM} = \vec{V}_W - \vec{V}_M$

$\vec{V}_{WM} = 5\sqrt{2}\,\hat{i} - (5\sqrt{2}\,\hat{i} + 5\sqrt{2}\,\hat{j})$

$\vec{V}_{WM} = -5\sqrt{2}\,\hat{j} = 5\sqrt{2}(-\hat{j})$

This implies direction of wind with respect to man in south.

152. Relative to lift initial velocity and acceleration of coin are 0 m/s and 1 m/s² downward

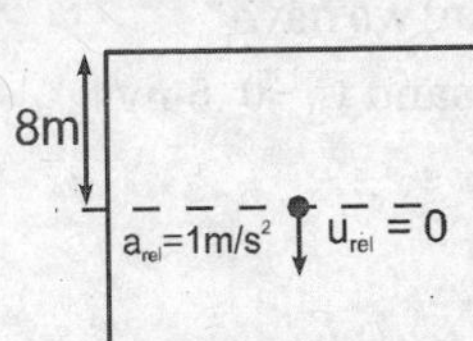

$\therefore\ 2 = \frac{1}{2}(1)\, t^2$ or t = 2 second

153. Relative velocity of stone = 5 m/s

Relative acceleration of stone = 10 + 5 = 15 m/s^2

$\therefore$ v = u + at = 5 + 15 × 2 = 35 m/s

$\therefore$ Relative velocity after t = 2 second is 35 m/s

154. $\vec{V}_{BG} = \vec{V}_{BR} + \vec{V}_{RG}$

$\therefore |\vec{V}_{BG}| = \sqrt{V_{BR}^2 + V_{RG}^2 + 2V_{BR}V_{RG}\cos\theta}$

$\because \theta$ is unknown $\therefore 6–4.8 \le |\vec{V}_{BG}| \le (6 + 4.8)$

$\Rightarrow 1.2 \le |\vec{V}_{BG}| \le 10.8$

155.

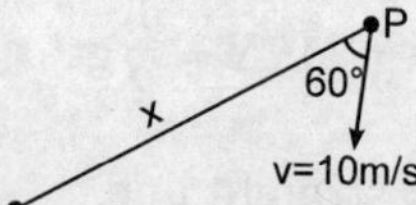

Velocity of approach of P and O is

$-\frac{dx}{dt} = v\cos 60° = 5$ m/s

It can be seen that velocity of approach is always constant.

$\therefore$ P reaches O after $= \frac{100}{5} = 20$ sec.

156. $\vec{V}_{O,M} = \vec{V}_O - \vec{V}_M$

$\vec{V}_{O,M} = \vec{V}_O - \vec{V}_{Train}$

$V_{O,M}$ = velocity of object with respect to man

V_O = velocity of object

V_M = velocity of man

Here velocity of object is zero.

So, $\vec{V}_{O,M} = -\vec{V}_M$

157. Let velocity of bodies be v_1 and v_2.

in first case

$u_1 = v_1 + v_2$ .... (i)

in second case

$u_2 = v_1 - v_2$ .... (i)

$\therefore v_1 = \frac{u_1 + u_2}{2}$ and $v_2 = \frac{u_1 + u_2}{2}$

Here $u_1 = \frac{16}{10}$ m/s and $u_2 = \frac{3}{5}$

After solving we have

v_1 = 1.1 m/sand v_2 =0 .5 m/s.

158. Velocity of approach = $\vec{V}_B - \vec{V}_A$.

159. Vertical Linear Motion

160. Relative to the person in the train, acceleration of the stone is 'g' downward, a (acceleration of train) backwards.

According to him : $x = \frac{1}{2}at^2$, $Y = \frac{1}{2}gt^2$

$\frac{X}{Y} = \frac{a}{g} \Rightarrow Y = \frac{g}{a}x \Rightarrow$ straight line.

161. W ← → E

$\vec{V}_A = -500\hat{i} \Rightarrow \vec{V}_{GA} + \vec{V}_A = V_{GAS}$

$\vec{V}_{GA} = 1500\hat{i} \Rightarrow 1500\hat{i} - 500\hat{i} = 1000\hat{i}$

162. $\vec{V}_{RG} = 3\hat{j} - 4\hat{i}$

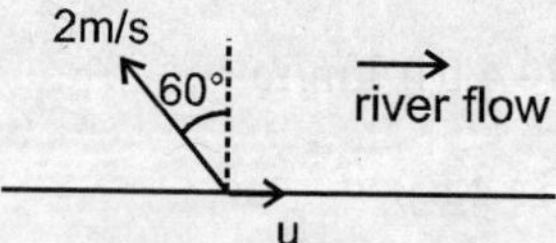

V_{RG} = 5 km/sec.

163. Then velocity of man w.r.t. ground $\vec{V}_M = 5\hat{i}$ m/s

velocity of rain w.r.t. ground $\vec{V}_R = -x\hat{j}$ m/s

$\vec{V}_{RM} = x\hat{j} - 5\hat{i}$,

$\tan 45° = \frac{x}{5}$

164.

2m/s 60° river flow u

Let speed of current be u.

For net velocity of man to be normal to river flow.

2 cos 60° = u

or u = 1 km/hr.

5

CHAPTER

Work, Energy and Power

WORK

In Physics, the term work is used in a specific sense which involves the displacement of a particle or a body under the action of force. It is measured by the product of force and displacement. It is scalar quantity with unit joule.

Work on an object is defined as the magnitude of the force multiplied by the distance moved by the object in the direction of the applied force.

Work done = force × distance = F × s

1 Joule = 1 Newton × 1 metre.

The unit of work is joule.

- Work done by a force acting obliquely is equal to W = F cos θ × s
- Work done on a body moving in circular path is zero.

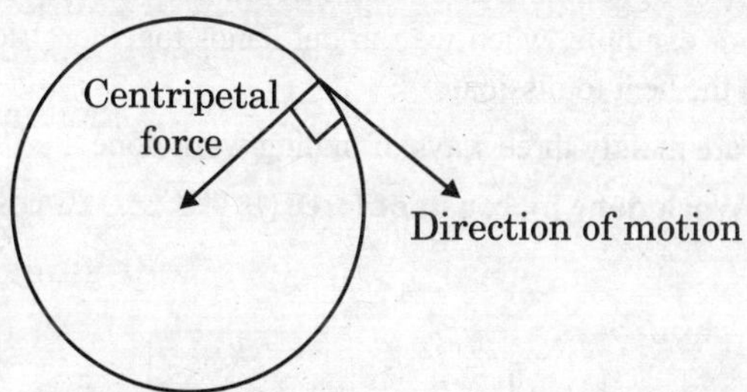

Units of Work:

The SI unit of work is the joule (J), which is defined as the work done by a force of one newton (N) causing a displacement of one meter (m).

Other units of work include:

- **Newton-meter (N·m) :** This unit is sometimes used as the measuring unit for work, but it can be confused with the measurement unit of torque.
- **Kilowatt-hour :** This unit is used to measure electrical energy and is equal to 3600 J.
- **Horsepower-hour :** This unit is used to measure the work done by a motor and is equal to 746 J.

  Which unit of work is used depends on the context. For example, joules are typically used in physics and engineering, while horsepower-hours are typically used in mechanics and thermodynamics.

Dimensions of Work:

The dimensions of work are $[M^1 L^2 T^{-2}]$, where:

- M is mass
- L is length
- T is time

This can be derived from the following equation:

Work = Force * Displacement

Force has the dimensions $[M^1 L^1 T^{-2}]$ and displacement has the dimensions $[L^1]$, so work must have the dimensions $[M^1 L^1 T^{-2}] * [L^1] = [M^1 L^2 T^{-2}]$.

The SI unit of work is the joule (J).

Work done in pulling and pulling and pushing an object:

The work done in pulling and pushing an object is the same, as long as the force applied and the distance moved are the same. However, there may be some differences in how much effort is required to pull versus push an object, depending on the object's weight, the surface it is moving on, and the angle at which it is being moved.

For example, it is generally easier to pull a heavy object on a smooth surface than it is to push it on a rough surface. This is because the frictional force between the object and the surface is lower when the object is being pulled.

It is also easier to push an object at a slight angle upwards than it is to pull it at the same angle. This is because the component of the force that is parallel to the ground is greater when the object is being pushed.

In general, the amount of work done in pulling and pushing an object can be calculated using the following equation:

Work = Force * Displacement

where:

- Force is the force applied to the object
- Displacement is the distance moved by the object

For example, if you pull a 100 kg object 10 meters, you will do 1000 joules of work. The same amount of work would be done if you pushed the object 10 meters.

However, if you were to push the object up a ramp at a 30 degree angle, you would do more work than if you pulled it on a level surface. This is because the displacement of the object is greater when it is being pushed up the ramp.

Work done by external force when spring is elongated from x_1 to x_2 :

The work done by an external force when a spring is elongated from x_1 to x_2 is given by the following equation:

$$W = \int x_2 x_1\ F(x)\ dx$$

where :

- W is the work done by the external force (in joules)
- F(x) is the force exerted by the spring on the external force (in newtons)
- x_1 and x_2 are the initial and final elongations of the spring (in meters)

The force exerted by the spring on the external force is given by Hooke's law :

$$F(x) = -kx$$

where :

- k is the spring constant (in newtons per meter)

Therefore, the work done by the external force can be written as follows:

$$W = \int x_2 x_1\ (-kx)\ dx$$

$$W = k\ (x_2^2 - x_1^2)/\ 2$$

This equation shows that the work done by the external force is proportional to the square of the change in elongation of the spring.

For example, if a spring with a spring constant of 100 N/m is elongated from 10 cm to 20 cm, the work done by the external force would be 500 J.

$$W = k\ (x_2^2 - x_1^2)\ /\ 2$$

$$= (100\ N/m) * ((0.2\ m)^2 - (0.1\ m)^2)\ /\ 2 = 500\ J.$$

Conservative & non conservative force :

Conservative forces are forces for which the work done is independent of the path taken. This means that the work done by a conservative force to move an object from one point to another is the same, regardless of the route taken.

Non-conservative forces are forces for which the work done depends on the path taken. This means that the work done by a non-conservative force to move an object from one point to another can vary depending on the route taken.

Examples of conservative forces include:

- Gravitational force
- Spring force
- Electric force
- Magnetic force

Examples of non-conservative forces include:

- Friction
- Air resistance
- Tension

Conservative forces can be associated with a potential energy function. The potential energy function is a function of the position of the object and gives the amount of work that a conservative force can do to move the object from one point to another.

The work done by a conservative force can be calculated by taking the negative of the change in potential energy of the object.

$$W = -\Delta U$$

Where;

- W is the work done by the conservative force
- ΔU is the change in potential energy of the object

Non-conservative forces do not have a potential energy associated with them. This is because the work done by a non-conservative force cannot be completely recovered as potential energy.

The work done by a non-conservative force is dissipated as heat, sound, or other forms of energy.

Conservative forces are important in physics because they allow us to conserve energy. For example, if we lift an object up in the air, we are doing work against the gravitational force. The work that we do is stored as potential energy in the object. When we let the object go, the potential energy is converted back into kinetic energy and the object falls back to the ground.

Non-conservative forces can also be useful. For example, friction allows us to walk and drive. Air resistance allows us to fly. However, non-conservative forces can also lead to energy loss. For example, when we rub our hands together, friction causes the heat to dissipate.

There are mainly three ways of finding work done.

1. **Work done by constant force** ($W = \vec{F}.\vec{s} = Fs\cos\theta$)

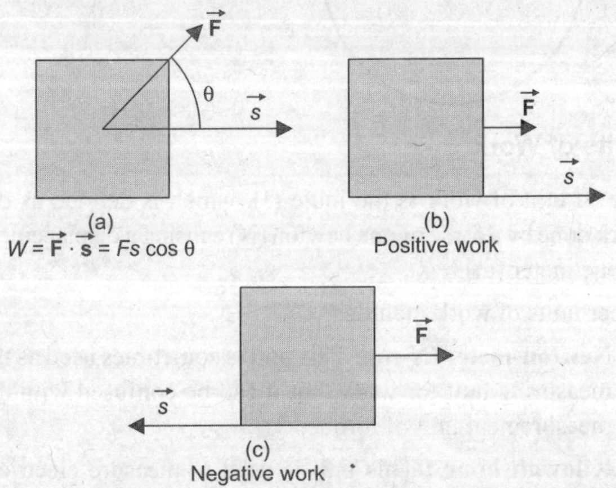

(a) $W = \vec{F}\cdot\vec{s} = Fs\cos\theta$ (b) Positive work (c) Negative work

- Work can be positive or negative or zero as θ is acute (< 90º) or obtuse (> 90º) or right (θ = 90°): positive work means that force (or its component) is parallel to displacement while negative work means that force (or its component) is opposite to displacement. Zero work done signify that force and displacement are perpendicular to each other.

- Work depends on frame of reference. With change of frame of reference inertial force does not change while displacement may change. So, the work done by a force will be different in different frames. For example, if a person is pushing a box inside a moving train, then work done as seen from the frame of reference of train is $\vec{F}.\vec{S}$ while as seen from the ground it is $\vec{F}.(\vec{S}+\vec{S}_0)$. Here $\vec{S}_0$ is the displacement of train relative to ground.

2. **Work done by variable force** When the force is variable, work obtained by integrating $\vec{F}.\vec{dx}$. Thus $W=\int \vec{F}.\vec{dx}$.

   If the work done by a force field along a closed path is zero, then force is said to be conservative otherwise it is called non-conservative. Under such forces, the work done depends only upon the initial and final positions and is path independent.

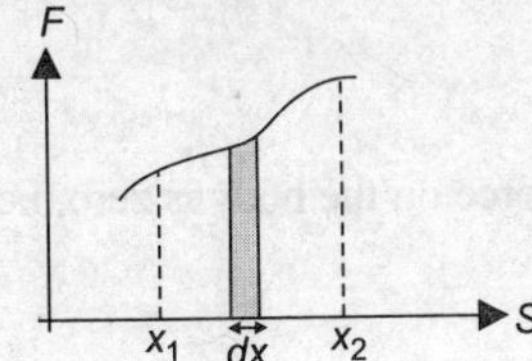

If number of forces act on a body or particle then, work is calculated by using

$$W=W_1+W_2+W_3+\ldots\ldots$$

or $\quad W=\int \vec{F_1}\cdot d\vec{s}+\int \vec{F_2}+\ldots d\vec{s}$

or $\quad W=\int(\vec{F_1}+\vec{F_2}+\ldots)\cdot d\vec{s}$

or $\quad W=\int \vec{F_R}\cdot d\vec{s} \qquad$ [as $\vec{F}_R=\Sigma\vec{F}$]

3. **Work done by F-S graph:** This is applicable in one dimensional motion. When force and displacement are parallel or anti-parallel to each other, then work done is obtained by area under F - S graph W = Area under F - S graph.

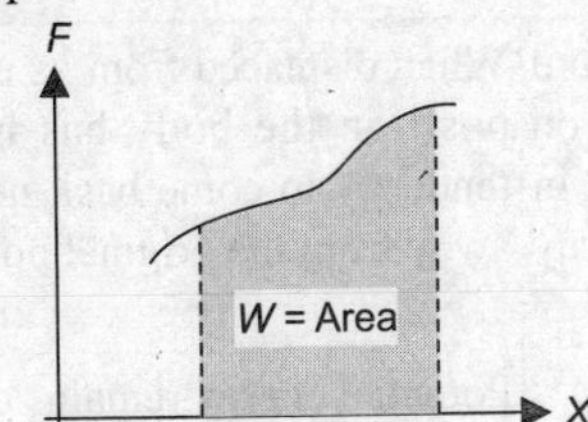

ENERGY

Energy is that physical quantity which enables a system to do work. In this section, we restrict ourselves to mechanical energy which consists of two forms:

(i) Kinetic energy

(ii) Potential energy

Kinetic Energy

The kinetic energy of a body is the energy possessed by the body by virtue of its motion. Mathematically, it is equal to $\frac{1}{2}mv^2$ where m is the mass of the body and v is the speed of the body.

$$K.E=\frac{1}{2}mv^2=\frac{p^2}{2m}$$

Hence, a body cannot have kinetic energy without having momentum and vice-versa.

Work-Energy Theorem

The increase in kinetic energy of a body is equal to the sum of the work done by all the forces acting on the body. In another words, we can say work done is always equal to change in kinetic energy

$$W=\frac{1}{2}mv^2-\frac{1}{2}mu^2=K_F-K_i=\Delta KE$$

Points to Remember:

- If work is positive, $K_f>K_i$, so, the kinetic energy will increase while if work is negative, $K_f<K_i$, so, the kinetic energy will decrease.
- This theorem is also valid for a system in presence of all types of forces (external or internal, conservative or nonconservative).

Potential Energy

The energy stored in a body or system by virtue of its configuration or its position in a field is called potential energy.

In case of conservative force as:

$F=-(dU/dr)$ i.e., $dU=-F\,dr$

So, $\int_{U_1}^{U_2} dU=-\int_{r_1}^{r_2}\mathbf{F}\cdot\vec{d\mathbf{r}}$

i.e., $U_2-U_1=-\int_{r_1}^{r_2}\mathbf{F}\cdot\vec{d\mathbf{r}}(=-W)$ ...(1)

Whenever and wherever possible, we generally take the reference point at ∞ and assume potential energy to be zero there, i.e., if we take $r_1=\infty$ and $U_1=0$

$U=-\int_{\infty}^{r}\vec{\mathbf{F}}\cdot\vec{dr}=-W$ ...(2)

Potential energy can be defined only for conservative forces. It does not exists for non-conservative forces. Potential energy can be positive or negative.

Law of Conservation of Mechanical Energy

The sum of potential energy and the kinetic energy is called mechanical energy:

From work-energy theorem

$$K_f-K_i=W$$

From definition of potential energy in a conservative field

$$U_f-U_i=-\int\vec{F}\,\vec{dr}=-W$$

$$\Rightarrow U_f-U_i=-(K_f-K_i)\Rightarrow U_f+K_f=U_i+K_i$$

$$\Rightarrow K+U=\text{constant}$$

Hence, total mechanical energy of a system always remains constant, if only conservative forces are acting on the system.

Energy of Spring

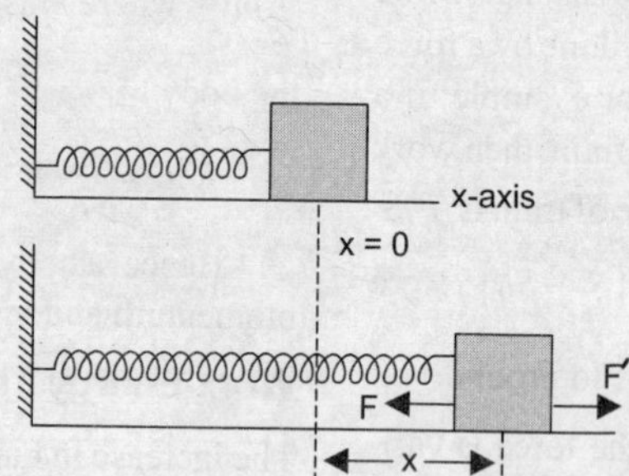

It is evident that the work done in compressing the spring by an amount x is given by $W = \frac{1}{2}kx^2$. The work done in stretching or compressing a spring is stored in it in the form of potential energy which is due to the changed configuration of the coils of the spring. Hence the potential energy of a massless elastic spring of force constant k when it is stretched or compressed by an amount x is given by

$$U = W = \frac{1}{2}kx^2$$

Equilibrium

When several forces act on a body simultaneously in such a way that the resultant force on the body is zero, i.e.,

$\vec{\mathbf{F}} = 0$ with $\vec{\mathbf{F}} = \sum \vec{\mathbf{F}}_i$

then the body is said to be in equilibrium. So for equilibrium $\vec{\mathbf{F}}_{\text{net}} = 0$.

If the forces are conservative $F = -\frac{dU}{dr}$.

For equilibrium $F = 0$, $\frac{-dU}{dr} = 0$, $\frac{dU}{dr} = 0$

Types of equilibrium are given in tabular form as given below.

Table 1: Types of Equilibrium

S.No.	Stable Equilibrium	Unstable Equilibrium	Neutral Equilibrium
1.	Net force is zero.	Net force is zero.	Net force is zero.
2.	$\frac{dU}{dr} = 0$ or slope of U-r graph is zero.	$\frac{dU}{dr} = 0$ or slope of U-r graph is zero.	$\frac{dU}{dr} = 0$ or slope of U-r graph is zero.
3.	When displaced from its equilibrium position a net restoring force starts acting on the body which has a tendency to bring the body back to its equilibrium position.	When displaced from its equilibrium position, a net force starts acting on the body which moves the body in the direction of displacement or away from the equilibrium position.	When displaced from its equilibrium position the body has neither the tendency to come back nor to move away from the original position.
4.	Potential energy in equilibrium position is minimum as compared to its neighbouring points. Or $\frac{d^2U}{dr^2}$ = positive	Potential energy in equilibrium position is maximum as compared to its neighbouring points. Or $\frac{d^2U}{dr^2}$ = negative	Potential energy remains constant even if the body is displaced from its equilibrium position. Or $\frac{d^2U}{dr^2} = 0$
5.	When displaced from equilibrium position the centre of gravity of the body goes up.	When displaced from equilibrium position the centre of gravity of the body comes down.	When displaced from equilibrium position the centre of gravity of the body remains at the same level.

POWER

Rate of doing work is called power. By definition, work done by a force does not depend on the time taken for a given displacement, i.e., work is independent of time. The time rate of doing work is defined as power and is given by

$$(\text{Power})_{\text{inst.}} = P = \frac{dW}{dt}$$

and $(\text{Power})_{\text{av.}} = \dfrac{W}{t}$

$$\text{Power } P = \frac{dW}{dt} = \frac{\vec{F}\cdot d\vec{s}}{dt} \quad [\text{as } dW = \vec{F}\cdot d\vec{s}]$$

i.e., $P = \vec{F}\cdot\vec{v}$ [as $d\vec{s}/dt = \vec{v}$]

i.e., power is equal to the scalar product of force and velocity.

Power is a scalar quantity with dimensions $[ML^2T^{-3}]$. The SI unit of power is J/s and is called watt (W). Practical unit of power is horse power with

1 hp = 746 watt = 550 ft-lb/s

Note: If force is variable, we calculate the average power as $P_{av} = \dfrac{\int_o^t P dt}{\int_o^t dt}$

COLLISION

Collision is an isolated event in which a strong force acts between two or more bodies for a short time. The collision is infact a redistribution of total momentum of the particles.

Types of Collision

(a) **Elastic Collision**: Collision is elastic i.e., = 1, where *e* = coefficient of restitution.

For elastic collision:

(i) Impulse of deformation = Impulse of reformation

(ii) Velocity of separation = Velocity of approach

(iii) KE before collision = KE after collision

(iv) Momentum before collision = Momentum after collision.

$\Rightarrow \quad m_1u_1 + m_2u_2 = m_1v_1 + m_2v_2$

Total energy before collision = Total energy after collision.

(v) $\frac{1}{2}m_1u_1^2 + \frac{1}{2}m_2u_2^2 = \frac{1}{2}m_1v_1^2 + \frac{1}{2}m_2v_2^2$

(vi) $v_1 = \dfrac{(m_1 - m_2)u_1}{m_1 + m_2} + \dfrac{2m_2u_2}{m_1 + m_2}$

(vii) $v_2 = \dfrac{2m_1u_1}{m_1 + m_2} + \dfrac{(m_2 - m_1)u_2}{m_1 + m_2}$

(b) **Inelastic Collision:** For $0 < e < 1$, collision is inelastic where e = coefficient of restitution

(i) Impluse of reformation < Impluse of deformation

(ii) Velocity of separation < Velocity of approach

(iii) KE is not conserved.

(iv) TE conserved. Momentum remains conserved.

(v) For e = 0, completely inelastic collision.

(vi) Impulse of reformation = 0

(vii) Velocity of separation = 0

(viii) KE in not conserved in inelastic collision

(ix) $v_1 = \left(\dfrac{m_1 - em_2}{m_1 + m_2}\right)u_1 + \left(\dfrac{(1+e)m_2}{m_1 + m_2}\right)u_2$

(x) $v_2 = \left(\dfrac{(1+e)m_1}{m_1 + m_2}\right)u_1 + \left(\dfrac{m_2 - em_1}{m_1 + m_2}\right)u_2$

(xi) In perfectly elastic collision both colliding bodies stick together and move with a common velocity

$$v = \frac{m_1u_1 + m_2u_2}{m_1 + m_2}$$

(c) **Head on collision or oblique collision**: Consider oblique collision of two particles as shown below here we have

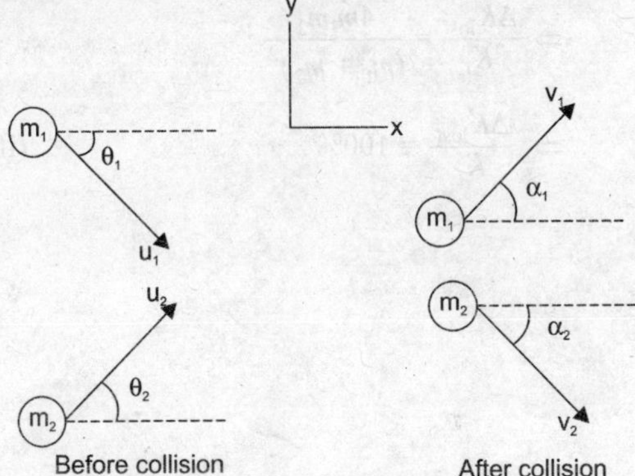

Before collision After collision

(i) Momentum conservation along c-axis :

$$m_1u_1\cos\theta + m_2u_2\cos\theta_1 + m_2u_2\cos\theta_2 = m_1v_1\cos\alpha_1 + m_2v_2\cos\alpha_2$$

(ii) Momentum conservation of y-axis :

$$-m_1u_1\sin\theta_1 + m_2u_2\sin\theta_2 = m_1v_1\sin\alpha_1 - m_2v_2\sin\alpha_2$$

(iii) Velocity of approach = $u_1\cos\theta_1 - u_2\cos\theta_2$

(iv) Velocity of separation = $v_2\cos\alpha_2 - v_1\cos\alpha_1$

$$\therefore \quad e = \frac{v_2\cos\alpha_2 - v_1\cos\alpha_1}{u_1\cos\theta_1 - u_2\cos\theta_2}$$

Consider the oblique collision as shown below. Here we have:

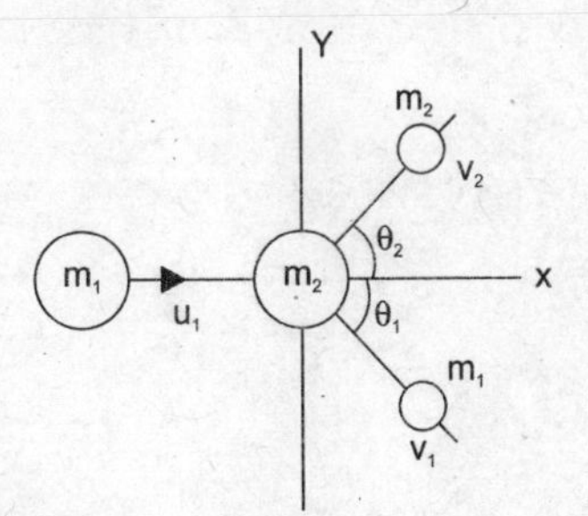

(i) $m_1u_1 = m_1v_1 \cos\theta_1 + m_2v_2 \cos\theta_2$ (along x-axis)

(ii) $m_1v_1 \sin\theta_1 - m_2v_2 \sin\theta_2 = 0$ (along Y-axis)

(iii) Momentum of the system is conserved along x-axis

(iv) Relative speed of separation = e (relative speed of approch)

Coefficient of restitution, $e = \dfrac{|v_2 - v_1|}{|u_1 - u_2|}$

$e = 1$ for elastic collision

$e = 0$ for completely inelastic collision.

$0 \leq e \leq 1$ for inelastic collision.

Energy Loss in Collision

(i) Elastic collision, for first (incident) particle

$$\frac{K_f}{K_i} = \left(\frac{m_1 - m_2}{m_1 + m_2}\right)^2$$

$$\Rightarrow \frac{\Delta K_{lost}}{K_i} = \frac{4m_1m_2}{(m_1 + m_2)^2}$$

$$\Rightarrow \frac{\Delta K_{lost}}{K_i} = 100\% \qquad (\text{if } m_1 = m_2)$$

(ii) Inelastic collision, loss in KE

$\Delta K_{lost} = K_i - K_f$

$$\frac{1}{2}\frac{m_1m_2}{m_1 + m_2}(u_1 - u_2)^2(1 - e^2)$$

On putting $e = 0$

$$\Delta K_{lost} = \frac{m_1m_2(u_1 - u_2)^2}{2(m_1 + m_2)}$$

Rebounding of a ball on Collision with Floor

(i) Speed of ball after nth rebound.

$v_n = e^n vo = e^n \sqrt{2gh}$

(ii) Height covered by the ball after nth rebound

$h_n = e^{2n}. h_o$

(iii) Total distance covered by the ball before comes to rest

$$h_0 = \left(\frac{1 + e^2}{1 - e^2}\right)$$

Objective Type Questions

1. A ball falling freely from height of 4.9 m hits a floor. If e = 3/4 then the ball will hit the surface second time after.
(a) 2.5 sec (b) 1.5 sec
(c) 3.5 sec (d) 3.6 sec

2. A body of mass m is moving towards east and another body of equal mass is moving towards north. If after collision both stick together, their speed after collision would be
(a) v (b) $v/2$
(c) $\sqrt{2}v$ (d) $v/\sqrt{2}$

3. A body of mass M moves with velocity v and collides elastically with another body of mass m ($M >> m$) at rest, then the velocity of body of mass m is
(a) v (b) $2v$
(c) $v/2$ (d) zero

4. An electron with kinetic 5 eV is incident on a H-atom in its ground state. The collision
(a) must be elastic
(b) may be partially elastic
(c) may be completely elastic
(d) may be completely inelastic

5. A bomb of mass 30 kg at rest explodes into two pieces of masses 18 kg and 12 kg. The velocity of 18 kg mass is 6 ms^{-1}. The kinetic energy of the other mass is
(a) 256 J (b) 486 J
(c) 524 J (d) 324 J

6. A ball is dropped from a height h. If the coefficient of restitution is e then to what height will it rise after jumping twice from the ground?
(a) $\frac{eh}{2}$ (b) $2eh$
(c) eh (d) e^4h

7. A particle of mass m moving with velocity v collides with a stationary particle of mass $2m$. The speed of the system, will be
(a) $3v$ (b) $v/2$
(c) $v/3$ (d) $2v$

8. A neutron makes a head-on elastic collision with a stationary deuteron. The fractional energy loss of the neutron in the collision is
(a) 16/81 (b) 8/9
(c) 8/27 (d) 2/3

9. A spring of force-constant k is cut into two pieces such that one piece is double the length of the other. Then the long piece will have a force-constant of:
(a) $\left(\frac{2}{3}\right)k$ (b) $\left(\frac{3}{2}\right)k$
(c) $3k$ (d) $6k$

10. A particle of mass m is moving in a circular path of constant radius r such that its centripetal acceleration a_c is varying with time t as $a_c = k^2rt^2$ where k is a constant. The power delivered to the particle by the force acting on it is:
(a) $2\pi mk^2r^2t$ (b) mk^2r^2t
(c) $\frac{(mk^4r^2t^5)}{3}$ (d) zero

11. A force $F = -K(y\hat{i} + x\hat{j})$ (where K is a positive constant) acts on a particle moving in the xy-plane. Starting from the origin, the particle is taken along the positive x-axis to the point $(a, 0)$ and then parallel to the y-axis to the point (a, a). The total work done by the force F on the particle is:
(a) $-2Ka^2$ (b) $2Ka^2$
(c) $-Ka^2$ (d) Ka^2

12. A wind powered generator converts wind energy into electrical energy. Assume that the generator converts a fixed fraction of the wind energy intercepted by its blades into electrical energy. For wind speed v, the electrical power output will be proportional to:
(a) v (b) v^2
(c) v^3 (d) v^4

13. At time $t = 0$ s, a particle starts moving along the x-axis. If its kinetic energy increases uniformly with time t, the net force acting on it must be proportional to:
(a) t (b) $1/\sqrt{t}$
(c) $\sqrt{t}$ (d) Constant

14. The potential energy function for a particle executing linear SHM is given by $V(x) = \frac{1}{2}kx^2$

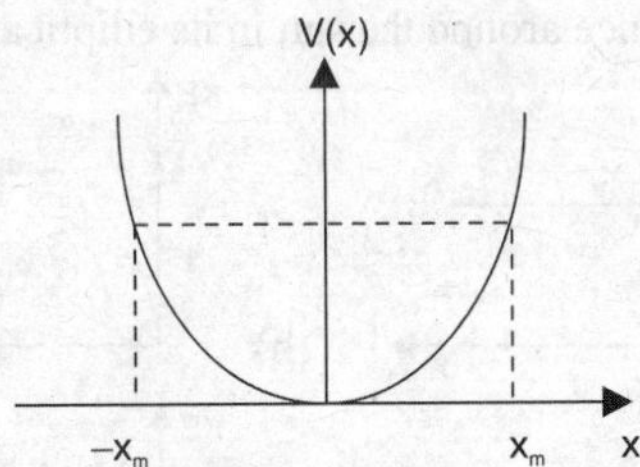

where k is the force constant of the oscillator. For $k = 0.5$ Nm^{-1}, the graph of $V(x)$ versus x is shown in the figure.

A particle of total energy E turns back when it reaches $x = \pm x_m$. If V and K indicate the potential energy and kinetic energy, respectively of the particle at $x = \pm x_m$, then which of the following is correct?

(a) $V = 0, K = E$ (b) $V = E, K = 0$

(c) $V < E, K = 0$ (d) $V = 0, K < E$

15. A body of mass m is accelerated uniformly from rest to a speed v in a time T. The instantaneous power delivered to the body as a function of time, is given by:

(a) $\frac{mv^2}{T^2}t$ (b) $\frac{mv^2}{T^2}t^2$

(c) $\frac{1}{2}\frac{mv^2}{T^2}t$ (d) $\frac{1}{2}\frac{mv^2}{T^2}t^2$

16. The potential energy of a 1 kg particle free to move along the x-axis is given by $V(x) = \left(\frac{x^4}{4} - \frac{x^2}{2}\right)$ J. The total mechanical energy of the particle is 2 J. Then, the maximum speed (in m/s) is:

(a) $\frac{3}{\sqrt{2}}$ (b) $\sqrt{2}$

(c) $\frac{1}{\sqrt{2}}$ (d) 2

17. Which of the diagrams shown in figure represents variation of total mechanical energy of a pendulum oscillating in air as function of time?

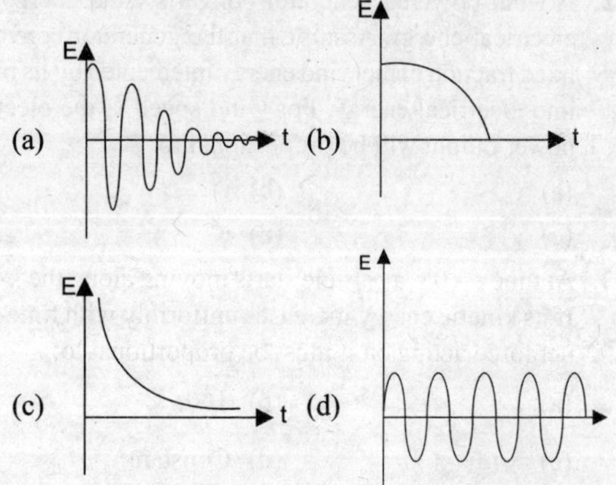

18. Which of the diagrams shown in figure most closely shows the variation in kinetic energy of the earth as it moves once around the sun in its elliptical orbit?

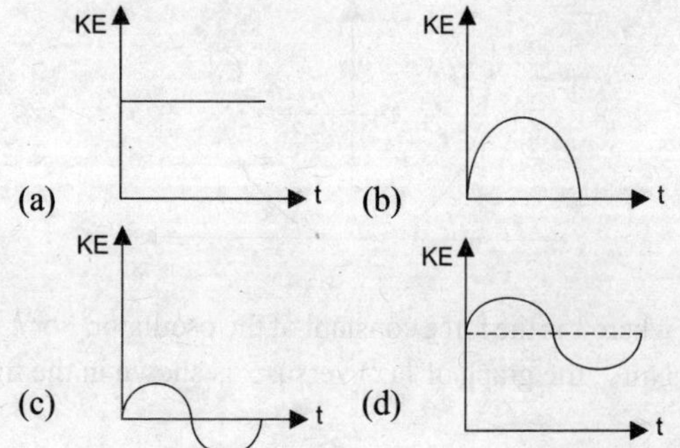

19. A body is moving unidirectionally under the influence of a source of constant power supplying energy. Which of the diagrams shown in figure correctly shows the displacement time curve for its motion?

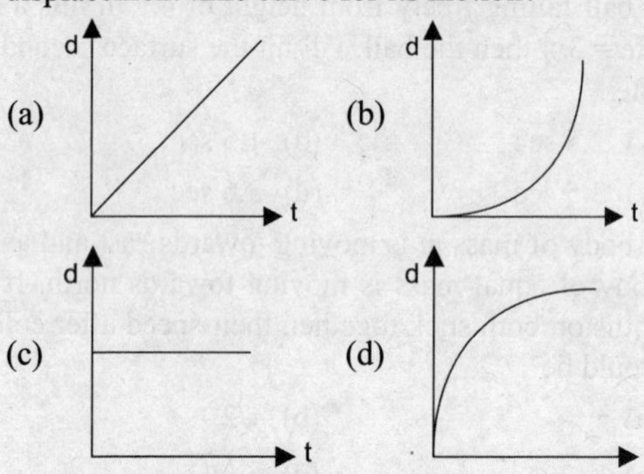

20. A raindrop falling from a height h above ground, attains a near terminal velocity when it has fallen through a height $\left(\frac{3}{4}\right)h$. Which of the diagrams shown in figure correctly shows the change in kinetic and potential energy of the drop during its fall up to the ground?

(a) (b) (c) (d)

21. A uniform chain of length L and mass M is lying on a smooth table and one-third of its length is hanging vertically down over the edge of the table. If g is acceleration due to gravity, the work required to pull the hanging part on to the table is

(a) MgL

(b) $MgL/3$

(c) $MgL/9$

(d) $MgL/18$

22. A force $\mathbf{F} = -k(y\hat{\mathbf{i}} + x\hat{\mathbf{j}})$ (where k is a positive constant) acts on a particle moving in the x - y plane. Starting from the origin, the particle is taken along the positive x-axis to the point $(a, 0)$ and then parallel to the Y-axis to the point (a, a). The total work done by the force F on the particle is

(a) $-2ka^2$ (b) $2ka^2$

(c) $-ka^2$ (d) ka^2

23. A mass of M kg is suspended by a weightless string. The horizontal force that is required to displace it until the string makes an angle of 45° with the initial vertical direction is:

(a) $Mg\left(\sqrt{2}+1\right)$ (b) $Mg\sqrt{2}$

(c) $\frac{Mg}{\sqrt{2}}$ (d) $Mg\left(\sqrt{2}-1\right)$

24. A particle, which is constrained to move along the x-axis, is subjected to a force in the same direction which varies with the distance x of the particle from the origin as $F(x) = -kx + ax^3$. Here k and a are positive constants. For $x \geq 0$, the functional graphically form of the potential energy $U(x)$ of the particle is:

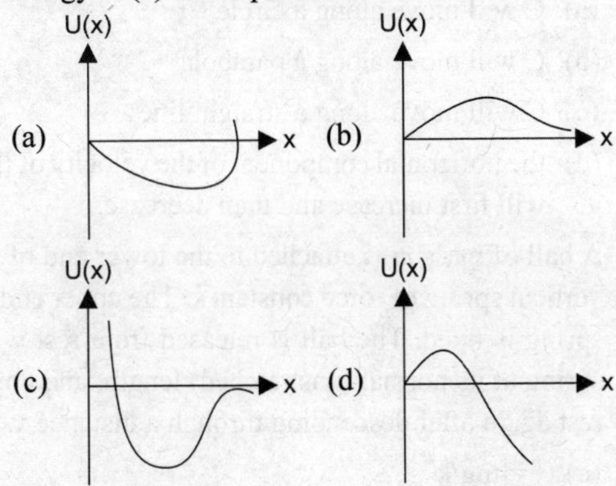

25. A smooth sphere of radius R is made to translate in a straight line with a constant acceleration $a = g$. A particle kept on the top of the sphere is released from there at zero velocity with respect to the sphere. The speed of the particle with respect to sphere as a function of θ as it slides down is

(a) $\sqrt{Rg(\sin\theta + \cos\theta)}$ (b) $\sqrt{Rg(1 + \cos\theta - \sin\theta)}$

(c) $\sqrt{4Rg\sin\theta}$ (d) $\sqrt{2Rg(1 + \sin\theta - \cos\theta)}$

26. A force $F = -k(y\hat{i} + x\hat{j})$, where k is a positive constant, acts on a particle moving in the xy plane. Starting from the origin, the particle is taken along the positive x-axis to the point $(a, 0)$, and the parallel to the y-axis to the point (a, a). The total work done by the force on the particle is

(a) $-2ka^2$ (b) $2ka^2$

(c) $-ka^2$ (d) ka^2

27. A stone tied to a string of length L is whirled in a vertical circle with the other end of the string at the centre. At a certain instant of time, the stone is at its lowest position, and has a speed u. The magnitude of the change in its velocity as it reaches a position where the string is horizontal is:

(a) $\sqrt{u^2 - 2gL}$ (b) $\sqrt{2gL}$

(c) $\sqrt{u^2 - 2gL}$ (d) $\sqrt{2\left(u^2 - gL\right)}$

28. A particle of mass m is moving in a circular path of constant radius r such that its centripetal acceleration a_c is varying with time as $a_c = k^2rt^2$, where k is a constant. The power delivered to the particle by the forces acting on it is

(a) $2\pi\, mk^2r^2t$ (b) mk^2r^2t

(c) $\frac{1}{3}mk^4r^2t^5$ (d) 0

29. A particle, which is constrained to move along the x-axis, is subjected to a force in the same direction which varies with the distance x of the particle from the origin as $F(x) = -kx + ax^3$. Here k and a are positive constants. For $x \geq 0$, the functional form of the potential energy $U(x)$ of particle is

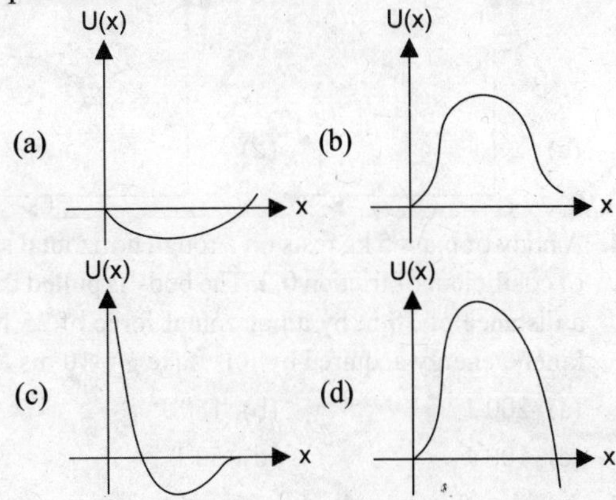

30. A wind – powered generator converts wind energy into electric energy. Assume that the generator converts a fixed fraction of the wind energy intercepted by its blades into electric energy. For wind speed V, the electrical power output will be proportional to

(a) V (b) V^2

(c) V^3 (d) V^4

31. A body is moved along a straight line by a machine delivering constant power. The distance moved by the body in time t is proportional to

(a) $t^{1/2}$ (b) $t^{3/4}$

(c) $t^{3/2}$ (d) t^2

32. A particle is acted by a force $F = kx$, where k is a positive constant. Its potential energy at $x = 0$ is zero. Which curve correctly represents the variation of potential energy of the block with respect to x?

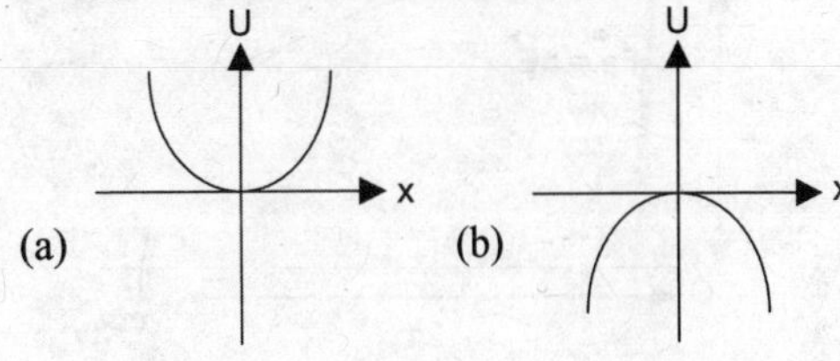

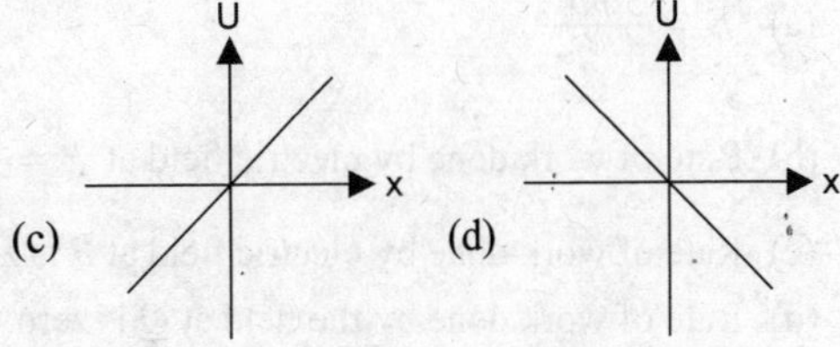

33. A ball is thrown up with a certain velocity at angle θ to the horizontal. The kinetic energy KE of the ball varies with horizontal displacement x as:

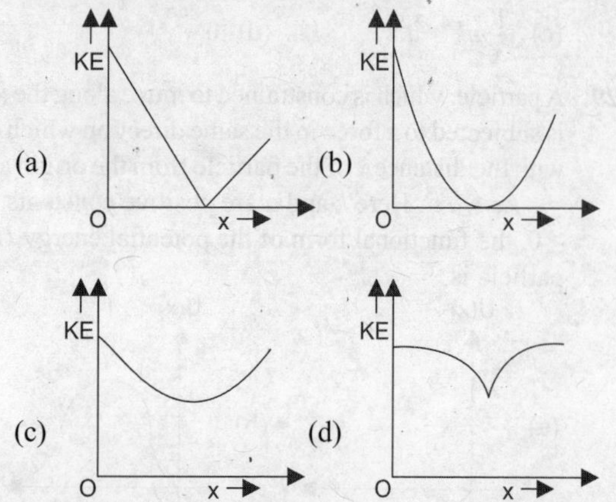

34. A body of mass 5 kg rests on a rough horizontal surface of coefficient of friction 0.2. The body is pulled through a distance of 10 m by a horizontal force of 25 N. The kinetic energy acquired by it is (take $g = 10\ ms^{-2}$)

(a) 200 J (b) 150 J

(c) 100 J (d) 50 J

35. A body of mass m, having momentum p, is moving on a rough horizontal surface. If it is stopped in a distance x, the coefficient of friction between the body and the surface is given by

(a) $\mu = \frac{p^2}{2gm^2x}$ (b) $\mu = \frac{p^2}{2gmx}$

(c) $\mu = \frac{p}{2gmx}$ (d) $\mu = \frac{p}{2gm^2x}$

36. A particle of charge +q and mass m, moving under the influence of uniform electric field $E\hat{i}$ and a uniform magnetic field $B\hat{k}$ follows a trajectory from P to Q as shown in figure. The velocity at P and Q are $\mathbf{V}\hat{i}$ and $-2\mathbf{v}\hat{j}$. Choose the correct statement.

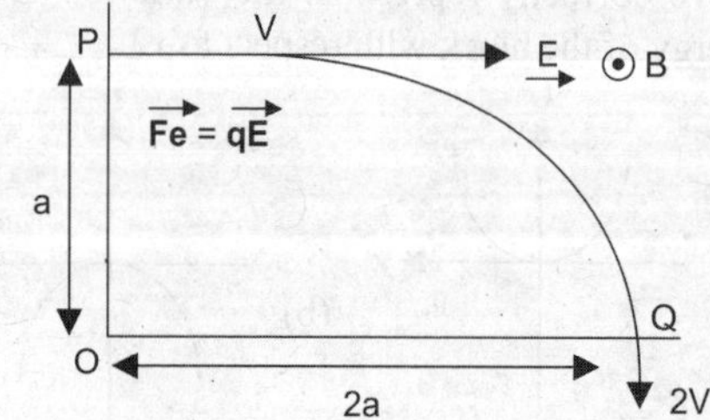

(a) $E = \frac{3}{4}\frac{mv^2}{qa}$

(b) Rate of work done by electric field at $P = \frac{3}{4}\frac{mv^3}{a}$

(c) Rate of work done by electric field at P is zero.

(d) Rate of work done by the field at Q is zero.

37. A small ball is connected to a block by light string of length l. Both are initially on the ground. There is sufficient friction on the ground to prevent the block from slipping. The ball is projected vertically up

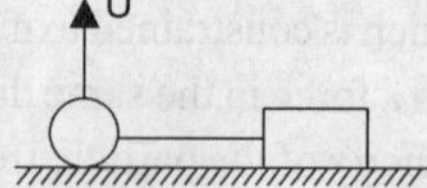

with a velocity u, where $2gl < u^2 < 3gl$. The centre of mass of the 'block + ball' system is C

(a) C will move along a circle

(b) C will move along a parabola

(c) C will move along a straight line

(d) the horizontal component of the velocity of the ball will first increase and then decrease.

38. A ball of mass m is attached to the lower end of a light vertical spring of force constant k. The upper end of the spring is fixed. The ball is released from rest with the spring at its normal (unstretched) length, and comes to rest again after descending through a distance x.

(a) $x = mg/k$

(b) $x = 2mg/k$

(c) The ball will have no acceleration at the position where it has descended through $x/2$

(d) The ball will have an upward acceleration equal to g at its lowermost position.

39. A long block A is at rest on a smooth horizontal surface. A small block B, whose mass is half of A, is placed on A at one end and projected along A with some velocity u. The coefficient of friction between the blocks is μ.

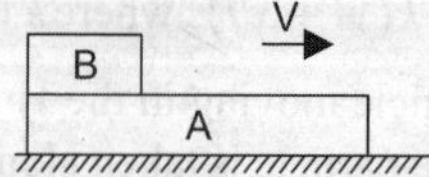

(a) the blocks will reach a final common velocity $\frac{u}{3}$

(b) the work done against friction is two-third of the initial kinetic energy of B.

(c) before the blocks reach a common velocity, the acceleration of A relative to B is $\frac{2}{3}\mu g$

(d) before the blocks reach a common velocity the acceleration of A relative to B is $\frac{3}{2}\mu g$

40. A particle is acted upon by a constant force which is always perpendicular to the velocity of the particle. The motion of the particle takes in a plane it follows that

(a) its velocity is constant

(b) its acceleration is constant

(c) its K.E is constant

(d) its moves in a circular path

41. A pendulum is released from point A as shown in figure. At some instant net force on the bob is making an angle θ with the string:

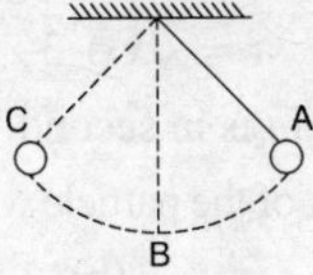

(a) for $\theta = 90^\circ$ particle is at A
(b) for $\theta = 0^\circ$ particle is at B
(c) for $\theta = 90^\circ$ particle at the position where string is horizontal
(d) For $\theta = 0^\circ$ particle is at A

42. A body of mass 1 kg is suspended from an inextensible string of length 1 m. When the string makes an angle 60° with vertical, speed of the bob is 4 m/s.
(a) net acceleration of the bob at the instant is 10 m/s^2.
(b) net acceleration of the bob at the instant is 18.2 m/s^2.
(c) the bob will rise to a maximum height with respect to bottom most point > 1.3 m
(d) the bob will rise to a maximum height with respect to bottom most point < 1.3m

43. A body is moved along a straight line by a machine delivering a power proportional to time t, then
(a) velocity is proportional to t
(b) displacement is proportional to t^3
(c) work done is proportional to t^2
(d) velocity is proportional to t^2

44. In the figure shown upper block is given a velocity of 6 m/s and lower block 3 m/s. When relative motion between them is stopped.

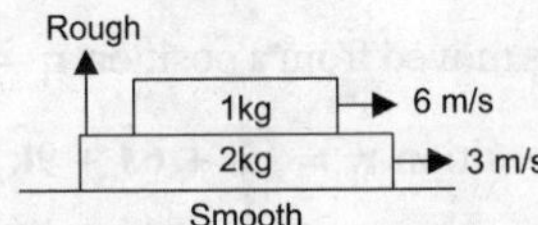

(a) work done by friction on upper block is negative
(b) work done by friction on both blocks is positive
(c) work done by friction on upper block is – 10 J
(d) net work done by friction is zero.

45. $U(r) = \frac{A}{r^2} - \frac{B}{r}$ where r is the distance from the centre of the force and A and B are positive constants then
(a) the equilibrium distance is given by $\frac{2A}{B}$
(b) the work required to move the particle from equilibrium distance to infinity is $\frac{B^2}{4A}$
(c) the work required to move the particle from equilibrium position to infinity is $\frac{B}{4A}$
(d) equilibrium distance is given by $\frac{B}{2A}$

46. Power of a force acting on a block varies with time t as shown in the figure. The angle between force acting on the block and its velocity is:

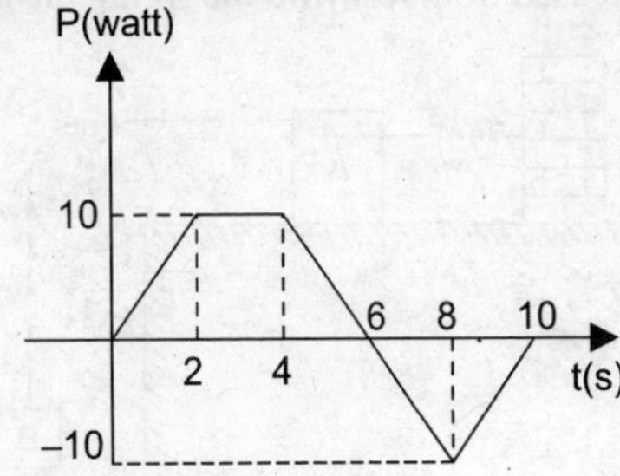

(a) acute at $t = 1$s
(b) 90° at $t = 3$ s
(c) obtuse at $t = 7$ s
(d) change in kinetic energy from $t = 0$, to $t = 10$ s is 20 J.

47. Displacement time graph of a particle moving in a straight line is as shown in figure. Select the correct alternative(s):

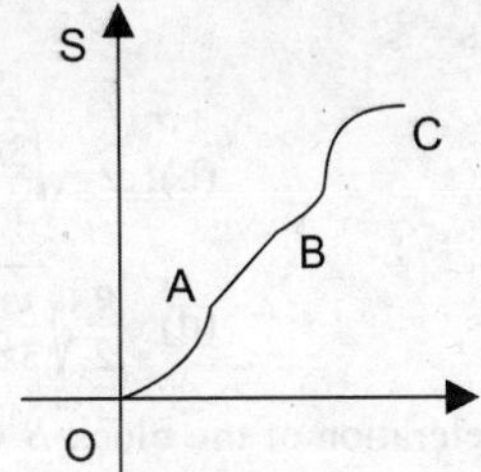

(a) Work done by all the forces in region OA and BC is positive
(b) Work done by all the forces in region AB is zero
(c) Work done by all the forces in region BC is negative
(d) Work done by all forces in region OA is negative

48. A block of mass 2 kg is hanging over a smooth and light pulley through a light string. The other end of the string is pulled by a constant force $F = 40$ N. The kinetic energy of the particle increases 40 J in a given interval of time. Then, ($g = 10$m/s^2)
(a) tension in the string is 40 N
(b) displacement of the block in the given interval of time is 2 m
(c) work done by gravity is –20 J
(d) work done by tension is 80 J.

49. Select the correct alternatives:
(a) work done by static friction is always zero
(b) work done by kinetic friction can be positive also
(c) kinetic energy of a system can not be increased without applying any external force on the system
(d) work energy theorem is valid in non-inertial frames also.

Directions (Q. 50 to 52) : Consider the situation shown in figure. Mass of block A is m and that of block B is $2\ m$. The force constant of spring is K. Friction is absent everywhere. System is released from rest with the spring unstretched.

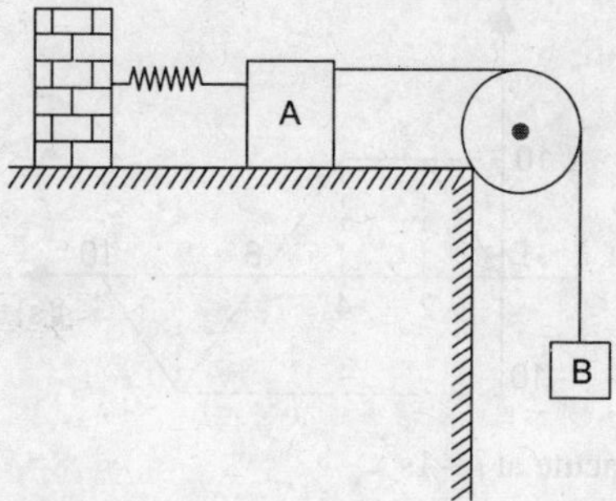

50. The maximum extension of the spring will be

(a) $\frac{mg}{k}$ (b) $\frac{2mg}{k}$

(c) $\frac{3mg}{k}$ (d) $\frac{4mg}{k}$

51. The speed of block A when the extension in the spring is $x = \frac{xm}{2}$ is

(a) $\frac{g}{2}\sqrt{\frac{3k}{m}}$ (b) $2g\sqrt{\frac{3k}{m}}$

(c) $2g\sqrt{\frac{m}{3k}}$ (d) $\frac{g}{2}\sqrt{\frac{m}{3k}}$

52. The net acceleration of the block B when extension in the spring is $x = \frac{xm}{4}$ is

(a) $\frac{g}{2}$ downward (b) $\frac{g}{3}$ upward

(c) $\frac{g}{2}$ upward (d) $\frac{g}{3}$ downward

Directions (Q. 53 to 55) : In a spring gun having spring constant 100 N/m, a small ball of mass 0.1 kg is put in its barrel by compressing the spring through 0.05 m as shown in figure.

53. The velocity of the ball when the spring is released will be

(a) $\sqrt{5/2}$ m/s (b) $\sqrt{2/5}$ m/s

(c) $5/2$ m/s (d) $2/5$ m/s

54. The time taken by the ball to reach the ground will be

(a) $2/5$ sec (b) $\sqrt{\frac{2}{5}}$ sec

(c) $5/2$ sec (d) $\sqrt{5/2}$ sec

55. Where should a box be placed on the ground so that the ball fall in it, if the ball leaves the gun horizontally at a height of 2 m above the ground is

(a) 0.5 m (b) 1 m

(c) 1.5 m (d) 2.0 m

Directions (Q. 56 to 58) : The displacement x of a particle moving in one dimension, under the action of a constant force is varying according to relation

$$t = \sqrt{x} + 3$$

where x is in metre and t is in second.

56. The displacement of the particle when its velocity is zero is

(a) zero (b) 1 m

(c) 2 m (d) 3 m

57. The acceleration of the particle

(a) increases with time

(b) decreases with time

(c) increases with time up to $t = 3$ s and then decreases with time.

(d) remains constant at 2 ms^{-2}

58. The work done by the force in first 6 s is

(a) 1 J (b) 3 J

(c) 6 J (d) zero

Directions (Q. 59 to 62) : The work done by a constant force acting on a body is given by

$$W = \mathbf{F} \cdot \mathbf{r}$$

where **F** is the force vector and **r** is displacement vector. The displacement vector $\mathbf{r} = \mathbf{r}_2 - \mathbf{r}_1$ where $\mathbf{r}_1$ is the initial position vector and $\mathbf{r}_2$ is the final position vector.

If the force is variable, the work done in moving a body from a position $\mathbf{r}_1$ to a position $\mathbf{r}_2$ is given by

$$W = \int_{r_1}^{r_2} \mathbf{F}.d\mathbf{r}$$

where $d\mathbf{r}$ is an infinitesimally small displacement.

59. A particle is moved from a position $\mathbf{r}_1 = (3\hat{\mathbf{i}} + 2\hat{\mathbf{j}} + 4\hat{\mathbf{k}})$ metre to a position $\mathbf{r}_1 = (5\hat{\mathbf{i}} + 6\hat{\mathbf{j}} + 9\hat{\mathbf{k}})$ metre under the action of a force $\mathbf{F} = (\hat{\mathbf{i}} + 3\hat{\mathbf{j}} + \hat{\mathbf{k}})$ newton. The work done is

(a) zero (b) 13 J

(c) 27 J (d) 35 J

60. A body of mass m is projected from a tower of height h at an angle θ above the horizontal. The work done by the gravitational force during the time it takes to hit the ground is

(a) $mgh\ (1 + \cos\theta)$ (b) $mgh\ (1 + \sin\theta)$

(c) mgh (d) zero

61. A body of mass m is projected from the ground with a velocity u at an angle θ above the horizontal. The work done by the gravitational force in time $t = \frac{u\sin\theta}{g}$ is

(a) $2mu^2\sin^2\theta$ (b) $mu^2\sin^2\theta$

(c) $\frac{mu^2\sin^2\theta}{2}$ (d) zero

62. If $\theta = 45°$, the work done by gravitational force in above question in time $t = \dfrac{2\mu \sin\theta}{g}$

(a) $\dfrac{mu^2}{4}$ (b) $\dfrac{mu^2}{2}$

(c) mu^2 (d) zero

Directions (Q. 63 to 65) : Work done by a constant force acting on a particle is defined as $W = \vec{F}.\Delta\vec{r}$ where $\Delta\vec{r} = \vec{r}_f - \vec{r}_i, \vec{r}_f$ is the final position of particle and $\vec{r}_i$ is the initial position of particle. If the force is variable work done is defined as $W = \int_{\vec{r}_i}^{\vec{r}_f} \vec{F}.\vec{d}r$, where $\vec{F}$ is the force at any general position $\vec{r}$ between $\vec{r}_i$ and $\vec{r}_f$ and $\vec{d}r$ is representing infinitely small displacement of particle. $\vec{d}r = dx\hat{\mathbf{i}} + dy\hat{\mathbf{j}} + dz\hat{\mathbf{k}}$.

63. A particle is thrown from a tower of height h at an angle θ above horizontal. Work done by gravity during its time of flights is (mass of particle is m)

(a) 0 (b) $mgh \cos\theta$

(c) $mgh \sin\theta$ (d) mgh

64. Given: $\vec{F} = 2\hat{i}+4\hat{j}$, $\vec{r}_i = 2\hat{i} + 3\hat{j}$ and $\vec{r}_f = 3\hat{i} + 4\hat{j}$ work done is (use SI units)

(a) 4 J (b) 6 J

(c) 10 J (d) zero

65. A particle thrown from ground with a velocity v at an angle θ above horizontal. Work done by gravity in $t = \dfrac{2v\sin\theta}{g}$ equals

(a) $\dfrac{mgv^2 \sin^2\theta}{2g}$ (b) $\dfrac{mgv^2 \sin^2\theta}{g}$

(c) zero (d) $\dfrac{2mgv^2 \sin^2\theta}{g}$

Directions (Q. 66 to 69) : A block of mass 0.5 kg is taken from the bottom of an inclined plane to its top and then allowed to slide down to the bottom. The length of the inclined plane is 2.5 m and its height is 1.5 m. The coefficient of friction between the block and the plane is 0.2.

66. Work done by the gravitational force over the round trip is

(a) 0 J (b) 0.5J

(c) 1 J (d) 1.5J

67. Work done by the applied force over the upward journey

(a) 0 J (b) 5.5 J

(c) 9.5 J (d) 8.5 J

68. Work done by the frictional force over the round trip

(a) 4.5 J (b) – 4 J

(c) – 4.5 j (d) 4 J

69. The kinetic energy of the block when it reaches the bottom of the plane is.

(a) 5.5 J (b) 6.5 J

(c) 4.5 J (d) 3.5 J

Directions (Q. 70 to 71) : An elastic ball of mass $\left(\dfrac{1}{2}\right)$ kg slides down along a smooth inclined plane having inclination angle 37° for a distance of $\left(\dfrac{100}{3}\right)$m along the incline and collides with a similar ball elastically, which is at rest on a horizontal smooth plane as shown in the figure. Then,

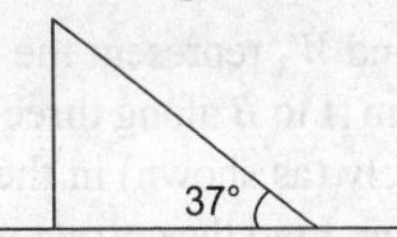

70. The velocity of two ball after collision will be.

(a) $v_1 = 0, v_2 = 10$ m/s

(b) $v_1 = 5$ m/s, $v_2 = 10$ m/s

(c) $v_1 = 0$ m/s, v2 = 20 m/s

(d) $v_1 = 10$ m/s, v2 = 0 m/s

71. Impulsive reaction produced on the second ball by the first ball will be.

(a) 10 N-s (b) 5 N-s

(c) 20 N-s (d) 2.5 N-s

72. A block of mass m is kept on a platform which starts from rest with constant acceleration g/2 upward, as shown in figure. Work done by normal reaction on block in time t is :

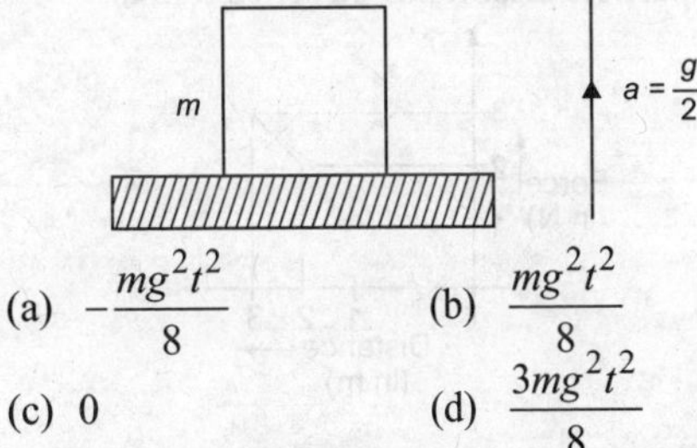

(a) $-\dfrac{mg^2t^2}{8}$ (b) $\dfrac{mg^2t^2}{8}$

(c) 0 (d) $\dfrac{3mg^2t^2}{8}$

73. A time dependent force $F = 6t$ acts on a particle of mass 1 kg. If the particle starts from rest, the work done by the force during the first 1 s will be

(a) 22J (b) 9 J

(c) 18 J (d) 4.5 J

74. When a rubber band is stretched by a distance x, it exerts a restoring force of magnitude $F = ax + bx^2$, where a and b are constants. The work done in stretching the unstretched rubber band by L is

(a) $aL^2 + bL^3$ (b) $\dfrac{1}{2}(aL^2 + bL^3)$

(c) $\dfrac{aL^2}{2} + \dfrac{bL^3}{3}$ (d) $\dfrac{1}{2}\left(\dfrac{aL^2}{2} + \dfrac{bL^3}{3}\right)$

75. The work done on a particle of mass m by a force, $K\left[\frac{x}{(x^2+y^2)^{3/2}}\hat{i}+\frac{y}{(x^2+y^2)^{3/2}}\hat{j}\right]$ (K being a constant of appropriate dimensions), when the particle is taken from the point $(a, 0)$ to the point $(0, a)$ along a circular path of radius a about the origin in the x - y plane is

(a) $\frac{2k\pi}{a}$ (b) $\frac{k\pi}{a}$

(c) $\frac{k\pi}{2a}$ (d) 0

76. If W_1, W_2 and W_3 represent the work done in moving a particle from A to B along three different paths 1, 2 and 3 respectively (as shown) in the gravitational field of a point mass m. Find the correct relation between W_1, W_2 and W_3

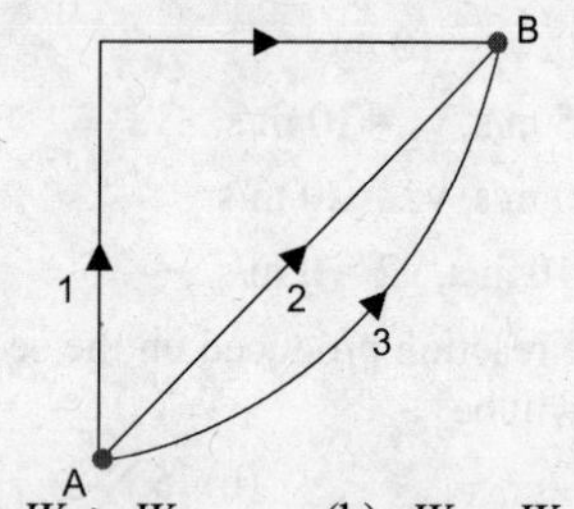

(a) $W_1 > W_2 > W_3$ (b) $W_1 = W_2 = W_3$

(c) $W_1 < W_2 < W_3$ (d) $W_2 < W_1 > W_3$

77. A particle moves in one dimension from rest under the influence of a force that varies with the distance travelled by the particle as shown in the figure. The kinetic energy of the particle after it has travelled 3 m is:

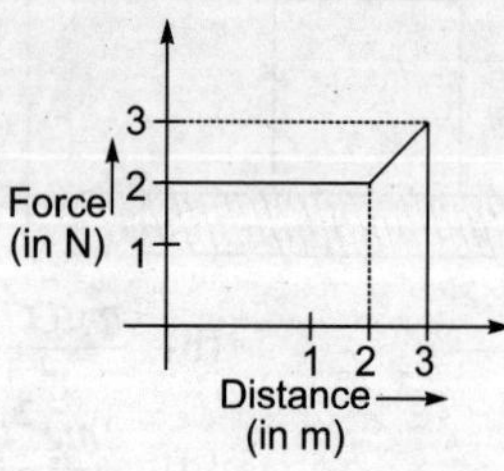

(a) 5 J

(b) 6.5 J

(c) 4 J

(d) 2.5 J

78. A particle is moving in a circular path of radius a under the action of an attractive potential $U = \frac{-k}{2r^2}$ its total energy is:

(a) zero

(b) $-\frac{3k}{2a^2}$

(c) $-\frac{K}{4a^2}$

(d) $\frac{K}{2a^2}$

79. A body of mass $m = 10^{-2}$kg is moving in a medium and experiences a frictional force $F = -kv^2$. Its initial speed is $v_0 = 10$ ms^{-1}. If, after 10 s, its energy is $\frac{1}{8}mv_0^2$, the value of k will be

(a) 10^{-3} kgs^{-1}

(b) 10^{-4} kgm^{-1}

(c) 10^{-1} kgm^{-1} s^{-1}

(d) 10^{-3} kgm^{-1}

80. A block of mass 2 kg is free to move along the x-axis. It is at rest and from $t = 0$ onwards it is subjected to a time dependent force $F(t)$ in the x-direction. The force $F(t)$ varies with t as shown in the figure. The kinetic energy of the block after 4.5 s is

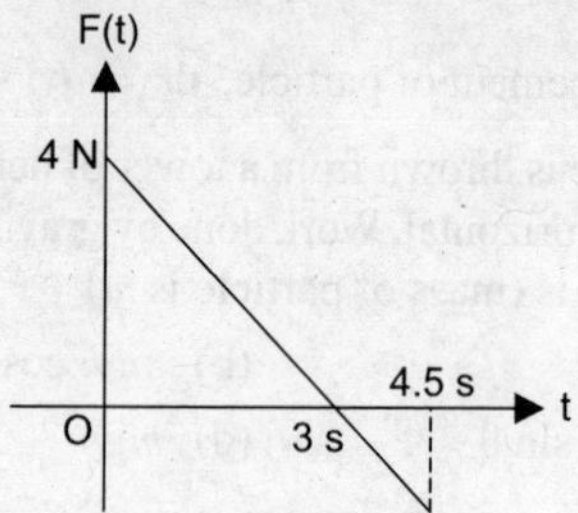

(a) 4.50 J

(b) 7.50 J

(c) 5.06 J

(d) 14.06 J

81. A block (B) is attached to two unstretched springs S_1 and S_2 with spring constants k and $4k$, respectively. The other ends are attached to two supports M_1 and M_2 not attached to the walls. The springs and supports have negligible mass. There is no friction anywhere.

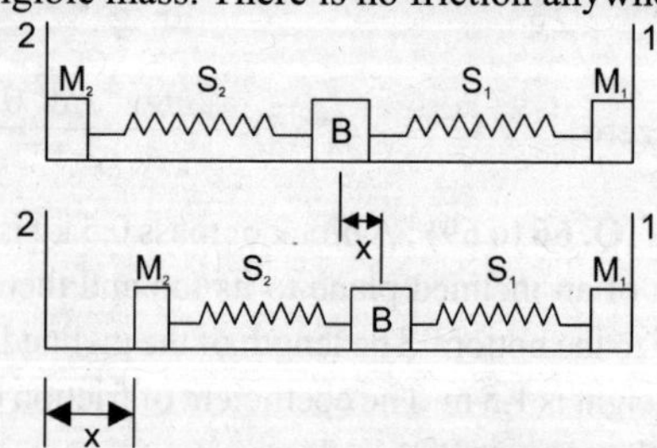

The block B is displaced towards wall 1 by a small distance x and released. The block returns and moves a maximum distance y towards wall 2. Displacements x and y are measured with respect to the equilibrium position of the block B. The ratio $\frac{y}{x}$ is

(a) 4

(b) 2

(c) $\frac{1}{2}$

(d) $\frac{1}{4}$

82. An ideal spring with spring constant k is hung from the ceiling and a block of mass M is attached to its lower end. The mass is released with the spring initially unstretched. Then the maximum extension in the spring is

(a) $\frac{4Mg}{k}$

(b) $\frac{2Mg}{k}$

(c) $\frac{Mg}{k}$

(d) $\frac{Mg}{2k}$

83. A particle is placed at the origin and a force $F = kx$ is acting on it (where, k is a positive constant). If $U(0) = 0$, the graph of $U(x)$ *versus* x will be (where, U is the potential energy function)

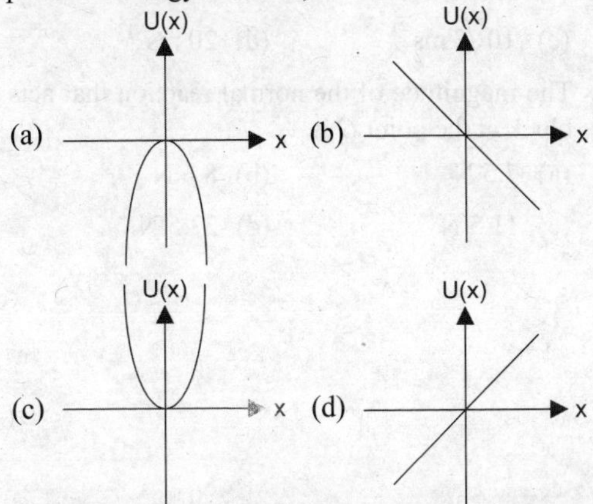

84. A particle of mass m is initially at rest at the origin. It is subjected to a force and starts moving along the x-axis. Its kinetic energy K changes with time as $dK/dt = \gamma t$, where γ is a positive constant of appropriate dimensions. Which of the following statements is (are) true?

(a) The force applied on the particle is constant
(b) The speed of the particle is proportional to time
(c) The distance of the particle from the origin increases linearly with time
(d) The force is conservative.

85. A person trying to loose weight by burning fat lifts a mass of 10 kg upto a height of 1 m 1000 times. Assume that the potential energy lost each time he lowers the mass is dissipated. How much fat will he use up considering the work done only when the weight is lifted up? Fat supplies 3.8×10^7 J of energy per kg which is converted to mechanical energy with a 20% efficiency rate. (Take, $g = 9.8 \text{ ms}^{-2}$)

(a) 2.45×10^{-3} kg
(b) 6.45×10^{-3} kg
(c) 9.89×10^{-3} kg
(d) 12.89×10^{-3} kg

86. It is found that if a neutron suffers an elastic collinear collision with deuterioum at rest, fractional loss of its energy is p_d, while for its similar collision with carbon nucleus at rest, fractional loss of energy is p_c. The value of p_d and p_c are respectively.

(a) (0, 0) (b) (0, 1)
(c) (0.89, 0.28) (d) (0.28, 0.89)

87. In a collinear collision, a particle with an initial speed v_0 strikes a stationary particle of the same mass. If the final kinetic energy 50% greater than the original kinetic energy, the magnitude of the relative velocity between the two particles, after collision, is

(a) $\frac{v_0}{2}$ (b) $\frac{v_0}{\sqrt{2}}$
(c) $\frac{v_0}{4}$ (d) $\sqrt{2}v_0$

88. A point particle of mass m, moves along the uniformly rough track PQR as shown in the figure. The coefficient of friction, between the particle and the rough track equals μ. The particle is released from rest, from the point P and it comes to rest at a point R. The energies lost by the ball, over the parts PQ and QR of the track, are equal to each other, and no energy is lost when particle changes direction from PQ to QR. The values of the coefficient of friction μ and the distance x (= QR), are respectively close to

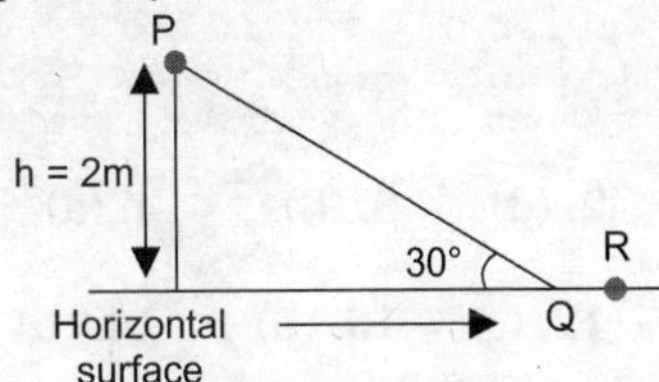

(a) 0.2 and 6.5 m
(b) 0.2 and 3.5 m
(c) 0.29 and 3.5 m
(d) 0.29 and 6.5 m

89. A wire, which passes through the hole in a small bead, is bent in the form of quarter of a circle. The wire is fixed vertically on ground as shown in the figure. The bead is released from near the top of the wire and it slides along the wire without friction. As the bead moves from A to B, the force it applies on the wire is

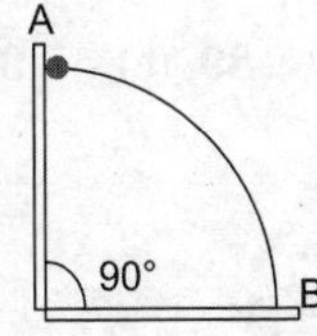

(a) always radially outwards
(b) always radially inwards
(c) radially outwards initially and radially inwards later
(d) radially inwards initially and radially outwards later

90. A bob of mass M is suspended by a massless string of length L. The horizontal velocity v at position A is just sufficient to make it reach the point B. The angle θ at which the speed of the bob is half of that at A, satisfies

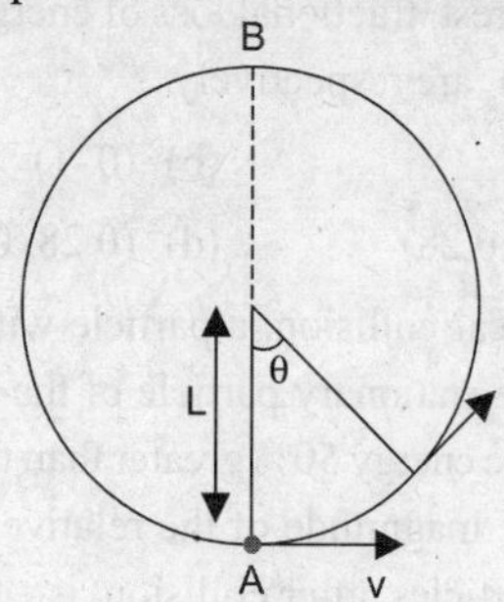

(a) $\theta = \frac{\pi}{4}$

(b) $\frac{\pi}{4} < \theta < \frac{\pi}{2}$

(c) $\frac{\pi}{2} < \theta < \frac{\pi}{4}$

(d) $\frac{3\pi}{4} < \theta < \pi$

Directions (Q. 91 to 92) :

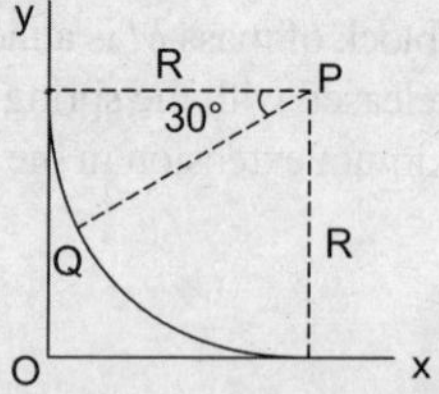

A small block of mass 1 kg is released from rest at the top of a rough track. The track is a circular arc of radius 40 m. The block slides along the track without toppling and a frictional force acts on it in the direction opposite to the instantaneous velocity. The work done in overcoming the friction up to the point Q, as shown in the figure, is 150 J. (Take the acceleration due to gravity, $g = 10\ ms^{-2}$)

91. The speed of the block when it reaches the point Q is

(a) $5\ ms^{-1}$ (b) $10\ ms^{-1}$

(c) $10\sqrt{3}\ ms^{-1}$ (d) $20\ ms^{-1}$

92. The magnitude of the normal reaction that acts on the block at the point Q is

(a) 7.5 N (b) 8.6 N

(c) 11.5 N (d) 22.5 N

Answers

1. (b)	**2.** (d)	**3.** (b)	**4.** (a)	**5.** (b)	**6.** (d)	**7.** (c)	**8.** (b)	**9.** (b)	**10.** (b)
11. (c)	**12.** (c)	**13.** (b)	**14.** (b)	**15.** (a)	**16.** (a)	**17.** (c)	**18.** (d)	**19.** (b)	**20.** (b)
21. (d)	**22.** (c)	**23.** (d)	**24.** (d)	**25.** (d)	**26.** (c)	**27.** (d)	**28.** (b)	**29.** (d)	**30.** (c)
31. (c)	**32.** (d)	**33.** (c)	**34.** (b)	**35.** (a)	**36.** (a,b,d)	**37.** (a,d)	**38.** (b,c,d)	**39.** (a,b,d)	
40. (c,d)	**41.** (a,b,c)		**42.** (b,d)	**43.** (a,c)	**44.** (a,c)	**45.** (a,b)	**46.** (a,c,d)	**47.** (b,d)	**48.** (a,b,d)
49. (b,d)	**50.** (d)	**51.** (c)	**52.** (a)	**53.** (a)	**54.** (b)	**55.** (b)	**56.** (a)	**57.** (d)	**58.** (d)
59. (c)	**60.** (c)	**61.** (c)	**62.** (d)	**63.** (d)	**64.** (b)	**65.** (c)	**66.** (a)	**67.** (c)	**68.** (b)
69. (a)	**70.** (c)	**71.** (a)	**72.** (d)	**73.** (d)	**74.** (c)	**75.** (d)	**76.** (b)	**77.** (b)	**78.** (a)
79. (b).	**80.** (c)	**81.** (c)	**82.** (b)	**83.** (a)	**84.** (a,b,c)	**85.** (d)	**86.** (c)	**87.** (d)	**88.** (c)
89. (c)	**90.** (d)	**91.** (b)	**92.** (a)						

Explanations

1. Where v is final velocity, u is initial velocity and h is height.

Given $h = 4.9\text{m}, g = 9.8 \text{ ms}^{-2}, u = 0$

$\therefore \ v = \sqrt{2gh} = \sqrt{2 \times 9.8 \times 4.9} = 9.8 \text{ ms}^{-1}$

Coefficient of restitution (e) of an object is a unit fraction value representing the ratio of velocities before and after an impact.

$v' = \frac{3}{4} \times 9.8$

Time taken from first bounce to second bounce is

$t = \frac{2v^l}{g} = 2 \times \frac{3}{4} \times 9.8 \times \frac{1}{9.8} = 1.5 \text{ sec}$

2. In inelastic collision most of the kinetic energy of the body is lost in other form of heat. Thus, in inelastic collision kinetic energy is not conserved but total energy and momentum are still conserved.

Hence, we have

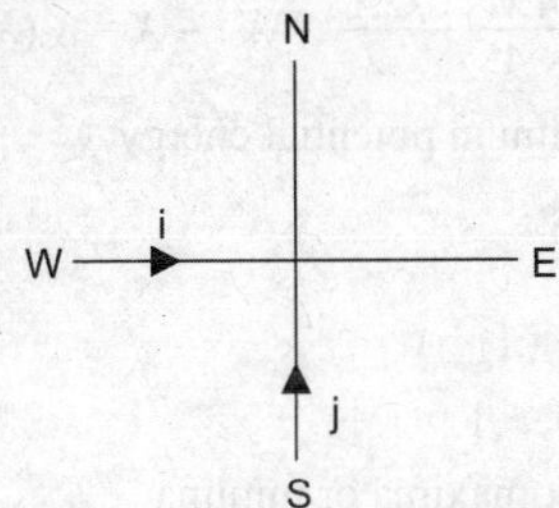

$mvi + mvj = 2mv'$

$\Rightarrow |2mv'| = m|vi + vj|$

$\Rightarrow 2mv' = m\sqrt{v^2 + v^2}$

$\Rightarrow v' = \frac{v\sqrt{2}}{2} = \frac{v}{\sqrt{2}}$

From equation of motion

$$v^2 = u^2 + 2gh$$

3. From law of conservation of linear momentum

$m_1u_1 + m_2u_2 = m_1v_1 + m_2v_2$

$M \times v + \text{m} \times 0 = M \times v_1 + mv_2$

$Mv = Mv_1 + mv_2$ .....(i)

$M(v - v_1) - mv_2$

In elastic collision kinetic energy is also conserved

$\frac{1}{2}m_1u_1^2 + \frac{1}{2}m_2u_2^2 = \frac{1}{2}m_1v_1^2 + \frac{1}{2}m_2v_2^2$

$Mv^2 = Mv_1^2 = mv_2^2$

$M(v + v_1)(v - v_1) = mv_2^2$ .....(ii)

Dividing Eq. (ii) by Eq. (i) we get

$v + v_1 \approx v_2$ as $M >> m$

So, $v_1 = v$

$\therefore \ v_2 = 2v$

4. In hydrogen atom $E_2 - E_1 = 10.2$ eV. Since, energy difference is 10.2 eV, which is greater that kinetic energy 5 eV the electron excites the hydrogen atom, hence collision is elastic.

5. Applying conservation of linear momentum, we write,

$m_1u_1 = m_2u_2$

here $m_1 = 18$ kg, $m_2 = 12$ kg

$u_1 = 6 \text{ ms}^{-1}, u_2 = ?$

$\therefore \ 18 \times 6 = 12u_2$

$\Rightarrow \quad u_2 = \frac{18 \times 6}{12} = 9 \text{ ms}^{-1}$

Thus, kinetic energy of 12 kg mass

$K_2 = \frac{1}{2}m_2u_2^2 = \frac{1}{2} \times 12 \times (9)^2 = 6 \times 81 = 486 \text{ J}$

6. Since, $e^n = \left(\frac{h_n}{h_0}\right)^{1/2}$

$\therefore \ h_n = e^{2n} h_0 = e^2 \times e^2 h = e^4 h$

7. According to conservation of momentum

$m_1v_1 + m_2v_2 = (m_1 + m_2)v'$

$\therefore \ mv + m_2 \times 0 = (m + 2m)v'$

or $\quad v' = \frac{v}{3}$

8. Let the two balls of mass m_1 and m_2 collide each other elastically with velocities u_1 and u_2. Their velocities become v_1 and v_2 after the collision.

Applying conservation of linear momentum, we get

$$m_1u_1 + m_2u_2 = m_1v_1 + m_2v_2 \quad ...(i)$$

Also from conservation of kinetic energy

$$\frac{1}{2}m_1u_1^2 + \frac{1}{2}m_2u_2^2 = \frac{1}{2}m_1v_1^2 + \frac{1}{2}m_2v_2^2 \quad ...(ii)$$

Solving Eqs. (i) and (ii), we get

$$v_1 = \left(\frac{m_1 - m_2}{m_1 + m_2}\right)u_1 + \left(\frac{2m_2}{m_1 + m_2}\right)u_2 \quad ...(iii)$$

and $$v_2 = \left(\frac{m_2 - m_1}{m_1 + m_2}\right)u_2 + \left(\frac{2m_2}{m_1 + m_2}\right)u_1 \quad ...(iv)$$

On taking approximate value the mass of deuteron is twice the mass of neutron.

Given $u_1 = u, u_2 = 0, m_1, m_2 = 2m$

Velocity of neutron $v_1 = \left(\frac{m - 2m}{m + 2m}\right)u = -\frac{u}{3}$

Velocity of deuteron $v_2 = \frac{2mu}{m + 2m} = \frac{2}{3}u$

Fractional energy loss $= \dfrac{\frac{1}{2}mu^2 - \frac{1}{2}\left(-\frac{u}{3}\right)^2}{\frac{1}{2}mu^2}$

$= 1 - \frac{1}{9} = \frac{8}{9}$

9. For a spring $k \propto \frac{1}{L}$. Thus we can say $k \times L$ = constant.

$$k \times L = k' \times \frac{2L}{3}$$

$$\therefore \quad k' = \left(\frac{3k}{2}\right)$$

10. $a_c = k^2 rt^2$ Hence, $\frac{v^2}{r} = k^2rt^2 \Rightarrow v^2 = k^2r^2t^2$

The kinetic energy $= \frac{1}{2}mv^2 = \frac{1}{2}mk^2r^2t^2$

The rate of change of kinetic energy is the power developed by all the forces.

$$\frac{d}{dt}(\text{KE}) = \frac{1}{2}mk^2r^2(2t) = mk^2r^2t$$

11. $F = -K(y\hat{i} + x\hat{j})$

$$\vec{ds} = dx(\hat{i}) + dy(\hat{j}) + dz(\hat{k})$$

$$dw = \vec{F}.\vec{ds} = -K[y\hat{i} + x\hat{j}].[dx\hat{i} + dy\hat{j} + dz\hat{k}]$$

$$= -K[y.dx + x.dy] = -K\,d(xy)$$

$$\therefore \quad w = \int dw$$

$$w = -K\int_{(0,0)}^{(a,a)} d(xy)$$

$$w = -Ka^2$$

12. $P = mv$

$$F = \frac{dP}{dt} = m\frac{dv}{dt} + v\frac{dm}{dt}$$

$$\because \frac{dv}{dt} = 0$$

$$F = v.\frac{dm}{dt} = (v).\{\text{Mass flow rate}\}$$

$F = (v).(\rho Av)$

$F = \rho Av^2$

Power = Force × Velocity

Power = ρAv^3

Hence, Power $\propto v^3$

13. $K \propto t$

$$\frac{P^2}{2m} \propto t$$

$P^2 = (2cm)\,t$ (where c is the constant of proportionality)

$$P = \sqrt{2cm}\,t^{1/2}$$

$$\frac{dp}{dt} = F = \sqrt{2cm}\,\frac{1}{2}(t^{\frac{1}{2}-1})$$

$$F = \sqrt{2cm}\,\frac{1}{2}t^{-\frac{1}{2}}$$

$$F = \sqrt{\frac{cm}{2}}\,\frac{1}{\sqrt{t}}$$

$$F \propto \frac{1}{\sqrt{t}}$$

14. At any instant, the total energy of an oscillator is the sum of kinetic energy and potential energy.

Total energy, $E = K + V$

$$E = \frac{1}{2}mv^2 + \frac{1}{2}kx^2$$

At $x = +x_m$ the particle turns back, therefore its velocity at this point is zero, i.e., $v = 0$

$\therefore K = 0$

$$\therefore \quad E = \frac{1}{2}kx^2 = V$$

15. We know that

$P = FV = mav = ma\,(at)$

$$P = ma^2t = \left(\frac{mv^2}{T^2}\right)t$$

As $a = \frac{v}{t}$

16. $V_{(x)} = \left(\frac{X^4}{4} - \frac{X^2}{2}\right)$ J

$$\frac{dV}{dX} = \frac{4X^3}{4} - \frac{2X}{2} = X^3 - X = X(X^2 - 1)$$

For minimum potential energy

$$\frac{dV}{dX} = 0$$

$\therefore X(X^2 - 1) = 0$

$X = 0, \pm 1$

To check maxima or minima

$$\frac{d^2V}{dX^2} = 3X^2 - 1$$

Putting $X = 0$

$$\frac{d^2V}{dX^2} = -1 \text{ (it is maxima)}$$

Putting $X = 1$ or -1

$$\frac{d^2V}{dX^2} = +2 \text{ (this is minima)}$$

$\therefore$ Minimum PE $V_{min} = \frac{1}{4} - \frac{1}{2} = -\frac{1}{4}$ J

$$\text{KE}_{max} = E_M - V_{min} = 2 - \left[-\frac{1}{4}\right] = \frac{9}{4}\text{ J}$$

$$\text{KE}_{max} = \frac{1}{2}MV_{max}^2$$

$$V_{max}^2 = \frac{2 \times 9}{4} = \frac{9}{2}$$

$$V_{max} = \frac{3}{\sqrt{2}}\text{ m/s}$$

17. When a pendulum is oscillating in air, its total mechanical energy decreases exponentially with time. Hence, option (c) represents correct diagram.

18. As the earth moves once around the sun in its elliptical orbit, its kinetic energy is maximum when it is closest to the sun and minimum when it is farthest from the sun. As kinetic energy is never zero during its motion, hence option (d) is correct.

19. For constant power, displacement $\propto t^{3/2}$.

20. At a height h above the gound, PE of raindrop is maximum and $KE = 0$. As the raindrop falls its PE goes on decreasing and KE goes on increasing upto a point $\frac{h}{4}$ above the gound. At this stage, rain drop has acquired near terminal velocity (= constant). Therefore, at this stage, KE tends to be constant. PE becomes zero when raindrop falls to the ground. Hence, option (b) is most appropriate.

21. Mass of hanging portion is $M/3$ (one - third) and centre of mass c, is at a distance $h = \frac{L}{6}$ below the table top. Therefore the required work done is,

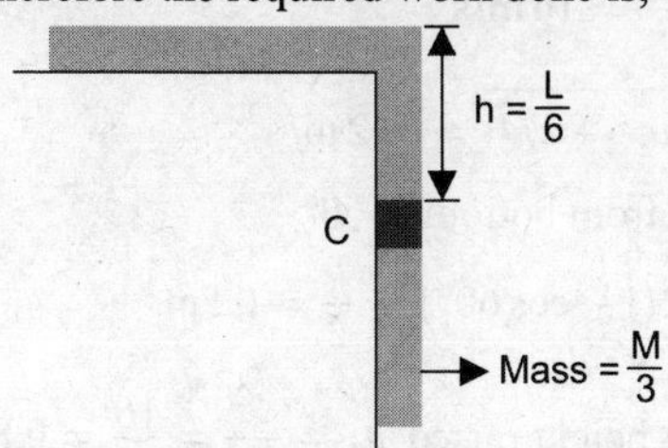

$$W = mgh = \left(\frac{M}{3}\right)(g)\left(\frac{L}{6}\right) = \frac{MgL}{18}$$

22. $dW = F.ds$, where $ds = dx\hat{i} + dy\hat{j} + dz\hat{k}$

and $F = -k(y\hat{i} + x\hat{j})$

$\therefore dW = -k\,(ydx + xdy)$

$= -kd\,(xy)$

$\therefore \quad W = \int_{0,0}^{a,a} dW = -k\int_{0,0}^{a,a} d(xy)$

$= -k[xy]_{0,0}^{a,a}$

$W = -ka^2$

23. On applying work-energy theorem

Work done by F from A to B = work done by Mg from A to B

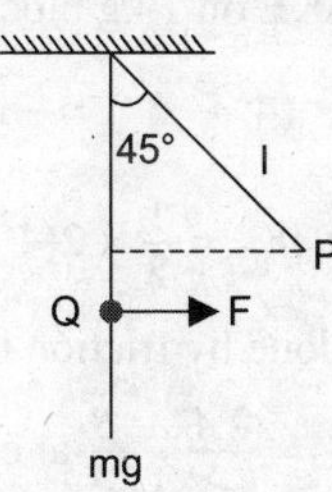

$Fl \sin 45° = mg\,[1 - \cos 45°]$

$F = mg\left(\sqrt{2} - 1\right)$

24. $F = -\frac{dU}{dx}$

$\therefore dU = -F.\,dx$

or $U(x) = -\int_0^x (-kx + ax^3)dx$

$U(x) = \frac{kx^2}{2} - \frac{ax^4}{4}$

$U(x) = 0$ at $x = 0$ and $x = \sqrt{\frac{2k}{a}}$

$U(x) =$ negative for $x > \sqrt{\frac{2k}{a}}$

From the given function, we can see that $F = 0$ at $x = 0$ i.e., slope of $U - x$ graph is zero at $x = 0$

25. $maR \sin\theta + mgR\,(1 - \cos\theta) = \frac{1}{2}mv^2$

On solving we get, $v = \sqrt{2Rg(1 + \sin\theta - \cos\theta}$

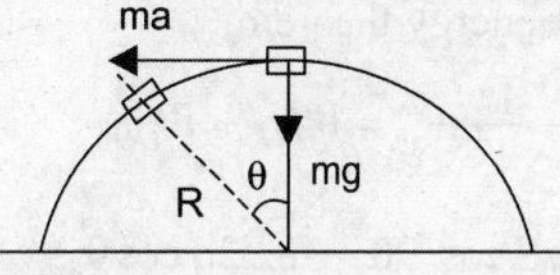

26. $W = -\int_{(0,0}^{(a,a)} \left(y\hat{i} + x\hat{y}\hat{j}\right)\left(dx\hat{i} + dy\hat{i}\right)$

$= -k\int_{(0,0)}^{(a,a)} ((ydx + xdy)$

$= -kxy \int_{(0,0)}^{(a,a)} d\,(xy) = -K\,[xy]_{(0,0)}^{(a,a)}$

27. Initial velocity $= u$. Final velocity $= \sqrt{u^2 - 2gl}$

So $|\Delta v| = \sqrt{u^2 + u^2 - 2gl} = \sqrt{2(u^2 - gl)}$

28. $P = F_t.v = ma_t.v;\, a_t = \frac{d|v|}{dt};\, a_c = k^2rt^2$

$\Rightarrow \frac{v^2}{r} = k^2rt^2$

$v = krt \Rightarrow \frac{d|v|}{dt} = kr;$

$a_t = kr\; P = mkr.krt = mk^2r^2t$

29. $F(x) = -kx + ax^3$; $F(x) = 0$ for $x = 0$

$\Rightarrow x = \sqrt{\frac{k}{a}};$

so slope is zero at $x = 0$ $x = \sqrt{\frac{k}{a}}$

30. $P_{wind} = F.v = \rho Av^2.v \quad P \propto v^3$

31. $P = Fv = mv\frac{dv}{dt}$

$v^2 \propto t$ or $v \propto t^{1/2}$

$\frac{dx}{dt} \propto t^{1/2}$ or $x \propto t^{3/2}$

32. $U = -\int Fdx \quad = -\frac{1}{2}kx^2$

33. Velocity is minimum but not zero at max. height also $\frac{dv}{dx} = 0$ hence $\frac{dk}{dx} = 0$

34. Friction force = $\mu mg = 0.2 \times 5 \times 10 = 10$ N. Effective force F = applied force – frictional force = 25 – 10 = 15 N. Kinetic energy = work done by force F in pulling the body through a distance S (= 10 m) = 15 × 10 = 150 J, which is choice (b).

35. Force of friction = μmg. Therefore, retardation $a = \mu mg/m = \mu g$ Also $2ax = v^2$ or $2am^2x = m^2v^2$.

But $p = mv$. Therefore, $2am^2 x = p^2$. But $a = \mu g$. Therefore, $2\mu g^2 x = p^2$ or $\mu = \frac{p^2}{2gm^2 x}$

Hence the correct choice is (a)

36. Work done in magnetic field is always zero as force is perpendicular to the field.

From work energy theorem

$$\frac{1}{2}m(2v)^2 - \frac{1}{2}mv^2 = W_{PO} + W_{OQ}$$

$$\frac{3}{2}mv^2 = qE\cos 90^\circ + qE2a\cos 0^\circ$$

$$2qEa = \frac{3}{2}mv^2 \text{ or } E = \frac{3}{4}\left(\frac{3v^2}{qa}\right) \text{ and } p = \text{F.v} = \text{qEv}$$

$$= qv\frac{3}{4}\frac{mv^2}{qa} = \frac{3}{4}\frac{mv^3}{a}$$

So (a, b, d) are correct.

37. As the block does not move, the ball moves along a circular path of radius l. The centre of mass of the system always lies some where on the string.

Let v = speed of the ball when the string makes an angle θ with the horizontal.

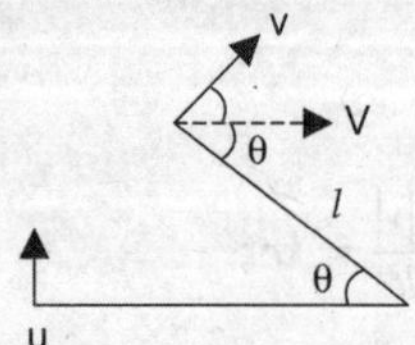

$$\frac{1}{2}mv^2 = \frac{1}{2}mu^2 - mg/\sin\theta$$

The horizontal component of

$$v = V = v\sin\theta = \sin\theta\sqrt{u^2 - 2gl\sin\theta}$$

For V to be maximum, $\frac{dV}{d\theta} = 0$,

which gives $\sin\theta = \frac{u^2}{3gl}$

38. $mgx = \frac{1}{2}kx^2$ or $x = \frac{2mg}{k}$

When the ball is at its lowest position, string force = kx = $2mg$

39. mu = $(m + 2m)\,v$, v is the final common velocity

$$\frac{1}{2}mu^2 - \frac{1}{2}(3m) - \frac{1}{2}(3m)\frac{u^2}{9}$$

$$= \frac{1}{2}mu^2\left[1 - \frac{1}{3}\right] = \frac{2}{3} \times \frac{1}{2}mu^2$$

The force of friction between the blocks is μmg.

Acceleration of A (to the right) = $a_1 = \frac{\mu mg}{2m} = \frac{\mu g}{2}$

Acceleration of B (to the left) = $a_2 = \frac{\mu mg}{m} = \mu g$

Acceleration of A relative to B = $a_1 - (-a_2) = \frac{3}{2}\mu g$.

40. Here velocity and acceleration keep on changing their direction. Their magnitude remains constant. KE remains constant.

41. (a, b, c)

42. $at = g\sin 60^\circ = 5\sqrt{3}\ \text{m/s}^2$

$$ar = \frac{v^2}{r} = 16\,\text{m/s}$$

$$a = \sqrt{at^2 + ar^2} = 18.2\,\text{m/s}^2$$

Height from bottom at 60°

$$h_1 = R(1 - \cos 60^\circ) = \frac{R}{2} = 0.5\text{m}$$

Further height raised $h_2 = \frac{v^2}{2g} = \frac{16}{20} = 0.8\,\text{m}$

Now $h_1 + h_2 = 1.3$ m > R

The bob will raise to θ = 90°

But there string will slack and height will be < 1.3 m.

43. P ∝ t $W = \int Pdt = \int \propto t\,dt$ or $W \propto t^2$

Hence, $v^2 \propto t^2$ or $v \propto t$ further, $v = \frac{ds}{dt}$

$$\therefore \frac{ds}{dt} \propto t$$

$ds \propto t\,dt$, $s \propto t^2$

44. From conservation of linear momentum (1 + 2)

$v = (6 \times 1) + (2 - 3)$

∴ v = 4 m/s (of both the blocks)

From work energy theorem

i.e., W_{total} = ΔKE on 1 kg block,

$$W_f = \frac{1}{2} \times 1 \times (4^2 - 6^2) = -10\text{J}$$

on 2 kg block $W_f = \frac{1}{2} \times 2(4^2 - 3^2) = +7\text{J}$

∴ Net work done by friction is – 3 J.

45. $\because F = -\frac{dU}{dr} = \frac{2A}{r^3} - \frac{B}{r^2}$ at equilibrium $f = 0$, or

$$r = \frac{2A}{B}$$

At infinity $U = 0$, $r = \frac{2A}{B}, U = -\frac{B^2}{4A}\ \Delta U = \frac{B^2}{4A}$

46. Power is the dot product of velocity. At 1s and 3s, power is positive. Hence, angle is acute. At 7s power is negative. Hence angle is obtuse.

47. In region OA particle is accelerated, in region AB particle has uniform velocity while in region BD particle is deceleration. Therefore, work done is positive in region OA, zero in region AB and negative in region BC.

48. $W_{net} = \Delta$ KE or $(40 - 20)\, s = 40$

$\therefore s = 2$m

Work done by gravity is $-20 \times 2 = -40$ J

and work done by tension is $40 \times 2 = 80$ J

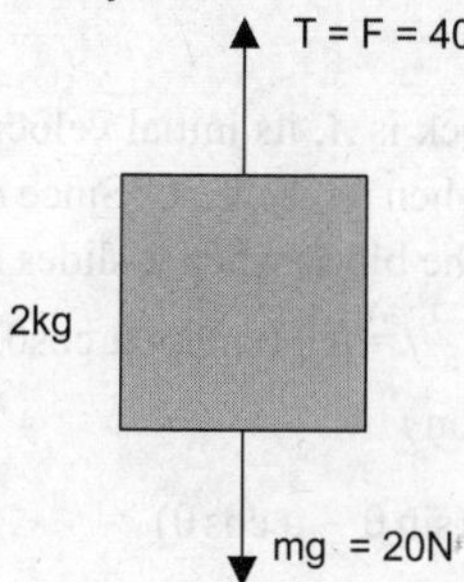

49. [b, d]

50. At maximum extension in the spring

$$v_A = v_B = 0 \text{ (momentarily)}$$

Therefore, applying conservation of mechanical energy: Decrease in gravitational potential energy of block B = increase in elastic potential energy of spring.

or $\quad m_B g x_m = \frac{1}{2} K x_m^2$

or $\quad 2mg x_m = \frac{1}{2} K x_m^2$

$\therefore \quad x_m = \frac{4mg}{K}$

51. At $x = \frac{x_m}{2} = \frac{2mg}{K}$

Let $\quad v_A = v_B = v$ (say)

Then, decrease in gravitational potential energy of block B = increase in elastic potential energy of spring + increase in kinetic energy of both the blocks.

$\therefore \quad m_B g x = \frac{1}{2} K x^2 + \frac{1}{2}(m_A + m_B)v^2$

or $\quad (2m)(g)\left(\frac{2gm}{K}\right) = \frac{1}{2} K \left(\frac{2mg}{K}\right)^2 + \frac{1}{2}(m + 2m)v^2$

$\therefore \quad v = 2g\sqrt{\frac{m}{3K}}$

52. At $x = \frac{x_m}{4} = \frac{mg}{K}$, net upward force on block B is Kx or mg and net downward force on block B is $2\,mg$

$\therefore \quad F_{net} = 2\,mg - mg = mg$ (downwards)

$\therefore \quad a = \frac{F_{net}}{m_B} = \frac{mg}{2m} = \frac{g}{2}$ downwards

53. When the spring is released its elastic potential energy $(1/2)\,kx^2$ is converted into kinetic energy $(1/2)mv^2$ of the ball; so, by conservation of ME, $\frac{1}{2}mv^2 = \frac{1}{2}kx^2$

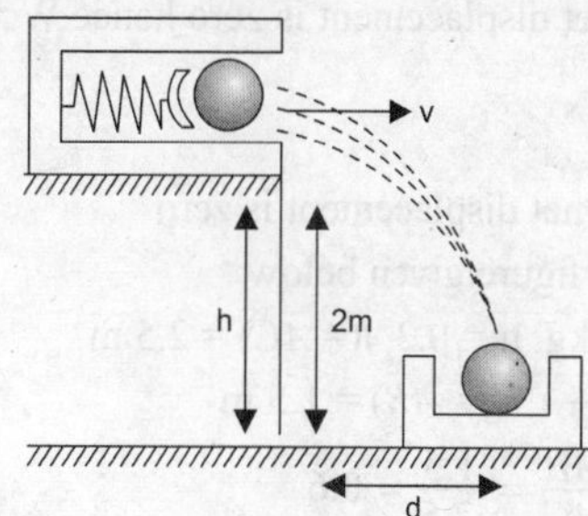

$v = x\sqrt{\frac{k}{m}}$

So $v = 0.05\sqrt{\frac{100}{0.1}}$ m/s $= \sqrt{\left(\frac{5}{2}\right)}$ m/s

54. As vertical component of velocity of ball is zero, time taken by the ball to reach the ground,

$t = \sqrt{\frac{2h}{8}} = \sqrt{\frac{2 \times 2}{10}} = \sqrt{\frac{2}{5}}$ s

55. So the horizontal distance travelled by the ball in this time

$d = vt = \sqrt{\frac{5}{2}} \times \sqrt{\frac{2}{5}} = 1$ m

56. Given $t = \sqrt{x} + 3$ or $\sqrt{x} = t - 3$

or $x = (t - 3)^2$ ...(i)

Differentiating (i) with respect to t, we get

$\frac{dx}{dt} = 2(t - 3)$ ...(ii)

or v = 2 $(t - 3)$

From (ii) it follows that v = 0 at $t = 3$ s. Using $t = 3$ s (ii) in (i), we get $x = 0$. Thus, the displacement of the particle is zero when its velocity is zero. Thus, the correct choice is (a).

57. From Eq. (2), we have

$a = \frac{dv}{dt} = \frac{d}{dt}[2(t - 3)] = 2\,\text{ms}^{-2}$

Hence the correct choice is (d).

58. From Eq. (2), the initial velocity, i.e., velocity at $t = 0$ is $V_0 = 2(0 - 3) = 6$ m/s^2

At $t = 6$ sec

$V = 2(6 - 3) = 6$ m/s

W.D = Final KE – Initial KE

$= \frac{1}{2}mv^2 - \frac{1}{2}mv_0^2 = \frac{1}{2}m(v^2 - v_0^2)$

$= \frac{1}{2}m\left[(6)^2 - (-6)^2\right] = 0$

59. (c) W = $F.(r_2 - r_1)$

$= (\hat{i} + 3\hat{j} + \hat{k}).(2\hat{i} + 4\hat{j} + 13\hat{j})$

$= 2 + 12 + 13 = 27$ J.

60. (c) $W = mgh$

61. (c) $W = mgh_{max} = \frac{mu^2 \sin^2 \theta}{2}$

62. (d) As net displacement is zero hence $W = 0$

63. (d) mgh

64. (b) 6 J

65. (c) 0 As net displacement is zero

Refer to figure given below.

$m = 0.5$ kg, $\mu = 0.2$, $l(= AC) = 2.5$ m

and $h (= AB) = 1.5$ m

$$\sin\theta = \frac{AB}{AC} = \frac{1.5}{2.5} = 0.6$$

$$\therefore \quad \cos\theta = \sqrt{1 - \sin^2\theta} = 0.8$$

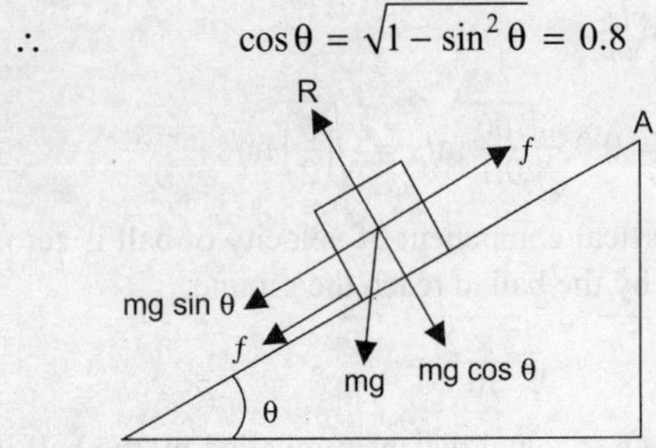

66. Work done by gravitational force to take the block from C to A is

$W_1 = (-mg \sin\theta)l$

The negative sign indicates that the gravitational force $mg \sin\theta$ is opposite to the displacement which is from C to A. Work done by the gravitational force to move the block from A to C is (because now the gravitational force is in the direction of the displacement)

$W_2 = (+mg \sin\theta)l$

$\therefore$ Total work done by the gravitational force over the round trip is

$W_G = W_1 + W_2 = 0$

This shows that gravitational force is conservative.

67. Frictional force $f = \mu R = \mu mg \cos\theta$. The applied force to move the block from C to A is

$F = mg \sin\theta + f = mg \sin\theta + \mu mg \cos\theta$

$= mg (\sin\theta + \mu\cos\theta)$

Work done by applied force to move the block from C to A is

$W_a = F \times AC = mg (\sin\theta + \mu\cos\theta) \times l$

$= 0.5 \times 10 (0.6 + 0.2 \times 0.8) \times 2.5$

$= 9.5$ J

68. Friction always opposes motion. When the block is moved from C to A, frictional force f is opposite to direction. Hence work done by frictional force in the upward journey is

$W_3 = -fl$

When the block slides from A to C, f acts upwards along the plane and is opposite to the displacement. Hence, work done by frictional force in the downward journey is

$W_4 = -fl$

$\therefore$ Total work done by frictional force over the round trip is

$W_f = W_3 + W_4 = -2fl$

$= -2\,\mu mg \cos\theta \times l$

$= -2 \times 0.2 \times 0.5 \times 10 \times 0.8 \times 2.5$

$= -4$ J

69. When the block is A, its initial velocity $u = 0$. Let v be the velocity when it reaches C. Since f acts upwards, the net force on the block when it slides down is

$F' = mg \sin\theta - f = mg (\sin\theta - \mu \cos\theta)$

$\therefore$ Acceleration

$$a = \frac{F'}{m} = g(\sin\theta - \mu\cos\theta)$$

$= 10 (0.6 - 0.2 \times 0.8) = 4.4$ ms^{-2}

From

$v^2 - u^2 = 2as$, we have

$v^2 - 0 = 2 \times 4.4 \times 2.5$

$\Rightarrow v^2 = 22$ m^2 s^{-2}

$\therefore$ Kinetic energy at $C = \frac{1}{2}mv^2$

$= \frac{1}{2} \times 0.5 \times 22 = 5.5$ J

70. (c) Applying COE,

$$mgh = \frac{1}{2}mv^2$$

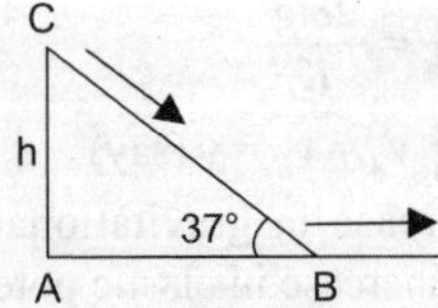

$v = \sqrt{2gh}$ ...(i)

But $\sin 37° = \frac{h}{100/3}$

$\frac{3}{5} = \frac{3h}{100} \Rightarrow h = 20$ m

Velocity before collision

$\therefore$ From Eq. (i)

$v = \sqrt{2(10(20))} = \sqrt{400} = 20$ m/s

Velocity after collision

$e = -\frac{(v_2 - v_1)}{(u_2 - u_1)}; 1 = \frac{v_2 - v_1}{20 - 0}$

$\Rightarrow v_2 - v_1 = 20$ ....(ii)

Applying COLM

$m(20) + 0 = mv_1 + mv_2$

$v_1 + v_2 = 20$ .....(iii)

From Eqs. (ii) and (iii),

$2v_2 = 40 \Rightarrow v_2 = 20$ m/s $\quad \therefore v_1 = 0$ m/s

71. (a) Impulse on the second ball $= m\,(v_2 - u_2)$

$= \frac{1}{2}(20 - 0) = 10$ N-s

72. Extension in spring will be

$$x_0 = \frac{mg}{k+k} = \frac{mg}{2k}$$

$$\Delta W = (\Delta E) = mg\left(\frac{mg}{4k}\right) + \frac{1}{2}k\left[\left(\frac{mg}{4k}\right)^2 - \left(\frac{mg}{2k}\right)^2\right] \times 2$$

$$\Delta W = \frac{m^2g^2}{16k}$$

On comparing given parameter we get $n = 4$.

73. As $N - mg = \frac{mg}{2}$

Normal force is given by $\frac{3mg}{2}$

Displacement of block is 't' sec is $\frac{1}{2}\frac{g}{2}t^2$

Work done by normal force is $\frac{3mg^2t^2}{8}$

74. From Newton's second law we get, $\frac{\Delta p}{\Delta t} = F$

$\Rightarrow \Delta p = F\Delta t$

$\therefore \quad p = \int dp = \int_0^1 F\ dt$

$\Rightarrow \quad p = \int_0^1 6t\,dt = 3\,\text{kg}\left(\frac{\text{m}}{\text{s}}\right)$

Also, $\Delta k = \frac{\Delta p^2}{2m} = \frac{3^2}{2 \times 1} = 4.5$

So, work done $= \Delta k = 4.5$ J

75. We know that change in potential energy of a system corresponding to a conservative internal force as

$U_f - U_i = -W = -\int_i^f \text{F}.dr$

Given, $\quad F = ax + bx^2$

We know that work done in stretching the rubber band by L is $|dW| = |Fdx|$

$$|W| = \int_0^L \left(ax + bx^2\right)dx = \left[\frac{ax^2}{2}\right]_0^L + \left[\frac{bx^3}{3}\right]_0^L$$

$$= \left[\frac{aL^2}{2} - \frac{a \times (0)^2}{2}\right] + \left[\frac{b \times L^3}{3} - \frac{b \times (0)^3}{3}\right]$$

$$= |W| = \frac{aL^2}{2} + \frac{bL^3}{3}$$

76. As, $r = OP = x\hat{i} + y\hat{j}$

$\therefore \quad$ Force, $\mathbf{F} = \frac{k}{(x^2+y^2)^{3/2}}(x\hat{\mathbf{i}} + y\hat{\mathbf{j}}) = \frac{k}{r^3}(\mathbf{r})$

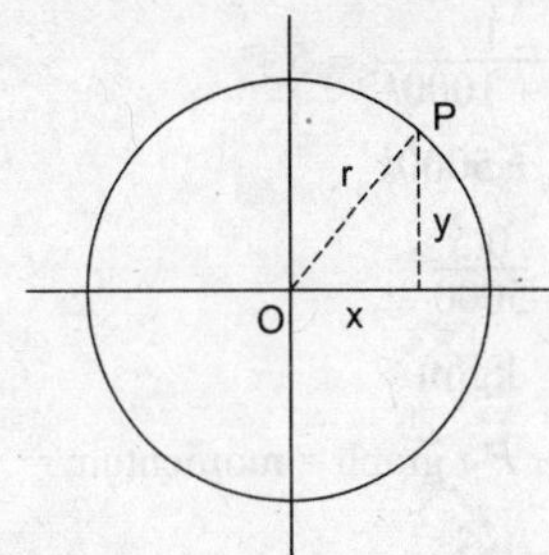

Since, **F** is along **r** or in radial direction. Therefore, work done is zero.

77. Gravitational field is a conservative force field. In a conservative force field work done is path independent

$\therefore W_1 = W_2 = W_3$

78. $W = (2\times 2) + \frac{1}{2}(1)(5) = 6.5$ J

Final K.E. = 6.5 J

79. $U = -\frac{K}{2r^3}$

$$F = -\frac{du}{dr} = \left(-\frac{K}{2}\left(-\frac{2}{r^3}\right)\right) = -\frac{K}{r^3}$$

$$\frac{K}{r^3} = \frac{mv^2}{r}$$

$$\Rightarrow mv^2 = \frac{K}{r^2}$$

$$\text{K.E.} = \frac{1}{2}mv^2 = \frac{K}{2r^2}$$

E = P.E. + K.E. = 0

80. Since, force, $F = -kv^2$

$\therefore \quad$ Acceleration, $a = \frac{-k}{m}v^2$

or $\quad \frac{dv}{dt} = \frac{-k}{m}v^2$

$\Rightarrow \quad \frac{dv}{v^2} = -\frac{k}{m}.dt$

Now, with limits, we have

$$\int_{10}^{v}\frac{dv}{v^2} = -\frac{k}{m}\int_0^t dt$$

$$\Rightarrow \quad \left(-\frac{1}{v}\right)_{10}^{v} = -\frac{k}{m}t$$

$$\Rightarrow \quad \frac{1}{v} = 0.1 + \frac{kt}{m}$$

$$\Rightarrow \quad v = \frac{1}{0.1 + \frac{kt}{m}} = \frac{1}{0.1 + 1000k}$$

$$\Rightarrow \frac{1}{2} \times m \times v^2 = \frac{1}{8} \times v_0^2$$

$$\Rightarrow \quad v = \frac{v_0}{2} = 5$$

$$\Rightarrow \quad \frac{1}{0.1 + 1000k} = 5$$

$$\Rightarrow 1 = 0.5 + 5000k$$

$$\Rightarrow \quad k = \frac{0.5}{5000}$$

$$\Rightarrow k = 10^{-4} \text{ kg/m}$$

81. Area under F-t graph = momentum = $p = \sqrt{2km}$

$$\therefore \quad k = \frac{A^2}{2m} \quad (A = \text{net area of } F\text{-}t \text{ graph})$$

$$= \frac{\left\{\left(\frac{4 \times 3}{2}\right) - \left(\frac{1.5 \times 2}{2}\right)\right\}^2}{2 \times 2}$$

$$= 5.0625 \text{ J}$$

82. Using energy conservation we get,

$$\frac{1}{2}kx^2 = \frac{1}{2}(4k)y^2$$

$$\therefore \quad \frac{y}{x} = \frac{1}{2}$$

83. If x be the maximum extension of the spring, then from conservation of mechanical energy we get,

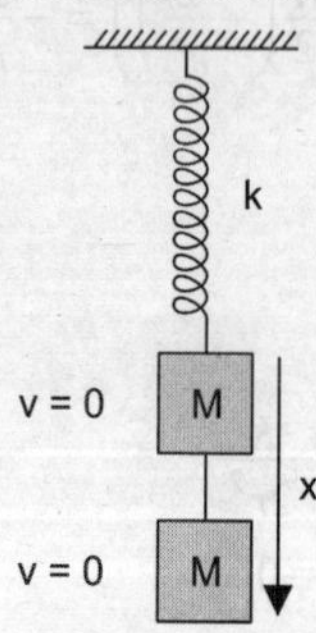

Decrease in gravitational potential energy = increase in elastic potential energy

$$\therefore \quad Mg\ x = \frac{1}{2}kx^2 \text{ or } x = \frac{2Mg}{k}$$

84. From $F = -\frac{dU}{dx}$

$$\int_0^{U(x)} dU = -\int_0^x F dx = -\int_0^x (kx)\, dx$$

$$\therefore \quad U(x) = -\frac{kx^2}{2} \text{ as } U(0) = 0$$

85. As, $K = \frac{1}{2}mv^2$

$$\Rightarrow \quad \frac{dK}{dt} = mv\frac{dv}{dt}$$

given, $\frac{dK}{dt} = \gamma t$

$$\Rightarrow \quad mv\frac{dv}{dt} = \gamma t$$

$$\Rightarrow \int_0^v v dv = \int_0^t \frac{\gamma}{m} t dt$$

$$\Rightarrow \frac{v^2}{2} = \frac{\gamma}{m}\frac{t^2}{2}$$

$$\Rightarrow \boxed{v = \sqrt{\frac{\gamma}{m}}\, t}$$

$$\Rightarrow a = \frac{dv}{dt} = \sqrt{\frac{\gamma}{m}}$$

$$F = ma = \sqrt{\gamma m} = \text{constant}$$

$$\frac{dS}{dt} = \sqrt{\frac{\gamma}{m}}\, t$$

$$\Rightarrow \boxed{S = \sqrt{\frac{\gamma}{m}}\frac{t^2}{2}}$$

86. Work done in lifting mass = (10 × 9.8 × 1) × 1000

If m is mass of fat burnt, then energy

$$= m \times 3.8 \times 10^7 \times \frac{20}{100}$$

Equating the two, we get

$$\therefore \quad m = \frac{49}{3.8} \approx 12.89 \times 10^{-3} \text{kg}$$

87. Case I:

JBC

(m) → V (2m)

JAC

V_1 ← (m) (2m) → V_2

$$2V_2 - V_1 = V$$

$$V_2 + V_1 = V$$

$$3V_2 = 2V$$

$$V_2 = \frac{2V}{3}$$

$$V_1 = \frac{V}{3}$$

$$P_d = \frac{\frac{1}{2}mV^2 - \frac{1}{2}mV_1^2}{\frac{1}{2}mV^2} = \frac{1 - \frac{1}{9}}{1} = \frac{8}{9} = 0.89$$

Case II:

JBC

(m) → V (12m)

JAC

V_1 ← (m) (12m) → V_2

$12V_2 - V_1 = V$

$V_2 + V_1 = V$

$13V_2 = 2V$

$V_2 = \frac{2V}{13}$

$V_1 = V - \frac{2V}{13} = \frac{11V}{13}$

$$\Rightarrow P_c = \frac{\frac{1}{2}mV^2 - \frac{1}{2}mV_1^2}{\frac{1}{2}mV^2} = \frac{1 - \frac{121}{169}}{1} = \frac{48}{169} = 0.28$$

88. Applying conservation of linear momentum

$mv_0 + 0 = mv_1 + mv_2$

$v_0 = v_1 + v_2$ ...(i)

$\frac{3}{2}\left[\frac{1}{2}mv_0^2\right] = \frac{1}{2}mv_1^2 + \frac{1}{2}mv_2^2$

$\frac{3}{2}v_0^2 = v_1^2 + v_2^2$ ...(ii)

Solving equation (i) and (ii)

$v_1 = \frac{v_0}{2}\left(1 + \sqrt{2}\right)$

$v_2 = \frac{v_0}{2}\left(1 - \sqrt{2}\right)$

$\vec{v}_{rel} = \vec{v}_1 - \vec{v}_2$

$\frac{v_0}{2}\left[1 + \sqrt{2} - 1 + \sqrt{2}\right] = \frac{v_0}{2} \times 2\sqrt{2} = \sqrt{2}v_0$

89. Since energy loss is same, thus

$\mu\, mg \cos\theta . (PQ) = \mu mg . (QR)$

$\therefore QR = (PQ) \cos\theta$

$\Rightarrow \quad QR = 4 \times \frac{\sqrt{3}}{2}$

$= 2\sqrt{3} \approx 3.5\text{m}$

Further, decrease in potential energy = loss due to friction

$\therefore mgh = (\mu mg \cos\theta)\, d_1 + (\mu mg)\, d_2$

$$m \times 10 \times 2 = \mu \times m \times 10 \times \frac{\sqrt{3}}{2} \times 4 + \mu \times m \times 10 \times 2\sqrt{3}$$

$\Rightarrow \quad 4\sqrt{3}\mu = 2$

$\Rightarrow \quad \mu = \frac{1}{2\sqrt{3}} = 0.288 = 0.29$

90. We have, $h = R - R\cos\theta$

Using conservation of energy

$mgR\,(1 - \cos\theta) = \frac{1}{2}mv^2$

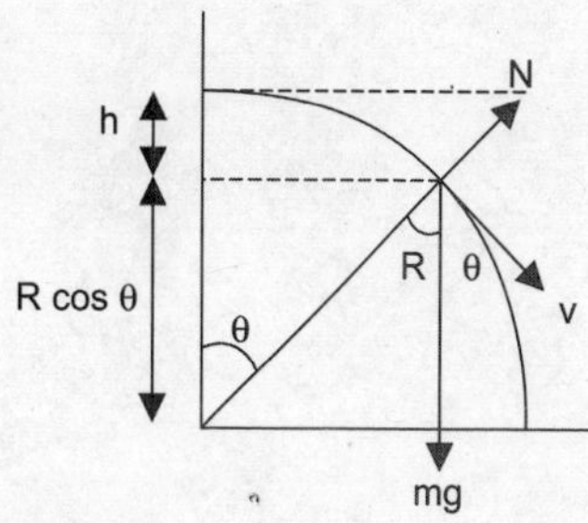

Radial force equation is

$mg\, \cos\theta - N = \frac{mv^2}{R}$

Here, N = nornal force on bead by wire

$N = mg\cos\theta - \frac{mv^2}{R} = mg\,(3\cos\theta - 2)$

$N = 0 \text{ at } \cos\theta = \frac{2}{3}$

$\Rightarrow$ Normal force act radially outward on bead, if $\cos\theta > \frac{2}{3}$ and normal force act radially inward on bead, if $\cos\theta < 2/3$

$\therefore$ Force on ring is opposite to normal force on bead.

91. As, $v = \sqrt{5gL}$ ...(i)

$\left(\frac{v}{2}\right)^2 = v^2 - 2gh$ ... (ii)

$h = L(1 - \cos\theta)$ ...(iii)

Solving Eqs. (i), (ii) and (iii), we get

$\cos\theta = -\frac{7}{8}$

or $\theta = \cos^{-1}\left(-\frac{7}{8}\right) = 151^\circ$

92. Height fallen up to point Q

$h = R\sin 30^\circ = 40 \times \frac{1}{2} = 20\,\text{m}$

Work done against friction = Initial mechanical energy – Final mechanical energy

$= mgh - \frac{1}{2}mv^2$

Putting the values, we get

$150 = 1 \times 10 \times 20 - \frac{1}{2} \times 1 \times v^2$

$\Rightarrow v = 10$ m/s

CHAPTER 6

Heat and Temperature

HEAT & TEMPERATURE

According to kinetic theory "Heat is a form of energy possess by a body due to motion of molecules.

Heat is measured in calorie or in kilocalorie.

It is the thermal state of body which determines the direction of flow of heat. Temperature can be regarded as the effect of cause of heat. If the bodies are at same temperature then they are said to be in thermal equilibrium.

Temperature Measuring Scales

Production and measurement of very low temperature (below B.P of liquid nitrogen i.e., 77°C) is called cryogenics. While measurement of very high temperature near about more than 1000 K is called pyrometry. Temperature is expressed by °C in Celsius, °F in Fahrenheit and K in Kelvin scale. While change in temperature is expressed by °C in Celsius and F° in Fahrenheit Scale. We don't use degree while reporting Kelvin temperature.

Temperature measuring scales are related as

$$\frac{C-0}{100-0} = \frac{F-32}{212-32} = \frac{R-0}{80-0} = \frac{K-273}{373-273}$$

$$\Rightarrow \quad \frac{C}{100} = \frac{F-32}{180} = \frac{R}{80} = \frac{K-273}{100}$$

Thermometers

These are temperature measuring devices. All thermometers are based on the principle that some physical properties of a system change with change in temperature. For example

(i) The volume of liquid.

(ii) Pressure of gas at constant volume.

(iii) Volume of gas at constant pressure.

(iv) Length of solid.

(v) Resistance of conductor etc.

Thermometric property is the property that can be used to measure the temperature. It is represented by any physical quantity such as length, volume, pressure, resistance etc.

Let x represents the thermometric of a physical quantity and x_0, x_{100} and x_t are its values at 0°C, 100°C and t°C respectively then

$$t = \left(\frac{x_t - x_0}{x_{100} - x_0}\right) \times 100$$

Hence,

(i) for constant volume gas thermometer we have to use

$$t = \left(\frac{p_t - p_0}{p_{100} - p_0}\right) \times 100$$

(ii) for platinum resistance thermometer we should use

$$t = \left(\frac{R_t - R_0}{R_{100} - R_0}\right) \times 100$$

(iii) and for mercury thermometer $t = \left(\frac{l_t - l_0}{l_{100} - l_0}\right) \times 100$

Apart from these, there are two more thermometers which are commonly used which are thermocouple thermometer and radiation thermometer.

Range of Thermometer

Thermometer	Lower Limit	Upper Limit
Radiation Thermometer	800°C	No limit
Thermocouple thermometer	– 200 °C	1600 °C
Platinum resistance thermometer	– 200 °C	1200 °C
Gas thermometer	– 268 °C	1500 °C
Mercury thermometer	– 30°C	300 °C

Triple Point

A substance is found to exists in three states solid, liquid and gas. For each substance there is a set of temperature and pressure at which all the three states may co-exists. This is known as triple point of substance. For water, the values of pressure and temperature corresponding to triple point are 4.58 mm of Hg and 273.15 K.

Thermal expansion

Every substance expands on heating, more or less depending on temperature and nature of substance.

Thermal expansion in solids can be classified in three ways.

(i) Linear expansion
(ii) Superficial expansion
(iii) Cubical expansion.

Linear Expansion

It is expressed as,

$$\alpha = \frac{\Delta L}{L} \times \frac{1}{\Delta\theta}$$

Here, L = original length

ΔL = change in length

$\Delta\theta$ = change in temperature

Coefficient of linear expansion is defined as fractional increase in length per C° increase in temperature.

Actually 'α' is the average value of coefficient of linear expansion over the temperature range θ °C to (θ + Δθ) so

$$\alpha = \lim_{\Delta\theta \to 0} \frac{1}{L}\frac{\Delta L}{\Delta\theta} = \frac{1}{L}\frac{dL}{d\theta}$$

S.I unit of $\alpha = K^{-1}$ or $°C^{-1}$

Superficial Expansion

It is defined as fractional increase in area per °C increase in temperature.

$$\therefore \quad \beta = \frac{\Delta S}{S\Delta\theta}$$

$$\Rightarrow \quad \Delta S = \beta S \Delta\theta$$

$$\Rightarrow \quad S = S_0(1 + \beta\Delta\theta)$$

S.I. unit of β is $°C^{-1}$ or K^{-1}

Cubical Expansion

It is defined as fractional increase in volume per °C increase in temperature.

$$\therefore \quad \gamma = \frac{\Delta V}{V\Delta\theta}$$

$$\Delta V = \gamma V \Delta\theta$$

$$\Rightarrow \quad V = V_0(1 + \gamma\Delta\theta)$$

S.I. unit = $°C^{-1}$ or K^{-1}

Relation Between α, β and γ

These are related as

$\alpha : \beta : \gamma :: 1 : 2 : 3$

For Isotropic solid

$$\alpha = \frac{\beta}{2} = \frac{\gamma}{3}$$

$$\Rightarrow \quad \beta = 2\alpha; \gamma = 3\alpha$$

For anisotropic solids

$\beta_{12} = \alpha_1 + \alpha_{21}$, $\beta_{23} = \alpha_2 + \alpha_3$ and $\beta_{31} = \alpha_1 + \alpha_3$

where β_{12}, β_{23} and β_{31} are coefficients of superficial expansions in XY, YZ and ZX plane and $\gamma = \alpha_1 + \alpha_2 + \alpha_3$.

Bimetallic Strip

If two strips of equal length but of different materials are placed on each other and riveted to form single strip. This arrangement is called bimetallic strip. This strip will bend with metal of greater co-efficient of linear expansion on outside i.e., convex side. These strips are used in auto-cut or thermostat in electric heating circuits.

The radius (R) of arc of bimetallic strip is given by

$$l_0(1 + \alpha_1\Delta\theta) = \left(R - \frac{d}{2}\right)\theta$$

For lower strip

$$l_0(1 + \alpha_2\Delta\theta) = \left(R + \frac{d}{2}\right)\theta$$

For upper strip

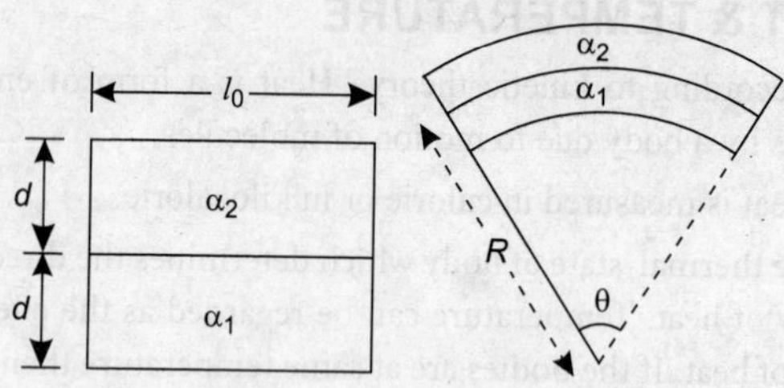

$$\Rightarrow \quad \frac{1 + \alpha_2\Delta\theta}{1 + \alpha_1\Delta\theta} = \frac{R + d/2}{R - d/2}$$

$$\Rightarrow \quad R = \frac{d}{(\alpha_2 - \alpha_1)\Delta\theta}$$

where, $\Delta\theta$ = Change in temperature.

Effect of Temperature on Scale Reading

(i) When only object expands

$l_2 = l_1[1 + \alpha(\theta_2 - \theta_1)]$

where l_1 = actual length of the object at θ_1 °C

l_2 = actual length of the object at θ_2 °C

α = co-efficient of linear expansion.

(ii) When only measuring instrument expands

In this situation scale reading = $l_1[(1 - \alpha_s)(\theta_2 - \theta_1)]$

where α_s = Co-efficient of linear expansion of measuring instrument.

(iii) When both an object and measuring instrument, a scale expands simultaneously.

In this situation scale reading = $l_1\{1 + (\alpha - \alpha_s)(\theta_2 - \theta_1)\}$

Now if, $\alpha > \alpha_s$ then scale reading is more than actual value at θ_1 °C and if $\alpha < \alpha_s$ the scale reading is less than actual value.

Hence time reading = scale reading $[1 + \alpha(\theta - \theta_0)]$

If $\theta > \theta_0$, time reading > scale reading

$\theta < \theta_0$, time reading < scale reading

Expansion of Liquid

In case of volume expansion of liquid.

$$V_L = V(1 + \gamma_L \Delta\theta)$$

whereas for volume expansion of container

$$V_C = V(1 + \gamma_C \Delta\theta)$$

So, change in volume of liquid relative to container

$$V_L - V_C = V(\gamma_L - \gamma_C)\Delta\theta$$

So, coefficient of apparent expansion of liquid, w.r.t container $\gamma_{app} = \gamma_L - \gamma_C$

$\Rightarrow \quad \Delta V_{app} = V\gamma_{app}\Delta\theta$ with $V_L - V_C = V_{app}$

Now following cases arises

(i) If $\gamma_L > \gamma_C$, $\gamma_{app} > 0$ so ΔV_{app} will be positive so level of liquid in container will rise on heating.

(ii) If $\gamma_L < \gamma_C$, $\gamma_{app} < 0$ so ΔV_{app} will be negative therefore level of liquid in the container will fall on heating.

(iii) If $\gamma_L = \gamma_C$, $\gamma_{app} = 0$ so ΔV_{app} will zero, hence level of liquid in container will be unchanged on heating. Therefore increase in height of liquid level is calculate by

$$h = \frac{\text{Volume of liquid over flow}}{\text{Area of container}}$$

$$= \frac{V_o(\gamma_L - \gamma_C)\Delta\theta}{S_o(1 + 2\alpha_C\Delta\theta)}$$

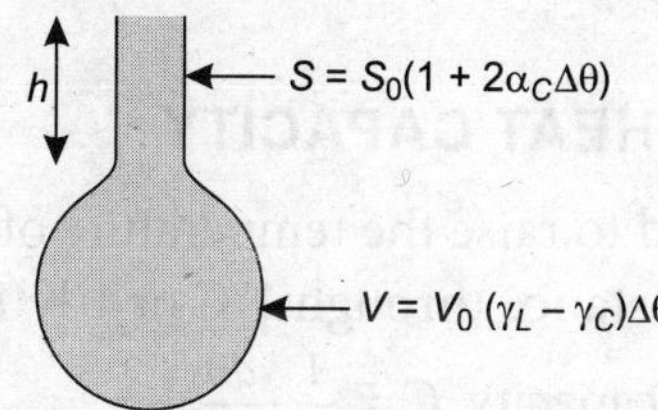

where α_c = linear expansion of container.

Variation in Density with Temperature

We know that density, $\rho = \frac{\text{Mass}}{\text{Volume}}$ or $\rho \propto \frac{1}{V}$

$$\frac{\rho'}{\rho} = \frac{V}{V'} = \frac{V}{V + \Delta V} = \frac{V}{V + \gamma V \Delta\theta} = \frac{1}{1 + \gamma\Delta\theta}$$

$$\Rightarrow \quad \rho' = \frac{\rho}{1 + \gamma\Delta\theta}$$

$$\Rightarrow \quad \rho' = \rho(1 + \gamma\Delta\theta)^{-1}$$

$$\Rightarrow \quad \rho' \approx \rho(1 - \gamma\Delta\theta)$$

Hence, with increase in temperature, density (ρ) of liquid decrease.

Effect of Temperature on Upthrust

When a solid body is completely immersed in a liquid, then there is apparent loss in its weight due to upthrust acting on it by the liquid. The apparent weight is given by $W - F$ where F = upthrust = $V_S \rho_L g$

Now with increase in temperature V_S increase while ρ_L decrease. So F may increase or decrease or remains same depending on the condition that which factor dominates on the other.

Here V_S = volume of solid.

ρ_L = density of liquid.

Now again $F \propto V_S \rho_L$

$$\Rightarrow \quad \frac{F'}{F} = \frac{V'_S \rho'_L}{V_S \rho_L} = \frac{V_S + \Delta V_S}{V_S} \cdot \left(\frac{1}{1 + \gamma_L \Delta\theta}\right)$$

$$= \left(\frac{V_S + \gamma_S V_S \Delta\theta}{V_S}\right)\left(\frac{1}{1 + \gamma_L \Delta\theta}\right)$$

$$\Rightarrow \quad F' = F\left(\frac{1 + V_S \Delta\theta}{1 + \gamma_L \Delta\theta}\right)$$

So if $\gamma_S > \gamma_L$, $F' > F$, $W_{app} < W_{app}$, fraction will increase.

If $\gamma_S < \gamma_L$, $F' < F$, $W'_{app} > W_{app}$

If $\gamma_S = \gamma_L$ $F' = F$, $W'_{app} = W_{app}$

Thus, immersed fraction will remain same.

Simply we can say

if $\quad F' > F$, body will move down

$F' < F$, body will move up

$F' = F$, body will remains at same position

Effect of Temperature on Time Period of Simple Pendulum

Let $T = 2\pi\sqrt{\frac{L}{g}}$ at a temperature θ and $T' = 2\pi\sqrt{\frac{L'}{g'}}$ at a temperature θ'.

$$\Rightarrow \quad \frac{T'}{T} = \sqrt{\frac{L'}{L}} = \sqrt{\frac{L(1 + \alpha\Delta\theta)}{L}}, (\theta' > \theta)$$

$$\Rightarrow \quad \frac{T'}{T} = (1 + \alpha\Delta\theta)^{1/2}$$

$$\Rightarrow \quad \frac{T'}{T} \approx 1 + \frac{1}{2}\alpha\Delta\theta$$

Therefore change (loss or gain) in time per unit time lapsed will be

$$\frac{T' - T}{T} = \frac{1}{2}\alpha\Delta\theta$$

Gain or loss is time, is duration of time period with $\Delta t = \frac{1}{2}\alpha\Delta\theta$ if T is the correct time period, so

(i) if $\theta' < \theta$, $T' < T$, clock becomes faster and there is gain in time

(ii) if $\theta' > \theta$, $T' > T$, clock will become slower and there is loss in time

Thermal Stress

We know that thermal strain = $\frac{\Delta L}{L} = \alpha\Delta\theta$

So, thermal stress = $Y\alpha\Delta\theta$ as $Y = \frac{\text{Stress}}{\text{Strain}}$

Also, $F = YA\alpha\Delta\theta$ as stress = $\frac{\text{Force}}{\text{Area}}$

Anomalous Expansion of Water

Water expands on heating if its temperature is greater than 4°C. In the range 0°C to 4°C water contracts on heating and expands on cooling as co-efficient of volume expansion is negative. Such a behaviour of water in the range of 0°C to 4°C is called anomalous expansion. This anomalous behaviour is due to presence of three types of molecules H_2O, $(H_2O)_2$, and $(H_2O)_3$ having different volume/mass at different temperatures. This anamalous behavior of water causes ice to form first at the surface of lake in cold weather. Different graphs related to variation of volume and density of water with temperature is shown in figures given below.

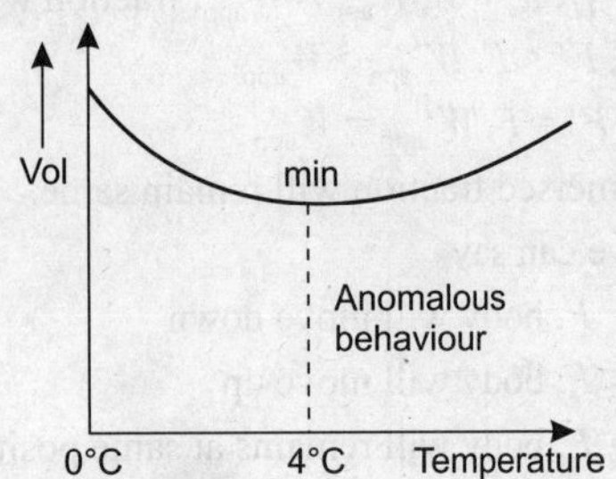

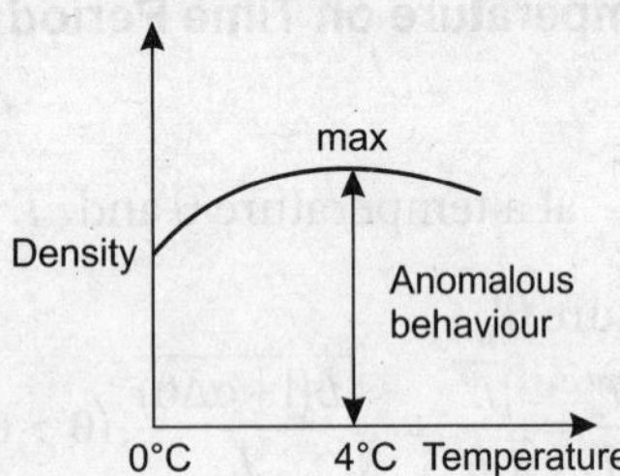

Points to Remember

(i) If α_x, α_y and α_z are co-efficients of linear expansions along x-axis, y-axis and z-axis (for anisotropic body) respectively then $\gamma = \alpha_x + \alpha_y + \alpha_z$

(ii) For water γ is negative between 0°C and 4°C.

(iii) Coefficient of apparent expansion (γ_a)

$$= \frac{\text{Apparent change in volume}}{\text{Initial vol.} \times \text{rise in temp.}}$$

In apparent expansion change in volume of container is not considered.

(iv) Coefficient of real expansion (γ_r)

$$= \frac{\text{Real change in volume}}{\text{Initial volume} \times \text{rise in temp}}$$

$$\gamma_r = \gamma_a + \gamma_c$$

(v) Increase in height of liquid level in container.

$$h = \frac{\text{Apparent change in volume of liquid}}{\text{Area of container}}$$

$$= \frac{V_0(\gamma_L - \gamma_C)\Delta\theta}{A_0(1 + 2\alpha_c\Delta\theta)}$$

(vi) Density of water is maximum at 4°C. Therefore water at the bottom of lake in winter is warmer than that at the surface.

(vii) The two rods of lengths L_1 and L_2 are placed side by side (one after other). If with increase in temperature, the difference in their lengths does not change i.e.

$$L'_2 - L'_1 = L_2 - L_1 \text{ where } L'_1 = L_1(1 + \alpha_1\Delta\theta)$$

and $L'_2 = L_2(1 + \alpha_2\Delta\theta)$

L_1, α_1

L_2, α_2

then $L_1\alpha_1 = L_2\alpha_2$

or $\dfrac{L_1}{L_1 - L_2} = \dfrac{\alpha_2}{\alpha_2 - \alpha_1}$

(viii) Coefficient of volume expansion of gas at constant temperature vary as $\gamma \propto \dfrac{1}{T}$

(ix) Let a solid body has a hole in it. Now if the temperature of the body increases, the size of hole also increases i.e., hole will expand, as every linear dimension of the body changes in the same way when the temperature changes.

SPECIFIC HEAT CAPACITY

Heat required to raise the temperature of unit mass of a substance through 1°C or 1 K, is called specific heat capacity, $C = \dfrac{1}{m} \cdot \dfrac{d\theta}{dt}$

Solid and liquid have single specific heat but gases has different specific heats ranging from negative to infinity (–ve, 0, +ve, ∞).

SI unit of specific heat is J/kg-K while practical unit is cal/gm °C.

Molar Specific Heat Capacity

It is given by, (C) $= \dfrac{1}{n} \cdot \dfrac{d\theta}{dt}$, where n = no. of moles with

$n = \dfrac{m}{M}$, where m = mass of substance, M = Molar mass of substance.

SI unit of Molar heat capacity is J/mol-K.

Some Important Terms Related to Specific Heat Capacity

(i) Specific heat of a substance depends on temperature.

(ii) Variation of specific heats with temperatures are shown in fig. (for water and metal).

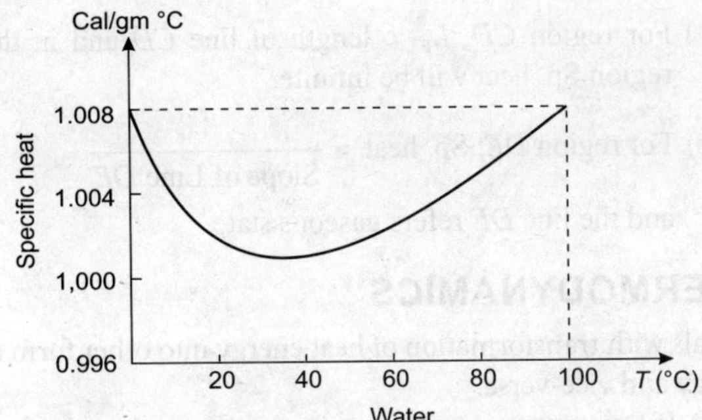

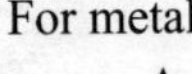

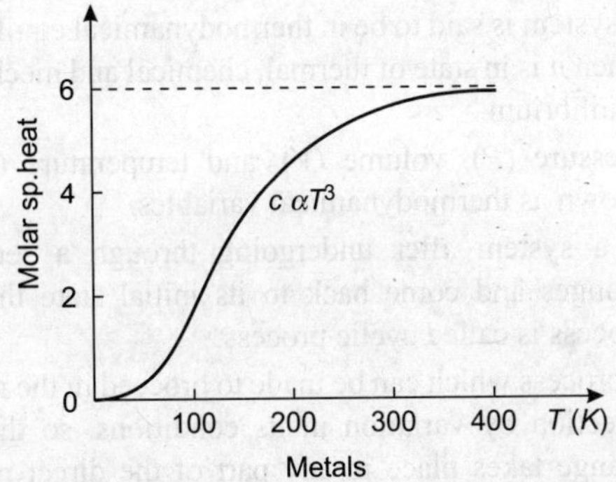

(iii) Specific heat is maximum for Hydrogen (3.5 cal/gm °C) then for water 1 cal/gm °C = 4200 J/kg K) and minimum for Radon and Actinium. For all other substances specific heat is less than 1 cal/gm °C.

(iv) Specific heat for ice (Solid) is 2100 J/kg K, for water (liquid) 4200 J/kg K and for steam (gas) it is 1970 J/kg K.

(v) For isothermal change, specific heat of gas is infinite while for adiabatic change it is zero.

(vi) If thermal capacity of a body is expressed in terms of mass of water it is called water equivalent of the body. If instead of unit mass we consider the mass of whole body then specific heat is termed as thermal capacity and is defined as amount of heat required to increase the temperature of a given body by 1°C is called its thermal capacity.

Thermal capacity = $mc = nc = \dfrac{Q}{\Delta T}$

Water-Equivalent = $(m \times c)$.

(vii) Gases has two specific heats one is specific heat at constant volume (C_V) and second is specific heat at constant pressure (C_P), such that

$C_P - C_V = R$ where R = Molar gas constant.

Note: The word capacity is misnomer as it is used for heat required per degree change in temperature and not the total amount of heat that a body can hold.

Heat of transformation

Amount of heat (Q) required to change the state of unit mass of a substance at a constant temperature is called the heat of transformation or latent heat i.e., $L = Q/m$ or $Q = mL$.

Here m = mass of the substance.

The heat of transformation during melting or freezing is called heat of fusion (L_F) while during boiling or condensation is called heat of vaporization (L_V).

It's SI unit is J/kg while practical unit is cal/gm.

Heat of transformation depends on nature and state of substance.

L_V = 540 cal/gm in C.G.S/practical units while in SI it is 2256×10^3 J/kg.

L_F = 80 cal/gm in C.G.S/practical while in SI it is 333×10^3 J/kg.

Heat of Evaporation

The amount of heat required to change unit mass of liquid into vapour at a given temperature is called heat of evaporation at that temperature. Liquid converts into gaseous phase (Vapour). Due to large heat of evaporation, water on sprinkling, produces cooling effect in a closed room.

Heat of sublimation

If a solid directly converts into gaseous phase at all temperatures then heat associated with the process is called heat of sublimation

Hoar Frost

If a vapour by releasing heat, directly comes to solid state without going through liquid phase, then the process is called Hoar Frost. Formation of snow by freezing water vapour in low temperature zone of atmosphere is an example of Hoar Frost. It is the reverse process of sublimation.

Change of state

In change of state, intermolecular distance changes. Also work is done against intermolecular force. If the molecules come closer in condensation, energy will be released and if go apart, energy will be absorbed (in boiling).

Clausius and clapeyron equations

It is given by $\dfrac{dp}{dT} = \dfrac{JL}{T_K(V_f - V_i)}$ where V_i and V_f are initial and final specific volume (cc/gm).

Important Conclusions

(i) Boiling point of every liquid rises with increase in pressure as $\dfrac{dp}{dT}$ is positive due to $V_f > V_i$.

(ii) Melting point of every substance which expands on melting (like sulphur, wax …) increases with increase in pressure as $V_f > V_i$.

(iii) Melting point of every substance which contracts on melting (Like rubber, ice….) decreases with increase in pressure as $\dfrac{dp}{dT}$ is negative due to $V_f < V_i$.

(iv) Melting of ice under the pressure and Its resolidification when pressure is released is called regelation.

CalorimetrY

It means measurement of heat. When a body is at higher temperature it releases heat while the body at lower temperature absorbs heat such that Heat lost = Heat gained.

Some Important Points

(i) Principle of calorimetry is the another form of conservation of heat energy.

(ii) Temperature of a mixture (T) can never be lesser than lower temperature (T_L) and greater than higher temperature (T_H).

$$T_L \leq T \leq T_H$$

(iii) The heat absorbed or released by a body of mass (m) is given by $Q = mC\Delta T$

where C = specific heat of body

ΔT = change in temperature in °C or K.

(iv) When state of a body changes, change of state takes place at constant temperature and heat absorbed or released is given by $Q = mL$, where L = latent heat

(v) If solid converts in liquid, heat is absorbed and if liquid converts in solid or vapour converts in liquid, heat is released.

(vi) No transfer of heat is possible if two bodies are at same temperature.

(vii) By calorimetry we are able to find specific heat and latent heat.

Heat Curve

Temperature time graph of a body as shown below is known as heat curve.

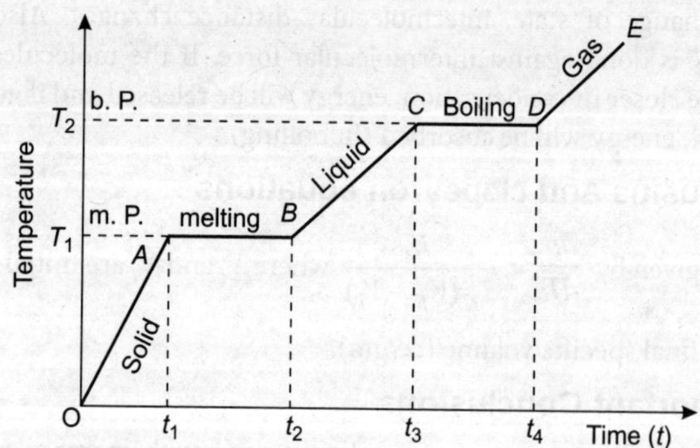

From the above graph we have

(i) For region OA,

$$C_S \propto \frac{1}{\text{Slope of Line } OA}$$ where C_S = specific heat of solid.

(ii) For region AB,

$L_F \propto$ Length of line AB. In this region specific heat will be infinite.

(iii) For region BC, $C_L \propto \dfrac{1}{\text{Slope of Line } BC}$ where C_L = specific heat of liquid.

(iv) For region CD, $L_V \propto$ length of line CD and in this region Sp. heat will be infinite.

(v) For region DE: Sp. heat $\propto \dfrac{1}{\text{Slope of Line } DE}$

and the line DE refers gaseous state.

THERMODYNAMICS

It deals with transformation of heat energy into other form of energy and vice-versa.

(i) If two systems are at same temperature, then they are in thermal equilibrium.

(ii) A system is said to be in thermodynamical equilibrium when it is in state of thermal, chemical and mechanical equilibrium.

(iii) Pressure (P), volume (V), and temperature (T) are known as thermodynamical variables.

(iv) If a system after undergoing through a series of changes and come back to its initial state then the process is called cyclic process.

(v) A process which can be made to proceed in the reverse direction by variation in its conditions, so that any change takes place in any part of the direct process are exactly reversed in the reverse process, called reversible process. Condensation and very slow evaporation are the examples of reversible process.

Conditions for Reversibility

(i) The direct and reverse processor must take place infinitely slow.

(ii) The temperature of system should not differ appreciably from its surroundings.

(iii) The dissipative forces such as friction, viscosity should be absent.

Thermodynamic Sign Conventions for Heat and Work

(i) Heat added to the system is positive ($Q > 0$).
(ii) Heat removed from the system is negative ($Q < 0$)
(iii) Work done by the system is positive ($W > 0$)
(iv) Work done on the system is negative ($W < 0$)

Zeroth law of thermodynamics

According to this law "If systems A and B are each in thermal equilibrium with a third system C separately, then A and B are also in thermal equilibrium with each other". It defines temperature as the property of the system which if equals to that of another system then two systems are in thermal equilibrium. Zeroth law of thermodynamics came to light in 1930. Later than Ist and IInd law of thermodynamics. Because the temperature is a fundamental concept for both laws, the laws that establishes temperature as a valid concept should have placed before Ist and IInd laws and hence it is called zeroth law of thermodynamics.

First Law of Thermodynamics

If we supply some heat (dQ) to a system so that the system may perform work (dW) then supplied heat is utilized in two ways, a part of supplied heat is consumed in increase the internal energy (dU, temperature) and remaining in performing work done such that,

$dQ = dU + dW$ (Heat supplied = increase in internal energy + work done by the gas)

Properties of Heat (dQ)

(i) It is path dependent.

(ii) It is the energy that is transfered between a system and its environment because of temperature difference.

(iii) It is a scalar quantity (Macroscopic).

(iv) It is taken to be positive if the system absorbs heat and negative if releases it.

(v) For solid and liquid $dQ = mL$ if there is a change of state and $dQ = mCdT$ if there is a change in temperature.

(vi) For gases when heat is absorbed and temperature changes $(dQ)_V = nC_VdT$, if volume is constant.

$(dQ)_P = nC_PdT$, if pressure is constant.

Internal Energy

It is the energy possessed by the system due to molecular motion (U_K) and molecular configuration (U_P). $U = U_K + U_P$.

Some properties of internal energy

These are

(i) Change in internal energy is path independent.

(ii) Change in internal energy depends only on the initial and final states of the system.

i.e., $dU = U_f - U_i$

(iii) For a gas $dU = nC_VdT = \dfrac{nRdT}{\gamma - 1}$ as $C_V = \dfrac{R}{\gamma - 1}$ whatever be the process no matter.

(iv) Change in internal energy of a cyclic process is always zero as for cyclic process $U_f = U_i$.

(v) As in ideal gas there is no intermolecular attraction so $U_P = 0$.

Therefore $U = U_K = \dfrac{3}{2}nRT$ with $\Delta U = \dfrac{3}{2}nRdT$

where R = molar gas constant, n = number of moles.

(vi) Change is internal energy dU of a system in case of gain is taken to be positive while it is taken to be negative if there is loss of energy.

(vii) For gas, $dU = nC_VdT = \dfrac{nRdT}{\gamma - 1} = \dfrac{P_fV_f - P_iV_i}{\gamma - 1}$

(viii) U (of an ideal gas) $= K_T + K_R$, at room temperature.

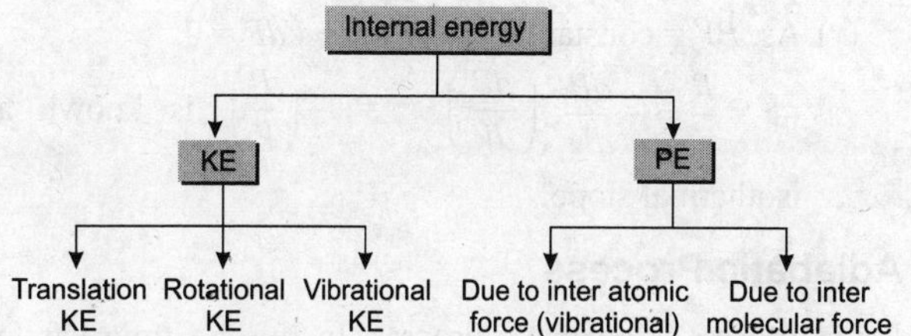

Work done (dW)

Work done by a system as it expands or contracts is given by

$$W = \int dW = \int_{V_i}^{V_f} PdV$$

(i) Work is path independent.

(ii) It is macroscopic and scalar quantity.

(iii) Work done by the system is taken to be positive while work done by the gas is taken to be negative.

(iv) For cyclic process, work done is equal to the area under the cycle and is positive if the cycle is clockwise and negative if anticlockwise.

THERMODYNAMICAL PROCESS

If state of a system changes in such a way that any of pressure (P), volume (V), temperature (T) changes, the process is called thermodynamical process.

It takes place, if the thermodynamic variables changes with time due to its interaction with its surroundings.

Isothermal Process

(i) In this, exchange of heat between system and surrounding is allowed.

(ii) Temperature remains constant or $dT = 0$.

(iii) Internal energy remain unchanged $dU = 0$.

(iv) As, $P \propto \dfrac{1}{V}$ or PV = constant, $P_iV_i = P_fV_f$.

(v) P-V graph is rectangular hyperbola.

(vi) Extremely very slow process is isothermal process.

(vii) As $dQ = dU + dW$ and here $dU = 0$ so $dQ = dW$.

(viii) Wiso $= nRT\log_e \dfrac{V_f}{V_i} = nRT\log_e \dfrac{P_i}{P_f}$

(ix) Heat supplied in an isothermal process is used to do work against external surroundings. Its PV-diagram is as shown below.

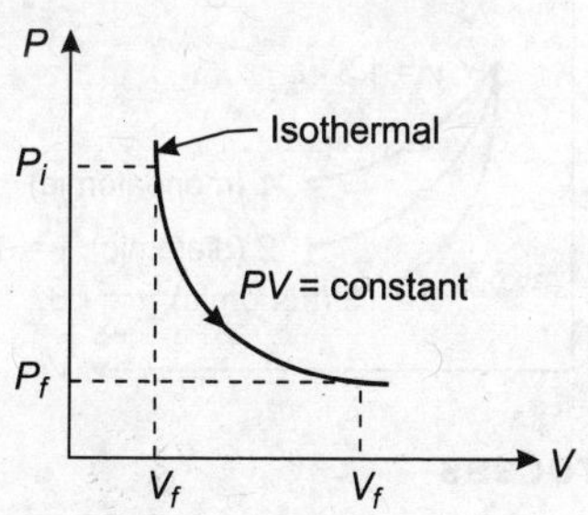

(x) As, PV = constant $\Rightarrow$ $PdV + VdP = 0$,

$$\Rightarrow \quad \frac{P}{V} = -\frac{dP}{dV}, \left(\frac{dP}{dV}\right)_{\text{iso}} = -\left(\frac{P}{V}\right)$$ is known as isothermal slope.

Adiabatic Process

Rapid process is adiabatic process. In this no time left for exchange of heat between system and surroundings ($dQ = 0$).

As $dQ = dU + dW$, and $dQ = 0$. So $dU = -dW$

$\therefore$ Work done in adiabatic process,

$$W_{\text{ad}} = \frac{nR}{\gamma - 1}\left(T_i - T_f\right) = \frac{P_iV_i - P_fV_f}{\gamma - 1}$$

State equations

These are

(i) PV^{γ} = constant with $\gamma = \dfrac{C_P}{C_V}$

(ii) $TV^{\gamma-1}$ = constant, $T_1V_1^{\gamma-1} = T_2V_2^{\gamma-1}$

(iii) $\dfrac{P^{\gamma-1}}{T^{\gamma}}$ constant, $T_1V_1^{\gamma-1} = T_2V_2^{\gamma-1}$

$$\Rightarrow \quad \frac{P_1^{\gamma-1}}{T_1^{\gamma}} = \frac{P_2^{\gamma-1}}{T_2^{\gamma}} \quad \text{where } \gamma = \frac{C_P}{C_V}$$

or $\quad T_1^{\gamma}P_1^{1-\gamma} = T_2^{\gamma}P_2^{1-\gamma}$

Slope of PV graph

These are

(i) Adiabatic slope $= -\gamma\left(\dfrac{P}{V}\right)$

(ii) Adiabatic curve is steeper than isothermal.

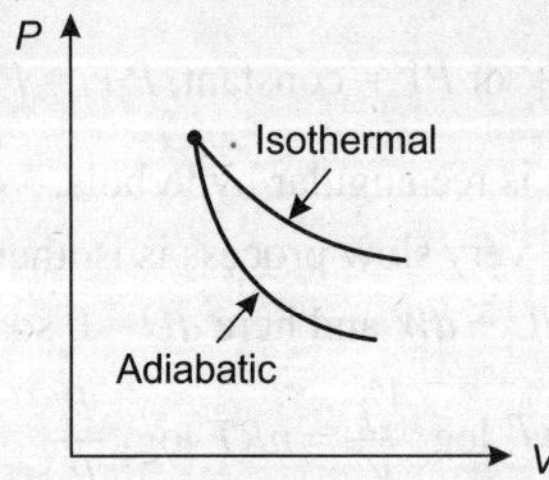

(iii) Adiabatic expansion for monoatomic, diatomic, and triatomic gases are shown in fig.

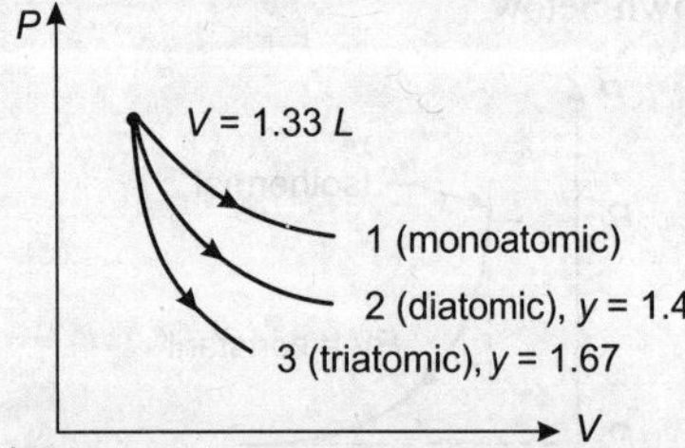

Isobaric Process

In this process, pressure is constant or $dp = 0$ (physical change at constant pressure)

State equations and work done

These are

(i) As, $V \propto T$ or $\dfrac{V}{T}$ = constant $\Rightarrow \dfrac{V_1}{T_1} = \dfrac{V_2}{T_2}$

(ii) V-T graph is straight line passing through origin.

$$\therefore \quad W_{\text{isobaric}} = \int_{V_i}^{V_f} PdV = P(V_f - V_i)$$

$$= nR\,(T_f - T_i)$$

As the temperature of the gas changes, so its internal energy also changes. Hence, in an isobaric process, the absorbed heat is utilized partly to increase internal energy and partly to do work.

Also, $dQ = nC_pdT$, $dU = nC_VdT$, $W = p\,(V_f - V_i)$

PV diagram

Isobaric expansion of a gas by PV diagram is shown in fig. given below.

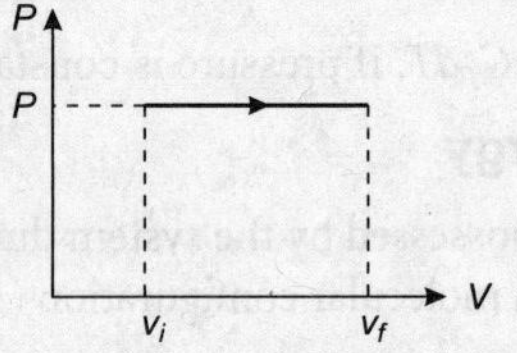

Isochoric Process

In this process volume is constant or $dV = 0$.

$$\Rightarrow \quad P \propto T \text{ or } \frac{P}{T} = \text{constant} \quad \Rightarrow \quad \frac{P_1}{T_1} = \frac{P_2}{T_2}$$

Work done and Graph

(i) P-T graph is straight line passing through origin.

(ii) As volume is constant so work done = 0, and $dQ = dU$. It means heat energy absorbed by the system goes entirely to change its internal energy. So $dQ = dU = nC_VdT$.

i.e., $\quad W = 0$

$\Rightarrow \quad dQ = dU = nC_VdT$.

(iii) Thermodynamical processes are shown in fig.

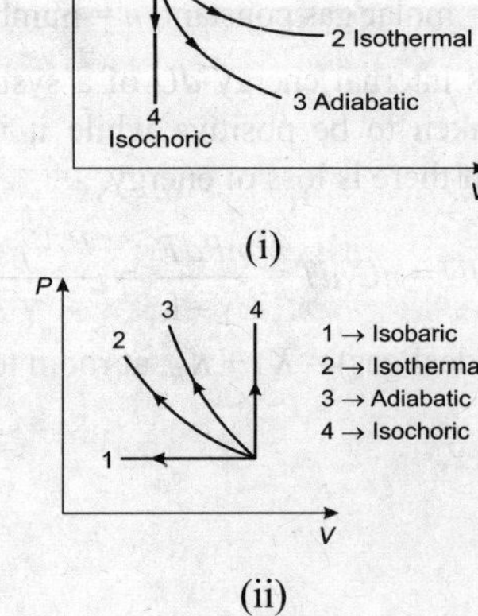

Cyclic Process

In a cyclic process, the system returns to its initial state

$\therefore \quad U_f = U_i$

$\Rightarrow \quad U_f - U_i = 0$

As $dQ = dU + dW$ and $dU = 0$ so $dQ = dW$ (heat supplied is equal to work done)

Work done

For cyclic process $W_{\text{clockwise}} = +\text{ve}$ (Shaded area)

$W_{\text{anticlockwise}} = -\text{ve}$ (Shaded area)

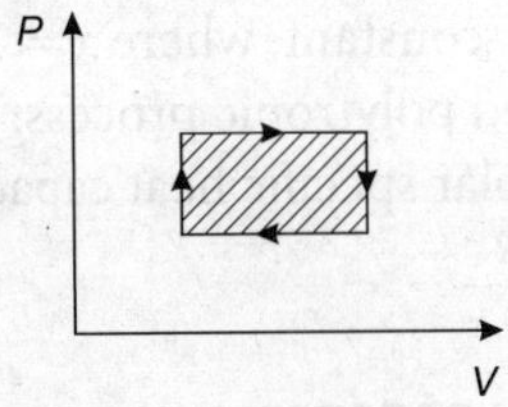

Second Law of Thermodynamics

Kelvin-Plank's Statement

It is impossible to construct an engine operating in a cyclic process to extract heat from a reservoir and convert it completely into work. In another words, whole heat can never be converted into work.

In simple way, it is not possible for an engine whose sole result is the absorption of heat from a reservoir and complete conversion of the heat into work.

Clausius Statement

It is impossible for a self acting engine unaided by any external agency to transfer heat from a cold reservoir to a hot reservoir. Simply we can say heat by itself cannot flow from a body at low temperature to a body at high temperature.

Heat engine

It is a device which converts heat into work continuously through a cyclic process. It consists of source of heat, working substance and sink as shown below.

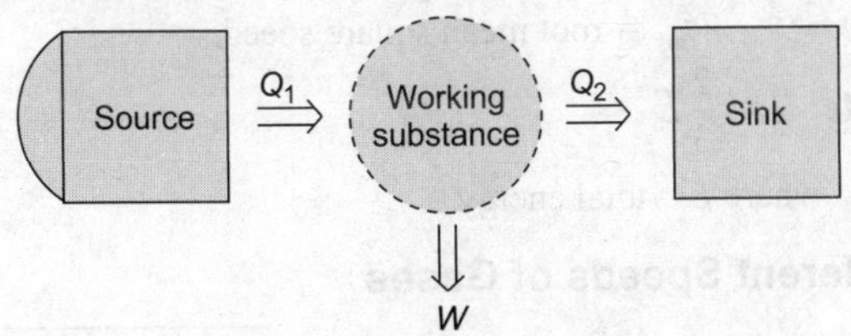

Efficiency of this engine, $\eta = 1 - \dfrac{Q_2}{Q_1}$

or $\eta = \dfrac{\text{Work done}}{\text{Heat obsorbed}} = \dfrac{W}{Q_1} = \dfrac{Q_1 - Q_2}{Q_1}$

PMM1 and PMM2

Any device (Machine) which violates the first law of thermodynamics (by creating energy) is called a perpetual motion machine of first type (PMM1) while the machine that violates the second law of thermodynamics by converting 100% of heat in work is called perpetual motion machine of second type (PMM2).

Types of Heat Engine

External combustion engine: Fuel is burnt outside the working substance. Steam engine is an example of external combustion engine. Efficiency of this engine is 12% to 20%.

Internal combustion engine: Fuel is burnt within the working substance. Diesel and petrol engines are examples of internal combustion engine. Efficiency of this engine is upto 52%.

Carnot engine

Essential parts of this engine are, source, working substance (cylinder) with perfectly non conducting wall, perfectly conducting fitted with non conducting friction-less piston. Sink and insulated pad.

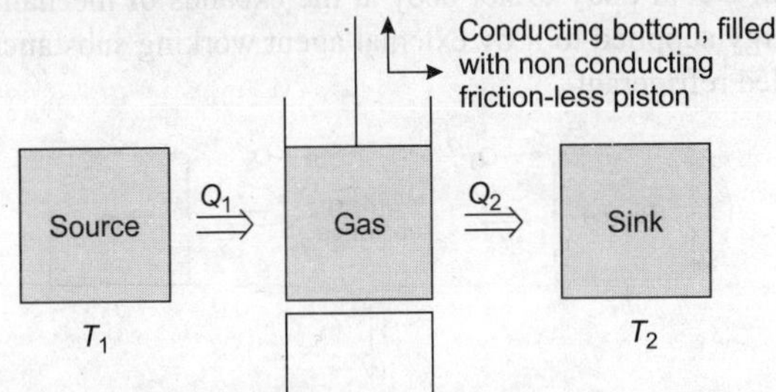

Work done

Carnot engine is taken through a reversible cyclic process through four steps as shown in figure.

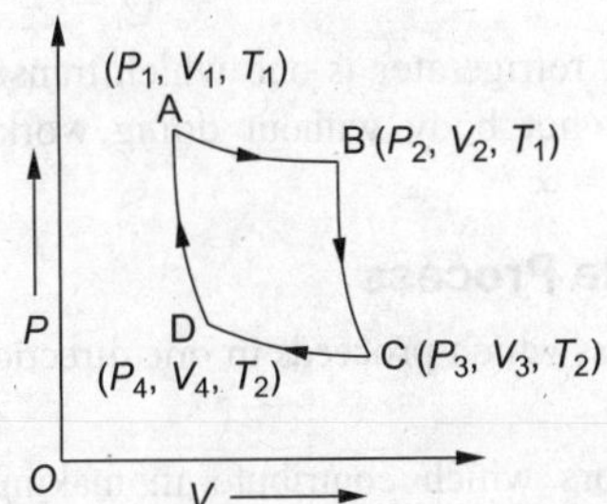

Work done during isothermal expansion (AB),

$$W_1 = Q_1 = nRT_1 \log_e \frac{V_2}{V_1} \text{ (Positive)}$$

Work done during adiabatic expansion (BC),

$$W_2 = -\Delta U = \frac{nR\Delta T}{1-\gamma}$$

Work done during isothermal compression (CD),

$$W_3 = Q_2\, nRT_2 \log_e\left(\frac{V_4}{V_3}\right) \text{ (– ve)}$$

Work done during adiabatic compression (DA),

$$W_4 = -\Delta U = \frac{nR\Delta T}{1-\gamma}$$

Efficiency

Efficiency of carnot engine $= 1 - \frac{T_2}{T_1}$

Also, Efficiency

$$= \frac{\text{Work done by working substance}}{\text{Heat supplied during the cycle}} \times 100$$

$$\Rightarrow \quad \eta = \frac{W_{\text{Total}}}{Q_{+\text{ve}}} \times 100$$

REFRIGERATOR

Refrigerator is also called heat pump. It is basically a heat engine runs in reverse direction.

In refrigerator working substance takes heat from a cold body (sink) and has a net amount of work done on it by an external agent (usually compressor) and gives large amount of heat to a hot body (usually atmosphere). It transfer heat from a cold body to hot body at the expands of mechanical energy supplied to it by external agent working substance is called refrigerant.

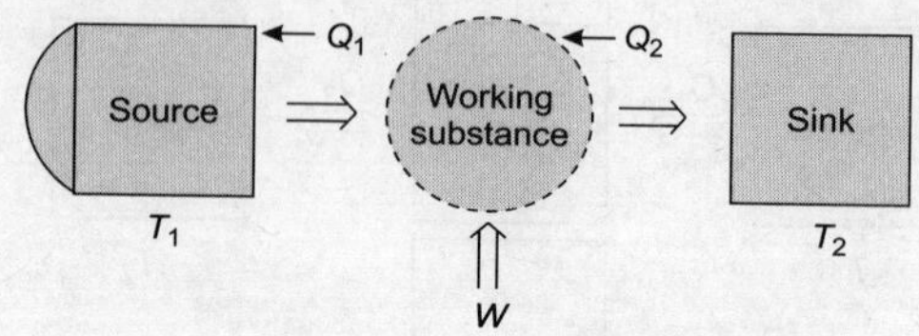

Coefficient of performance $= \frac{\text{heat external}}{\text{W.D}}$

Coefficient of performance $(k) = \frac{Q_2}{Q_1 - Q_2}$

A perfect refrigerator is one which transfers heat from cold body to hot body without doing work. i.e., $w = 0$ so $Q_1 = Q_2, K = \infty$

IRreversible Process

It is the process which proceeds in one direction and cannot be reversed.

The factors which contribute in making the process irreversible are friction, heat transfer through a finite temperature difference, mixing of two different substances and unrestrained expansion of fluid.

Thermodynamic parameters for a mixture of gases

(i) When n_1 moles of a gas with molar mass M_1 are mixed with n_2 moles of a gas with molar mass M_2 then equivalent molar mass will be

$$M = \frac{n_1 M_1 + n_2 M_2}{n_1 + n_2}$$

(ii) Internal energy of mixture $U = U_1 + U_2$

(iii) C_V of mixture $= \frac{n_1 C_{V_1} + n_2 C_{V_2}}{n_1 + n_2}$

(iv) C_P of mixture $= \frac{n_1 C_{P_1} + n_2 C_{P_2}}{n_1 + n_2}$

(v) γ of mixture will be

$$\gamma_{\text{mix}} = \frac{n_1 + n_2}{\gamma - 1} = \frac{n_1}{\gamma_1 - 1} + \frac{n_2}{\gamma_2 - 1}.$$

Polytropic process

When pressure (P) and volume (V) bears the relation PV^x = constant, where $x \neq 1$ then the process is called polytropic process. For polytropic process the molar specific heat capacity $C = C_V + \frac{R}{1-x} = \frac{R}{\gamma - 1} + \frac{R}{1-x}$.

Kinetic theory of gases

Assumptions of an ideal gas

(i) The number of particles in the gas is very large which are tiny, spherical, neutral and elastic.

(ii) Gaseous molecules are free to more in all possible directions, as intermolecular force is negligible.

(iii) Inter molecular distance is much larger as compared to their size.

(iv) The pressure of gas is due to the elastic collision of gas molecules with the wall of container.

(v) The gaseous molecules are identical in all respect.

(vi) The volume occupied by the gaseous molecules is much smaller than the volume of the gas.

Pressure of an Ideal Gas

Pressure of an ideal gas is given by,

$$P = \frac{1}{3}\frac{mN}{V} = \frac{1}{3}\frac{M}{V}V_{\text{rms}}^2$$

$$\Rightarrow \quad P = \frac{1}{3}\rho . V_{\text{rms}}^2$$

where M = Mass of the enclosed gas.

V = volume of container.

ρ = density of gas.

V_{rms}^2 = root mean square speed.

Note: $P = \frac{2}{3}E$

where E = total energy

Different Speeds of Gases

(i) Root mean square speed $V_{\text{rms}} = \sqrt{\frac{V_1^2 + V_2^2 + \cdots V_n^2}{n}}$

$$\Rightarrow \quad V_{\text{rms}} = \sqrt{\frac{3RT}{M}} = \sqrt{\frac{3P}{\rho}} = \sqrt{\frac{3K_BT}{m}} \quad \text{as } M = N_A \cdot m$$

(ii) Average speed $(V_{av}) = \dfrac{V_1 + V_2 + \cdots + V_n}{n}$

According to kinetic theory of gas.

$$V_{av} = \sqrt{\frac{8RT}{\pi M}} = \sqrt{\frac{8P}{\pi\rho}} = \sqrt{\frac{8K_BT}{\pi m}} \quad \text{where, } K_B = \text{Boltzman's constant ; } V_{av} = 0.92\ V_{rms}.$$

(iii) Most probable speed (V_{mp}) – It is the speed possessed by maximum number of gas molecules.

$$V_{mp} = \sqrt{\frac{2P}{\rho}} = \sqrt{\frac{2K_BT}{m}} = \sqrt{\frac{2RT}{M}} = \sqrt{\frac{2}{3}}\ V_{rms}$$

$$\Rightarrow \quad V_{rms} : V_{av} : V_{mp} = \sqrt{3} : \sqrt{\frac{8}{\pi}} : \sqrt{2}$$

$$\therefore \quad V_{rms} > V_{av} > V_{mp}.$$

Ideal gas equation

It is given by

$PV = RT$ for 1 mole

$\Rightarrow$ $PV = nRT$ for n moles

$PV = NK_BT$ for N moles of gas.

Values of few constants for an ideal gas

Name of Constant	Relation	Value	Dimension
(Molar gas constant)	$R = \dfrac{PV}{nT}$	8.31 J/mol-K	$[ML^2 T^{-2} k^{-1} \mu^{-1}]$
Boltzman Constant (K_B)	$\dfrac{R}{N_A}$	1.38×10^{-23} J/K	$[ML^2 T^{-2} k^{-1}]$
Avogadro's Number	$\dfrac{R}{K_B}$	6.023×10^{23} mol^{-1}	μ^{-1}

Kinetic Energy of an Ideal Gas

(i) Translational KE of molecules $= \dfrac{3}{2} K_BT$

(ii) KE of 1 mole of gas $= \dfrac{3}{2} RT$

(iii) KE of 1 gm of gas $= \dfrac{3}{2}\dfrac{R}{M} T$; where M = Molar mass of gas in gram.

Degree of freedom

(i) The total number of co-ordinates required to completely specify the position and configuration of a dynamical system is called degree of freedom (DF).

(ii) The total number of independent ways in which the position and configuration of a mechanical system may change is called degree of freedom.

(iii) The total number of independent ways in which the particle of a system can take up energy is called degree of freedom.

(iv) For 1-D motion DF will be one, For 2-D motion DF will be two and For 3-D motion DF will be three.

(v) Degree of freedom is given by $N = 3A - R$, where N = no. of degree of freedom, A = no. of atom, and R = no. of independent relation between them.

(vi) For mono atomic DF = 3

For diatomic DF = 5

For triatomic linear DF = 7

For triatomic non linear DF = 6

Note: No rotational motion is associated with point mass.

Law of Equipartion of Energy

For a dynamical system in thermal equilibrium, the energy of the system in equally distributed amongst the various degrees of freedom and the energy associated with each degree of freedom per molecule is $\frac{1}{2}K_BT$ when K_B is Boltzman constant.

Various parameters in tabular form

S.No.	Physical quantity	Monoatomic gas	Diatomic gas	Triatomic gas	
				Liners	Non-liners
1.	Atomicity	1	2	3	3
2.	Relations	0	1	2	3
3.	Degree of freedom $N = 3A - R$	3	5	7	6
4.	C_V	$3/2R$ or 2.97 cal/mol K.	$5/2R$ or 4.95 cal/mol K.	$7/2R$ or 6.92 cal/mol K.	$3R$ or 5.91 cal/mol K.
5.	C_P	5/2R or 4.95 cal/mol K.	$7/2R$ or 6.92 cal/mol K.	$9/2R$ or 8.86 cal/mol K.	$4R$ 7.88 cal/mol K.
6.	$\gamma = \frac{C_P}{C_V}$	5/3 = 1.67	7/5 = 1.4	9/7 = 1.2	4/3 = 1.33

Note: For Polyatomic $C_V = \frac{n}{2}R$

$$C_P = \left(\frac{n}{2}+1\right)R$$

$$\gamma = \frac{C_P}{C_V} = 1+\frac{2}{n}.$$

Mean free path

It is the distance travelled by molecules on an average between two successive collision of a gas molecules Mean free path is given by $\lambda = \frac{1}{\sqrt{2}\pi d^2 n}$ where d = diameter of molecules and n = no. of molecules/volume. Mean free path is also given by

$$\lambda = \frac{1}{\sqrt{2}}\cdot\frac{K_BT}{\pi d^2 P}$$

As $PV = nRT = n\,NK_BT$

So $n = \frac{N}{V} = \frac{P}{K_BT}$

$$\therefore \quad \lambda \propto \frac{1}{p} \Rightarrow \lambda \propto T \Rightarrow \lambda \propto \frac{1}{p}.$$

Points to Remember

1. The mean free path depends on nature of molecules
2. With increase in n, l decrease
3. At NTP mean free path for air molecules is 0.01 μm.

Gas law

(i) Boyle's law $V \propto \frac{1}{P}$, T is constant

(ii) Charle's law $V \propto T$, P is constant

Gas equation $PV = RT$, at constant volume $P \propto T$.

(iii) *Avogadro's law*: Equal volume of all the gases under the same condition of temperature and pressure contains the same number of molecules.

From this law $V \propto n$, P and T are constants.

(iv) *Avogadro's number* $(N_A) = 6.023 \times 10^{23}\ \text{mol}^{-1}$

(v) *Grahm's law of diffusion*: According to this law relative rates of diffusion of gases are inversely proportional to square root of their densities.

i.e., $r \propto \frac{1}{\sqrt{\rho}}$

$$\Rightarrow \quad \frac{r_1}{r_2} = \sqrt{\frac{\rho_2}{\rho_1}}$$

(vi) *Dalton's law of partial pressure*: The total pressure exerted by a mixture of non-reacting gases occupying a vessel is equal to sum of the individual partial pressure which each gas exerts, if it alone occupied that volume.

$$\therefore \quad P = P_1 + P_2 + P_3 + \ldots + P_n$$

where P = Pressure exerted by mixture and P_1, P_2 ... are partial pressures of individual gases.

Van der waal's equation

It is given by,

$$\left(P + \frac{a}{V^2}\right)(v - b) = RT$$

Here a and b are positive constants.

Critical Temperature, Pressure and Volume

(i) Gases can't be liquified above a temperature called critical temperature (T_C) how large the pressure be no matter.

(ii) The pressure required to liquified the gas at critical temperature is called critical pressure (P_C)

(iii) The volume of gas at critical temperature and pressure is called critical volume (V_C)

(iv) The values of critical constant in terms of Vander-waal's constants a and b is given by

$$V_C = 3b,\ P_C = \frac{a}{27b^2} \text{ and } T_C = \frac{8a}{27Rb}.$$

Also, $\frac{RT_C}{P_C V_C} = 8/3$ are called critical co-efficients and is same for all gases.

Heat transfer

Heat can be transferred from one place to other by three different process namely conduction, convection and radiation. Conduction usually takes place in solid, convection in fluid (liquid and gases) and no medium is required for radiation.

Heat Conduction

In this heat conduction in conductors takes place due to molecular collisions. Consider conductor through a thermal conducting rod as shown below.

L

Q_1 → Q Q_2

(i) In steady state $Q = \frac{KA(Q_1 - Q_2)}{L}t$

(ii) Rate of flow $\frac{dQ}{dt} = -KA\frac{dQ}{dx}$

(iii) Thermometric conductivity $(D) = \frac{K}{\rho_C}$, where

K = thermal conductivity, ρ_C = thermal capacity

(iv) According to Wiedemann-Franz law, $\frac{K}{\sigma T}$ = constant.

where K = thermal conductivity

σ = electrical conductivity.

This law signifies that a substance which is good conductor of heat is also a good conductor of electricity and a substance which is bad conductor of heat is also a bad conductor of electricity.

(v) Thermal resistance $R = \frac{L}{KA}$

(vi) Greater the thermal resistance, better will be the insulation and poorer will be the conduction.

(vii) For thermal resistances in series $R = R_1 + R_2$ with

$$R = \frac{L}{KA} \text{ and } H = \frac{Q_1 - Q_2}{R}$$

(viii) For thermal resistances in parallel

$$\frac{1}{R} = \frac{1}{R_1} + \frac{1}{R_2}$$

and $H = \frac{Q_1 - Q_2}{R}$

(*ix*) Time taken by ice to grow a thickness x,

$$t = \frac{\rho L}{K\theta}\int_0^x x\,dx = \frac{1}{2}\frac{\rho L}{K\theta}.x^2$$

where L = Latent heat.

(*x*) Time taken to double and triple the thickness will be in the ratio of $t_1 : t_2 : t_3 :: 1^2 : 2^2 : 3^2$

Convection

(i) In this, rate of flow of heat, $\left(\frac{dQ}{dt}\right)_{\text{Convection}} = hAd\theta$

where h = constant of proportionality called convection coefficient.

(ii) Natural convection plays an important role in ventilation, in changing climate and weather and in forming land and sea breezes and trade wind.

(iii) Forced convection of blood in our body by the pump (heart) helps in keeping the temperature of body constant.

Radiation

(i) In this heat is transferred directly from one body to another without requiring any medium.

(ii) It is the fastest mode of heat transfer.

(iii) Absorptive power (a) = $\frac{\text{Energy absorbed}}{\text{Energy incident}}$

$a \leq 1$, $a = 1$ for perfectly black body.

(iv) Spectral absorptive power

$$a_\lambda = \int_0^\infty a_\lambda d_\lambda$$

$$a_\lambda \leq 1$$

$a_\lambda = 1$ for perfectly black body

(v) Emissive power (e) is energy radiated per unit area per unit time is called emissive power with SI unit wm^{-2}

(vi) Spectral emissive power (e)

$$e = \int_0^\infty e_\lambda d_\lambda$$

(vii) According to Kirchoff's law the ratio of emissive power to absorptive power is same for all surfaces at the same temperature and is equal to the emissive power of a perfectly black body at that temperature.

$$\frac{e}{a} = \frac{E}{A}$$

For perfectly black body $A = 1$

$$\Rightarrow \quad \frac{e}{a} = E.$$

(viii) According to Stefan's law

$$E = e\,\sigma\,T^4$$

where σ = Stefan's constant = 5.67×10^{-8} W/m^2 K^4

(ix) Total energy radiated is given by

$$E = eA\,\sigma\,T^4$$

(x) Cooling by radiation is given by

$$-\frac{dT}{dt} = \frac{eA\sigma}{mc}\left(T^4 - T_0^4\right)$$

Wein's Displacement Law

According to this law the wavelength (λ_m) corresponding to the maximum intensity radiated is inversely proportional to the absolute temperature (T).

i.e. $\lambda_m \propto \frac{1}{T}$

$\Rightarrow \quad \lambda_m = \frac{b}{T}$, where $b = 2.89 \times 10^{-3}$ m-K

Variation of intensity

Intensity variation of radiation with wavelength is shown below.

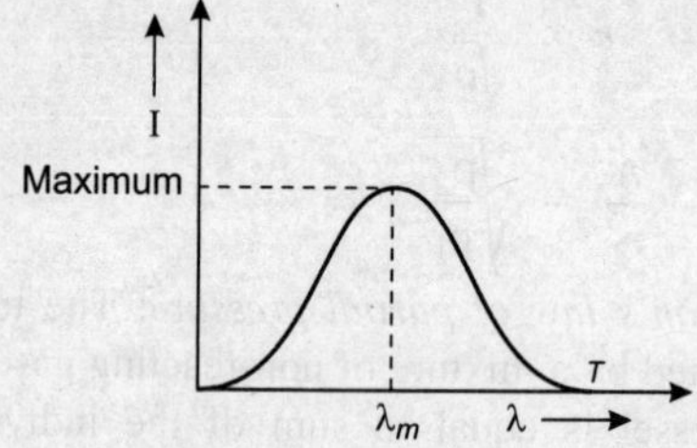

At the given wavelength (λ_m) the radiated intensity is maximum.

Newton's Law of Cooling

According to this law rate of cooling is directly proportional to the temperature difference between body and surroundings provided temperature difference should be small.

Mathematically $\frac{d\theta}{dt} \propto (\theta - \theta_0)$

$$\Rightarrow \quad \frac{\theta_1 - \theta_2}{t} = \left(\frac{\theta_1 + \theta_2}{2} - \theta_0\right)$$

Fall of temperature

The rate of fall of temperature (θ) is graphically shown below.

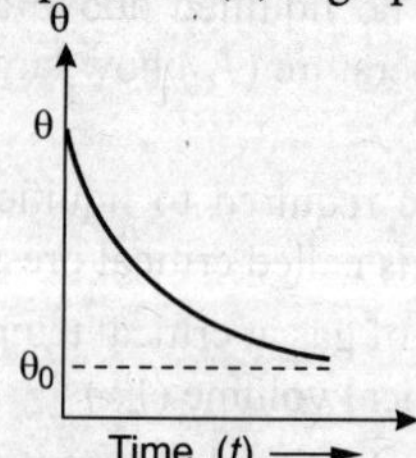

Objective Type Questions

1. Two rigid boxes containing different ideal gases are placed on a table. Box *A* contains one mole of nitrogen at T_0. While box *B* contain one mole of He at 7/3 T_0. The boxes are then put into thermal contact with each other and heat flows between them till the gases reach a common final temperature T_f. Ignore the heat capacity of boxes. Then T_f in terms of T_0 is

(a) $T_f = \frac{7}{3}T_0$ (b) $T_f = \frac{5}{2}T_0$

(c) $T_f = \frac{14}{9}T_0$ (d) $Tf = \frac{3}{2}T_0$

2. The molar specific heat at constant pressure of an ideal gas is (7/2 *R*). The ratio of specific heat at constant pressure to that at constant volume is

(a) 9/7 (b) 7/5

(c) 5/7 (d) 8/7

3. At what temperature is the rms velocity of a hydrogen molecule equal to that of an oxygen molecule at 47°C?

(a) 80 K (b) –73 K

(c) 3 K (d) 20 K

4. The average translational kinetic energy of O_2 (molar mass 32) molecules at a particular temperature is 0.048 eV. The translational kinetic energy of N_2 (molar mass 28) molecules in eV at the same temperature is

(a) 0.0015 (b) 0.003

(c) 0.048 (d) 0.768

5. A vessel contains 1 mole of O_2 gas (molar mass 32) at a temperature *T*. The pressure of the gas is *P*. An identical vessel containing one mole of He gas (relative molar mass 4) at a temperature 2*T* has a pressure of

(a) *P*/8 (b) *P*

(c) 2*P* (d) 8*P*

6. Given is the graph between $\frac{PV}{T}$ and *P* for 1 gm of oxygen gas at two different temperatures T_1 and T_2, as shown in fig. Given, density of oxygen = 1.427 kg m^{-3}. The value of *PV*/*T* at the point *A* and the relation between T_1 and T_2 are respectively :

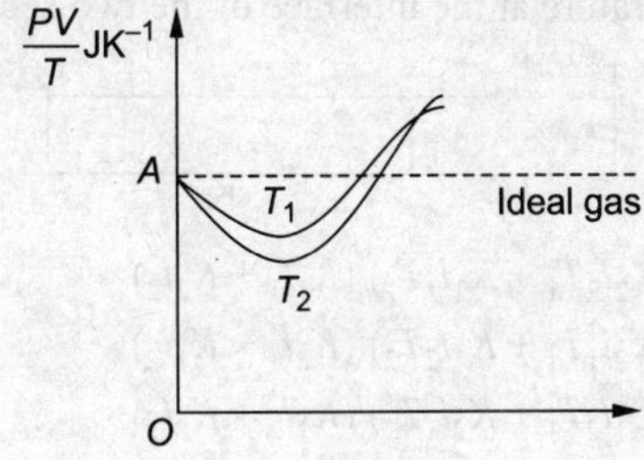

(a) 0.256 JK^{-1} and $T_1 < T_2$

(b) 8.314 J mol^{-1} K^{-1}and $T_1 > T_2$

(c) 0.256 JK^{-1} and $T_1 > T_2$

(d) 4.28 JK^{-1} and $T_1 < T_2$

7. A gas mixture consists of 2 mole of oxygen and 4 mole of argon at temperature *T*. Neglecting all vibrational modes, the total internal energy of the system is

(a) 4*RT* (b) 15*RT*

(c) 9*RT* (d) 11*RT*

8. The average translational kinetic energy and the root mean square speed of molecules in a sample of oxygen gas at 300 K are 6.21 × 10^{-21} J and 484 m/s respectively. The corresponding values at 600 K are nearly (assuming ideal gas behaviour)

(a) 12.42 × 10^{-21} J, 968 m/s

(b) 8.78 × 10^{-21} J, 684 m/s

(c) 6.21 × 10^{-21} J, 968 m/s

(d) 12.42 × 10^{-21} J, 684 m/s

9. A container with insulating walls is divided into two equal parts by a partition fitted with a valve. One part is filled with an ideal gas at *a* pressure *P* and temperature *T*, whereas the other part is completely evacuated. If the valve is suddenly opened, the pressure and temperature of the gas will be:

(a) *P*, *T* (b) $P, \frac{T}{2}$

(c) $\frac{P}{2}, T$ (d) $\frac{P}{2}, \frac{T}{2}$

10. A cylinder of radius *R* made of a material of thermal conductivity K_1 is surrounded by a cylindrical shell of inner radius *R* and outer radius 2*R* made of a material of thermal conductivity K_2. The two ends of the combined system are maintained at two different temperatures. There is no loss of heat across the cylindrical surface and the system is in steady state. The effective thermal conductivity of the system is

(a) $K_1 + K_2$ (b) $K_1K_2/(K_1 + K_2)$

(c) $(K_1 + 3K_2)/4$ (d) $(3K_1 + K_2)/4$

11. Three rods of identical cross-sectional area and made from the same metal from the sides of an isosceles triangle *ABC*, right angled at *B*. The points *A* amd *B* are maintained at temperatures *T* and $(\sqrt{2})T$ respectively. In the steady state, the temperatures of the point *C* is T_C/T. Assuming that only heat conduction takes place, T_C/T is

(a) $\frac{1}{2(\sqrt{2}-1)}$ (b) $\frac{3}{\sqrt{2}+1}$

(c) $\frac{1}{\sqrt{3}(\sqrt{2}-1)}$ (d) $\frac{1}{(\sqrt{2}-1)}$

12. Two metallic spheres S_1 and S_2 are made of the same material and have got identical surface finish. The mass of S_1 is thrice that of S_2. Both the spheres are heated to the same high temperature and placed in the same room having lower temperature but are thermally insulated from each other. The ratio of the initial rate of cooling of S_1 to that of S_2 is

(a) $\frac{1}{3}$ (b) $\frac{1}{\sqrt{3}}$

(c) $\frac{\sqrt{3}}{1}$ (d) $\left(\frac{1}{3}\right)^{1/3}$

13. A spherical black body with a radius of 12 cm radiates 450 W power at 500 K. If the radius were halved and the temperature doubled, the power radiated in watt would be

(a) 225 (b) 450

(c) 900 (d) 1800

14. A black body is at a temperature of 2880 K. The energy of radiation emitted by this body with wavelength between 499 nm and 500 nm is U_1, between 999 nm and 1000 nm is U_2 and between 1499 nm and 1500 nm is U_3. The Wien constant $b = 2.88 \times 10^6$ nm-K. Then,

(a) $U_1 = 0$ (b) $U_3 = 0$

(c) $U_1 > U_2$ (d) $U_2 > U_1$

15. The intensity of radiation emitted by the sun has its maximum value at a wavelength of 510 nm and that emitted by north star has the maximum value at 350 nm. If these stars behave like black bodies, then the ratio of the surface temperature of the sun and the north star is

(a) 1.46 (b) 0.69

(c) 1.21 (d) 0.83

16. Which one of the following is $v_m - T$ graph for perfectly black body? v_m is the frequency of radiation with maximum intensity. T is the absolute temperature

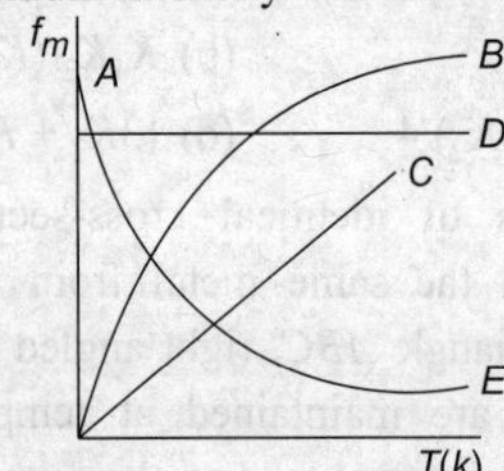

(a) A (b) B

(c) C (d) D

17. The plots of intensity (I) of radiation versus wavelength (λ) of three black bodies at temperatures T_1, T_2 and T_3 are shown in Fig. Then,

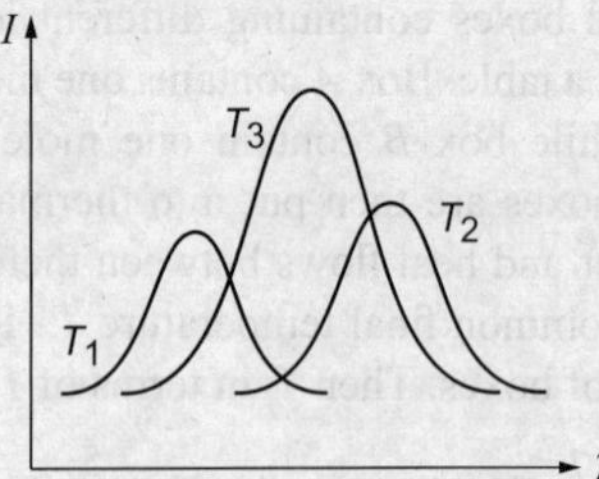

(a) $T_3 > T_2 > T_1$ (b) $T_1 > T_2 > T_3$

(c) $T_2 > T_3 > T_1$ (d) $T_1 > T_3 > T_2$

18. A black body at 1227°C emits radiation with maximum intensity at a wavelength of 5000 Å. If the temperature of the body is increased by 1000°C, the maximum intensity will be observed at

(a) 3000 Å (b) 4000 Å

(c) 5000 Å (d) 6000 Å

19. Three identical rods A, B and C are placed end to end. A temperature difference is maintained between the free ends of A and C. The thermal conductivity of B is thrice that of C and half that of A. The effective thermal conductivity of the system will be (K_A is the thermal conductivity of rod A)

(a) $\frac{1}{3} K_A$ (b) $3 K_A$

(c) $2 K_A$ (d) $\frac{2}{3} K_A$

20. Three identical thermal conductors are connected as shown in Fig. Considering no heat is lost due to radiation, the temperature of the junction is

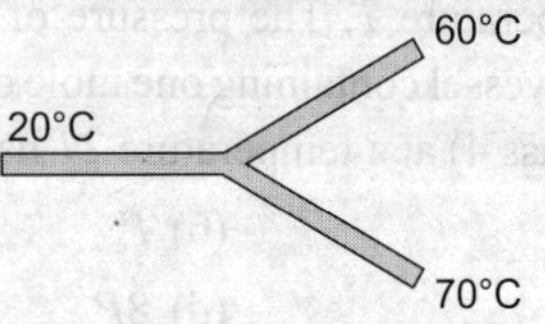

(a) 60°C (b) 20°C

(c) 50°C (d) 10°C

21. One end of a thermally insulated rod is kept at a temperature T_1 and the other at T_2. The rod is composed of two sections of lengths l_1 and l_2 and thermal conductivities K_1 and K_2 respectively. The temperature at the interface of the two sections is :

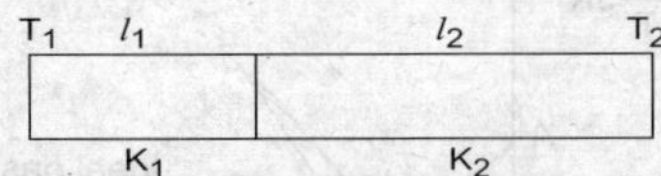

(a) $(K_2 l_2 T_1 + K_1 l_1 T_2)/(K_1 l_1 + K_2 l_2)$

(b) $(K_2 l_1 T_1 + K_1 l_2 T_2)/(K_2 l_1 + K_1 l_2)$

(c) $(K_1 l_2 T_1 + K_2 l_1 T_2)/(K_1 l_2 + K_2 l_1)$

(d) $(K_1 l_1 T_1 + K_2 l_2 T_2)/(K_1 l_1 + K_2 l_2)$

22. A long metallic bar is carrying heat from one of its ends to the other end under steady-state. The variation of temperature θ along the length x of the bar from its hot end is best described by which of the following figures?

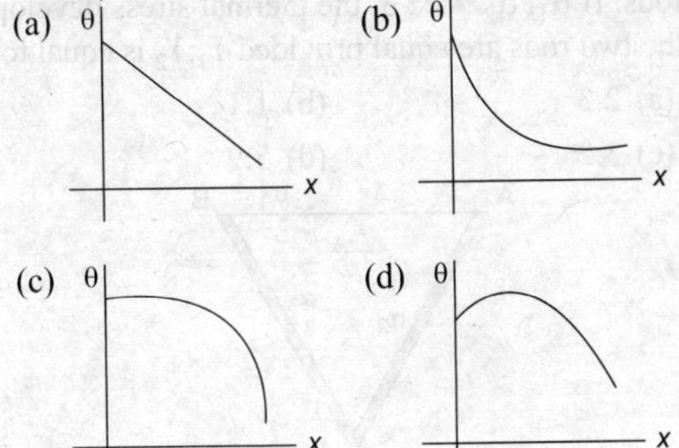

23. A Carnot engine takes 3×10^6 cal of heat from reservoir at 627°C and it to a sink at 27°C.

The work done by the engine is

(a) 4.2×10^6 J (b) 8.4×10^6 J
(c) 16.8×10^6 J (d) 2×10^6 J

24. The temperature inside and outside of a refrigerator are 273 K and 303 K respectively Assuming that the refrigerator cycle is reversible the heat delivered to surround for every joule of work done will be

(a) 20.1 J (b) 5.1 J
(c) 10.1 J (d) 30.1 J

25. The specific heat capacity of a metal at low temperature (T) is given as

$$C_P\,(\text{kJK}^{-1}\,\text{kg}^{-1}) = 32\left(\frac{T}{400}\right)^3$$

A 100 gram vessel of this metal is to be cooled from 20° K to 4° K by a special refrigerator operating at room temperature (27°C). The amount of work required to cool the vessel is

(a) equal to 0.002 kJ (b) greater than 0.148 kJ
(c) between 0.148 kJ and 0.028 kJ
(d) less than 0.028 kJ

26. Stream at 100°C is passed into 20 g of water at 10°C. When water acquires a temperature of 80°C, the mass of water present will be [Take specific heat of water = cal g^{-1}°C^{-1} and latent heat of steam = 540 cal g^{-1}]

(a) 24 g (b) 31.5 g
(c) 42.5 g (d) 22.5 g

27. A diatomic ideal gas is used in a Carnot engine as the working substance. If during the adiabatic expansion part of the cycle the volume of the gas increases from V to 32 V, the efficiency of the engine is :

(a) 0.25% (b) 0.5%
(c) 0.75% (d) 0.99%

28. 100 g of water is heated from 30°C to 50°C. Ignoring the slight expansion of the water, the change in its internal energy is (Specific heat of water is 4184 J/kg/K):

(a) 2.1 KJ (b) 4.2 KJ
(c) 8.4 KJ (d) 84 KJ

29. A Carnot engine operating between temperature T_1 and T_2 has efficiency $\frac{1}{6}$. When T_2 is lowered by 62 K its efficiency increases to $\frac{1}{3}$. Then T_1 and T_2 are, respectively :

(a) 310 K and 248 K (b) 372 K and 310 K
(c) 372 K and 330 K (d) 330 K and 268 K

30. A thermally insulated vessel contains an ideal gas of molecular mass M and ratio of specific heats γ. It is moving with speed v and is suddenly brought to rest. Assuming no heat is lost to the surroundings, its temperature increases by:

(a) $\frac{(\gamma-1)}{2R}Mv^2K$ (b) $\frac{(\gamma-1)}{2(\gamma+1)R}Mv^2K$
(c) $\frac{(\gamma-1)}{2\gamma R}Mv^2K$ (d) $\frac{\gamma Mv^2}{2R}K$

31. If 4 gram of hydrogen and 4 gram of helium are mixed and given a heat of 32 calories, such that their volume does not change. The rise in temperature of the mixture will be

(a) 1°C (b) 2°C
(c) 3°C (d) 4°C

32. A Carnot engine, having an efficiency of $\eta = \frac{1}{10}$ as heat engine, is used as a refrigerator. If the work done on the system is 10 J, the amount of energy absorbed from the reservoir at lower temperature is :

(a) 99 J (b) 90 J
(c) 1 J (d) 100 J

33. A rod of length 20 cm made of metal A expands by 0.075 cm when its temperature is raised from 0°C to 100°C. Another rod of a different metal B having the same length expands 0.045 cm for the same change in temperature. A third rod of the same length is composed of two parts, one of metal A and other of metal B. This rod expands by 0.065 cm for the same change in temperature. They portion made of metal A has the length

(a) 10 cm (b) 13.3 cm
(c) 15 cm (d) 6.7 cm

34. A pendulum clock (fitted with small heavy bob that is connected with metal rod) is 5 seconds fast each day at a temperature of 30°C and 10 seconds slow each day at temperature of 15°C. The temperature at which it is designed to give correct time is

(a) 18°C (b) 20°C
(c) 24°C (d) 25°C

35. A sphere of radius 0.049 m and mass 0.596 kg floats in a liquid bath at 0°C. The density of liquid is 1.25×10^3 kg/m^3. Assume that the sphere does not expand. If the temperature of 30°C. The temperature of the bath is raised to 40°C, the sphere just begins to sink. The volume coefficient of liquid is

(a) 8.1×10^{-4}/°C (b) 1.3×10^{-4}/°C
(c) 4.15×10^{-4}/°C (d) 2.8×10^{-4}/°C

36. A steel tape measured the length of copper rod as 90.00 cm when both are 10°C, the calibration temp-erature, for the tape. When both are at 30°C given, $\alpha_{steel} = 1.2 \times 10^{-5}$/°C and $\alpha_{Cu} = 1.7\times10^{-5}$/°C

(a) 89.00 cm (b) 90.21 cm
(c) 89.90 cm (d) 90.01 cm

37. A brass wire 2 m long at 27°C is held taut with negligible tension between two rigid supports If the wire is cooled to a temperature of –33°C, the tension developed in the wire, its diameter being 2 mm, will be (coefficient of linear expansion of brass = 2.0×10^{-5}C^{-1} and Young's modulus of brass = 0.91×10^{11} pa

(a) 680 N (b) 3400 N
(c) 6800 N (d) 340 N

38. A pendulum clock, made of a material having coefficient of linear expansion $\alpha = 9 \times10^{-7}$/°C has a period of 0.500 sec at 20°C. If the clock is used in a climate where temperature average 30°C, what correction is necessary at the end of 30 days to the time given by clock.

(a) 11.6 s (b) 3.88 s
(c) 0.100 s (d) 2.0 s

39. An iron tyre to be fitted on a wooden wheel 1.0 m in diameter. The diameter of the tyre is 6 mm smaller than that of the wheel. The tyre should be heated by a temperature of (coefficient of volume expansion of iron is 3.6×10^{-5}/°C)

(a) 400°C (b) 500°C
(c) 350°C (d) 250°C

40. A composite bar of length $L = L_1 + L_2$ is made up from a rod materials 1 and of length L_1 attached to a rod of material 2 and of length L_2 as shown. If α_1 and α_2 are their respective coefficient of linear expansion, then equivalent coefficient of linear expansion of the composite rod is

(a) $\dfrac{\alpha_1 L_2 + \alpha_2 L_1}{L}$ (b) $\dfrac{\alpha_1 L_2^2 + \alpha_2 L_1^2}{L^2}$

(c) $\dfrac{\alpha_1 L_1 + \alpha_2 L_2}{L}$ (d) $\dfrac{\alpha_1 \alpha (L_1^2 + L_2^2)}{(\alpha_1 L_1 + \alpha_2 L_2)}$

41. Two rods of different materials having coefficients of linear expansion α_1, α_2 and Young's modulii Y_1 and Y_2 respectively are fixed between two rigid massive walls. The rods are heated such that they undergo the same increase in temperature. There is no bending of rods. If $\alpha_1 : \alpha_2 = 2 : 3$, the thermal stress developed in the two rods are equal provided $Y_1 : Y_2$ is equal to.

(a) 2:3 (b) 1:1
(c) 3:2 (d) 5:9

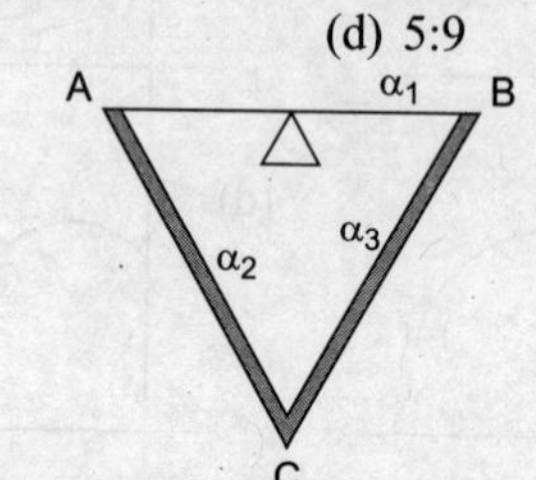

42. A vessel of volume V and linear coefficient of expansion α contains a liquid. The level of liquid does not change on heating. The volume coefficient of real expansion of the liquid is

(a) $\dfrac{V+\alpha}{V}$ (b) $\dfrac{V-\alpha}{V}$

(c) $\dfrac{V}{V-\alpha}$ (d) 3α.

43. A faulty Celsius thermometer has its fixed points marked at 5°C and 95°C respectively. What is the actual temperature of a liquid, if this thermometer reads 59°C?

(a) 64°C (b) 54°C
(c) 60°C (d) 68°C

44. The Fahrenheit and Kelvin scales in temperature will give the same reading at

(a) –40 (b) 313
(c) 574.25 (d) 732.75

45. Two thermometers, one and the other Fahrenheit are put in a hot bath. The reading on Fahrenheit thermometer is just three times the reading on Celsius thermometer. The temperature of the bath

(a) 100°C (b) (80/3)°C
(c) 80°C (d) 70°C

46. At a certain temperature dependent property of y varies according to law $y = \dfrac{\alpha(t_2 - t_1)}{1+\alpha t_2}$ where t is in °C and α is constant, and $y > 1$ is not permitted. Then the absolute zero of temperature scale based on this property in °C is

(a) $\dfrac{1}{\alpha}$ (b) 0

(c) $\dfrac{\alpha}{1+\alpha}$ (d) $-\dfrac{1}{\alpha}$

47. Three rods of equal length are joined to form an equilateral triangle ABC as shown in figure. D is the midpoint of AB. The coefficient of linear expansion is α_1 for AB, and α_2 for AC and BC.
If the distance DC remains constant for small change in temperature, then

(a) $\alpha_1 = \alpha_2$ (b) $\alpha_1 = 2\alpha_2$

(c) $\alpha_1 = 4\alpha_2$ (d) $\alpha_1 = \frac{1}{2}\alpha_2$

48. In a vertical U–tube containing a liquid the two arms are maintained at different temperatures, t_1 and t_2. The liquid columns in the two arms have height l_1 and l_2 respectively. The coefficient of volume expansion of the liquid is equal to

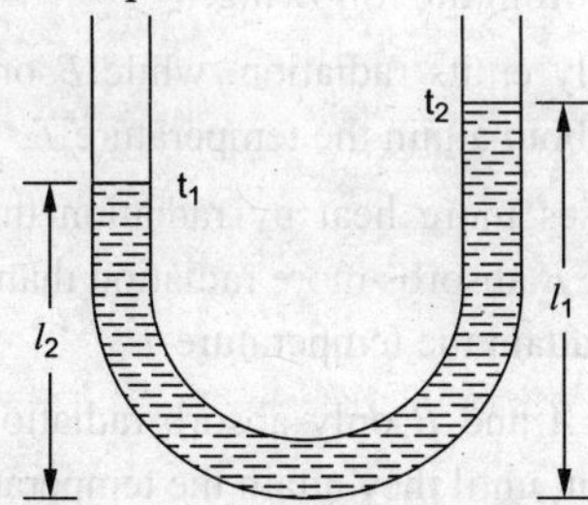

(a) $\frac{l_1 - l_2}{l_2 t_1 - l_1 t_2}$ (b) $\frac{l_1 + l_2}{l_2 t_1 + l_1 t_2}$

(c) $\frac{l_1 - l_2}{l_1 t_1 - l_2 t_2}$ (d) $\frac{l_1 + l_2}{l_1 t_1 + l_2 t_2}$

49 When a block of iron floats in mercury at 0°C, a fraction k_1 of its volume is submerged, while at the temperature 60°C, a fraction k_2 is seen to be submerged. if the coefficient of volume expansion of iron is γ_{Fe} and that of mercury is γ_{Hg}, then the ratio k_1/k_2 can be expressed as

(a) $\frac{1+60\gamma_{Fe}}{1+60\gamma_{Hg}}$ (b) $\frac{1-60\gamma_{Fe}}{1+60\gamma_{Hg}}$

(c) $\frac{1+60\gamma_{Fe}}{1-60\gamma_{Hg}}$ (d) $\frac{1+60\gamma_{Hg}}{1+60\gamma_{Fe}}$

50 The volume thermal expansion coefficient of an ideal gas at constant pressure is

(a) T (b) T^2

(c) $\frac{1}{T}$ (d) $\frac{1}{T^2}$

51. A cylindrical metal rod of length Lo is shaped into a ring with a small gap as shown. On heating the system

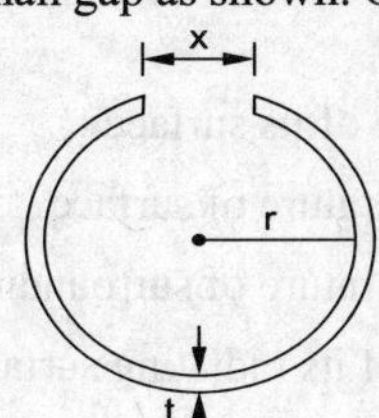

(a) x decreases, r and t increase

(b) x and r increase, t decrease

(c) x, r and t all increase

(d) data insufficient to arrive at a conclusion

52 The radius of ring is R and its coefficient of linear expansion is α. If the temperature of ring increases by θ, then its circumference will increase by.

(a) $\pi R\alpha\theta$ (b) $2\pi R\alpha\theta$

(c) $\pi R\alpha\theta/2$ (d) $\pi R\alpha\theta/4$

53. Two rods of length l_1 and l_2 are made of materials whose coefficients of linear expansion are α_1 and α_2. If the difference between the two lengths is independent of temp., then

(a) $\frac{l_1}{l_2} = \frac{\alpha_1}{\alpha_2}$ (b) $\frac{l_1}{l_2} = \frac{\alpha_2}{\alpha_1}$

(c) $l_2^2\alpha_2 = l_1^2\alpha_2$ (d) $\frac{\alpha_1^2}{l_1} = \frac{\alpha_2^2}{l_2}$

54. Two iron spheres of the same diameter are heated to the same temperature. One is solid and other is hollow. Which will expand more

(a) hallow

(b) Solid

(c) Same for hollow and solid

(d) data insufficient

55. An ideal gas is taken from the state A (P, V) to the state B $(P/2, 2V)$ along a straight line path as shown in fig. Choose the correct option

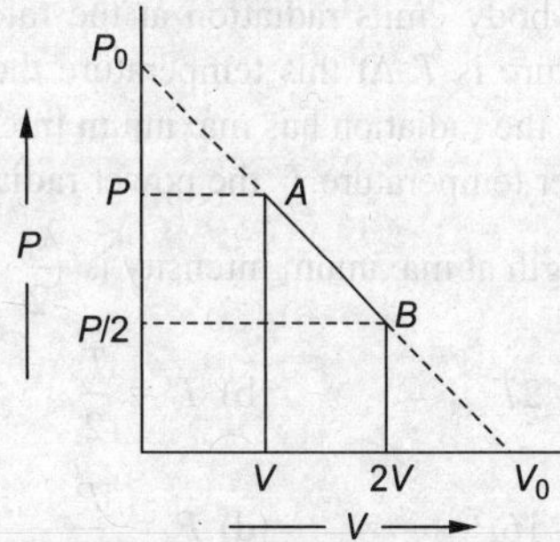

(a) In the T-V diagram, Path AB would becomes a Parabola

(b) In tP-T diagram, path would be part of hyperbola

(c) In going from A to B the temperature T of gas first increase to maximum value and then decreases.

(d) Work done by the gas in going from A to B exceeds the work done in going from A to B under constant temperature

56. Which of the following diagrams, depicts ideal gas behaviour?

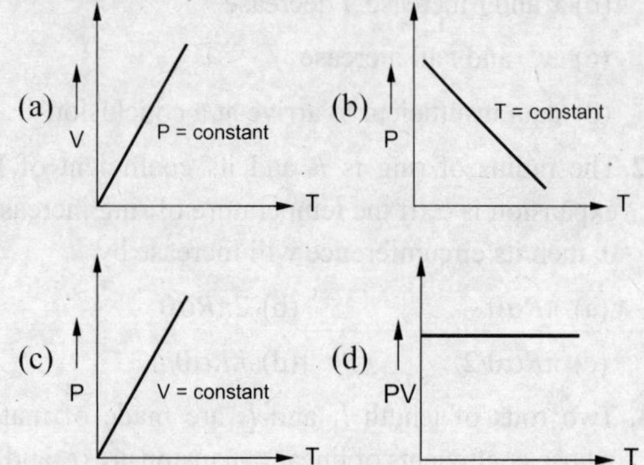

57. *ABCDEFGH* is a hollow cube made of an insulator, in the given figure. Face *ABCD* has positive charge on it. Inside the cube, we have ionized hydrogen.

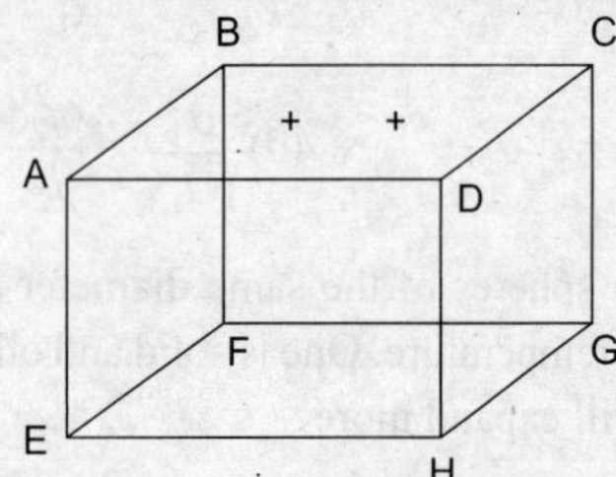

The usual kinetic theory expression for pressure
(a) will be valid.
(b) will not be valid since the ions would experience forces other than due to collision with the walls.
(c) will not be valid since collisions with walls would not be elastic.
(d) will not be valid because isotropy is lost.

58. A black body emits radiation at the rate P when its temperature is T. At this temperature the wavelength at which the radiation has maximum intensity is λ_0. If at another temperature T' the power radiated is P' and wavelength at maximum intensity is $\frac{\lambda_0}{2}$ then :

(a) $T' = 2T$ (b) $T' = \frac{T}{2}$
(c) $P' = 16P$ (d) $P' = \frac{P}{16}$

59. A black body is at a temperature of 2880 K. The energy of radiation emitted by this object between wavelength 4990 Å and 5000 Å is U_1, between 9990 Å and 10000 Å is U_2 and between 14990 Å and 15000 Å is U_3. The Wien's constant $b = 2.88 \times 10^{-3}$ mK, then
(a) $U_2 > U_1$ (b) $U_2 > U_3$
(c) $U_1 = U_3 < U_2$ (d) $U_1 < U_2 < U_3$

60. A hot body emits radiation which has maximum intensity at frequency ν_m. If the temperature of the body is doubled.
(a) the maximum intensity radiation will be at frequency $2\nu_m$
(b) the maximum intensity radiation will be at frequency $(1/2)\ \nu_m$
(c) the total emitted energy will increase by a factor 16
(d) the total emitted energy will increase by a factor 2

61. Two identical objects A and B are at temperature T_A and T_B respectively. Both objects are placed in a room with perfectly absorbing walls maintained at temperature T ($T_A > T > T_B$). The objects A and B attain the temperature T eventually. Select the correct statement from the following.
(a) A only emits radiation, while B only absorbs it until both attain the temperature T.
(b) A loses more heat by radiation than it absorbs while B absorbs more radiation than it emits until they attain the temperature T.
(c) Both A and B only absorb radiation, but do not emit it, until they attain the temperature T.
(d) Each objects continues to emit and absorb radiation even after attaining the temperature T.

62. Two Plates A and B of equal surface area are placed one on top of the other to form a composite plate of the same surface area. The thickness of A and B are 4.0 cm and 6.0 cm respectively. The temperature of the exposed surface of plate A is –10°C and that of the exposed surface of plate B is 10°C. Neglect heat loss from the edges of the composite plate, the temperature of the contact surface is T_1 if the plates A and B are made of the same material and T_2 if their thermal conductivities are in the ratio 2 : 3 then
(a) $T_1 = -4°C$ (b) $T_1 = -2°C$
(c) $T_2 = -3°C$ (d) $T_2 = 0$

63. A star appears red if the wavelength of maximum emission is in the range 620 nm to 780 nm. The corresponding temperatures of the star for maximum emission are T_1 and T_2 respectively. If Wien's constant is $b = 2.9 \times 10^{-3}$ m-K, then
(a) $T_1 = 3718$ K (b) $T_1 = 2690$ K
(c) $T_2 = 2318$ K (d) $T_2 = 4677$ K

64. The rate at which energy is radiated by hot body depends on
(a) The nature of its surface
(b) The temperature of surface
(c) The temperature of surroundings
(d) The area of its radiating surface

65. Two bodies A and B have thermal emissivities of 0.01 and 0.81 respectively. The outer surface areas of the two bodies are the same. The two bodies emit total radiant power of the same rate. The wavelength λ_B corresponding to maximum spectral radiancy in the radiation from B shifted from the wavelength corresponding to maximum spectral radiancy in the radiation from A, by 1.00 μm. If the temperature of A is 5802 K.
(a) the temperature of B is 1934 K
(b) $\lambda_B = 1.5$ μm
(c) the temperature of B is 11604 K
(d) the temperature of B is 2901 K.

66. Two spheres A and B have same radius but heat capacity of A is greater than that of B. The surface of both one painted black. They are heated to the same temperature and allowed to cool then
(a) A cools faster than B
(b) Both A and B cools at the same rate
(c) B cools faster than A
(d) at any temperature the ratio of their rates of cooling is a constant.

67. A Spherical black body of radius 'r' radiates power 'P' and its rate of cooling is R then
(a) $P \propto r$ (b) $P \propto r^2$
(c) $R \propto r^2$ (d) $R \propto \frac{1}{r}$

68. A vessel is partly filled with a liquid. When the vessel is heated, the space in the vessel, unoccupied by the liquid remains constant. The volume of the liquid (V_L), Volume of the vessel (V_V), the coefficient of cubical expansion of the material of the vessel (γ_V) and of the liquid (γ_L) are related as
(a) $\gamma_L > \gamma_V$ (b) $\gamma_L < \gamma_V$
(c) $\gamma_V/\gamma_L = V_V/V_L$ (d) $\gamma_V/\gamma_L = V_L/V_V$

69. Three bars each of length L are connected with the help of three springs as shown in fig. Coefficients of linear expansion of A,B and C are 2α, α and 4α respectively. The surface on which the arrangement is kept is smooth. If the temperature of rods have been increased by ΔT (assume there is no effect of change in temperature on springs), then mark out the correct statement (Assume that thermal stress is negligible

k 8k 4k
A B C

(a) The compression in spring having spring constant 8k is $(7/11)\alpha\, L\Delta T$
(b) The force exerted by C on the wall is $(56/11)\alpha k\, L\Delta T$
(c) The compression in all the three springs are different
(d) The compression in all the three springs is same.

70. A bimetallic strip is formed out two identical strips one of copper and the other of brass. The coefficient of linear expansion of the two metals are α_C and α_B. On heating, the temperature of the strip goes up by ΔT and the strip bends to form an arc of radius of curvature R. Then R is
(a) proportional to ΔT
(b) inversely proportional to ΔT
(c) proportional to $|\alpha_B - \alpha_C|$
(d) inversely proportional to $|\alpha_B - \alpha_C|$

71. When the temperature of a copper coin is raised by 80°C, its diameter increase by 0.2% Then.
(a) percentage rise in the area of a face is 0.4%
(b) percentage rise in the thickness is 0.4%
(c) percentage rise in the volume is 0.6%
(d) coefficient of linear expansion of copper is 0.25×10^{-4}/°C.

72. The temperature of an isotropic cubical solid of length L, density d and coefficient of expansion α per degree kelvin is raised by 10°C. Then, at this temperature, to good approximation
(a) length is $L(1 + 10\alpha)$
(b) total surface area is $6L_2(1 + 20\alpha)$
(c) density is $d(1 + 30\alpha)$
(d) density is $d/(1 + 30\alpha)$.

73. A metallic circular disc having a circular hole at its centre rotates about an axis is passing through its centre and perpendicular to its plane. When the disc is heated
(a) its angular velocity will decrease
(b) its diameter will decrease
(c) its moment of inertia will increase
(d) its speed will increase.

74. Due to thermal expansion with rise in temperature,
(a) metallic scale reading becomes less than the actual value
(b) pendulum clock becomes slow
(c) a floating body may sink if $\gamma_{liquid} > \gamma_{body}$
(d) a floating body may sink if $\gamma_{liquid} < \gamma_{body}$

Directions (Q. 75 to 77) : Solids and liquids both expand on heating. The density of substance decreases on expanding according to the relation $\rho_2 = \frac{\rho_1}{1+\gamma(T_2 - T_1)}$ where, ρ_1 and ρ_2 are the densities of substance at temperatures T_1 and T_2 respectively, when a solid is submerged in a liquid, the liquid exerts an upward force on solid which is equal to the weight of liquid displaced by submerged part of solid. Solid will float or sink depends on relative densities of solid and liquid.

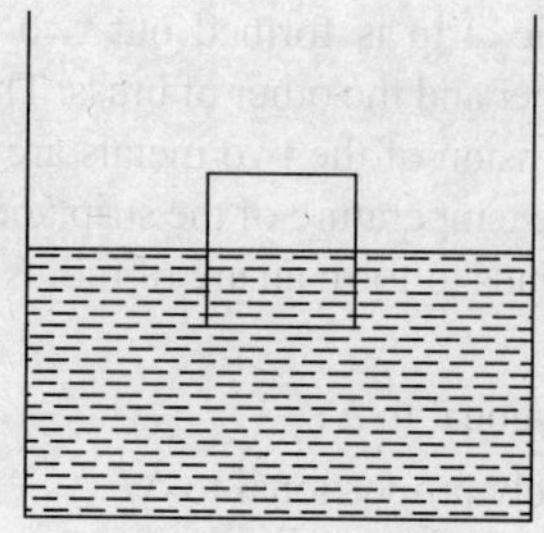

A cubical block of solid at temperature T floats in a liquid with half of its volume submerged in liquid as shown in figure. It is given that

α_s = coefficient of linear expansion of solid

γ_L = coefficient of volume expansion of solid

ρ_s = density of solid at temperature T

ρ_L = density of liquid at temperature T

75. The relation between densities of solid and liquid at temperature T is

(a) $\rho_s = 2\rho_L$ (b) $\rho_s = (1/2)\rho_L$

(c) $\rho_s = \rho_L$ (d) $\rho_s = (1/4)\rho_L$

76. If temperature of system increases, then fraction of solid submerged in liquid.

(a) increases (b) decreases

(c) remains unchanged (d) insufficient information

77. Imagine fraction submerged does not both change on increasing temperature. The relation between γ_L and α_s is.

(a) $\gamma_L = 3\alpha_s$ (b) $\gamma_L = 2\alpha_s$

(c) $\gamma_L = 4\alpha_s$ (d) $\gamma_L = (3/2)\alpha_s$.

Directions (Q. 78 to 79) : An ideal gas (monoatomic) is confined in a cylinder by a spring loaded piston of cross-section 8×10^{-3} m^2. Initially the gas is at 300 K and occupies a volume of 2.4×10^{-3} m^3 and spring is in its relaxed position. The gas is heated by a small electric heater until the piston moves out slowly by 0.1m force constant of spring is 8000 N/m and atmospheric pressure is 1×10^5 N/m^2.

78. The final temperature of the gas is

(a) 400 K (b) 350 K

(c) 800 K (d) 700 K

79. The heat supplied by the heater in joule is

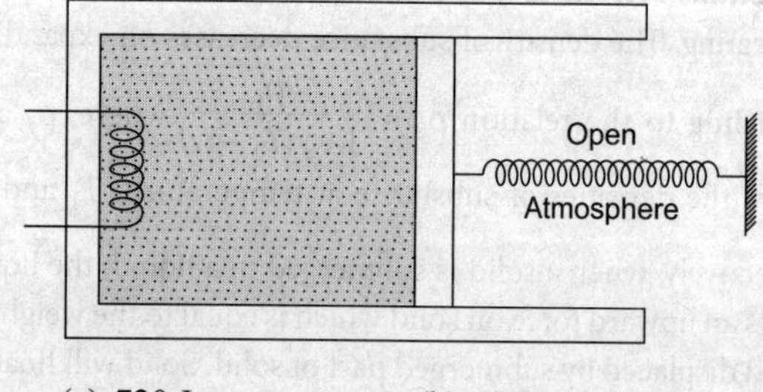

(a) 720 J (b) 520 J

(c) 620 J (d) 320 J

Directions (Q. 80 to 82) : Two moles of helium gas ($\gamma = 5/3$) are initially at temperature 27°C and occupy a volume 20 litre, The gas is first expanded at constant pressure until its volume is doubled. Now it undergoes an adiabatic change until the temperature back to its initial value.

80. The process on $P - V$ diagram is

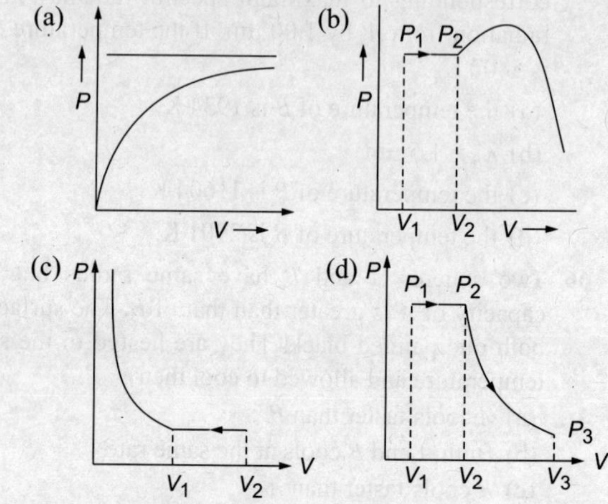

81. The final volume of gas will be

(a) 210.12×10^{-3} m^3 (b) 113.12×10^{-3} m^3

(c) 213.4×10^{-3} m^3 (d) 2.13×10^{-3} m^3

82. The find pressure of the gas will be.

(a) 0.11×10^5 N/m^2 (b) 0.22×10^5 N/m^2

(c) 0.33×10^5 N/m^2 (d) 0.44×10^5 N/m^2

Directions (Q. 83 to 85) : One mole of monoatomic ideal gas is taken through a cyclic process as shown in fig.

$A \to B$ adiabatic expansion

$B \to C$ Cooling at constant Volume

$C \to D$ adiabatic compression

$D \to A$ heating at constant volume.

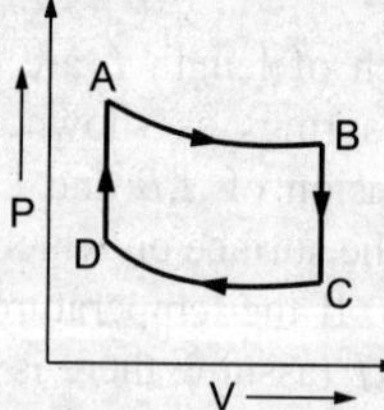

The pressure and temperature at A, B are P_A, T_A, P_B, T_B respectively. Given that $T_A = 1000$ K, $P_B = \dfrac{2}{3} P_A$, $P_C = \dfrac{1}{3} P_A$.

$(2/3)^{2/5} = 0.85$ and $R = 8.31$ J/mol K.

83. The work done by the gas in the process $A \to B$ will be

(a) 1869.75 J (b) 1069.75 J

(c) 1569.75 J (d) 1950.75 J

84. The heat lost by the gas in the process $B \to C$ will be.

(a) 5367.6 J (b) 5297.6 J

(c) 4237.6 J (d) 830.6 J

85. The temperature at D will be

(a) 400 K (b) 300 K
(c) 500 K (d) 200 K

Directions (Q. 86 to 89) : Two moles of an ideal monoatomic gas is taken through cyclic process ($ABCA$) such that pressure is inversely proportional to temperature.
The temperature $T = 300$ k.

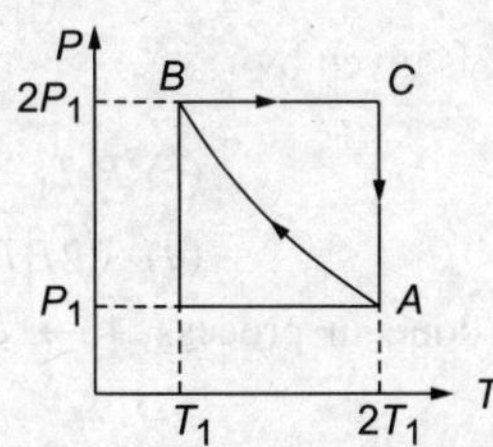

86. The work done on the gas in the process AB will be

(a) –1200 R (b) –600 R
(c) 1200 R (d) 600 R

87. Heat energy absorbed or released by the gas during the process AB will be

(a) –2100 R (b) 2100 R
(c) 1450 R (d) –1450 R

88. Heat energy absorbed or released by the gas during the process BC will be

(a) 300 R (b) 600 R
(c) 900 R (d) 1500 R

89. Heat energy absorbed or released during the process CA will be

(a) 831.6 R (b) 931.6 R
(c) 10.31 R (d) –831.6 R

Directions (Q. 90 to 92) : Two moles of a monoatomic ideal gas occupy a volume V at 27°C. The gas is expanded adiabatically to volume $2\sqrt{2}\ V$. Gas constant $R = 8.3$ JK^{-1} mol^{-1}.

90. The final temperature of the gas is

(a) $\frac{150}{\sqrt{2}}$ K (b) 150 K
(c) 150°C (d) 13.6°C

91. The change in the internal energy of the gas in this process is

(a) –3735 J (b) 1245 J
(c) –2490 J (d) +3735 J

92. The work done by the gas during the process is

(a) 1245 J
(b) 1660 J
(c) 2490 J
(d) 3735 J

Directions (Q. 93 to 95) : A sample of 2 kg of monoatomic helium (assumed ideal) is taken through the process ABC and another sample of 2 kg of the same gas is taken through the process ADC as shown in Fig. The molecular mass = 4 and R = 8.3 J K^{-1} mol^{-1}.

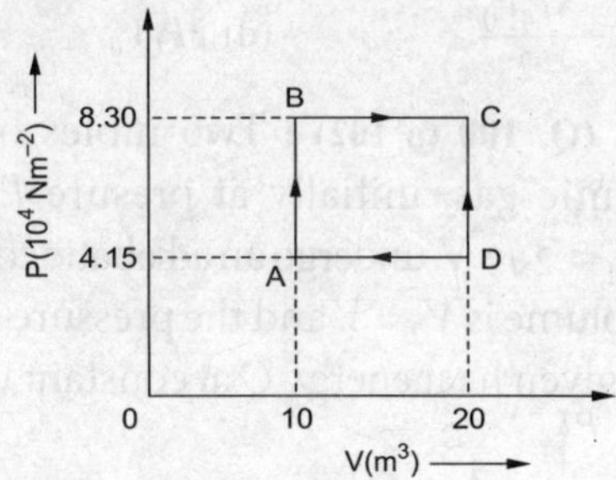

93. The temperature of state A is

(a) 100 K (b) 200 K
(c) 300 K (d) 415 K

94. The temperature state B is

(a) 150 K (b) 200 K
(c) 415 K (d) 830 K

95. The temperature of state C is

(a) 150 K (b) 300 K
(c) 400 K (d) 415 K

Directions (Q. 96 to 99) : One mole of an ideal monoatomic gas is taken round the cyclic process $ABCA$ as shown in fig.

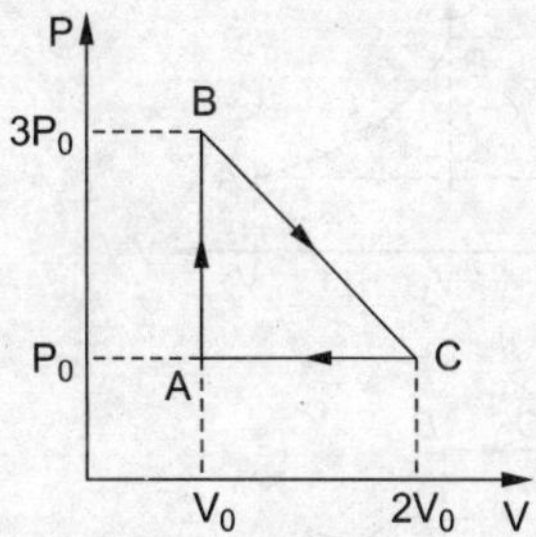

96. The work done by the gas is

(a) P_0V_0 (b) $2P_0V_0$
(c) $3P_0V_0$ (d) $4P_0V_0$

97. The heat energy rejected by the gas in the process $C \rightarrow A$ is

(a) $-\frac{P_0V_0}{2}$ (b) $-\frac{3P_0V_0}{2}$
(c) $-\frac{5P_0V_0}{2}$ (d) $-3P_0V_0$

98. The heat energy absorbed by the gas in the process $A \rightarrow B$ is

(a) P_0V_0 (b) $\frac{3P_0V_0}{2}$
(c) $\frac{5P_0V_0}{2}$ (d) $3P_0V_0$

99. The net heat energy rejected or absorbed by the gas in the process $B \to C$ is

(a) $\frac{P_0V_0}{2}$ (b) $-2P_0V_0$

(c) $-\frac{5P_0V_0}{2}$ (d) $3P_0V_0$

Directions (Q. 100 to 102) : Two moles of an ideal monoatomic gas, initially at presure $P_1 = P$ and volume $V_1 = 2\sqrt{2}$ V, undergo an adiabatic compression until its volume is $V_2 = V$ and the pressure is P_2. Then the gas is given heat energy Q at constant volume V_2.

(a)

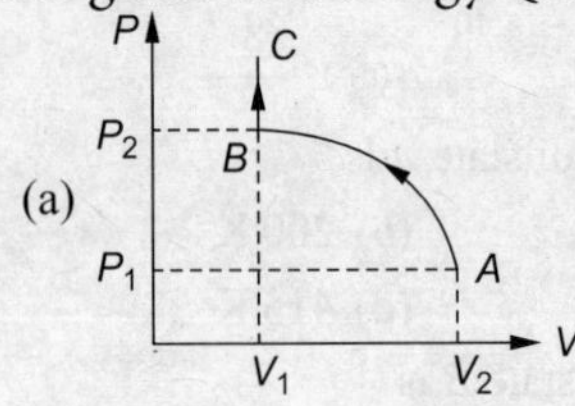

(b)

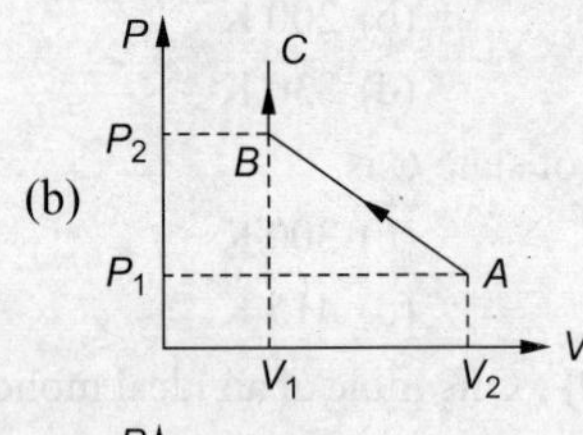

(c)

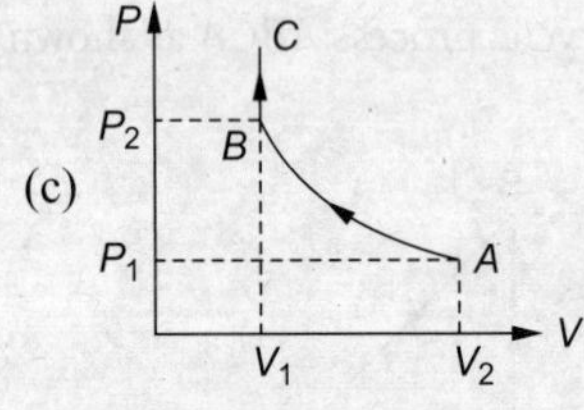

(d)

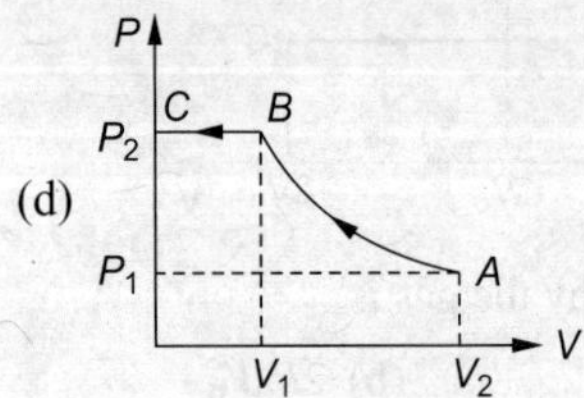

100. Which of the graphs shown in Fig. represents the $P - V$ diagram of the complete process.

101. Pressure P_2 is

(a) $\sqrt{2}\ P$ (b) $2\ P$

(c) $2\sqrt{2}\ P$ (d) none of these

102. The total work done by the gas is

(a) $-PV$ (b) $-2\sqrt{2}\ PV$

(c) $-3\sqrt{2}\ PV$ (d) $-3PV$

Directions (Q. 103 to 105) : Two moles of an ideal mono-atomic gas is taken through cycle $ABCA$ as shown in the P-T diagram During the process AB, pressure and temperature of the gas vary such that $PT = K$, where K is constant.

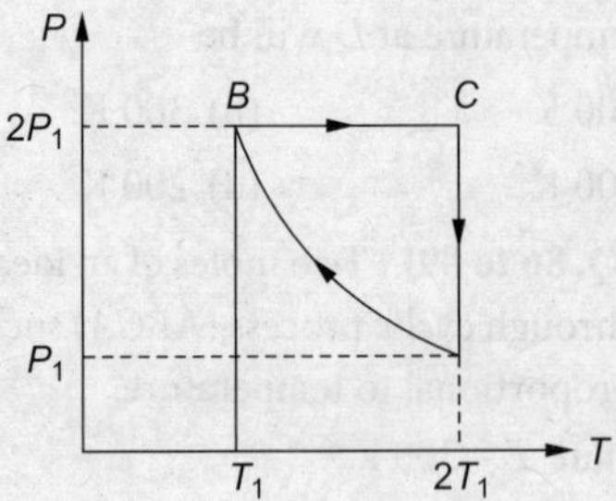

103. Constant K is given by

(a) $\frac{P_1T_1}{2}$ (b) P_1T_1

(c) $2P_1T_1$ (d) $\sqrt{2}P_1T_1$

104. The work done in process $A \to B$ is (R is the gas constant)

(a) $-RT_1$ (b) $-2RT_1$

(c) $-3RT_1$ (d) $-4RT_1$

105. The heat energy released in process $A \to B$ is

(a) $-3RT_1$ (b) $-5RT_1$

(c) $-7RT_1$ (d) $-9RT_1$

Directions (Q. 106 to 108) :

Stellar Spectra: Like the solar spectrum, the spectra of stars show a continuous spectrum on which dark aborption lines are superimposed. The inner layer (called the photosphere) of the star emits radiations of all wavelengths, producing a continuous spectrum. When these radiations pass through the outer, relatively cooler, layer of the star, the radiations of certain wavelength are selectively absorbed by this layer. This explains the dark lines in the spectrum of a star. The dark lines are characteristics of the substance present in the outer layer of the star.

The surface temperature T of a star can be estimated by measuring the wavelengths λ_m at which the intensity of the emitted radiation is maximum and then using Wien's displacement law which states that

$$\lambda_m \times T = b$$

where b is a constant called Wien's constant and the above relation is called Wien's Displacement Law which states that as the temperature increases, the maximum intensity of emission shifts (or is displaced) towards the shorter wavelengths. The value of constant b has been found experimentally to be 2.89×10^{-3} mK.

106. The spectrum of light received from a star is a

(a) continuous emission spectrum

(b) emission line spectrum

(c) emission band spectrum

(d) absorption line spectrum

107. The dark lines in the solar spectrum are due to the

(a) absence of corresponding wavelength from the light emitted by the core of the sun

(b) absorption of corresponding wavelengths by the outer layers of the sun

(c) absorption of corresponding wavelengths by the prism used in the spectrograph

(d) destructive interference between waves of certain definite wavelengths

108. The study of dark lines in the spectra of stars has revealed that the atmospheres of stars contains

(a) oxygen (b) nitrogen

(c) uranium (d) helium

Directions (Q. 109 to 111) : Three cylindrical rods *A*, *B* and *C* of equal lengths and equal diameters are joined in series as shown in the following figure. Their thermal conductivities are 2 *k*, *k* and 0.5 *k* respectively.

100°C A B C 0°C

In the steady state, the free ends of rods *A* and *C* are at 100°C and 0°C respectively. Neglect loss of heat from the curved surfaces of rods.

109. The temperature of the junction between rods *A* and *B* is

(a) 55.7°C (b) 65.7°C

(c) 75.7°C (d) 85.7°C

110. The temperature of the junction between rods *B* and *C* is

(a) 57.1°C (b) 47.1°C

(c) 37.1°C (d) 27.1°C

111. The equivalent thermal conductivity of the combination is

(a) $\frac{7k}{3}$ (b) $\frac{2k}{7}$

(c) $\frac{5k}{3}$ (d) $\frac{3k}{5}$

112. An external pressure p is applied on a cube at 0°C so that it is equally compressed from all sides. K is the bulk modulus of the material of the cube and α is its coefficient of linear expansion. Suppose we want to bring the cube to its original size by heating. The temperature should be raised by

(a) $\frac{p}{\alpha K}$ (b) $\frac{3\alpha}{pK}$

(c) $3\,pK\alpha$ (d) $\frac{p}{3\alpha K}$

113. A pendulum clock loses 12 s a day if the temperature is 40°C and gains 4 s a day if the temperature is 20°C. The temperature at which the clock will show correct time, and the coefficient of linear expansion α of the metal of the pendulum shaft are, respectively.

(a) 25°C, $\alpha = 1.85 \times 10^{-5}$/°C

(b) 60°C, $\alpha = 1.85 \times 10^{-4}$/°C

(c) 30°C, $\alpha = 1.85 \times 10^{-3}$/°C

(d) 55°C, $\alpha = 1.85 \times 10^{-2}$/°C

114. The ends Q and R of two thin wires, PQ and RS, are soldered (joined) together. Initially, each of wire has a length of 1 m 10°C. Now, the end P is maintained at 10°C, while the end S is heated and maintained at 400°C. The system is thermally insulated from its surroundings. If the thermal conductivity of wire PQ is twice that of the wire RS and the coefficient of linear thermal expansion of PQ is $1.2 \times 10^{-5}K^{-1}$, the change in length of the wire PQ is

(a) 0.78 mm (b) 0.90 mm

(c) 1.56 mm (d) 2.34 mm

115. Two identical beakers *A* and *B* contain equal volumes of two different liquids at 60°C each and left to cool down. Liquid in *A* has density of 8×10^2 kg/m^3 and specific heat of 2000J kg^{-1} k^{-1} while liquid in *B* has density of 10^3 kg m^{-3} and specific heat of 4000J kg^{-1}k^{-1}. Which of the following beat describes their temperature vtersus time graph schematically? (Assume the emissivity of both the beakers to be the same)

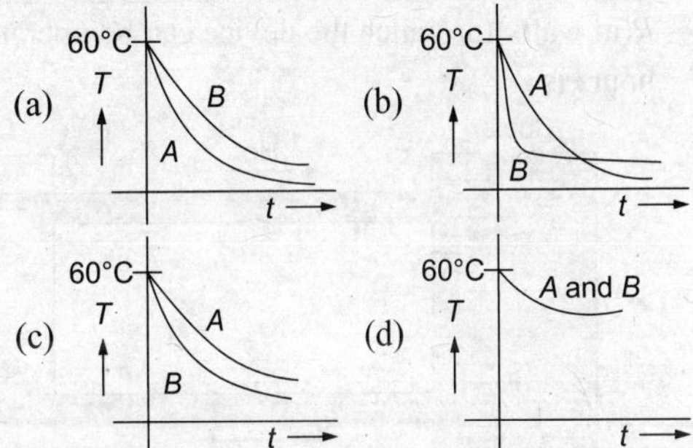

116. A thermally insulated vessel contains 150 g of water at 0°C. Then the air from the vessel is pumped out adiabatically. A fraction of water turns into ice and the rest evaporates at 0°C itself. The mass of evaporated water will be closest to :

(Latent heat of vaporization of water = 2.10 × 106 J kg^{-1})

(a) 35 g (b) 20 g

(c) 130 g (d) 150 g

117. Two moles of an ideal monoatomic gas occupies a volume V at 27°C. The gas expands adiabatically to a volume $2V$. Calculate (a) the final temperature of the gas and (b) change in its internal energy.

(a) (i) 189 K (ii) – 2.7 K

(b) (i) 195 K (ii) – 2.7 kJ

(c) (i) 189 K (ii) 2.7 kJ

(d) (i) 195 K (ii) – 2.7 kJ

118. C_p and C_v are specific heats at constant pressure and constant volume, respectively. It is observed that $C_p - C_v = a$ for hydrogen gas $C_p - C_v = b$ for nitrogen gas. The correct relation between a and b is

(a) $a = b$ (b) $a = 14b$

(c) $a = 28b$ (d) $a = \frac{1}{14}b$

119. A copper ball of mass 100 g is at a temperature T. It is dropped in a copper calorimeter of mass 100 g, filled with 170 g of water at room temperature. Subsequently, the temperature of the system is found to be 75°C. T is (Given, room temperature = 30°C, specific heat of copper = 0.1 cal/g°C)

(a) 885°C (b) 1250°C

(c) 825°C (d) 800°C

120. A water cooler of storage capacity 120 litres can cool water at a constant rate of P watts. In a closed circulation system (as shown schematically in the figure), the water from the cooler is used to cool an external device that generates constantly 3 kW of heat (thermal load). The temperature of water fed into the device cannot exceed 30°C and the entire stored 120 litres of water is initially cooled to 10°C. The entire system is thermally insulated. The minimum value of P(in watts)for which the device can be operated for 3 hours is

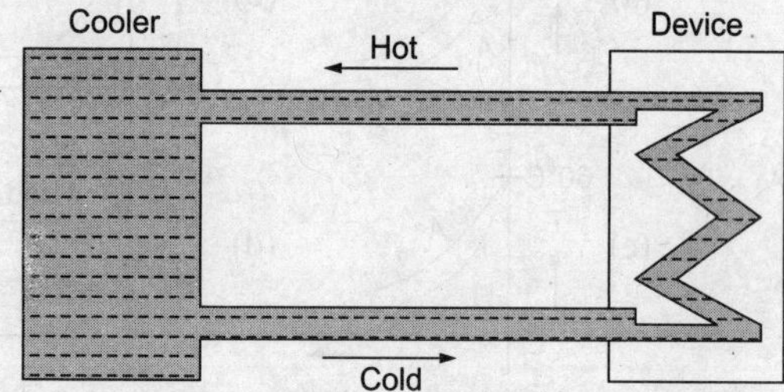

(Specific heat of water is 4.2 kJ kg^{-1}K^{-1} and the density of water is 1000 kg m^{-3})

(a) 1600 (b) 2067

(c) 2533 (d) 3933

121. n moles of an ideal gas undergoes a process A and B as shown in the figure. The maximum temperature of the gas during the process will be

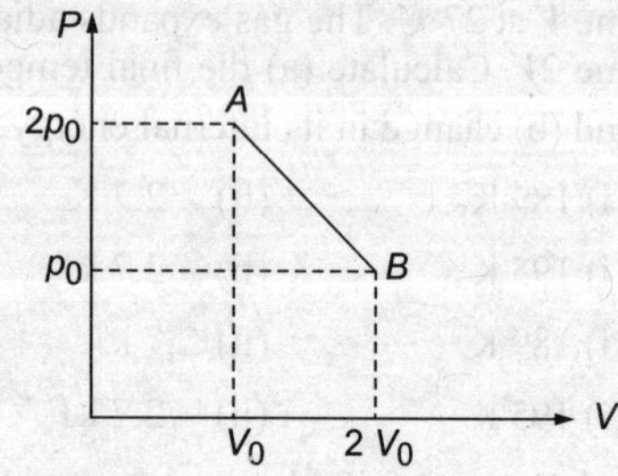

(a) $\dfrac{9p_0v_0}{4nR}$ (b) $\dfrac{3p_0v_0}{2nR}$

(c) $\dfrac{9p_0v_0}{2nR}$ (d) $\dfrac{9p_0v_0}{nR}$

122. A gas is enclosed in a cylinder with a movable frictionless piston. Its initial thermodynamic state at pressure $p_i = 10^5$ pa and volume $V_1 = 10^{-3}$ m^3 changes to a final state at $P_f = (1/32) \times 10^5$ pa and $V_f = 8 \times 10^{-3}$m^3 in adiabatic Quasi–static process, such that p^3V^5 = constant. Consider another thermodynamic process that brings the system from the same initial state to the same final state in two steps: an isobaric expansion at p_i followed by an isochoric (isovolumetric) process at volume V_f. The amount of heat supplied to the system in the two-step process is approximately

(a) 112 J (b) 294 J

(c) 588 J (d) 813 J

123. Consider a spherical shell of radius R at temperature T. The black body radiation inside it can be considered as an ideal gas of photons with internal energy per unit volume $u = \dfrac{U}{V} \propto T^4$ and pressure $p = \dfrac{1}{3}\left(\dfrac{U}{V}\right)$. If the shell now undergoes an adiabatic expansion, the relation between T and R is

(a) $T \propto e^{-R}$ (b) $T \propto \dfrac{1}{R}$

(c) $T \propto e^{-3R}$ (d) $T \propto \dfrac{1}{R^3}$

124. A solid body of constant heat capacity 1 J/°C being heated by keeping it in contact with reservoirs in two ways

(i) Sequentially keeping in contact with 2 reservoirs such that each reservoir supplies same amount of heat

(ii) Sequentially keeping in contact with 8 reservoirs such that each reservoir supplies same amount of heat.

In both the cases, body is brought from initial temperature 100°C to final temperature 200°C. Entropy change of the body in the two cases respectively, is

(a) In (2), In 2 (b) In 2, 2 In 2

(c) 2 In 2, 8 In 2 (d) In 2, 4 In 2

125. One mole of diatomic ideal gas undergoes a cyclic process ABC as shown in figure. The process BC is adiabatic. The temperature at A, B and C are 400 K, 800 K and 600 K respectively. Choose the correct statement.

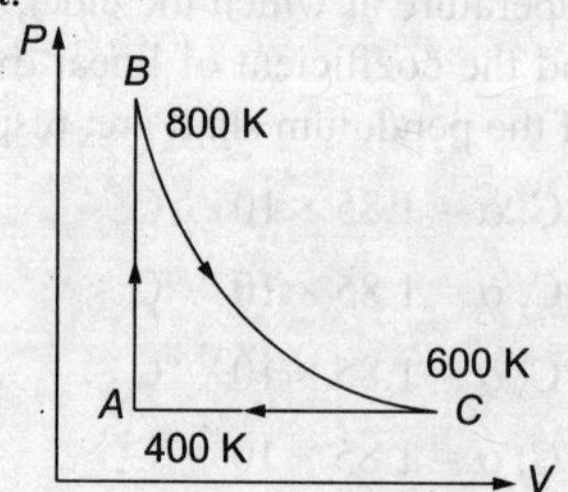

(a) The change in internal energy in whole cyclic process is 250 R

(b) The change in internal energy in the process CA is 700 R

(c) The change in internal energy in the process AB is −350 R

(d) The change in internal energy in the process BC is − 500 R

126. The shown p-V diagram represents the thermodynamic cycle of an engine, operating with an ideal monoatomic gas. The amount of heat, extracted from the source in a single cycle is

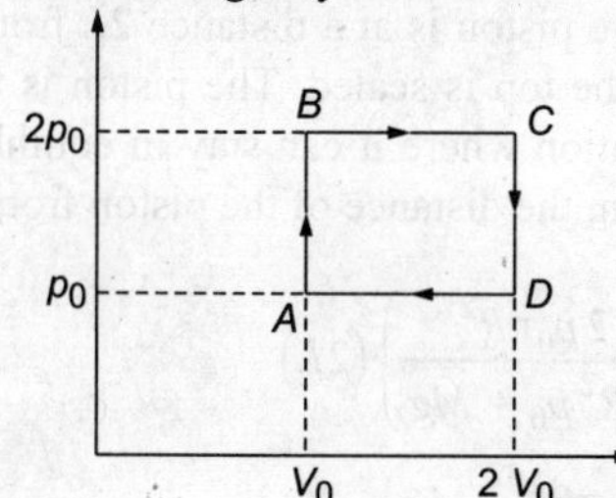

(a) p_0V_0 (b) $\left(\frac{13}{2}\right)p_0V_0$

(c) $\left(\frac{11}{2}\right)p_0V_0$ (d) $4\,P_0V_0$

127. One mole of a monoatomic ideal gas is taken along two cyclic processes $E\to F\to G\to E$ and $E\to F\to H\to E$ as shown in the p–V diagram.

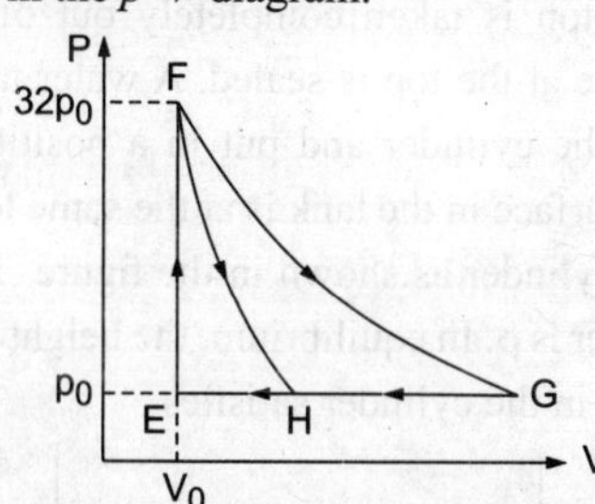

The processes involved are purely isochoric, isobaric, isothermal or adiabatic.

Match the paths in List I with the magnitudes of the work done in List II and select the correct answer using codes given below lists.

List I		List II	
P.	$G\to E$	1.	$160\,p_0V_0$ In 2
Q.	$G\to H$	2.	$36\,p_0V_0$
R.	$F\to H$	3.	$24\,p_0V_0$
S.	$F\to G$	4.	$31\,p_0V_0$

Codes

	P	Q	R	S
(a)	4	3	2	1
(b)	4	3	1	2
(c)	3	1	2	4
(d)	1	3	2	4

128. Two moles of ideal helium gas are in a rubber balloon at 30°C. The balloon is expandable and can be assumed to require no energy in its expansion. The temperature of the gas in the balloon is slowly changed to 35°C. The amount of heat required in raising the temperature is nearly (take R = 8.31 J/mol-K)

(a) 62 J (b) 104 J

(c) 124 J (d) 208 J

129. 5.6 L of helium gas at STP is adiabatically compressed to 0.7 L. Taking the initial temperature to T_1, the work done in the process is

(a) $\frac{9}{8}RT_1$ (b) $\frac{3}{2}RT_1$

(c) $\frac{15}{8}RT_1$ (d) $\frac{9}{2}RT_1$

130. Calorie is defined as the amount of heat required to raise temperature of 1 g of water by 1°C and it is defined under which of the following conditions?

(a) From 14.5°C to 15.5°C at 760 mm of Hg

(b) From 98.5°C to 99.5°C at 760 mm of Hg

(c) From 13.5°C to 14.5°C at 76 mm of Hg

(d) From 3.5°C to 4.5°C at 76 mm of Hg

131. Water of volume 2 L in a container is heated with a coil of 1 kW at 27°C. The lid of the container is open and energy dissipates at rate of 160 J/s. In how much time temperature will rise from 27°C to 77°C?

[Specific heat of water is 4.2 kJ/kg]

(a) 8 min 20 s

(b) 6 min 2 s

(c) 7 min

(d) 14 min

132. Liquid oxygen at 50 K is heated to 300 K at constant pressure of 1 atm. The rate of heating is constant. Which of the following graphs represent the variation of temperature with time?

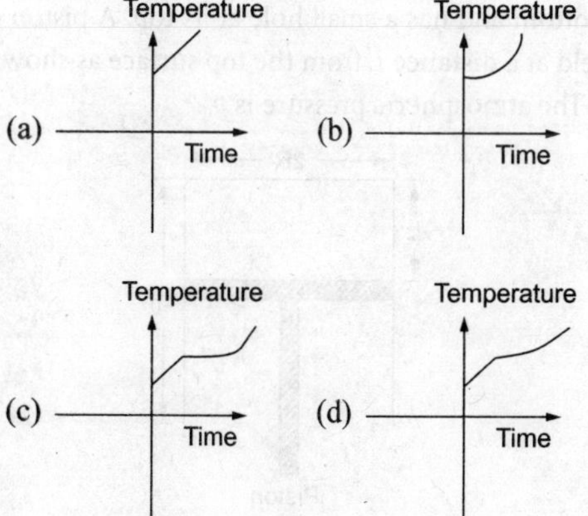

Directions (Q. 210 to 211)

In the figure a container is shown to have a movable (without friction) piston on top. The container and the piston are all made of perfectly insulating material allowing no heat transfer between outside and inside the container. The container is divided into two compartments by a rigid partition made of a thermally conducting material that allows slow transfer of heat.

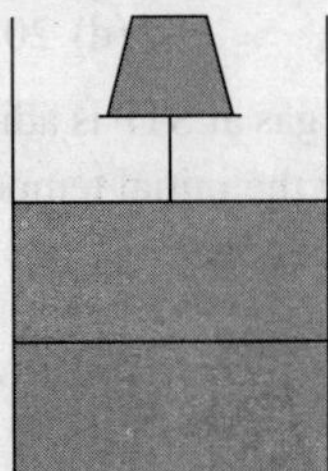

The lower compartment of the container is filled with 2 moles of an ideal monoatomic gas at 700 K and the upper compartment is filled with 2 moles of an ideal diatomic gas at 400 K. The heat capacities per mole of an ideal monoatomic gas are $C_v = \frac{3}{2}R$, $C_p = \frac{5}{2}R$, and those for ideal diatomic gas are $C_v = \frac{5}{2}R$, $C_p = \frac{7}{2}R$.

133. Consider the partition to be rigidly fixed so that it does not move. When equilibrium is achieved, the final temperature of the gases will be

(a) 550 K (b) 525 K

(c) 513 K (d) 490 K

134. Now consider the partition to be free to move without friction so that the pressure of gases in both compartments is the same. Then total work done by the gases till the time they achieve equilibrium will be

(a) 250 R (b) 200 R

(c) 100 R (d) – 100 R

Directions (Q. 212 to 214) : A fixed thermally conducting cylinder has a radius R and height L_0. The cylinder is open at its bottom and has a small hole at its top. A piston of mass M is held at a distance L from the top surface as shown in the figure. The atmospheric pressure is p_0.

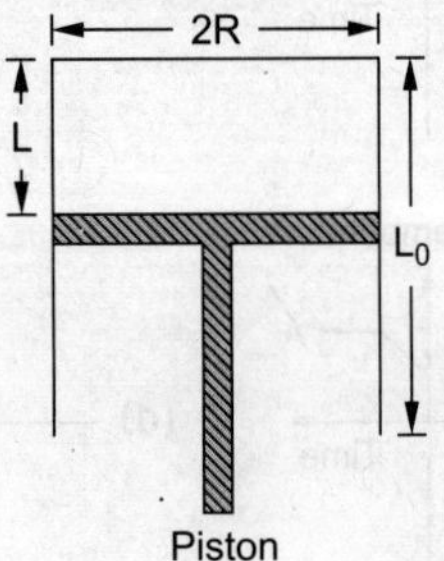

135. The piston is now pulled out slowly and held at a distance $2L$ from the top. The pressure in the cylinder between its top and the piston will then be

(a) p_0

(b) $\frac{p_0}{2}$

(c) $\frac{p_0}{2} + \frac{Mg}{\pi R^2}$

(d) $\frac{p_0}{2} - \frac{Mg}{\pi R^2}$

136. While the piston is at a distance $2L$ from the top, the hole at the top is sealed. The piston is then released, to a position where it can stay in equilibrium. In this condition, the distance of the piston from the top is

(a) $\left(\frac{2p_0\pi R^2}{\pi R^2 p_0 + Mg}\right)(2L)$

(b) $\left(\frac{p_0\pi R^2 - Mg}{\pi R^2 p_0}\right)(2L)$

(c) $\left(\frac{p_0\pi R^2 + Mg}{\pi R^2 p_0}\right)(2L)$

(d) $\left(\frac{p_0\pi R^2}{\pi R^2 p_0 - Mg}\right)(2L)$

137. The piston is taken completely out of the cylinder. The hole at the top is sealed. A water tank is brought below the cylinder and put in a position so that the water surface in the tank is at the same level as the top of the cylinder as shown in the figure. The density of the water is ρ. In equilibrium, the height H of the water column in the cylinder satisfies

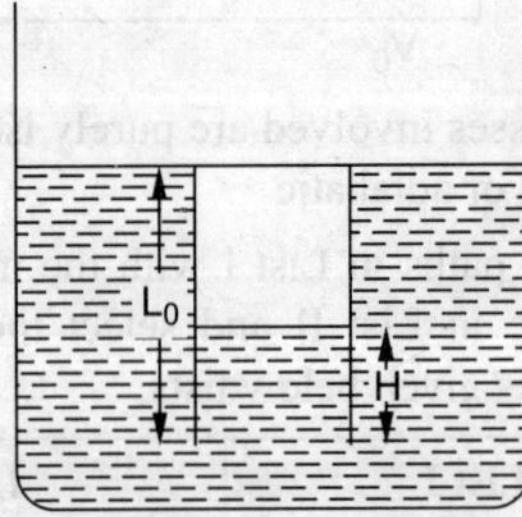

(a) $\rho g(L_0 - H)^2 + p_0(L_0 - H) + L_0p_0 = 0$

(b) $\rho g(L_0 - H)^2 - p_0(L_0 - H) - L_0p_0 = 0$

(c) $\rho g(L_0 - H)^2 + p_0(L_0 - H) - L_0p_0 = 0$

(d) $\rho g(L_0 - H)^2 - p_0(L_0 - H) + L_0p_0 = 0$

Directions (Q. 216 to 218) : An ideal gas undergoing a cyclic thermodynamic process in different ways as shown in the corresponding p–V diagrams in column 3 of the table. Consider only the path from state 1 to state 2. W denotes the corresponding work done on the system. The equations and plots in the table have standards notations and used in thermodynamic processes. Here γ is the ratio of heat capacities at constant pressure and constant volume. The number of moles in the gas is n.

Column 1		Column 2		Column 3	
(i)	$W_{1\to 2} = \frac{1}{\gamma - 1}(P_2V_2 - P_1V_1)$	(i)	Isothermal	(P)	p–V diagram (1, 2)
(ii)	$W_{1\to 2} = -pV_2 + pV_1$	(ii)	Isochoric	(Q)	p–V diagram (1, 2)
(iii)	$W_{1\to 2} = 0$	(iii)	Isobaric	(R)	p–V diagram (2)
(iv)	$W_{1\to 2} = -nRT\ln\left(\frac{V_2}{V_1}\right)$	(iv)	Adiabatic	(S)	p–V diagram (1, 2)

138. Which one the following options correctly represents a thermodynamic process that is used as a correction in the determination of the speed of sound in an ideal gas?

(a) (iv) (ii) (R) (b) (i) (ii) (Q)
(c) (i), (iv) (Q) (d) (iii) (iv) (R)

139. Which of the following options is the only correct representation of a process in which $\Delta U = \Delta Q - p\Delta V$?

(a) (ii) (iii) (S) (b) (ii) (iii) (S)
(c) (iii), (iii) (P) (d) (ii) (iv) (R)

140. Which one of the following options is the correct combination?

(a) (ii) (iv) (P) (b) (iii) (ii) (S)
(c) (ii) (iv) (R) (d) (iv) (ii) (S)

141. A heat source at $T = 10^3$ K is connected to another heat reservoir at $T = 10^2$ K by a copper slab which is 1 m thick. Given that the thermal conductivity of copper is 0.1 $WK^{-1}m^{-1}$, the energy flux through it in the steady state is :

(a) 90 Wm^{-2} (b) 120 Wm^{-2}
(c) 65 Wm^{-2} (d) 200 Wm^{-2}

142. Parallel rays of light of intensity I = 912 Wm^{-2} are incident on a spherical black body kept in surroundings of temperature 300 K. Take stefan constant $\sigma = 5.7 \times 10^{-8}$ Wm^{-2} K^{-4} and assume that the energy exchange with the surroundings is only through radiation. The final steady state temperature of black body is close to

(a) 330 K (b) 660 K
(c) 990 K (d) 1550 K

143. Three rods of copper, brass and steel are welded together to form a Y–shaped structure. Area of cross-section of each rod is 4 cm^2. End of copper rod is maintained at 100°C whereas ends of brass and steel are kept at 0°C. Lengths of the copper, brass and steel rods are 46, 13 and 12 cm respectively. The rods are thermally insulated from surroundings except at ends. Thermal conductivities of copper, brass and steel are 0.92, 0.26 and 0.12 in CGS units, respectively. Rate of heat flow through copper rod is

(a) 1.2 cal/s (b) 2.4 cal/s
(c) 4.8 cal/s (d) 6.0 cal/s

144. If a piece of metal is heated to temperature θ and then allowed to cool in a room which is at temperature θ_0. The graph between the temperature T of the metal and time t will be closed to

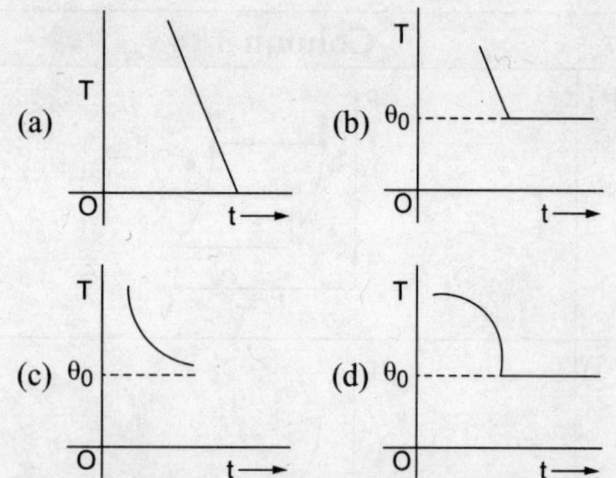

145. Two rectangular blocks, having identical dimensions, can be arranged either in configuration I or in configuration II as shown in the figure. One of the blocks has thermal conductivity K and the other $2K$. The temperature difference between the ends along the X-axis is the same in both the configurations. It takes 9 s to transport a certain amount of heat from the hot end to the cold end in the configuration I. The time to transport the same amount of heat in the configuration II is

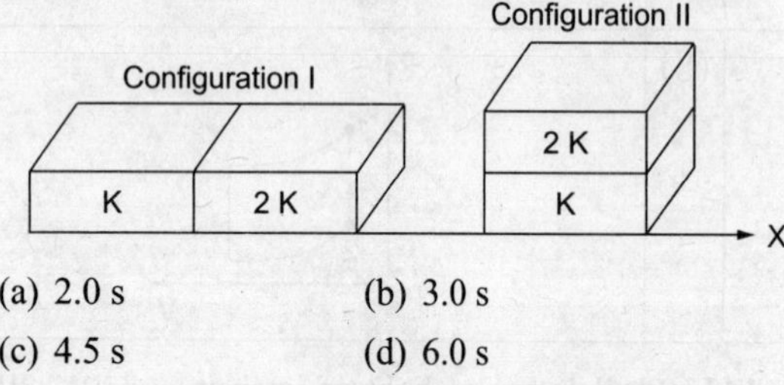

(a) 2.0 s (b) 3.0 s

(c) 4.5 s (d) 6.0 s

146. Three very large plates of same area kept parallel and close to each other. They are considered as ideal black surfaces and have very high thermal conductivity. The first and the third plates are maintained at temperature $2T$ and $3T$ respectively. The temperature of the middle (i.e. second) plate under steady state condition is

(a) $\left(\frac{65}{2}\right)^{\frac{1}{4}}T$ (b) $\left(\frac{97}{4}\right)^{\frac{1}{4}}T$

(c) $\left(\frac{97}{2}\right)^{\frac{1}{4}}T$ (d) $(97)^{\frac{1}{4}}T$

147. Variation of radiant energy emitted by sun, filament of tungsten lamp and welding arc as a function of its wavelength is shown in figure. Which of the following option is the correct match?

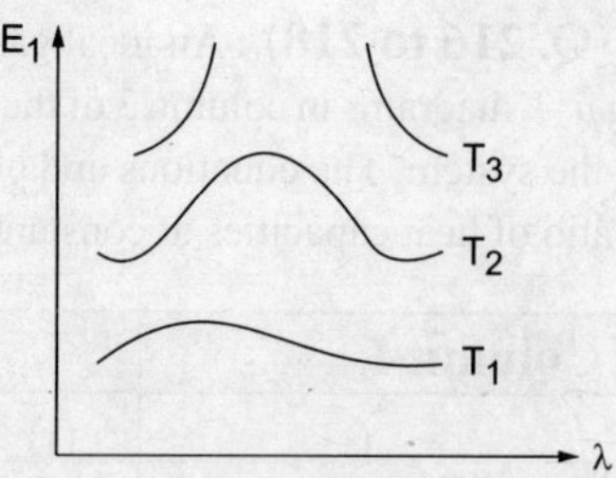

(a) Sun–T_1, tungsten filament–T_2, welding arc–T_3

(b) Sun–T_2, tungsten filament–T_1, welding arc–T_3

(c) Sun–T_3, tungsten filament–T_2, welding arc–T_1

(d) Sun–T_1, tungsten filament–T_3, welding arc–T_2

148. In which of the following process, convection does not take place primarily?

(a) Sea and land breeze

(b) Boiling of water

(c) Warming of glass of bulb due to filament

(d) Heating air around a furnace

149. Three discs, A, B and C having radii 2 m, 4 m and 6 m respectively are coated with carbon black on their outer surfaces. The wavelengths corresponding to maximum intensity are 300 nm, 400 nm and 500 nm, respectively. The power radiated by them are Q_A, Q_B and Q_C respectively

(a) Q_A is maximum (b) Q_B is maximum

(c) Q_C is maximum (d) $Q_A = Q_B = Q_C$

150. Two identical conducting rods are first connected independently to two vessels, one containing water at 100°C and the other containing ice at 0°C. In the second cases, the rods are joined end to end and connected to the same vessels. Let q_1 and q_2 gram per second be the rate melting of ice in the two cases respectively. The ratio $\frac{q_1}{q_2}$ is

(a) $\frac{1}{2}$ (b) $\frac{2}{1}$

(c) $\frac{4}{1}$ (d) $\frac{1}{4}$

151. If 10^{22} gas molecules each of mass 10^{-26} kg collide with a surface (perpendicular to it) elastically per second over an area 1 m^2 with a speed 10^4 m/s, the pressure exerted by the gas molecule will be of the order of :

(a) 4 N/m^2 (b) 2 N/m^2

(c) 3 N/m^2 (d) 6 N/m^2

152. The temperature of an open room of volume 30 m^3 increases from 17°C to 27°C due to the sunshine. The atmospheric pressure in the room of remains 1×10^5 pa. If n_i and n_f are the number of molecules in the room before and after heating, then $n_f - n_i$ will be

(a) 1.38×10^{23} (b) 2.5×10^{25}

(c) -2.5×10^{25} (d) -1.61×10^{23}

153. An ideal gas undergoes a quasi-static, reversible process in which its molar heat capacity C remains constant. If during this process the relation of pressure P and volume V is given by pV^n = constant, then n is given by (Here, C_p and C_v are molar specific heat at constant pressure and constant volume, respectively)

(a) $n = \dfrac{C_p}{C_v}$ (b) $n = \dfrac{C - C_p}{C - C_v}$

(c) $n = \dfrac{C_p - C}{C - C_v}$ (d) $n = \dfrac{C - C_v}{C - C_p}$

154. Two non-reactive monoatomic ideal gases have their atomic masses in the ratio 2 : 3. The ratio of their partial pressures, when enclosed in a vessel kept at a constant temperature, is 4 : 3. The ratio of their densities is

(a) 1 : 4 (b) 1 : 2

(c) 6 : 9 (d) 8 : 9

155. An ideal gas enclosed in a vertical cylindrical container supports a freely moving piston of mass M. The piston and the cylinder have equal cross–sectional area A. When the piston is in equilibrium the volume of the gas in V_0 and its pressure is p_0. The piston is slighting displaced from the equilibrium position and released. Assuming that the system is completely isolated from its surrounding, the piston executes a simple harmonic motion with frequency

(a) $\dfrac{1}{2\pi}\dfrac{A\gamma p_0}{V_0 M}$ (b) $\dfrac{1}{2\pi}\dfrac{V_0 M p_0}{A^2\gamma}$

(c) $\dfrac{1}{2\pi}\sqrt{\dfrac{A^2\gamma p_0}{MV_0}}$ (d) $\dfrac{1}{2\pi}\sqrt{\dfrac{MV_0}{A\gamma p_0}}$

156. A mixture of 2 moles of helium gas (atomic mass = 4 amu) and 1 mole of argon gas (atomic mass = 40 amu) is kept at 300 K in a container. The ratio of the rms speeds $\left(\dfrac{v_{rms}\,(\text{helium})}{v_{rms}\,(\text{argon})}\right)$ is

(a) 0.32 (b) 0.45

(c) 2.24 (d) 3.16

157. A real gas behaves like an ideal gas if its

(a) Pressure and temperature are both high

(b) Pressure and temperature are both low

(c) Pressure is high and temperature is low

(d) Pressure is low and temperature is high

158. An ideal gas is expanding such that pT^2 = constant. The coefficient of volume expansion of the gas is

(a) $\dfrac{1}{T}$ (b) $\dfrac{2}{T}$

(c) $\dfrac{3}{T}$ (d) $\dfrac{4}{T}$

Answers

1. (c) **2.** (b) **3.** (d) **4.** (c) **5.** (c) **6.** (c) **7.** (d) **8.** (d) **9.** (c) **10.** (c)

11. (b) **12.** (d) **13.** (b) **14.** (d) **15.** (d) **16.** (c) **17.** (d) **18.** (a) **19.** (a) **20.** (c)

21. (c) **22.** (a) **23.** (b) **24.** (c) **25.** (a) **26.** (d) **27.** (c) **28.** (c) **29.** (b) **30.** (b)

31. (a) **32.** (b) **33.** (b) **34.** (b) **35.** (a) **36.** (d) **37.** (d) **38.** (a) **39.** (b) **40.** (c)

41. (c) **42.** (d) **43.** (c) **44.** (c) **45.** (b) **46.** (d) **47.** (c) **48.** (a) **49.** (a) **50.** (c)

51. (c) **52.** (b) **53.** (b) **54.** (c) **55.** (a,d) **56.** (a,c) **57.** (b,d) **58.** (a,c) **59.** (a,d) **60.** (a,c)

61. (b,d) **62.** (b,d) **63.** (a,b) **64.** (a,b,c,d) **65.** (a,b) **66.** (c,d) **67.** (b,d) **68.** (a,d) **69.** (a,b,d)

70. (a,c) **71.** (a,b,c) **72.** (a,b,c) **73.** (a,b,c) **74.** (a,b,c) **75.** (b) **76.** (d) **77.** (a) **78.** (c)

79. (a) **80.** (d) **81.** (b) **82.** (d) **83.** (a) **84.** (b) **85.** (c) **86.** (a) **87.** (a) **88.** (d)

89. (a) **90.** (b) **91.** (a) **92.** (d) **93.** (a) **94.** (b) **95.** (c) **96.** (a) **97.** (c) **98.** (d)

99. (a) **100.** (c) **101.** (d) **102.** (c) **103.** (c) **104.** (c) **105.** (d) **106.** (d) **107.** (b) **108.** (d)

109. (d) **110.** (a) **111.** (b) **112.** (d) **113.** (a) **114.** (a) **115.** (a) **116.** (b) **117.** (a) **118.** (b)

119. (a) **120.** (b) **121.** (a) **122.** (c) **123.** (b) **124.** (a) **125.** (d) **126.** (b) **127.** (a) **128.** (d)

129. (a) **130.** (a) **131.** (a) **132.** (c) **133.** (d) **134.** (d) **135.** (a) **136.** (d) **137.** (c) **138.** (c)

139. (b) **140.** (b) **141.** (a) **142.** (c) **143.** (c) **144.** (a) **145.** (c) **146.** (c) **147.** (c) **148.** (b)

149. (c) **150.** (d) **151.** (c) **152.** (b) **153.** (d) **154.** (c) **155.** (d) **156.** (d) **157.** (c) **158.** (b,c,d)

Explanations

1. Here, $n_1 = 1$ mole, $n_2 = 1$ mole

For nitrogen, $C_{p_1} = \frac{7}{2}R$

For helium, $C_{p_2} = \frac{5}{2}R$

$$T_1 = T_0, T_2 = \frac{7}{3}T_0, T_f = ?$$

When gases are put into thermal contact, heat is exchanged between them till final temperature T_f is reached.

Now as we know that heat gain by Nitrogen = heat lost by helium

So, $n_1 C_{p_1}(T_f - T_i) = n_2 C_{p_2}(T_2 - T_f)$

$(n_1 C_{p_1} + n_2 C_{p_2}) T_f = n_2 C_{p_2} T_2 + n_1 C_{p_1} T_1$

$(1 \times \frac{7}{2}R + 1 \times \frac{5}{2}R) T_f$

$$= 1 \times 5/2\, R\, \frac{7}{3} T_0 + 1 \times \frac{7}{2} RT_0$$

$$6\, RT_f = \left(\frac{35}{6} + \frac{7}{2}\right) RT_0$$

$$T_f = \frac{56}{36} T_0 = \frac{14}{9} T_0$$

2. $C_p = \frac{7}{2} R$

$$C_v = C_p - R = \frac{7}{2}R - R = \frac{5}{2}R$$

$$\Upsilon = \frac{C_p}{C_v} = \frac{7/2R}{5/2R} = \frac{7}{5}$$

3. $v_{rms} = \sqrt{\frac{3RT_H}{M_H}} = \sqrt{\frac{3RT_{OXY}}{M_{OXY}}}$

$$\frac{T_H}{M_H} = \frac{T_{OXY}}{M_{OXY}}$$

or $T_H = T_{OXY} \frac{M_H}{M_{OXY}}$

$$= (47 + 273)\frac{2}{32} = \frac{320}{16} = 20 \text{ K}$$

4. Average $K.E.\ (\overline{K}) = kT$

It depends on temperature and does not depend on molar mass.

∴ For both the gases, average translational kinetic energy will be same viz 0.048 eV.

5. $PV = nRT$

$$\frac{P_1}{P_2} = \frac{T_1}{T_2} \quad (\because V, n \text{ and } R \text{ are same})$$

$$\frac{P}{P_2} = \frac{T}{2T} \text{ or } P_2 = 2P$$

6. $PV = nRT = \frac{m}{M}RT$

where m = mass of the gas

and $\frac{m}{M} = n$ = number of moles.

$\frac{PV}{T} = nR = a$ constant for all values of P.

That is why, ideally it is a straight line.

$$\therefore \frac{PV}{T} = \frac{1\text{gm}}{32\text{gm}} \times 8.31 \text{ J mol}^{-1}\text{K}^{-1}$$

$= 0.256 \text{ JK}^{-1}$. Also, $T_1 > T_2$

7. Internal energy $= \frac{nfRT}{2}$

where n = number of mole of the gas

f = number of degree of freedom

∴ For 2 mole of oxygen, $U_0 = \frac{2 \times 5 \times RT}{2} = 5\,RT$

Again for 4 mole of argon, $U_a = \frac{4 \times 3 \times RT}{2} = 6\,RT$

∴ Total internal energy $= U_0 + U_a = 5RT + 6RT$

$= 11RT$

8. Average $K.E(\overline{K}) = \frac{3}{2}kT$

$$\frac{\overline{K_1}}{\overline{K_2}} = \frac{T_1}{T_2} \text{ or } \overline{K_2} = \frac{T_2}{T_1} \times \overline{K_1}$$

$$= \frac{600}{300} \times (6.21 \times 10^{-21})$$

or $\overline{K_2} = 12.42 \times 10^{-21}$ J ..(i)

$$v_{rms} = \sqrt{\frac{3kT}{m}}, \frac{v_2}{v_1} = \sqrt{\frac{T_2}{T_1}}$$

or $v_2 = \sqrt{\frac{T_2}{T_1}} \times v_1 = \sqrt{\frac{600}{300}} \times 484$

$= \sqrt{2} \times 484 = 1.414 \times 484$

$= 684$ m/s ...(ii)

9. Since on the other side of the partition vacuum is present offering no pressure; hence no work is done.

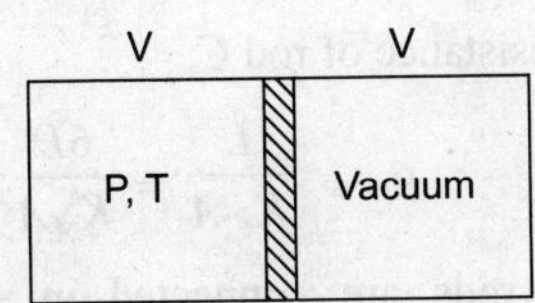

So, Heat supplied $\Delta\theta = 0$ [As vessel is insulating]

Work done $\Delta W = 0$

Hence $\Delta U = 0$

$$U_i = U_f$$

$$MC_V T_i = nC_V T_f$$

$$T_{final} = T_{initial}$$

Also $P_1 V_1 = P_2 V_2$

$$P_2 = \frac{P_1 V_1}{V_2} = \frac{P_1 V_1}{2V_1} = \frac{P_1}{2}$$

$$P_f = \frac{P_i}{2}; T_f = T_i$$

10. Let R_1 and R_2 be the thermal resistance of inner and outer portions. Since, temperature difference at both ends is same, the resistance are in parallel. Hence,

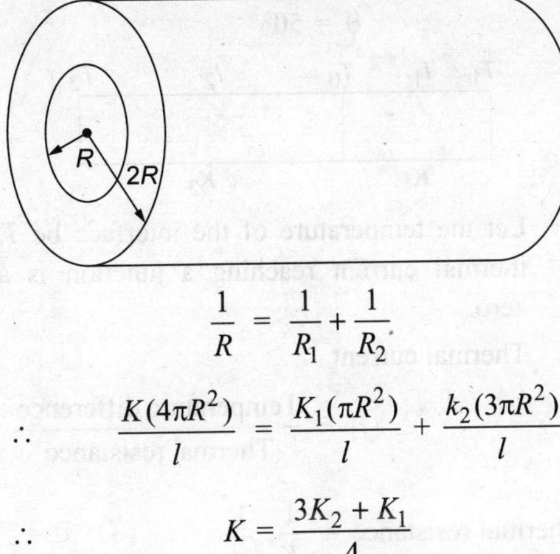

$$\frac{1}{R} = \frac{1}{R_1} + \frac{1}{R_2}$$

$$\therefore \quad \frac{K(4\pi R^2)}{l} = \frac{K_1(\pi R^2)}{l} + \frac{k_2(3\pi R^2)}{l}$$

$$\therefore \quad K = \frac{3K_2 + K_1}{4}$$

11. The diagrammatic representation of the given problem is shown in figure. Since, $T_B > T_A$ the heat will flow from B to A.

Similarly, heat will also flow from B to C and C to A.

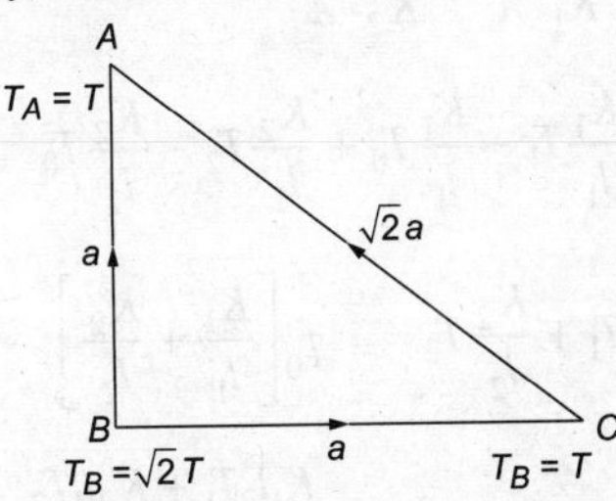

Applying the conduction formula

$$\frac{\Delta Q}{\Delta t} = \frac{KA}{l}(\Delta T)$$

$$= \left(\frac{\Delta T}{\sqrt{2}a}\right)_{CA} = \left(\frac{\Delta T}{a}\right)_{BC}$$

$$\Rightarrow \quad \frac{T_C - T}{\sqrt{2}a} = \frac{\sqrt{2}T - T_C}{a}$$

$$\Rightarrow \quad 3T = T_C(\sqrt{2} + 1)$$

$$\Rightarrow \quad \frac{T_C}{T} = \frac{3}{(\sqrt{2}+1)}$$

12. The rate at which energy radiates from the object is

$$\frac{\Delta Q}{\Delta t} = e\sigma AT^4$$

Since, $\Delta Q = mc\Delta T$, we get

$$\frac{\Delta T}{\Delta t} = \frac{e\sigma AT^4}{mc}$$

Also, since $m = \frac{4}{3}\pi r^3 \rho$ for a sphere, we get

$$A = 4\pi r^2 = 4\pi \left(\frac{3m}{4\pi\rho}\right)^{2/3}$$

Hence, $$\frac{\Delta T}{\Delta t} = \frac{e\sigma T^4}{mc}\left[4\pi\left(\frac{3m}{4\pi\rho}\right)^{2/3}\right] = K\left(\frac{1}{m}\right)^{1/3}$$

For the given two bodies

$$\frac{(\Delta T/\Delta t)_1}{(\Delta T/\Delta t)_2} = \left(\frac{m_2}{m_1}\right)^{1/3} = \left(\frac{1}{3}\right)^{1/3}$$

13. From Wein's displacement law

$$\lambda_m T = \text{constant}$$

or $$T = \frac{1}{\lambda_m}$$

$$\therefore \quad \frac{T_{sun}}{T_{north\ star}} = \frac{(\lambda_m)_{north\ star}}{(\lambda_m)_{sun}}$$

$$= \frac{350}{510} \approx 0.69$$

14. Power radiated (surface area) $(T)^4$. Thus radius is halved, hence, surface area will become $\frac{1}{4}$ times.

Temperature is doubled, therefore, T^4 becomes 16 times.

$$\text{New power} = (450)\left(\frac{1}{4}\right)(16) = 1800 \text{ W.}$$

15. Wien's displacement law is

$$\lambda_m T = b \quad (b = \text{Wien's constant})$$

$$\lambda_m = \frac{b}{T} = \frac{2.88 \times 10^6 \text{ nm-K}}{2800 \text{ K}}$$

$$\lambda = 1000 \text{ nm}$$

Energy distribution with wavelength will be as follows:

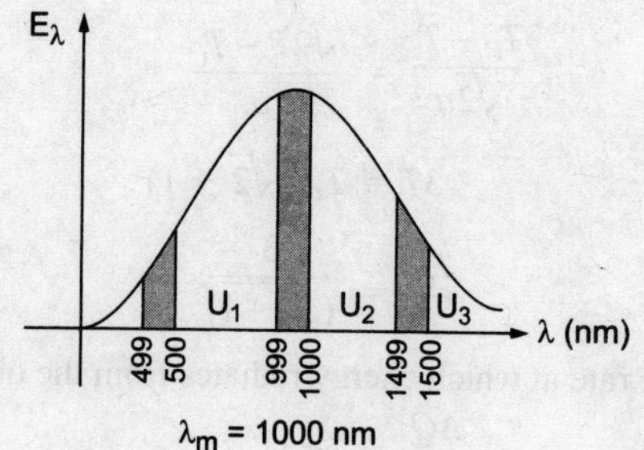

From the graph it is clear that

$$U_2 > U_1 \quad \text{(In fact } U_2 \text{ is maximum)}$$

16. According to Wein's displacement law

$$\lambda_m T = b = \text{Wein constant}$$

If ν_m is the frequency corresponding to wavelength

λ_m then $\left(\dfrac{c}{\nu_m}\right) T = b$ or $\nu_m = \dfrac{c}{b} T$, i.e., $\nu_m \propto T$

$\therefore$ $\nu_m - T$ graph is a straight line shown by line C.

Thus, option (c) is true.

17. For black body radiation, $\lambda_m T$ = a constant = b or $\lambda_m \propto \dfrac{1}{T}$. The wavelength λ_m is less for curve T_1, more for curve T_3 and maximum for curve T_2.

Hence, $T_1 > T_3 > T_2$

18. According to Wein's displacement law

$$\lambda_m T = \text{a constant}$$

$$\therefore \quad \lambda_{m_2} T_2 = \lambda_{m_1} T_1$$

or

$$\lambda_{m_2} = \lambda_{m_1} \frac{T_1}{T_2}$$

$$= \frac{5000 \times (1227 + 273)}{(1500 + 1000)}$$

$$= 3000 \text{ Å}$$

19. Let L be the length and A be the area of cross-section of each rod. Given

$$K_B = 3K_c, K_B = \frac{1}{2} K_A$$

$$\therefore \quad K_C = \frac{1}{3} K_B = \frac{1}{3} \times \frac{1}{2} K_A = \frac{1}{6} K_A$$

Thermal resistance of rod A,

$$R_A = \frac{L}{K_A A}$$

Thermal resistance of rod B,

$$R_B = \frac{L}{K_B A} = \frac{2L}{K_A A}$$

Thermal resistance of rod C,

$$R_C = \frac{L}{K_C A} = \frac{6L}{K_A A}$$

Here, the rods are connected in series. If K is effective thermal conductivity of the system, and R_S is the total thermal resistance of the system then $R_S = R_A + R_B + R_C$

$$\therefore \quad \frac{3L}{KA} = \frac{L}{K_A A} + \frac{2L}{K_A A} + \frac{6L}{K_A A}$$

$$= \frac{9L}{K_A A}$$

or

$$\frac{3}{K} = \frac{9}{K_A} \text{ or } K = \frac{K_A}{3}$$

20. Let θ be the temperature of junction

$$\frac{KA(60° - \theta)}{x} + \frac{KA(70° - \theta)}{x} = \frac{KA(\theta - 20°)}{x}$$

$$60° - \theta + 70° - \theta = \theta - 20°$$

$$\theta = 50°$$

21.

Let the temperature of the interface be T_0. The thermal current reaching a junction is always zero.

Thermal current

$$(I) = \frac{\text{Temperature difference}}{\text{Thermal resistance}}$$

$$\text{Thermal resistance} = \frac{1}{K}\frac{1}{A}$$

Applying it on the interface T_0, we get

$$\frac{T_1 - T_0}{\frac{1}{K_1}\frac{l_1}{A}} + \frac{T_2 - T_0}{\frac{1}{K_2}\frac{l_2}{A}} = 0$$

$$\Rightarrow \quad \frac{K_1}{l_1}T_1 - \frac{K_1}{l_1}T_0 + \frac{K_2}{l_2}T_2 - \frac{K_2}{l_2}T_0 = 0$$

$$\Rightarrow \quad \frac{K_1}{l_1}T_1 + \frac{K_2}{l_2}T_2 = T_0\left[\frac{K_1}{l_1} + \frac{K_2}{l_2}\right]$$

$$\Rightarrow \quad T_0 = \frac{K_1 l_2 T_1 + K_2 l_1 T_2}{K_1 l_2 + K_2 l_1}$$

22. In steady state, the rate of flow of heat is constant and it is given as

$$\frac{dQ}{dt} = -KA\frac{d\theta}{dx}$$

$$\Rightarrow \quad \frac{d\theta}{dx} = \frac{1}{-KA}\left(\frac{dQ}{dt}\right)$$

Let $\frac{1}{KA}\left(\frac{dQ}{dt}\right) = B = A$ constant

$$\Rightarrow \quad \frac{d\theta}{dx} = -B$$

$$\Rightarrow \quad \int_{\theta_1}^{\theta_2} d\theta = -B\int_0^x dx$$

$$\Rightarrow \quad \theta_2 - \theta_1 = -Bx$$

$$\Rightarrow \quad \theta_2 = \theta_1 - Bx$$

$$\Rightarrow \quad \theta_2 = -Bx + \theta_1$$

The θ vs x graph will be a straight line with negative slope and positive intercept on y-axis.

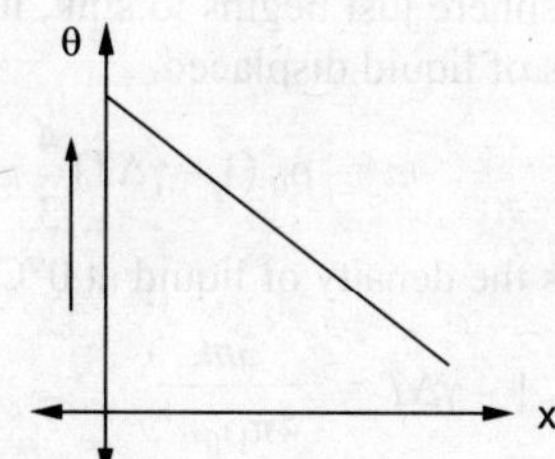

23. $\eta = \frac{W}{Q_1} = 1 - \frac{T_2}{T_1} \Rightarrow W = \left(\frac{T_1 - T_2}{T_1}\right)Q_1$

$$W = \frac{(627+273)-(27+273)}{(627+273)} \times 3\times10^6$$

$$= \frac{600}{900}\times 3\times10^6 \text{cal} = 2\times10^6 \text{ cal}$$

$$= 8.4\times10^6 \text{J}$$

24. Coefficient of performance of Carnot refrigerator is given

by $\quad \beta = \frac{Q_2}{W} = \frac{T_2}{T_1 - T_2}$

So $\quad \frac{Q_2}{1} = \frac{273}{303-273}$

$$= \frac{273}{30} = 9.1 \text{ J}$$

Heat delivered to the surrounding

$$Q = Q_2 + W = 9.1 + 1 = 10.1 \text{ J}$$

25. $W = \int_{20}^{4} mCpdT = \int_{20}^{4} 0.1\left(32\frac{T^3}{400^3}\right)dT = 0.002$ kJ.

26. Heat gain by water = heat lost by steam

$$20\times1\times(80-10) = m\times540 + m\times1\times(100-80)$$

$$1400 = 560 \text{ m}$$

or $\quad m = 2.5$ gm

Total mass of water = 20 + 2.5 = 22.5 gm

27. $\gamma_{\text{diatomic molecule}} = \frac{7}{5}$

Applying the adiabatic equation, i.e.,

$$T_1V_1^{\gamma-1} = T_2V_2^{\gamma-1}$$

$$T_1V^{2/5} = T_2(32V)^{2/5}$$

$$\frac{T_1}{T_2} = (32)^{2/5} = 4$$

Efficiency of a Carnot engine

$$= 1 - \frac{T_2}{T_1} = 1 - \frac{1}{4} = \frac{3}{4} = 0.75\%$$

28. As the question assumes no expansion, hence heat is supplied at constant volume; So heat supplied = change in internal energy.

Change in internal energy = $mS\Delta T$

$$= 0.1\times4184\times(50–30)$$

$$= 2\times4184 = 8368\text{J} = 8.4 \text{ kJ}$$

29. Let η is the efficiency of heat engine and β is the corresponding coefficient of performance of a refrigerator working between the same temperatures. The relation between η and β is

$$\beta = \frac{1}{\eta} - 1 = 10 - 1 = 9$$

Also $\quad \beta = \frac{\text{Output}}{\text{Input}}$

$$= \frac{\text{Energy absorbed from the reservoir at lower temp.}}{\text{Work done on the system}}$$

$$\beta = 9 = \frac{\text{Energy absorbed}}{10 \text{ J}}$$

Hence, energy absorbed = 90 J

30. $\quad \eta_1 = \frac{1}{6} = 1 - \frac{T_2}{T_1}$

$$\Rightarrow \quad \frac{T_2}{T_1} = 1 - \frac{1}{6} = \frac{5}{6} \quad \text{...(i)}$$

$$\eta_2 = \frac{1}{3} = 1 - \frac{(T_2 - 62)}{T_1}$$

$$\Rightarrow \quad \frac{T_2 - 62}{T_1} = 1 - \frac{1}{3} = \frac{2}{3} \quad \text{...(ii)}$$

On dividing equation (ii) by equation (i); we get

$$\frac{T_2 - 62}{T_2} = \frac{2}{3}\times\frac{6}{5} = \frac{4}{5}$$

$$5T_2 - 310 = 4T_2$$

$$T_2 = 310 \text{ K}$$

On replacing T_2 in equation number (i); we get

$$\frac{T_2}{T_1} = \frac{5}{6}$$

$$T_1 = \frac{6}{5} T_2 = \frac{6}{5} \times 310$$

$$= 6 \times 62 = 372 \text{ K}$$

$$T_1 = 372 \text{ K}$$

$$T_2 = 310 \text{ K}$$

31. Molecular mass of gas = M

Let these are N number of molecules;

Hence, total mass of the gas = NM

As the vehicle is brought to rest; the orderly kinetic energy for the gas becomes the disorderly kinetic energy of the molecules. It is this disorderly kinetic energy of the molecules which increases the temperature the gas.

Hence, $\frac{1}{2}(NM)\,v^2 = n\,C_v(\Delta T)$

$$\frac{1}{2}(NM)\,v^2 = \frac{N}{N_A}\left(\frac{R}{\gamma - 1}\right)\Delta T$$

$$\Delta T = \left[\frac{1}{2}\frac{Mv^2(\gamma-1)}{R}\right]N_A$$

32. As C_V for hydrogen $= \frac{5}{2}R$ (diatomic)

C_V for helium $= \frac{3}{2}R$ (monoatomic)

$$C_V \text{ of mixture} = \frac{\frac{4}{2}\times\frac{5}{2}R + \frac{4}{2}\times\frac{3}{2}R}{4/2 + 4/2}$$

$$= \frac{(5+3)R}{4} = 2R$$

$$= 2 \times 2 \text{ cal/mol}$$

Hence, rise in temperature T will be

$$32 = 4 \times 4 \times T$$

$$T = 2°\text{C}$$

33. $\Delta LA = \alpha_A L \Delta T$ and $\Delta L_B = \alpha_B L \Delta T$

Let x be the length of metal A in the composite rod. Then, $\Delta L = \alpha_A x\,\Delta T + \alpha_B\,(L - x)\Delta T$

$$\Rightarrow \quad \Delta L = \frac{x\Delta L_A}{L} + (L-x)\frac{\Delta L_B}{L}$$

$$\Rightarrow \quad 0.065 \times 20 = x\,(0.075) + (20 - x) \times 0.045$$

$$\therefore \quad x = 13.3 \text{ cm}$$

34. If n is number of seconds in a day and T is the time period of pendulum, then nT = constant.

$$\Rightarrow \quad n \times 2\pi\sqrt{\frac{1}{g}} = \text{constant}$$

$$\Rightarrow \quad \frac{\Delta n}{n} + \frac{1}{2}\frac{\Delta l}{l} = 0$$

$$\frac{\Delta n}{n} = -\frac{1}{2}\frac{\Delta l}{l} = -\frac{1}{2}\alpha\Delta\theta$$

Let θ be the temperature at which the clock gives correct time. Then, we have

$$\Rightarrow \quad \frac{5}{n} = -\frac{1}{2}\alpha(15-\theta)$$

and $$\frac{-10}{n} = -\frac{1}{2}\alpha(30-\theta)$$

$$\Rightarrow \quad \frac{5}{-10} = \frac{15-\theta}{30-\theta}$$

$$\therefore \quad \theta = 20°\text{C}$$

35. When the sphere just begins to sink, its mass is equal to the mass of liquid displaced.

$$\Rightarrow \quad m = \rho_0\,(1 - \gamma\Delta T)\frac{4}{3}\pi r^3$$

where ρ_0 is the density of liquid at 0°C temperature

$$\Rightarrow \quad 1 - \gamma\Delta T = \frac{3m}{4\pi\rho_0 r^3}$$

$$= \frac{3 + 0.596}{4\pi \times (1.25\times10^3)\times 0.049^3}$$

$$= 0.9675$$

$$\therefore \quad \gamma = \frac{1-0.9675}{40} = 8.1\times10^{-4}/°\text{C}$$

36. The apparent increase in length of the rod is

$$\Delta L = (\alpha_{cu} - \alpha_{steel})L\Delta T$$

$$= (1.7\times10^{-5} - 1.2\times10^{-5}) \times 90 \times 20$$

$$= 9\times10^{-3} \text{ cm}$$

$$L + \Delta L = 90 + 0.009 = 90.009 \text{ cm}$$

Therefore, tape will read 90.01 cm

37. $$Y = \frac{F/A}{\Delta L/L}$$

$$\Rightarrow \quad F = AY\frac{\Delta L}{L} = AY\alpha\Delta T$$

$$F = \pi \times (10^{-3})^2 \times (0.91 \times 10^{11}) \times (2 \times 10^{-5}) \times 60$$

$$= 340 \text{ N}$$

38. $$T = 2\pi\sqrt{\frac{1}{g}}$$

$$\Rightarrow \quad \frac{\Delta T}{T} = -\frac{\Delta l}{l} = \frac{1}{2}\alpha\Delta\theta$$

If n is the number of second in 30 days,

then $$nT = \text{constant} \quad \frac{\Delta n}{n} + \frac{\Delta T}{T} = 0$$

$$\Delta n = -n\frac{\Delta T}{T} = -\frac{n}{2}a\Delta\theta$$

$$= -\frac{(30\times24\times3600)}{2}\times(\times10^{-7})\times10$$

$$= -11.66 \text{ sec.}$$

39. The diameter (d) of iron tyre must be expanded by 6 mm.

Now, $\quad Dd = adDT = (g/3)dDT.$

$$\Delta T = \frac{3\Delta d}{\gamma d} = \frac{3\times6\times10^{-3}}{3.6\times10^{-5}\times1} = 500°\text{C}$$

40. $$\Delta L = \Delta L_1 + \Delta L_2$$

$$\alpha(L_1+L_2)\Delta T = \alpha_1L_1\Delta T + \alpha_2L_2\Delta T$$

$$\alpha = \frac{\alpha_1L_1+\alpha_2L_2}{L}$$

41. $$Y = \frac{\sigma}{\Delta L/L} = \frac{\sigma}{\alpha\Delta T}$$

$$\Rightarrow \quad \frac{Y_1}{Y_2} = \frac{a_2}{a_1} = \frac{3}{2}$$

42. Since the level does not change on heating

$$\gamma_{liquid} = \gamma_{vessel} = 3\alpha$$

43. (c) Let the actual temperature be T.

Then, $$\frac{T-0}{100-0} = \frac{59-5}{95-5}$$

$\therefore \quad T = 60°\text{C}$

44. (c): Let the actual temperature (x) $K = (x)°\text{F}$

Then, $\frac{5}{9}(x-32) + 273 = x$

$\therefore \quad x = 574.25$

45. Let the temperature of bath be x°C

Then, $$3x = \frac{9}{5}x + 32$$

$$x = 80/3$$

46. As $y > 1$ is not allowed so maximum value of γ should be 1

$$\gamma_{max} = 1$$

$$\gamma = \frac{\alpha(t_2-t_1)}{1+\alpha t_2} = 1$$

$$\alpha(t_2 - t_1) = 1 + \alpha t_2$$

$$\Rightarrow \quad \alpha t_2 - \alpha t_1 = 1 + \alpha t_2$$

$$t_1 = -\frac{1}{\alpha}$$

47. $$\Delta C^2 = l^2 - \left(\frac{l}{2}\right)^2$$

$$= l^2(1+\alpha_2 t)^2 - \left[\frac{l}{2}(1+\alpha_1 t)\right]^2$$

Neglecting α_2^2 and α_1^2 and solving above we get $\alpha_1 = 4\alpha_2$

48. Let ρ_0, ρ_1 and ρ_2 be the densities of the liquid at temperatures t_0, t_1 and t_2 respectively.

To balance Pressure, $P_1l_1g = P_2l_2g$

or $$\left(\frac{\rho_o}{1+\gamma t_1}\right)l_1 = \left(\frac{\rho_o}{1+\gamma t_2}\right)t_2$$

$$l_1 + l_1\gamma t_2 = l_2 + l_2\gamma t_1$$

$$\gamma = \left(\frac{l_1-l_2}{l_2t_1 - l_1t_2}\right)$$

49. $$K_1 = \frac{(d_{Fe})_0}{(d_{Hg})_0}$$

$$K_2 = \frac{(d_{Fe})_{60°}}{(d_{Hg})_{60°}} = \frac{\dfrac{(d_{Fe})_0}{1+\gamma_{Fe}60}}{\dfrac{(d_{Hg})_0}{1+\gamma_{Hg}60}}$$

$$\therefore \quad \frac{K_1}{K_2} = \frac{1+60\gamma_{Fe}}{1+60\gamma_{Hg}}$$

50. $$PV = nRT$$

$$PdV = nRdT \quad (P = \text{constant})$$

$$dV = \left(\frac{nR}{P}\right)dT$$

$$dV = \left(\frac{V}{T}\right)dT \quad \text{...(i)}$$

Further $\quad dV = \gamma V dt \quad$ ...(ii)

From equation (i) and (ii) we get $\gamma = \frac{1}{T}$

51. x, r and t all increase.

52. If new radius is R'

then $$R' = R(1+\alpha\theta)$$

$$2\pi R' = 2\pi R + 2\pi R\alpha\theta$$

$\therefore$ Change in circumference $= 2\pi R' - 2\pi R = 2\pi R\alpha\theta$

53. $$L_1 = l_1[1+\alpha_1\Delta T]$$

$$L_2 = l_2[1+\alpha_2\Delta T]$$

$$L_1 - L_2 = (l_1 - l_2) + (\Delta T)(l_1\alpha_1 - l_2\alpha_2)$$

If $L_1 - L_2$ is to be independent of ΔT, then

$$l_1\alpha_1 - l_2\alpha_2 = 0$$

$$\Rightarrow \quad \frac{l_1}{l_2} = \frac{\alpha_2}{\alpha_1}$$

54. Both will shown same expansion. Expansion of sphere does not depend on internal construction.

55. Isothermal curve from A to B will be parabolic with lesser area under the curve than the area under st. line AB. Therefore, work done by the gas in going straight from A to B is more. If P_o, V_o be the intercepts of the curve on P or V axis then from $y = mx + c$

$$p = \frac{p_o}{V_o}V + p_o$$

or $$\frac{RT}{V} = \frac{p_o V}{V_o} + p_o$$

$$T = \frac{p_o}{V_o R} V^2 + \frac{p_o V}{R}.$$

Hence $V - T$ curve is Parabola.

56. In an ideal gas, when P is constant, $V \propto T$ (Charle's Law) Choice (a) is correct.

Again, when V is constant, $P \propto T$ (Regnault's Law) Choice (c) is correct.

57. As face $ABCD$ has positive charge on it and the gas consists of ionized hydrogen, therefore, isotropy is lost. The usual expression for pressure on the basis of kinetic theory will not be valid as ions would also experience forces other than the forces due to collisions with the walls of container. Choices (b) and (d) are correct.

58. Since wavelength $|\lambda_0|$ becomes half, temperature will become double and power radiated will become 16 times

$$\therefore \quad T = 2T \text{ and } P' = 16P$$

59. $\lambda m = \frac{b}{T} = \frac{2.88 \times 10^{-3}}{2880} = 10{,}000$ Å, So maximum emission corresponds to wavelength around 10,000 Å

60. (a) According to Wien's displacement law ($\lambda_m T =$ Constant),

When temperature is made double, the wavelength corresponding to maximum emission becomes half and, therefore, frequency corresponding to maximum emission becomes double (i.e., $2V_m$).

61. (b) As $T_A > T$, the body A loses more heat than it absorbs. As $T > T_B$, the body B absorb more radiation then it emits.

(d) Even if the two bodies acquire temperature T, each body continues to emit and absorb heat.

62. Let T be the temperature of the contact surface

Then, in the steady state, we have

$$\frac{Q}{t} = \frac{K_A A(-10 - T)}{4.0} = \frac{K_B A(T - 10)}{6.0}$$

or $$\frac{K_A A(-10 - T)}{4} = \frac{K_B A(T - 10)}{6} \quad \text{...(1)}$$

(a) If $K_A = K_B$, Eq. (1) gives $T_1 = -2°C$

(b) If $\frac{K_A}{K_B} = \frac{2}{3}$, Eq. (1) gives $T_2 = 0°C$

Thus the Correct choices are (b) and (d).

63. From Wein's law, $\lambda_{max} T = b$, Thus

$$T_1 = \frac{2.9 \times 10^{-3}}{7.8 \times 10^{-7}} = 3718 \text{ K}$$

$$T_2 = \frac{2.9 \times 10^{-3}}{6.2 \times 10^{-3}} = 4677 \text{ K}$$

So, the correct choice are (a) and (b)

64. To calculate temperature of B

Power of body $A = e_A \sigma T_A^4 \times$ (area)

Power of body $B = e_B \sigma T_B^4 \times$ (area)

The two powers are equal.

$$\therefore \quad e_B \sigma T_B^4 \times (\text{area}) = e_A \sigma T_A^4 \times (\text{area})$$

or $$T_B^4 = \left(\frac{e_A}{e_B}\right) T_A^4$$

or $$T_B^4 = \left(\frac{0.01}{0.81}\right) \times (5802)^4$$

or $$T_B^4 = \left(\frac{1}{3}\right)^4 \times (5802)^4$$

or $$T_B = \left(\frac{5802}{3}\right)$$

or $T_B = 1934$ K Option (a) is correct.

(d) According to Wein's displacement law,

$$\lambda T = \text{constant } \lambda_A T_A = \lambda_B T_B$$

$$\frac{\lambda_A}{\lambda_B} = \frac{T_B}{T_A} = \frac{1934}{5802}$$

or $$\frac{\lambda_A}{\lambda_B} = \frac{1}{3} \text{ or } \lambda_B = 3\lambda_A$$

Given: $\lambda_B - \lambda_A = 1.0 \times 1.0^{-6}$ m

$$3\lambda_A - \lambda_A = 10^{-6}$$

or $2\lambda_A = 10^{-6}$ m

or $\lambda_A = 0.5 \times 10^{-6}$

and $\lambda_B = 3 \times 0.5 \times 10^{-6}$

or $\lambda_B = 1.5 \times 10^{-6}$ m.

Hence option (b) is correct

Options (c) and (d) are incorrect as option (a) is correct

Hence option (a) and (b) are correct.

65. At any temperature, they lose heat at the same rate

So $$\left(\frac{-d\theta}{dt}\right)_A = \left(\frac{-d\theta}{dt}\right)_B$$

or $$\frac{\left(\frac{-d\theta}{dt}\right)_A}{\left(\frac{-d\theta}{dt}\right)_B} = \text{Constant}$$

66. $$P = 4\pi r^2 \sigma T^4 = -mc\left(\frac{dT}{dt}\right)$$

$$= \frac{-4}{3} \pi r^3 \rho s \frac{dT}{dt}$$

Given $R = \frac{dT}{dt}$

$$\therefore \quad P \propto r^2 \text{ and } R \propto \frac{1}{r}$$

67. If the space unoccupied by liquid remains the same, it means the expansion of both liquid and vessel is same at all temperature.

$\Rightarrow \quad \gamma_L V_L \Delta T = \gamma_V V_V \Delta T$

$\therefore \quad \gamma_V/\gamma_L = V_L/V_V$

Also since $V_V > V_L$, we have $\gamma_L > \gamma_L$

68. Let the springs of constant k,$8k$ and $4k$ be compressed by x_1, x_2 and x_3 respectively.

Then $x_1 + x_2 + x_3 = 2\alpha L\Delta T + \alpha L\Delta T + 4\alpha L\Delta T = 7\alpha L\Delta T$

The force F exerted by block C on the wall and force developed in all the springs in equal.

$\Rightarrow \quad kx_1 = 8kx_2 = 4kx_3$

$\Rightarrow \quad \frac{x_1}{8} = x_2 = \frac{x_3}{2} = C$ (say)

Then, $\quad x_1 = 8C, x_2 = C, x_3 = 2C$

$\Rightarrow \quad 8C + C + 2C = 7\alpha L\Delta T$

$\Rightarrow \quad C = \frac{7\alpha L\Delta T}{11}$

$\therefore \quad x_1 = \frac{56\,\alpha L\Delta T}{11}$

$x_2 = \frac{7\alpha L\Delta T}{11}$

$x_3 = \frac{28 L\Delta T}{11}$

$F = kx_1 = \frac{56\,\alpha KL\Delta T}{11}$

69.

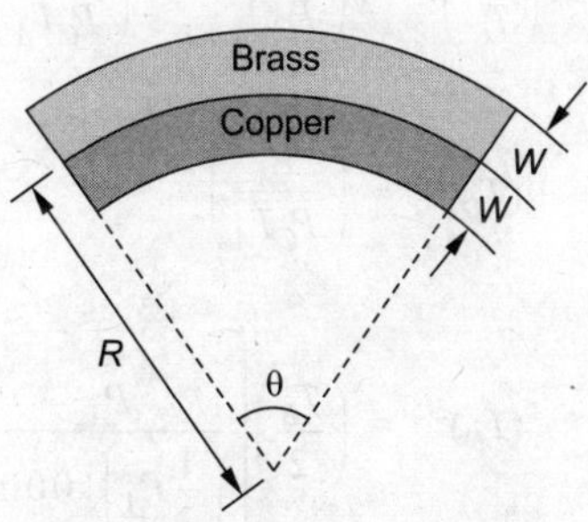

If W is the width of each strip and L_0 is their original length, then

$$\left(R + \frac{W}{2}\right)\theta = L_0(1 + \alpha_B \Delta T)$$

$$\left(R - \frac{W}{2}\right)\theta = L_0(1 + \alpha_C \Delta T)$$

On subtracting 2nd equation from 1st equation, we get

$$W\theta = L_0(\alpha_B - \alpha_C)\Delta T$$

Since, $\theta = L_0/R$, where have $R = \frac{W}{(\alpha_B - \alpha_C)\Delta T}$

$\therefore R \propto \frac{1}{|\alpha_B - \alpha_C|}$ and $R \propto \frac{1}{\Delta T}$

70. $\quad \frac{\Delta d}{d} = \alpha\Delta T = 0.2\%$

$\therefore \quad \alpha = \frac{0.2}{100} \times \frac{1}{80}$

$= 0.25 \times 10^{-4}/°C$

$\frac{\Delta A}{A} = 2\alpha\Delta T = 0.4\%$

$\frac{\Delta V}{V} = 3\alpha\Delta T = 0.6\%$

71. New length $L' = L(1 + \alpha\Delta T) = L(1 + 10\alpha)$

New surface are, $A' = A(1 + 2\alpha\Delta T) = 6L^2(1 + 20\alpha)$

New density. $\quad d' = \frac{d}{1 + 3\alpha\Delta T} = \frac{d}{1 + 30\alpha}$

72. On heating, diameter will increase.

Hence, moment of inertia will increase.

Since, $I\omega$ = constant angular velocity will decreased

75. $\rho_s Vg = \rho_L(V/2) \quad \therefore g\rho_s(1/2)\rho_L$

76. The fraction of solid submerged in liquid depends on whether $\gamma_L > 3\alpha_s$ or $\gamma_L < 3\alpha_s$

77. If $\gamma_L = 3\alpha_s$, there is no change in fraction submerged.

78. $\quad P_I = P_0 = 1 \times 10^5$ N/m^2,

$V_I = V_0 = 2.4 \times 10^{-3}$ m^3,

$T_I = T_0$ 300 k.

Finally, $\quad P_F = P_0 + \frac{Kx}{A}$

$= 1 \times 10^5 + \frac{8000 \times 0.1}{8 \times 10^{-3}}$

$= 2 \times 10^5$ N/m^2

$V_F = V_0 + Ax$

$= 2.4 \times 10^{-3} + 0.1 \times 8 \times 10^{-3}$

$= 3.2 \times 10^{-3}$ m^3.

Now from gas equation

$$\frac{P_I V_I}{T_I} = \frac{P_F V_F}{T_F}$$

$$T_F = \frac{P_F}{P_I} \times \frac{V_F}{V_I} \times T_I$$

$$= \frac{2 \times 10^5}{1 \times 10^5} \times \frac{3.2 \times 10^{-3}}{2.4 \times 10^{-3}} \times 300$$

$= 800$ K

79. We known that $dw = \int PdV, P = P_0 + \frac{Kx}{A}$

$$dw = \int_0^{0.1} \left(P_0 + \frac{kx}{A}\right) A\,dx = \int_0^{0.1} (P_0 A + Kx)dx$$

$$= P_0 Ax + \frac{1}{2}Kx^2$$

$$= 10^5 \times 8 \times 10^{-3} \times 0.1 + \frac{1}{2} \times 8000 \times (0.1)$$

$$= 80 + 40 = 120 \text{ J.}$$

Here 80 J of work is done against atmosphere and 40 J against spring

Now, $dU = nc_v\, dT$

$$= \frac{nRdT}{\gamma - 1} = \frac{P_F V_F - P_I V_I}{\gamma - 1}$$

$$= \frac{(2\times10^5)(3.2\times10^{-3}) - (1\times10^5)\times(2.4\times10^{-3})}{5/3 - 1}$$

$$\Delta U = \frac{3}{2}\times 10[6.4 - 2.4] = 600 \text{ J}$$

Hence total heat supplied

$$Q = dU + dW$$

$$= 600 + 120 = 720 \text{ J}$$

80. As the process is partly isobaric expansion and partly adiabatic

81. As for isobaric process P = constant

$$\frac{T_2}{T_1} = \frac{V_2}{V_1} = \frac{2V}{V} = 2$$

$$T_2 = 2T_1 = 2\times 300 = 600\ k \ldots(1)$$

Now $T_2 V_2^{\gamma-1} = T_3 V_3^{\gamma-1}$

$T_3 = T_1$ 300 K, $T_2 = 600$ K, $V_2 = 40\times10^{-3}\text{m}^3$

$$V_3 = 40 \times 10^{-3} \times \left(\frac{600}{300}\right)^{3/2} = 113.12\times10^{-3} \text{ m}^3.$$

82. $P_3 V_3 = nRT_3$

So, $$P_3 = \frac{2\times 8.3\times 300}{113.12\times10^{-3}}$$

$$= 0.44 \times 10^5 \text{ N/m}^2$$

83. As we know that adiabatic relation between pressure and temperature is $\frac{T^\gamma}{P^{\gamma-1}}$ = constant

So, $$\left(\frac{T_B}{T_A}\right)^\gamma = \left(\frac{P_B}{P_A}\right)^{\gamma-1} \quad \text{with } \gamma = 5/3$$

$$T_B = T_A\left(\frac{2}{3}\right)^{1-\frac{1}{\gamma}}$$

$$= 1000\left(\frac{2}{3}\right)^{2/5} = 850 \text{ K} \quad \ldots\text{(i)}$$

Hence, work done $= \frac{nR(T_I - T_F)}{\gamma - 1}$

$$= \frac{1\times 8.31(1000 - 850)}{5/3 - 1}$$

$$= \frac{3}{2}\times 8.31\times 150 = 1869.75 \text{ J}$$

84. For the process $B \to C$, V = Constant, So $dW = 0$

Now from first law of thermodynamics

$$dQ = dU + dW = nC_V dT + 0$$

$$dQ = 1\times\frac{3}{2}R(T_C - 850)$$

Here, $P \propto T$

$$\frac{P_C}{P_B} = \frac{T_C}{T_B}$$

$$\therefore \quad T_C = \frac{\frac{1}{3}P_A}{(2/3)P_A}\times T_B = \frac{T_B}{2}$$

$$= \frac{850}{2} = 425 \text{ K} \quad \ldots\text{(ii)}$$

$$dQ = 1\times\frac{3}{2}\times 8.31(425 - 850)$$

$$= -5297.6 \text{ J.}$$

Negative sign refers that heat is lost.

85. Here A and D lie at same isochoric

So, $$\frac{P_D}{P_A} = \frac{T_D}{T_A},\ P_D = P_A \times \frac{T_D}{T_A}$$

B and C lie on the same adiabatic

$$\left(\frac{T_D}{T_C}\right)^\gamma = \left(\frac{P_D}{P_C}\right)^{\gamma-1} = \left(\frac{P_A T_D}{P_C T_A}\right)^{\gamma-1}$$

$$(T_D)^{1/\gamma} = \left(\frac{P_A}{P_C T_A}\right)^{1-\frac{1}{\gamma}}$$

$$(T_D)^{3/5} = \left(\frac{T_B}{2}\right)\left(\frac{P_A}{\left(\frac{1}{3}P_A\right)1000}\right)^{2/5}$$

$$(T_D)^{3/5} = \frac{1}{2}\left(\frac{2}{3}\right)^{2/5}\times 1000\times\left(\frac{3}{1000}\right)^{2/5},$$

$$T_D = 500 \text{ K}$$

86. $W = \int PdV$

$$PV = nRT$$

On differentiating

$$PdV + VdP = nRdT$$

According to question along AB

$$PT = \text{constant}$$

So, $PdT + TdP = 0$

$$dP = -\frac{PdT}{T}$$

$$\text{Hence, } PdV + V\left(-\frac{PdT}{T}\right) = nRdT$$

$$PdV + \left(\frac{-nRTdT}{T}\right) = nRdT$$

$$PdV = 2nRdT$$

$$W_{AB} = \int_{2T_1}^{T_1} 2nRdT = -2nRT_1$$

$$= -2 \times 2R \times 300 = -1200R \text{ Joule}$$

87. $$(dQ)_{AB} = dU + dW = nC_V dT + dW$$

$$= -2\times \frac{3R}{2}\times 300 - 1200R = -2100\ R$$

88. $$dQ = 2\times\frac{3R}{2}\times 300 + 2P_1(V_C - V_B)$$

$$V_C = \frac{nR_2T_1}{2P_1},\ V_B = \frac{nRT_1}{2P_1}$$

$$V_C - V_B = \frac{nR2T_1}{2P_1}$$

$$(dQ)_{BC} = 900\ R + 2P_1 \times \frac{nRT_1}{2P_1}$$

$$= 900\ R + 2 \times R \times 300 = 1500\ R$$

89. $$(dQ)C_A = 2\times\frac{3R}{2}\times 0 + nR(2T_1)\log e^{V_A/V_C}$$

$$= 2nRT_1 \log e\frac{P_C}{P_A} = 2nRT_1 \log e^2$$

$$= 2 \times 2 \times 2 \times 300 \times 0.693 = 831.6\ R$$

90. $T_1 = 300$ K, $V_1 = V$, $V_2 = 2\sqrt{2}\ V$.

Let T_2 be the final temperature of the gas. T_2 is obtained from the adiabatic relation

$$T_1V_1^{\gamma-1} = T_2V_2\,(\gamma - 1)$$

or $$T_2 = T_1 \times \left(\frac{V_1}{V_2}\right)^{(\gamma-1)}$$

For a monoatomic gas, $\gamma = \frac{5}{3}$. Therefore,

$$T_2 = 300 \times \left(\frac{1}{2\sqrt{2}}\right)^{2/3} = 150 \text{ K}$$

So, the correct choice is (b).

91. $U = nC_v(T_2 - T_1)$

For a monoatomic gas $C_v = \frac{3R}{2}$. Therefore,

$$\Delta U = 2 \times \frac{3}{2} \times 8.3 \times (150 - 300) = -3735 \text{ J}$$

The negative sign implies that the internal that the internal energy decreases in this process.

So, the correct choice is (a).

92. For a adiabatic process, $\Delta Q = 0$, Hence $\Delta W = -\Delta U =$ 3735 J, which is choice (d).

93. Number of moles of helium is

$$n = \frac{\text{mass in gram}}{\text{molecular mass}} = \frac{2000}{4} = 500$$

From eqution state at A,

$$P_AV_A = nRT_A$$

$$T_A = \frac{P_AV_A}{nR} = \frac{4.15\times 10^4 \times 10}{500 \times 8.3} = 100 \text{ K}$$

So, the correct choice is (a).

94. For isobaric process $A \rightarrow B$,

$$\frac{T_B}{T_A} = \frac{P_B}{P_A} = \frac{8.3\times 10^4}{4.15\times 10^4} = 2$$

Thus, $T_B = 2\ T_A = 200$ K, which is choice (b).

95. For isobaric process $B \rightarrow C$,

$$\frac{T_C}{T_B} = \frac{V_C}{V_B} = \frac{20}{10} = 2$$

Thus, $T_C = 2\ T_B = 400$ K which is choice (c)

96. Work done by the gas in the cyclic process $ABCA$ is W = area enclosed in the $P - V$ diagram

$$= \text{area of triangle } ABC$$

$$= \frac{1}{2} \times AB \times AC$$

$$= \frac{1}{2}(3P_0 - P_0) \times (2V_0 - V_0)$$

$$= P_0V_0.$$

which is choice (a).

97. In the isobaric process CA, the heat energy rejected by the gas is given by

$$Q_{CA} = nC_\pi\Delta T = n(T_A - T_C) \quad \text{...(1)}$$

Using ideal gas equation $PV = nRT$ for points A and C, we have

$$P_AV_A = nRT_A \text{ or } P_0V_0 = nRT_A \quad \text{...(2)}$$

and $$P_CV_C = nRT_C \text{ or } P_0(2V_0) = nRT_C \quad \text{...(3)}$$

Subtracting (2) and (3), we have

$$P_0V_0 = nR(T_C - T_A)$$

or $$T_A - T_C = -\frac{P_0V_0}{nR} \quad \text{...(4)}$$

Using (4) in (1), we get

$$Q_{CA} = \frac{C_pP_0V_0}{R}, \text{ which is choice (c).} \quad \text{...(5)}$$

98. The heat energy absorbed in the isochoric process AB is given by

$$Q_{AB} = nC_v\Delta T = nC_v(T_B - T_A) \quad \text{...(6)}$$

Using the ideal gas equation for points A and B, we have

$$P_AV_A = nRT_A \text{ or } P_0V_0 = nRT_A$$

and $$P_BV_B = nRT_B \text{ or } (3\ P_0)V_0 = nRT_B$$

which give $T_B - T_A = \dfrac{2P_0V_0}{nR}$ ...(7)

Using (7) in (6), we get

$$Q_{AB} = \frac{2C_vP_0V_0}{R}$$

Now, for a monoatomic gas,

$$C_v = \frac{3R}{2}. \text{ Therefore}$$

$$Q_{AB} = 3P_0V_0, \text{ which is choice (d)} \quad ...(8)$$

99. From the first law of thermodynamics, the heat energy absorbed by the gas is given by

$$\Delta Q = \Delta U + \Delta W$$

where $\Delta W = W =$ work done by the gas $= P_0V_0$.

Since the process is cyclic, there is no change in the internal energy of the gas, i.e., $\Delta U = 0$. Hence

$$\Delta Q = \Delta W = P_0V_0 \quad ...(9)$$

If Q_{BC} is the heat absorbed the process BC, then

$$Q = Q_{AB} + Q_{BC} + Q_{CA} \quad ...(10)$$

Using (5), (8) and (9) in (10), we have

$$P_0V_0 = 3P_0V_0 + Q_{BC} - \frac{5P_0V_0}{2}$$

or $$Q_{BC} = \frac{P_0V_0}{2}$$

∴ Correct choice is (a)

100. The correct choice is (c).

101. For an adiabatic change, $P_1V_1 = P_2V_2$. Therefore

$$P_2 = P_1\left(\frac{V_1}{V_2}\right)^{\gamma}$$

For a monoatomic gas, $\gamma = 5/3$. Hence

$$P_2 = P\left(\frac{2\sqrt{2}V}{V}\right)^{5/3} = P(2\sqrt{2})^{5/3}.$$

So, the correct choice is (d).

102. In an adiabatic process, $\Delta Q = 0$. Hence from the first law of thermodynamics, we have

$$W = -\Delta U_1 = -nC_v\Delta T$$

$$= -2\,C_v \times (T_2 - T_1) \quad (\because n = 2)$$

Now for 2 moles $P_1V_1 = 2RT_1$ and $P_2V_2 = 2RT_2$

Thus, $T_1 = \dfrac{P_1V_1}{2R}$ and $T_2 = \dfrac{P_2V_2}{2R}$

Using these, we have

$$W = -\frac{C_v}{R}(P_2V_2 - P_1V_1)$$

$$= -\frac{C_v}{R}\left(\frac{P_1V_1^{\gamma}}{V_2^{\gamma}} \times V_2 - P_1V_1\right)$$

$$= -\frac{C_v}{R} \times P_1V_1\left[\left(\frac{V_1}{V_2}\right)^{\gamma-1} - 1\right]$$

$$= \frac{3P_1V_1}{2}\left[\left(\frac{V_1}{V_2}\right)^{2/3} - 1\right] \quad \left(\because C_v = \frac{3R}{2}\right)$$

$$= -\frac{3P \times 2\sqrt{2}V}{2}[(2\sqrt{2})^{2/3} - 1]$$

$$= -3\sqrt{2}\,PV$$

The work done at constant volume = 0. Hence the correct choices is (c).

103. Using the ideal gas equation $PV = nRT$, the volumes of the gas is states A, B and C are

$$V_A = \frac{nRT_A}{P_A} = \frac{nR(2T_1)}{P_1} = \frac{2nRT_1}{P_1} \quad ...(1)$$

$$V_B = \frac{nRT_B}{P_B} = \frac{nR(T_1)}{2P_1} = \frac{1}{2}\frac{n\,RT_1}{P_1} \quad ...(2)$$

and $$V_C = \frac{nRT_C}{P_C} = \frac{nR(2T_1)}{2P_1} = \frac{nR2T_1}{P_1} \quad ...(3)$$

It is given that in the process $A \to B$, the pressure and temperature of the gas such that

$$PT = K$$

where K is a constant. Thus for point A, we have

$$K = P_AT_A = P_1(2T_1) = 2\,P_1T_1 \quad ...(4)$$

So, the correct choice is (c).

104. For the process $A \to B$, we have

$$PV = nRT \quad ...(5)$$

$$PT = K \quad ...(6)$$

Eliminating T from (5) and (6) we get

$$PV = nR \times \frac{K}{P} \text{ or } P^2V = nRK \quad ...(7)$$

or $$P = \left(\frac{nRK}{V}\right)^{1/2} \quad ...(8)$$

The work done in process $A \to B$ is given by

$$W_{AB} = \int_{V_A}^{V_B} PdV = \int_{V_A}^{V_B}\left(\frac{nRK}{V}\right)^{1/2} dV$$

$$= \sqrt{nRK}\int_{V_A}^{V_B}\frac{dV}{\sqrt{V}} = 2\sqrt{nRK}\,(\sqrt{V_B} - \sqrt{V_A})$$

Using (1), (2) and (4), we get

$$W_{AB} = 2\sqrt{nR(2P_1T_1)}\left[\sqrt{\frac{1}{2}\frac{nRT_1}{P_1}} - \sqrt{\frac{2nRT_1}{P_1}}\right]$$

$$= 2\sqrt{2}\,nRT_1\left(\frac{1}{\sqrt{2}} - \sqrt{2}\right)$$

$$= -2nRT_1 = -4RT_1$$

The negative sign indicates that heat is absorbed in this process. The correct choice is (d)

105. For a monoatomic gas $C_v = 3R/2$. The internal energy of the gas in the process $A \to B$ is

$$(\Delta U)_{AB} = nC_v\Delta T = nC_v(T_B - T_A)$$

$$= 2 \times \frac{3R}{2} \times (T_1 - 2T_1)$$

$$= 3R \times (-T_1) = -3RT_1$$

From the first law of thermodynamics.

$$Q_{AB} = (\Delta U)AB + W_{AB}$$

$$= -3RT_1 - 4RT_1 = -7\,RT_1$$

which is choice (c).

109. In the steady state, the rate of flow of heat is the same for all rods. If T_1 and T_2 are the temperatures at the junction points between A and B and between B and C respectively, then

$$\frac{Q}{t} = \frac{k_A A(100 - T_1)}{d} = \frac{k_B A(T_1 - T_2)}{d} = \frac{k_C A(T_2 - 0)}{d}$$

Given $k_A = 2k$, $k_B = \text{k}$

and $k_c = 0.5\,k$. Hence

$$2(100 - T_1) = (T_1 - T_2) = 0.5(T_2 - 0)$$

which gives $200 - 2T_1 = T_1 - T_2$ (1)

and $T_1 - T_2 = 0.5\,T_2$ (2)

Equation (1) and (2) gives $T_1 = 85.7°\text{C}$. So the correct choice is (d).

110. Putting $T_1 = 85.7°\text{C}$ in Eq. (1) or (2), we get $T_2 = 57.1°\text{C}$, which is choice (a).

111. Since the rods have the same lengths and the same diameters, the equivalent thermal conductivity of the series combination is given by

$$\frac{1}{k_e} = \frac{1}{k_A} + \frac{1}{k_B} + \frac{1}{k_C} = \frac{1}{2k} + \frac{1}{k} + \frac{1}{0.5k}$$

which gives $k_e = \frac{2k}{7}$. So, the correct choice is (b).

112. $$K = \frac{p}{(-\Delta V / V)} \Rightarrow \frac{\Delta V}{V} = \frac{p}{K}$$

$$\Rightarrow \quad -\Delta V = \frac{pV}{K}$$

$$\Rightarrow \quad \frac{pV}{K} = V\,(3\alpha)\,\Delta T$$

$$\therefore \quad \Delta T = \frac{p}{3\alpha K}$$

113. $$T_0 = 2\pi\sqrt{\frac{L}{g}}$$

$$T' = T_0 + \Delta T = 2\pi\sqrt{\frac{L + \Delta L}{g}}$$

$$\therefore \quad T' = T_0 + \Delta T$$

$$= 2\pi\sqrt{\frac{L(1 + \alpha\,\Delta\theta)}{g}}$$

$$= \left\{2\pi\sqrt{\frac{L}{g}}\right\}(1 + \alpha\Delta\theta)^{\frac{1}{2}}$$

$$\approx T_0\left(1 + \frac{\alpha\Delta\theta}{2}\right)$$

$$\therefore \quad \Delta T = T' - T_0 = \frac{\alpha\Delta\theta T_0}{2} \qquad \text{...(i)}$$

$$\text{or} \quad \frac{\Delta T_1}{\Delta T_2} = \frac{\alpha\Delta\theta_1 T_0}{\alpha\Delta\theta_2 T_0}$$

$$\Rightarrow \quad \frac{12}{4} = \frac{40 - \theta}{\theta - 20}$$

$$\Rightarrow \quad 3\,(\theta - 20) = 40 - \theta$$

$$\Rightarrow \quad 4\theta = 100$$

$$\Rightarrow \quad \theta = 25°\text{C}$$

Time gained or lost is given by

$$\Delta T = \left(\frac{\Delta T}{T_0 + \Delta T}\right) t \approx \frac{\Delta t}{T_0} t$$

From Eq. (i), $$\frac{\Delta T}{T_0} = \frac{\alpha\Delta\theta}{2}$$

$$\therefore \quad \Delta t = \frac{\alpha(\Delta\theta)t}{2}$$

$$12 = \frac{\alpha(40 - 25)(24 \times 3600)}{2}$$

$$\therefore \quad \alpha = 1.85 \times 10^{-5}/°\text{C}$$

114.

P S
Q, R
10°C 2K K 400°C
1 m 1 m

Rate of heat flow from P to Q

$$\frac{dQ}{dt} = \frac{2KA(T - 10)}{1}$$

Rate of heat flow from Q to S

$$\frac{dQ}{dt} = \frac{KA(4000 - T)}{1}$$

At steady state rate of heat flow is same

$$\therefore \quad \frac{2KA(T - 10)}{1} = KA\,(400 - T)$$

$$\text{or} \quad 2T - 20 = 400 - t \quad \text{or} \quad 3T = 420$$

$$\therefore \quad T = 140°$$

P S
Q, R
10°C K 400°C
x dx
Junction

Temperature of junction is 140°C

Temperature at a distance x from end P is

$Tx = (130x + 10°)$

Change in length dx is suppose dy

Then, $dy = \alpha dx\,(Tx - 10)$

$$\int_0^{\Delta y} dy = \int_0^1 \alpha dx\,(130x + 10 - 10)$$

$$\Delta y = \left[\frac{\alpha x^2}{2} \times 130\right]_0^1$$

$$\Delta y = 1.2 \times 10^{-5} \times 65$$

$$\Delta y = 78.0 \times 10^{-5}\text{ m} = 0.78\text{ mm}$$

115. By using stefan's law

$$\frac{-dT}{dt} = \frac{\sigma A(T^4 - T_0^4)}{ms} = \frac{\sigma A(T^4 - T_0^4)}{V(\rho s)}$$

ρs is more for B.

116. $mL_v = (150 - m)L_f$

$m \times 2.1 \times 10^6 = (150 - m)(3.36 \times 10^5)$

$m \approx 20$ g

117. For adiabatic process

$$T_1V_1^{\gamma-1} = T_2V_2^{\gamma-1}$$

$$\gamma = \frac{5}{3}$$

$$\Rightarrow\ 300(V)^{2/3} = T_2(2V)^{2/3}$$

$$\Rightarrow\ T_2 = \frac{300}{2^{2/3}} \approx 189\text{ K}$$

$$\Delta U = \frac{f}{2}nR\Delta T = \frac{3}{2}.2\frac{25}{3}(189 - 300)$$

$$= -2.7\text{ kJ}$$

118. By Mayor's relation for 1 g mole of a gas,

$$C_p - C_v = R$$

So, when n gram moles are given

$$C_p - C_v = \frac{R}{n}$$

As per given question,

$$a = C_p - C_v = \frac{R}{2};\ \text{for } H_2$$

$$b = C_p - C_v = \frac{R}{28};\ \text{for } N_2$$

$$a = 14b$$

119. Heat gained (water + calorimeter) = Heat lost copper ball

$$\Rightarrow\ m_w s_w \Delta T + m_c s_c \Delta T = m_B s_B \Delta T$$

$$\Rightarrow\ 170 \times 145 + 100 \times 0.1 \times 45$$

$$= 100 \times 0.1 \times (T - 75)$$

$$\therefore\ T = 885°\text{C}$$

120. Heat generated in device 3 h = time × power = 3 × 3600 × 3 × 10^3 = 324 × 10^5 J

Heat used to heat water = $ms\Delta\theta$

$= 120 \times 1 \times 4.2 \times 10^3 \times 20$ J

Heat absorbed by coolant = Pt

$= 324 \times 10^5 - 120 \times 1 \times 4.2 \times 10^3 \times 20$ J

$= (325 - 100.8) \times 10^5$ J

$$P = \frac{223.2 \times 10^8}{3600} = 2067\text{ W}$$

121. p–V equation for path AB

$$p = -\left(\frac{p_0}{V_0}\right)V + 3p_0$$

$$\Rightarrow\ pV = 3p_0V - \frac{p_0}{V_0}V^2$$

or $$T = \frac{pV}{nR} = \frac{1}{nR}\left(3p_0V - \frac{p_0}{V_0}V^2\right)$$

For maximum temperature,

$$\frac{dT}{dV} = 0$$

$$\Rightarrow\ 3p_0 - \frac{2p_0V}{V_0} = 0$$

$$\Rightarrow\ V = \frac{3}{2}V_0$$

and $$p = 3p_0 - \frac{p_0}{V_0} = \frac{3p_0}{2}$$

Therefore, at these values:

$$\therefore\ T_{\max} = \frac{\left(\frac{3p_0}{2}\right)\left(\frac{3V_0}{2}\right)}{nR} = \frac{9p_0V_0}{4nR}$$

122. In the first process: $p_iV_i^\gamma = p_fV_f^\gamma$

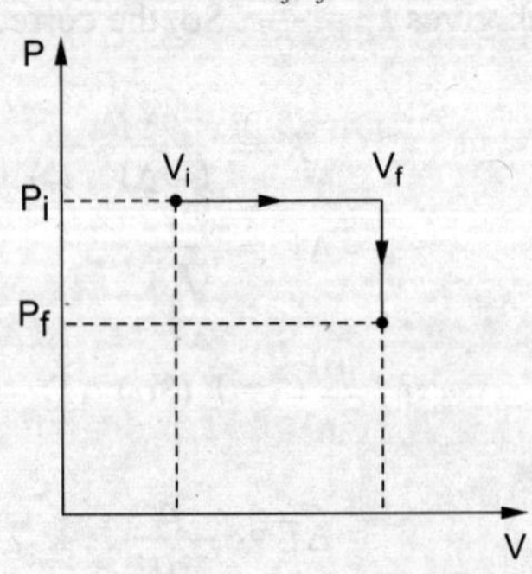

$$\Rightarrow\ \frac{p_i}{p_f} = \left(\frac{V_f}{V_i}\right)^\gamma$$

$$\Rightarrow\ 32 = 8^\gamma$$

$$\gamma = \frac{5}{3} \quad \text{...(i)}$$

For the two step process

$$W = p_i (V_f - V_i) = 10^5(7 \times 10^{-3})$$

$$W = 7 \times 10^2 \text{ J}$$

$$\Delta U = \frac{f}{2} (p_f V_f - p_i V_i)$$

$$= \frac{1}{\gamma - 1}\left(\frac{1}{4} \times 10^2 - 10^2\right)$$

$$\Delta U = -\frac{3}{2}\cdot\frac{3}{4} \times 10^2 = -\frac{9}{8} \times 10^2 \text{ J}$$

$$Q - W = \Delta U$$

$$\Rightarrow \quad Q = 7 \times 10^2 - \frac{9}{8} \times 10^2$$

$$= \frac{47}{8} \times 10^2 \text{ J} = 588 \text{ J}$$

123. Given, $\frac{U}{V} \propto T^4$

$$\frac{U}{V} = \alpha T^4$$

It is also given that, $P = \frac{1}{3}\left(\frac{U}{V}\right)$

$$\Rightarrow \quad \frac{nR_0 T}{V} = \frac{1}{3}\left(\alpha T^4\right) \quad (R_0 = \text{Gas constant})$$

or $$VT^3 = \frac{3nR_0}{\alpha} = \text{constant}$$

$$\therefore \quad \left(\frac{4}{3}\pi R^3\right) T^3 = \text{constant or } RT = \text{constant}$$

$$\therefore \quad T \alpha \frac{1}{R}$$

124. Entropy is a state functions. Therefore in both cases answer should be same.

125. According to first law of thermodynamics, we get

(i) Change in internal energy from A to B i.e. ΔU_{AB}

$$\Delta U_{AB} = nC_v (T_B - T_A) = 1 \times \frac{5R}{2} (800 - 400)$$
$$= 1000 \text{ R}$$

(ii) Change in internal energy from B to $\Delta U_{BC} = nC_v$ $(T_c - T_B) = 1 \times \frac{5R}{2} (600 - 800) = -500 \text{ R}$

(iii) $\Delta U_{\text{isothermal}} = 0$

(iv) Change in internal energy from C to A i.e.

$$\Delta U_{CA}\, \Delta U_{CA} = nC_v (T_A - T_C)$$

$$= 1 \times \frac{5R}{2} (400 - 600) = -500 \text{ R}$$

126. Heat is extracted from the source means heat is given to the system (or gas) or Q is positive. This is positive only along the path ABC.

$\therefore$ Heat supplied,

$$Q_{ABC} = \Delta U_{ABC} + W_{ABC}$$

$$= nC_v (T_f - T_i) + \text{Area under } p\text{–}V \text{ graph}$$

$$= n\left(\frac{3}{2}R\right) (T_C - T_A) + 2p_0V_0$$

$$= \frac{3}{2} (nRT_C - nRT_A) + 2p_0V_0$$

$$= \frac{3}{2} (p_CV_C - P_AV_A) + 2p_0V_0$$

$$= \frac{3}{2} (4\, p_0V_0 - p_0V_0) + 2p_0V_0$$

$$= \frac{13}{2} p_0V_0$$

127.

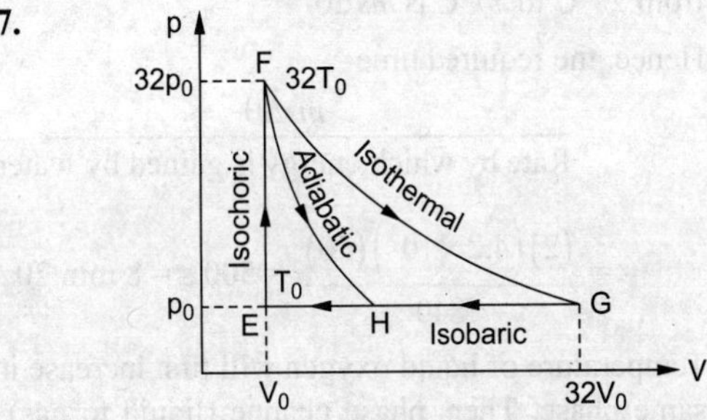

In $F \to G$ work done in isothermal process is nRT In $\left(\frac{V_f}{V_i}\right) = 32\, p_0V_0$ In $\left(\frac{32V_0}{V_0}\right)$

$$= 32\, p_0V_0 \ln 2^5 = 160\, p_0V_0 \ln 2$$

In $G \to E$, $\Delta W = p_0\Delta V = p_0\,(31V_0) = 31\, p_0V_0$

In $G \to H$ work done is less than $31\, p_0V_0$ i.e., $24\, p_0V_0$

In $F \to H$ work done is $36\, p_0V_0$

128. The process may be assumed to be isobaric.

$$\therefore \quad Q = nC_p\Delta T = (2)\left(\frac{5}{2}R\right)(5)$$

$$= 5 \times 8.31 \times 5 = 207.75 \text{ J} \approx 208 \text{ J}$$

129. At STP. 22.4 L of any gas is 1 mole.

$$\therefore 5.6 \text{ L} = \frac{5.6}{22.4} = \frac{1}{4} \text{ moles} = n$$

In adiabatic process,

$$TV^{\gamma-1} = \text{constant}$$

$$\therefore \quad T_2V_2^{\gamma-1} = T_1V_1^{\gamma-1}$$

or $$T_2 = T_1\left(\frac{V_1}{V_2}\right)^{\gamma-1}$$

$$\gamma = \frac{C_p}{C_v} = \frac{5}{3} \text{ for monoatomic He gas.}$$

$$\therefore \quad T_2 = T_1\left(\frac{5.6}{0.7}\right)^{\frac{5}{3}-1} = 4T_1$$

Further in adiabatic process, $Q = 0$

$$\therefore \quad W + \Delta U = 0$$

or $$W = -\Delta U = -nC_v\Delta T$$

$$= -n\left(\frac{R}{\gamma - 1}\right)(T_2 - T_1)$$

$$= -\frac{1}{4}\left(\frac{R}{\frac{5}{3}-1}\right)(4T_1 - T_1) = -\frac{9}{8}RT_1$$

130. 1 calorie is the heat required to raise the temperature of 1 g of water from 14.5°C to 15.5°C at 760 mm of Hg.

Hence correct option is (a).

131. Energy gained by water (in 1 s) = energy supplied – energy lost = 1000 J – 160 J = 840 J

Total heat required to raise the temperature of water from 27°C to 77°C is $ms\Delta\theta$

Hence, the required time

$$t = \frac{ms\Delta\theta}{\text{Rate by which energy is gained by water}}$$

$$= \frac{(2)(4.2\times10^3)(50)}{840} = 500 \text{ s} = 8 \text{ min } 20 \text{ s}$$

132. Temperature of liquid oxygen will first increase in the same phase. Then, phase change (liquid to gas) will take place. During which temperature will remain constant. After that temperature of oxygen in gaseous state will further increase.

133. Let final equilibrium temperature of gases in T

Heat rejected by gas by lower compartment

$$= nC_V\Delta T = 2\times\frac{3}{2}R(700-T)$$

Heat received by the gas in above compartment

$$= nC_P\Delta T = 2\times\frac{7}{2}R(T-400)$$

Equating the two, we get

$$2100 - 3T = 7T - 2800$$

$$\Rightarrow \quad T = 490 \text{ K}$$

134. $\Delta W_1 + \Delta U_1 = \Delta Q_1$ (i)

$\Delta W_2 + \Delta U_2 = \Delta Q_2$ (ii)

$\Delta Q_1 + \Delta Q_2 = 0$

$\therefore \quad (nC_P\Delta T)_1 + (nC_P\Delta T)_2 = 0$

But $\quad n_1 = n_2 = 2$

$$\therefore \quad \frac{5}{2}R(T-700)+\frac{7}{2}R(T-400) = 0$$

Solving, we get $T = 525$ K

Now, from Eqs. (i) and (ii), we get

$$\Delta W_1 + \Delta W_2 = -\Delta U_1 - \Delta U_2$$

as $\quad \Delta Q_1 + \Delta Q_2 = 0$

$$\therefore \quad \Delta W1 + \Delta W_2 = -[(nC_V\Delta T)_1 + (nC_V\Delta T)_2]$$

$$= -\left[2\times\frac{3}{2}R\times(525-700)+2\times\frac{5}{2}R\times(525-400)\right]$$

$$= -100 \text{ R}$$

135. Since it is open from top, pressure will be p_0

136. Let p be the pressure in equilibrium.

pA

Mg $\quad p_0A$

Then, $\quad pA = p_0A - Mg$

$$p = p_0 - \frac{Mg}{A} = p_0 - \frac{Mg}{\pi R^2}$$

Applying, $\quad p_1V_1 = p_2V_2$

$\therefore \quad p_0(2AL) = (p)(AL')$

$$\therefore \quad L' = \frac{2p_0L}{p} = \left(\frac{p_0}{p_0 - \frac{Mg}{\pi R^2}}\right)(2L)$$

$$= \left(\frac{p_0\pi R^2}{\pi R^2 p_0 - Mg}\right)(2L)$$

$\therefore$ Correct option is (d).

137. $p_1 = p_2$

$$p_0 + \rho g(L_0 - H) = p \quad \text{...(i)}$$

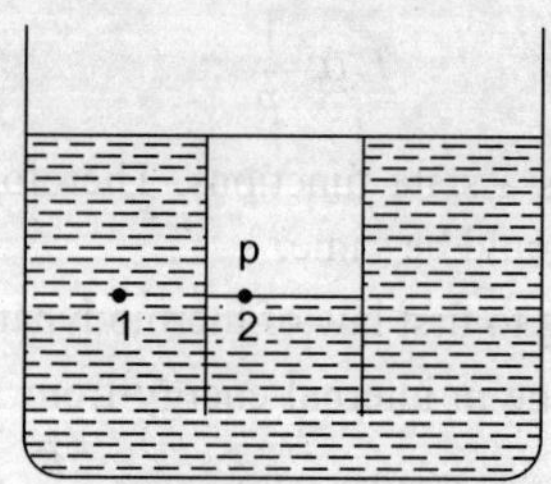

Now, applying $p_1V_1 = p_2V_2$ for the air inside the cylinder,

we have $\quad p_0(L_0) = p(L_0 - H)$

$$\therefore \quad p = \frac{p_0L_0}{L_0 - H}$$

Substituting in Eq. (i), we have

$$p_0 + \rho g(L_0 - H) = \frac{p_0L_0}{L_0 - H}$$

or $\quad \rho g(L_0 - H)^2 + p_0(L_0 - \text{H}) - p_0L_0 = 0$

$\therefore$ correct option is (c).

138. $v_{\text{sound}} = \sqrt{\frac{\gamma RT}{M}}$. As the sound wave propagates, the air in a chamber undergo compression and rarefaction very fastly hence undergo a adiabatic process.

So curves are steeper than isothermal.

$$\left(\frac{dp}{dV}\right)_{\text{Adi}} = -\gamma\left(\frac{p}{V}\right) \quad ...(i)$$

$$\left(\frac{dp}{dV}\right)_{\text{Iso}} = -\left(\frac{p}{V}\right) \quad ...(ii)$$

Graph 'Q' satisfies Eq. (i)

139. $\Delta U = \Delta Q - p\Delta V$; $\Delta U + p\Delta V = \Delta Q$

As $\Delta U \neq 0$, $W \neq 0$, $\Delta Q \neq 0$. The process represents, isobaric process

$$W_{\text{gas}} = -p(\Delta V) = -p(V_2 - V_1) = pV_2 + pV_1$$

Graph 'P' satisfies isobaric process.

140. Work done in isochoric process is zero.

$$W_{12} = 0 \text{ as } \Delta V = 0$$

Graph 'S' represents isochoric process.

141. Heat flow rate $= KA\dfrac{\Delta T}{l}$

Heat flux $= K\left(\dfrac{\Delta T}{l}\right)$

142. In steady state

Energy incident per second

= Energy radiated per second

$\therefore \quad I\pi R^2 = \sigma(T^4 - T_0^4)4\pi R^2 \Rightarrow I = \sigma(T^4 - T_0^4)4$

$\Rightarrow \quad T_4 = 121 \times 10^8 \Rightarrow T = 300$ K

143. In thermal conduction

$$\frac{\Delta G}{\Delta t} = \frac{KA(T_1 - T_2)}{x}$$

$$\frac{dQ_1}{dt} = \frac{dQ_2}{dt} + \frac{dQ_3}{dt}$$

$$\frac{0.92(100 - T)}{46} = \frac{0.26(T - 0)}{13} + \frac{0.12(T - 0)}{12}$$

$\Rightarrow \quad T = 40°C$

$$\frac{dQ_1}{dt} = \frac{0.92 \times 4(100 - 40)}{40} = 4.8 \text{ cal/s.}$$

145. Since thermal resistance R_{II} is 4.5 less than thermal resistance R_{I}.

$$\therefore \quad t_{\text{II}} = \frac{t_{\text{I}}}{4.5} = \frac{9}{4.5} \text{ s} = 2 \text{ s}$$

146. Let temperature of middle plate in steady state is T_0

$$Q_1 = Q_2$$

Q = net rate of heat flow

$\therefore \sigma A(3T)^4 - \sigma A{T^4}_0 = \sigma A{T^4}_0 - \sigma A\,(2T)^4$

Solving this equation, we get

$$T_0 = \left(\frac{97}{2}\right)^{1/4} T$$

147. $\lambda_m T$ = constant

From the graph $T_3 > T_2 > T_1$

Temperature of sun will be maximum.

Therefore, (c) is the correct option.

148. Glass of bulb heats due to filament by radiation.

149. $Q \propto AT^4$ and $\lambda m T$ = constant

Hence, $\quad Q \propto \dfrac{A}{(\lambda_m)^4} \propto \dfrac{r^2}{(\lambda_m)^4}$

$$Q_A : Q_B : Q_C = \frac{(2)^2}{(3)^4} : \frac{(4)^2}{(4)^4} : \frac{(6)^2}{(5)^4} = \frac{4}{18} : \frac{1}{16} : \frac{36}{625}$$

$= 0.05 : 0.0625 : 0.05$

i.e. Q_B is maximum.

150. $$\frac{dQ}{dt} = L\left(\frac{dm}{dt}\right)$$

or $$\frac{\text{Temperature difference}}{\text{Thermal resistance}} = L\left(\frac{dm}{dt}\right)$$

or $$\frac{dm}{dt} \propto \frac{1}{\text{Thermal resistance}} \propto \frac{1}{R}$$

In the first case rods are in parallel and thermal resist $\dfrac{R}{2}$ while in second case rods are in series and t resistance is $2R$.

$$\therefore \quad \frac{q_1}{q_2} = \frac{2R}{R/2} = \frac{4}{1}$$

151. As we know force

$$F = 2\frac{dN}{dt} \times mv = 2 \times 10^{22} \times 10^{-26} \times 10^4 = 2N$$

Pressure = 2 Nm^{-2}

152. From $pV = nRT = \dfrac{N}{N_A}RT$

We have, $n_f - n_i = \dfrac{pVN_A}{RT_f} - \dfrac{pVN_A}{RT_i}$

$$n_f - n_i = \frac{10^5 \times 30}{8.3} \times 6.02 \times 10^{23} \cdot \left(\frac{1}{300} - \frac{1}{290}\right)$$

$= -2.5 \times 10^{25}$

$\therefore \quad \Delta n = -2.5 \times 10^{25}$

153. $\Delta Q = \Delta U + \Delta W$

In the precess pV^n = constant, molar heat capacity is given by

$$C = \frac{R}{\gamma - 1} + \frac{R}{1 - n} = C_v + \frac{R}{1 - n}$$

$$\Rightarrow \quad 1 - n = \frac{C_p - C_v}{C - C_v}$$

$$\Rightarrow \quad n = 1 - \left(\frac{C_p - C_v}{C - C_v}\right) = \frac{C - C_p}{C - C_v}$$

154. $\rho = \dfrac{pM}{RT}$ $\rho \propto p_M$

or $\dfrac{\rho_1}{\rho_2} = \left(\dfrac{p_1}{P_2}\right)\left(\dfrac{M_1}{M_2}\right) = \left(\dfrac{2}{3}\right)\left(\dfrac{4}{3}\right) = \dfrac{8}{9}$

155. In equilibrium,

$$p_0 A = Mg \quad \text{...(i)}$$

when slightly displayed downwards,

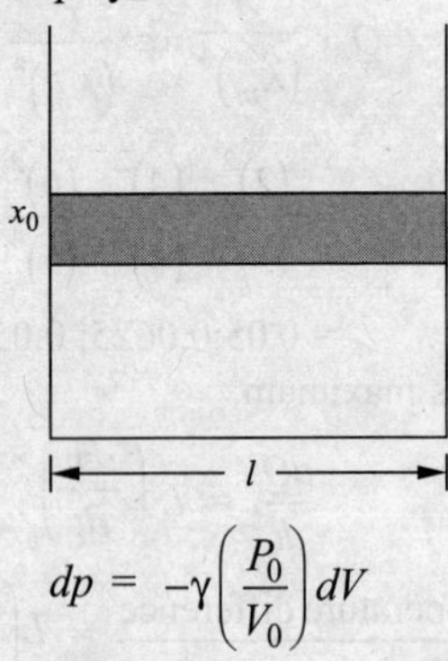

$$dp = -\gamma\left(\frac{P_0}{V_0}\right)dV$$

(As in adiabatic process,

$$\frac{dp}{dV} = -\gamma\frac{P}{V})$$

$\therefore$ Restoring force,

$$F = (dp)A = -\left(\frac{\gamma P_0}{V_0}\right)(A)(Ax)$$

$$F \propto -x$$

Therefore, motion is simple harmonic comparing with $F = -kx$ we have

$$k = \frac{\gamma p_0 A^2}{V_0} \quad \therefore f = \frac{1}{2\neq}\sqrt{\frac{k}{m}} = \frac{1}{2\pi}\sqrt{\frac{\gamma p_0 A^2}{MV_0}}$$

156. $v_{rms} = \sqrt{\dfrac{3RT}{M}}$ or $v_{rms} \propto \dfrac{1}{\sqrt{M}}$

$$\therefore \frac{(v_{rms})_{He}}{(v_{rms})_{Ar}} = \sqrt{\frac{M_{Ar}}{M_{He}}} = \sqrt{\frac{40}{4}} = \sqrt{10} \approx 3.16$$

157. A real gas behaves like an ideal gas at low pressure high temperature.

158. pT^2 = constant

$$\therefore \left(\frac{nRT}{V}\right)T^2 = \text{constant or } T^3V^{-1} = \text{constant}$$

Differentiating the equation, we get

$$\frac{3T^2}{V}.dT - \frac{T^3}{V^2}dV = 0 \text{ or } 3dT = \frac{T}{V}.dV \quad \text{...(i)}$$

From the equation

$$dV = V\gamma dT$$

γ =coefficient of volume expansion of gas = $\dfrac{dV}{V.dT}$

From Eq. (i) $\gamma = \dfrac{dV}{V.dT} = \dfrac{3}{T}$

7 CHAPTER

Basic Electricity

ATOM

An atom is a particle of matter that uniquely defines a chemical element. An atom consists of a central nucleus that is surrounded by one or more negatively charged electrons. The nucleus is positively charged and contains one or more relatively heavy particles known as protons and neutrons.

Atoms are the basic building blocks of matter. Anything that takes up space and anything with mass is made up of atoms. Protons and neutrons are subatomic particles that make up the center of the atom, or its atomic nucleus.

- A **proton** is positively charged. The number of protons in the nucleus of an atom is the atomic number for the chemical element. Different elements' atomic numbers are found in the Periodic Table of Elements. For example, sodium has 11 protons, and its atomic number is 11. A proton has a rest mass, denoted mp, of approximately 1.673 x 10-27 kilogram (kg).
- A **neutron** is electrically neutral and has a rest mass, denoted mn, of approximately 1.675 x 10-27.

The mass of a proton or neutron increases when the particle attains extreme speed, for example in a cyclotron or linear accelerator.

The structure of an atom:

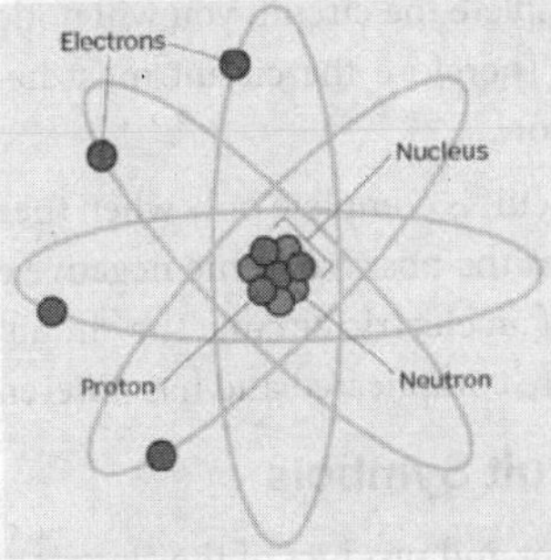

The total mass of an atom, including the protons, neutrons and electrons, is the atomic mass or atomic weight. The atomic mass or weight is measured in atomic mass units. Electrons contribute only a tiny part to the mass of the atomic structure; however, they play an important role in the chemical reactions that create molecules. For most purposes, the atomic weight can be thought of as the number of protons plus the number of neutrons. Because the number of neutrons in an atom can vary, there can be several different atomic weights for most elements. Protons and electrons have equal and opposite charges. Protons have a positive charge and electrons a negative charge. Normally, atoms have equal numbers of protons and electrons, giving them a neutral charge. An ion is an atom with a different number of electrons than protons and is electrically charged. An ion with extra electrons has a negative charge and is called an anion and an ion deficient in electrons has a positive charge and is called a cation. Atoms having the same number of protons but different numbers of neutrons represent the same element and are known as isotopes of that element. An isotope for an element is specified by the sum of the number of protons and neutrons.

Electricity:

Electricity is a fundamental property of matter that is the source of many physical phenomena, including electromagnetic fields, magnetism, and light. It is also the basis for a wide range of technological applications, including power generation, transmission, and distribution.

Electricity is produced by the movement of charged particles, such as electrons. When an object is charged, it has either an excess or a deficiency of electrons. If two objects with opposite charges are brought close together, the electrons will flow from the object with the excess electrons to the object with the deficiency. This flow of electrons is what we call electricity.

Electricity can be generated in a number of ways, including :

- **Chemical reactions:** Batteries generate electricity by using chemical reactions to create a flow of electrons.
- **Mechanical energy:** Generators convert mechanical energy into electrical energy by turning a coil of wire in a magnetic field.
- **Solar energy:** Solar panels convert sunlight into electrical energy using the photovoltaic effect.

- **Wind energy:** Wind turbines generate electricity by converting the kinetic energy of the wind into electrical energy.

Electricity is transmitted and distributed through a network of power lines. Power lines are made of conductive materials, such as copper or aluminum, that allow electrons to flow freely. The electrons are pushed through the power lines by an electric field, which is created by a voltage difference between the two ends of the line. The voltage difference is what we call electricity.

Electricity is used in a wide variety of applications, including :

- **Power generation :** Electricity is the primary source of power for most of the world's homes and businesses.
- **Transportation :** Electric vehicles are becoming increasingly popular as a way to reduce pollution from gasoline-powered vehicles.
- **Lighting :** Electric lights are the most common type of lighting in the world.
- **Communication :** Electricity is used to power a wide variety of communication devices, such as telephones, computers, and televisions.
- **Manufacturing :** Electricity is used to power a wide variety of manufacturing processes, such as metal working, plastics production, and food processing.

Electricity is a powerful and versatile form of energy that is essential to our modern way of life. As we continue to develop new technologies, electricity will continue to play an even more important role in our lives.

Basic electricity concepts:

Here are some basic electricity concepts that you should know:

- **Electric charge :** Electric charge is a property of matter that determines its electromagnetic interactions. There are two types of electric charge: positive and negative. Objects with the same charge repel each other, while objects with opposite charges attract each other.
- **Electric field :** An electric field is a region of space that is influenced by the presence of electric charges. Electric fields exert forces on charged particles.
- **Electric potential :** Electric potential is the amount of work that must be done to move a unit of electric charge from one point to another in an electric field. Electric potential is measured in volts (V).
- **Electric current :** Electric current is the flow of electric charge. Electric current is measured in amperes (A).
- **Resistance :** Resistance is a measure of how difficult it is for electric charge to flow through a material. Resistance is measured in ohms (Ω).
- **Voltage :** Voltage is the difference in electric potential between two points in an electric circuit. Voltage is measured in volts (V).
- **Ohm's law :** Ohm's law is a fundamental principle of electricity that states that the current flowing through a conductor between two points is directly proportional to the voltage difference across the two points and inversely proportional to the resistance between the two points.
- **Power :** Power is the rate at which energy is transferred. Power is measured in watts (W).
- **Circuits :** A circuit is a closed loop of conductors through which electric current flows. Circuits can be series circuits, parallel circuits, or combinations of both.
- **Batteries :** Batteries are devices that store chemical energy and convert it into electrical energy. Batteries are used to power a wide variety of devices, from portable electronics to electric vehicles.
- **Generators :** Generators are devices that convert mechanical energy into electrical energy. Generators are used to produce electricity for power grids.

Electric Circuits :

The electric circuits are closed-loop or paths, forming a network of electrical components where electrons can flow. This path is made using electrical wires and is powered by a source, like a battery. The start of the point from where the electrons start flowing is called the source, whereas the point where electrons leave the electrical circuit is called the return. Let's conduct a small experiment; you would need the following; Electric bulb, Wire, Electrical tape and a battery.

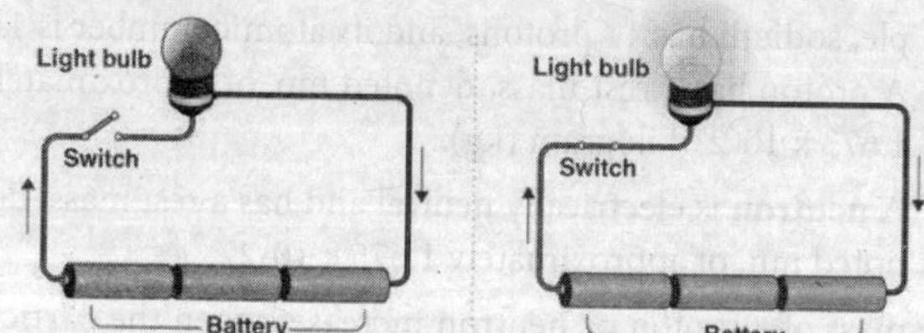

Connect the wires to the bulb and connect one end of the wire to the battery. Notice what happens, there won't be any change in the bulb, but when you connect the free wire to the battery and complete the circuit, you will notice that the bulb starts glowing. Therefore the circuit must be completed for the current to flow.

An electrical circuit is complete only when there is at least one closed loop from the positive to the negative end. This is the simplest form of an electric circuit. The circuit found inside a television is more complicated and has different components.

Electric Circuit Symbols

Every component and product of the electric circuit contains a symbol. The symbols represent parts of the circuit in a circuit diagram. Beneath are the basic set of symbols that are present in a circuit diagram.

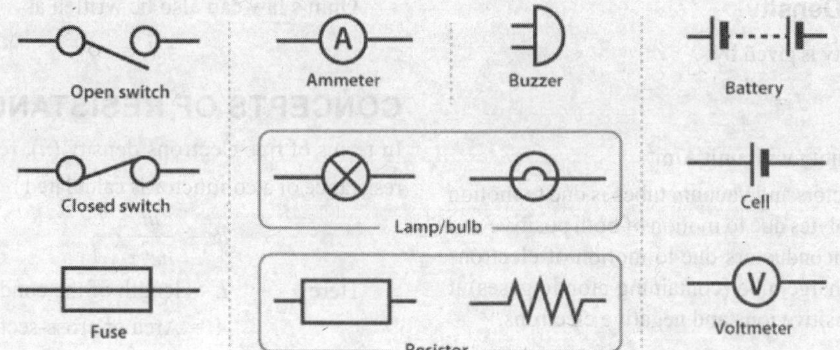

Basic components of an electrical circuit :

An electrical circuit is a closed loop path that allows electrons to flow continuously. It contains a source of electromotive force (EMF), such as a battery or generator, which drives current through the circuit.

The basic components of an electrical circuit are:

- **Source of EMF :** This provides the energy to drive the current in the circuit.
- **Conductor :** This is a material that allows electrons to flow freely through it.
- **Load :** This is a device that consumes electrical energy, such as a light bulb or motor.
- **Control devices :** These are devices that can switch or regulate the flow of current in the circuit, such as switches, relays, and transistors.

There are two main types of electrical circuits:

- **Series circuits :** In a series circuit, all the components are connected in a single loop, so the current must flow through each component in succession.
- **Parallel circuits :** In a parallel circuit, the components are connected in multiple branches, so the current can flow through each branch independently.

Electrical circuits are used in a wide variety of applications, including:

- **Power generation and transmission :** Electrical circuits are used to generate, transmit, and distribute electricity to homes and businesses.
- **Electronics :** Electrical circuits are used to create a wide variety of electronic devices, such as computers, smartphones, and televisions.
- **Industrial control :** Electrical circuits are used to control machinery and equipment in industrial settings.
- **Transportation :** Electrical circuits are used to power electric vehicles and trains.
- **Communication :** Electrical circuits are used to transmit and receive communication signals, such as telephone calls and internet traffic.
- **Medical devices :** Electrical circuits are used to power a wide variety of medical devices, such as pacemakers and MRI machines.

ELECTRIC CURRENT

The time rate of flow of charge through any cross-section is called current. So through a cross-section, Δq charge passes in time Δt is

$$\therefore \quad I_{av} = \frac{\Delta q}{\Delta t}$$

And hence instantaneous current

$$I = \lim_{\Delta t \to 0} \frac{\Delta q}{\Delta t} = \frac{dq}{dt}$$

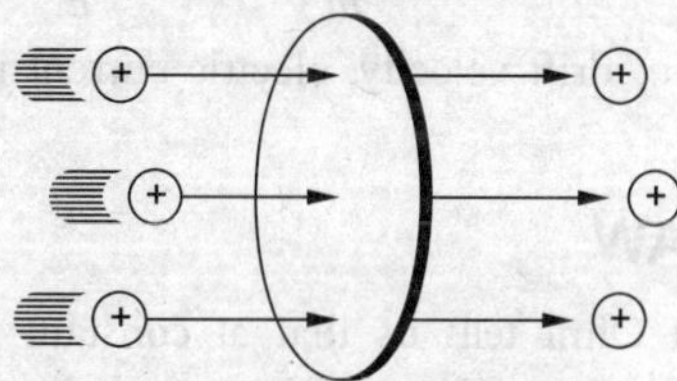

SI unit of electric current is Ampere.

Electric Current for Different Situations

(i) If there are n-particles, each of charge q passing through given area in time t then $I = \frac{\Delta q}{\Delta t} = \frac{nq}{t}$.

(ii) If n particles, each having a charge q, pass per sec per unit area, the current associated with cross-sectional area A is

$$I = \frac{\Delta Q}{\Delta t} = nqA$$

(iii) If there are n particles per unit volume, each having a charge q and moving with velocity v, the current through cross-sectional area A is

$$I = \frac{\Delta Q}{\Delta t} = nqA\frac{\Delta}{\Delta t} = nqvA \qquad \text{...(i)}$$

(iv) Electric current due to rotational motion is given by,

$$\frac{qv}{2\pi r} = qf.$$

Electric Current Density

Electric current density is given by,

$$J = \frac{I}{A}$$

It is a vector quantity with unit A/m^2.

Current in conductors and vacuum tubes is due to motion of electrons, in electrolytes due to motion of both positive and negative ions, in semiconductors due to motion of electrons and holes and in discharge tube (containing atomic gases) it is due to motion of positive ions and negative electrons.

DRIFT VELOCITY

It is the average velocity acquired by free electrons inside a metal under the influence of electric field which is responsible for current through it.

i.e., $$V_d = \frac{-eE}{m}\tau$$

$\Rightarrow$ $$V_d \propto E$$

where τ = Relaxation time and defined as the time interval between two successive collisions.

m = mass of electron

and e = elementary charge

Drift velocity per unit electric field is called mobility of electron (μ_e)

i.e., $$\mu_e = \frac{e}{m}\tau \text{ as } \mu_e = \frac{V_d}{E}$$

In terms of drift velocity, electric current is calculated by $I = AneV_d$.

OHM'S LAW

Georg Simon Ohm tells us that at constant temperature potential difference (V) across a conductor is directly proportional to its resistance (R).

i.e., $$V = IR$$

Conductors obeying Ohm's law are called ohmic conductors for example metal and their alloys. V-I graph for ohmic conductor is straight line as shown below.

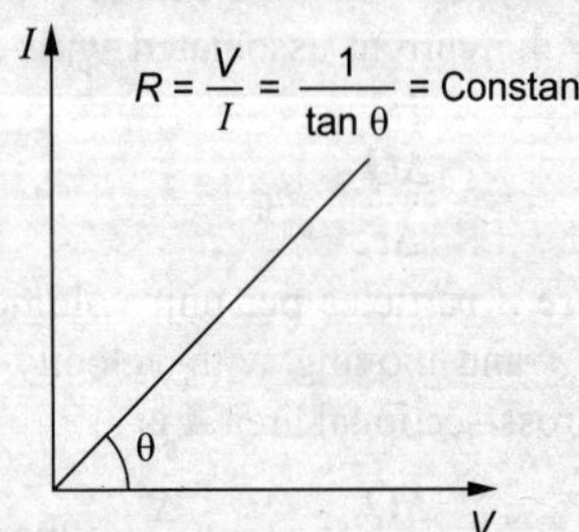

Conductivity or resistivity of a material is independent of the electric field existing in the material.

Conductors which do not obey Ohm's law are non ohmic conductors for example, electrolytes, gases thermionic tubes, transistors, rectifiers etc. V-I graphs for these materials are non-linear.

Ohm's law can also be written as

$$\vec{J} = \sigma\vec{E}$$

CONCEPTS OF RESISTANCE

In terms of free electrons density (n), relaxation time (τ) the resistance of a conductor is calculated by

$$R = \frac{m}{ne^2\tau}\cdot\frac{L}{A}$$

Here L = length of the conductor

A = Area of cross-section of the conductor

In terms of free electrons density and relaxation time resistivity of material is $\rho = \dfrac{m}{ne^2\tau}$

$$\therefore \quad J = \sigma E = \frac{1}{\rho}E = \frac{ne^2\tau E}{m}$$

Resistance and resistivity increases with increase in temperature according to relation

$$R_t = R_0(1 + \alpha\Delta\theta)$$
$$\rho_t = \rho_0(1 + \alpha\Delta\theta)$$

Here α = temperature coefficient

and $\Delta\theta$ = increase in temperature

Grouping of Resistance; Resistances in Series

Series combination of resistances is shown below:

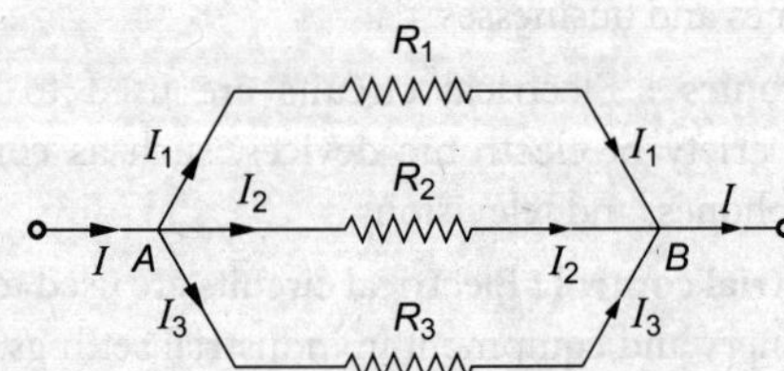

For this combination equivalent resistance

$$R_{eq} = R_1 + R_2 + R_3$$

Voltages are in the ratio

$$V_1 : V_2 : V_3 :: R_1 : R_2 : R_3$$

(i) $V_1 = \dfrac{V R_1}{R_1 + R_2 + R_3}$, (ii) $V_2 = \dfrac{V R_2}{R_1 + R_2 + R_3}$

(iii) $V_3 = \dfrac{V R_3}{R_1 + R_2 + R_3}$

Resistances in Parallel

Parallel combination of resistances is shown below:

R_1, R_2, R_3; I_1, I_2, I_3; I; A, B

For this combination equivalent resistance is,

$$\frac{1}{R_{eq}} = \frac{1}{R_1} + \frac{1}{R_2} + \frac{1}{R_3}$$

Ratio of currents, $I_1 : I_2 : I_3 :: \dfrac{1}{R_1} : \dfrac{1}{R_2} : \dfrac{1}{R_3}$

When two resistors are in parallel then

$$I_1 = \frac{IR_2}{R_1 + R_2}$$

and $$I_2 = \frac{IR_1}{R_1 + R_2}$$

Points to Remember

(i) Ratio of equivalent resistances of series and parallel combinations of equal resistance, $\frac{R_s}{R_p} = n^2$

(ii) If a skeleton cube is made with 12 equal resistances, each having a resistance R, then the net resistance across

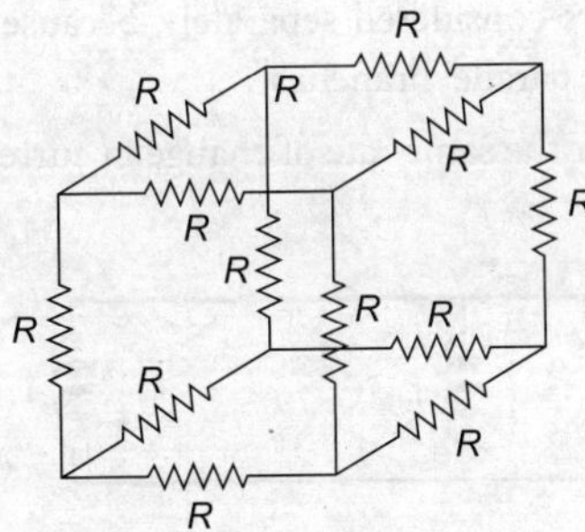

(a) the diagonal of cube $= \frac{5}{6}R$,

(b) the diagonal of a face $= \frac{3}{4}R$, and

(c) along a side $= \frac{7}{12}R$.

CONCEPTS OF CAPACITOR

Capacitors are passive electronic components that store electrical energy in the form of an electric field. They are used in a wide variety of applications, including filtering, timing, and energy storage.

A capacitor consists of two conducting plates separated by a dielectric material. The dielectric material can be a solid, liquid, or gas. When the plates are charged, an electric field is created between them. This electric field stores energy. The capacitance of a capacitor is the amount of charge it can store per unit of voltage. The capacitance of a capacitor is measured in farads (F).

The capacitance of a capacitor is calculated using the following formula:

$$C = \varepsilon A/d$$

where :

- C is the capacitance in farads (F)
- ε is the permittivity of the dielectric material in farads per meter (F/m)
- A is the area of each plate in square meters (m^2)
- d is the distance between the plates in meters (m)

The permittivity of a dielectric material is a measure of its ability to store electrical energy. The permittivity of free space is approximately 8.85 × 10-12 F/m. The permittivity of a dielectric material is always greater than the permittivity of free space.

Grouping of Capacitors:

Capacitors can be grouped together in two ways: in series and in parallel.

Series Capacitors:

Capacitors are connected in series when their terminals are connected together in a chain. The equivalent capacitance of a series combination of capacitors is calculated using the following formula :

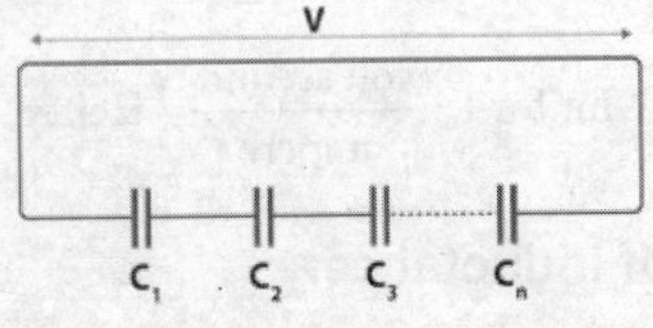

$$1/C_{eq} = 1/C_1 + 1/C_2 + ... + 1/C_n$$

Where, C_{eq} is the equivalent capacitance of the series combination $C_1, C_2, ..., C_n$ are the capacitances of the individual capacitors.

Parallel Capacitors:

Capacitors are connected in parallel when their plates are connected together. The equivalent capacitance of a parallel combination of capacitors is calculated using the following formula:

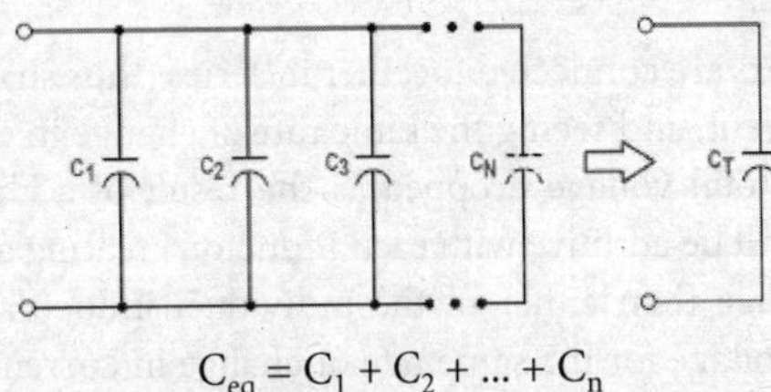

$$C_{eq} = C_1 + C_2 + ... + C_n$$

The equivalent capacitance of a group of capacitors is the capacitance of a single capacitor that would store the same amount of energy at the same voltage.

Applications of Capacitors

Capacitors are used in a wide variety of applications, including:

- **Filtering :** Capacitors can be used to remove unwanted frequencies from a signal. This is because capacitors block alternating current (AC) but allow direct current (DC) to pass through.
- **Timing :** Capacitors can be used to create time delays. This is because it takes time for a capacitor to charge and discharge.
- **Energy storage :** Capacitors can be used to store electrical energy. This is because capacitors can store an electric field.
- **Power factor correction :** Capacitors can be used to improve the power factor of a load. This is because capacitors reduce the amount of reactive power that a load consumes.

- **Coupling and decoupling :** Capacitors can be used to couple two circuits together or to decouple two circuits from each other. This is because capacitors block DC but allow AC to pass through.
- **Tuning :** Capacitors can be used to tune circuits. This is because capacitors can change the resonant frequency of a circuit.

CONCEPTS OF INDUCTANCE

Inductance is typified by the behavior of a coil of wire in resisting any change of electric current through the coil. Arising from Faraday's law, the inductance L may be defined in terms of the emf generated to oppose a given change in current :

$$\text{Emf} = -L\frac{\Delta I}{\Delta t}$$

$$\text{Unit for L} : \frac{\text{volt second}}{\text{ampere}} = \text{Henry}$$

Grouping of inductance:

Inductors can be grouped together in two ways: in series and in parallel.

Series inductors :

When inductors are connected in series, the total inductance is the sum of the individual inductors' inductances. To understand why this is so, consider the following: the definitive measure of inductance is the amount of voltage dropped across an inductor for a given rate of current change through it.

If inductors are connected together in series (thus sharing the same current, and seeing the same rate of change in current), then the total voltage dropped as the result of a change in current will be additive with each inductor, creating a greater total voltage than either of the individual inductors alone. Greater voltage for the same rate of change in current means greater inductance.

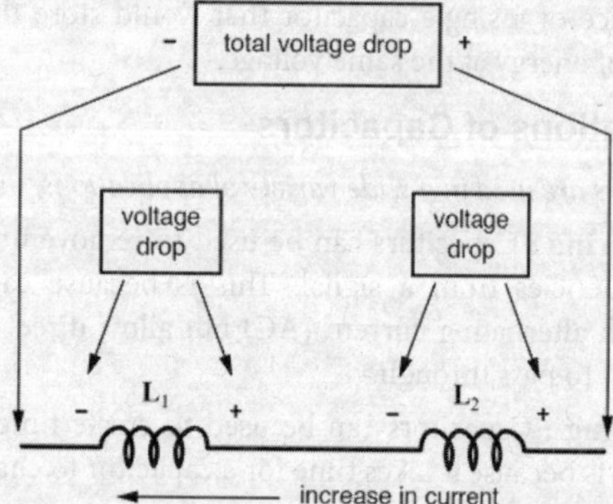

Thus, the total inductance for series inductors is more than any one of the individual inductors' inductances. The formula for calculating the series total inductance is the same form as for calculating series resistances :

$$L_{total} = L_1 + L_2 + ... L_n$$

Parallel inductors :

When inductors are connected in parallel, the total inductance is less than any one of the parallel inductors' inductances. Again, remember that the definitive measure of inductance is the amount of voltage dropped across an inductor for a given rate of current change through it.

Since the current through each parallel inductor will be a fraction of the total current, and the voltage across each parallel inductor will be equal, a change in total current will result in less voltage dropped across the parallel array than for any one of the inductors considered separately. In other words, there will be less voltage dropped across parallel inductors for a given rate of change in current than for any of those inductors considered separately, because total current divides among parallel branches.

Less voltage for the same rate of change in current means less inductance.

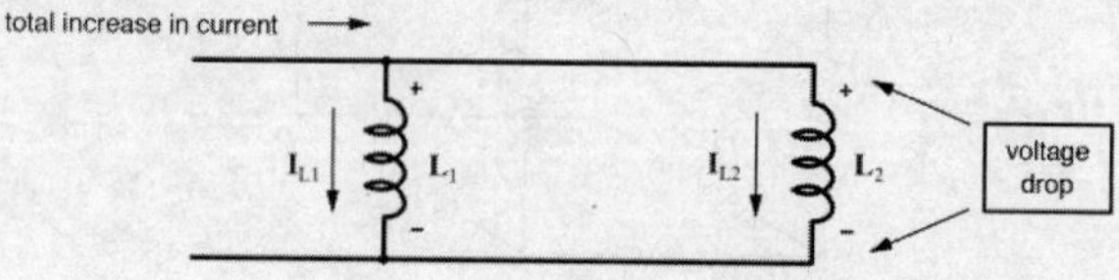

Thus, the total inductance is less than any one of the individual inductors' inductances. The formula for calculating the parallel total inductance is the same form as for calculating parallel resistances:

Parallel Inductances

$$L_{total} = \frac{1}{\frac{1}{L_1} + \frac{1}{L_2} + ... \frac{1}{L_n}}$$

Electric voltage:

Electric voltage, also known as electric pressure, electric tension, or (electric) potential difference, is the difference in electric potential between two points. In a static electric field, it corresponds to the work needed per unit of charge to move a test charge between the two points.

Voltage is typically provided by a power source, such as a battery or a generator, and it is distributed through electrical circuits to power various devices and systems. In an electrical circuit, voltage is often represented by the symbol "V," and it is measured in volts (V).

Ohm's Law is a fundamental principle in electrical circuits that relates voltage (V), current (I), and resistance (R). The relationship is given by the formula:

$$V = I \cdot R$$

Where;

- V is the voltage (in volts),
- I is the current (in amperes), and
- R is the resistance (in ohms).

This formula indicates that voltage is equal to the product of current and resistance. Understanding voltage is crucial for designing and analyzing electrical circuits.

Voltage is often measured with a voltmeter. A voltmeter is a device that measures the potential difference between two points in a circuit. Voltmeters can be either analog or digital. Analog voltmeters have a needle that moves along a scale, while digital voltmeters display the voltage on a screen.

Voltage is an important concept in electronics. It is used to drive current through a circuit, and it is also used to measure the amount of energy that is transferred by a circuit.

There are two types of voltage: AC voltage and DC voltage. AC voltage is an alternating voltage, which means that it changes direction periodically. DC voltage is a direct voltage, which means that it does not change direction.

Most household appliances use AC voltage. This is because AC voltage can be easily transmitted over long distances. DC voltage is often used in electronic devices, such as computers and cell phones. This is because DC voltage is more stable than AC voltage.

RMS Voltage equation:

Root Mean Square (RMS) voltage is a measure of the effective voltage of an alternating current (AC) waveform. For a sinusoidal waveform, the RMS voltage is related to the peak voltage (V_peak) by the following equation :

$$V_{RMS} = \frac{V_{peak}}{\sqrt{2}}$$

Where :

- V_{RMS} is the RMS voltage,
- V_{peak} is the peak voltage.

For example, if you know the peak voltage of a sinusoidal AC waveform, you can use this formula equivalent basis. Note that this formula specifically applies to sinusoidal waveforms.

The RMS voltage is a useful concept in electrical engineering because it is a measure of the average power that a sinusoidal AC waveform can deliver to a load.

Power calculations :

The RMS voltage is used to calculate the power delivered to a load by an AC circuit. The formula for power is:

$$P = VI$$

where:

- P is the power,
- V is the RMS voltage,
- I is the current.
- **Voltage ratings :** The RMS voltage is used to rate the voltage of AC circuits and devices. For example, a household AC outlet is rated at 120 V RMS.
- **AC circuit analysis :** The RMS voltage is used to analyze AC circuits. For example, the impedance of an AC circuit can be calculated using the formula:

$$Z = V/I$$

Where;

- Z is the impedance,
- V is the RMS voltage,
- I is the current.

Basic circuit:

A basic circuit is a closed loop that allows electricity to flow from one point to another. It consists of a power source, a conductor, and a load. The power source provides the electrical energy to drive the current through the circuit. The conductor is a material that allows electricity to flow through it. The load is the device that uses the electrical energy to do work.

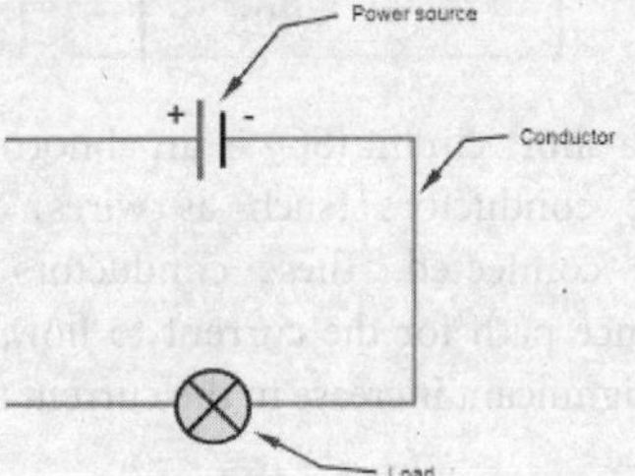

There are two types of basic circuits: series and parallel. In a series circuit, the components are connected in a single line, so the current has only one path to flow through. In a parallel circuit, the components are connected in separate branches, so the current can flow through multiple paths.

Basic circuits are used in a wide variety of applications, from household appliances to electronic devices. They are the building blocks of more complex circuits, and they are essential for understanding the principles of electricity.

Here are some examples of basic circuits :

- **A light switch :** A light switch is a series circuit that consists of a switch, a light bulb, and a power source. When the switch is turned on, the current flows from the power source to the light bulb, and the light bulb turns on.
- **A battery :** A battery is a series circuit that consists of two or more cells. Each cell contains a chemical reaction that produces electricity. The cells are connected in series so that the voltage of the battery is equal to the sum of the voltages of the cells.
- **A fuse :** A fuse is a series circuit that consists of a fuse wire and a power source. The fuse wire is made of a material that melts when the current through it exceeds a certain limit. If the current through the circuit is too high, the fuse wire will melt and open the circuit, protecting the other components from damage.
- **A transistor :** A transistor is a semiconductor device that can be used to amplify or switch electronic signals. Transistors are the building blocks of integrated circuits, which are used in a wide variety of electronic devices.

- **A light-emitting diode (LED) :** An LED is a semiconductor device that emits light when an electric current is passed through it. LEDs are used in a wide variety of applications, including displays, lighting, and communications.

These are just a few examples of the many different types of basic circuits. Basic circuits are an essential part of our everyday lives, and they are used in a wide variety of applications.

Short circuit :

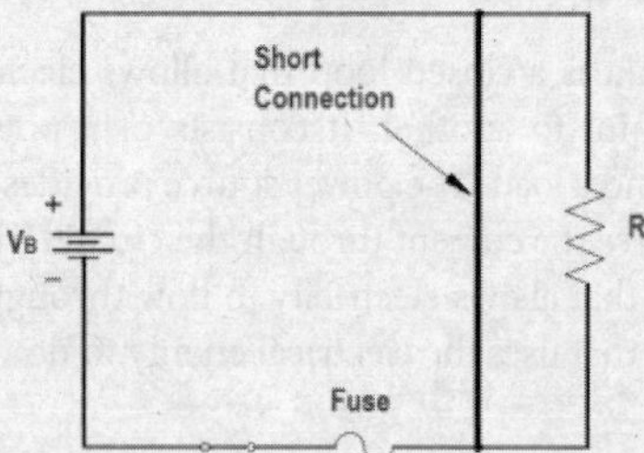

In a circuit, a short circuit (SC) is an abnormal connection between two conductors (such as wires) that normally shouldn't be connected. These conductors then provide a low-resistance path for the current to flow, resulting in a sudden and significant increase in the current flow beyond its intended value.

Short circuits can cause serious damage to electrical equipment and even start fires. They are often caused by accidental wire damage or by faulty insulation.

Here are some of the dangers of short circuits :

- Overheating: The sudden increase in current flow can cause the wires and other components in the circuit to overheat. This can lead to insulation failure, which can in turn cause fires.
- Electrical shock: The high current flow can also create a dangerous electrical shock hazard.
- Damage to equipment: The excessive current can damage electrical equipment, such as motors, transformers, and appliances.

There are a number of things that can be done to prevent short circuits, including :

- Using properly insulated wires: Proper insulation will prevent wires from touching each other and causing a short circuit.
- Inspecting wires regularly: Regularly inspecting wires for damage can help to identify potential problems before they cause a short circuit.
- Using fuses and circuit breakers: Fuses and circuit breakers are designed to protect circuits from short circuits. They will trip and cut off the power to the circuit if the current flow exceeds a certain limit.

By following these safety precautions, you can help to prevent short circuits and protect your electrical equipment from damage.

Here are some examples of how short circuits can occur :

- **A frayed wire :** A frayed wire can touch another wire or a grounded object, causing a short circuit.
- **A loose connection :** A loose connection can create a spark, which can ignite nearby flammable materials.
- **A nail or screw driven through a wire :** A nail or screw can pierce the insulation of a wire, causing a short circuit.
- **Water or other liquids :** Water or other liquids can conduct electricity and cause a short circuit if they come into contact with exposed wires.

Circuit protection :

Circuit protection is a crucial aspect of electrical engineering, as it safeguards electrical circuits from potential damage caused by overcurrent, overvoltage, or ground faults. By implementing appropriate protective devices, one can prevent electrical fires, equipment malfunctions, and personal injuries.

Types of Circuit Protection Devices:

1. **Fuses :** Fuses are among the oldest and most basic circuit protection devices. They consist of a thin metal wire that melts when the current exceeds a predetermined threshold, interrupting the circuit and preventing further damage.
2. **Circuit Breakers :** Circuit breakers operate on a similar principle to fuses, but they are resettable. When an overcurrent occurs, a circuit breaker trips, cutting off the power to the circuit. Once the fault is cleared, the circuit breaker can be manually reset to restore power.
3. **GFCIs (Ground Fault Circuit Breakers) :** GFCIs are specifically designed to protect against ground faults, which occur when electrical current leaks to the ground instead of following its intended path. GFCIs are particularly important in areas where electrical equipment is exposed to water, such as kitchens, bathrooms, and outdoor outlets.
4. **RCDs (Residual Current Devices) :** RCDs, also known as earth leakage protection (ELP), are similar to GFCIs but offer a higher level of sensitivity. They can detect even small leakage currents, providing protection against both ground faults and electrical shocks.
5. **Surge Protectors :** Surge protectors safeguard electrical devices from damage caused by power surges, which are sudden spikes in voltage. These spikes can be caused by lightning strikes, utility switching operations, or other events.
6. **Overcurrent Protection Relays :** Overcurrent protection relays are used in industrial settings to protect large electrical circuits. They monitor the current flow and trip when it exceeds a safe level, preventing damage to expensive equipment.

In addition to these devices, there are various other circuit protection methods employed in specific applications, such as thermal fuses, motor protection relays, and arc flash protection systems.

Selecting Appropriate Circuit Protection :

The choice of circuit protection devices depends on several factors, including the type of circuit, the current rating, the potential hazards, and the desired level of protection. Electrical engineers carefully consider these factors when designing and installing electrical systems to ensure the safety and reliability of electrical installations.

ELECTROCHEMICAL CELL

An electrochemical cell is a device which, by converting chemical energy into electrical energy, maintains the flow of charge in a circuit. It consists of two electrodes of different materials and an electrolyte. The electrode at higher potential is called positive terminal, or anode while at lower potential negative terminal, or cathode. When a cell is in use, i.e., discharging, current outside the cell is from anode to cathode while inside it from cathode to anode as shown in Fig.

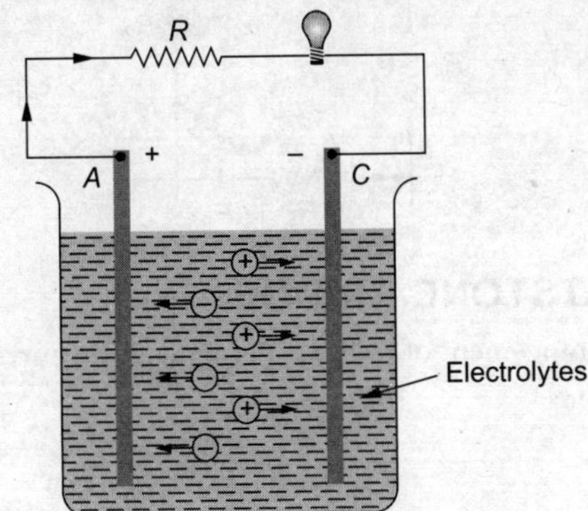

Some important terms related to the cell are:

(i) E.m.f of cell is $\frac{W}{q}$ with unit J/C, called volt.

$E = E_1 + E_2$ $E = E_1 - E_2$ $E = E_2 - E_1$

(ii) Internal resistance of cell is given by

$$r = \left(\frac{E - V}{V}\right) R$$

(iii) When cell is charging terminal potential difference, $V = E - Ir$

(iv) When cell is discharging $V = E + Ir$.

GROUPING OF CELLS

(a) In series as shown above.

(i) $E_{eq} = nE$

(ii) $r_{eq} = nr$

(iii) $I = \frac{nE}{R + nr}$.

(iv) If in series grouping of 'n' cells, 'm' cells are reversed then $I = \frac{(n - 2m)E}{R + nr}$

(v) If the cells are not identical then $I = \frac{\Sigma E_i}{R + \Sigma r_i}$

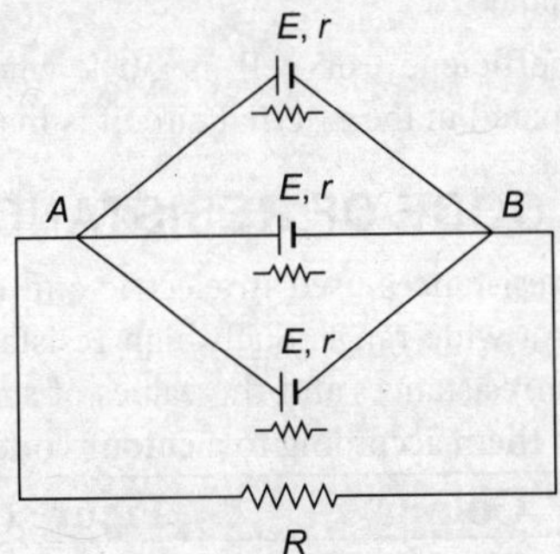

(b) In parallel as shown above,

(i) $r_{eq} = \frac{r}{n}$

(ii) $E_{eq} = E$

(iii) $I = \frac{E}{R + \frac{r}{n}}$

If the cells are not identical then

$$I = \frac{\frac{E_1}{r_1} - \frac{E_2}{r_2} + \frac{E_3}{r_3}}{1 + R\left(\frac{1}{r_1} + \frac{1}{r_2} + \frac{1}{r_3}\right)}$$

(c) In mixed grouping

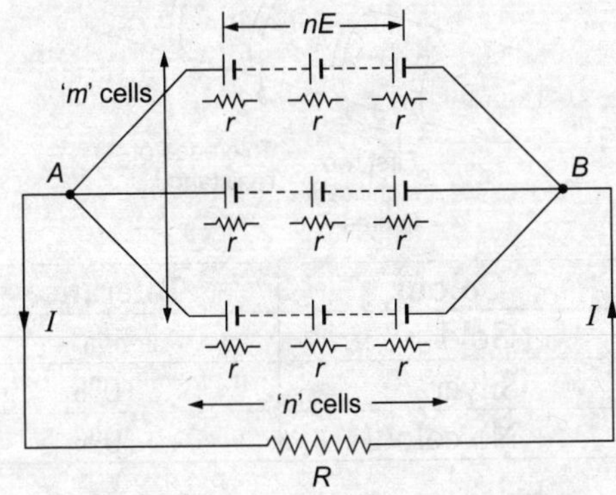

(i) $E_{eq} = nE$

(ii) $r_{eq} = \frac{nr}{m}$

(iii) $I = \frac{nE}{R + \frac{nr}{m}} = \frac{mnE}{mR + nr}$

(iv) For maximum current in circuit $\frac{m}{n} = \frac{r}{R}$.

Points to Remember

(i) Charging current for a secondary cell

$$= \frac{\text{emf of charge} - \text{emf of cell}}{\text{total resistance of the circuit}}$$

(ii) Efficiency of a cell is given by $\eta = \frac{R}{r + R}$

where R is external resistance and r is internal resistance.

(iii) The efficiency of cell is 50% when the power dissipated in the external circuit is maximum.

COLOUR CODE OF RESISTANCES

The value of resistances used in electric and electronic circuit vary over a wide range. Such high resistances used are usually carbon resistances and the values of such resistances are marked on them according to a **colour code** given below.

Colour	Figure (Code)
Black	0
Brown	1
Red	2
Orange	3
Yellow	4
Green	5
Blue	6
Violet	7
Grey	8
White	9

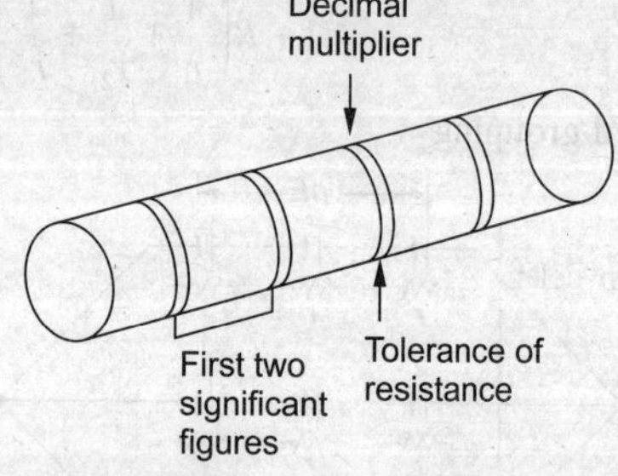

Colour	Tolerance
Gold	5%
Silver	10%
No colour	20%

KIRCHOFF'S LAW

***First law (Junction law)*:** The algebraic sum of currents meeting at a junction is zero.

i.e., $\sum I = 0$

$\Rightarrow$ $I_1 - I_2 - I_3 = 0$

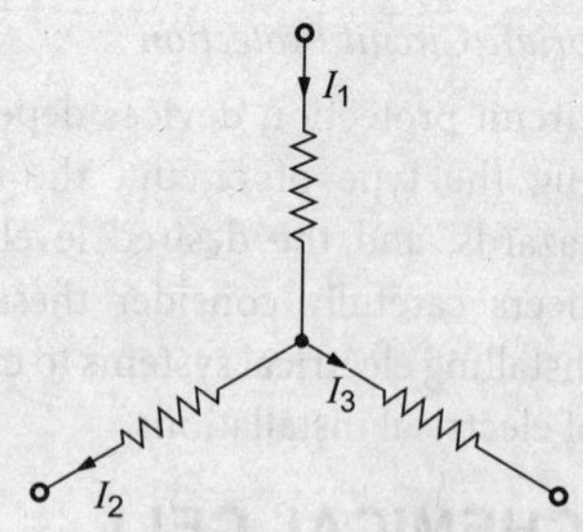

This law is based on conservation of charge.

***Second law (loop law)*:** The algebraic sum of all the potentials in a loop is zero.

i.e., $I_1R_1 + I_2R_2 - E_1 + I_3R_3 - I_4R_4 + E_2 = 0.$

This law is based on conservation of energy.

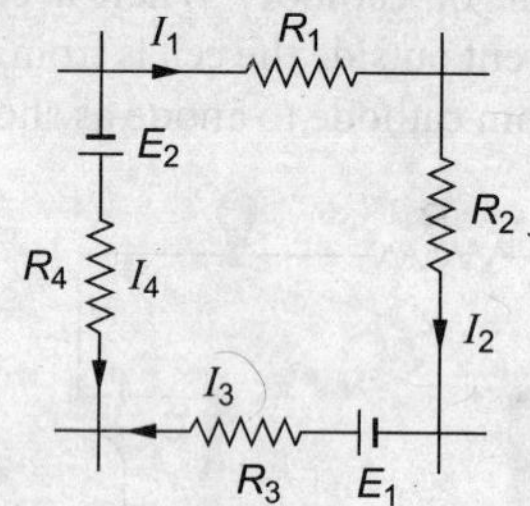

WHEATSTONE BRIDGE

In this arrangement of resistors (as shown), no current flows through R_0 i.e.,

$$V_A = V_B, \text{ if } \frac{P}{Q} = \frac{R}{S}$$

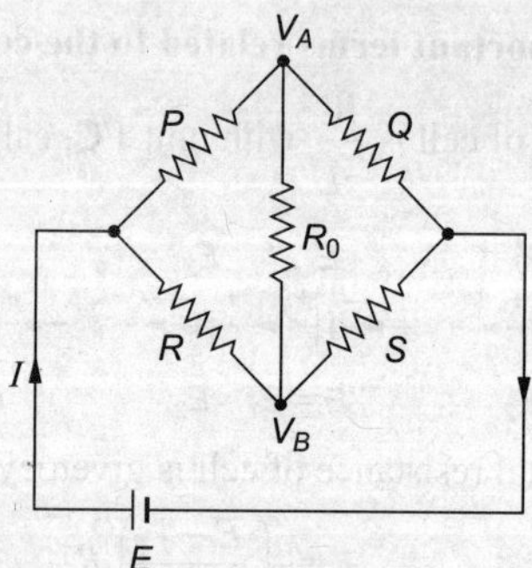

AMMETER

This instrument is used for measuring current in a circuit. In an ammeter, a resistor having a small resistance (r) is connected in parallel with the coil (R_c). This resistor is called the shunt.

$$R_{eq} = \frac{R_c \cdot r}{R_c + r}$$

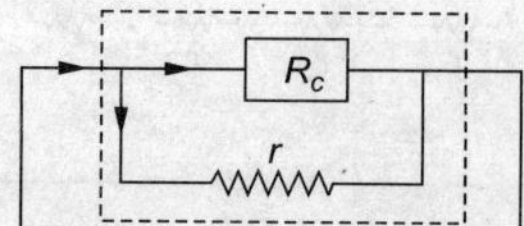

Network of resistances, connected across the battery, is actually a Wheatstone bridge in balanced condition. The equivalent circuits are shown below:

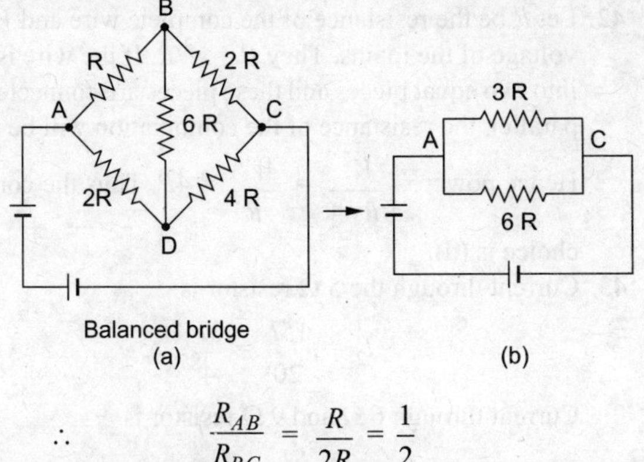

Balanced bridge
(a) (b)

$$\therefore \quad \frac{R_{AB}}{R_{BC}} = \frac{R}{2R} = \frac{1}{2}$$

$$\text{and} \quad \frac{R_{AD}}{R_{DC}} = \frac{2R}{4R} = \frac{1}{2}$$

$$\therefore \quad \frac{R_{AB}}{R_{BC}} = \frac{R_{AD}}{R_{DC}}$$

Wheatstone bridge is therefore balanced. Hence the resistance of arm *BD* becomes ineffective.

Now *ABC* ($3R\Omega$) and *ADC* ($6R\Omega$) are in parallel

$$\therefore \quad R_{\text{eq}} = \frac{(3R)(6R)}{3R+6R} = \frac{3R \times 6R}{9R} = 2R \qquad \text{...(ii)}$$

For maximum power, $2R = 4\Omega$

$\therefore R = 2\Omega$.

25. The minimum potential difference across the given galvanometer is

$$V = IR$$

$$V = 10^{-5} \times 40$$

$$V = 400\ \mu\text{V}$$

For each 25 μV thermo emf the temperature difference measured is 1°C.

For 400 μV temperature difference is 16°C

So, measured temperature difference detected by galvanometer is 16°C.

26. For a given volume, the resistance of the wire is expressed as

$$R = \frac{\rho l^2}{\text{Volume}} \quad \Rightarrow \quad R \propto l^2$$

$$\frac{R_2}{R_1} = \left(\frac{2l}{l}\right)^2 = 4 \quad \Rightarrow \quad \frac{R_2}{R_1} - 1 = 4 - 1$$

$$\frac{R_2 - R_1}{R_1} = 3$$

So, the change in resistance of wire will be 300%.

27. $$E = a\theta + b\theta^2$$

Given $$\frac{a}{b} = 700°\text{C}$$

$$\frac{dE}{d\theta} = a + 2b\theta$$

At neutral temperature, $\dfrac{dE}{d\theta} = 0$

$$\theta_n = \frac{-a}{2b} = \frac{-700}{2} = -350°\text{C}$$

As this temperature is below the temperature of cold Junction, hence no neutral temperature is possible for this thermocouple.

28. Power dissipation for a given value of voltage is

$$P = \frac{V^2}{R}$$

$$\frac{P_2}{P_1} = \frac{R_1}{R_2}$$

When the coil is cut into two halves; then the value of resistance for each half is $\dfrac{R}{2}$. When these two halves are put in parallel then

$$R_{\text{eff}} = \frac{R}{4}$$

$$\frac{P_2}{P_1} = \frac{R_1}{R_2} = \frac{R}{(R/4)} = 4$$

29.

On redrawing the diagram, we get

$$I = \frac{6}{1.5} = 4\ \text{A}$$

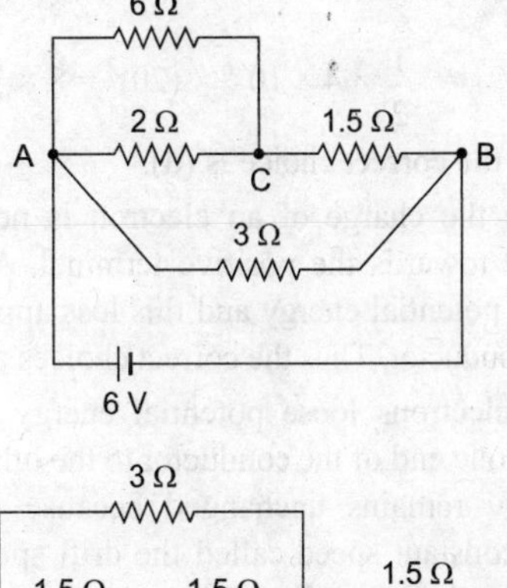

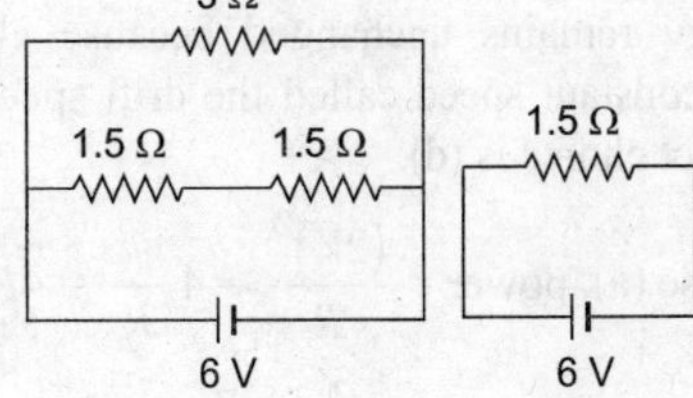

30. The correct choices are (b), (c) and (d). The free electrons in a metal are never at rest. At room temperature, they move randomly in all directions at speeds of the order of 10^5 ms^{-1}, even when no potential difference is applied across the conductor.

31. The correct choices are (a), (c) and (d).

32. The correct choices is (d). Drift speed and resistance change along the length of the conductor due to varying cross-section. Electric field is given by

$$E = -\frac{dV}{dx}$$

Since the resistance is changing along the length of the conductor dV/dx will change and hence electric field also changes along the length of the conductor.

33. Since $I = 1$ A, the charge passing through any cross-section of wire in 1 second is C. In 1.6 s, the charge transferred is $q = 1.6$ C. Now, $q = Ne$. Hence

$$N = \frac{q}{e} = \frac{1.6\text{C}}{1.6\times10^{-19}\text{C}}$$

$$= 10^{19} \text{ electrons}$$

Hence the correct choice is (a).

34. $v_d = \frac{I}{neA} = \frac{1.6}{10^{28}\times1.6\times10^{-19}\times10^{-7}}\ 10^{-2}\ \text{ms}^{-1} =$ 10 mms^{-1}, which is choice (c).

35. Applying Kirchhoff's junction rule to junction A, we have $i_1 = 2 + 1 = 3$ A, which is choice (c).

36. At junction B, $i_2 + 1 = 2$ or $i_2 = 1$ A, which is choice (a).

37. At junction D, $i_1 = i_2 + i_3$

$\Rightarrow i_3 = i_1 - i_2 = 3 - 1 = 2$ A.

So the correct choice is (b).

38. Potential drop along $AEDB$ is given by

$$V = 5\,i_1 + 1\,i_1 + 2\,i_2 = 15 + 3 + 2 = 20 \text{ V}$$

$\therefore$ Potential difference across the capacitor $C = 20$ V

Energy stored in the capacitor $= \frac{1}{2}CV^2$

$$= \frac{1}{2}\times 4\times10^{-6}\times(20)^2 = 8\times10^{-4}\text{J}$$

Thus the correct choice is (d).

39. Since the charge of an electron is negative, it will move towards the positive terminal. As it moves, it loses potential energy and this loss appears as heat in the conductor. Thus the correct choices are (b) and (c).

40. The electrons loose potential energy as they move from one end of the conductor to the other. The kinetic energy remains unchanged because electrons drift at a constant speed called the drift speed. Hence the correct choice is (d).

41. In case (a), power $= \frac{(2V)^2}{R} = 4\frac{V^2}{R} = 4P$

In case (b), power $= \frac{V^2}{2R} = \frac{P}{2}$

In case (c), power $= I^2(2R) = 2I^2R = 2P$

In case (d), power $= \frac{(2V)^2}{2R} = 2\frac{V^2}{R} = 2P$

42. Let R be the resistance of the complete wire and V the voltage of the mains. They $P = V^2/R$. If the wire is cut into two equal pieces and these pieces are connected in parallel, the resistance of the combination will be $R/4$.

Hence power $= \frac{V^2}{R/4} = \frac{4V^2}{R} = 4P$. Thus the correct choice is (d).

43. Current through the 5 Ω resistor is

$$I_2 = \frac{15I}{20} = \frac{3I}{4}$$

Current through 6 Ω and 9 Ω resistor is

$$I_1 = \frac{5I}{20} = \frac{I}{4}$$

Heat energy developed per second in the 5 Ω resistor is $I_2^2 \times 5 = 45$ or

$$\left(\frac{3I}{4}\right)^2 \times 5 = 45 \Rightarrow I = 4\text{ A}.$$

So the correct choice is (d).

44. Power developed in the 2 Ω resistor $= I^2 \times 2 = (4)^2 \times 2 = 32$ W, which is choice (c).

45. Potential difference across the 6 Ω resistor $= I_1 \times 6 = \frac{I}{4}\times 6 = \frac{4}{4}\times 6 = 6$ V, which is choice (c).

When switch S_1 is closed, the capacitor is charged to the voltage of the battery. Energy stored in the capacitor is

$$U = \frac{1}{2}CV^2 = \frac{1}{2}\times 500\times10^{-6}\times(120)^2 = 3.6\text{ J}.$$

When S_1 is opened and switch S_2 is closed, no current flows through R_4. Hence power developed in $R_4 = 0$, i.e., $P_4 = 0$. Let I_1 be the current through the 4 Ω resistor at an instant of time t. This current divides into I_2 flowing through R_2 and I_3 flowing through R_3 such that $I_1 = I_2 + I_3$. Since the potential difference across R_2 and R_3 is the same, we have, $I_2R_2 = I_3R_3$ or $6I_2 = 12\,I_3$ or $I_2 = 2I_3$. But $I_1 = I_2 + I_3$. Therefore,

$$I_1 = I_3 + I_3 \text{ or } I_3 = \frac{I_1}{3}.$$

Similarly $I_2 = \frac{2I_1}{3}$

Thus, $I_1 : I_2 : I_3 = I_1 : \frac{2I_1}{3} : \frac{I_1}{3}$

$$= 1 : \frac{2}{3} : \frac{1}{3} = 3 : 2 : 1$$

Now $P = I^2R$. Therefore,

$$= P_1 : P_2 : P_3 : I_1^2R_1 : I_2^2R_2 : I_3^2R_3$$

$$= (3)^2\times 4 : (2)^2\times 6 : (1)^2\times 12$$

$$= 36 : 24 : 12 = 3 : 2 : 1$$

Thus energy $U = 3.6$ J stored in the capacitor is distributed among resistors R_1, R_2 and R_3 in the ratio 3 : 2 : 1.

46. $P_1 = \dfrac{3.6\times 3}{6} = 1.8$ W, which is choice (a).

47. $P_2 = \dfrac{3.6\times 2}{6} = 1.2$ W, which is choice (d).

48. $P_3 = \dfrac{3.6\times 1}{6} = 0.6$ W, which is choice (c).

49. As resistance of each side is 6 Ω.

So 12Ω and 6Ω will be parallel

So resistance between any two corners $\dfrac{6\times 12}{18} = 4\Omega$

50. $$\frac{1}{R_{eq}} = \frac{1}{R_{Al}} + \frac{1}{R_{Fe}} = \left(\frac{A_{Al}}{\rho_{Al}} + \frac{A_{Fe}}{\rho_{Fe}}\right)\frac{1}{\ell}$$

$$= \left[\frac{(7^2 - 2^2)}{2.7} + \frac{2^2}{10}\right]\frac{10^{-6}}{10^{-8}} \times \frac{1}{50\times 10^{-3}}$$

Simplify above we get,

$$R = \frac{1875}{64}\times 10^{-6}\ \Omega = \frac{1875}{64}\ \mu\Omega$$

51. As, we know that $i = neAv_d$

So $$\frac{V}{R} = neAv_d$$

or $$\frac{V}{\left(\dfrac{\rho l}{A}\right)} = neAv_d$$

∴ $$\rho = \frac{V}{nelv_d} = \text{resistivity of the wire}$$

On putting the values we have

$$\rho = \frac{5}{(8\times 10^{28})(1.6\times 10^{-19})(0.1)(2.5\times 10^{-4})}$$

$\approx 1.6 \times 10^{-5}$ Ω-m

52. From law of resistance we have

$$R = \frac{\rho(L)}{A} = \frac{\rho L}{tL} = \frac{\rho}{t}$$

i.e., R is independent of L.

Thus, the correct option is (c)

53. As resistance of PQ $\quad R_{PQ} = \dfrac{5}{11}r$,

Resistance of QR $\quad R_{QR} = \dfrac{4}{11}r$

and resistance of PR $\quad R_{PR} = \dfrac{3}{11}r$

∴ R_{PQ} is maximum.

Therefore, the correct option is (a).

54. Since the potential drop across each resistor is zero, so the current through each of resistor is zero.

55. If we exchange the battery and galvanometer, then in a balanced Wheatstone bridge, there is no effect on position of null point.

56.

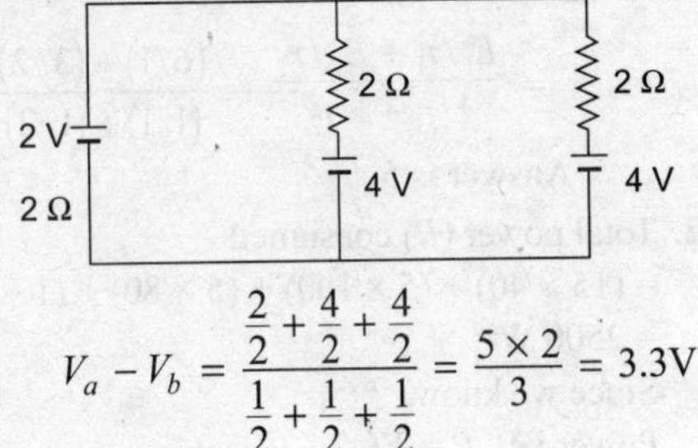

$$V_a - V_b = \frac{\dfrac{2}{2}+\dfrac{4}{2}+\dfrac{4}{2}}{\dfrac{1}{2}+\dfrac{1}{2}+\dfrac{1}{2}} = \frac{5\times 2}{3} = 3.3\text{V}$$

57. Potential drop across R_1 is 10 V,

Current in $R_1 = 0.5$ A, Current in $R_2 = 0$ A

58.

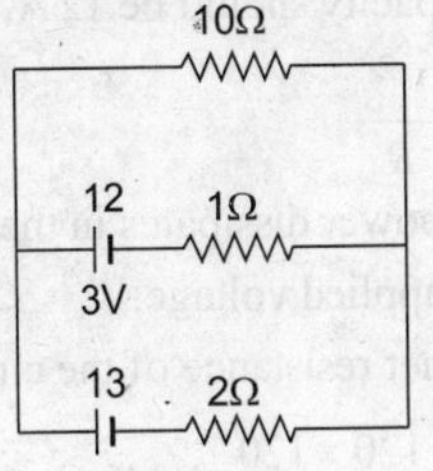

As $$E_{eq} = \frac{\dfrac{12}{1}+\dfrac{13}{2}}{\dfrac{1}{1}+\dfrac{1}{2}} = \frac{\dfrac{37}{2}}{\dfrac{3}{2}} = \frac{37}{3}$$

$$Y_{eq} = \frac{2}{3}$$

$$I = \frac{\dfrac{37}{3}}{\dfrac{2}{3}+10} = \frac{\dfrac{37}{3}}{\dfrac{32}{3}} = \frac{37}{32}$$

Voltage across load = IR = $\left(\dfrac{37}{32}\right)(10) = 11.56$ V.

59.

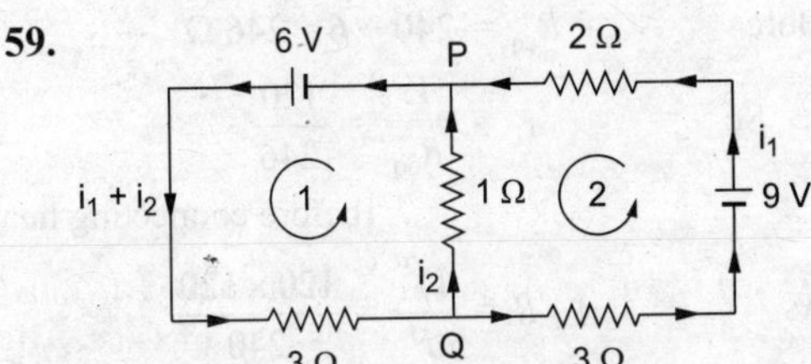

Using Kirchhoff's loop law in loops 1 and 2 in the directions shown in figure we get

$$6 - 3(i_1 + i_2) - i_2 = 0 \quad \text{...(i)}$$

and $$9 - 2i_1 + i_2 - 3i_1 = 0 \quad \text{...(ii)}$$

Solving Eqs. (i) and (ii) we get,

$$i_2 = 0.13\ \text{A}$$

Thus, the current in 1 Ω resistor is 0.13 A from Q to P.

60. Current in the respective loop will remain confined in the loop itself.

Thus, current through 2 Ω resistance = 0

∴ Correct answer is (c).

61. V_{AB} = Equivalent emf of two batteries in parallel.

$$= \frac{E_1/r_1 + E_2/r_2}{1/r_1 + 1/r_2} = \frac{(6/1)+(3/2)}{(1/1)+(1/2)} = 5 \text{ V}$$

∴ Answer is 5.

62. Total power (P) consumed

= (15 × 40) + (5 × 100) + (5 × 80) + (1 × 1000)

= 2500 W

Since we know,

Power i.e., $P = VI$

$$\Rightarrow \quad I = \frac{2500}{220} \text{A} = \frac{125}{11} = 11.3 \text{ A}$$

Minimum capacity should be 12 A.

63. As, $\quad P = \dfrac{V^2}{R}$

where, P = power dissipates in the circuit,

V = applied voltage,

R = net resistance of the circuit

$$R = \frac{120 \times 120}{60} = 240\ \Omega \text{ [resistance of bulb]}$$

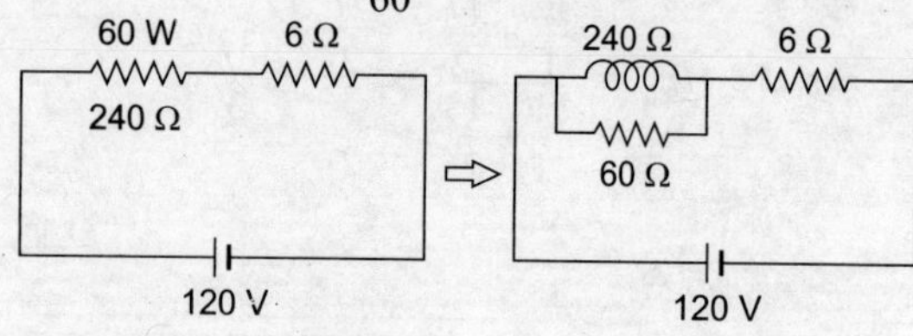

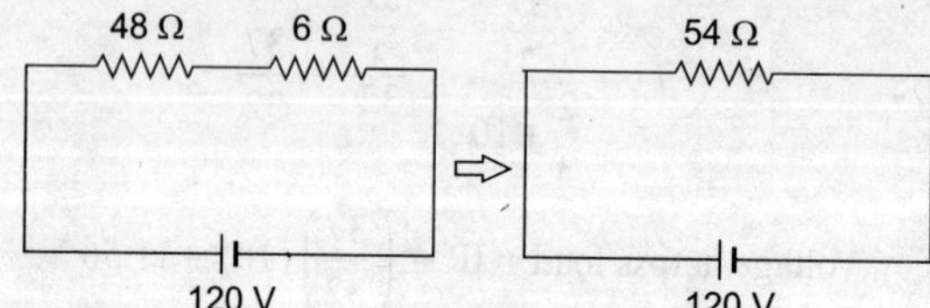

Here $\quad R_{eq} = 240 + 6 = 246\ \Omega$

$$\Rightarrow \text{So} \quad i_1 = \frac{V}{R_{eq}} = \frac{120}{246}$$

[before connecting heater]

$$\text{As} \quad R = \frac{V^2}{P} = \frac{120 \times 120}{240}$$

$\Rightarrow \quad R = 60\ \Omega \quad$ [resistance of heater]

So, tfrom figure, we have

$$V_1 = \frac{240}{246} \times 120 = 117.073 \text{ V} \quad [\because V = IR]$$

$$\Rightarrow \quad i_2 = \frac{V}{R_2} = \frac{120}{54}$$

$$V_2 = \frac{48}{54} \times 120 = 106.66 \text{ V}$$

$$V_1 - V_2 = 10.41 \text{ V}$$

64. $R = \dfrac{V^2}{P}$ so $R \propto \dfrac{1}{P}$

Therefore $\quad \dfrac{1}{R_{100}} > \dfrac{1}{R_{60}} > \dfrac{1}{R_{40}}$

Thus, the correct option is (d).

65. Using formula $P = \dfrac{V^2}{R}$, $R_1 = 1\ \Omega$, $R_2 = 0.5\ \Omega$

and $\quad R_3 = 2\ \Omega$

$V_1 = V_2 = V_3 = 3$ V

$$\therefore \quad P_1 = \frac{(3)^2}{1} = 9 \text{ W}$$

$$P_2 = \frac{(3)^2}{0.5} = 18 \text{ W}$$

$$\text{and} \quad P_3 = \frac{(3)^2}{2} = 4.5 \text{ W}$$

∴ $\quad P_2 > P_1 > P_3$

∴ Correct option is (c).

66. Current flowing through both the bars is equal.

Now, the heat produced is given by

$$H = I^2Rt$$

or $\quad H \propto R$

$$\text{or} \quad \frac{H_{AB}}{H_{BC}} = \frac{R_{AB}}{R_{BC}} = \frac{(1/2r)^2}{(1/r)^2} \qquad \left(\text{as } R \propto \frac{1}{A} \propto \frac{1}{r^2}\right)$$

$$= \frac{1}{4}$$

or $\quad H_{BC} = 4\,H_{AB}$

67. $W = 0$. Hence, from first law of thermodynamics,

$$\Delta U = \Delta Q = i^2Rt = (1)^2\,(100)\,(5 \times 60) \text{ J} = 30 \text{ kJ}.$$

∴ Correct answer is (d).

68. Potential gradient across wire is $\dfrac{12E}{13L}$

For null deflection $\dfrac{12E}{13L} \times l = E/2 \quad l = \dfrac{13L}{24}$

69.

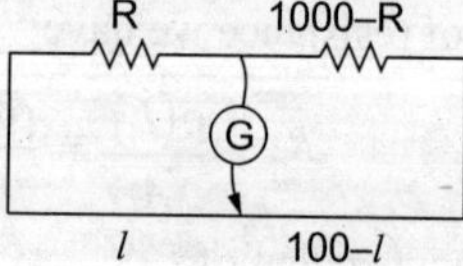

Let resistances are R and $1000 - R$

$$\text{For case-I} \quad \frac{R}{l} = \frac{1000 - R}{100 - l} \quad \text{...(i)}$$

$$\text{For case-II} \quad \frac{1000 - R}{l - 10} = \frac{R}{110 - l} \quad \text{...(ii)}$$

Multiplying equation (i) and (ii) we have,

$$\frac{R(1000 - R)}{l(l - 10)} = \frac{(1000 - R)R}{(100 - l)(110 - l)}$$

$$\Rightarrow \quad l^2 - 10\,l = 11000 + l^2 - 210\,l$$

$$\Rightarrow \quad 200\,l = 11000$$

$$\Rightarrow \quad l = 55 \text{ cm}$$

Putting in equation (i) we have,

$$\frac{R}{55} = \frac{1000 - R}{45}$$

$$\Rightarrow \quad 45\,R = 55000 - 55\,R$$

$$\Rightarrow \quad R = 550\,\Omega$$

70. For a Voltmeter,

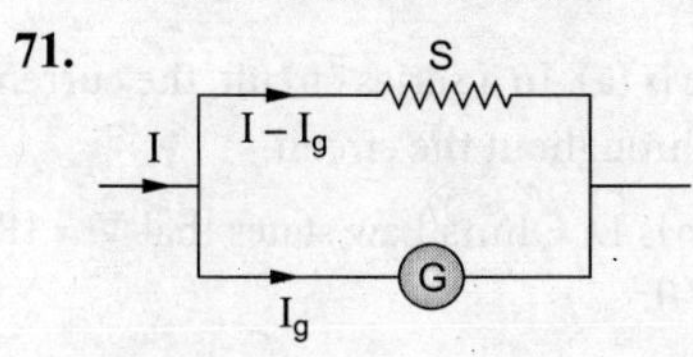

$$V = I_g G + I_g R_s$$

$$\text{So } I_g (G + R_s) = V \Rightarrow R = \frac{V}{I_g} - G$$

$$\Rightarrow \quad R = 1985 = 1.985\text{ k}\Omega \quad \text{or} \quad R = 1.985 \times 10^3\,\Omega$$

71.

In parallel, current distributes in inverse ratio of resistance.

$$\text{As} \quad I_g G = (I - I_g)S$$

$$\text{Hence,} \quad \frac{I - I_g}{I_g} = \frac{G}{S}$$

$$\text{So} \quad S = \frac{G I_g}{I - I_g}$$

Since I_g is very small, so that

$$S = \frac{G I_g}{I}$$

$$b = \frac{(100)(1 \times 10^{-3})}{10} = 0.01\,\Omega$$

72. For balanced meter bridge

$$\frac{X}{R} = \frac{l}{(100 - l)} \quad (\text{where, } R = 90\,\Omega)$$

$$\therefore \quad \frac{X}{90} = \frac{40}{100 - 40}$$

$$\therefore \quad X = 60\,\Omega$$

$$\Rightarrow \quad X = R\frac{l}{(100 - l)}$$

$$\Rightarrow \quad \frac{\Delta X}{X} = \frac{\Delta l}{l} + \frac{\Delta l}{100 - l} = \frac{0.1}{40} + \frac{0.1}{60}$$

$$\Delta X = 0.25$$

$$\text{So,} \quad X = (60 \pm 0.25)\,\Omega$$

73. Applying the concept of balanced Wheatstone bridge, we get,

$$\frac{P}{Q} = \frac{R}{S}$$

$$\therefore \quad \frac{X}{(52 + 1)} = \frac{10}{(48 + 2)}$$

$$\therefore \quad X = \frac{10 \times 53}{50}$$

$$= 10.6\,\Omega$$

$\therefore$ Correct option is (b).

74. We will require a voltmeter, an ammeter, a test resistor and a variable battery to verify Ohm's law.

Voltmeter which is made by connecting a high resistance with a galvanometer is connected in parallel with the test resistor.

Further, an ammeter which is formed by connecting a low resistance in parallel with galvanometer is required to measure the current through test resistor.

The correct option is (c).

75. $R > 2\,\Omega$

$$\Rightarrow \quad 100 - x > x$$

$$\text{Using} \quad \frac{P}{Q} = \frac{R}{S}$$

$$\text{We get} \quad \frac{2}{R} = \frac{x}{100 - x} \quad \text{...(i)}$$

$$\frac{R}{2} = \frac{x + 20}{80 - x} \quad \text{...(ii)}$$

On solving Eqs.(i) and (ii), we get, $R = 3\,\Omega$

$\therefore$ Correct option is (a).

76. $V_{ab} = i_g.G = (i - i_g)S$

$$\Rightarrow \quad i = \left(1 + \frac{G}{S}\right) i_g$$

On putting the given i values, we get

$$i = 100.1 \text{ mA}$$

Therefore, if X is increasing R, should also increase.

$\therefore$ Correct answer is (a).

77. BC, CD and BA are known resistances.

The unknown resistance is connected between A and D.

Hence, the correct option is (c).

78. In the given resistance 200 Ω, 2 stands for red. If it is replaced by green, then the resistance becomes 500 Ω. As 5 stands for green, so multiple will be 10^5.

79. Resistance $= 50 \times 10^2 \pm 1\%$ $\quad i_{max} = 20$ mA

80. The unit of electric current is the ampere, represented by the symbol "A."

81. Copper is a good conductor of electricity due to its high electrical conductivity.

82. The unit of electric potential difference is the volt, represented by the symbol "V."

83. In a series circuit, adding more resistors increases the total resistance, leading to a decrease in current.

84. Ohm's Law states that voltage (V) is equal to the product of current (I) and resistance (R), expressed as V = IR.

85. The unit of electrical power is the watt, represented by the symbol "W."

86. Conventional current flows from the positive terminal to the negative terminal.

87. A capacitor stores electrical energy in an electric field.

88. An ideal conductor has zero resistance.

89. A transformer is used to change the voltage level in an electrical circuit.

90. Household circuits typically use alternating current.

91. The unit of electric charge is the coulomb, represented by the symbol "C."

92. Ohm's Law describes the relationship between voltage, current, and resistance in a conductor.

93. A fuse is a safety device that interrupts the flow of excessive current to protect the circuit.

94. A diode allows current to flow in one direction and blocks it in the opposite direction, controlling the flow of current in a circuit.

95. Electrons are negatively charged subatomic particles orbiting the nucleus of an atom.

96. The coulomb is the unit of electric charge, representing the amount of charge transported by a current of one ampere in one second.

97. Resistance is the measure of opposition to the flow of electric current in a material.

98. In a series circuit, the current has only one pathway to follow.

99. DC stands for Direct Current, where the electric charge flows in one direction.

100. An ammeter is used to measure electric current in a circuit.

101. A conductor is a material that allows the flow of electric current.

102. Kirchhoff's Current Law states that the total current entering a junction in a circuit is equal to the total current leaving the junction.

103. Power is the rate at which electrical energy is used or produced, measured in watts.

104. A capacitor is a component used to store electrical energy in an electric field.

105. The correct answer is (c). The unit of electric current is the Ampere (a).

106. The correct answer is (a). In a series circuit, the current remains constant throughout the circuit.

107. The correct answer is D. Ohm's Law states that V = IR, I = V/R, and R = V/I.

108. The correct answer is (d). A diode allows current to flow in one direction and blocks it in the opposite direction.

109. The correct answer is (d). Power can be calculated using P = IV, P = I^2R, and P = V^2/R.

110. The correct answer is (b). In a parallel circuit, as more resistors are added, the total resistance decreases.

111. The correct answer is (a). A capacitor stores electrical energy in an electric field.

112. The correct answer is (c). A resistor is used to limit the flow of current in a circuit.

113. The correct answer is (c). Silicon is commonly used as a semiconductor in electronic devices.

114. The correct answer is (b). A transformer is used to regulate voltage in an electrical circuit.

115. The correct answer is (b). The transistor is the basic building block of digital circuits, acting as a switch or amplifier.

116. The correct answer is (c). "IC" stands for Integrated Circuit, which is a miniaturized assembly of electronic components.

117. The correct answer is (b). In a NAND gate, the output is low only when both inputs are high.

118. The correct answer is (b). A flip-flop is used to store binary information in digital circuits.

119. The correct answer is (b). An operational amplifier is used for signal amplification in electronic circuits.

120. The correct answer is (c). "CMOS" stands for Complementary Metal-Oxide-Semiconductor, a technology used in integrated circuits.

121. The correct answer is (c). A diode is primarily used for rectifying current in electronic circuits.

122. The correct answer is (d). A resistor network is used for voltage division in electronic circuits.

123. The correct answer is (c). A comparator is used to compare two input signals in electronic circuits.

124. The correct answer is (b). In a DAC, the binary input controls the output voltage.

125. A fuse is designed to protect against overcurrent by breaking the circuit when the current exceeds a specified value.

126. In a short circuit, current takes an unintended low-resistance path, bypassing the normal load.

127. Copper is a common material for fuse elements due to its low melting point and good conductivity.

128. The main function of a circuit breaker is to interrupt the circuit in case of overcurrent, providing protection against short circuits and overloads.

129. A circuit breaker is reusable, as it can be reset after tripping, while a fuse typically needs to be replaced after it blows.

130. The unit of electrical resistance is ohm (Ω).

131. In a series circuit, the total resistance is equal to the sum of the individual resistances.

8

CHAPTER

Machine & Its Types

MACHINE

A machine is a device or apparatus that uses energy or power to perform a specific task or work. Machines are designed to make tasks easier, more efficient, or possible in the first place.

Parts of Machine

Machine parts are individual components or elements that make up a machine and contribute to its overall functionality. They can vary depending on the type of machine and its intended purpose. Here are some common machine parts:

1. **Motor :** The motor is an essential part of many machines, providing power and generating mechanical motion.
2. **Bearings :** Bearings reduce friction and facilitate smooth movement between two moving parts, such as shafts or axles.
3. **Gears :** Gears transmit motion and power between rotating shafts. They can change the speed, torque, and direction of rotation.
4. **Belts and Pulleys :** Belts and pulleys are used to transfer power from one shaft to another when the two shafts are not in direct contact.
5. **Shafts :** Shafts are long, cylindrical components that transmit torque and rotational motion between various machine parts.
6. **Springs :** Springs store mechanical energy and release it when needed, providing suspension, cushioning, or tension in a machine.
7. **Valves :** Valves control the flow of fluids or gases within a machine, regulating the movement and pressure of the medium.
8. **Cylinders :** Cylinders convert fluid or air pressure into linear motion, often used in hydraulic or pneumatic systems.
9. **Control panels :** Control panels consist of switches, buttons, displays, and other interfaces that allow users to operate and control the machine.
10. **Sensors :** Sensors detect and measure physical quantities such as temperature, pressure, position, or speed, providing feedback and enabling automation in machines.
11. **Circuit boards :** Circuit boards, also known as PCBs (Printed Circuit Boards), contain electronic components and conductive pathways that control electrical functions within a machine.
12. **Housings and enclosures :** Housings and enclosures provide protection and support for the internal components of a machine, ensuring safety and durability.
13. **Actuators :** Actuators convert electrical, hydraulic, or pneumatic energy into mechanical motion, enabling machines to perform specific tasks or movements.
14. **Filters :** Filters remove contaminants or unwanted particles from fluids or gases flowing through a machine, ensuring clean and efficient operation.
15. **Control valves :** Control valves regulate the flow rate, pressure, or direction of a fluid or gas within a machine, allowing precise control over its operation.

Types of Machines :

They can be simple, consisting of a few basic parts, and complex, involving intricate mechanisms and systems.

Simple Machines

Simple machines are fundamental mechanical devices that have few or no moving parts and are used to perform work. They are the building blocks of more complex machines and are based on basic principles of physics.

There are six main types of simple machines :

I. Lever : "Lever" is a term that can have different meanings depending on the context.

A lever is a rigid bar that pivots around a fixed point called a fulcrum. It can be used to amplify force or change the direction of the force applied. Examples of levers include seesaws, crowbars, and scissors.

Here are a few common uses of the word "lever":

1. **Mechanical device :** A lever is a simple machine consisting of a rigid bar or beam that is used to transmit and amplify force. It typically has a fulcrum or pivot point, an effort or input force, and a load or output force. Levers are used in various applications, such as in tools, machines, and mechanisms.
2. **Financial Term :** In finance and investing, a lever refers to the use of borrowed funds (debt) to increase the potential return of an investment. This practice is known as leverage, and it can amplify both gains and losses. Using leverage involves taking on additional risk, as the investor is liable for the borrowed funds.
3. **Strategic Advantage :** In a broader sense, the term "lever" can also refer to a strategic advantage or tool that can be used to achieve a desired outcome. For example, in business or negotiations, someone may have a lever or leverage over another party if they possess information, resources, or influence that can be used to exert pressure or gain an advantage.

Types of Lever

In the context of mechanical devices, levers can be classified into three different types based on the relative positions of the fulcrum, effort (input force), and load (output force). These types are :

1. **First-class lever :** In a first-class lever, the fulcrum is positioned between the effort and the load. This means that the effort and the load are on opposite sides of the fulcrum..

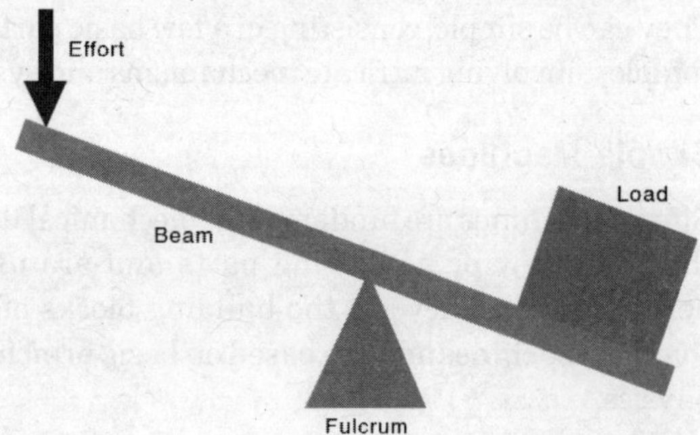

Examples of first-class levers include a see-saw, scissors, and a crowbar.

2. **Second-class lever :** In a second-class lever, the load is positioned between the fulcrum and the effort. This means that the load and the effort are on opposite sides of the fulcrum.

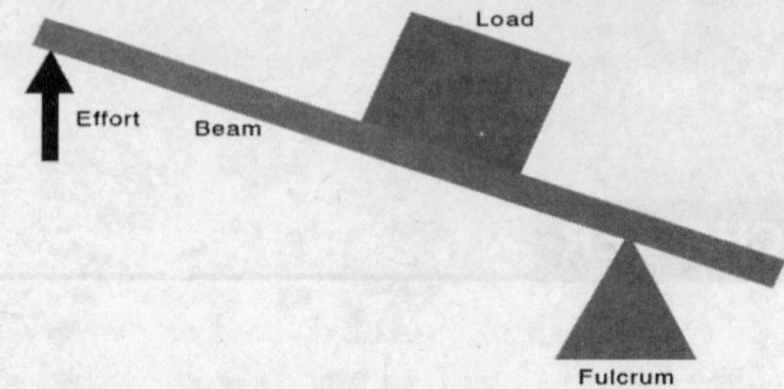

Examples of second-class levers include a wheel barrow and a nutcracker.

3. **Third-class lever :** In a third-class lever, the effort is positioned between the fulcrum and the load. This means that the effort and the load are on the same side of the fulcrum, with the effort closer to the fulcrum.

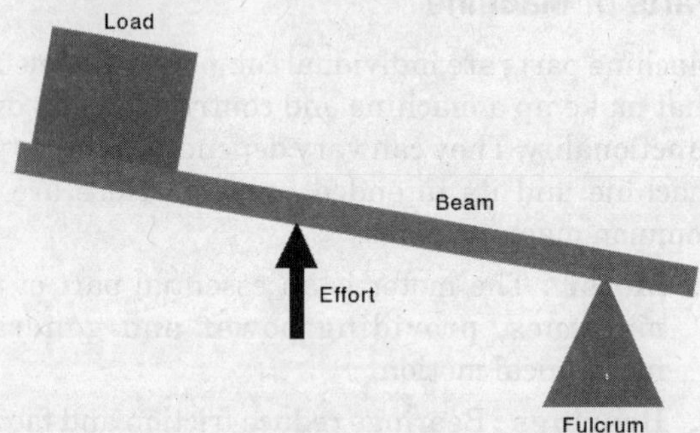

Examples of third-class levers include tweezers, tongs, and a baseball bat.

Applications and uses of Lever

Because of their high mechanical advantage, levers are used in many applications in everyday life. Here are some of them.

- Lifting and moving objects using a wheelbarrow
- Removing nails using a claw hammer
- Lifting small particles using a tweezers
- Cutting or separating materials using scissors
- Stripping wires using pliers or wire cutter

Besides, many parts of the human body function like a lever. The joints behave like a fulcrum, and the bones act as a beam.

II. Pulley : A pulley is a simple machine consisting of a wheel with a groove along its edge and a rope or cable that runs along the groove. Pulleys are used to change the direction or magnitude of a force and can be found in various applications, such as lifting heavy objects or transmitting power.

A pulley consists of a wheel with a groove and a rope or cable. It is used to change the direction of force and can also provide a mechanical advantage by allowing a person to lift heavy loads with less effort. Examples of pulleys include flagpole pulleys and cranes.

There are three main types of pulleys based on their configuration and functionality :

1. **Fixed Pulley :** A fixed pulley is attached to a fixed point, such as a beam or a ceiling. It changes only the direction of the force applied and does not provide any mechanical advantage. The load is lifted by pulling down on the rope, and the effort force required is equal to the weight of the load. Fixed pulleys are commonly used in flagpoles and blinds.
2. **Movable Pulley :** A movable pulley is attached to the load being lifted and moves with it. When using a movable pulley, the load is suspended from a fixed point, and the effort force is applied in the opposite direction. This type of pulley reduces the amount of force required to lift the load. The mechanical advantage of a movable pulley is equal to 2, meaning the effort force is half the weight of the load. Movable pulleys are often used in block and tackle systems for lifting heavy objects.
3. **Compound Pulley :** A compound pulley combines multiple fixed and movable pulleys to provide an increased mechanical advantage. In a compound pulley system, the rope is threaded through several pulleys in a way that allows the effort force to be divided over multiple segments of the rope. This arrangement enables a significant reduction in the force required to lift heavy loads. Compound pulleys are commonly used in cranes and hoists.

III. Wheel and axle : The wheel and axle is another simple machine that consists of a circular wheel attached to a cylindrical axle. The wheel and axle work together to transmit force and motion and the wheel is the larger, outer part that rotates around the axle, which is the smaller, central part.

Wheel and axles consist of a circular object (the wheel) that rotates around a shaft (the axle). It is used to transmit force or torque and to change the direction of force. Examples include wheels on vehicles, gears, and doorknobs.

There are three main types of wheel and axle based on their application and design :

1. **Ordinary Wheel and Axle :** In the ordinary wheel and axle configuration, the wheel and axle have a uniform diameter throughout their length. This type of wheel and axle is commonly found in everyday objects such as car wheels, bicycle wheels, and doorknobs. When force is applied to the wheel, it rotates around the axle, enabling the movement or transmission of force.
2. **Steering Wheel and Axle :** The steering wheel and axle configuration is specifically designed for steering vehicles. In this type, the steering wheel is connected to the axle through a mechanism such as a steering column. When the steering wheel is turned, it causes the axle to rotate, which in turn controls the direction of the vehicle's wheels.
3. **Capstan :** A capstan is a specialized type of wheel and axle used for winding ropes or cables. It consists of a cylindrical drum (the axle) around which a rope or cable is wound, and a handle or lever attached to the drum. Capstans are commonly used on ships for tasks like raising anchors or hoisting sails. By turning the handle or lever, force is applied to the drum, causing the rope to wind or unwind.

The wheel and axle is a versatile simple machine that can be found in numerous applications, ranging from transportation to mechanical systems. It provides a mechanical advantage by increasing the distance over which a force can be applied, making it easier to move or lift heavy objects.

IV. Inclined plane : An inclined plane is a simple machine that consists of a flat surface set at an angle to the horizontal plane. It allows objects to be moved up or down with less force than would be required to lift them vertically. The inclined plane is one of the six classical simple machines, and it can be found in various forms and applications.

An inclined plane is a sloping surface that allows objects to be raised or lowered with less force. It reduces the amount of work required by increasing the distance over which the force is applied. Examples include ramps, staircases, and slides.

Here are some common types of inclined planes:

1. **Ramp :** A ramp is a type of inclined plane that is commonly used for loading and unloading objects from a higher level to a lower level. It provides a sloping surface that allows for easier movement of heavy objects, such as when loading furniture into a moving truck.

2. **Wedge :** A wedge is a double-inclined plane that is thick at one end and tapers to a thin edge at the other. It is often used for splitting or cutting objects. Examples of wedges include axes, knives, and chisels. The sharp edge of the wedge concentrates the force over a smaller area, making it easier to penetrate or separate materials.
3. **Screw :** Although it may not be immediately apparent, a screw is actually a type of inclined plane wrapped around a cylinder. It consists of an inclined plane (the thread) spiraling up the shaft. Screws are used for fastening objects together, and they convert rotational motion into linear motion. Examples of screws include those used in woodworking, as well as in machinery and construction.

   These are three common types of inclined planes. Each type serves a specific purpose and offers mechanical advantages in different applications.

Features of Simple Machines:

1. **Few Moving Parts :** Simple machines are characterized by their simplicity, often consisting of only a few moving parts. They are designed to perform basic functions using minimal components.
2. **Basic Mechanisms :** Simple machines are based on fundamental mechanical principles, such as levers, inclined planes, wheels and axles, pulleys, wedges, and screws. Each type of simple machine operates on a specific mechanism to achieve a particular purpose.
3. **Mechanical Advantage :** Simple machines provide a mechanical advantage, allowing the user to accomplish tasks with less force or effort. They leverage forces to make work easier, either by amplifying force or by changing the direction of the force applied.
4. **Versatility :** Simple machines have a wide range of applications and can be used individually or in combination to create more complex systems. They can be found in everyday objects and activities, as well as in various industries.

Importance of Simple Machines :

1. **Efficiency :** Simple machines provide mechanical advantage, allowing us to accomplish tasks more easily and with less effort. They help increase efficiency in performing work by reducing the amount of force required or by enabling us to apply force in a more favorable direction.
2. **Basic Understanding of Mechanics :** Simple machines serve as the building blocks for understanding more complex principles of physics and mechanics. By studying and applying the concepts of levers, inclined planes, pulleys, and other simple machines, we gain a fundamental understanding of how forces, motion, and energy work.
3. **Everyday Applications :** Simple machines are present in numerous everyday objects and activities. From using scissors and opening doors to riding a bicycle or using a wheelbarrow, we rely on simple machines to make our daily tasks easier and more efficient.
4. **Education and Learning :** Simple machines are often used as educational tools to teach students about fundamental mechanical concepts and principles. They offer hands-on learning experiences and help develop problem-solving skills and critical thinking.

Complex Machines

Complex machines are composed of multiple simple machines and often involve intricate mechanisms and systems. They are designed to perform more sophisticated tasks and typically require an energy source or power input to function. Examples of complex machines include:

- **Automobiles :** Cars are complex machines that combine multiple simple machines like wheels and axles, levers in the braking system, pulleys in the engine, and inclined planes in the transmission.
- **Industrial Machinery :** Various complex machines are used in manufacturing and industrial processes, such as conveyor belts, robotic arms, CNC machines, and assembly lines. These machines involve a combination of mechanical, electrical, and computer systems.
- **Aircraft :** Aircraft are complex machines that incorporate numerous mechanical systems, such as engines, landing gear, control surfaces, and hydraulic or pneumatic systems.
- **Computers :** Computers are complex machines that consist of intricate electronic circuits and components, including processors, memory modules, hard drives, and input/output devices.
- **Medical Equipment :** Complex machines in the medical field include MRI scanners, X-ray machines, surgical robots, and dialysis machines, which involve advanced mechanical, electrical, and imaging systems.

  Complex machines are designed to perform specialized functions, achieve high precision, automate tasks, or accomplish complex operations that would be difficult or impossible with simple machines alone.

Features of Complex Machines :

1. **Multiple Components :** Complex machines are characterized by their intricate design, often involving numerous components and subsystems. They are composed of interconnected parts that work together to perform complex tasks.
2. **Advanced Mechanisms :** Complex machines employ a combination of simple machines, mechanical systems, electrical components, computer systems, and other technologies to achieve their functions. They may incorporate complex mechanisms like gears, linkages, actuators, sensors, and control systems.
3. **Specialized Functions :** Complex machines are designed to perform specific tasks or functions that require advanced capabilities. They are often developed for specialized applications in industries such as manufacturing, healthcare, transportation, and aerospace.
4. **Power Source :** Complex machines typically require an energy source or power input to operate. This can be in the form of electricity, hydraulic power, pneumatic power, thermal energy, chemical reactions, or a combination of these sources.
5. **Precision and Control :** Complex machines are designed for high precision and control. They often incorporate advanced sensors, feedback systems, and algorithms to ensure accurate operation, safety, and optimization of performance.
6. **Automation and Integration :** Many complex machines are automated or computer-controlled, reducing the need for human intervention. They can be integrated into larger systems or networks, enabling communication, data exchange, and coordination with other machines or devices.

Importance of Complex Machines:

1. **Specialized Functions :** Complex machines are designed to perform specific and often intricate tasks that would be difficult or impossible with simple machines alone. They enable us to achieve high precision, automation, and advanced operations in various industries.
2. **Industrial Production and Manufacturing :** Complex machines are at the heart of modern manufacturing processes. They enable large-scale production, increase productivity, and improve the quality and consistency of manufactured goods. Complex machines like CNC machines, robotic arms, and conveyor systems revolutionize industrial production.
3. **Technological Advancements :** Complex machines drive technological advancements in fields such as transportation, aerospace, healthcare, and telecomm-unications. They enable the development of advanced vehicles, medical equipment, communication systems, and more.
4. **Research and Innovation :** Complex machines are essential for conducting research and experime-ntation in various scientific and engineering disciplines. They allow scientists and engineers to study complex phenomena, simulate real-world scenarios, and push the boundaries of knowledge and innovation.
5. **Enhancing Human Capabilities :** Complex machines can augment human capabilities, enabling us to perform tasks beyond our natural abilities. Examples include exoskeletons that enhance strength and mobility, surgical robots that assist in precision surgeries, and advanced imaging equipment that aids in medical diagnoses.

Objective Type Questions

1. Which of the following is not a class of lever?

(a) First-class lever

(b) Second-class lever

(c) Third-class lever

(d) Fourth-class lever

2. In a first-class lever, where is the fulcrum located in relation to the effort and load?

(a) Between the effort and load

(b) At one end of the lever

(c) At the midpoint of the lever

(d) It can be anywhere along the lever

3. Which of the following is an example of a second-class lever?

(a) Pliers (b) Wheelbarrow

(c) Baseball bat (d) Crowbar

4. Which class of lever provides the greatest mechanical advantage?

(a) First-class lever

(b) Second-class lever

(c) Third-class lever

(d) They all provide the same mechanical advantage

5. In a third-class lever, where is the effort located in relation to the fulcrum and load?

(a) Between the fulcrum and load

(b) At one end of the lever

(c) At the midpoint of the lever

(d) It can be anywhere along the lever

6. Which of the following is an example of a first-class lever?

(a) Nutcracker (b) Shovel

(c) Fishing rod (d) Wheelbarrow

7. Which class of lever provides the least mechanical advantage?

(a) First-class lever

(b) Second-class lever

(c) Third-class lever

(d) They all provide the same mechanical advantage

8. Which of the following is an example of a third-class lever?

(a) Scissors (b) Bottle opener

(c) See-saw (d) Tweezers

9. A lever is in equilibrium when :

(a) The effort arm is longer than the load arm

(b) The load arm is longer than the effort arm

(c) The effort and load are equal

(d) The fulcrum is located at the midpoint

10. Which class of lever is most commonly found in the human body?

(a) First-class lever (b) Second-class lever

(c) Third-class lever (d) Fourth-class lever

11. Which class of lever allows for the greatest range of motion?

(a) First-class lever (b) Second-class lever

(c) Third-class lever (d) Fourth-class lever

12. Which of the following is an example of a first-class lever in the human body?

(a) Elbow joint

(b) Hip joint

(c) Ankle joint

(d) Shoulder joint

13. A lever with a mechanical advantage greater than 1:

(a) Increases the effort required

(b) Increases the load it can lift

(c) Decreases the distance the load can be moved

(d) Decreases the distance the effort has to travel

14. Which class of lever is commonly used to pry open objects?

(a) First-class lever

(b) Second-class lever

(c) Third-class lever

(d) Fourth-class lever

15. The length of the effort arm compared to the length of the load arm determines the:

(a) Mechanical advantage

(b) Distance the load can be moved

(c) Efficiency of the lever

(d) Weight of the load

16. Which class of lever is a pair of scissors?

(a) First-class lever

(b) Second-class lever

(c) Third-class lever

(d) Fourth-class lever

17. Which of the following is an example of a second-class lever in the human body?
(a) Bicep curl
(b) Knee extension
(c) Sitting down in a chair
(d) Opening and closing your hand

18. Which class of lever is a catapult?
(a) First-class lever (b) Second-class lever
(c) Third-class lever (d) Fourth-class lever

19. A lever with a mechanical advantage of less than 1:
(a) Increases the effort required
(b) Increases the load it can lift
(c) Decreases the distance the load can be moved
(d) Decreases the distance the effort has to travel

20. Which class of lever is a push-up exercise?
(a) First-class lever (b) Second-class lever
(c) Third-class lever (d) Fourth-class lever

21. Which of the following is not a common application of levers?
(a) Opening a door (b) Lifting weights
(c) Rowing a boat (d) Cooking food

22. Levers are commonly used in which field?
(a) Engineering
(b) Medicine
(c) Agriculture
(d) All of the above

23. The primary advantage of using levers is:
(a) Increased speed
(b) Increased force
(c) Increased distance
(d) Increased precision

24. Levers can be used to:
(a) Transfer motion
(b) Change the direction of motion
(c) Increase or decrease force
(d) All of the above

25. Which feature of a lever determines its mechanical advantage?
(a) Length of the lever
(b) Weight of the load
(c) Position of the fulcrum
(d) Material of the lever

26. A longer effort arm in a lever will result in:
(a) Increased mechanical advantage
(b) Decreased mechanical advantage
(c) No change in mechanical advantage
(d) Mechanical advantage depends on the load arm

27. Which type of lever has the fulcrum located between the effort and the load?
(a) First-class lever
(b) Second-class lever
(c) Third-class lever
(d) Fourth-class lever

28. Which class of lever is commonly used in wheel barrows?
(a) First-class lever (b) Second-class lever
(c) Third-class lever (d) Fourth-class lever

29. Which class of lever provides speed and range of motion but sacrifices force?
(a) First-class lever (b) Second-class lever
(c) Third-class lever (d) Fourth-class lever

30. Which class of lever is commonly used in tweezers?
(a) First-class lever (b) Second-class lever
(c) Third-class lever (d) Fourth-class lever

31. Which class of lever is commonly used in scissors?
(a) First-class lever (b) Second-class lever
(c) Third-class lever (d) Fourth-class lever

32. Levers are used in construction machinery for:
(a) Lifting heavy objects
(b) Digging trenches
(c) Excavating soil
(d) All of the above

33. Which class of lever is commonly used in nutcrackers?
(a) First-class lever
(b) Second-class lever
(c) Third-class lever
(d) Fourth-class lever

34. Which feature of a lever affects the ease of control and stability?
(a) Length of the lever
(b) Weight of the load
(c) Position of the fulcrum
(d) Material of the lever

35. Which class of lever is commonly used in fishing rods?
(a) First-class lever (b) Second-class lever
(c) Third-class lever (d) Fourth-class lever

36. Which class of lever is commonly used in tongs?
(a) First-class lever (b) Second-class lever
(c) Third-class lever (d) Fourth-class lever

37. Levers are used in gym equipment for:
(a) Weightlifting (b) Leg presses
(c) Rowing machines (d) All of the above

38. The concept of levers is based on which fundamental principle of physics?
(a) Newton's first law of motion
(b) Newton's second law of motion
(c) Archimedes' principle
(d) Pascal's principle

39. Which class of lever is commonly used in a stapler?
(a) First-class lever (b) Second-class lever
(c) Third-class lever (d) Fourth-class lever

40. Which class of lever is commonly used in a crowbar?
(a) First-class lever (b) Second-class lever
(c) Third-class lever (d) Fourth-class lever

41. What type of simple machine is a shovel?
(a) Lever (b) Wheel and axle
(c) Inclined plane (d) Pulley

42. How does a lever make work easier?
(a) By increasing force
(b) By increasing speed
(c) By changing direction
(d) By amplifying the effort applied

43. Which of the following is an example of a complex machine?
(a) Screw (b) Wheelbarrow
(c) Pulley (d) Wedge

44. What type of simple machine is a pair of scissors?
(a) Screw (b) Inclined plane
(c) Lever (d) Wedge

45. How does a pulley make work easier?
(a) By increasing force
(b) By increasing speed
(c) By changing direction
(d) By reducing friction

46. What type of simple machine is a screw?
(a) Inclined plane (b) Wheel and axle
(c) Lever (d) Wedge

47. How does an inclined plane make work easier?
(a) By increasing force
(b) By increasing speed
(c) By changing direction
(d) By reducing effort over a longer distance

48. Which of the following is an example of a complex machine?
(a) Hammer (b) Wedge
(c) Scissors (d) Pulley

49. What type of simple machine is a wheel and axle?
(a) Screw (b) Inclined plane
(c) Lever (d) Wheel and axle

50. How does a wedge make work easier?
(a) By increasing force
(b) By increasing speed
(c) By changing direction
(d) By splitting or separating objects

51. How does a pulley make work easier?
(a) By increasing force
(b) By increasing speed
(c) By changing direction
(d) By reducing friction

52. Which of the following is an example of a complex machine?
(a) Screwdriver (b) Scissors
(c) Hammer (d) Wrench

53. What type of simple machine is a seesaw?
(a) Screw (b) Inclined plane
(c) Lever (d) Pulley

54. How does an inclined plane make work easier?
(a) By increasing force
(b) By increasing speed
(c) By changing direction
(d) By reducing effort over a longer distance

55. Which of the following is an example of a complex machine?
(a) Screw (b) Wedge
(c) Crane (d) Pulley

56. What type of simple machine is a ramp?
(a) Screw (b) Inclined plane
(c) Lever (d) Wheel and axle

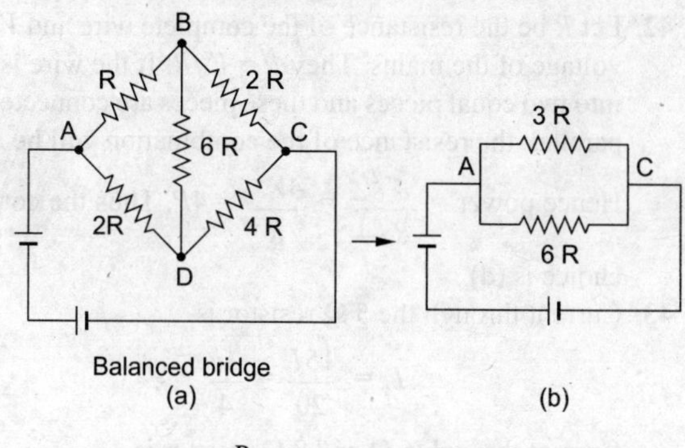

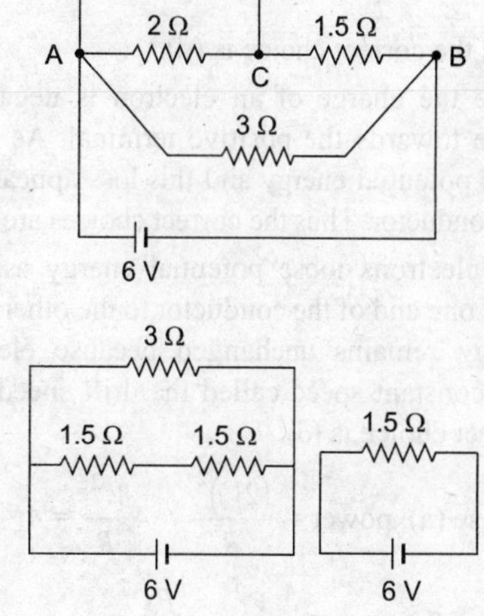

In case (b), power $= \dfrac{V^2}{2R} = \dfrac{P}{2}$

$$I_1 = I_3 + I_3 \quad\text{or}\quad I_3 = \frac{I_1}{3}.$$

Similarly $\quad I_2 = \dfrac{2I_1}{3}$

Thus, $\quad I_1 : I_2 : I_3 = I_1 : \dfrac{2I_1}{3} : \dfrac{I_1}{3}$

As $\quad E_{eq} = \dfrac{\frac{12}{1}+\frac{13}{2}}{\frac{1}{1}+\frac{1}{2}} = \dfrac{\frac{37}{2}}{\frac{3}{2}} = \dfrac{37}{3}$

$$\text{Therefore} \quad \frac{1}{R_{100}} > \frac{1}{R_{60}} > \frac{1}{R_{40}}$$

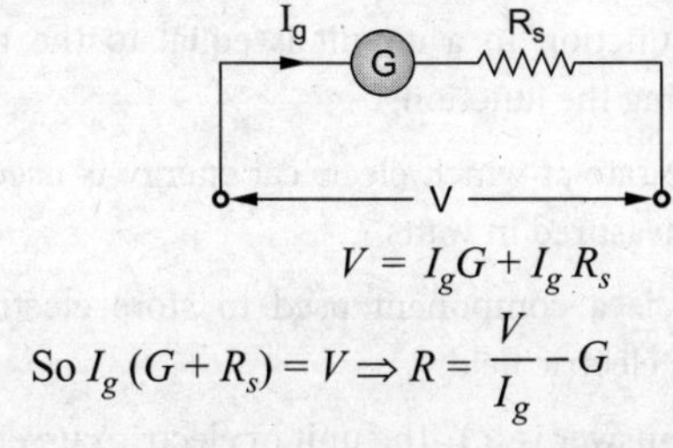

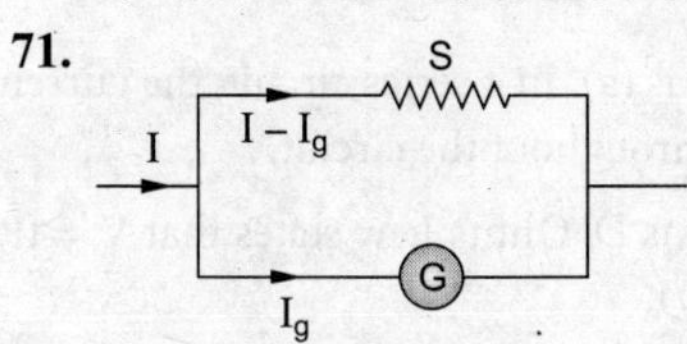

Hence, $\quad \dfrac{I - I_g}{I_g} = \dfrac{G}{S}$

$\Rightarrow \quad \dfrac{\Delta X}{X} = \dfrac{\Delta l}{l} + \dfrac{\Delta l}{100 - l} = \dfrac{0.1}{40} + \dfrac{0.1}{60}$

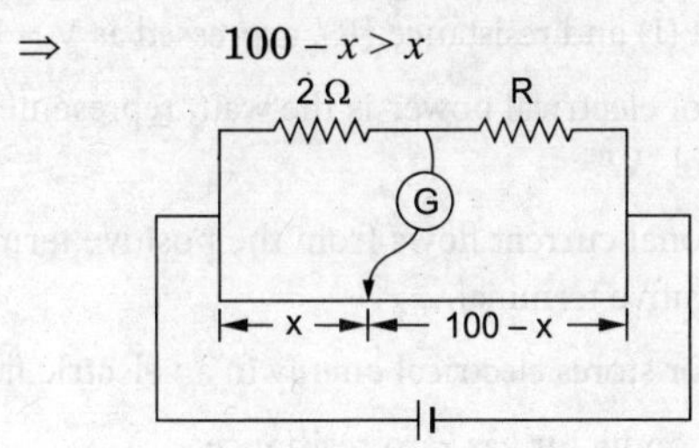

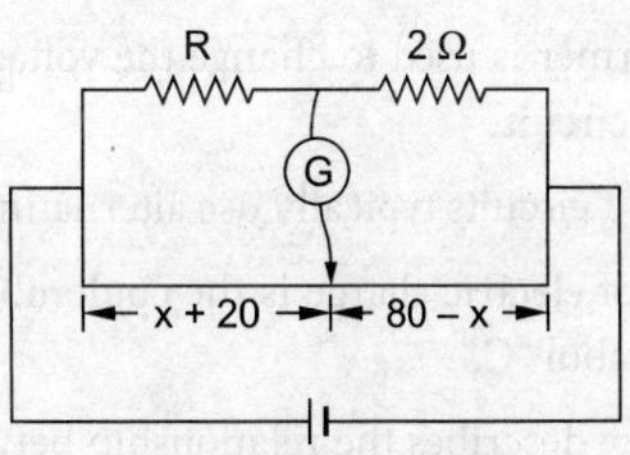

Using $\quad \dfrac{P}{Q} = \dfrac{R}{S}$

We get $\quad \dfrac{2}{R} = \dfrac{x}{100 - x}$ ...(i)

$\dfrac{R}{2} = \dfrac{x + 20}{80 - x}$ ...(ii)

57. How does a lever make work easier?
(a) By increasing force
(b) By increasing speed
(c) By changing direction
(d) By amplifying the effort applied

58. Which of the following is an example of a complex machine?
(a) Screw (b) Wheel and axle
(c) Hammer (d) Scissors

59. What type of simple machine is a screw?
(a) Wedge (b) Inclined plane
(c) Lever (d) Pulley

60. How does a wedge make work easier?
(a) By increasing force
(b) By increasing speed
(c) By changing direction
(d) By splitting or separating objects

61. Which of the following is an example of a complex machine?
(a) Scissors (b) Lever
(c) Wheelbarrow (d) Inclined plane

62. What type of simple machine is a nutcracker?
(a) Screw (b) Wedge
(c) Lever (d) Pulley

63. How does a pulley system with multiple pulleys make work easier?
(a) By increasing force
(b) By increasing speed
(c) By changing direction
(d) By providing mechanical advantage

64. Which of the following is an example of a complex machine?
(a) Screwdriver (b) Wedge
(c) Bicycle (d) Wheel and axle

65. What type of simple machine is a doorknob?
(a) Screw (b) Wedge
(c) Lever (d) Wheel and axle

66. How does a lever system with a longer lever arm make work easier?
(a) By increasingforce
(b) By increasing speed
(c) By changing direction
(d) By providing mechanical advantage

67. Which of the following is an example of a complex machine?
(a) Screw (b) Wedge
(c) Elevator (d) Pulley

68. What type of simple machine is a pair of tweezers?
(a) Screw (b) Wedge
(c) Lever (d) Pulley

69. How does an inclined plane with a steeper slope make work harder?
(a) By increasing force
(b) By increasing speed
(c) By changing direction
(d) By requiring more effort over a shorter distance

70. Which of the following is an example of a complex machine?
(a) Screw (b) Wedge
(c) Bicycle (d) Hammer

71. What type of simple machine is a screwdriver?
(a) Screw (b) Wedge
(c) Lever (d) Pulley

72. How does a pulley with a greater number of ropes make work easier?
(a) By increasing force
(b) By increasing speed
(c) By changing direction
(d) By distributing the load

73. Which of the following is an example of a complex machine?
(a) Screw (b) Wedge
(c) Scissors (d) Pulley

74. What type of simple machine is a jar lid?
(a) Screw (b) Wedge
(c) Lever (d) Pulley

75. How does a lever system with the fulcrum closer to the load make work easier?
(a) By increasing force
(b) By increasing speed
(c) By changing direction
(d) By providing mechanical advantage

76. Which of the following is an example of a complex machine?
(a) Screwdriver (b) Wedge
(c) Crane (d) Wheel and axle

76. What type of simple machine is a pair of pliers?

(a) Screw (b) Wedge

(c) Lever (d) Pulley

78. How does an inclined plane with a longer length make work easier?

(a) By increasing force

(b) By increasing speed

(c) By changing direction

(d) By reducing effort over a longer distance

79. Which of the following is an example of a complex machine?

(a) Screw (b) Wedge

(c) Bicycle (d) Wheelbarrow

80. What type of simple machine is a faucet valve?

(a) Screw (b) Wedge

(c) Lever (d) Pulley

81. How does a wheel and axle make work easier?

(a) By increasing force

(b) By increasing speed

(c) By changing direction

(d) By reducing friction

82. Which of the following is an example of a complex machine?

(a) Screw (b) Wedge

(c) Hammer (d) Pulley

Answers

1. (d)	**2.** (c)	**3.** (b)	**4.** (b)	**5.** (a)	**6.** (c)	**7.** (c)	**8.** (d)	**9.** (c)	**10.** (c)
11. (c)	**12.** (d)	**13.** (b)	**14.** (b)	**15.** (a)	**16.** (c)	**17.** (b)	**18.** (a)	**19.** (a)	**20.** (c)
21. (d)	**22.** (d)	**23.** (b)	**24.** (d)	**25.** (c)	**26.** (a)	**27.** (a)	**28.** (b)	**29.** (c)	**30.** (c)
31. (a)	**32.** (d)	**33.** (a)	**34.** (c)	**35.** (c)	**36.** (c)	**37.** (d)	**38.** (b)	**39.** (a)	**40.** (a)
41. (c)	**42.** (d)	**43.** (b)	**44.** (c)	**45.** (c)	**46.** (a)	**47.** (d)	**48.** (c)	**49.** (d)	**50.** (d)
51. (c)	**52.** (b)	**53.** (c)	**54.** (d)	**55.** (c)	**56.** (b)	**57.** (d)	**58.** (d)	**59.** (b)	**60.** (d)
61. (c)	**62.** (c)	**63.** (d)	**64.** (c)	**65.** (d)	**66.** (d)	**67.** (c)	**68.** (c)	**69.** (a)	**70.** (c)
71. (c)	**72.** (d)	**73.** (c)	**74.** (a)	**75.** (d)	**76.** (c)	**77.** (c)	**78.** (d)	**79.** (d)	**80.** (a)
81. (b)	**82.** (c)								

Explanations

1. There are only three classes of levers, namely, first-class, second-class, and third-class levers.

2. In a first-class lever, the fulcrum is located at the midpoint, with the effort applied on one side and the load on the other side.

3. In a second-class lever, the load is located between the fulcrum and the effort. In a wheelbarrow, the wheel serves as the fulcrum, the load is placed in the container, and the effort is applied to the handles.

4. Second-class levers provide the greatest mechanical advantage because the load is positioned between the fulcrum and the effort, allowing for efficient force multiplication.

5. In a third-class lever, the effort is applied between the fulcrum and the load, with the fulcrum closer to the load than the effort.

6. In a first-class lever, the fulcrum is located in the middle, with the effort applied at one end and the load (fish) being lifted at the other end.

7. Third-class levers provide the least mechanical advantage because the effort is applied closer to the fulcrum than the load, resulting in a lower force multiplication.

8. In a pair of tweezers, the effort is applied between the fulcrum (the hinge) and the load (the object being picked up).

9. In order for a lever to be in equilibrium, the effort and load forces must be balanced, meaning they are equal in magnitude.

10. Third-class levers are the most common type found in the human body, such as the system of bones, muscles, and joints that create a lever mechanism.

11. Third-class levers provide a greater range of motion because the effort is applied closer to the fulcrum than the load, allowing for increased speed and mobility.

12. The shoulder joint acts as a first-class lever, with the fulcrum at the joint, the effort provided by muscles, and the load being the weight or resistance being moved.

13. A lever with a mechanical advantage greater than 1 allows for a smaller effort force to lift a larger load.

14. Second-class levers are commonly used for prying actions, such as using a crowbar to lift a heavy object by applying effort at one end and the load at the other end.

15. The ratio of the effort arm length to the load arm length determines the mechanical advantage of a lever.

16. A pair of scissors is an example of a third-class lever, where the effort is applied between the fulcrum (the pivot) and the load (the material being cut).

17. The knee joint acts as a second-class lever in the human body, with the effort provided by the quadriceps muscles, the fulcrum at the knee joint, and the load being the weight of the lower leg.

18. A catapult is an example of a first-class lever, where the fulcrum is located between the effort (the tension in the catapult's arm) and the load (the projectile being launched.

19. A lever with a mechanical advantage of less than 1 means that the load arm is longer than the effort arm, requiring a larger effort force to lift a smaller load.

20. A push-up exercise is an example of a third-class lever, where the effort is applied by the muscles between the hands (fulcrum)and the feet (load on the ground.

21. While levers are not directly involved in cooking food, they are commonly used in tasks such as opening doors, lifting weights, and rowing boats.

22. Levers are widely used in various fields, including engineering, medicine (e.g., for prosthetics), and agriculture (e.g., in machinery).

23. Levers allow for the multiplication of force, enabling the lifting of heavier loads or the application of greater force with less effort.

24. Levers are versatile tools that can transfer motion, change the direction of motion, and modify the amount of force applied.

25. The mechanical advantage of a lever is determined by the position of the fulcrum, which affects the ratio of the effort arm to the load arm.

26. A longer effort arm in a lever increases the lever's mechanical advantage, as it allows for more leverage and force multiplication.

27. In a first-class lever, the fulcrum is positioned between the effort and the load, allowing for a variety of applications.

28. Wheel barrows typically use a second-class lever design, with the load between the fulcrum (wheel) and the effort (handles).

29. Third-class levers sacrifice force in exchange for speed and a wider range of motion, making them suitable for tasks requiring agility.

30. Tweezers operate as third-class levers, with the effort (squeezing the handles) between the fulcrum (pivot point)and the load (object being picked).

31. Scissors operate as first-class levers, where the fulcrum is located at the pivot point, and the effort and load are on opposite sides.

32. Construction machinery, such as cranes, excavators, and backhoes, utilize levers to lift heavy objects, dig trenches, and excavate soil.

33. Nutcrackers operate as first-class levers, with the fulcrum at the pivot point and the effort applied at one end to crack the nut.

34. The position of the fulcrum in a lever affects the ease of control and stability, as it determines the distribution of forces and torques.

35. Fishing rods function as third-class levers, where the effort is applied through the angler's hand, between the fulcrum (reel) and the load (fish).

36. Tongs operate as third-class levers, with the effort applied between the fulcrum (hinge) and the load (object being gripped).

37. Gym equipment often incorporates levers for various exercises, such as weightlifting machines, leg presses, and rowing machines.

38. Levers operate based on Newton's second law of motion, which states that force is equal to mass multiplied by acceleration. Levers allow for the application of force to overcome resistance.

39. A stapler operates as a first-class lever, where the fulcrum is located at the pivot point, and the effort (squeezing the handles)is applied on one side to drive the staple into the paper.

40. A crowbar is an example of a first-class lever, where the fulcrum is positioned between the effort (applied force on one end and the load (object being pried).

41. A shovel has a flat, sloping surface that allows for the lifting and moving of materials, making it an inclined plane.

42. A lever is a simple machine that uses a rigid bar and a fulcrum to multiply the force applied, making it easier to move or lift heavy objects.

43. A wheelbarrow is an example of a complex machine as it combines multiple simple machines like a lever, wheel and axle, and an inclined plane.

44. Scissors consist of two levers connected at a fulcrum, making them an example of a lever.

45. A pulley is a simple machine that uses a wheel with a grooved rim and a rope or chain to lift or move objects. It changes the direction of the force applied, making it easier to lift heavy objects.

46. A screw is an inclined plane wrapped around a cylinder, making it a type of inclined plane.

47. An inclined plane is a simple machine that allows objects to be moved from a lower to a higher level with less force, but over a longer distance.

48. Scissors are considered a complex machine because they consist of two levers (blades) connected at a fulcrum.

49. A wheel and axle is a simple machine that consists of a wheel attached to a smaller axle. It allows for the transmission of force and rotation.

50. A wedge is a simple machine with a thick end and a thin, sharp end. It is used to split or separate objects apart with less force.

51. A pulley is a simple machine that uses a wheel with a grooved rim and a rope or chain to lift or move objects. It makes work easier by changing the direction of the force required to lift the object.

52. Complex machines are made up of multiple simple machines working together. Among the given options, scissors are an example of a complex machine, as they consist of two levers (blades) connected at a fulcrum.

53. A seesaw is an example of a lever, which is a simple machine. It consists of a long beam (board) that pivots on a fulcrum, with two people sitting on opposite ends.

54. An inclined plane is a simple machine that is a sloping surface used to move objects between different heights. It makes work easier by reducing the effort required to lift an object over a longer distance.

55. Among the given options, a crane is an example of a complex machine. It consists of various simple machines such as pulleys, levers, and gears working together to lift heavy loads.

56. A ramp is an example of an inclined plane, which is a simple machine. It is a flat, sloping surface that allows objects to be moved from a lower level to a higher level with less force.

57. A lever is a simple machine that consists of a rigid bar that pivots around a fixed point called a fulcrum. It makes work easier by amplifying the effort applied, allowing heavy objects to be moved with less force.

58. Among the given options, scissors are an example of a complex machine. They consist of two levers (blades) connected at a fulcrum, allowing for cutting or shearing actions.

59. A screw is an example of an inclined plane wrapped around a cylinder. Therefore, it is considered a type of inclined plane and is classified as a simple machine.

60. A wedge is a simple machine that has a thick end and a thin, sharp end. It makes work easier by splitting or separating objects apart with less force.

61. Among the given options, a wheelbarrow is an example of a complex machine. It combines various simple machines, such as levers and wheels, to facilitate the movement of heavy loads.

62. A nutcracker is an example of a lever, which is a simple machine. It consists of two arms connected by a fulcrum, allowing for the application of force to crack nuts.

63. A pulley system with multiple pulleys makes work easier by providing mechanical advantage. It allows for the distribution of the load among multiple ropes, reducing the effort required to lift heavy objects.

64. Among the given options, a bicycle is an example of a complex machine. It incorporates various simple machines, including levers, wheels and axles, pulleys, and gears, to enable motion and transportation.

65. A doorknob is an example of a wheel and axle, which is a simple machine. It consists of a wheel (the knob) attached to an axle (the spindle), allowing for the rotation and opening/closing of the door.

66. A lever system with a longer lever arm makes work easier by providing mechanical advantage. The longer lever arm allows for the application of force at a greater distance from the fulcrum, resulting in a greater mechanical advantage and requiring less force to perform the same task.

67. Among the given options, an elevator is an example of a complex machine. It involves the integration of multiple simple machines, including pulleys, levers, and gears, to move people or objects between different levels or floors.

68. A pair of tweezers is an example of a lever, which is a simple machine. It consists of two arms connected at a fulcrum, allowing for the precise grasping and manipulation of small objects.

69. An inclined plane with a steeper slope makes work harder by requiring more force to overcome gravity and move an object up the slope. It increases the vertical height that needs to be overcome, resulting in a higher required force.

70. Among the given options, a bicycle is an example of a complex machine. It incorporates various simple machines, including levers, wheels and axles, pulleys, and gears, to enable motion and transportation.

71. A screwdriver is an example of a lever, which is a simple machine. It consists of a long handle (lever arm)that can be rotated to apply torque to a screw, enabling tightening or loosening.

72. A pulley with a greater number of ropes makes work easier by distributing the load among multiple ropes. This reduces the force required to lift the load, as it is distributed among multiple strands.

73. Among the given options, scissors are an example of a complex machine. They consist of two levers (blades) connected at a fulcrum, allowing for cutting or shearing actions.

74. A jar lid is an example of a screw, which is a simple machine. It consists of an inclined plane wrapped around a cylinder, allowing for the tightening or loosening of the lid.

75. A lever system with the fulcrum closer to the load makes work easier by providing mechanical advantage. The closer the fulcrum is to the load, the greater the mechanical advantage, requiring less for to lift or move the load.

76. Among the given options, a crane is an example of a complex machine. It incorporates multiple simple machines, such as pulleys, levers, and gears, to enable the lifting and movement of heavy loads.

77. A pair of pliers is an example of a lever, which is a simple machine. It consists of two arms connected at a fulcrum, allowing for the application of force to grip, hold, or manipulate objects.

78. An inclined plane with a longer length makes work easier by reducing the effort required to move an object over a longer distance. It allows for a smaller applied force over a greater distance to achieve the same displacement.

79. Among the given options, a wheelbarrow is an example of a complex machine. It combines various simple machines, such as levers and wheels, to facilitate the movement of heavy loads.

80. A faucet valve is an example of a screw, which is a simple machine. It uses an inclined plane wrapped around a cylinder to control the flow of water, allowing for opening or closing the valve.

81. A wheel and axle is a simple machine that consists of a wheel (a circular object) attached to an axle (a cylindrical rod. It makes work easier by increasing speed or mechanical advantage when rotational motion is involved.

82. Among the given options, a hammer is an example of a complex machine. It combines a lever (handle) and a wedge (the head) to exert force and drive nails or perform other tasks.

9

CHAPTER

Occupational Health and Safety

OCCUPATIONAL HEALTH AND SAFETY (OHS)

Occupational health and safety (OHS) refers to the practices and procedures implemented in the workplace to ensure the physical, mental, and social well-being of employees and to prevent work-related injuries, illnesses, and accidents. OHS encompasses a broad range of measures and regulations designed to create a safe and healthy working environment for all workers.

Some key aspects of occupational health and safety:

1. Risk Assessment: Employers are responsible for identifying and assessing potential hazards in the workplace. This involves examining the work environment, equipment, and tasks performed to determine any risks to employee safety and health.
2. Hazard Prevention and Control: Once hazards are identified, steps should be taken to eliminate or control them. This can involve implementing safety protocols, providing personal protective equipment (PPE), modifying equipment or processes, and creating safe work practices.
3. Training and Education: Employers are required to provide proper training and education to employees to ensure they understand the hazards and know how to work safely. This includes training on specific tasks, emergency procedures, proper use of equipment, and recognizing and reporting potential hazards.
4. Health Promotion: Occupational health and safety is not limited to physical safety; it also involves promoting overall employee health and well-being. This may include initiatives such as wellness programs, ergonomic assessments, mental health support, and promoting work-life balance.
5. Compliance with Regulations: Employers must comply with relevant local, national, and international regulations and standards related to occupational health and safety. These regulations often cover areas such as workplace design, ventilation, hazardous substance handling, noise control, and emergency preparedness.
6. Incident Reporting and Investigation: When accidents, injuries, or near-miss incidents occur in the workplace, they should be reported and thoroughly investigated to determine the cause and prevent future occurrences. This helps identify underlying issues and implement corrective measures.
7. Continuous Improvement: Occupational health and safety is an ongoing process that requires regular evaluation and improvement. Employers should encourage feedback from employees, conduct safety audits, and implement measures to address any identified shortcomings.

Importance of occupational health and safety

Occupational health and safety (OHS) is of paramount importance in any workplace. It refers to the measures and practices put in place to ensure the well-being, health, and safety of employees, as well as the prevention of accidents, injuries, and illnesses in the workplace. Here are some key reasons why occupational health and safety is crucial:

1. Protecting workers' lives and well-being: The primary objective of OHS is to safeguard the lives and physical well-being of employees. By implementing safety protocols, providing appropriate training, and maintaining a hazard-free work environment, employers can reduce the risk of accidents, injuries, and illnesses among their workforce.
2. Reducing workplace accidents and injuries: Occupational accidents and injuries not only cause physical harm to employees but also lead to financial losses for companies. By prioritizing safety measures, companies can significantly reduce the number of accidents, resulting in fewer injuries, medical expenses, and legal liabilities.
3. Enhancing productivity and efficiency: A safe and healthy work environment positively impacts productivity and efficiency. When employees feel safe, they are more focused, motivated, and productive. Moreover, fewer accidents mean fewer disruptions in workflow and decreased downtime due to injuries.
4. Compliance with legal requirements: Governments across the world have established regulations and

standards to ensure occupational health and safety in workplaces. Complying with these regulations is not only a legal requirement but also demonstrates a company's commitment to its employees' well-being. Failure to comply with OHS laws can lead to legal consequences, penalties, and damage to a company's reputation.

5. Boosting employee morale and engagement: When employees see that their employer values their safety and well-being, it fosters a positive work environment and boosts morale. Employees are more likely to be engaged, satisfied, and loyal to a company that prioritizes their health and safety. This, in turn, leads to increased employee retention and a more positive company culture.
6. Attracting and retaining talent: In today's competitive job market, potential employees consider occupational health and safety as a crucial factor when evaluating job opportunities. Companies that have a strong OHS program in place are more likely to attract top talent and retain skilled employees who prioritize their well-being.
7. Reputation and public image: Companies that prioritize occupational health and safety earn a positive reputation in the industry and among the public. Demonstrating a commitment to employee safety can enhance the company's public image, attract customers, investors, and partners who value ethical and responsible business practices.

Cost of occupational injury:

The cost of occupational injuries can vary depending on various factors such as the severity of the injury, the industry, the country, and the specific circumstances surrounding the incident. Here are some of the costs associated with occupational injuries:

1. Direct Costs: These are the immediate costs incurred as a result of an occupational injury. They typically include medical expenses, emergency response costs, hospitalization, surgeries, and medication. The direct costs also include the cost of rehabilitation and physical therapy required for the injured worker.

Here are some examples of direct costs:

- Raw materials: The cost of purchasing the materials and components that are directly used in the production of a product.
- Labor costs: Wages, salaries, and benefits of employees directly involved in the production or delivery of a product or service.
- Manufacturing equipment: The cost of machinery and equipment specifically used in the manufacturing process.
- Packaging materials: Expenses for packaging materials that are directly used for a product, such as boxes, labels, or containers.
- Direct labor: Wages and benefits paid to employees who work directly on a specific project or provide direct services to clients.
- Subcontractor costs: Payments made to external contractors or vendors who are hired to perform specific tasks or provide specialized services.
- Sales commissions: Commissions or incentives paid to sales personnel for selling specific products or services.
- Shipping and transportation: The cost of shipping and transporting goods or materials directly associated with a product or project.
- Direct utilities: Expenses for utilities directly related to the production process, such as electricity, water, or fuel used in manufacturing.
- Prototype development: Costs incurred during the development and creation of a prototype or sample product.

2. Indirect Costs: Indirect costs are the long-term or hidden costs that arise from occupational injuries. These costs are not as visible as direct costs but can be significant. They include lost productivity due to the absence of the injured worker, training and hiring replacement workers, reduced efficiency during the injured worker's recovery period, and administrative costs associated with workers' compensation claims.

Here are some examples of indirect costs:

- Rent and utilities: The cost of leasing or renting office space, as well as expenses for electricity, water, heating, and other utilities.
- Administrative salaries: Salaries and benefits for employees who provide administrative support, such as human resources, accounting, and management personnel.
- Office supplies and equipment: Expenses for purchasing and maintaining office supplies, computers, printers, furniture, and other necessary equipment.
- Insurance: Costs associated with various insurance policies, including general liability insurance, property insurance, workers' compensation insurance, and professional liability insurance.
- Depreciation: The reduction in value of assets over time, such as buildings, vehicles, or machinery, as they are used in the business.
- Maintenance and repairs: Expenses for routine maintenance and repairs of equipment, machinery, and facilities.
- Communication and technology: Costs related to internet services, phone systems, software licenses, and other communication and technology infrastructure.
- Training and development: Expenses for employee training programs, workshops, seminars, and professional development activities.
- Marketing and advertising: Costs associated with promoting products or services, including advertising campaigns, marketing materials, and online marketing efforts.

- Legal and professional fees: Payments made to attorneys, accountants, consultants, and other professional service providers for legal advice, tax preparation, auditing, or other specialized services.

3. Workers' Compensation: Many countries have workers' compensation programs in place to provide benefits to workers who suffer occupational injuries. The costs of workers' compensation insurance premiums are borne by employers and are based on factors such as the industry's risk level and the employer's safety record.
4. Legal Costs: In cases where an occupational injury leads to legal disputes, there may be additional costs associated with legal representation, court fees, and potential settlements or judgments.
5. Intangible Costs: Occupational injuries can also have intangible costs that are difficult to quantify. These include pain and suffering endured by the injured worker, emotional distress, damage to the company's reputation, and decreased employee morale.

Cost of occupational disease:

The cost of occupational diseases can be significant and have various impacts on individuals, employers, and society as a whole. Here are some factors to consider when assessing the cost of occupational diseases:

1. Healthcare Expenses: Occupational diseases often require medical treatment, including doctor visits, diagnostic tests, medication, and specialized care. The cost of healthcare can be substantial, particularly for chronic or long-term conditions.
2. Lost Productivity: When workers become ill due to occupational diseases, they may need time off work or be unable to perform their job duties effectively. Lost productivity can result in reduced output, decreased efficiency, and the need for temporary or permanent replacements, which can all have financial implications for employers.
3. Workers' Compensation: Many countries have workers' compensation systems in place to provide financial support to employees who suffer from occupational diseases. This includes covering medical expenses, providing disability benefits, and compensating for lost wages. Employers often bear the cost of workers' compensation insurance premiums, which can increase with higher rates of occupational diseases.
4. Legal Costs: In some cases, occupational diseases may lead to legal disputes, such as claims for compensation or lawsuits against employers. These legal processes can involve legal fees, settlements, and court costs, adding to the overall cost of the disease.
5. Rehabilitation and Disability Support: Depending on the severity of the occupational disease, affected individuals may require rehabilitation services or ongoing support to manage their condition and reintegrate into the workforce. These services can involve additional expenses.
6. Social and Economic Impact: Occupational diseases can have broader societal and economic consequences. They can lead to decreased productivity at a national level, increased strain on healthcare systems, and higher social welfare costs if individuals are unable to work and require financial support.

Poor working conditions impact on worker health and safety:

Poor working conditions can indeed have a significant impact on worker health and safety. When employees are subjected to unfavorable working conditions, it can lead to a range of negative consequences for their well-being. Here are some ways in which poor working conditions can affect worker health and safety:

1. Physical health hazards: Inadequate ventilation, exposure to harmful substances or toxins, noise pollution, improper ergonomics, and lack of personal protective equipment (PPE) can all contribute to physical health issues. These conditions may lead to respiratory problems, hearing loss, musculoskeletal disorders, skin irritations, and other occupational illnesses.
2. Accidents and injuries: Poorly maintained equipment, insufficient training, lack of safety protocols, and overcrowded or cluttered workspaces can increase the risk of accidents and injuries. Workers may be exposed to hazards such as falls, machinery accidents, electrical shocks, or being struck by falling objects.
3. Mental and emotional well-being: Unfavorable working conditions, including long working hours, excessive workload, lack of support or recognition, poor management, and workplace harassment, can take a toll on employees' mental and emotional health. It may lead to stress, anxiety, depression, burnout, and decreased job satisfaction.
4. Occupational diseases: Some industries expose workers to specific risks that can result in occupational diseases. For example, workers in construction, mining, or manufacturing may be at risk of developing lung diseases due to asbestos exposure, or those working with chemicals may experience long-term health effects.
5. Fatigue and sleep disturbances: Extended working hours, night shifts, irregular schedules, and high-stress environments can disrupt sleep patterns and lead to fatigue. Fatigue not only affects worker performance but also increases the likelihood of accidents and errors.
6. Lack of work-life balance: Poor working conditions can make it challenging for employees to maintain a healthy work-life balance. Long hours, inflexible schedules, and excessive work demands can result in heightened stress levels, strained relationships, and reduced time for self-care or leisure activities.

Challenges and issues related to occupational health and safety:

There are some common challenges and issues related to occupational health and safety such as:

1. Work-related accidents and injuries: Many industries and occupations pose inherent risks to workers, leading to accidents and injuries. These can include slips, trips,

falls, exposure to hazardous substances, machinery accidents, and more. The extent of these incidents varies across sectors, but they contribute to lost productivity, increased medical costs, and human suffering.

2. Occupational diseases: Workers may be exposed to various occupational hazards, such as chemicals, noise, radiation, or biological agents, which can lead to long-term health issues or occupational diseases. Examples include respiratory conditions, skin disorders, hearing loss, occupational cancers, and musculoskeletal disorders.
3. Psychological and psychosocial issues: Occupational health and safety concerns extend beyond physical hazards. Psychological factors such as stress, long working hours, bullying, and workplace violence can have a significant impact on employee well-being and mental health. These issues can lead to decreased productivity, absenteeism, and turnover.
4. Compliance and enforcement: Ensuring compliance with occupational health and safety regulations can be challenging for employers and regulatory agencies. Some organizations may prioritize productivity over safety, leading to inadequate safety measures or non-compliance with regulations. Additionally, enforcement efforts and resources may vary across jurisdictions, resulting in inconsistent adherence to OHS standards.
5. Emerging risks: As workplaces evolve with technological advancements and new industries, new risks to occupational health and safety may emerge. For example, the increasing use of automation, robotics, and artificial intelligence may introduce unique hazards that require specialized safety measures and training.

Identifying the cause of an accident in occupational health and safety:

Identifying the cause of an accident in the context of occupational health and safety also involves a systematic investigation. Here are the key steps typically followed in such investigations:

1. Ensure immediate safety: The first priority is to ensure the safety and well-being of the individuals involved in the accident and to prevent further harm or injuries. This may involve providing medical assistance, securing the area, and addressing any immediate hazards.
2. Form an investigation team: A team or an individual is assigned the responsibility of conducting the accident investigation. This team should ideally have relevant expertise and knowledge in occupational health and safety.
3. Collect information: Gather all available information related to the accident. This includes incident reports, witness statements, photographs, video footage, equipment data, and any other relevant documentation. If applicable, review safety policies, procedures, and training records.
4. Interview involved parties: Interview the individuals directly involved in the accident, such as the injured employees or witnesses. Collect their accounts of the incident, focusing on the sequence of events, activities being performed, equipment used, and any potential hazards they observed.
5. Examine the accident scene: Visit and thoroughly examine the accident scene. Look for physical evidence, such as equipment damage, environmental conditions, layout, lighting, or any other factors that may have contributed to the accident.
6. Identify underlying factors: Analyze the information collected to identify the underlying causes and contributing factors of the accident. These factors can include unsafe work practices, inadequate training, equipment failure, lack of maintenance, communication issues, or deficiencies in safety procedures.
7. Conduct root cause analysis: Use various tools and techniques, such as the "5 Whys" method or Fishbone (Ishikawa) diagrams, to delve deeper into the factors identified in the previous step. This helps identify the underlying root causes that led to the accident.
8. Determine preventive measures: Based on the identified root causes, develop recommendations for corrective actions and preventive measures to mitigate the risk of similar accidents in the future. These recommendations may include improvements in training, policies, procedures, equipment maintenance, or communication systems.
9. Document and communicate findings: Prepare a detailed report that outlines the investigation process, findings, and recommendations. This report should be shared with relevant stakeholders, such as management, supervisors, and workers' representatives. It can serve as a learning tool for improving occupational health and safety practices within the organization.

The range of hazards in occupational health and safety:

Occupational health and safety hazards encompass a wide range of risks that workers may face in their work environments. These hazards can vary depending on the nature of the job, industry, and specific workplace conditions. Here are some common categories of hazards in occupational health and safety:

1. Physical Hazards: These hazards involve conditions or factors that can cause physical harm to workers. They include:
   - Noise: Excessive noise levels that can lead to hearing loss or communication difficulties.
   - Vibration: Prolonged exposure to vibration from tools or machinery, leading to musculoskeletal disorders.
   - Temperature Extremes: Extreme heat or cold that can cause heatstroke, hypothermia, or frostbite.
   - Radiation: Exposure to ionizing radiation, such as X-rays or radioactive materials, leading to health issues.

- Ergonomic Hazards: Poorly designed workstations or repetitive tasks that can cause musculoskeletal disorders.

2. Chemical Hazards: These hazards arise from exposure to harmful substances in the workplace. Examples include:
   - Toxic Chemicals: Exposure to substances like solvents, pesticides, or heavy metals that can cause acute or chronic health effects.
   - Carcinogens: Substances that have the potential to cause cancer, such as asbestos or certain chemicals.
   - Irritants: Chemicals that can cause irritation or damage to the skin, eyes, or respiratory system.
3. Biological Hazards: These hazards involve exposure to biological agents such as viruses, bacteria, fungi, or parasites. Examples include:
   - Infectious Diseases: Exposure to pathogens in healthcare settings or laboratories.
   - Animal-borne Diseases: Risks associated with working with animals, including zoonotic diseases.
   - Allergens: Substances that can cause allergic reactions, such as pollen, mold, or certain chemicals.
4. Psychosocial Hazards: These hazards are related to the psychological and social aspects of work that can impact mental well-being. They include:
   - Work-related Stress: High workloads, long hours, or job insecurity that can lead to stress and burnout.
   - Workplace Violence: Threats, harassment, or physical violence from co-workers, customers, or the public.
   - Bullying: Persistent mistreatment, intimidation, or humiliation by colleagues or supervisors.
   - Organizational Culture: Poor communication, lack of support, or inadequate leadership leading to low job satisfaction.
5. Safety Hazards: These hazards pertain to conditions that can directly cause accidents, injuries, or fatalities. They include:
   - Falls: Working at heights without proper fall protection or tripping hazards.
   - Machinery Hazards: Unguarded machinery, faulty equipment, or lack of safety procedures.
   - Electrical Hazards: Exposed wiring, improper grounding, or electrical shocks.
   - Fire and Explosions: Inadequate fire prevention measures or handling of flammable materials.

Key features of a national policy in occupational safety and health:

A national policy in occupational safety and health is designed to protect workers and promote a safe working environment. While specific policies may vary from country to country, here are some key features commonly found in such policies:

1. Legal Framework: A national policy typically includes a legal framework that sets out the rights and responsibilities of employers, employees, and regulatory authorities. It may include laws, regulations, and standards related to workplace safety and health.
2. Hazard Identification and Risk Assessment: The policy emphasizes the importance of identifying workplace hazards and assessing the associated risks. It encourages employers to conduct regular inspections and risk assessments to identify potential dangers and implement appropriate control measures.
3. Prevention and Control Measures: The policy emphasizes preventive measures to eliminate or minimize workplace hazards. It promotes the use of engineering controls, administrative controls, and personal protective equipment (PPE) to mitigate risks. It may also encourage employers to implement safety management systems and provide training to employees on hazard recognition and control.
4. Occupational Health Services: The policy may advocate for the establishment of occupational health services to promote the well-being of workers. This may include access to medical examinations, health surveillance, counseling, and rehabilitation services. The policy may also emphasize the importance of promoting mental health in the workplace.
5. Worker Participation and Consultation: The policy recognizes the importance of worker involvement in decision-making processes related to occupational safety and health. It encourages employers to establish mechanisms for workers to participate in identifying hazards, assessing risks, and developing safety policies. It may also promote the establishment of worker safety committees or representatives.
6. Training and Education: The policy highlights the need for training and education programs to increase awareness and knowledge of occupational safety and health among employers, employees, and other relevant stakeholders. It may emphasize the development of training materials, guidelines, and certification programs.
7. Enforcement and Compliance: The policy establishes mechanisms for enforcement and compliance with occupational safety and health regulations. It may outline penalties and sanctions for non-compliance and the roles and responsibilities of regulatory bodies responsible for inspections, investigations, and enforcement.
8. Research and Data Collection: The policy may encourage research and data collection to improve understanding of occupational safety and health issues. It may promote the collection and analysis of occupational injury and illness data to identify trends, emerging risks, and areas requiring further attention.
9. International Cooperation: The policy may recognize the importance of international cooperation and collaboration in addressing occupational safety and health issues. It may encourage participation in international initiatives, sharing of best practices, and alignment with international standards and guidelines.
10. Continuous Improvement: The policy emphasizes the need for continuous improvement in occupational safety and health. It may require regular reviews and updates of policies and regulations based on changing technologies, work practices, and emerging risks. It may also promote the sharing of lessons learned and best practices within and across industries.

National Occupational health and safety system model

The national occupational health and safety (OHS) system model refers to the framework or structure implemented by a country to promote and regulate workplace health and safety. While specific details and components of the model can vary between countries, there are certain common elements typically found in an effective OHS system.

Here is a general outline of the elements of a national OHS system model:

1. **Legislative Framework**: A comprehensive set of laws and regulations is established to provide the legal basis for occupational health and safety. These laws define the rights and responsibilities of employers, employees, and other stakeholders, and they cover various aspects of workplace safety, such as hazard identification, risk assessment, and control measures.
2. **Regulatory Authorities**: Government agencies or bodies are designated to oversee and enforce the OHS laws and regulations. These authorities are responsible for monitoring compliance, conducting inspections, investigating accidents, and issuing penalties or sanctions for non-compliance.
3. **Occupational Health and Safety Standards**: Specific standards are developed and enforced to address various occupational hazards and risks. These standards may include requirements for safe working conditions, equipment, machinery, processes, and protective measures. They serve as guidelines for employers and employees to ensure compliance with OHS regulations.
4. **Hazard Identification and Risk Assessment**: Employers are required to identify potential hazards in the workplace and assess the associated risks. This process involves evaluating the likelihood and severity of harm resulting from exposure to hazards and taking necessary steps to eliminate or control those risks.
5. **Training and Education**: Employers are responsible for providing appropriate training and education to employees regarding workplace hazards, safe work practices, and emergency procedures. This ensures that workers are aware of the risks they may encounter and are equipped with the knowledge and skills to protect themselves and their colleagues.
6. **Consultation and Participation**: The OHS system promotes worker participation and consultation in decision-making processes that affect their health and safety. Employers are encouraged to involve employees and their representatives in OHS committees, safety meetings, and the development of policies and procedures.
7. **Incident Reporting and Investigation**: A system for reporting and investigating workplace incidents, accidents, and near misses is established. This helps identify the causes of incidents, implement corrective actions, and prevent future occurrences. Employers are required to maintain records of incidents and report serious accidents to the regulatory authorities.
8. **Enforcement and Compliance**: Regulatory authorities have the power to enforce OHS regulations through inspections, audits, and penalties for non-compliance. This ensures that employers fulfill their responsibilities and provides a deterrent against unsafe practices.
9. **Continuous Improvement**: The OHS system encourages ongoing improvement through periodic reviews, evaluations, and feedback mechanisms. Lessons learned from incidents and changes in technology or work processes are used to update standards and regulations, ensuring that the OHS system remains effective and up to date.

Fundamental principles of occupational health and safety model:

According to Convention No. 187, to be functional and effective in addressing the OSH needs of both employers and workers, a national system must include at the least the following key elements:

- Laws, regulations, collective agreements where appropriate, and any other relevant instruments on occupational safety and health;
- An authority or authorities responsible for occupational safety and health, designated in accordance with national law and practice;
- Mechanisms for ensuring compliance with national laws and regulations, including systems of inspection;
- Arrangements to promote, at the level of the undertaking, cooperation between management, workers and their representatives as an essential element of workplace-related prevention measures;
- A national tripartite body on occupational safety and health;
- Information and advisory services on occupational safety and health and Research on occupational safety and health;
- The provision of occupational health services in accordance with national law and practice, provision of OSH training;
- Mechanisms for the collection and analysis of data on occupational accidents and diseases, taking into account relevant ILO instruments;
- Provisions for collaboration with relevant insurance and compensation schemes covering occupational accidents and diseases;
- support mechanisms for a progressive improvement of occupational safety and health conditions in micro-, small and medium-sized enterprises and in the informal economy;

Other additional elements are also required to complete a system adequate to deal with so complex an area as occupational safety and health. A national OSH system designed to incorporate all these elements is illustrated in below figure:

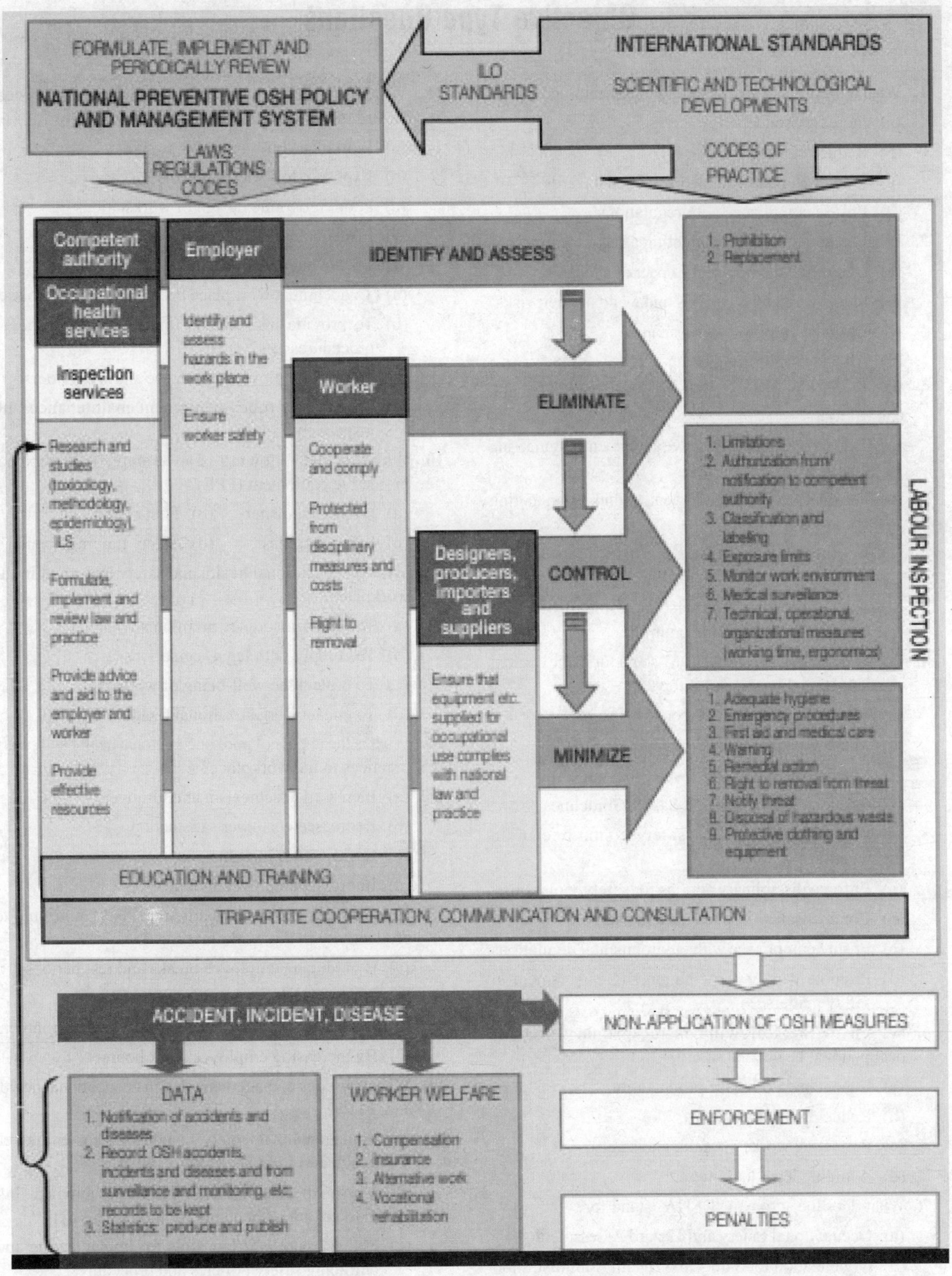
FORMULATE, IMPLEMENT AND PERIODICALLY REVIEW
NATIONAL PREVENTIVE OSH POLICY AND MANAGEMENT SYSTEM
ILO STANDARDS
INTERNATIONAL STANDARDS
SCIENTIFIC AND TECHNOLOGICAL DEVELOPMENTS
LAWS REGULATIONS CODES
CODES OF PRACTICE
Competent authority
Occupational health services
Inspection services
Research and studies (toxicology, methodology, epidemiology), ILS
Formulate, implement and review law and practice
Provide advice and aid to the employer and worker
Provide effective resources
Employer
Identify and assess hazards in the work place
Ensure worker safety
IDENTIFY AND ASSESS
Worker
Cooperate and comply
Protected from disciplinary measures and costs
Right to removal
Designers, producers, importers and suppliers
Ensure that equipment etc. supplied for occupational use complies with national law and practice
ELIMINATE
CONTROL
MINIMIZE
1. Prohibition
2. Replacement
1. Limitations
2. Authorization from/ notification to competent authority
3. Classification and labeling
4. Exposure limits
5. Monitor work environment
6. Medical surveillance
7. Technical, operational, organizational measures (working time, ergonomics)
1. Adequate hygiene
2. Emergency procedures
3. First aid and medical care
4. Warning
5. Remedial action
6. Right to removal from threat
7. Notify threat
8. Disposal of hazardous waste
9. Protective clothing and equipment
LABOUR INSPECTION
EDUCATION AND TRAINING
TRIPARTITE COOPERATION, COMMUNICATION AND CONSULTATION
ACCIDENT, INCIDENT, DISEASE
NON-APPLICATION OF OSH MEASURES
ENFORCEMENT
PENALTIES
DATA
1. Notification of accidents and diseases
2. Record: OSH accidents, incidents and diseases and from surveillance and monitoring, etc; records to be kept
3. Statistics: produce and publish
WORKER WELFARE
1. Compensation
2. Insurance
3. Alternative work
4. Vocational rehabilitation

Objective Type Questions

1. What is the primary goal of occupational health and safety?
   (a) Increase productivity
   (b) Reduce costs
   (c) Protect workers from work-related hazards
   (d) Ensure compliance with regulations
2. What is the purpose of conducting a risk assessment?
   (a) Determine the financial impact of accidents
   (b) Identify potential hazards and evaluate their risks
   (c) Evaluate employee performance
   (d) Allocate safety equipment
3. What is the hierarchy of controls in occupational health and safety?
   (a) Training, personal protective equipment, engineering controls
   (b) Personal protective equipment, training, engineering controls
   (c) Engineering controls, administrative controls, personal protective equipment
   (d) Administrative controls, personal protective equipment, engineering controls
4. What does the acronym "MSDS" stand for in the context of occupational health and safety?
   (a) Material Safety Data Sheet
   (b) Management System Development Strategy
   (c) Mandatory Safety Disclosure Standards
   (d) Occupational Health and Safety Guidelines
5. What is the purpose of a safety committee in an organization?
   (a) Enforce disciplinary actions for safety violations
   (b) Conduct safety inspections and audits
   (c) Ensure compliance with environmental regulations
   (d) Promote worker participation and engagement in safety matters
6. Which of the following is the primary goal of occupational health and safety?
   (a) Enhancing workplace productivity
   (b) Reducing healthcare costs
   (c) Protecting workers' health and safety
   (d) Avoiding legal liabilities
7. What does the acronym "OSHA" stand for?
   (a) Occupational Safety and Hazard Assessment
   (b) Organization for Safety and Health Administration
   (c) Occupational Safety and Health Act
   (d) Occupational Security and Health Association
8. Which of the following is an example of a physical hazard in the workplace?
   (a) Workplace bullying
   (b) Exposure to toxic chemicals
   (c) Poor ergonomic design of workstations
   (d) Inadequate training programs
9. What is the purpose of a safety data sheet (SDS)?
   (a) To document workplace accidents and near misses
   (b) To provide instructions for emergency response procedures
   (c) To track employee attendance and work hours
   (d) To ensure proper equipment maintenance and inspection
10. Which of the following is an example of a personal protective equipment (PPE)?
    (a) Fire extinguisher (b) First aid kit
    (c) Safety goggles (d) Safety training manual
11. Why is occupational health and safety important in the workplace?
    (a) To reduce insurance premiums
    (b) To comply with legal regulations
    (c) To protect the well-being of workers
    (d) To enhance organizational reputation
12. What is the impact of poor occupational health and safety practices in the workplace?
    (a) Increased absenteeism and turnover
    (b) Decreased customer satisfaction
    (c) Higher profit margins
    (d) Improved employee morale
13. How can occupational health and safety contribute to productivity in the workplace?
    (a) By reducing employee breaks and rest periods
    (b) By minimizing workplace distractions
    (c) By promoting a safe and healthy work environment
    (d) By increasing employee work hours
14. What role does management play in occupational health and safety?
    (a) Management is solely responsible for employee health and safety.
    (b) Management should provide safety equipment, but workers are responsible for their own safety.
    (c) Management is responsible for implementing and enforcing safety policies and procedures.
    (d) Management is responsible for conducting regular safety inspections.

15. How does occupational health and safety contribute to cost savings for organizations?
    (a) By reducing workers' salaries
    (b) By minimizing the need for employee benefits
    (c) By lowering insurance premiums and healthcare costs
    (d) By increasing productivity and profits
16. Why is it important to prioritize occupational health and safety in the workplace?
    (a) To improve employee morale
    (b) To reduce legal liabilities
    (c) To enhance productivity
    (d) All of the above
17. What is the primary reason for implementing occupational health and safety programs?
    (a) Compliance with legal regulations
    (b) Cost savings for the organization
    (c) Preservation of workers' well-being
    (d) Improvement of workplace aesthetics
18. How can occupational health and safety contribute to employee retention?
    (a) By increasing salary packages
    (b) By providing career advancement opportunities
    (c) By creating a safe and healthy work environment
    (d) By implementing strict disciplinary measures
19. What is the impact of occupational health and safety on organizational reputation?
    (a) Positive impact on brand image
    (b) Decreased customer loyalty
    (c) Increased competition in the market
    (d) Improved financial performance
20. Why is training an essential component of occupational health and safety programs?
    (a) To meet legal requirements
    (b) To develop employees' skills and knowledge
    (c) To reduce insurance premiums
    (d) To minimize workplace accidents caused by employees
21. How does occupational health and safety impact worker productivity?
    (a) By reducing employee work hours
    (b) By minimizing workplace stress
    (c) By increasing workload expectations
    (d) By enforcing strict performance evaluations
22. What is the role of employees in occupational health and safety?
    (a) To enforce safety rules and regulations
    (b) To report hazards and incidents
    (c) To conduct workplace inspections
    (d) To monitor compliance with legal standards
23. How can occupational health and safety programs contribute to cost savings for organizations?
    (a) By reducing employee salaries
    (b) By eliminating employee benefits
    (c) By lowering insurance premiums
    (d) By increasing revenue through higher sales
24. Why is risk assessment an important aspect of occupational health and safety?
    (a) To identify potential hazards and their associated risks
    (b) To implement strict disciplinary measures
    (c) To improve employee motivation and engagement
    (d) To increase revenue through cost-cutting measures
25. How does occupational health and safety contribute to legal compliance?
    (a) By minimizing workplace accidents
    (b) By providing emergency response plans
    (c) By enforcing disciplinary actions
    (d) By conducting regular safety audits
26. Which of the following is a potential cost associated with occupational injuries and diseases?
    (a) Medical treatment expenses
    (b) Lost productivity
    (c) Legal fees and fines
    (d) All of the above
27. Which of the following factors contributes to the cost of occupational injuries and diseases?
    (a) Workers' compensation claims
    (b) Absenteeism and presenteeism
    (c) Increased insurance premiums
    (d) All of the above
28. What is the significance of indirect costs related to occupational injuries and diseases?
    (a) They are easier to quantify than direct costs.
    (b) They include medical expenses and rehabilitation costs.
    (c) They are not directly associated with the injured worker.
    (d) They account for lost productivity and increased training costs.
29. How can occupational injuries and diseases impact an organization's productivity?
    (a) By increasing absenteeism and turnover rates
    (b) By decreasing healthcare expenses
    (c) By improving employee morale
    (d) By reducing insurance premiums

30. How can organizations mitigate the costs of occupational injuries and diseases?
   (a) Implementing effective workplace safety measures
   (b) Providing comprehensive employee training on safety protocols
   (c) Encouraging a culture of reporting near misses and hazards
   (d) All of the above

31. Which of the following is a potential health risk associated with poor working conditions?
   (a) Musculoskeletal disorders
   (b) Improved immune system
   (c) Increased energy levels
   (d) Enhanced mental well-being

32. Which of the following is a potential safety hazard resulting from poor working conditions?
   (a) Fire safety measures
   (b) Safety training programs
   (c) Adequate lighting
   (d) Slippery floors

33. How can poor ventilation impact worker health?
   (a) Improved air quality
   (b) Reduced respiratory issues
   (c) Increased exposure to harmful substances
   (d) Enhanced concentration

34. How can excessive noise in the workplace affect worker well-being?
   (a) Improved hearing ability
   (b) Reduced stress levels
   (c) Increased risk of hearing loss
   (d) Enhanced communication skills

35. What is the potential consequence of inadequate personal protective equipment (PPE)?
   (a) Enhanced workplace aesthetics
   (b) Reduced risk of injuries
   (c) Increased exposure to hazards
   (d) Improved productivity

36. What is the impact of poor working conditions on worker health and safety?
   (a) Increased risk of accidents and injuries
   (b) Improved productivity and job satisfaction
   (c) Decreased absenteeism and turnover
   (d) Enhanced employee engagement and motivation

37. How can poor working conditions affect worker health?
   (a) Improved physical fitness and well-being
   (b) Reduced stress levels and improved mental health
   (c) Increased vulnerability to occupational diseases
   (d) Enhanced work-life balance and job satisfaction

38. How can poor working conditions impact worker safety?
   (a) Enhanced safety protocols and procedures
   (b) Reduced risk of accidents and injuries
   (c) Increased likelihood of workplace hazards
   (d) Improved emergency response systems

39. What are the potential consequences of poor working conditions on worker health?
   (a) Improved employee morale and job satisfaction
   (b) Decreased healthcare costs for the organization
   (c) Increased sick leaves and medical expenses
   (d) Enhanced teamwork and collaboration

40. How can poor working conditions impact worker morale and job satisfaction?
   (a) Increased job security and stability
   (b) Improved work-life balance and flexibility
   (c) Decreased job satisfaction and motivation
   (d) Enhanced career growth opportunities

41. What is a common challenge related to occupational health and safety?
   (a) Lack of awareness and training
   (b) Excessive regulations and restrictions
   (c) High cost of implementing safety measures
   (d) Limited access to healthcare facilities

42. What is a potential issue regarding occupational health and safety regulations?
   (a) Insufficient enforcement mechanisms
   (b) Excessive leniency in penalties
   (c) Lack of flexibility in compliance requirements
   (d) Limited scope of covered industries

43. What is a significant challenge in promoting occupational health and safety in small businesses?
   (a) Limited financial resources
   (b) Lack of governmental support
   (c) Decreased employee motivation
   (d) Inadequate regulatory framework

44. What is a common issue related to occupational health and safety in high-risk industries?
   (a) Excessive employee turnover
   (b) Inadequate safety equipment availability
   (c) Insufficient training programs
   (d) Lack of emergency response plans

45. What is a potential challenge related to occupational health and safety in remote or mobile work settings?
   (a) Lack of communication and coordination
   (b) Decreased work flexibility and autonomy
   (c) Inadequate access to healthcare facilities
   (d) Reduced exposure to workplace hazards

46. What is a common issue associated with occupational health and safety for temporary or contract workers?
(a) Lower risk of workplace accidents
(b) Lack of safety training and orientation
(c) Higher job security and stability
(d) Inclusion in regular employee benefits

47. What is a challenge related to occupational health and safety for multinational corporations operating in different countries?
(a) Consistency in regulatory compliance
(b) Lower risk of workplace hazards
(c) Standardization of safety protocols
(d) Access to universal healthcare

48. What is an issue associated with occupational health and safety in physically demanding occupations?
(a) Excessive employee benefits
(b) Inadequate rest breaks and recovery time
(c) Reduced risk of musculoskeletal disorders
(d) Availability of ergonomic workstations

49. What is a challenge related to occupational health and safety in the agricultural sector?
(a) Advanced technology implementation
(b) Limited exposure to hazardous substances
(c) Lack of awareness about pesticide safety
(d) Availability of comprehensive insurance coverage

50. What is a potential challenge associated with occupational health and safety for night shift workers?
(a) Increased social interactions and support
(b) Availability of well-lit workspaces
(c) Higher risk of fatigue and sleep disorders
(d) Greater access to recreational facilities

51. Which of the following is an example of a physical hazard in the workplace?
(a) Exposure to toxic chemicals
(b) Repetitive motion injuries
(c) Noise pollution
(d) Poor lighting conditions

52. What is the primary concern when dealing with chemical hazards in the workplace?
(a) Ergonomic injuries
(b) Fires and explosions
(c) Noise-induced hearing loss
(d) Heat stress

53. Which of the following is an example of a biological hazard?
(a) Chemical spills (b) Slippery floors
(c) Bacterial infections (d) Heavy machinery

54. What type of hazard is associated with prolonged computer use and repetitive tasks?
(a) Physical hazard (b) Chemical hazard
(c) Ergonomic hazard (d) Biological hazard

55. Which of the following is an example of a psychosocial hazard?
(a) Fall from height (b) Exposure to toxic fumes
(c) Workplace violence (d) Electric shock

56. What is the primary concern with radiation hazards in the workplace?
(a) Exposure to ionizing radiation
(b) Electrocution risks
(c) Noise-induced hearing loss
(d) Slips, trips, and falls

57. Which of the following is an example of a fire hazard?
(a) Noise pollution (b) Chemical spills
(c) Confined spaces (d) Faulty electrical wiring

58. What is the primary concern when dealing with heat-related hazards?
(a) Exposure to hazardous substances
(b) Musculoskeletal injuries
(c) Falls from heights
(d) Heat exhaustion or heat stroke

59. Which of the following is an example of a mechanical hazard?
(a) Exposure to loud noises
(b) Inhalation of toxic gases
(c) Fall from a ladder
(d) Exposure to infectious diseases

60. What type of hazard is associated with inadequate ventilation or poor air quality in the workplace?
(a) Physical hazard (b) Biological hazard
(c) Chemical hazard (d) Radiological hazard

61. What is the key feature of a national policy in occupational safety and health?
(a) Voluntary compliance
(b) Mandatory regulations
(c) Employee training programs
(d) Workplace inspections

62. Which of the following is a key feature of a national policy in occupational safety and health?
(a) Continuous improvement
(b) Ad hoc decision-making
(c) Minimal oversight
(d) Reactive measures

63. What is a key feature of a national policy in occupational safety and health related to worker participation?

(a) Employee empowerment

(b) Solely management decision-making

(c) Limited worker involvement

(d) Lack of communication channels

64. Which of the following is a key feature of a national policy in occupational safety and health regarding risk assessment?

(a) Reactive response

(b) Absence of risk evaluation

(c) Proactive risk assessment

(d) Minimal risk control measures

65. What is a key feature of a national policy in occupational safety and health related to enforcement?

(a) Lack of penalties for non-compliance

(b) Inconsistent enforcement measures

(c) Encouragement of self-regulation

(d) Strong enforcement mechanisms

66. Which of the following is a key feature of a national policy in occupational safety and health regarding training and education?

(a) Limited access to training programs

(b) Exclusion of employers from training

(c) Emphasis on continuous training

(d) Lack of awareness campaigns

67. What is a key feature of a national policy in occupational safety and health related to monitoring and evaluation?

(a) Irregular evaluation processes

(b) Limited data collection

(c) Reactive approach to monitoring

(d) Regular monitoring and evaluation

68. Which of the following is a key feature of a national policy in occupational safety and health regarding research and development?

(a) Absence of research initiatives

(b) Inadequate funding for research

(c) Collaboration with academic institutions

(d) Lack of technological advancements

69. What is a key feature of a national policy in occupational safety and health related to communication and awareness?

(a) Limited dissemination of information

(b) Exclusion of stakeholders from communication

(c) Promotion of open communication channels

(d) Lack of awareness campaigns

70. Which of the following is a key feature of a national policy in occupational safety and health regarding international cooperation?

(a) Isolationist approach

(b) Limited collaboration with other countries

(c) Adherence to international standards

(d) Lack of information sharing

71. What does the National Occupational Health and Safety (OHS) system model aim to achieve?

(a) Promote employee wellness

(b) Ensure workplace safety and health

(c) Increase productivity

(d) All of the above

72. Which of the following is NOT a key element of the National OHS system model?

(a) Hazard identification and risk assessment

(b) Employee training and education

(c) Incident reporting and investigation

(d) Performance appraisal and rewards

73. What is the purpose of hazard identification and risk assessment in the National OHS system model?

(a) To eliminate all workplace hazards

(b) To assess the severity of workplace hazards

(c) To identify and assess workplace hazards

(d) To mitigate the impact of workplace hazards

74. Which of the following is an example of a control measure in the National OHS system model?

(a) Providing personal protective equipment (PPE)

(b) Conducting regular safety inspections

(c) Training employees on emergency procedures

(d) All of the above

75. What is the role of employee training and education in the National OHS system model?

(a) To ensure compliance with OHS regulations

(b) To develop specialized OHS expertise

(c) To increase employee awareness and knowledge

(d) To establish communication channels

76. What is the purpose of incident reporting and investigation in the National OHS system model?

(a) To assign blame to individuals responsible for incidents

(b) To meet legal reporting requirements

(c) To identify the root causes of incidents and implement corrective actions

(d) To minimize insurance costs for the organization

77. Which of the following is a key principle of the National OHS system model?

(a) Continuous improvement
(b) Employee discipline
(c) Cost reduction
(d) Short-term focus

78. What is the role of management commitment in the National OHS system model?

(a) To allocate resources for OHS initiatives
(b) To develop OHS policies and procedures
(c) To lead by example in promoting safety culture
(d) All of the above

79. What is the purpose of OHS performance measurement in the National OHS system model?

(a) To compare organizations' safety performance
(b) To identify areas for improvement
(c) To comply with regulatory requirements
(d) All of the above

80. Which entity is responsible for the development and implementation of the National OHS system model?

(a) International Labor Organization (ILO)
(b) World Health Organization (WHO)
(c) National OHS authority or agency
(d) Occupational Safety and Health Administration (OSHA)

81. Which principle of the occupational health and safety model emphasizes the responsibility of employers to provide a safe working environment?

(a) Risk assessment
(b) Hierarchy of controls
(c) Prevention through design
(d) Employer commitment and responsibility

82. Which principle of the occupational health and safety model focuses on identifying and evaluating potential hazards in the workplace?

(a) Risk assessment
(b) Worker participation
(c) Incident investigation
(d) Hierarchy of controls

83. Which principle of the occupational health and safety model promotes the involvement of workers in decision-making processes related to health and safety?

(a) Worker participation
(b) Prevention through design
(c) Continuous improvement
(d) Incident investigation

84. Which principle of the occupational health and safety model emphasizes the need to eliminate or minimize hazards through the use of engineering controls?

(a) Hierarchy of controls
(b) Risk assessment
(c) Prevention through design
(d) Incident investigation

85. Which principle of the occupational health and safety model focuses on investigating and analyzing incidents to prevent their recurrence?

(a) Incident investigation
(b) Continuous improvement
(c) Worker participation
(d) Employer commitment and responsibility

86. Which principle of the occupational health and safety model promotes the integration of health and safety considerations into the design and redesign of work processes, systems, and equipment?

(a) Prevention through design
(b) Continuous improvement
(c) Risk assessment
(d) Hierarchy of controls

87. Which principle of the occupational health and safety model emphasizes the need for ongoing evaluation and enhancement of health and safety practices?

(a) Continuous improvement
(b) Risk assessment
(c) Worker participation
(d) Incident investigation

88. Which principle of the occupational health and safety model emphasizes the use of administrative controls, such as training and procedures, to reduce risks?

(a) Hierarchy of controls
(b) Prevention through design
(c) Worker participation
(d) Incident investigation

89. Which principle of the occupational health and safety model emphasizes the need to provide workers with information and training to enable them to work safely?

(a) Worker participation
(b) Continuous improvement
(c) Risk assessment
(d) Employer commitment and responsibility

90. Which principle of the occupational health and safety model focuses on the collaboration between employers, workers, and other stakeholders to achieve and maintain a safe work environment?

(a) Worker participation
(b) Prevention through design
(c) Incident investigation
(d) Continuous improvement

Answers

1. (c)	**2.** (b)	**3.** (c)	**4.** (a)	**5.** (d)	**6.** (c)	**7.** (c)	**8.** (b)	**9.** (b)	**10.** (c)
11. (c)	**12.** (a)	**13.** (c)	**14.** (c)	**15.** (c)	**16.** (d)	**17.** (c)	**18.** (c)	**19.** (a)	**20.** (b)
21. (b)	**22.** (b)	**23.** (c)	**24.** (a)	**25.** (a)	**26.** (d)	**27.** (d)	**28.** (d)	**29.** (a)	**30.** (d)
31. (a)	**32.** (d)	**33.** (c)	**34.** (c)	**35.** (c)	**36.** (a)	**37.** (c)	**38.** (c)	**39.** (c)	**40.** (c)
41. (a)	**42.** (a)	**43.** (a)	**44.** (b)	**45.** (a)	**46.** (b)	**47.** (a)	**48.** (b)	**49.** (c)	**50.** (c)
51. (d)	**52.** (b)	**53.** (c)	**54.** (c)	**55.** (c)	**56.** (a)	**57.** (d)	**58.** (d)	**59.** (c)	**60.** (c)
61. (b)	**62.** (a)	**63.** (a)	**64.** (c)	**65.** (d)	**66.** (c)	**67.** (d)	**68.** (c)	**69.** (c)	**70.** (c)
71. (d)	**72.** (d)	**73.** (c)	**74.** (d)	**75.** (c)	**76.** (c)	**77.** (a)	**78.** (d)	**79.** (d)	**80.** (c)
81. (d)	**82.** (a)	**83.** (a)	**84.** (a)	**85.** (a)	**86.** (a)	**87.** (a)	**88.** (a)	**89.** (d)	**90.** (a)

Explanations

1. The primary goal of occupational health and safety is to ensure the well-being and safety of workers by identifying and mitigating workplace hazards, preventing occupational injuries and illnesses, and promoting a safe working environment. So, the correct answer is (c) Protect workers from work-related hazards.

2. Conducting a risk assessment involves systematically identifying workplace hazards, evaluating the associated risks, and determining appropriate control measures to minimize or eliminate those risks. It helps in preventing accidents and injuries by proactively addressing potential hazards. So, the correct answer is (b) Identify potential hazards and evaluate their risks.

3. The hierarchy of controls is a framework used to prioritize and implement measures for hazard control. It starts with engineering controls, which involve modifying the workplace or equipment to remove or reduce hazards. If engineering controls are not feasible or sufficient, administrative controls such as work procedures and policies are implemented. Personal protective equipment (PPE) is the last line of defense and is used when other controls are not adequate to mitigate the risks. So, the correct answer is (c) Engineering controls, administrative controls, and personal protective equipment.

4. An MSDS (or SDS - Safety Data Sheet) is a document that provides detailed information about potentially hazardous substances or chemicals used in the workplace. It includes information about physical properties, health effects, handling precautions, and emergency response procedures, helping workers and employers understand and manage the risks associated with the substances.

5. A safety committee is a group composed of workers and management representatives who collaborate to identify and address safety concerns in the workplace. The committee promotes communication, involvement, and consultation with workers, fostering a proactive safety culture and improving overall occupational health and safety performance. So, the correct answer is (d) Promote worker participation and engagement in safety matters.

6. While enhancing workplace productivity, reducing healthcare costs, and avoiding legal liabilities are important secondary goals, the primary goal of occupational health and safety is to ensure the well-being and safety of workers in the workplace. So, the correct answer is (c) Protecting workers' health and safety.

7. OSHA stands for Occupational Safety and Health Act, which is a federal law in the United States that establishes and regulates workplace health and safety standards.

8. Physical hazards refer to hazards that can cause harm through physical contact or exposure, such as noise, radiation, temperature extremes, and exposure to toxic substances. Workplace bullying, poor ergonomic design, and inadequate training programs are examples of other types of hazards (psychological, ergonomic, and training-related, respectively). So, the correct answer is (b) Exposure to toxic chemicals.

9. A safety data sheet (SDS) is a document that provides detailed information about hazardous chemicals, including their properties, handling procedures, storage requirements, and emergency response measures. So, the correct answer is (b) To provide instructions for emergency response procedures.

10. Personal protective equipment (PPE) refers to equipment or clothing designed to protect workers from hazards in the workplace. Safety goggles are a type of PPE that protects the eyes from flying debris, chemicals, or other potential eye hazards. Fire extinguishers, first aid kits, and safety training manuals are not considered PPE.

11. While reducing insurance premiums, complying with legal regulations, and enhancing organizational reputation are potential benefits of occupational health and safety, the primary and most important reason for its importance is to ensure the health, safety, and well-being of workers. So, the correct answer is (c) To protect the well-being of workers.

12. Poor occupational health and safety practices can result in higher rates of workplace injuries, illnesses, and accidents, which can lead to increased absenteeism and turnover as employees may need time off for recovery or may seek employment elsewhere due to safety concerns. Decreased customer satisfaction, higher profit margins, and improved employee morale are not directly associated with poor occupational health and safety practices. So, the correct answer is (a) Increased absenteeism and turnover.

13. Occupational health and safety measures create a work environment that is free from hazards, promotes employee well-being, and reduces the risk of accidents and injuries. When employees feel safe and healthy, they are more likely to be engaged, motivated, and productive. Reducing breaks, minimizing distractions, and increasing work hours are not effective or ethical ways to enhance productivity. So, the correct answer is (c) By promoting a safe and healthy work environment.

14. While employees also have a responsibility to follow safety protocols, management plays a crucial role in establishing a safe work environment, providing necessary safety equipment, training employees, and enforcing safety policies. Conducting regular safety inspections is part of management's responsibility, but it is not the sole role they play in occupational health and safety. So, the correct answer is (c) Management is responsible for implementing and enforcing safety policies and procedures.

15. Effective occupational health and safety practices can lead to a reduction in workplace accidents and illnesses, resulting in lower insurance premiums and healthcare costs for organizations. While occupational health and safety can indirectly contribute to productivity and profits, reducing workers' salaries and minimizing employee benefits are not ethical or effective strategies in promoting a safe and healthy work environment. So, the correct answer is (c) By lowering insurance premiums and healthcare costs.

16. Prioritizing occupational health and safety in the workplace has multiple benefits, including improving employee morale, reducing legal liabilities, and enhancing productivity. A safe and healthy work environment leads to higher employee satisfaction, lower risk of accidents and lawsuits, and increased efficiency and effectiveness.

17. While compliance with legal regulations, cost savings, and workplace aesthetics can be additional benefits, the primary reason for implementing occupational health and safety programs is to protect the well-being and safety of workers. It ensures that employees can perform their tasks without unnecessary risks to their health and safety. So, the correct answer is (c) Preservation of workers' well-being.

18. Occupational health and safety programs contribute to employee retention by fostering a workplace culture that values the well-being of employees. When workers feel safe and secure, they are more likely to stay with the organization. While salary, career advancement, and discipline play a role in retention, they are not directly related to occupational health and safety. So, the correct answer is (c) By creating a safe and healthy work environment.

19. Occupational health and safety practices demonstrate an organization's commitment to the well-being of its employees, which can enhance its brand image and reputation. It showcases the organization as a responsible employer and can attract customers, investors, and talented employees. Decreased customer loyalty, increased competition, and improved financial performance are not direct outcomes of occupational health and safety practices. So, the correct answer is (a) Positive impact on brand image.

20. Training is crucial in occupational health and safety programs to equip employees with the necessary skills and knowledge to identify and mitigate workplace hazards. While meeting legal requirements, reducing insurance premiums, and minimizing accidents are important, the primary goal of training is to empower employees to contribute to a safe work environment. So, the correct answer is (b) To develop employees' skills and knowledge.

21. Occupational health and safety measures contribute to worker productivity by creating a safe and healthy work environment that reduces stress and potential hazards. When employees feel safe, supported, and motivated, their productivity levels tend to increase. Reducing work hours, increasing workload expectations, and implementing strict performance evaluations are not effective or ethical means to enhance productivity. So, the correct answer is (b) By minimizing workplace stress.

22. While employees should be aware of safety rules and regulations and comply with them, their primary role in occupational health and safety is to report hazards and incidents to the appropriate channels. This helps in identifying risks, addressing concerns, and improving safety measures. Enforcing safety rules, conducting inspections, and monitoring compliance are typically the responsibility of management and designated safety personnel. So, The correct answer is (b) To report hazards and incidents.

23. Effective occupational health and safety programs can lead to a decrease in workplace accidents and illnesses, resulting in lower insurance premiums for organizations. While occupational health and safety can indirectly contribute to revenue through increased productivity and employee well-being, reducing employee salaries and eliminating benefits are not ethical or effective means of cost savings. So, the correct answer is (c) By lowering insurance premiums.

24. Risk assessment is a systematic process of identifying, evaluating, and controlling workplace hazards. It helps in understanding the potential risks to employee health and safety, allowing organizations to implement appropriate preventive measures. While disciplinary measures, employee motivation, and cost-cutting measures can be influenced by risk assessment, the primary purpose is to identify hazards. So, the correct answer is (a) To identify potential hazards and their associated risks.

25. Occupational health and safety measures, such as hazard identification, risk assessment, safety training, and the provision of appropriate equipment, help in minimizing workplace accidents and injuries. By preventing accidents, organizations can comply with legal regulations and requirements. While emergency response plans, disciplinary actions, and safety audits are essential components of occupational health and safety, they are not directly related to legal compliance. So, the correct answer is (a) By minimizing workplace accidents.

26. Occupational injuries and diseases can lead to various costs. Medical treatment expenses arise from providing necessary healthcare and rehabilitation services to injured or ill workers. Lost productivity refers to the decreased efficiency or absence of affected workers, resulting in reduced output and increased workload on other employees. Legal fees and fines may be incurred if an employer is found responsible for a workplace injury or illness due to negligence or non-compliance with safety regulations.

27. Workers' compensation claims are filed by employees seeking compensation for work-related injuries or illnesses. These claims can result in financial payouts and increased insurance costs for employers. Absenteeism occurs when workers are absent from work due to injuries or illnesses, leading to decreased productivity and increased costs. Presenteeism refers to the situation when workers come to work despite being unwell or injured, which can result in reduced productivity and potential exacerbation of the condition.

28. Indirect costs are the intangible expenses associated with occupational injuries and diseases that are not directly linked to the injured or ill worker. They include factors such as lost productivity due to absence or reduced efficiency, the need for temporary or permanent replacement workers, and expenses related to training new employees. Indirect costs are often more challenging to quantify compared to direct costs like medical expenses, but they can have a significant impact on an organization's overall financial burden. So, the correct answer is (d) They account for lost productivity and increased training costs.

29. Occupational injuries and diseases can lead to increased absenteeism as injured or ill workers may need time off to recover. Additionally, a high incidence of workplace injuries can contribute to higher turnover rates, as employees may become dissatisfied with safety conditions or perceive their workplace as unsafe. These factors can have a detrimental impact on productivity, as the organization may experience reduced workforce capacity and the need for frequent recruitment and training of new employees. So, the correct answer is (a) By increasing absenteeism and turnover rates.

30. Organizations can reduce the costs associated with occupational injuries and diseases by implementing effective workplace safety measures, such as installing safety equipment, conducting regular safety inspections, and enforcing safety protocols. Providing comprehensive training to employees on safety procedures and hazard recognition can help prevent accidents and injuries. Encouraging a culture of reporting near misses and hazards allows for early identification and rectification of potential risks, further minimizing the occurrence of injuries and illnesses in the workplace.

31. Poor working conditions such as repetitive movements, awkward postures, and lack of ergonomics can contribute to musculoskeletal disorders like back pain, carpal tunnel syndrome, and tendonitis.

32. Poor working conditions, such as inadequate housekeeping or failure to address spills and leaks, can lead to slippery floors, increasing the risk of slip and fall accidents in the workplace.

33. Poor ventilation can lead to the accumulation of hazardous substances, pollutants, and contaminants in the air, exposing workers to respiratory problems, allergies, and other health issues. So, the correct answer is (c) Increased exposure to harmful substances.

34. Excessive noise levels in the workplace can damage workers' hearing over time, leading to hearing loss and related health problems. It is important to implement measures like hearing protection and noise control to mitigate this risk. So, the correct answer is (c) Increased risk of hearing loss.

35. Inadequate or insufficient PPE can expose workers to various workplace hazards such as chemical splashes, impact injuries, and respiratory issues. Properly fitting and appropriate PPE is essential for safeguarding worker health and safety. So, the correct answer is (c) Increased exposure to hazards.

36. Poor working conditions, such as inadequate safety measures, lack of proper training, or faulty equipment, can significantly increase the likelihood of accidents and injuries in the workplace. Workers may be exposed to hazardous substances, unsafe machinery, or insufficient safety protocols, leading to an elevated risk of harm. So, the correct answer is (a) Increased risk of accidents and injuries.

37. Poor working conditions can expose workers to various health hazards, such as toxic chemicals, excessive noise, repetitive motion injuries, or inadequate ventilation. These factors can contribute to the development of occupational diseases, including respiratory problems, musculoskeletal disorders, and mental health issues. So, the correct answer is (c) Increased vulnerability to occupational diseases.

38. Poor working conditions often mean a lack of proper safety protocols, inadequate training, or insufficient maintenance of equipment and infrastructure. These factors increase the chances of workplace hazards, such as slips, falls, machinery malfunctions, or electrical accidents, jeopardizing the safety of workers. So, the correct answer is (c) Increased likelihood of workplace hazards.

39. Poor working conditions can lead to a decline in worker health, resulting in higher rates of sick leaves, medical expenses, and reduced productivity. Workers may require medical treatment, rehabilitation, or time off work to recover from work-related injuries or illnesses, imposing financial burdens on both the individual and the organization. So, the correct answer is (c) Increased sick leaves and medical expenses.

40. Poor working conditions, characterized by factors such as excessive work hours, lack of recognition, unsafe environment, or poor management, can significantly impact worker morale and job satisfaction. Workers may feel demotivated, undervalued, and dissatisfied with their work, leading to decreased productivity and higher turnover rates. So, the correct answer is (c) Decreased job satisfaction and motivation.

41. Many workers and employers may not have sufficient knowledge or understanding of occupational health and safety practices. This lack of awareness can lead to unsafe work conditions, inadequate safety protocols, and increased risk of accidents and injuries.

42. Occupational health and safety regulations may exist, but their effectiveness depends on proper enforcement. If enforcement mechanisms are weak or inadequate, employers may not prioritize compliance, leading to ongoing hazards and unsafe working conditions. So, the correct answer is (a) Insufficient enforcement mechanisms.

43. Small businesses often face financial constraints, making it challenging to invest in occupational health and safety measures. They may struggle to allocate funds for training, safety equipment, or workplace modifications, increasing the risk of accidents and injuries. So, the correct answer is (a) Limited financial resources.

44. High-risk industries, such as construction or manufacturing, require specialized safety equipment to protect workers from potential hazards. However, the availability or accessibility of such equipment can be limited, exposing workers to unnecessary risks. So, the correct answer is (b) Inadequate safety equipment availability.

45. In remote or mobile work settings, maintaining effective communication and coordination regarding occupational health and safety measures can be challenging. Workers may be geographically dispersed, making it difficult to ensure consistent adherence to safety protocols and provide immediate assistance in case of emergencies. So, the correct answer is (a) Lack of communication and coordination.

46. Temporary or contract workers often have limited exposure to comprehensive safety training and orientation programs. Due to the temporary nature of their employment, employers may overlook investing time and resources in ensuring their safety, leading to increased vulnerability to workplace accidents. So, the correct answer is (b) Lack of safety training and orientation.

47. Multinational corporations must navigate different occupational health and safety regulations across various countries. Ensuring consistent compliance with varying standards and requirements can be complex and requires dedicated efforts to prioritize the safety of workers across different geographical locations. So, the correct answer is (a) Consistency in regulatory compliance.

48. Physically demanding occupations often involve repetitive tasks or prolonged periods of physical exertion. Inadequate rest breaks and insufficient recovery time can contribute to fatigue, overexertion, and an increased risk of injuries or accidents. So, the correct answer is (b) Inadequate rest breaks and recovery time.

49. In the agricultural sector, workers often handle pesticides and other chemicals without proper training or awareness of safety protocols. This lack of knowledge can lead to pesticide exposure, posing risks to both the workers' health and the surrounding environment. So, the correct answer is (c) Lack of awareness about pesticide safety.

50. Night shift work disrupts the body's natural circadian rhythm, leading to increased fatigue and a higher risk of sleep disorders among workers. These conditions can impair concentration, reaction times, and decision-making abilities, elevating the likelihood of workplace accidents and injuries.

51. Physical hazards refer to conditions or factors within the work environment that can cause harm through physical contact or exposure. Poor lighting conditions can lead to trips, falls, and other accidents.

52. Chemical hazards involve the presence of substances that can cause harm through skin contact, inhalation, or ingestion. Certain chemicals can be flammable or reactive, posing a risk of fires and explosions.

53. Biological hazards involve exposure to living organisms or their byproducts that can cause harm, such as bacteria, viruses, fungi, or parasites. In the workplace, this can include exposure to infectious diseases.

54. Ergonomic hazards relate to factors that can lead to musculoskeletal disorders and injuries, such as repetitive tasks, poor posture, inadequate workstations, or improper lifting techniques.

55. Psychosocial hazards involve factors that affect the psychological well-being of workers, including workplace violence, stress, bullying, harassment, and inadequate social support.

56. Radiation hazards involve exposure to ionizing or non-ionizing radiation, which can cause harm to the body's cells, leading to health issues such as cancer or genetic mutations.

57. Fire hazards refer to conditions or factors that can ignite fires or contribute to their spread. Faulty electrical wiring can lead to short circuits and electrical fires.

58. Heat-related hazards involve exposure to high temperatures or extreme heat, which can cause heat-related illnesses, such as heat exhaustion or heat stroke.

59. Mechanical hazards are physical factors associated with machinery, tools, or equipment that can cause harm through contact, entanglement, or impact, such as falls, caught-in/between accidents, or machinery malfunctions.

60. Inadequate ventilation or poor air quality can lead to the accumulation of harmful chemical substances or irritants in the air, posing a risk to the health and well-being of workers.

61. A key feature of a national policy in occupational safety and health is the establishment of mandatory regulations. These regulations set specific standards and requirements that employers must follow to ensure a safe and healthy working environment for their employees.

62. A national policy in occupational safety and health should promote continuous improvement in workplace safety and health conditions. This involves regularly assessing and revising policies and practices to adapt to changing hazards and technologies, with the goal of achieving higher levels of safety and reducing the risk of workplace accidents and illnesses.

63. A key feature of a national policy in occupational safety and health is the promotion of worker participation and empowerment. This involves creating mechanisms and platforms for workers to actively participate in decision-making processes, share their knowledge and concerns, and contribute to the development and implementation of safety and health measures in the workplace.

64. A national policy in occupational safety and health should emphasize proactive risk assessment. This involves identifying and evaluating potential hazards and risks in the workplace before they result in accidents or illnesses. Through risk assessment, appropriate control measures can be implemented to mitigate or eliminate hazards, ensuring the safety and well-being of workers.

65. A key feature of a national policy in occupational safety and health is the establishment of strong enforcement mechanisms. This includes the implementation of penalties and sanctions for non-compliance with safety and health regulations, as well as the provision of adequate resources for inspections and monitoring to ensure employers adhere to the prescribed standards.

66. A national policy in occupational safety and health should emphasize the importance of continuous training and education for both employers and employees. This includes providing access to training programs, promoting ongoing learning opportunities, and ensuring that individuals have the necessary knowledge and skills to identify and manage workplace hazards effectively.

67. A key feature of a national policy in occupational safety and health is the establishment of regular monitoring and evaluation processes. This involves collecting data, conducting inspections, and assessing the effectiveness of safety and health measures to identify areas for improvement and ensure the policy's objectives are being met.

68. A national policy in occupational safety and health should promote collaboration with academic institutions and research organizations to encourage research and development activities. This can lead to the discovery of innovative approaches, technologies, and best practices that enhance workplace safety and health.

69. A key feature of a national policy in occupational safety and health is the promotion of open communication channels. This includes disseminating information about safety and health practices, regulations, and initiatives to stakeholders, facilitating dialogue between employers and workers, and promoting awareness campaigns to foster a culture of safety in the workplace.

70. A key feature of a national policy in occupational safety and health is the adherence to international standards and cooperation with other countries. This involves aligning national regulations with international guidelines, participating in international forums and initiatives, and sharing best practices to ensure a global approach to workplace safety and health.

71. The National OHS system model aims to promote employee wellness, ensure workplace safety and health, and increase productivity by providing a framework for managing occupational health and safety in the workplace.

72. While employee performance appraisal and rewards are important aspects of overall management, they are not considered key elements of the National OHS system model. The other options listed are key elements that contribute to an effective OHS system. So, the correct answer is (d) Performance appraisal and rewards.

73. Hazard identification and risk assessment are crucial steps in the National OHS system model as they help in identifying potential hazards and evaluating their associated risks in order to implement appropriate control measures. So, the correct answer is (c) To identify and assess workplace hazards.

74. Providing personal protective equipment, conducting regular safety inspections, and training employees on emergency procedures are all examples of control measures that can be implemented to prevent or minimize workplace hazards.

75. Employee training and education play a vital role in the National OHS system model by enhancing employees' understanding of workplace hazards, safe work practices, and their responsibilities in maintaining a safe and healthy work environment. So, the correct answer is (c) To increase employee awareness and knowledge.

76. To identify the root causes of incidents and implement corrective actions. Incident reporting and investigation are essential in the National OHS system model to understand why incidents occurred, identify underlying factors, and implement measures to prevent similar incidents in the future.

77. Continuous improvement is a key principle of the National OHS system model, emphasizing the need for ongoing evaluation, monitoring, and enhancement of occupational health and safety practices to achieve better outcomes over time.

78. Management commitment in the National OHS system model involves allocating resources, developing policies and procedures, and leading by example to create a positive safety culture and ensure that OHS initiatives are effectively implemented.

79. OHS performance measurement in the National OHS system model serves multiple purposes, including benchmarking safety performance, identifying areas for improvement, and ensuring compliance with regulatory requirements.

80. The development and implementation of the National OHS system model typically fall under the jurisdiction of the national OHS authority or agency in each respective country. While international organizations like the ILO and WHO may provide guidance and support, the national authority or agency takes the lead in establishing the model within their jurisdiction

81. Employer commitment and responsibility principle emphasizes that employers have a duty to provide a safe workplace and protect the health and safety of their employees.

82. Risk assessment principle involves the systematic identification and evaluation of workplace hazards to determine the level of risk they pose to workers' health and safety.

83. Worker participation principle recognizes that involving workers in health and safety decision-making leads to better outcomes, as they possess valuable insights and experiences regarding the work environment.

84. Hierarchy of controls principle suggests that hazards should be eliminated or minimized at their source through engineering controls, such as installing safety guards or implementing ventilation systems.

85. Incident investigation principle involves conducting thorough investigations into workplace incidents to determine their root causes and implement measures to prevent similar incidents in the future.

86. Prevention through design principle encourages the consideration of health and safety aspects during the design and redesign stages of work processes, systems, and equipment to minimize hazards and risks.

87. Continuous improvement principle highlights the importance of regularly reviewing and improving health and safety practices to adapt to changes in the workplace and enhance overall safety performance.

88. Principle suggests that when it is not feasible to eliminate hazards through engineering controls, administrative controls should be implemented, such as training programs, standard operating procedures, and work permits.

89. Employer commitment and responsibility principle highlights the employer's responsibility to provide workers with the necessary information, training, and resources to perform their work safely and protect their health.

90. Worker participation principle emphasizes the importance of fostering collaboration and active involvement of all stakeholders to create a safe and healthy work environment.

10 CHAPTER

Environment Education & Engineering

ENVIRONMENTAL EDUCATION

Environmental education (EE) is a process that allows individuals to develop the knowledge, values, skills, experiences, and commitment to make informed decisions and take responsible actions for the environment. It is a lifelong learning process that begins early in life and continues throughout adulthood. EE can be formal or informal. Formal EE takes place in schools, colleges, and universities, while informal EE occurs in community centers, museums, and nature centers. EE can also take place outdoors, through activities such as hiking, camping, and fishing.

The goals of EE are to :

- Increase public awareness and knowledge about environmental issues.
- Promote sustainable lifestyles.
- Develop citizens who are informed and engaged in environmental decision-making.
- Empower individuals to take action to protect the environment.

EE is essential for creating a sustainable future. By educating people about the environment, we can help them make choices that protect the planet for future generations.

Benefits to Environmental Education :

Environmental education (EE) is a process that allows individuals to develop the knowledge, values, skills, experiences, and commitment to make informed decisions and take responsible actions for the environment. It is a lifelong learning process that begins early in life and continues throughout adulthood.

There are many benefits to environmental education. Some of the most important benefits include:

- Increased awareness and understanding of environmental issues and challenges. EE can help people understand the interconnectedness of all living things and the impact of human activities on the environment.
- Improved critical thinking and problem-solving skills. EE can help people develop the skills to analyze environmental problems, identify potential solutions, and make informed decisions about environmental issues.
- Enhanced social and emotional development. EE can help people develop a sense of empathy and compassion for the environment and other living things.
- Increased sense of responsibility for the environment. EE can help people develop a sense of stewardship for the environment and a commitment to taking action to protect it.
- Greater participation in environmental stewardship activities. EE can encourage people to get involved in environmental activities, such as volunteering for environmental organizations or participating in community cleanup projects.
- Improved mental and physical health. Spending time in nature has been shown to have a number of positive benefits for mental and physical health, such as reducing stress levels, improving mood, and boosting the immune system.

Components of Environment Education

Environmental education (EE) is a process that allows individuals to develop the knowledge, values, skills, experiences, and commitment to make informed decisions and take responsible actions for the environment. It is a lifelong learning process that begins early in life and continues throughout adulthood.

There are three main components of EE:

- Awareness and sensitivity to the environment and environmental challenges. This includes understanding the interconnectedness of all living things and the impact of human activities on the environment.

- Knowledge and understanding of the environment and environmental challenges. This includes learning about the natural world, environmental issues, and the principles of sustainability.
- Attitudes of concern for the environment and motivation to improve or maintain environmental quality. This includes developing a sense of stewardship for the environment and a commitment to taking action to protect it.

All three of these components are essential for effective EE. Without awareness and sensitivity, individuals may not be motivated to learn about environmental issues or take action to protect the environment. Without knowledge and understanding, individuals may not be able to make informed decisions about environmental issues. And without attitudes of concern, individuals may not be motivated to take action to protect the environment, even if they have the knowledge and skills to do so.

EE can be delivered in a variety of ways, including:

- **Formal education :** This includes teaching about environmental issues in schools, colleges, and universities.
- **Non-formal education :** This includes teaching about environmental issues through community centers, museums, and nature centers.
- **Informal education :** This includes learning about environmental issues through everyday experiences, such as hiking, camping, and fishing.

EE can also be delivered to a variety of audiences, including :

- **Children :** EE can help children develop a lifelong love of the environment and a sense of responsibility for protecting it.
- **Adults :** EE can help adults learn about environmental issues and take action to protect the environment.
- **Communities :** EE can help communities develop sustainable practices and protect their local environment.
- **Businesses :** EE can help businesses reduce their environmental impact and become more sustainable.

EE is a powerful tool for addressing environmental challenges. By educating people about the environment, we can help them make choices that protect the planet for future generations.

Concept of environment education:

Environmental education is a holistic, interdisciplinary field that focuses on raising awareness, understanding, and appreciation of the environment. It encompasses a wide range of topics related to the natural world, ecosystems, sustainability, and the intricate relationships between humans and their environment.

Key aspects of environmental education include :

1. **Awareness and Knowledge :** Educating individuals about the environment, ecosystems, biodiversity, climate change, natural resources, pollution, and other relevant topics. This involves understanding the interconnections between various environmental factors.
2. **Promoting Environmental Stewardship :** Encouraging individuals to become responsible and active stewards of the environment. This includes fostering a sense of responsibility and care for the natural world.
3. **Sustainability and Conservation :** Highlighting the importance of sustainable practices and conservation efforts to protect natural resources, reduce environmental degradation, and preserve ecosystems for future generations.
4. **Interdisciplinary Approach :** Environmental education often draws on knowledge from various disciplines such as biology, ecology, chemistry, geology, sociology, economics, and more to provide a comprehensive understanding of environmental issues.
5. **Hands-On Learning :** It often involves practical, experiential learning methods such as field trips, hands-on activities, and outdoor experiences to facilitate a deeper understanding of environmental concepts.
6. **Critical Thinking and Problem-Solving :** Encouraging individuals to think critically about environmental issues, analyze problems, and come up with solutions to address them.
7. **Policy and Advocacy :** Empowering individuals to engage in policy discussions and advocate for environmental policies and practices that support sustainability and conservation.

The scope of environmental education (EE):

The scope of Environmental Education (EE) is broad and multifaceted, encompassing various aspects related to the environment, sustainability, and the interconnectedness of ecosystems. Its primary goal is to foster an understanding of environmental issues, promote the development of critical thinking skills, and encourage responsible and informed decision-making about environmental concerns. The scope of EE typically includes the following areas :

1. **Awareness and Understanding :** Educating individuals about the environment, its ecosystems, biodiversity, natural resources, and the impact of human activities on the environment.
2. **Sustainability :** Promoting the concept of sustainability, that is involves the responsible use of resources to meet the need of the present without compromising the ability of future generations to meet their own needs.
3. **Conservation and Preservation :** Highlighting the importance of preserving natural habitats, protecting endangered species, and conserving biodiversity.
4. **Environmental Ethics:** Encouraging the development of ethical principles that guide responsible behavior towards the environment.
5. **Climate Change Education :** Addressing the causes and effects of climate change, as well as strategies for mitigation and adaptation.
6. **Waste Management and Recycling :** Educating about proper waste disposal, recycling practices, and the reduction of waste to minimize environmental impact.
7. **Environmental Policies and Governance:** Understanding local and global environmental policies, regulations, and governance structures to advocate for sustainable practices and policies.
8. **Outdoor Education and Experiential Learning :** Providing hands-on experiences in nature to foster a deeper connection with the environment and promote active learning.
9. **Interdisciplinary Approach :** Incorporating various disciplines such as science, social studies, geography, economics, and ethics to provide a comprehensive understanding of environmental issues.
10. **Community Engagement and Action :** Encouraging individuals and communities to take action, participate in environmental initiatives, and become advocates for positive environmental change. The scope of EE is not limited to formal education systems; it extends to informal education, community programs, advocacy, and policy-making. It aims to empower individuals to become environmentally literate, take informed actions, and contribute to the sustainable development of society.

ENVIRONMENTAL ENGINEERING

Environmental education is an important part of environmental engineering. It helps to teach people about the environment and how to protect it.

Components of Environmental Engineering

I. Water Resources

Water resources engineers design and manage systems for the collection, treatment and distribution of water. In the context of environmental engineering, Water Supply is the process of providing clean and safe drinking water to a community or population.

Water is extremely useful to man, providing him luxuries and conterts, in addition to fulfilling his basic necessities of life. It has been estimated that two third of human body is constituted of water.

Sutiable system should be designed for collecting, transporting , and treating water.

Public Water Supply Scheme

Essential elements.

(1) *Intake and reservoir* : To collect water.

(2) *Water treatment plant* : Screening, sedimentations, filteration, disinfection units etc.

(3) *Elevated tanks and stand pipes* : It provide storage to meet peak demands occuring for limited periods.

(4) *Valves* : It control the flow of water in the pipe system.

(5) *Hydrants* : It provide a connection with the water in the main for fighting fires, flushing streeets etc.

(6) *Distribution system* : mains, submains, and branch lines which carry the water to the streets.

(7) *Servies* : It carry the water to the individual house etc.

Water Demand

In fact the first requirement is to consider the demand, and the second requirement is to find sources to fulfil that demand.

Types of water demands.

(1) Domestic water demand 55% to 60% of total water consumption.

(2) Industrial water demand 50 lpcd :

(3) Institutional and commercial water demand – 20 lpcd

(4) Demand for public uses – 10 lpcd

(5) Fire demand; – 1 lpcd

(6) Water required to compensate losses in wastes and thefts–55 lpcd

As per is 1172-1983 as well as National building code, the domestic consumption under normal conditions in an Indian city is expected to be around 135 letre/head/day

Table : Break up of 135 lpcd

Use	*Consumption in litres per capita per day*
Drinking	5
Cooking	5
Bathing	55
Washing of clothes	20
Washing of utensils	10
Washing and cleaning of houses and residences	10
Flushing of latrines, etc.	30
Total	135

(2) *Industrial water demand – 50 lpcd :*

The ordinary per capital consumption for industrial needs of a city is generally taken as 50 litres/capita/day.

(3) On an average, per capita demand of 20 l/h/d is usually considered to be enough to meet such commercial and institutional water requirements, although this demand may be as high as 50 l/h/d for highly commercialised cities.

(4) Demand for public uses is generally taken as 10 l/h/day.

(5) *Fire demand* :

- Fire hydrants are usually fitted in the water mains at about 100 to 150 metres apart.
- The per capita fire demand is thus generally ignored while computing the total per capita water requirement of a city.
- Kilo litre of water required = $100\sqrt{P}$ when population exceeding 50,000

  where, P = population in thousand.
- Rate of fire demand is worked out on the basis of certain empirical formula.

Kuichling's formula

$$Q = 3182\sqrt{P}$$

where, P = Population in thousand.

Freeman's formula

Amount of water required in litres/min,

$$Q = 1136\left[\frac{1}{10}+10\right]$$

For a central congested high value city

$$Q = 4637\sqrt{P}\,[1-0.01\sqrt{P}\,]$$

(6) *Wastes and thefts*, etc.

Per Capita Demand

q = Total yearly water requirement of the city in litres/365 × Design population

For an Indian city, as per recommendation of IS. code, per capita demand, q = 270 l/h/d.

Factors affecting per capita demand.

(1) Size of the city
(2) Climate conditions
(3) Types of gentry and habits of people.
(4) Industrial and commercial activities.
(5) Quality of water supplies.
(6) Pressure in the distribution system.
(7) Development of sewerage facilities
(8) System of supply.
(9) Cost of water
(10) Policy of metering and Method of charging.

Variation in the demand

(1) Maximum daily consumptions

= 180% of the annual average daily demand

= 1.8 × Average daily demand

= $1.8q$

(2) Maximum hourly consumption= 150 % of the average houry demand of the month day.

$$= \frac{150}{100} \times \frac{\text{Maximum daily demand}}{24}$$

$$= \frac{150}{100} \times \frac{1.8q}{24}$$

$$= \frac{1.8 \times 1.5}{24}q$$

$$= 2.7\left(\frac{q}{24}\right)$$

= 2.7 × Annual average hourly demand

(3) Maximum hourly demand of maximum day = $2.7\,q$

(4) Goodrich's formula

$$P = 180 + t^{-0.10}$$

where, P = % of the annual average draft for the time t in days.

t = time in days from $\frac{1}{24}$ to 365

When t = 1 day (for daily variations), then

$$P = 180 \times (1)^{-0.10} = 180$$

$$\therefore \frac{\text{Maximum daily demand}}{\text{Average daily demand}} = 180\%$$

When t = 7 days (for weekly variations), then

$$P = 180 \times (7)^{-0.10} = 148\ \%$$

$$\therefore \frac{\text{Maximum weekly demand}}{\text{Average weekly demand}} = 148\%$$

Similarly, $\frac{\text{Maximum monthly demand}}{\text{Average monthly demand}} = 128\%$

(5) The pipe mains carrying water from the source to the reservior is designed for the maximum daily demand.

(6) Distribution system is designed for maximum hourly demand 5.5

(7) The filters and other units of the treatment plant are desinged for a 2 times the average daily demand.

(8) Coincident demand : The maximum daily demand when added to fire demands for working out total demand is known as *coincident demand*.

Water Supply Schemes

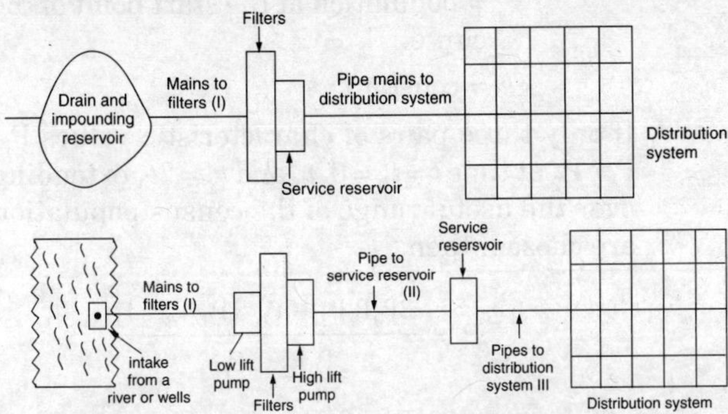

- In case of dams and reservoirs—Generally no needs of pumps.
- In case a river is used as a source, is required dumping equipment is required

Design Periods

The future period or the number of years for which a provision is made in designing the capacities of the various components of the water supply scheme is known as **design period.**

Water supply projects, under normal circumstances, may be designed for a design period of 30 years. This 30 years is to be counted after the completion of the project.

POPULATION FORECASTS

Factor affecting population growth.

(1) Birth

(2) Deaths

(3) Migrations

Besides these some other factors like wars, nature havoc and disasters may also bring about sharp reduction in the pupulations.

Population forecasting methods

(1) Arithmatical increase method.

$$P_n = [P_0 + n\bar{x}]$$

where, P_n = forcasted population after n decades from the present

P_0 = population at present (*i.e.* last known census)

n = number of decades between present and future

$\bar{x}$ = average population increase in the known decades

(2) Geometrical increase method or Uniform increase method.

In arithmatic method, no compounding is done but, in geometric method comounding is done every decade.

$$P_n = P_o\left(1 + \frac{r}{100}\right)^n$$

where, P_o = initial population

P_n = future population after n decades

r = assumed growth rate (%)

Computation of assumed growth rate (r) from the past known population data.

$$r = \sqrt[t]{\frac{P_2}{P_1}} - 1$$

where, P_1 = intial known population

P_2 = final known population

t = number of decades between P_1 and P_2

Note : Arithmetic mean,

$$r = \frac{r_1 + r_2 + r_3 + \ldots\ldots\ r_t}{t}$$

Geometric mean,

$$r = \sqrt[t]{r_1 + r_2 + r_3 \ldots\ldots\ r_t}$$

where, $r_1, r_2, r_3 \ldots\ldots\ r_t$ are % growth rates of the several known decades of past.

Arithmetic mean is slightly higher than geometric mean

Also r can be calculated as

$$r = \text{increase}\ \frac{\text{in population}}{\text{original population}} \times 100$$

Note : In geometric method computing is done every decade

(3) Incremental increase method or Method of varying increment.

$$P_n = P_o + n\bar{x} + \frac{n(n+1)}{2}\bar{y}$$

where, P_n = population after n decades from present

P_o = present population

$\bar{x}$ = average increase of population of known decades.

$\bar{y}$ = average of incremental increase of the known decades.

- Population obtained by

  Arithmatic increase method < Incremental increase method < Geometrical increment method.

- Incremental method gives quite satisfactory results.
- For newyounger cities expanding at faster rates → Geometrical increment method is applied.
- For old cities → Arithmetic method is better.
- Incremental method is applied for any type of city.

(4) Decreasing rate method.

This method is applicable only in cases where the rate of growth shows a downward manner.

In this method, the average decreases in the percentage increases is worked out, and is then substracted from the latest percentage increase for each successive decade.

(5) Simple graphical method.

In this method, a graph is plotted from the available data, between time and population. The curve is then smoothly extended upto the desired year.

(6) Comparative graphical method.

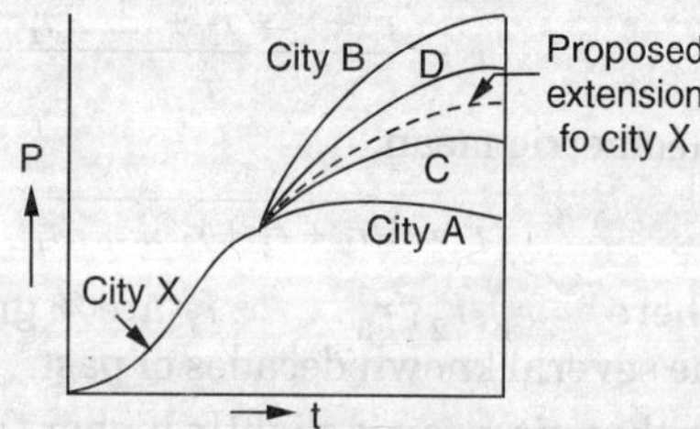

(7) Master plan method.

It is very easy to access precisely the design population, because the master plan will give us as to when and where the given number of houses, industries and commercial establishment would be developed.

(8) Apportionment method or Ratio Method.

The local population and the country population for the last four or five decades is obtained from the census method.

(9) Logistic curve method.

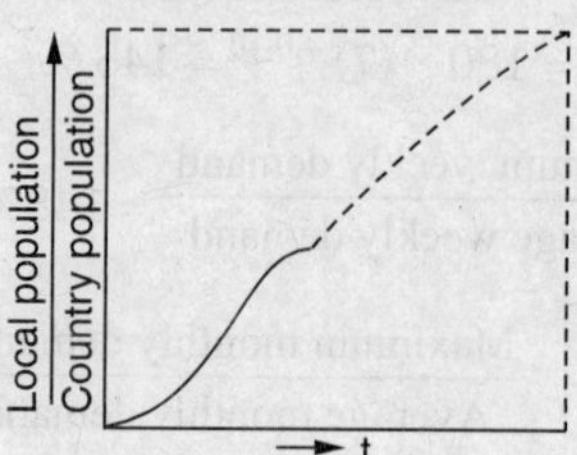

Equation of the logistic curve is

$$P = \frac{P_s}{1 + m\log_e^{-1}(nt)}$$

where, P = population at any time t from the origin A

P_s = saturated population

$$m = \frac{P_s\ P_0}{P_0} \text{ (a constant)}$$

$n = kp_s$ (another constant)

P_0 = population at the start point of the curve.

k = constant

- If only three pairs of characteristic values P_0, P_1, P_2 at time $t = t_0 = 0$, t_1 and $t_2 = 2t_1$ extending over the useful range of the census population are chosen, then

$$P_s = \frac{2P_0P_1P_2 - P_1^2\,(P_0 + P_2)}{P_0P_2 - P_1^2}$$

$$m = \frac{P_s - P_0}{P_0}$$

$$n = \frac{1}{t_1}\log_e\left[\frac{P_0\,(P_s - P_1)}{P_1\,(P_s - P_0)}\right]$$

Note :

(i) Methods 1 to 5 are based on the assumption that factors and conditions which were responsible for population increase in the past and continue even in the future also, with the intensity. This is a vague assumption.

(ii) Methods 6 to 9 are advanced and time consuing methods which gives fair results.

(iii) None of these methods is exact, and they are all based on the laws of probability, and thus, only approximate estimation for possible future population can be made.

Sources of Water

After calculating the demand of water, the main job is to search the source of water.

Classification of sources of water available on earth.

(1) Surface sources.

(i) Ponds and lakes

(ii) Streams and rivers

(iii) Storage reservoirs; impounding reservior

(iv) Ocean, generally not used for water supplies

(2) Sub-surface sources or Underground sources.

(i) Spring

(ii) Infiltration galleries

(iii) Infiltration wells

(iv) Wells and tube-wells.

- The yield which correspond to the worst or most critical year on record is called **firm yield** or **safe yield**.

Hydrologic Principles.

- The precipitation and evaporation continues forever, and thereby a balance is maintained between the two. This process is known as **hydrological cycle**.
- The evaporated water comes back to the surface of the earth is in its various forms like rain, show, hail, mist, sleet etc. is known as **precipitation**
- A major part of the precipitation occurs in the form of rain, and a minor part occurs in the form of snow.

Types of Precipitations.

(i) Cyclonic precipitation :

It is caused by the lifting of the air mass due to the pressure difference. If low pressure occurs in an area, air will flow horizontal from the surrounding area, causing the air in the low pressure area to lift. The precipitation that results, is called *non-frontal cyclonic precipitation.* If one air mass lifts over another air mass, then the precipitation is called **frontal or cyclonic precipitation.**

- The boundry between these two air masses of different temperatures and densities is known as a **front** or a **frontal surface**.
- The large whirling mass of air, at the centre of which the barometric pressure is low, is known as a **cyclone**.

(ii) Convective precipitation :

Convective precipitation is due to the upward movement of air that is warmer than its surroundings. Precipitation occurs of high intensity and short duration.

(iii) Orographic precipitation :

Orographic precipitation is the most important precipitation which is responsible for most of the heavy rains in India. Orographic precipitation is caused by air masses which strike some natural topographic barriers like mountains, and cannot move forward, and hence rise up, causing condentation and precipitation.

Note : The usual mechanism by which the air is cooled to cause precipitation is the lifting of the air mass.

Rainfall and it's Distribution

Rainfall interception (P_i).

The rain interrupted by buildings and trees.

Ground rainfall (P_g).

Total rainfall = $P—P_i$

Infiltration (F).

The ground rainfall infiltrated by the soil.

Infiltration capacity (f).

The maximum rate at which the soil in a given condition can absorp water is known as **infiltration capacity.**

Depression storage (S_d).

None of it appear as surface runoff.

Rainfall excess (P_e).

P_e = rainfall rate (P)-infiltration capacity (f)

Measurement of Railfall

Two types of raingauges are used :

(1) Non-recording type rain gauge

(only collect the rain)

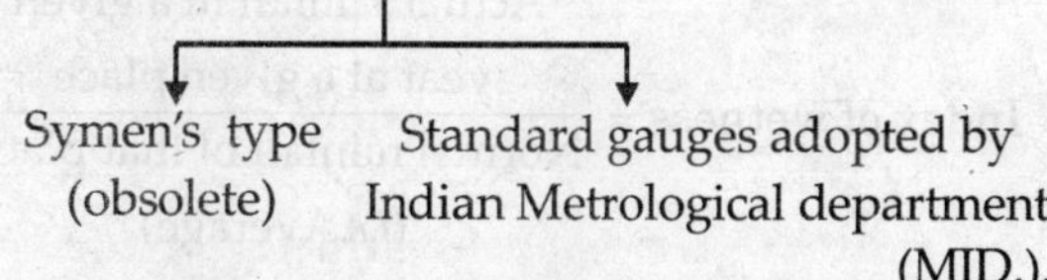

Symen's type (obsolete)

Standard gauges adopted by Indian Metrological department (MID.).

(2) Recording type rain gauge.

It gets rcorded automatically on a graph paper. This gauge thus produces a record of cumulative rain Vs. time in the form of graph, which is known as the **mass curve of rainfall.**

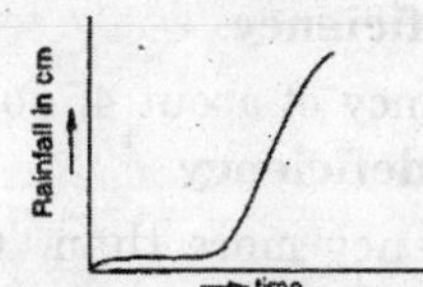

It is also known as *integrating raingauges or continuous rain-gauges.*

Type of recording raingauges :

(i) Tipping bucket type–operated through telecommounication system.

(ii) Weighing type

(iii) Floating type, etc. (most widely used in India).

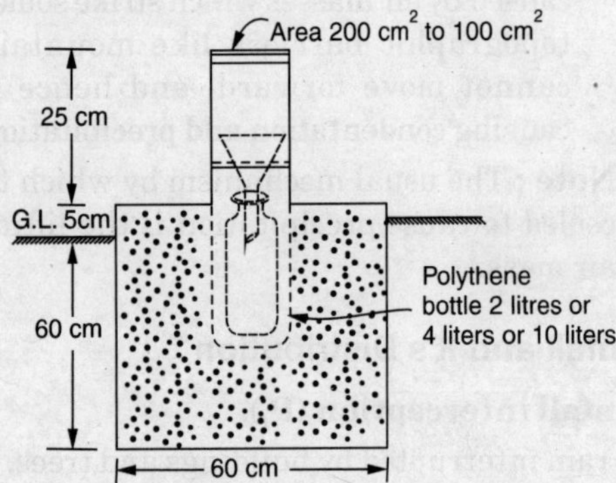

Fig. Standard non-recording raingauge.

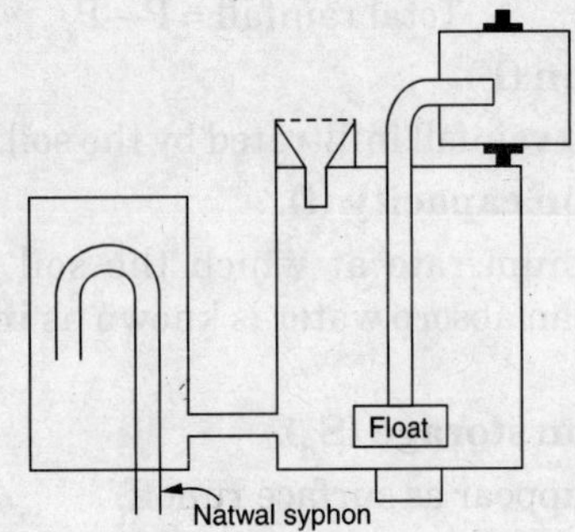

Fig. Float type automatic raingauge.

The rotating drum completes one revolution in 24 hours or sometimes in 7 days.

$$\text{Average annual rainfall} = \frac{\text{Annual rainfall at a given station should be recorded over a number of years (35 years)}}{\text{Number of years}}$$

Index of wetness.

$$\text{Index of wetness} = \frac{\text{Actual rainfall in a given year at a given place}}{\text{Normal rainfall of that place (\textit{i.e.} Average)}}$$

- Index of wetness, gives us an idea of the wetness of the year.
- 60% index of wetness means a rain deficiency of 40%.
- A deficiency of about 30 to 45% is known as **large deficiency**
- A deficiency of about 45 to 60% is known as **serious deficiency**
- A deficiency more than 60% is known as **disastrous deficiency.**

The year in which the rainfall is less than the average annual, is called a **bad year** or a **sub normal year**; and the year in which the rainfall is more than the average, is called a **good year**. If the rainfall in a particular year is a approximately equal to the annual average value, then it is known as a **normal year**.

The average annual rainfall of a given place is very useful for planning water supply schemes at that place, because it direct gives us an idea of the probable amount of water that may be available at that place.

Estimating Run-off and yield of a Basin

(1) English formula :

$$Q_y = 0.85\,P_y - 304 \text{ for hilly canctchment}$$

$$Q_y = P_y\left[\frac{P_y - 17.8}{254}\right] \text{ for plane catchment}$$

(Used in South India.)

where, Q_y = yearly runoff in cm depth over the basin

P_y = yearly precipitation or annual rainfall in cm.

(2) Khosla's Formula :

$$Q_y = P_y - 0.4813\,T_m \quad (T_m > 4.5°C)$$

(3)

$$Q_y = KP_y$$

where, K = impervious factor.

This runoff is helpful in evaluating the amount of water available in the river over long periods. They are, therefore, useful for estimating the storage capacity of the reservoir, and this fixed the height. of the dam required to be constructed for that storage. These determinations are hence useful when storage reservoir is to be used as a source of water. However, when a river or a stream is to be directly used as a source of water, we must determine the day to day quantities of flow in that river or stream.

Surface Sources of Water Supplies

(1) Ponds and Lakes : If size of the depression is comparatively small, it may be termed as a **pond**, and when the size of depression is larger, it many be termed as a **lake**.

Due to the smaller quantity of water available from them, lakes are not considered as principal source of water supplies.

(2) Streams and Rivers : Small stream channels feed their waters to the lakes or rivers.

Rivers are the most important sources of water supply schemes.

(i) Perennial river : water is available throughout the year.

(ii) Non-perennial rivers : The quality of water obtained from these rivers is not reliable.

(3) Storage Reservoirs : A water supply scheme drawing water directly from a river or a stream may fail to satisfy the consumers demands during extremely low flows. To avoid such problem we construct a dam across a river for storage of water. The artificial lake is formed on the up stream side is known as **storage reservoir.**

- The subject of design and planning of dams and reservoirs is a big topic in itself, and is generally dealt under the subject of irrgation.
- Surface waters are, however, generally soft and less corrosive than ground waters. On the whole it can be stated that the surface supplies are generally contaminated and cannot be used without treatment.

Subsurface or Underground Water Sources

Sometimes, the ground water is brought to the surface by some natural processes like **springs**, and sometimes the water is tapped by artificial means by constructing wells, tubewells, infiltration galleries etc.

Since the ground water is largely tapped in our country for water supplies and there is a scope for its development in future also.

Factors affecting the selection of a particular source of water:

(i) Quantity of available water.
(ii) Quality of available water.
(iii) Distance of the source of supply.
(iv) General topography of the interveing area.
(v) Elevation of the source of supply.

- The dead storage zone in a reservoir is provided for storage of sand and silt.
- Trap efficiency = $\dfrac{\text{Total sediment deposited in the reservoir}}{\text{Total sediment flowing in the river.}}$
- With the redution in the reservoir capacity, the quantum of sediment trapped by it decreases.

Development of Ground Water

Geological factors governing the occurrance of ground water.

Possibility of occurrance of the underground water mainly depends upon two properties of the underground soil

(i) Porosity of the soil
(ii) Permeability of the soil.

Rock Formations

Porosity values of some rock formations.

Granite, Quartzite	—	1.5%
Slate, Shale	—	4 %
Limestone	—	5 to 10 %
Sandstone	—	10 to 15 %
Sand and Gravel	—	20 to 30 %
Only gravel	—	25%
Only sand	—	35%
Clay and Soil	—	45%

Permeability and transmissibility.

- The porosity of the rock is defined the maximum amount of water that can be stored in the rock. This porosity, however, in itself, does not ensure the storage of underground water, because the water can enter into a rock only if the rock permits the flow of water through it.
- A rock which is porous, may or may not be permeable.
- The capability of the entire soil of full width and depth is represented by **permeability**; while that of the soil of unit width and full depth is known as **transmissibility**.
- The permeability is measured in terms of coefficient of permeability.

Zones of Underground Water

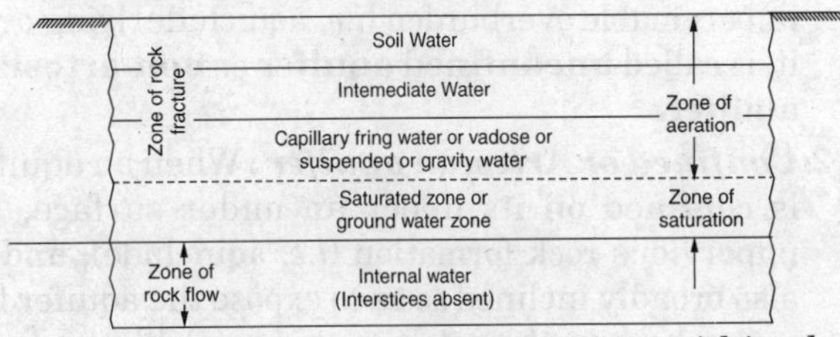

In the zone of saturation, water exists within the interstices and is known as *ground water*. This is the most important zone for a ground water hydrolic engineering because it has to tap out this water. Water in this zone is under hydrostatic pressure.

$$Q = kiA$$

$$V = ki$$

where, V is discharge velocity not the actual velocity (V_a) through the soil medium.

$$A_v V_a = A \times V$$

where, A_v = cross-sectional area of void

$$V = \frac{A_v}{A} V_a$$

$$V = \eta\, V_a$$

$$V_a = \frac{V}{n} = \frac{ki}{n}$$

Intrinsic permeability or specific permeability,

$$k_o = \frac{kv}{g} = k\left(\frac{\mu}{\gamma w}\right)$$

Relation between coefficient of permonability (k) and coefficient of transmissibility (T).

$$T = kd$$

where, d = mean particle size of porous medium.

Drainage of Ground Water

It means extracting the water from below the water lable through well, infiltration galleries, springs, etc.

Porosity = Specifie yield + Specific retention

$$= \frac{\text{Volume of water obtained by gravity drainage}}{\text{total weight of the material drained}} + \frac{\text{volume of water held against gravity drainage}}{\text{total weight of the material drained}}$$

- Large particles of soils like coarse gravels, the specific retention would be small and it would result in large specific yields.
- Water bearing formation of coars gravel would supply large quantities of water to wells, whereas clay formations, although saturated and of high porosity, would be of little value in this respect.

Aquifers

Types of aquifers.

1. ***Unconfined or non-artesian aquifers :*** The top most water bearing stratum having no confined imperemable overburden (*i.e.* aquiclude) lying over it, is called **unconfined aquifer** or **non-artesian aquifer.**
2. ***Confined or Artesian aquifer*** **:** When an aquifer is confined on its upper an under surface, by impervious rock formation (*i.e.* aquiclude), and is also broadly inclined so as to expose the aquifer for somewhere to the catchment area at higher level for the creation of sufficient hydraulic head, it is called a **confined aquifer** or an **artesion aquifer**.

Perched aquifer

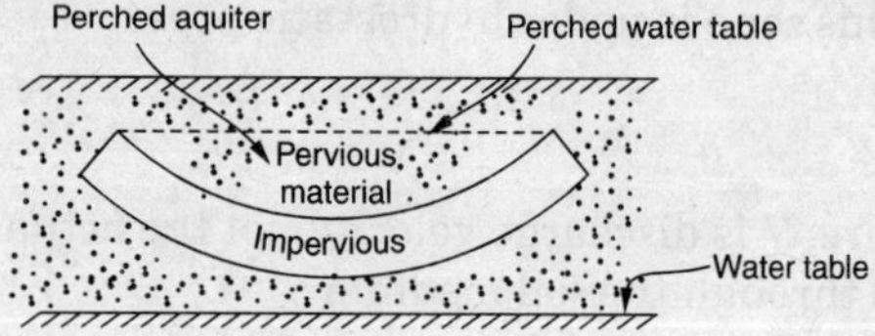

Aquifuse : It is that geological formation which is, neither porous nor permeable.

e.g. granite rock

Aquitard : It is that geological formation, which does not yield water problems to wells due to its lesser permeability. The yield from such a formation is, thus insignificant.

e.g., sandy clay.

Aquiclude : It is highly porous, containing large quantities of water, but essentially impervious.

e.g. clay layer.

Storage co-efficient (A) : It is defined as the volume of water that an aquifer release or storage per unit surface area of the aquifer per unit change in the component of head normal to that surface. The storage co-efficient (A) for an artesian aquifer is equal to the volume of water released from the aquifer of full height and unit area when the piezometricf surface declines by unity.

Ground Water Specific Yield

It is the ratio of volume of water obtained by gravity-drainage to the total volume of the sub-soil.

$$\text{Specific yield} = \frac{\text{Volume of water obtained by gravity drainage}}{\text{Total volume of the sub-soil}} \times 100$$

$$\text{Specific retention} = \frac{\text{Volume of water held against gravity drainage}}{\text{Total volume of the material}} \times 100$$

Porosity = Specific yield + specific retention

Ground Water Velocity

Slichter's formula :

$$v = \frac{k' SD^2}{\mu}$$

where, v = velocity of ground water in m/day

k' = constant (approx. 400)

s = slope of hydraulic gradient line

D = effective size of the particle in aquifer (in mm)

μ = dynamic viscosity

Hazen's formula:

$$v = \frac{k'' SD^2}{60}(1.8T + 42)$$

where, K" = constant (approx. 1000)

T = temperature (in °C)

Specific yield of well in recuperating test

It can be determined from the following formula:

$$\frac{C'}{A} = \frac{2.3}{T} \log_{10} \frac{S_1}{S_2}$$

where, S_1 = depression head in the well immediately after the pumping was stopped.

S_2 = depression head in well at time *'T'* after the pumping was stopped.

T = time after which S_2 was measured

$\frac{C'}{A}$ = specific yield.

$$\text{Discharge, } Q = \left(\frac{C'}{A}\right) \cdot AS$$

where, A = cross-sectional area of well

Yield of a well,

$$Q = \frac{\pi \rho k}{2.3} \frac{(H^2 - h^2)}{\log_{10} R/r} m^3/\text{day}$$

$$= \frac{\pi \rho k \times 1000}{2.3 \times 24 \times 60} \frac{H^2 - h^2}{\log_{10}(R/r)} \text{ litres/minute}$$

$$= \frac{k_m(H^2 - h^2)}{\log_{10}(R/r)} lpm$$

where, $k_m = \frac{\pi p k \times 1000}{2.3 \times 24 \times 60}$ is known as transmission constant of the acquifer.

The above formula is known as **Thiem's formula.**

Yield of tubewell when equilibrium conditions have not reached can be determined using following formula :

$$s = \frac{Q}{4\pi\mu}\left[\log e\left(\frac{4T\mu}{r^2 A}\right) - 0.5772\right]$$

where, s = draw down in observation well after time T.

r = radial distance of the observation well from the main well.

Q = yield or constant discharge pumped out from the well.

A = coefficient of storage of measured drawdown.

μ = coefficient of transmissibility.

$$s_1 - s_2 = \frac{2.3Q}{4\pi\mu} \log_{10}\left(\frac{T_2}{T_1}\right)$$

Forms of Underground Sources :

(1) Infiltration galleries

(2) Infiltration wells

(3) Springs

(4) Wells including tubewells.

INTAKE FOR COLLECTING SURFACE WATER

The basic function of the intake structure is to help in safely withdrawing water from the source over a predetermined range of pool levels and then to discharge this water into the withdrawal condict, through which it flows upto the water treatment plant.

Site selection of intake depends on

(i) availability of water is all seasons

(ii) quality and quantity of water

(iii) away from the pollution

(iv) nearer to the city

(v) upstream side of the river

(vi) costs and reliability

Types of Intakes

(1) Simple submerged intakes:

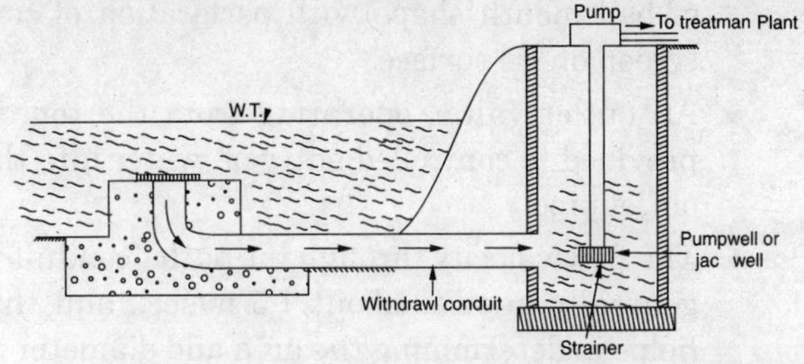

These intakes are not used on bigger projects on river and reservoir, as their main disadvantage is the fact that they are not easily accessible for cleaning, repairing, etc.

(2) Intake tower.

(i) Wet intake towers } Standing in the river or reservoir

(ii) Dry intake towers.

The essential difference between a dry intake tower and a wet intake tower is that, in a wet intake tower, the water enters from the entry ports into the tower and then it enters into the conduit pipe through separate gate conrolled opening; but in a dry intake tower, the water is directly drawn into the withdrawal conduit through the gated entry ports.

(3) Medium sized intake wells (River intake) :

(i) **Medium sized river intake :** The water from the intake chamber is taken through a withdrawal conduit (called intake conduit) to a sump well, from where it is lifted and taken to the treatment plant.

(ii) Canal intake well

Design criteria :

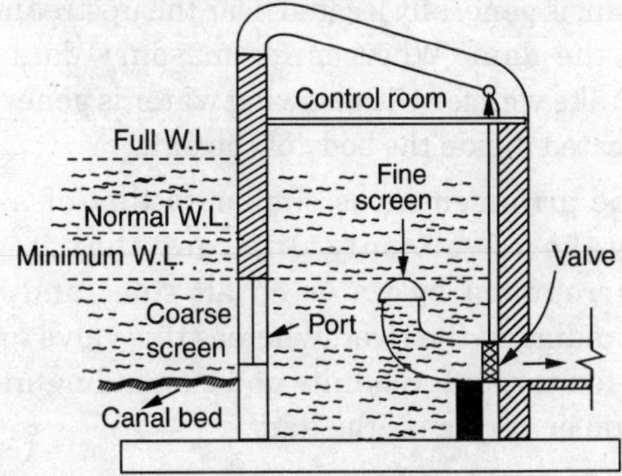

Fig. Canal intake well

- The entry of water in the intake well takes through a coarse screen, the top of which is generally provided at minimum water level in the canal, and bottom is about 0.45 m above the canal bed to avoid entry of bed load.

- An additions fine screen is provided at the inlet end of the withdrawal conduit. This inlet end of bell mouth shape with perforation of fine screen on its surface.
- An outlet value, operating from the top, is provided to controlled entry of water into the outlet pipe.
- The flow velocity through the outlet conduit is generally kept as about 1.5 m/sec., and this helps in determining the area and diameter of the withdrawal conduit.
- The area of coarse screen is designed by limiting the flow velocity to as low as 0.15 m/ sec or so. The flow velocity through the bell mouth inlet is limited to about 0.3 m/sec. or so.
- The head loss in the intake conduit upto treatment works, can be determined by using Darcy Weisback formula

$$H_L = \frac{f\,L\,V^2}{2gd}$$

or by using Házen William's formula.

$$V = 0.85\ C_H + R^{0.63}\ S^{0.54}$$

where, $S = \frac{H_L}{L}$ = slope of the energy line

C_H = 130 for C.I. pipe.

(4) Intake for sluiceways of dam :

In case a reservoir developed by constructing a dam, it is a common practice to fetch water through the sluiceways from inside the dam.

- In case of earthen dams, the intake for withdrawing water into the sluiceway of the dam, is generally located near the upstream toe of the dam. Whereas for masonry dam the intake well for withdrawing water is generally located inside the body of the dam.
- The arrangement is similar to that of a dry intake tower, only different that it was surrounded by water on all sides and was standing in the river, whereas this valve tower is fed through conduits and is standing in the dam or very near the dam.

Design of canal intake.

(1) Q and then assume D.T. and get volume of intake.

(2) Design of coarse screen.

(3) Design of bell mouth entry.

(4) Design of intake conduit.

(5) Head loss.

Conduits for Transporting Water

Types of conduits.

(1) Gravity conduits.

(*i*) Canal (often used for irrigation)

(*ii*) Flumes

(*iii*) Aquaducts (are closed, rectangular, circular or horse shoe sections). They are generally designed as $\frac{1}{2}$ to $\frac{3}{4}$ th full.

- In gravity conduit, the hydraulic gradient line will concide with the water surface and will be parallel to the bed of the conduit.
- These conduits cannot, therefore, go up and down hills and valleys as desired by existing topography of the area.
- From hydraulic point of view, a circular section provides the maximum hydraulic mean depth or maximum area per unit of wetted perimeter $\left(i.e.\ R = \frac{A}{P}\right)$ and is, therefore, the most efficient. Moreover, since the perimeter per unit of cross section is less the construction cost or material required is also the least. But circular sections cannot be easily supported on ground and, therefore seldom used.
- A rectangular shape is hydraulically inefficient and requires more material for construction, but is more stable to support on the ground, and therefore widely used.
- Horse shoe shape may be used with great advantage.
- The bed or the invert of the conduit in pressure flows is thus independent of the grade of the hydraulic gradient line which really governs the flow velocities.

(2) Pressure conduits (Pressure above the atmospheric pressure)

- The pressure pipes can, therefore, follow the natural, available ground surface and can freely go up and down hills or can dip beneath valleys or mountains, sometimes even rising above the H.G. Lines and thusrequiring lesser length of conduit.

Water borne diseases and their control

Water borne diseases are those diseases which spread primarily through contaminated water.

(1) Disease caused by bacterial infections.

(*i*) Typhoid fever and paratyphoid fever (caused by salmonella typhi becteria)

(*ii*) Cholera (caused by vibrio-cholera bacteria)

(*iii*) Bacillary dysentery (caused by shiga bacillus or flexner bacillus.

(2) Disease caused by viral infections.

(i) Infectious hepatitis or infectious jaundice (caused by hepatitis virus).

(ii) Poliomyelitis (caused by polio virus).

(iii) Gastroentritis.

(3) Disease caused by protozoal infections.

Amoebic dysentery (caused by entamoeba hystolytic germ).

WATER QUALITY STANDARDS FOR DRINKING WATER

S.No.	Type of Characterstic	Type of imputrity	Permissible limit	Absolute maximum limit	Remark
1.	Physical	Turbidity	5	25	On silica scale
		Colour	5	50	Colour number on cobalt scale
		Taste & odour	1	3	Threshold odour number
2.	Chemical	pH value	7—8.5	6.5—9.2	
		Hardness	75 mg./l.	110 mg./l.	Hardness expenssed as $CaCO_3$
		Total solids	500 mg./l.	1500 mg./l.	As per WHO standards
		Magnesium & Sodium	500	1000 mg./l.	As per WHO standards
		Chlorides	200	600 mg./l.	As per WHO standards
		Sulphates	200	400 mg./l.	As per WHO standards
		Calcium	75	200 mg./l.	As per WHO standards
		Zinc	5	15 mg./l.	As per WHO standards
		Copper	1	1.5 mg./l.	As per WHO standards
		Iron	0.3	1.0	As per WHO standards
		Maganese	0.1	0.5	As per WHO standards
		Arsenic	Nil	0.2	As per WHO standards
		Lead	Nil	0.1	As per WHO standards
		Selenium	Nil	0.05	As per WHO standards
		Chromium	Nil	0.05	As per WHO standards
		Phenolic compounds as phenole	0.001	0.002	As per WHO standards
		Cynide	Nil	0.01	As per WHO standards
		Fluoride	0.5 mg./l.	1.5 mg./l.	As per WHO standards
		Cadmium	–	0.05 mg/l	As per WHO standards
3.	Biological and Micro-organic		Coliform bacteria	Nil colony per 100 ml. or MPN of B coli is limited to 1 per 100 ml.	1 coliform
4.	Radiological	α-emitters	Nil	1 μμc/litre.	W.H.O. standard
	β-emitters		Nil	10 μμc/litres.	W.H.O. standard

- Water used in pulp or paper industries, must be free from iron, maganese, and hardness.
- Water required for breweries, distilleries, and bakeries should preferably be hard.
- For steel rolling mills, the chloride content of water must be less than 150 mg./l.
- The water (prevention and control of pollution) Act enacted by the Indian Parliament in 1974.

Methods of Purfication of Water

(i) Plain Sedimentation

Principle behind sedimentation is to reduce the flow velocity by providing tank called settling tank, or **clarifier** or **sedimentation basin.**

Detention period : Theoretical average time for which the water is detained in the tank is called the detention period.

Settling velocity of spherical particle :

$$V_s = \frac{g}{18}(G-1)\frac{d^2}{\nu} \quad \text{for } d < 0.1 \text{ mm.} \quad [Re < 0.5]$$

where, V_s = velocity of settlement of particle
d = diameter of the particle
G = specific gravity of the particle
ν = kinematic viscosity of water

$$R_e = \text{Reynold number} = \frac{V_s d}{\upsilon}$$

Since, viscosity depend upon the temperature, the above equation can be modified as

$$V_s = 418\,(G-1)\,d^2\left(\frac{3T+70}{100}\right)$$

for $d < 0.1$ mm.

where, T = temperature of water in degree centigrades
V_s = velocity of settlement in mm/sec
d = diameter of the particle in mm.

$$V_s = 1.8\sqrt{gd\,(G-1)}$$

for $d > 1.0$ mm (turbulent settling)

In transition zone, settling velocity is given by Hazen as :

$$V_s = 418\,(G-1)\,d\left(\frac{3T+70}{100}\right)$$

when d lies between 0.1 mm. and 1 mm

The above formula represent the theoretical setling velocities of discrete spherical particles. The actual settling velocities in the sedimentation basins, will be much less than that calculated by these formulae, because of :

(i) non-sphericity of the particles
(ii) upward displacement of the fluid caused by the settling of other particles
(iii) convection currents.

Note : A plain sedimentation tank under normal conditions may remove as much as 70% of the suspended impurities present in water.

Types of sedimentation tank.

(i) Intermittenly function sedimentation tank : not preferred these day.

(ii) Continuously function sedimentation tank.

The velocity is so adjusted that the time taken by the particle to travel from one end to another is slightly more than the time required for settling of that particle.

Design of confinuous flow type of sedimentation tank

***(i)* Flow velocity:** $V = \frac{Q}{BH}$

where, Q = discharge entering the basin
B = width of the basin
H = depth of water in the tank.

***(ii)* Permissible velocity (V_s) :** $\frac{V}{V_s} = \frac{L}{H}$

$$\Rightarrow V_s = \frac{VH}{L} = \frac{Q}{BH} \times \frac{H}{L} = \frac{Q}{BL}$$

$$\Rightarrow V_s = \frac{Q}{BL}$$

It shows that all those particles having a settling velocity equal to or greater than $\frac{Q}{BL}$ will settle down and be removed.

***(iii)* Overflow rate :**

Discharge per unit of plan area (surface area), i.e. the $\frac{Q}{BL}$ is a very important term for the design of continuous flow type settling tanks; and is known as the **overflow rate** or the **surface loading** or the **overflow velocity**.

For plain sedimentation tanks overflow velocity = 500 – 700 litres/hr./m² of plan area

For plain sedimentation tanks using coagulants as aids overflow velocity = 1000 – 1250 litres/hr./m². of plan area.

Smaller particles will also settle down, if the overflow rate is reduced.

***(iv)* Depth of sedimentation tank :** Usual values of depth ranges between 3.0 to 4.5 m.

***(v)* Detention period or Retention period *(t)* :**

It is the average time for which the water is detained in the tank.

Detention time for rectangular tank,

$$t = \frac{\text{Volume of the tank}}{\text{Rate of flow}} \quad i.e.\ t = \frac{BLH}{Q}$$

Detention time for a circular tank,

$$t = \frac{d^2(0.011d + 0.785H)}{Q}$$

where, d = diameter of the tank.
H = side water depth.

For plain sedimentation, detention time = 4 to 8 hr.
When the coagulants are used, detention time = 2 to 4 hr.

***(vi)* Dimensions of the tank :** $B \approx 10$ to 12 m.

Length of the tank is not generally allowed to exceed four times the width.

(vi) Normally kept flow velocity at about 0.3 m/min.

(vii) In actual practice, certain amount of short circuting always exist and therefore, the actual average time which a batch of water takes in passing through a settling tank, is called the **flowing through period**.

$$\text{Displacement efficiency} = \frac{\text{Flowing through period}}{\text{Detention period}} \approx 0.25 \text{ to } 0.5$$

***(viii)* Sludge zone :** For tanks without mechanical sludge removal equipment, an additional minimum depth of about 0.8 to 1.2 m. should be provides for storage of sediment, and is called the **sludge zone**.

(ii) Sendimentation Aided with coagulation

Certain chemical compounds called **coagulants** are added to the water, which on thorough mixing from a gelatenous precipitate called **'floc'**. The very fine mud particles and the colloidal matter present in water get attracted and absorbed in these flocs, forming the bigger sized floculated particles. The process of addition and mixing of the chemicals (*i.e,* the coagulants) is called the **coagulation**. The coagulated water is then made to pass through the sedimentation tank, where the floculated particles settle down and, are, thus removed.

The coagulation before sedimentation is almost universally adopted in all the major water treatment plants, and is followed by rapid sand filtration.

Chemicals used for coagulation.

***(i)* Aluminium sulphate :**

$$Al_2(SO_4)\cdot 18H_2O + \underset{\text{Bicarbonte alkalinity}}{3\,Ca(HCO_3)_2} \longrightarrow 3\,CaSO_4 + \underset{\text{(floc)}}{2Al(OH)_3\downarrow} + \underset{\text{present in raw water}}{6CO_2\uparrow + 18\,H_2O}$$

- Average normal does is about 17 mg./l. (5 mg/l – 55 mg/l.)
- If raw water supplies are not sufficiently alkaline, then the external alkalies like lime *i.e.* $Ca(OH)_2$ or soda ash (Na_2CO_3) are generally added.

(i) $Al_2(SO_4)_3\cdot 18H_2O + 3\,Ca(OH)_2 \rightarrow 3\,CaSO_4 + Al(OH)_3\downarrow + 18\,H_2O$

(ii) $Al_2(SO_4)_3\cdot 18H_2O + 3\,Na_2CO_3 \rightarrow 3\,Na_2SO_4 + 2Al(OH)_3\downarrow + 3\,CO_2\uparrow + 15\,H_2O$

- Aluminium sulphate is very effective coagulant, and is now extensively used throughout the world.

***(ii)* Ferrous sulphate (copperas) ($FeSO_4\cdot 7H_2O$) :**

(a) *When copper as is added earlier to lime* :

$FeSO_4\cdot 7H_2O + Ca(HCO_3)_2 \rightarrow Fe(HCO_3)_2 + CaSO_4 + 7H_2O$

$Fe(HCO_3)_2 + 2\,Ca(OH)_2 \rightarrow Fe(OH)_2 + 2\,CaCO_3 + 2H_2O$

$4\,Fe(OH)_2 + O_2 + 2H_2O \rightarrow 4\,Fe(OH)_3\downarrow$ (Ferric hydroxide precipitate)

(b) *When lime is added first* :

$FeSO_4\cdot 7H_2O + Ca(OH)_2 \rightarrow CaSO_4 + Fe(OH)_2 + 7H_2O$

$$4Fe(OH)_2 + O_2 + 2H_2O \rightarrow \underset{\text{(floc)}}{4Fe(OH)_3\downarrow}$$

Copperas are used when the raw waters are not coloured and high pH (8 to 10).

***(iii)* Chlorinated copperas**

$$6\,(FeSO_4\cdot 7H_2O) + 3Cl_2 \rightarrow \underset{\text{Ferric sulphate}}{2Fe_2(SO_4)_3} + \underset{\text{Ferric chloride}}{2\,FeCl_3} + 42\,H_2O$$

know as chlorinated copperas

$Fe(SO_4)_3 + 3\,Ca(OH)_2 \rightarrow 3\,CaSO_4 + 2Fe(OH)_3\downarrow$

$2FeCl_3 + 3Ca(OH)_2 \rightarrow 3CaCl_2 + 2Fe(OH)_3\downarrow$

It remove colour and effective in low & high pH range.

***(iv)* Sodium Aluminate ($Na_2H_2O_4$) :**

$$Na\,Al_2O_4 + Ca(HCO_3)_2 \rightarrow \underset{\text{Cal. aluminate}}{CaAl_2O_4\downarrow} + Na_2CO_3 + CO_2\uparrow + H_2O$$

$Na_2Al_2O_4 + CaCl_2 \rightarrow CaAl_2O_4\downarrow + 2NaCl$

$Na_2Al_2O_4 + CaSO_4 \rightarrow CaAl_2O_4\downarrow + Na_2SO_4$

Iron salts are used as coagulants more frequently for treating sewage, and alum is used more frequently for treating raw water.

Parts of a coagulation sedimentation plant

(i) Feeding device:

These are of two types:

(a) Dry feeding

(b) Wet feeding.

Feeding depends on following factors

(a) Characteristics of coagulant and convenience.

(b) Amount of coagulant

(c) Cost of coagulant and size of plan

Note. Large plants use wet feeding and smaller plants use dry feeding, unless objected to by characteristics of coagulant.

(ii) Mixing devices:

Centrifugal pumps, compressed air, mixing basins etc.

Mixing Basings.

(a) With baffle walls

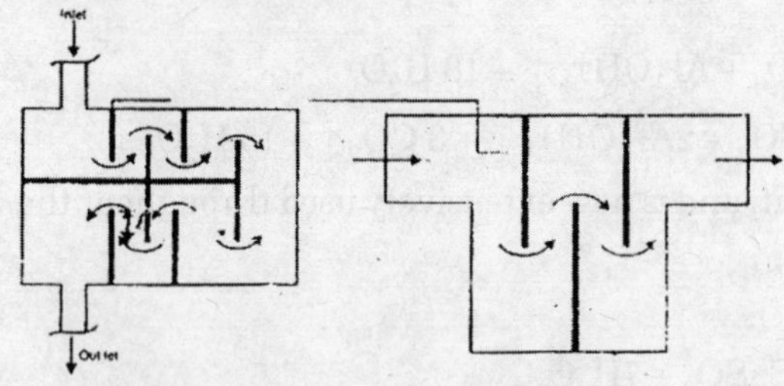

Fig. Mixing basin with baffel Walls

Design criteria

Velocity of flow in channels

= 1.15 to 0.045 m/sec.

Detention peirod = 20-50 min.

Hence length of flow is known.

Clear opening between end of each baffle and the tank wall should be kept about 1.5 × distance between baffles.

Minimum value = 60 cm

Note:

- Around the end baffles should not be used when the computed depth < 1m.
- In over and under baffles; depth is normally kept (2 to 3) × distance between baffles.
- In basins, loss of head ≈ 3.2× velocity head in channel
- Baffle type mixing basins are not used in modern day or on large plants.

(b) With Mechanical devices:

These use Flash mixer

Impeller¢s speed = 100–120 rpm.

Detention period = 2-3 minutes.

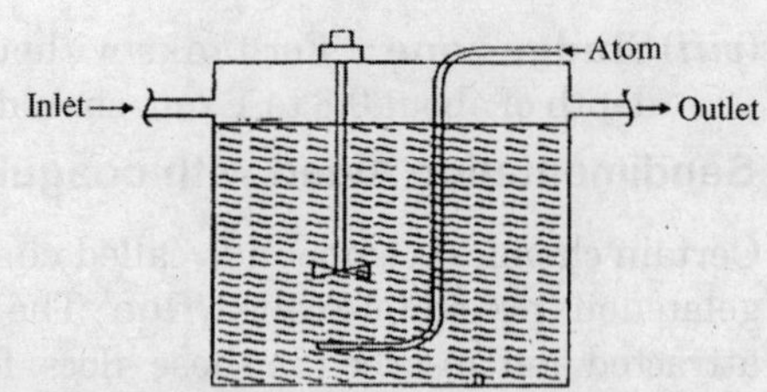

(iii) Flocculator:

Paddles rotated at speed of 2-3 rpm.

Detention period = 30 to 60 minutes (ave. 40 min.)

Clear distance between paddles and wall is about 15 to 30 cm.

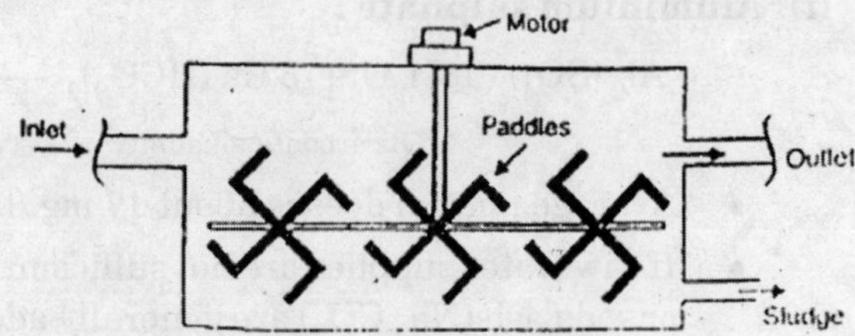

(iv) Sedimentation tank:

The complete process of coagulation sedimentation may help in removing turbidities upto as low values as 10-20 mg./l. It may also help in reducing the bacteria from the water, and thus to reduce the B-coli index by as much as 70%.

Large plant uses wet feeding while smaller plants uses dry feeding.

Detention period = 2 – 4 hrs.

Overflow rate = 1000 – 1250 lit/hr./m^2

Combined co-agulation-cum-sedimentation tank:

Detention period = 15 – 40. in floc-chamber

= 2-4 hrs. in settling tank.

Optimum coagulant quantities determination:

Jar test is made. Large number of jars are used for good results.

The amount of coagulant in jar which produces a good floc with the least amount of co-agulant, indicates optimum dosage.

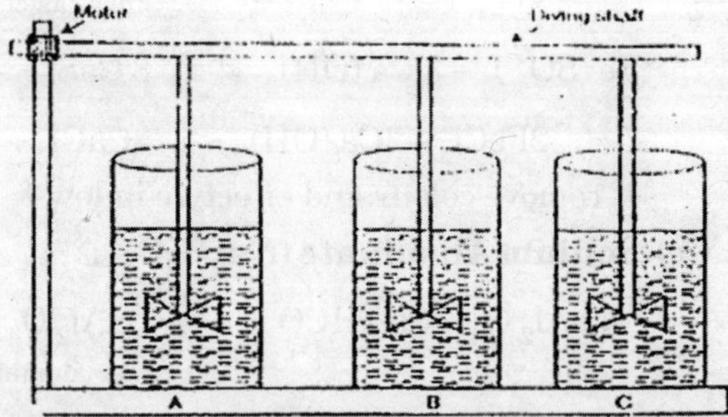

Fig. Jar Test

Production of sludge:

Alum, which s cheifly used has been found to be generating sludge equal to 0.24 times of its own weight.

Dry sludge produced in mg/day = Q in lit/day [suspended solids removed in mg/l + 0.24 × Alum does in mg/l + misc. chemicals added like carbon, clay, polymer in mg/l]

Dewatering and Disposal of sludge from water treatment plants :

Wet or watery sludge is produced in a water treatment plant in its following units :

(i) Sedimentation flocculation tank or clariflocculator

(ii) Filters

Methods for disposing of wastes obtained from above plants :

(i) Ponding in artificial or natural lagoons

(ii) Sand drying bed

(iii) Gravity thickners

(iv) High speed centrifuges

The dewatered sludge is finally disposed off either by incineration or by burial in trenches.

(iii) Filtration of Water

The process of passing the water through the beds of granular materials is know as **Filtration**. Filtration may help in removing colour, odour, turbidity and pathogenic bacteria from the water.

Types of filters.

(*i*) Slow sand filters.

Construction of slow sand filters : Parts of slow sund filter are :

(*a*) Enclosure tank or basin :

Depth of tank = 2.5 to 3.5 m.

Plan area of the tank = 100 to 2000 m^2

(*b*) Filter media :

Sand layers go to 110 cm. in depth.

(*c*) Base material :

30 to 75 cm. thick gravels of different sizes placed in layers.

(*d*) Under drainage system.

(*e*) Inlet and outlet arrangements.

(*f*) Other appurtenances.

(*ii*) Rapid sand filters or mechanical sand filters.

These filters employ coarse sand, with effective size as 0.5 mm or so. On an average, these filters may yield as high as 30 times the yield given by the slow sand filters. Water from the clariflocculator are used in these filters, and filtered water is treated with disinfectants, so as to obtain potable supplies.

Construction of rapid gravity filters : *Parts of rapid sand filter*:

(*a*) Enclosure tank or basin :

Depth of tank = 2.5 to 3.5 m.

Plan area of tank = 10 to 50 m^2 for each unit.

(*b*) Number of units at a filter plant, $N = 1.22\sqrt{Q}$

where, Q = plant capacity in million litres per day.

(*c*) *Filter media* : sand layer 60 to 90 cm. in depth.

(*d*) *Base material* : gravel layer 60 to 90 cm. thick gravels of different sizes placed in layers.

(*e*) Under drainage system

(*f*) Other appurtenances.

Working and Cleaning of Rapid gravity filters :

The amount of water required for washing a rapid gravity filter may very from 21.5% of the total amount of water filtered. The rapid gravity filters get clogged very frequently and have to be washed every 24 to 48 hours.

The rapid gravity filters are conventionally cleaned by back washing.

Rate of Filtration or Rate of loading for Rapid gravity filters.

3000 to 6000 litres/hr/m^2 of filter area.

Rate of filtration of pressure filter :

6000 to 15000 l/h/m^2 of filter media.

3000 to 6000 litres/hr/m^2 of filter area.

- The pressure filter are less efficient than the rapid gravity filter.
- Pressure filters are generally not used for treating municipal surface supplies.
- Pressure filters are used for small plants such as for individual industrial supplies, not adopted for treating large scale municipal supplies.
- Slow sand filters remove larger percentage of impurities and bacteria as compare to rapid sand filters but slow sand filters are obsolete these days due to slow rate of filtration.
- In the modern treatment plants, rapid sand gravity filters are now a days almost universally adopted. The water from the coagulation sedimentation plant is directly fed into the rapid sand gravity filters, and the resultant supplies are disinfected for complete killing of germs and colour removal.

Comparison of slow sand and Rapid sand filters :

S.No.	Item	Slow sand filters	Rapid gravity filters
1.	Pre treatment requirements	Effluents either from plain sedimentation tanks or raw waters without any treatment are generally fed into them; and coagulation is not at all required.	Coagulation, flocculation, and sedimentation is a must.
2.	Base material	The gravel base supports the sand. It varies from 3 to 65 mm in size and 30 to 75 cm. in depth.	The gravel base supports the sand and also distributes the wash water uniformly on the surface of sand. It varies from 3 to 40 mm. in size and its depth is slightly more, *i.e.* about 60 to 90 cm.
3.	Filter sand	The effective size (D_{10}) of filter sand ranges between 0.2 to 0.4 mm. and uniformity co-efficient between 1.8 to 2.5 or 3.0. The grain size distribution is generally uniform throughout the depth of filter media, except that top 10 to 15 cm. may be laid of finer variety.	The effective filter sand ranges between 0.35 to as and unformity co-efficient between 1.2 to 1.8. The sand is laid in layers with smallest grain size at top and coarsest grain size at the bottom.
4.	Underdrainage system	Laid in order to receive filtered water.	Laid in order to receive filtered water and also to pass water for back washing at a very high rate. Small, such as 5m × 8m. The area varying from 10 to 80 sq. m.
5.	Size of each unit	Large such as (30 m to 60 m). The area varying from 100 to 2000 sq. m. or more.	Large such as 3000 to 6000 lit./hr./m². of filter area.
6.	Rate of filtration	Small such as 100 to 200 lit./hr./m² of filter area.	
7.	Economy	High intial cost of both land and material but low cost of operation and maintenance.	Low initial cost, but higher cost of operation and maintenance overall , it is cheaper and economical.
8.	Depreciation cost	Relatively low.	Relatively high.
9.	Efficiency	Very efficient in removing bacteria (98 to 99%) but less efficient in removing colour. Overall turbidity removal in these filters using plain sedimentation is also low. They cannot handle turbid water containing turbidities more than 50 mg/l.	Less efficient in removing bacteria (80 to 90%) but very efficient in removing colour. The overall turbidity removal in these fill using coagulation sedimentation, is also high. They can threrefore, handle very turbid waters.
10.	Flexibility	Not flexible for meeting variations in demand.	Quite flexible for meeting reasonable variations in demand.
11.	Suitability and adaptability	May be adopted for treating smaller village supplies or for individual industrial supplies. They are absolete these day.	They are widely and almost univers adopted for treating public supplies especially at all major cities and town.
12.	Post treatment requirement, if any	Almost pure water is obtained. However; it may be disinfected slightly to make it completely safe. Other miscellaneous may or may not be required.	Disinfection is must and some other miscellaneous treatment may be given, if needed.
13.	Ease in construction	Simple	Complicated, as under drainage is properly designed.
14.	Skilled supervision, if required	Not required.	Essential.
15.	Method of cleaning	(*a*) Scrapping and removing the top 1.5 to 3 cm. thick layer and washing down by hoses. (*b*) Laborious method.	(*a*) Agitating the sand grains and back washing with or without compressed air. (*b*) Short and easy methode.
16.	Period of cleaning	Cleaned at intervels of 1 to 3 months.	Cleaned frequently at intervals of 1 to 3 days.
17.	Loss of head	Approximately 10 cm is the initial loss, and 0.8 to 1.2 m is the final limit when cleaning is required	Approximately 0.3m is the initial loss, and 2.5 to 3.5 m. is the final limit when cleaning is required.
18.	Quantity of wash water required	0.2 to 0.6% of the total water filtered.	1 to 5% of the total water filters.

(iv) Disinfection or Sterilisation

Chlorine has been found to be the best and the most ideal disinfectant and is now invariably used throughout the world. Disinfection means killing of only the discase producing bacteria, whereas sterilisation means killing of are the bacteria of all types. Disinfection, chlorination and sterilisation are used as synonymous to each other.

Minor methods of disinfection.

(*i*) **Boiling of water :** It can only kill the existing germs but cannot take care of the future possible contaminaions, hence it is not used for disinfecting public supplies. However, during water borne epidemics, public is advised to drink water only after boiling.

(*ii*) **Treatment with excess lime :** Lime is generally used as a water purification plant for softening (i.e. reducing hardness), but excess lime may kill the bacteria also.

- The excess lime when added to water, in fact, raises the pH value of water.
- This method is quite practical for complete removal of bacteria, yet needs the removal of excess lime from the water before it can be supplied to the general public (called recarbonation). Moreover,it cannot protect the water from the possible dangers of recontamination, and hence not used these days.

(*iii*) **Treatment with Ozone :**

$$3O_2 \xrightarrow[\text{arc voltage}]{\text{under high electric}} 2O_3$$

$$O_3 \rightarrow O_2 + O_{\text{nascent oxygen}}$$

- The nascent oxygen, so produced, is a powerful oxidising agent and removes the organic matter as well as the bacteria from the water.
- Ozone being unstable, nothing remain in water, by the time it reaches the distribution system.
- Ozone remove colour, taste and odour from water, in addition to removing the bacteria from it.
- The Ozonised water becomes tasty and pleasant unlike the chlorinated water which becomes bitter to tongue.

(*iv*) **Treatment with Pottasium permanganate ($KMnO_4$) :**

It is used for disinfecting well water supplies in village; which are generaly contaminated with lesser amount of bacteria. It also produce taste.

If the pink colour disappears, it shows that organic matter is present in water.

(*v*) **Treatment with iodine and bromine**

(*vi*) **Treatment with ultraviolet rays :** suitable for swimming pool water

(*vii*) **Treatment with silver :** called Eleipa-katadyn process.

(v) Chlorination

The teratment of waterby chlorine water is called **chlorination.**

$$Cl_2 + H_2O \xrightarrow{pH > 5} \underset{\text{Hypochlorous acid}}{HOCl} + HCl$$

$$HOCl \underset{pH < 7}{\overset{pH > 8}{\rightleftarrows}} H^+ + OCl^- \text{ (Hypochlorite ions)}$$

Free available chlorine.

The sum of hypochlorous acid, hypochlorite ions, and molecular chlorine existing in a sample of water is termed as **free available chlorine.**

Out of these form of free available chlorine, the hypochlorous acid is the most destructive, being about 80 times more effective than OCl. For this reason, the pH value of water during chlorination is generally maintained slightly less than 7, so as to keep the dissociation of HOCl to minimum and thereby keeping more HOCl in solution compared to OCl ions.

- Moreover, the chlorine will immedialqtely react with ammonia present in water to form various chloramines, as given below :

$$NH_3 + HOCl \xrightarrow{pH > 7.5} \underset{\text{Monochloramine}}{NH_2Cl} + H_2O$$

$$NH_2Cl + HOCl \xrightarrow{pH\ 5\ to\ 6.5} \underset{\text{Di-chloramine}}{NHCl_2} + H_2O$$

$$NHCl_2 + HOCl \xrightarrow{pH < 4} \underset{\text{Nitrogen. Trichloramine}}{NCl_3} + H_2O$$

In usual chlorine treatment, when pH is kept slightly less than 7, $NHCl_2$ is the most predominant.

- If all NH_3 is consumed by added Cl_2, then it would persist as free **chlorine**.
- Chloramine is less effective than free chlorine.
- Correct sequence of formation of residual chlorine compound is NH_2Cl, $NHCl_2$, HOCl, OCl

Dose of chlorine : The amount of Chlorine used in reducing organic and inogranic impurities is called the **chlorine demand of water**. After the Cl_2demand is fulfilled, Chlorine will appear as free chlorine residual (hypochlorites). This residue Chlorine will serve as disinfectant to kill pathogens.

Chlorine dose required for killing isolated virus.

Types of virus to be killed	Quantity of free chlorine required in mg/l with about 30 minutes contact period for water of pH lower than 7 or so.
Poliomyelitis virus	0.1
Hepatitis virus	0.4
Cysts of E. histolytica, *i.e.* organism causing ameobic dysentery.	3.0 or even lower.
Tuberculosis organisms	3.0
Coxsaickie Virus	Very huge does varying from 21 to 138 mg/l

Forms in which chlorine can be applied.

(*i*) As free chlorine :

In the form of liquid chlorine or as chlorine gas. ($HOCl$, OCl^-)

(*ii*) As combined chlorine :

(*a*) **Use of hypochlorites or bleaching powder** (not used these days)

$$Ca(OCl)_2 \xrightleftharpoons{H_2O} \underset{\text{Hypochlorite ions}}{Ca^{++} + 2OCl^-}$$

$$OCl^- + H^+ \underset{pH>8}{\overset{pH<7}{\rightleftharpoons}} \underset{\text{Hypochlorans acid}}{HOCl}$$

This process is known as *hypochlorination.* The hypochlorite ions as well as hypochlorous acid both causing disinfection of water.

(*b*) **Use of chloramines or use of chlorine with ammonia**

(*c*) **Use of chloramine dioxide :**

Disinfecting power is 2½ times stronger than chlorine but is very useful.

Types of Chlorination

(*i*) **Plain chlorination :** It indicates that only chlorine treatment and no other treatment has been given to the raw water.

The used quantity of chlorine requred is about 0.5 mg/l or more

(*ii*) **Pre-chlorination :** Pre-chlorination is the process of applying chlorine to the water before filtration or rather before sedimentation.

The normal doses are as 5 to 10 mg/l so that 0.1 to 0.5 mg/l of residual chlorine comes to the filter plant.

(*iii*) **Post-chlorination :** It is the process of applying chlorine after filtration and before enter the distribution sytem. The dosage of chlorine should be such as to leave a residual chlorine of start 0.1 to 0.2 mg/l after a contact period of about 20 minutes. This residual will ensure the disinfection of water, if at all any future recontamination occurs in the distribution system.

(*iv*) **Double chlorination :** It indicates that water has been chlorinated twice. The prechlorination and post-chlorination are generally used in double chlorination. Post chlorination, however, is generally always used, while the pre-chlorination is also used when the waters are highly turbid and contaminated.

(*v*) **Break-point chlorination :**

- Some Cl_2 is consumed for killing bacteria and thus the amount of residual Cl_2 shall be slightly less than that added as shown by the curve AB.

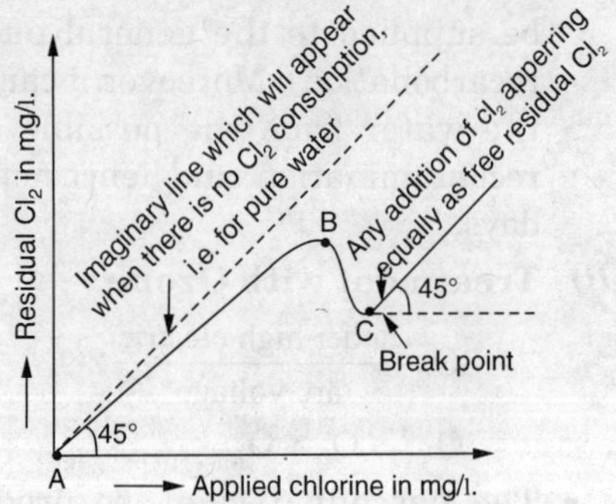

Fig:- Break point Chlorination

- If the addition of Cl_2 is continued beyond the point B, the organic matter present in water gets oxidised and therefore, the residual Cl_2 content suddenly falls down as shown by curve BC.
- Break point chlorination is a term which gives us an idea of the extent of chlorine added to water, beyond which any further addition of chlorine will appear as free residual chlorine.
- The D.P.D. test will indicate the quantum of total residual chlorine **"combined"** as well as **"free"**.
- The point C is the point beyond which any further addition of Cl_2 will appear equally as free chlorine. This point **"C"** is called the **break point**. The addition of Cl_2 beyond break point is called **break point chlorination**.
- It is a general practice to add Cl_2 beyond break point, and thus to ensure a residual of 0.2 to 0.3 mg/l of free chlorine.

(vi) **Super chlorination :** It indicates the addition of excessive amount of chlorine (*i.e.*, 5 to 15 mg./l.) to the water. This may be required in some special cases of highly polluted water, or during epidemics of water borne diseases.

- The huge quantity of Cl_2 is added in super chlorination is such as to give about 1 to 2 mg./l. of residual beyond the break point in the treated water.
- Sometimes, even higher doses may be used and the resultant water is dechlorinated after the end of the desired contact period, by using dechlorinating agent. This ensures the removal of bad tastes and odour caused by the presence of excess chlorine. Since residual Cl_2 is zero, so again chlorinate the water by a dose of about 0.1 to 0.2 mg./l.

(vii) **Dechlorination :** It means removing of chlorine from water. The dechlorination may be carried out by adding **certain chemicals** to water or by **simple aerating the water**. These chemicals are called **dechlorinating agents.**

Some common dechlorinating agents :

(a) Sulphur dioxide gas (SO_2);
(b) Activated carbon;
(c) Sodium thiosulphate (Na_2, S_2, O_3), cheapest dechlorinating agent
(d) Sodium metabisulphate ($Na_2S_2O_5$);
(e) Sodium sulphite (Na_2SO_3);
(f) Sodium bisulphite ($NaH\ SO_3$); and
(g) Ammonia (NH_4OH).

Testing of chlorine residuals.

(i) Orthotolidine test *(ii)* D.P.D. test
(iii) Chlorotex test *(iv)* Starch iodine test.

(vi) Water Softening

The reduction or removal of hardness from water is known as water softening.

Methods of removing temporary hardness.

(i) **Boiling :** When water is boiled, it leads to the peccipitation of $CalO_3$, which can be sedimented out in settling tank. But boiling cannot remove hardness caused by magnesium as $MgCO_3$ is fairly soluble in water

$$Ca(HCO_3)_2 \xrightarrow[+CO_2H_2O]{Heat} CaCO_3 \downarrow \text{insoluble}$$

(ii) **Addition of lime :**

$$MgCO_3 + Ca(OH)_2 \rightarrow \underset{(insoluble)}{Mg(OH)_2 \downarrow} + \underset{(insoluble)}{CaCO_3 \downarrow}$$

$$Mg(HCO_3)_2 + Ca(OH)_2 \rightarrow Ca(HCO_3) + Mg(OH)_2 \downarrow$$

$$Ca(HCO_3) + Ca(OH)_2 \rightarrow 2\,CaCO_3 \downarrow + 2H_2O$$

The calcuim carbonate and magenisum hydroxide are precipitated, and can be removed in the seidmentation tank.

Method of removing permanent hardness

Following three methods, which are commonly adopted for softening waters containing either permanent hardness or permanent as well as temporary hardness both

(i) **Lime-Soda process :** In this process lime $[Ca(OH)_2]$ and soda ash $[Na_2CO_3]$ are added to the hard water, which react with the Ca and Mg salts, to form insoluble precipitates of $CaCO_3$ and $Mg(OH)_2$ These precipitates can be sedimented out in sedimentation tank.

$$Ca(HCO_3)_2 + Ca(OH)_2 \rightarrow 2\,CaCO_3 \downarrow + 2H_2O$$

(a) $Mg(HCO_3)_2 + Ca(OH)_2 \rightarrow Ca(HCO_3)_2 + Mg(OH)_2 \downarrow$

(b) $MgCO_3 + Ca(OH)_2 \rightarrow Ca(OH)_2 + CaCO_3 \downarrow$

$$MgCl_2 + Ca(OH)_2 \rightarrow Mg(OH)_2 \downarrow + CaCl_2$$

$$MgSO_4 + Ca(OH)_2 \rightarrow Mg(OH)_2 \downarrow + CaSO_4$$

$$CO_2 + Ca(OH)_2 \rightarrow CaCO_3 \downarrow + H_2O$$

(free dissolved CO_2)

$$CaCl_2 + Na_2CO_3(Soda) \rightarrow CaCO_3 \downarrow + 2NaCl$$

$$CaSO_4 + Na_2CO_3 \rightarrow CaCO_3 + Na_2SO_4 \downarrow$$

- After sedimentation of $CaCO_3$ and $Mg(OH)_2$, a little quantity may remain as finely divided particles and may cause trouble by getting deposited on the filter or in the pipes of the distribution system. To present this, water be recarbonated by passing CO_2 gas through it if leaves the sedimentation tank.

$$CaCO_3 \downarrow + CO_2 + H_2O \rightarrow \underset{\text{soluble cal. bicarbonate.}}{Ca(HCO_3)_2}$$

$$Mg(OH)_2 + CO_2 \rightarrow MgCO_3 + H_2O$$

$$MgCO_3 + CO_2 + H_2O \rightarrow Mg(HCO_3)_2$$

- Many of the hard water contain the carbonate hardnes and very low amounts of non-carbonate hardness.
- For treating all such waters, lime is often the only chemical required.
- The equipment required for lime soda treatment is similar to that required for chemical coagulation.
- The effluents from the recarbonation plant are finally passed through a rapid gravity filter.

Dry sludge produced in mg/l = $[Ca_R + 0.58\,Mg_R + Li_A]$

where, Ca_R = calcium hardness removed in mg./l. (expressed as ($CaCO_3$)

Mg_R = magnesium hardness removed in mg./l. (expressed as $CaCO_3$)

Li_A = lime added in mg./l. (expressed as $CaCO_3$)

Alkalinity : It may be defined as the quantity of ions in water that will react to neutralise the hydrogen ion (H^+).

Alkalinity = $[HCO_3] + [2CO_3^{--} + [OH^-] - [H^+]$

where, [ ] refers the concentration in moles/L.

- The carbonate hardness can be considered to be equal to the alkalinity, provided there is no sodium alkalinity in water.
- It follows that if non-carbonate hardness is present in water, then its carbonate hardness will be equal to its alkalinity, since sodium alkalinity will be zero.
- When $pH > 11.5$, the entire alkalinity is in the form of CO_3^{--} and OH^-.

  When $7.5 < pH < 8.3$ the entire alkalinity is in the form of HCO^-_{3}.

  When $pH < 4.5$ the entire alkalinity is in the form Carbonic acid H_2CO_3.

***(ii)* Zeolite process or Base-exchange or Cation-exchange process.**

- General formula of zolites are $Na_2O\ Al_2O_3\ x\ SiO_2\ y\ H_2O$. The usual value of x is 2 or more and that of y of ranging amounts.
- During softening operation, the sodium ions of the zeolite get replaced by the calcium and magnesium ions present in hard waters. The Co and Mg zeolite can be regenerated into active sodium zeolite by titrating it with 5 – 10% solution of sodium chloride.
- Zeolite softeners may be either gravity or pressure filters; pressure filter type zeolite softeners being more common. The rate of filteration through a zeolite softener is about 300 l/minute/m^2 *i.e.* 18000 l./h./m^2.
- The zeolite process will result in a water of zero hardness, which generally is not suitable for public supplies. Therefore, only a portion of the water passing through the treatment plant is to be softenq and then mixed with unsoftened water to obtain the desired water quality.

Comparison of Lime-Soda and Zeolite processes of softening water supplies :

	Item	*Lime Soda Process*	*Zeolite Process*
1.	Size of plant	Bulky and Large	Compact and small.
2.	Skilled supervision if required.	Careful and skilled supervision is necessary for obtaining results.	Automatic and easy to operate.
3.	Sludge troubles, if any.	Large quantity of sludge is formed.	No sludge is formed.
4.	Post treatment if needed.	Recarbonation is a must after sedimentation and filtration.	No such post treatment is required.
5.	Results obtained	It can produce water of hardness not less than about 50 mg./l. Therefore, useful for public supplies only.	Water of zero hardness can be obtained.
6.	Removal of colour due to iron and manganese.	Can remove the colour due to iron and manganese, but only to a very small extent.	Can remove the colour due to Fe & Mn, although very costly for treating such waters, because the exhausted Mn and Fe zeolite cannot be regenerated.
7.	Effects on bacteria	The increased causticity may help in killing pathgenic bacteria.	No such advantage is offered by this process.
8.	pH of the treated water	Increases the pH value of water, which reduces the corrosion of distribution pipes.	pH value of the water is not affected.
9.	Economy.	Process is economical and can be easily combined with usual water treatment methods at slight extra cost.	Process is costlier.
10.	Hardness which can be treated	Excessively hard waters can be treated.	Raw waters with hardness greater than 800 mg./l. cannot be easily and economically treated.
11.	Allowable turbidity in raw waters.	Highly turbid and acidic water can be treated.	Highly turbid waters are difficult to be treated.

***(iii)* Demineralisation process for removing hardness:** It means removing the minerals from the water. This demineralised water, sometimes called *de-ionised water*, is as pure as distilled water, and is very suitable for industrial purposes.

This complete removal of minerals present in water can be carried out by first passing the water through a bed of cation exchange resins, and then through a bed of anion exchange resins.

(vii) Miscellaneous Treatments

The flouride content of the water should neither be less as to cause dental caries (early tooth decay) in children, during the calcination of their permanent teeth, nor it should be too high as to cause fauorisis (discolouration of teeth) and even deformation of bones (in extreme cases).

(i) **Removal of colours, odours and tastes from water.**

(a) **Aeration :** Under the process of aeration, water is brought in intimate contact with air, so as to absorb oxygen and to remove CO_2 gas. It may also help in killing bacteria, removing H_2S gas, iron and manganese to a certain extent, from the treated water.

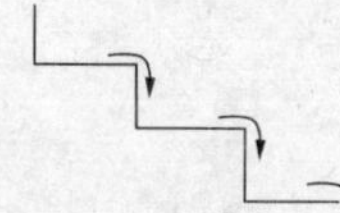

The aeration of water can be carried out in one of the following ways :

- By using spray nozzles
- By permitting water to trickle over cascades;
- By air diffusion;
- By using trickling beds : More efficient than casades.

(b) **Treatment with activated carbon :** It posses the property of absorbing and attracting impurities, such as gases, liquids and finely divided solids. It is widely used for removing testes and odours from public supplies. It is very useful for removing phenol type impurities.

- The activated carbon is available under various potential trade names, such as **Darco**, Nuchar etc. It is available in granular as well as powder forms.
- The activated carbon is mostly used in the powdered form and may be added to the water either before or after the coagulation, but before filtration.
- Activated carbon may also be used in the granular form as a filter media.

Advantage of activated carbon :

- It reduces the chlorine demand of treated water.
- It removes the organic matter present in water.
- It removes the tastes, odours and colours caused by the presence of Fe, Mn, phenols, excess chlorine, H_2S etc.
- It's overdose is not harmful.

(c) **Treatment with copper sulphate ($CuSO_4 \cdot 7\,H_2O$) :** Algae control compound.

The solution of $CuSO_4$ may be prepared and added just at the entry of water into the distribution system.

(d) **Treatment with oxidising agents :** The oxidising agents commonly used are $KMnO_4$, Cl_2, O_3 etc.

(ii) **Removal of iron and manganese from water.**

When present without combination with organic matter, they can be easily removed by aeration. On the other hand, when iron and maganese are present in combination with organic matter, it becomes difficult to break the bond between them and removal.

Manganese can be removed by activated alumina.

(iii) **Fluoridation and Defluoridation of water.**

Fluoridation : The process of adding fluoride compounds is called fluoridation.

Compounds used are : Sodium fluoride (NaF) (mostly used), sodium silico fluoride ($Na_2\,Si\,F_2$), hydrofluosilic acid ($H_2Si\,F_6$) etc.

Defluoridation : The process of removal of fluorine is called defluoridation process.

Process used are :

Lime soda process, cation exchange etc.

Fluorides is removed by manganese zeolite.

(iv) **Removal of radiotivity from water.**

(a) By phosphate coagulation method;

(b) By electrolysis method;

(c) By adding of clay materials to water; and

(d) By adding of metallic dusts of water.

(v) **Desalination of brackish water.**

The process of removing salts such as NaCl from water is known as **desalination.**

- Scarcity of water – Hongkong (import from other country)
- Desalination is a very costly process.
- National Chemical Laboratory (Poona), and Central Arid zones Research Institute (Jodhpur) are busy on this subject.

Methods of desalination :

(a) Desalination by evaporation and distillation

(b) Electrodialysis method

(c) Reverse osmosis method

(d) Freezing process

(e) Solar distillation method

(f) Other methods.

II. AIR POLLUTION

Air pollution is defined as "the presence in the outdoor atmosphere of one or more contaminants, such as dust, fumes, gas, mist, odour, smoke or vapour, in quantities, of characteristics, and of duration such as to injurious to human, plant or animal life or to property, or which unreasonably interferas with the comfortable enjoyment of life and property".

Composition of dry air at MSL in percentage.

Nitrogen	78.08
Oxygen	20.94
Argon	0.9340
Carbon dioxide	0.0315
Neon	0.0018
Helium	0.0005
Methane	0.0001 to 0.00015
Krypton	0.00011
Nitrous oxide	0.00005
Hydrogen	0.00005
Xenon	0.000008

Aerosol

Aerosol is a dispersion of solid or liquid particles of microscopic size in gaseous media, such as smoke, fog or mist.

Dust

Dust is a loose term applied to solid particles larger than colloidal particles and capable of temporary suspension in air or other gases. Dusts do not tend to flocculate except under electrostatic forces; they do not diffuse but settle under the influence of gravity. (Size : 1 – 200 μm)

Droplet

A droplet is a small liquid particle of such size and density as to fall under still conditions but which may remain suspended under turbulent conditions.

Fly-ash

Fly-ash is the finely divided particles of ash entrained in fuel gases arising from the combustion of fuel. The term is generally applied to the gas-borne ash from boilers using pulverised fuel (coal) firing.

Fog

Fog is a loose term applied to liquid dispersed aerosols in air by condensation.

Fume

Fume is the solid particles generated by condensation from the gaseous state, generally after volatization from melted substances, and often accompanied by a chemical reaction such as oxidation.
(Size: 0.1 to 1 μm)

Mist

Mist is a loose term applied to dispersions of liquid particles in atmosphere, the dispersion large size. (Size: 5 – 100 μm)

Particle

A particle is a small discrete mass of solid or liquid matter.

Smoke

Smoke is finely divided aerosol particles resulting from incomplete combustion. It consists mainly of carbon and other combustible material.
(Size: 0.01 to 1 μm)

Soot

Soot is collection of particles of carbon impregnated with 'tar' formed in the incomplete combustion of carbonaceous material.

Vapour

Vapour is the gaseous form of matter which normally exists in a liquid or solid state.

Classification of Air Pollution

Air pollution exists in three distinct categories

(1) Personal air pollution.
This refers to exposure of an individual to dust, fumes and gases. For example, when a person indulges in cigarette, cigar or pipe smoking.

(2) Occupational air pollution.
This represents the type of exposure of individuals to potentially harmful concentration of aerosols, vapours and gases in their working environment.

(3) Community air pollution.
This represents the most complex of the three varieties since it involves pollution from a variety of sources and contaminants and factors which cause adverse social, economic and health effects. Not only does community air pollution affect many individuals, but it can also exert a significant impact on man's total environment including plants, animals, property and the weather itself.

Sources of Air Pollution

There are two main sources of air pollution.

(1) Natural air pollution sources.

The atomosphere is polluted due to following natural causes.

(*i*) Wind-blown dust

(*ii*) Somke, fly-ash, gases from forest fires

(*iii*) Micro-organisms

(*iv*) Gases and odours from swamps and marshes

(*v*) Fog

(*vi*) Volcanic ash and gases

Pollutants from various natural sources :

- Pollutant Natural sources
- SO_2 Volcanoes
- H_2S Volcanoes, biological action in swamp areas
- CO Forest fires, ocean
- NO-NO_2 Bacterial action in soil
- NH_3 Biological decay
- Hydrocarbons
- (CH_4, etc.) Biological processes
- CO_2 Biological decay, release from oceans
- O_3 Oxygen and ozone in stratosphere and their downward transport

(2) Man-Made Sources.

Sources of pollution due to man's activities.

Source	*Category*	*Examples*	*Pollutants*
Dust-producing process	Crushing, grinding, screening Demolition Milling	Road mix plants Construction work Grain elevators	Mineral and organic particulates
Combustion	Fuel burning	Home oven, power plants	Oxides of sulphur, oxides of nitrogen.
	Motor vehicles	Cars, buses and trucks	Carbon monoxide, Smoke, flyash, organic vapour, metal oxide, particles and odours
	Refuse burning	Open burning of refuse	
Manufacturing processes	Metallurgical plant	Smelters, steel mills, non-ferrous industries, etc. of sulphur.	Metal fumes, lead, arsenic and zinc fluorides and oxides
Chemical plants	Petroleum refineries, pulp mills, fertiliser plants, cement mills	H_2S, oxides of sulphur, fluorides, organic vapour, particles, odours	
Agricultural activities	Crop spraying, dusting dusting	Pest and weed control	Organic phosphates, chlorinated hydrocarbons, arsenic, lead
	Field burning		Smokes, fly-ash and soot
Nuclear energy activities	Ore preparations	Crushing, grinding, screening	Uranium and dust beryllium
	Nuclear fissions Nuclear device testing	Nuclear reactors Atmospheric explosions	Agron-41 Radioactive fallous

Effects of Air Pollution

(1) Effect on vegetation : Vegetation exposed to atmosphere containing heavy amounts of sulphur dioxide is severly damaged. It is also affected by ozone and nitrogen dioxide.

(2) Effect on human beings and animals : People suffer from respiratory diseases when exposed to atmosphere in which the concentration of sulphur dioxide is in excess of safe limits, and their visibility is affected when exposed to higher temperature. The death rate of people suffering with cardiac or pulmonary diseases, when exposed to atmosphere contaminated with sulphur dioxide, is found to be higher.

Due to incomplete combustion of fuels from petrol engines, industrial operations, etc., carbon monoxide is liberated. When air containing CO is inhaled, the CO combines with the haemoglobin of the blood, depriving the tissues of oxygen. It has been found that when the carbonyl haemoglobin saturation level of blood is about 20%, it harms the heart and also impairs tissues restricting the oxygen. When in excess of 10%, it is found to cause headaches.

When the nitrogen dioxide level in the air is above tolerable limits, respiratory illness among children has been observed.

When oxygen content in the air is above 500 mg/m^3 and photochemical action is high, people have been found to have asthmatic attacks. Irritation of throat, nose or eyes are some other minor problems experienced in these conditions.

In general, air pollution decreases visibility. It is also found that it makes the town or city more cloudy, more foggy and is subjected to more acid rains.

(3) Effect on materials.

Air pollutants affect materials in the following ways and cause economic losses

(*i*) Abrasion

(*ii*) Deposition of materials

(*iii*) Direct chemical attack

(*iv*) Indirect chemical attack

(*v*) Corrosion

Effects of air pollution on materials.

S.No	*Material*	*Air Pollutants*	*Effect on materials*
1.	Metals	SO_2, acids, gases	Tarnishing of surface, loss of metal, etc.
2.	Paints	SO_2, H_2S and particulates	Discolouration
3.	Textiles	SO_2, acid, gases	Reduction in tensile strength
4.	Ceramics	-do-	Discolouration

AIR-POLLUTION CONTROL

The following methods are useful in controlling air pollution

(1) Control of air pollution by zoning.

In this method adopt the zoning system at the planning stage itself. A separate zone or area is set aside for industries thereby reducing the ill effects of air pollution on the urban dwellers.

The zoning of the industries is done based on the type of industries, their functions, etc. Every city has its own zoning rules.

Zoning of the industries may be based on

(*i*) **Functions :** These include industries such as linkages for industry, sidings, etc.

(*ii*) **Performance :** Here the industries are classified according to their nuisance value.

(*a*) Traffic congestion

(*b*) Abnoxious and hazardous

(*c*) Industrial nuisance such a smoke, noise, dust, odour, etc.

Separate areas may be earmarked according to their performance as stated.

In India, the zoning system varies from city to city. For instance, in Industrial Estate of Bangalore, three zones are provided for light, medium and large industries. Further, large industries are not encouraged. In Delhi also large industries are not permitted.

(2) Air-pollution control at the source.

The air-pollution problems can be minimised at the source by the following four ways:

(*i*) **Raw material substitution :** If one raw material results in a pollution problem while a substitute material does not, obviously the substitute would be more desirable. The raw material may contain an ingredient which is not essential but is a pollution source. If the non-essential ingredients can be removed prior to processing the raw material, the pollution pzotential can be minimised.

e.g. use low-sulphur fuels to replace high-sulphur fuels.

(*ii*) **Process modifications.** Pollution reduction can frequently be achieved by new or modified processes.

e.g. use of exhaust hoods and ducts over several types of industrial ovens has allowed the recovery of valuable solvents that could have become air pollutants.

(*iii*) **Equipment alterations.**

Equipment alterations such as the use of floating roof tanks rather than vented tanks can cut down on evaporation losses. Newer types of equipment are less pollution-prone.

e.g. basic oxygen furnaces that are replacing the open-hearth furnaces in the steel industry, pose less of a pollution problem.

(*iv*) **Removal of pollutants at source:** Sometime costly control equipment is necessary to remove pollutants from the main gas stream. In such cases it is simpler to remove pollutants at the source. It is normally more economical to remove these pollutants while they are present in relatively higher concentrations rather than at some point away from the source where the pollutants are diluted by gases from other processes or air.

(3) Controlling Air Pollution by Devices.

Due to different process in industries, various type of gases are liberated alongwith particulates. To arrest these entering the atmosphere, control devices are used depending on the collection capacity and processes used by the particular industry.

Types of devices used for dust collections based on the method of their removal.

(*i*) **Internal separators.**

These devices separate the dust in the gases. These are manufactured in various shapes and sizes.

Following types are commonly used :

(*a*) ***Gravity-settling chamber.*** This consists of a chamber in which the dust is separated from the gas by reducing the velocity of the gas.

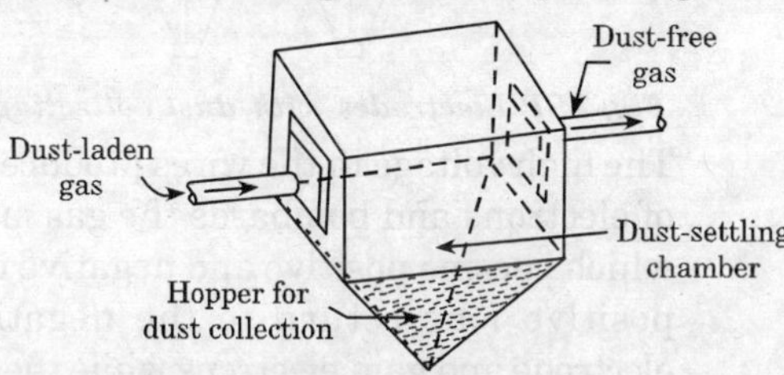

Fig. Gravity settling chamber

Due to this, the dust particles settle down in the chamber. As the size of the chamber for very low velocities of the gas required is very large and cost is prohibitive, the velocity in the chamber is generally kept between 0.3 to 3.0 m/sec. By this the coarser particles are removed. The gravity-settling chamber are capable of removing only the large particles of size 25 to 50 μm dia.

(*b*) ***Cyclone:*** When a gas travels in a double vertex, the particles contained in the it are separated. The cyclone works on this principle.

The gas is first allowed to spiral down at the inner surface and then it spirals upwards at the central portion of the cyclone. Due to inertia, the dust particles tend to settle on the surface of the cyclone wall. From here they are led away to the receiver.

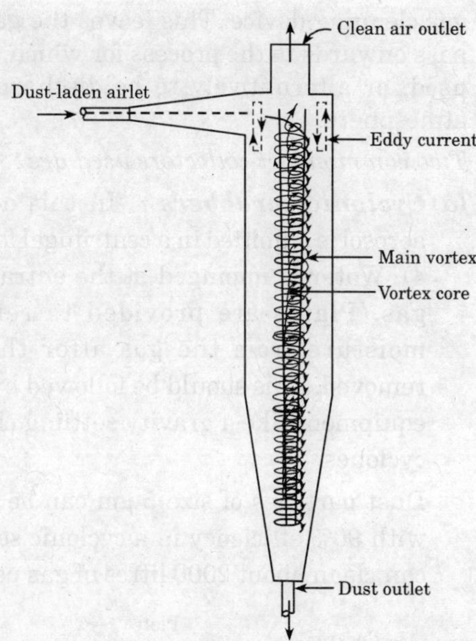

Cyclones are very efficient and can handle a number of operations. They are suitable for removing particles of size of 10–40 μm.

(*c*) ***Fabric filters :*** Here, the gas with the dust is allowed to pass through a fabric (cloth) to which the dust gets attached. If the gas is flowing at low velocity and contains considerable amount of larger particulates, these settle down by sedimentation. Fine particles are also attached to the fabric due to electrostatic charges.

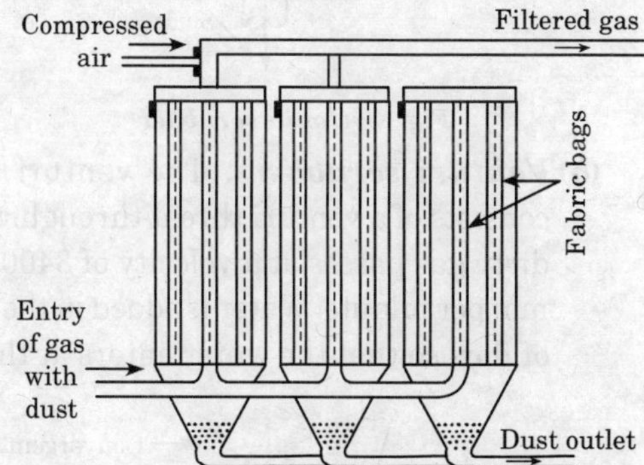

These bags are fitted with hopper at bottom. The gas enters from the bottom through the hopper. The heavy particles settle down in the hopper due to gravity. Finer particles are deposited on the fabric of the bag. For clearing the bags, compressed air is blown in the reverse direction.

(*ii*) **Wet-collection devices:**

Wet washers and scrubbers are devices using mixed phases of gas and liquid. The object of the scrubber or washing device is to transfer suspended particulate matter in the gas to the scrubbing liquid which can readily removed by the gas cleaning device. This leaves the gas clean to pass onwards to the process for which it is being used, or alternatively to be discharged to the atmosphere.

Two common wet-collectors used are :

(a) *Cyclonic scrubbers :* In this device, the aerosol is admitted in a centrifugal fashion (Fig 4). Water is impinged at the entrance of the gas. Plates are provided to remove the moisture from the gas after the dust is removed. This should be followed by a control equipment like a gravity-settling chamber or cyclones.

Dust particles of size 5 μm can be separated with 90% efficiency in a cyclonic scrubber. It can clean about 2000 litres of gas per minute.

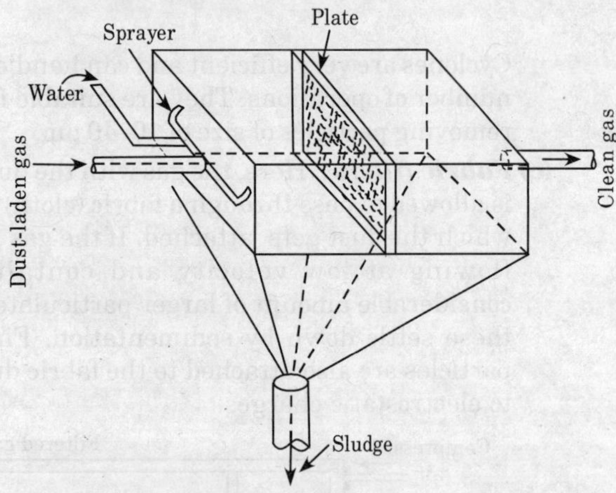

Fig. Cyclonic scrubber

(b) *Venturi scrubbers.* The venturi scrubber consists of a venturi throat through which the dirty gas passes at a velocity of 3400 to 12600 mm per minute. Water is added in the direction of flow so that the water enters at the throat.

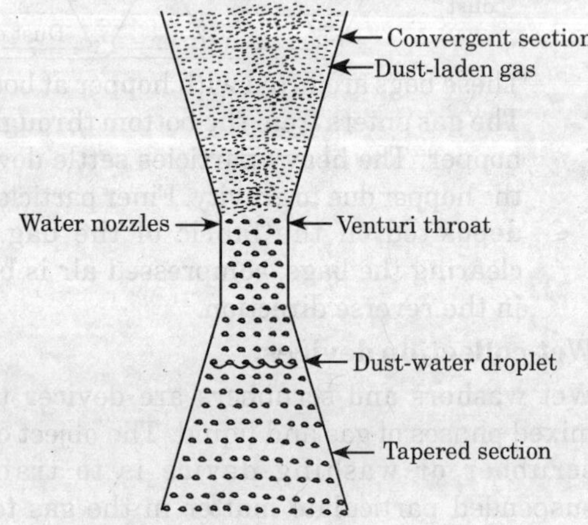

Fig. Venturi scrubber

The venturi scrubber can clean about 4000 litres of gas per minute. The efficiency is about 99% and can clean very fine particles.

If the moisture has to be removed from the gas, a cyclonic separator is used after the venturi scrubber.

***(iii)* Electrostatic precipitator.**

The electrostatic precipitator is a device by which the dust in a gas is removed by electrostatic attractions.

The gas is allowed to enter the electrostatic precipitator through narrow vertical gas passages which are formed by parallel rows of grounded collecting electrodes. Insulated high-voltage wires of about 40-50 kV are placed in the centre of each passage. The dirty gas thus passes between the high-voltage wires and the grounded plates.

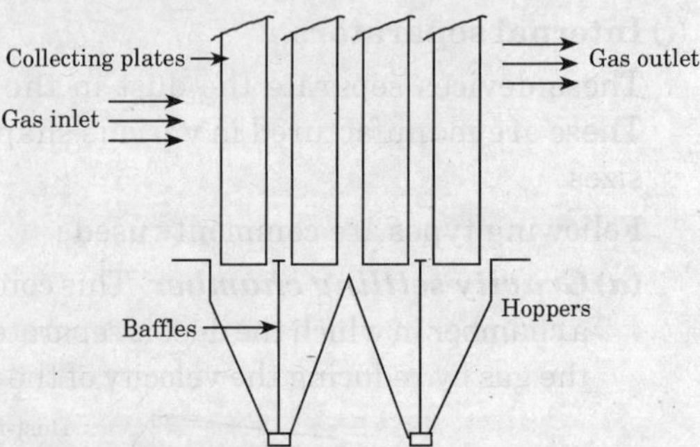

Fig. ESP Electrodes with dust collecting hoppers

The high voltage in the wires produces billions of electrons and bombards the gas molecules, which become positive and negative ions. The positive ions return to the negative wire electrode and gain electrons while the negative ions combine with the dust particles and make them negative ions.

The negatively charged dust particles collect at the positively charged plates.

When the thickness of the dust layer increases to more than 6 mm, the electrical attraction becomes weak. A sharp gap is given which causes the dust layer to separate and fall down into the hopper.

The electrostatic precipitator has an efficiency of 99.9% and can clean up to 150,000 litres of gas per minute at a temperature of 600° C.

(4) Air pollution control by stacks.

When small quantities of air pollutants are released at a source, these can be absorbed without producing noticeable pollution. However, if the quantity of pollutants released is large, and the air has a limited capacity, the pollution becomes high. If the pollutants are carried away to some distance or taken to high altitudes, they are reduced in concentration by diffusion and dilution. The pollutants are taken to high altitudes by means of stacks.

Diffusion of pollutant in air depends on the following factors :

(*i*) Atmospheric temperature

(*ii*) Speed and direction of wind

The height and diameter of stack required is designed to keep the ground level concentration within permissible limits. The concentration at ground level varies inversely with the square of the stack height and is maximum at a distance of 5-10 m stack height.

Some authors suggest the following

(a) The height of the stack must be 2.5 times the height of the surrounding buildings and

(b) The velocity of the exit gases should not be more than 20 m/sec.

(5) Air pollution control by vegetation.

To reduce the spreading of air pollutant emanating from industrial sources, growing green vegetation around the industry has been recommended by many scientists. Studies (Waren 1973, Fleming 1967) indicate that there are large differences among species vis-a-vis the response to air pollutants. Hence cultivation of pollution resistant species represents the best possibility of reducing injury by air pollutants. The degree of resistance depends on type of pollutant.

III. Noise Pollution

Noise is a characteristic of an environment, and is usually defined as unwanted sound. The unwanted sound certainly produces several undesirable effects on our body health, and it can therefore, be called a pollutant.

Noise can also be defined as that unwanted sound pollutant which produces undesirable physiological and psychological effects in an individual, by interfering with one's social activities like work, rest, recreation, sleep, etc.

It is a generalised fact that noise of sufficient intensity and duration can induce health problems like temporary and some-times permanent hearing loss, besides causing several other diseases like general annoyance, irritation, disturbance, headaches, insomnia, fatigue, mental torture, nausea, high blood pressure, high pulse rate, greater perspiration, etc.*

Characteristics of Sound and its Measurement.

We know that sound is produced in the environment by alternating pressure changes in the air, and is caused by the vibrations of solid objects or separation of fluids, as they pass over, around, or through holes in solid objects. These vibrations cause the surrounding air to undergo compression, then rarefaction, again compression, then rarefaction, and so on. Such alternating compression and rarefaction of the surrounding air produces sound waves which propagate in the form of sinusoidal path, as shown in Fig. (a) and (b).

Fig. *(a)* shown the time between the successive peaks or troughs of oscillation is called **the period** (P), and its inverse, which represents the number of times a peak arrives in one second, is called the **frequency** (*f*). Hence

$$P = \frac{1}{f}$$

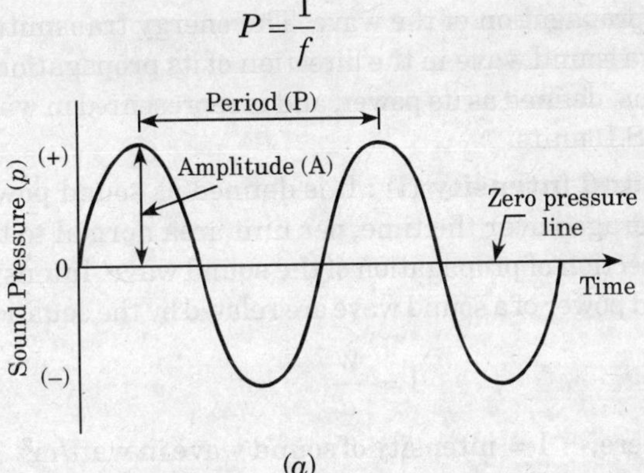

(a)

Fig. *(b)* shows the distance between successive peaks or troughs is called the **wave length** (λ), which is related to frequencey (*f*) by the relation

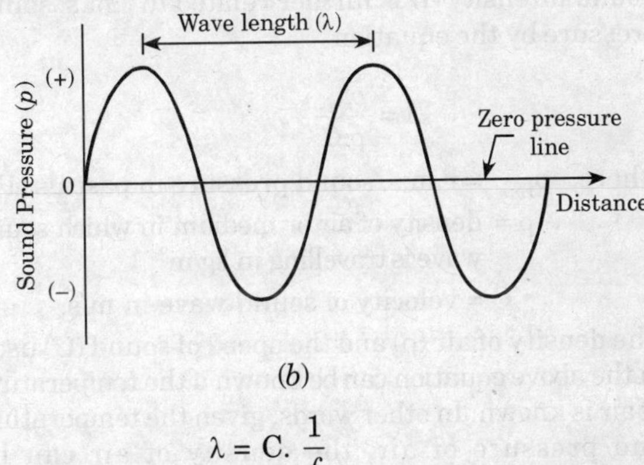

(b)

$$\lambda = C.\,\frac{1}{f}$$

where C = velocity of the sound wave.

The amplitude (A) of the wave is the height of the peak sound pressure measured above or below the zero pressure line. The equivalent pressure of such a sine wave is represented by root mean square pressure (p_{rms}) as

$$p_{rms} = \sqrt{p_{(t)}^2} = \sqrt{\frac{1}{T} \cdot \int_0^T p_{(t)}^2 dt}$$

where $p_{(t)}$ = pressure at any time t.

The r.m.s. sound pressure is, thus, obtained by adding the squares of amplitude values at small time intervals, and dividing the total by the averaging time, and finally taking the square root of the total. This works out equal $\frac{A}{\sqrt{2}}$ for a regular sine wave.

The sound pressure (p_{rms}) is further related to atmospheric pressure and barometric pressure by the equation

Sound pressure

= Total atmospheric pressure — barometric pressure

Power of sound (W) : It is defined as the rate of doing work by a travelling sound wave in the direction of propagation of the wave. The energy transmitted by a sound wave in the direction of its propagation is thus, defined as its power, and is represented in watts in S.I. units.

Sound intensity (I) : It is defined as sound power averaged over the time, per unit area normal to the direction of propagation of the sound wave. Intensity and power of a sound wave are related by the equation.

$$I = \frac{W}{a}$$

where, I = intensity of sound wave in watt/m^2

W = power of sound wave in watts

a = unit area perpendicular to the direction of wave motion.

Sound intensity *(I)* is further related to r.m.s. sound pressure by the equation

$$I = \frac{p_{rms}^2}{\rho . C}$$

where, p_{rms} = r.m.s. sound pressure in pascals (Pa)

ρ = density of air or medium in which sound wave is travelling in kg/m^3

C = velocity of sound wave in m/s.

The density of air (ρ) and the speed of sound (C) used in the above equation can be known if the temperature of air is known. In other words, given the temperature and pressure of air, the density of air can be determined from the standard tables; and the speed of sound in air at 101.325 kPa may be determined by the equation

$$C = 20.05 \sqrt{T}$$

where, T = absolute temperature in kelvin (K) and C is in m/s.

Levels of Noise :

The sound pressure of the faintest sound that can be heard by a normal healthy individual is about 20 micro-pascal (μ - Pa), and the loudest sound produced by a Saturn rocket at the lift off stage is about 200 Pa. This astronomical variation in sound pressure (varying from 20 μ - Pa to 200 Pa) is usually avoided by expressing sound pressure on a scale based on the log of the ratio of the measured sound pressure and a reference standard pressure. Measurements on this scale are called **levels**.

sound level, $L = \log_{10} \frac{Q}{Q_0}$ (bels)

where, Q = measured quantity of sound pressure, or sound power, or sound intensity

Q_o = reference standard quantity of sound pressure, or sound power, or sound intensity, as case may be

L = sound level in bels (B)

The unit of sound level is turns out to be a rather large unit, a smaller unit of **decibels (dB)** is generally used.

$$1 \text{ dB} = \frac{1}{10} \text{B}$$

Hence, when sound level is expressed in decibels, the above equation reduces to

$$L = 10. \log_{10} \frac{Q}{Q_o} \text{ (dB)}$$

- The reference standard quantity Q_0 in the above equation is taken to be equal to 20 μ Pa, when sound pressure is measured.

  Sound pressure level,

$$L_p = 10 \,.\, \log_{10} \left(\frac{p_{rms}}{20\mu Pa}\right)^{2*}$$

or $$L_p = 20 \log_{10} \left(\frac{p_{rms}}{20\mu Pa}\right)$$

  The sound pressure levels so measured are reported as dB *re* : 20 μ*Pa*.

- Similarly, the reference standard quantity Q_0 in the above equation is taken to be equal to 10^{-12} watts, when sound power is measured.

  Sound power level,

$$L_w = 10 \log_{10} \left(\frac{W}{10^{-12}}\right)$$

  The sound power levels so computed are reported as dB *re* : 10^{-12} W.

- Similarly, the reference standard quantity Q_0 is taken to be equal to $10^{-12}\ \frac{W}{m^2}$, when sound intensity level is measured.

Sound intensity level,

$$L_I = 10 \log_{10}\left(\frac{I}{10^{-12}}\right)$$

Out of the three terms given above, *sound pressure level* on reference scale of 20 μ*Pa*, is usually adopted to express sound levels in decibels.

Averaging Sound Pressure Levels :

The average value of the various recorded sound pressure levels (L_p) at a particular place over a given period cannot be computed by simple averaging due to log scale involved in their values.

Average pressure level,

$$\overline{L}_p = 20 \log \frac{1}{N} \sum_{n=1}^{n=N} (10)^{L_n/20}$$

where, $\overline{L}_p$ = Average sound pressure level in dB re : 20μPa

N = Number of measurement readings.

L_n = *n*th sound pressure level in dB *re.* 20 μPa.

n = 1, 2, 3......... N.

Types of Sound :

(*i*) **Continuous noise :** It is an uninterrupted sound level that varies less than 5 dB during the entire period of observation. A running fan is an example of such a sound.

(*ii*) **Intermittent noise :** It is a noise which continues for more than 1 second and is then interrupted for more than 1 second. A drilling machine used by a dentist produces such type of sound.

(*iii*) **Impulse noise :** It is characterised by a change of sound pressure of atleast 40 dB within 0.5 second with a duration of less than one second. The noise produced from firing of a weapon would fall in this category.

Noise Rating Systems :

A noise may consist of different types of sounds with different pressure levels operating for different time intervals. The frequencies of these sounds may also vary. The combined resultant noise will infact be responsible for determining the human response and degree of annoyance caused by it. The combined impact of different sound pressures lasting for different periods is therefore attempted to be worked out by using some statistical measures, such as L_N and L_{eq} systems.

L_N Concept :

The parameter L_N is a statistical measure indicating how frequently a particular sound level is exceeded. The value of L_N will represent the sound pressure level that will exceed for N% of the gauging time. When L_N is plotted against N (where N = 1, 2, 3, ... 100%), a cumulative distribution curve, is obtained.

L_{eq} Concept :

L_{eq} is defined as the constant noise level, which, over a given time, expands the same amount of energy, as is expanded by the fluctuating levels over the same time. This value is expressed by the equation:

$$L_{eq} = 10 \log \sum_{i=1}^{i=n} (10)^{\frac{L_i}{10}} \times t_i$$

where, n = total number of sound samples

L_i = noise level of any *i*th sample

t_i = time duration of *i*th sample, expressed as fraction of total sample time.

The *equivalent noise level* (L_{eq}) constitutes an important parameter for evaluating the impact of fluctuating noises of all kinds, such as from aircraft, street and road traffic, rail traffic, industrial machines, sports stadiums, play grounds, etc.

Moreover, the duration in hours, over which L_{eq} is worked out for a given site, is further mentioned in bracket, such as $L_{eq(8)}$ which means that L_{eq} is based on 8-hour measurement; when, however, no such time is mentioned, then L_{eq} always corresponds to one hour measurement.

Noise Level Standards

The prescribed noise standards generally put a limit either on L_{eq} or L_N values. Different such limiting values are then prescribed for different areas.

e.g. example, VIP and serene areas will impose lower limiting values as compared to those for commercial or industrial areas within a city. The usually prescribed limiting L_{eq} values for different areas of a city is of the order of 40 to 70 decibels.

Table (*a*) and (*b*) show two sets of noise standards, which have been laid down in USA. The first standards developed by *U.S. Federal Highway Administration* are the levels prescribed for newly planned highways through different types of areas. These levels are above those that would be absolutely harmless, but are below those of many existing highways.

Table *(a)*. Noise standards laid down by U.S. federal highway administration for highways in new delopments

Land use category	***Exterior design noise level dB(A)****		***Description of land use category***
	L_{eq} ***or*** L_{10}		
A	57	60	VIP and other protected areas, where serenity and quietness is to be maintained
B	67	70	Residence, hotels, schools, hospitals, picnic areas, play grounds, parks, etc.
C	72	75	Developed lands and properties not included in A and B category, such as commercial and industrial areas.
D	No limit	No limit	Undeveloped lands
E	52 (interior)	55 (interior)	Public meeting halls, schools, libraries, churches, hospitals, etc.
*Either L_{eq} or L_{10}, based on 1 hour samples, is to be used.			

Table *b*. has been evolved by U.S. *Environmental Protection Agency* and shows the limiting noise levels for different types of areas for indoor as well as outdoor noises, that should be maintained for adequately safeguarding public health over long periods (accounting annual average levels in L_{eq} values).

Table (*b*). Average yearly energy Levels (L_{eq}) identified as requisite to protect public health and welfare with an adequate margin of safety.

Types of areas	*Measure*	*Indoor*		*To protect against both effects (b)*	*Outdoor*		*To protect against both effects (b)*
		Activity interference	*Hearing loss consideration*		*Activity interference*	*Hearing loss consideration*	
(1)	(2)	(3)	(4)	(5)	(6)	(7)	(8)
Residential with out side space and farm residences	L_{dn} $L_{eq}(24)$	45	70	45	55	70	55
Residential with no outside space	L_{dn} $L_{eq}(24)$	45	70	45			
Commercial	$L_{eq}(24)$	(*a*)	70	70(*c*)	(*a*)	70	70(*c*)
Inside transportation	$L_{eq}(24)$	(*a*)	70	(*a*)			
Industrial	$L_{eq(24)}(d)$	(*a*)	70	70(*c*)	(*a*)	70	70(*c*)
Hospitals	L_{dn} $L_{eq(24)}$	45	70	45	55	70	55
Educational area	$L_{eq(24)}$ $L_{eq(24)}(d)$	45	70	45	55	70	55
Recreational areas	$L_{eq(24)}$	(*a*)	70	70(c)	(*a*)	70	70(*c*)
Farm land and general unpopulated land	$L_{eq(24)}$				(*a*)	70	70(*c*)

Codes:

(*a*) Since different types of activites appear to be associated with different levels, identification of a maximum level for activity interference may be difficult except in those circumstances where speech communication is a critical activity.

(*b*) Based on lowest level.

(*c*) Based only on hearing loss.

(*d*) An $L_{eq(8)}$ of 75 *d*B may be identified in these situations so long as the exposure over the remaining 16 hour per day is low enough to result in negligible contribution to the 24-hour average, that is, no greater than an L_{eq} of 60 *d*B.

- Explanation of identified level for hearing loss. The exposure period that results in hearing loss at the identified level is a period of 40 years.

Table (*c*). Acceptable noise levels for residential areas, as per I.S. code.

S. No.	*Acceptable outdoor noise levels in residential areas*		*S. No.*	*Acceptable indoor levels for various types of buildings*	
	Location	*Noise levels dB(A)*		*Location*	*Noise levels dB(A)*
1.	Rural areas	25 – 35	1.	Radio and TV studios	25 – 30
2.	Suburban areas	30 – 40	2.	Music rooms	30 – 35
3.	Urban Residential areas	35 – 45	3.	Hospitals, class rooms, auditoria	35 – 40
4.	Residential and business urban areas	40 – 50	4.	Apartments, hotels, homes Conference rooms, small offices	35 – 40
5.	City areas	45 – 55	5.	Court rooms, private offices, libraries	45 – 50
6.	Industrial areas	50 – 60	6.	Large public offices, banks, stores, etc.	45 – 50
			7.	Restaurants	50 – 55

The acceptable outdoor noise levels in different types of residential areas, as well as the acceptable indoor noise levels for various types of buildings, as recommended by *Indian standard code* IS: 4954 – 1968, are given in table *c*.

In order to legally enforce control on noise levels, the GOI has notified **the Noise Pollution (Regulation and Control) Rules 2000,** under *the Environment (Protection) Act, 1986,* Under these Rules, Ambient Air Quality Standards in respect of Noise, have been specified in respect of different types of areas uses (such as industrial area, commercial area, residential area and silence zones), as shown in Table (*d*)

Table (*d*). Ambient air quality standards in respect of noise.

Area Code	*Category of Area / Zone*	*Limits in dB (A) Leq*	
		Day Time	*Night Time*
A	Industrial Area	75	70
B	Commercial Area	65	55
C	Residential Area	55	45
D	Silence Zone	50	40

Note:

1. Day time shall mean from 6.00 a.m. to 10.00 p.m.
2. Night time shall mean from 10.00 p.m. to 6.00 a.m.

3. Silence zone is an area comprising not less than 100 metres around hospitals, educational institutions, courts, religious places or any other area which is declared as such by the competent authority.

4. Mixed categories of areas may be declared as one of the four above mentioned categories by the competent authority.

Sources of Noise and their Noise Levels :

Outdoor noise is usually produced by the following sources:

(1) *Traffic* including air traffic, road traffic, and sea-shore and inland water traffic

(2) *Industries*

(3) *Other miscellaneous activities*

Traffic Noise :

The amount and type of noise produced by traffic is largely dependent upon the type of traffic.

Table *(e)*. Noise levels of different sources of traffic.

S.No.	*Source of Noise*	*Noise level in dB*
1.	Air traffic	
	(*i*) Jet aircraft at take off stage at about 300m	100 – 110
	(*ii*) Propeller type aircraft at take off stage at about 300 m	90 – 100
2.	Rail traffic (at about 30 m)	90 – 110
3.	Heavy road traffic (highway)	80 – 90
4.	Medium road traffic (main streets)	70 – 80
5.	Light road traffic (side streets)	60 – 70

Table *(f)*. GOI noise standards for different types of vehicles.

S. No.	*Type of vehicles*	*Noise level in dB*
1	Two wheelers	80
2	Cars	82
3	Passenger or commercial vehicles	
	(*i*) upto 4 MT (Tonnes)	85
	(*ii*) between 4 MT to 12 MT	89
	(*iii*) More than 12 MT	91

Industrial Noise :

Noise is the essential by-product of industry; its intensity and nature being dependent upon the type of the industry. Industrial noises are usually produced by rotating, reciprocating or any other types of machinery, or by high pressure high velocity gases, liquids or vapour involved in the industrial processes. The usual noise level of the industries is of the order of 60 to 95 decibels.

Noise Produced by Other Sources :

Several other human activities, such as blarring of loud-speakers and sirens, shouting of hawkers, playing of children, general life and activity, ringing of temple and church bells, etc. do produce noises of different levels, tones and spectra.

Noise Abatement and Control :

Exposure of mankind to the day by day increasing noise. Nuisance must be reduced and abated, if its adverse effects on human health are to be controlled. The society must therefore be protected from the harmful effects of noise by devising and implementing ways and means for the abatement of noises.

There are certain noises which can be kept under control by legal laws and ordinances, and there are others which have to be damped and attenuated by the use of good technology and town planning. For example, the noises produced by motor vehicles can be controlled to some extent by proper maintenance of vehicles, which can be ensured only by prescribing maximum permissible noise levels for different types of automobiles, through Motor Vehicles Act. Similarly, Industrial noises, can be brought under the control of Factories Act by specifying maximum permissible noise levels and other checks. Similarly, public blarring of loud-speakers and playing of radio sets at loud levels can be prevented by general legal laws of public nuisance or laws specifically made for noise pollution. Yet however, there exist several other noises which have become part and parcel of our modern life. All such noises are to be reduced by better design technology to be used in the modern day gadgets like fans, air-conditioners, washing machines, refrigeratiors, mixers and grinders, etc.

Another very important method for abating noise effects on mankind is to use proper town planning techniques, and thus, to ensure construction of houses and offices away from the major sources of noise. Proper segregation, zoning and separation of residential complexes from the commercial and industrial ones, by means of physical barriers, roads, railway lines, parks or green belts, do constitute an important aspect of such good town-planning.

The noises produced by automobiles and trains, being the biggest noise nuisance in a modern city life, can be abated by construction of walls on both sides of roads and railway lines. Raising of such obstructions and barriers in between the noise sources (automobiles) and residences, may considerably reduce the noise levels reaching the residences. Attenuation of up to 15 decibels is possible in this manner.

When $D \geq R$ and $R >> H$, the noise reduction may also be calculated by the equation:

$$\text{Noise reduction (dB)} = 10 \log_{10}\left(\frac{20\,H^2}{\lambda R}\right)$$

where, H = height of the barrier wall.

λ = wavelength of sound.

D = distance between barrier and the receiving point.

Raising of thick and high vegetation and tree growing along sides of roads and railway lines, offers offer cheaper barriers to cause such noise reductions.

Locating the noisy sources on the downwind side of the residences, may be another important consideration in good town planning, because noise will then travel farther in the downwind direction away from the residences.

Noise levels in residential buildings can be reduced to some extent by offsetting the building from the main or street roads by a suitable distance. The farther is this distance, the better will be the attenuation, because the intensity of noise gets reduced with increase in distance.

Objective Type Questions

1. The chlorine demand of a water sample was found to be 0.5 mg/lt. The amount of bleaching powder containing 30% available chloride to be added to treat one litre of such a water sample is

(*a*) 1.67 (*b*) 1.92

(*c*) 1.01 (*d*) 1.36

2. A water treatment work treats 6000 m^3 of water per day. If it consumes 20 kg chlorine per day, then chlorine desage would be

(*a*) 2.33 mg/lit (*b*) 5 mg/lit

(*c*) 4 mg/lit (*d*) 3.33 mg/lit

3. A city supply of 16000 cubic metres of water per day treated with chlorine with dosage of 0.6 ppm. For this purpose the requirement of 30% bleaching powder per day would be

(*a*) 32 kg (*b*) 16 kg

(*c*) 18 kg (*d*) 22 kg

4. If the average daily consumption of a city is 100,000 m^3, the maximum daily consumption on peak hourly demand will be

(*a*) 100, 000 m^3 (*b*) 150,000 m^3

(*c*) 180,000 m^3 (*d*) 270,000 m^3

5. The polluted water is one which

(*a*) contains pathogenic bacteria

(*b*) consists of undesirable substances rendening it unfit for drinking and domestic use.

(*c*) is safe and suitable for drinking and domestic use.

(*d*) is contaminated.

6. The population of a town in three consecutive years are 5000, 7000 and 8400 respectively. The population of the town in the fourth consecutive year according to geometrical increase method is

(*a*) 9500 (*b*) 9800

(*c*) 10100 (*d*) 10920

7. If the total hardness of water is greater than its total alkalinity, the carbonate hardness will be equal to

(*a*) total alkalinity

(*b*) total hardness

(*c*) total hardness–total alkalinity

(*d*) non-carbonate hardness

8. The dissolved oxygen level in natural unpolluted waters, at normal temperature is found to be of the order of

(*a*) 1 mg/litre (*b*) 10 mg/litre

(*c*) 100 mg/litre (*d*) 1000 mg/litre

9. The most common cause of acidity in water is

(*a*) carbon dioxide (*b*) oxygen

(*c*) hydrogen (*d*) nitrogen

10. Standard EDTA (Ethylene Diamine Tetra Acetic Acid) solution is used to determine the

(*a*) hardness in water

(*b*) turbidity in water

(*c*) dissolved oxygen in water

(*d*) residual chlorine in water

11. The process in which the chlorination is done beyond the break point is

(*a*) pre chlorination

(*b*) post chlorination

(*c*) super chlorination

(*d*) break point chlorination

12. The rate of filtration of pressure filters is

(*a*) less than that of slow sand filters

(*b*) in between the filtration rate of slow sand filters and rapid sand filters

(*c*) greater than that of rapid sand filters

(*d*) equal to that of slow sand filters

13. The effective size of sand particles used in slow sand filters is

(*a*) 0.25 to 0.35 mm (*b*) 0.35 to 0.60 mm

(*c*) 0.60 to 1.00 mm (*d*) 1.00 to 1.80 mm

14. Which of the following methods of analysis of water distribution system is most suitable for long and narrow pipe system ?

(*a*) Circle method

(*b*) Equivalent pipe method

(*c*) Hardy cross method

(*d*) Electrical analysis method

15. The type of valve which is provided to control the flow of water in the distribution system at street corners and where the pipe lines intersect is

(*a*) check valve (*b*) sluice valve

(*c*) safety valve (*d*) scour valve

16. If the diameter of the main pipe is taken less than economic diameter, then

1. head loss will be high
2. cost of pipe will be less
3. cost of pumping will be less of these statements.

(*a*) only 1 is correct
(*b*) 1 and 2 are correct
(*c*) 1 and 3 are correct
(*d*) 1, 2 and 3 are correct

17. What is the primary purpose of the Basel Convention?

(*a*) Protecting wetlands
(*b*) Managing hazardous waste
(*c*) Regulating air quality
(*d*) Conserving marine biodiversity

18. Two samples of water A and B have pH values of 4.4 and 6.4 respectively. How many times more acidic sample A is than sample B ?

(*a*) 0 (*b*) 50
(*c*) 100 (*d*) 200

19. When the coefficient of rugosity is increased from 0.01 to 0.02, the gradient of a pipe of a given diameter to carry the same flow at the same velocity will be

(*a*) increased by 4 times
(*b*) increased by 2 times
(*c*) decreased by $\sqrt{2}$ times
(*d*) decreased by 4 times

20. A city supply of 1500 cubic metres of water per day is treated with a chlorine dosage of 0.5 ppm. For this purpose, the requirement of 25% bleaching powder per day would be

(*a*) 300 kg (*b*) 75 kg
(*c*) 30 kg (*d*) 7.5 kg

21. Figure given below shows roughly, the daily mass curves of supply to and demand from an elevated service reservoir (ESR).

The minimum required capacity of the reservoir is given by

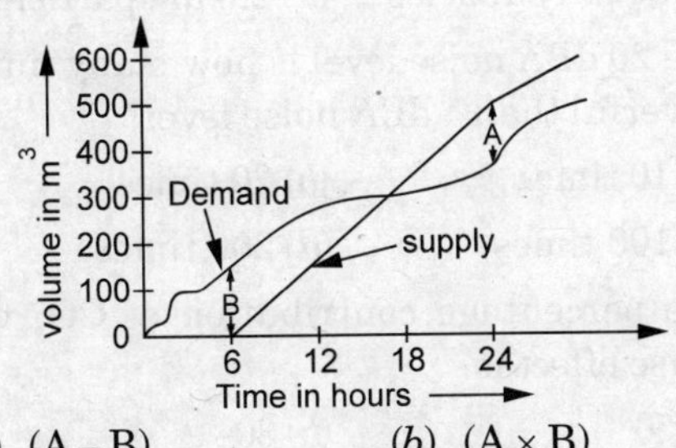

(*a*) (A – B) (*b*) (A × B)
(*c*) (A + B) (*d*) Larger of A or B

22. The water supply to a house begins with the connection of the service pipe with the municipal water mains. The connection comprises

1. Stop cock
2. Goose neck
3. Ferrule
4. Water meter

The correct sequence of these connections is

(*a*) 1, 2, 3, 4 (*b*) 3, 1, 2, 4
(*c*) 3, 2, 1, 4 (*d*) 1, 2, 4, 3

23. The chlorine demand of a water sample was found to be 0.2 mg/l. The amount of bleaching powder containing 30% available chlorine to be added to treat one litre of such a water sample is

(*a*) 0.67 mg (*b*) 0.06 mg
(*c*) 1.33 mg (*d*) 0.14 mg

24. When two identical centrifugal pumps are operating in series on a common rising main, then

(*a*) the pressure in the rising main will be nearly doubled, while the discharge will remain the same.
(*b*) the discharge will be nearly doubled, while the pressure remains the same.
(*c*) discharge as well as the pressure in the rising main will be doubled.
(*d*) discharge as well as the pressure in the rising main will increase but not become double.

25. An aeration basin with a volume of 400 m^3 contains mixed liquor with suspended solid concentration of 1000 mg/l. The amount of mixed liquor suspended solids in the tank is

(*a*) 500 kg (*b*) 250 kg
(*c*) 600 kg (*d*) 400 kg

26. Under natural conditions of flow an unpolluted river would contain

(*a*) more dissolved oxygen in summer than in winter
(*b*) less dissolved oxygen in summer than in winter
(*c*) more or less the same amount of dissolved oxygen in winter and summer.
(*d*) the least amount of dissolved oxygen during the floods.

27. Traps are used in household drainage system to

(*a*) prevent entry of foul gases in the house
(*b*) restrict the flow of water
(*c*) provide a partial vacuum
(*d*) trap the solid wastes

28. Two reservoirs at different levels are connected by two parallel pipes of diameter 2d and d. The ratio of the flows in the two pipes (large smaller) is

(*a*) $\sqrt{2}:1$ (*b*) 2 : 1

(*c*) 4 : 1 (*d*) $4\sqrt{2}$: 1

29. Area method of land filling is most suitable when

(*a*) area is unsuitable for excavation of trenches.

(*b*) adequate depth of cover material is available at the site.

(*c*) the water table is near the surface

(*d*) natural or artificial depressions exist in the vicinity.

30. If the total hardness and alkalinity of a sample of water are 300 mg/l and 100 mg/l($CaCo_3$ scale) respectively, then its carbonate and non-carbonate hardness (in units of mg/l) will be respectively

(*a*) 100 and 200 (*b*) 400 and 300

(*c*) 100 and 400 (*d*) 400 and zero

31. What is carbon footprint?

(*a*) measure of radioactivity from a fossil

(*b*) environmental impact because of used cells and batteries

(*c*) total sets of green house gas emissions by organization, individual etc.

(*d*) amount of carbon content in the organic compounds

32. Thermochemical decomposition of organic materials at high temperatures, in the absence of oxygen is called

(*a*) Pyrolysis (*b*) Thermolysis

(*c*) Caramelization (*d*) Catagenesis

33. Acid rain is caused by presence of which of the following gases in the atmosphere

(*a*) Nitrogen and oxygen

(*b*) Sulfur dioxide and Nitrogen oxide

(*c*) Carbon dioxide and Carbon-mono-oxide

(*d*) Ozone and argon

34. One of the main reason for depletion of ozone layer in the Earth's atmosphere is

(*a*) Green house gases

(*b*) Colloidal impurities

(*c*) CFC and halons

(*d*) Rockets and satellite launching vehicles

35. What is the value of total hardness acceptable in potable water as per Indian Standards?

(*a*) 0.3 (*b*) 3

(*c*) 30 (*d*) 300

36. Preventing rain water to run-off and its accumulation and deposition for re-use on site is called

(*a*) rain water collection

(*b*) micro-dams

(*c*) micro-accumulation

(*d*) rain water harvesting

37. Which of the following is biodegradable pollutant?

(*a*) DDT (*b*) BHC

(*c*) Cotton cloth (*d*) Mercury

38. BOD (Bio Chemical Oxygen Demand) of safe drinking water must be :

(*a*) 0 (*b*) 50 ppm

(*c*) 100 ppm (*d*) 200 ppm

39. Large scale deforestation decreases :

(*a*) Soil Erosion (*b*) Rain fall

(*c*) Drought (*d*) Global warming

40. The prescribed per capita water demand for small cities and towns is

(*a*) 135 litres per capita per day

(*b*) 200 litres per capita per day

(*c*) 150 litres per capita per day

(*d*) 180 litres per capita per day

41. In small water supplies such as army troops, private plants and swimming pools, the most common disinfectants used are

(*a*) chlorine dioxide and potassium permanganate

(*b*) ozone and uv rays

(*c*) iodine and bromine

(*d*) chlorine and bromine

42. The air pollution control device, cyclone is used for the removal of

(*a*) 100 μm particles (*b*) 10 μm particles

(*c*) 50 μm particles (*d*) 2.5 μm particles

43. The 20 dBA noise level is how many times more powerful than 1 dBA noise level?

(*a*) 10 times (*b*) 20 times

(*c*) 100 times (*d*) 200 times

44. The percentage contribution of CO_2 to green house effect is

(*a*) 50 (*b*) 30

(*c*) 18 (*d*) 10

45. Per capita water demand is
(*a*) average amount of daily water required by one person
(*b*) monthly average amount of daily water required by one person
(*c*) annual average amount of daily water required by one person
(*d*) weekly average amount of daily water required by one person

46. The permissible/desirable drinking water standard for total hardness is
(*a*) 200 mg/l (*b*) 300 mg/l
(*c*) 250 mg/l (*d*) 500 mg/l

47. In BOD_5 determination of sewage, the initial dissolved oxygen is measured to be 8.3 mg/l. However, after 5 day incubation at 20 °C temperature, the dissolved oxygen is found to be 2.3 mg/l. If the dilution factor is 1:60, the BOD_5 of the sewage would be
(*a*) 360 mg/l
(*b*) 260 mg/l
(*c*) cannot be determined
(*d*) 6.0 mg/l

48. The suspended solids present in surface water can be determined by
(*a*) gravimetric test
(*b*) colourimetric test
(*c*) titrimetric test
(*d*) spectrophotometric test

49. Length to width ratio of rectangular sedimentation tank should be
(*a*) 3 : 4 (*b*) 3 : 1
(*c*) 4 : 1 (*d*) 1 : 5

50. In PERT analysis, event means
(*a*) Start or finish of a task
(*b*) Time taken for a task
(*c*) End of an activity
(*d*) Work involved in the project

51. In potable water, the dissolved oxygen is stipulated as-
(*a*) <6μg/l (*b*) >6μg/l
(*c*) <6mg/l (*d*) >6mg/l

52. In reference to Acid rain, what is correct statement
(*a*) The pH value is below 5.6
(*b*) It occurs due to presence of sulphuric acid or nitric acid in the atmosphere
(*c*) Maximum acid is due to strong Carbonic Acid
(*d*) Acid rain affects ecosystem

53. The working principle of turbidimeter is based on
(*a*) reflection of light (*b*) refraction of light
(*c*) scattering of light (*d*) adsorption of light

54. The major source of carcinogenic hydrocarbon, benzo (*a*) pyrene present in urban atmosphere is
(*a*) construction activities
(*b*) road traffic
(*c*) bursting of crackers
(*d*) domestic burning

55. The prescribed permissible noise level, Leq for commercial area at day time is
(*a*) 75 dBA (*b*) 50 dBA
(*c*) 55 dBA (*d*) 65 dBA

56. The global warming is caused by green house gases, which are
(*a*) CO, N_2O, CH_4 and CFC
(*b*) CO_2, NO_2, CH_4 and H_2O
(*c*) CO_2, N_2O, CH_4 and H_2O
(*d*) CO_2, NO_2, CH_4 and CFC

57. Which of the following roles fly ash does not play in concrete
(*a*) Improving the workability
(*b*) Accelerating the strength gain
(*c*) Delaying the setting time of concrete
(*d*) Helps in long-term strength gain

58. One turbidity unit NTU is equal to
(*a*) 1.0 mg/l farmazin (*b*) 1.0 meq/l SiO_2
(*c*) 1.0 mg/l SiO_2 (*d*) 1.0 meq/l kaolin

59. The prescribed permissible noise level, Leq for residential area at day time is
(*a*) 65 dBA (*b*) 45 dBA
(*c*) 50 dBA (*d*) 55 dBA

60. Which of the following is not used as a supplementary cementations material?
(*a*) Fly ash (*b*) Gypsum
(*c*) Rice husk ash (*d*) Silica fume

61. According to IS 456, if the maximum aggregate size is increased from 20 mm to 40 mm, the minimum cement content requirement changes (in kg/cum) by
(*a*) –20 (*b*) 20
(*c*) –30 (*d*) 30

62. The turbidity in surface water is due to presence of
(*a*) dissolved organics
(*b*) colloidal material
(*c*) dissolved in organics
(*d*) dissolved colors

63. The prescribed permissible noise level, for residential area at night time is

(*a*) 45 dBA (*b*) 50 dBA
(*c*) 40 dBA (*d*) 55 dBA

64. The continuous exposure of high concentration of reparable suspended particulate matter may cause

(*a*) eye irritation
(*b*) kidney damage
(*c*) failure of respiratory system
(*d*) cardiac disease

65. The prescribed permissible noise level, Leq for commercial area at night time is

(*a*) 45 dBA (*b*) 65 dBA
(*c*) 50 dBA (*d*) 55 dBA

66. The pH of acid rain should always be less than

(*a*) 5.6 even after precipitation
(*b*) 7.0 after precipitation
(*c*) 6.5 after precipitation
(*d*) 4.2 after precipitation

67. The exposure of gaseous pollutant sulphur dioxide may cause

(*a*) bronchitis and pulmonary emphysema
(*b*) lungs failure and kidney damage
(*c*) gastrointestinal problem
(*d*) the irritation in alveoli of the lungs

68. The machine 'A' and machine 'B' produce equal noise levels, i.e., 60 dBA each. The summation of these two noise levels is

(*a*) 100 dBA (*b*) 66 dBA
(*c*) 63 dBA (*d*) 55 dBA

69. In stratosphere, the temperature increases with altitude due to presence of

(*a*) radicals (*b*) chlorofluorocarbons
(*c*) HCFCs (*d*) Ozone

70. Nuclear density guage can be used for all the following purposes, except

(*a*) Moisture content
(*b*) Wet density
(*c*) Dry density
(*d*) Standard penetration reading

71. What is the main goal of environmental education?

(*a*) To teach people about the environment.
(*b*) To help people protect the environment.
(*c*) To make people aware of the benefits of environmental protection.
(*d*) All of the above.

72. What are the three main components of environmental education?

(*a*) Knowledge, skills, and attitudes.
(*b*) Science, technology, and engineering.
(*c*) Economics, politics, and social justice.
(*d*) All of the above.

73. What are some examples of environmental education activities?

(*a*) Reading books about the environment.
(*b*) Visiting a nature center or museum.
(*c*) Participating in a community clean-up project.
(*d*) All of the above.

74. What are some of the benefits of environmental education?

(*a*) It can help people make informed decisions about their environmental impact.
(*b*) It can help people develop a sense of stewardship for the environment.
(*c*) It can help people build a stronger connection to nature.
(*d*) All of the above.

75. What is the role of environmental education in sustainability?

(*a*) It can help people understand the limits of the planet's resources.
(*b*) It can help people develop ways to live more sustainably.
(*c*) It can help people create a more sustainable future.
(*d*) All of the above.

76. Which of the following is NOT a goal of environmental education?

(*a*) To increase environmental awareness
(*b*) To teach people about environmental problems
(*c*) To promote sustainable lifestyles
(*d*) To make money

77. Which of the following is one of the three main components of environmental education?

(*a*) Knowledge (*b*) Skills
(*c*) Attitudes (*d*) All of the above

78. What is one of the most important things that environmental education can teach us?

(*a*) That we are all connected to the environment
(*b*) That our actions have a ripple effect on the planet
(*c*) That we need to take responsibility for our environmental impact
(*d*) All of the above

79. What is one way that environmental education can be used to promote sustainability?

(*a*) By teaching people about the importance of recycling and composting

(*b*) By encouraging people to conserve water and energy

(*c*) By promoting the use of public transportation

(*d*) All of the above

80. How can we make environmental education more accessible to everyone?

(*a*) By making it more affordable

(*b*) By making it more inclusive

(*c*) By making it more engaging

(*d*) All of the above

81. What is one of the most important challenges facing environmental education?

(*a*) Reaching a wide audience

(*b*) Making it effective

(*c*) Measuring its impact

(*d*) All of the above

82. What is one way that we can make environmental education more effective?

(*a*) By using real-world examples

(*b*) By making it hands-on

(*c*) By making it relevant to students' lives

(*d*) All of the above

83. How can we measure the impact of environmental education?

(*a*) By tracking students' knowledge and understanding of the environment

(*b*) By assessing students' attitudes towards the environment

(*c*) By measuring students' behavior towards the environment

(*d*) All of the above

84. What is one way that we can make environmental education more inclusive?

(*a*) By using culturally relevant materials

(*b*) By providing translations in multiple languages

(*c*) By making it accessible to people with disabilities

(*d*) All of the above

85. What is one way that we can make environmental education more engaging?

(*a*) By using games and activities

(*b*) By using technology

(*c*) By taking students on field trips

(*d*) All of the above

86. What is the primary goal of environmental education?

(*a*) To instill fear about environmental problems

(*b*) To teach people how to live in harmony with nature

(*c*) To provide scientific knowledge about the environment

(*d*) To promote specific environmental solutions

87. Which of the following is NOT a key component of environmental education?

(*a*) Awareness and sensitivity to the environment

(*b*) Knowledge and understanding of environmental issues

(*c*) Skills to identify and solve environmental problems

(*d*) Emotional detachment from the environment

88. What is the role of environmental education in promoting sustainable development?

(*a*) It provides scientific data for decision-making.

(*b*) It raises awareness about environmental consequences.

(*c*) It empowers individuals to make sustainable choices.

(*d*) It dictates specific environmental policies.

89. How can environmental education be made more effective in addressing environmental challenges?

(*a*) By focusing on academic knowledge and memorization

(*b*) By emphasizing hands-on experiences and real-world applications

(*c*) By adopting a one-size-fits-all approach

(*d*) By tailoring education to specific contexts and communities

90. What is the importance of incorporating cultural perspectives into environmental education?

(*a*) It promotes a universal understanding of environmental issues.

(*b*) It recognizes the diverse relationships between cultures and the environment.

(*c*) It establishes a single set of environmental values and practices.

(*d*) It prioritizes Western scientific knowledge over traditional ecological knowledge.

91. How can environmental education promote environmental justice?

(*a*) By focusing on individual actions and behaviors

(*b*) By addressing the disproportionate impact of environmental issues on marginalized communities

(*c*) By promoting economic development at the expense of environmental protection

(*d*) By blaming individuals for environmental problems without addressing systemic issues

92. What is the role of environmental education in promoting sustainable consumption patterns?

(*a*) It encourages the consumption of more goods and services.

(*b*) It promotes responsible consumer choices and reduces environmental impact.

(*c*) It emphasizes the need for economic growth over environmental protection.

(*d*) It prioritizes the production of environmentally harmful goods.

93. How can environmental education foster a sense of stewardship for the environment?

(*a*) By instilling fear and guilt about environmental problems

(*b*) By promoting a sense of responsibility and connection to nature

(*c*) By imposing strict regulations and restrictions

(*d*) By emphasizing individual consumer choices without addressing broader systemic issues

94. What is the primary objective of environmental engineering?

(*a*) Resource extraction

(*b*) Pollution prevention

(*c*) Energy production

(*d*) Urban planning

95. Which of the following is a greenhouse gas?

(*a*) Oxygen (O2) (*b*) Carbon dioxide (CO2)

(*c*) Nitrogen (N2) (*d*) Hydrogen (H2)

96. What is the purpose of a wastewater treatment plant?

(*a*) Energy production

(*b*) Water conservation

(*c*) Treating and purifying sewage

(*d*) Agricultural irrigation

97. What is the primary function of a landfill?

(*a*) Water storage (*b*) Waste disposal

(*c*) Air purification (*d*) Energy generation

98. Which air pollutant is a major contributor to acid rain?

(*a*) Carbon monoxide (CO)

(*b*) Sulfur dioxide (SO2)

(*c*) Nitrogen oxides (NOx)

(*d*) Particulate matter (PM)

99. What is the purpose of an environmental impact assessment (EIA)?

(*a*) Identifying endangered species

(*b*) Assessing the potential environmental effects of a project

(*c*) Monitoring air quality

(*d*) Analyzing geological formations

100. Which of the following is a renewable energy source?

(*a*) Coal (*b*) Natural gas

(*c*) Solar power (*d*) Nuclear energy

101. What is the primary purpose of the Clean Water Act?

(*a*) Regulating air quality

(*b*) Protecting water resources

(*c*) Controlling noise pollution

(*d*) Managing hazardous waste

102. Which of the following is a characteristic of sustainable development?

(*a*) Depleting natural resources

(*b*) Meeting current needs without compromising future generations

(*c*) Maximizing short-term profits

(*d*) Ignoring social equity

103. What is the primary role of wetlands in environmental engineering?

(*a*) Waste disposal (*b*) Flood control

(*c*) Habitat for wildlife (*d*) Industrial production

104. What is the main source of indoor air pollution in homes?

(*a*) Radon

(*b*) Carbon monoxide

(*c*) Volatile organic compounds (VOCs)

(*d*) Mold

105. Which of the following is a non-point source of water pollution?

(*a*) Industrial discharge pipe

(*b*) Wastewater treatment plant

(*c*) Urban stormwater runoff

(*d*) Sewage outfall

106. What is the purpose of a septic system?

(*a*) Electricity generation

(*b*) Solid waste disposal

(*c*) Wastewater treatment for individual homes

(*d*) Flood control

107. Which process is commonly used for groundwater remediation?

(*a*) Incineration (*b*) Bioremediation

(*c*) Desalination (*d*) Composting

108. What is the primary purpose of the Montreal Protocol?

(*a*) Banning nuclear weapons testing

(*b*) Protecting the ozone layer

(*c*) Regulating greenhouse gas emissions

(*d*) Managing marine pollution

109. What is the primary goal of the Kyoto Protocol?

(*a*) Reducing carbon dioxide emissions

(*b*) Protecting biodiversity

(*c*) Addressing deforestation

(*d*) Controlling marine pollution

110. Which air pollutant is associated with respiratory problems and asthma?

(*a*) Carbon dioxide (CO2)

(*b*) Ozone (O3)

(*c*) Nitrogen dioxide (NO2)

(*d*) Methane (CH4)

111. What is the primary function of a bioswale in stormwater management?

(*a*) Electricity generation

(*b*) Flood control

(*c*) Treating wastewater

(*d*) Filtering and slowing stormwater runoff

112. Which of the following is a sustainable transportation option?

(*a*) Single-occupancy vehicles

(*b*) Electric scooters

(*c*) Diesel-powered buses

(*d*) Large SUVs

Answers

1. (*a*)	**2.** (*d*)	**3.** (*a*)	**4.** (*d*)	**5.** (*b*)	**6.** (*d*)	**7.** (*a*)	**8.** (*b*)	**9.** (*a*)	**10.** (*a*)
11. (*d*)	**12.** (*c*)	**13.** (*a*)	**14.** (*b*)	**15.** (*b*)	**16.** (*b*)	**17.** (*b*)	**18.** (*c*)	**19.** (*a*)	**20.** (*c*)
21. (*b*)	**22.** (*c*)	**23.** (*a*)	**24.** (*a*)	**25.** (*d*)	**26.** (*b*)	**27.** (*a*)	**28.** (*d*)	**29.** (*c*)	**30.** (*d*)
31. (*c*)	**32.** (*a*)	**33.** (*b*)	**34.** (*c*)	**35.** (*d*)	**36.** (*d*)	**37.** (*c*)	**38.** (*a*)	**39.** (*b*)	**40.** (*a*)
41. (*c*)	**42.** (*b*)	**43.** (*c*)	**44.** (*a*)	**45.** (*c*)	**46.** (*b*)	**47.** (*c*)	**48.** (*a*)	**49.** (*b*)	**50.** (*a*)
51. (*a*)	**52.** (*b*)	**53.** (*c*)	**54.** (*b*)	**55.** (*d*)	**56.** (*c*)	**57.** (*b*)	**58.** (*c*)	**59.** (*d*)	**60.** (*b*)
61. (*c*)	**62.** (*b*)	**63.** (*a*)	**64.** (*c*)	**65.** (*d*)	**66.** (*a*)	**67.** (*a*)	**68.** (*c*)	**69.** (*d*)	**70.** (*d*)
71. (*d*)	**72.** (*a*)	**73.** (*d*)	**74.** (*d*)	**75.** (*d*)	**76.** (*d*)	**77.** (*d*)	**78.** (*d*)	**79.** (*d*)	**80.** (*d*)
81. (*d*)	**82.** (*d*)	**83.** (*d*)	**84.** (*d*)	**85.** (*d*)	**86.** (*b*)	**87.** (*d*)	**88.** (*c*)	**89.** (*b*)	**90.** (*b*)
91. (*b*)	**92.** (*b*)	**93.** (*b*)	**94.** (*b*)	**95.** (*b*)	**96.** (*c*)	**97.** (*b*)	**98.** (*b*)	**99.** (*b*)	**100.** (*c*)
101. (*b*)	**102.** (*b*)	**103.** (*c*)	**104.** (*c*)	**105.** (*c*)	**106.** (*c*)	**107.** (*b*)	**108.** (*b*)	**109.** (*a*)	**110.** (*c*)
111. (*d*)	**112.** (*b*)								

Explanations

1. 1 mg m of bleaching powder contains – 0.3 mgm of chlorine

1 mg m of chlorine will be = $\frac{1}{0.3}$ mgm of bleaching

$\therefore$ 0.5 mg m of chlorine will be = $\frac{1}{0.3} \times [0.5] = \mathbf{1.667}$

2. Chlorine dosage = $\left[\frac{20\times10^6}{6000}\right]\frac{mgm}{\text{lit}}$

= **3.33 mg m/lit**

3. Chlorine required= $16000 \times 10^3 \times 0.6 = 9.6$ kg

$\therefore$ Amount of bleaching powder required

$= \left[\frac{9.6}{0.3}\right] = \mathbf{32\ kg}$

4. The maximum daily consumption on peak hourly day or maximum day

= 2.7 × (Average demand)

= 2.7 × 100,000

= **2.70,000 m^3**

5. It contains undesirable substance and unfit for domestic use.

6. Average of percentage increase in previous year = $\frac{40+20}{2}$ = 30%

Population next year = $8400 + \frac{30}{100} \times 8400 = \mathbf{10920}$

7. The carbonate hardness is equal to total hardness if total hardness is equal to or less than total alkalinity.

The non carbonate harness = Total hardness – total alkanity.

8. Minimum required for aquatic life is 4 ppm

10. Hardness of water removed by zeolite process ; while bicarbonate hardness can be removed by boiling.

11. *Methods by which chlorination may be done :*

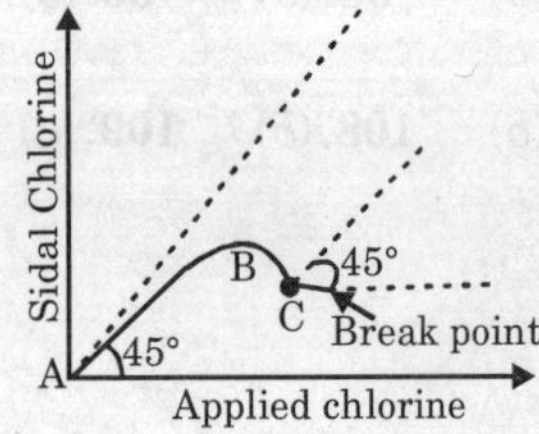

(*a*) Plain chlorination (*b*) Prechlorination

(*c*) Post chlorination (*d*) Double chlorination

(*e*) Break point chlorination

(*f*) Super chlorination (*g*) Dechlorination

12. It works on high pressure with pressure slightly above rapid sand filters.

13. In slow sand filters, rate of filtration is very slow and one of the major reason being its minute size. For rapid sand filters, the effective size of sand particles used is 0.35 to 0.60 mm.

14. In equivalent pipe system, first of all different small loops are replaced by single equivalent pipes having the same discharging capacities and causing the same head loss.

15. Sluice valves are usually placed at corners summits (3 – 5 km) interval.

16. If diameter is less than economic diameter, then cost of pipe will be less but head loss will be high. Hence cost of pumping will be more.

17. The Basel Convention aims to control the transboundary movement and disposal of hazardous waste.

18. Difference of pH = 6.4 – 4.4 = 2

Quantum of acidity = $(10)^2$ = 100 times more acidic

19. Velocity $\propto$ [R^2]

i.e. increased by 4 times.

20. Amount of chlorine required daily

$= \left[\frac{0.5 \times 15000 \times 10^3}{10^6}\right] = 7.5$ kg

Amount of bleaching powder required daily

$= \frac{7.5 \times 100}{25} = \mathbf{30\ kg}$

22.

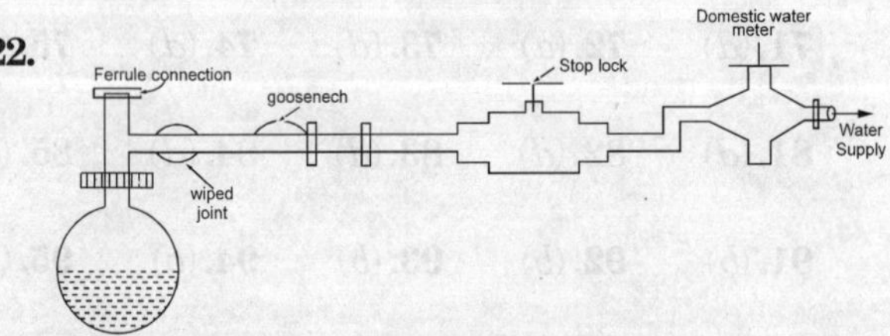

26. Dissolved oxygen in an unpolluted river will be equal to saturation D.O. which reduces with increase in temperature. Since temperature is more in summer than winter, an unpolluted river would contain less D.O. in summer than in winter.

31. A carbon footprint is historically defined as the total emissions caused by an individual, event, organisation, or product, expressed as carbon dioxide equivalent.

32. Pyrolysis is the thermal decomposition of materials at elevated temperatures in an inert atmosphere. It involves the change of chemical composition and is irreversible. The word is coined from the Greek-derived elements pyro "fire" and lysis "separating".

33. Sox and NOx are responsible for acid rain.

34. Chlorofluorocarbons (CFCs) and other halogenated **ozone depleting** substances (ODS) are mainly responsible for man-made chemical **ozone depletion**. The total amount of effective halogens (chlorine and bromine) in the stratosphere can be calculated and are known as the equivalent effective stratospheric chlorine (EESC).

35. 300 mg/l is the acceptable standard.

36. **Rainwater** harvesting is **the accumulation** and storage of **rainwater** for **reuse** on-**site**, rather than allowing it to **run off**.

37. Biodegradable pollutants: Those pollutants which can be broken down into simpler, harmless, substances in nature in due course of time (by the action of micro-organisms like certain bacteria) are called biodegradable pollutants. Cotton cloth is biodegradable pollutant.

38. A **water** supply with a **BOD** level of 1-2 ppm is considered to be very clean.

A **water** supply with a **BOD** level of 3-5 ppm is considered moderately **clean**. In **water** with a **BOD** level of 6-9 ppm, the **water** is considered somewhat polluted because there is usually organic matter present and bacteria are decomposing this waste.

39. Large scale deforestation decreases rain fall. **Drop in rainfall** occurs because **deforestation reduces** the natural recycling of moisture from soils, through vegetation, and into the atmosphere, from where it returns as□**rainfall.**

40. The prescribed per capita water demand for small cities and towns is 135 litres per capita per day.

41. The most common disinfectants are iodine and bromine. **Bromine** does not oxidize ammonia or other nitrogen substances. Hypobromous acid reacts with sunlight. When the pH value is between 7 and 8,5 dibromoamine is **the most common** form of **bromine**. Dibromoamine is almost as effective as free chlorine in killing microorganisms.

42. The most frequently used **Air Pollution Control Devices** for controlling **air pollution** emissions are Fabric filters (also called bag houses), **Cyclones** (or Multi **cyclones**), Wet scrubbers, Electrostatic Precipitator. Cyclone removes 10 mm particles.

43. On the **decibel** scale, the smallest audible **sound** (near total silence) is 1 dB. A**sound** 10 **times more powerful** is 10 dB. A **sound** 100 **times more powerful than** near total silence is **20** dB. A **sound** 1,000 **times more powerful than** near total silence is 30 dB.

44. They estimated that water vapor accounts for about 50% of Earth's greenhouse effect, with clouds contributing 25%, carbon dioxide 20%, and the minor greenhouse gases and aerosols accounting for the remaining 5%. In the study, the reference **model** atmosphere is for 1980 conditions.

45. Generally, it **means** the average amount of **water** each person in a particular area uses on a daily basis, expressed as "gallons **per capita per** day."

46. 300 mg/l is the permissible limit of the hardness.

47. Cannot be determined.

48. **Gravimetric analysis** is a technique through which the amount of an analyte (the ion being analyzed) can be determined through the measurement of mass.**Gravimetric** analyses depend on comparing the masses of two compounds containing the analyte.

49. A typical long **rectangular** tank have **length** ranging from 2 to 4 times their **width**.

50. *PERT event*: a point that marks the start or completion of one or more activities. It consumes no time and uses no resources. When it marks the completion of one or more activities, it is not "reached" (does not occur) until *all* of the activities leading to that event have been completed.

51. $<6 \mu g/l$

52. pH value is generally less than 4 and it occurs due to presence of sulphuric and nitric acid.

53. The Turbidity meter uses the principle of Nephelometry. As light of a known intensity is passed through a sample some of the light will be scattered by particles in the sample. A detector is placed at 90° to the sample to collect the scattered light. The intensity of the scattered light is compared to that of the source. This value is reported as a Nephelometric Turbidity Unit, or NTU. The meter is calibrated with Formazine standards of a known NTU.

54. Road traffic is the major source of carcinogenic hydrocarbon present in urban atmosphere.

55. The prescribed permissible noise level, Leq for commercial area at day time is 65 dBA.

According to Central Pollution Control Board,

Area Code	Category of Area	Limits in dB(A), Leq	
		Day time	Night time
A	Industrial area	75	70
B	Commercial area	65	55
C	Residential area	55	45
D	Silence Zone	50	40

56. Green house gases are the gas mixed in the atmosphere that absorbs the infrared radiation emitted by the earth's surface.

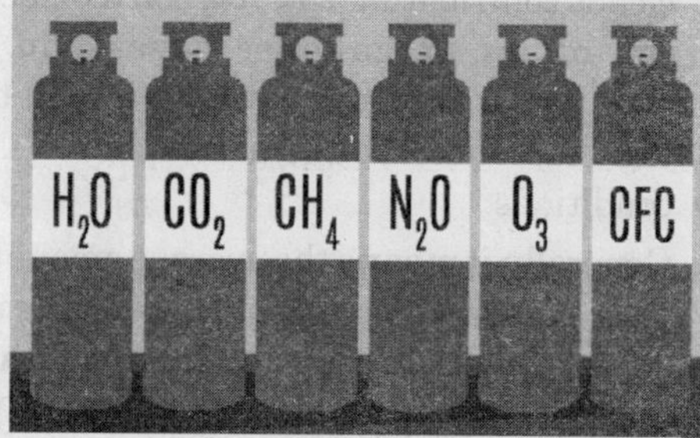

We are not accustomed to these gases because neither nitrogen nor oxygen, the two most abundant gases of the atmosphere (78% and 21%, respectively), that many of us have heard of, have this ability to intercept infrared radiation.

57. Fly ash never improves strength of concrete.

The advantages of using fly ash far outweigh the disadvantages. The most important benefit is reduced permeability to water and aggressive chemicals. Properly cured concrete made with fly ash creates a denser product because the size of the pores are reduced.

58. One turbidity unit NTU is equal to 1.0 mg/l SiO2.

59. The prescribed permissible noise level, Leq is 55 dBA.

According to Central Pollution Control Board,

Area Code	Category of Area	Limits in dB(A),	
		Day	Night
A	Industrial area	75	70
B	Commercial area	65	55
C	Residential area	55	45
D	Silence Zone	50	40

60. Gypsum is not used as a supplementary cementations material.

61. Turbidity in surface water is due to colloidal material.

63. The prescribed permissible noise level, Leq is 45 dBA.

According to Central Pollution Control Board,

Area Code	Category of Area	Limits in dB(A), Leq	
		Day time	Night time
A	Industrial area	75	70
B	Commercial area	65	55
C	Residential area	55	45
D	Silence Zone	50	40

64. Continuous exposure to suspended particles are harmful to the lungs and can cause failure of respiratory system.

65. The prescribed permissible noise level, Leq for commercial area at night time is 55 dBA.

According to Central Pollution Control Board,

Area Code	Category of Area	Limits in dB(A), Leq	
		Day time	Night time
A	Industrial area	75	70
B	Commercial area	65	55
C	Residential area	55	45
D	Silence Zone	50	40

66. pH of acid rain should always be less than 5.6 even after precipitation.

67. The exposure of gaseous pollutant sulphur dioxide may cause bronchitis and pulmonary emphysema.

69. In the stratosphere, temperature increases with altitude. The reason is that the direct heat source for the stratosphere is the Sun. A layer of ozone molecules absorbs solar radiation, which heats the stratosphere. The amount of ozone present in the ozone layer is tiny, only a few molecules per million air molecules.

70. Nuclear density gauge can be used for all the following purposes except standard penetration reading.

71. The main goal of environmental education is to help people understand and appreciate the environment, and to take action to protect it.

72. Environmental education should provide people with the knowledge they need to understand the environment, the skills they need to take action to protect it, and the attitudes they need to support environmental protection.

73. There are many different ways to learn about the environment. Environmental education activities can be formal or informal, and they can take place at home, in school, or in the community.

74. Environmental education can have a positive impact on individuals, communities, and the planet.

75. Environmental education is essential for achieving sustainability. It can help people understand the challenges we face, and it can help us find solutions to those challenges.

76. Environmental education is not a business venture. Its primary goal is to educate people about the environment and to promote sustainable practices.

77. Environmental education should provide people with the knowledge they need to understand the environment, the skills they need to take action to protect it, and the attitudes they need to support environmental protection.

78. Environmental education can teach us many important things about the environment and our relationship to it. By understanding the interconnectedness of all living things, we can learn to make more sustainable choices that will benefit the planet.

79. Environmental education can play a vital role in promoting sustainability by teaching people about the importance of environmental protection and by providing them with the tools they need to make sustainable choices.

80. Environmental education should be accessible to everyone, regardless of their age, background, or income level. By making it more affordable, inclusive, and engaging, we can ensure that everyone has the opportunity to learn about the environment and to make a positive impact on the planet.

81. Environmental education faces a number of challenges, including reaching a wide audience, making it effective, and measuring its impact. However, these challenges can be overcome with careful planning and implementation.

82. Environmental education is most effective when it is relevant to students' lives and when it provides them with opportunities to learn through experience.

83. The impact of environmental education can be measured in a number of ways, including tracking students' knowledge, attitudes, and behavior.

84. Environmental education should be inclusive and accessible to everyone, regardless of their background or ability.

85. Environmental education can be made more engaging by using a variety of teaching methods and techniques. By making it fun and interactive, we can encourage students.

86. Environmental education aims to foster a deeper understanding of the environment and our relationship to it, encouraging individuals to make informed decisions and adopt sustainable practices to protect and conserve natural resources.

87. While environmental education provides knowledge and skills, it also seeks to cultivate a sense of empathy and connection to the natural world, motivating individuals to take action and advocate for environmental protection.

88. Environmental education plays a crucial role in sustainable development by equipping individuals with the knowledge, skills, and values to make informed decisions that minimize their environmental impact and contribute to a more sustainable future.

89. Effective environmental education goes beyond classroom lectures and rote learning. It provides opportunities for students to engage with the environment through field trips, experiments, and community projects, fostering a deeper understanding and appreciation for the natural world.

90. Environmental education should be inclusive and culturally sensitive, acknowledging the unique perspectives, knowledge, and practices that different cultures have developed in their interactions with the natural world.

91. Environmental education should recognize and address the unequal distribution of environmental burdens, empowering communities to advocate for environmental justice and equitable access to a healthy environment.

92. Environmental education empowers individuals to make informed decisions about their consumption habits, encouraging them to reduce waste, choose sustainable products, and adopt eco-friendly practices.

93. Environmental education cultivates a sense of stewardship by fostering understanding, empathy, and appreciation for the natural world, encouraging individuals to take proactive steps to protect and conserve the environment for future generations.

94. Environmental engineering focuses on preventing and controlling pollution to protect the environment and human health.

95. CO2 is a significant greenhouse gas contributing to climate change.

96. Wastewater treatment plants remove contaminants from sewage before releasing it into the environment.

97. Landfills are designated areas for the disposal of solid waste.

98. SO2 emissions can lead to the formation of acid rain.

99. EIAs help identify and mitigate potential environmental impacts of development projects.

100. Solar power is derived from the sun and is considered a renewable energy source.

101. The Clean Water Act is aimed at regulating and protecting water quality in the United States.

102. Sustainable development seeks to balance economic, social, and environmental goals.

103. Wetlands play a crucial role in supporting biodiversity and providing habitat for various species.

104. VOCs released from household products can contribute to indoor air pollution.

105. Non-point sources are diffuse and arise from various sources, such as runoff from streets and agricultural fields.

106. Septic systems treat and dispose of household wastewater on-site.

107. Bioremediation involves using microorganisms to break down and remove contaminants from the environment.

108. The Montreal Protocol aims to phase out the production and consumption of ozone-depleting substances.

109. The Kyoto Protocol is an international treaty focused on mitigating climate change by reducing greenhouse gas emissions.

110. NO2 is a common air pollutant that can irritate the respiratory system.

111. Bioswales are designed to capture and treat stormwater, promoting infiltration and reducing runoff.

112. Electric scooters are a more sustainable transportation option compared to traditional gasoline-powered vehicles.

CHAPTER 11 Basics of Computers and Applications

PERSONAL COMPUTERS

Personal computers can be categorized by size and portability as :

1. Desktop computers
2. Laptop or notebooks
3. Personal Digital Assistants (PDAs)
4. Portable computers
5. Tablet computers
6. Wearable computers

Uses.

Personal computers are normally operated by one user at a time to perform such general purpose tasks as word processing, Internet browsing, Internet faxing, e-mail and other digital messaging , multimedia playback, computer game play, computer programming, etc. The user of modern personal computer may have significant knowledge of the operating environment and application programs, but is not necessarily interested in programming not even able to write programs for the computer. Therefore, most software written primarily for personal computers tends to be designed with simplicity of use, or "user-friendliness" in mind. However, the software industry continuously provide a wide range of new products for use in personal computers, targeted at both the expert and the non-expert user.

COMPUTER COMPONENTS

1. Computer case with power supply (usually sold together)
2. Motherboard
3. Processor with fan (usually sold together)
4. At least one memory card
5. Mass storage
6. Keyboard and mouse for input
7. Monitor for output

The motherboard connects everthing together. The memory card(s), graphics card and processor are mounted directly onto the motherboard (the processor in a socket an the memory and graphics cards in an expansion slot). The mass storage is connected to it with cables. Same for keyboard and mouse, except that they are external and connect to the back plate. The monitor is also connected to the back plate, except not (usually) directly to the motherboard, but to a connector in the graphics card.

Mass storage.

It can be

(*i*) Hard disk
(*ii*) Floppy drive or zip drive (both with media)
(*iii*) Optical drive (CD or DVD)

The operating system (e.g., Microsoft Windows, Linux or many others) can be located on either of these, but typically it son one of the hard disks. Alive CD is also possible, but very slow and used for either installation of the OS or problem solving.

A *typical* computer also has

(*i*) Sound card (*ii*) Network card
(*iii*) Modern and possibly router

Common additions, connected on the outside (peripherals).

Printer; Scanner; Webcam; Speakers; Microphone; Headset; Card reader; Gaming devices such as a joystick Several functions (implemented by chipsets) can be integrated into the motherboard, such as typically USB and network, but also graphics and sound. But even if these are present, a separate card can be added if what is available isn't sufficient.

The graphics and sound card can have a break out box to keep the analog parts away from the electromagnetic radiation inside the computer case. For really large amounts of data, a tape drive can be used or (extra) hard disks can be put together in an external case.

These components can usually be put together with little knowledge, to build a computer. If something shouldn't go somewhere, it usually doesn't fit (this used to not always be the case in the past) and if it does fit it can usually do little harm.

Most personal computers are standardized to the point that purchased software is expected to run with little or no customization for the particular computer. Many PCs are also user-upgradeable, especially desktop and workstation class computers. Devices such as main memory, mass storage, even the motherboard and central processing unit may be easily replaced by an end user. This upgradeability is, however, not idefinite due to rapid changes in the personal computer industry, A PC that was considered top-of-the-line five or six years prior may be impractical to upgrade due to changes in industry standards. Such a computer usually must be totally replaced once it's no longer suitable for its purpose. This upgrade and replacement cycle is partially related to new releases of the primary mass-market operated system, which tends to drive the acquisition of new hardware and tends of obsolete previously serviceable hardware (see planned obsolescence).

The hardware capabilities of personal computers can sometimes be extended by the addition of expansion cards connected via an expansion bus. Some standard peripheral buses often used for adding expansion cards in personal computers as of 2005 are PCI, AGP (a high-speed PCI bus dedicated to graphics adapters), and PCI Express. Most personal computers as of 2005 have multiple physical PCI expansion slots. Many also include an AGP bus and expansion slot or a PCI Express bus and one or more explansion slots, but few PCs contain both buses.

Motherboard

The motherboard (or mainboard) is the primary circuit board within a personal computer. Many other components connect directly or indirectly to the motherboard. Motherboards usually contain one or more CPUs, supporting circuitry - usually integrated circuits (ICs) providing the interface between the CPU memory and input/output peripheral circuits, main memory, and facilities for initial setup of the computer immediately after being powered on (often called boot firmware or, in IBM PC compatible computers, a BIOS). In many portable and embedded personal computers, the motherboard houses nearly all of the PC's core components. Often a motherboard will also contain one or more peripheral buses and physical connectors for expansion purposes. Sometimes a secondary daughter board is connected with the motherboard to provide further expandibility or to satisfy space constraints.

Main Memory

A PC's main memory (i.e., its primary store) is fast storage that is directly accessible by the CPU, and is used to store the currently executing program and immidiately needed data. PCs use semiconductor Random Access Memory (RAM) of various kinds such as DRAM or SRAM as their primary storage. Which exact kind depends on cost/performance issues at any particular time. Main memory is much faster than mass storage devices like hard disks or optical discs, but is usually volatile, meaning it does not retain its contents (instructions or data) in the absence of power, and is much more expensive for a given capacity than is most mass storage. Main memory is generally not suitable for long-term or archival data storage.

Mass storage devices store programs and data even when the power is off; they do require power to perform read/write functions during usage. Although semiconductor flash memory has dropped in cost, the prevailing form of mass storage in personal computers is still the electromechanical hard disk.

The disk drives use a sealed Head/Disk Assembly (HDA) which was first introduced by IBM's "Winchester" disk system. The use of a sealed assembly allowed the use of the positive air pressure to drive out particles from the surface of the disk, which improves reliability.

Video Card

The video card- otherwise called a graphics card, graphics adapter or video adapter - processors and renders the graphics output from the computer to the computer display, also called the Visual Display Unit (VDU), and is an essential part of the modern computer.

MICROPROCESSOR

A microprocessor is a multipurpose programmable logic device that reads binary instructions from a storage device called memory, accepts binary data as input and process data according to those instructions and provides results as output. A typical programmable machine can be represent with three components : microprocessor, memory, and I/O.

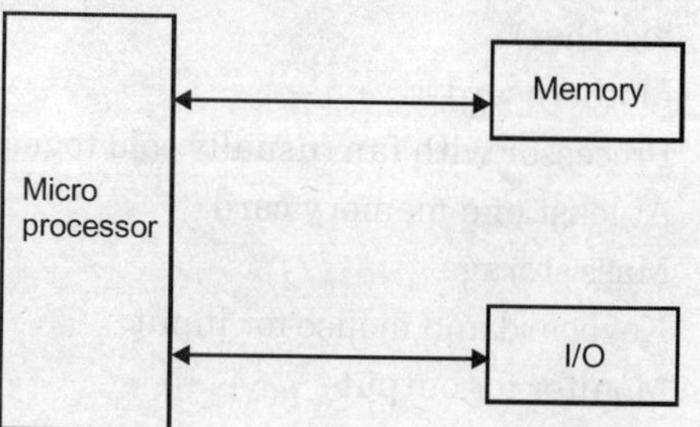

These three components work together or interact with each other to perform a given task, thus they comprise a system

Hardware

The physical components of this system are called hardware.

Software

A set of instructions written for the microprocessor to perform a task is called *a program* and a group of programs is called software.

APPLICATIONS.

The microprocessor applications are classified primarily in two categories

(*i*) In Re-programmable systems.

Such as microcomputers, the microprocessor is used for computing and data processing. These systems, include general purpose microprocessor capable of handling large data. Mass storage device (disks), and peripherals such as I/O device (printer).

(*ii*) Embedded system.

In embedded systems, the microprocessor is part of a final product and is not available for reprogrammable to the end user. A copying machine is a typical example of an embedded system. The microprocessors used in these systems are generally categorised as

(*a*) Microcontrollers that include all the components like microprocessor, memory and I/O.

(*b*) Integrated microprocessor that include various devices such as timers and various types of I/O on a chip.

(*c*) General purpose microprocessor with discrete components such as microprocessor, memory and I/O.

Embedded systems can also be increased as products that use microprocessor to perform their operations they are called as microprocessor based products.

e.g. washing machines, dish washers, automobile dashboard controls, traffic light controllers, and automatic testing instruments.

BINARY DIGIT.

The microprocessor operates in binary digits 0 and 1, also known as bits. Bit is an abbreviation for the term binary digit. Those digits are represented in terms of electrical voltages in the machine : generally 0 represents one voltage level and 1 represents another. The digits 0 and 1 are also synonyms with low and high respectively.

Each microprocessor recognizes and processes a group of bits called the word and microprocessor are classified according to their word length.

Memory

Memory is like the pages of a notebook with space for a fixed number of binary numbers on each line. However these pages are generally made of semi-conductor material. Each line in 8 bit register that can store 8 bit binary bits, and several of these registers are arranged in a sequence called memory.

Input/Output

The user can enter instructions and data into memory through devices such as keyboard or simple switches. These devices are called input devices.

The microprocessor reads instructions from the memory and processes the data according to those instructions. The result can be displayed by a device such as seven segment LED (light emitting diodes) or printed by a printer. These devices are called output devices.

MICROPROCESSOR AS A CPU

The central processing unit (CPU) consists of the Arithmetic Logic Unit (ALU) and Control Unit (CU). The CPU contains various registers to store data, ALU to perform Arithmetic and logical, operations, instruction decoders, counters and control lines. The CPU reads instructions from the memory and perform the tasks specified. It communicates with input/output devices either to accept or to send data. These devices are also known as peripherals. The CPU is the primary and central player in communicating with devices such as memory, input and output. However, the timing of the communication process is controlled by the group of circuit called control unit. CPU on single chip called microprocessor.

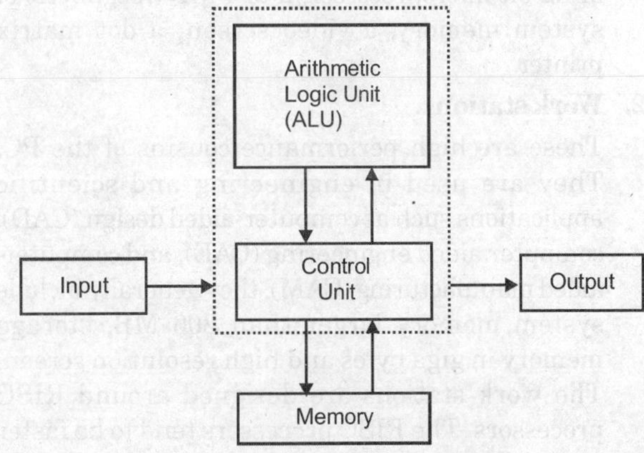

Fig. (a) Traditional block diagram of

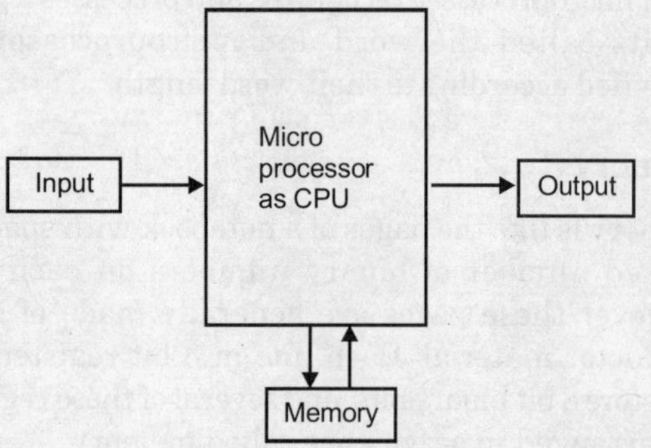

Fig. (b) Block diagram of a computer with the a computer microprocessor as CPU

1. **bit microprocessor.**

   The Intel 4004 was the first 4 bit programmable device that was primarily used in calculators.

2. **bit microprocessor.**

   The intel 8008 is 8 bit microprocessor, which was in turn superseded by the Intel 8080. Intel 8080 widely used in control applications, and small computers also were designed using the 8080 as the CPU. Within a few years after the emergence of the 8080, the Motorola 6800 and Zilog Z80 and Intel 8085 microprocessor were developed as improvements

3. **16 bit microprocessor.** 8086/88
4. **32 bit microprocessor.** 80380/486 and Pentium
5. **64 bit microprocessor.** Motorola 68000 series

MICROCOMPUTERS

Microcomputer is classified in four groups.

1. **Personnel computers.**

   These microcomputers are single user systems and being used for variety of purposes, such as payroll, business accounts, word processing, legal and medical record keeping, personnel finance and instructions. A typical configuration includes a 16 or 32 bit microprocessor, 2 to 4 MB (megabyte) of system memory, a video screen, a dot matrix printer.

2. **Work stations.**

   These are high performance cousins of the PC. They are used in engineering and scientific applications such as computer-aided design (CAD), computer aided engineering (CAE), and computer-aided manufacturing (CAM), they generally include system memory larger than 200 MB, storage memory in giga bytes and high resolution screen. The work stations are designed around RISC processors. The RISC processors tend to be faster and more efficient than the processors used in personnel computer.

3. **Single board microcomputers.**

   These microcomputers are primarily used in college, laboratories and industries for instructional purposes or to evaluate the performance of a given microprocessor. They can also be part of some larger systems. Typically these microcomputers include 8 or 16 bit microprocessor.

   e.g. These computers include such systems as Intel SDK85, SDK86, Motorola Evaluation kits, these are generally used to write and execute assembly language programs and to perform interfacing experiments

4. **Single chip microcomputers (micro-controllers)**

   These microcomputers are designed on a single chip, which typically includes a chip of 64 bytes of R/W memory from 4K to 2K bytes of ROM and several single lines to connect I/Os. These are complete microcomputers on a chip, they are also known as microcontrollers. These are used primarily for such functions as controlling appliances and traffic lights. *e.g.* Zilog Z8, Intel MCS51 and 96 series, and Motorola 68H C11.

COMPUTER LANGUAGES. Nibble

It is a group of four bits

Mnemonic : A combination of letters to suggest the operation of an instruction.

Compiler : A program that translates english like words of high language in the machine language of a computer. A complier reads a given program, called a source code and then translates the program into the machine language which is called an object code.

Assembler : A computer program that translates an assembly language program from mnemonics to the binary machine code of a computer.

Monitor program : A program that interprets the input from a keyboard and converts the input into its binary equivalent.

COMPUTER SYSTEM.

8085 Programming Model.

The 8085 programming model includes six registers, one accumulator and one flag register. It has two 16 bit register the stack pointer and the program counter.

Registers : The 8085 has six general purpose registers to store 8 bit data. These are identical as B, C, D, E, H and L. They can be combined as Registers pairs BC, DE, and HL to perform some 16 bit operations. The programmer can use these registers to store or copy data into the registers by using data copy instructions.

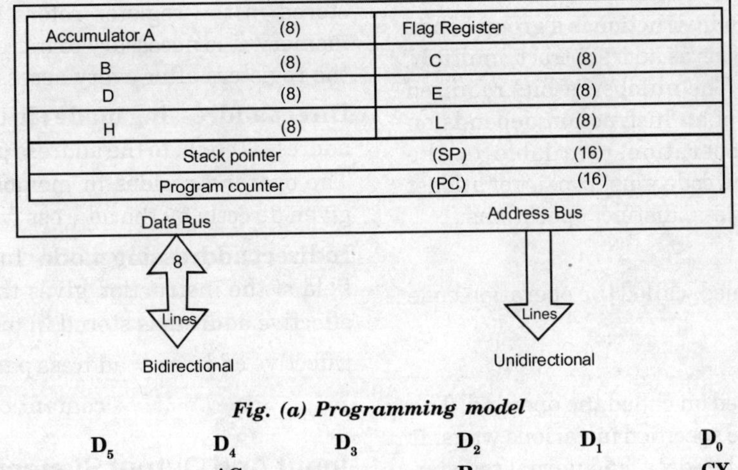

Fig. (a) Programming model

D_7	D_6	D_5	D_4	D_3	D_2	D_1	D_0
S	Z		AC		P		CY

Fig. (b) Flab Register

Accumulator

The Accumulator is an 8 bit register that is part of the arithmetic/logic unit (ALU). This register is used to store 8 bit data and to perform arithmetic/logic unit (ALU). This register is used to store 8-bit data and to perform arithmetic and logical operations. The result of an operation is stored in the accumulator. The accumulator is also identified as register A.

FLAGS

The ALU includes five flip-flops, which are set or reset after an operation according to data conditions of the result in the accumulator and other registers. They are called zero (Z), carry (CY); sign (S), parity (P) and Auxiliary carry (AC) flags.

The most commonly used flags are zero, carry, and sign. The microprocessor uses these flags to test data conditions.

After an addition of two numbers, if the sum in the accumulator is larger than eight bits, the flip-flop used to indicate a carry called carry flag (CY) is set to one. When an arithmetic operation is zero the flip flop called the zero (Z) flag is set to one.

The flags have critical importance in the decision making process of the microprocessor. The conditions (set or reset) of the flags are tested through software instructions.

PROGRAM COUNTER (PC).

This 16 bit register deals with sequencing the execution of instruction. This register is a memory pointer. Memory locations have 16 bit addresses, and that is why this is a 16-bit register. The microprocessor uses this register to sequence the execution of the instructions. The function of the program counter is to point to the memory addresses from which the next byte is to be fetched. When a byte (machine code) is being fetched, the program counter is incremented by one to point to the next memory location.

STACK POINTER (SP)

The stack pointer is also a 16 bit register used as memory pointer. It points to a memory location in R/W memory, called the stack. The beginning of stack is defined by loading a 16-bit address in the stack pointer.

OPCODE FORMAT

In the design of the 8085 microprocessor chip, all operations, registers and status flags are identified with a specific code.

All internal registers are identified as follows :

Code	Registers	Code	Register pairs
000	B	00	BC
001	C	01	DE
010	D	10	HL
011	E	11	A F or S P
100	F		
101	G		
110	Reserved for Memory Related Operation		
111	A		

INSTRUCTION CODES

An instruction code is a group of bits that instruct the computer to perform a specific operation. It is usually divided into parts, each having its own particular interpretation. The most basic part of an instruction codes is its operation part.

Operation Code

The operation code of an instruction is a group of bits that define such operations as add, subtract, multiply, shift and complement. The number of bits required for the operation code of an instruction depends on the total number of operations available in the computer. The operation code must consist of atleast n bits for a given 2^n (or less) distinct operations.

OP Code.

What task to be performed, called the operation code (OPcode).

Operand.

When data to be operated on called the operand. The operand (or data) can be specified in various ways. It may include 8-bit or (16 bit) data, an internal register, a memory location, or 8 bit (or 16 bit) address. In some instructions, the operand is implicit.

ADDRESSING MODES

The control unit of a computer is designed to go through an instruction cycle that is divided into three major phases.

(i) Fetch the instruction from memory

(ii) Decode the instruction

(iii) Execute the instruction

Implied mode : All register reference instructions that use an accumulator are implied mode instructions. Zero address instructions in a stack-organized computer are implied mode instructions since the operands are implied to be on top of the stack.

Immediate mode : The operand is specified in the instruction itself. In other words, an immediate mode instruction has an operand field rather than an address field. The operand field contains the actual operand to be used in conjunction with the operation specified in the instructions.

Register mode : In this mode the operands are in registers, that reside within the CPU. The particular register is selected from a register field in the instruction. A K bit field can specify any one of 2^k registers.

Register indirect mode : In this mode the instruction specifies a register in the CPU, whose content gives the address of the operand in memory. The advantage of a register indirect mode instruction is that the address field of the instruction uses fewer bits to select a register than would have been required to specify a memory address directly,

Auto Increment or Decrement mode : This is similar to register indirect mode except that the register is incremented or decremented after or before its value is used to access memory. When the address stored in the register refers to a table of data in memory, it is necessary to increment and decrement the registers after every access to the table

Direct addressing mode : In this mode the effective address is equal to the address part of the instruction. The operand resides in memory and its address is given directly by the address field of the instruction.

Indirect addressing mode : In this mode the address field of the instruction gives the address where the effective address is stored in memory.

Effective address = address part of instruction

+ content of CPU register

Input And Output System

Input/output devices are the means through which the MPU communicates with the outside world. The MPU accepts binary data as input from devices such as keyboards and A/D converters and send data to output devices such as LEDs or printers. There are two different methods by which I/O devices can be identified. One uses an 8 bit address and the other uses a 16 bit address.

PERIPHERAL MAPPED I/O

In this type of I/O, the MPU uses eight address lines to identify an input or an output device; this is known as peripheral mapped I/O. The eight address lines can have 256 (2^8 combinations) addresses; thus the MPU can identify 256 input devices and 256 output devices with addresses ranging from 00H to FFH input and output devices are differentiated by the control signals. The MPU uses the I/O Read Control Signal for input devices and the I/O Write Control Signal for output devices. The entire range of I/O addresses from 00 to FF is known as an I/O map, and individual addresses are referred to as I/O devices addresses 8 I/O port numbers.

MEMORY MAPPED I/O (I/O WITH 16 BIT ADDRESSES).

I/O is connected as if it is memory register. This is known as memory mapped I/O. The MPU uses the same control signal (Memory Read or Memory Write) and instructions as those of memory. In some microprocessor such as motorola 6800, all I/O have 16 bit addresses. I/Os and memory share the same memory map (64K). In memory mapped I/O, the MPU follows the same steps as if it is accessing a memory register.

INPUT DEVICES

These include a mouse, track ball, space ball, joystick, digitizers, dials and button boxes. Some other input devices used in particular applications are data glove, touch panels, image scanners and voice systems.

1. **Keyboards :** An alphanumeric keyboard on a graphics system is used primarily as a device for entering text strings. The keyboard is an efficient device for inputting such non graphics data as picture labels associated with graphics display. Keyboards can also be provided with feature to facilitate entry of screen coordinates, menu selectors or graphics functions.

2. **Mouse :** A mouse is small hand held box used to position the screen cursor. Wheels or rollers on the button of the mouse can be used to record the amount and direction of movements. Another method for detecting mouse motion is with an optical sensor. For these systems, the mouse is moved over a special mouse pad that has grid of horizontal and vertical lines. The optical sensor detects movements across the lines in the grid. Since mouse can be picked up and put down at another position without change in cursor movement. It is used for making relative changes in the position of the screen cursor. One, two or three buttons are usually included on the top of the mouse for signalling the execution of some operation, such as recording cursor position or invoking a function. Most general purpose graphics system now included a mouse and keyboard as major input devices.

3. **Track Ball and Space Ball :**A track ball is a ball that can be rotated with the fingers or palm of the hand to produce screen-cursor movement, potentiometers attached to the ball measure the amount and direction of rotation. Trackballs are often mounted on keyboards or other devices such as the mouse.

   While a track ball is two dimensional posting device, a space ball provides six degree of freedom. Unlike the track ball, space ball does not actually move. Strain gauges measure the amount of pressure applied to the spaceball to provide input for spatial positioning and orientation as the ball is pushed or pulled in various directions. Space balls are used for three-dimensional positioning and selection operations in virtual reality systems, modelling, animation, CAD, and other applications.

4. **Joysticks :** A joystick consists of a small, vertical lever called stick mounted on a base that is used to steer and screen cursor around. Most joysticks select screen position with actual stick movement. Others respond to pressure on the stick. Some joysticks are mounted on keyboard, others function as stand alone units. Potentiometer mounted at the base of joystick measures the amount of movement, and springs return the stick to the center position when it is released one or more buttons can be programmed to act as input switches to signal certain actions once a screen position has been selected.

5. **Data Glove :** Data glove that can be used to grasp a "virtual" object. The glove is constructed with a series of sensors that detect hand and finger motions. Electromagnetic coupling between transmitting antennas and receiving antennas is used to provide information about the position and orientation of the hand. The transmitting and receiving antennas can each be structured as a set of three mutually perpendicular coils, forming a three dimensional cartesian co-ordinate system.

6. **Digitizers :** A common device for drawing, painting or interactively selecting co-ordinate positions on an object is a digitizer. These devices can be used to input co-ordinate values in either a two dimensional or three dimensional space. Typically, a digitizer is used to scan over a drawing or object and to input a set of discrete co-ordinate positions, which can be joined with straight-line segments to approximate the curve or surface shapes. One type of digitizer is the graphics tablet, also referred to as a data tablet which is used to input two dimensional coordinates by activating a hand cursor or styles at selected positions on a flat surface.

7. **Image Scanners :** Drawing, graphs, color and black and white photos or text can be stored for computer processing with an image scanner by passing an optical scanning mechanism over the information to be stored. The gradations of gray scale or color are then recorded and stored in an array. Once we have the internal representation of a picture, we can apply transformations to rotate, scale or crop the picture to a particular screen area. We can also apply various image processing methods to modify the array representation of the picture. For scanned text input, various editing operations can be performed on stored documents. Some scanners are able to scan either graphical representation or text, and they come in a variety of sizes and capabilities.

8. **Touch Panels :** Touch panels allow displayed objects or screen positions to be selected with the touch of a finger. A typical application of touch panels is for the selection of processing options that are represented with graphical icons. Some

systems, such as the plasma panels are designed with touch screens. Other system can be adapted for touch input by fitting a transparent device with a touch-sensing mechanism over the video monitor screen. Touch input can be recorded using optical, electrical or acoustical methods.

9. Light Pens.

Light pen is pencil-shaped devices are used to select screen positions by detecting the light coming from points on the CRT screen. They are sensitive to the short burst of light emitted from the phosphor coating at the instant the electron beam strikes a particular point. Other light sources, such as the background light in the room, are usually not detected by a light pen.

PRINTERS

Printers produce output by either impact or non-impact methods. Impact printers press formed character faces against an inked ribbon onto the paper. A line printer is an example of impact device with the type faces mounted on bands, chains, drums or wheels. Non-impact printers and plotters use laser techniques, inkjet sprays, xerographic processes as used in photocopying machine, electrostatic methods and electrothermal methods to get images on to paper.

Character impact printers often have a dot matrix print head containing a rectangular array of protruding wire pins, with the number of pens depending on the quality of the printer.

In a laser device, laser beam creates a charge distribution on a rotating drum coating with a photoelectric material, such as selenium. Toner is applied to the drum and then transferred to paper.

Inkjet methods produce output by squirting ink in horizontal rows across a roll of paper wrapped on a drum. The electrically charged ink stream *is* deflected by an electric field to produce dot matrix patterns. A desktop inkjet plotter with resolution of 360 dots per inch.

An electrostatic device places a negative charge on the paper, one complete row at a time along the length of the paper. Then the paper is exposed to a toner. The toner is positively charged and so it is attracted to the negatively charged, areas, where it adheres to produce the specified output. Electrothermal methods use heat in a dot matrix print head to output patterns on heat sensitive paper. We can get limited color output on an impact printer by using different colored ribbons.

Non impact devices use various techniques to combine three color pigments (cyan, magneta and yellow) to produce a range of color patterns.

Parallel printers use :

(*a*) RS-232C interface

(*b*) Centronics interface

(*c*) Handshake mode

Storage Unit

It consists of main memory and secondary memory.

Main Memory :

1. A flip-flop made of electronic semiconductor devices is used to fabricate a memory cell. These memory cells organized as a Random Access Memory (RAM). Each cell has a capability to store one bit of information. A main memory or store of a computer is organized using a large number of cells. Each cell stores a binary digit.
2. A memory cell, which does not loose the bit stored in it when no power is supplied to the cell, is known as a non-volatile cell.
3. A word is a group of bits, which are stored and retrieved as a unit. A memory system is organized to store a number of words.
4. A Byte consists of 8 bits. A word may store one or more bytes.
5. The storage capacity of a memory is the number of bytes it can store.
6. The address of the location from where a word is to be retrieved or to be stored is entered in a Memory Address Register (MAR).
7. The data retrieved from memory or to be stored in memory are placed in a Memory Data Register (MDR).
8. The time taken to write a word is known as the Write time.
9. The time to retrieve information is called the Access time of the memory.
10. The time taken to access a word in a memory is independent of the address of the word and hence it is know as a Random Access Memory (RAM).
    - The main memory used to store programs and data in a computer is a RAM.
11. A RAM may be fabricated with permanently stored information, which cannot be erased. Such a memory is called a Read Only Memory (ROM).
    - For more specialized uses, a user can store his won special functions or programs in a ROM. Such ROM's are called Programmable ROM (PROM).
12. A serial access memory is organized by arranging memory cells in a linear sequence.

- Information is retrieved or stored in such a memory by using a read/write head.
- Data is presented serially for writing and is retrieved serially during read.

Secondary / Auxiliary storage devices : Magnetic surface recording devices used in computers as Hard disks, Floppy disks, CD-ROMs and Magnetic tapes.

1. **Floppy Disk Drive (FDD) :** In this device, the medium used to record the data is called as floppy disk. It is a flexible circular disk of diameter 3.5 inches made of plastic coated with a magnetic material. This is housed in a square plastic jacket. Data recorded on a floppy disk is read and stored in a computer's memory by a device called a floppy disk is read and stored in a computer's memory by a device called a floppy disk drive (FDD). A floppy disk is inserted in a slot of the FDD. Floppy Disks with various capacities are as follow:
   - $5^{1/4}$ drive- 360KB, 1.2MB (1 KB= 2^{10} = 1024 bytes)
   - $3^{1/2}$ drive- 1.44 Mb, 2.88 MB (1MB= 2^{20} bytes)
2. **Compact Disk Drive (CDD) :** CD-ROM (Compact Disk Read Only Memory) used a laser beam to record and read data along spiral tracks on a 51/4 disk. A disk can store around 650 MB of information. CD-ROMs are normally used to store massive text data. Recently CD writers have come in the market. Using a CD writer, lot of information can be written on CD-ROM and stored for future reference.
3. **Hard Disk Drive (HDD) :** Unlike a floppy disk that is flexible and removable, the hard disk used in the PC is permanently fixed. The data transfer rate between the CPU and hard disk is much higher as compared to the between the CPU and the floppy disk drive. The CPU can use the hard disk to load programs and data as well as to store data.

CLASSIFICATION OF COMPUTERS

Computers come in sizes from tiny to monstrous, in both appearance and power. The size of a computer that a person or an organization needs depends on the computing requirements.

Supercomputers : The mightiest computers-and, of course, the most expensive-are known as supercomputers. Supercomputers process billions of instructions per second. One uses supercomputers for tasks that require mammoth data manipulation, such as worldwide weather forecasting and weapons research.

Mainframes : In the jargon of the computer trade, large computers are called mainframes. Mainframes are capable of processing data at very high speeds-millions of instructions per second-and have access to billions of characters of data. Their principal use of it is for processing vast amounts of data quickly, some of the obvious customers are banks, insurance companies, and manufacturers.

Personal Computers : Personal computers are often called PCs. A PC usually comes with a tower that holds the main circuit boards and disk drives of the computer, and a collection of peripherals, such as a keyboard, mouse, and monitor. The term "PC" often means machines that are compatible to IBM other than a Macintosh.

Personal Computers (PC) and MAC : A PC is based on a microprocessor originally made by the Intel Company (Intel's Pentium) with other companies such as AMD. The computers made by Macintoshes which uses, PowerPC processor, made by Motorola are referred as Mac. Also, the operating system software that runs these two kinds of computers is different. PCs usually use an Operating System made by Microsoft, i.e., Windows. Macintoshes use operating system, called Mac OS, made by Apple.

Notebook Computers : A computer that fits in a briefcase?. Notebook computers, also known as Laptop computers, are portable and popular with travelers who need a computer that can go with them. Most notebooks accept diskettes or network connections, so it is easy to move data from one computer to another.

INTERNET

The **Internet** is a global system of interconnected computer networks that use the standard Internet Protocol Suite (TCP/IP) to serve billions of users worldwide. It is a *network of networks* that consists of millions of private, public, academic, business, and government networks, of local to global scope, that are linked by a broad array of electronic, wireless and optical networking technologies. The Internet carries a vast range of information resources and services, such as the inter-linked hypertext documents of the World Wide Web (WWW) and the infrastructure to support electronic mail.

NETWORKS

A **computer network**, often simply referred to as a network, is a collection of computers and devices interconnected by communications channels that facilitate communications and allows sharing of resources and information among interconnected devices. **Computer networking** or **Data communications** (**Datacom**) is the engineering discipline concerned with the computer networks.

The three types of networks are:

(*i*) the Internet

(*ii*) the intranet

(*iii*) the extranet.

Examples of different network methods are :

1. Local area network (LAN), which is usually a small network constrained to a small geographic area. An example of a LAN would be a computer network within a building.
2. Metropolitan area network (MAN), which is used for medium size area. examples for a city or a state.
3. Wide area network (WAN) that is usually a larger network that covers a large geographic area.
4. Wireless LANs and WANs (WLAN & WWAN) are the wireless equivalent of the LAN and WAN.

IP ADDRESS

An **Internet Protocol address** (**IP address**) is a numerical label assigned to each device (e.g., computer, printer) participating in a computer network that uses the Internet Protocol for communication.[1] An IP address serves two principal functions: host or network interface identification and location addressing. Its role has been characterized as follows: *"A name indicates what we seek. An address indicates where it is. A route indicates how to get there.*

Important Devices Used in Network

1. **Modem :** A **modem** (**mo**dulator-**dem**odulator) is a device that modulates an analog carrier signal to encode digital information, and also demodulates such a carrier signal to decode the transmitted information. The goal is to produce a signal that can be transmitted easily and decoded to reproduce the original digital data. Modems can be used over any means of transmitting analog signals, from light emitting diodes to radio.
2. **Router :** A **router** is a device that forwards data packets across computer networks. Routers perform the data "traffic directing" functions on the Internet. A router is connected to two or more data lines from different networks. When data comes in on one of the lines, the router reads the address information in the packet to determine its ultimate destination.
3. **Bridge :** A **network bridge** connects multiple network segments. **Bridging** is a forwarding technique used in packet-switched computer networks. Unlike routing, bridging makes no assumptions about where in a network a particular address is located. Instead, it depends on flooding and examination of source addresses in received packet headers to locate unknown devices. Once a device has been located, its location is recorded in a table where the MAC address is stored so as to preclude the need for further broadcasting.
4. **Hub : hub** is a device for connecting multiple twisted pair or fiber optic Ethernet devices together and making them act as a single segment. The device is a form of multiport repeater.
5. **Repeater :** A **repeater** is an electronic device that receives a signal and retransmits it at a higher level and/or higher power, or onto the other side of an obstruction, so that the signal can cover longer distances.
6. **Server :** A **server computer** is a computer, or series of computers, that link other computers or electronic devices together. They often provide essential services across a network, either to private users inside a large organization or to public users via the internet. For example, when you enter a query in a search engine, the query is sent from your computer over the internet to the servers that store all the relevant web pages. The results are sent back by the server to your computer.

EMAIL

Electronic mail, commonly called **email** or **e-mail**, is a method of exchanging digital messages from an author to one or more recipients. Modern email operates across the Internet or other computer networks. Some early email systems required that the author and the recipient both be online at the same time, *a la* instant messaging. Today's email systems are based on a store-and-forward model. Email servers accept, forward, deliver and store messages. Neither the users nor their computers are required to be online simultaneously; they need connect only briefly, typically to an email server, for as long as it takes to send or receive messages.

EMAIL ADDREES

An **email address** identifies an email box to which email messages are delivered. An example format of an email address is lewis @ example .com which is read as *lewis at example dot net*. It has two parts. The part before the @ sign is the *local-part* of the address, often the username of the recipient *lewis* and the part after the @ sign is a *domain name i.e.* example.com to which the email message will be sent.

MS OFFICE

Microsoft Office is a proprietary commercial office suite of inter-related desktop applications, servers and services for the Microsoft Windows and Mac OS X operating systems, introduced by Microsoft in 1989. Initially a marketing term for a bundled set of applications, the first version of Office contained Microsoft Word, Microsoft Excel, and Microsoft PowerPoint.

WORD

Microsoft Word is a word processor and was previously considered to be the main program in Office. Its proprietary DOC format is considered a *de facto* standard, although Word 2007 can also use a new XML-based, Microsoft Office-optimized format called .DOCX which has been standardized by Ecma International as Office Open XML and its SP2 update will support ODF and PDF. Word is also available in some editions of Microsoft Works. It is available for the Windows and Mac platforms. The first version of Word, released in the autumn of 1983, was for the MS-DOS operating system and had the distinction of introducing the mouse to a broad population. Word 1.0 could be purchased with a bundled mouse, though none was required. Following the precedents of LisaWrite and MacWrite, Word for Macintosh attempted to add closer WYSIWYG features into its package. Word for Mac was released in 1985. Word for Mac was the first graphical version of Microsoft Word. Despite its bugginess, it became one of the most popular Mac applications.

EXCEL

Microsoft Excel is a spreadsheet program which originally competed with the dominant Lotus 1-2-3, but eventually outsold it. It is available for the Windows and Mac platforms. Microsoft released the first version of Excel for the Mac in 1985, and the first Windows version (numbered 2.05 to line up with the Mac and bundled with a standalone Windows run-time environment) in November 1987.

OUTLOOK

Microsoft Outlook (not to be confused with Outlook Express) is a personal information manager and e-mail communication software. The replacement for Windows Messaging, Microsoft Mail and Schedule+ starting in Office 97, it includes an e-mail client, calendar, task manager and address book.

On the Mac, Microsoft offered several versions of Outlook in the late 1990s, but only for use with Microsoft Exchange Server. In Office 2001, it introduced an alternative application with a slightly different feature set called Microsoft Entourage. It reintroduced Outlook in Office 2011, replacing Entourage.

POWERPOINT

Microsoft PowerPoint is a popular presentation program for Windows and Mac. It is used to create slideshows, composed of text, graphics, movies and other objects, which can be displayed on-screen and navigated through by the presenter or printed out on transparencies or slides.

Objective Type Questions

1. Which of the following is the fastest ?
(*a*) CPU
(*b*) magnetic tapes and disks
(*c*) video terminal
(*d*) sensors, mechanical controllers

2. The input unit of a computer
(*a*) feeds data to the CPU or memory
(*b*) retrieves data from CPU
(*c*) directs all other units
(*d*) all of these

3. Offline device is
(*a*) a device which is not connected to CPU
(*b*) a device which is connected to CPU
(*c*) a direct access storage device
(*d*) an I/O device

4. Which of the following is a set of general purpose internal registers ?
(*a*) Stack (*b*) Scratchpad
(*c*) Address register (*d*) Status register

5. A single bus structure is primarily found in
(*a*) main frames
(*b*) super computers
(*c*) high performance machines
(*d*) mini-and micro-computers

6. Which of the following registers is used to keep track of address of the memory location where the next instruction is located ?
(*a*) Memory Address Register
(*b*) Memory Data Register
(*c*) Instruction Register
(*d*) Program Counter

7. Which of the following registers is loaded with the contents of the memory location pointed by the PC ?
(*a*) Memory Address Register
(*b*) Memory Data Register
(*c*) Instruction Register
(*c*) Program counter

8. In a generic microprocessor, instruction cycle time is
(*a*) shorter than machine cycle time
(*b*) larger than machine cycle time
(*c*) exactly double the machine cycle time
(*d*) exactly the same as the machine cycle time

9. Program Status Word (PSW) contains various (different) status of
(*a*) CPU (*b*) ALU
(*c*) program (*d*) registers

10. When an interrupt occurs, CPU saves the value of——in a stack,
(*a*) accumulator
(*b*) program status word (PSW) only
(*c*) Instruction Address Counter (IAC)only
(*d*) both PWS and IAC

11. Bus Arbitration is
(*a*) clearing the bus
(*b*) latching information on the bus
(*c*) deciding the controller of the bus
(*d*) controlling the bus

12. Control Memory Address Register is present in
(*a*) ALU
(*b*) Instruction Register Unit
(*c*) Control Unit
(*d*) Disk Control Interface Unit

13. Which of the following is not one of the three primary functions that on-line direct access system can serve?
(*a*) inquiry (*b*) backup
(*c*) update (*d*) programming

14. Which of the following is not true of punched cards as data entry media?
(*a*) They can be used as turn around documents
(*b*) They are inexpensive
(*c*) Input is slow compared with other media
(*d*) They are easily damaged

15. Magnetic tape can serve as
(*a*) input media
(*b*) output media
(*c*) secondary storage media
(*d*) all of these

16. In the context of Information Technology, OCR means
(*a*) Optical Character Recognition
(*b*) Octagonal Cyclic Recharge
(*c*) Octadecimal Cyclic Regeneration
(*d*) Optical Character Regeneration

17. In Boolean algebra $\left(\overline{1+1\cdot 0+0}\right)=?$

(*a*) 0 (*b*) 1

(*c*) 2 (*d*) –1

18. Which of the followingis not an I/O device of the computer?

(*a*) Keyboard (*b*) Joy stick

(*c*) ALU (*d*) Printer

19. What is floating point with reference to computers?

(*a*) It is a software subroutine around which other subroutines are built

(*b*) It is a representation of real numbers to facilitate computing

(*c*) It is the main algebraic formula of the software

(*d*) It is the voltage point given to various operating units of the computer

20. A system of digital rules for exchange and processing of data between various devices is called

(*a*) software programme

(*b*) algorithm

(*c*) protocol

(*d*) information processing

21. A theoretical computer with infinite type and memory, used in analysis of problems of computation, is called

(*a*) Tape calculator

(*b*) Babbage machine

(*c*) Turing machine

(*d*) Theoretical machine

22. ASCII coding allocated binary codes to English alphabets and symbols for computer use. More recently a new standard has been adopted which allocates code to almost all the languages of the world and also to symbols covering more than a lakh characters. The new standard is called

(*a*) CCS

(*b*) Unicode

(*c*) Standard CCS code

(*d*) Universal CCS code

23. For using passwords on the Internet a software is used so that the password is not intercepted easily. It is called

(*a*) Coding

(*b*) Malware

(*c*) Virus

(*d*) Encryption

24. A software, coding of which is available freely on Internet and is open for users for further use and improvement and which is generally developed in a collaborative manner is called

(*a*) open source software

(*b*) unlicensed software

(*c*) free software

(*d*) community software

25. Which of the following are machine level languages?

(*a*) C++ (*b*) Java

(*c*) Python (*d*) None of these

26. Which of the following statements is incorrect?

(*a*) Microsoft windows is GUI

(*b*) Linux is GUI

(*c*) More than 5000 kB data can be stored in a DVD

(*d*) A 1 TB flash drive can store 2 million files each of size 1 MB

27. The terms ALU, CPU, I/O devices pertain to

(*a*) computers

(*b*) environmental engineering

(*c*) diesel engine

(*d*) engineering drawing and orthogonal projections

28. In a computing device 'MHz' is mentioned in the specifications. It refers to

(*a*) size of memory

(*b*) speed of computation

(*c*) clock speed

(*d*) none of the above

29. The value of binary 1111 is :

(*a*) 2^3 (*b*) $2^3 - 1$

(*c*) 24 (*d*) $2^4 - 1$

30. The term 'Operating System' means :

(*a*) A set of programmes which controls computer working

(*b*) The way a computer operator works

(*c*) Conversion of high level language into machine level language

(*d*) None of these

31. Which of these is NOT an Operating System?

(a) Android (b) iOS

(c) Linux (d) Power point

32. A software user interface feature that allows the user to view something very similar to the end result while the document is being created is called-

(a) Format creator (b) Format fidelity

(c) WYSIWYG (d) WYGIWYS

33. In a computer system there are softwares and languages at various levels, like High level Language (HL), Machine Language (ML), Compiler (C). Which of the following is the correct indicative representation from user (U) to the computer (COMP)?

(a) $U \rightleftharpoons HL \rightleftharpoons C \rightleftharpoons ML \rightleftharpoons Comp$

(b) $U \rightleftharpoons C \rightleftharpoons ML \rightleftharpoons HL \rightleftharpoons Comp$

(c) $U \rightleftharpoons C \rightleftharpoons HL \rightleftharpoons ML \rightleftharpoons Comp$

(d) $U \rightleftharpoons ML \rightleftharpoons HL \rightleftharpoons C \rightleftharpoons Comp$

34. Which of these devices performs the function of both input device and output device for a computer?

(a) Joy Stick (b) Mouse

(c) Modem (d) Printer

35. Who wrote/invented the Linux software?

(a) Microsoft (b) Apple INC

(c) IBM (d) None of these

36. A technique of anonymous communication over a computer network using encryption of messages and splitting between the nodes, is called-

(a) Spice routing (b) Onion routing

(c) Cabbage routing (d) Flower routing

37. Processing speed of computer is measured in-

(a) MIPS(Million Instruction Per Second)

(b) MHz of clock

(c) Both (a) and (b)

(d) None of these

38. To close a presentation and quit PowerPoint, one must click the close button on the :

(a) menu bar (b) title bar

(c) standard tool bar (d) common tasks toolbar

39. Expression + + i is equivalent in 'C' to :

(a) i = i + 1 (b) i = i + 2

(c) i = 2i (d) None of these

40. Which of the following rational relation operations in 'C means "not equal to" ?

(a) # (b) ==

(c) ! = (d) < =

41. Microsoft Windows is a/an :

(a) Word-processing program

(b) Database program

(c) Operating system

(d) Graphics program

42. _________will translate the complete program at once from a High Level Language to the Machine Language.

(a) Compiler (b) Joy stick

(c) Ports (d) Light pen

43. The word function that corrects text as we type is referred to as :

(a) Auto insert (b) Auto correct

(c) Auto summarize (d) Track changes

44. Primary Storage, in computer terminology, refers to :

(a) Hard Disc Drive

(b) Random Access Memory (RAM)

(c) Read Only Memory (ROM)

(d) The storage device where the operating system is stored

45. What does an electronic spreadsheet consist of ?

(a) Rows (b) Columns

(c) Cells (d) All of the above

Answers

1. (*a*)	**2.** (*a*)	**3.** (*a*)	**4.** (*b*)	**5.** (*d*)	**6.** (*d*)	**7.** (*c*)	**8.** (*b*)	**9.** (*a*)	**10.** (*d*)
11. (*c*)	**12.** (*c*)	**13.** (*d*)	**14.** (*b*)	**15.** (*d*)	**16.** (*a*)	**17.** (*a*)	**18.** (*c*)	**19.** (*b*)	**20.** (*c*)
21. (*c*)	**22.** (*b*)	**23.** (*d*)	**24.** (*a*)	**25.** (*d*)	**26.** (*d*)	**27.** (*a*)	**28.** (*c*)	**29.** (*d*)	**30.** (*a*)
31. (*d*)	**32.** (*c*)	**33.** (*a*)	**34.** (*c*)	**35.** (*d*)	**36.** (*c*)	**37.** (*b*)	**38.** (*b*)	**39.** (*b*)	**40.** (*c*)
41. (*c*)	**42.** (*a*)	**43.** (*b*)	**44.** (*b*)	**45.** (*d*)					

Explanations

16. Optical Character Reader is full form of OCR, which can read a character and convert its bitmap image to equivalent ASCII codes.

17. It is equivalent to 0.1 = 0

18. Arithmetic Logical Unit is not an Input device while all the other three are.

19. Floating point numbers are used in computers to represent real numbers. Since real numbers can not be accurately represented in computers through binàry numbers.

20. Protocols are rules developed for exchanging and processing of data between various devices. Examples include HTTP, IP, FTTP etc.

21. Turing machine is a mathematical model of a hypothetical computing machine which can use a predefined set of rules to determine a result from a set of input variables.

22. The new standard which allocates codes to almost all languages and symbols, totaling more than a lakh is called Unicode. It makes transfer and reuse of translated data etc. very easy. Also it represents each character with 16 bits.

23. To protect passwords etc. Encryption is used which is coding each data point in a particular pattern which is not easy to decode.

24. Open source softwares like Unix have their source code freely available and these are developed through collaboration of coders from across the world. Many developers as a principle use only open source softwares.

25. All the languages mentioned here are high level languages, in which it is easier to write code.

26. 1 TB flash drive can store approximately 1 million file sizes each of 1 MB.

27. All these devices are related to computers. CPU is Central Processing Unit, while ALU is Arithmetic and Logical unit, while I/O is Input Output devices.

28. MHz is used to measure the number of operations that can be done by the CPU in 1 second. So it refers to clock speed.

29. 1111 of binary is $2^4 - 1$. It is $2^3 + 2^2 + 2^1 + 2^0$

30. An operating system (OS) is system software that manages computer hardware and software resources and provides common services for computer programs.

31. Powerpoint is not an operating system but an application to make presentation slides.

32. When users can see something very similar to end result while document creation, it is called WYSIWYG.

33. It is the correct representation where user gives input in high level language, it is then compiled and becomes machine language which is computed and the output is similarly provided to the user.

34. The modem is an input and an output device. It is used for sending and receiving information and data over telephone lines.

35. LINUX software was invented by Linus Torvalds while studying computer science at University of Helsinki in 1991.

37. Processing speed is measured in MHz. Nowadays it is even measured in GHz i.e. Giga Hertz. Basically it represents how many operations can be processed in 1 second.

38. To close applications such as Powerpoint, MS-word etc. one must click the close button on the title bar which is at the top right hand corner.

39. ++I in C means i = i + 2. This was a way developed to write smaller lines in code.

40. != means not equal to in C.

41. Microsoft Windows is the world's most popular commercial operating system for PCs.

42. Compilers are used to translate entire programs from High level language to machine language, so that computer can understand and execute it.

43. When we type text, Auto correct feature corrects the word's spelling or any other portion of the text.

44. Primary storage, also known as main storage or memory, is the area in a computer in which data is stored for quick access by the computer's processor. The terms random access memory (RAM) and memory are often used as synonyms for primary or main storage.

45. An electronic spreadsheet like MS-Excel consists of Cells which are arranged in Rows and Columns. So all are present.

Mechanical/Automobile

CHAPTER 1

Engineering Mechanics and Strength of Materials

MECHANICAL PROPERTIES OF SOLIDS

(i) Elasticity : *Property by which a body returns to its original shape after the removal of external load is called elasticity.* If the body regains completely its original shape, it is said to be *perfectly elastic*. A material is said to be *isotropic* if it is equally elastic in all directions. Steel, copper, aluminium, stone etc., may be considered to be perfectly elastic, within certain limits. For any particular material, a critical value of the load, known as the *elastic limit*, marks the partial breakdown of elasticity beyond which removal of the load results in the degree of permanent defomation.

(ii) Plasticity : Plasticity is the property of a material by which no strain disappears when it is relieved from the stress. Plasticity is thus the converse of elasticity. Most of the materials become plastic under the action of the large forces, and behave in a manner similar to a viscous fluid.

(iii) Ductility : Ductility is the property of a material by which it can be drawn out by tension to a small section. In a ductile material, therefore, large deformation is possible before the absolute failure or rupture takes place. During ductile extension, a material shows a certain degree of elasticity, together with a considerable degree of plasticity. This property is utilised in wire-drawing.

(iv) Brittleness : A material is said to be brittle when it cannot be drawn out by tension to smaller section. Brittleness is, therefore, lack of ductility. In a brittle material, failure takes place with a relatively small deformaton. This property is generally considered to be highly undesirable.

(v) Malleability : Malleability is the property by which a material can be uniformly extended in a direction without rupture. A malleable material possesses a high degree of plasticity. The property is utilised in many operations, such as forging, hot rolling, drop stamping etc.

(vi) Toughness : Toughness is the property of a material which enables it to absorb energy fracture. This property is very desirable in components subject to cyclic or shock loading.

(vii) Hardness : Hardness is the ability of a material to resist indentation or surface abrasion.

STRESS

When a body is acted upon by external force or load, internal resisting forces are set up and it is then said to be in a *state of stress*. *Stress is the resistance offered by the body to deformation.* Stress is usually measured by the intensity of force per unit area.

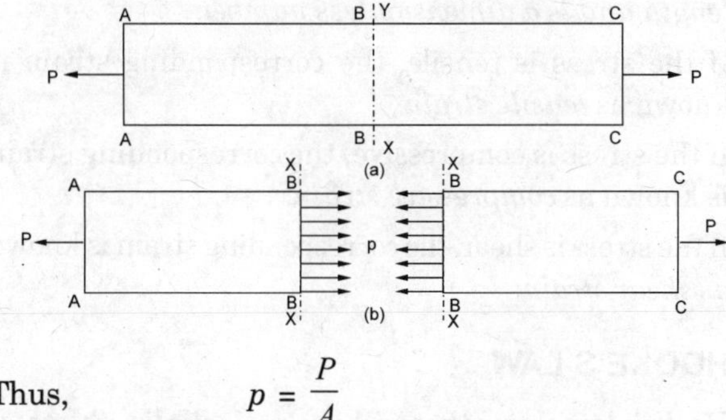

Thus, $p = \dfrac{P}{A}$

where p = Internal resistance = intensity of stress, or simply, *stress*.

A = Area of cross-section normal to its axis.

The state of stress is *simple* when the stress acts in one direction only. The state of stress is compound when two or more stresses are acting in different directions.

There are five kinds of stress :

(a) Tensile Stress
(b) Compressive Stress } Direct Stresses
(c) Shear Stress or Tangential Stress
(d) Transverse Stress or Bending Stress
(e) Twisting or Torsional Stress

However, the *average shear stress q* is given by

$$q = \frac{Q}{A}$$

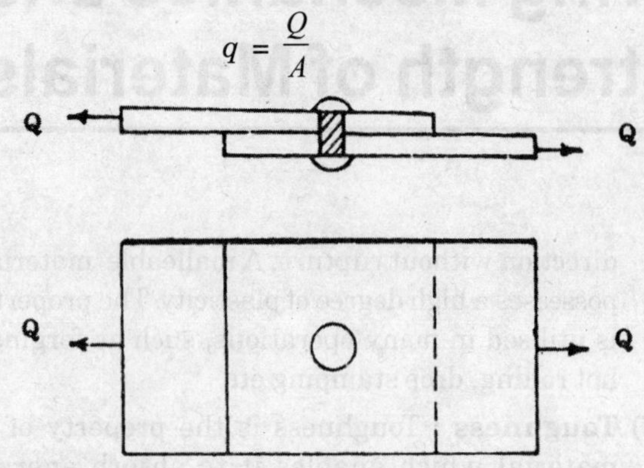

SI Unit of Stress. N/m^2 (Pascal).

STRAIN

Strain is the measure of the deformation caused due to external loading. If a load P is applied to a body, the body deforms. Let ΔL be the deformation of the body and L be its original length. The strain e is given by

$$e = \frac{\Delta L}{L}$$

Thus, *strain is the ratio of deformation to the original length and is a dimensionless number.*

If the stress is tensile, the corresponding strain is known as *tensile strain.*

If the stress is compressive, the corresponding strain is known as *compressive strain.*

If the stress is shear, the corresponding strain is known as *shear strain.*

HOOKE'S LAW

Hooke's law states that within the elastic limits, stress is proportional to strain. Thus

$$\text{Stress} \propto \text{Strain}$$

Thus, $\frac{p}{e} = E$

Now $p = \frac{P}{A}$, and $e = \frac{\Delta L}{L}$

$$\therefore \quad \frac{PL}{A\Delta L} = E, \text{ or } \Delta L = \frac{PL}{AE}$$

Shear Stress

Shear stress is tangential to the area

$$\tau = \frac{P}{A}$$

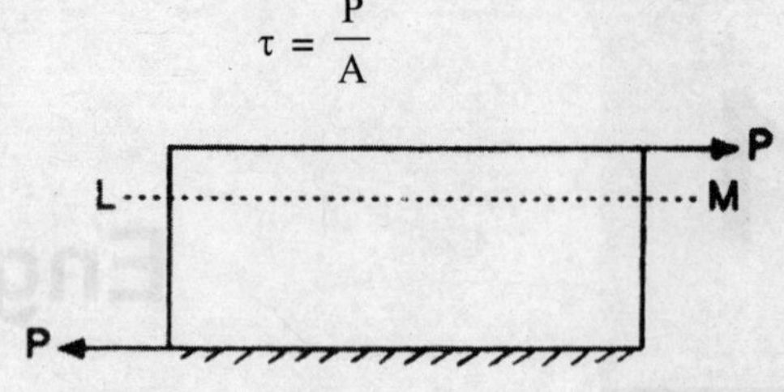

Shear Strain

Shear strain or slide ϕ, measured in radians and is dimension ( ) less

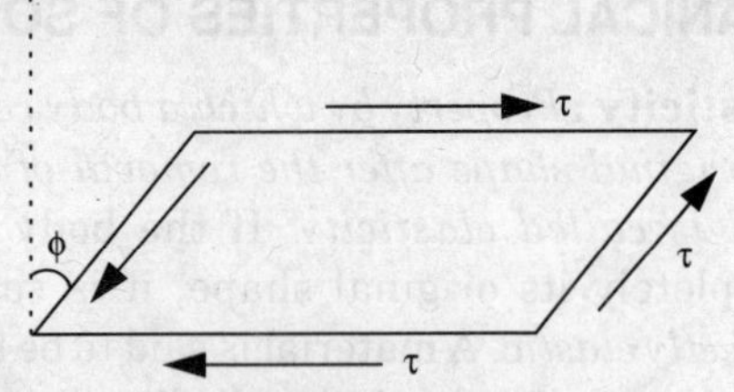

TENSILE TEST DIAGRAM

In this test a piece of ductile material is subjected to gradually increasing pull in a tension test machine.

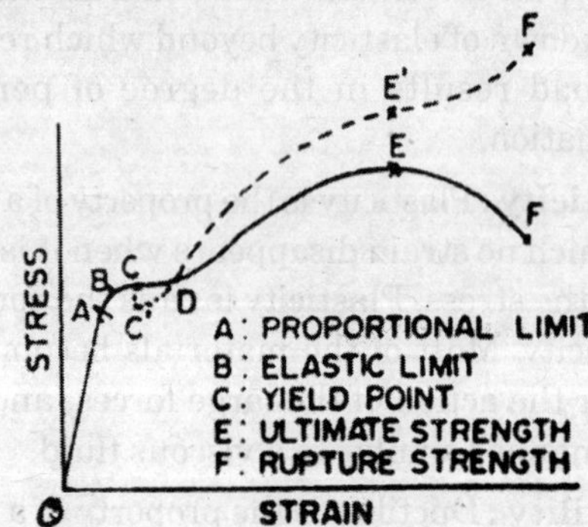

Given Figure represents a stress-strain diagram in which the stress (calculated on the basis of original area) is plotted against strain. The straight line from O to A represents that part of the test where the extension remains proportional to the load and is termed the *line of proportionality*. Hooke's law is valid for this range. The stress at A is known as the *proportional limit*. If the load is increased beyond this, elongation increases more rapidly and the diagram becomes as represented by A to C. At a point B, between A and C, the elastic limit is reached and after that permanent set or deformation takes place. C is the point of sudden large extension.

COMPOSITE SECTIONS

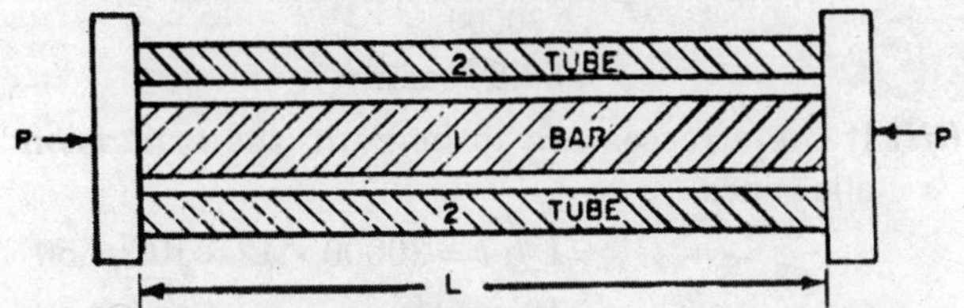

Let us take the case of solid bar enclosed in the hollow tube and subjected to a compressive force P through rigid collars as shown in Fig. the above figure Using suffix 1 for the bar and 2 for the tube, we get from the conditions of equilibrium,

$$P_1 + P_2 = P \qquad \text{...... } (i)$$

Since the whole assembly is composite, the deformation of bar is equal to the deformation of the tube.

Thus, $\Delta_1 = \Delta_2$

or $$\frac{P_1L}{A_1E_1} = \frac{P_2L}{A_2E_2} \qquad \text{..... } (ii)$$

The second equation is known as the *equation of compactibility.*

Now from (*ii*), $P_1 = P_2 \dfrac{A_1E_1}{A_2E_2}$

Substituting in (*i*), we get $P_2 \left\{1+\dfrac{A_1E_1}{A_2E_2}\right\} = P$

or $$P_2 = \frac{P}{1+\dfrac{A_1E_1}{A_2E_2}}$$

Substituting the value of P_2 in (*ii*), we get

$$P_1 = \frac{P}{1+\dfrac{A_1E_1}{A_2E_2}} \times \frac{A_1E_1}{A_2E_2}$$

Example. *A copper rod, 25 mm in diameter is encased in steel tube 30 mm internal diameter and 35 mm external diameter. The ends are rigidly attached. The composite bar is 500 mm long and is subjected to an axial pull of 30 kN. The stressed induces in the rod and the tube will be*

Take E for steel = 2×10^5 N/mm² and E for copper as 1×10^5 N/mm².

Ans. Let us use suffix 1 for rod (copper) and 2 for be (steel). Therefore

$$A_1 = \frac{\pi}{4}(25)^2 = 490.9 \text{ mm}^2\text{; and}$$

$$A_2 = \frac{\pi}{4}\left[(35)^2 - (30)^2\right] = 255.3 \text{ mm}^2$$

Now $\quad p_1A_1 + p_2A_2 = P = 30000 \text{ N} \qquad \text{... } (i)$

Also, $$\frac{p_1L}{E_1} = \frac{p_2L}{E_2}$$

or $$p_1 = p_2 \frac{E_1}{E_2} = \frac{2\times 10^5}{1\times 10^5} p_2 = 2p_2 \text{ ...} (ii)$$

From equation (*i*), $2p_2(490.9) + p_2(255.3) = 30000$

From which $\quad p_2 = \mathbf{24.25\ N/mm^2}$

and $\quad p_1 = 2p_2 = \mathbf{48.5\ N/mm^2}$

THERMAL STRESSES

Hooke's law, $\quad \Delta L = \dfrac{pL}{E}$

where $\ p$ = temperature stress

or $$p = \frac{\Delta L}{L}E = \alpha\, t\, E$$

where, α is coefficient of thermal expansion

Similarly, if the temperature falls, the tensile stress is $\alpha\, t\, E$.

Again, let us consider the case when the ends yield by an amount *a*. In this case,

the total amount of expansion checked = $\Delta L - a$.

Therefore, $$p = (\Delta L - a)\frac{E}{L} = (L\,\alpha\, t - a)\frac{E}{L}$$

COMPOSITE SECTION

$$\Delta = \Delta_c = \Delta_s$$

Tensile force in steel = Compressive force in copper

or $\quad P_s = P_c = P \qquad \text{...... } (i)$

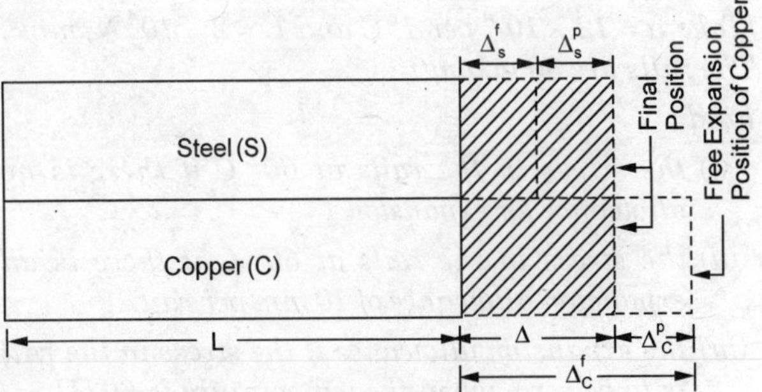

From the compatibility equation,

Extension of steel = Extension in copper

$$\Delta_s = \Delta_c = \Delta \text{ (say)} \qquad \text{...... } (ii)$$

From Figure, $\quad \Delta_s = \Delta_s^t + \Delta_s^p$

$$\Delta_c = \Delta_c^t - \Delta_c^p \qquad \text{..... } (iii)$$

where $\Delta_s = \Delta_c = \Delta$ = Final expansion

Δ_s^t = Free expansion of steel due to temperature

Δ_c^t = Free expansion of copper due to temperature

Δ_s^p = Expansion of steel due to temperature stress

Δ_c^p = Compression of copper due to temperature stress.

Substituting these value in (*ii*), we get

$$\Delta_s^t + \Delta_s^p = \Delta_c^t - \Delta_c^p$$

or $$\Delta_s^p + \Delta_c^p = \Delta_c^t - \Delta_s^t$$

or $$\Delta_s^p + \Delta_c^p = \text{L}.t\,(\alpha_c - \alpha_s)$$

$$\text{PL}\left(\frac{1}{\text{A}_s\text{E}_s} + \frac{1}{\text{A}_c\text{E}_c}\right) = \text{L}.t\,(\alpha_c - \alpha_s) \quad \text{...... (iv)}$$

or $$\text{P} = \frac{t(\alpha_c - \alpha_s)}{\frac{1}{\text{A}_s\text{E}_s} + \frac{1}{\text{A}_c\text{E}_c}}$$

Knowing the value of *P*, the individual stresses in the material will be

$$p_s = \frac{\text{P}}{\text{A}_s}; \quad p_c = \frac{\text{P}}{\text{A}_c}$$

Equation (*iv*) can also be written in the form,

$$\frac{\text{P}}{\text{A}_s\text{E}_s} + \frac{\text{P}}{\text{A}_c\text{E}_c} = t\,(\alpha_c - \alpha_s)$$

or $$\frac{p_s}{\text{E}_s} + \frac{p_c}{\text{E}_c} = t\,(\alpha_c - \alpha_s)$$

or $$e_s + e_c = (\alpha_c - \alpha_s)\,t$$

which relates the strains in the two materials.

Example. *A railway is laid so that there is no stress in the rails at 10°C.*

[Take $\alpha = 12 \times 10^{-6}$ per 1°C and $E = 2 \times 10^5$ N/mm². The rails are 30 m long]

Find :

(*i*) *the stress in the rails at 60° C if there is no allowance for expansion.*

(*ii*) *the stress in the rails at 60° C if there is an expansion allowance of 10 mm per rail.*

(*iii*) *the expansion allowance if the stress in the rail is to be zero when the temperature is 60° C.*

(*iv*) *the maximum temperature to have no stress in the rails, if the expansion allowance is 13 mm per rails.*

Ans. Rise of temperature = t = 60 – 10 = 50° C

(*i*) Stress = $\alpha\, t\, \text{E} = 12 \times 10^{-6} \times 50 \times 2 \times 10^5$

= **120 N/mm²**

(*ii*) $$\frac{p\text{L}}{\text{E}} = \Delta\text{L} = (\text{L}\,\alpha\, t - 10)$$

$$= \left(30000 \times 12 \times 10^{-6} \times 50 - 10\right)$$

$$= 18 - 10 = 8\text{mm}$$

$$\therefore \quad p = \frac{2 \times 10^5}{30000} \times 8$$

= **53.3 N/mm²**

(*iii*) If the stresses are to be zero, the expansion allowance

$$= \text{L}\,\alpha\, t = 30000 \times 12 \times 10^{-6} \times 50$$

= **18 mm**

(*iv*) If the stresses are to be zero, we have

$$p = \frac{\text{E}}{\text{L}}(\text{L}\,\alpha\, t - 13) = 0$$

$$\therefore \quad \text{L}\,\alpha\, t = 13$$

or $$t = \frac{13}{\text{L}\alpha} = \frac{13}{12 \times 10^{-6} \times 30000} = 36°$$

Allowable temperature = 10 + 36 = **46°C**

EQUIVALENT MODULUS OF A COMPOUND BAR

Let us consider a compound bar of length *L* consisting of two materials of modulus E_1 and E_2 and having areas of cross-section A_1 and A_2 as shown in Fig. (*a*). Fig. (*b*) shows an equivalent bar.

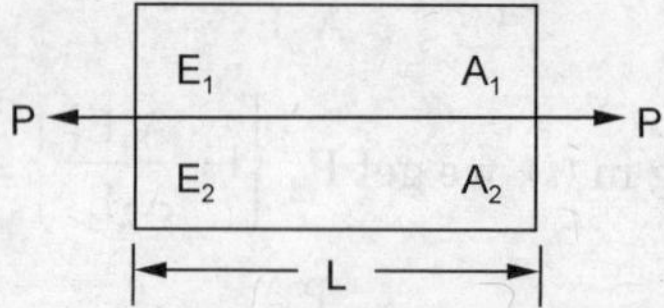

Fig. (a) Compound Bar

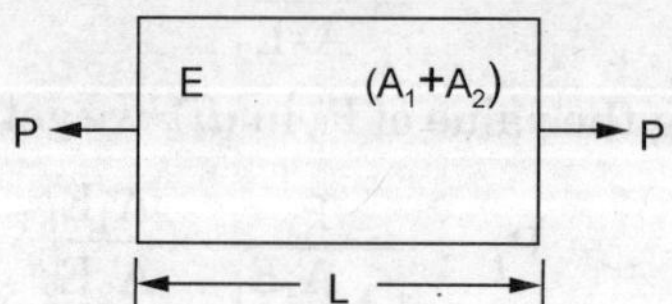

Fig. (b) Equivalent Bar

For the equivalent bar

$$\text{Extension, } \Delta\text{L} = \frac{\text{PL}}{\text{AE}}$$

But $$\text{A} = (\text{A}_1 + \text{A}_2)$$

$$\therefore \quad (\text{A}_1 + \text{A}_2)\,\text{E} = \frac{\text{PL}}{\Delta\text{L}}$$

$$\Rightarrow \quad \text{E} = \frac{\text{PL}}{\Delta\text{L}\,(\text{A}_1 + \text{A}_2)} \quad \text{...... (i)}$$

For the compound bar

Since the strain in both the materials is equal, therefore

$$\frac{p_1}{\text{E}_1} = \frac{p_2}{\text{E}_2}$$

or $$\frac{p_1}{p_2} = \frac{\text{E}_1}{\text{E}_2} \quad \text{...... (ii)}$$

Also $p_1A_1 + p_2A_2 = P$

$$\therefore \quad \left(p_2 \frac{E_1}{E_2}\right) A_1 + p_2A_2 = P$$

or $$p_2 = \frac{P}{\frac{E_1}{E_2} A_1 + A_2} \quad ......(iii)$$

Now, common extension ΔL is given by

$$\Delta L = \frac{p_2 L}{E_2}$$

Substituting the value of p_2 from *(iii)*,

$$\Delta L = \frac{PL}{A_1E_1 + A_2E_2}$$

or $$\frac{PL}{\Delta} = A_1E_1 + A_2E_2 \quad ......(iv)$$

Equating equations *(i)* and *(iv)*, we get

$$(A_1 + A_2)\,E = A_1\,E_1 + A_2\,E_2$$

$$\therefore \quad E = \frac{A_1E_1 + A_2E_2}{A_1 + A_2}$$

which is the required expression for the equivalent or *apparent* modulus elasticity.

ELASTIC CONSTANTS

Poisson's Ratio : Lateral Strain

When a bar of uniform length is subjected to force then its length is increased or the width and breadth is decreased. *Thus, any direct stress produces a strain in its own direction and an opposite kind of strain in every direction at right angles to this.* The ratio of the lateral strain to the longitudinal strain is constant for a given material and is known as *Poisson's Ratio.*

Thus, $$\frac{\text{Lateral strain}}{\text{Longitudinal strain}} = \text{Contant} = \frac{1}{m} = \mu$$

or $$\text{Lateral strain} = \frac{1}{m} \times \text{Longitudinal strain}$$

Poisson's ratio is denoted by $\frac{1}{m}$ or μ, and its value lies between 0.25 to 0.42 for most of the metal. For rubber its value ranges from 0.45 to 0.50.

SINGLE DIRECT STRESS ALONG THE LONGITUDINAL AXIS

Let p be the stress (tensile).

Longitudinal strain e_1 (say) $= \frac{p}{E}$ (tensile)

Lateral strain $e_2 = -\frac{1}{m} e_1 = -\frac{1}{m}\frac{p}{E} = \frac{p}{mE}$ (compressive)

For a rectangular bar of length L, width b and thickness d, we have

Volumetric strain $e_v = \frac{\delta V}{V} = \frac{p}{E}\left(1 - \frac{2}{m}\right)$

If the bar is circular, of diameter d, we get

$$e_v = \frac{\delta V}{V} = \frac{p}{E}\left(1 - \frac{2}{m}\right)$$

Stress p_1 along the Axis and p_2 and p_3 Perpendicular to IT

Gernalised Hook's Law : Let p_1, p_2 and p_3 be all tensile.

Longitudinal strain $e_1 = \frac{p_1}{E} - \frac{p_2}{mE} - \frac{p_3}{mE}$

Similarly, $$e_2 = \frac{p_2}{E} - \frac{p_3}{mE} - \frac{p_1}{mE}$$

and $$e_3 = \frac{p_3}{E} - \frac{p_1}{mE} - \frac{p_2}{mE}$$

These equations are known as the *general equations of Hooke's Law.*

If some of the stresses are of opposite sign, necessary change in the algebraic signs of the above expressions will have to be made.

UPPER LIMIT OF POISSON'S RATIO

Adding the above three expressions of equations, we get

$$e_1 + e_2 + e_3 = \left(1 - \frac{2}{m}\right)\left(\frac{p_1 + p_2 + p_3}{E}\right)$$

The sum of the three strains on the left is known as *dilatation* and, for small strains, it represents change in volume per unit volume.

In case of hydrostatic tension, we have $p_1 = p_2 = p_3 = p$ and the resulting strains are

$$e_1 = e_2 = e_3 = e.$$

$$\therefore \quad Ee = p\left(1 + \frac{2}{m}\right)$$

In the above expression, Ee and p are positive numbers. Hence $\left(1 - \frac{2}{m}\right)$ must also be positive. This limits $\frac{1}{m}$ to a maximum of 0.5. No material is known to have a higher value for Poisson's ratio $\frac{1}{m} = 0.5$, although $\frac{1}{m}$ for rubber approaches this value.

Strain Energy

Strain energy U is the work done by the stresses in straining the material. It is sufficiently general to consider a unit cube acted on by the principal stresses σ_1, σ_2, and σ_3. If the corresponding strains are ε_1, ε_2 and ε_3, then the total work done, since the stresses are gradually applied from zero,

i.e. $U = \frac{1}{2}\sigma_1\varepsilon_1 + \frac{1}{2}\sigma_2\varepsilon_2 + \frac{1}{2}\sigma_3\varepsilon_3 = \left(\frac{1}{2E}\right)$

$[\sigma_1(\sigma_1 - \upsilon\sigma_2 - \upsilon\sigma_3) + \sigma_2(\sigma_2 - \upsilon\sigma_3 - \upsilon\sigma_1) + \sigma_3(\sigma_3 - \upsilon\sigma_1 - \upsilon\sigma_2)]$

$$= \left(\frac{1}{2E}\right)\left[\sigma_1^2 + \sigma_2^2 + \sigma_3^2 - 2\nu(\sigma_1\sigma_2 + \sigma_2\sigma_3 + \sigma_3\sigma_1)\right]$$

per unit volume.

For a two-dimensional stress system $\sigma_3 = 0$

and $U = \left(\frac{1}{2E}\right)\left[\sigma_1^2 + \sigma_2^2 - 2\nu\sigma_1\sigma_2\right]$ per unit volume.

Example. *The principal stresses at a point in an elastic material are 60 N/mm² tensile, 20 N/mm² tensile and 50 N/mm² compressive. Find :*

(i) The volumetric strain $v = 0.35$

(Given $E = 100{,}000$ N/mm².)

(ii) The resilience in Nmm/mm³

Ans. $\sigma_1 = 60,\quad \sigma_2 = 20,\quad \sigma_3 = -50$

(i) Volumetric strain $= (\sigma_1 + \sigma_2 + \sigma_3)\frac{(1-2v)}{E}$

$$= (60 + 20 - 50)\frac{(1-0.7)}{100{,}000}$$

$$= 9 \times 10^{-5}$$

(ii) Resilience

$= [1/(2 \times 100{,}000)]$

$\times\left[60^2 + 20^2 + (-50)^2 - 2 \times 0.35(60\times20 - 20\times50 - 50\times60)\right]$

$= 8460/200{,}000$

$= \mathbf{0.0423\ N\ mm/mm^3}$

Shear Strain Energy

Writing $\sigma_1 = \frac{1}{3}(\sigma_1 + \sigma_2 + \sigma_3) + \frac{1}{3}(\sigma_1 - \sigma_2) + \frac{1}{3}(\sigma_1 - \sigma_3)$

$$\sigma_2 = \frac{1}{3}(\sigma_1 + \sigma_2 + \sigma_3) + \frac{1}{3}(\sigma_2 - \sigma_1) + \frac{1}{3}(\sigma_2 - \sigma_3)$$

$$\sigma_3 = \frac{1}{3}(\sigma_1 + \sigma_2 + \sigma_3) + \frac{1}{3}(\sigma_3 - \sigma_1) + \frac{1}{3}(\sigma_3 - \sigma_2),$$

then under the action of the mean stress $\frac{1}{3}(\sigma_1 + \sigma_2 + \sigma_3)$ there will be volumetric strain with no distortion of shape, (i.e. no shear stress any where). The strain energy under this mean stress acting in each direction is obtained from the general formula, and may be called *volumetric strain energy,*

$$= \left(\frac{3}{2}E\right)\left[\frac{\sigma_1 + \sigma_2 + \sigma_3}{3}\right]^2 (1 - 2\nu)$$

SHEARING FORCE AND BENDING MOMENT

Shearing Force

The shear represents the tendency for the action to slide or shear laterally F acting downwards. F is called the *Shearing Force* (abbrev. S.F.) at the section AA and may be defined as follows : *the shearing force at any section of a beam is the algebraic sum of the lateral components of the forces acting on either side of the section.*

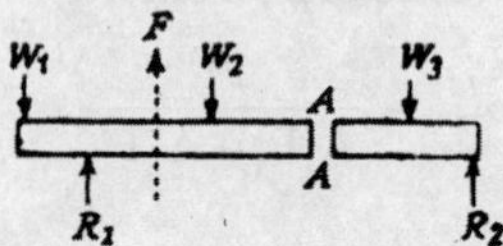

Where a force is in neither the axial nor lateral direction it must be resolved in the usual way, the lateral component being taken into account in the shearing force.

Shearing force will be considered positive when the resultant of the forces to the left is upwards, or to the right is downwards.

A shearing force diagram is one which shows the variation of shearing force along the length of the beam.

Bending Moment

In a similar manner it can be argued that if the momemt about the section AA of the forces to the left is M clock-wise, then the momemt of the forces to the right of AA must be M anticlockwise. M is called the *Bending moment* (abbrev. B.M.) at *AA*, and *is defined as the algebraic sum of the moments about the section of all the forces acting on either side of the section.*

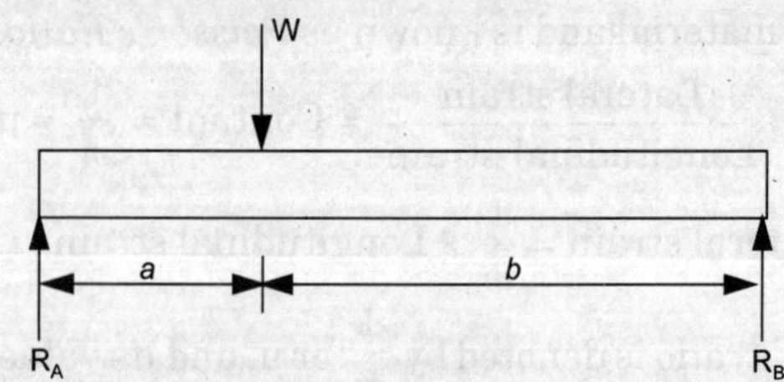

Bending moment will be considered positive when the moment on the left.

Taking moments about B, we get

$$R_B \times L = + Wa$$

$$R_B = + \frac{Wa}{L}$$

$$R_A + R_B = W$$

$$R_A = W - \frac{Wa}{L}$$

$$= \frac{W(L-a)}{L} = \frac{Wb}{L}$$

S.F.D.

Between C and A, S.F. = – W = constant

Between A and B, S.F. = – W + R_A

$$= -W + \frac{W(L+a)}{L} = \frac{Wa}{L}$$

The S.F.D. is shown in Fig. (*b*).

B.M.D.

Between C and A, M_x = W*x*, which gives $M_C = 0$; $M_A = Wa$.

Between A and B, $M_x = Wx - R_A(x-a)$

$$= Wx - \frac{W(L+a)}{L}(x-a)$$

which gives $M_A = Wa$ and $M_B = 0$.

The B.M.D. diagram is shown in Fig. (*c*).

Freely Supported Beam with Couples to Both Ends

Let us take the case of a beam AB, hinged at both the ends and subjected to couples M_A and M_B at the ends.

Let $M_B > M_A$

From statics, $\Sigma V = 0$

Hence $R_A = -R_B = R$ (say)

Again, the net unbalanced moment (external) is $(M_B - M_A)$ (in the anti-clockwise direction).

Since $\Sigma M = 0$, we have $(R \times L) = (M_B - M_A)$

$$\therefore \quad R = \frac{M_B - M_A}{L}$$

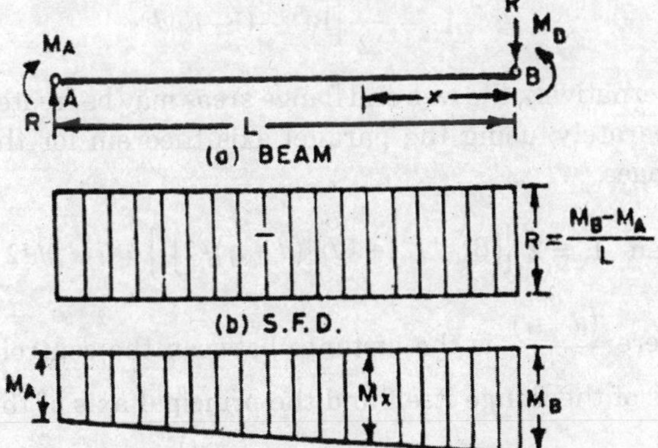

Thus the reaction at A will be R acting upwards and that at B will also be R, acting downwards.

S.D.F. : For any section *x* from B, we have

$$F_x = -R = \frac{M_B - M_A}{L}$$

which is constant from B to A. Hence the S.F.D. will be a rectangle, shown in Fig. (*b*).

B.D.M. : $M_x = -M_B + Rx = M_B + (M_B - M_A)\frac{x}{L}$

At $x = 0$, $M = -M_B$, which decreases linearly

At $x = L$, $M = -M_B + (M_B - M_A)\frac{L}{L} = -M_A$

Thus the B.M.D. will be a trapezium, as shown in Fig. (*c*).

Beam with an Intermediate Couple

Consider a beam AB, hinged at A and supported at B, subjected to couple μ at a distance *a* from A and *b* from B.

Since $\Sigma V = 0$, we get $R_A = -R_B = R$ (say).

The external couple is in the clockwise direction. Hence, the reaction at A will be acting downwards and that at R acting upwards, such that

$$R \times L = \mu$$

or
$$R = \frac{\mu}{L}$$

S.F.D. At any distance *x* from B

$F_x = +R = \frac{\mu}{L}$, which is constant from B to A. Hence, the S.F.D. will be a rectangular, as shown in Fig. (*b*).

B.M.D. For B.C. $M_x = -Rx = -\frac{\mu}{L}x$

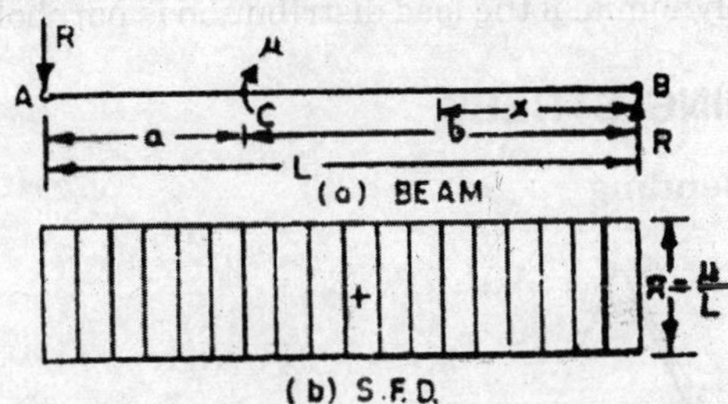

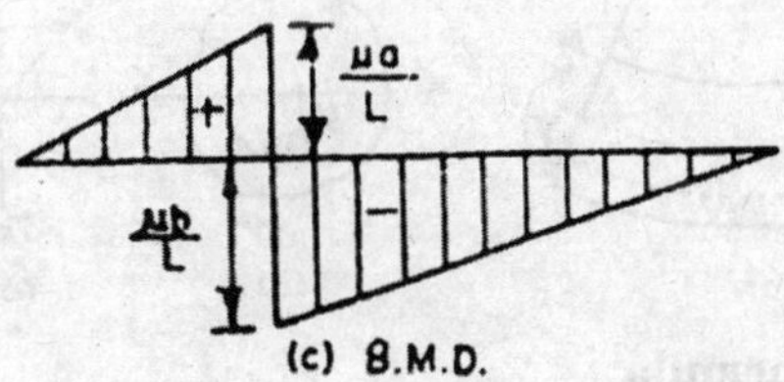

$$\therefore \quad M_C\,(\text{right}) = -\frac{\mu b}{L}$$

For CA, $M_x = -R.x + \mu = -\frac{\mu}{L}x + \mu$

$$\therefore \quad M_C\,(\text{left}) = -\frac{\mu b}{L} + \mu = +\frac{\mu a}{L}$$

$$M_A = 0$$

The variation is linear.

The B.M.D. and S.F.D. have been shown in Fig. (*b*) and (*c*) respectively.

Loading and B.M. Diagrams from S.F.D.

If the S.F.D. for beam is given (or the B.M.D. is given), the loading diagram for the beam can very easily be drawn, if the following points are remembered :

(i) The S.F.D. will consist of rectangle (or series of rectangles) if the beam is loaded with point loads.

(ii) The S.F.D. will consist of inclined lines for the portion on which U.D.L. is acting.

(iii) This S.F.D. will consist of parabolic lines for the portion over which triangular or trapezium load distribution is acting.

(iv) The S.F.D. will consist of 'cubics' for the portion over which parabolic load distribution is acting.

(v) The B.M.D. will consist of inclined lines, if the beam is loaded with point loads.

(vi) The B.M.D. will consist of parabolic lines for the portion over which U.D.L. is acting.

(vii) The B.M.D. will consist of 'cubic' or third degree polynomials if the load distribution is triangular.

(viii) The B.M.D. will consist of fourth degree polynomial if the load distribution is parabolic.

BENDING STRESS

Pure Bending

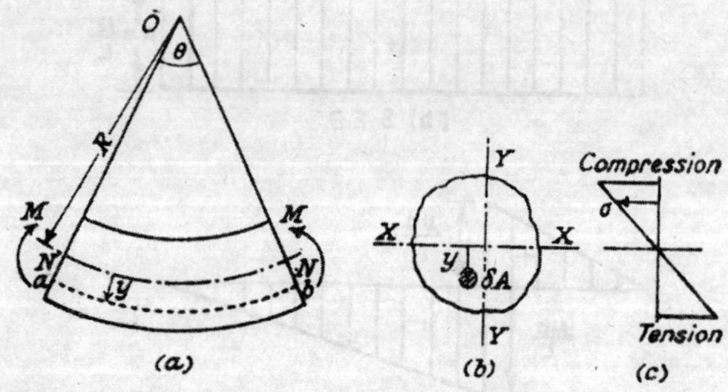

Flexural Formula

$$\frac{\sigma}{y} = \frac{M}{I} = \frac{E}{R}$$

The ratio $I/\hat{y}$ is called the *section modulus* Z, so that $\hat{\sigma} = M/Z$. The bending moment which can be carried by a given section for a limiting maximum stress is called the *moment of resistance*.

$$\int \sigma x dA = 0$$

or $$\int xy dA = 0$$

This integral is referred to as the *product of inertia*, and the axes for which it is zero are called the *Principal Axes* of the cross-section.

Rectangular Section

For bending about the XX' axis, let the width be b and the depth d.

Then $$I_X = \int_{-d/2}^{d/2} y^2 .bdy = b\left[\frac{y^3}{3}\right]_{-d/2}^{d/2} = \frac{bd^3}{12}$$

For the hollow rectangular section, of outside dimensions B,D, and inside dimensions b,d,

$$I_X = \frac{1}{12}(BD^3 - bd^3)$$

1 - Section

In the case of standard sections the moments of inertia are computed graphically from the actual shape of the cross-section as rolled but a reasonable approximation may be obtained by estimating a mean flange thickness and working from a series of rectangles as shown in the figure

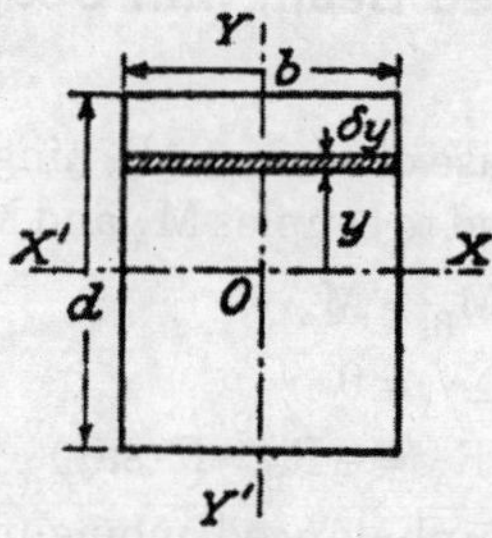

Using the dimensions shown, the moment of inertia about XX' may be obtained by subtracting that for rectangles $(B - t_2)$ wide and d deep from the overall figure B by D, i.e.

$$I_X = \frac{1}{12}\left[BD^3 - (B - t_2)d^3\right]$$

Alternatively, the web and flange areas may be treated separately, using the parallel axis theorem for the flanges.

Then $$I_X = 2\left\{(Bt_1^3/12) + Bt_1\left[(d + t_1)/2\right]^2\right\} + (t_2 d^3/12)$$

where $\frac{(d+t_1)}{2}$ is the distance between the centroid axis of the flange itself and the principal axis of the whole cross-section XX'. The term $\frac{Bt_1^3}{12}$ is very small and can usually be neglected.

$$I_Y = \frac{1}{12}(2t_1B^3 + dt_2^3)$$

Combined Bending and Direct Stress

Consider the case of a column acted on by a thrust P whose line of action cuts the cross-section at a point on the XX axis at a distance h from the centroid O.

Then P is equivalent to an equal load at O, which produces a uniform direct stress, together with a bending moment Ph about YY, which produces a varying bending stress.

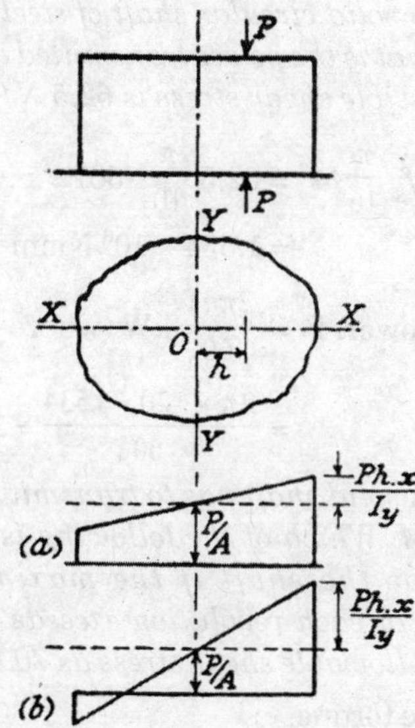

The combined stress, at any point at a distance x from YY, is given by

$$\sigma = \frac{P}{A} + Ph \cdot \frac{x}{I_y}$$

where A is the cross-sectional area.

If x is *reckoned positive on the same side of YY as the load,* so that the bending stress of the same type as the direct stress, the equation for compressive loads will give a positive value for compressive stress. The same notation used for tensile loads will produce a positive value for tensile stresses.

Proceeding with the case under consideration, it is clear that the maximum compressive stress will occur at the right-hand edge of the section. At the left-hand edge of the section x is negative, and if $\frac{P}{A} > Ph.\,x / I_Y$ the stress will remain of a same type, i.e. compressive (Fig. (*a*)). If the bending stress is greater than the direct stress, then the tensile stress at the left-hand edge may be written $Ph.x/I_Y - P/A$ (Fig. (*b*)).

Other points to note from the stress variation diagrams are that the stress at the centroid is P/A, and the usual bending stress diagrams is then plotted about this base. Whether there is a reversal of stress depends on the magnitude of the eccentricity h.

Composite Beams

In the case of beams made up of two different materials, such as timber beams reinforced by steel plates, if the parts are assumed to be rigidly connected together the strain at the common surfaces will be the same for both. Then, if transverse sections remain plane after bending, strain will be proportional to the distance from the common neutral axis.

Denoting the two materials by suffixes 1 and 2, the following equations are obtained from these assumptions.

$$\text{Strain} = \frac{\sigma_1}{E_1} = \frac{\sigma_2}{E_2} \text{ at any common surface} \quad ......(i)$$

In general, as stress = E × strain, and strain is proportional to distance from neutral axis.

$$\frac{\sigma_1'}{\sigma_2'} = \frac{E_1 y_1}{E_2 y_2} \quad .....(ii)$$

where σ'_1 is the stress in material 1 at a distance y_1 from the neutral axis, and σ'_2 is the stress in material 2 at y_2 from the neutral axis.

$$M_1 = \frac{\sigma_1 I_1}{y} \quad .....(iii)$$

and $$M_2 = \frac{\sigma_2 I_2}{y} \quad .....(iv)$$

where y is the distance from the neutral axis to the common surface and σ_1 and σ_2 are as equation (*i*).

Total moment of resistance,

$$M = M_1 + M_2$$

From equations (*iii*) and (*iv*),

$$M = (\sigma_1 I_1 + \sigma_2 I_2)/y$$

From equation (*i*),

$$M = \frac{\sigma_1}{y}\left[I_1 + \frac{E_2}{E_1} I_2\right] = \frac{\sigma_1}{y}(I_1 + mI_2)$$

where m = modular ratio $\frac{E_2}{E_1}$

$I_1 + mI_2$ can be treated as the *equivalent moment of inertia* of the cross-section, as if all made of material 1, which will give the same moment of resistance as the composite beam. It is frequently convenient to produce an *equivalent section* with $I = I_1 + mI_2$, which can be achieved by *multiplying by m the dimensions of material 2 in the direction parallel to the neutral axis*. The equivalent figure can be used for finding the position of the neutral axis and the equivalent moment of inertia, but equation (*ii*) should be used for the stresses, taking care to relate corresponding σ and y values for the separate materials.

TORSION

We know, $$\frac{T}{J} = \frac{\tau}{r} = \frac{c\theta}{l}$$

Showing that, for a given torque, the **shear stress is proportional to the radius.**

For a solid shaft : $T = \frac{\pi D^4}{32}$

and the maximum stress,

$$T = \frac{16T}{\pi D^3}, \quad \text{at } r = D/2$$

For a hollow shaft :

$$\tau = \frac{\pi}{32}(D^4 - d^4)$$

and $\hat{\tau} = \frac{16D.T}{\pi\left(D^4 - d^4\right)}$, at $r = D/2$

Torsional stiffness k is defined as torque per radian twist, i.e.

$$k = \frac{T}{\theta} = \frac{CJ}{l}$$

Design of Shafts

In SI system, power (P) is measured in watts (W).

1W = 1 Joule/sec = 1 N-m/sec.

Let the power be P kW.

Work done in transmitting P kilo watts

$= 1 \times P \times 10^3$ Nm/sec

$= P \times 60 \times 10^6$ Nm/min

$= 60$ P kNm/min ......(*i*)

If T = torque in kNm,

Work supplied = (average couple)

× (angle turned through one minute) ......(*ii*)

$= T . 2\pi n$

From equations (*i*) and (*ii*), we get

$$60\,P = 2\pi n T$$

or $P = \frac{2\pi n T}{60}$ kW

and $T = \frac{60\,P}{2\pi n}$ kNm ......(*iii*)

[It should be noted that 1 H.P. (metric) = 0.75 kW.]

The resistance torque (T_r) of the shaft must atleast be equal to T above, so that maximum stress f_s is not exceeded.

$\therefore \quad T = T_r = f_s \cdot \frac{J}{R}$

or $\frac{J}{R} = \frac{T}{f_s}$

In the above equation, T is known from Eq. (*ii*) and f_s is the allowable stress. Hence the section modulus $\frac{J}{R}$ can be determined. Knowing $\frac{J}{R}$, the diameter of the shaft can be calculated.

$$T = f_s \cdot \frac{J}{R} = f_s \frac{\pi}{16} d^3$$

In the above equation, T must be substituted in Nmm units if f_s is in N/mm² units.

Example. *A solid circular shaft of steel is 50 mm in diameter. What is the power transmitted at 120 R.P.M. If the permissible shear stress is 62.5 N/mm² ?*

Ans. $T_r = f_s \frac{\pi}{16} d^3 = 62.5 \frac{\pi}{10} (50)^2$

$= 1.534 \times 10^6$ Nmm = 1.534 kNm

Power, $P = \frac{2\pi n T}{60}$ kW (where T is in kNm)

$\therefore \quad = \frac{2\pi \times 120 \times 1.534}{60} = \mathbf{19.28\ kW}$

Example. *A solid shaft has to transmit 90 kW power at 160 R.P.M. Which of the following is the suitable diameter for the shaft if the maximum torque transmitted in each revolution exceeds the mean by 25% ? Take allowable shear stress as 70 N/mm².*

Ans. Average torque,

$T_{av} = \frac{60\,P}{2\pi n}$ kNm

$= \frac{60 \times 90}{2\pi \times 160} = 5.37$ kNm

$T_{max} = 1.25\,T_{av}$

$= 1.25 \times 5.37$

$= 6.71$ kNm

$= 6.71 \times 10^6$ Nmm

But $T = f_s \frac{\pi}{16} d^3$

or $d^3 = \frac{16T}{f_s . \pi}$

$= \frac{16 \times 6.71 \times 10^6}{70 \times \theta}$

$= 488542$ mm³

$\therefore \quad d = 78.86$ mm $\simeq$ **80 mm**

Combined Bending and Torsion : Principal Stresses

At any point in the shaft, the component stresses are

(i) the shear stress due to torsion,

(ii) the bending stress (tensile or compressive) and

(iii) the shear stress due to bending forces.

In shafts which are not very long, the principal stresses will be maximum at the surface point (such as A or B).

Thus, at A or B the stresses will be :

1. The shear stress f_s due to torsion.
2. The bending stress f_b due to bending.

The shear stress due to bending will be zero at point A or B.

Thus we have $$f_s = \frac{T}{J} R = \frac{16T}{\pi d^3}$$

and $$f_b = \frac{M}{I} R = \frac{32M}{\pi d^3}$$

And the principal stresses are

$$\sigma = \frac{f_b}{2} \pm \sqrt{\frac{f_b^2}{4} + f_s^2}$$

$$= \frac{16}{\pi d^3}\left\{M \pm \sqrt{M^2 + T^2}\right\}$$

The position of principal planes are given by

$$\tan 2\theta = \frac{2 f_s}{f_b} = \frac{T}{M}$$

It is to be noted that the principal stresses σ_1 and σ_2 will be of opposite sign.

In the case of a very short shaft, the effect of bending stress may be very small in comparison to the component shear caused by bending forces. In such cases, the maximum principal stress may occur within the shaft. Usually, however, the maximum principal stress is at the circumference.

Torsional Strain Energy

$$\therefore \quad \delta U = \frac{f_s^2 r^2}{2R^2 N}(2\pi r dr) = \frac{f_s^2 r^3}{2R^2 N} 2\pi l dr$$

$$U \simeq \frac{f_s^2}{2N} \times \text{volume of the shaft}$$

Shafts in Series and Parallel

When two dissimilar shafts are connected together to form one shaft, the shaft is known as a *composite shaft*. If the driving torque is applied at one end, and the resisting torque at the other end, the shafts are said to be connected in *series* (Fig. (*a*)]. In such a case both the shafts carry the same torque T, and the total angle of twist at the fixed or resisting end is the sum of the separate angles of twist of the two shafts :

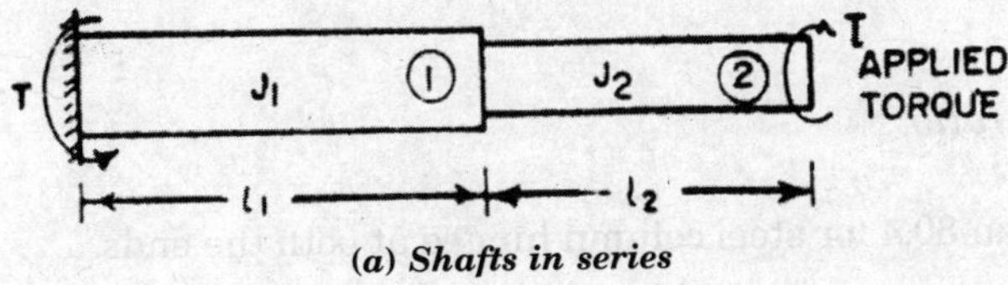

(*a*) *Shafts in series*

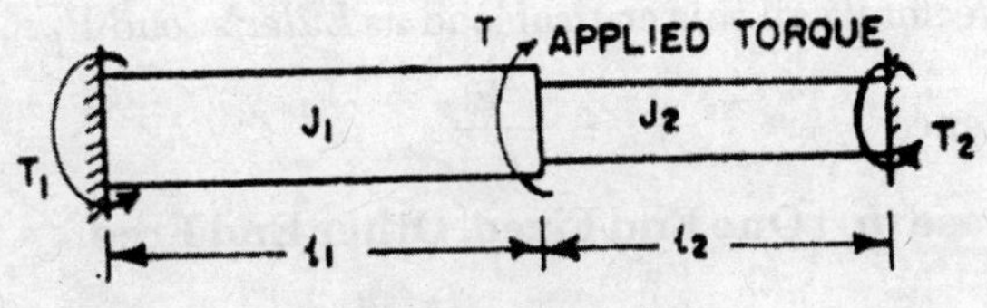

(*b*) *Shafts in parallel*

$$\theta = \theta_1 + \theta_2 = \frac{Tl_1}{N_1 J_1} + \frac{Tl_2}{N_2 J_2}$$

If $N_1 = N_2 = N$ (i.e both shafts of the same material)

$$\theta = \frac{T}{N}\left(\frac{l_1}{J_1} + \frac{l_2}{J_2}\right)$$

If the torque T is applied at the junction of the two shafts and the resisting torques T_1 and T_2 at their remote ends, the shafts are said to be connected in parallel. In such a case, the angle of twist is the same for both the shafts, *i.e.*, $\theta_1 = \theta_1$

$$\therefore \quad \frac{T_1 l_1}{N_1 J_1} = \frac{T_2 l_2}{N_2 J_2}$$

or $$\frac{T_1}{T_2} = \frac{l_2}{l_1} \cdot \frac{N_1}{N_2} \cdot \frac{J_1}{J_2}$$

If both the shafts are of the same material, then

$$\frac{T_1}{T_2} = \frac{J_1}{J_2} \cdot \frac{l_2}{l_1}.$$

Columns

Euler's Theory : Long Columns

At critical load causing neutral equilibrium, a compression member may buckle in any direction if its I is same about both the axes. Generally, a compression member does not possess equal flexural rigidity in all directions. The *significant* flexural rigidity EI of a column depends on the *minimum* I, and at the critical load a column buckles either to one side or the other in that plane about which I is minimum.

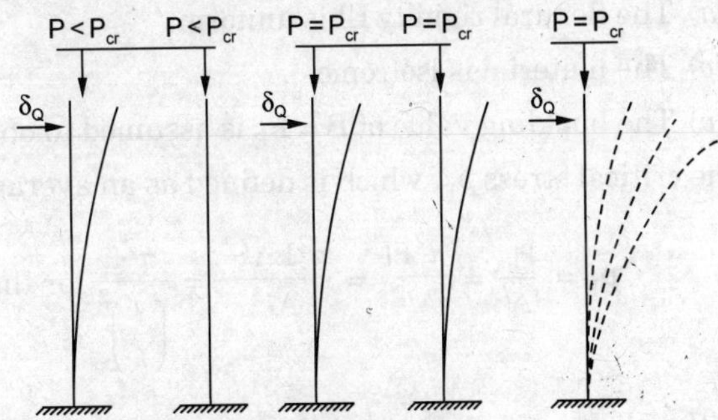

Case (*a*) : Both Ends Hinged

$$P = \frac{\pi^2 EI}{l^2}$$

We shall call this critical load as *Euler's load* P_E.

Hence $$P_E = \frac{\pi^2 EI}{l^2}$$

Case (*b*) : One End Fixed, Other End Free

$$P = P_E = \frac{\pi^2 EI}{4l^2}$$

Case (*c*) : Both Ends Fixed

$$P = \frac{4\pi^2 EI}{l^2}$$

Case (*d*) : One End Fixed, the Other Hinged

$$P = P_E = \frac{2\pi^2 EI}{l^2}$$

The Equivalent Length

In all the four cases, we have deduced the Euler's crippling load.

In general, Euler's crippling load can be expressed in the form $P_E = \frac{\pi^2 EI}{Cl^2}$ in which C is a constant which takes into account the method of fixing the ends (i.e. whether the ends are fixed or hinged or free).

For a column hinged at both the ends are represented in Fig. (*a*), C = 1, and hence will be called the standard case. For case (*b*), C = 4; for case (*c*), $C = \frac{1}{4}$ and for case (*d*), $C = \frac{1}{2}$.

In the place of using the actual length l of the column, we can use that length of the column which is *equivalent* to that of a pin jointed column. Thus

$$P_E = \frac{\pi^2 EI}{I_E^{\,2}}$$

The above expression is applicable for all end conditions. L_E in the above formula is equal to $l\sqrt{C}$ and is known as *equivalent length*. The equivalent length of different columns is given below :

End conditions	*Both ends hinged*	*One end fixed other free*	*Both ends fixed*	*One end fixed other hinged*
Equivalent length $L_E = l\sqrt{C}$	l	$2l$	$\frac{l}{2}$	$\frac{l}{\sqrt{2}}$

It is to be noted that no factor of safety is included in the Euler's equations.

Limitations of Euler's Formula

The Euler's theory is based on the following assumptions :

(*i*) The axis of the strut is perfectly straight when unloaded.

(*ii*) The line of thrust coincides exactly with the unstrained axis of the strut.

(*iii*) The flexural rigidity EI is uniform.

(*iv*) The material is isotropic.

(*v*) The buckling value of $P = P_E$ is assumed to obtain for all degrees of flexure.

The critical stress p_E, which is defined as an average stress over the cross-section is given by

$$p_E = \frac{P_E}{A} = \frac{\pi^2 EI}{Al^2} = \frac{\pi^2 EAk^2}{Al^2} = \frac{\pi^2 E}{\left(\frac{l}{k}\right)^2} \text{ for the standard case.}$$

In the above expression, $\frac{l}{k}$ is known as the *slenderness ratio*.

The Euler's formula is applicable only if $\frac{l}{k}$ is greater than 80.4 for steel column hinged at both the ends.

Rankine's Formula

We have seen that Euler's formula is valid only for long columns, i.e., for column having $\frac{l}{k}$ ratio greater than a certain value for a particular material. Also, short columns fail in direct compression only. Euler's formula valid for $\frac{l}{k}$ higher than 80.4 (for Mild Steel), does not take into account the direct compressive stress, and hence gives correct results only for very long columns. For columns intermediate between very long and short ones, Euler's formula, though applicable, does not give correct results.

Rankine proposed an empirical formula for columns which cover all cases ranging from very short to very long struts. He proposed the relation.

$$\frac{1}{P} = \frac{1}{P_C} + \frac{1}{P_E}$$

where $P_C = f_C A$ = ultimate load for a strut, and $P_E = \frac{\pi^2 EI}{l^2}$ Eulerian crippling load for the standard case.

In the above relation, $\frac{1}{P_C}$ is constant for a material. For short columns, P_E is very large and hence $\frac{1}{P_E}$ is small in comparison to $\frac{1}{P_C}$, thus making the crippling load P approximately equal to P_C. For long columns, P_E is extremely small and hence $\frac{1}{P_E}$ is large as compared to $\frac{1}{P_C}$, thus making the crippling load P approximately equal to P_E. Thus the value of P obtained from the above relation covers all cases ranging from short to long columns or struts.

The above relation can be re-arranged as

$$P = \frac{P_C P_E}{P_E + P_C} = \frac{P_C}{1 + \frac{P_C}{P_E}} = \frac{f_C A}{1 + \frac{f_C A l^2}{\pi^2 EI}} = \frac{f_C \cdot A}{1 + \left(\frac{f_C}{\pi^2 E}\right)\left(\frac{l}{k}\right)^2} = \frac{f_C \cdot A}{1 + a\left(\frac{l}{k}\right)^2}$$

In the above equation, f_C is crushing stress for the material and a is the Rankine's constant for the material. Though the formula is empirical, the value of the constant a is not calculated from the values of f_C, π^2 and E, but is determined experimentally.

The following table gives the values of f_C and a for the materials most commonly used for columns and struts.

No.	*Material*	f_C		*a for ends hinged*
		kg/cm²	*N/mm²*	
1.	Wrought Iron	2550	255	$\frac{1}{9000}$
2.	Cast Iron	5670	567	$\frac{1}{1600}$
3.	Mild Steel	3300	330	$\frac{1}{7500}$
4.	Strong Timber	550	50	$\frac{1}{750}$

Equation (*i*) is the Rankine's formula for the standard case of two hinged columns. It is sometimes known as Rankine-Gordon formula. For columns with other end conditions, the value of the constant will be changed accordingly. However, since a is a constant for a particular material used as a hinged column, it is not convenient to remember the values of a for other end conditions. It is, therefore, better to modify the Rankine's formula and remember it in the form :

$$P = \frac{f_C A}{1 + a\left(\frac{L_E}{k}\right)^2} \quad \text{...... (ii)}$$

in which a is the Rankine's constant for a particular material and for the standard case of column and L_E is the equivalent length of the column. Since equivalent length is generally known, it can be substituted in the above formula to get the Rankine's formula for a particular case of end conditions. Equations (6) and (*ii*) do not include the factor of safety.

Gordon's Formula

Gordon proposed the following formula :

$$P = \frac{f_A}{1 + a' \dfrac{l^2}{b^2}}$$

in which a' = Gordon's constant = $\dfrac{ab^2}{k^2}$

b = Overall lesser dimension

a = Rankine's constant.

Gordon's constant a' is not a mathematical constant like Rankine's but its value depends upon the properties of the material and the shape of the section.

Johnson's Formula

Johnson proposed the following two formulae :

$$P = A\left(f - n\frac{l}{k}\right) \text{ straight line } \quad ......(i)$$

$$P = A\left(f - r\frac{l^2}{k^2}\right) \text{ parabolic } \quad ......(ii)$$

Equation (*i*) is a *straight line* formula, as a straight line will be obtained if $\dfrac{P}{A}$ is plotted against $\dfrac{l}{k}$. The constant n depends on the material and upon the end conditions of the column, f is the allowable stress of the material and therefore, P is the safe load for the column.

For mild steel, f = 1125 kg/cm^2 and n = 5.625 for both ends hinged and n = 4.219 for both ends fixed. Thus, Johnson's straight line formula becomes

$$P = A\left(1125 - 5.625\frac{l}{k}\right) \text{ for both ends hinged}$$

$$\text{and } P = A\left(1125 - 4.219\frac{l}{k}\right) \text{ for both ends fixed}$$

Equation (*ii*) is a parabolic formula, as a parabola will be obtained if $\dfrac{P}{A}$ is plotted against $\dfrac{l}{k}$. The constant r depends on the material and upon the end conditions of the column.

Objective Type Questions

1. During a tensile test on a specimen of 1 cm^2 cross-section, maximum load observed was 8 tonnes and area of cross-section at neck was 0.5 cm^2. Ultimate tensile strength of specimen is
   (a) 4 tonnes/cm^2 (b) 8 tonnes/cm^2
   (c) 16 tonnes/cm^2 (d) 22 tonnes/cm^2
2. Young's modulus of a wire is defined as the stress which will increase the length of wire compared to its original length by
   (a) half (b) same amount
   (c) double (d) one-fourth
3. A material obey's Hooke's law up to
   (a) Plastic limit
   (b) Elastic limit
   (c) Yield point
   (d) Limit of proportionality
4. After reaching the yielding stage while testing a mild steel specimen, strain
   (a) becomes contant
   (b) starts decreasing
   (c) increases without any increase in load
   (d) none of the above
5. True stress-strain curve for materials is plotted between
   (a) load/original cross-sectional area and change in length/original length
   (b) load/instantaneous cross-sectional area and $\log_e\left(\frac{\text{original area}}{\text{instantaneous area}}\right)$
   (c) load/instanataneous cross-sectional area and change in length/original length
   (d) load/instantaneous area and instantaneous area/ original area
6. Strain energy per unit volume due to principle stress σ_1, σ_2 and σ_3 is
   (a) $\frac{2}{E}\left[\sigma_1^2+\sigma_2^2+\sigma_3^2+\frac{2}{m}(\sigma_1\sigma_2+\sigma_2\sigma_3+\sigma_3\sigma_1)\right]$
   (b) $\frac{2}{2E}\left[\sigma_1^2+\sigma_2^2+\sigma_3^2-\frac{2}{m}(\sigma_1\sigma_2+\sigma_2\sigma_3+\sigma_3\sigma_1)\right]$
   (c) $\frac{2}{2E}\left[(\sigma_1^2-\sigma_2^2)+\sigma_3^2+\frac{2}{m}(\sigma_1\sigma_2+\sigma_2\sigma_3+\sigma_3\sigma_1)\right]$
   (d) $\frac{2}{2E}\left[\sigma_1^2-\sigma_2^2-\sigma_3^2-\frac{2}{m}(\sigma_1\sigma_2+\sigma_2\sigma_3+\sigma_3\sigma_1)\right]$
7. A cube subjected to three mutually perpendicular stress of equal intensity p expenses a volumetric strain
   (a) $\frac{3p}{E}\left(\frac{2}{m}-1\right)$ (b) $\frac{3p}{E}(2-m)$
   (c) $\frac{3p}{E}\left(1-\frac{2}{m}\right)$ (d) $\frac{E}{3p}\left(\frac{2}{m}-1\right)$
8. Impact strength of a material is an index of its
   (a) toughnesss
   (b) tensile strength
   (c) capability of being cold worked
   (d) hardness
9. Volumetric strain for a rectangular specimen of length 1, breadth b and thickness t subjected to a pull of p is given by
   (a) $e\,(1-2m)$ (b) $e\left(1-\frac{2}{m}\right)$
   (c) $e\,(m-2)$ (d) $e\left(\frac{2}{m}-1\right)$
10. A hollow shaft of same cross-section area as solid shaft transmits
    (a) same toruqe (b) less torque
    (c) more torque (d) unpredictable
11. The intensity of stress which causes unit strain is called
    (a) unit stress (b) modulus of rigidity
    (c) bulk modulus (d) modulus of elasticity
12. In a block subjected to normal stresses σ_x and σ_y and shear stress τ along two mutually perpendicular planes, the normal stress on plane making angle 0 with σ_x is given by
    (a) $\sigma_x \cos^2\theta + \sigma_y \sin^2\theta + \cos 2t$
    (b) $\sigma_x \sin^2\theta + \sigma_y \sin^2\theta + \tau \cos 2t$
    (c) $\sigma_x \sin^2\theta - \sigma_y \sin^2\theta + \cos 2t$
    (d) $\sigma_x \cos^2\theta + \sigma_y \sin^2\theta + \tau \sin 2\theta$
13. A composite bar made up of steel and copper bars of equal length are heated through 100°C. The stresses developed shall be
    (a) tensile in both the materials
    (b) tensile in steel and compressive in copper
    (c) compressive in steel and tensile in copper
    (d) compressive in both the materials

14. Whitin elastic limit stress is
(*a*) inversely proportional to strain
(*b*) directly proportinal to strain
(*c*) square root of strain
(*d*) equal to strain

15. Modulus of rigidity is defined as the ratio of
(*a*) longitudinal stress and longitudinal strain
(*b*) volumetric stress and volumetric strain
(*c*) lateral stress and lateral strain
(*d*) shear stress and shear strain

16. The shape of cantilever for uniformly distributed load will be
(*a*) straight line (*b*) parabolic
(*c*) parabolic (*d*) elliptical

17. The ultimate tensile stress of mild steel compared to ultimate compressive stress is
(*a*) same (*b*) more
(*c*) less (*d*) unpredictable

18. A bar when subjected to an axial pull P
(*a*) decrease in length and width and increase in thickness
(*b*) decrease in length and increase in width and thickness
(*c*) increase in length and decrease in width and thickness.
(*d*) increase in length, width and thickness.

19. Deflection of the centre of simply supported beam of length/carrying a uniformly distributed load w kg/m will be
(*a*) $\dfrac{wl^3}{8EI}$ (*b*) $\dfrac{5wl^3}{384\ EI}$
(*c*) $\dfrac{5wl^3}{8\ EI}$ (*d*) $\dfrac{5}{384}\dfrac{wl^3}{EI}$

20. Percentage reduction of area in performing tensile test on cast iron may be of the order of
(*a*) 50%
(*b*) 25%
(*c*) 0%
(*d*) 15%

21. Poissons's ratio is the ratio of
(*a*) stress and strain
(*b*) modules of elasticity and strain
(*c*) lateral strain and longitudinal strain
(*d*) none of these

22. Modular ratio of two materials is the ratio of
(*a*) strains
(*b*) stress and strain
(*c*) sheaz stress and shear strain
(*d*) modulii and elasticity

23. A coil is cut into two halves, the stiffness of cut coils will be
(*a*) double (*b*) half
(*c*) same (*d*) none of these

24. Elasticity of a M.S. specimen is defined by
(*a*) Hooke's law (*b*) yield point
(*c*) plastic flow (*d*) proof stress

25. If the radius of wire streched by a load is doubled, then its Young's modulus will
(*a*) be doubled (*b*) be halved
(*c*) become four times (*d*) none of these

26. In a uniform bar supported at one end in position, the maximum stress under self weight of bar shall occur at the
(*a*) middle of bar (*b*) supported end
(*c*) bottom end (*d*) none of the above

27. The extension of a uniforme tapering bar from dia D_2 at top to dia D_1 at bottom and having length l, under an axial load P is given by
(*a*) $\dfrac{4\pi P\ell}{ED_1D_2}$ (*b*) $\dfrac{4E\pi P\ell}{D_1D_2}$
(*c*) $\dfrac{4\pi D_1D_2}{EP\ell}$ (*d*) $\dfrac{4P\ell}{\pi ED_1D_2}$

28. When both ends of a column are fixed, the effective length is
(*a*) its own length (*b*) twice its length
(*c*) half its length (*d*) $1/\sqrt{2}\ \times$ its length

29. The extension of a mild steel bar 4m long, 2000 mm^2 cross section under the action of an axial load of 20 kN, if $E = 2 \times 10^{-5}$ N/ mm^2, is
(*a*) 2 mm
(*b*) 0.2 mm
(*c*) 0.5 mm
(*d*) 0.05 mm

30. Stenderness of a column is zero when
(*a*) ends are firmly fixed
(*b*) column is supported on all sides throughout the length
(*c*) length is equal to radius of gyration
(*d*) length is twice the radius of gyration.

31. Formula adopted for IS codes is based on
(*a*) Straight line formula
(*b*) Euler's formula
(*c*) Rankine's formula
(*d*) Secant formula

32. Ratio of maximum deflection of a simply supported beam of span L carrying
(*i*) A concentrated load w at wid point and
(*ii*) total load w_1 uniformly distributed over the entire span, is
(*a*) 1 : 16 (*b*) 1.6 : 1
(*c*) 1 : 1 (*d*) None of the above

33. Deflection at the mid span of a rectangular point beam under a concentrated load acting there shall become ..... if the length, width and depth of beam are all doubled
(*a*) 2 times (*b*) 8 times
(*c*) same (*d*) half

34. Principal planes are planes having
(*a*) maximum shear stress
(*b*) no shear stress
(*c*) minimum shear stress
(*d*) none of the above

35. Figure below shows the relationship of various scales of hardness w.r.t. Brinell Numbers. Curve A is for

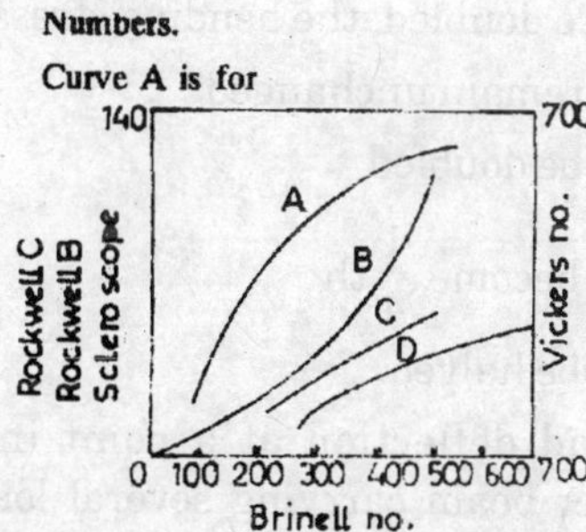

(*a*) Rockwell C (*b*) Vickers
(*c*) Rockwell B (*d*) Scleroscope

36. In above fig. curve D is for
(*a*) Rockwell C (*b*) Vickers
(*c*) Rockwell B (*d*) Scleroscope

37. In above fig. curve B is for
(*a*) Rockwell C (*b*) Vickers
(*c*) Rockwell B (*d*) Scleroscope

38. In fig. above curve C is for
(*a*) Rockwell C (*b*) Vickers
(*c*) Rockwell B (*d*) Scleroscope

39. For a cantilever of span L carrying a moment M at free end, deflection at free end is
(*a*) $\frac{ML^3}{6EI}$ (*b*) $\frac{ML^3}{2EI}$
(*c*) $\frac{ML^3}{8EI}$ (*d*) none of the above

40. Length of a column having Euler's crippling load and Rankine's crippling load of same magnitude, is given by
(*a*) $\sqrt{\frac{\pi E\, r}{\pi^2 Ea - fa}}$ (*b*) $\sqrt{\frac{\pi E\, r^2}{\pi^2 Ea - fa}}$
(*c*) $\sqrt{\frac{\pi^2 E\, r}{fa - \pi^2 Ea}}$ (*d*) none of the above

r = minimum radius of gyration
E = Young's Modulus of elasticity
a = Rankine's a

41. The force acting along the circumferece will cause stress in the walls in a direction normal to the longitudinal axis of cylinder, this stress is called
(*a*) longitudinal stress (*b*) hoop stress
(*c*) yield stress (*d*) ultimate stress

42. A simply supported beam of length L and flexural rigidity EI, loaded with a central point load W shall have a maximum deflection of
(*a*) $\frac{WL^3}{187EI}$ (*b*) $\frac{WL^3}{48\,EI}$
(*c*) $\frac{WL^3}{9\sqrt{3}\,EI}$ (*d*) $\frac{WL^3}{107\,EI}$

43. A boiler shell 200 cm diameter and plate thickness 1.5 cm is subjected to internal pressure of 1.5 MN/m^2, then the hoop stress will be
(*a*) 30 MN/m^2 (*b*) 50 MN/m^2
(*c*) 100 MN/m^2 (*d*) 200 MN/m^2

44. In a cantilever, maximum deflection occurs where
(*a*) bending moment is zero
(*b*) bending moment is maximum
(*c*) shear force is zero
(*d*) slope is zero

45. Euler's crippling load formula is valid for a columns having slenderless ratio (in terms of effective length and minimum radius of gyration)
(*a*) upto 12 (*b*) upto 30
(*c*) between 30 to 80 (*d*) Above 80 only

46. Dampling capacity of material is its ability to

(*a*) absorb shock

(*b*) absorb vibrations

(*c*) withstand compression

(*d*) absorb impact loads.

47. A beam encastered at both the ends is known as

(*a*) simply supported beam

(*b*) over hanging beam

(*c*) a fixed beam

(*d*) a continuous beam

48. At the principal planes

(*a*) normal stress is maximum or minium and the shear stress is zero

(*b*) tensile and compressive stresses are zero

(*c*) tensile stress is zero and the shear stress is maximum.

(*d*) no stress acts.

49. Relationship between modulus of elasticity E, modulus of rigidity G is

(*a*) $E = G(1 + \mu)$ (*b*) $G = E(2 - \mu)$

(*c*) $G = \frac{E}{2(1+\mu)}$ (*d*) $G = \frac{E}{1+\mu}$

where μ = Poisson's ratio

50. Torsional rigidity of a solid circular shaft of diameter '*d*' is proportional to

(*a*) d (*b*) d^2

(*c*) $\frac{1}{d^2}$ (*d*) d^4

51. The resistance offered by internal stresses to bending is known as

(*a*) shear stress

(*b*) compressive stress

(*c*) modulus of elasticity

(*d*) moment of resistance

52. A cylindrical section having no joint is known as

(*a*) jointless section

(*b*) homogeneous section

(*c*) perfect section

(*d*) seamless section

53. Bending stress at any section in a beam is

(*a*) equal to section Modulus

(*b*) inversely proportional to section modulus

(*c*) directly proportional to section modulus

(*d*) none of the above.

54. The Rankine's crippling load is given by

(*a*) $PR = \frac{f_c A}{1 + a\left(\frac{l}{r}\right)^2}$ (*b*) $PR = \frac{f_c \times a}{1 + \left(\frac{l}{r}\right)^2}$

(*c*) $PR = \frac{f_c \times A}{1 + \left(\frac{l}{r}\right)^2}$ (*d*) none of the above

55. A sudden change in shear force diagram between and two points indicates that there is

(*a*) point load at both the points

(*b*) no loading between two points

(*c*) u.d.l. between two point

(*d*) uniformly varying load between two points.

56. If b is the width of a plate joined by diamond riveting of diameter (d), the efficiency of the joint is given by

(*a*) $\frac{b+d}{b}$ (*b*) $\frac{b-d}{b}$

(*c*) $\frac{d-b}{d}$ (*d*) $\frac{b-d}{d}$

57. Effective length of a column of length L fixed at one end and hinged at the other end is

(*a*) L (*b*) 2L

(*c*) $\sqrt{2L}$ (*d*) $\frac{L}{\sqrt{2}}$

58. In a rectangular beam, when width, depth and length are doubled, the bending stress

(*a*) shall remain unchanged

(*b*) shall be doubled

(*c*) shall become $\frac{1}{4}$ th

(*d*) shall be halved.

59. Slope and deflection at a point in a loaded cantilever beam carrying several loads can be found out by the

(*a*) principle of least work

(*b*) moment area method

(*c*) double integration method

(*d*) Macualay's method

60. A circular bar is subjected to an axial force of 1000 kg. The components of force normal and tangent to a plane inclined at 45° to the axis of bar will be

(*a*) 1003 kg each

(*b*) 707 kg each

(*c*) 500 kg each

(*d*) not possible to determine with these data

61. A composite bar made of steel and copper is heated up. The stresses developed in steel and copper will be

(a) compressive and tensile
(b) compressive and bending
(c) bending and tensile
(d) tensile and compressive

62. Diagram showing the variation of axial load a long the span is

(a) Shear force diagram
(b) Normal thrust diagram
(c) Influence line diagram
(d) Bending moment diagram

63. The factor of safety considered in Euler's formula for crippling load is

(a) 1 (b) 3
(c) 5 (d) 6

64. Rankines crippling load formula is valid for

(a) long columns only
(b) short columns
(c) for all columns
(d) intermediate columns

65. Hoop stress in a thin cylinder of diameter d and thickness t subjected to pressure p will be

(a) $\frac{pd}{4t}$ (b) $\frac{pd}{t}$
(c) $\frac{pd}{2t}$ (d) $\frac{2pd}{t}$

66. Longitudinal strain for a specimen is 0.01 and it is found to undergo 1 mm change in its thickness. Its thickness will be

(a) 100 mm (b) 200 mm
(c) 400 mm (d) 800 mm

67. In I-section, the bending moment is resisted mainly by

(a) flanges only
(b) web only
(c) both by flanges and web
(d) none of the above

68. A simply supported beam of span l carrying a uniformly varying load from zero at one end to w at the other end undegroes a maximum bending of

(a) $\frac{4wl^2}{125}$ (b) $\frac{8wl^2}{125}$
(c) $\frac{2wl^2}{125}$ (d) $\frac{12wl^2}{125}$

69. Maximum deflection in a beam supported freely at both ends due to a central load p at middle is

(a) $\frac{Pt^3}{48EI}$ (b) $\frac{Pt^3}{32EI}$
(c) $\frac{Pt^3}{96EI}$ (d) $\frac{Pt^3}{64EI}$

70. The rate of change of shear force at any section is equal to

(a) bending moment (b) loading
(c) deflection (d) intensity of loading

71. The section modulus of a circular section about an axis through its c.g. is

(a) $\frac{\pi d^3}{16}$ (b) $\frac{\pi d^3}{32}$
(c) $\frac{\pi d^3}{64}$ (d) $\frac{\pi d^2}{32}$

72. If the depth of a recrtangular beam is halved the deflection for a beam carrying a mid point load shall be

(a) Halved (b) Doubled
(c) Four times (d) Eight times

73. A simply supported rectangular beam 200 mm wide, 300 mm deep, 4m long carrying a u.d.l. of 10 kN/m experiences a maximum bending stress of

(a) 66.67 N/mm²
(b) 0.667 N/mm²
(c) 6.67 N/mm²
(d) none of the above

74. The depth of breadth ratio for the strongest rectangular beam that can be cur out of a cylindrical wooden log is

(a) 3 : 1 (b) $\sqrt{2}$: 1
(c) 2 : 3 (d) 2 : 1

75. Beams of uniform strength are better as compared to beams of uniform cross section as they are economical

(a) for short spans
(b) for large spans
(c) for heavy weight beams
(d) for light weight beams

76. A point of contraflexure occurs in a

(a) simply supported beam
(b) fixed beam
(c) cantilever
(d) none of the above

77. Shape of bending moment diagram for a simply supported beam carrying a number of concentrated loads is a

(*a*) series of straight lines
(*b*) straight line
(*c*) a parabola
(*d*) none of the above

78. Shear force diagram for a cantilever beam carrying a uniformly distributed load over its length is a

(*a*) triangle (*b*) rectangle
(*c*) hyperbola (*d*) parabola

79. Minimum thickness of a flange forged at the end of shaft is determined by

(*a*) compression between two flanges
(*b*) tightening of bolts
(*c*) fact that it must be sufficient to prevent the shaft from shearing out of the flange on the cylindrical surface
(*d*) all of the above

80. Shear stress in a rectangular beam exhibits a

(*a*) parabolic variation (*b*) linear variation
(*c*) cubic variation (*d*) none of the above

81. Deflection at mid pint of a simply supported beam carrying a u.d.i. w/m run is

(*a*) $\frac{wL^3}{48\,EI}$ (*b*) $\frac{w \times L^4}{48\,EI}$
(*c*) $\frac{5wL^4}{384EI}$ (*d*) none of these

EI = flexural rigidity of the beam

82. In T-section

(*a*) both flange and web resists in the ratio of the their areas of cross-section
(*b*) only flanges resists shear
(*c*) most of the shear is resisted by web only
(*d*) none of these

83. A beam of span L is simply supported at both the ends is having eaual overhangs beyond both the supports. The beam carries a u.d.i. throughout. Distance between the supports for mid span moment to be numerically equal to support moment, is

(*a*) 0.25 L (*b*) 0.50 L
(*c*) 0.586 L (*d*) 0.15 L

84. Mohr's circle can be used to determine following stress on inclined surface

(*a*) principal stress (*b*) normal stress
(*c*) tangential stress (*d*) all of the above

85. A structure, made up of sereval bars, joined together is known as

(*a*) beam (*b*) column
(*c*) strut (*d*) frame

86. For a beam of uniform strength, keeping depth constant, width varies

(*a*) $\sqrt{M}$ (*b*) M
(*c*) M^2 (*d*) $m^{\frac{2}{3}}$

87. If the width (*b*) and depth (*d*) of a simply supported beam are interchanged, the mid point deflection shall change in the ratio of

(*a*) d^2/b^2 (*b*) d^3/b^3
(*c*) d/b (*d*) none of the above

88. A riveted joint in which the spacing of the rivets is staggered in suclr a way that every rivet is in the middle of the two rivets of the opposite row, is known as

(*a*) zig-zag riveted joint
(*b*) diamond riveted joint
(*c*) butt riveted joint
(*d*) chain riveted joint

89. Section modulus Z is expressed as

(*a*) I/y (*b*) E/I
(*c*) M/I (*d*) EI

90. A member is subjected to tensile force F and its normal cross-section perpendicular to line of force is A. The resulting normal stress in an oblique plane inclined at angle 0 to traverse plane will be

(*a*) $\frac{P}{A}\cos^2\theta$ (*b*) $\frac{P}{2A}\sin 2\,\theta$
(*c*) $\frac{P}{A}\sin^2\theta$ (*d*) $\frac{P}{2A}\cos 2\,\theta$

91. For eccentrically loaded strut, the section preferred is

(*a*) solid (*b*) hollow
(*c*) reinforced (*d*) composite

92. Maximum strain energy that can be stored in a body is known as

(*a*) impact energy (*b*) resilience
(*c*) proof resilience (*d*) none of these

93. Shear stress in beam occurs due to

(*a*) bending moment only
(*b*) pure shear force only
(*c*) torsional force only
(*d*) transverse shear and torsonal moments

94. Coaxing is the method of increasing

(*a*) strength by reversible cycling

(*b*) corrosion resistance by spraying

(*c*) hardness by surface treatment

(*d*) fatigue resistance over-stressing the metal by successively increasing loadings.

95. The elongation produced in a tapered shaft with end diameters d_1 and d_2 due to tensile or compressive axial load is proportional to

(*a*) $d_1 + d_2$ (*b*) $\frac{1}{d_1 + d_2}$

(*c*) $d_1 d_2$ (*d*) $\frac{1}{d_1\ d_2}$

96. Parry's formula for columns take into account

(*a*) accentricity

(*b*) initial curvature

(*c*) both (*a*) and (*b*)

(*d*) none of the above

97. A frame in which the number of members is just sufficient to keep it in equilibrium is known as

(*a*) theoretical frame (*b*) perfect frame

(*c*) ideal frame (*d*) deficient frame

98. Diamond riveted joint can be adopted in

(*a*) butt joint

(*b*) double riveted lap joints

(*c*) lap joint

(*d*) all types of joints

99. Proof stress

(*a*) is the safest stress

(*b*) causes a specified permanent deformation in a material, usually 0.01% or less

(*c*) is used in connection with materials like mild steel

(*d*) does not exist

100. The hoop stress of a thick cylinder is considered (i.e. it is maximum)

(*a*) near centre

(*b*) at outer radius

(*c*) at inner radius

(*d*) depending on the type of loading

101. Distribution of stress in a beam of rectangular cross-section will be

(*a*) triangular (*b*) rectangular

(*c*) parabolic (*d*) elliptical

102. The extension of a circular bar tapering uniformly from diameter d_1 to d_2 is same as of uniform circular bar of diameter

(*a*) $\frac{d_1 + d_2}{2}$ (*b*) $\frac{d_1 - d_2}{2}$

(*c*) $\sqrt{d_1 d_2}$ (*d*) $\sqrt{d_1^2 d_2^2}$

103. Stress concentration in a flat bar having a hole of radius r as compared to a flat bar having same dimension but having circular fillets of radius r at both ends will be

CIRCULAR HOLE CIRCULAR FILLETS

(*a*) same (*b*) more

(*c*) less (*d*) unpredictable

104. If a material is subjected to a tensile load, then to avoid shear failure of a material along a plane inclined at 45° to the direction of tensile stress, the material should have its shear strength at least equal to

(*a*) its tensile strength

(*b*) half the tensile strength

(*c*) its compressive strength

(*d*) principle stress

105. A uniformally strong beam is one having

(*a*) equal bending stress at all sections

(*b*) equal deflection throughout

(*c*) constant bending moment throughout

(*d*) uniform shear stress

106. It is assumed that the longitudinal strain is constant at any point in the thinckness of the cylinder, the radial stress s_r and hoop stress s_h are related as

(*a*) $s_r - s_h$ = constant

(*b*) $\frac{s_r}{s_h}$ = constant

(*c*) $s_r + s_h$ = constant

(*d*) none of these

107. Compression members tend to buckle in the direction of

(*a*) axis of load

(*b*) perpendicular of the axis of load

(*c*) minimum cross-section

(*d*) least radius of gyration

108. The radius taken into consideration in calculating the stress in a hollow shaft subjected to torsion is

(*a*) inner radius

(*b*) outer radius

(*c*) mean radius

(*d*) both inner and outer radii

109. A flat plate with fillets of radius r shown in given fig is subjected to tensile loading. With the increase in the value of $\frac{h}{r}$ the stress concentration factor will

Flat plate fillets in tension

(*a*) decrease (*b*) increase

(*c*) remain same (*d*) unpredictable

110. Longitudinal stress in a thin cylinder is

(*a*) equal to the hoop stress

(*b*) twice the hoop stress

(*c*) half of the hoop stress

(*d*) one-fourth the hoop stress

111. The longtudinal stress induced in a thin walled cylindrical vessel is

(*a*) $\frac{pD}{t}$ (*b*) $\frac{pD}{2t}$

(*c*) $\frac{pD}{3t}$ (*d*) $\frac{pD}{4t}$

112. A material having same properties in all directions is known as

(*a*) Orthotropic meterial

(*b*) Isotropic material

(*c*) Elastic material

(*d*) Homogenous material

113. If A_1 and A_2 be areas of shear force diagram and bending moment diagram respectively over the portion of the beam, then the change of slope over any portion of a loaded beam is equal to

(*a*) $\frac{A_1}{EI}$ (*b*) $\frac{A_2}{EI}$

(*c*) $\frac{A_1 A_2}{EI}$ (*d*) $\frac{A_1 \times A_2}{EI}$

114. A material subjected to reversal of stresses does not fail at a stress known as

(*a*) Fatiuge stress (*b*) Proof stress

(*c*) Safe stress (*d*) Endurance stress

115. Maximum stress produced in a rectangular bar under its own weights will .... if all the dimensions of the bar are halved

(*a*) remain unchanged (*b*) doubled

(*c*) halve (*d*) none of the above

116. When a rectangular beam is loaded longitudinally, shear develops on

(*a*) every horizontal plane

(*b*) top fibre

(*c*) every vertical plane

(*d*) bottom fibre

117. The reactions of each support of beam can be determined from following conditions of equilibrium

(*a*) algebraic sum of all vertical forces is zero

(*b*) algebraic sum of all horizontal forces is zero

(*c*) algebraic sum of moments about any point is zero

(*d*) all of the above

118. A beam of length l, having uniform load of w kg per unit length, is supported freely at the ends. The bending moment at mid span will be

(*a*) $\frac{wl}{4}$ (*b*) $\frac{wl^2}{2}$

(*c*) $\frac{wl^2}{4}$ (*d*) $\frac{wl^2}{8}$

119. The moment diagram for a cantilever beam whose free end is subjected to a bending moment will be

(*a*) triangle (*b*) rectangle

(*c*) parabola (*d*) cubic parabola

120. When the external forces and moments that support an object can be found by the equations of statics alone, object is said to be

(*a*) free body

(*b*) statically determinate

(*c*) statically indeterminate

(*d*) homgeneous

121. Maximum bending moment in a cantilever of length L carrying a uniformly varying load of zero intensity at one end wN/m at the other end is

(*a*) $\frac{wL^4}{24}$ (*b*) $\frac{wL}{24}$

(*c*) $\frac{wL^2}{6}$ (*d*) none of the above

122. Shear force is

(*a*) rate of change of loading

(*b*) sum of bending moments

(*c*) rate of change of bending moment

(*d*) none of the above

123. Number of independent elastic constant for an isotropic, homogeneous and elastic material obeying Hookes law is

(*a*) 1 (*b*) 2
(*c*) 5 (*d*) 6

124. If a beam of constant section is subjected throughout its length to a uniform bending moment, it will bend to

(*a*) a circular arc (*b*) a parabolic arc
(*c*) a catenary (*d*) elliptical shape

125. A reinforced cement concrete beam is said to be made of

(*a*) homogeneous material
(*b*) heterogeneous material
(*c*) isotropic material
(*d*) all of the above

126. The steel bars in reinforced cement concrete beam are located at

(*a*) top (*b*) bottom
(*c*) centre (*d*) neutral axis

127. In case of an eccentric loading on a bracket subjected to moment (M), the tangential force developed in any rivet, at right angles to its radius vector (*r*) is

(*a*) $\frac{Mr}{\sum r^2}$ (*b*) $\frac{\sum r^2}{Mr}$
(*c*) $\frac{Mr^2}{\sum r^2}$ (*d*) $\frac{\sqrt{Mr}}{\sum r^2}$

128. Twisting couple in a shaft introduces in it

(*a*) bending moment (*b*) deflection
(*c*) shear strain (*d*) shear stress

129. If the rivets in adjacent rows are staggered and the outermost row has only one rivet, the arrangement of the rivet is called

(*a*) chain riveting (*b*) zig zag riveting
(*c*) diamond riveting (*d*) criss-cross riveting

130. Rankine-Gorden formula is applicable for determining the buckling load for

(*a*) long columns
(*b*) intermediate columns
(*c*) medium size columns
(*d*) intermediate columns, but with certain amendments it can be used for short as well as long columns

131. The rate of change of bending moment at any section is equal to the

(*a*) shear force at that section
(*b*) rate of change of shearing force at that section
(*c*) deflection at that section
(*d*) rate of change deflection at that section

132. Torsion bars are in parallel

(*a*) if same torque acts on each
(*b*) if they have equal angles of twist and applied torque apportioned between them
(*c*) are not possible
(*d*) if their ends are connected together

133. A rigid beam of negligible weight is supported in a horizontal position by two rods of steel and aluminium, 2 m and 1 m long having values of cross-sectional areas 1 cm^2 and 2 cm^2 and E of 2 × 10^6 kg/cm^2 and 1× 10^6 kg/cm^2 respectively. What is the guide line for placing a load P on beam such that it remains horizontal

(*a*) forces on both rods should be equal
(*b*) force on aluminium rod should be twice the force on steel
(*c*) force on steel rod should be twice the force on aluminium
(*d*) unpredictable

134. A load of 20,000 kg applied to a brass cylinder 40 cm long and 10 cm in diameter caused the length to increase 0.8 cm and the diameter to decrease 0.005 cm. Poisson's ratio of brass is

(*a*) 0.25 (*b*) 0.925
(*c*) 0.4 (*d*) 2.5

135. A composite bar of copper and steel is heated. The ratio of tensile force in steel and the compressive stress in copper will be

(*a*) 1.0 (*b*) 0.5
(*c*) 2.0 (*d*) 2.5

136. Two beams have same width but one beam has double the depth of the other. The elastic strength of double depth beam compared to other beam will be

(*a*) double (*b*) four times
(*c*) eight times (*d*) same

137. The strain energy stored in a body of volume V due to shear stress S_s and shear modulus C is

(*a*) $\frac{S_s^2 V}{2C}$ (*b*) $\frac{S_s V^2}{2C}$
(*c*) $\frac{S_s^2 V}{C}$ (*d*) $\frac{2C}{S_s^2 V}$

138. Ratio of maximum shear stress to the average shear stress in case of a circular beam trasmitting power is equal to

(*a*) $\frac{3}{2}$ (*b*) $\frac{4}{3}$
(*c*) $\frac{7}{4}$ (*d*) 2

139. When a strip made of iron and copper is heated, it

(*a*) does not bend

(*b*) gets twisted

(*c*) bends with iron on concave side

(*d*) bends with iron on convex side

140. The diameter of rivets in mm for a plate of thickness '*t*' mm is taken as

(*a*) t (*b*) $2t$

(*c*) $\sqrt{t}$ (*d*) $6.05\sqrt{t}$

141. Ratio of maximum shear stress to the average shear stress in a rectangular beam subjected to torsion is

(*a*) $\frac{3}{2}$ (*b*) $\frac{4}{3}$

(*c*) $\frac{7}{4}$ (*d*) 2

142. A load W acting at a distance 'a' from left hand support of a simply supported beam of span L causes a bending moment of

(*a*) $\frac{Wa(L-a)}{L}$ (*b*) $\frac{Wa(L-a)^2}{L^2}$

(*c*) $\frac{Wa(L-a)L}{L^2}$ (*d*) none of above

143. Ratio of thickness to diameter for thin cylinder is

(*a*) $\frac{1}{10}$ (*b*) $\frac{1}{15}$

(*c*) $\frac{1}{20}$ (*d*) $\frac{1}{40}$

144. The value of Poisson's ratio for cast iron is

(*a*) 0.1 to 0.2 (*b*) 0.23 to 0.27

(*c*) 0.25 to 0.33 (*d*) 0.4 to 0.6

145. The stress induced in a body due to suddenly applied load compared to when it is applied gradually is

(*a*) same (*b*) half

(*c*) two times (*d*) four times

146. Ratio of maximum bending stress and maximum shear and maximum shear stress for a circular shaft subjected to combined action of bending moment (M) and torque (T) is

(*a*) $\frac{2T}{M}$ (*b*) $\frac{(2M)}{T}$

(*c*) $\frac{M}{(2T)}$ (*d*) $\frac{M}{T}$

147. If the rate of loading is zero, the shear force curve shall

(*a*) vary linearly (*b*) vary parabolically

(*c*) remain constant (*d*) none of the above

148. Rankine's theory is valid to

(*a*) long column (*b*) short column

(*c*) both (*d*) None of the above

149. Poisson's ratio is used in

(*a*) one-dimensional body

(*b*) two dimensional body

(*c*) three dimensional body

(*d*) both two and three dimensional body

150. Which is the correct expression?

(*a*) $E = 2C\left(1-\frac{1}{m}\right)$ (*b*) $E = 3C\left(1-\frac{1}{2m}\right)$

(*c*) $E = 3C\left(2-\frac{1}{m}\right)$ (*d*) $E = 3C\left(1-\frac{1}{3m}\right)$

151. The cripling load for both ends fixed long column is given by

(*a*) $\frac{\pi^2 EI}{l^2}$ (*b*) $\frac{\pi^2 EI}{4l^2}$

(*c*) $\frac{4\pi^2 EI}{l^2}$ (*d*) $\frac{2\pi^2 EI}{l^2}$

152. At the point of contraflexure

(*a*) shear force changes its behaviour

(*b*) bending moment changes its behaviour

(*c*) shear force is maximum

(*d*) shear force is minimum

153. Proof resilience in a member is stored strain energy

(*a*) per unit volume (*b*) in whole volume

(*c*) per unit area (*d*) per unit length

154. For simple supported beam having load at the centre the bending moment will be

(*a*) minimum at the support

(*b*) minimum at the centre

(*c*) maximum at the support

(*d*) None of the above

155. The effective length of the column with one end fixed and the other end free is

(*a*) its own length (*b*) twice its length

(*c*) half its length (*d*) None of the above

156. Hooke's law holds good upto

(*a*) yield point (*b*) limit of proportionality

(*c*) breaking point (*d*) elastic limit

157. The percentage reduction in area in case of cast iron when it is subjected to tensile test is of the order of

(*a*) 0% (*b*) 10%
(*c*) 20% (*d*) 25%

158. A cantilever beam is deflected by d due to load P. If load is doubled, then deflection compared to earlier case will be changed by a factor of:

(*a*) 2 (*b*) $\frac{1}{2}$
(*c*) $\frac{1}{8}$ (*d*) 8

159. Principle plane is one which carries

(*a*) no shear stress
(*b*) maximum shear stress
(*c*) no normal stress
(*d*) maximum resultant of stresses

160. When a wire is stretched to double in length, the longitudinal strain produced in it is

(*a*) 0.5 (*b*) 1.0
(*c*) 1.5 (*d*) 2.0

161. Resilience of a material is considered when it is subjected to

(*a*) Frequent heat treatment
(*b*) Fatigue
(*c*) Creep
(*d*) Shock loading

162. If equal and opposite forces applied to a body tend to elongate it, the stress so produced is called

(*a*) Internal resistance
(*b*) Tensile stress
(*c*) Transverse stress
(*d*) Compressive stress

163. The strain enegy stored in a body due to direct stress 'f' is

(*a*) f/2E × vol (*b*) f^2/E × vol
(*c*) f^2/2E × vol (*d*) 2f/E × vol

164. The shear force at certain section of a beam is stated to be zero. The bending moment at that section will be

(*a*) Minimum
(*b*) Maximum
(*c*) Either minimum or maximum
(*d*) Zero

165. The polar section modulus of a solid circular shaft of diameter 'd' about an axis through its centre of gravity is

(*a*) $(\pi/8)/d^3$ (*b*) $(\pi/16)/d^3$
(*c*) $(\pi/32)/d^3$ (*d*) $(\pi/64)/d^3$

166. An idler pulley is used

(*a*) For frequent stoppage of motion
(*b*) To maintain requisite tension in the belt
(*c*) To change the direction of motion of the belt
(*d*) To run only during non-load periods

167. Modules of rigidity is the ratio of

(*a*) Axial stress to lateral strain
(*b*) Linear stress to longitudinal strain
(*c*) Shear stress to shear strain
(*d*) Hydrostatic stress to volumetric strain

168. The elastic constants E, G and K are related by the expression

(*a*) E = GK/K + G (*b*) E = GK/2K + G
(*c*) E = 3GK/K + 2G (*d*) E = 9GK/3K + G

169. A cylindrical rod of length '*l*' and diameter '*d*' is rigidly fixed at its upper end and hangs vertically. The elongation produced in rod due to its self weight 'W' is

(*a*) W*l*/AE (*b*) W*l*/2AE
(*c*) 2AE/W*l* (*d*) 3W*l*/2AE

170. True stress represents the ratio of

(*a*) Average load and average area
(*b*) Average load and maximum area
(*c*) Maximum load and maximum area
(*d*) Instantaneous load and the instantaneous area

171. A structure made up of several bars, revitted or welded together, is known as

(*a*) Strut (*b*) Column
(*c*) Frame (*d*) Tie

172. The coupling which is the inversion of the double slider crank chain is

(*a*) Flange coupling (*b*) Oldham's coupling
(*c*) Universal coupling (*d*) Box coupling

173. The deformation per unit length in the direction of the force is known as

(*a*) linear stress (*b*) shear stress
(*c*) linear strain (*d*) lateral strain

174. Which material has the highest value of Poisson's ratio ?

(*a*) Rubber (*b*) Copper
(*c*) Steel (*d*) Concrete

175. In order to produce bending and shear stresses of equal magnitudes at the extreme fibres of a circular cross-section under the action of combined bending and torsion, the ratio of bending to twisting moments must be

(*a*) $\frac{1}{4}$ (*b*) 1
(*c*) 2 (*d*) $\frac{1}{2}$

176. The ratio of Euler's buckling loads of columns with same parameters having (i) both ends fixed (ii) one end fixed and the other end free, is

(*a*) 1 (*b*) 4

(*c*) 8 (*d*) 16

177. A hollow pipe of OD = 80 mm and thickness = 16 mm is used as a simply supported beam over a span of 2 m. What maximum point load can be applied at the center of the span if the permissible bending stress is 800 N/mm^2 ?

(*a*) 4.021 N (*b*) 40.21 N

(*c*) 8.042 N (*d*) 80.42 N

178. The longitudinal stress in a thin thicknesst cylinder pressure vessel of diameter d and internal pressure p, is

(*a*) $\frac{pd}{t}$ (*b*) $\frac{pd}{2t}$

(*c*) $\frac{pd}{4t}$ (*d*) $\frac{pd}{8t}$

179. A solid shaft transmits a torque T. The allowable shear stress is T. The diameter of the shaft is

(*a*) $\sqrt[3]{\frac{16T}{\pi\tau}}$ (*b*) $\sqrt[3]{\frac{32T}{\pi\tau}}$

(*c*) $\sqrt[3]{\frac{4T}{\pi\tau}}$ (*d*) $\sqrt[3]{\frac{64T}{\pi\tau}}$

180. A machine part is designed as a strut, when it is subjected to

(*a*) an axial tensile stress

(*b*) an axial compressive stress

(*c*) a tangential force

(*d*) any one of the above

181. A simply supported beam is subjected to point load P at the middle of the beam. The correct normal stress distribution across its cross-section is given by which figure?

(*a*) 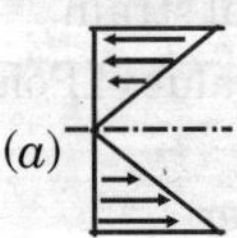 (*b*) 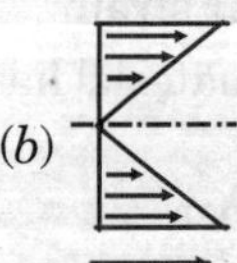

(*c*) 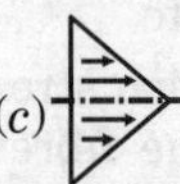 (*d*)

182. The shear strength, tensile strength and, compressive strength of a rivet joint are 100 N, 120 N and 150 N respectively. If strength of the unrivetted plate is 200 N, the efficiency of rivet joint is

(*a*) 75% (*b*) 80%

(*c*) 50% (*d*) 60%

183. A simply supported beam carries a uniformly distributed load of w kgf per unit length over the whole span (l). The shear force at the centre is

(*a*) $Wl/4$ (*b*) zero

(*c*) $Wl/2$ (*d*) $Wl^2/8$

184. The strain energy stored in a cantilever beam loaded as shown, will be

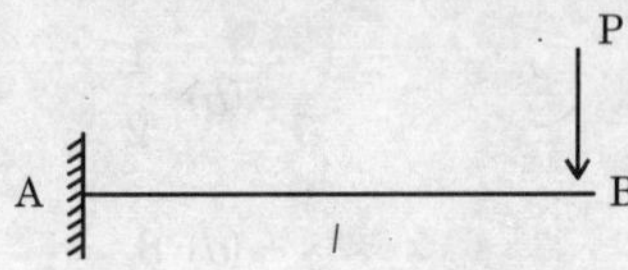

(*a*) $\frac{P^2l^3}{3EI}$ (*b*) $\frac{P^2l^3}{2EI}$

(*c*) $\frac{P^2l^3}{6EI}$ (*d*) $\frac{P^2l^3}{4EI}$

185. The torque producing a unit twist in shaft of unit length is

(*a*) Maximum torque (*b*) Torsional rigidity

(*c*) Normal torque (*d*) Nominal torque

186. For a helical spring, spring index is

(*a*) the ratio of the wire diameter to the pitch of helix.

(*b*) the difference between the mean coil diameter and the wire diameter.

(*c*) the ratio of mean coil diameter to wire diameter.

(*d*) the ratio of the mean coil diameter to the pitch of helix.

187. Rankine formula (for a column) takes into account which of the following?

(*a*) The eccentricity of loading.

(*b*) The effect of direct compressive stress.

(*c*) The effect of slenderness ratio.

(*d*) The initial curvature of the column.

188. A circular shaft of length L and diameter D is fixed in one end. The other end of the shaft is subjected to a twisting moment T. The angle of rotation of the free end with respect to the fixed end is θ. What will be the angle of rotation of the free end if length is doubled and diameter is reduced to $\frac{D}{2}$?

(*a*) 16 θ

(*b*) 32 θ

(*c*) $\frac{\theta}{2}$

(*d*) 2 θ

189. Two simply supported beam A and B has the same length L and subjected to equal bending moment M. The stress induced in the beam A and B are σ_A and σ_B respectively. If the cross section of beam A is $b \times \frac{b}{2}$ and that of beam B is $\frac{b}{2} \times b$, then correct relation between σ_A and σ_b is

(*a*) $\sigma_A = \frac{\sigma_B}{2}$ (*b*) $\sigma_A = \frac{\sigma_B}{4}$

(*c*) $\sigma_A = \sigma_B$ (*d*) $\sigma_A = 2\sigma_B$

190. In a tensile test of a specimen, the ratio of maximum load to the original cross-sectional area of the test piece is called

(*a*) Safe stress (*b*) Breaking stress

(*c*) Yield stress (*d*) Ultimate stress

191. Which one of the following assumptions in the theory of pure torsion is false?

(*a*) The shaft is of uniform circular section throughout.

(*b*) Cross-section plane before torsion remain plane after torsion.

(*c*) All radii get twisted due to torsion.

(*d*) The twist is uniform along the length.

192. If a beam is supported on more than two supports, is called a

(*a*) Simply supported beam

(*b*) Encastered beam

(*c*) Built-in beam

(*d*) Continuous beam

193. If a beam of constant section is subjected throughout its length to a uniform bending moment, it will bend to

(*a*) A triangular shape (*b*) A catenary

(*c*) A parabolic curve (*d*) A circular arc

194. A steel bar is fixed at both ends. If the bar is heated, it will develop

(*a*) Compressive stress (*b*) Tensile stress

(*c*) Bending stress (*d*) None of the above

195. A slider crank chain is a four bar linkage consisting of

(*a*) one sliding pair and two turning pairs

(*b*) one sliding pair and three turning pairs

(*c*) two sliding pairs and two rotating pairs

(*d*) two sliding pairs and two turning pairs

196. If two shafts of the same length, one of which is hollow, transmit equal torques and have equal maximum stress, then they should have equal

(*a*) polar moment of inertia

(*b*) polar modulus of section

(*c*) diameter

(*d*) angle of twist

197. In case of cantilever, irrespective of the type of loading, the maximum bending moment and maximum shear force occur at

(*a*) fixed end (*b*) free end

(*c*) middle (*d*) any point

198. Ratio of moment of inertia of a circle and that of a square having same area about their centroidal axis is

(*a*) $\frac{3}{\pi}$ (*b*) $\frac{3}{2\pi}$

(*c*) $\frac{4}{\pi}$ (*d*) $\frac{4}{\pi}$

199. A circular shaft can transmit a torque of 13 kN-m. If the torque is reduced to 12 kN-3, then the maximum value of bending moment that can be applied to the shaft is

(*a*) 1 kN-m (*b*) 3 kN-m

(*c*) 5 kN-m (*d*) 7 kN-m

200. Assertion (A): The preferred cross-section of a beam subjected to transverse loading is I section.

Reason (R): Section modulus of I section is low

(*a*) Both A and R are true and R is a correct explanation of A

(*b*) Both A and R are true but R is not a correct explanation of A

(*c*) A is true but R is false

(*d*) R is true but A is false

201. Tension in the tight side of a belt drive is 100 N and that in the slack side 60 N. If the belt breadth is 10 cm and thickness 4 cm, what is the maximum stress induced in the belt?

(*a*) 2.5 N/cm^2 (*b*) 1.5 N/cm^2

(*c*) 4 N/cm^2 (*d*) 2 N/cm^2

202. A uniform simply supported beam of span (l) carries a point load (W) at the centre. The downward deflection at the centre will be

(*a*) $Wl^2/8$ EI (*b*) $Wl^3/3$ EI

(*c*) 5 $Wl^3/384$ EI (*d*) $Wl^3/48$ EI

203. The power transmitted by a circular shaft rotating at N rpm under action of Torque T is

(*a*) 2π NT/750 (*b*) 2π NT/60

(*c*) 2π NT/450 (*d*) 2π NT/4500

204. A cylinder is said to be thin if the thickness to diameter ratio is less than

(*a*) 1/5 (*b*) 1/10

(*c*) 1/15 (*d*) 1/20

205. The bending moment on a section is maximum where shearing force is

(*a*) Minimum (*b*) Maximum
(*c*) Zero (*d*) Changing sign

206. Strut is defined as a

(*a*) Member of a structure which carries a tensile load
(*b*) Member of a structure which carries an axial compressive load
(*c*) Vertical member of a structure which carries a tensile load
(*d*) Vertical member of a structure which carries no load

207. The value of Poisson's ratio is always less than

(*a*) 1 (*b*) 0.2
(*c*) 0.4 (*d*) 0.5

208. The spindle of a machine tool is subjected to the following type of load:

(*a*) Torsional load
(*b*) Bending load
(*c*) Axial compressive load
(*d*) Axial tensile load

209. The cross-section of a member is subjected to a uniform shear stress τ. The strain energy stored per unit volume is equal to (G = modulus of rigidity)

(*a*) $\frac{2\tau^2}{G}$ (*b*) $\frac{\tau^2}{G}$
(*c*) $\frac{\tau^2}{2G}$ (*d*) $\frac{2G}{\tau^2}$

210.

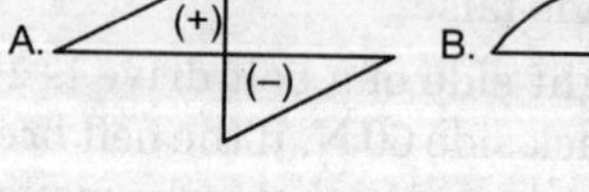

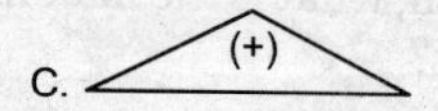

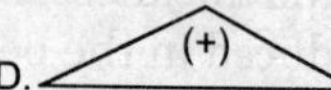

Figures A, B, C and D are bending moment distributions of a simply supported beam for some particular shear stress distribution. Which figure is the correct bending moment diagram corresponding to the shear stress distribution given below:

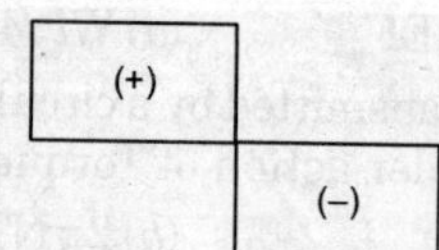

(*a*) A is correct bending moment distribution
(*b*) B is correct bending moment distrubiton
(*c*) C is correct bending moment distribution
(*d*) D is correct bending moment distribution

211. A body of weight 30 N rests on a horizontal floor. A gradually increasing horizontal for applied to the body which just starts moving when the force is 9 N. The coefficient of friction between the body and the floor will be

(*a*) 10/3 (*b*) 3/10
(*c*) 1/3 (*d*) 1/9

212. A body of weight W is placed on a rough inclined plane. The inclination of the plane with the horizontal is less than the angle of friction. The body will

(*a*) be in equilibrium
(*b*) move downwards
(*c*) move upwards
(*d*) None of the above

213. A ball is dropped vertically downwards, it hits the floor with a velocity of 9 m/s and bounces to a distance of 1.2 m. Coefficient of restitution between the floor and the ball is

(*a*) 0.54 (*b*) zero
(*c*) 1 (*d*) 0.27

214. For a material with Poisson's ratio 0.25, ratio of modulus of rigidity to modulus elasticity will be

(*a*) 0.4 (*b*) 1.2
(*c*) 2.0 (*d*) 3.6

215. If equal and opposite forces applied to a body tend to elongate it, then the stress produced

(*a*) tensile stress (*b*) bending stress
(*c*) compressive stress (*d*) shear stress

216. The direction of frictional force acting on a body which can slide on a fixed surface is

(*a*) in the direction of motion
(*b*) normal to the direction of motion
(*c*) unpredictable
(*d*) opposite to the direction of motion

217. What strength of the material is to be considered for design of a ductile component under cyclic load?

(*a*) Ultimate strength
(*b*) Yield strength
(*c*) Endurance strength
(*d*) Fracture strength

218. For any given power and permissible shear stress, the rotational speed of shaft and its diameter are correlated by the expression

(*a*) ND^3 = constant (*b*) ND^2 = constant
(*c*) ND = constant (*d*) $\sqrt{ND}$ = constant

219. Which law of motion (of Newton) gives the measure of force ?

(*a*) Newton's first law

(*b*) Newton's second law

(*c*) Newton's third law

(*d*) None of these

220. The shear stress at the centre of a circular shaft under torsion is

(*a*) maximum (*b*) minimum

(*c*) zero (*d*) unpredictable

221. The friction between objects that are stationary is called

(*a*) static friction (*b*) rolling friction

(*c*) kinetic friction (*d*) dynamic friction

222. Fatigue of a component is due to

(*a*) cyclic load (*b*) static load

(*c*) constant heating (*d*) collision

223. The angle turned by a wheel while it starts from rest and accelerates at constant rate of 3 rad/s^2 for an interval of 20 sec is

(*a*) 900 rad (*b*) 600 rad

(*c*) 1200 rad (*d*) 300 rad

224. Stress due to change in temperature developed in a bar depends upon

(*a*) coefficient of thermal expansion

(*b*) thermal conductivity

(*c*) density

(*d*) Poisson's ratio

225. Strength of the beam depends on

(*a*) Bending moment (*b*) Density

(*c*) Section modulus (*d*) c.g. of the section

226. Poisson's ratio is defined as the ratio of :

(*a*) Shear stress to shear strain

(*b*) Longitudinal strain to lateral strain

(*c*) Lateral strain to longitudinal strain

(*d*) Axial stress to axial strain

227. A body of mass 5 kg is pushed up to 2 m on a smoth 30° incline by a force of 60 N acting parallel to the plane. The work done- on the body is :

(*a*) Zero (*b*) 70.95 J

(*c*) 141.9 J (*d*) 35.47 J

228. The ratio of equivalent length of the column to minimum radius of gyration is called as :

(*a*) Bulking factor

(*b*) Factor of safety

(*c*) Poisson's ratio

(*d*) Co-efficient restitution

229. Two Tensile forces, each of magnitude F are acting at a point perpendicular to each other, then their resultant force will be :

(*a*) $\sqrt{2}$ F (*b*) Zero

(*c*) $\sqrt{F}$ (*d*) $\sqrt{2F}$

230. Which cross-section of a cantilever beam which is loaded with UDL can give economical design :

(*a*) Square (*b*) Circular

(*c*) I-Section (*d*) Rectangular

231. A long circular cylinder has a diameter D and length L. The slenderness ratio of the column is :

(*a*) $\sqrt{\frac{L}{D}}$ (*b*) $\left(\frac{L}{D}\right)$

(*c*) $\left(\frac{2L}{D}\right)$ (*d*) $\left(\frac{4L}{D}\right)$

232. A beam is fixed at one end and free at the other end. A load acts in the centre. The maximum bending moment will occur at :

(*a*) between centre and fixed end

(*b*) under the load

(*c*) fixed end

(*d*) free end

233. Bending moment at the supports in case of simply supported beam is :

(*a*) > 1 (*b*) Zero

(*c*) 1 (*d*) < 1

234. A simply supported beam of 1 m length is subjected to a distributed load of 0.4 N/m. The maximum bending moment occurring in the beam is :

(*a*) 1.0 N-m (*b*) 0.1 N-m

(*c*) 0.05 N-m (*d*) 0.025 N-m

235. If the *x*-component of a force is negative and the *y*-component is positive, the direction of that force must lie in the :

(*a*) Fourth quadrant (*b*) First quadrant

(*c*) Second quadrant (*d*) Third quadrant

236. The quantity, which is equal to rate of change of momentum is known as :

(*a*) impulse (*b*) displacement

(*c*) acceleration (*d*) force

237. What is the ratio at maximum tangential stress (σ_t) and maximum radial stress (σ_r) of a solid disk flywheel?

(*a*) $\frac{\sigma_t}{\sigma_r} = 0.5$ (*b*) $\frac{\sigma_t}{\sigma_r} = 1.0$

(*c*) $\frac{\sigma_r}{\sigma_r} = 1.5$ (*d*) $\frac{\sigma_t}{\sigma_r} = 2.0$

238. A structural member subjected to an axial compressive force is called

(*a*) beam (*b*) Column

(*c*) frame (*d*) strut

239. Volumetric strain of a rectangular body subjected to an axial force, in terms of linear strain *e* and Poisson's ratio μ, is equal to

(*a*) $e(1-2\mu)$ (*b*) $e(1-\mu)$

(*c*) $e(1-3\mu)$ (*d*) $e(1+\mu)$

240. Torsional rigidity of a solid circular shaft of diameter d is proportional to

(*a*) d (*b*) d^2

(*c*) d^4 (*d*) $1/d^2$

241. Two shafts, one solid and the other hollow, are made of the same materials and are having same length and weight. The hollow shaft as compared to solid shaft is

(*a*) More strong

(*b*) Less strong

(*c*) Have same strength

(*d*) None of the above

242. The point of contra-flexure occurs only in

(*a*) Continuous beams

(*b*) Cantilever beams

(*c*) Overhanging beams

(*d*) Simply supported beams

243. Which of the following theorem is used for the equilibrium of the body applied with three concurrent coplanar forces?

(*a*) Varignon's theorem

(*b*) Lame's theorem

(*c*) Pythagoras theorem

(*d*) Hamilton theorem

244. A body of mass 5 kg accelerates at a constant rate of 2 m/s² on a smooth horizontal surface due to an external force acting at 30° with horizontal. The magnitude of the force is

(*a*) 10 cos 30 N (*b*) 10 sin 30 N

(*c*) 10/cos 30 N (*d*) 10/sin 30 N

245. In case of a circular section the section modulus is given as

(*a*) $\pi d^2/16$ (*b*) $\pi d^3/16$

(*c*) $\pi d^3/32$ (*d*) $\pi d^4/64$

246. Leaf springs are subjected to

(*a*) bending stress (*b*) tensile stress

(*c*) shear stress (*d*) compressive stress

247. The strength of the beam mainly depends on

(*a*) centre of gravity of the section

(*b*) its weight

(*c*) section modulus

(*d*) bending moment

248. In a homogeneous, isotropic elastic material the modulus of elasticity E in terms of G and K is equal to

(*a*) $\dfrac{9KG}{G+3K}$ (*b*) $\dfrac{9KG}{3G+K}$

(*c*) $\dfrac{3K+G}{3G+K}$ (*d*) $\dfrac{6KG}{K+3G}$

249. In a composite bar the resultant strain produced will be

(*a*) sum of the strain produced by the individual bars

(*b*) same as the strain produced in each bar

(*c*) difference of strain produced by the individual bars

(*d*) same as the stress produced in each bar

250. Two springs of stiffness k_1 and k_2 respectively are connected in series, what will be the stiffness of the composite spring?

(*a*) $k = \dfrac{k_1 k_2}{k_1 + k_2}$ (*b*) $k = \dfrac{k_1 + k_2}{k_1 k_2}$

(*c*) $k = k_1 + k_2$ (*d*) $k = k_1 k_2$

251. A solid shaft transmits 44 kW power at 700 rps. Calculate the torque produced

(*a*) 10 Nm (*b*) 100 Nm

(*c*) 600 Nm (*d*) 60 Nm

252. What are the equilibrium conditions to be satisfied for a particle applied with a system of non-coplanar concurrent forces?

(*a*) $\Sigma F_x = 0$ and $\Sigma F_y = 0$

(*b*) $\Sigma F_x = 0$, $\Sigma F_y = 0$ and $\Sigma M_{z\text{-axis}} = 0$

(*c*) $\Sigma F_x = 0$, $\Sigma F_y = 0$ and $\Sigma F_z = 0$

(*d*) $\Sigma F_x = 0$, $\Sigma F_y = 0$, $\Sigma F_z = 0$ $\Sigma M_x = 0$, $\Sigma M_y = 0$ and $\Sigma M_z = 0$

Answers

1. (*b*) 2. (*b*) 3. (*b*) 4. (*c*) 5. (*b*) 6. (*b*) 7. (*c*) 8. (*a*) 9. (*b*) 10. (*b*)

11. (*d*) 12. (*d*) 13. (*b*) 14. (*b*) 15. (*d*) 16. (*c*) 17. (*b*) 18. (*c*) 19. (*d*) 20. (*c*)

21. (*c*) 22. (*d*) 23. (*a*) 24. (*b*) 25. (*d*) 26. (*b*) 27. (*d*) 28. (*c*) 29. (*b*) 30. (*b*)

31. (*d*) 32. (*b*) 33. (*d*) 34. (*b*) 35. (*c*) 36. (*a*) 37. (*a*) 38. (*d*) 39. (*d*) 40. (*d*)

41. (*b*) 42. (*b*) 43. (*c*) 44. (*a*) 45. (*d*) 46. (*b*) 47. (*c*) 48. (*a*) 49. (*c*) 50. (*d*)

51. (*d*) 52. (*d*) 53. (*b*) 54. (*a*) 55. (*a*) 56. (*b*) 57. (*d*) 58. (*d*) 59. (*d*) 60. (*b*)

61. (*d*) 62. (*b*) 63. (*a*) 64. (*c*) 65. (*c*) 66. (*c*) 67. (*b*) 68. (*b*) 69. (*a*) 70. (*d*)

71. (*b*) 72. (*d*) 73. (*c*) 74. (*b*) 75. (*b*) 76. (*b*) 77. (*a*) 78. (*a*) 79. (*c*) 80. (*a*)

81. (*c*) 82. (*c*) 83. (*c*) 84. (*e*) 85. (*d*) 86. (*b*) 87. (*b*) 88. (*a*) 89. (*a*) 90. (*a*)

91. (*d*) 92. (*b*) 93. (*d*) 94. (*d*) 95. (*d*) 96. (*a*) 97. (*b*) 98. (*a*) 99. (*b*) 100. (*c*)

101. (*a*) 102. (*c*) 103. (*b*) 104. (*b*) 105. (*a*) 106. (*a*) 107. (*d*) 108. (*d*) 109. (*b*) 110. (*c*)

111. (*d*) 112. (*d*) 113. (*d*) 114. (*d*) 115. (*b*) 116. (*a*) 117. (*d*) 118. (*d*) 119. (*b*) 120. (*b*)

121. (*d*) 122. (*c*) 123. (*a*) 124. (*a*) 125. (*b*) 126. (*b*) 127. (*a*) 128. (*d*) 129. (*c*) 130. (*d*)

131. (*a*) 132. (*b*) 133. (*b*) 134. (*a*) 135. (*a*) 136. (*a*) 137. (*a*) 138. (*b*) 139. (*c*) 140. (*d*)

141. (*a*) 142. (*a*) 143. (*c*) 144. (*b*) 145. (*c*) 146. (*b*) 147. (*c*) 148. (*c*) 149. (*d*) 150. (*)

151. (*c*) 152. (*b*) 153. (*b*) 154. (*a*) 155. (*b*) 156. (*b*) 157. (*a*) 158. (*a*) 159. (*a*) 160. (*b*)

161. (*d*) 162. (*b*) 163. (*c*) 164. (*c*) 165. (*b*) 166. (*c*) 167. (*c*) 168. (*d*) 169. (*b*) 170. (*d*)

171. (*c*) 172. (*b*) 173. (*c*) 174. (*a*) 175. (*) 176. (*d*) 177. (*) 178. (*c*) 179. (*b*) 180. (*)

181. (*a*) 182. (*c*) 183. (*b*) 184. (*c*) 185. (*b*) 186. (*c*) 187. (*b*) 188. (*b*) 189. (*d*) 190. (*d*)

191. (*c*) 192. (*d*) 193. (*d*) 194. (*a*) 195. (*d*) 196. (*b*) 197. (*a*) 198. (*a*) 199. (*c*) 200. (*a*)

201. (*a*) 202. (*b*) 203. (*b*) 204. (*b*) 205. (*d*) 206. (*b*) 207. (*d*) 208. (*a*) 209. (*c*) 210. (*c*)

211. (*b*) 212. (*a*) 213. (*a*) 214. (*a*) 215. (*a*) 216. (*d*) 217. (*c*) 218. (*a*) 219. (*b*) 220. (*c*)

221. (*a*) 222. (*a*) 223. (*b*) 224. (*a*) 225. (*c*) 226. (*c*) 227. (*b*) 228. (*a*) 229. (*a*) 230. (*c*)

231. (*d*) 232. (*c*) 233. (*b*) 234. (*c*) 235. (*c*) 236. (*d*) 237. (*b*) 238. (*b*) 239. (*a*) 240. (*c*)

241. (*a*) 242. (*a*) 243. (*b*) 244. (*b*) 245. (*c*) 246. (*d*) 247. (*c*) 248. (*a*) 249. (*b*) 250. (*a*)

251. (*a*) 252. (*d*)

Explanations

148. Rankine theory is valid for both long column.

149. Poison's ratio is defined as the ratio of transverse strain to the longitudinal strain. Hence Poison's ratio is used for both two and the dimensional body.

150. None of the option is correct. The correct expression may be:

$$E = 2G\,(1 + 1/m)$$

Where E & G are elastic constant and 1/m is poison's ratio.

151. Cripling load is given by $P_{cr} = \dfrac{\pi^2 EI}{l_e^2}$

Where l_e is the effective length and effective length for both end fixed is l/2.

So cripling load will be $P_{cr} = \dfrac{4\pi^2 EI}{l^2}$

152. In a bending beam, a point is known as point of contraflexure if it is a location at which no bending occurs. In bending moment diagram it is a point at which bending moment curve intersect with zero line.

153. Proof resilience is defined as the maximum energy that can be absorbed within the elastic limit, without creating a permanent distortion. The modulus of resilience is defined as the maximum energy that can be absorbed per unit volume without creating a permanent distortion.

154. The simple support beam having load at the centre the bending moment will be minimum at the centre.

155. The effective length of column for one end fixed and other end free is given by:

$$L_e = 2\,L$$

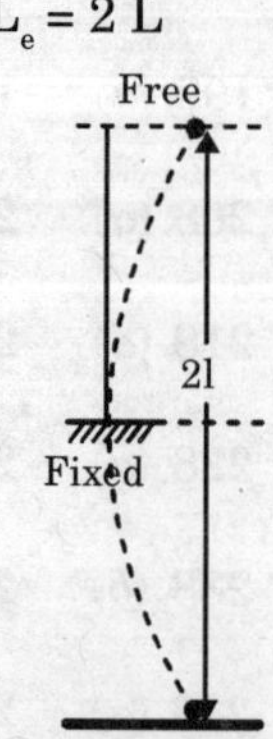

156. Hooks law state that within elastic limits (Proportional) limits, strain is directly proportional to stress.

157. There is no reduction in area of cast iron when it is subjected to tensile test is observed.

158. Deflection of cantilever beam having concentrated load at the free end is given by

$$\delta = \frac{PL^3}{3EI}$$

So if load is doubled the deflection will also doubled.

159. Principle plane is one which doesn't have any shear stress.

160. Longitudinal strain

= Change in length/original length

= l/l = 1

161. **Resilience** is the ability of a material to absorb energy when it is *deformed elastically*, and release that energy upon unloading. So when a material is subjected to shock loading Resilience is considered.

162. If equal and opposite forces applied to body tends to elongate it, the stress so produces is known as tensile stress.

163. Strain Energy stored in a body due to direct stress f is given by

$$\text{Strain energy} = \frac{1}{2E}\sigma^2 \text{X Volume}$$

164. The relation between shear force and bending moment is given by:

$$\frac{\partial M}{\partial x} = F$$

When shear force is zero at any section then the bending moment will be either **maximum** or **constant** at that section.

165. The polar section modulus of solid circular shaft of diameter d about its C.G. $= \dfrac{\left(\dfrac{\pi}{16}\right)}{d^3}$.

166. An idler pulley is used to change the direction of belt drive system.

167. Modulus of rigidity is defined as the ratio of shearing stress to shearing strain.

$$G = \frac{\tau}{\gamma}$$

168. Three elastic constant E, G and K are related by

$$E = \frac{9KG}{3K + G}$$

169. Elongation of rod due to self weight:

$$\delta = \frac{WL}{2AE}$$

170. True stress the **stress** determined by the instantaneous load acting on the Instantaneous cross-sectional area. **True stress** is related to engineering **stress.**

175. Both ends fixed $P_1 = \frac{4\pi^2 EI}{l^2}$

one end box and other end free

$$P_2 = \frac{\pi^2 EI}{4l^2}$$

$$\therefore \frac{P_1}{P_2} = \frac{\frac{4\pi^2 EI}{l^2}}{\frac{\pi^2 EI}{4l^2}} = 16$$

194. When bar is heated it will tend to grow in longitudinal direction due to thermal expansion but due to restriction from fixed ends, it will experience compressive stress.

195. Two turning and two sliding pairs.

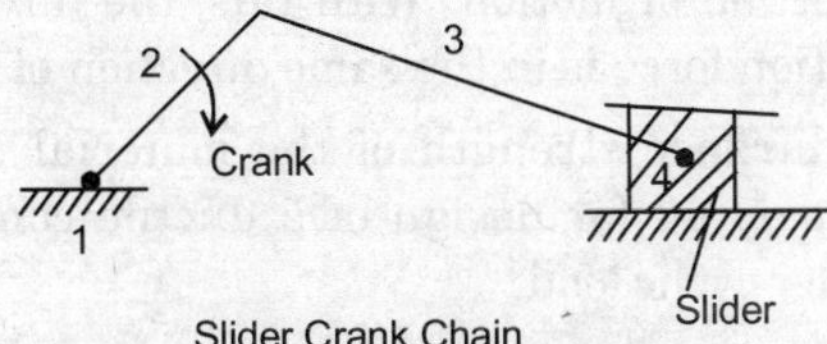

Slider Crank Chain

196. For shafts transmitting torques.

Shear stress is given by $\tau = \frac{T \times r}{J}$

r = Radius of shaft

J = Polar moment of Inertia

T = Torque transmitted

τ = Shear stress maximum

$\frac{J}{r} = t_P \rightarrow$ polar section modulus

197. As reaction force in given at fixed end only hence it experiences maximum shear force.

198. Moment of Inertia of square

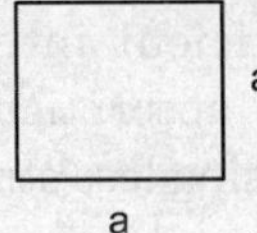

$$I_n = \frac{a^4}{12}$$

Moment of Inertia of circle

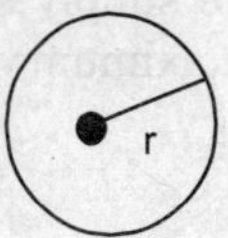

$$I_c = \frac{\pi r^4}{4}$$

For area to be same

$$a^2 = \pi r^2$$

$$\therefore \quad \text{Ratio} = \frac{I_C}{I_{sq.}} = \frac{\pi r^4 \times 12}{4a^4} = \frac{3}{\pi}$$

200.

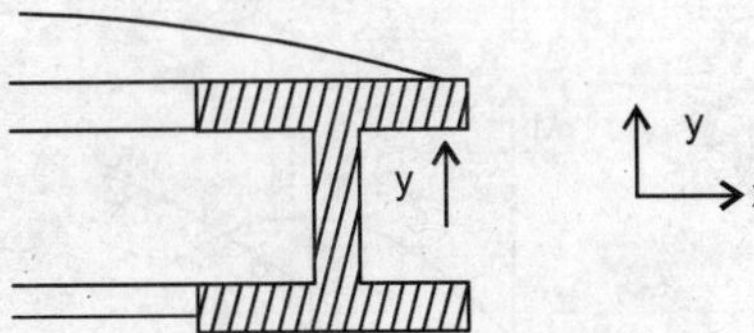

Section modulus

$$\boxed{Z_x = \frac{I_{xx}}{y}}$$

Low for I cross section

$$\text{Stress bending } \sigma_b = \frac{M}{Z_{xx}}$$

201. Maximum stress will be on tight side of belt.

$$\therefore \sigma_{max.} = \frac{T(\text{tigh side})}{\text{Cross-section area of belt}}$$

$$= \frac{160\text{ N}}{40 \times 10\text{ cm}^2} = 2.5\text{ N/cm}^2$$

202.

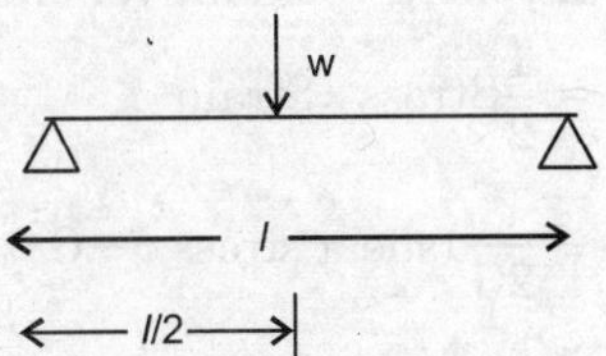

Using governing differential equation for beam deflection.

$$EI\frac{d^4y}{dx^4} = -W_0 \text{ or } EI\frac{d^2y}{dx^2} = M$$

$$\boxed{W_0 = \frac{W}{L}}$$

and boundary condition

We can derive $y_{max} = \frac{Wl^3}{3EI}$

203. Power = $T_w = \frac{2\pi N}{60}T$

204. For thin cylinders radius to thickness ratio r/t = 10 for error in stress predicted when compared to thick cylinder is around 4%.

205. For example simply supported beam bending moment is maximum where shear force changes sign

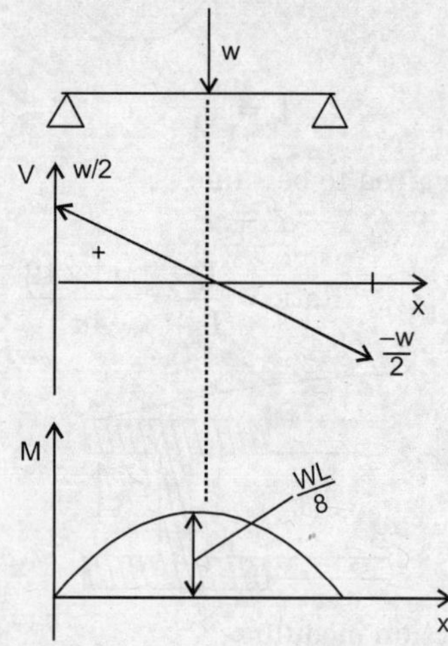

206. Strut are member of structure which carries axial compressive load. For example column in buildings.

207. Poisson's ratio have value from −1 to 0.5

$$\boxed{-1 < v < 0.5}$$

This comes from requirement that young's modulus shear modulus and bulk modulus must be positive.

208. Spindle of machine tool is subjected to torsionel load generally as during machining tool experience resisting torque.

209. Strain energy per unit volume

$$= \frac{1}{2}\text{Stress} \times \text{Strain}$$

$$= \frac{\tau^2}{2G} \text{ (shear stress } \tau = Gr)$$

210.

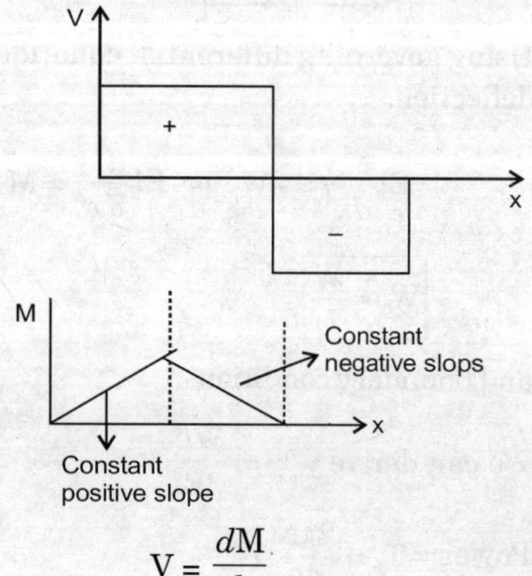

$$V = \frac{dM}{dx}$$

211. F = μ.N or μ = F/N. Here, Friction Force (limiting, F) = 9 N and Reaction (N) = 30 N.

So, μ = 9/30 = 3/10

212. The body will be in equilibrium as angle is less than angle of friction. At this, value is less than limiting friction.

213. Coefficient of restitution (e) = Velocity after rebound (v) / Velocity before rebound (u) ;

and $v = (2.g.H)^{1/2}$; So, $e = [\,(2gH)^{1/2} / u\,]$.

Thus, $e = (2 \times 9.81 \times 1.2)^{1/2} / 9$

$= 4.85/9 = 0.54$

214. The relationship between modulus of elasticity (E) and modulus of rigidity (G) is expressed by relation → E = 2G (μ + 1) where μ is the Poisson's Ratio (Ratio of secondary or lateral strain to primary or longitudinal or axial strain).

So, (G / E) = 1 / [2 (μ +1)] ; (G/E)

= 1 / [(2 × 1 + 0.25)]

= 1 / 2.5 = 0.40

215. Elongating forces are tensile forces and thus developed stress is known as tensile stress.

216. The direction of force of friction is opposite to cause and at the time of sliding of a body on a fixed surface, the force is applied opposite to direction of motion. With this, the direction of friction force is in the same direction of motion.

217. Endurance strength of the material is being considered for design of a ductile component under cyclic load.

219. Newton's second law of motion gives the measure of force as F = m.a

220. Shear stress at the centre of a circular shaft under torsion is zero and varies to maximum at its extreme surface.

221. The friction between objects that are stationary is called Static Friction.

222. Fatigue of a component is due to cyclic loading for large no. of cycles.

223. Using equation of motion for circular path as

$\theta = \omega_0 + \frac{1}{2}\alpha\, t^2$; $\theta = 0 + \frac{1}{2} \times 3 \times 20^2$

= 600 rad /s

224. Stress due to change in temperature developed in a bar depends upon Density as low density provide sufficient inter-molecular space for adjustment / absorption of force / dimensional change - causing less stress generation.

225. Strength of the beam depends on Section Modulus (Z = I/y)

237. The ratio of maximum tangential stress (σ_t) and maximum radial stress (σ_r) of a solid disk flywheer is 1.0

238. The structural member subjected to an axial compressive force is called column.

239. Volumetric strain = $\frac{\sigma_x + \sigma_y + \sigma_z}{E}(1 - 2\mu)$

For one axial = $\frac{\sigma}{E}$ (1 – 2μ) = e(1 – 2μ)

So, the Poisson's ratio μ is given by $e(1-\mu)$

240.

$$g = \frac{T}{3} \times \frac{\ell}{Q}$$

$$g = \frac{32}{\pi d^4} = \frac{1}{d^4}$$

Torsional rigidity of a solid circular shaft is inversely proportional to d^4.

241.

$$\frac{T_{hollow}}{T_{solid}} = \frac{b^4 - a^4}{br^3}$$

$$\frac{T_{hollow}}{T_{solid}} = \frac{1 + c^2}{\sqrt{1 - c^2}}$$

Hence the hollow shaft as compared to solid shaft is more strong.

242. The point of contra-flexure only in overhanging beams.

243. Lame's theorem is used for the equilibrium of the body applied with three concurrent coplanar forces.

244. The magnitude of force

$$|\vec{F}| = m.a \sin\theta$$

$$= 5.2 \sin 30° \text{ N}$$

$$= 10 \sin 30° \text{ N}$$

245. In case of a circular section, the section modulus is given by $\pi d^3/32$.

246. Leaf springs an subjected to compressive stress.

247. The strength of the beam mainly depends on section modulus.

248. In a homogeneous isotropic elastic material the modulus of elasticity E in terms of G and K is equal to $\frac{9KG}{G + 3K}$

249. In a composite bar the resultant strain produced will be same as the strain produced in each bars

250.

k1

k2

$$\frac{1}{k_{eq}} = \frac{1}{k_1} + \frac{1}{k_2} = \frac{k_1 \times k_2}{k_1 + k_2}$$

251.

$$P = T \times \omega, \; T = \frac{P \times 60}{2\pi N}$$

$$\frac{N}{60} = 700 \text{ rps}, \; T = \frac{44 \times 1000}{2\pi \times 700} = 10 \text{ Nm}$$

252. The equilibrium conditions to be satisfied for a particle applied with a system of non-coplaner concurrent forces are $\Sigma F_x = 0$, $\Sigma F_y = 0$, $\Sigma F_z = 0$

$\Sigma M_x = 0$, $\Sigma M_y = 0$ and $\Sigma F_z = 0$

Theory of Machines and Machines Design

DEFINITION

A *machine* is a device which receives energy in some available form and utilises it to do some particular type of work.

Sub-Divisions of Theory of Machines

Theory of Machines may be *sub-divided* into the following four branches :

1. **Kinematics:** It is that branch of Theory of Machines which deals with the *relative motion* between the various parts of the machines.
2. **Dynamics :** It is that branch of Theory of Machines which deals with the *forces and their effects*, while *acting upon the machine parts in motion.*
3. **Kinetics :** It is that branch of Theory of Machines which deals with *inertia forces* which arise from the *combined effect of the mass and motion* of the machine parts.
4. **Statics :** It is that branch of Theory of Machines which deals with the *forces* and *their effects* while the machine parts are at *rest*. The mass of the parts is assumed to be negligible.

Kinematic Link or Element

Each part of a machine, which moves relative to some other part, is known as a *kinematic link* (or simply link) or *element*.

A *link* or element need not to be a rigid body, but it must be a *resistant body*. A body is said to be a resistant body if it is capable of transmitting the required forces with negligible deformation. Thus a link should have the following two characteristics :

(*i*) It should have relative motion, and

(*ii*) It must be a resistant body.

Types of Links

In order to transmit motion, the driver and the follower may be connected by the following three types of links:

(*i*) **Rigid link :** A rigid link is one which does not undergo any deformation while transmitting motion. Strictly speaking, rigid links do not exist. However, as the deformation of a *connecting rod*, crank etc. of a reciprocating steam engine is not appreciable, they can be considered as rigid links.

(*ii*) **Flexible link :** A flexible link is one which is partly deformed in a manner not to affect the transmission of motion. *e.g.*, *belts, ropes, chains* and *wires* are flexible links and transmit tensile forces only.

(*iii*) **Fluid link :** A fluid link is one which is formed by having a fluid in a receptacle and the motion is transmitted through the fluid by pressure or compression only, as in the case of hydraulic presses, jacks and brakes.

STRUCTURE

It is an assemblage of a number of resistant bodies (known as members) having *no relative motion* between them and meant *for carrying loads having straining action e.g.*, railway bridge, a roof truss, machine frames etc.,

Difference between a machine and a structure

The following difference between a machine and a structure are important from the subject point of view :

(*i*) The parts of a machine move relative to one another, whereas the members of a structure do not move relative to one another.

(*ii*) A machine transforms the available energy into some into some useful work, whereas in a structure no energy is transformed into useful work.

(*iii*) The link of a machine may transmit both power and motion, while the members of a structure transmit forces only.

Kinematic Pair

The two links or elements of a machine, when in contact with each other, are said to form a *pair*. If the relative motion between them is *completely or successfully constrained* (*i.e.* in a definite direction), the pair is known as *kinematic pair*.

TYPES OF CONSTRAINED MOTIONS

Following are the three types of constrained motions :

(*i*) **Completely constrained motion :** When the motion between a pair is limited to a definite direction *irrespective of the direction of force applied*, then the motion is said to be a *completely constrained motion*. *e.g.*, the *piston* and *cylinder* (in a steam engine) form a pair and the motion of the piston is limited to a definite direction (*i.e.* it will only reciprocate) relative to the cylinder irrespective of the direction of motion of the crank, as shown in Fig. (*a*) *e.g.,* The motion of a square bar in a square hole, as shown in Fig. (*b*), and the motion of a shaft with collars at each end in a circular hole, as shown in Fig. (*c*).

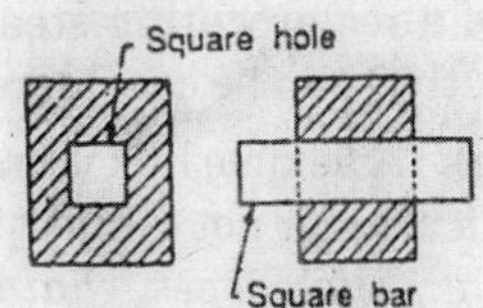

Fig. (a) Square bar in a square hole.

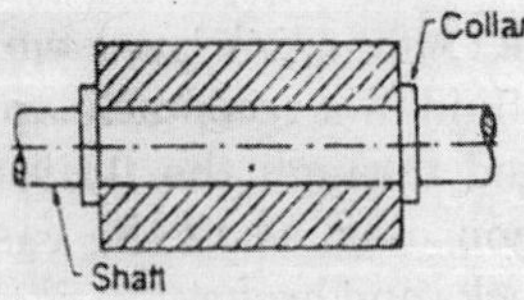

Fig. (b) Shaft with collars in a circular hole.

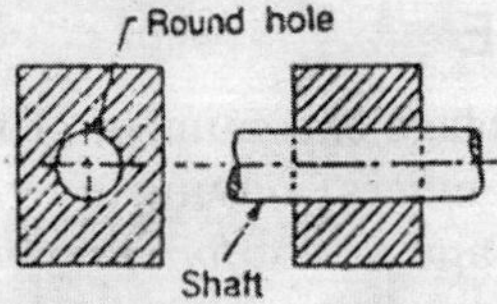

Fig. (c) Shaft in a circular hole

(*ii*) **Incompletely constrained motion :** When the motion between a pair can take place *in more than one direction*, then the motion is called an incompletely constrained motion. The change in the direction of impressed force may alter the direction of relative motion between the pair.

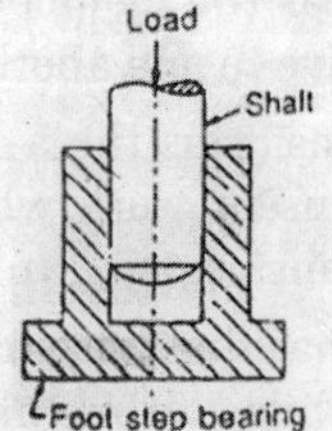

Fig. Shaft in a foot step bearing

e.g., A circular bar or shaft in a circular hole, as shown in Fig., as it may either rotate or slide in a hole. These both motions have no relationship with the other.

(*iii*) **Successfully constrained motion :** When the motion between the elements, forming a pair, is such that the constrained motion is *not completed* by *itself*, but *by some other means*, then the motion is said to be successfully constrained motion.

TYPES OF KINEMATIC PAIRS

Kinematic pairs can be classified according to

(*i*) nature of contact

(*ii*) nature of mechanical constraint, and

(*iii*) nature of relative motion.

(*i*) Kinematic Pairs according to Nature of Contact

(*a*) **Lower Pair.** A pair of links having *surface or area contact* between the members is known as a lower pair. The *contact surfaces* of the two *links are similar.*

e.g. *Nut turning on a screw, shaft rotating in a bearing, all pairs of a slider-crank mechanism, universal joint,* etc.

(*b*) **Higher Pair.** When a pair has a *point or line contact* between the links, it is known as a higher pair. The *contact-surfaces* of the two links are *dissimilar*.

e.g. *Wheel rolling on a surface, cam and follower pair, tooth gears, ball and roller bearings,* etc.

(*ii*) Kinematic Pairs according to Nature of Mechanical Constraint

(*a*) **Closed Pair.** When the *elements* of a pair are held together mechanically, it is known as a closed pair. The two elements are geometrically identical; one is solid and full and the other is hollow or open. The latter not only envelops the former but also encloses it. The *contact* between the two *can be broken only by destruction of at least one of the members.*

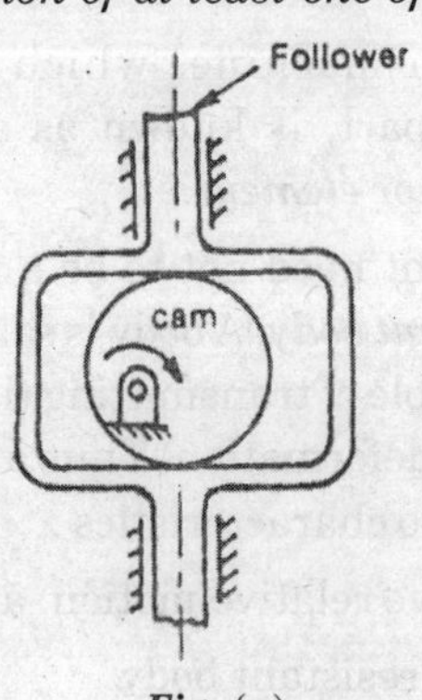

Fig. (a)

All the lower pairs and some of the higher pairs are closed pairs. A cam and follower pair (higher pair) shown in Fig. (*a*) and a *screw pair* (lower pair) belong to the *closed pair category.*

(*b*) Unclosed Pair. When two links of a pair are in *contact either due to force of gravity or some spring action*, they constitute an unclosed pair. In this, the links are not held together mechanically.

e.g. cam and flollower pair of Fig. (*b*).

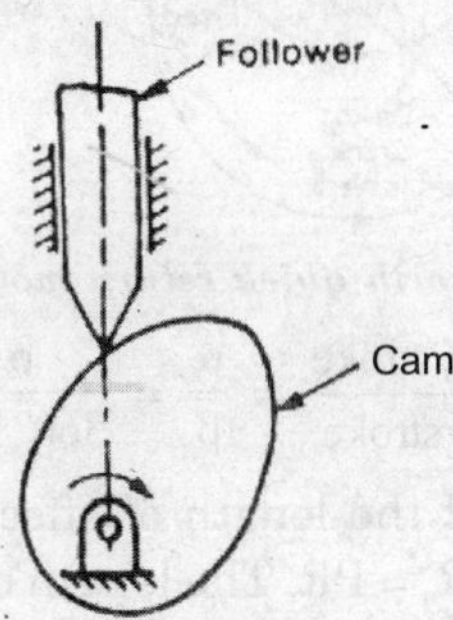

***Fig.* (*b*)**

(*iii*) Kinematic Pairs according to Nature of Relative Motion

(*a*) Sliding Pair. If two links have a *sliding motion relative* to each other, they form a sliding pair.

A rectangular rod in a rectangular hole in a prism is a sliding pair [Fig. (*c*)].

(*b*) Turning Pair. When one link has a *turning or revolving motion* relative to the other, they constitute a turning or revolving pair [Fig. (*d*)].

In a slider-crank mechanism, all pairs except the slider and guide pair are turning pairs. A circular shaft revolving inside a bearing is a turning pair.

(*c*) Rolling Pair. When the links of a pair have a rolling motion relative to each other, they form a rolling pair. *e.g.*, a *rolling wheel on a flat surface*, ball and roller bearings, etc. In a *ball bearing* [Fig. (*e*)], the ball and the shaft constitute one rolling pair whereas the ball and the bearing is the second rolling pair.

(*d*) Screw Pair (Helical Pair). If two mating links have a *turning as well as sliding motion* between them, they form a screw pair. This is achieved by cutting matching threads on the two links.

The *lead screw* and the *nut* of a lathe is a screw pair [Fig.(*f*)].

(*e*) Spherical Pair. When one link in the form of a *sphere turns* inside a fixed link, it is a spherical pair. The ball and socket joint is a spherical pair [Fig.(*g*)].

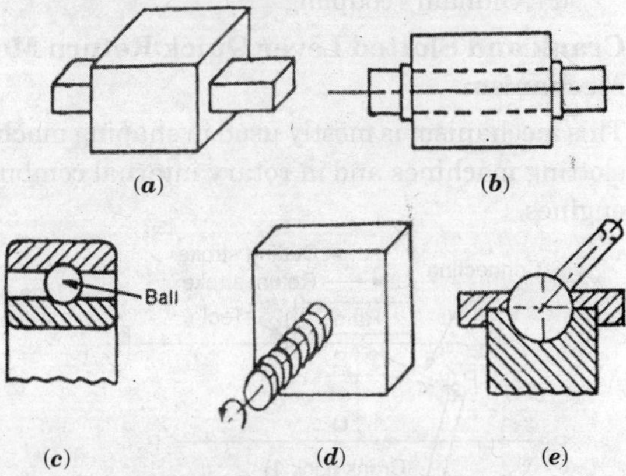

Inversion of Mechanism

When one of links is fixed in a kinematic chain, it is called a mechanism. So we can obtain as many mechanisms as the number of links in a kinematic chain by fixing, in turn, different links in a kinematic chain. This method of obtaining different mechanisms by fixing different links in a kinematic chain, is known as *inversion of the mechanism.*

Types of Kinematic Chains

The most important kinematic chains are those which consist of four lower pairs, each pair being a sliding pair or a turning pair. The following three types of kinematic chains with four lower pairs are important :

(*i*) Four bar chain or quadric cyclic chain,

(*ii*) Single slider crank chain, and

(*iii*) Double slider crank chain.

INVERSIONS OF MECHANISMS

(*i*) Four Bar Mechanism

(*a*) Beam Engine

(*b*) Coupling Rod of Locomotive

(*c*) Watts Indicator Mechanism

(*ii*) Single Slider Crank Chain

(*a*) Pendulum pump or Bull engine

(*b*) Oscittating cylinder engine

(*c*) Rotary internal combustion engine

(*d*) Crank and Slotted lever quick return mechanism

(*e*) Whitworth quick return mechanism

(*iii*) Double Slider Crank Chain

(*a*) Elliptical trammel

(*b*) Scotch-yoke mechanism

(*c*) Oldham's coupling.

Crank and Slotted Lever Quick Return Motion Mechanism

This mechanism is mostly used in shaping machines, slotting machines and in rotary internal combustion engines.

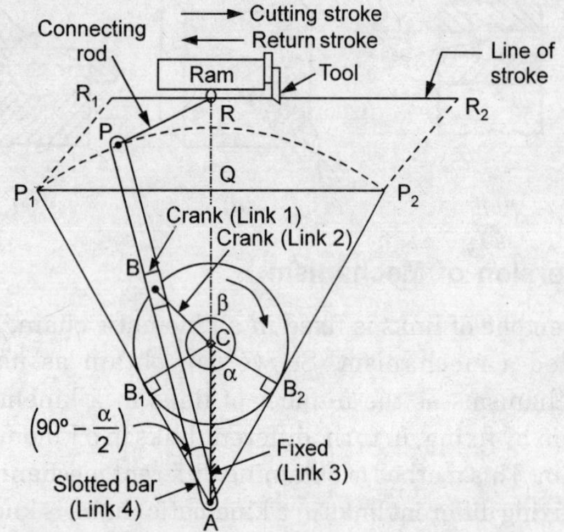

Fig. (a) Crank and slotted lever quick return motion mechanism.

$$\frac{\text{Time of cutting stroke}}{\text{Time of return stroke}} = \frac{\beta}{\alpha} = \frac{\beta}{360^\circ - \beta} \text{ or } \frac{360^\circ - \alpha}{\alpha}$$

Since the tool travels a distance of $R_1 R_2$ during cutting and return stroke, therefore travel of the tool or length of stroke = $R_1R_2 = P_1P_2 = 2\,P_1Q = 2\,AP_1 \sin \angle P_1AQ$

$$= 2\,AP_1 \sin\left(90^\circ - \frac{\alpha}{2}\right)$$

$$= 2\,AP \cos\frac{\alpha}{2} \quad \ldots (\because AP_1 = AP)$$

$$= 2\,AP \times \frac{CB_1}{AC} \ldots \left(\because \cos\frac{\alpha}{2} = \frac{CB_1}{AC}\right)$$

$$= 2\,AP \times \frac{CB}{AC} \quad \ldots (\because CB_1 = CB)$$

From above figure (*a*), we see that the *angle β made* by the forward or cutting stroke is *greater than the angle* α described by the return stroke. Since the crank rotates with uniform angular speed, therefore the *return stroke is completed within shorter time.* Thus it is called *quick return motion mechanism.*

Whitworth Quick Return Motion Mechanism

This mechanism is mostly used in *shaping* and *slotting* machines. In this mechanism, the link CD (link 2) forming the turning pair is fixed, as shown in Fig. (*b*) The link 2 corresponds to a crank in a reciprocating steam engine. The driving crank CA (link 3) rotates at a uniform angular speed. The slider (link 4) attached to the crank pin at A slides along the slotted bar PA (link 1) which oscillates at a pivoted point D. The connecting rod PR carries the ram at R to which a cutting tool is fixed. The motion of the tool is constrained along the line RD produced, *i.e.* along a line passing through D and perpendicular to CD.

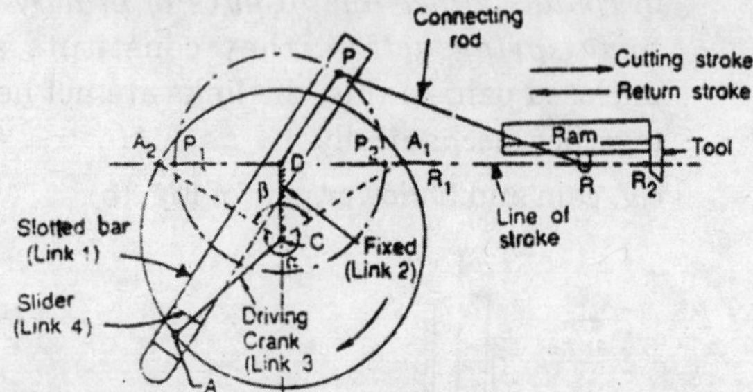

Fig. (b). Whitworth quick return motion mechanism.

$$\frac{\text{Time of cutting stroke}}{\text{Time of return stroke}} = \frac{\alpha}{\beta} = \frac{\alpha}{360^\circ - \alpha} \text{ or } \frac{360^\circ - \beta}{\beta}$$

In order to find the length of effective stroke R_1R_2, mark $P_1R_1 = P_2R_2 = PR$. The length of effective stroke is also equal to 2 PD.

SLIDER-CRANK MECHANISM

The configuration and the velocity diagrams of a slider-crank mechanism is shown in Figs. (*a*) and (*b*).

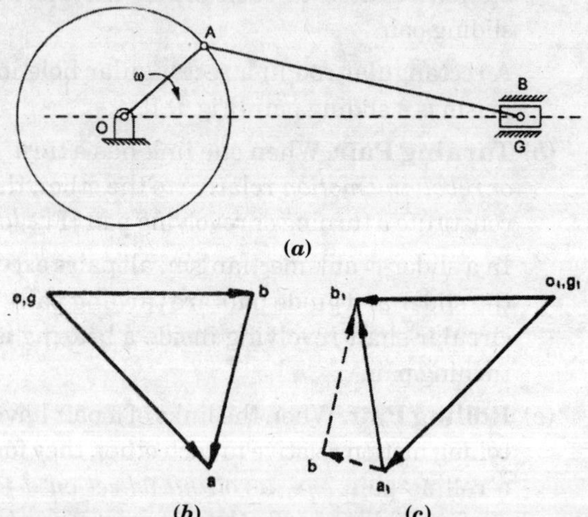

Writing the acceleration equation,

Acceleration of B relative to O = Acceleration of B relative to A + Acceleration of A relative to O

$$f_{bo} = f_{ba} + f_{ao}$$

$$f_{bg} = f_{ao} + f_{ba} = f_{ao} + f^{c}_{ba} + f^{t}_{ba}$$

$$g_1\,b_1 = o_1\,a_1 + a_1\,b_a + b_a\,b_1$$

The crank OA rotates at a uniform velocity, therefore, the acceleration of A relative to O has only the centripetal component. Similarly, the slider moves in a linear direction and thus has no centripetal component.

Setting the vector table :

S. N.	*Vector*	*Magnitude*	*Direction*	*Sense*
1.	f_{ao} or $o_1 a_1$	$\frac{(oa)^2}{OA}$	parallel to OA	$\rightarrow$ O
2.	$f^c{}_{ba}$ or $a_1 b_a$	$\frac{(ab)^2}{AB}$	parallel to AB	$\rightarrow$ A
3.	$f^t{}_{ba}$ or $b_a b_1$	—	perpendicular AB	—
4.	f_{bg} or $g_1 b_1$	—	parallel to line of motion of B	—

Construct the acceleration diagram as follows :

1. Take the first vector f_{ao}.
2. Add the second vector to the 1st.
3. For the third vector, draw a line perpendicular to AB through the head b_a of the second vector.
4. For the fourth vector, draw a line through g_1 parallel to the line of motion of the slider.

This completes the velocity diagram.

Acceleration of the slider B = $o_1 b_1$ (or $g_1 b_1$)

Total acceleration of B = $a_1 b_1$

Note that for the given configuration of the mechanism, the direction of the acceleration of the slider is opposite to that of the velocity. Therefore, the acceleration is negative or the slider is decelerating while moving to the right.

KLEIN'S CONSTRUCTION

Slider Crank Mechanism

In Klein's construction, the velocity and the acceleration diagrams are made on the configuration diagram itself. The line that represents the crank in the configuration diagram also represents the velocity and the acceleration of its moving end in the velocity and the acceleration diagrams respectively.

In the figs (*a*) and (*b*) OAB represents the configuration of a slider-crank mechanism. Its velocity and acceleration diagrams are as shown in Figs. (*b*) and (*c*).

Length of the crank = OA = r

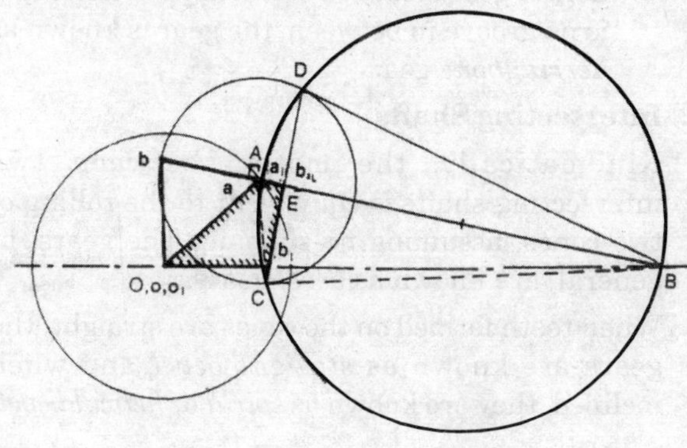

Velocity Diagram

For velocity diagram, let r represents v_{ao}, to some scale. Then for the velocity diagram,

$$\text{length} \quad oa = \omega r = OA.$$

From this, the scale for the velocity diagram is known. Produce BA and draw a line perpendicular to OB through O. The intersection of the two lines locates point b. The figure oab is the velocity diagram which is similar to the velocity diagram of Fig. (*b*) rotated through 90° in a direction opposite to that of the crank.

Acceleration Diagram

For acceleration diagram, let r represents f_{ao}.

$$\therefore \quad o_1 a_1 = \omega^2 r = OA$$

This provides the scale for the acceleration diagram.

Make the following constructions :

1. Draw a circle with ab as the radius and a as the center.
2. Draw another circle with AB as diameter.
3. Join the points of intersections C and D of the two circles. Let it meet OB at b_1 and AB at E.

Then $o_1 a_1 b_a b_1$ is the required acceleration diagram which is similar to the acceleration diagram of Fig. (*c*) rotated through 180°.

Proof: Join AC and BC. AEC and ABC are two right-angled triangles in which angle CAB is common. Therefore, the triangles are similar.

$$\frac{AE}{AC} = \frac{AC}{AB}$$

or

$$AE = \frac{(AC)^2}{AB}$$

or

$$a_1 b_a = \frac{(ab)^2}{AB} = f^c_{ba}$$

Thus this acceleration diagram has all the sides parallel to that of acceleration diagram of Fig. (*c*) and also has two sides $o_1 a_1$ and $a_1 b_a$ representing the corresponding magnitudes of the acceleration. Thus the two diagrams are similar.

GEAR TOOTH PROFILE

Gears are toothed wheels used for transmitting motion and power from one shaft to another when they are not too far apart and when a constant velocity ratio is desired. In comparision with belt, chain drives and friction drives, gear drives are more compact, can operate at high speeds and can be used where precise timing is required.

Classification of Gears

Gears can be classified *according to the relative positions of their shaft axes* as follows :

(*i*) Gears with *parallel axes*, *e.g.* spur gears, helical and herringbone gears, rack and pinion and internal gears.

(*ii*) Gears in which the shaft *axes intersects* if prolonged, *e.g.* bevel gears.

(*iii*) Gears in which the axes are *neither parallel* nor intersecting. *e.g.* Worm, hypoid and spiral gears.

I. Parallel Shafts

Regardless of the manner of contact, uniform rotary motion between two parallel shafts is equivalent to the rolling of two cylinders, assuming no slipping. Depending upon the teeth of the equivalent cylinders, *i.e.* straight or helical, following are the main types of gears to join parallel shafts :

(*i*) Spur Gears : They have straight teeth parallel to the axes and thus are not subjected to axial thrust due to tooth load (Fig. *a*).

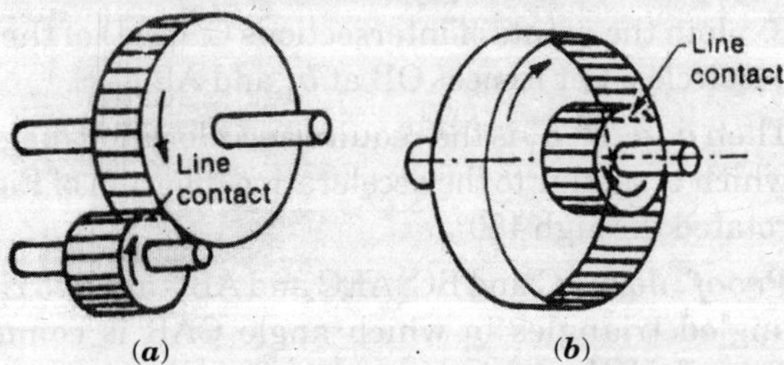

(*ii*) Spur Rack and Pinion : Spur rack is a special case of a spur gear where it is made of infinite diameter so that the pitch surface is a plane. The spur rack and pinion combination converts rotary motion into translatory motion, or vice-versa. It is used in a *lathe* in which the rack transmits motion to the saddle.

(*iii*) Helical Gears or Helical Spur Gears : In helical gears, the teeth are curved, each being helical in shape. Two mating gears have the same helix angle, but have teeth of opposite hands.

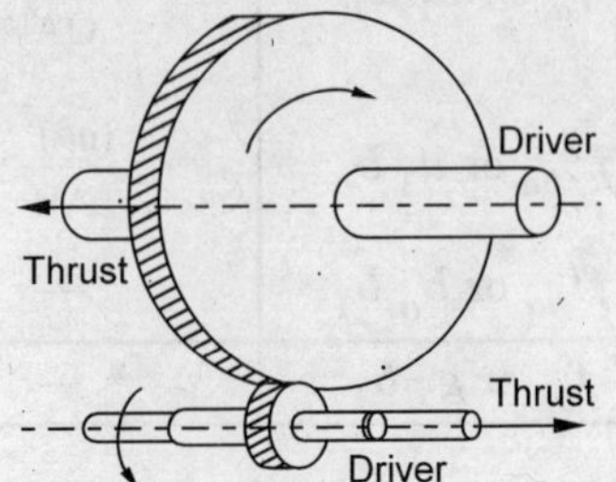

Helical gears can be used at higher velocities than the spur gears and have greater load-carrying capacity.

Helical gears have the disadvantage of having end thrust as there is a force component along the gear axis. The bearings and the assemblies mounting the helical gears must be able to withstand thrust loads.

(*iv*) Double-helical and Herringbone Gears : A double-helical gear is equivalent to a pair of helical gears secured together, one having a right-hand helix and the other a left-hand helix. The teeth of the two rows are separated by a groove used for tool runout. Axial thrust which occurs in case of single-helical gears is eliminated in double-helical gears. This is because the axial thrusts of the two rows of teeth cancel each other out. These can be run at high speeds with less noise and vibrations.

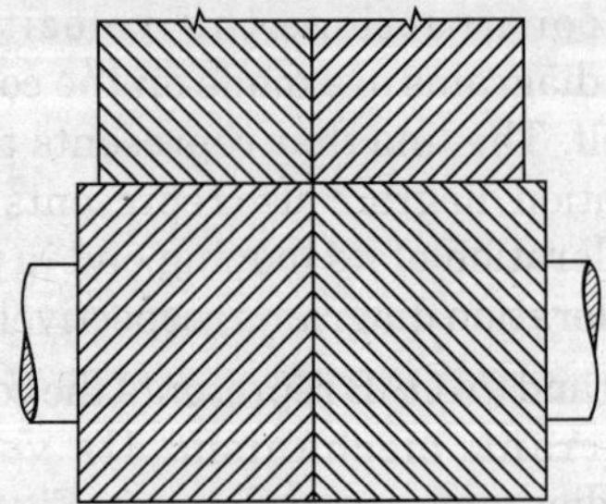

If the left and the right inclinations of a double-helical gear meet at a common apex and there is no groove in between, the gear is known as *herringbone* gear.

II. Intersecting Shafts

Kinematically, the motion between two intersecting shafts is equivalent to the rolling of two cones, assuming no slipping. The gears, in general, are known as *bevel* gears.

When teeth formed on the cones are straight, the gears are known as *straight bevel* and when inclined, they are known as *spiral* or *helical bevel*.

(i) Straight Bevel Gears : The teeth are straight, radial to the point of intersection of the shaft axes and vary in cross-section throughout their length. Usually, they are used to connect shafts at right angles which run at low speeds. Gears of the same size and connecting two shafts at right angle to each other are known as *mitre gears*.

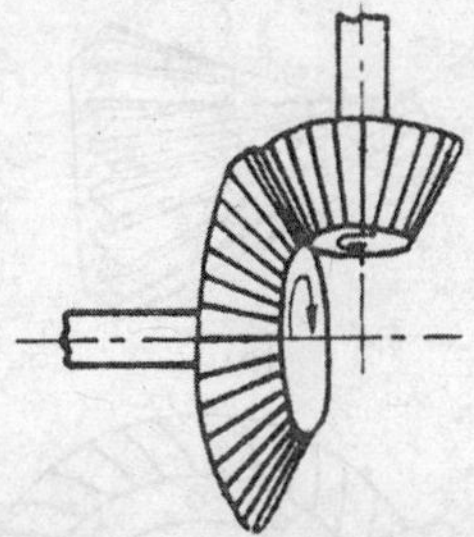

At the beginning of engagement, straight bevel gears make the *line contact* similar to spur gears. There can also be internal bevel gears analogous to internal spur gears.

(ii) Spiral Bevel Gears : When the teeth of a bevel gear are inclined at an angle to the face of the bevel, they are known as *spiral bevels gears* or *helical bevels gears*. They are *smoother* in action and quieter than straight tooth bevels as there is gradual load application and low impact stresses. There exists an axial thrust calling for stronger bearings and supporting assemblies.

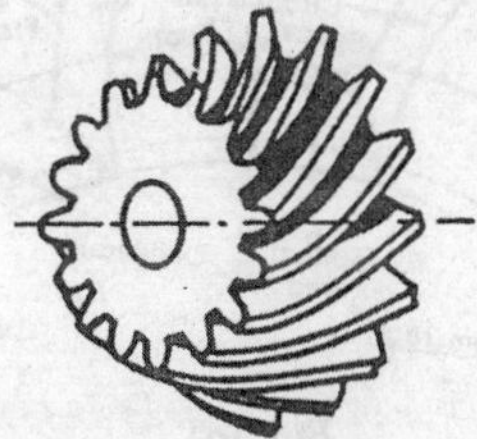

These are used for the drive to the differential of an automobile.

(iii) Zerol Bevel Gears : Spiral bevel gears with curved teeth but with a zero degree spiral angle are known as *zerol bevel gears*. Their tooth action and the end thrust are the same as that of straight bevel gears and, therefore, can be used in the same mountings. However, they are quieter in action than the straight bevel type as the teeth are curved.

III. Skew Shafts

In case of parallel and intersecting shafts, a uniform rotary motion is possible by pure rolling contact. But in case of skew (non-parallel, non-intersecting) shafts, this is not possible.

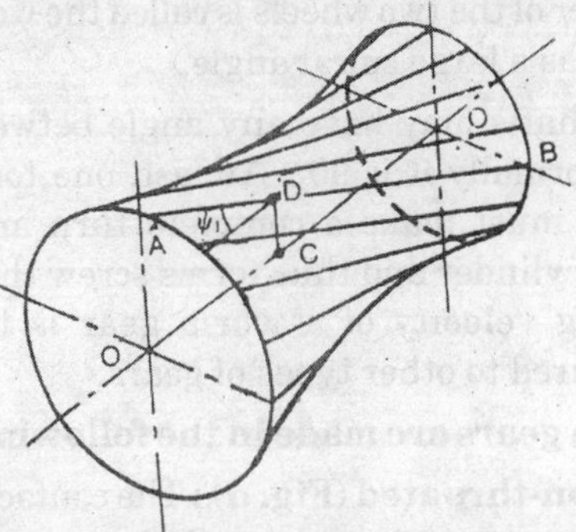

Fig. (a) One Hyperboloid

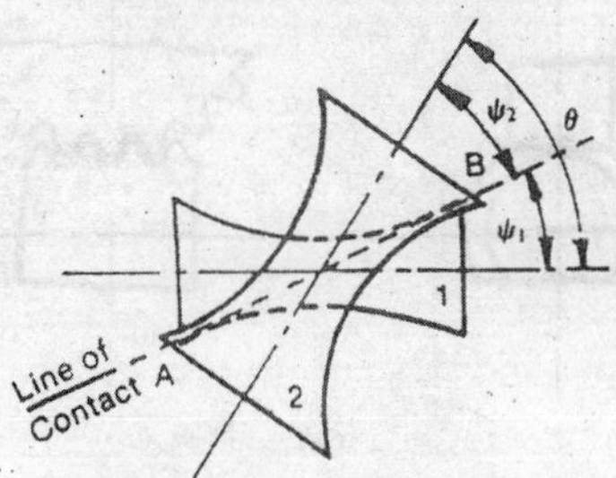

Fig. (b) Two Hyperboloids

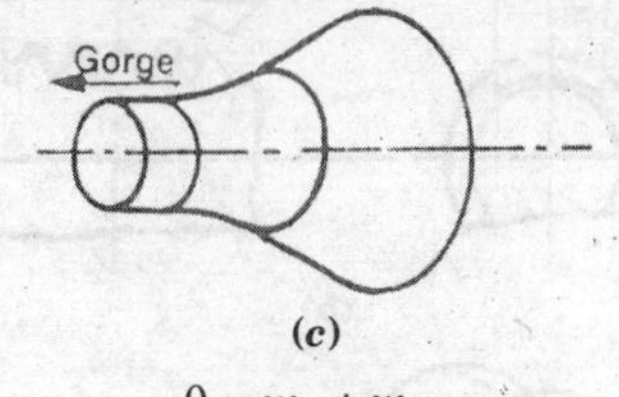

(c)

$$\theta = \psi_1 + \psi_2$$

Main Types of Gears used for skew shafts are

(i) Crossed-helical Gears

The use of crossed-helical gears or spiral gears is limited to light loads. By a suitable choice of helix angle for the mating gears, the two shafts can be set at any angle.

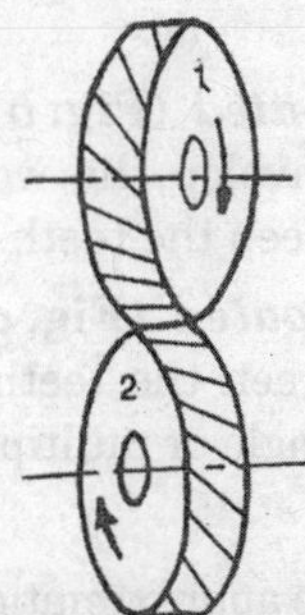

These gears are used to drive feed mechanisms on machine tools, camshafts and oil pumps on small IC engines, etc.

(ii) Worm Gears

Worm gear is a special case of a spiral gear in which the larger wheel, usually, has a hollow or concave shape such that a portion of the pitch diameter of the other gear is enveloped on it. The smaller of the two wheels is called the worm which also has a large spiral angle.

The shafts may have any angle between them, but normally it is 90°. Atleast, one tooth of the worm must make a complete turn around the pitch cylinder and thus forms screw thread. The sliding velocity of a worm gear is higher as compared to other types of gears.

Worm gears are made in the following forms :

(a) Non-throated (Fig. a) : The contact between the teeth is concentrated at a point.

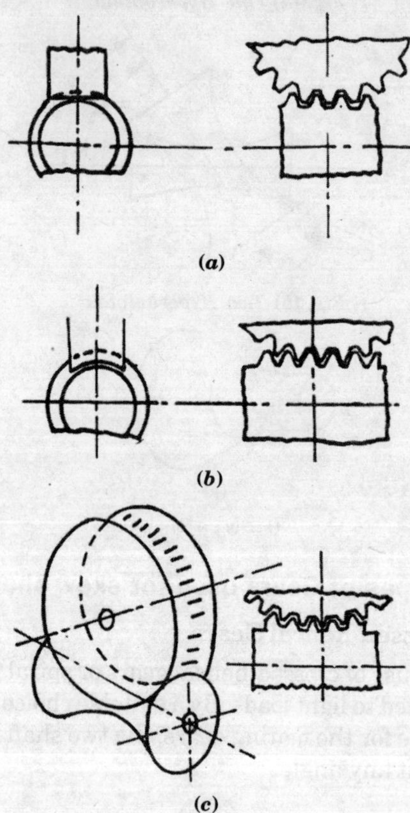

(a)

(b)

(c)

(b) *Single-throated* (Fig. b) : Gear teeth are curved to envelop the worm. There is line contact between the teeth.

(c) *Double-throated* (Fig. c) : There is area contact between the teeth. A worm may be cut with a single or multiple thread cutter.

(iii) Hypoid Gears

Hypoid gears are approximations of hyperboloids though they look like spiral bevel gears (Fig. *a*). A hypoid pinion is larger and stronger than a spiral bevel pinion. A hypoid pair has a quite and smooth action. Moreover, the shafts can pass each other so that bearings can be used on both sides of the gear and the pinion (Fig. *b*).

There is continuous pitch line contact of the two mating hypoid gears while in action and they have larger number of teeth in contact than straight tooth bevel gears. These can wear well if properly lubricated.

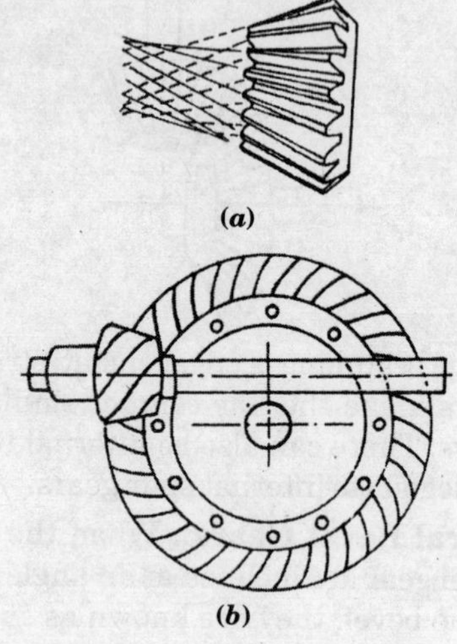

(a)

(b)

Gear Terminology

1. Refer Figs. (a) and (b)

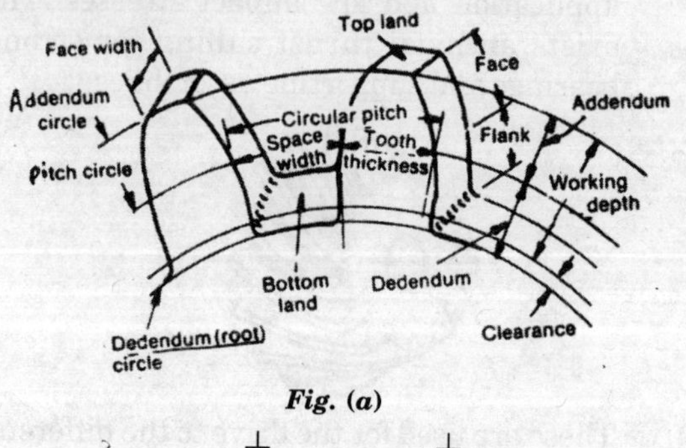

Fig. (a)

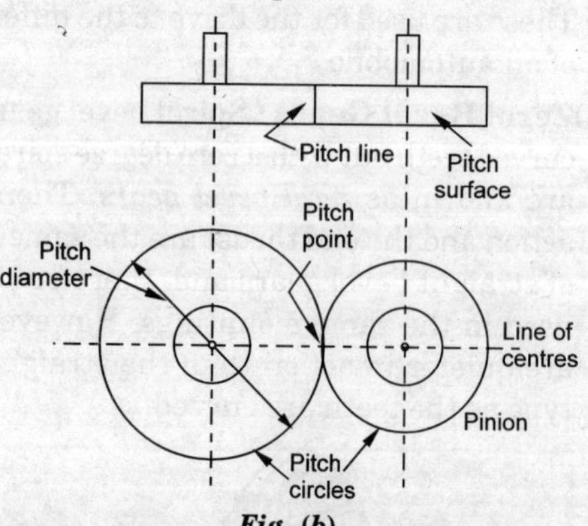

Fig. (b)

(i) **Pitch Cylinders :** Pitch cylinders of a pair of gears in mesh are the imaginary friction cylinders, which by pure rolling together, transmit the same motion as the pair of gears.

(ii) **Pitch Circle :** It is the circle corresponding to a section of the equivalent pitch cylinder by a plane normal to the wheel axis.

(iii) **Pitch Diameter :** It is the diameter of the pitch cylinder.

(iv) **Pitch Surface :** It is the surface of the pitch cylinder.

(v) **Pitch Point :** The point of contact of two pitch circles is known as the pitch point.

(vi) **Pinion :** It is the smaller and usually the driving gear of a pair of mated gears.

2. Refer Fig. (c)

(i) **Rack :** It is a part of a gear wheel of infinite diameter.

(ii) **Pitch Line :** It is a part of the pitch circle of a rack and is a straight line.

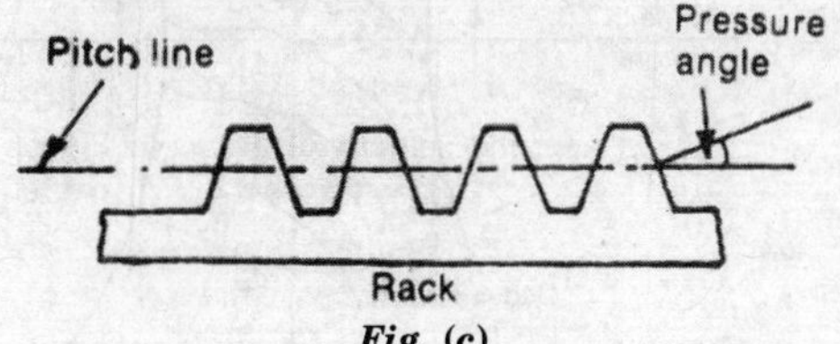

Fig. (c)

3. Pitch : Pitch of two mating gears *must be same*. It is defined as follows :

(i) **Circular Pitch (p) :** It is the distance measured along the circumference of the pitch circle from a point on one tooth to the corresponding point on the adjacent tooth.

$$p = \frac{\pi d}{T}$$

where p = circular pitch,

d = pitch diameter,

and T = number of teeth.

As the expression for p involves π, an indeterminate number, p cannot be expressed precisely.

The angle subtended by the circular pitch at the centre of the pitch circle is known as the *pitch angle* (γ).

(ii) **Diametral Pitch (P) :** It is the number of teeth per unit length of the pitch circle diameter in inches.

$$P = \frac{T}{d}$$

Limitations of the diametral pitch is that it is not in terms of units of length, but in terms of teeth per unit length.

Also, it can be seen that $p\,P = \frac{\pi d}{T}\,\frac{T}{d} = \pi$

The term diametral pitch is not used in S.I. units.

(iii) **Module (m) :** It is the ratio of the pitch diameter in mm to the number of teeth. The term is used in S.I. units in place of diametral pitch.

$$m = \frac{d}{T}$$

Also, $p = \frac{\pi d}{T} = \pi m$

4. (i) **Gear Ratio (G) :** It is the ratio of the number of teeth on the gear to that on the pinion.

$$G = \frac{T}{t}$$

where, T = number of teeth on the gear

t = number of teeth on the pinion.

(ii) **Velocity Ratio (VR) :** The velocity ratio is defined as the ratio of the angular velocity of the follower to the angular velocity of the driving gear.

Let d = pitch diameter,

T = number of teeth

ω = angular velocity (rad/s)

and N = angular velocity (rpm)

Subscript 1 = driver

and 2 = follower

$$VR = \frac{\text{angular velocity of follower}}{\text{angular velocity of driver}}$$

$$= \frac{\omega_2}{\omega_1}$$

$$= \frac{N_2}{N_1} \quad \ldots\ldots (\because \omega = 2\pi N)$$

$$= \frac{d_1}{d_2} \quad \ldots\ldots (\because \pi d_1 N_1 = \pi d_2 N_2)$$

$$= \frac{T_1}{T_2} \quad \ldots\ldots \left(p = \frac{\pi d_1}{T_1} = \frac{\pi d_2}{T_2}\right)$$

5. Refer to fig. (a)

(i) (a) **Addendum Circle :** It is a circle passing through the tips of teeth.

(b) **Addendum :** It is the radial height of a tooth above the pitch circle. Its standard value is one module.

(c) **Dedendum or Root Circle :** It is a circle passing through the roots of the teeth.

(d) **Dedendum :** It is the radial depth of a tooth below the pitch circle. Its standard value is 1.157 m.

(e) **Clearance :** Radial difference between the addendum and the dedendum of a tooth.

Thus

Addendum circle diameter = $d + 2m$

Dedendum circle diameter = $d - 2 \times 1.157\,m$

Clearance = $1.157\,m - m = 0.157\,m$

(ii) (a) Full Depth of Teeth : It is the total radial depth of the tooth space.

Full depth = Addendum + Dedendum

(b) Working Depth of Teeth : The maximum depth to which a tooth penetrates into the tooth space of the mating gear is the working depth of teeth.

Working depth = Sum of addendums of the two gears.

(c) Space Width : It is the width of the tooth space along the pitch circle.

(d) Tooth Thickness : It is the thickness of the tooth measured along the pitch circle.

(e) Backlash : It is the difference between the space width and the tooth thickness along the pitch circle.

Backlash = Space width – Tooth thickness

(f) Face Width : The length of the tooth parallel to the gear axis is the face width.

(iii) (a) Top Land : It is the surface of the top of the tooth.

(b) Bottom Land : The surface of the bottom of the tooth between the adjacent fillets.

(c) Face : Tooth surface between the pitch circle and the top land.

(d) Flank : Tooth surface between the pitch circle and the bottom land including fillet.

(e) Fillet : It is the curved portion of the tooth flank at the root circle.

6. Refer to (a)

(i) (a) Line of Action or Pressure Line : The force, which the driving tooth exerts on the driven tooth, is along a line from the pitch point to the point of contact of the two teeth. This line is also the common normal at the point of contact of the mating gears and is known as *the line of action* or *the pressure line*.

The component of the force along the common tangent at the pitch point is responsible for the power transmission.

The component of the force perpendicular to the common tangent at the pitch point produces thrust which tends to make the shafts apart.

(b) Pressure Angle or Angle of Obliquity (ϕ) : The angle between the pressure line and the common tangent to the pitch circles is known as *the pressure angle* or *the angle of obliquity*.

For more power transmission and lesser pressure on the bearings, pressure angle must be kept small. Standard pressure angles are 20° and 25°. Gears with 14.5° pressure angles have become almost obsolete.

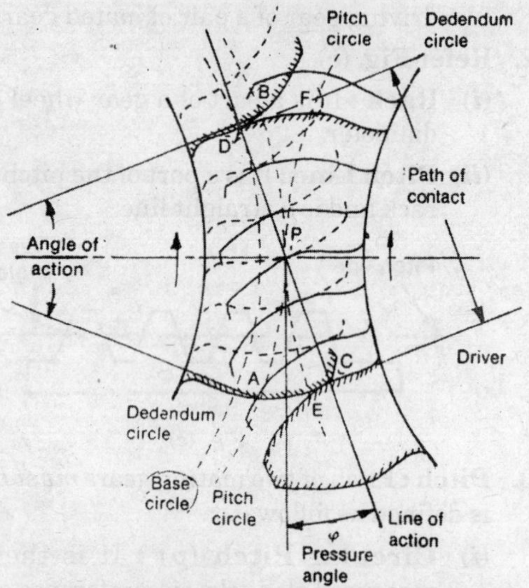

Fig. (d)

(ii) (a) Path of Contact or Contact Length : Locus of the point of contact of two mating teeth from the beginning of engagement to the end of engagement is known as *the path of contact* or *the contact length*. It is CD in the figure. Pitch point P is always one point on the path of contact. It can be subdivided as follows :

Path of Approach : Portion of the path of contact from the beginning of engagement to the pitch point, *i.e.* the length CP.

Path of Recess : Portion of the path of contact from the pitch point to the end of engagement *i.e.* length PD.

(b) Arc of Contact : Locus of a point on the pitch circle from the beginning to the end of engagement of two mating gears is known as the *arc of contact*. In Fig. APB or EPF is the arc of contact. It has also been divided into sub-portions.

Arc of Approach : It is the portion of the arc of contact from the beginning of engagement to the pitch point, *i.e.* length AP or EP.

Arc of Recess : Portion of the arc of contact from the pitch point to the end of engagement is the arc of recess *i.e.* length PB or PF.

(*c*) **Angle of Action** (δ) **:** It is the angle turned by a gear from the beginning of engagement to the end of engagement of a pair of teeth, *i.e.* the angle turned by arcs of contact of respective gear wheels.

Similarly, angle of approach (α) and angle of recess (β) can be defined.

$$\delta = \alpha + \beta$$

The angles will have different values for the driving and the driven gears.

7. **Contact Ratio :** It is the angle of action divided by the pitch angle, *i.e.*

$$CR = \frac{\delta}{\gamma} = \frac{\alpha + \beta}{\gamma}$$

LAW OF GEARING

The common normal at the point of contact between a pair of teeth must always pass through the pitch point.

TYPES OF TEETH PROVIDED ON GEARS

Cycloidal Teeth

A *cycloid* is the curve traced by a point on the circumference of a circle which rolls without slipping on a fixed straight line. When a circle rolls without slipping on the outside of a fixed circle, the curve traced by a point on the circumference of a circle is known as *epi-cycloid*. On the other hand, if a circle rolls without slipping on the inside of a fixed circle, then the curve traced by a point on the circumference of a circle is called *hypo-cycloid*.

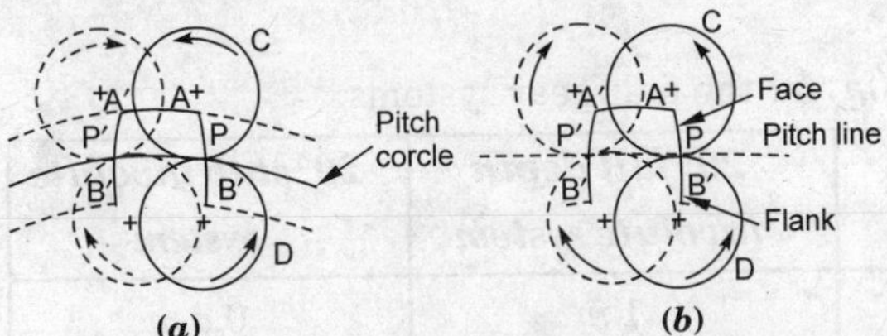

Fig. Construction of cycloidal teeth of a gear

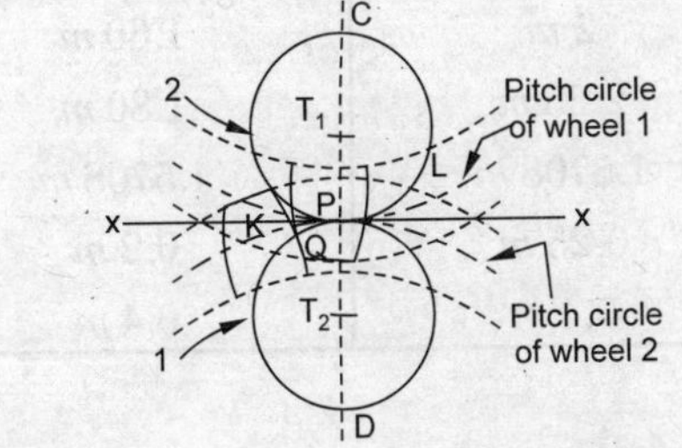

Fig. Construction of two mating cycloidal teeth.

Involute Teeth

An involute of a circle is a plane curve generated by a point on a tangent, which rolls on the circle without slipping or by a point on a taut string which in unwrapped from a reel as shown in the figure (*a*) below.

If F is the maximum tooth pressure as shown in the fig (*b*), then

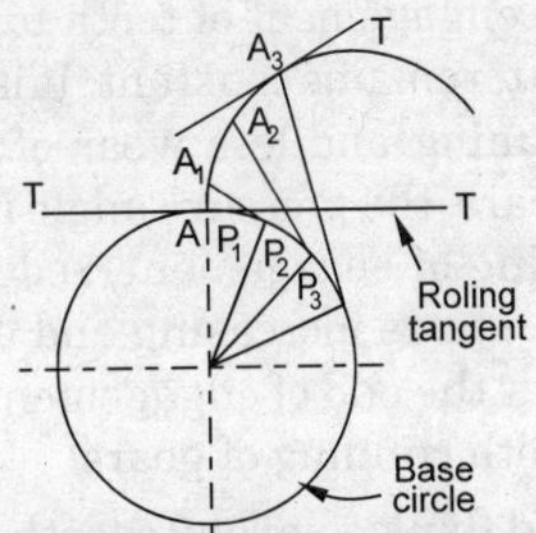

Fig. Construction of involute

Tangential force, $F_T = F \cos \phi$

and radial or normal force, $F_R = F \sin \phi$

∴ Torque exerted on the gear shaft = $F_T \times r$

where *r* is the pitch circle radius of the gear.

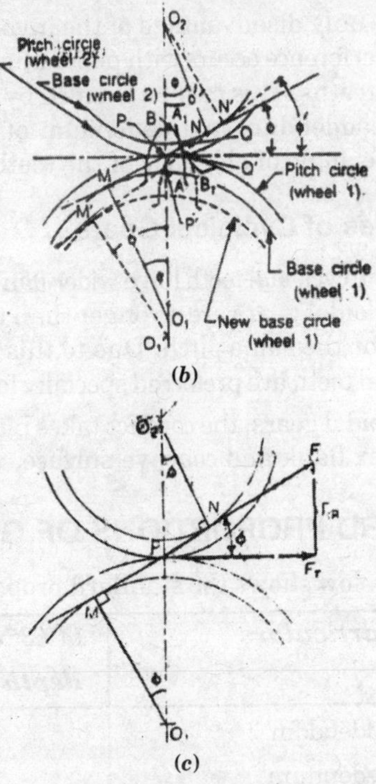

Fig. Involute teeth

Note : The tangential force provides the driving torque and the radial or normal force produces radial deflection of the rim and bending of the shafts.

Comparison between Involute and Cycloidal Gears

In actual practice, the involute gears are more commonly used as compared to cycloidal gears, due to the following advantages :

Advantages of Involute Gears

(*i*) The most important advantage of the involute gears is that the centre distance for a pair of involute gears can be varied within limits without changing the velocity ratio. This is not true for cycloidal gears which requires exact centre distance to be maintained.

(*ii*) In involute gears, the pressure angle, from the start of the engagement of teeth to the end of the engagement, remains constant. It is necessary for smooth running and less wear of gears. But in cycloidal gears, the pressure angle is maximum at the beginning of engagement, reduces to zero at pitch point, starts increasing and again becomes maximum at the end of engagement. This results in less smooth running of gears.

(*iii*) The face and flank of involute teeth are generated by a single curve whereas in cycloidal gears, double curves (*i.e.* epi-cycloid and hypo-cycloid) are required for the face and flank respectively. Thus the involute teeth are easy to manufacture than cycloidal teeth. In involute system, the basic rack has straight teeth and the same can be cut with simple tools.

Note : The only disadvantage of the involute teeth is that the interference occurs with pinions having smaller number of teeths. This may be avoided by altering the heights of addendum and dedendum of the mating teeth or the angle of obliquity of the teeth.

Advantages of Cycloidal Gears

(*i*) Since the cycloidal teeth have wider flanks, therefore the cycloidal gears are stronger than the involute gears for the same pitch. Due to this reason, the cycloidal teeth are preferred specially for cast teeth.

(*ii*) In cycloidal gears, the contact takes place between a convex flank and concave surface, where as in involute gears, the convex surfaces are in contact. This condition results in less wear in cycloidal gears as compared to involute gears. However the difference in wear is negligible.

(*iii*) In cycloidal gears, the interference does not occur at all. Though there are advantages of cycloidal gears but they are outweighed by the greater simplicity and flexibility of the involute gears.

SYSTEMS OF GEAR TEETH

The following four systems of gear teeth are commonly used in practice :

(*i*) $14\frac{1}{2}^\circ$ Composite system,

(*ii*) $14\frac{1}{2}^\circ$ Full depth involute system,

(*iii*) 20° Full depth involute system, and

(*iv*) 20° Stub involute system.

The $14\frac{1}{2}^\circ$ *composite system* is used for general purpose gears. It is stronger but has no interchangeability. The tooth profile of this system has cycloidal curves at the top and bottom and involute curve at the middle portion. The teeth are produced by formed milling cutters or hobs. The tooth profile of the $14\frac{1}{2}^\circ$ *full depth involute system* was developed for use with gear hobs for spur and helical gears.

The tooth profile of the *20° full depth involute system* may be cut by hobs. The increase of the pressure angle from $14\frac{1}{2}^\circ$ to 20° results in a stronger tooth, because the tooth acting as a beam is wider at the base. The *20° stub involute system* has a strong tooth to take heavy loads.

STANDARD PROPORTIONS OF GEAR SYSTEMS

The table below shows the standard proportions in module (*m*) for the four gear systems.

S. No.	*Particulars*	*14½3° composite or full depth involute system*	*20° full depth involute system*	*20° stub involute system*
1.	Addenddm	1 *m*	1 *m*	0.8 *m*
2.	Dedendum	1.25 *m*	1.25 *m*	1 *m*
3.	Working depth	2 *m*	2 *m*	1.60 *m*
4.	Minimum total depth	2.25 *m*	2.25 *m*	1.80 *m*
5.	Tooth thickness	1.5708 *m*	1.5708 *m*	1.5708 *m*
6.	Minimum clearance	0.25 *m*	0.25 *m*	0.2 *m*
7.	Fillet radius at root	0.4 *m*	0.4 *m*	0.4 *m*

LENGTH OF PATH OF CONTACT

Consider pinion driving the wheel as shown in the given figure

Length of the part of the path of contact, or the path of approach,

$$KP = KN - PN$$

$$= \sqrt{(R_A)^2 - R^2 \cos^2 \phi} - R \sin \phi$$

Length of the part of the path of contact, or path of recess,

$$PL = ML - MP$$

$$= \sqrt{(r_A)^2 - r^2 \cos^2 \phi} - r \sin \phi$$

Length of the path of contact,

$$KL = KP + PL$$

$$= \sqrt{(R_A)^2 - R^2 \cos^2 \phi} + \sqrt{(r_A)^2 - r^2 \cos^2 \phi} - (R + r) \sin \phi$$

LENGTH OF ARC OF CONTACT

The arc of contact is the path traced by a point on the pitch circle from the beginning to the end of engagement of a given pair of teeth. In the above figure, the arc of contact is EPF or GPH. Considering the arc of contact GPH, it is divided itno two parts *i.e.* arc GP and arc PH. The arc GP is known as *arc of approach* and the arc PH is called *arc of recess.* The angles subtended by these arcs at O_1 are called *angle of approach* and *angle of recess* respectively.

length of the arc of approach (arc GP)

$$= \frac{\text{Length of path of approach}}{\cos \phi} = \frac{KP}{\cos \phi}$$

and, length of the arc of recess (arc PH)

$$= \frac{\text{Length of path of recess}}{\cos \phi} = \frac{PL}{\cos \phi}$$

Since the length of the arc of contact GPH is equal to the sum of the length of arc of approach and arc of recess, therefore

Length of the arc of contact = arc GP + arc PH

$$= \frac{KP}{\cos \phi} + \frac{PL}{\cos \phi}$$

$$= \frac{KL}{\cos \phi}$$

$$= \frac{\text{Length of path of contact}}{\cos \phi}$$

Contact Ratio (or number of pairs of teeth in contact)

The contact ratio or the number of pairs of teeth in contact is defined as the ratio of the length of the arc of contact to the circular pitch. Mathematically,

Contact ratio or number of pairs of teeth in contact

$$= \frac{\text{Length of the arc of contact}}{p_c}$$

where p_c = circular pitch = πm and m = module.

Note:

1. The contact ratio, usually, is not a whole number. *e.g.*, if the contact ratio is 1.6, it does not mean that there are 1.6 pairs of teeth in contact. It means that there are alternately one pair and two pairs of teeth in contact and on a time basis the average is 1.6.
2. The theoretical minimum value for the contact ratio is one, *i.e.* there must always be atleast one pair of teeth in contact for continuous action.
3. Larger the contact ratio, more quietly the gears will operate.

Minimum Number of Teeth on the Pinion on order to Avoid Interference

Let t = Number of teeth on the pinion;

T = Number of teeth on the wheel

m = Module of the teeth;

r = Pitch circle radius of the pinion

$$= \frac{m . t}{2}$$

G = Gear ratio

$$= \frac{T}{t} = \frac{R}{r};$$

ϕ = Pressure angle or angle of obliquity.

$$\therefore \quad t = \frac{2 A_p}{\sqrt{1 + \frac{T}{t}\left(\frac{T}{t} + 2\right) \sin^2 \phi} - 1}$$

$$= \frac{2 A_p}{\sqrt{1 + G(G + 2) \sin^2 \phi} - 1}$$

This equation gives the miniumum number of teeth required on the pinion in order to avoid interference.

Note :

1. If the pinion and wheel have equal teeth, then G = 1.

Therefore the above equation reduces to

$$t = \frac{2\,A_p}{\sqrt{1+3\sin^2\phi}\ -1}$$

2. The minimum number of teeth on the pinion which will mesh with any gear (also rack) without interference are given in the following table :

S. No.	*System of gear teeth*	*Minimum number of teeth on the pinion*
1.	14½° Composite	12
2.	14½° Full depth involute	32
3.	20° Full depth involute	18
4.	20° Stub involute	14

Minimum Number of Teeth on the Wheel in Order to Avoid Interference

Let T = Minimum number of teeth required on the wheel in order to avoid interference

and $A_w.m$ = Addendum of the wheel,

where A_w is a fraction by which the standard addendum for the wheel should be multiplied.

$$\therefore \quad T = \frac{2\,A_w}{\sqrt{1+\frac{t}{T}\left(\frac{t}{T}+2\right)\sin^2\phi}\ -1}$$

$$= \frac{2\,A_w}{\sqrt{1+\frac{1}{G}\left(\frac{1}{G}+2\right)\sin^2\phi}-1}$$

$$= \frac{2\,A_w}{\sqrt{1+\left(\frac{2G+1}{G^2}\right)\sin^2\phi}-1}$$

If wheel and pinion have equal teeth, then G = 1, and

$$T = \frac{2\,A_w}{\sqrt{1+3\sin^2\phi}-1}$$

COMPARISON OF CYCLOIDAL AND INVOLUTE TOOTH FORMS

Cycloidal Teeth	*Involute Teeth*
(*i*) Pressure angle varies from maximum at the beginning of engagement, reduces to zero at the pitch point and again increases to maximum at the end of engagement resulting in less smooth running of the gears.	(*i*) Pressure angle is constant throughout the engagement of teeth. This results in smooth running of the gears.
(*ii*) It involves double curve for the teeth, epicycloid and hypocycloid, this complicates the manufacture.	(*ii*) It involves single curve for the teeth resulting in simplicity of manufacturing and of tools.
(*iii*) Owing to difficulty to manufacture, these are costlier.	(*iii*) These are simple to manufacture and thus are cheaper.
(*iv*) Exact centre-distance is required to transmit a constant velocity ratio.	(*iv*) A little variation in the centre distance does not affect the velocity ratio.
(*v*) Phenomenon of interference does not occur at all.	(*v*) Interference can occur if the condition of minimum number of teeth on a gear is not followed.
(*vi*) The teeth have spreading flanks and thus are stronger.	(*vi*) The teeth have radial flanks and thus are weaker as compared to cycloidal form for the same pitch.
(*vii*) A convex flank always has contact with a concave face resulting in less wear.	(*vii*) Two convex surfaces are in contact and thus there is more wear.

Here it can be deduced that the advantages of involute system are more real. Therefore, the use of involute teeth have become almost universal rendering the cycloidal system obsolete.

GOVERNORS

The function of a governor is to regulate the mean speed of an engine, when there are variations in the load, *e.g.* when the load on an engine increases, its speed decreases, therefore it becomes necessary to increase the supply of working fluid. On the other hand, when the load on the engine decreases, its speed increases and thus less working fluid is required. The governor automatically controls the supply of working fluid to the engine with the varying load conditions and keeps the mean speed within certain limits.

Type of Governors

The governors may, broadly, be classified as

(*i*) Centrifugal governors, and

(*ii*) Inertia governors.

The centrifugal governors, may further be classified as follows :

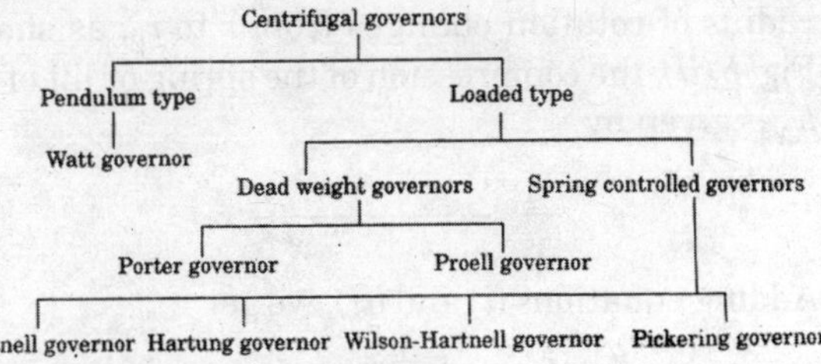

(*i*) Centrifugal Governor.

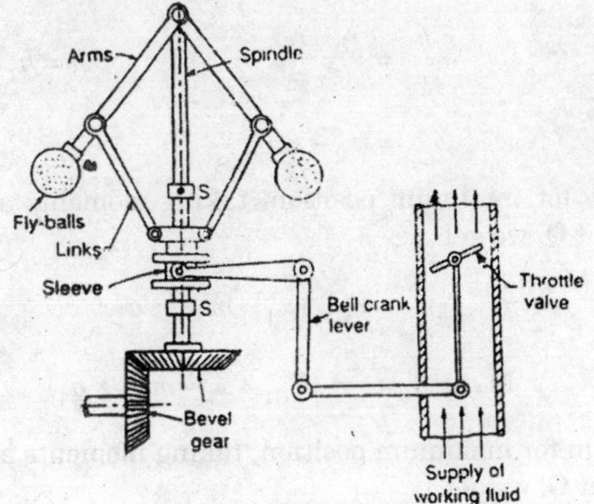

Fig. Centrifugal governor

When the balls rotate at uniform speed, controlling force is equal to the centrifugal force and they balance each other.

Terms Used in Governors

(*i*) **Height of a Governor :** It is the vertical distance from the centre of the ball to a point where the axes of the arms (or arms produced) intersect on the spindle axis. It is usually denoted by *h*.

(*ii*) **Equilibrium Speed :** It is the speed at which the governor balls, arms etc., are in complete equilibrium and the sleeve does not tend to move upwards or downwards.

(*iii*) **Mean Equilibrium Speed :** It is the speed at the mean position of the balls or the sleeve.

(*iv*) **Maximum and Minimum Equilibrium Speeds :** The speeds at the maximum and minimum radius of rotation of the balls, without tending to move either way are known as maximum and minimum equilibrium speeds respectively.

Note : There can be many equilibrium speeds between the mean and the maximum and the mean and the minimum equilibrium speeds.

(*v*) **Sleeve lift :** It is the vertical distance which the sleeve travels due to change in equilibrium speed.

Watt Governor

The simplest form of a centrifugal governor is a Watt governor, as shown in the figure below. It is basically a conical pendulum with links attached to a sleeve of negligible mass. The arms of the governor may be connected to the spindle in the following three ways :

(*i*) The pivot P, may be on the spindle axis as shown in Fig. (*a*).

(*ii*) The pivot P, may be offset from the spindle axis and the arms when produced intersect at O, as shown in Fig. (*b*).

(*iii*) The pivot P, may be offset, but the arms crosses the axis at O, as shown in Fig. (*c*).

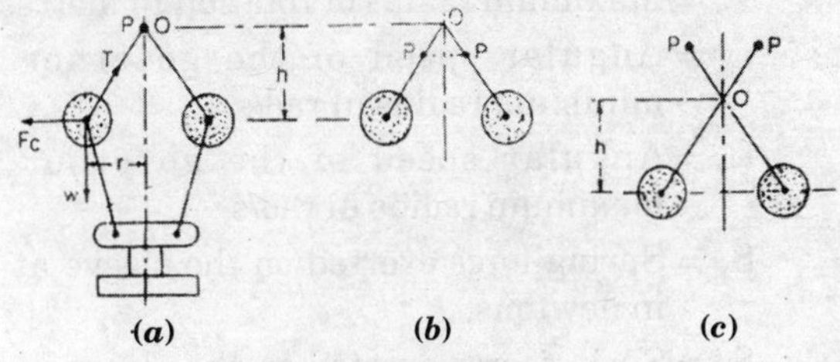

Fig. Watt governor

Let m = Mass of the ball in kg

w = Weight of the ball in newtons = $m.g.$

T = Tension in the arm in newtons

ω = Angular velocity of the arm and ball about the spindle axis in rad/s

r = Radius of the path of rotation of the ball, *i.e.* horizontal distance from the centre of the ball to the spindle axis in metres

F_C = Centrifugal force acting on the ball in newtons

$= m.\omega^2.r,$

Height of the governor in metres,

$$h = \frac{9.81}{(2\pi N/60)^2}$$

$$= \frac{895}{N^2} \text{ metres}$$

Hartnell Governor

A Hartness governor is a spring loaded governor as shown in the figure (*a*). It consists of two bell crank levers pivoted at the points O, O' to the frame. The frame is attached to the governor spindle and therefore rotates with it. Each lever carries a ball at the end of the vertical arm OB and a roller at the end of the horizontal arm OR. A helical spring in compression provides equal downward forces on the two rollers through a collar on the sleeve. The spring force may be adjusted by screwing a nut up or down on the sleeve.

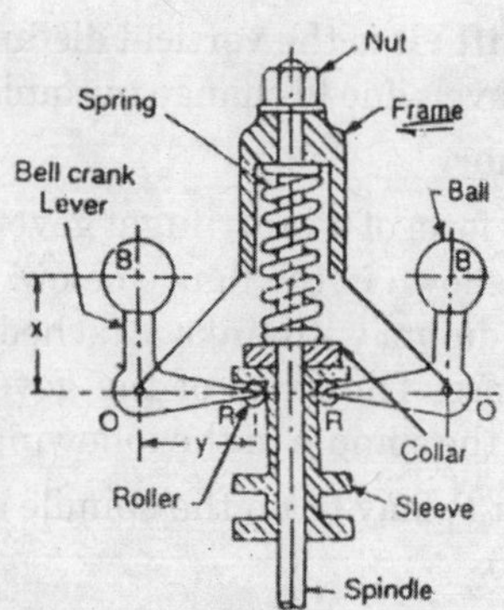

Hartness Governor

Let m = Mass of each ball in kg,

M = Mass of sleeve in kg,

r_1 = Minimum radius of rotation in metres,

r_2 = Maximum radius of rotation in metres,

ω_1 = Angular speed of the governor at minimum radius in rad/s,

ω_2 = Angular speed of the governor at maximum radius in rad/s,

S_1 = Spring force exerted on the sleeve at ω_1 in newtons,

S_2 = Spring force exerted on the sleeve at ω_2 in newtons,

F_{C1} = Centrifugal force at ω_1 in newtons $= m(\omega_1)^2 r_1$,

F_{C2} = Centrifugal force at ω_2 in newtons $= m(\omega_2)^2 r_2$,

s = Stiffness of the spring or the force required to compress the spring by one mm

x = Length of the vertical or ball arm of the lever in metres,

y = Length of the horizontal or sleeve arm of the lever in metres, and

r = Distance of fulcrum O from the governor axis or the radius of rotation when the governor is in mid-position, in metres.

Consider the forces acting at one bell crank lever. The minimum and maximum position is shown in Fig. (*b*) Let h be the compression of the spring when the radius of rotation changes from r_1 to r_2.

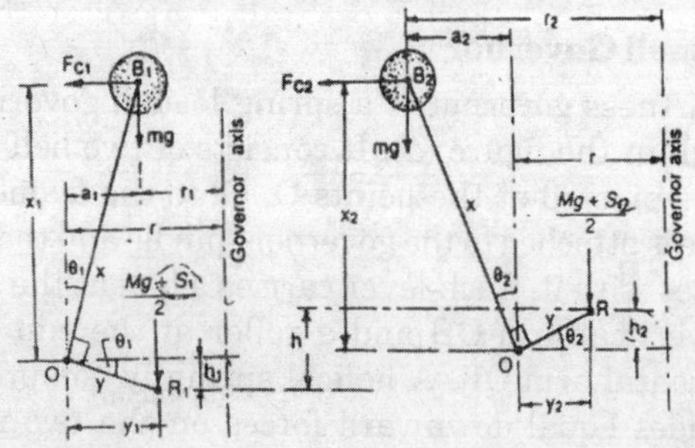

(i) Minimum position *(ii) Maximum position*

Fig. (b)

For the minimum position, *i.e.* when the radius of rotation changes from r to r_1, as shown in Fig. *b (i)*, the compression of the spring or the lift of sleeve h_1 is given by

$$\frac{h_1}{y} = \frac{a_1}{x} = \frac{r - r_1}{x} \quad \text{... (i)}$$

Similarly, for the maximum position, *i.e.* when the radius of rotation changes from r to r_2, as shown in Fig. *b (ii)*, the compression of the spring or lift of sleeve h_2 is given by

$$\frac{h_2}{y} = \frac{a_2}{x} = \frac{r_2 - r}{x} \quad \text{... (ii)}$$

Adding equations (*i*) and (*ii*), we get

$$\frac{h_1 + h_2}{y} = \frac{r_2 - r_1}{x}$$

or

$$\frac{h}{y} = \frac{r_2 - r_1}{x} \quad (\because h = h_1 + h_2)$$

$$\therefore \quad h = (r_2 - r_1)\frac{y}{x} \quad \text{... (iii)}$$

Now for minimum position, taking moments about point O, we get

$$\frac{M \cdot g + S_1}{2} \times y_1 = F_{C1} \times x_1 - m.g. \times a_1$$

or

$$M.g + S_1 = \frac{2}{y_1}(F_{C1} \times x_1 - m.g. \times a_1) \quad \text{... (iv)}$$

Again for maximum position, taking moments about point O, we get

$$\frac{M.g + S_2}{2} \times y_2 = F_{C2} \times x_2 + m.g. \times a_2$$

or

$$M.g + S_2 = \frac{2}{y_2}(F_{C2} \times x_2 - m.g. \times a_2) \quad \text{... (v)}$$

Subtracting equation (*iv*) from equation (*v*), we get

$$S_2 - S_1 = \frac{2}{y_2}(F_{C2} \times x_2 + m.g. \times a_2) - \frac{2}{y_1}(F_{C1} \times x_1 - m.g. \times a_1)$$

We know that $S_2 - S_1 = h.s.$

and

$$h = (r_2 - r_1)\frac{y}{x}$$

$$\therefore \quad s = \frac{S_2 - S_1}{h} = \left(\frac{S_2 - S_1}{r_2 - r_1}\right)\frac{x}{y}$$

Neglecting the obliquity effect of the arms (*i.e.* $x_1 = x_2 = x$, and $y_1 = y_2 = y$) and the moment due to weight of the balls (*i.e., m.g.*), we have for minimum position,

$$\frac{M.g + S_1}{2} \times y = F_{C1} \times x$$

or

$$M.g + S_1 = 2F_{C1} \times \frac{x}{y} \quad \text{... (vi)}$$

Similarly for maximum position,

$$\frac{M\cdot g + S_2}{2} \times y = F_{C2} \times x$$

or $$M.g + S_2 = 2F_{C2} \times \frac{x}{y} \quad ...(vii)$$

Subtracting equation (*vi*) from equation (*vii*), we get

$$S_2 - S_1 = 2\,(F_{C2} - F_{C1})\,\frac{x}{y} \quad ...(viii)$$

We know that $S_2 - S_1 = h.s.$

and $$h = (r_2 - r_1)\,\frac{x}{y}$$

$$\therefore \quad s = \frac{S_2 - S_1}{h}$$

$$= 2\left(\frac{F_{C2} - F_{C1}}{r_2 - r_1}\right)\left(\frac{x}{y}\right)^2 \quad ...(ix)$$

Note :

1. Unless otherwise stated, the obliquity effect of the arms and the moment due to the weight of the balls is neglected, in actual practice.
2. When friction is taken into account, the weight of the sleeve (M.*g*) may be replaced by (M.*g* ± F).
3. The centrifugal force (F_C) for any intermediate position (*i.e.* between the minimum and maximum position) at a radius of rotation (*r*) may be obtained as discussed below :

Since the stiffness for a given spring is constant for all positions, therefore for minimum and intermediate position,

$$s = 2\left(\frac{F_C - F_{C1}}{r - r_1}\right)\left(\frac{x}{y}\right)^2 \quad ...(x)$$

and for intermediate and maximum position

$$s = 2\left(\frac{F_{C2} - F_C}{r_2 - r}\right)\left(\frac{x}{y}\right)^2 \quad ...(xi)$$

From equations (*ix*), (*x*) and (*xi*),

$$\frac{F_{C2} - F_{C1}}{r_2 - r_1} = \frac{F_C - F_{C1}}{r - r_1} = \frac{F_{C2} - F_C}{r_2 - r}$$

or $$F_C = F_{C1} + (F_{C2} - F_{C1})\left(\frac{r - r_1}{r_2 - r_1}\right)$$

$$= F_{C2} - (F_{C2} - F_{C1})\left(\frac{r_2 - r}{r_2 - r_1}\right)$$

Sensitiveness of a Governor

A governor is said to be sensitive when it readily responds to a small change of speed. The movement of the sleeve for a fractional change of speed is the measure of sensitivity.

As a governor is used to limit the change of speed of the engine between zero to full-load conditions, the sensitiveness of a governor is also defined as

$$\text{Sensitiveness} = \frac{\text{Mean speed}}{\text{Range of speed}} = \frac{N}{N_2 - N_1}$$

$$= \frac{1}{2}\,\frac{N_2 + N_1}{N_2 - N_1}$$

where N = mean speed

N_1 = minimum speed corresponding to full load conditions

N_2 = maximum speed corresponding to no-load conditions

Hunting

Sensitiveness of a governor is desirable quality. However, if a governor is too sensitive, it may fluctuate continuously, because when the load on the engine falls, the sleeve rises rapidly to a maximum position. This shuts off the fuel supply to the extent to affect a sudden fall in the speed. As the speed falls to below the mean value, the sleeve again moves rapidly and falls to a minimum position to increase the fuel supply. The speed subsequently rises and becomes more than the average with the result that the sleeve again falls to reduce the fuel supply. This process continues and is known as hunting.

Isochronism

A governor with a range of speed zero is known as an *isochronous governor.*

$$\text{Sensitiveness} = \frac{\text{Mean speed}}{\text{Range of speed}} = \infty$$

i.e. such a governor is infinitely sensitive. This means that for all positions of the sleeve or the balls, the governor has the same speed. Any change of speed results in moving the balls and the sleeve to their extreme positions. However, an isochronous governor is not practical due to friction at the sleeve.

For a Porter governor, with all arms equal in length and intersecting on the axis (neglecting friction),

$$h_1 = \frac{g}{\omega_1^2}\left(1 + \frac{M}{m}\right),$$

and $$h_2 = \frac{g}{\omega_2^2}\left(1 + \frac{M}{m}\right)$$

For isochronism, $\omega_1 = \omega_2$ and thus $h_1 = h_2$. However, from the configuration of a Porter governor, it can be judged that it is impossible to have two positions of the balls at the same speed. Thus a pendulum type of governor connot possibly be isochronous.

In the case of a Hartnell governor (neglecting friction),

At ω_1, $mr_1\,\omega_1^2\,a = \frac{1}{2}\,(Mg + F_{s1})\,b$

At ω_2, $mr_2\,\omega_2^2\,a = \frac{1}{2}\,(Mg + F_{s2})\,b$

For isochronism, $\omega_1 = \omega_2$

$$\therefore \quad \frac{Mg + F_{s1}}{Mg + F_{s2}} = \frac{r_1}{r_2}$$

which is the required condition of isochronism.

Stability

A governor is said to be stable if it brings the speed of the engine to the required value and there is not much hunting. The ball masses occupy a definite position for each speed of the engine within the working range.

Obviously, the stability and the sensitivity are two opposite characteristics.

Effort of a Governor

$$\text{Effort, } \frac{E}{2} = \frac{(c^2 - 1)}{2}\,(Mg + F_s)$$

Power of a Governor

The power of a governor is the work done at the sleeve for a given percentage change of speed, i.e. it is the product of the effort and the displacement of the sleeve.

For a Porter governor, having all equal arms which intersect on the axis or pivoted at points equidistant from the spindle axis,

$$\text{Power} = \frac{E}{2} \times (2 \times \text{height of governor})$$

$$\text{Power} = \frac{c^2 - 1}{2}\,(m + M)\,g \times 2h\left(\frac{c^2 - 1}{c^2}\right)$$

$$= (m + M)\,g\,h\left(\frac{c^2 - 1}{c}\right)^2$$

Turning Moment Diagram and Fly wheel

The turning moment diagram (also known as *crank-effort diagram*) is the graphical representation of the turning moment or crank effort for various positions of the crank. It is plotted on cartesian co-ordinates, in which the turning moment is taken as the ordinate and crank angle as abscissa.

Turning Moment Diagram for a Single Cylinder Double Acting Steam Engine

A turning moment diagram for a single cylinder double acting steam engine is shown in the figure below. The vertical ordinate represents the turning moment and the horizontal ordinate represents the crank angle.

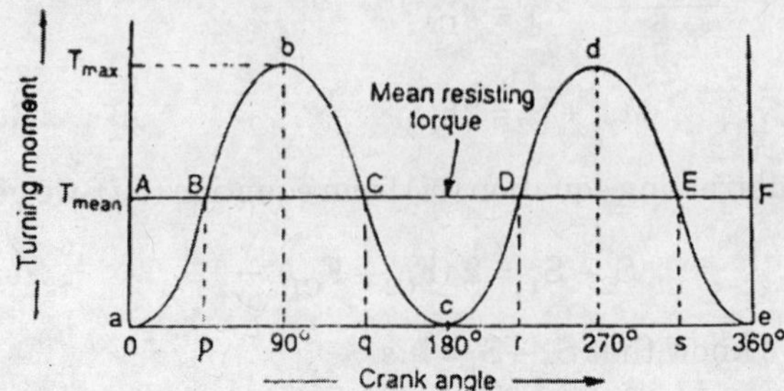

Fig. Turning moment diagram for a single cylinder, double acting steam engine.

Turning moment of the crankshaft,

$$T = F_P \times r\left(\sin\theta + \frac{\sin 2\theta}{2\sqrt{n^2 - \sin^2\theta}}\right)$$

Where F_P = Piston effort,

r = Radius of crank

n = Ratio of the connecting rod length and radius of crank, and

θ = Angle turned by the crank from inner dead centre.

Note:

1. When the turning moment is positive (i.e., when the engine torque is more than the mean resisting torque) as shown between points B and C (or D and E) in the above figure the crankshaft accelerates and the work is done by the steam.
2. When the turning moment is negative (i.e. when the engine torque is less than the mean resisting torque) as shown between points C and D in the above figure, the crankshaft retards and the work is done on the steam.
3. If T = Torque on the crankshaft at any instant, and

   T_{mean} = Mean resisting torque.

   then acclerating torque on the rotating parts of the engine = $T - T_{mean}$
4. If $(T - T_{mean})$ is positive, the flywheel accelerates and if $(T - T_{mean})$ is negative, then the flywheel retards.

Turning Moment Diagram for a Four Stroke Cycle Internal Combustion Engine

A turning moment diagram for a four stroke cycle internal combustion engine is shown in the figure below. In a four stroke cycle internal combustion engine, there is one working stroke after the crank has turned through two revolutions, i.e. 720° (or 4 π radians).

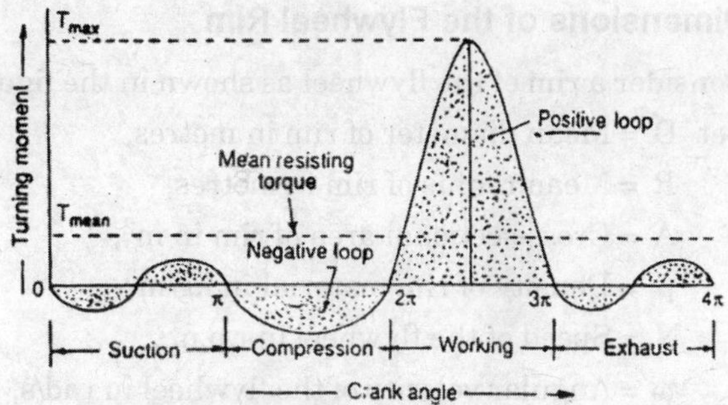

Fig. Turning moment diagram for a four stroke cycle internal combustion engine.

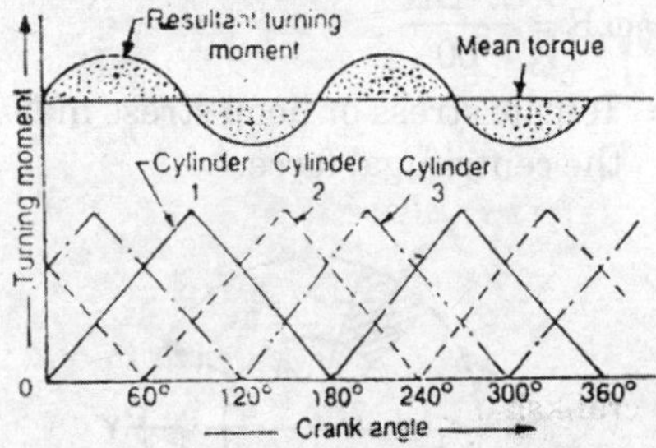

Fig. Turning moment diagram for a multi-cylinder engine.

Determination of Maximum Fluctuation of Energy

A turning moment diagram for a multi-cylinder engine is shown by a wavy curve in the figure below. The horizontal line AG represents the mean torque line. Let a_1, a_3, a_5 be the areas above the mean torque line and a_2, a_4 and a_6 be the areas below the mean torque line. These areas represent some quantity of energy which is either added or subtracted from the energy of the moving parts of the engine.

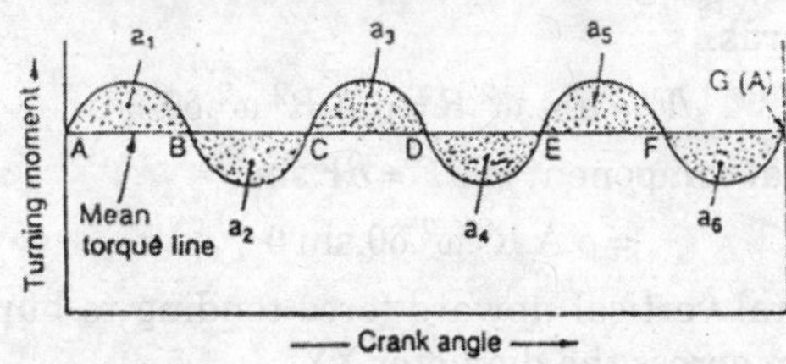

Fig. Determination of maximum fluctuation of energy

Let the energy in the flywheel at A = E, then from Fig., we have

$$\text{Energy at B} = E + a_1$$

$$\text{Energy at C} = E + a_1 - a_2$$

$$\text{Energy at D} = E + a_1 - a_2 + a_3$$

$$\text{Energy at E} = E + a_1 - a_2 + a_3 - a_4$$

$$\text{Energy at F} = E + a_1 - a_2 + a_3 - a_4 + a_5$$

$$\text{Energy at G} = E + a_1 - a_2 + a_3 - a_4 + a_5 - a_6 = \text{Energy at A}$$

(*i.e.* cycle repeats after G)

Suppose that the greatest of these energies is at B and least at E. Therefore,

Maximum energy in flywheel = $E + a_1$

Minimum energy in the flywheel = $E + a_1 - a_2 + a_3 - a_4$

∴ Maximum fluctuation of energy,

$$\Delta E = \text{Maximum energy} - \text{Minimum energy}$$

$$= (E + a_1) - (E + a_1 - a_2 + a_3 - a_4)$$

$$= a_2 - a_3 + a_4$$

Co-efficient of Fluctuation of Energy

It may be defined as the ratio of the maximum fluctuation of energy to the workdone per cycle. Mathematically, coefficient of fluctuation of energy,

$$C_E = \frac{\text{Maximum fluctuation of energy}}{\text{Workdone per cycle}}$$

The workdone per cycle (in N-m or joules) may be obtained by using the following two relations :

(*i*) Workdone per cycle = $T_{mean} \times \theta$

where, T_{mean} = Mean torque, and

θ = Angle turned (in radians), in one revolution.

= 2π, in case of steam engine and two stroke internal combustion engines

= 4π, in case of four stroke internal combustion engines.

The mean torque (T_{mean}) in N-m may be obtained by using the following relation :

$$T_{mean} = \frac{P \times 60}{2\pi N} = \frac{P}{\omega}$$

where, P = Power transmitted in watts,

N = Speed in r.p.m., and

ω = Angular speed in rad/s = $2\pi N/60$

(*ii*) The workdone per cycle may also be obtained by using the following relation :

$$\text{Work done per cycle} = \frac{P \times 60}{n}$$

where, n = Number of working strokes per minute.

= N, in case of steam engines and two stroke internal combustion engines,

= N/2, in case of four stroke internal combustion engines.

Co-efficient of Fluctuation of Speed of Flywheel

The difference between the maximum and minimum speeds during a cycle is called the *maximum fluctuation of speed*. The ratio of the maximum fluctuation of speed to the mean speed is called the *coefficient of fluctuation of speed*.

Let N_1 and N_2 = Maximum and minimum speeds in r.p.m. during the cycle,

and $N = \text{Mean speed in r.p.m.} = \dfrac{N_1 + N_2}{2}$

$\therefore$ Coefficient of fluctuation of speed,

$$C_s = \frac{N_1 + N_2}{N} = \frac{2(N_1 - N_2)}{N_1 + N_2}$$

$$= \frac{\omega_1 - \omega_2}{\omega} = \frac{2(\omega_1 - \omega_2)}{\omega_1 + \omega_2}$$

... (In terms of angular speeds)

$$= \frac{v_1 - v_2}{v} = \frac{2(v_1 - v_2)}{v_1 + v_2}$$

... (In terms of linear speeds)

The coefficient of fluctuation of speed is a limiting factor in the design of flywheel. It varies depending upon the nature of service to which the flywheel is employed.

Note : The reciprocal of the coefficient of fluctuation of speed is known as *coefficient of steadiness* and is denoted by *m*.

$$\therefore \quad m = \frac{1}{C_s} = \frac{N}{N_1 - N_2} = \frac{N_1 + N_2}{2(N_1 - N_2)}$$

Energy Stored in a Flywheel

When a flywheel absorbs energy, its speed increases and when it gives up energy, its speed decreases. Mean kinetic energy of the flywheel,

$$E = \frac{1}{2} \times I.\omega^2 = \frac{1}{2} \times m.k^2\omega^2 \text{ (in N-m or joules)}$$

As the speed of the flywheel changes from ω_1 to ω_2, the maximum fluctuation of energy,

$$\Delta E = \text{Maximum K.E.} - \text{Minimum K.E.}$$

$$= 2\,E.\,C_s \quad \text{(in N-m or joules)}$$

The radius of gyration (*k*) may be taken equal to the mean radius of the rim (R), because the thickness of rim is very small as compared to the diameter of rim. Therefore

$$\Delta E = m{\cdot}R^2.\omega^2.C_S = m.v^2.C_S$$

where v = Mean linear velocity (*i.e.* at the mean radius) in m/s = ω.R

Dimensions of the Flywheel Rim

Consider a rim of the flywheel as shown in the figure

Let D = Mean diameter of rim in metres,

R = Mean radius of rim in metres,

A = Cross-sectional area of rim in m^2,

ρ = Density of rim material in kg/m^3,

N = Speed of the flywheel in r.p.m.,

ω = Angular velocity of the flywheel in rad/s,

v = Linear velocity at the mean radius in m/s

$$= \omega.R = \frac{\pi \cdot DN}{60},$$

and σ = Tensile stress or hoop stress in N/m^2 due to the centrifugal force.

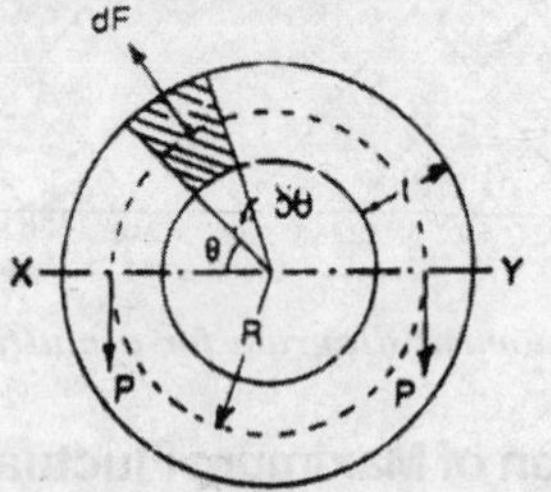

Fig. Rim of a flywheel

Consider a small element of the rim as shown shaded in Fig. Let it subtends an angle $\delta\theta$ at the centre of the flywheel.

Volume of the small element = A × R.$\delta\theta$

$\therefore$ Mass of the small element dm

$$= \text{Density} \times \text{volume} = \rho.A.R.\delta\theta$$

and centrifugal force on the element, acting radially outwards,

$$dF = dm.\omega^2.R = \rho.A.R^2.\omega^2.\delta\theta$$

Vertical component of $dF = dF.\sin\theta$

$$= \rho.A.R^2.\omega^2.\delta\theta.\sin\theta$$

$\therefore$ Total vertical upward force tending to burst the rim across the diameter XY.

$$= \rho.A.R^2.\omega^2 \int_0^{\pi} \sin\theta.d\theta$$

$$= \rho.A.R^2.\omega^2 \left[-\cos\theta\right]_0^{\pi}$$

$$= 2\rho.A.R^2.\omega^2 \quad \text{... (i)}$$

This vertical upward force will produce tensile stress or hoops stress (also called centrifugal stress or circumferential stress), and it is resisted by 2P, such that

$$2P = 2\,\sigma\,A \quad \text{... (ii)}$$

Equating equations (*i*) and (*ii*), we have

$$2\,\rho.A.R^2.\omega^2 = 2\sigma A$$

or $\sigma = \rho.R^2.\omega^2 = \sigma.v^2$ ... $(\because v = \omega.R)$

$$\therefore \quad v = \sqrt{\frac{\sigma}{\rho}} \quad \text{... (iii)}$$

Now mass of the rim,

$$m = \text{Volume} \times \text{density}$$

$$= \pi\,D.A.\rho$$

$$\therefore \quad A = \frac{m}{\pi\,D.\rho} \quad \text{... (iv)}$$

From equations (*iii*) and (*iv*), we may find the value of the mean radius and cross-sectional area of the rim.

Note : If the cross-section of the rim is a rectangular, then

$$A = b \times t$$

where b = Width of the rim, and

t = Thickness of the rim.

We know that, workdone per cycle

$= P \times 60/N.$

Objective Type Questions

1. When nature of contact between the elements of a pair is such that they only slide relative to each other, the pair is known as
(*a*) sliding pair (*b*) rolling pair
(*c*) turning pair (*d*) cylindrical pair

2. Piston and cylinder in a slider crank mechanism form a
(*a*) sliding pair (*b*) rolling pair
(*c*) turning pair (*d*) cylindrical pair

3. Ball bearing and roller bearing form a
(*a*) sliding pair (*b*) turning pair
(*c*) rolling pair (*d*) cylindrical pair

4. A pulley in a belt drive acts as
(*a*) sliding pair (*b*) rolling pair
(*c*) turning pair (*d*) cylindrical pair

5. When nature of contact between elements of a pair is such that it can turn or revolve about a fixed axis, the pair is known as
(*a*) sliding pair (*b*) rolling pair
(*c*) turning pair (*d*) cylindrical pair

6. Shaft with collars at both ends fitted into a circular hole forms a
(*a*) sliding pair (*b*) rolling pair
(*c*) turning pair (*d*) cylindrical pair

7. Hammer blow in locomotives causes
(*a*) uneven speed
(*b*) uniform torque
(*c*) pulsating torque
(*d*) tendency to lift wheels from rails

8. A nut and bolt form a
(*a*) turning pair (*b*) spherical pair
(*c*) screw pair (*d*) rolling pair

9. A ball and socket joint form a
(*a*) turning pair (*b*) spherical pair
(*c*) screw pair (*d*) rolling pair

10. When the two elements of a pair have surface contact when relative motion takes place and surface of one element slides over the surface of the other, the pair formed is known as
(*a*) higher pair (*b*) lower pair
(*c*) force-closed pair (*d*) none of the above

11. The contact between the two elements while in the motion in lower pairs is
(*a*) line contact (*b*) point contact
(*c*) surface contact (*d*) none of the above

12. A shaft revolving in a bearing forms a
(*a*) lower pair (*b*) higher pair
(*c*) sliding pair (*d*) turning pair

13. Lower pair is
(*a*) ball and roller baring
(*b*) cam & follower
(*c*) belt and chain drives
(*d*) all of the above

14. Lower pair is
(*a*) sliding pair (*b*) turning pair
(*c*) screw pair (*d*) all of the above

15. When two elements of a pair have a line or point contact when in motion, they are said to form a
(*a*) lower pair (*b*) higher pair
(*c*) force-closed pair (*d*) none of the above

16. Higher pair is an
(*a*) closed pair
(*b*) point contact pair
(*c*) both (*a*) and (*b*) above
(*d*) none of the above

17. When the relative motion between the elements of a pair is partly turning and partly sliding, the pair is known as a
(*a*) lower pair (*b*) higher pair
(*c*) force closed pair (*d*) none of the above

18. When there is only line or point contact between the two elements while in motion, the pair formed is
(*a*) higher pair (*b*) lower pair
(*c*) force closed pair (*d*) none

19. When the connection between the two elements is such that only required kind of relative motion occurs, it is known as
(*a*) force-closed pair (*b*) self-closed pair
(*c*) lower pair (*d*) higher pair

20. Two elements of a pair is held together mechanically in
(*a*) force-closed pair (*b*) self-closed pair
(*c*) lower pair (*d*) higher pair

21. When two elements of a pair are not held together mechanically, it is known as
(*a*) kinematic pair (*b*) open-pair
(*c*) closed pair (*d*) none of the above

22. When motion between a pair is limited to a definite direction, irrespective of the direction of force applied, it is known as

(*a*) completely constrained motion
(*b*) incompletely constrained motion
(*c*) successfully constrained motion
(*d*) none of the above

23. Completely constrained motion is, motion of a

(*a*) square bar in a square hole
(*b*) piston in the cylinder of a steam engine
(*c*) shaft with collars at each end in a circular hole
(*d*) all of the above

24. When motion between a pair takes place in more than one direction, it is known as

(*a*) completely constrained motion
(*b*) incomplete constrained motion
(*c*) successfully constrained motion
(*d*) none of the above

25. When the connection between the elements of a pair is such that the constrained motions not completed by itself, but by some other means, the motion is known as

(*a*) completely constrained motion
(*b*) incompletely constrained motion
(*c*) successfully constrained motion
(*d*) none of the above

26. Successfully constrained motion is

(*a*) motion of an I.C. engine valve
(*b*) motion of the shaft between foot-step bearing
(*c*) piston reciprocating inside an engine cylinder
(*d*) all the above

27. When kinematic pairs are joined in such a way that the relative motion between the links is completely restrained, it is known as

(*a*) mechanism (*b*) kinematic chain
(*c*) structure (*d*) inversion

28. A kinematic chain requires minimum of

(*a*) 2 links and 2 turning pairs
(*b*) 3 links and 3 turning pairs
(*c*) 4 links and 4 turning pairs
(*d*) 5 links and 5 turning pairs

29. The relation between number of pairs (*p*) forming a kinematic chain and the number of links (L) is

(*a*) $L = 2p - 2$ (*b*) $L = 2p - 3$
(*c*) $L = 2p - 4$ (*d*) $L = 2p - 5$

30. For kinematic chain formed by lower pair, the relation between the number of link (L) and number of joints (J) is

(*a*) $L = \frac{3}{2}(J+2)$ (*b*) $L = \frac{2}{3}(J+2)$
(*c*) $L = \frac{2}{3}(J+3)$ (*d*) $L = \frac{3}{2}(J+3)$

31. For kinematic chains formed by lower pairs the relationship between the number of link L and number of joints J, may be expressed as $L = \frac{2}{3}(J+2)$. If this relation is applied to chains formed by higher pairs, then each higher pair must be taken equivalent to

(*a*) one lower pair and two additional links
(*b*) two lower pairs and one additional link
(*c*) two lower pairs and two additional links
(*d*) one lower pair and one additional link

32. A chain consisting of three links and three joints is known as

(*a*) locked chain (*b*) constrained chain
(*c*) kinematic chain (*d*) unconstrained chain

33. A mechanism consisting of four links is known as

(*a*) simple mechanism (*b*) compound mechanism
(*c*) pantograph (*d*) none of the above

34. A point on the pitch curve having maximum pressure angle, is known as

(*a*) pitch point (*b*) centre of the cam
(*c*) trace point (*d*) none of the above

35. A kinematic chain is known as a mechanism when

(*a*) no link is fixed
(*b*) one of the links is fixed
(*c*) two of the links is fixed
(*d*) none of the above

36. A pantograph is a mechanism or a kinematic arrangement consisting of

(*a*) one lower pair (*b*) two lower pairs
(*c*) three lower pair (*d*) four lower pairs

37. If there are L number of links in a mechanism, then the number of possible inversions would be

(*a*) L (*b*) L – 1
(*c*) L – 2 (*d*) (L + 2)

38. In a kinematic chain with four lower pairs, if all the four lower pairs are turning pairs, the mechanism is known as

(*a*) four bar chain
(*b*) slider crank chain
(*c*) crossed slider crank chain
(*d*) double slider crank chain

39. In a kinematic chain with four lower pairs, if one is sliding pair and three are turning pairs, the mechanism is known as
(*a*) four bar chain
(*b*) slider crank chain
(*c*) double slider crank chain
(*d*) crossed slider crank chain

40. In a kinematic chain with four lower pairs, if there are two sliding pairs and two turning pairs and two similar pairs adjacent, the mechanism is known as
(*a*) four bar chain
(*b*) slider crank chain
(*c*) double crank chain or elliptical trammel
(*d*) crossed crank chain

41. A point on a link connecting double slider crank chain traces a
(*a*) straight line path (*b*) circular path
(*c*) parabolic path (*d*) elliptical path

42. In case of an elliptical trammel
(*a*) one pair slides and three pairs turn
(*b*) two pair slides and two pairs turn
(*c*) three pairs slides and one pair turn
(*d*) all four pairs turns
(*e*) all four pairs slides

43. In a kinematic chain with four lower pairs, if there are two sliding pairs and two turning pairs and two similar pairs are not adjacent, the mechanism is known as
(*a*) four bar chain (*b*) sliding crank chain
(*c*) double crank chain (*d*) crossed crank chain

44. The Ackermann steering gear consists of a four bar mechanism with
(*a*) all four pairs sliding
(*b*) all four pairs turning
(*c*) three pairs turning and one pair sliding
(*d*) one pair turning and three pairs sliding

45. The Ackermann steering gear is the inversion of a
(*a*) four bar chain
(*b*) slider crank chain
(*c*) double slider crank chain
(*d*) cross slider crank chain

46. Whitworth quick return motion mechanism consists of
(*a*) one sliding pair and three turning pairs
(*b*) three sliding pairs and one turning pair
(*c*) all four pairs sliding
(*d*) all four pairs turning

47. Whitworth quick return mechanism is an inversion of
(*a*) four bar chain
(*b*) single slider crank chain
(*c*) double slider crank chain
(*d*) crossed slider crank chain

48. The distance between two parallel shafts, whose axes is small and variable, may be connected by
(*a*) Oldham's coupling (*b*) knuckle joint
(*c*) universal joint (*d*) none of the above

49. Oldham's coupling and elliptical trammels are the inversion of
(*a*) four bar chain
(*b*) single slider crank chain
(*c*) double slider crank chain
(*d*) crossed slider crank chain

50. Rapson's slide is an inversion of
(*a*) four bar chain
(*b*) single slider crank chain
(*c*) double slider crank chain
(*d*) crossed slider crank chain

51. Quick return mechanism is an inversion of
(*a*) four bar chain
(*b*) single slider crank chain
(*c*) double slider crank chain
(*d*) crossed slider crank chain

52. Inversion of slider crank chain is
(*a*) reciprocating internal combustion engine
(*b*) crank and slotted level mechanism
(*c*) Whitworth and quick return mechanism
(*d*) all of the above

53. A Scott-Russel mechanism consists of
(*a*) Turning pairs only
(*b*) rotary pairs only
(*c*) sliding and turning pairs
(*d*) sliding and rotary pairs

54. Periodic time of simple pendulum is given by
(*a*) $2\pi\sqrt{\frac{l}{g}}$ (*b*) $2\pi\sqrt{\frac{g}{l}}$
(*c*) $\frac{1}{2\pi}\sqrt{\frac{g}{l}}$ (*d*) $\frac{1}{2\pi}\sqrt{\frac{l}{g}}$

55. Time period of a compound pendulum is equal to
(*a*) $2\pi\sqrt{\frac{gh}{k^2+h^2}}$ (*b*) $2\pi\sqrt{\frac{k^2+h^2}{gh}}$
(*c*) $\frac{1}{2\pi}\sqrt{\frac{k^2+h^2}{gh}}$ (*d*) $\frac{1}{2\pi}\sqrt{\frac{gh}{k^2+h^2}}$

56. Equivalent simple pendulum means a simple pendulum having

(*a*) time period of one second

(*b*) time period of two seconds

(*c*) the same periodic time of oscillation as given compound pendulum

(*d*) all of the above

57. Secondary unbalance force is maximum, when the angle of inclination of crank with the line of stroke is

(*a*) 0° (*b*) 90°

(*c*) 180° (*d*) 360°

(*e*) all of the above

58. In one revolution of crank, the primary unbalanced force is maximum

(*a*) once (*b*) twice

(*c*) four times (*d*) eight times

59. Equivalent length of a simple pendulum depends upon the distance between

(*a*) point of suspension and C.G.

(*b*) point of suspension and radius of gyration

(*c*) radius of gyration and C.G.

(*d*) none of the above

60. Minimum periodic time of a compound pendulum is

(*a*) $2\pi\sqrt{\frac{k}{g}}$ (*b*) $2\pi\sqrt{\frac{2k}{g}}$

(*c*) $2\pi\sqrt{\frac{k}{2g}}$ (*d*) $2\pi\sqrt{\frac{2g}{k}}$

61. Centre of suspension is interchangeable with

(*a*) centre of gravity

(*b*) centre of percussion

(*c*) both (*a*) and (*b*) above

(*d*) none of the above

62. When the body is suspended at point of suspension, its periodic time and frequency as compared to the body suspended at the point of percussion, is

(*a*) more (*b*) less

(*c*) same (*d*) none of the above

63. Frequency of oscillation of a compound pendulum having the same distance between points of suspension and the C.G. of mass as a simple pendulum will be

(*a*) more (*b*) less

(*c*) same (*d*) none of the above

64. If frequency of oscillation on earth is n, then the frequency of oscillation on the moon will be

(*a*) n (*b*) $6n$

(*c*) $\frac{n}{\sqrt{6}}$ (*d*) $n\sqrt{6}$

65. Total number of instantaneous centres for a mechanism of n links is

(*a*) n (*b*) $n - 1$

(*c*) $\frac{(n-1)}{2}$ (*d*) $\frac{n(n-1)}{2}$

66. Total number of instantaneous centers for a 4 – bar chain mechanism will be

(*a*) 1.5 (*b*) 4

(*c*) 6 (*d*) 8

67. According to Kennedy's theorem, if three bodies move relative to each other, having three instantaneous centers lie on a

(*a*) straight line

(*b*) different planes

(*c*) plane perpendicular to the plane of motion

(*d*) none of the above

68. Instantaneous centers which remain in the same plane for all congifurations of the mechanism, are known as

(*a*) fixed instantaneous centers

(*b*) permanent instantaneous centres

(*c*) neither fixed nor permanent instantaneous centers

(*d*) none of the above

69. Two links are said to have a pure rolling contact if their instantaneous center lies

(*a*) on their point of contact

(*b*) at the center of curvature

(*c*) at the pin joint

(*d*) at infinity

70. When a slider moves on a fixed link having curved surface, their instantaneous centre lies

(*a*) on their point of contact

(*b*) at the center of curvature

(*c*) at the pin joint

(*d*) at infinity

71. When two links are connected by a pin joint, their instantaneous center lies

(*a*) on their point of contact

(*b*) at the center of curvature

(*c*) at the pin joint

(*d*) at infinity

72. When a slider moves on a fixed link having straight surface, their instantaneous center lies

(*a*) on their point of contact

(*b*) at the center of curvature

(*c*) at the pin joint

(*d*) at infinity

73. A slider moving on a fixed link having constant radius of curvature will have its instantaneous centre

(*a*) at the pin joint

(*b*) at infinity

(*c*) at centre of circle

(*d*) on their point of contact

74. Linear velocity of a point on a link relative to any other point on the link will be

(*a*) parallel to line joining the two points

(*b*) perpendicular to the line joining the twc points

(*c*) perpendicular to lower end of the link

(*d*) none of the above

75. Component of acceleration parallel to the velocity of the particle at the given instant is known as

(*a*) radial component

(*b*) tangential component

(*c*) coriolis component

(*d*) none of the above

76. When a point on a link moves along a straight line, its acceleration will only have

(*a*) radial component

(*b*) tangential component

(*c*) coriolis component

(*d*) all of the above

77. The sense of tangential acceleration of a link

(*a*) is same as that of velocity

(*b*) is opposite to the velocity

(*c*) can be either same or opposite to velocity

(*d*) none of the above

78. Direction of tangential acceleration is

(*a*) along the angular velocity

(*b*) opposite to the angular velocity

(*c*) both (*a*) and (*b*) above

(*d*) perpendicular to the angular velocity

79. Radial and tangential components of a particle at any instant will be

(*a*) parallel to each other

(*b*) perpendicular to each other

(*c*) opposite to each other

(*d*) at 45 to each other

80. When end point of a link moves with constant angular velocity, its acceleration will have only

(*a*) radial component (*b*) tangential component

(*c*) coriolis component (*d*) all of the above

81. A point B on a rigid link moves with respect to A with angular velocity ω rad/sec, of link AB about A. The radial component of the acceleration of B with respect to A, is

(*a*) $\frac{V_{BA}^2}{AB}$ (*b*) $\frac{V_{BA}}{AB}$

(*c*) $V_{BA} \cdot AB$ (*d*) $V_{BA}^2 \cdot AB$

where V_{BA} is linear velocity of B with respect to A

82. In a rigid link AB, the point B moves with respect to A. The angular acceleration of link AB will be equal to

(*a*) (radial acceleration)/AB

(*b*) (tangential acceleration)/AB

(*c*) (total acceleration)/AB

(*d*) none of the above

83. If a particle of a link has a velocity which changes both in magnitude and direction at any instant, then it must have components of acceleration

(*a*) centripetal and tangential

(*b*) centripetal, centrifugal and tangential

(*c*) centripetal, centrifugal and gravitational

(*d*) centripetal, centrifugal, gravitational and tangential

84. The coriolis component of acceleration acts

(*a*) parallel to the sliding surface

(*b*) perpendicular to the sliding surface

(*c*) at 45° to the sliding surface

(*d*) none of the above

85. The coriolis component of acceleration will exist only if the two coincidental points

(*a*) have same centre of rotation

(*b*) have relative angular velocity of sliding

(*c*) have linear relative velocity of sliding accompanied by the rotation about fixed centres

(*d*) none of the above

86. According to the coriolis law if a point moves along a path having rotation, the absolute acceleration of the point is equal to the

(*a*) absolute acceleration of the point relative to coincident point in the path

(*b*) absolute acceleration of the coincident point in the path

(*c*) coriolis component acceleration

(*d*) vector sum of (*a*), (*b*) and (*c*) above

87. The direction of coriolis component of acceleration is the direction of relative velocity vector for the two coincidental points

(*a*) rotated by 90° in the direction of angular velocity of rotation of the link

(*b*) rotated by 180° in the direction of angular velocity of rotation of the link

(*c*) in the direction directly opposite to that of angular velocity

(*d*) none of the above

88. The coriolis component of acceleration leads the sliding velocity by

(*a*) 30° (*b*) 45°

(*c*) 90° (*d*) 180°

89. The coriolis component of acceleration exist when a point moves along a path which has

(*a*) rotational motion

(*b*) linear motion

(*c*) tangential acceleration

(*d*) gravitation acceleration

90. If a slider moves with a velocity v on a link revolving at angular velocity ω, the magnitude of coriolis component of acceleration is

(*a*) $v\,\omega$ (*b*) $2\,v\,\omega$

(*c*) $\sqrt{2}\,v\,\omega$ (*d*) $\frac{v\,\omega}{2}$

91. The coriolis component exists in

(*a*) shaper mechanism

(*b*) tangent cam mechanism

(*c*) link sliding in a swivelling pin

(*d*) all of the above

92. In Scotch Yoke mechanism, the coriolis component is

(*a*) involved (*b*) not involved

(*c*) generally involved (*d*) sometime involved

93. Klein's construction gives a graphical construction for

(*a*) acceleration polygon

(*b*) velocity polygon

(*c*) angular acceleration

(*d*) all of the above

94. Klein rs construction is used to determine

(*a*) displacement of various parts

(*b*) acceleration of various parts

(*c*) velocity of various parts

(*d*) angular acceleration of various parts

95. Klein's construction can be used when crank has a

(*a*) uniform angular velocity

(*b*) non-uniform angular velocity

(*c*) non-uniform angular acceleration

(*d*) uniform angular acceleration

96. Biflar suspension method is used to determine

(*a*) natural frequency of vibration

(*b*) angular accelration

(*c*) moment of inertia

(*d*) centripetal acceleration

97. Number of links in a pantograph is equal to

(*a*) 3 (*b*) 4

(*c*) 5 (*d*) 6

98. Mechanism used to enlarge or reduce the size of a drawing is

(*a*) clinometer (*b*) pantograph

(*c*) oscillograph (*d*) all of the above

99. Maximum fractional force experienced by a body, when it just begins to side over the surface of other body, is known as

(*a*) static friction (*b*) dynamic friction

(*c*) limiting friction (*d*) none of the above

100. Friction force experienced by a body, when in motion, is known as

(*a*) static friction (*b*) dynamic friction

(*c*) limiting friction (*d*) none of the above

101. Angle which the normal reaction makes with the resultant reaction, is known as

(*a*) angle of friction

(*b*) angle of repose

(*c*) coefficient of friction

(*d*) angle of projection

102. Angle of inclination of the plane, at which the body begins to move down the plane, is known as

(*a*) angle of friction

(*b*) angle of repose

(*c*) coefficient of friction

(*d*) angle of projection

103. The ratio of the limiting friction to the normal reaction between the two bodies, is known as

(*a*) angle of friction

(*b*) angle of repose

(*c*) coefficient of friction

(*d*) angle of projection

104. If ϕ is the angle of friction, the value of tan ϕ can not be

(*a*) 0.1 μ (*b*) 0.5 μ

(*c*) μ (*d*) 1.5 μ

105. A dynamometer is used for the measurement of

(*a*) kinetic energy of the machine

(*b*) speed of the machine

(*c*) torque exerted by or on a machine

(*d*) all of the above

106. Transmission type dynamometer is used to measure power of

(*a*) hydraulic dynamometer

(*b*) prony brake dynamometer

(*c*) torsion dynamometer

(*d*) Electrical dynamometer

107. In solid friction when tan $\phi = \mu$, then

(*a*) body A will move on surface B, irrespective of magnitude of force applied on the body

(*b*) body A will not move on surface B, irrespective of magnitude of force applied on the body

(*c*) tan ϕ has no bearing on the value of μ

(*d*) none of the above

108. If angle of friction is ϕ, then limiting value of tan ϕ will be

(*a*) 0.1 μ (*b*) 0.5 μ

(*c*) μ (*d*) 1.5 μ

109. If ϕ is angle of friction, the efficiency of an inclined plane at α^0 to the vertical is expressed for horizontal direction applied force will be

(*a*) $\dfrac{\tan(\alpha+\phi)}{\tan\alpha}$ (*b*) $\dfrac{\tan\alpha}{\tan(\alpha+\phi)}$

(*c*) $\dfrac{\tan\alpha}{\tan(\alpha-\phi)}$ (*d*) $\dfrac{\tan(\alpha-\phi)}{\tan\alpha}$

110. Radius of a friction circle for a shaft rotating inside a bearing is

(*a*) $r \sin\phi$ (*b*) $r \cos\phi$

(*c*) $r \tan\phi$ (*d*) $r \cot\phi$

111. Radius of friction circle of any rotating surface is

(*a*) $r \sin\phi$ (*b*) $r \cos\phi$

(*c*) $r \tan\phi$ (*d*) $r \cot\phi$

112. Radius of friction circle increases with the increase of

(*a*) radius of journal

(*b*) co-efficient of sliding friction

(*c*) speed

(*d*) both (*a*) and (*b*) above

113. For a square threaded screw, maximum efficiency of screw jack will be

(*a*) $\dfrac{1-\sin\phi}{1+\sin\phi}$ (*b*) $\dfrac{1-\tan\phi}{1+\tan\phi}$

(*c*) $\dfrac{1+\tan\phi}{1-\tan\phi}$ (*d*) none of the above

114. For a square threaded screw jack, maximum efficiency will occur, when the angle of helix of the thread is

(*a*) $\dfrac{\pi}{4}$ (*b*) $\left(\dfrac{\pi}{4}+\dfrac{\phi}{2}\right)$

(*c*) $\left(\dfrac{\pi}{4}-\dfrac{\phi}{2}\right)$ (*d*) $\left(\dfrac{\pi}{4}-\phi\right)$

115. Maximum efficiency of a screwjack is a function of

(*a*) angle of friction (*b*) load lifted

(*c*) helix angle (*d*) effort

116. By using large thread angles in a lifting machine

(*a*) mechanical advantage decreases

(*b*) mechanical advantage increases

(*c*) the load will be easily lifted

(*d*) none of the above

117. Maximum efficiency of square threaded screw jack having angle of friction 30° will be

(*a*) 25% (*b*) 30%

(*c*) 33% (*d*) 60%

118. For a machine to be self sustaining the relation between angle of friction 4> and slope of the thread a should be

(*a*) $\alpha = \phi$ (*b*) $\alpha > \phi$

(*c*) $\alpha < \phi$ (*d*) none of the above

119. If μ is actual co-efficient offrictioin and β is semi-angle of the thread, then the equivalent coefficient for angular threads is

(*a*) $\mu \sin\beta$ (*b*) $\mu \cos\beta$

(*c*) $\dfrac{\mu}{\sin\beta}$ (*d*) $\dfrac{\mu}{\cos\beta}$

120. As compared to actual co-efficient of friction, the equivalent co-efficient of friction for V threads is

(*a*) more (*b*) less

(*c*) same (*d*) none of the above

121. In flat pivot bearing, the rubbing velocity is

(*a*) uniform throughout

(*b*) zero at the centre and maximum at the outer radius

(*c*) maximum at the centre and zero at the outer radius

(*d*) none of the above

122. In flat pivot bearing, rate of wearing is directly proportional to the

(*a*) rubbing velocity

(*b*) pressure intensity

(*c*) both (*a*) and (*b*) above

(*d*) none of the above

123. Assumption made for the calculation of friction power of bearing is

(*a*) pressure intensity is uniform

(*b*) rate of wearing at the surface is uniform

(*c*) both (*a*) and (*b*) above

(*d*) rubbing velocity is constant

124. Ratio of the actual damping co-efficient to the critical damping co-efficient is known as

(*a*) damping factor

(*b*) critical damping co-efficient

(*c*) logrithmic decrement

(*d*) magnification factor

125. Ratio of the maximum displacement of the forced vibration to the deflection due to static force, is known as

(*a*) damping factor

(*b*) critical damping co-efficient

(*c*) logrithmic decrement;

(*d*) magnification factor

126. In under damped vibrating system, the natural logrithm of the ratio of any two successive amplitudes is known as

(*a*) damping factor

(*b*) critical damping co-efficient

(*c*) logrithmic decrement

(*d*) magnification factor

127. Frictional torque transmitted in a flat pivot bearing with assumption of uniform pressure as compared to assumption of uniform wear is

(*a*) more

(*b*) less

(*c*) same

(*d*) none of the above

128. Multiple collars are provided on a flat collar pivot bearing to

(*a*) bistribute the frictional load because of limiting friction

(*b*) distribute the axial load because of limiting bearing pressure on a collar

(*c*) increase frictional resistance

(*d*) establish self locking bearing condition

129. Frictional torque transmitted in a flat collar pivot bearing, considering uniform pressure is

(*a*) $\frac{1}{2}\mu W(r_1 + r_2)$ (*b*) $\frac{2}{3}\mu W(r_1 + r_2)$

(*c*) $\frac{3}{4}\mu W\left(\frac{r_1^3 - r_2^3}{r_1^3 - r_2^2}\right)$ (*d*) $\frac{1}{2}\mu W\left(\frac{r_1^3 - r_2^3}{r_1^2 - r_2^2}\right)$

130. When the phase difference between displacement and centrifugal force is 0°, the shaft is rotating at a speed which as compared to critical speed is

(*a*) more (*b*) less

(*c*) same (*d*) none of the above

131. When the phase difference between displacement and centrifugal force is 180., the shaft is rotating at a speed which as compared to critical speed is

(*a*) more (*b*) less

(*c*) same (*d*) none of the above

132. Fractional torque transmitted in a flat collar pivot bearing considering uniform wear, may be assumed to act at

(*a*) $\frac{1}{2}\mu W(r_1 + r_2)$ (*b*) $\frac{2}{3}\mu W(r_1 + r_2)$

(*c*) $\frac{1}{2}\mu W\left(\frac{r_1^3 - r_2^3}{r_1^3 - r_2^2}\right)$ (*d*) none of the above

133. Frictional torque transmitted in a multi-collared shaft as compared to single collared shaft is

(*a*) more (*b*) less

(*c*) same (*d*) none of the above

134. In flat collar bearing, if axial load carried by the shaft is large, then number of collars are provided on the shaft to

(*a*) reduce pressure intensity

(*b*) reduce frictional torque

(*c*) both (*a*) and (*b*) above

(*d*) none of the above

135. Frictional torque transmitted in a conical pivot bearing considering uniform pressure is

(*a*) $\frac{1}{2}\mu$ WR cosec α (*b*) $\frac{3}{4}\mu$ WR cosec α

(*c*) $\frac{2}{3}\mu$ WR cosec α (*d*) μ WR cosec α

136. A vibrometer is used to indicate vibration

(*a*) amplitude (*b*) frequency

(*c*) nature (*d*) all of the above

137. Vibration measurement is done by

(*a*) vibrometer (*b*) accelerometer

(*c*) balometer (*d*) photometer

138. Frictional torque transmitted in a conical pivot bearing considering runiform wear is

(a) $\frac{1}{2}\mu$ WR cosec α (b) $\frac{2}{3}\mu$ WR cosec α

(c) $\frac{3}{4}\mu$ WR cosec α (d) μ WR cosec α

139. Ratio of the force transmitted to the force applied is known as

(a) damping factor (b) damping co-efficient

(c) transmissibility (d) magnification factor

140. Frictional torque transmitted in a conical pivot bearing considering uniform pressure as compared to uniform wear is

(a) more (b) less

(c) same (d) none of the above

141. Frictional torque transmitted in a truncated conical pivot bearing having radius $r_1 > r_2$ considering uniform wear is

(a) $\frac{1}{2}\mu$ W cosec $\alpha(r_1 + r_2)$

(b) $\frac{2}{3}\mu$ W cosec $\alpha(r_1 + r_2)$

(c) $\frac{2}{3}\mu$ W cosec $\alpha\left(\frac{r_1^3 - r_2^3}{r_1^2 - r_2^2}\right)$

(d) $\frac{1}{2}\mu$ W cosec $\alpha\left(\frac{r_1^3 - r_2^3}{r_1^2 - r_2^2}\right)$

142. Frictional torque transmitted by a conical pivot collar bearing as compared to flat collar bearing is

(a) more (b) less

(c) same (d) none of the above

143. If in a disc clutch, number of discs on the driving shaft is n_1 and on driven shaft is n_2, then number of pairs of contact surfaces will be

(a) $n_1 + n_2$ (b) $n_1 + n_2 + 1$

(c) $n_1 + n_2 - 1$ (d) $n_1 - n_2 + 1$

144. In a belt drive the pulley acts as

(a) sliding pair (b) rolling pair

(c) turning pair (d) none of the above

145. When two pulleys are connected by a crossbelt drive, then both the pulleys rotate in the

(a) same direction

(b) opposite direction

(c) not necessary

(d) none of the above

146. If for power transmission a gear train consisting of 11 gears is used, then the motion of the driver and follower will be in the

(a) same direction

(b) opposite directions

(c) both (a) and (b) above

(d) none of the above

147. If for a power transmission, a gear train consisting of 12 gears is used, then the motion of the driver and follower will be in the

(a) same direction

(b) opposite directions

(c) both (a) and (b) above

(d) none of the above

148. Length of an open belt connecting two pulleys of radii r_1 and r_2 and at a centre distance D apart, is

(a) $\pi(r_1 + r_2) + \frac{(r_1 - r_2)^2}{D} + 2D$

(b) $\pi(r_1 + r_2) + \frac{(r_1 + r_2)^2}{D} + 2D$

(c) $\pi(r_1 - r_2) + \frac{(r_1 + r_2)^2}{D} + 2D$

(d) $\pi(r_1 - r_2) + \frac{(r_1 - r_2)^2}{D} + 2D$

149. Length of a crossed open belt connecting two pulleys of radii r_1 and r_2 and at a centre distance D apart, is

(a) $\pi(r_1 + r_2) + \frac{(r_1 - r_2)^2}{D} + 2D$

(b) $\pi(r_1 + r_2) + \frac{(r_1 + r_2)^2}{D} + 2D$

(c) $\pi(r_1 - r_2) + \frac{(r_1 + r_2)^2}{D} + 2D$

(d) $\pi(r_1 - r_2) + \frac{(r_1 - r_2)^2}{D} + 2D$

150. Length of cross belt between two pulleys of diameters D_1 and D_2 in addition to centre length, depends on

(a) sum of diameters of pulleys only

(b) difference of diameters of pulleys only

(c) $\left(D_1^2 + D_2^2\right)$

(d) none of the above

151. Angular velocities of the two pulleys, connected either by an open belt or crossed belt drive are proportional

(*a*) directly to their diameters
(*b*) inversely to their diameters
(*c*) directly to square of their diameters
(*d*) directly to square root of their diameters

152. Angle of contact in crossed belt drive as compared to open belt drive is

(*a*) more (*b*) less
(*c*) same (*d*) none of the above

153. When two pulleys of different diameters are connected by means of an open belt, the angle of contact considered must be on the

(*a*) smaller pulley
(*b*) larger pulley
(*c*) average of two pulleys
(*d*) none of the above

154. Due to slip of belt, the velocity ratio of the belt drive

(*a*) increases (*b*) decreases
(*c*) remains constant (*d*) none of the above

155. Slip in timing belt is

(*a*) less than 1% (*b*) less than 5%
(*c*) maximum allowed (*d*) zero

156. If T is belt tension and W is weight per unit length of belt, then velocity of the belt for maximum power is

(*a*) $\sqrt{\frac{T.g}{3w}}$ (*b*) $\sqrt{\frac{3T.g}{w}}$

(*c*) $\sqrt{\frac{3w.g}{T}}$ (*d*) $\sqrt{\frac{3T.g}{w}}$

157. If T_1 and T_2 are tensions on tight and slack slide of belt, θ is the angle of contact and μ is co-efficient of friction between belt and pulley, then ratio of tensions is

(*a*) $\frac{T_1}{T_2} = \mu\theta$ (*b*) $\frac{T_1}{T_2} = e^{\mu\theta}$

(*c*) $\frac{T_1}{T_2} = \mu e^{\theta}$ (*d*) $\frac{T_1}{T_2} = e^{1/\mu\theta}$

158. If T_1 and T_2 are tensions on tight and slack slide of belt and v is linear velocity of belt, the horsepower transmitted by a belt is

(*a*) $\frac{(T_1 - T_2)v}{75}$ (*b*) $\frac{(T_1 + T_2)v}{75}$

(*c*) $\frac{1}{2}\frac{(T_1 - T_2)v}{75}$ (*d*) none of the above

159. If w is weight of belt per unit length, v is velocity of belt and r is radius of bigger pulley, the tension caused by centrifugal force on the belt is

(*a*) $\frac{w}{g} \cdot \frac{v^2}{r}$ (*b*) $\frac{w}{g} \cdot \frac{v}{r}$

(*c*) $\frac{w}{g} \cdot v$ (*d*) $\frac{w}{g} \cdot v^2$

160. Initial tension in a belt allowing for centrifugal tension T_c is

(*a*) $\frac{T_1 + T_2 + T_c}{2}$ (*b*) $\frac{T_1 + T_2}{2} + T_c$

(*c*) $\frac{T_1 + T_2 + 2T_c}{2}$ (*d*) $(T_1 + T_2) + \frac{T_c}{2}$

161. Sum of tensions when the belt is running on the pulley is

(*a*) half the initial tension
(*b*) twice the initial tension
(*c*) more than twice the initial tension
(*d*) less than twice the initial tension

162. For maximum power transmission, the maximum tension T_{max} in the belt is equal to

(*a*) T_c (*b*) $2\,T_c$

(*c*) $3\,T_c$ (*d*) $\frac{1}{3}T_c$

where T_c is centrifugal tension in the belt.

163. For maximum power transmission, the tension on the tight side should be equal to

(*a*) $\frac{1}{4}T_{max}$ (*b*) $\frac{1}{3}T_{max}$

(*c*) $\frac{2}{3}T_{max}$ (*d*) $\frac{3}{4}T_{max}$

where T_{max} is maximum tension in the belt,

164. The initial ratio of tensions in the belt is 5. If the coefficient of friction between pulley and belt is reduced to half, the ratio of tensions in the belt will become

(*a*) 2.5
(*b*) 5
(*c*) 10
(*d*) none of the above

165. Creep in belt drive is due to

(*a*) elasticity of belt material
(*b*) elongation of belt due to tension
(*c*) differential elongation of belt due to difference in tension on two sides of a pulley
(*d*) plasticity of belt material

166. In cross-belt drive, creep

(*a*) increases the power transmitted

(*b*) increases the speed of driven pulley

(*c*) decreases the speed of driven pulley and consequently decreases the power output

(*d*) none of the above

167. Crowing of flat pulley is done

(*a*) to reduce belt friction

(*b*) to prevent belt from running off the pulley

(*c*) to enable pulley rigidly fixed to the shaft

(*d*) all of the above

168. To avoid belt running off the pulley

(*a*) it should be properly tightened

(*b*) the centre line of the belt as it approaches the pulley must lie in a plane perpendicular to the axis of that pulley

(*c*) the belt should be provided with friction material

(*d*) all of the above

169. If T is the maximum permissible tension, v is linear velocity of the belt and w is weight per meter length of the belt, then the maximum permissible velocity is given by

(*a*) $T = \frac{wv^2}{g}$ (*b*) $T = \frac{2wv^2}{g}$

(*c*) $T = \frac{3wv^2}{g}$ (*d*) $T = \frac{wv^2}{3g}$

170. If centrifugal tension T_c is considered, the belt is designed for the tension

(*a*) T_1 (*b*) $T_1 + T_c$

(*c*) $T_1 + T_c$ (*d*) none of the above

171. Included angle of V-belt is generally

(*a*) 10° to 20° (*b*) 20° to 30°

(*c*) 30° to 40° (*d*) 50° to 60°

172. Ratio of the actual damping co-efficient to the critical damping co-efficient is known as

(*a*) damping factor

(*b*) critical damping co-efficient

(*c*) logrithmic decrement

(*d*) magnification factor

173. In V-belts

(*a*) belts should touch the bottom of groove in pulley

(*b*) belts should not touch the bottom of groove in pully

(*c*) transmission efficiency is less

(*d*) tension in belt remains constant throughout

174. Two parallel and coplanar shafts are connected gearing arrangement having teeth parallel to the axis of the shaft known as

(*a*) spur gearing (*b*) helical gearing

(*c*) spiral gearing (*d*) bevel gearing

175. Size of the gear is generally specified by

(*a*) circular pitch module

(*b*) module

(*c*) pitch circle diameter

(*d*) pressure angle

176. The radial distance of tooth from the pitch circle to the top of the tooth, is known as

(*a*) module (*b*) dedendum

(*c*) addendum (*d*) circular pitch

177. In gears, the module is

(*a*) length of the pitch circle diameter per tooth

(*b*) number of teeth per unit length on pitch circle diameter

(*c*) distance measured along pitch circle from a point on one tooth to a corresponding point on the adjacent tooth

(*d*) none of the above

178. Critical damping depends upon

(*a*) mass only

(*b*) mass and stiffness

(*c*) mass and natural frequency

(*d*) none of the above

179. Module is expressed in

(*a*) mm/mm

(*b*) mm

(*c*) mm/number of teeth

(*d*) none of the above

180. Two meshing gears must have same

(*a*) number of teeth (*b*) dedendum

(*c*) addendum (*d*) module

181. Pressure angle varies from

(*a*) 14° to 20° (*b*) 20° to 30°

(*c*) 30° to 40° (*d*) 40° to 45°

182. Module is reciprocal of

(*a*) circular pitch (*b*) diametral pitch

(*c*) dedendum (*d*) addendum

183. Standard pressure angle is generally

(*a*) $10\frac{1°}{2}$ (*b*) $12\frac{1°}{2}$

(*c*) $14\frac{1°}{2}$ (*d*) $17\frac{1°}{2}$

184. High pressure angle causes

(*a*) bigger size of gear teeth

(*b*) wider base ang stronger teeth

(*c*) weaker teeth

(*d*) narrow base

185. Stub tooth as compared to standard tooth depth is

(*a*) long (*b*) short

(*c*) same (*d*) none of the above

186. Incorrect relation is

(*a*) Addendum = module

(*b*) Dedendum = 15.7 . module

(*c*) Circular pitch . diameteral pitch = π

(*d*) none of the above

187. In gears, the tooth fillet is

(*a*) surface of the top of the tooth

(*b*) radius that connects the root circle to the profile of the tooth

(*c*) curve forming face and flank

(*d*) none of the above

188. Gear having minimum axial thrust is

(*a*) spur gears (*b*) bevel gears

(*c*) helical gears (*d*) double helical gears

189. The minimum number of teeth on a pinion of a gear is calculated with consideration,

(*a*) to minimise clearance

(*b*) to avoid interference

(*c*) to minimise diameter of the pinion

(*d*) all of the above

190. Ratio of length of arc of contact to the circular pitch is known as

(*a*) diametral pitch (*b*) contact ratio

(*c*) dedendum (*d*) addendum

191. Contact ratio of gear should be

(*a*) equal to one (*b*) more than one

(*c*) less than one (*d*) not definite

192. If ϕ is the pressure angle, then dedendum circle diameter is equal to cos ϕ times the

(*a*) addendum circle diameter

(*b*) clearance circle diameter

(*c*) pitch circle diameter

(*d*) none of the above

193. When tip of tooth undercut the roots on its mating gear, it is known as

(*a*) clearance (*b*) interface

(*c*) dedendum (*d*) addendum

194. In spur gears, the profile is

(*a*) surface of top of tooth

(*b*) curve forming face and flank

(*c*) part of tooth surface below pitch surface

(*d*) none of the above

195. In spur gears, top land is

(*a*) surface of top of tooth

(*b*) curve forming face and flank

(*c*) part of tooth surface below pitch surface

(*d*) none of the above

196. According to law of gearing

(*a*) minimum clearance should be 0.15 mm

(*b*) gears should be cut with cutter having same module

(*c*) common normal at the point of contact between a pair of teeth must always pass through the pitch point

(*d*) all of the above

197. Advantage of involute teeth over cycloidal teeth is

(*a*) the profile for the flank and face is a single curve

(*b*) the pressure angle is constant from commencement to end of engagement

(*c*) straight teeth of the basic rack admits of simple tools

(*d*) variation in the centre distance within limits does not affect the two mating gears

(*e*) all of the above

198. Curve traced by the end of a thread as it is unwound from a stationary cylinder is known as

(*a*) circle (*b*) cycloid

(*c*) involute (*d*) epicycloid

199. In gears, the involute function [Inv, (ϕ)] in terms of pressure angle (ϕ), is expressed as

(*a*) Inv. (ϕ) = tan (ϕ – 1) (*b*) Inv. (ϕ) = tan (ϕ + 1)

(*c*) Inv. (ϕ) = 1 – tan ϕ (*d*) Inv. (ϕ) = tan ϕ – ϕ

200. In involute gears

(*a*) interference is inherently absent

(*b*) pressure angle is constant throughout

(*c*) convex flank is always in contact with the concave flank

(*d*) none of the above

201. Normal at any point of an involute is

(*a*) normal to the base circle

(*b*) tangent to the base circle

(*c*) inclined to tangent to the base circle

(*d*) inclined to normal to the base circle

202. Path of contact in involute gears is a

(*a*) straight line (*b*) circle

(*c*) curved line (*d*) all of the above

203. When two involutes are in mesh, the angular velocity ratio is

(*a*) proportional to the radius of base circle

(*b*) inversely proportional to the radius of base circle

(*c*) equal to the radius of base circle

(*d*) does not depend on the radius of base circle

204. Centre line distance between two meshing involute gears is directly proportional to the

(*a*) $\frac{1}{\cos\phi}$

(*b*) sum of base circle radii of the meshing gears

(*c*) both (*a*) and (*b*) above

(*d*) none of the above

205. In cycloid gears

(*a*) interference is inherently absent

(*b*) pressure angle is constant throughout the teeth engagement

(*c*) centre line distance variation within limits does not affect velocity ratio

(*d*) all of the above

206. In hypocycloid gears, the mutual position of shaft will be

(*a*) parallel

(*b*) non parallel

(*c*) intersecting

(*d*) non parallel, non intersecting

207. If P_c is circular pitch and α is helix angle, then

(*i*) the axial of helical gears is equal to

(*a*) $p_c \tan\alpha$ (*b*) $\frac{P_C}{\tan\alpha}$

(*c*) $\frac{\tan\alpha}{P_C}$ (*d*) $\frac{1}{P_c \cos\alpha}$

(*ii*) the normal circular pitch of helical gears is equal to

(*a*) $P_c \cos\alpha$ (*b*) $\frac{P_C}{\cos\alpha}$

(*c*) $\frac{\cos\alpha}{P_c}$ (*d*) $\frac{1}{P_c \cos\alpha}$

208. In a simple train of wheels, if numbers of intermediate wheels is odd, the follower will rotate in the

(*a*) same direction as the driver

(*b*) opposite to the direction of the driver

(*c*) any direction

(*d*) none of the above

209. In a simple train of wheels, the velocity ratio

(*a*) depend on intermediate wheels

(*b*) is independent of intermediate wheels

(*c*) can be dependnt or independent of intermediate wheels

(*d*) none of the above

210. In a reverter gear train first and last gear

(*a*) are on the same shaft

(*b*) are on the parallel but separate shafts

(*c*) rotate in the same direction

(*d*) rotate in the opposite directions

211. Negative sign of speed ratio means

(*a*) driver and driven wheels rotate in the opposite directions

(*b*) driver and driven wheels rotate in the same direction

(*c*) driver speed is more than driven speed

(*d*) driver speed is less than driven speed

212. The distance by which the outer edge of the D-slide valve overlaps the steam port in a steam engine, is known as

(*a*) lead (*b*) exhaust lap

(*c*) steam lap (*d*) none of the above

213. The distance by which the displacement of the D-slide valve is more than the steam lap, is known as

(*a*) lead (*b*) exhaust lap

(*c*) steam lap (*d*) none of the above

214. The distance by which the inner edge of the D-slide valve overlaps the steam port, is known as

(*a*) lead (*b*) exhaust lap

(*c*) steam lap (*d*) none of the above

215. A D-slide valve is also known as

(*a*) piston slide valve

(*b*) inside admission valve

(*c*) outside admission valve

(*d*) none of the above

216. A piston slide valve is a

(*a*) inside admission valve

(*b*) outside admission valve

(*c*) both (*a*) and (*b*) above

(*d*) none of the above

217. Distance moved by the valve from one end to the other end is known as

(*a*) valve travel

(*b*) throw of the eccentric

(*c*) angle of advance

(*d*) none of the above

218. With the increase or decrease of load on the engine, it is necessary to increase or decrease the supply of working fluid accordingly. This is done by

(*a*) D-slide valve (*b*) governor

(*c*) fly wheel (*d*) all of the above

219. The function of a governor is

(*a*) to keep the engine speed constant

(*b*) to maintain the engine speed within prescribed limits of varying load conditions

(*c*) to control the en gine speed

(*d*) all of the above

220. The mean speed of an engine caused by the variations in load, is controled by a

(*a*) D-slide valve

(*b*) governor

(*c*) fly wheel

(*d*) Mayor's expansion valve

221. The speed variation of the engine caused by the fluctuations of the engine turning moment is controlled by a

(*a*) D-slide valve

(*b*) governor

(*c*) flywheel

(*d*) Mayer's expansion valve

222. A flywheel

(*a*) is provided to minimise engine vibrations

(*b*) is provided to control engine speed

(*c*) controls output fluctuations and input accordingly

(*d*) all of the above

223. The speed variations of the engine during a cycle for constant output load is reduced by a

(*a*) D-slide valve

(b) governor

(*c*) flywheel

(*d*) Mayer's expansion valve

224. As the speed range decreases, the sensitiveness of the governor

(*a*) increases (*b*) decreases

(*c*) remains same (*d*) none of the above

225. Frequency of damped vibrations with viscous damping as compared to undamped vibrations is

(*a*) more (*b*) less

(*c*) same (*d*) none of the above

226. Ratio of the force transmitted to the force applied is known as

(*a*) damping factor (*b*) damping co-efficient

(*c*) transmissibility (*d*) magnification factor

227. A gover is said to be stable, when

(*a*) there is minimum change of the radius of the governor weights at a operating speed

(*b*) there is one radius of the governor weights for each equilibrium speed

(*c*) the position of balls does not change within the operating speed

(*d*) the position of balls changes within permissible limits

228. A governor is said to be stable, if the radius of rotation of balls

(*a*) increase as the equilibrium speed increases

(*b*) increase as the equilibrium speed decreases

(*c*) decreases as the equilibrium speed decreases

(*d*) decreases as the equilibrium speed increases

229. A governor is said to be isochronous, when

(*a*) equilibrium ball radii is constant for a given speed

(*b*) there is only one equilibrium speed which is constant for all radii of rotation of the balls within the working range

(*c*) there is only one radius of the governor weights for each equilibrium speed

(*d*) none of the above

230. Isochronism in a governor is desired when

(*a*) one speed is required for all loads

(*b*) one speed is required under one load

(*c*) engine runs at high speeds

(*d*) engine rans at low speeds

231. When a governor is over sensitive, the sleeve will oscillate between two extreme positions on slight change of speed. The governor is said to be

(*a*) isochronus (*b*) stable

(*c*) ustable (*d*) hunting

232. Hunting in a governor occurs due to

(*a*) worn out guides of the sleeve

(*b*) fixed position of balls for each speed within working range

(*c*) friction

(*d*) none of the above

233. A vibrometer is used to indicate vibration

(*a*) amplitude (*b*) frequency

(*c*) nature (*d*) all of the above

234. Mean force exerted by the governor on the sleeve for a given variation of speed, is known as
(*a*) stability of governor
(*b*) sensitiveness of governor
(*c*) effort of governor
(*d*) none of the above

235. The work done at the sleeve for a given percentage change of speed, is known as
(*a*) effort of governor
(*b*) power of governor
(*c*) stability of governor
(*d*) sensitiveness of governor

236. A very sensitive governor may
(*a*) cause hunting
(*b*) not be very stable
(*c*) both (*a*) and (*b*) above
(*d*) none of the above

237. Critical speed of a shaft depends on its
(*a*) mass
(*b*) stiffness
(*c*) eccentricity
(*d*) both (*a*) and (*b*) above

238. For stability of governor, the rate of increase of controlling force as compared to rate of increase of radius must be
(*a*) more (*b*) less
(*c*) same (*d*) none of the above

239. The sensitiveness of the governor, due to friction at the sleeve of a governor
(*a*) increases (*b*) decreases
(*c*) remains same (*d*) none of the above

240. Gravity controlled governor is
(*a*) Hartnell governor (*b*) Watt governor
(*c*) Hartung governor (*d*) none of the above

241. Spring controlled governor is
(*a*) Hartnell governor
(*b*) Hartung governor
(*c*) Pickering governor
(*d*) Wilson Hartnell governor
(*e*) all of the abovee

242. Dead weight governor is
(*a*) Porter governor
(*b*) Watt governor
(*c*) Hartnell governor
(*d*) all of the above

243. Spring controlled governors as compared to gravity controlled governors
(*a*) are much smaller in size
(*b*) can be operated at very high speed
(*c*) can be revolved about a vertical or inclined axis
(*d*) all of the above

244. Governor preferred for gramophones is
(*a*) Watt governor (*b*) Hartnell governor
(*c*) Pickering governor (*d*) Hartung governor

245. Pendulum type governor is
(*a*) Hartnell governor (*b*) Watt governor
(*c*) Porter governor (*d*) all of the above

246. Centrifugal type governor is
(*a*) Watt governor
(*b*) Hartnell governor
(*c*) Pickering governor
(*d*) all the above

247. If N is speed of arm and ball about the spindle axis, the height of a Watt's governor (in meters) is given by
(*a*) $\frac{8.95}{N^2}$ (*b*) $\frac{89.5}{N^2}$
(*c*) $\frac{895}{N^2}$ (*d*) $\frac{895}{N}$

248. Inertia and fly wheel governors as compared to centrifugal governors are
(*a*) more sensitive
(*b*) less simple
(*c*) less sensitive
(*d*) both (*a*) and (*b*) above

249. Height of a Watt's governor is proportional
(*a*) inversely to speed
(*b*) inversely to square of speed
(*c*) directly to square of speed
(*d*) directly to speed

250. If w is weight of the ball, W is weight on the sleeve and the upper and lower arms are equal and pivoted either on the governor axis or at equal distance from it, the height of a Porter governor is equal to
(*a*) $\left(\frac{w+W}{w}\right)\frac{895}{N^2}$ (*b*) $\left(\frac{w}{w+W}\right)\frac{895}{N^2}$
(*c*) $\left(\frac{w+W}{w}\right)\frac{N^2}{895}$ (*d*) $\left(\frac{w}{w+W}\right)\frac{N^2}{895}$

251. Ratio of height of Porter governor (if length of arms and links are equal) to the height of Watt's governor is

(*a*) $\frac{w}{w+W}$ (*b*) $\frac{w+W}{w}$

(*c*) $\frac{w+W}{w}$ (*d*) $\frac{W}{w+W}$

252. Satisfactory working range of Watt's governor is

(*a*) 40 to 60 rpm (*b*) 60 to 80 rpm

(*c*) 80 to 100 rpm (*d*) 100 to 150 rpm

253. With increase in the speed of governor

(*a*) height of governor increases

(*b*) height of governor decreases

(*c*) radius of rotation increases

(*d*) both (*b*) and (*c*) above

254. As the sleeve of a Porter governor moves upwards, the governor speed

(*a*) increases (*d*) decreases

(*c*) remains same (*d*) none of the above

255. The balls are attached to the extension of lower links in

(*a*) Hartnell governor (*b*) Watt's governor

(*c*) Porter governor (*d*) Proell governor

256. Porter governor as compared to Proell governor

(*a*) requires weights of bigger size

(*b*) is less sensitive

(*c*) is less sensitive of smaller size

(*d*) both (*a*) and (*b*) above

257. In Hartnell governor, the compression of the spring as compared to lift of the sleeve is

(*a*) more (*b*) less

(*c*) same (*d*) none of the above

258. If r_1 and r_2 are maximum and minimum radii of rotation, *x* and *y* are lengths of ball arm and sleeve arm of the lever respectively, then the lift of the sleeve in a Hartnell governor is equal to

(*a*) $\frac{x}{y}(r_1+r_2)$ (*b*) $\frac{y}{x}(r_1+r_2)$

(*c*) $\frac{x}{y}(r_1-r_2)$ (*d*) $\frac{y}{x}(r_2-r_1)$

259. If S_1 and S_2 are spring forces exerted on the sleeve at maximum and minimum radii of rotation o n respectively, *h* is lift of sleeve, then the stiffness of spring in a Hartnell governor is equal to

(*a*) $\frac{S_1+S_2}{2h}$ (*b*) $\frac{S_1-S_2}{2h}$

(*c*) $\frac{S_1-S_2}{h}$ (*d*) $\frac{S_1+S_2}{h}$

260. If the stiffness of spring is increased, the Hartnell governor will become

(*a*) more sensitive

(*b*) less sensitive

(*c*) remain same sensitive

(*d*) none of the above

261. If r_1 and r_2 are maximum and minimum radius of rotation of balls, S_1 and S_2 are maximum and minimum force exerted on the sleeve respectively and W is weight on the sleeve, then for an isochronous Hartnell governor

(*a*) $\frac{r_1}{r_2}=\frac{S_1}{S_2}$ (*b*) $\frac{r_1}{r_2}\frac{S_2}{S_1}$

(*c*) $\frac{r_1}{r_2}=\frac{W+S_1}{W+S_2}$ (*d*) $\frac{r_1}{r_2}\frac{W-S_1}{W-S_2}$

262. If C is percentage increase in speed, S is spring force exerted on the sleeve and the moments due to weight of arms and ball are neglected, the effort of a Hartnell governor is equal to

(*a*) $\frac{S}{C}$ (*b*) $\frac{C}{S}$

(*c*) SC (*d*) $\frac{1}{CS}$

263. In Hartnell governor, the controlling force is provided by

(*a*) springs (*b*) weight of balls

(*c*) dead weight (*d*) none of the above

264. In Porter governor, the controlling force is provided by

(*a*) springs (*b*) weight of balls

(*c*) deadweight (*d*) none of the above

265. If *w* and W are weights of ball and sleeve respeceively, C is percentage increase in speedy then

(*i*) the effort of a Porter governor is equal to

(*a*) $C(w+W)$ (*b*) $C(w-W)$

(*c*) $C(W-w)$ (*d*) $\frac{C}{w+W}$

(*ii*) the power of a Porter governor is equal to

(*a*) $\frac{C^2}{1+2C}(w+W)h$ (*b*) $\frac{4C^2}{1+2C}(w+W)h$

(*c*) $\frac{2C^2}{1+2C}(w+W)h$ (*d*) $\frac{4C^2}{1+2C}(w+W)h$

where *h* is height of the governor.

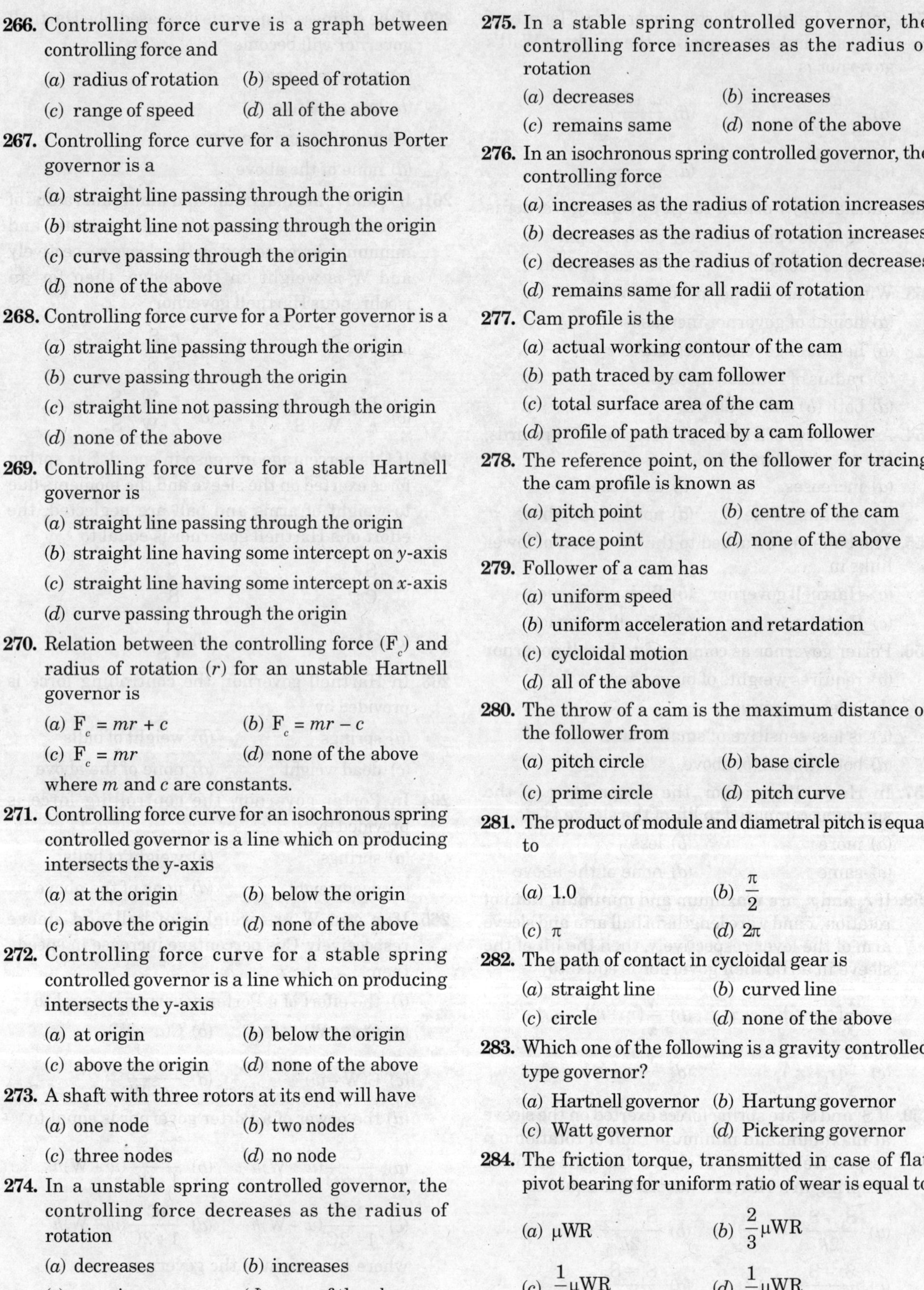

266. Controlling force curve is a graph between controlling force and

(*a*) radius of rotation (*b*) speed of rotation

(*c*) range of speed (*d*) all of the above

267. Controlling force curve for a isochronus Porter governor is a

(*a*) straight line passing through the origin

(*b*) straight line not passing through the origin

(*c*) curve passing through the origin

(*d*) none of the above

268. Controlling force curve for a Porter governor is a

(*a*) straight line passing through the origin

(*b*) curve passing through the origin

(*c*) straight line not passing through the origin

(*d*) none of the above

269. Controlling force curve for a stable Hartnell governor is

(*a*) straight line passing through the origin

(*b*) straight line having some intercept on *y*-axis

(*c*) straight line having some intercept on *x*-axis

(*d*) curve passing through the origin

270. Relation between the controlling force (F_c) and radius of rotation (r) for an unstable Hartnell governor is

(*a*) $F_c = mr + c$ (*b*) $F_c = mr - c$

(*c*) $F_c = mr$ (*d*) none of the above

where m and c are constants.

271. Controlling force curve for an isochronous spring controlled governor is a line which on producing intersects the y-axis

(*a*) at the origin (*b*) below the origin

(*c*) above the origin (*d*) none of the above

272. Controlling force curve for a stable spring controlled governor is a line which on producing intersects the y-axis

(*a*) at origin (*b*) below the origin

(*c*) above the origin (*d*) none of the above

273. A shaft with three rotors at its end will have

(*a*) one node (*b*) two nodes

(*c*) three nodes (*d*) no node

274. In a unstable spring controlled governor, the controlling force decreases as the radius of rotation

(*a*) decreases (*b*) increases

(*c*) remains same (*d*) none of the above

275. In a stable spring controlled governor, the controlling force increases as the radius of rotation

(*a*) decreases (*b*) increases

(*c*) remains same (*d*) none of the above

276. In an isochronous spring controlled governor, the controlling force

(*a*) increases as the radius of rotation increases

(*b*) decreases as the radius of rotation increases

(*c*) decreases as the radius of rotation decreases

(*d*) remains same for all radii of rotation

277. Cam profile is the

(*a*) actual working contour of the cam

(*b*) path traced by cam follower

(*c*) total surface area of the cam

(*d*) profile of path traced by a cam follower

278. The reference point, on the follower for tracing the cam profile is known as

(*a*) pitch point (*b*) centre of the cam

(*c*) trace point (*d*) none of the above

279. Follower of a cam has

(*a*) uniform speed

(*b*) uniform acceleration and retardation

(*c*) cycloidal motion

(*d*) all of the above

280. The throw of a cam is the maximum distance of the follower from

(*a*) pitch circle (*b*) base circle

(*c*) prime circle (*d*) pitch curve

281. The product of module and diametral pitch is equal to

(*a*) 1.0 (*b*) $\frac{\pi}{2}$

(*c*) π (*d*) 2π

282. The path of contact in cycloidal gear is

(*a*) straight line (*b*) curved line

(*c*) circle (*d*) none of the above

283. Which one of the following is a gravity controlled type governor?

(*a*) Hartnell governor (*b*) Hartung governor

(*c*) Watt governor (*d*) Pickering governor

284. The friction torque, transmitted in case of flat pivot bearing for uniform ratio of wear is equal to

(*a*) μWR (*b*) $\frac{2}{3}\mu WR$

(*c*) $\frac{1}{3}\mu WR$ (*d*) $\frac{1}{2}\mu WR$

285. In double slider crank chain, the number of revolute pairs is/are

(a) 1 (b) 2
(c) 3 (d) 4

286. Oldham's coupling is inversion of

(a) 4-bar chain
(b) 6-bar chain
(c) single slider crank chain
(d) double slider crank chain

287. Cam size depends upon

(a) base circle (b) pitch circle
(c) prime circle (d) outer circle

288. Hartnell governor could be classified under the head of

(a) inertia type governors
(b) pendulum type governors
(c) centrifugal type governors
(d) dead weight type-governors

289. Which of the following clutches is positive type?

(a) Cone (b) Disc
(c) Jaw (d) Centrifugal

290. Creep in belt is due to

(a) material of the pulley
(b) material of the belt
(c) larger size of driver pulley
(d) uneven extensions and contractions due to varying tension

291. Kinetic pairs are those which have two elements that

(a) have line contact
(b) have surface contact
(c) permit relative motion
(d) are held together

292. Governor is used in automobile to

(a) decrease the variation of speed
(b) control $\delta N/\delta t$
(c) control δN
(d) All the above

293. Which of the following machines does not require quick return mechanism?

(a) Slotter (b) Planer
(c) Shaper (d) Broaching

294. The height 'h' and angular speed 'ω' for the Watt governor and Portar governor are related by the identity

(a) $h \alpha \omega$ (b) $h \alpha 1/\omega$
(c) $h \alpha \omega^2$ (d) $h \alpha 1/\omega^2$

295. The surface of gear tooth below pitch surface is called

(a) bottom tooth (b) face
(c) flank (d) dedendum portion

296. For maximum power transmitted by belt, the maximum permissible tension in the belt is

(a) Equal to centrifugal tension
(b) Twice the centrifugal tension
(c) Thrice the centrifugal tension
(d) Four-times the centrifugal tension

297. A simple mechanism has

(a) 1 link (b) 2 links
(c) 3 links (d) 4 links

298. A universal joint is an example of

(a) Lower pair (b) Higher pair
(c) Rolling pair (d) Sliding pair

299. In automobiles the power is transmitted from gear box to differential through

(a) Bevel gear (b) Universal joint
(c) Hooke's joint (d) Knuckle joint

300. Inversion of a mechanism is

(a) Changing of a higher pair to lower pair
(b) Obtained by fixing different links in a kinematic chain
(c) Turning it upside down
(d) Obtained by reversing the input and output motion

301. For a slider crank mechanism, the velocity and acceleration of the piston at inner dead centre will be

(a) 0 and 0 (b) 0 and $\omega^2 r$
(c) 0 and $< \omega^2 r$ (d) 0 and $> \omega^2 r$

where 'ω' is angular velocity of the crank and 'r' its radius.

302. Crank, connecting rod, cylinder and piston of steam engine constitute

(a) One link (b) Two links
(c) Three links (d) Four links

303. The number of links I and the number of pairs p in a kinematic chain conform to the relation

(a) $l = p - 4$ (b) $l = 2p - 4$
(c) $l = 2p + 1$ (d) $l = 2(p - 1)$

304. For a flat open-belt drive, the belt speed is 880 m/min and the power transmitted is 22.5 kW. What is the difference between the tight side as slack side tensions of the belt drive ?

(a) 900 N (b) 6450 N
(c) 1540 N (d) 1000 N

305. The power transmitted by means of belt depends upon

(*a*) velocity of the belt

(*b*) tension on the belt

(*c*) arc of contact between the belt and the smaller pulley

(*d*) All of the above

306. Herringbone gears are

(*a*) spur gears (*b*) single helical gears

(*c*) double helical gears (*d*) bevel gears

307. For an involute gear, the ratio, pitch circle radius/ base circle radius =

(*a*) cos ϕ (*b*) sin ϕ

(*c*) sec ϕ (*d*) cossec ϕ

308. The difference between tensions on the tight and slack slides of a belt drive is 3000 N. If the belt speed is 15 m/sec, the transmitted power, in kW, is

(*a*) 45 (*b*) 22.5

(*c*) 90 (*d*) 100

309. The maximum efficiency of worm and worm wheel system is

(*a*) $\eta_{max} = \dfrac{1-\cos\phi}{1+\cos\phi}$ (*b*) $\eta_{max} = \dfrac{1-\sin\phi}{1+\cos\phi}$

(*c*) $\eta_{max} = \dfrac{1-\sin\phi}{1+\sin\phi}$ (*d*) $\eta_{max} = \dfrac{1-\tan\phi}{1+\tan\phi}$

where ϕ is the friction angle.

310. In gear drive, addendum angle.

(*a*) diametral pitch

(*b*) circular pitch

(*c*) module of the gear

(*d*) 1.57 times the module of the gear

311. For helical gears, the helix angle generally ranges from

(*a*) 45 to 60 degrees (*b*) 30 to 75 degrees

(*c*) 0 to 30 degrees (*d*) 30 to 45 degrees

312. The crank radius of a slider crank mechanism is 10 cm. If the crank radius is increased to 12 cm, the stroke length will increase by

(*a*) 20% (*b*) 12%

(*c*) 5% (*d*) 10%

313. Assertion (A) : A clutch is the best means to connect a driving shaft with a driven shaft for regular power transmission.

Reason (R) : A clutch can be frequently engaged and disengaged at operators will.

(*a*) (A) is true, but (R) is false.

(*b*) (R) is true, but (A) is false.

(*c*) Both (A) and (R) are true and (R) is the correct explanation of (A).

(*d*) Both (A) and (R) are true, but (R) is not the correct explanation of (A).

314. A spur gear with pitch circle diameter D has number of teeth T. The module m is defined as

(*a*) m = DT (*b*) $m = \dfrac{T}{D}$

(*c*) $m = \dfrac{\pi D}{T}$ (*d*) $m = \dfrac{D}{T}$

315. A ball and socket joint forms a

(*a*) Sliding pair (*b*) Spherical pair

(*c*) Turning pair (*d*) Rolling pair

316. ABCD is a four-bar mechanism in which AB = 30 cm and CD = 45 cm. At an instant, both AB and CD are perpendicular to fixed link AD. If velocity of B at this condition is V, then velocity of C is

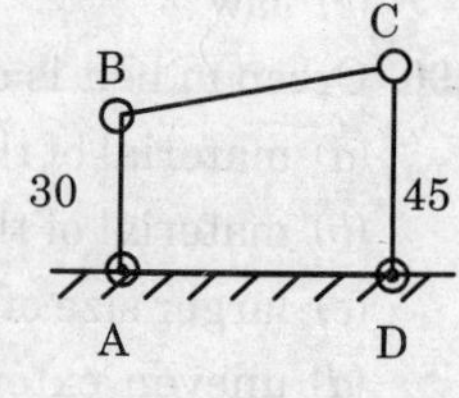

(*a*) $\dfrac{9}{4}$V

(*b*) $\dfrac{3}{2}$V

(*c*) V

(*d*) $\dfrac{4}{3}$V

317. The inner and outer radius of friction surface of a plate clutch are 50 mm and 100 mm respectively. What is the ratio of maximum intensity of pressure to minimum intensity of pressure on clutch plate if magnitude of axial force is 4 kN? Assume uniform wear theory.

(*a*) 2 (*b*) 6

(*c*) 8 (*d*) 4

318. The thickness of a boiler plate is 16 mm, the diameter of rivet used in the boiler joint is

(*a*) 28 mm (*b*) 10 mm

(*c*) 20 mm (*d*) 24 mm

319. Lewis equation in spur gear design is applied to

(*a*) Stronger of the pinion or gear

(*b*) Weaker of the pinion or gear

(*c*) Pinion

(*d*) Gear

320. Degree of freedom of a slider crank mechanism is

(*a*) 2 (*b*) 3

(*c*) 0 (*d*) 1

321. Match the List-I with the List-II and select the correct match using the codes below:

List-I	List-II
(A) Governor	1. Dunkerleymethod
(B) Flywheel	2. Turning moment
(C) Critical speed	3. D'Alembert's principle
(D) Inertia force	4. Speed control

Codes:

	(A)	(B)	(C)	(D)
(a)	1	2	3	4
(b)	3	2	1	4
(c)	4	2	1	3
(d)	2	3	4	1

322. The relation between number of lower pair (P) and number of links (L) in a four link kinematic chain is given by

(a) L = 2P – 6 (b) L = 2(P – 1)
(c) L = 2P – 4 (d) L = P + 4

323. The stiffness of the spring in a Hartnell governor is equal to, where

S_1 = Spring force exerted on the sleeve at maximum radius of rotation.

S_2 = Spring force exerted on the sleeve at minimum radius of rotation.

h = lift of sleeve

(a) $S_1 - S_2/2h$ (b) $S_1 + S_2/h$
(c) $S_1 - S_2/h$ (d) $2(S_1 - S_2)/h$

324. The differential gear in the automobiles is used to

(a) Assist in changing speed
(b) Provide balancing
(c) Reduce speed
(d) Help in turning

325. Which of the following gear system have minimum axial thrust?

(a) Helical gears (b) Double helical gears
(c) Spur gears (d) Bevel gears

326. A sliding bearing which can support steady loads without any relative motion between the journal and the bearing is called

(a) Zero film bearing
(b) Hydrodynamic lubricated bearing
(c) Hydrodynamic lubricated bearing
(d) Boundary lubricated bearing

327. From the Lewis equation $F_b = f.p.y.b$, the strength factor of the gear is given by the product

(a) p · y (b) p · b
(c) f · b (d) f · y

328. Mass per unit length of the belt of an open belt drive is 1.5 kg/m. If the linear velocity of the belt is 10 m/s and radius of driving pulley 0.5 m, centrifugal tension in the belt is

(a) 600 N (b) 400 N
(c) 300 N (d) 150 N

329. In wheel and differential axle, the velocity ratio is given by

(a) $\frac{d_1 - d_2}{2D}$ (b) $\frac{d_1 - d_2}{4D}$
(c) $\frac{2D}{d_1 - d_2}$ (d) $\frac{3D}{d_1 - d_2}$

330. Acme threads are generally used in

(a) railway carriage couplings
(b) spindles of bench vices
(c) screw cutting lathes
(d) feed mechanism of machine tools

331. In a Hartnell governor, 800 N force is exerted on the sleeve at minimum radius and 1200 N force is exerted at maximum radius. If sleeve lift is 20 mm, the value of spring-stiffness (s) is

(a) 10 N/mm (b) 20 N/mm
(c) 15 N/mm (d) 18 N/mm

332. The maximum and minimum speeds of a flywheel during a cycle are N_1 and N_2 r.p.m. respectively. The coefficient of steadiness of the flywheel is

(a) $\frac{N_1 - N_2}{2(N_1 + N_2)}$ (b) $\frac{N_1 + N_2}{2(N_1 - N_2)}$
(c) $\frac{2(N_1 + N_2)}{N_1 - N_2}$ (d) $\frac{N_1 + N_2}{N_1 - N_2}$

333. The angle of Vee belts is

(a) 30° (b) 85°
(c) 40° (d) 45°

334. Which of the following statements is ***not*** true for couplings?

(a) Couplings are meant for transmitting torque
(b) Couplings keep the mating shafts in alignment
(c) Couplings are used in shafts
(d) Couplings connect parallel shafts

335. The sum of the tensions when the belt is running on the pulley is

(a) less than the initial tension
(b) more than the initial tension
(c) more than twice the initial tension
(d) half the initial tension

336. For a screw, the angle of helix (α) is related to the lead (L) and mean screw thread diameter (d) as

(*a*) $\tan \alpha = \frac{L}{d}$ (*b*) $\tan \alpha = \frac{d}{L}$

(*c*) $\tan \alpha = \frac{L}{\pi d}$ (*d*) $\tan \alpha = \frac{\pi d}{L}$

337. A point an a link connecting double slider cran chain traces a/an

(*a*) Straight line path (*b*) Circular path

(*c*) Parabolic path (*d*) Elliptical path

338. The angular speed of a Wall's governor, when its height is 20 cm, will be equal to

(*a*) 20 rad/sec (*b*) 10 rad/sec

(*c*) 6 rad/sec (*d*) 7 rad/sec

339. The efficiency in case of worm gear drives is generally in the range of

(*a*) 10 – 25 percent (*b*) 40 – 60 percent

(*c*) 50 – 70 percent (*d*) 70 – 85 percent

340. In a kinematic chain, the minimum number of kinematic pairs required is

(*a*) one (*b*) two

(*c*) three (*d*) four

341. For a key to be equally strong in shearing and crushing, the width of the key, assuming that the allowable crushing stress is twice the allowable shear stress, should be

(*a*) 2.5 times its thickness

(*b*) 2 times its thickness

(*c*) 1.5 times its thickness

(*d*) equal to its thickness

342. The twining moment (T) delivered by a flywheel with respect to its angular displacement is given by the following expression :

$T = 14000 + 7000 \sin \theta$

The values of θ for which delivered torque is equal to mean torque for a single cycle are

(*a*) 0°, 180°, 360° (*b*) 90°, 270°, 360°

(*c*) 90°, 270°, 180° (*d*) 0°, 270°, 360°

343. The shearing strength of a rivet is 50 N/mm². If the diameter of the rivet is doubled, then its shearing strength will be

(*a*) 100 N/mm²

(*b*) 200 N/mm²

(*c*) 50 N/mm²

(*d*) 300 N/mm²

344. Figure shows a four bar chain and the number indicates the respective link lengths in cm. The type of the mechanism is known as

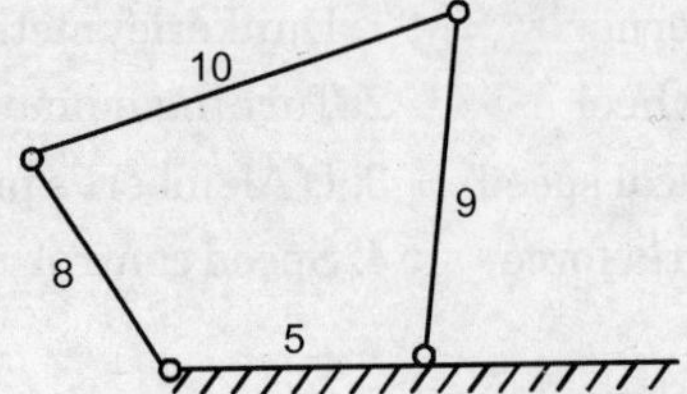

(*a*) slider crank (*b*) double crank

(*c*) crank rocker (*d*) double rocker

345. A slider sliding at 10 cm/s on a link which is rotating at 60 rpm, is subjected to Coriolis acceleration of magnitude, in cm²/s,

(*a*) 20π (*b*) 10π

(*c*) 40π (*d*) 80π

346. Name the mechanism in which the Coriolis component of acceleration is to be considered

(*a*) Quick return motion mechanism

(*b*) Four-bar mechanism

(*c*) Slider crank mechanism

(*d*) Beam engine

347. Bevel gears are used to transmit rotary motion between two shafts whose axes are

(*a*) Perpendicular (*b*) Parallel

(*c*) Non-intersecting (*d*) Non-coplanar

348. A differential gear in an automobile is a

(*a*) simple gear train

(*b*) epicyclic gear train

(*c*) compound gear train

(*d*) speed reducer

349. Creep in belt drive is due to

(*a*) weak material of the belt

(*b*) weak material of the pulley

(*c*) uneven extensions and contractions of the belt when it passes from tight to slack side

(*d*) expansion of the belt

350. The crank shaft turning in a journal bearing forms a

(*a*) turning pair (*b*) sliding pair

(*c*) rolling pair (*d*) helical pair

351. What type of contact occurs during meshing of helical gears ?

(*a*) Point (*b*) Line

(*c*) Area (*d*) Volume

352. Which one of the following drives is used for transmitting power without slip ?

(*a*) Belt drives (*b*) Rope drives

(*c*) Cone pulleys (*d*) Chain drives

353. The contact between cam and follower is to form a

(*a*) lower pair (*b*) higher pair

(*c*) sliding pair (*d*) rolling pair

354. Which of the following is antifriction bearing ?

(*a*) Needle bearing (*b*) Pedestal bearing

(*c*) Collar bearing (*d*) Hydrostatic bearing

355. Helical gears have their teeth

(*a*) inclined to wheel rim

(*b*) straight over the wheel rim

(*c*) curved over the wheel rim

(*d*) cut on the surfaces of the frusta of cones

356. When the speed of governor increases, then

(*a*) height of governor and radius of rotation increase

(*b*) height of governor and radius of rotation decrease

(*c*) height of governor decreases but radius of rotation increases

(*d*) height of governor increases but radius of rotation decreases

357. The power transmitted by a belt is maximum when the maximum tension in the belt compared to centrifugal tension is :

(*a*) 3-5 times (*b*) 2 times

(*c*) 3 times (*d*) 4 times

358. Effort lost in friction in a simple machine is :

(*a*) $P - 2P_0$ (*b*) $2P - P_0$

(*c*) $P_0 - P/2$ (*d*) $P - P_0$

359. The crank pin is to be connected in the bush and the dimensions for the bush and crank are given respectively of in mm-

are $16^{+0.017}_{+0.000}$, $16^{-0.035}_{-0.062}$

Maximum clearance between bush and crank pin is :

(*a*) 0.079 mm (*b*) 0.0079 mm

(*c*) 0.035 mm (*d*) 0.062 mm

360. How many links does a pantograph mechanism contain ?

(*a*) Ten (*b*) Two

(*c*) Four (*d*) Nine

361. The total number instantaneous centres for a mechanism consisting of '*n*' links are :

(*a*) $\frac{n(n-1)}{2}$ (*b*) $\frac{n}{2}$

(*c*) n (*d*) $\frac{(n-1)}{2}$

362. The product of circular pitch and diametral pitch is equal to :

(*a*) π (*b*) Module

(*c*) Unity (*d*) $1/\pi$

363. The purpose of the flywheel in an IC engine is :

(*a*) To regulate the fuel supply

(*b*) To keep the output power constant at the crank shaft

(*c*) To increase the power capacity of the engine

(*d*) To reduce the vibration in an engine

364. The device which permits the connection and disconnection of shaft is :

(*a*) Bearing (*b*) Connector

(*c*) Clutch (*d*) Pulley

365. The circular pitch of a toothed wheel having 24 teeth and module of 4.25 mm will be :

(*a*) 8.50 mm (*b*) 1.35 mm

(*c*) 4.25 mm (*d*) 6.67 mm

366. The size of the gear is usually specified by :

(*a*) Pitch circle diameter

(*b*) Pressure angle

(*c*) Circular pitch

(*d*) Diameter pitch

367. Rivets are generally specified by :

(*a*) Diameter of head

(*b*) Thickness of plates to be riveted

(*c*) Length of rivet

(*d*) Nominal diameter

368. Herring bone gears are :

(*a*) Double helical gears

(*b*) Spur gears with small teeth

(*c*) Large worm gears

(*d*) Spiral gears

369. A fan rotates at a constant speed of 60 rpm. The total angular displacement it makes in 10 sec is :

(*a*) Zero (*b*) 10π rad

(*c*) 40π rad (*d*) 20π rad

370. The maximum speed and minimum speed in r.p.rn. at a Watt governor are 72 and 68 respectively. The range of speed of the governor is :

(*a*) 4 (*b*) 2

(*c*) 8 (*d*) 6

371. Fan belt in automobiles is :

(*a*) E-Section V belt

(*b*) A three layer flat belt

(*c*) A five layer flat belt

(*d*) B-SectionV belt

372. In a gear drive, module is equal to :

(*a*) $\dfrac{1}{\text{Diametral pitch}}$ (*b*) $\dfrac{1}{\text{Circular pitch}}$

(*c*) $\dfrac{\text{Circular pitch}}{\pi}$ (*d*) $\dfrac{\text{Diametral pitch}}{\pi}$

373. The relation between the number of links (L) and number of pairs (P) is :

(*a*) L = 2P – 3 (*b*) L = 2P – 2

(*c*) L = 2P – 4 (*d*) L = 3 – 2P

374. The cone angle of a pivot bearing is increased by 2%. The maximum load carrying capacity at the bearing will increase by

(*a*) 0.05% (*b*) 1%

(*c*) 0.5% (*d*) 0%

375. Why are gear teeth made harder?

(*a*) To avoid wear

(*b*) To avoid pitting

(*c*) to avoid abrasion

(*d*) To avoid tensile strength

376. The centre of gravity of a complex link in a four bar chain mechanism will experience.

(*a*) No acceleration

(*b*) Only linear acceleration

(*c*) Only angular acceleration

(*d*) Both linear and angular acceleration

377. The power from the engine to the rear axle of an automobile is transmitted by means of

(*a*) Worm and worm wheel

(*b*) Spur gears

(*c*) Bevel gears

(*d*) Hooke's joint

378. The included angle for the v-belt is usually

(*a*) 10° to 20° (*b*) 20° to 30°

(*c*) 30° to 40° (*d*) 60° to 80°

379. In railway axle boxes, the bearing used is

(*a*) Cylindrical roller bearing

(*b*) Deep groove ball bearing

(*c*) Double row spherical roller bearing

(*d*) Double row self-aligning ball bearing

380. When the sleeve of a Porter govenor moves upwards, the govenor speed

(*a*) Increases

(*b*) Decreases

(*c*) Remains unaffected

(*d*) First increases and then decreases

381. When the load on engine increases, it becomes necessary to increase the supply of working fluid and when the load decreases, less working fluid is required. The supply of the working fluid to the engine is controlled by a

(*a*) D-slide valve

(*b*) Governor

(*c*) Meyer's expansion valve

(*d*) Fly wheel

382. For high speed engine the cam follower should move with

(*a*) Uniform velocity

(*b*) Simple harmonic motion

(*c*) Uniform acceleration and retardation

(*d*) Cycloidal motion

383. The minimum required centre distance of two mating spur gears is decided based on

(*a*) Surface compressive strength of the gear material

(*b*) Bending strength of the gear material

(*c*) Ultimate strength of the gear material

(*d*) Fatigue strength of the gear material

384. Which of the following bearings can take large thrust loads?

(*a*) Deep-Groove ball bearing

(*b*) Filling-Notch ball bearing

(*c*) Self-aligning ball bearing

(*d*) Angular-Contact bearing

385. A cotter joint is used to connect two rods which are in

(*a*) Tension only

(*b*) Compression only

(*c*) Tension and Compression only

(*d*) Shear only

386. Which of the following statements regarding 'mitre gears' is correct?

These are employed for

(*a*) minimum back-lash

(*b*) great speed reduction

(*c*) equal speed

(*d*) minimum axial thrust

387. Regarding journal bearing under film lubrication condition which of the following statements is correct?

Frictional resistance is

(*a*) directly proportional to the pressure

(*b*) independent of the area

(*c*) proportional to the speed of rotation

(*d*) inversely proportional to the viscosity of the lubricant

388. According to Indian standard specifications, a plain carbon steel designated by 40C8 means that the percentage of carbon content is

(*a*) 0.04 (*b*) 0.35 to 0.45

(*c*) 0.4 to 0.6 (*d*) 0.6 to 0.8

Answers

1. (*a*)	**2.** (*a*)	**3.** (*c*)	**4.** (*b*)	**5.** (*c*)	**6.** (*c*)	**7.** (*d*)	**8.** (*c*)	**9.** (*b*)	**10.** (*b*)
11. (*c*)	**12.** (*a*)	**13.** (*)	**14.** (*d*)	**15.** (*b*)	**16.** (*c*)	**17.** (*b*)	**18.** (*a*)	**19.** (*b*)	**20.** (*a*)
21. (*c*)	**22.** (*a*)	**23.** (*d*)	**24.** (*b*)	**25.** (*c*)	**26.** (*d*)	**27.** (*b*)	**28.** (*c*)	**29.** (*c*)	**30.** (*b*)
31. (*b*)	**32.** (*a*)	**33.** (*a*)	**34.** (*a*)	**35.** (*b*)	**36.** (*b*)	**37.** (*b*)	**38.** (*a*)	**39.** (*a*)	**40.** (*c*)
41. (*d*)	**42.** (*b*)	**43.** (*d*)	**44.** (*b*)	**45.** (*a*)	**46.** (*a*)	**47.** (*b*)	**48.** (*a*)	**49.** (*c*)	**50.** (*d*)
51. (*b*)	**52.** (*d*)	**53.** (*c*)	**54.** (*a*)	**55.** (*b*)	**56.** (*c*)	**57.** (*e*)	**58.** (*b*)	**59.** (*a*)	**60.** (*b*)
61. (*b*)	**62.** (*c*)	**63.** (*b*)	**64.** (*c*)	**65.** (*d*)	**66.** (*c*)	**67.** (*a*)	**68.** (*a*)	**69.** (*a*)	**70.** (*b*)
71. (*c*)	**72.** (*d*)	**73.** (*c*)	**74.** (*c*)	**75.** (*b*)	**76.** (*b*)	**77.** (*c*)	**78.** (*c*)	**79.** (*b*)	**80.** (*a*)
81. (*b*)	**82.** (*c*)	**83.** (*a*)	**84.** (*b*)	**85.** (*c*)	**86.** (*d*)	**87.** (*a*)	**88.** (*c*)	**89.** (*a*)	**90.** (*b*)
91. (*d*)	**92.** (*b*)	**93.** (*a*)	**94.** (*b*)	**95.** (*a*)	**96.** (*c*)	**97.** (*b*)	**98.** (*b*)	**99.** (*c*)	**100.** (*b*)
101. (*a*)	**102.** (*b*)	**103.** (*c*)	**104.** (*d*)	**105.** (*c*)	**106.** (*c*)	**107.** (*a*)	**108.** (*c*)	**109.** (*b*)	**110.** (*a*)
111. (*b*)	**112.** (*d*)	**113.** (*a*)	**114.** (*c*)	**115.** (*a*)	**116.** (*a*)	**117.** (*c*)	**118.** (*c*)	**119.** (*d*)	**120.** (*a*)
121. (*b*)	**122.** (*c*)	**123.** (*c*)	**124.** (*d*)	**125.** (*d*)	**126.** (*d*)	**127.** (*d*)	**128.** (*b*)	**129.** (*b*)	**130.** (*c*)
131. (*b*)	**132.** (*a*)	**133.** (*c*)	**134.** (*a*)	**135.** (*c*)	**136.** (*a*)	**137.** (*d*)	**138.** (*a*)	**139.** (*b*)	**140.** (*a*)
141. (*c*)	**142.** (*a*)	**143.** (*c*)	**144.** (*b*)	**145.** (*b*)	**146.** (*a*)	**147.** (*b*)	**148.** (*a*)	**149.** (*b*)	**150.** (*c*)
151. (*b*)	**152.** (*a*)	**153.** (*a*)	**154.** (*b*)	**155.** (*d*)	**156.** (*a*)	**157.** (*b*)	**158.** (*a*)	**159.** (*d*)	**160.** (*c*)
161. (*c*)	**162.** (*c*)	**163.** (*c*)	**164.** (*c*)	**165.** (*d*)	**166.** (*c*)	**167.** (*c*)	**168.** (*b*)	**169.** (*c*)	**170.** (*c*)
171. (*c*)	**172.** (*c*)	**173.** (*a*)	**174.** (*a*)	**175.** (*c*)	**176.** (*c*)	**177.** (*a*)	**178.** (*d*)	**179.** (*b*)	**180.** (*d*)
181. (*a*)	**182.** (*b*)	**183.** (*c*)	**184.** (*b*)	**185.** (*b*)	**186.** (*d*)	**187.** (*b*)	**188.** (*b*)	**189.** (*b*)	**190.** (*b*)
191. (*d*)	**192.** (*c*)	**193.** (*b*)	**194.** (*b*)	**195.** (*a*)	**196.** (*c*)	**197.** (*e*)	**198.** (*c*)	**199.** (*d*)	**200.** (*b*)

201. (*b*)	**202.** (*a*)	**203.** (*b*)	**204.** (*c*)	**205.** (*a*)	**206.** (*d*)	**207.** (*a*)	**208.** (*a*)	**209.** (*b*)	**210.** (*a*)
211. (*a*)	**212.** (*c*)	**213.** (*a*)	**214.** (*b*)	**215.** (*c*)	**216.** (*a*)	**217.** (*a*)	**218.** (*b*)	**219.** (*b*)	**220.** (*b*)
221. (*c*)	**222.** (*d*)	**223.** (*c*)	**224.** (*a*)	**225.** (*a*)	**226.** (*b*)	**227.** (*b*)	**228.** (*a*)	**229.** (*b*)	**230.** (*a*)
231. (*d*)	**232.** (*d*)	**233.** (*a*)	**234.** (*c*)	**235.** (*b*)	**236.** (*c*)	**237.** (*c*)	**238.** (*a*)	**239.** (*b*)	**240.** (*c*)
241. (*e*)	**242.** (*a*)	**243.** (*d*)	**244.** (*c*)	**245.** (*b*)	**246.** (*b*)	**247.** (*c*)	**248.** (*d*)	**249.** (*b*)	**250.** (*a*)
251. (*b*)	**252.** (*b*)	**253.** (*d*)	**254.** (*a*)	**255.** (*d*)	**256.** (*d*)	**257.** (*c*)	**258.** (*d*)	**259.** (*c*)	**260.** (*b*)
261. (*c*)	**262.** (*c*)	**263.** (*a*)	**264.** (*c*)	**265.** (*d*)	**266.** (*a*)	**267.** (*c*)	**268.** (*b*)	**269.** (*b*)	**270.** (*a*)
271. (*a*)	**272.** (*b*)	**273.** (*b*)	**274.** (*a*)	**275.** (*d*)	**276.** (*a*)	**277.** (*b*)	**278.** (*d*)	**279.** (*c*)	**280.** (*a*)
281. (*a*)	**282.** (*a*)	**283.** (*c*)	**284.** (*a*)	**285.** (*b*)	**286.** (*d*)	**287.** (*a*)	**288.** (*c*)	**289.** (*c*)	**290.** (*d*)
291. (*c*)	**292.** (*c*)	**293.** (*a*)	**294.** (*d*)	**295.** (*c*)	**296.** (*c*)	**297.** (*d*)	**298.** (*a*)	**299.** (*c*)	**300.** (*b*)
301. (*d*)	**302.** (*d*)	**303.** (*b*)	**304.** (*c*)	**305.** (*d*)	**306.** (*c*)	**307.** (*c*)	**308.** (*a*)	**309.** (*c*)	**310.** (*c*)
311. (*c*)	**312.** (*a*)	**313.** (*b*)	**314.** (*d*)	**315.** (*b*)	**316.** (*b*)	**317.** (*a*)	**318.** (*d*)	**319.** (*b*)	**320.** (*d*)
321. (*c*)	**322.** (*c*)	**323.** (*c*)	**324.** (*d*)	**325.** (*b*)	**326.** (*c*)	**327.** (*d*)	**328.** (*d*)	**329.** (*c*)	**330.** (*c*)
331. (*b*)	**332.** (*b*)	**333.** (*c*)	**334.** (*d*)	**335.** (*c*)	**336.** (*c*)	**337.** (*d*)	**338.** (*d*)	**339.** (*c*)	**340.** (*d*)
341. (*d*)	**342.** (*a*)	**343.** (*b*)	**344.** (*b*)	**345.** (*c*)	**346.** (*a*)	**347.** (*a*)	**348.** (*b*)	**349.** (*c*)	**350.** (*a*)
351. (*a*)	**352.** (*d*)	**353.** (*b*)	**354.** (*a*)	**355.** (*a*)	**356.** (*c*)	**357.** (*c*)	**358.** (*d*)	**359.** (*a*)	**360.** (*c*)
361. (*a*)	**362.** (*a*)	**363.** (*b*)	**364.** (*c*)	**365.** (*c*)	**366.** (*a*)	**367.** (*d*)	**368.** (*a*)	**369.** (*d*)	**370.** (*a*)
371. (*d*)	**372.** (*a*)	**373.** (*c*)	**374.** (*d*)	**375.** (*b*)	**376.** (*a*)	**377.** (*c*)	**378.** (*c*)	**379.** (*d*)	**380.** (*a*)
381. (*b*)	**382.** (*d*)	**383.** (*d*)	**384.** (*b*)	**385.** (*c*)	**386.** (*c*)	**387.** (*c*)	**388.** (*b*)		

Explanations

281. Module × Diametrical pitch = m × π/p

Where m is module = p/π

So module diametrical pitch = p/π × π/p = 1

282. The path of contact in cycloidal gear is a straight line.

283. Watt governor is a gravity controlled governor.

284. The frictional torque in case of flat pivot bearing for uniform wear ratio is

$$T = \mu WR$$

285. In a double slider crank mechanism there is two revolute pair.

286. Oldham's coupling is an inversion of double slider crank mechanism.

287. Cam size determination is related to the determination of the base circle of the cam.

288. Centrifugal governors are mainly divided in two types they are :

Pendulum type, Loaded type

The Loaded type governors are mainly divided in to two types they are

Dead weight governor

Spring controlled governor

The Hartnell governor is type of spring loaded governor.

289. The **positive clutches** are used when a **positive** drive is required. The simplest type of a **positive clutch** is a jaw or claw **clutch.**

290. Creap can be defined as the slow and progressive deformation of a material with time under constant stress. So creap in belt is due to uneven extension and contraction due to varying load.

291. The two links or elements of a machine, when in contact with each other are said to form a pair. If relative motion between them is completely or successfully constrained, the pair is known as kinematic pair.

292. The governor is used in automobile to regulate the mean speed of an engine, when there are variations in load.

293. Planner , Shaper and Broaching are the example of quick return motion mechanism.

294. For Watt Governor : Height of Governor, $h = g/\omega^2$

And for Porter Governor, $\dfrac{m + \dfrac{M}{2}(1+q)}{m}\dfrac{g}{\omega^2}$

So $h \,\alpha\, 1/\omega^2$

295. The Flank of tooth is the surface of the gear tooth below the pitch surface.

296. Condition for Maximum power transmitted by belt is: $T = 3T_C$ i.e. when power transmitted is maximum tension is equal to three time centrifugal tension.

297. A mechanism with four links is known as simple mechanism, and mechanism with more than four link is known as compound mechanism.

298. When two elements of a pair have surface contact when relative motion take place, the pair formed is known as lower pair. Universal joint is an example of lower pair.

299. In automobiles power is transmitted from gear box to differential through Hooks Joint.

300. The method of obtaining different mechanisms by fixing different links in a kinematic chain, is known as inversion of mechanism.

301. For Slider crank:

Velocity of piston is $v_p = \omega r\left(\sin\theta + \dfrac{\sin 2\theta}{2n}\right)$

Acceleration of piston $a_p = \omega^2 r\left(\cos\theta + \dfrac{\cos 2\theta}{n}\right)$

So when piston is at inner dead centre $\theta = 0$

Velocity = 0 and Acceleration is greater than $\omega^2 r$.

302. Crank, connecting rod, cylinder and piston of steam engine are an example of single slider crank mechanism so it constitute of four links.

304. Velocity = 880m/min = $\dfrac{880}{60}$ = 14.66 m/s

Power transmission by a belt

$= (T_1 - T_2)\,V$ watt.

$$T_1 - T_2 = \frac{22.5\times10^3}{14.66} = 1534.8\text{ N.}$$

308. Given

$T_1 - T_2 = 3000$ N

Speed of belt, V = 15 m/sec

$P = (T_1 - T_2)V$

$= 3000 \times 15 = 45Kw$

329.

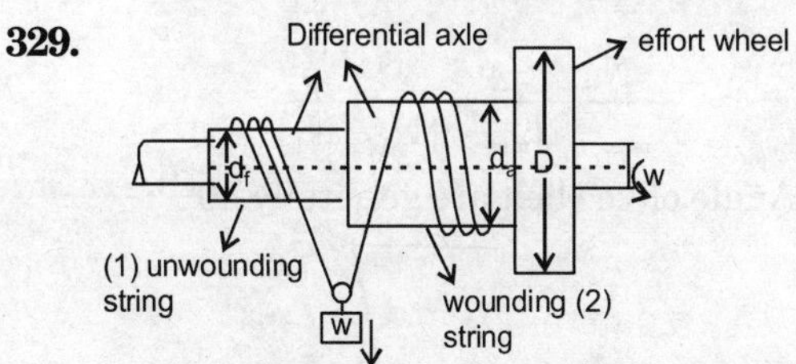

Total unwounding

= Unwounding (1) – wounding (2)

$= \pi d_1 - \pi d_2$

Distance moved by weigh W $= \dfrac{1}{2}\pi(d_1 - d_2)$

Distance moved by effort wheel = πD

$$\text{Velocity ratio} = \frac{\text{Velocity effort wheel}}{\text{Velocity of weight}}$$

$$= \frac{\pi D}{(1/2)\pi(d_1 - d_2)} = \frac{2D}{d_1 - d_2}$$

330.

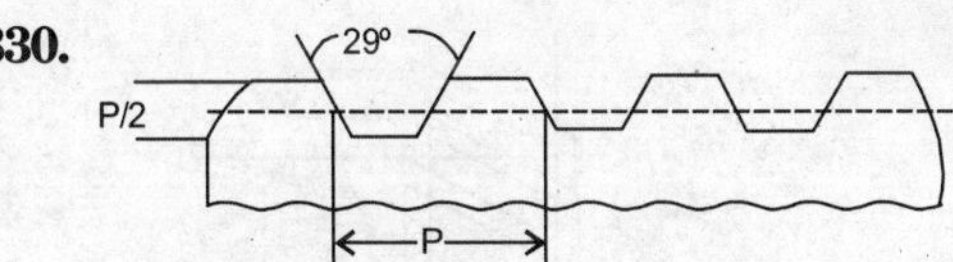

For Acme thread

Thread height

$= \dfrac{1}{2}$(Pitch) and thread angle = 29°

They are generally used in screw cutting lathes

331.

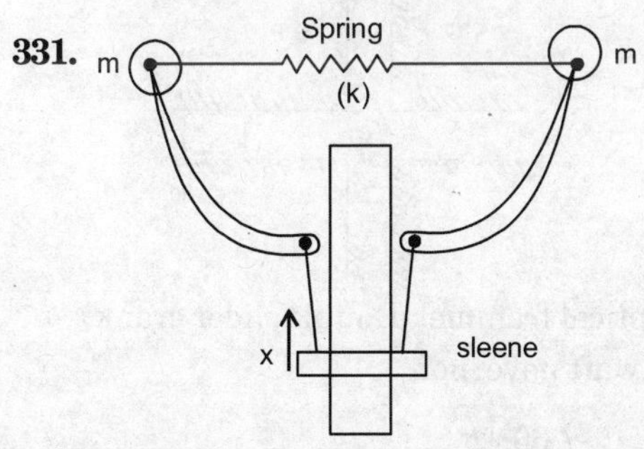

Spring force F = R(x)

For Hartnell governor

$$\boxed{F_{r_1} - F_{r_2} = R(x)}$$

$$1200 - 800 = R(20)$$

Spring stiffness $\boxed{R = 20\ \text{N/m}}$

332. For fly wheel coefficient of steadiness

coefficient of steadiness

$$= \frac{1}{\text{Coeff. of fluctuation of speed}}$$

$$= \frac{N_{mean}}{N_{max} - N_{min}} = \frac{(N_1+N_2)/2}{(N_1 - N_2)}$$

333. Angle of vee belt are generally 40º

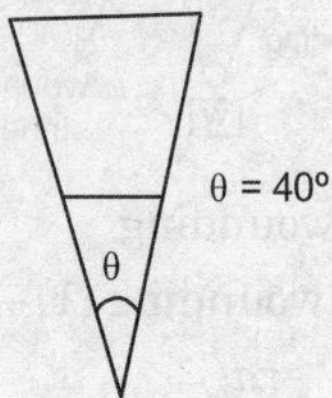

334. Coupling connects parallel shafts which intersect at an angle.

335. When pulley is running the belt in transmitting torque or power from one pulley to another, hence the net tension $(T_1 + T_2)$ is greater than the net tension $(2T_0)$ when pulley are stationary.

$$\text{Power} = (T_1 - T_2)v$$

336. $\tan \alpha = \dfrac{L}{\pi d}$

337. Print 'P' as shown in double slider crank chain or mechanism tracess and ellipse.

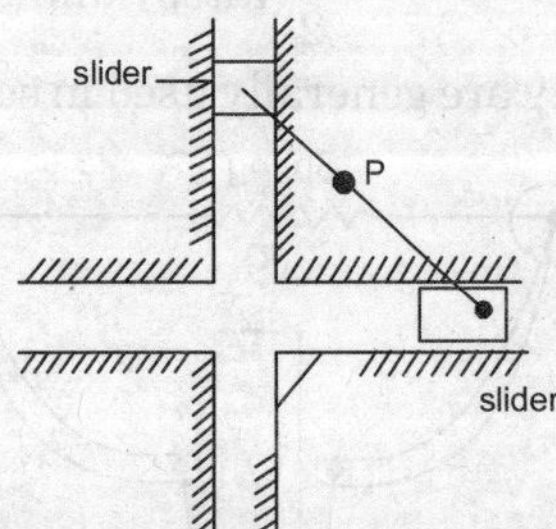

Elliptical frammel (Double slider crank)

338. For watt governor

$$N^2 = \left(\frac{60}{2\pi}\right)\frac{g}{h} \text{ or } w\sqrt{\frac{g}{h}} = 7 \text{ rad/sec.}$$

339. Efficiency of warm gear drives are generally in the range of 50-70%

340. For crushing stress = 2 × (shearing stress)

341.

t → thickness of key
w → width of key
p → load
L → length of key

$$\frac{\text{Load}}{\text{Crushing area}} = 2 \times \left(\frac{\text{load}}{\text{shearing area}}\right)$$

$$\frac{1}{\left(\frac{t}{2} \times L\right)} = 2\left(\frac{1}{(W \times L)}\right), \quad \boxed{t = W}$$

343. Shearing strength of rivet is directly proportional to square of diameter. When diameter has been doubled, the value of shear strength will raise by 4 times [$(2d)^2 = 4.\ d^2$]

344. If S is the smallest link, L is the largest link and P,Q are the intermediate links, then there will be at least one link which will be able to revolve/ rotate if [S + L < P + Q]. The four bar mechanisms that satisfy this criteria, are known as grashofian mechanism. For grashofian mechanism, if S is the ground link, then it is double crank mechanism. Here, S = 5, L = 10, P = 8, Q = 9; S + L = 15 which is less than P + Q = 8 + 9 =17 and S = 5 is the ground link.

346. Quick return motion mechanism is the mechanism in which the Coriolis component of acceleration is being considered.

347. Bevel gears are used to transmit rotary motion between two perpendicular shafts.

348. A differential gear in an automobile is a epicyclic gear train as in this, one gear assembly rotates inside the other gear assembly.

349. Creep in belt drive is due to uneven extensions and contractions of the belt when it passes from tight to slack side.

350. The crank shaft turning in a journal bearing forms a turning pair.

351. The initial contact of helical gear teeth is a point which changes into a line as the teeth come into more engagement.

352. Except chain drives / gear drives, all the above mentioned drives have slip.

353. The contact between cam and follower is to form a higher pair. A higher pair is a kinematic pair in which the links have point or line contact. Ball bearings, cam and follower are examples of higher pair.

354. Needle bearing is antifriction bearing. Antifriction bearings minimize friction by removing any possible sliding between bearing surfaces and replacing all contacts with rolling interfaces. They substitute balls or rollers for a hydrodynamic or hydrostatic fluid film to carry loads with reduced friction. The types of antifriction bearing are grouped by the shape of the rolling element and they are ball bearings, cylindrical roller bearings, tapered roller bearings and needle roller bearings.

355. The teeth of helical gears are inclined to wheel rim. Helical gears are circular gears with angled rather than straight teeth. The angled design of the teeth causes them to engage other gears differently than spur gears, which have straight teeth. As properly matched helical gears come in contact with one another, their level of contact increases gradually, rather than engaging the entire tooth at once.

356. When the speed of governor increases, then height of governor decreases but radius of rotation increases. When speed increases, centrifugal force increases that increased radius of rotation of arm and with this, sleeve moves downward - reducing the height of governor.

The function of governor is to increase the supply of working fluid going to the prime-mover when the load on the prime-mover increases and to decrease the supply when the load decreases so as to keep the speed of the prime-mover almost constant at different loads. The balls and the sleeve rises when the spindle speed increases, and falls when the speed decreases.

374. The maximum load carrying capacity at bearing will increased by 0%

375. Gear teeth made harder to avoid pitting.

376. The centre of gravity of a complex link in a four bar. Chain mechanism will experience no acceleration.

377. Bevel gear are used when axis are intersecting.

378. The included angle for the v-belt is usually 30° to 40°.

379. In railway axle boxes, the bearing used is double row self-aligning ball bearing.

380. Sleeve → move down → Throttle open

Sleeve → move up → Throttle closed.

381. The supply of the working fluid to the engine is controlled by a governor.

382. For high speed engine the cam follower should move with cycloidal motion.

383. The minimum required centre distance of two mating spur gears is decided based on fatigue strength of the gear material.

384. Due to ball compliment, high radial load carrying capacity than bearing without filling shot.

385. A cotter is a form of key used to fasten together two m/c parts which tend to become separate through the action of force → axial force only.

386. Mitre gear → Two similar gear.

$$\frac{W_1}{W_2} = 1$$

387. Frictional resistance is proportional to the speed of rotation.

388. A plain carbon steel designated, by 40C8 means the percentage of carbon content is 0.35 to 0.45.

3

CHAPTER

Thermal Engineering

BASIC CONCEPTS AND LAWS OF THERMODYNAMICS

System, Surrounding and Boundary

A system is defined as qnantity of matter or a region in space chosen for study. Everything external to the system is *surrounding*. Thermodynamic system and surrounding is always separated by the *boundary.*

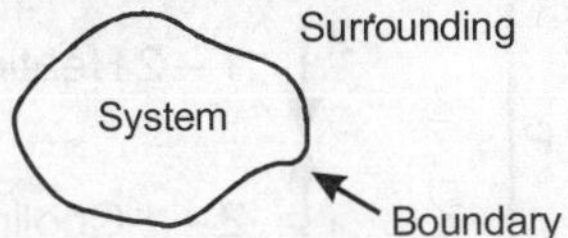

Universe = System + Surrounding

Closed System. The system in which only energy transfer can take place and no mass can cross the boundary.

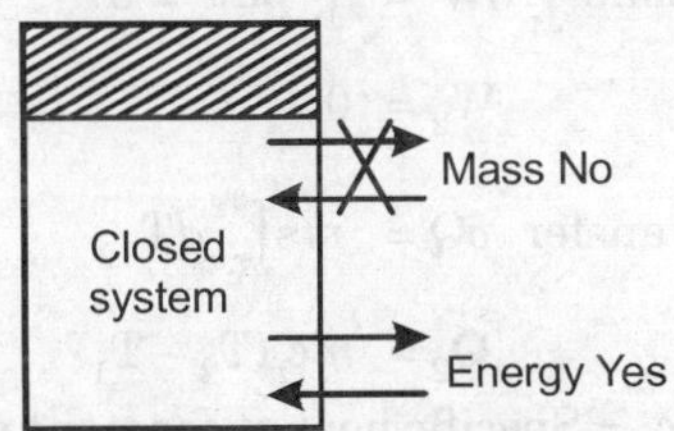

Open System. The system in which both energy and mass can cross the boundary.

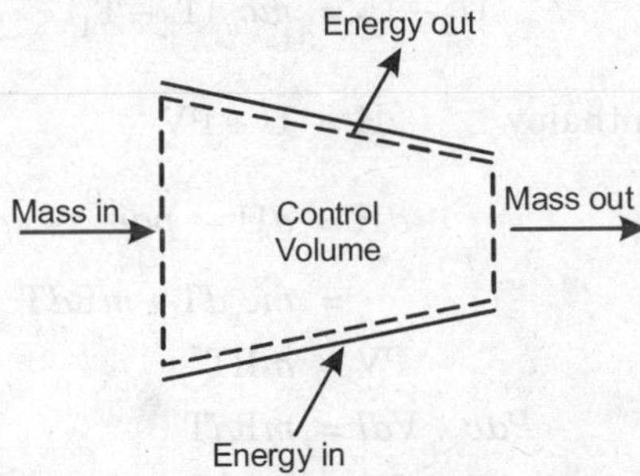

Note : Most of the engineering devices are generally open system.

Isolated System. The system in which neither energy nor mass cross the boundary.

Thermodynamic Properties

Intensive properties are those properties that are independent of mass of a system.

Extensive properties are those whose value depends upon the mass of a system.

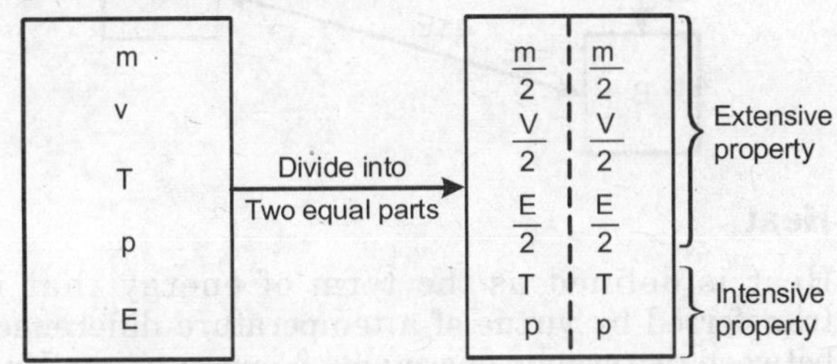

Note : Extensive Property per unit mass is always Intensive property

State Process, and Cycle

Consider a system not undergoing any change and at this point all the properties can be measured and gives us a set of properties, describes **state.**

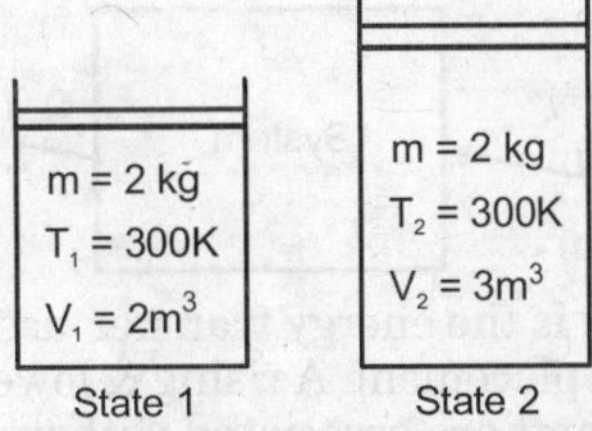

Any change that a system undergoes from one equilibrium state to the another equilibrium state is called ***process***. And series of state through which a system passes is known as ***path of a system***.

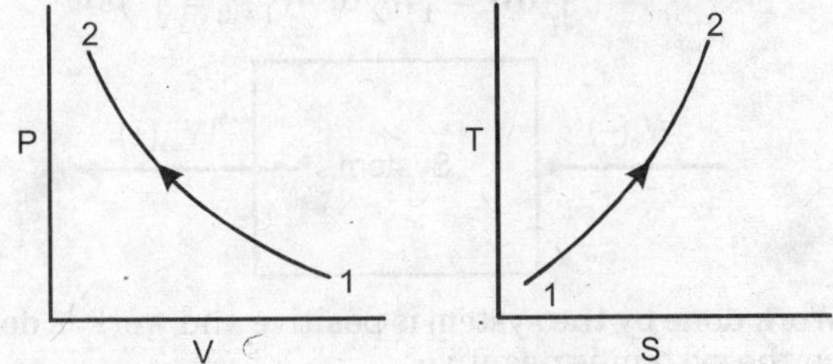

If the initial and end state are identical in a series of processes, it becomes thermodynamic **cycle**.

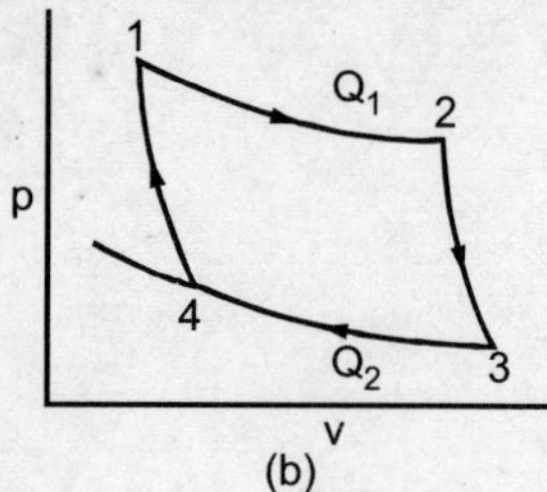

(b)

Zeroth Law of Thermodynamics

If two bodies are in thermal equilibrium (TE) with third body separately then they will also be in thermal equilibrium. This law of thermodynamics defines temperature.

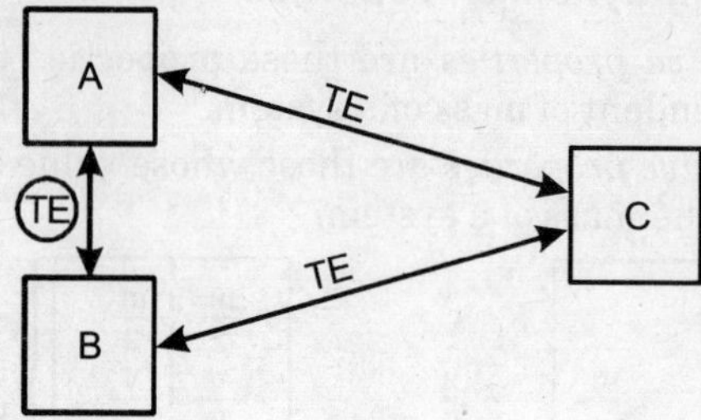

Heat

Heat is defined as the term of energy that is transferred by virtue of a temperature differenace between two system or systems & surrounding. Unit of heat is J. It is a path function and a transient phenomenon.

We represent heat by δQ (Inexact differential) or Q.

$$\delta Q = ms\Delta T \text{ or } Q$$

$$\int_1^2 \delta Q = {}_1Q_2 \text{ or } Q_{1-2}$$

Sign convention for Heat transfer

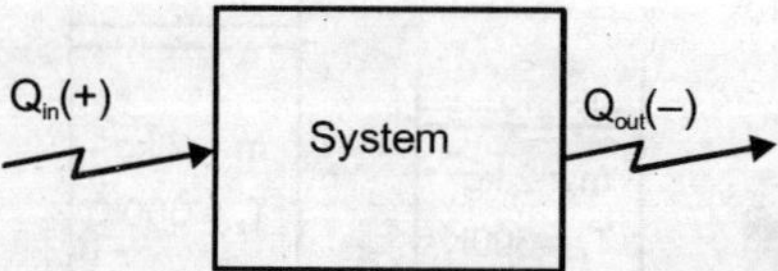

Work. Work is the energy transfer associated with a force and displacement. A rising & lowering of piston, a rotating shaft are associated with work transfers. Unit of work is J. This is also a path function.

We represent work by δW or W

$$\int_1^2 \delta W = {}_1W_2 \text{ or } W_{1-2} = \int_1^2 pdv$$

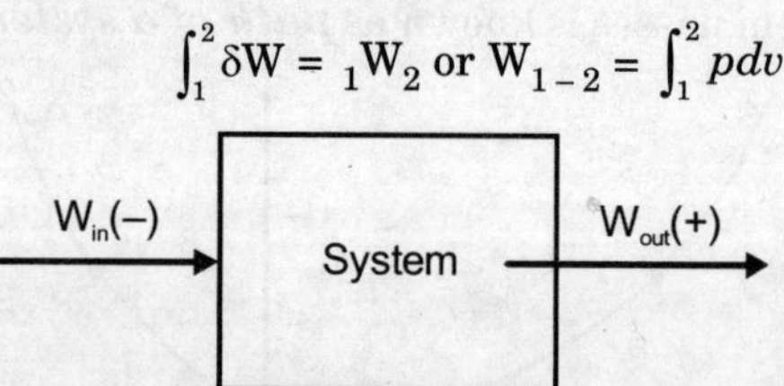

Work done by the system is positive and work is done on the system is negative

First Law of Thermodynamics

State that energy can neither be created nor be destroyed during a process, it can change the forms

Mathematical expression :

$$\delta Q - \delta W = dU \text{ for a process}$$

$$\oint \delta Q = \oint \delta W \text{ for a cycle}$$

Where dU = change in internal energy, unit is J

For an ideal gas the internal energy is the function of temperature only, $U = f(T)$

Enthalpy. Enthalpy is the total energy of a system, this property is introduced to simplify the problem solving.

Enthalpy $\quad H = U + PV$ kJ

Specific enthalpy, $\quad h = u + pv$ kJ/kg

Thermodynamic Processes

1. Constant volume process (or isochoric process)

(*a*) PVT Relation V = constant, $\frac{P}{T}$ = constant.

(*b*) PV diagram

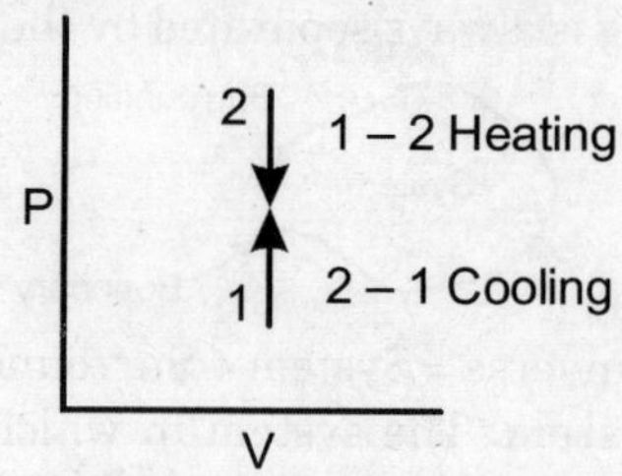

(*c*) Work done $\int_1^2 \delta W = \int_1^2 pdv = 0$

$${}_1W_2 = 0$$

(*d*) Heat transfer $\delta Q = ms\int_{T_1}^{T_2} dT$

$${}_1Q_2 = mc_v(T_2 - T_1)$$

where c_v = Specific heat at constant volume.

(*e*) Internal energy $dU = \delta Q - \delta W$

$$U_2 - U_1 = mc_v(T_2 - T_1) \qquad \because \delta W = 0$$

(*f*) Enthalpy $\quad H = U + PV$

$$dH = dU + \cancel{pdv}^{0} + vdp$$

$$= mc_v dT + mRdT$$

$$PV = mRT$$

$$Pdv + Vdl = mRdT$$

$$H_2 - H_1 = mc_p(T_2 - T_1)$$

$$\because \quad c_p = c_v + R$$

Processes	PVT Relation	PV Diagram	Work done ${}_1W_2$	Heat transfer ${}_1Q_2$	Change in I.E, dU	Change is Enthalpy, dh
Constant Volume Process (Isochoric)	V = const. $\frac{P}{T}$ = const.	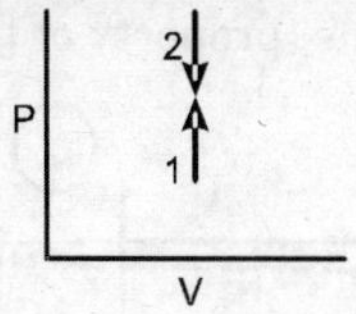	0	$mc_v(T_2 - T_1)$	$mc_v(T_2 - T_1)$	$mc_p(T_2 - T_1)$
Constant Pressure from (Isobaric)	P = const. $\frac{V}{T}$ = const.	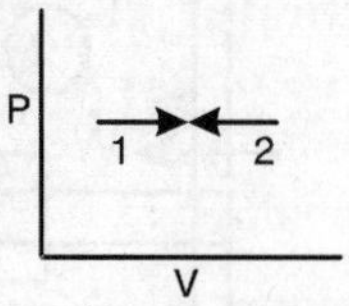	$P(V_2 - V_1)$	$mc_p(T_2 - T_1)$	$mc_v(T_2 - T_1)$	$mc_p(T_2 - T_1)$
Constant Temperature Processes (Isothermal)	PV = const. T = const.	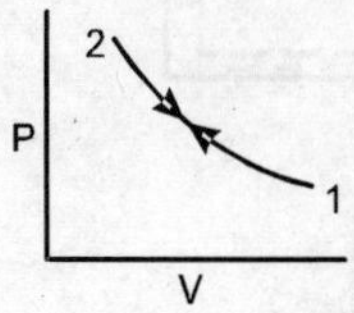	$P_1V_1 \ln \frac{v_2}{v_1}$ $P_1V_1 \ln \frac{P_2}{P_1}$ $mRT_1 \ln \frac{v_2}{v_1}$	$P_1V_1 \ln \frac{v_2}{v_1}$ $P_1V_1 \ln \frac{P_2}{P_1}$	0	$mc_p(T_2 - T_1) = 0$
Reversible Adibatic Process (Isentropic process) Adibatic index = r $r = \frac{c_p}{c_v}$	$PV^\gamma = k$ $TV^{\gamma-1} = k$ $\frac{T}{P^{\frac{\gamma-1}{\gamma}}} = k$	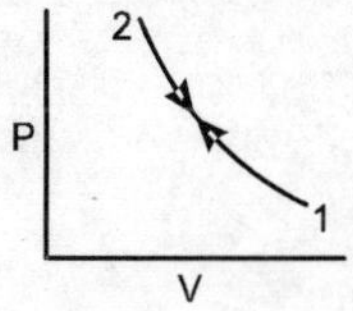	$\frac{P_1V_1 - P_2V_2}{\gamma - 1}$ $\frac{mR(T_1 - T_2)}{r-1}$	0	$mc_v(T_2 - T_1)$	$mc_p(T_2 - T_1)$
Polytropic Process Polytropic index = n $\infty \leq n \geq 0$	$PV^n = k$ $TV^{n-1} = k$ $\frac{T}{P^{\frac{n-1}{n}}} = k$	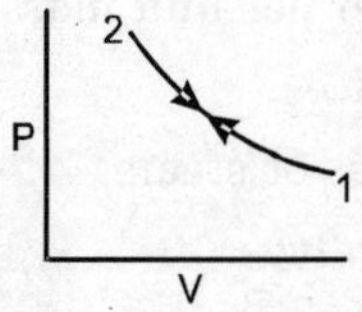	$\frac{P_1V_1 - P_2V_2}{n-1}$ $\frac{mR(T_1 - T_2)}{n-1}$	$\frac{n-r}{n-1} \times dU$	$mc_v(T_2 - T_1)$	$mc_p(T_2 - T_1)$

First law of thermodynamics applied to open system

Steady flow energy system

Steady flow process means at any point in the control volume, property of flow does not change with time.

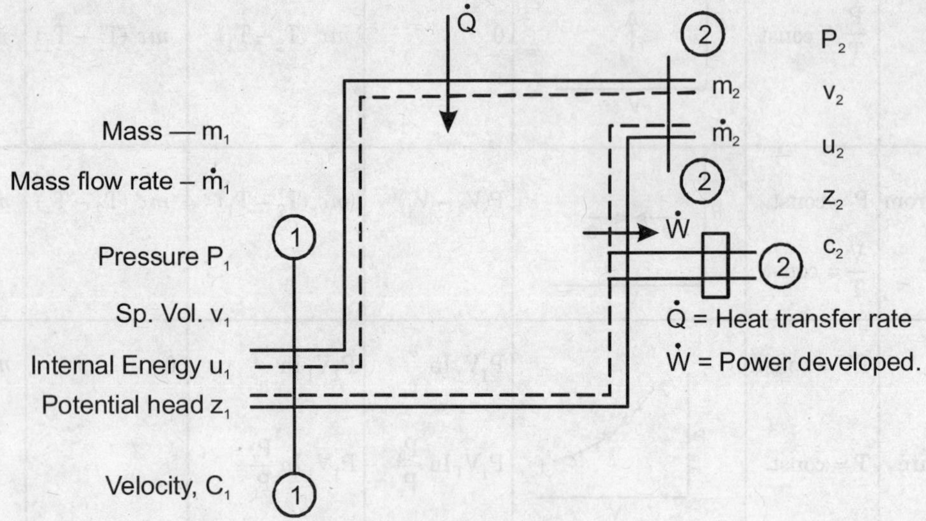

From Ist law of thermodynamics.

$$\text{Energy in} = \text{Energy out}$$

From mass balance equation

$$m_1 = m_2 = m$$

$$\dot{m}_1\left(p_1v_1 + u_1 + gz_1 + \frac{C_1^2}{2}\right) + \dot{Q} = \dot{m}_2\left(p_2v_2 + u_2 + gz_2 + \frac{C_2^2}{2}\right) + \dot{W}$$

We know $p_1v_1 + u_1 = h_1$ & $\dot{m}_1 = \dot{m}_2 = \dot{m}$

$p_2v_2 + u_2 = h_2$, specific enthalpy

In kW units

SFEE $\dot{Q} - \dot{W} = \dot{m}\left[(h_2 - h_1) + \left(\frac{c_2^2 - c_1^2}{2}\right) + g(z_2 - z_1)\right]$

Where $\dot{Q}$ = Heat transfer rate and $\dot{W}$ = Work transfer rate or Power developed

In kJ units

SFEE $Q - W = m\left[(h_2 - h_1) + \left(\frac{c_2^2 - c_1^2}{2}\right) + g(z_2 - z_1)\right]$

Where Q = Work done and W = Heat transfer

In kJ/kg unit, SFEE $q - w = (h_2 - h_1) + \frac{c_2^2 - c_1^2}{2} + g(z_2 - z_1)$

Where w = Work done per unit mass and q = Heat transfer per unit mass.

We normally apply SFEE to the following steady flow devices.

1. Nozzles and diffusers
2. Turbines (gas or steam)
3. Compressors
4. Throttling valves
5. Mixing chambers
6. Heat exchangers
7. Pipe or duct flow

Application of Steady Flow Processes

(i) Nozzle and Diffusor

A nozzle is a device which increases the velocity or kinetic energy of a fluid at the expense of its pressure drop, whereas a diffusor increases the pressure of a fluid at the expense of its kinetic energy

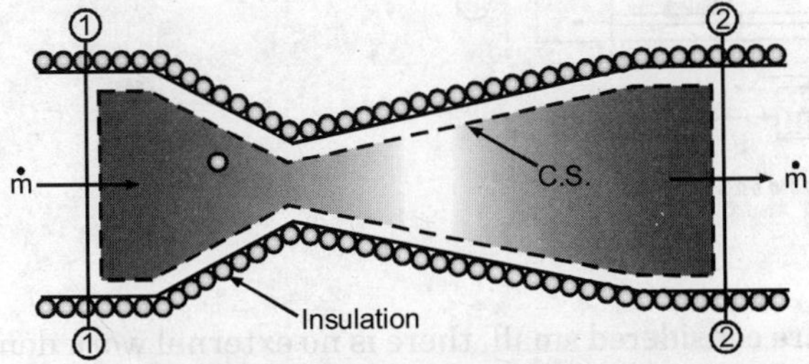

Fig. shows a nozzle which is insulated. The steady flow energy equation of the control surface gives

$$h_1 + \frac{V_1^2}{2} + Z_1 g + q = h_2 + \frac{V_2^2}{2} + Z_2 g + w$$

Here $q = 0$, $w = 0$, and the change in potential energy is zero.

$$h_1 + \frac{V_1^2}{2} = h_2 + \frac{V_2^2}{2} \quad \text{... (i)}$$

The continuity equation gives

$$\dot{m} = \frac{A_1 V_1}{v_1} = \frac{A_2 V_2}{v_2} \quad \text{... (ii)}$$

When the inlet velocity or the *'velocity of approach'* V_1 is very small compared to the exit velocity V_2, then V_1 is neglected and equation *(i)* becomes

$$h_1 = h_2 + \frac{V_2^2}{2}$$

or $\quad V_2 = \sqrt{2 \times 1000 (h_1 - h_2)}\ m/s$

where $(h_1 - h_2)$ is in kJ/kg.

(ii) Throttling Device

When a fluid flows through a constricted passage, like a partially opened valve, an orifice, or a porous plug, there is an appreciable drop in pressure, and the flow is said to be throttled. Figure shows the process of throttling by a partially opened valve on a fluid flowing in an insulated pipe.

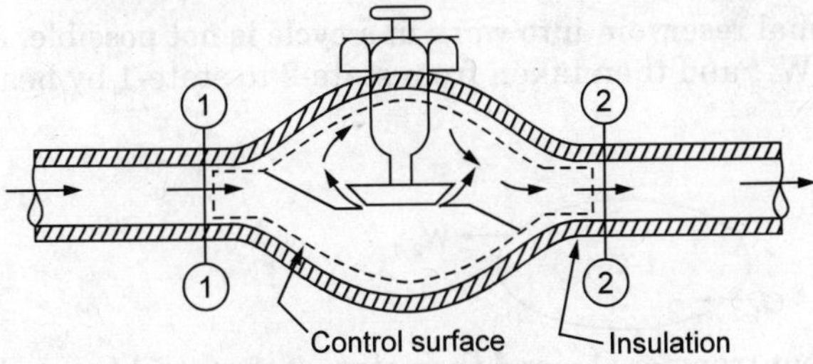

Fig. Flow through a valve

In the steady-flow energy equation,

$$q = 0, \qquad w = 0$$

and the changes in P.E. are very small and ignored. Thus the steady flow energy equation reduces to

$$h_1 + \frac{V_2^2}{2} = h_2 + \frac{V_2^2}{2}$$

Often the pipe velocities in throttling are so low that the kinetic energy terms are also negligible.

$$\therefore \quad h_1 = h_2$$

or enthalpy of the fluid before throttling is equal to the enthalpy of the fluid after throttling.

(iii) Turbine and Compressor

Turbines and engines give positive power output, whereas compressors and pumps require power input.

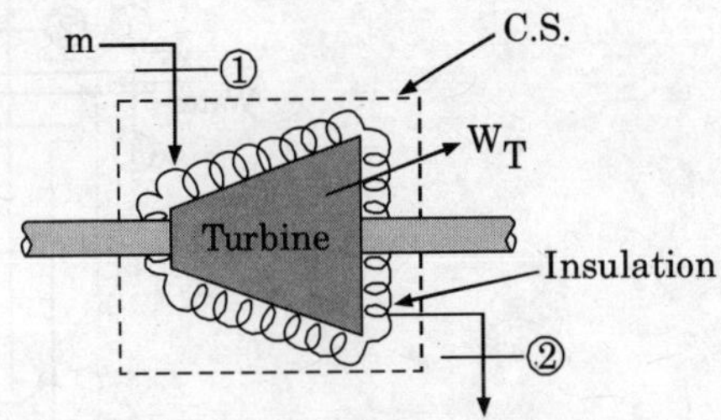

Fig. Flow through a turbine

For a turbine (Fig.) which is well insulated, the flow velocities are often small, and the kinetic energy terms can be neglected. The steady flow energy equation then becomes

$$h_1 = h_2 + w$$

or $\quad w = (h_1 - h_2)$

It is seen that in turbines work is done by the fluid at the expense of its enthalpy.

Similarly, for an adiabatic pump or compressor, work is done upon the fluid and W is negative. Thus the steady flow energy equation becomes

$$h_1 = h_2 - \frac{W}{m}$$

or $\quad \frac{W}{m} = h_2 - h_1$

In compressor the enthaply of the fluid increases by the amount of work input.

(iv) Heat exchanger

A heat exchanger is a device in which heat is transferred from one fluid to another.

The steady flow energy equation for the cross-section gives

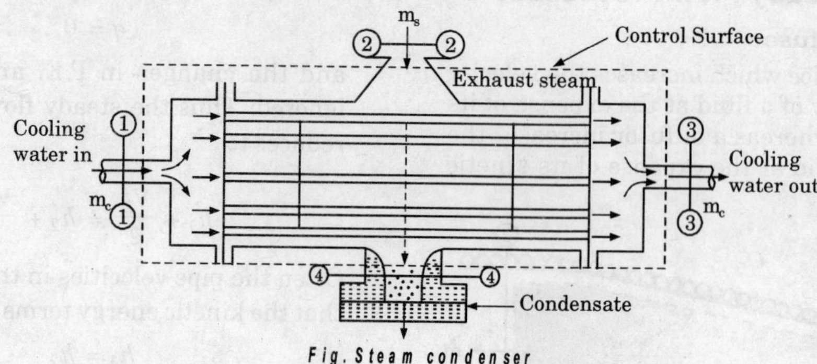

Fig. Steam condenser

$$m_c h_1 + m_s h_2 = m_c h_3 + m_s h_4$$

or $$m_s (h_2 - h_4) = m_c (h_3 - h_1)$$

Here the kinetic energy and potential energy terms are considered small, there is no external work done, and *energy exchange* in the form of heat is confined only between the two fluids, *i.e.*, there is no external heat interaction or heat loss.

(v) Steam desuperheater

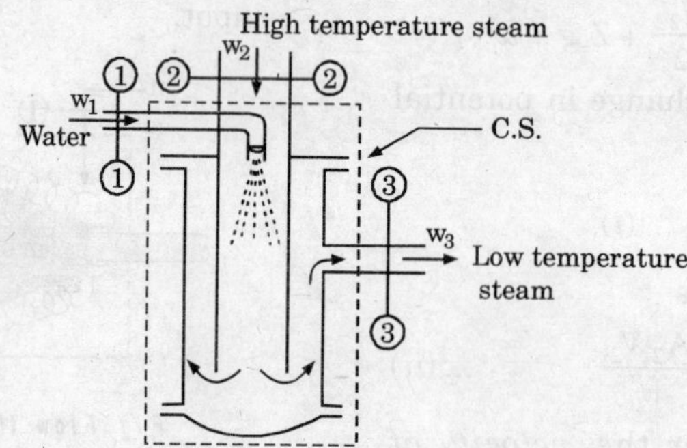

Figure shows a *steam desuperheater* where the temperature of the superheated steam is reduced by spraying water. If w_1, w_2 and w_3 are the mass flow of the injected water, of the steam entering, and of the steam leaving, respectively, and h_1, h_2 and h_3 are the corresponding enthalpies, and if K.E. and P.E. terms are neglected as before, the steady flow energy equation becomes

$$w_1 h_1 + w_2 h_2 = w_3 h_3$$

and the mass balance gives

$$w_1 + w_2 = w_3$$

SECOND LAW OF THERMODYNAMICS

The first law of thermodynamic states that a certain energy balance will hold when a system undergoes a change of state or a thermodynamic process. But it does not provide any information on whether that change of state or the process is at all feasible or not. *The second law of thermodynamic provides the criterion to the probability of various processes.*

Joule's experiments shows that when energy supplied to a system in the form of work, then it can be converted in heat as follows :

Work transfer → Internal energy increase → Heat transfer

The complete conversion of heat taken from a single thermal reservoir, into work in a cycle is not possible. A system is taken from state-1 to state-2 by work transfer $W_{1\text{-}2}$ and then taken from state-2 to state-1 by heat transfer $Q_{2\text{-}1}$ to complete the cycle.

then $$W_{1\text{-}2} = Q_{2\text{-}1}$$

1–2–1 $\quad Q_{2-1}$, W_{1-2} $\qquad$ 1–2–1 $\quad W_{2-1}$, Q_{1-2}

But when the system is taken from state-1 to state-2 by heat transfer $Q_{1\text{-}2}$ and then state-2 to state-1 by work transfer $W_{2\text{-}1}$ to complete the cycle then it is always found that

$$Q_{1\text{-}2} > W_{2\text{-}1}$$

Hence heat can not be converted completely and continuously into work. Work is said to be high grade energy and heat a low grade energy. The complete conversion of low grade energy to high grade energy in a cycle is not possible.

Heat Engine Cycle

Cyclic heat engine works under a thermodynamic cycle in which there is a net heat transfer to the system and net work transfer from the system. The system which executes under this thermodynamic cycle is called a heat engine.

Let Q is heat transferred to the system, W_E is work done by the system, the work W_C is done upon the system then heat Q_2 is rejected from the system as shown in Fig. *(a)*.

The net heat transfer in a cycle to either of the heat engines

$$Q_{net} = Q_1 - Q_2 \qquad ...(i)$$

(a) Heat engine cycle performed by a closed system undergoing four successive energy interactions with the surroundings

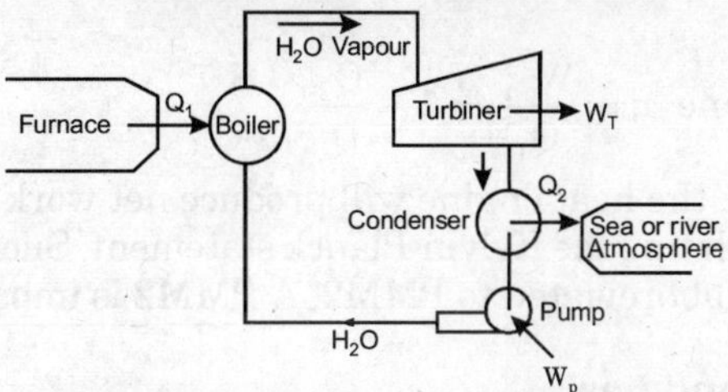

(b) Heat engine cycle performed by a steady flow system interacting with the surroundings as shown

and the net work transfer in a cycle

From Fig *(a)* $\quad W_{net} = W_T - W_P \quad ...$ *(ii)*

From Fig *(b)* $\quad W_{net} = W_E - W_C$

By the first law of thermodynamics, we have

$$\sum_{cycle} Q = \sum_{cycle} W$$

$$\therefore \quad Q_{net} = W_{net}$$

or $\quad Q_1 - Q_2 = W_T - W_P \quad ...$ *(iii)*

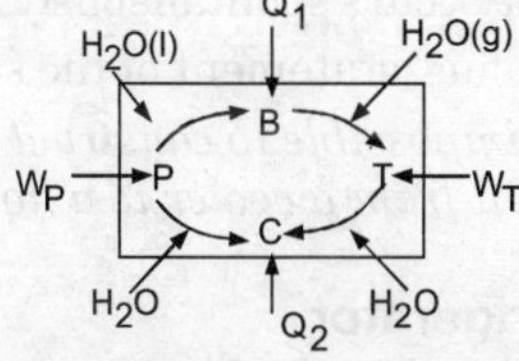

Fig. Cyclic heat engine with energy interactions represented in a block diagram

Figure represents a cyclic heat engine in the form of a block diagram indicating the various energy interactions during a cycle. Boiler (B), turbine (T), condenser (C), and pump (P), all four together constitute a heat engine.

The function of heat engine cycle is to produce work continuously at the expense of heat input to the system, the efficiency of heat engine is

$$\eta = \frac{\text{Network output of the cycle}}{\text{Total heat output to the cycle}} = \frac{W_{net}}{Q_1} \qquad ...(iv)$$

From equations *(i)*, *(ii)*, *(iii)*, and *(iv)*, we have

$$\eta = \frac{W_{net}}{Q_1} = \frac{W_T - W_P}{Q_1} = \frac{Q_1 - Q_2}{Q_1} = 1 - \frac{Q_2}{Q_1}$$

This is also known as the *thermal efficiency of a heat engine cycle.*

Heat Reservoirs

A *heat reservoir* is defined as a body of infinite heat capacity, which is capable of absorbing or rejecting an unlimited quantity of heat without suffering any change in its temperature.

Let Q_1 is the heat transferred to the system from source Q_2 is heat rejected from system

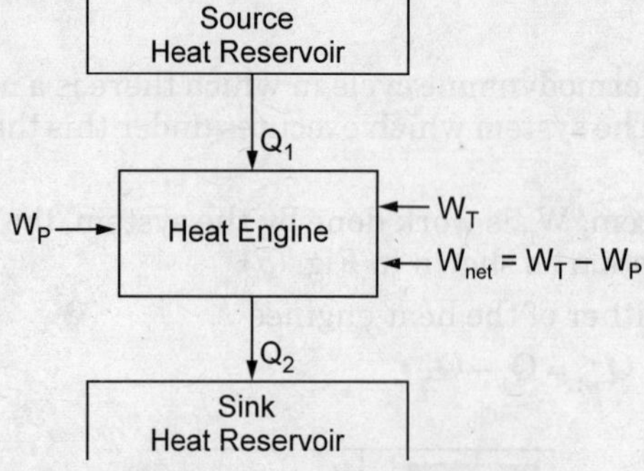

Figure show cyclic heat engine exchanging heat with source and a sink and producing

$$W_{net} = W_T - W_P$$

Kelvin-planck Statement of Second Law

The *Kelvin-Planck* statement of the second law states :

It is impossible for a heat engine to produce net work in a complete cycle if it exchanges heat only with bodies at a single fixed temperature.

$$\text{Efficiency of a heat engine } \eta = \frac{W_{net}}{Q_1} = 1 - \frac{Q_2}{Q_1}$$

If $Q_2 = 0$ (*i.e.*, $W_{net} = Q_1$, or $\eta = 1.00$), the heat engine will produce net work in a complete cycle by exchanging heat with only one reservoir, thus violating the Kelvin-Planck statement. Such a heat engine is called a *perpetual motion machine of the second kind,* abbreviated to PMM2. A PMM2 is impossible.

Clausius' Statement of the Second Law

Heat always flows from a body at a higher temperature to a body at a lower temperature. The reverse process never occurs spontaneously.

Clausius' statement of the second law states :

It is impossible to construct a device which, operating in a cycle, will produce no effect other than the transfer of heat from a cooler to a hotter body.

Refrigerator

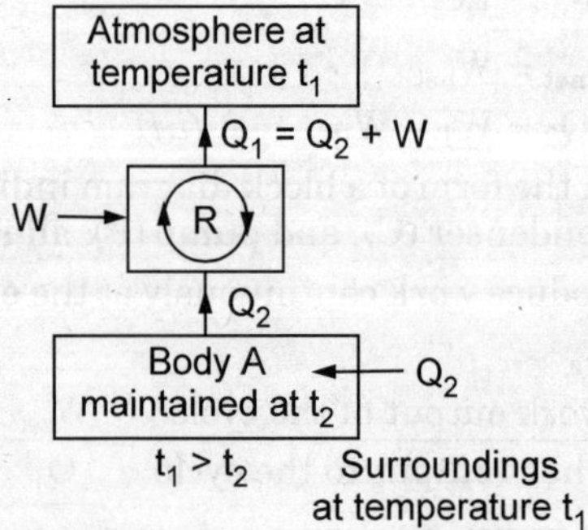

A *refrigerator* is a device which, operating in a cycle, maintains a body at a temperature lower than the temperature of the surroundings. Let the body A (Fig.) be maintained at t_2, which is lower than the ambient temperature t_1. Even though A is insulated, there will always be heat leakage Q_2 into the body from the surroundings by virtue of the temperature difference. In body A, Q_2 and W are of primary interest. there is a performance parameter in a refrigerator cycle, called the *coefficient* of performance abbreviated to COP, is defined as

$$\text{COP} = \frac{\text{Desired effect}}{\text{Work input}} = \frac{Q_2}{W}$$

since

$$Q_1 = Q_2 + W$$

$$\therefore \quad [\text{COP}]_{ref} = \frac{Q_2}{Q_1 - Q_2} \quad \text{... (i)}$$

Heat Pump

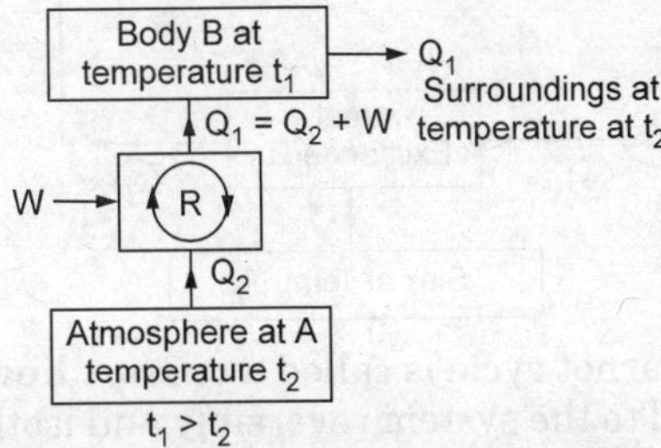

A heat pump is a device which operating in a cycle, maintains a body say B at a temperature higher than the temperature of the surroundings. Due to temperature difference, there will be heat leakage Q_1 from the body to the surroundings.

$$\text{COP} = \frac{Q_1}{W}$$

$$\therefore \quad [\text{COP}]_{H.P} = \frac{Q_1}{Q_1 - Q_2} \quad \text{... (ii)}$$

From equations *(i)* and *(ii)*, we get

$$[\text{COP}]_{H.P.} = [\text{COP}]_{ref.} + 1$$

The COP of a heat pump is greater than COP of a refrigerator by unity. At steady state, the electrical energy W supplied to an electric heater is dissipated as heat to the space, but when supplied to a heat pump dissipates Q_1 (>W) giving a thermal advantage.

For heat to flow from a cooler to a hotter body, W cannot be zero, and hence, the COP (both for refrigerator and heat pump) cannot be infinity. Therefore

$$W > 0,$$

and

$$\text{COP} < \infty.$$

Carnot Cycle

Carnot cycle is an ideal cycle in which all the processes constituting a reversible cycle.

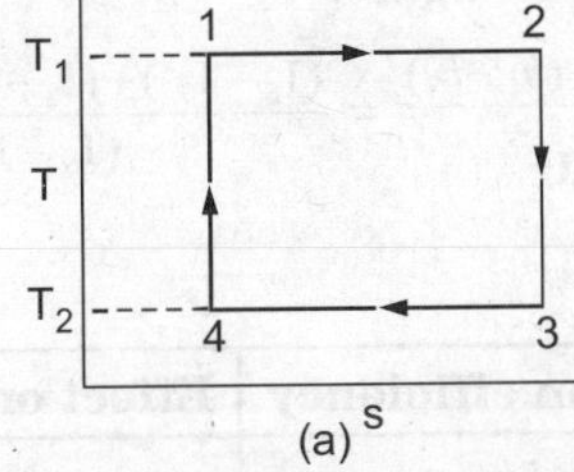

(a)

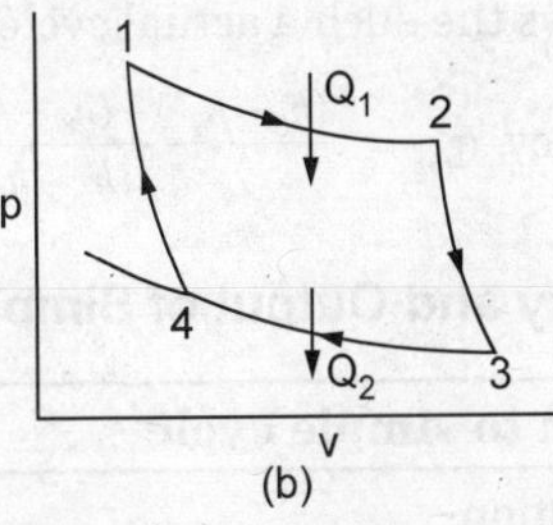

(b)

(i) **Reversible isothermal process** (1-2) in which heat Q_1 enters the system at temperature T_1 reversibly from a constant temperature at T_1. The internal energy of the system increases.

(ii) **Reversible adiabatic process** (2-3) in which work W_E is done by the system adiabatically and reversibly at the expense of its internal energy and the temperature of the system decreases from T_1 to T_2, the internal energy decreases during this process.

(iii) **Reversible isothermal process** (3-4)-in which heat Q_2 is rejected at constant temperature. In this process the internal energy of the system further decreases.

(iv) **Reversible adiabatics process** (4-1) in which work W_P is done upon the system reversibly and adiabatically and the internal energy of the system increases, and the temperature rises from T_2 to T_1.

Carnot Heat Engine

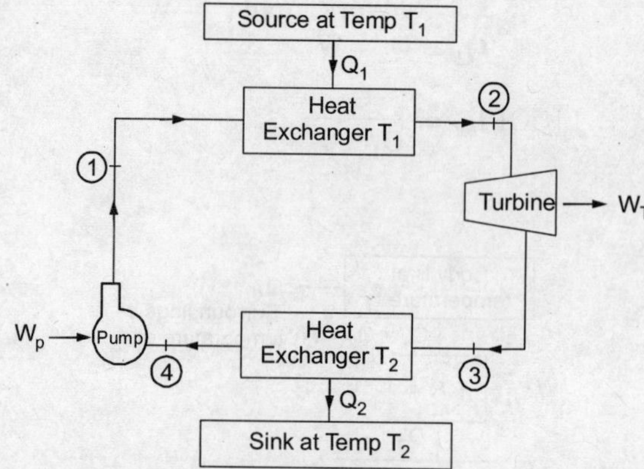

A *cyclic heat* engine operating on the carnot cycle is called a **carnot heat engine.** The carnot cycle is shown in the figure. The heat Q_1 is transferred to the system reversibly and isothermally at T_1 in the heat exchanger. The work is done by the system reversibly and adiabatically in the turbine, then heat Q_2 is transferred from the system reversibly and isothermally at temperature T_2 in the heat exchanger, and W_P is done upon the system reversibly and adiabatically by the pump.

Reserved Heat Engine

Since all the processes are reversible in the carnot heat engine, it is possible to imagine that the processes are individually reversed and carried out in the reversed order

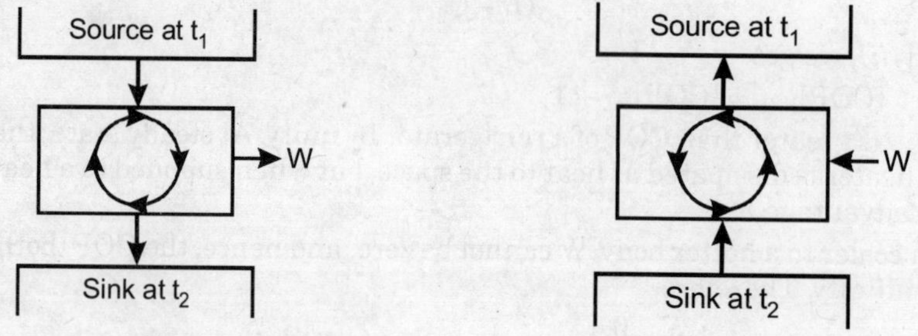

(a) Carnot heat Engine *(b) Reversed heat engine*

The heat pump and refrigerator are applied to the reversed heat engine.

Actual Brayton Cycle with Intercooling Reheat and Intercooling

1-2'-3'-4'-6-7'-8-9'10' shows the such a actual cycle as shown in the figure.

$$\text{Actual thermal efficiency, } \eta_{tha} = \frac{(h_6 - h_7') + (h_8 - h_9') - (h_2' - h_1) - (h_4' - h_3)}{(h_6 - h_5') + (h_8 - h_7')} = \frac{(T_6 - T_7') + (T_8 - T_2') - (T_9' - T_1) - (T_4' - T_3)}{(T_6 - T_5') + (T_8 - T_7')}$$

Improvent in Efficiency and Output of Simple Cycle

Addition to simple cycle	Effect on efficiency	Effect on output
1. Regeneration	+ 50%	Nil
2. Intercooling	– 6.5%	+ 10.2%
3. Reheat	– 10.4%	+ 24.5%
4. Reheat + Regeneration	66.7%	+ 24.0%
5. Intercooling + Regeneration	68%	+ 10.2%
6. Reheat + Intercooling	– 18.2%	+ 34.7%
7. Reheat + Intercooling Regeneration	+ 80%	34.7%

IC ENGINE

1. Air Standard Cycle

1. Working substance is air
2. Cycles are mathematical models
3. Used in I.C. Engine and Gasturbine

Assumption

1. It follows the law pV = mRT
2. The physical constants of the working medium are the same as of air at standard ambient i.e., molecular weight= 29, C_p = 1.005, C_v = 0.718 and r = 1.4
3. Constant specific heats C_p and C_v does not through out the cycle.
4. The working medium does not under go any chemical change through out the cycle.
5. Compresion and expansion processes are reversible adiabatic i.e., there is no gain and loss of entropy.
6. The operation of engine is frictionless.
7. The K.E and P.E of the working fluid air negligible.

Air Standard Cycle Parameters

1. Air standard Efficiency (or Thermal Efficiency)

$$\eta_{th} = \frac{W}{H.S} = \frac{\text{Net W.D}}{\text{Heat supplied to the system}}$$

2. Specific Work done (or work transfer)

It is the W.D per unit mass of working substance *i.e.*, size of plant needed to perform the task (or job)

$$w = \frac{W}{m} = \frac{W.D}{\text{mass}} \text{ where W.D is work done}$$

3. Specific Air consumption

It is the reverse of specific W.D = $\frac{m}{W} = \frac{\text{mass}}{W.D}$

4. Work ratio (r_w) $\quad r_w = \frac{\text{Net W.D in the cycle}}{+ve\text{ W.D in a cycle}}$

Note: Ideal cycle have high η_{th}, wigh w and high r_w.

Cycles

1. Otto cycle (constant volume cycle) (used for Petrol engine or Gas Engine)
2. Diesel cycle (constant pressure cycle) (used for slow speed Diesel Engine)
3. Dual cycle (mixed or limited pressure cycles) (used for high speed disel engine) Dual combustion cycle
4. Brayton cycle (Jouble cycle) (used for gas tasbine plants)

2. Otto Cycle

A very common type of internal combustion engine is the spark ignition used in automobile. The otto cycle is the air standard cycle of such an engine.

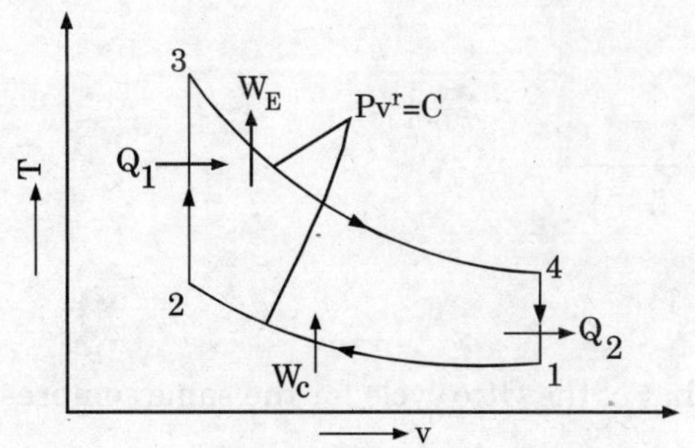

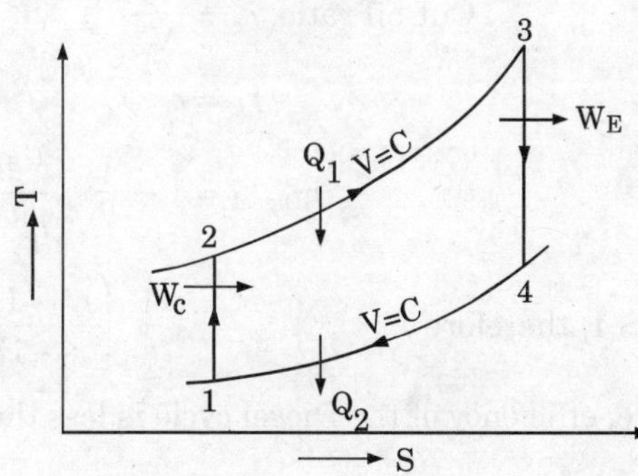

Let m be the fixed mass of air undergoing the cycle of operations

$$\text{Heat supplied, } Q_1 = Q_{2-3} = m\,c_v\,(T_3 - T_2)$$

$$\text{Heat rejected, } Q_2 = Q_{4-1} = m\,c_v\,(T_4 - T_1)$$

$$\text{Efficiency, } \eta = 1 - \left(\frac{V_2}{V_1}\right)^{\gamma-1} \quad \text{or} \quad \eta_{otto} = 1 - \frac{1}{r_k^{\gamma-1}}$$

where r_k = compression ratio and given by

$$r_k = \frac{\text{Volume at the beginning of compression}}{\text{Volume at the end of compression}} = \frac{V_1}{V_2}$$

Efficiency of the air standard Otto cycle is thus a function of compression ratio only. The higher the compression ratio, the higher the efficiency.

3. Diesel Cycle

It consist of two reversible adibatics one reversible isobar *i.e.* constant pressure and one reversible isochore, *i.e.* constant-volume process. Air is compressed in process 1-2. Heat is then added to it from an external source at constant pressure process (2-3). Air expends in process (3-4). Then heat is rejected at constant volume in process (4-1) and cycle repeats itself.

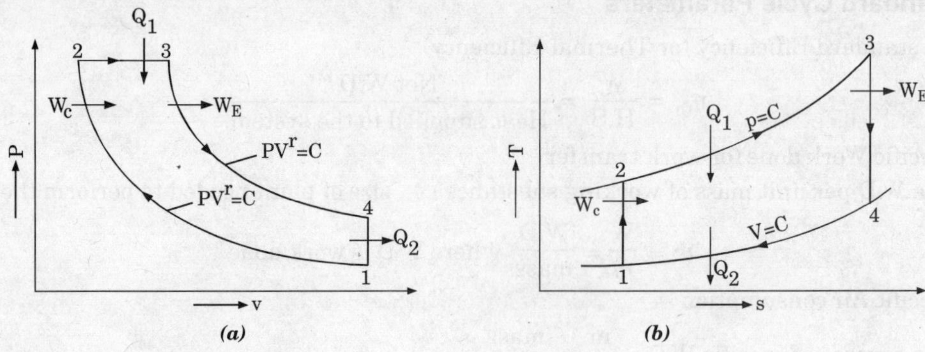

(a) *(b)*

Consider m kg of air in the cylinder.

$$\text{Heat supplied, } Q_1 = Q_{2-3} = m\,c_p\,(T_3 - T_2)$$

$$\text{Heat rejected, } Q_2 = Q_{4-1} = m\,c_v\,(T_4 - T_1)$$

$$\text{Efficiency, } \eta = 1 - \frac{Q_2}{Q_1} = 1 - \frac{m\,c_v\,(T_4 - T_1)}{m\,c_p\,(T_3 - T_2)} = 1 - \frac{T_4 - T_1}{\gamma\,(T_3 - T_2)}$$

Efficiency may be expressed in terms of any two of the following three ratios.

$$\text{Compression ratio, } r_k = \frac{V_1}{V_2}$$

$$\text{Expansion ratio, } r_e = \frac{V_4}{V_3}$$

$$\text{Cut-off ratio, } r_c = \frac{V_3}{V_2}$$

We know,

$$r_k = r_e \cdot r_c$$

$$\eta_{Diesel} = 1 - \frac{1}{\gamma} \cdot \frac{1}{r_k^{\gamma-1}} \cdot \frac{r_c^{\gamma} - 1}{r_c - 1}$$

Since $r_c > 1$, therefore

$$\frac{1}{\gamma}\left(\frac{r_c^{\gamma} - 1}{r_c - 1}\right) > 1$$

Therefore, efficiency of the Diesel cycle is less than that of the Otto cycle for the same compression ratio.

4. Limited Pressure Cycle, Mixed Cycle or Dual Cycle

Heat is added reversibly partly at constant volume and partly at constant pressure. Remaining cycle is same as diesel cycle.

$$\text{Heat supplied,}\quad Q_1 = m\,c_p\,(T_3 - T_2) + m\,c_p\,(T_4 - T_3)$$

$$\text{Heat rejected,}\quad Q_2 = m\,c_v\,(T_5 - T_1)$$

$$\text{Efficiency,}\quad \eta = 1 - \frac{Q_2}{Q_1} = 1 - \frac{m\,c_v\,(T_5 - T_1)}{m\,c_v\,(T_3 - T_2) + m\,c_p\,(T_4 - T_3)}$$

$$= 1 - \frac{T_5 - T_1}{(T_3 - T_2) + \gamma\,(T_4 - T_3)}$$

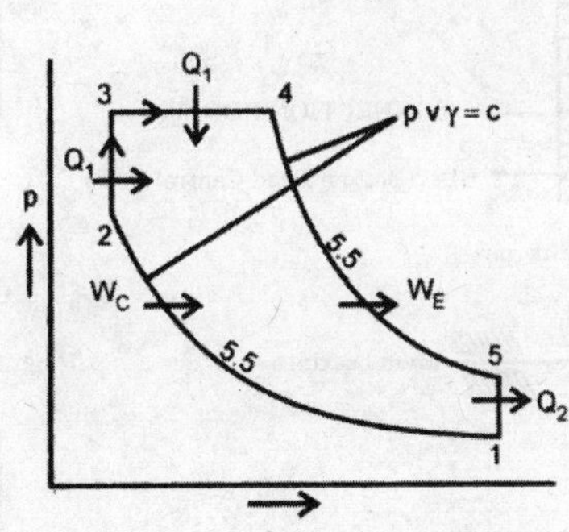

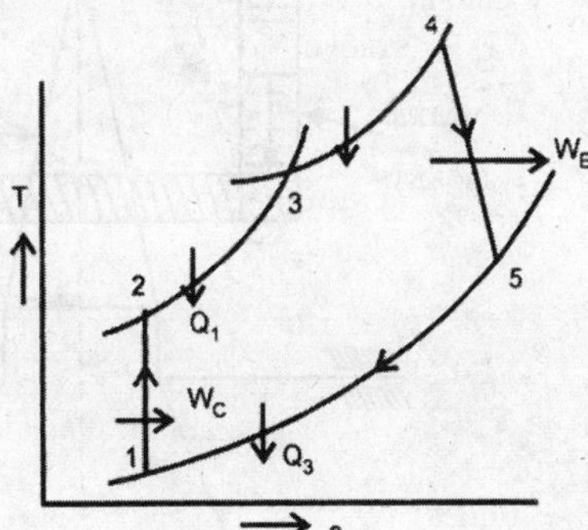

Efficiency of the cycle can be expressed in terms of the following ratios

$$\text{Compression ratio,}\quad r_k = \frac{V_1}{V_2}$$

$$\text{Expansion ratio,}\quad r_e = \frac{V_5}{V_4}$$

$$\text{Cut-off ratio,}\quad r_c = \frac{V_4}{V_3}$$

$$\text{Constant volume pressure ratio,}\quad r_p = \frac{p_3}{p_2}$$

$$\therefore\quad r_k = r_c \cdot r_e$$

$$\therefore\quad \eta_{Dual} = 1 - \frac{1}{r_k^{\gamma-1}}\;\frac{r_p \cdot r_e - 1}{r_p - 1 + \gamma r_p\,(r_c - 1)}$$

Q For the same compression ratio and for the same amount of heat supplied, discuss the η of Otto cycle, diesel cycle and Dual cycle.

$$\eta = \frac{W.D}{H.S} = \frac{H.S - H.R}{H.S} = 1 - \frac{H.R}{H.S}$$

$$\delta_1 = T.ds$$

H.S = Area under 2 – 3

= Area under 2 – 3′

= Area under 2 – 3‴

1 – 2 – 3 – 4 – 1 → Otto cycle

1 – 2 – 3′ – 4′ – 1 → Diesel cycle

1 – 2 – 3′ – 3‴ – 4‴ – 1 → Dual cycle

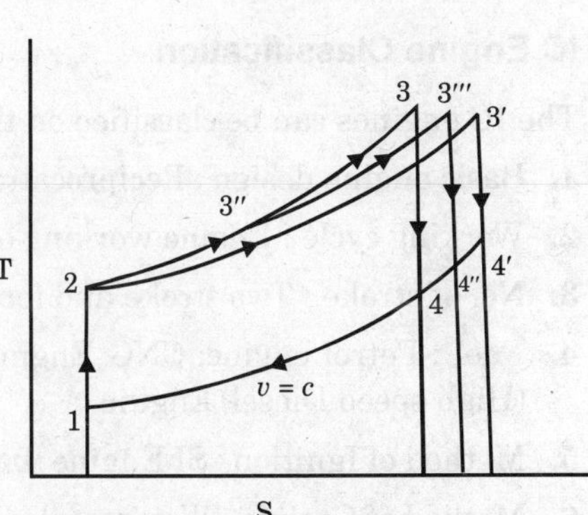

H.S is same in all 3 cycles

And below If H.R is less, then η will be more from the curve

From the curve

Otto cycle – Area under 1 – 4 is heat rejection which is less than other cycles. So η of Otto cycle will be more.

IInd dual cycle → H.R less than Diesel cycle but more then Otto cycle

$$\eta_{otto} > \eta_{Dual} > \eta_{Diesel}$$

I.C. Engine

Engine Compoents and Basic Engine Nomenclatures (Single Cylinder)

Vertical Engine

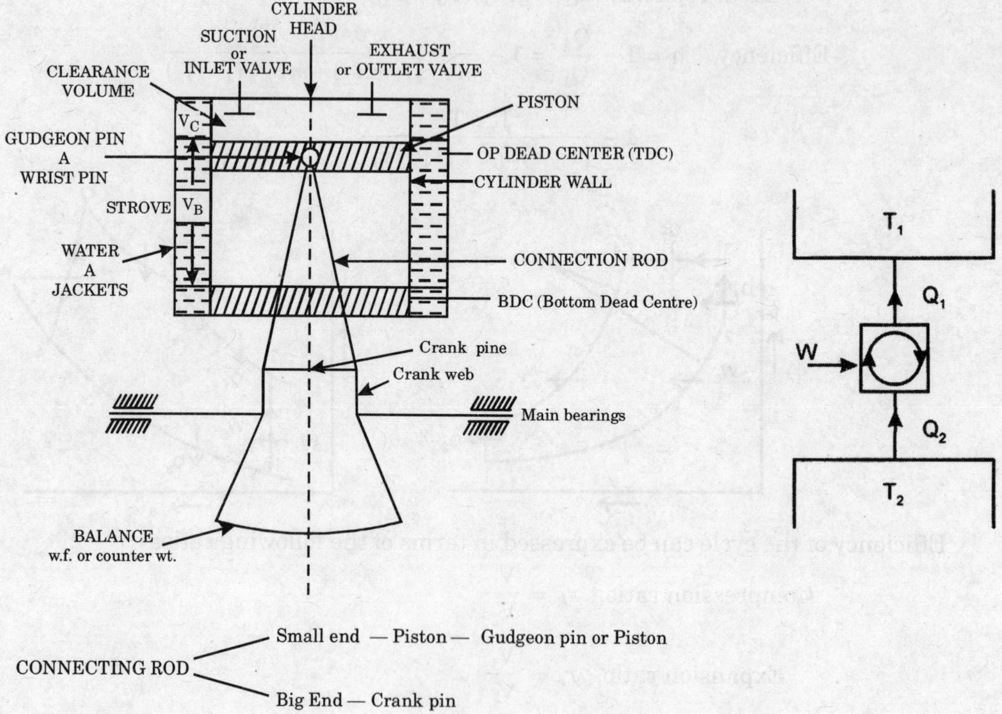

Horizontal Engine

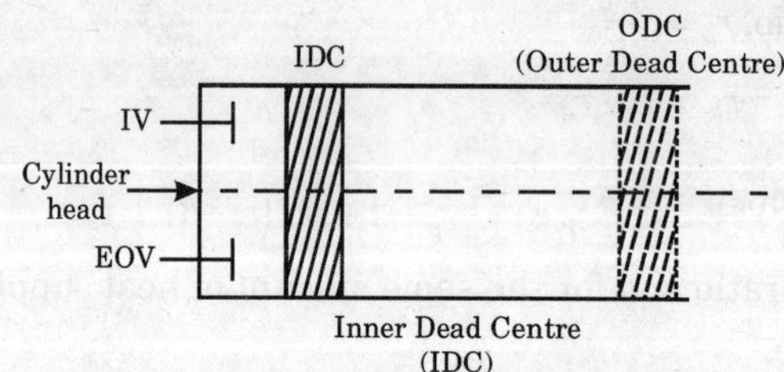

IC Engine Classification

The IC engines can be classified on the basis of cycle operation in cylinder, type of fluid, type of ignition etc.

1. Basic engine design : Reciprocating engines, Rotary engines
2. Working cycle : Engine working on Otto cycle (SI engines), working Diesel cycle (C I Engine)
3. No. of stroke : Two stroke and four stroke Engine
4. Fuel : Petrol engine; CNG Engine, LPG (Liquefed Petroleum Gas) Engine, LDO (light Diesel oil), HSD (High speed Diesel) Engine
5. Method of Ignition : SI Engine (battery ignition), CI Engine (Compression Ignition)
6. Method of Cooling : Water cooled and Air cooled Engine
7. Cylinder arrangement : Vertical Engine, Horizontal Engine

FOUR STROKE PETROL ENGINE

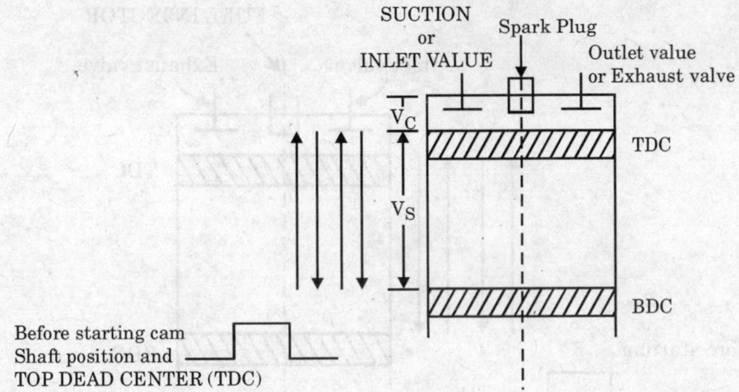

1. SUCTION STROKE

INLET valve open (or suction value pens)

TDC → BDC, Charge (Petrol and air) is admited and the carge is supplied by Carburettor.

BDC, Suction valve gets closed.

$\frac{1}{2}$ REV or 180° rotation of shaft

2. COMPRESSION STROKE BDC

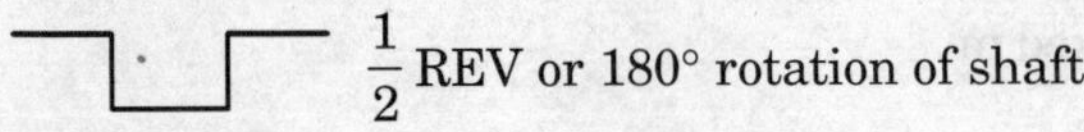

Both the valve reamin closed

BDC → TDC. Charge is being compresed (compression takes place). Pressure and Temp. increased charge partionsprepars themselves for ignition.

TDC $\frac{1}{2}$ Rev. or 180° rotation.

At the end of the compression stroke, spark is attained at the spark plug and igniation occuss.

There is sort of explosion in the cylinder.

So it is the spak ignition engine (SI Engine)

3. EXPANSION STROKE TDC

Both the valve remain closed

TDC → BDC,

Gas expands. Work is obtained working stroke or power stroke

BDC $\frac{1}{2}$ Rev. or 180°

4. EXHAUST STROKE BDC

Exhaust valve opens

BDC → TDC Gases are exhausted out.

TDC $\frac{1}{2}$ Rev. or 180°

Exhaust value closed.

It number of revolutions are N then the number of cycles will be $\frac{N}{2}$

Range of compression ratio $r = 6 - 9$

$r = 9$ (is preferable)

$$r = \frac{V_1}{V_2} = \frac{V_c + V_s}{V_c} = 1 + \frac{V_s}{V_c}$$

Four Stroke Diesel Engine

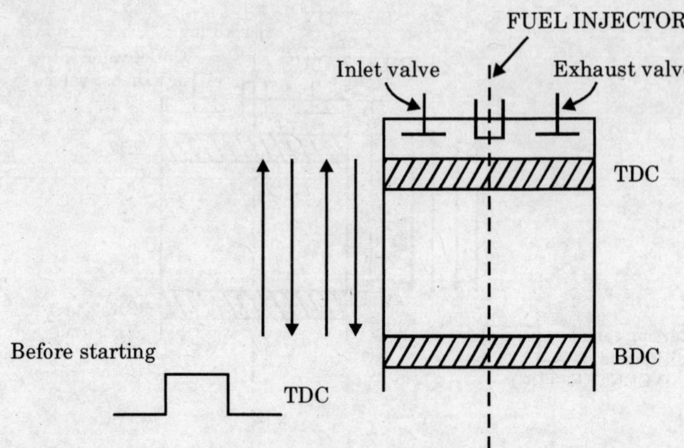

1. SUCTION STROKE 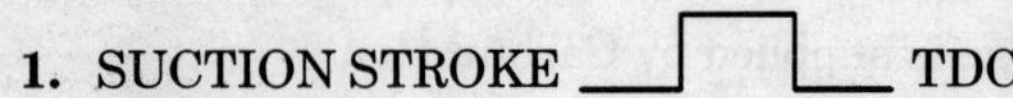 TDC

   Suction value opens

   TDC → BDC, Charge (pure air) sucked in

   BDC $\frac{1}{2}$ Rev. or 180°

   Suction valve closes

2. Compression stroke BDC

   Both the value remain closed

   BDC → TDC Process of campression takes place, pressure and temp. increases

   TDC $\frac{1}{2}$ Rev. or 180° rotation of shaft

   Range of compression ratio, r = 14 to 22 (M used in veryt strong for extra ondirary and engine mfg)

   In buses and trucks r = 18

   At the end of the compression, Diesel is injected into the cylinder at a pressure higher than the pressure insdie the cylinder. As soon as diesel gets injected it ignites.

   It is the compression ignition engine (CI Engine) fuel injector and fuel injection pump is used.

3. Expansion stroke TDC

   Both the valves remains closed

   TDC → BDC Gas expands

   Work is obtained working stroke or power stroke

   BDC $\frac{1}{2}$ Rev. or 180°

4. EXHAUST STROKE BDC

   Exhaust valve opens

   BDC → TDC Gases are exhausted out

   TCD $\frac{1}{2}$ Rev. or 180°

   Exhaust valve closes.

Fuel Consumption

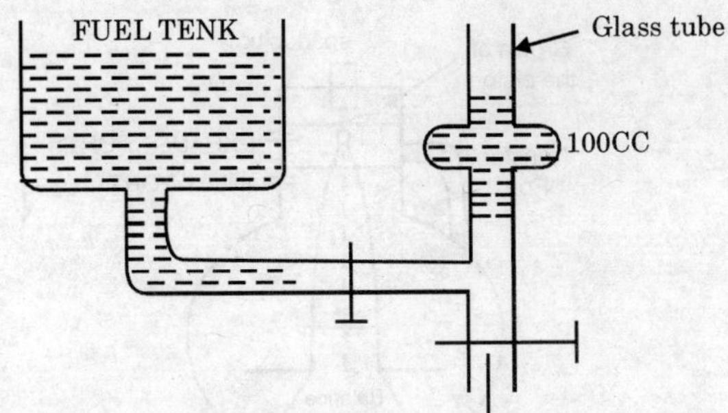

Amount of fued compresed in kg/sec

$$m_f = \frac{100\text{C.C} \times \rho\text{gm/c.c}}{1000 \times t} \text{kg/sec}$$

where ρ for Petrol = 0.72 to 0.78 ⇒ 0.75

ρ for Diesel = 0.82 to 087 ⇒ 0.85

$t \rightarrow$ time in seconds taken for combiustion of 100 c.c. fuel

Brake Dynamometer

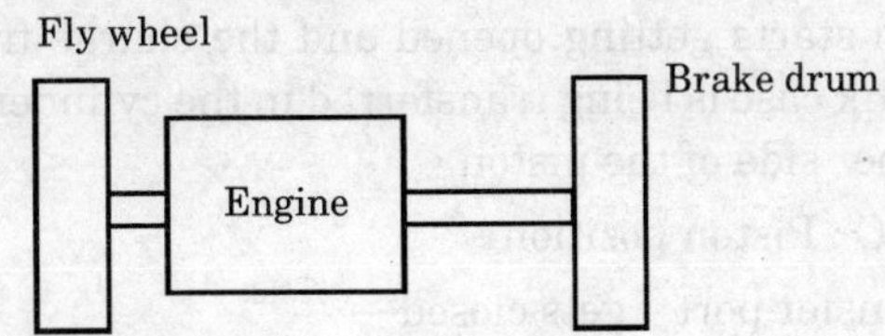

Net balancing fore

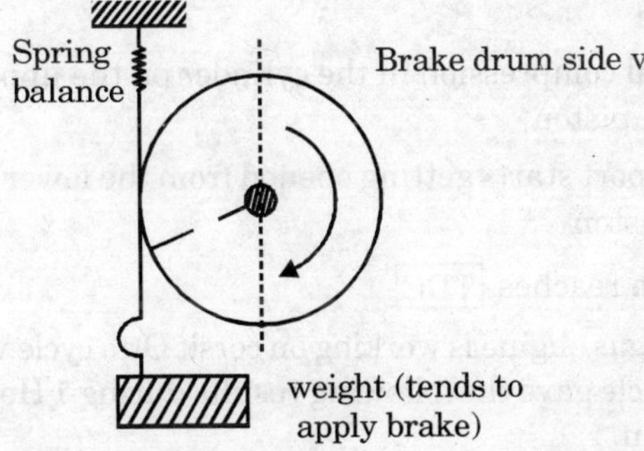

W = (*w* – *s*) Newtons effective redius of break drum

= r meters

Braking Torque = W × *r*

$$\text{B.P} = \text{T} \times w = \text{T} \times 2\pi\text{N} \frac{\text{N}-m}{s}$$

$$\text{Brake Power, B.P} = \frac{2\pi\text{NT}}{1000} \text{kW}$$

1. For Solving the Problems

$$\text{Brake Power, B.P} = \frac{2\pi\text{NT}}{1000} \text{kW}$$

where N → *r.p.s* T → Torque in kN-m

2. Indicated Power

From the Indicated diagram·

I.P = Gross Power – Pumping power

Let area of the diagram = a cm^2

Length of the diagram = l cm

Spring No. or Pressure scale or spring stiffinessd in bar /cm = s

∴ Indicated mean effective pressure (i.m.e.p)

$$\text{or} \quad \text{P}_{mi} = \frac{a}{l} \times s$$

$$\text{where} \quad \frac{a}{l} = \text{Average } ht. \text{ of the diagram}$$

Work done/sec = force × Displacement

$= (\text{P}_{mi} \times \text{A}) \times \text{L}$

$$\text{Work done/sec} = \text{P}_{mi} \times \text{A} \times \text{L} \times \frac{\text{N}}{2} \quad \text{(Fours stroke)}$$

$$\text{Indicated power I}_p = \frac{\text{P}_{mi} \text{ LAN}}{2} \times n$$

Average velocity = LN

n → No. of cylinders

$\text{I}_p = \text{P}_{mi}\text{LAN} \times \text{n}$ Two stroke

where P_{mi} → i.m.e.p in k Pa

L → stroke or length of the stroke in m

A → Cross-sectional area of the cylinder = $\frac{\pi}{4} d^2 \; m^2$

d → bore or dia of the cylinder

n → No. of cylinders

3. Brake Mean Effective Pressure (b.m.e.p) = b_{bi}

$$\text{B.P} = \frac{\text{P}_{bi} \times \text{LAN}}{2} \quad \text{(four stroke)}$$

$$\text{B.m.e.p} = \frac{2 \text{ BP}}{\text{LAN}}$$

4. Friction Power (F.P)

F.P = I.P – B. P

5. Mechanical Efficiency η_{mach}

$$\eta_{mech} = \frac{\text{B.P}}{\text{I.P}}$$

6. Indicated Thermal Efficiency (η_{th})

$$\eta_{mech} = \frac{\text{Energy equivalent to B.P}}{\text{Energy supplied by fuel}}$$

Energy supplied by fuel = m_f × C.V

m_f → Mass of fuel per second

C.V= Calorific value or heating value in kJ/kg

$$\eta_{ith} = \frac{\text{I}_p}{m_f \times \text{C.V}}$$

7. Brake Thermal Efficiency η_{bth}

$$\eta_{bth} = \frac{\text{B.P}}{m_f \times \text{C.V}}$$

8. Mechanical Efficiency (η_{mech})

$$\eta_{mech} = \frac{\eta_{bth}}{\eta_{ith}}$$

9. Volumetric Efficiency (η_v)

$$\eta_v = \frac{\text{Volume of air at ambient condition}}{\text{Swept Volume}}$$

$$= \frac{\text{Mass of charge sucked in}}{\text{Mass of charge represented by cylinder volume}}$$

$$\eta_v = \frac{V_a}{V_s}$$

10. *b.s.f.c* (Brake Specific Fuel Consumption)

$$b.s.f.c = \frac{\text{fuel used in kg/hr}}{b.p\,kw} = \frac{m_f}{b.p}\frac{kg}{kwn}$$

$$\eta_{mech} = \frac{isfc}{bsfc}$$

11. $i.s.f.c = \frac{m_f}{I_p}$ kg/kwh

12.Fuel – Air (F/A) or Air – Fuel (A/F)Ratio

$$\frac{F}{A} = \frac{m_f}{m_a}, \quad \frac{A}{F} = \frac{m_a}{m_f}$$

13. Relative Fuel – Air Ratio (f_r)

$$f_r = \frac{\text{Acutal fuel–air ratio}}{\text{Stoichiometric fuel –air ration}}$$

14. Relative Efficiency or Efficiency Ratio (η_{rel})

$$\eta_{rel} = \frac{\eta_{ith}}{\eta_{\text{air starded}}}$$

$$\text{Brake relative } \eta = \frac{\eta_{bth}}{\eta_{\text{air starded}}}$$

15. Air Supply to Engine by Orifice is Given by

$Q = A\,V\ m^3$/sec

$V = C_d\sqrt{2gH}$

whereA → area of orifice

C_d → Coeff. of discharge of orifice

H → Head

$Q = A.C_d\sqrt{2gH}$

Weight of the air supplied = $Q.W_a$

W_a → Weight of one m^3 of air in kg

Two Stroke Petrol Engine

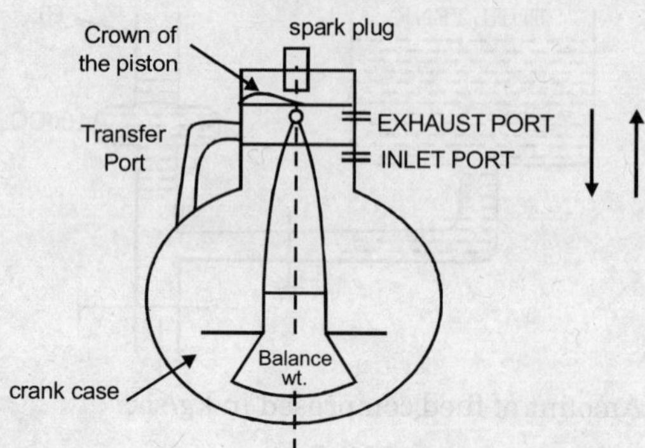

TDC

Suction on the lower side of the piston spark occurs, ignition takes place on the upper side of the piston

Expansion

Inlet part closed prelimanery compression of the charge in the crank case (crank case campression) Exhaust port starts getting opended. Transfer part also starts getting opened and the charge from the crank case is being transferred in the cylinder on the upper side of the piston.

BDC : Piston position

Transfer port – gets closed

Scavanging – wastage of charge Exhaust port gets closed

Actual compression in the cylinder on the upper side of the piston

Inlet port starts getting opened from the lower side of the piston

Piston reaches TDC

Q. A gas engine is working on corslt Otto cycle volume cycle gave the following results during 1 Hour test run.

Cylinder diameter = 24 cm

Stroke = 48 cm

Effcetive dia of the brake wheel = 1.25 m

Net load on the break = 1236 N

Average speed = 226 rpm

Average explosions/ min = 77

m.e.p = 73.57 N/cm^2

Super Gas used = 13 m^3 at 15°C and 771 min of Hg

C.V of the gas = 16727 kj/m3

Cooling water based, mw = 625 kg

Inlet temp of the water Twi = 25°C

Out let = Two

Determine

η_{mech}, η_{ith} = ? and

Heat balance

$$B.P = 2\pi N T$$

$$= \frac{2\pi \times \frac{226}{60} \times 1236 \times \frac{1.25}{2}}{1000} \text{ kw}$$

$$= 18.25W$$

$$\text{Explosion} = 77 \text{ but theortically} = \frac{236}{2}$$

$$= 113$$

$\therefore$ 113 – 77 = 36 explsions are missed

36 × 2 = 72 cycles are missed

$$I_p = P_m LA \frac{N}{2}$$

N = Number of cycles are excuted/second

REFRIGERATION AND PSYCHROMETRY

Refrigeration Cycles

Refrigeration by Non-cyclic Processes

Refrigeration is the cooling of a system below the temperature of its surroundings.

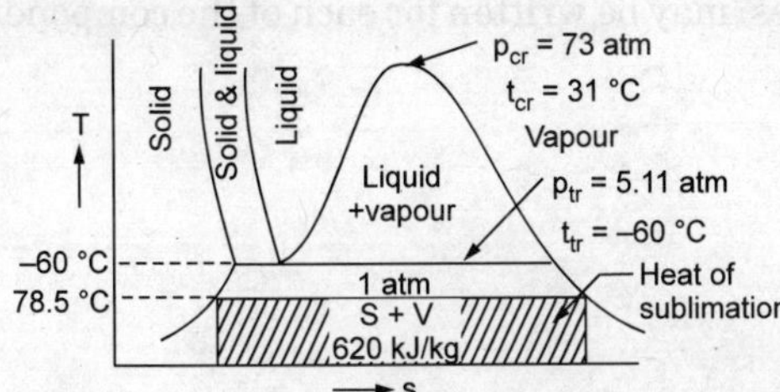

Another medium of refrigeration is solid carbon dioxide or dry ice. At atmospheric pressure CO_2 cannot exist in a liquid state, and consequently, when solid CO_2 is exposed to atmosphere, it sublimates, i.e. it goes directly from solid to vapour, by absorbing the latent heat of sublimation (620 kJ/kg at 1 atm., –78.5°C) from the surroundings. Thus dry ice is suitable for low temperature refrigeration.

REVERSED HEAT ENGINE CYCLE

A reversed heat engine cycle, is visualised as an engine operating in the reverse way, i.e. receiving heat from a low temperature region, discharging heat to a high temperature region, and receiving a net inflow of work. Under such conditions the cycle is called *heat pump cycle* or *refrigeration cycle*.

For a heat pump, $(COP)_{H.P.} = \frac{Q_1}{W} = -\frac{Q_1}{Q_1 - Q_2}$

For a refrigerator, $(COP)_{ref.} = \frac{Q_2}{W} = \frac{Q_2}{Q_1 - Q_2}$

Here, $Q_1 = T_1 (s_2 - s_3)$

$Q_2 = T_2 (s_1 - s_4)$

$$\therefore \quad W_{net} = W_C - W_E = Q_1 - Q_2$$

$$= (T_1 - T_2)(s_1 - s_4)$$

where T_1 = temperature of heat rejection,

T_2 = temperature of heat absorption.

$$(COP_{ref.})_{rev.} = \frac{Q_2}{W_{net}} = \frac{T_2}{T_1 - T_2}$$

$$\text{and} (COP_{H.P.})_{rev.} = \frac{Q_1}{W_{net}} = \frac{T_1}{T_1 - T_2}$$

Vapour Compression Refrigeration Cycle

In an actual vapour refrigeration cycle, an expansion engine, as shown in the figure is not used, since power recovery is small and does not justify the cost of engine. A throttling valve or a capillary tube is used for expansion in reducing the pressure from p_1 to p_2.

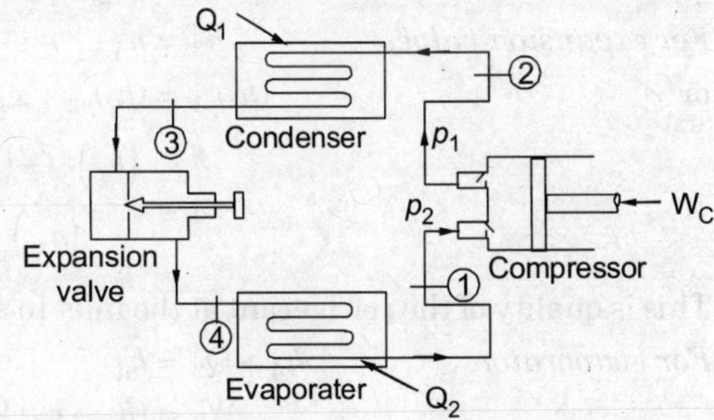

Operations Represented for an Idealized Plant

The basic operations involved in a vapour compression refrigeration plant are shown in the flow diagram, and the property diagrams.

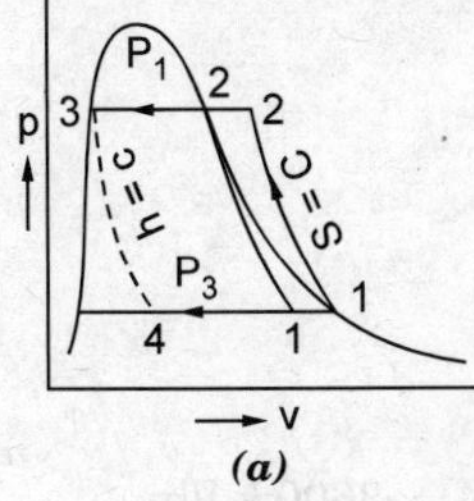

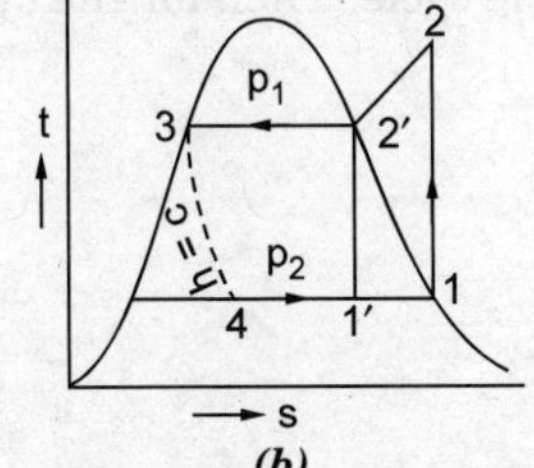

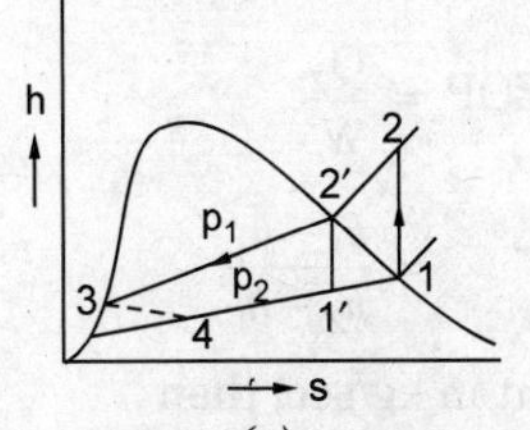

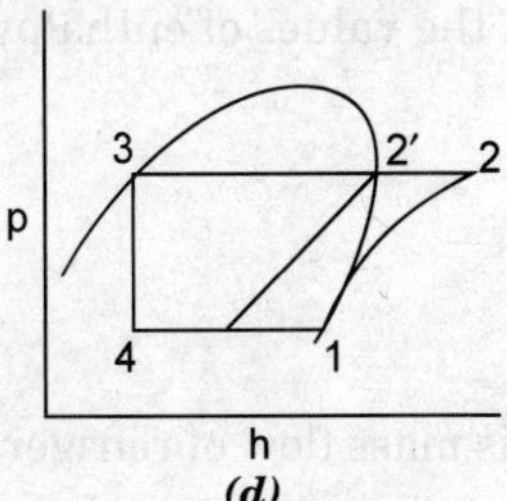

Fig. Vapour compression refrigeration cycle property diagrams

(*i*) **Compression :** A reversible adiabatic process 1-2 or 1′- 2′either starting with saturated vapour (state 1), called *dry compression*, or starting with wet vapour (state 1), called *wet compression.* Dry compression (1-2) is always preferred to wet compression (1-′ 2′), because with wet compression there is a danger of the liquid refrigerant being trapped in the head of the cylinder by the rising piston which may damage the valves or the cylinder head, and the droplets of liquid refrigerant may wash away the lubricating oil from the walls of the cylinder, thus accelerating wear.

(*ii*) **Cooling and Condensing :** A reversible constant pressure process, 2-3, first desuperheated and then condensed, ending with saturated liquid. Heat Q_1 is transferred out.

(*iii*) **Expansion :** An adiabatic throttling process 3-4, for which enthalpy remains unchanged. States 3 and 4 are equilibrium points. Process 3-4 is adiabatic (then only $h_3 = h_4$), but not isentropic.

$$Tds = dh - vdp \quad \text{or} \quad s_4 - s_3 = -\int_{p_1}^{p_2} \frac{vdp}{T}$$

Hence it is irreversible and cannot be shown in property diagrams. States 3 and 4 have simply been joined by a dotted line.

(*iv*) **Evaporation :** A constant pressure reversible process, 4-1, which completes the cycle. The refrigerant is throttled by the expansion valve to a pressure, the saturation temperature at this pressure being below the temperature of the surroundings. Heat then flows, by virtue of temperature difference, from the surroundings, which gets cooled or refrigerated, to the refrigerant, which then evaporates, absorbing heat of evaporation. The evaporator thus produces cooling or *refrigerating effect,* absorbing heat Q_2 from the surroundings by evaporation.

In refrigeration practice, enthalpy is the most sought-after property. The diagram in *p-h* coordinates is found to be the most convenient.

When steady state has been reached, for 1 kg flow of refrigerant through the cycle, the steady flow energy equations (neglecting kinetic and potential energy and P.E. changes) may be written for each of the components in the cycle as given below.

For compressor, $h_1 + W_c = h_2$

$\therefore$ $W_c = (h_2 - h_1)$ kJ/kg

For condenser, $h_2 = Q_1 + h_3$

$\therefore$ $Q_1 = (h_2 - h_3)$ kJ/kg

For expansion valve, $h_3 = h_4$

or $(h_f)_{p1} = (h_f)_{p2} + x_4 (h_{fg})_{p2}$

$$\therefore \quad x_4 = \frac{(h_f)_{p1} - (h_f)_{p2}}{(h_{fg})_{p2}}$$

This is quality of the refrigerant at the inlet to the evaporator (mass fraction of vapour in liquid-vapour mixture).

For evaporator, $h_4 + Q_2 = h_1$

$\therefore$ $W_2 = (h_1 - h_4)$ kJ/kg

This is called **refrigerating effect**. It is the amount of heat removed from the surroundings per unit mass flow of refrigerant.

If *p-h* chart for a particular refrigerant is available with the given parameters, it is possible to obtain from the chart the values of enthalpy at all the cardinal points of the cycle. Then for the cycle

$$COP = \frac{Q_2}{W_c}$$

$$= \frac{h_1 - h_4}{h_2 - h_1}$$

If $\dot{m}$ is mass flow of refrigerant in kg/sec, then

rate of heat removal from the surroundings = $\dot{m}\ (h_1 - h_4)$ kJ/sec = $m\ (h_1 - h_4) \times 3600$ kJ/hr

One Tonne of Refrigeration

It is defined as the rate of heat removal from the surroundings equivalent to the heat required for melting 1 tonne of ice in one day.

If latent heat of fusion of ice is taken as 336 kJ/kg, then 1 tonne is equivalent to heat removal at the rate of

$\frac{1000 \times 336}{24}$ or 14,000 kJ/hr.

$$\therefore \quad \text{Capacity of the refrigerating plant} = \frac{\dot{m}(h_1 - h_4) \times 3600}{14{,}000} \text{ tonnes}$$

$$\text{Rate of heat removal in the condenser, } Q_1 = m\,(h_2 - h_3) \text{ kJ/s}$$

If condenser is water-cooled, $\dot{m}_c$ the flow-rate of cooling water in kg/s, and $(t_{c_2} - t_{c_1})$ the rise in temperature of water, then

$$Q_1 = m\,(h_2 - h_3) = \dot{m}_c\,(t_{c_2} - t_{c_1}) \text{ kJ/s}$$

provided heat transfer is confined only between refrigerant and water, and there is no heat interaction with the surroundings.

Rate of work input to the compressor,

$$W_c = m\,(h_2 - h_1) \text{ kJ/s} = m\,(h_2 - h_1) \text{ kW}$$

where h_1 and h_2 are in kJ/kg.

Actual Vapour Compression Cycle

In order to ascertain that there is no droplet of liquid refrigerant being carried over into the compressor, some superheating of vapour is recommended after the evaporator.

A small degree of subcooling of the liquid refrigerant after the condenser is also used to reduce the mass of vapour formed during expansion, so that too many vapour bubbles do not impede the flow of liquid refrigerant through the expansion valve.

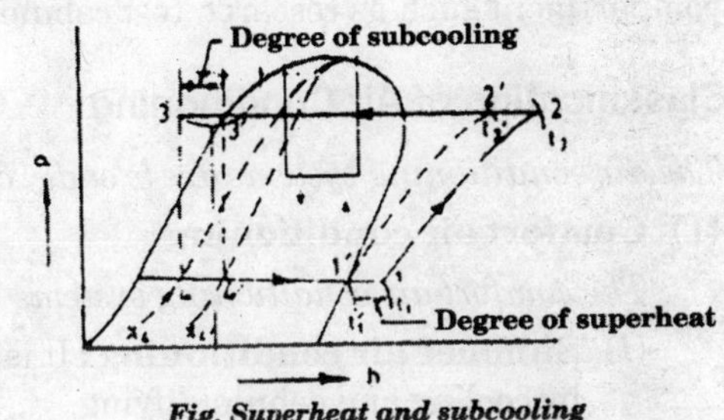

Fig. Superheat and subcooling in a vapour compression cycle

Both superheating of vapour at the evaporator outlet and subcooling of liquid at the condenser outlet contribute to an increase in the refrigerating effect, as shown in the figure. The compressor discharge temperature, however, increases due to superheat, from t'_2 to t_2, and load on the condenser also increases.

Sometimes, a liquid-line heat exchanger is used in the plant, as shown in the figure. The liquid is subcooled in the heat exchanger, reducing the load on the condenser and improving the COP.

For 1 kg flow,

$$Q_2 = h_6 - h_5,\; Q_1 = h_2 - h_3$$

$$W_c = h_2 - h_1 \text{ and } h_1 - h_6 = h_3 - h_4$$

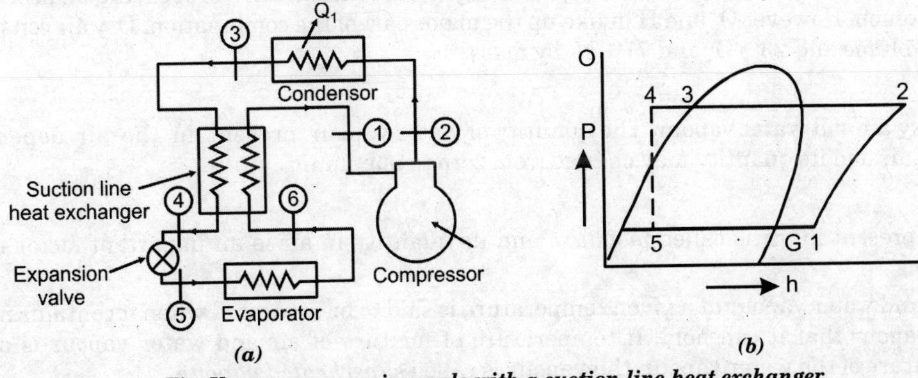

Fig. Vapour compression cycle with a suction-line heat exchanger.

Volumetric Efficiency of Compressor

In refrigerant compressors which may be single cylinder or multi cylinder, due to clearance, leakage past the piston and valves the throttling effects at the suction and discharge valve, the actual volume of gas drawn into the cylinder is less than the volume displaced by the piston, the ratio of these two is called *volumetirc efficiency*.

$$\eta_{vol} = \frac{\text{Actual volume of gas drawn at evaporator pressure and temperature}}{\text{Piston displacement volume}}$$

$$= \frac{mv_1}{\frac{\pi}{4} D^2 L \frac{N}{60} n}$$

where m = refrigerant mass flow rate; D and L = diameter and stroke of compressor

n = number of cylinders; N = r.p.m.

AIR CONDITIONING

Air conditioning means the automatic control of an atomospheric environment either for comfort of human beings or animals or for the proper performance of some industrial or scientific process. The purpose of air conditioning is to supply sufficient volume of clean air containing a specific amount amount of water vapour and at a temperature capable of maintaining predetermined atmospheric conditions. The space may be small compartment such as research test cabinet or a cinema hall.

Classification of Air Conditioning

The air conditioning systems are broadly classified into two group :

(1) Comfort air conditioning

The comfort air conditioning systems are further subdivided into three groups.

(i) **Summer air conditioning :** It is used to reduce the sensible heat and water vapour content of the air by cooling and dehumidifying.

(ii) **Winter air conditioning :** It is used to increase the sensible heat and water vapour content of the air by heating and humdification.

(iii) **Year-round air conditioning :** This system assures the control of temperature and humidity of air in an enclosed space throught the year when the atomospheric conditions are changing as per the season.

(2) Industrial air conditioning

Propertiesof Moist Air

Dry Air

Dry air is the mechanical mixture of gases like, oxygen, nitrogen, carbondioxide, hydrogen, argon, neon, krypton, helium, ozone and xenon. However O_2 and H_2 make up the major part of the combination. Dry air consist of 21% O_2 and 79% N_2 by volume and 23% O_2 and 77% N_2 by mass.

Moist Air

It is a mixture of dry air and water vapour. The quantity of water vapour present in the air depends upon temperature of the air and its quantity may change from zero to maximum.

Water Vapour

The water vapour present in air is called *moisture* and its quantity in air is an important factor in all air-conditioning systems.

The mixture of air and water vapour at a given temperature is said to be saturated when it contains maximum amount of water vapour that it can hold. If temperature of mixture of air and water vapour is above the saturation temperature of the water vapour, the vapour is called *superheated vapour*.

Dry-bulb Temperature

The temperature of air measured by ordinary thermometer called *dry-bulb-temperature*.

Wet-bulb Temperature

The temperature measured by the thermometer when its bulb is covered with wet cloth and is exposed to a current of moving air is called *wet bulb temperature*. The difference between dry-bulb and wet-bulb temperature is called *wet-bulb-depression*. Wet bulb depression becomes zero when the air is fully saturated.

Dew-bulb Temperature

The temperature of the air is reduced by continuous cooling than the water vapour in the air will start condensing at a particular temperature. The temperature at which the condensing starts is called *dew-point temperature*. Dew point temperature is equal to the steam table saturation temperature corresponding to the actual partial pressure of the water vapour in the air. The difference between dry bulb-temperature and dew-point temperature is *called dew-point depression*.

Specific Humidity (Humidity Ratio)

It is the mass of water vapour present per kg of dry air. It is given in grams per kg of dry air.

Absolute Humidity

The weight of water vapour present in unit volume of air is called *absolute humidity*.

Degree of Saturation

It is defined as the ratio of mass of water vapour associated which unit mass of dry air to mass of water vapour associated with unit mass of dry air saturated at the same termperature.

Relative Humidity

It is defined as the ratio of actual mass of water vapour in a given volume to the mass of water vapour if the air is saturated at the same temperature.

Sensible Heat of Air

The quantity of heat which can be measured by measuring the dry bulb temperature of the air is called sensible heat.

Total Heat

The total heat of the himid air is the sum of the sensible heat of the dry air and sensible and latent heat of water vapour associated with dry air.

Humid Specific Volume

The volume of the mixture per kg of dry air in the mixture, expressed in cubic metres, is called *humid specific volume*.

Dalton's Law of Partial Pressure

It states that, total pressure of a mixture of gases is equal to sum of the partial pressures exerted by each gas when it occupies the mixture volume at the mixture temperature.

As per the Dalton's law of partial pressure

$$p_t = p_a + p_b + p_c$$

If this is applied to the moist air which contains dry air and water vapour, then

$$p_t = p_a + p_v$$

where, p_t = total pressure of moist air

p_a = partial pressure of dry air

p_v = partial pressure of water vapour

Specific Humidity (w)

$$w = \frac{\text{mass of water vapour in mixture}}{\text{mass of dry air in mixture}} = \frac{m_v}{m_a}$$

Mass of the mixture is $(m_a + m_v)$.

Here, $$m_a = \frac{p_a V}{R_a T}$$

where, p_a = partial pressure of dry air ; V = volume of mixture ; R_a = gas constant for dry air

and
$$m_v = \frac{p_v V}{R_v T}$$

where, p_v = partial pressure of water vapour ; R_v = gas constant for water vapour.

$$\therefore \quad w = \frac{p_v V}{R_v T} \cdot \frac{R_a T}{p_a V} = \frac{R_a}{R_v} \cdot \frac{p_v}{p_a}$$

But
$$R_a = \frac{\overline{R}}{M_a} \quad \text{and} \quad R_v = \frac{\overline{R}}{M_v}$$

where $\overline{R}$ = universal gas constant

M_a and M_v = molecular weights of air and water vapour respectively

$$\therefore \quad w = \frac{M_v}{M_a} \cdot \frac{p_v}{p_a} = \frac{18}{29} \cdot \frac{p_v}{p_a} = 0.622 \frac{p_v}{p_a} = 0.622 \frac{p_v}{p_t - p_v} \quad ....(i)$$

Masses of air and water vapour in terms of specific volumes are given by

$$m_a = \frac{V}{v_a} \quad \text{and} \quad m_v = \frac{V}{v_v}$$

where v_a and v_v are specific volumes of dry air and water vapour at the given mixture temperature and at respective partial pressure.

$$\therefore \quad w = \frac{v_a}{v_v}$$

Degree of Saturation (μ)

$$\mu = \frac{\text{mass of water vapour associated with unit mass of dry air}}{\text{mass of water vapour associated with saturated unit mass of dry air}} = \frac{w}{w_s}$$

where, w_s = specific humidity of air when air is fully saturated.

$$\therefore \quad \mu = \frac{0.622\left(\frac{p_v}{p_t - p_v}\right)}{0.622\left(\frac{p_{vs}}{p_t - p_{vs}}\right)} = \frac{p_v}{p_{vs}}\left(\frac{p_t - p_{vs}}{p_t - p_v}\right) = \frac{p_v}{p_{vs}}\left[\frac{1-\frac{p_{vs}}{p_t}}{1-\frac{p_v}{p_t}}\right]$$

where, p_{vs} = partial pressure of water vapour when air is fully saturated at the same temperature of air.

Relative Humidity (ϕ)

Relative humidity can be defined as the ratio of partial pressure of water vapour in a given volume of mixture to the partial pressure of water vapour when same volume of mixture is saturated at the same temperature.

$$\phi = \frac{\text{mass of water vapour in a given volume}}{\text{mass of water vapour in same volume if saturated at the same temperature}} = \frac{m}{m_{vs}} = \frac{\frac{p_v V}{R_v T}}{\frac{p_{vs} V}{R_v T}} = \frac{p_v}{p_{vs}}$$

$$\phi = \frac{\mu}{1-(1-\mu)\frac{p_{vs}}{p_t}}$$

When $p_{vs} << p_t$ $\qquad \phi \approx \mu$

Relative humidity plays more important part in comfort air conditioning and industrial air-conditioning than specific humidity. Relative humidity signifies the absorption capacity of the air. More moisture will be absorbed by the air if the initial relative humidity of the air is less.

$$\phi = \frac{p_a w}{0.622} \cdot \frac{1}{p_{vs}} = 1.6 w \cdot \frac{p_a}{p_{vs}}$$

Enthalpy of Moist Air

It is sum of the enthalpy of dry air and enthalpy of the water vapour assciated with dry air.

$\therefore$ Enthalpy of moist air = enthalpy of one kg of dry air + enthalpy of water vapour associated with one kg of dry air

or $$h = 1.005\ T_{db} + w\ [2500 + 1.88\ T_{db}]\ \text{kJ/kg of dry air}$$

or $$h = (1 + 1.88\ w)\ T_{db} + w\ [(h_{fg})_{dp} + 2.3\ T_{dp}]$$
$$= (1 + 1.88\ w)\ T_{db} + w\ [(h_{fg})_{dp} + 2.3\ T_{dp}]$$
$$= C_{pma} \times T_{db} + w\ [(h_{fg})_{dp} + 2.3\ T_{dp}]$$

where C_{pma} is called *mean humid specific heat of air*.

As $1.88\ w << 1$, therefore value of C_{pma} is always taken as 1.0216 kJ/kg of dry air-K for all practical purposes in air-conditioning calculations

$$\therefore \quad h = 2.0216\ t_{db} + w\ [(h_{fg})_{dp}] + 2.3\ T_{dp}]$$

AIR COMPRESSORS

Air compressors are used for supplying high-pressure air. There are many uses of high-pressure air in the industry. The main uses of high-pressure (compressed) air are :

- to drive compressed air engines (air motors) used in coal mines,
- to inject or spray fuel into the cylinder of a Diesel engine (air injection Diesel engine),
- to operate drills, hammers, air brakes for locomotives and railway carnages, water pumps and paint sprays,
- to start large (heavy) Diesel engines,
- to clean workshop machines, generators, automobile vehicles, etc.,
- to operate blast furnaces, gas turbine plants, Bessemer convertors used in steel plants, etc.,
- to cool large buildings and air crafts, and
- to supercharge I.C. engines.

There are mainly two types of air compressors viz. reciprocating air compressors and rotary air compressors. Reciprocating air compressors are similar to reciprocating engines where a piston reciprocates inside a cylinder. In rotary air compressors, air is compressed due to rotation of impeller or blades inside a casing. Air compressors are driven by engines or electric motors.

Reciprocating Air Compressor

The reciprocating air compressor may be single-acting (air is admitted to one side of the piston only) or double-acting (air is admitted to each side of the piston alternatively), and may be single-stage or multi-stage. Single-stage compressors are used for delivery pressures upto 10 bar, three-stage compressors for pressure upto 200 bar and two-stage compressors for pressures in between 10 to 200 bar. The average piston speed of a reciprocating air compressor is limited to about 300 to 400 metres per minute to reduce friction wear.

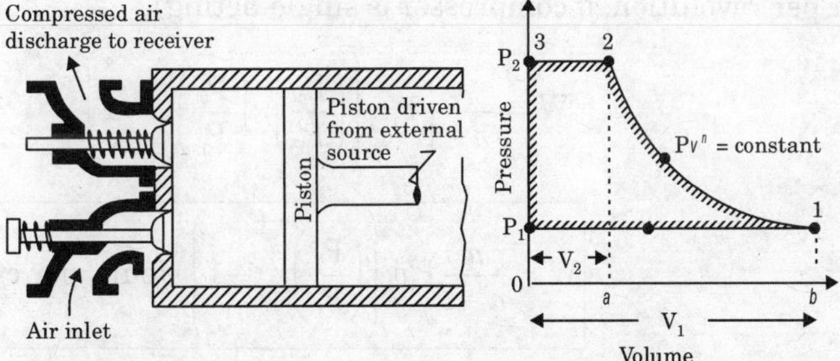

Single-stage air compressor without clearance.

Single-Stage Air Compressor

Indicator Diagram: The events described above can be conveniently represented by P-V diagram shown above figure. The diagram is drawn for a compressor without clearance.

line 4-1- suction stroke

line 1-2- compression stroke

line 2-3- delivery of the compressed air

The net work required for compression and delivery of the air per cycle is represented by the area 1-2 -3 -4.

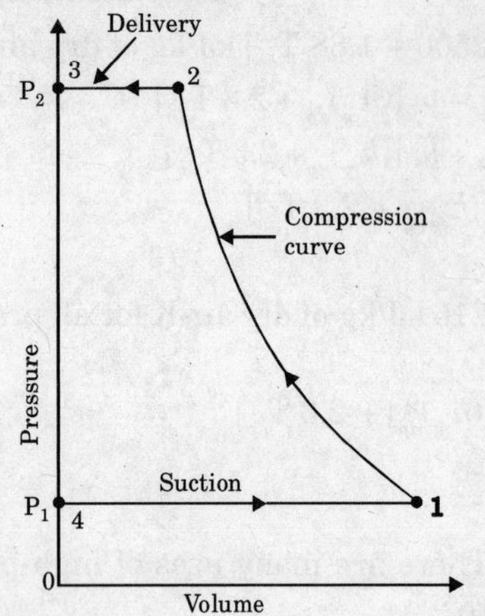

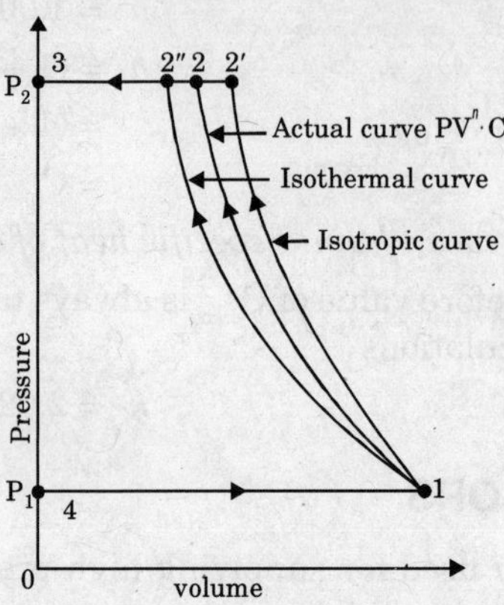

The amount of work done on the air will depend upon the nature of the compression curve. If the compression occurs very rapidly in a non-conducting cylinder so that there is no heat transfer, the compression will be practically isentropic. If it is carried out slowly so that the heat of the compression is extracted from the air by the jacket cooling water, the compression will approach isothermal. However, in actual practice neither of these conditions can be fulfilled and the actual compression will be between isentropic and isothermal as shown in figure.

Let pressure P_1 is in N/m² and volume v_1 is in m^3 represent initial condition of the air before compression. If the compression is polytropic

Indicated Work required to be done on the air W, per cycle assuming compression curve to be polytropic $PV^n = C$, is given by area 1-2-3-4 of indicator diagram.

$$W = p_2 V_2 + \frac{P_2 v_2 - P_1 v_1}{n-1} - P_1 v_1$$

$$W = \frac{n}{n-1}(P_2 v_2 - P_1 v_1) \text{ by ideal gas relation we get}$$

$$W = \frac{n}{n-1} mR(T_2 - T_1)$$

$$W = \frac{n}{n-1} P_1 v_1 \left(\frac{P_2 v_2}{P_1 v_1} - 1\right)$$

But for polytropic compression $P_1 v_1^n = P_2 v_2^n$. Hence $\frac{v_2}{v_1} = \left(\frac{P_2}{P_1}\right)^{\frac{1}{n}}$

Work required per cycle (or per revolution, if compressor is single-acting),

$$W = \frac{n}{n-1} P_1 v_1 \left(\left(\frac{P_2}{P_1}\right) \times \left(\frac{P_2}{P_1}\right)^{-\frac{1}{n}} - 1\right)$$

$$\boxed{W = \frac{n}{n-1} P_1 v_1 \left(\left(\frac{P_2}{P_1}\right)^{\frac{n-1}{n}} - 1\right) \text{ Joule per cycle}}$$

This equation gives the work required in Joules per cycle (or per revolution, if the compressor is single-acting) in compressing and delivering the air.

Indicated power of the compressor = $\frac{W \times N}{60}$ *J/s* or Watt; where W = work required in Joules per cycle, and N – No. of cycles performed per minute (r.p.m.) for single-acting compressor, if p_1v_1 in above equation is substituted by mRT_1, then work required per cycle,

$$W = \frac{n}{n-1} mRT_1 \left[\left(\frac{P_2}{P_1}\right)^{\frac{n-1}{n}} - 1\right] \text{ Joule per cycle}$$

Work required per kg of air,

$$W = \frac{n}{n-1} RT_1 \left[\left(\frac{P_2}{P_1}\right)^{\frac{n-1}{n}} - 1\right] \text{ Joule per cycle}$$

Indicated power of the compressor = W × mass of air delivered per second J/sec. or Watt B. If the compression is isentropic.

$$W = \frac{\gamma}{\gamma-1} P_1v_1 \left[\left(\frac{P_2}{P_1}\right)^{\frac{\gamma-1}{\gamma}} - 1\right] \text{ Joule per cycle}$$

Work required per kg of air,

$$W = \frac{\gamma}{\gamma-1} RT_1 \left[\left(\frac{P_2}{P_1}\right)^{\frac{\gamma-1}{\gamma}} - 1\right] \text{ Joule per cycle}$$

If the compression is isothermal ($pv = C$), then work required

W = area under 1-2-3-4

$$W = P_1v_1 \log_e\left(\frac{v_1}{v_2}\right) + P_2v_2 - P_1v_1$$

$$W = P_1v_1 \log_e\left(\frac{v_1}{v_2}\right)$$

$$W = P_1v_1 \log_e\left(\frac{P_2}{P_1}\right) \text{ Joule per cycle}$$

Work required per kg of air

$$W = RT_1 \log_e\left(\frac{P_2}{P_1}\right) \text{ Joule per cycle}$$

Work Input to the Compressor with Clearance Volume

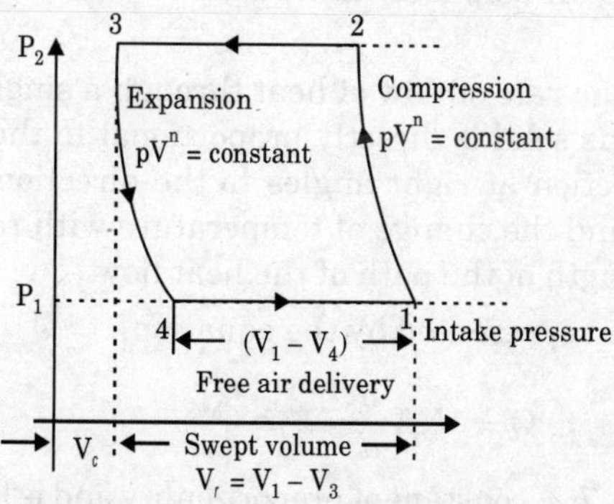

From indicator diagram shown in figure.

$$W_{Input} = W_{compression}(W_c) - W_{expansion}(W_e)$$

$$W_c = \frac{n}{n-1} P_1v_1 \left[\left(\frac{P_2}{P_1}\right)^{\frac{n-1}{n}} - 1\right]$$

$$W_e = \frac{n}{n-1}(P_3v_3 - P_{41}v_4)$$

$$W_e = \frac{n}{n-1} P_4v_4 \left(\frac{P_3v_3}{P_4v_4} - 1\right)$$

As $P_3v_3^{\,n} = P_4v_4^{\,n}$

$$\frac{v_3}{v_4} = \left(\frac{p_4}{p_3}\right)^{1/n} = \left(\frac{p_1}{p_2}\right)^{1/n} = \left(\frac{p_2}{p_1}\right)^{-1/n}$$

$$W_e = \frac{n}{n-1} P_1v_4 \left[\left(\frac{P_2}{P_1}\right)^{\frac{n-1}{n}} - 1\right]$$

$$W_{Input} = W_c - W_e$$

$$W_{Input} = \frac{n}{n-1} P_1(v_1 - v_4) \left[\left(\frac{P_2}{P_1}\right)^{\frac{n-1}{n}} - 1\right]$$

$$W_{Input} = \frac{n}{n-1} P_1v_{actual} \left[\left(\frac{P_2}{P_1}\right)^{\frac{n-1}{n}} - 1\right]$$

Note : Clearance volume does not affect the work input.

Multi-stage Air Compressor

High Pressure required by Single – Stage:

1. Requires heavy working parts.
2. Has to accommodate high pressure ratios.
3. Increased balancing problems.
4. High Torque fluctuations.
5. Requires heavy Flywheel installations.

This demands for Multi-staging.

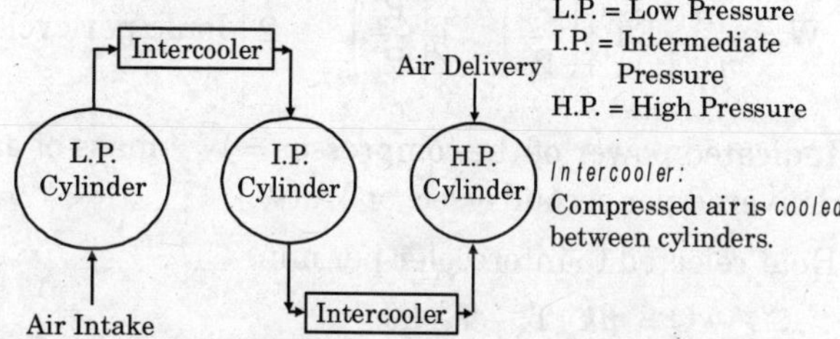

A multi-stage air compressor with intercooler is shown in fig.. Series arrangement of cylinders, in which the compressed air from earlier cylinder (i.e. discharge) becomes the intake air for the next cylinder (i.e. *inlet*). When cooling is perfect, i.e., when air is cooled to intake temperature in the intercooler (T1 = T2), the point 2 will lie on the isothermal line 1 - 3" as shown in fig.. It may be noted that each stage will increase the pressure of air while the intake temperature T1 (corresponding to point 1) is maintained same at the end. The isothermal line during the process has been approximated as shown by the diagram, and the shaded area 2-3-3'-2' shows the saving of work as a result of this approximated isothermal.

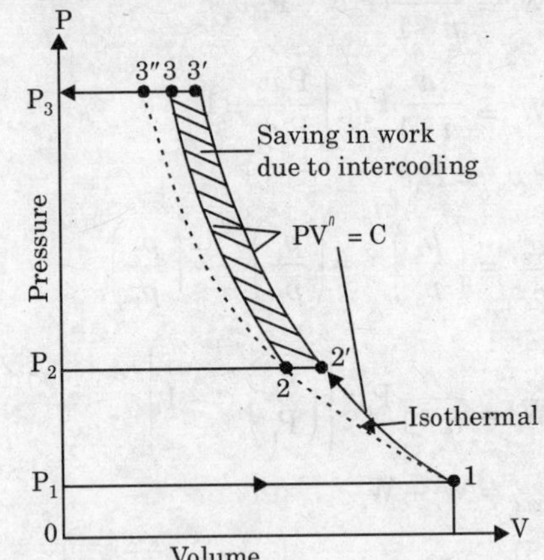

Combined ideal indicator diagram of two-stage compression with perfect-intercooling.

Perfect-intercooling

If intercooling is perfect or complete, the point 2 will lie on the isothermal line, i.e., point 2 will coincide with point 2", then $P_1V_1 = P_2V_2$.

Total work required per cycle,

$$W = \frac{n}{n-1} P_1 v_1 \left[\left(\frac{P_2}{P_1}\right)^{\frac{n-1}{n}} + \left(\frac{P_3}{P_2}\right)^{\frac{n-1}{n}} - 2 \right] \text{ Joule per cycle}$$

Indicated power of the compressor $= \frac{W \times N}{60}$ J/s or Watt

If P_1v_1 in above eqn. is substituted by mRT_1, then work required per kg of air may be written as

$$W = \frac{n}{n-1} RT_1 \left[\left(\frac{P_2}{P_1}\right)^{\frac{n-1}{n}} + \left(\frac{P_3}{P_2}\right)^{\frac{n-1}{n}} - 2 \right] \text{ Joule per cycle}$$

Indicated power of the compressor = W × mass of air delivered per second J/sec. or Watt

Heat rejected to intercooler per min.

$$Q = mk_p(T_2 - T_2) \text{ kJ}$$

where, m = mass of air compressed per minute,

k_p = specific heat of air at constant pressure,

T_2' = temperature of air before entering the intercooler, and

T_2 = temperature of air after leaving the intercooler

CONDUCTION

Modes of Heat Transfer

Heat transfer may be defined as the transmission of energy from one region to another as a result of temperature gradient and it takes place by three modes :

(i) **Conduction :** Conduction is the transfer of heat from one part of a substance to another part of the same substance, or from one substance to another in physical contact with it, without appreciable displacement of molecules forming the substance.

(ii) **Convection :** Convection is the transfer of heat within a fluid by mixing of one portion of the fluid with another.

(a) **Free or natural convection :** It occurs when the fluid circulated by virtue of the natural difference in densities of hot and cold fluids, the denser portions of the fluid move downward because of the greater force or gravity, as compared with the force on the less dense.

(b) **Forced convection :** When work is done to blow of pump the fluid, it is said to be forced convection.

(iii) **Radiation :** Radiation is the transfer of heat through space or matter by means other than conduction or convection. Radiation of heat is thought of as electromagnetic waves or quanta (as convenient) an emanation of the same nature as light and radio waves. All bodies radiate heat, so a transfer of heat by radiation occurs because hot body emits more heat than it receives and a cold body recives more heat than it emits. Radiant energy (being electromagnetic radiation) requires no medium for propagation, and will pass through a vacuum.

HEAT TRANSMISSION BY CONDUCTION

Fourier's Law of Conduction

This is an empirical law based on observation and states.

That the rate of flow of heat through a single homogeneous solid is directly proportional to the area of the section at right angles to the direction of heat flow, and the change of temperature with respect to the length of the path of the heat flow.

It is be represented by the equation, $Q \propto A$.

Thus, $Q = -k.A \frac{dt}{dx}$

where k = constant of proportionlity and is known as *thermal conductivity of the body*

The –ve sign of k is to take care of the decreasing temperature along with the direction of increasing thickness of the direction of heat flow. The temperature gradient $\frac{dt}{dx}$ is always negative along positive x direction and therefore the value of Q becomes + ve.

Now, $$k = \frac{Q}{A} \cdot \frac{dx}{dt}$$

Unit of k : $$W \times \frac{1}{m^2} \times \frac{m}{K} = \frac{W}{mK}$$

From the above equation, meterials with high thermal conductivities are good conductors of heat, whereas materials with low thermal conductivities are good themal insulators. Conduction of heat occurs most readily in pure metals, less so in alloys, and mush less readily in non-metals. The very low thermal conductivities of certain thermal insulators, *e.g.* cork is due to their porosity, the air trapped within the material acting as an insulator.

Sequence of Materials of Decreasing Thermal Conductivity

(*i*) Pure metal
(*ii*) Metal alloys
(*iii*) Non-metallic crystalline and amorphous substance
(*iv*) Liquid
(*v*) Gases

Thermal Conduction in Liquids

Heat conduction in liquids and gases are based on the movemoment of atoms in a molecule. In case of liquids, the random translatory motion is small and it appears that translation of energy occurs by longitudinal vibration, similar to the propagation of sound.

Bridgman assumptions for the conductivity of liquids.

(*i*) Adjacent molecules are arranged in a simple cubical fashion.

(*ii*) When the energy from one molecule to another is transferred at the velocity of sound, then thermal conductivity in liquid is given by the expression,

$$k = 3\,\frac{R}{A_0} \cdot \frac{v_s}{\lambda^2} = 3.\,\sigma \frac{v_s}{\lambda^2}$$

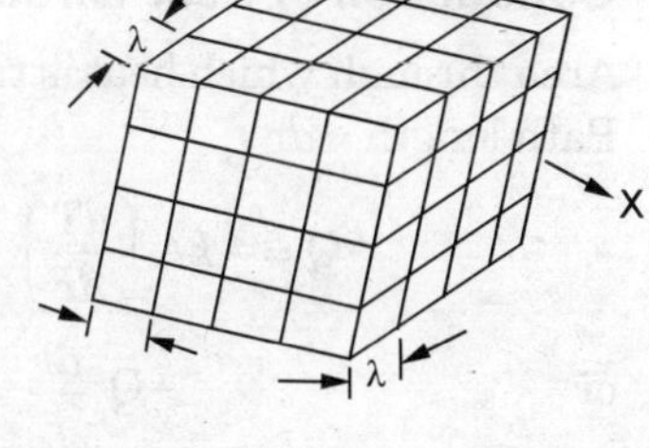

where $\sigma = \frac{R}{A_0}$ is known as Boltzmann constant per molecule

R = universal gas constant

A_0 = avogadro's number

v_s = sonic velocity

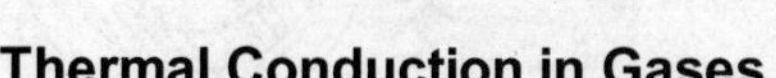

Thermal Conduction in Gases

Heat conduction in a gas is explained in term of the net of transport of energy across imaginary surface by molecule psssing in both direction through the surface. When temperature gradient exists in a gas as shown in the figure between two parallel surface, molecules in the regions of higher temperatures must have higher random velocity than in the lower temperature regions.

Thermal conductivity, $$k = \frac{1}{6} . n . \overline{v}_s . f . \sigma . \lambda$$

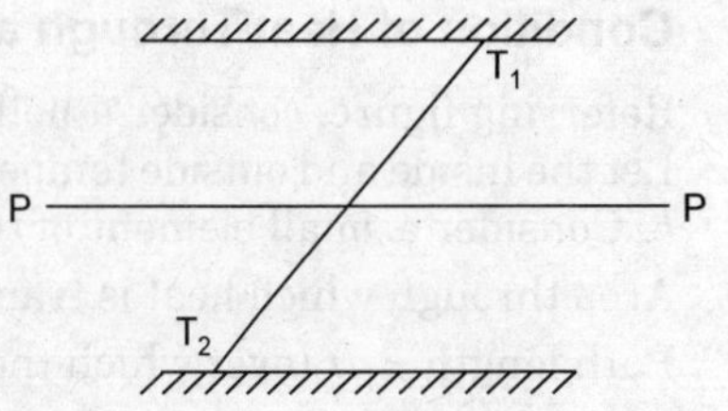

where n = number of molecules per unit volumes

$\overline{v}_s$ = arithmatic mean molecular velocity

f = number of degree of freedom

σ = boltzmann's constant

λ = molecular mean depth path

Gases with the higher molecular weights have smaller thermal conductivity than those with lower molecular weights. This is due to fact that molecular path of the gas molecules decrease with increase in density and k is directly proportional to mean free path of the molecule. This can be explained by the comparison of two gases as follows :

At STP, k for $N_2 = 0.021\ W/mk$

k for $H_2 = 0.15\ W/mk$

Conductivity of the liquid can also be explained in terms of dynamic viscosity μ as

$$k = \left[1 + \frac{4.5}{2n}\right]\mu c_v$$

where, n = number of atoms in a molecule

ONE DIMENSIONAL HEAT CONDUCTION

Conduction of Heat Through Slabs

Consider the transmission of heat through area A of a wall (thickness x) consisting of a number of slabs. Let conductivities of different slabs (wall materials) be k_1, k_2 and k_3, thickness of slabs (also called as 'path' length)be x_1, x_2 and x_3 and temperatures at the wall surfaces be T_1, T_2, T_3 and T_4 ($T_1 > T_4$) respectively.
Since quantity of heat transmitted per unit time through each slab is the same, therefore

$$\frac{Q}{A} = \frac{k_1(T_1 - T_2)}{x_1} = \frac{k_2(T_2 - T_3)}{x_2} = \frac{k_3(T_3 - T_4)}{x_3}$$

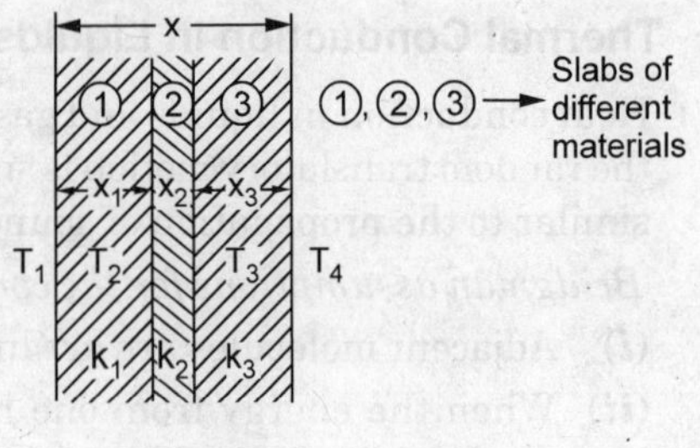

$$\therefore \quad T_1 - T_4 = \frac{Q}{A}\left[\frac{x_1}{k_1} + \frac{x_2}{k_2} + \frac{x_3}{k_3}\right]$$

or
$$Q = \frac{A(T_1 - T_4)}{\left[\frac{x_1}{k_1} + \frac{x_2}{k_2} + \frac{x_3}{k_3}\right]}$$

Conduction of Heat Through Pipe Walls

Area through which heat is transmitted, $A = 2\pi rl$
Path length = dr

$$\therefore \quad Q = -kA\left(\frac{dT}{dr}\right) = -k.\ 2\pi rl\ \frac{dT}{dr} \text{ per unit time}$$

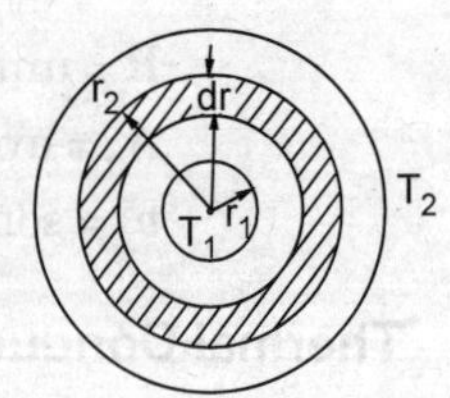

or
$$Q\ \frac{dr}{r} = -k.\ 2\pi l.dT$$

Integrating
$$Q\int_{r_1}^{r_2}\frac{dr}{r} = -\ k.\ 2\pi l\int_{T_1}^{T_2} dT$$

$$\therefore \quad = \frac{T_1 - T_2}{\frac{1}{2\pi l}\left[\frac{1}{k}\log_e\frac{r_2}{r_1}\right]}$$

Condition of Heat Through a Hollow Sphere

Referring figure, consider a hollow sphere of internal radius r_1 and external radius r_2.
Let the inside and outside temperatures be T_1 and T_2 and let the thermal conductivity be k. Consider a small element of thickness of dr at any radius r.
Area through which heat is transmitted, $A = 4\pi r^2$
Path length = dr (over which the temperature fall in temperature is dT)

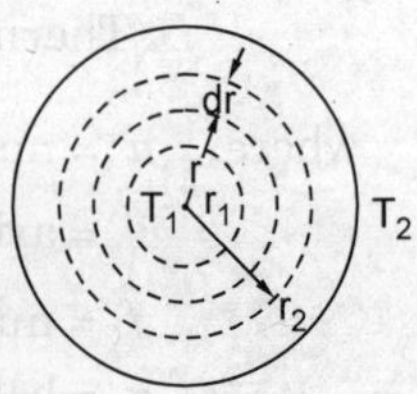

$$\therefore \quad Q = -k.\ 4\pi r^2\ \frac{dT}{dr}$$

Integrating, $$Q \int_{r_1}^{r_2} \frac{dr}{r^2} = -4\pi k \int_{T_1}^{T_2} dT$$

or $$Q = \frac{4\pi k r_1 r_2 (T_1 - T_2)}{(r_2 - r_1)} = \frac{T_1 - T_2}{\left(\frac{r_2 - r_1}{4\pi k r_1 r_2}\right)}$$

The term $\frac{r_2 - r_1}{4\pi k r_1 r_2}$ is known as *thermal resistance of the sphere.*

Heat Transfer at The Interface of Two Solids

Fig. (*a*) shows the temperature distribution through a composite wall which is linear through each of its component. This means that at the interface of two solids, there is a discontinuity in the temperature gradient although the temperature itself is continuous.

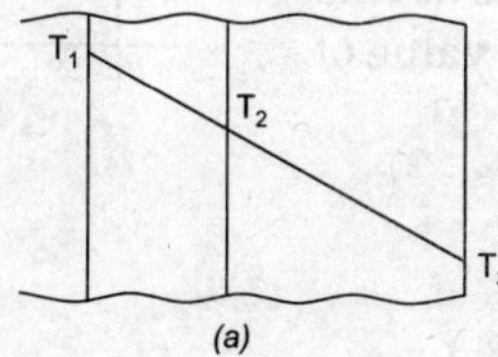

(a)

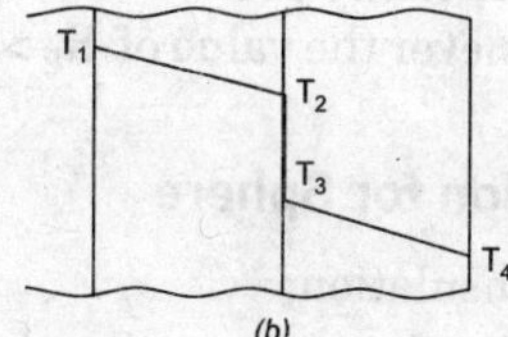

(b)

At the interface, $$k_1 \left(\frac{dT}{dx}\right)_1 = k_2 \left(\frac{dT}{dx}\right)_2$$

INSULATION

The insulation is a material which retards the heat flow with reasonable effectiveness. It is not necessary to have low thermal conductivity for insulating material. The purpose of insulation is to prevent the flow of heat from the system to the surrounding as in case of steam and hot water pipes which are used for air conditioning in winter and to prevent the flow of heat from the surrounding to the system as in the case of brine pipes which are used for air conditioning in summer and domestic refrigerators and water coolers.

Uses of insulations for industrial purposes.

(i) Air conditioning system
(ii) Refrigerators and food preserving stores
(iii) Preservation of liquid gases
(iv) Boiler and steam pipes

Critical Thickness of Insulation

When a solid cylinder radius R_1 is insulated with an insulation thickness $R_2 - R_1$ as shown in the figure, then heat flow from the surface of the solid cylinder to the surrounding is given by

$$Q = \frac{2\pi L(T_1 - T_a)}{\frac{1}{k_2}\log_e\left(\frac{R_2}{R_1}\right) + \frac{1}{R_2 h_0}}$$

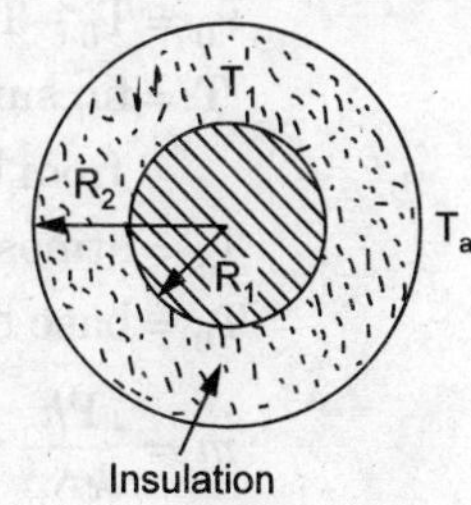

where L = length of the cylinder

k_2 = conductivity of insulation

h_0 = combined heat transfer coefficient (convection and radiation) on the outer surface of the insulation.

In the above expression as R_2 increases, the factor $\frac{1}{k_2}\log_e\left(\frac{R_2}{R_1}\right)$ increases but the factor $\frac{1}{R_2 h_0}$ decreases.

Therfore Q becomes maximum when $\frac{1}{k_2}\log\left(\frac{R_2}{R_1}\right) + \frac{1}{R_2 h_0}$ becomes minimum.

The required condition is

$$\frac{d}{dR_2}\left[\frac{1}{k_2}\log_e\left(\frac{R_2}{R_1}\right)+\frac{1}{R_2 h_0}\right]=0$$

$$\therefore \quad \frac{1}{k_2}\frac{1}{R_2}+\frac{1}{h_0}\left(-\frac{1}{R_2^2}\right)=0 \text{ or } R_2=\frac{k_2}{h_0}$$

where R_2 is known as *critical radius of insulation* as Q becomes maximum at the value of R_{2c}.

The critical thickness of insulation = $R_2 - R_1$

The variation of Q with respect to R_2 is shown in the figure below When $R_2 = R_1$ it indicates bare cylinder without insulation.

The critical value of R_2 is represented by point 2 and the radius at this point is represented by R_{2c}, Whenever the value of $R_2 > R_{2c}$ the value of Q decreases.

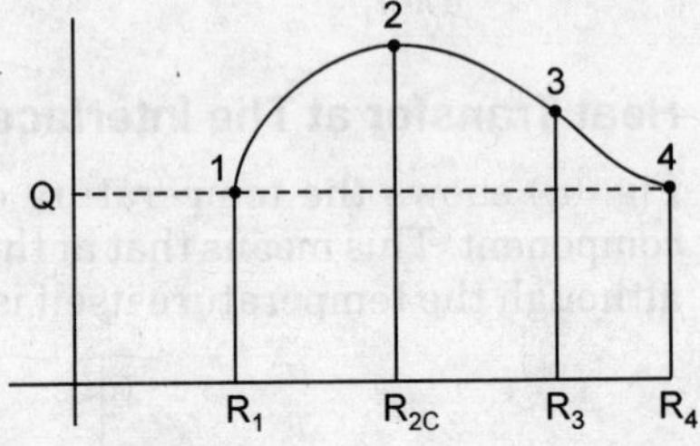

Critical Thickness of Insulation for Sphere

Heat flow through sphere with insulation,

$$Q=\frac{T_1-T_2}{\frac{R_2-R_1}{4\pi R_2 R_1 k}+\frac{1}{4\pi R_2^2 h_0}}=\frac{4\pi(T_1-T_2)}{\left[\frac{1}{R_1 k}-\frac{1}{R_2 k}+\frac{1}{R_2^2 h_0}\right]}$$

$$\therefore \quad \frac{d}{dR_2}\left[\frac{1}{R_1 k}-\frac{1}{R_2 k}+\frac{1}{R_2^2 h_0}\right]=0 \quad \text{or} \quad R_2=\frac{2k}{h_0}$$

FINS

Fins are commonly used for increasing the heat transfer rates from surface whenever it is not possible to increase the rate of heat transfer either by increasing the heat transfer co-efficient on the surface or by increasing the temperature difference between the surface and surrounding fluids. The fins are commonly used in engines used for scooters and motorcycles as well as small capacity compressors.

The circumferential fins of rectangular or triangular profile are commonly used on the engine cylinder of scooters and motorcycles. The pin type fins are used on the condenser of a domestic refrigerator.

Heat Transfer through Fin

Figure shows a rectangular fin of length L, which is perpendicular to surface from which heat is to be removed, 2 δ is the thickness of the fin, W is width of fin which is parallel to the surface from which heat is to be removed.

Then $$\frac{\theta}{\theta_0}=\left[\frac{\cosh m(L-x)+(h/mk)\sinh m(L-x)}{\cosh mL+(h/mk)\sinh mL}\right]$$

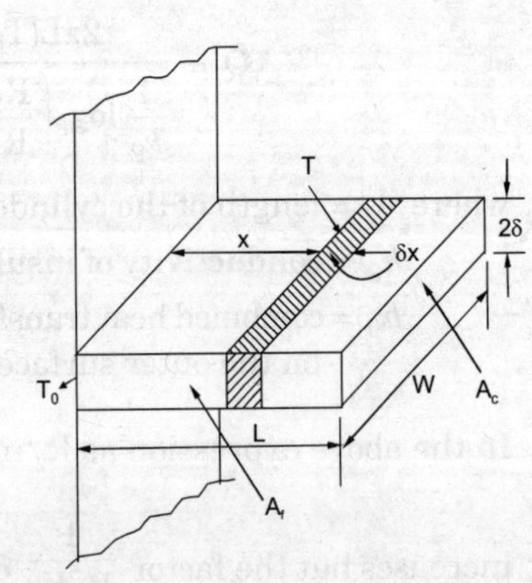

where $\theta = T - T_a$

$\theta_0 = T_0 - T_a$

T = fin surface temperature at a distance x measured from base of the fin.

T_a = atmosphere temperature

T_0 = base temperature

$$m=\frac{Ph}{kA_c}$$

P = perimeter of the fin = 2W + 4δ

A_c = cross sectional area of the fin

k = conductivity of fin material

h = convection heat transfer coefficient

Heat lost by the fin, $Q = kA_c\, m\, \theta_0 \left[\dfrac{h \cosh mL + km \sinh mL}{km \cosh mL + h \sinh mL}\right] = kA_c\, m\, \theta_0 \left[\dfrac{1 + \dfrac{mk}{h}\tanh mL}{\dfrac{mk}{h} + \tanh mL}\right]$

For rectangular fin, $m = \sqrt{\dfrac{h.P}{kA_c}} = \sqrt{\dfrac{h(2W + 4\delta)}{kW.2\delta}} = \sqrt{\dfrac{h}{k\delta}}$

For circular fin, $m = \sqrt{\dfrac{hP}{kA_c}} = \sqrt{\dfrac{h\pi d}{k.\dfrac{\pi}{4}d^2}} = \sqrt{\dfrac{4h}{kd}}$

where, d = diameter of the fin

If end of the fin is insulated, then $\theta = \theta_0\left[\dfrac{\cosh m(L - x)}{\cosh mL}\right]$

and $Q = kA_c\, m\theta_0$

If the fin is sufficiently long, then

$$\frac{\theta}{\theta_0} = e^{-mx} = \cosh mx - \sinh mx$$

$$Q = kA_c\, m\, \theta_0$$

Effectiveness of the Fin $(\in)$. $\in = \dfrac{\text{Heat lost with fin}}{\text{Heat lost without fin}}$

Effectiveness $\in$ should be more than 1 $\in = \dfrac{\dfrac{kA_c\, m.\theta_0[h\cosh mL + mk\sinh mL]}{mk\cosh mL + h\sinh mL}}{hA_c.\theta_0} = \dfrac{km}{h}\left[\dfrac{1 + \dfrac{mk}{h}\tanh mL}{\dfrac{mk}{h} + \tanh mL}\right]$

where, $m = \sqrt{\dfrac{Ph}{kA_c}} = \sqrt{\dfrac{2W.h}{k.W.2\delta}} = \sqrt{\dfrac{h}{k\delta}}$

When $2\delta << W$, a non-dimensional number (Biot number) is

$$Bi = \frac{h\delta}{k} = \frac{\dfrac{\delta}{k}}{\dfrac{1}{h}} \quad \frac{\text{Internal resistance of the fin material}}{\text{External resistance of the fluid on fin material}}$$

$$\in = \frac{1}{\sqrt{Bi}}\left[\frac{\sqrt{Bi} + \tanh(\sqrt{Bi}.\bar{L})}{1 + \sqrt{Bi} + \tanh(\sqrt{Bi}.\bar{L})}\right]$$

where, $\bar{L} = \dfrac{L}{\delta}$ = non-dimensional length

Now there are three important cases :

(i) If $Bi = 1$, then $\in = 1$. This is possible when poor conducting material is used for fin.

(ii) If $Bi > 1$, then $\in < 1$. There is an adverse effect on heat flow and fin works as insulator. This is possible if the value of h is quite high this is the main cause for not using the fins on the steam condenser tubes.

(iii) If $Bi < 1$, then $\in > 1$ which is the most desirable case. This is possible in the case of high conductivity materials like Cu, Al. Therefore fins are desirable in all types of heat exchangess.

Variation of Heat Loss From Fins with Length of Fin

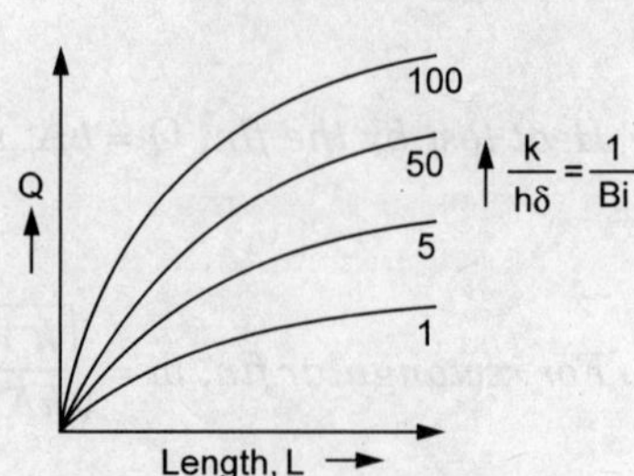

It can be seen from the graph that the rate of increase of Q with increase of L is quite less as compared with the rate of increase of Q with increase of $\frac{k}{h\delta}$.

Efficiency of Fin

$$\eta_f = \frac{\text{Heat lost from the fin}}{\text{Heat lost from the fin, if the whole surface of the fin is maintained at base temperature}}$$

$$= \frac{1}{L} \cdot \sqrt{\frac{k\,\delta}{h}} \tan h\, mL \qquad \text{.....} \because m = \sqrt{\frac{h}{K\delta}}$$

Temperature error of thermometer

Temperature distribution along the fin is given by

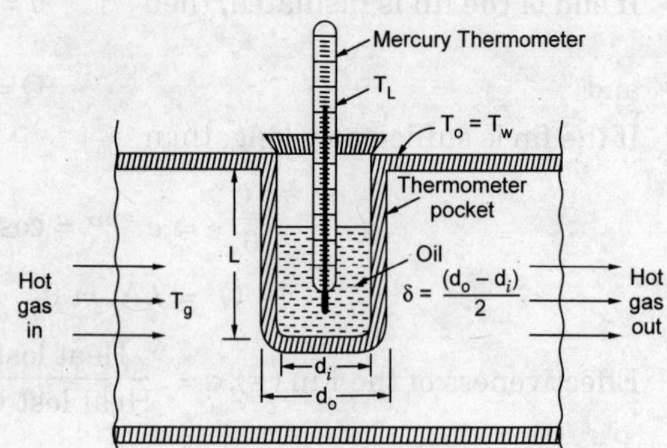

$$\frac{\theta}{\theta_0} = \frac{T_x - T_a}{T_0 - T_a} = \frac{\cosh m(L - x)}{\cosh mL}$$

In this case, $T_a = T_g$, $T_o = T_w$, $T_x = T_L$,

At $x = L$

$$\frac{\theta}{\theta_o} = \frac{T_x - T_a}{T_o - T_a} = \frac{T_L - T_g}{T_w - T_g} = \frac{1}{\cos h\, mL}$$

CONVECTION

Heat Transfer By convection

A process of heat transfer by the combined action of heat conduction and mixing motion is known as *convection*. Heat is transferred by convection due to mass movement and mixing of macroscopic element or gas. The actual process of energy transfer from one fluid particle to another is by conduction, but the energy may be transported from one point to another by the displacement of fluid. As the motion of the fluid is involved, the heat transfer by convection is partly governed by the law of fluid mechanics.

From the Newton's law of cooling,

$$q = hA\Delta T = hA(T_w - T_\infty)$$

$$Q = hA(T_w - T_f)$$

where T_w = temperature of wall

T_f = temperature of fluid

h = heat transfer co-efficient

Unit of heat transfer co-efficient : W/m^2K

Types of Convection Heat Transfer

(i) **Natural convection :** The flow of fluid take place when the hot or cold body comes in contact with the fluid. The heat flow from the hot body to fluid due to temperature difference between the body and the fluid and fluid density in the vicinity of the hot body decreases. The difference in density of the hot and cold fluid cause the fluid to flow in the upward direction. The force causing this flow is known as buoyancy force. Whenever the motion of the fluid is caused only due to the difference in density resulting from temperature gradient without the use of pump or fan, then the mechanism of heat transfer is known as natural or free convection.

(ii) **Force convection :** It may be caused by some external agency such as pump or a blower. The motion of fluid in force convection will be faster than in the free or natural convection, therefore, rate of heat transfer increases. As the convection process depends upon the motion of the fluid particles also, so the heat transfer by convection depends upon the law of heat conduction, geometry of the system and law of fluid dynamics.

Some Useful Ratios

(i) Reynold number, (R_e). It is the ratio of inertia force to the viscous force.

$$Re = \frac{\rho v L}{\mu} \qquad \rho - \text{fluid density, } v - \text{mean velocity}$$

L – characteristic length, μ – dynamic viscosity

(ii) Prandtl number, (P_r). It is the ratio of kinetic viscosity to thermal diffusity.

$$P_r = \frac{\mu c_p}{k} \qquad c_p - s_p \text{ heat, } k - \text{thermal conductivity}$$

(iii) Nusselt number, (N_u). It is a dimensionless heat transfer coefficient which gives a measure of the ratio of the heat transfer rate q to the rate at which heat would be conducted within the fluid under a temperature gradient $\frac{\Delta\theta}{L}$.

$$Nu = \frac{hL}{k} = \frac{q}{\Delta\theta}.\frac{L}{k} = \frac{q}{\frac{\Delta\theta}{L}.k}$$

(iv) Stanton number,(S_t). It is the ratio of wall heat transfer rate (h) to the mass heat flow rate ($\rho v c_p$). It gives a measure of the ratio of the heat transfer coefficient h or $\left(\frac{q}{\Delta\theta}\right)$ to the flow of heat per unit temperature rise due to the velocity and heat capacity of the fluid.

$$S_t = \frac{Nu}{RePr} = \frac{\frac{hL}{k}}{\frac{\rho v L}{\mu} \times \frac{\mu c_p}{k}} = \frac{h}{\rho v c_p}$$

(v) Peclet number (p_e). It is the ratio of mass heat flow rate to the heat flow rate by the conduction under a unit temperature gradient and through a thickness L $\left(q = \frac{k}{L}\right)$.

$$\text{Mass flow rate} = \rho V c_p$$

$$\therefore \qquad Pe = \frac{\rho V C_p}{q} = \frac{\rho V C_p}{\frac{k}{L}} = \frac{\frac{LV}{k}}{\rho c_p} = \frac{LV}{\alpha}$$

Again,

$$Pe = \frac{\rho V c_p L}{K} = \frac{\rho V L}{\mu}.\frac{\mu c_p}{K}$$

$$\therefore \qquad Pe = Re \,.\, Pr$$

(vi) Graetz number (Gr). It is the ratio of heat capacity of the fluid flowing through the pipe per unit length of the pipe to the conductivity of the pipe. So this number is related only for the heat flow to the fluid passing through circular pipes.

$$\therefore \qquad Gr = \frac{mc_p/L}{k} = \frac{\frac{\pi}{4}D^2 \times \rho V.\frac{c_p}{L}}{k} = \frac{\pi}{4}\frac{D^2 \rho V c_p}{kL} = \frac{\pi}{4}.\frac{\rho VD}{\mu}.\frac{\mu c_p}{k}.\frac{D}{L} = \frac{\pi}{4} Re.Pr.\frac{D}{L}$$

$$\therefore \qquad = Pe\frac{\pi D}{4L}$$

(vii) Grashaff number (Gr). It is only used in the natural convection heat transfer. It is defined as the ratio of product of Inertia force and buoyancy force to the square of viscous force.

$$Gr = \frac{\text{Inertia force} \times \text{Buoyance force}}{(\text{Viscous force})^2} = \frac{\rho^2 \beta g \Delta\theta.L^3}{\mu^2} = \frac{\beta g \Delta\theta L^3}{\nu^2} \qquad \ldots\left(\because \nu = \frac{\mu}{\rho}\right)$$

Formulae for Solving the Problems of Natural and Forced Convections

(1) Natural Convection

(i) $\text{Nu} = \dfrac{h_a L}{k} = 0.13\,(Gr\,Pr)^{\frac{1}{3}}$ for vertical surfaces when $10^8 < GrPr < 10^{12}$

$= \dfrac{h_a L}{k} = 0.56\,(GrPr)^{\frac{1}{4}}$ for vertical surfaces when $10^5 < GrPr < 10^8$

(ii) $\text{Nu} = \dfrac{h_a d}{k} = 0.13\,(GrPr)^{\frac{1}{3}}$ for horizontal cylinders when $10^9 < GrPr < 10^{12}$

$= \dfrac{h_a d}{k} = 0.53\,(GrPr)^{\frac{1}{4}}$ for horizontal cylinder when $10^4 < GrPr < 10^9$

(iii) $\text{Nu} = \dfrac{h_a d}{k} = 0.17\,(GrPr)^{\frac{1}{3}}$ for horizontal hot circular plate facing upward when $GrPr > 10^9$

$= \dfrac{h_a d}{k} = 0.71\,(GrPr)^{\frac{1}{4}}$ for $10^3 < GrPr < 10^9$

(iv) $\text{Nu} = 0.667\,Pr^{\frac{1}{2}}\,(Pr + 0.952)^{-\frac{1}{4}}\,(Gr)^{\frac{1}{4}}$ for vertical plate

(2) Forced Convection

(i) $\text{Nu} = \dfrac{h_a L}{k} = 0.664\,Re^{\frac{1}{2}}\,Pr^{\frac{1}{3}}$ for the flow over flat plate

(ii) $\text{Nu} = \dfrac{h_a d}{k} = 0.023\,Re^{0.8}Pr^{0.4}$ for the flow through tube

(3) Model Testing

(i) $\dfrac{v_m}{v_p} = \dfrac{\rho_p}{\rho_m} \cdot \dfrac{\mu_m}{\mu_p} \cdot \dfrac{L_p}{L_m}$

$\dfrac{v_m}{v_p} = \dfrac{L_p}{L_m} \cdot \dfrac{\nu_m}{\nu_p}$

(ii) $\dfrac{v_m}{v_p} = \sqrt{\dfrac{L_m}{L_p}}$ (testing for resistance in the same fluid)

(iii) $\dfrac{F_m}{F_p} = \dfrac{\rho_m}{\rho_p} \cdot \left(\dfrac{v_m}{v_p}\right)^2 \left(\dfrac{L_m}{L_p}\right)^2$ (testing for thrust for propeller

(iv) $\text{H.P.} = \dfrac{F_p v_p}{75}$

$$Q = hA(T_w - T_f)$$

where T_w = temperature of wall

T_f = temperature of fluid

h = heat transfer co-efficient

Unit of heat transfer co-efficient : W/m^2K

Under steady heat flow conduction.

Heat conducted = Heat convected from solid boundary to adjacent fluid

$$\therefore \quad Q = -kA\left(\frac{dT}{dx}\right)_{x=L} = hA(T_w - T_a) \text{ or } h = \frac{-k\left(\dfrac{dT}{dx}\right)_{x=L}}{T_w - T_a}$$

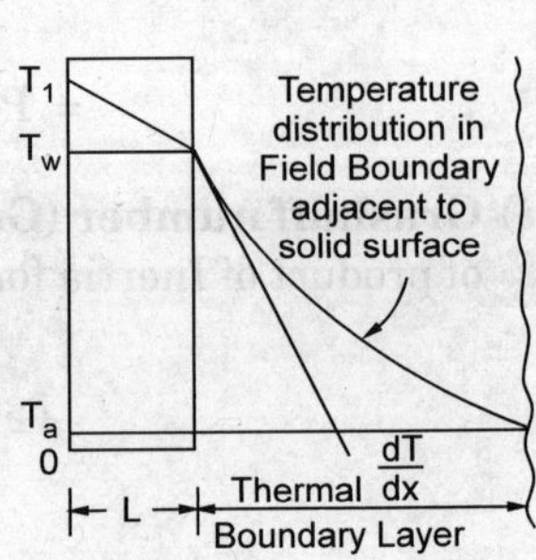

From the above equation, for a system in which the wall temperature T_w, the ambient temperature T_a and thermal conductivity of solids, k are constant, then any change in h mean change in $\left(\dfrac{dT}{dx}\right)_{x=L}$

i.e. heat transfer co-efficient can be considered fundamentally as a slope of the temperature destribution in the fluid.

RESISTANCE CONCEPT

Overall Heat Transfer Co-Efficient

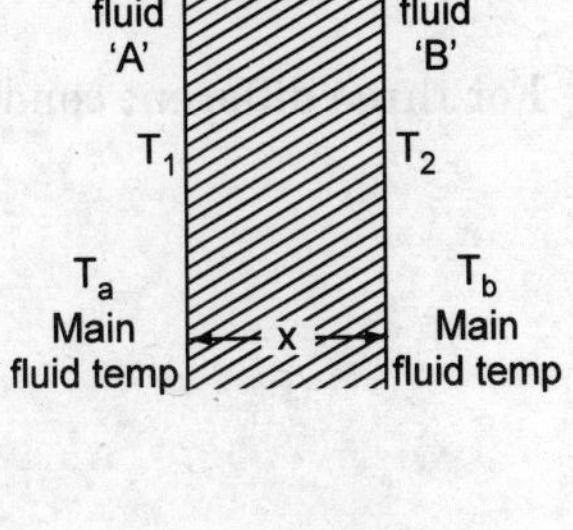

If U is overall co-efficient of the heat transfer, then

$$Q = UA(T_a - T_b) = \frac{A(T_a - T_b)}{\frac{1}{h_a} + \frac{x}{k} + \frac{1}{h_b}}$$

$$\therefore \quad U = \frac{1}{\frac{1}{h_a} + \frac{x}{k} + \frac{1}{h_b}}$$

Here, h_a = heat transfer co-efficient from hot fluid to metal surface

h_b = heat transfer co-efficient from metal surface to cold fluid

k = thermal conductivity of metal wall.

Heat Transfer Through Composite Cylinder

When a hot fluid at a temperature T_a flowing through a pipe is separated by two layers from cold fluid at temperature T_b(say atmosphere). (notations carry the usual meaning), then

$$\therefore \quad Q = \frac{T_a - T_b}{\frac{1}{2\pi l}\left[\frac{1}{r_1 h_a} + \frac{1}{k_1}\log_e\frac{r_2}{r_1} + \frac{1}{k_2}\log_e\frac{r_3}{r_2} + \frac{1}{r_4 h_b}\right]}$$

here, $\quad r_1 < r_2 < r_3$

If U_a and U_b are the overall co-efficients of heat transfer referred to inside and the outside area of tube respectively, then

$$Q = U_a A_a (T_a - T_b) = U_b A_b (T_a - T_b)$$

Heat Transfer Through Composite Spherical Shell

Proceeding in the same way as in the previous case, the heat transfer in this case will be given by the expression

$$Q = \frac{T_a - T_b}{\frac{1}{h_a A_a} + \frac{r_2 - r_1}{4\pi k_1 k_2 r_1 r_2} + \frac{r_3 - r_2}{4\pi k_2 r_2 r_3} + \frac{1}{h_b A_b}}$$

Prandtl Number

If the free stream velocity is low and temperature difference between free stream and the plate is small, then the frictional heat generation can be neglected and energy equation becomes

$$u.\frac{\partial T}{\partial x} + v.\frac{\partial T}{\partial y} = \alpha.\frac{\partial^2 T}{\partial y^2} \quad \ldots (i)$$

where, $\quad \alpha = \frac{k}{\rho c_p} = \frac{\text{Thermal conductivity}}{\text{Thermal capacity}}$

and this ratio is known as *thermal diffusivity*

Hydrodynamic equation or momentum equation for boundary layer is

$$u.\frac{\partial u}{\partial x} + v.\frac{\partial u}{\partial y} = \nu.\frac{\partial^2 u}{\partial y^2} \quad \ldots (ii)$$

In this case the temperature and velocity distribution would be identical

$$\therefore \quad \frac{\theta}{\theta_m} = \frac{T_\eta - T_w}{T_\infty - T_w} = \frac{u}{U} = \frac{df}{d\eta} \text{ where } \eta = y\sqrt{\frac{v}{\nu x}} = \text{stretching factor}$$

The result is of considerable practical importance because all the gases have $\alpha \approx \nu$.

Also if $\frac{\nu}{\alpha} > 1$, greater will be the difference between temperature and velocity profile.

$$\frac{\nu}{\alpha} = \frac{\mu C_p}{k} = \frac{\mu}{\frac{k}{c_p}} = \frac{\text{Viscous nature of fluid}}{\frac{\text{Heat conducting capacity}}{\text{Heat storage capacity}}}$$

For three different conditions of Pr, the thermal and hydraulic boundary layers are shown in the figure.

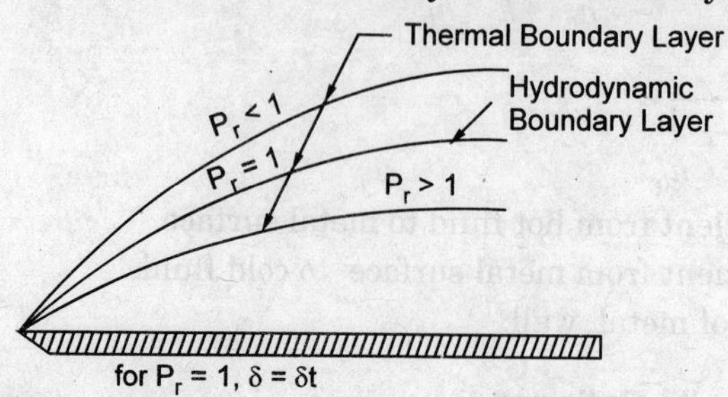

Formulae Used For Solving Problems

For laminar flow

(i) $\frac{\delta}{x} = \frac{4.64}{\sqrt{Re_x}}$ (Von-Karman equation) $= \frac{5}{\sqrt{Re_x}}$ (Blasius equation)

(ii) $\frac{\delta}{\delta_t} = (Pr)^{\frac{1}{3}}$

(iii) (Mass flow through boundary layer at a section $x = m_x$), $m_x = \frac{5}{8}\rho U\delta$

(iv) Mass flow between two sections), $\delta_m = \frac{5}{8}\rho U(\delta_2 - \delta_1)$ where $\delta_2 > \delta_1$

(v) $C_{fx} = 0.664 (Re_x)^{-\frac{1}{2}}$

(vi) $C_{fa} = 1.328\ (Re_l)^{-\frac{1}{2}}$

(vii) $\tau_a = C_{fa} \frac{\rho U^2}{2}$

(viii) $\tau_x = 0.332\ \frac{\mu U}{L}\ \sqrt{Re_x}\ = 0.332\ \rho U^2 (Re_x)^{-\frac{1}{2}}$

(ix) $\tau_x = 0.664\ \frac{\mu U}{L}\ \sqrt{Re_l}\ = 0.664\ \rho U^2 (Re_l)^{-\frac{1}{2}}$

(x) $F = \tau_a.A = 0.664\ \mu UW (Re_l) = 0.664\ A\rho U^2\ (Re_l)^{-\frac{1}{2}}$

(xi) $F_x = \tau_x.A$

(xii) $Nu_x = 0.332\ (Re_x)^{\frac{1}{2}}\ (Pr)^{\frac{1}{3}}$

(xiii) $Nu_a = 0.664 (Re_l)^{\frac{1}{2}}\ (Pr)^{\frac{1}{3}}$

(xiv) $St_x (Pr)^{\frac{2}{3}} = \left(\frac{h_x}{\rho U c_p}\right) (Pr)^{\frac{2}{3}} = \frac{C_{fx}}{2}$

(xv) $St_a (Pr)^{\frac{2}{3}} = \left(\frac{h_a}{\rho U c_p}\right)(Pr)^{\frac{2}{3}} = \frac{C_{fa}}{2}$; where, $Re_x = \frac{x \cdot U}{\nu}$ and $Re_l = \frac{LU}{\nu}$

$Nu_x = \frac{h_x \cdot x}{k}$ and $Nu_a = \frac{h_a \cdot L}{k}$

For turbulent flow :

(i) $\frac{\delta}{x} = \frac{0.39}{(Re_x)^{1/5}}$

(ii) $C_{fx} = 0.0576\ (Re_x)^{-\frac{1}{5}}$

(iii) $C_{fa} = 0.072\ (Re_l)^{-\frac{1}{5}}$

(iv) $\tau_a = C_{fa} \cdot \frac{\rho U^2}{2}$

(v) $F = \tau_a \cdot A$

(vi) $Nu_x = 0.0288\ (Re_x)^{0.8}\ (Pr)^{\frac{1}{3}}$

(vii) $Nu_a = 0.036\ (Re_l)^{0.8}\ (Pr)^{\frac{1}{3}}$

(viii) $St_x \cdot (Pr)^{\frac{2}{3}} = 0.0288 (Re_x)^{-\frac{1}{5}}$

(ix) $St_a \cdot (Pr)^{\frac{2}{3}} = 0.036\ (Re_l)^{-\frac{1}{5}}$

For laminar and turbulent flows :

(i) $Nu_a = 0.664\ (Re_c)^{\frac{1}{2}}\ (Pr)^{\frac{1}{3}}$

where, $Re_c = 5 \times 10^5$ and $L_c = \frac{5 \times 10^5 \cdot \nu}{U}$

(ii) Turbulent region : $\frac{h_a(L - L_c)}{k} = 0.036\ [(Re_l)^{0.8} - (Re_c)^{0.8}](Pr)^{\frac{1}{3}}$

(iii) Overall heat transfer co-efficient for both regions $h_a = \frac{k}{L}[0.036\ (Re_l)^{0.8} - 836] \cdot (Pr)^{\frac{1}{3}}$

RADIATION

Heat Transfer By radiation

The heat transfer by radiation does not require any medium and it is more effective in vaccum rather than in a medium. There are two theories which explain the transfer of heat by radiation.

(i) Wave Theory : According to this theory, it is assumed that all the space in a universe is filled up by a hypothetical medium called ether. It was stated that the radiation heat transfer take place because of propagation of electromagnetic wave through the ether. A hot body emits electromagnetic wave due to the vibration of molecules and gives out its stored energy. These waves travel through space until they strike another body where part of their energy is absorbed and reconverted back into external energy. The radiaton in the form of electromagnetic wave cause a decrease in internal energy of the emitting body unless the heat is generated within that body equivalent to the decrease in internal energy.

(ii) Quantum Theory : Some of the atoms and molecules of a solid body are raised to excited states when they are heated and there is tendency for these atom and molecules to return to lower energy levels spontaneously. During this process, energy in the form of electromagnetic radiation is emitted. This emitted energy is not continuous but in the form of successive and separate quantities called "*quanta*".

Max planck has given the equation

$$E = hf$$

where h = Planck's constant

f = frequency of vibration

Reflection, Absorption and Transmission of Radiation

Radiation is the property of all substances and each emits energy and amount of energy emitted depends upon the temperature level.

In general, radiation energy falling on a body partly reflected, partly transmitted and partly absorbed.

For a particular wave length, the amount of reflected energy depends upon

(*i*) type of the material

(*ii*) surface finish

(*iii*) angle of incidence

For a given finish, the portion reflected depends on wave length.

If the total incident energy Q_i is falling on an object as shown in the figure and Q_a is absorbed, Q_r is reflected and Q_t is transmitted, then

$$Q_a + Q_r + Q_t = Q_i$$

$$\therefore \quad \frac{Q_a}{Q_i} + \frac{Q_r}{Q_i} + \frac{Q_t}{Q_i} = 1$$

$$\therefore \quad \alpha + r + \tau = 1$$

where α is known as *absorbivity*

r is known as *reflectivity*

τ is known as *transmissivity*

The values of α, r, τ in above equation are dimensionless and vary from 0 to 1.

For most of the solids and liquids, $\tau = 0$ except few as glass etc.

$$\therefore \quad \alpha + r = 1$$

Most solid bodiesas well as liquids are strong absorbers of the thermal radiation. The absorption occurs in a very thin region near the surface of solids. For good conductors of electricity this is of the order of one micron and in electrical insulators this thickness may be as much as thousands of microns.

Opaque Body

The bodies which do not transmit any radiation energy are known as *opaque bodies*. All engineering materials are considered opaque.

Black Body

If $r = 0$ and $\tau = 0$, then $\alpha = 1$

This means that incident energy is entirely absorbed by the body. Such body is defined as a "Black body".

White Body

If $\alpha = 0$ and $\tau = 0$, then $r = 1$

This means that entire incident radiant energy is reflected by the body and such body is called "White body".

Transparent Body

If $\alpha = 0$ and $r = 0$, then $\tau = 1$

This means that entire incident radiant energy passes through the body and such bodies are called *transparent bodies*.

Note : Since for most of the gases $r = 0$, therefore $\alpha + \tau = 1$

There are no absolutely black, white and transparent bodies in nature.

Reflection of Radiation

Specular Reflection

The reflection of the radiation energy is known as *"specular reflection"* when the angle of reflection (β_2) is equal to the angle of incidence β_1 as shown in the figure.

Diffused Reflection

The reflection of the radiation energy is known as *"diffused reflection"* when it is reflected in all direction as shown in the figure.

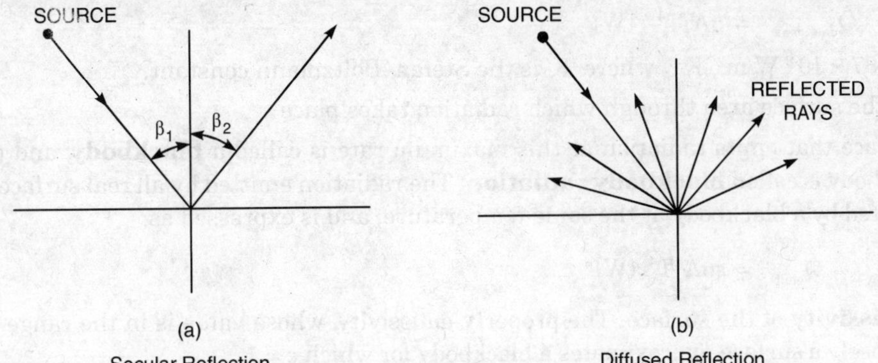

Secular Reflection

Diffused Reflection

Specular reflection occurs on a highly polished surface while the diffused reflection occurs on a rough surface.

Absorption and Transmission

The non-reflected part of incident radiation is partly absorbed and partly transmitted through the body. The absorption and transmission depend on the material and geometry of the body receiving the energy as well as on the wavelength of the incident radiation.

Normal glass is transparent to light rays but non-transparent to ultraviolet rays and it only transmits a small part of thermal radiation. The word transparent is used within some limits because a thin layer of water is transparent to light radiation but it does not reach the bottom of the sea.

Black and GrEy Surface

A black body which absorbs all the incident radiation and none is reflected or transmitted. In other words, a black body is one whose absorptivity is 100%.

Plank's Law of Radiation

The total emissive power of a grey body varies with the wavelength at a given temperature and also varies with a temperature.

$$\therefore \quad E_b = f(\lambda, T)$$

For the monochromatic emissive power of black body,

$$E_{b\lambda} = \frac{C_1 \lambda^{-5}}{e^{\frac{C_2}{\lambda T}} - 1}$$

Source

Circular caruity

where $\quad C_1 = \dfrac{3.21 \times 10^{-8}}{10^{-16}} = 37.45 \times 10^{-17}$ J-m^2/sec

and $\quad C_2 = 1.438$ cm-K $= 14380$ μ–K.

Total emissive power of the black body is given by Boltzmann as

$$E_b(0 - \infty) = \int_0^\infty E_{b\lambda}\, d\lambda = \int_0^\infty \frac{C_1 \lambda^{-5}}{e^{C_2/\lambda T} - 1}\, d\lambda$$

Solving the above equation and substituting the values of C_1 and C_2, we have

$$E_b = \sigma T^4 \text{ (Stefan Boltzmann's law)}$$

where, $\sigma = 5.67 \times 10^{-8}$ J/m^2-sec-K^4

Stefan–Boltzmann Law

The maximum rate of radiation that can be emitted from a surface at an absolute temperature T_s (in K) is given by the **Stefan–Boltzmann law** as

$$\dot{Q}_{emit, max} = \sigma A_s T_s^4 \quad (W)$$

where $\sigma = 5.67 \times 10^{-8}$ W/m$^2 \cdot$K^{-4} where 'K' is the Stefan–Boltzmann constant.

A_s is the surface area through which radiation takes place

The idealized surface that emits radiation at this maximum rate is called a **blackbody,** and the radiation emitted by a blackbody is called **blackbody radiation.** The radiation emitted by all real surfaces is less than the radiation emitted by a blackbody at the same temperature, and is expressed as

$$\dot{Q}_{emit} = \varepsilon\sigma A_s T_s^4 \quad (W)$$

where ε is the **emissivity** of the surface. The property emissivity, whose value is in the range $0 \le \varepsilon \le 1$ is a measure of how closely a surface approximates a blackbody for which $\varepsilon = 1$.

When a surface of emissivity and surface area As at an absolute temperature Ts is completely enclosed by a much larger (or black) surface at absolute temperature Tsurr separated by a gas (such as air) that does not intervene with radiation, the net rate of radiation heat transfer between these two surfaces is given by shown in figure.

$$Q_{rad} = \varepsilon\sigma A_s (T_s^4 - T_{surr}^4)$$

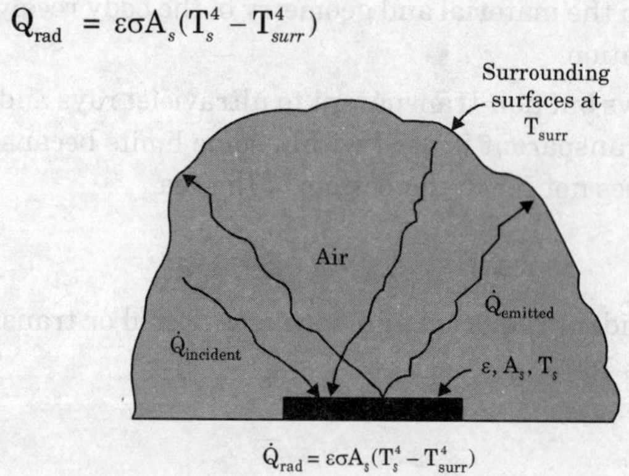

Fig : Radiation heat transfer between a surface and the surfaces surrounding it

Grey Body

The body which absorbs a definite percentage of incident radiation waves irrespective of their wavelengths, the body is known as **grey body**. When the absorptivity of a body varies with wavelength of radiation waves, the body is known as **coloured body**.

Emissive Power of Grey Body

The emissive power of the body is always less than the black body. The ratio of emissive power of grey body to that of black body at given temperature is constant for all wave lengths.

$$\text{Emissivity of a grey body, } \in = \frac{\text{Emissive power of grey body at a temperature}}{\text{Emissive power of black body at same temperature}} = \frac{E_g}{E_b}$$

For monochromatic radiation,

$$\text{Emissivity, } \in_\lambda = \frac{E_{g\lambda}}{E_{b\lambda}}$$

$$E_g = \int_0^\infty E_{g\lambda}.d\lambda \text{ and } E_b = \int_0^\infty E_{b\lambda}.d\lambda$$

$$\therefore \quad \in = \frac{\int_0^\infty E_{g\lambda}.d\lambda}{\int_0^\infty E_{b\lambda}.d\lambda} = \frac{\int_0^\infty E_{b\lambda}.\in_\lambda.d\lambda}{\int_0^\infty E_{b\lambda}.d\lambda}$$

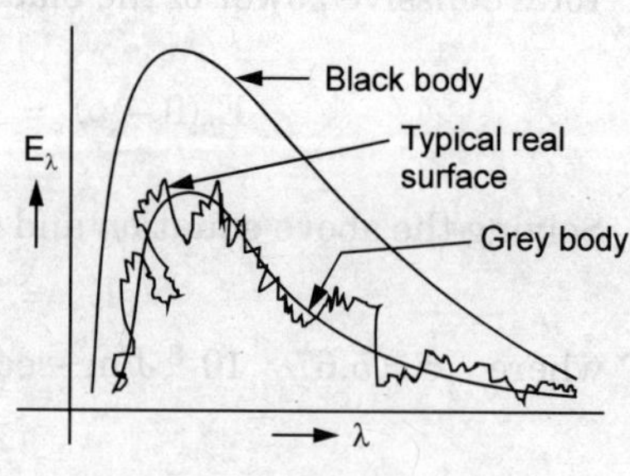

Hence *emissivity* of surface is property of the surface and only depends on the characteristie of the surface and independent on the wavelength of the incident radiation waves, while absorptivity of the surface is not property of the surface because it depends on the wavelength of the incident radiation waves.

Kirchoff's Law

Kirchoff's law states that the ratio of total emissive power to absorptivity is constant for all the substances which are in the thermal equilibrium with the surroundings.

Applying this law on three bodies whose emissive powers are E_1, E_2, and E_3 and absorptivities are α_1, α_2, and α_3 respectively.

$$\frac{E_1}{\alpha_1} = \frac{E_2}{\alpha_2} = \frac{E_3}{\alpha_3} = \text{constant} = \frac{E_b}{\alpha_b}$$

Since absorptivity for black body, $\alpha_b = 1$

$$\therefore \quad \frac{E_1}{E_b} = \alpha_1, \quad \frac{E_2}{E_b} = \alpha_2 \quad \text{and} \quad \frac{E_3}{E_b} = \alpha_3$$

But according to the definition of emissivity of a body

$$\frac{E_1}{E_b} = \in_1, \quad \frac{E_2}{E_b} = \in_2 \quad \text{and} \quad \frac{E_3}{E_b} = \in_3$$

Comparing both above equations, we get

$$\alpha_1 = \in_1, \quad \alpha_2 = \in \quad \text{and} \quad \alpha_3 = \in_3$$

In general form we can write, $\alpha = \in$

Hence this law state that the emissivity of a body is equal to its absorptivity when the body remains in thermal equilibrium with its surroundings.

Wien's Displacement Law

$$\lambda_m T = 2.9 \text{ mm-K}$$

where λ_m is that wavelength at which monochromatic emissive power of the black body becomes maximum at a temperature T.

As the body is heated, the maximum intensity is shifted to the shorter wave lengths and first visible sign of increase in temperature of the body is a dark red colour. With further increase in temperature, the colour appears as bright red, then bright yellow and finally white.

Solid Angle

It is defined as the angle covered by unit area on a surface of a sphere of unit radius when joined with the centre of sphere and it is measured in the *steradians*.

$$\text{Solid angle, } \omega = \frac{A}{R^2}$$

where A is area on a surface of a sphere of radius R which is cut out from the issuing centre of a sphere.

Intensity of Radiation

It is defined as the rate of emission of radiation in a given direction from a surface per unit solid angle and per unit projected area of a radiating surface on a plane perpendicular to the direction of radiation.

$$E_b = \pi I_b$$

Radiosity

It refers to all the radiant energy leaving surface. The radiation leaving the surface includes the reflected portion as well as emission as shown in the figure. Therefore, radiosity is different from the emissive power.

Types of Radiosity

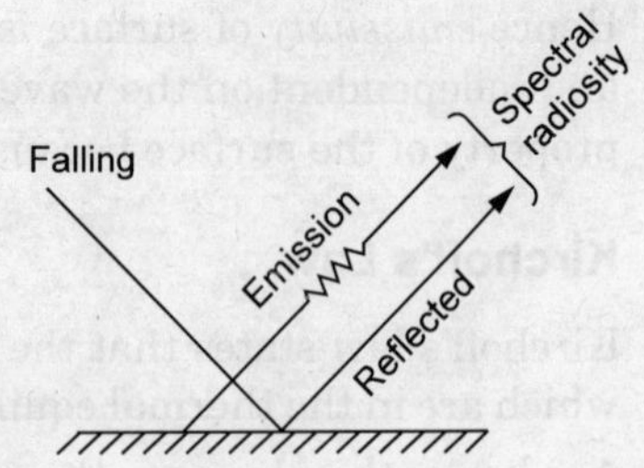

(*i*) **Spectral radiosity**. It is the rate at which radiation leaves per unit area of the surface at a wavelength λ per unit wavelength. It is related to the intensity of radiation associated with emission also shown in figure.

(*ii*) **Total radiosity**. It is associated with the entire spectrum of wave length. The intensity of radiation is based on projected area while the radiosity is based on the actual surface area.

RADIATION BETWEEN TWO INFINITELY LONG CYLINDERS

Two concentric cylinder of radius R_1 and R_2 are shown in figure. T_1 and T_2 are temperaturers of inner and outer surface of inner and outer cylinder respectively and their relative emissivities are $\in_1$ and $\in_2$.

Then net heat transfer between the inner and outer concentric cylinders is given by

$$Q_{net} = \frac{A_1\sigma(T_1^4 - T_2^4)}{\frac{1}{\in_1} + \frac{A_1}{A_2}\left(\frac{1}{\in_2} - 1\right)} = \frac{\sigma A_1(T_1^4 - T_2^4)}{\frac{1}{\in_1} + \frac{R_1}{R_2}\left(\frac{1}{\in_2} - 1\right)}$$

For concentric sphere, net heat flow, $Q_{net} = \dfrac{\sigma A_1(T_1^4 - T_2^4)}{\frac{1}{\in_1} + \left(\frac{R_1}{R_2}\right)^2\left(\frac{1}{\in_2} - 1\right)}$

NETWORK ANALYSIS

Consider two bodies A and B radiating heat as shown in figure. It emissivity of body A is $\in_a$, then amount of energy radiated by A is $\in_a \cdot E_{ba}$ and if G is the amount of energy falling on A from B, then out of G, the amount of energy reflected by A is $r_a G$, where r_a is the reflectivity of the surface A.

Total energy going away from the body A is,

$$\tau = \in_a E_{ba} + r_a G \quad \text{.... }(i)$$

Since transmissivity is assumed to be zero for solid bodies, therefore

$$\alpha_a + r_a = 1$$

$\Rightarrow$ $\quad r_a = 1 - \alpha_a$

From Kirchhoff's law, $\quad \alpha_a = \in_a$

$\therefore$ $\quad J = \in_a E_{ba} + (1 - \in_a)G$

Net energy lost by the body A, $\quad q = J - G$

$$q = \in_a E_{ba} - \in_a G \quad \text{... }(ii)$$

From equation (*i*) and (*ii*), we get

$$q = \frac{E_{ba} - J}{\frac{1 - \in_a}{\in_a}} \text{ Joule per unit area}$$

Total heat lost from A is given by, $\quad Q = \dfrac{E_{ba} - J}{\left(\frac{1 - \in_a}{\in_a}\right)\frac{1}{A_a}}$

where $\dfrac{1 - \in_a}{\in_a A_a}$ is the surface resistance of the body as it is related to the surface properties of the body.

When two surface resistance of the two bodies and space resistance between them is considered, then net heat flow can be given by an electric circuit as shown in figure.

E_{b1} $\frac{1-\epsilon_1}{A_1\epsilon_1}$ $\frac{1}{A_1F_{1-2}}$ $\frac{1-\epsilon_2}{A_2\epsilon_2}$ E_{b2}

$$\therefore \quad Q = \frac{E_{b1} - E_{b2}}{\dfrac{1-\epsilon_1}{A_1\epsilon_1} + \dfrac{1}{A_1F_{1-2}} + \dfrac{1-\epsilon_2}{A_2\epsilon_2}} = \frac{\sigma A_1(T_1^4 - T_2^4)}{\dfrac{1-\epsilon_1}{\epsilon_1} + \dfrac{1}{F_{1-2}} + \left(\dfrac{1-\epsilon_2}{\epsilon_2}\right)\dfrac{A_1}{A_2}}$$

(i) If two bodies are infinite parallel plate, then $A_1 = A_2$ and $F_{1-2} = 1$

$$\therefore \quad Q = \frac{\sigma A_1(T_1^4 - T_2^4)}{\dfrac{1}{\epsilon_1} + \dfrac{1}{\epsilon_2} - 1}$$

(ii) If two bodies are concentric cylinder or sphere, then $F_{1-2} = 1$

$$\therefore \quad Q = \frac{\sigma A_1(T_1^4 - T_2^4)}{\dfrac{1}{\epsilon_1} + \left(\dfrac{1-\epsilon_2}{\epsilon_2}\right)\dfrac{A_1}{A_2}}$$

(iii) For concentric cylinders, $\dfrac{A_1}{A_2} = \dfrac{\pi D_1 L}{\pi D_2 L} = \dfrac{D_1}{D_2} = \dfrac{R_1}{R_2}$

$$Q = \frac{\sigma A_1(T_1^4 - T_2^4)}{\dfrac{1}{\epsilon_1} + \left(\dfrac{1-\epsilon_2}{\epsilon_2}\right)\dfrac{R_1}{R_2}}$$

(iv) For concentric sphere, $\dfrac{A_1}{A_2} = \left(\dfrac{R_1}{R_2}\right)^2$

$$\therefore \quad Q = \frac{\sigma A_1(T_1^4 - T_2^4)}{\dfrac{1}{\epsilon_1} + \left(\dfrac{1-\epsilon_2}{\epsilon_2}\right)\left(\dfrac{R_1}{R_2}\right)^2}$$

In all the above case when the grey surface are replaced by the black body, the surface resistance becomes zero.

Objective Type Questions

1. A closed system is one, which
(*a*) permits the passage of energy and matter across the boundaries
(*b*) does not permit the passage of energy and matter across the bandaries
(*c*) permits the passage of energy across the boundary but does not permit the passage of matter
(*d*) permits the passage of matter across the boundary but does not permit the passage of energy

2. An isolated system is one, which
(*a*) permits the passage of energy and matter across the boundaries
(*b*) permits the passage of energy only
(*c*) does not permit the passage of energy and matter across it
(*d*) permits the passage of matter only

3. A system comprising of a single phase, is known as
(*a*) open system (*b*) closed system
(*c*) homogeneous system (*d*) heterogeneous system

4. The characteristic of a control volume is/are
(*a*) the volume, shape and position with respect to an observer are fixed
(*b*) material flow across the boundary
(*c*) both (*a*) and (*b*)
(*d*) none of theses

5. Control volume refers to a
(*a*) specified mass
(*b*) fixed region in the space
(*c*) closed system
(*d*) none of the above

6. Specific heat is the amount of heat required to raise the temperature
(*a*) by unit degree of a substance
(*b*) by unit degree of a unit mass
(*c*) of a unit mass by 10°
(*d*) none of the above

7. The ratio of specific heats of a gas at constant pressure and at constant volume
(*a*) varies with temperature
(*b*) varies with pressure
(*c*) is always constant
(*d*) none of the above

8. Internal energy of a perfect gas depends upon
(*a*) temperature only
(*b*) temperature and pressure
(*c*) temperature, pressure and specific heats
(*d*) none of the above

9. With rise of temperature, the specific heat of water
(*a*) increases
(*b*) decreases
(*c*) first decreases to minimum then increases
(*d*) remains constant

10. For a closed system, difference between the heat added to the system and work done by the gas, is equal to the change in
(*a*) enthalpy (*b*) entropy
(*c*) internal energy (*d*) temperature

11. Which of the following is not an extensive property of a thermo-dynamic system ?
(*a*) Total mass (*b*) Total internal energy
(*c*) Total volume (*d*) Temperature

12. Thermal equilibrium between two or more bodies exists, when they are brought together, there is no change in
(*a*) density (*b*) pressure
(*c*) temperature (*d*) all of these

13. The sequence of process that eventually returns the working substance to its original state, is known as
(*a*) event
(*b*) thermodynamic cycle
(*c*) thermodynamic property
(*d*) none of these

14. A system consisting of more than one phase is called
(*a*) isolated system (*b*) open system
(*c*) non-uniform system (*d*) heterogeneous system

15. Kelvin-Plank's law deals with
(*a*) conversion of work into heat
(*b*) conversion of heat into work
(*c*) conservation of work
(*d*) conservation of heat

16. According to Kelvin-Plank's statement, a perpetual motion machine of
(*a*) first kind is possible
(*b*) first kind is impossible
(*c*) second kind is impossible
(*d*) second kind is possible

17. A perpetual motion machine of the first kind i.e. a machine which produces power without consuming any energy is

(*a*) possible according to first law of thermo-dynamics

(*b*) impossible according to first law of thermo-dynamics

(*c*) impossible according to second law of thermo-dynamics

(*d*) possible according to second law of thermo-dynamics.

18. According to kinetic theory of gases, at absolute zero

(*a*) specific heat of molecules reduces to zero

(*b*) kinetic energy of molecules reduces to zero

(*c*) volume of gas reduce to zero

(*d*) pressure of gas reduce to zero.

19. In an isothermal process, internal energy

(*a*) increases (*b*) remains constant

(*c*) decreases (*d*) none of the above

20. For the same expansion ratio, work done by the gas in case of adiabatic process as compared to work done in case of isothermal process is

(*a*) same (*b*) more

(*c*) less (*d*) none of the above

21. In isothermal expansion, work done by gas depends upon

(*a*) atomicity of gas only

(*b*) expansion ratio only

(*c*) adiabatic index

(*d*) both (*a*) and (*b*)

22. A process, in which no heat is supplied or rejected from the system and entropy is not constant, is called

(*a*) isothermal (*b*) isentropic

(*c*) polytropic (*d*) hyperbolic

23. A process, in which the working substance neither receives nor gives out heat to its surroundings during its expansion or contraction, is called

(*a*) isothermal process (*b*) isentropic process

(*c*) polytropic process (*d*) adiabatic process

24. If v_1 is volume at the begining and v_2 is volume at the end of expansion, then expansion ratio (r) is given by

(*a*) $\frac{v_1}{v_2}$ (*b*) $\frac{v_2}{v_1}$

(*c*) $\frac{v_1 + v_2}{v_1}$ (*d*) $\frac{v_1 + v_2}{v_2 - v_1}$

25. The net work done in a polytropic process is given by

(*a*) $\frac{p_1 V_1 - p_2 V_2}{(n-1)}$ (*b*) $\frac{p_2 V_2 - p_1 V_1}{(n-1)}$

(*c*) $\frac{p_1 V_1 - p_2 V_2}{n}$ (*d*) $\frac{p_2 V_2 - p_1 V_1}{n}$

26. The polytropic index (n) is given by

(*a*) $\frac{\log\left(\frac{p_2}{p_1}\right)}{\log\left(\frac{V_1}{V_2}\right)}$ (*b*) $\frac{\log\left(\frac{V_1}{V_2}\right)}{\log\left(\frac{p_1}{p_2}\right)}$

(*c*) $\frac{\log\left(\frac{p_1}{p_2}\right)}{\log\left(\frac{V_1}{V_2}\right)}$ (*d*) None of the above

27. In a throttling process

(*a*) W = 0 (*b*) E = 0

(*c*) H = 0 (*d*) all of the above

28. In a reversible polytropic process

(*a*) enthalpy remains constant

(*b*) entropy remains constant

(*c*) some heat transfer occurs

(*d*) internal energy remains constant

29. In the polytropic equation,

pV^n = constant,

if value of n is infinite, then process is called

(*a*) constant pressure process

(*b*) constant volume process

(*c*) constant temperature process

(*d*) none of

30. In the polytropic process equation, pV^n = constant, if n = 0, the process is called

(*a*) constant pressure process

(*b*) constant volume process

(*c*) constant temperature process

(*d*) none of these

31. In the polytropic process equation, pV^n = constant, if n = 1, the process is called

(*a*) constant pressure process

(*b*) constant volume process

(*c*) constant temperature process

(*d*) none of these

32. In the polytropic process equation, pV^n = constant, the process will be adiabatic, if n in the euqtion is

(*a*) zero (*b*) one

(*c*) γ (*d*) infinite

33. In a reversible adiablatic process, the ratio of T_1/T_2 is equal to

(*a*) $\left(\frac{p_1}{p_2}\right)^{\frac{\gamma-1}{\gamma}}$ (*b*) $\left(\frac{p_2}{p_1}\right)^{\frac{\gamma-1}{\gamma}}$

(*c*) $\left(\frac{V_1}{V_2}\right)^{\frac{\gamma-1}{\gamma}}$ (*d*) $\left(\frac{V_2}{V_1}\right)^{\frac{\gamma-1}{\gamma}}$

34. A reversible process

(*a*) must pass through a continuous series of equlibrioum states.

(*b*) leaves no history of the events in surroundings.

(*c*) must pass through the same states on the reversed path as on the forward path.

(*d*) all of these.

35. Isentropic flow is

(*a*) reversible adiabatic flow

(*b*) irreversible adiabatic flow

(*c*) frictionless fluid flow

(*d*) none of the above.

36. Non quasi-static process is

(*a*) free expansion of gas

(*b*) expansion of a gas in a cylinder under constant pressure

(*c*) rapid compression of a gas in a cylindder.

(*d*) gradual compression of a gas in a cylinder.

37. For an ideal gas, the change in enthalpy (ΔH) for an elemental change in temperature ΔT is given by

(*a*) $C_p \cdot \Delta T$ (*b*) $C_v \cdot \Delta T$

(*c*) $\frac{C_p}{C_v} \Delta T$ (*d*) $\frac{C_v}{C_p} \Delta T$

38. One hundredth of a kilogram of air is compressed in a piston-cylinder device. At an instant of time when T = 400 K, the rate at which work is being done on the air is 8.165 kW, and heat is being removed at a rate of 1.0 kW, the rate of temperature rise will be

(*a*) 10 K/s (*b*) 100 K/s

(*c*) 1000 K/s (*d*) 10000 K/s.

39. For which of the following situations, zeroth law of thermodynamics will not be valid ?

(*a*) 50 cc of water at 25°C are mixed with 150 cc of water at 25°C

(*b*) 500 cc of milk at 15°C are mixed with 100 cc of water at 15°C

(*c*) 5 kg of wet steam at 100°C is mixed with 50 kg of dry and saturated steam at 100°C

(*d*) 10 cc of water at 20°C are mixed with 10 cc of sulphuric acid at 20°C.

40. Figure shows a vessel divided into two parts by a diaphragm. The space A contains a gas and space B is evacuated. These two spaces are separated by a diaphragm. Now if the diaphragm is punctured, the gas will expand into the evacuated space B. Which of the following statement is invalid ?

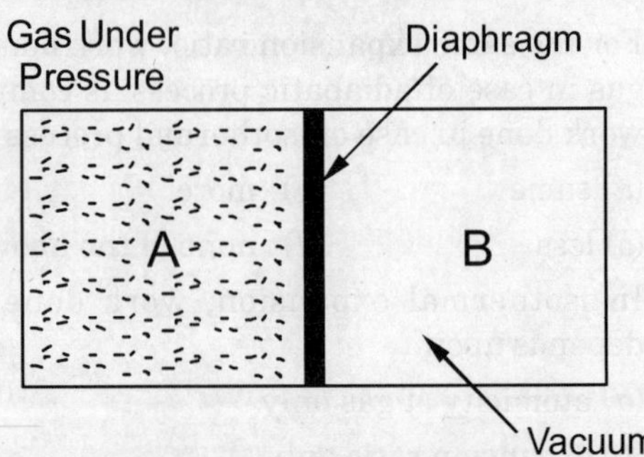

(*a*) A free expansion is a non-quasistatic process

(*b*) The pressure and volume of gas are not related through the equation of states

(*c*) The process is irreversible

(*d*) The energy is transferred to the system.

41. In a thermodynamic system, a process in which volume remains constant is called____process.

(a) isobaric (b) isometric

(c) adiabatic (d) isentropic

42. Coefficient of performance of a commercially used refrigerator would be close to

(a) 40% (b) 85%

(c) 1.5 (d) 3.5

43. In a thermodynamic system, thermal equilibrium is achieved when two bodies reach

(a) same thermal energy

(b) same entropy

(c) same temperature

(d) same molecular energy

44. A hot body follows Newton's law of cooling. Typical temperature-time graph of the cooling body would be

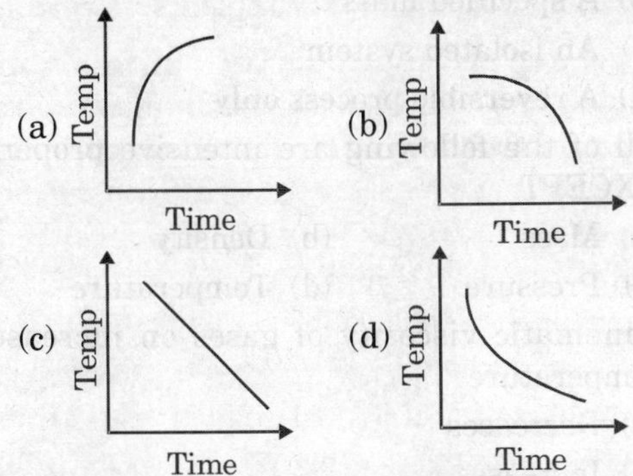

45. Consider the following graph :

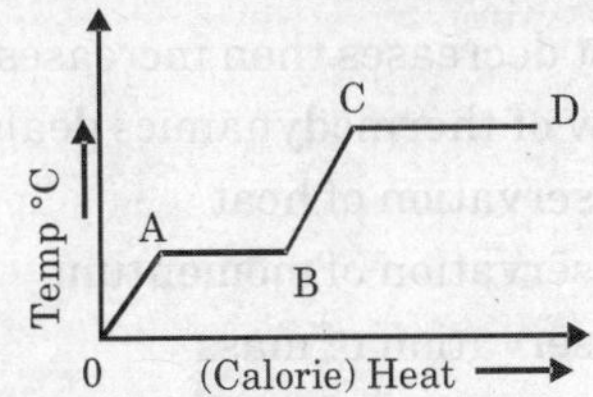

Which portion represents the 'Latent heat of fusion"?

(a) OA (b) AB

(c) BC (d) CD

46. Which of the following does not sublimate?

(a) Ice (b) Ammonium chloride

(c) Naphthalene (d) Camphor

47. The pressure exerted on the walls of a container by a gas is due to the fact that Gas molecules :

(a) Stick to the walls of the container

(b) Lose their kinetic energy

(c) Get accelerated towards the wall

(d) Change their momentum due to collision with the wall.

48. Zeroth Law of thermodynamics forms the basis of measurement.

(a) Pressure (b) Temperature

(c) Work (d) Momentum

49. Boyle's law states that:

(a) The pressure of a gas varies directly with temperature at constant volume i.e. PαT.

(b) The product of pressure and volume of a given mass of a gas is constant at constant temperature i.e. PV = constant.

(c) The volume of a gas varies directly with temperature at constant pressure i.e. VαT.

(d) The pressure of a gas varies directly with volume at constant temperature i.e. PαV.

50. The entropy of universe tends to be :

(a) Minimum (b) Zero

(c) Average (d) Maximum

51. At what temperature, both Celsius and Fahrenheit scales will show the identical readings?

(a) 100° (b) 0°

(c) –40° (d) 40°

52. A closed thermodynamic system is one in which

(a) There is no energy or mass transfer across the boundary

(b) There is no mass transfer, but energy transfer exists

(c) There is no energy transfer, but mass transfer exists

(d) Both energy and mass transfer take place across the boundary, but mass transfer is controlled by valves

53. Pressure reaches a value of absolute zero

(a) at a temperature of –273 K

(b) under vacuum condition

(c) at the earth's centre

(d) when molecular momentum of system becomes zero

54. Zeroth Law of Thermodynamics states that

(a) Two thermodynamic systems are always in thermal equilibrium with each other

(b) If two systems are in thermal equilibrium, then the third system will also be in thermal equilibrium

(c) Two systems not in thermal equilibrium with a third system will also not be in thermal equilibrium with each other

(d) When two systems are in thermal equilibrium with a third system they are in thermal equilibrium with each other

55. In fluid flow, the line of constant piezometric head passes through two points which have the same

(a) Elevation

(b) Pressure

(c) Velocity

(d) Velocity potential

56. A man is standing on a boat in still water. If he walks in the boat towards the shore, the boat will

(a) move away from the shore

(b) remain stationary

(c) move towards the shore

(d) Sink

57. Relative Humidity is the percentage of the

(a) absolute humidity value to the amount of humidity actually present

(b) increase of humidity/absolute humidity

(c) amount of humidity actually present to the absolute humidity

(d) None of these

58. Which of the following is an extensive property?

(a) Pressure (b) Heat capacity

(c) Temperature (d) Specific volume

59. Kelvin Planck's law deals with

(a) Conservation of heat

(b) Conservation of heat

(c) Conservation of heat into work

(d) Conservation of work into heat

60. Turbine used for low head is

(a) Kaplan turbine

(b) Francis turbine

(c) Pelton Wheel turbine

(d) Propeller turbine

61. A system and its environment put together constitute

(a) An adiabatic system

(b) An isolated system

(c) A segregated system

(d) A homogeneous system

62. Slope of constant volume line on temperature entropy diagram is given by

(a) Cp/T (b) T/Cp

(c) Cv/T (d) T/Cv

63. Zeroth law of thermodynamics forms the basis of measurement of

(a) Pressure (b) Temperature

(c) Heat exchange (d) Work

64. Internal energy is defined by

(a) Zeroth law of thermodynamics

(b) First law of thermodynamics

(c) Second law of thermodynamics

(d) Law of entropy

65. The given P-V diagram indicates following cycle

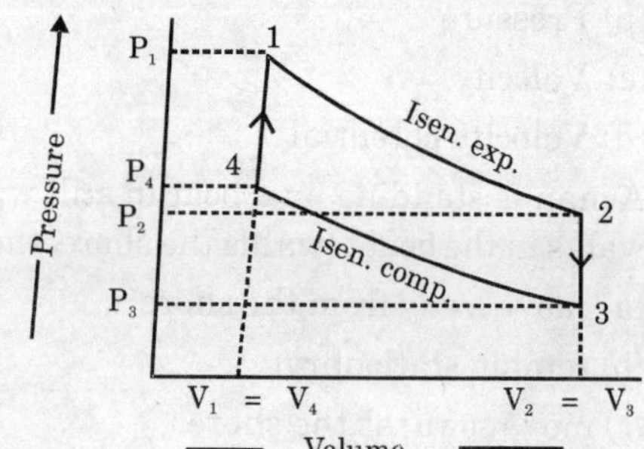

(a) Carnot cycle (b) Otto cycle

(c) Diesel cycle (d) Dual cycle

66. Control volume refers to

(a) A fixed region in space

(b) A specified mass

(c) An isolated system

(d) A reversible process only

67. All of the following are intensive properties EXCEPT

(a) Mass (b) Density

(c) Pressure (d) Temperature

68. Kinematic viscosity of gases on increase of temperature

(a) Decreases

(b) Increases

(c) Remains the same

(d) First decreases then increases

69. First law of thermodynamics deals with

(a) Conservation of heat

(b) Conservation of momentum

(c) Conservation of mass

(d) Conservation of energy

70. An isothermal process is governed by

(a) Boyle's law (b) Charle's law

(c) Gay-lussac's law (d) Avogadro's law

71. Heat is closely related with

(a) Energy (b) Temperature

(c) Entropy (d) Enthalpy

72. An engine operates between temperature limits of 900 K and T2: and another between T2 and 400 K. For both the engines to be equally efficient. T2 should be equal to

(a) 600 K (b) 650 K

(c) 625 K (d) 700 K

73. Work done in a free expansion process is

(a) Zero (b) Positive

(c) Negative (d) Maximum

74. The internal energy of an ideal gas is

(a) A function of temperature only

(b) A function of pressure

(c) A function of volume

(d) Both pressure and volume

75. The process in which no heat enters or leaves the system is called

(a) Isobaric (b) Isothermal

(c) Isentropic (d) Isochoric

76. Economiser used in power plants is used to heat

(a) flue gases (b) intake air

(c) steam (d) feed water

77. Which of the following is a high head turbine

(a) Propeller turbine (b) Francis turbine

(c) Kaplan turbine (d) Pelton wheel turbine

78. Which one of following expression is true for Tds equation

(a) du – PdV (b) du + PdV

(c) du – VdP (d) du + VdP

79. PMM1 is closely related with

(a) First law of thermodynamics

(b) Second law of thermodynamics

(c) Third law of thermodynamics

(d) Zeroth law of thermodynamics

80. Isolated system indicates

(a) Mass of substance cross the boundary

(b) Energy of substance cross the boundary

(c) Both mass and energy of substance cross the boundary

(d) Both mass and energy substance does not cross the boundary

81. The thermal diffusivity of a substance is given by :

(a) $\frac{K\rho}{C}$ (b) $\frac{K}{\rho C}$

(c) $\frac{KC}{\rho}$ (d) $\frac{\rho C}{K}$

[Where K = Thermal conductivity; p = Mass density; C = Specific heat]

82. Fins are provided on heat transferring surface in order to increase :

(a) Heat transfer area

(b) Heat transfer coefficient

(c) Temperature gradient

(d) Mechanical strength of the equipment

83. Heat is mainly transferred by conduction, convection and radiation in

(a) Insulated pipes carrying hot water

(b) Refrigerator freezer coil

(c) Boiler furnaces

(d) Condensation of steam in a condenser

84. Heat transfer in liquids and gases is essentially due to

(a) Conduction

(b) Convection

(c) Radiation

(d) Conduction and Radiation put together

85. In which of the following mechanisms, is heat conducted in liquid and gas

(a) Lattice vibration

(b) Transportation of free electrons

(c) Collisions and diffusion

(d) No heat conducted

86. An essential requirement for the transfer of heat from one body to another body is that

(a) Both bodies must be solids

(b) Both bodies must be in contact

(c) Temperatures of the two bodies must be different

(d) Temperatures of the two bodies must be same

87. Stefen Boltzman law is applicable to

(a) Gray body (b) White body

(c) Black body (d) Blue body

88. Heat is transferred by conduction, convection and radiation in

(a) Insulated pipe carrying hot water

(b) Refrigerator freezer coils

(c) Melting of ice

(d) Boiler furnaces

89. The concept of overall heat transfer is used in the heat transfer in the case of

(a) Conduction

(b) Convection

(c) Radiation

(d) Combined mode of heat transfer of conduction and convection

90. The unit of thermal conductivity in S.I. unit is

(a) W/mK (b) W^2/mK

(c) W/m^2K (d) W/m

91. All radiations in a black body are

(a) Reflected (b) Refracted

(c) Transmitted (d) Absorbed

92. Fourier's law of heat conduction gives the heat flow for

(a) Irregular surfaces

(b) Non-uniform temperature surfaces

(c) One dimensional cases only

(d) Two dimensional cases only

93. Absorptivity of a body is equal to its emissivity

(a) For a polished body

(b) Under thermal equilibrium

(c) At one particular temperature

(d) At shorter wavelengths

94. Metals are good conductor of heat because
(a) Their atoms collide frequently
(b) Their atoms are relatively far apart
(c) They contain free electron
(d) They have high density

95. Heat conduction in gases is due to
(a) Electromagnetic waves
(b) Motion of electrons
(c) Mixing motion of the different layers of the gas
(d) Elastic impact of molecules

96. The heat flow through solids only by
(a) Conduction (b) Convection
(c) Radiation (d) Does not flow

97. A perfect black body is
(a) One which absorbs total radiant energy
(b) Black in colour
(c) One which does not reflect the radiant energy
(d) One which absorbs all radiant energy at all wavelengths

98. Heat transfer by molecular collision in
(a) Conduction (b) Convection
(c) Radiation (d) Scattering

99. Which one of the following have a highest thermal conductivity
(a) Boiling water (b) Steam
(c) Solid ice (d) Rain water

100. The ratio of thermal conductivity to electrical conductivity is equal to
(a) Prandtl number (b) Schmidt number
(c) Lorentz number (d) Lewis number

101. The effectiveness of a fin will be maximum in an environment with
(a) Free convection
(b) Forced convection
(c) Radiation
(d) Convection and radiation

102. Which one of the following modes of heat transfer would takes place predominantly from boiler furnace to water wall
(a) Convection
(b) Conduction
(c) Radiation
(d) Conduction and Convection

103. Heat pipe is widely used now a days, use
(a) It acts as an insulator
(b) It acts as conductor and insulator
(c) It acts as a superconductor
(d) It acts as afin

104. Ice is very close to a
(a) Gray body
(b) Black body
(c) White body
(d) Specular body

105. In which one of the following materials is the heat propagation minimum due to conduction heat transfer?
(a) Lead (b) Copper
(c) Water (d) Air

106. Assume that a 1 ton air conditioner is required to cool a room of size 14' × 14' × 14'. How many 1 ton ACs would be required for a hall of size of 24' × 24' of the same roof height as that of the previous room?
(a) 2 *(b)* 3
(c) 4 *(d)* 5

107. Efficiency of Carnot cycle is:
(a) $1-\frac{Q_1}{Q_1+Q_2}$ *(b)* $1-\frac{T_1}{T_2}$
(c) $1-\frac{T_1}{T_1+T_2}$ *(d)* $1-\frac{Q_1}{Q_2}$

108. In a building, water is to be pumped to a height of 10m at the rate of 1 litre/second. Power requirement would be approx:
(Take 'g' 10 m/scc^2)
(a) 10 Watts *(b)* 100 Watts
(c) 500 Watts *(d)* 1 kW

109. Which law of thermodynamics defines Entropy?
(a) Zeroth *(b)* First
(c) Second *(d)* Third

110. If a system in equilibrium is subjected to a change of concentration; temperature or pressure, the equilibrium shifts in a direction that tends to undo the effect of the change imposed. This is known as:
(a) Le Chatelier's Principle
(b) Law of Mass Action
(c) Van der Waals Principle
(d) None of these

111. The value of $\sum \frac{dQ}{T}$ for an irreversible process is:

(*a*) Less than zero (*b*) Greater than zero

(*c*) Equal to zero (*d*) Any one of these

112. Which of the following cycles is used in thermal power plants ?

(*a*) Rankine (*b*) Carnot

(*c*) Otto (*d*) Joule

113. The characteristic equation of Gases PV = nRT holds good for :

(*a*) Monoatomic Gases

(*b*) Diatomic Gases

(*c*) Ideal Gases

(*d*) Real Gases

114. For an Ideal Gas, the change in Enthalpy (ΔH) for an elemental change in temperature (ΔT) is given by:

(where C_p = Heat capacity at Constant Pressure; C_V = Heat capacity at Constant Volume)

(*a*) $C_V.\Delta T$ (*b*) $\frac{C_P}{C_V}.\Delta T$

(*c*) $\frac{C_V}{C_P}.\Delta T$ (*d*) $C_P.\Delta T$

115. A perfect gas at 27 °C is heated at constant pressure till its volume is doubled. The final temperature is :

(*a*) 54°C (*b*) 108°C

(*c*) 327°C (*d*) 600°C

116. Zeroth law of thermodynamics is the basis of

(*a*) Pressure measurement

(*b*) Temperature measurement

(*c*) Density measurement

(*d*) Viscosity measurement

117. A process in which no heat crosses the boundary of the system is called

(*a*) Ideal process

(*b*) Adiabatic process

(*c*) Isothermal process

(*d*) Isobaric process

118. The enthalpy of a substance is defined as

(*a*) h = pv+RT (*b*) h = u+pT

(*c*) h = u+pv (*d*) h = u-pv

119. Cyclic integral of any property is

(*a*) Zero (*b*) One

(*c*) Infinite (*d*) Two

120. The machine which violates the first law of thermodynamics is known as

(*a*) PMM-I (*b*) PMM-II

(*c*) PMM-III (*d*) Heat engine

121. The device in which the work is done by the fluid at the expense of its enthalpy is known as

(*a*) Compressor (*b*) Throttling device

(*c*) Turbine (*d*) Heat exchanger

122. A device which increases the velocity of a fluid at the expense of its pressure drop is known as

(*a*) Diffuser (*b*) Nozzle

(*c*) Throttling device (*d*) Heat transfer

123. The Prandtl number for liquid, which has velocity boundary layer much thicker than thermal boundary layer, is

(*a*) Pr >> 1 (*b*) Pr<<1

(*c*) Pr ≈ 1 (*d*) Pr = 0

124. A fluid flow in which the density of the fluid does not change during flowing is called as

(*a*) Incompressible (*b*) Uniform

(*c*) Compressible (*d*) Non-linear

125. The formation of bubbles of vapour in a flowing fluid is called as

(*a*) Cavitation (*b*) Corrosion

(*c*) Gasification (*d*) Boiling

126. A large body of infinite heat capacity is known as

(*a*) Thermal Energy Reservoir (TER)

(*b*) Mechanical energy reservoir (MER)

(*c*) Thermometer

(*d*) Heat pump

127. "Heat always flows from a body at a higher temperature to a body at a lower temperature" is the statement of

(*a*) First law of thermodynamics

(*b*) Second law of thermodynamics

(*c*) Third law of thermodynamics

(*d*) Zeroth law of thermodynamics

128. The network output for any heat engine is given by

(*a*) $Q_L - Q_H$ (*b*) $Q_L + Q_H$

(*c*) $Q_H - Q_L$ (*d*) $2Q_L$

Where, Q_H = magnitude of heat transfer between heat engine and source

Q_L = magnitude of heat transfer between heat engine and sink

129. A cyclic device which produces work continuously at the expense of heat input is known as

(*a*) Refrigerator (*b*) Heat pump

(*c*) Heat engine (*d*) Throttling

130. A liquid forms an interface with another liquid or gas; the surface energy per unit area of the interface is known as

(*a*) Surface tension (*b*) Specific energy

(*c*) Specific heat (*d*) Suction energy

131. According to Darcy's law, for laminar flow in a saturated soil, the rate of flow is proportional to the

(*a*) Cross sectional area

(*b*) Hydraulic gradient

(*c*) Coefficient of permeability

(*d*) Porosity of the soil

132. The efficiency of perpetual motion machine-ll (PMM-II) is

(*a*) 0% (*b*) 50%

(*c*) 75% (*d*) 100%

133. A thermal energy reservoir that supplies the heat is known as

(*a*) Refrigerator (*b*) Source

(*c*) Sink (*d*) Heat engine

134. Thermal efficiency of heat engine may be defined as

(*a*) $1 - (Q_2/Q_1)$ (*b*) $1 - Q_1/Q_2)$

(*c*) (Q_1/Q_2) 1 (*d*) $(Q_2/Q_1) - 1$

Where, O_1 = magnitude of heat transfer between heat engine and source

Q_2 = magnitude of heat transfer between heat engine and sink.

135. "Theoretical limits" for the performance of commonly used engineering systems is determined by

(*a*) Zeroth law of thermodynamics

(*b*) First law of thermodynamics

(*c*) Second law of thermodynamics

(*d*) Third law of thermodynamics

136. Radiation of a black body, in terms of its temperature follows:

(*a*) Newton's law of cooling

(*b*) Plank's law

(*c*) Stefan's law

(*d*) Einstein Bose equation

137. Consider that two solid bodies A and B are touching each other and transmitting heat through conduct ion. In the graph below, OX represents the first body and XY represents the second body.

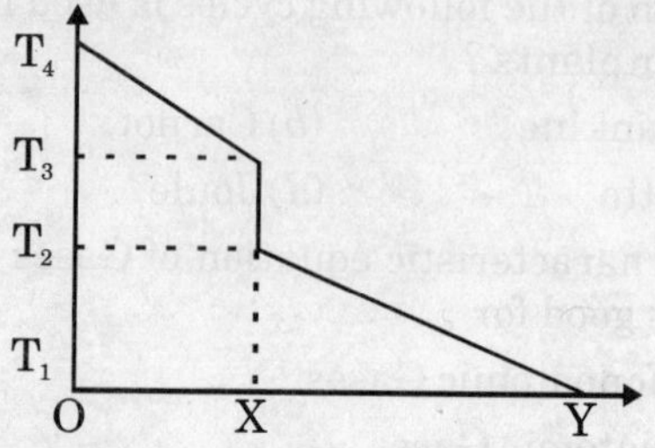

State True (T) or False(F).

1) Temperature gradient is more in A than in B

2) The heat flow is determined by Fourier's law

3) Area under the curve represents heat dissipation rate.

(*a*) T, T, T (*b*) T, T, F

(*c*) T, F, T (*d*) F, F, T

138. Stefan Boltzmann Law is applicable for heat Transfer by :

(*a*) Conduction (*b*) Convection

(*c*) Radiation (*d*) All of these

139. The bending of bimetallic strips during rise in temperature is due to difference in their :

(*a*) Coefficient of linear expansion

(*b*) Thickness

(*c*) Thermal conductivities

(*d*) Elastic properties

140. Steady State Heat flow implies

(*a*) negligible flow of heat

(*b*) no difference of temperature between the bodies

(*c*) constant heat flow rate i.e. heat flow rate independent of time

(*d*) uniform rate in temperature rise of a body

141. Which of the following fluid flow conditions has high heat transfer coefficient?

(*a*) Free convection in air

(*b*) Forced convection in air

(*c*) Free convection in water

(*d*) Condensation of steam

142. The value solar constant is

(*a*) 1353 kW/m^2 (*b*) 1353 W/m^2

(*c*) 1353 J/m^2 (*d*) 135 kJ/m^2

143. "At thermal equilibrium, the ratio of the total emissive power to the total absorptivity is constant for all bodies" is known as

(*a*) Kirchhoff's law

(*b*) Wien's displacement law

(*c*) Maxwell's theory

(*d*) Stefan Boltzmann law

144. The substance for which Prandtl number (Pr) << 1 is characterized by

(*a*) High rate of heat diffusion

(*b*) Low rate of heat diffusion

(*c*) High rate of mass diffusion

(*d*) Low rate of mass diffusion

145. The critical radius of insulation of cylinder is given by

(*a*) k/h (*b*) 2k/h

(*c*) k/2h (*d*) k/4h

146. Maximum spectral emissive power at temperature (T) is proportional to

(*a*) T^4 (*b*) T^5

(*c*) $T^{5/2}$ (*d*) T^3

147. The radiation energy emitted by the Sun between the wavelength of 0.4 μn to 0.76 μm is known as

(*a*) ultraviolet radiation

(*b*) infrared radiation

(*c*) thermal radiation

(*d*) visible radiation

148. To reduce the heat loss with insulation in sphere the following condition should be satisfied

(*a*) $r_{\text{insulation thickne}} >> r_{\text{critical}}$

(*b*) $r_{\text{insulation thickness}} << r_{\text{critical}}$

(*c*) $r_{\text{insulation thickness}} = r_{\text{critical}}$

(*d*) $r_{\text{insulation thickness}} = 0$

149. The peak frequency at which energy is radiated from a blackbody radiator is dependent on

(*a*) color (*b*) distance

(*c*) intensity (*d*) temperature

150. Heat transfer takes place according to

(*a*) Zeroth Law of Thermodynamics

(*b*) First Law of Thermodynamics

(*c*) Second Law of Thermodynamics

(*d*) Third Law of Thermodynamics.

Answers

1. (c)	**2.** (c)	**3.** (c)	**4.** (c)	**5.** (b)	**6.** (b)	**7.** (c)	**8.** (a)	**9.** (c)	**10.** (c)
11. (d)	**12.** (c)	**13.** (b)	**14.** (d)	**15.** (b)	**16.** (c)	**17.** (b)	**18.** (b)	**19.** (b)	**20.** (c)
21. (d)	**22.** (c)	**23.** (d)	**24.** (b)	**25.** (a)	**26.** (a)	**27.** (d)	**28.** (c)	**29.** (b)	**30.** (a)
31. (c)	**32.** (c)	**33.** (a)	**34.** (d)	**35.** (a)	**36.** (a)	**37.** (a)	**38.** (c)	**39.** (d)	**40.** (d)
41. (b)	**42.** (c)	**43.** (c)	**44.** (d)	**45.** (b)	**46.** (a)	**47.** (d)	**48.** (b)	**49.** (b)	**50.** (d)
51. (c)	**52.** (b)	**53.** (d)	**54.** (b)	**55.** (c)	**56.** (a)	**57.** (d)	**58.** (b)	**59.** (c)	**60.** (a)
61. (b)	**62.** (d)	**63.** (b)	**64.** (a)	**65.** (b)	**66.** (a)	**67.** (a)	**68.** (b)	**69.** (d)	**70.** (a)
71. (b)	**72.** (a)	**73.** (a)	**74.** (a)	**75.** (c)	**76.** (d)	**77.** (d)	**78.** (b)	**79.** (a)	**80.** (d)
81. (b)	**82.** (a)	**83.** (c)	**84.** (b)	**85.** (c)	**86.** (c)	**87.** (c)	**88.** (d)	**89.** (d)	**90.** (a)
91. (d)	**92.** (c)	**93.** (b)	**94.** (a)	**95.** (d)	**96.** (a)	**97.** (d)	**98.** (b)	**99.** (c)	**100.** (c)
101. (a)	**102.** (c)	**103.** (c)	**104.** (b)	**105.** (d)	**106.** (b)	**107.** (b)	**108.** (b)	**109.** (c)	**110.** (a)
111. (a)	**112.** (a)	**113.** (c)	**114.** (d)	**115.** (c)	**116.** (b)	**117.** (b)	**118.** (c)	**119.** (a)	**120.** (a)
121. (c)	**122.** (b)	**123.** (a)	**124.** (a)	**125.** (a)	**126.** (a)	**127.** (b)	**128.** (c)	**129.** (c)	**130.** (a)
131. (b)	**132.** (d)	**133.** (b)	**134.** (a)	**135.** (c)	**136.** (c)	**137.** (c)	**138.** (c)	**139.** (a)	**140.** (c)
141. (d)	**142.** (b)	**143.** (a)	**144.** (a)	**145.** (a)	**146.** (b)	**147.** (d)	**148.** (a)	**149.** (d)	**150.** (c)

Explanations

1. An isochoric process, also called a constant-volume process, an isovolumetric process, or an isometric process, is a thermodynamic process during which the volume of the closed system undergoing such a process remains constant.
2. Coefficient of performance of a commercially used refrigerator would be close to 1.5
3. Thermal equilibrium means that there is no heat transfer going on between the bodies, which simply means that the bodies are at the same temperature. Heat content is a whole different concept - it is the amount of heat contained in a body, which is crucially dependent on mass.
4. Newton's law of cooling applies to convective heat transfer; it does not apply to thermal radiation.Newton's law of cooling states that the rate of heat exchange between an object and its surroundings is proportional to the difference in temperature between the object and the surroundings.

Temperature
100
80
60
40
20
0 10 20 30 40 50 60 Time

5. Latent heat process is a process in which temperature remains constant and phase change takes place.
6. Ice will not sublimate at atmospheric conditions.
7. Due to change in momentum.
8. The Zeroth law of thermodynamics is the basis for measurement of temperature and setting its scale. In simple word, Zeroth law of thermodynamics says that "When two bodies are separately in thermal equilibrium with the third body, then the two are also in thermal equilibrium with each other."
9. Boyle's law (sometimes referred to as the Boyle-Mariottelaw, or Mariotte's law) is an experimental gas law that describes how the pressure of a gas tends to increase as the volume of the container decreases.
10. Entropy seems to tend to some maximum value.
11. The formulas for converting between degree Celsius and degree Fahrenheit are:

    $°F = (°C - 9/5) + 32$

    $°C = (°F - 32) - 5/9$

    To find the temperature when both are equal, we use an old algebra trick and just set °F = °C and solve one of the equations.

    $°C = (°C \times 9/5) + 32$

    $°C - (°C \times 9/5) = 32$

    $-4/5 \times °C = 32$

    $°C = -32 \times 5/4$

    $°C = -40$

    $°F = (°F \times 9/5) + 32$

    $°F - (°F \times 9/5) = 32$

    $-4/5 - °F = 32$

    $°F = -32 - 5/4$

    $°F = -40$

    So the temperature when both the Celsius and Fahrenheit scales are the same is -40 degrees.
12. There are mainly three types of system:

    Open System: Both mass transfer and energy transfer can take place.

    Closed System: Only energy transfer can take place.

    Isolated System: Both mass transfer and energy transfer can not take place.
13. Absolute pressure becomes zero when molecular momentum of the system becomes zero.
14. The zeroth law of thermodynamics states that if two thermodynamic systems each are in thermal equilibrium with a third, then they are in thermal equilibrium with each other. Accordingly, thermal equilibrium between systems is a transitive relation.
15. In fluid flow, the line of constant piezometric head passes through two points which have the same Velocity.
16. The boat will start moving away from the shore.
17. Relative humidity is the ratio of the partial pressure of water vapor to the equilibrium vapor pressure of water at a given temperature. Relative humidity depends on temperature and the pressure of the system of interest. The same amount of water vapor results in higher relative humidity in cool air than warm air.

18. Pressure, temperature and specific volume are intensive property. Heat capacity is an extensive property. Extensive property is a property of matter that changes as the amount of matter changes.

19. Kelvin Planck's law deals with conservation of heat into work.

20. Kaplan turbine is used for low head. Low head turbines are those turbines with a head of 20 metres (66 ft) or less to produce energy.

21. An isolated system does not exchange energy or matter with its surroundings. A system and its environment put together constitute an isolated system.

22. $\frac{dT}{ds} = \frac{T}{C_v}$

23. Zeroth law of thermodynamics forms the basis of measurement of temperature. It states that when two bodies are in thermal equilibrium with a third body, then they are also in thermal equilibrium with each other.

24. The first law of thermodynamics makes the use of the key concepts of internal energy, heat and system work.

$\Delta U = Q - W$

$\Delta U \rightarrow$ Change in internal energy

$Q \rightarrow$ Heat added to the system

$W \rightarrow$ Work done by system

25. Otto cycle is an idealized thermodynamic cycle which consists of two isentropic (reversible adiabatic) processes and two isochoric (constant volume) processes.

26. Control volume: Control volume is a volume fixed in space or moving with constant velocity through which the fluid (gas or liquid) flows.

27. Mass and volume are extensive properties. Intensive properties are those properties that does not depend on the system size or the amount of material in the system, such as density, pressure etc.

28. If temperature increases, the kinematic viscosity of gases increases.

29. First law of thermodynamics deals with conservation of energy. The law of conservation of energy states that the total energy of an isolated system is constant; energy can be transformed from one form to another, but can be neither created nor destroyed.

30. Boyle's law: According to Boyle's law, the pressure (P) of a given mass of gas is inversely proportional to its volume (V), provided that the temperature of the gas remains constant.

31. Heat is closely related with temperature.

32. $\frac{T_1 - T_2}{T_1} = \frac{T_1 - T_2}{T_1}$ [Both engines equally efficient]

$$\Rightarrow \frac{900 - T_2}{900} = \frac{T_2 - 400}{T_2}$$

$$\Rightarrow T_2 = 600 \text{ Kelvin}$$

33. Work done in free expansion process is always zero.

34. Internal energy of an ideal gas depends only on temperature, not on pressure and volume.

35. An isentropic process is an idealized thermodynamic process that is both adiabatic and reversible. The work transfers of the system are frictionless and there is no transfer of heat or matter.

36. Economiser: Economizers are generally heat exchangers which are designed to exchange heat with the fluid, generally water.

37. Pelton wheel turbine, turgo turbines are high head turbine.

38. $du = \delta Q - \delta W$

$\Rightarrow du = Tds - pdv$

$\Rightarrow Tds = du + pdv$ q1

39. PMM1 is closely related with first law of thermodynamics. It violates the first law of thermodynamics.

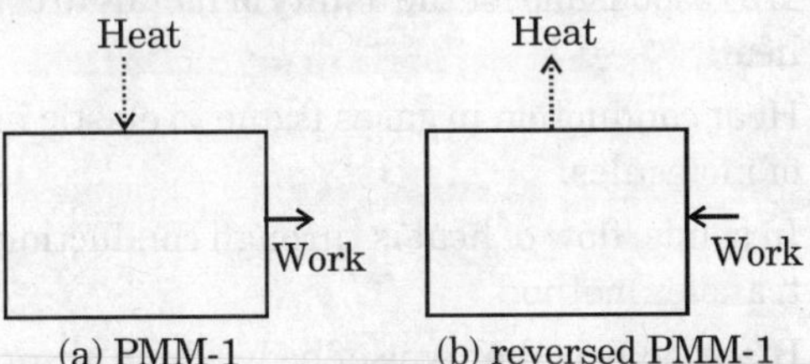

(a) PMM-1 (b) reversed PMM-1

40. Isolated system is a system that can not exchange either energy or matter outside the boundaries of the system.

41. In heat transfer analysis, thermal diffusivity is the thermal conductivity divided by density and specific heat capacity at constant pressure. It measures the rate of transfer of heat of a material from the hot side to the cold side. It has the SI derived unit of m²/s.

$$\alpha = \frac{\text{heat conducted}}{\text{heat stored}} = \frac{k}{\rho c_p}$$

42. Fins are used to increase heat transfer rate.

43. Heat is mainly transferred by conduction, convection and radiation in Boiler furnaces.

44. Heat can be transferred from one place to another by three methods: conduction in solids, convection of fluids (liquids or gases), and radiation through anything that will allow radiation to pass. The method used to transfer heat is usually the one that is the most efficient.

45. Collisions and diffusion.

46. Heat transfer between two bodies only takes place when temperature of one body is different from temperature of other body.

47. Stephan Boltzman law is applicable to black body, theoretical surfaces that absorb all incident heat radiation.

48. Heat transfer takes place in boiler furnaces through three modes, namely conduction, convection and radiation.

49. Overall heat transfer concept is used in the cobined mode of heat transfer of conduction and convection.

50. Unit of thermal conductivity in S.I. unit i W/mk.

51. An object that absorbs all radiation falling on it, at all wavelength is called a black body.

52. Fourier's law of heat conduction is applicable only for one dimensional cases.

53. When the body is under thermal equilibrium, then its absorptivity is equal to its emissivity.

54. Metallic bonds are made from a lattice of irons in a 'cloud' of free electrons. These free electrons are responsible for the ability of metals to conduct heat.

55. Heat conduction in gases is due to elastic impact of molecules.

56. In solids, flow of heat is through conduction heat transfer method.

57. Black body is that type of body which absorbs all radiant energy at all wavelengths.

58. Convection is the heat transfer due to bulk movement of molecules within fluids such as gases and liquids.

59. Solid ice has highest thermal conductivity than boiling water, steam and rain water. Thermal conductivity is evaluated primarily in terms of the Fourier's law for heat conduction.

60. Lorentz number is defined as the ratio of thermal conductivity to electrical conductivity at a given temperature.

$$L = \frac{K}{\sigma T}$$

Where,

L = Lorentz number

σ = electrical conductivity

K = Thermal conductivity

61. Effectiveness of fin: Effectiveness of fin is defined as the ratio of actual heat transfer that takes place from the fin to the heat that would be dissipated from the same surfaces area without fin. It will be maximum with free convection.

62. Radiation is the heat transfer due to emission of electromagnetic waves. From boiler furnace to water wall, radiation modes of heat transfer takes place.

63. Heat pipe acts as a superconductor. Heat pipes are transport mechanisms that can carry heat fluxes ranging from 10 w/cm^2 to 20 kw/cm^2 at nearly the speed of sound (340 m/sec.)

64. Ice is very close to black body because ice is a very good absorber of radiation outside the visible region.

65. Because air has lowest value of thermal conductivity amongst given options.

106. 1 tonne AC's required

for size of room = 14 × 14 × 14 = 2744 unit

Now, for size of room = 24 × 24 × 14 = 8064 unit

So, number of tonne of AC's required

$$\text{for this } = \frac{8064}{2744} = 2.938 = 3 \text{ unit(Approx)}$$

107. T_2 is source temperature

T_1 is sink temperature

Carnot cycle efficiency is a function of temperature limits only.

$$\therefore \eta_{carnot} = 1 - \frac{T_1}{T_2}$$

108. Given:

Height = 10 m

Discharge(Q) Rate = 1 litre/second

$$= \frac{1}{1000} \text{ m}^3\text{/sec } 1$$

$$\text{Here, Power} = \frac{\text{Work}}{\text{Time}} = \frac{mgh}{t} = Qgh$$

$$= \frac{PVgh}{t} = PQgh$$

$$= 10000 \times \frac{1}{1000} \times 10 \times 10$$

$$= 100 \text{ watt}$$

109. The second law of thermodynamics states that the state of entropy of the entire universe, as an isolated system, will always increase overtime. The second law also states that the changes in the entropy in the universe can never be negative.

110. Le-chatelier's principle: A principle stating that if a constraint (such as a change in pressure, temperature or concentration of a reactant) is applied to a system in equilibrium the equilibrium will shift so as to tend to counteract the effect of the constraint.

111. Value of $\Sigma \frac{dQ}{T}$ for an irreversible process is less than zero.

112. Rankine cycle is used in thermal power plants.

113. Ideal Gas equation is given by $PV = nRT$

114. The change in enthalpy(ΔH) is given by, Cp. ΔT.

115. $T_1 = 27 + 273 = 300K$

$V_1 = V$

$V_2 = 2V$

$T_2 = ?$

By using,

$$\frac{P_1 V_1}{T_1} = \frac{P_2 V_2}{T_2}$$

Given, $P_1 = P_2$

So, $\frac{V_1}{T_1} = \frac{V_1}{T_2}$

$\Rightarrow \frac{V}{300} = \frac{2V}{T_2}$

$\Rightarrow T_2 = 300 \times 2 = 600K$

$= (600 - 273)\ °C$

$= 327°C$

116. The zeroth law is incredibly important as it allows us to define the concept of temperature scale. If two systems are each in thermal equilibrium with third, they are also in thermal equilibrium with each other.

117. In thermodynamics, an adiabatic process is one that occurs without transfer of heat or mass of substances between a thermodynamic system and its surroundings. In an adiabatic process, energy is transferred to the surrounding only as work.

118. Enthalpy of a system is equal to the system's internal energy plus the product of its pressure and volume.

$h = u + pv$

119. Cyclic integral of any property is zero.

120. PMM-I → PMM-I stands for perpetual motion machine-I. It is a hypothetical machine which can produce useful energy (work) without any source or which can produce more energy than consumed. It violates the first law of thermodynamics.

121. Turbine is a device designed to do work at the expense of a decrease in either the enthalpy of a fluid or the kinetic energy of the fluid or both.

122. Nozzle increases the velocity of the fluid at the expense of its pressure drop.

123. Prandtl number for liquid, which has velocity boundary layer much thicker than thermal boundary layer, is given by "Pr >> 1".

124. Incompressible fluid is a fluid whose density does not change when the pressure changes. In incompressible flow, the material density is constant within a fluid parcel.

125. Formation of bubbles of vapour in a flowing fluid is called as cavitation.

126. Thermal Energy Reservoir: A thermal energy reservoir (TER) is defined as a large body of infinite heat capacity, which is capable of absorbing or rejecting an unlimited quantity of heat without suffering appreciable changes in its thermodynamic co-ordinates.

127. Second law of thermodynamics states that heat flows naturally from an object at a higher temperature to an object at a lower temperature, and heat does not flow in the opposite direction of its own.

128. $Q_H - Q_L$

where,

Q_H = Magnitude of heat transfer between heat engine and source.

Q_L = magnitude of heat transfer between heat engine and sink.

129. Heat Engine: A heat engine is a device that converts chemical energy to heat or thermal energy and then to mechanical energy or to electrical energy. It is a cyclic device which produces work continuously at the expense of heat input.

130. Surface Tension: Surface tension is measured as the energy required to increase the surface area of a liquid by a unit of area. The surface tension of a liquid results from an imbalance of intermolecular attractive forces, the cohesive forces between the molecules.

131. Hydraulic Gradient: The hydraulic gradient is a vector gradient between two or more hydraulic head measurements over the length of the flow path. According to darcy's law, for laminar flow in a saturated soil, the rate of flow is proportional to hydraulic gradient.

132. P M M – II Machines are those machines which violate the second law of thermodynamics because such machines will absorb continuously heat energy from a single thermal reservoir and will convert the aborbed heat energy completely into work energy.

P M M II efficiency is approximately 100%

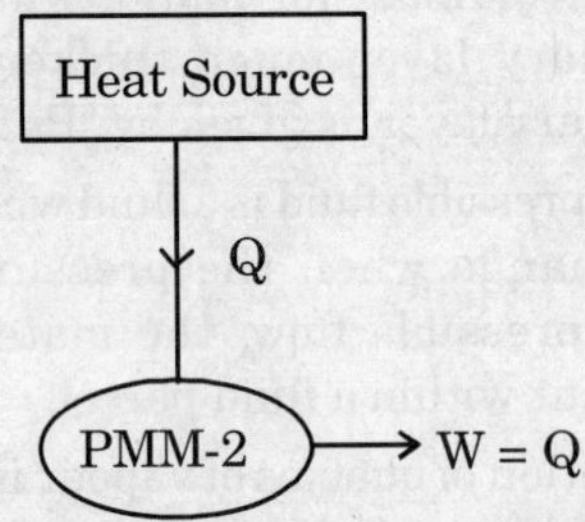

133. Source is a thermal energy reservoir that supplies the heat and Sink is a thermal energy reservoir that receives the heat.

134. Thermal efficiency of Heat engine,

$$\eta_{th} = \frac{Wnet}{Q_1} = \frac{Qnet}{Q_1} = 1 - \frac{Q_2}{Q_1}$$

where, $Q_2 \rightarrow$ Heat rejected

$Q_1 \rightarrow$ Heat supplied

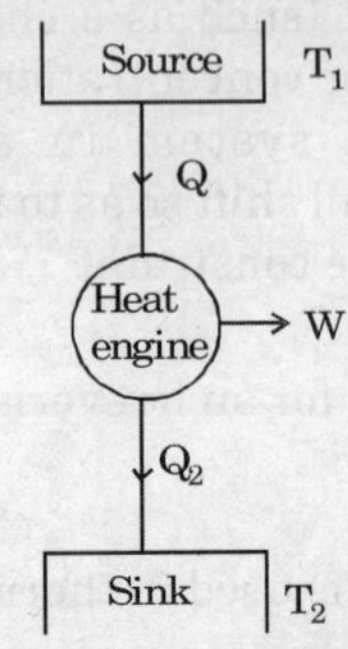

Also, η th (rev.cycle) $= 1 \frac{-T_2}{T_1}$

135. Second law of thermodynamics is used in determining the therrical limits for the the performance of commonly used engineering systems, such as heat engines and refrigerators etc.

Fluid Mechanics and Hydraulic Machinery

FLUID PROPERTIES

(i) **Mass density (ρ).**

It is mass per unit volume.

$$\rho = \frac{\text{Mass of the fluid}}{\text{Volume of the fluid}}$$

Dimensionally, $\rho = ML^{-3}$

In MKS unit, it is expressed in metric slugs per meter cube (slug/m^3).

In SI units, it is expressed in Newtons per meter cube (N/m^3).

Density of liquid may be considered as constant but density of gases varies with the variation of pressure and temperature.

(ii) **Specific weight.**

It is weight of fluid per unit volume.

$$\gamma = \frac{\text{weight of fluid}}{\text{volume of the fluid}}$$

In MKS system, it is measured in kg/m^3.

In SI system, it is measured in N/m^3.

To convert γ in SI units multiply ρ (MKS) by 9.81. The specific weight of water is 9810 N/m^3.

Specific weight of a fluid varies due to

(a) change of gravity

(b) effect of pressure and temeperature

(iii) **Specific volume (v_s).**

It is defined as volume per unit mass.

In MKS unit it is measured in m^3/slug.

In SI system it is measured in m^3/kg.

(iv) **Specific gravity (S).**

It is defined as the ratio of weight density (or density) of a fluid to the weight density (or density) of a standard fluid. The standard liquid is water and the standard gas is air. It is a dimensionless quantity.

Mathematically,

For liquids, $$S = \frac{\text{weight density (or density) of liquid}}{\text{weight density (or density) of water}}$$

For gases, $$S = \frac{\text{weight density (or density) of gas}}{\text{weight density (or density) of air}}$$

***(v)* Viscosity (Dynamic viscosity).**

It is defined as the property of fluid which offers resistance to the movement of one layer of fluid over another adjacent layer of the fluid.

Let two fluid layers at distances y and $(y + dy)$ from the surface have velocity values u and $(u + du)$ as shown in the figure.

The top layer causes a shear stress on the adjacent lower layer while the lower layer causes a shear stress on the adjacent top layer. The shear stress (τ) is proportional to the rate of change of velocity with respect to y.

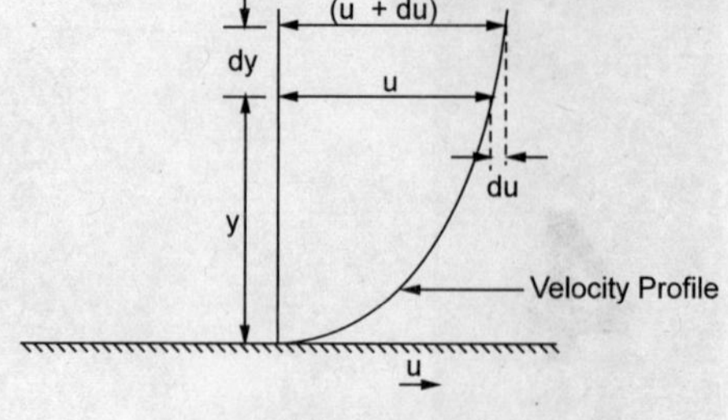

Fig. Velocity variation near a solid boundary

Mathematically, $$\tau \propto \frac{du}{dy}$$

or $$\tau = \mu \cdot \frac{du}{dy}$$

where, μ is constant of proportionality known as *coefficient of dynamic viscosity*

$\frac{du}{dy}$ is called *velocity gradient.*

$$\therefore \qquad \mu = \frac{\tau}{\left(\frac{du}{dy}\right)}$$

Unit of viscosity.

In MKS system : kgf – sec/m^2

In C.G.S. system : dyne – sec / cm^2. 1 dyne-sec/cm^2 is called **one poise.**

In S.I. system : Newton – sec / m^2 = Ns / m^2

***(vi)* Kinematic viscosity (ν).**

It is the ratio of two physical properties of a fluid. It is defined as the ratio between dynamic viscosity and density of the fluid

Mathematically, $$\nu = \frac{\mu}{\rho} = \frac{\text{viscosity}}{\text{density}}$$

Unit of kinematic viscosity .

$$\nu = \frac{\text{unit of } \mu}{\text{unit of } \rho} = \frac{\frac{FT}{L^2}}{\frac{M}{L^3}} = \frac{M \cdot \frac{L}{T^2} \cdot \frac{T}{L^2}}{\frac{M}{L^3}} = \frac{L^2}{T}, \text{ where } F = \frac{ML}{T^2}$$

In MKS and SI system : m^2/s.

In CGS system : cm^2/s. One cm^2/s is known as *one Stoke.*

$$\text{One stoke} = \text{one cm}^2/\text{sec} = \left(\frac{1}{100}\right)^2 = 10^{-4} \text{ m}^2/\text{sec}$$

The practical unit of kinematic viscosity is centi stoke.

$$1 \text{ centistoke} = \frac{1}{100} \text{ stoke.}$$

Newton's law of viscosity.

It states that, shear stress on a fluid element layer is directly proportional to the rate of shear strain.

Mathamatically, $$\tau = \mu\left(\frac{du}{dy}\right)$$

CLASSIFICIATION OF FLUIDS

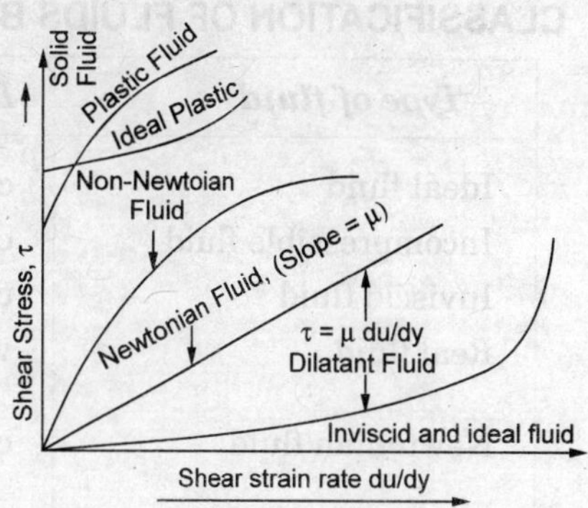

(i) **Ideal fluid:** This fluid is incompressible and possesses no viscosity. Such a fluid is only an imaginary fluid. All existing fluids have some viscosity.

(ii) **Real fluid:** A fluid that possesses viscosity is called a real fluid. In actual practice, all fluids are real fluids.

(iii) **Newtonian fluids:** A real fluid in which the shear stress is directly proportional to the rate of shear strain (or velocity gradient) is called Newtonian fluid.

(iv) **Non-Newtonian fluids:** A real fluid in which the shear stress is not proportional to the rate of shear strain (or velocity gradient) is called non-Newtonian fluid.

(v) **Ideal plastic fluid:** A fluid in which the shear stress is more than the yield value and the shear stress is proportional to the rate of shear strain (or velocity gradient) is called ideal plastic fluid.

RHEOLOGICAL CLASSIFICATION OF FLUIDS.

Newtonian fluids	Non-Newtonian fluids : $\tau \neq \mu \dfrac{du}{dy}$		
$\tau = \mu \dfrac{du}{dy}$			
e.g. air, water and many other engineering fluids behave as Newtonian fluids under normal circumstances.	*Purely viscous fluids*		*Viscoelastic fluids*
	Time-Independent	*Time-Dependent*	
	(i) Pseudoplastic fluids	*(i)* Thixotropic fluids	Viscoelastic fluids
	$\tau = \mu\left(\dfrac{du}{dy}\right)^n, n < 1$	$\tau = \mu\left(\dfrac{du}{dy}\right)^n + f(t)$	$\tau = \mu\dfrac{du}{dy} + \alpha E$
	e.g. fine particle suspensions	***e.g.*** crude oils bentonitic	where E is modulus of elasticity
	(ii) Dilament fluids	*(ii)* Rheopectic fluids	Liquid solid
	$\tau = \mu\left(\dfrac{du}{dy}\right)^n, n < 1$	$\tau = \mu\left(\dfrac{du}{dy}\right)^n + f(t),$	***e.g.*** combinations in pipe flow and
	e.g. ultrafine irregular suspensions	*f(t)* increases particle drag reduction features.	polymerised fluids with
	(iii) Ideal plastics or Bingham fluids	*(iii)* Rare liquid-solid suspensions.	
	$\tau = \tau_0 + \mu\left(\dfrac{du}{dy}\right)^n$		
	e.g. water suspensions of clay and fly ash.		

VARIATION OF VISCOSITY WITH TEMPERATURE.

Viscosity of liquids decreases with the increase of temperature while viscosity of the gases increases with the increase of temperature.

For liquids, $\mu = \mu_0 \left[\dfrac{1}{1+\alpha t+\beta t^2}\right]$

For gases, $\mu = \mu_0 + \alpha t - \beta t^2$

CLASSIFICATION OF FLUIDS BASED ON DENSITY AND VISCOSITY.

Type of fluid	*Density*	*Viscosity*
Ideal fluid	constant	zero
Incompressible fluid	constant	non-zero
Inviscid fluid	constant or variable	zero
Real fluid	variable	non-zero
Newtonian fluid	constant or variable	$\tau = \mu \dfrac{du}{dy}$
Non-Newtonian fluid	constant or variable	$\tau \neq \mu \dfrac{du}{dy}$
Perfect gas	$\dfrac{p}{RT}$	zero or non-zero

CLASSIFICATION OF FLOWS BASED ON MACH NUMBER.

Type of flow	*Mach number,* M
Incompressible flow	M less than 0.3
Compressible subsonic flow	M between 0.3 and 1
Transonic flow	M ranging between values less than 1 and more than 1
Supersonic flow	M grater than 1 but less than 5
Hypersonic flow	M greater than 5

COMPRESSIBILITY

It is the reciprocal of bulk modulus of elasticity '*k*' and is defined as the ratio of compressive stress to volumetric strain.

Let V = volume of gas enclosed in a cylinder

p = pressure of gas when the volume is V

Let pressure be increased to $(p + dp)$, so that corresponding volume decrease to $(V - dV)$

V
dV
Cylinder
Piston

$$\therefore \quad \text{Volumetric strain} = -\left(\frac{dV}{V}\right)$$

[negative sign is due to decrease of volume when pressure value increases]

$$\text{Bulk modulus, K} = \frac{\text{Increase of pressure}}{\text{Volumetric strain}} = \frac{dp}{\left(-\dfrac{dV}{V}\right)} = -\left(\frac{dp}{dV}\right)V$$

$$\text{Compressibility} = \frac{1}{K}$$

Surface Tension (σ)

It is defined as the tensile force acting on the surface of a liquid in contact with a gas or on the surface between two immiscible liquids such that the contact surface behaves as if it is a membrane under tension. The value of this force per unit length of the free surface is same as the surface energy per unit area.

It is expressed in S. I. system as N/m.

- *Surface tension on a liquid droplet :*

$$p \times \frac{\pi d^2}{4} = \sigma \times \pi d$$

$$\Rightarrow \quad p = \frac{4\sigma}{d}$$

where, d = diameter of droplet

p = pressure inside the droplet.

With decrease of diameter of the droplet, the pressure intensity inside the droplet increases.

- *Surface tension on a hollow bubble :*

$$p = \frac{8\sigma}{d}$$

- Surface tension on a liquid jet :

$$p = \frac{2\sigma}{d}$$

CAPILLARITY

It is defined as a phenomenon of rise or fall of a liquid surface in a small tube relative to the adjacent general level of liquid when the tube is held vertically in the liquid. The term used is capillary rise or capillary fall. Its value depends upon specific weight of the liquid, diameter of the tube and surface tension of the liquid.

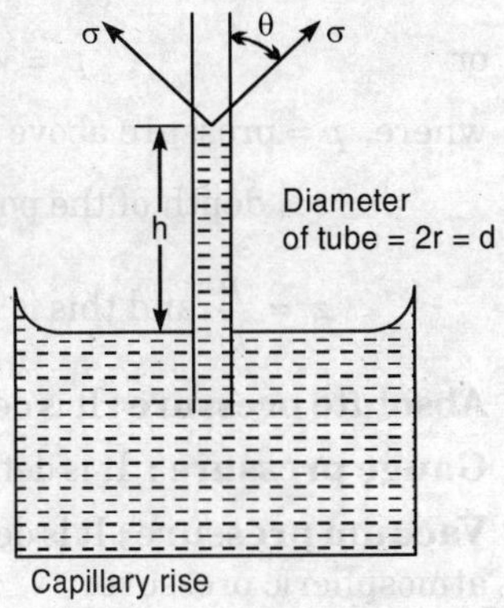

Capillary rise

For equilibrium, $\frac{\pi d^2}{4} \times h \times w = \sigma \times \pi d \cos\theta$

where θ = angle made by surface layer in the glass tube with glass tube

w = specific weight of the liquid

$$\therefore \quad h = \frac{4\,\sigma\cos\theta}{wd}$$

For water, the value of θ is nearly zero.

If a glass is dipped in mercury, the level of mercury in the tube will be lower than the general level of the outside liquid.

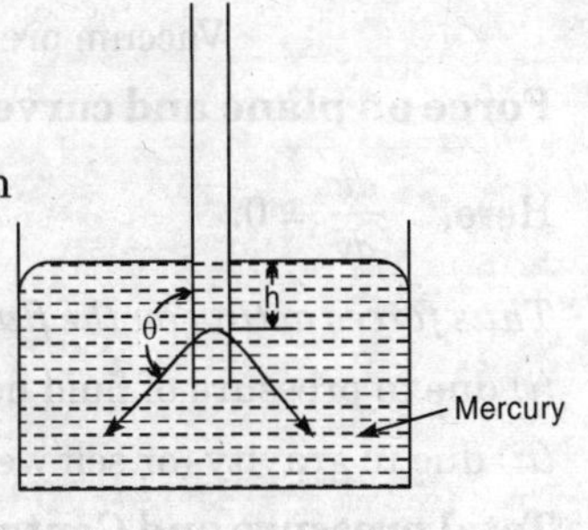

For equilibrium, $\sigma \pi d \cos\theta = wh\frac{\pi}{4}d^2$

or $$h = \frac{4\,\sigma\cos\theta}{wd}$$

Value of θ for mercury $\approx 128°$

FLUID STATICS

In fluid statics, fluids (liquids and gases) are at rest. There is no relative motion between adjacent or neighbouring fluid layers. The velocity gradient, which is equal to change of velocity between two adjacent fluid layers divided by the distance between the layers i.e. $\frac{du}{dy}$ will be equal to zero.

Shear stress which is equal to $\left(\mu\frac{\partial u}{\partial y}\right)$ will also be zero.

Forces acting on the fluid particles.

(*i*) Due to pressure of fluid normal to the surface

(*ii*) Due to gravity (or self weight of fluid particles)

Vapour pressure : Pressure exerted by the vapour formed at the free surface of a liquid is called *vapour pressure*. This phenomenon of vaporisation is due to the surface molecules escaping the liquid by overcoming the molecular attractive forces by virtue of their translational momentum.

Difference between vaporisation and boiling : Vaporisation occurs if vapour pressure < pressure above a liquid surface at a temperature.

Boiling occurs if vapour pressure = pressure above a liquid surface at a temperature.

Pascal's law : This law states that intensity of pressure at a point in a static fluid is same in all the directions.

Pressure variation in a fluid at rest.

$$p\Delta A - \left(p + \frac{\partial p}{\partial z}.\Delta z\right)\Delta A + w(\Delta A \times \Delta z) = 0$$

$$\therefore \qquad \frac{\partial p}{\partial z} = w$$

or $$p = wz$$

where, p = pressure above atmospheric pressure

z = depth of the point from free surface

$z = \frac{p}{w}$ and this is known as *pressure head.*

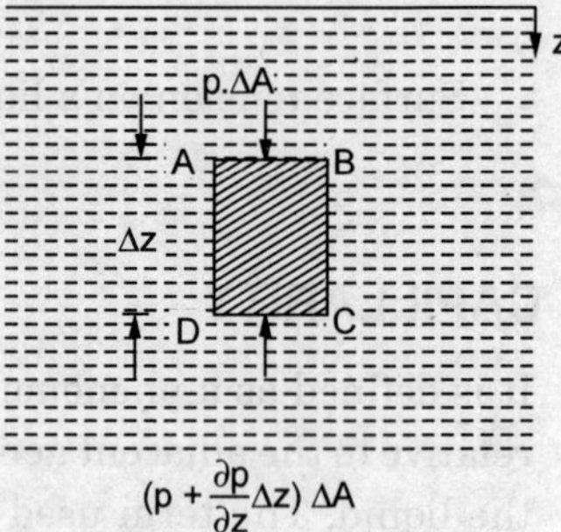

Fig. Forces on a fluid element

Absolute pressure : It is defined as the pressure which is measured with reference to absolute vacuum pressure.

Gauge pressure : It is defined as the pressure which is measured taking atmospheric pressure as the datum.

Vacuum pressure : It is defined as the pressure below the atmospheric pressure. The datum in this case is the atmospheric pressure.

Mathematically, Absolute pressure = Atmospheric pressure + Gauge pressure

i.e. $$p_{abs} = p_{atm} + p_{gauge}$$

Vaccum pressure = Atmospheric pressure – Absolute pressure

Force on plane and curved surfaces.

Here, $\frac{du}{dy} = 0.$

Thus forces acting on the fluid particles will be

(*i*) due to pressure of fluid normal to the surface

(*ii*) due to gravity (or self weight of fluid particles).

Total pressure and Centre of pressure.

Total pressure is defined as the force exerted by a static fluid on a surface either plane or curved, when the fluid comes into contact with the surface. This force acts always normal to the surface.

where, A = total area of the surface

$\bar{x}$ = distance of centre of gravity of the area from free surface of fluid

G = centre of gravity of the plane surface

P = centre of pressure (a point)

$\bar{h}$ = distance of centre of pressure from free surface of fluid

w = specific weight of the fluid

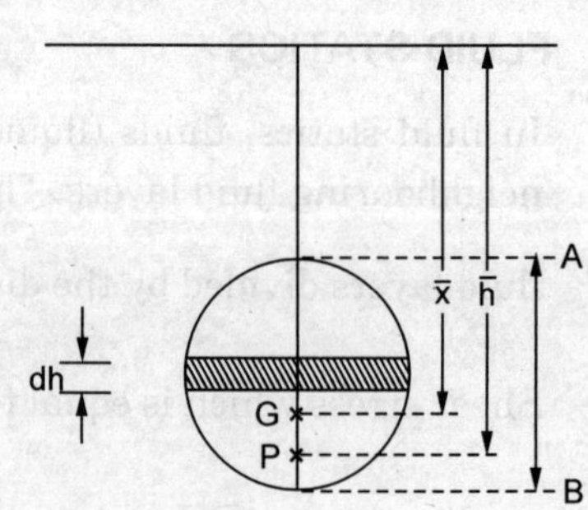

Total pressure over the area, $P = wA\bar{x}$

Distance of centre of pressure from fluid surface,

$$\bar{h} = \bar{x} + \frac{I_G}{A\bar{x}}$$

$$= \bar{x} + \frac{k_G^2}{\bar{x}}$$

where I_G and K_G are moment of inertia of the surface about an axis passing through the centre of gravity of the surface lying on its plane parallel to the fluid surface and radius of gyration of the body. Centre of pressure lies below the centre of gravity of the vertical surface.

Inclined plane surface submerged in a fluid.

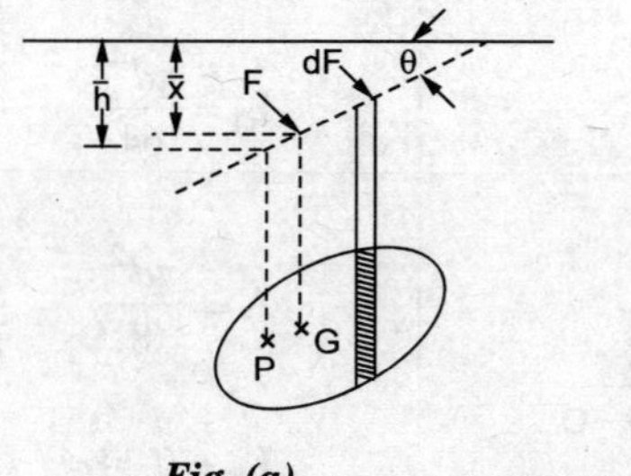

Fig. (a)

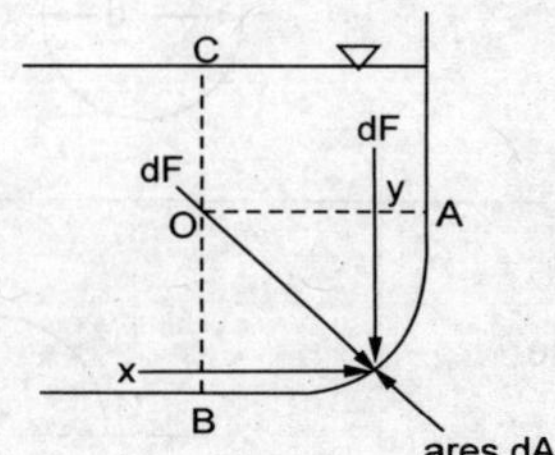

Fig. (b)

Consider Fig.(a). Total pressure on one face of the lamina, $P = wA\bar{x}$

Vertical depth of the centre of pressure from the fluid surface

$$\bar{h} = \bar{x} + \frac{I_G \sin^2\theta}{A\bar{x}}$$

$$= \bar{x} + \frac{k_G^2 \sin^2\theta}{\bar{x}}$$

- When $\theta = 0°$, then $\frac{k_G^2 \sin^2\theta}{\bar{x}} = 0$, and centre of gravity (G) and centre of pressure (P) coincide.
- When $\theta = 90°$, the value of $\bar{h} = \bar{x} + \frac{k_G^2}{\bar{x}}$ which is same as for vertical submersion.

Consider Fig. *(b)* to find total pressure and the centre of pressure of a curved surface submerged in a fluid.

The curved surface AB lies submerged inside the fluid.

Consider a small area *d*A at a depth of *h* from water surface. Total pressure *p* over this small area *d*A acts normal to the surface.

Total pressure over the whole curved area, $P = \int_{area} wh \cdot dA$

Total force on the curved surface, $p = \sqrt{p_x^2 + p_y^2}$

and inclination of resultant with horizontal is given by, $\tan\theta = \frac{p_y}{p_x}$

Geometric properties of plane figures.

S. No.	*Figure*	*Figure with C.G. shown on it*	*Area and Moment of Inertia*
1.	Rectangle	d/2, G, d, G, b, C.G.	$A = bd$ $I_G = \frac{bd^3}{12}$
2.	Circle	C.G., d, $\bar{x} = d/2$	$A = \frac{\pi d^2}{4}$ $I_G = \frac{\pi d^4}{64}$
3.	Semicircle	r, G, G, 4r/3π, O, O, C.G.	$A = \frac{\pi d^2}{8}$ $I_G = 0.11r^4$; $I_0 = \frac{\pi d^4}{8}$
4.	Triangle	d, G, G, O, O, b, d/3	$A = \frac{1}{2}\ bd$ $I_G = \frac{bd^3}{36}$; $I_0 = \frac{bd^3}{12}$
5.	Trapezium	a, G, G, $\bar{x}$, C.G., $\bar{x} = \frac{(2a+b)\,d}{(a+b)\,3}$	$A = \frac{d}{2}\ (a + b)$ $I_G = \frac{a^2 + 4ab + b^2}{a + b}\left(\frac{d^3}{36}\right)$
6.	Parabola	G, C.G., d, G, (2/5) d, O, O	$A = \frac{2bd}{3}$; $I_G = \frac{8}{175}\ bd^3$ $I_0 = \frac{16}{105}\ bd^3$; $I_{01} = \frac{2}{7}\ bd^3$
7.	Ellipse	G, C.G., G, d, b	$A = \frac{\pi\ bd}{4}$; $I_G = \frac{\pi\ bd^3}{64}$ Perimeter (approximately) $\frac{\pi}{2}\ (b + d)$ or $\frac{\pi}{2}\ \{1.5\ (b + d) - \sqrt{bd}\}$

BUOYANCY AND FLOTATION

A body may float in liquid in fully immersed state or in a partly immersed state.

Centre of buoyancy.

It is the centroid of the displaced fluid. It is the point where buoyant force is supposed to act.

Metacentre.

When a floating body is tilted by a small angle, the point of intersection of line joining previous buoyant centre and centre of gravity G, and vertical through the new buoyant centre is called *Metacentre*. Thus metacentre is the intersection of buoyant force and centreline of the body. It is the point about which a floating body oscillates when it is tipped or made unstable.

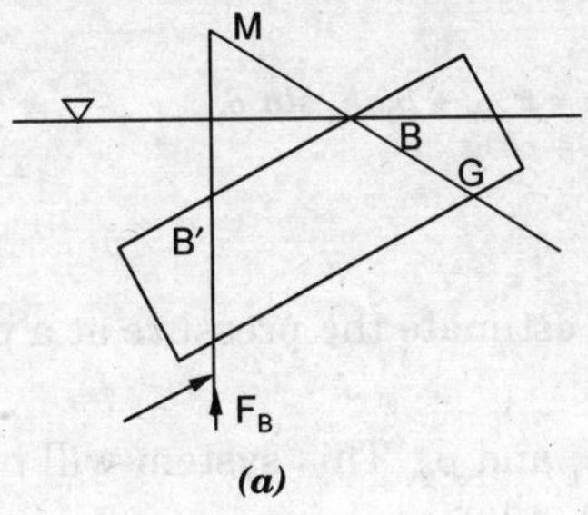

(a)

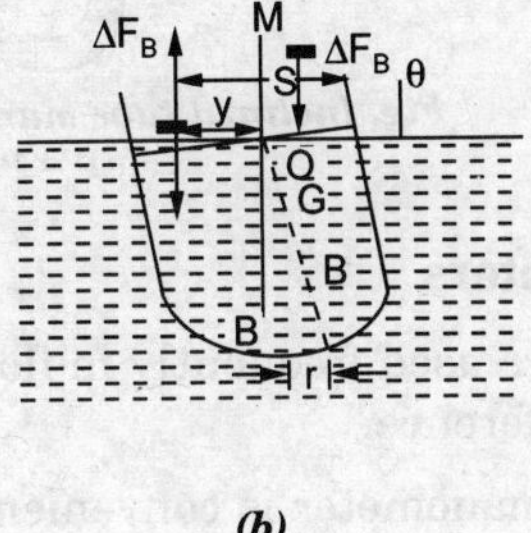

(b)

Notations used :

F_B = buoyant force

V = volume of floating body

x = x coordinate of centre of elementary area from reference axis

$\bar{x}$ = distance from the axis to the line of action of buoyant force

Refer figures *(a)* and *(b)*

BM = distance between metacentre and the buoyant centre

GM = metacentric height, *i.e.* distance between centre of gravity and metaceentre.

We have, $BM = \frac{I}{V}$, and $GM = \frac{I}{V} - BG$

$\therefore$ $GM = \frac{P_0 x}{W \tan \theta}$ [for P_0 and x refer Fig. *(b)*]

The body is in

(a) stable equilibrium if M is above G or GM is positive.

(b) unstable equilibrium if M is below G or GM is negative.

(c) neutral equilibrium if M coincides with G or GM = 0.

Larger is the metacentric height (GM), more stable is the body.

MANOMETRY

Manometers are used for the measurement of fluid pressure by measuring height of the same or another constant density fluid at rest.

Referring figure below, a liquid under pressure is contained in a pipe of diameter D. Another tube is fitted on to this pipe with the end of tube opening to atmosphere.

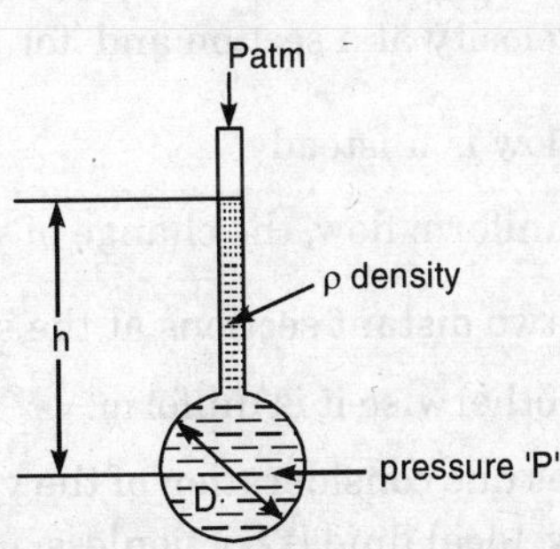

Fig. direct vertical tube manometer, i.e. piezometer

$$P = \rho g h + P_{atm}$$

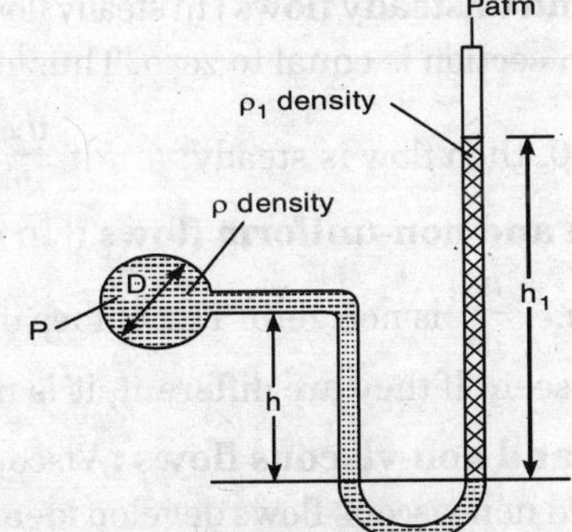

Fig. U tube manometer

$$P + \rho g h = P_{atm} + \rho_1 g h_1$$

$$\Rightarrow \quad (P - P_{atm}) = (\rho_1 h_1 - \rho h) g$$

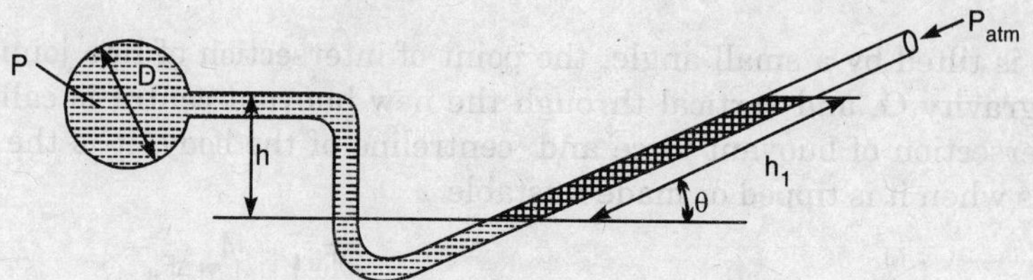

Fig. Inclined tube manometer $P + \rho gh = P_{atm} + \rho_1 gh_1 \sin\theta$,
$\Rightarrow (P - P_{atm}) = (\rho_1 h_1 \sin\theta - \rho h)g$

Differential Manometers

These manometers are used frequently in flow systems to estimate the pressure at a point with respect to that at another by difference.

Upright differential manometer is convenient when $\rho_3 > \rho_1$ and ρ_2. This system will be adopted when the fluids A and B are not allowed to come in contact with each other.

Manometer fluid with density ρ_3 is permitted to have contact with both the fluids A and B.

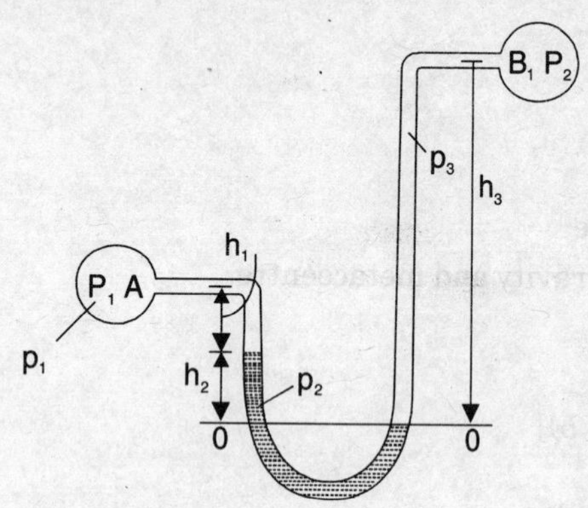

Upright differential manometer
Pressure balance across O – O
$P_1 + \rho_1 gh_1 + \rho_2 gh_2 = P_2 + \rho_3 gh_3$
$\Rightarrow (P_1 - P_2) = (\rho_2 h_2 - \rho_1 h_1 - \rho_2 h_3)g$

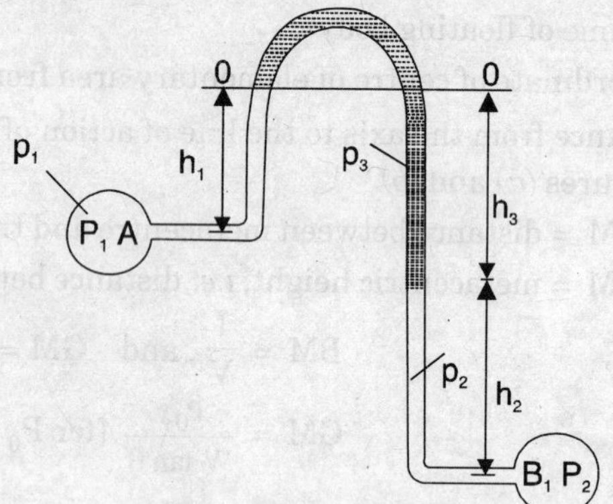

Inverted differential manometer
Pressure balance across O – O
$P_1 - \rho_1 gh_1 = P_2 - \rho_2 gh_2 - \rho_3 gh_3$
$\Rightarrow (P_1 - P_2) = (\rho_3 h_2 - \rho_1 h_1 - \rho_3 h_3)g$

FLUID KINEMATICS

Types of Fluid Flow.

(i) Laminar and turbulent flows : Main difference in *laminar and turbulent flows* is the randomness and impracticability of turbulent flow as compared to that in laminar flow. A turbulent flow comprises of more irreversibility. Turbulent losses are proportional to V^2 whereas laminar losses are proportional to V.

(ii) Steady and unsteady flows : In steady flow, time rate of change of a particular property (or flow parameter) at a given section is equal to zero. Thus if u is point velocity at a section and for all instants of time,

if $\frac{du}{dt} = 0$, then flow is steady; if $\frac{du}{dt} \neq 0$, then flow is unsteady.

(iii) Uniform and non-uniform flows : In case of non-uniform flow, the change of say velocity per unit distance *i.e.* $\frac{du}{dx}$ is non zero. The values of velocity at two distant sections at the same instant of time are to be seen. If they are different, it is non-uniform otherwise it is uniform.

(iv) Viscous and non-viscous flows : Viscous flow makes due consideration of the viscosity effects (real fluids) and non viscous flows develop ideal fluid theory. Ideal fluid is frictionless, incompressible fluid, but a perfect gas should not be confused with an ideal fluid. In ideal fluid, the flow process is reversible. In adiabatic flow, no heat is transferred to and from the fluid. Reversible adiabatic flow is isentropic.

(*v*) **Compressible and incompressible flows :** When variation of mass density of a fluid is considered, the treatment is that of compressible flows otherwise it is incompressible. Water at pressure more than 600 kPa is to be treated as compressible.

(*vi*) **One two and three dimensional flows :** If changes of velocity, pressure etc. are neglected in transverse to main flow direction, the treatment is that of one-dimensional flow and if considered, it is that of two mensional flow, *i.e.*

if $\frac{du}{dy} = 0$, it is one-dimensional

if $\frac{du}{dy} \neq 0$, it is two-dimensional.

A three dimensional flow is a flow in which the velocity components u, v, ω in three mutually perpendicular directions are functions of space coordinates x, y, z and time t.

(*vii*) **Rotational and irrotational flows :** If $\frac{du}{dy} = \frac{dv}{dx}, \frac{dw}{dy} = \frac{dv}{dz}, \frac{du}{dz} = \frac{dw}{dx}$; the flow is irrotational otherwise it is rotational.

For rotational flow, the cross derivatives of velocity components in two mutually perpendicular directions are unequal.

Also symbolically, if V refers to velocity.

	Steady	***Unsteady***
One dimensional flow	$V = f(x)$	$V = f(x, t)$
Two dimensional flow	$V = f(x, y)$	$V = f(x, y, t)$
Three dimensional flow	$V = f(x, y, z)$	$V = f(x, y, z, t)$

(*viii*) **Sub-critical, critical or super-critical (for open channel) flow**

(*ix*) **Sub-sonic, sonic or super sonic (for compressible fluids) flow**

Note: All the above types of flow can exist independent of each other, making it possible to have various combinations.

STREAM LINES

It is an imaginary line drawn in a flow field such that a tangent drawn at any point on this line represents the direction of velocity vector. From the definition, it follows that there can be no flow across a stream line.

Consider a particle moving along a stream line for a short distance *ds*, having its components *dx, dy* and *dz* along the three mutually perpendicular axes.

Let velocity components of V_s in x, y, and z directions be u, v and w respectively.

Time taken by a fluid particle to move through a distance *ds* along a stream line with a velocity V_s is

$$t = \frac{ds}{V_s}$$

which is the same as
$$t = \frac{dx}{u} = \frac{dy}{v} = \frac{dz}{w}$$

Hence differential equation for a stream line is, $\frac{dx}{u} = \frac{dy}{v} = \frac{dz}{w}$

Forms of energy present in the fluid.

(*i*) Elevation (*ii*) Kinetic (*iii*) Pressure head (*iv*) Internal energy

General equation is, $$\frac{P_1}{\gamma_1} + z_1 + \frac{V_1^2}{2g} + H_m = \frac{P_2}{\gamma_2} + z_2 + \frac{V_2^2}{2g} + J\,[I_2 - I_1 + q] \quad \ldots (1)$$

where J = mechanical equivalent of heat

$(I_2 - I_1)$ = change of internal energy

H_m = external source of energy supplied at a certain rate

q = heat units per unit weight of flowing fluid transferred out of the fluid to the surroundings.

In equation (1)

(i) If rate of loss of heat is such that temperature of the system remains constant, then $I_2 = I_1$

(ii) For well insulated systems, $q = 0$

(iii) If there is no external supply of heat energy, $H_m = 0$

(iv) For incompressible flow, $\gamma_1 = \gamma_2 = \gamma$

(v) The quantity $[J\,(I_2 - I_1) + Jq]$ refers, to frictional head loss = h_L

Equation (1) then reduces to, $$\frac{P_1}{\gamma} + z_1 + \frac{V_1^2}{2g} = \frac{P_2}{\gamma} + z_2 + \frac{V_2^2}{2g} + h_L$$

Sometimes, h_L is neglected being small, then $\left[\frac{P}{\gamma} + z + \frac{V^2}{2g}\right]$ becomes a constant value.

The above general energy equation is applicable for

(i) ideal and real fluids

(ii) liquid and gases or vapours and

(iii) compressible and incompressible fluids

VELOCITY AND ACCELERATIONS.

Let V be the resultant velocity at any point in a fluid flow. Let u, v and w be its components in the x, y and z directions. The velocity components are functions of space co-ordinates and time.

Mathematically, the velocity components are given as :

$$u = f_1\,[x, y, z, t], \quad v = f_2\,[x, y, z, t], \quad \text{and} \quad w = f_3\,[x, y, z, t]$$

$$\text{Resultant velocity, } V = |ui + vj + wk| = \sqrt{u^2 + v^2 + w^2}$$

$$a_x = \frac{du}{dt} = \frac{\partial u}{\partial x}\cdot\frac{dx}{dt} + \frac{\partial u}{\partial y}\cdot\frac{dy}{dt} + \frac{\partial u}{\partial z}\cdot\frac{dz}{dt} + \frac{\partial u}{\partial t}$$

But $$\frac{dx}{dt} = u, \quad \frac{dy}{dt} = v, \quad \text{and} \quad \frac{dz}{dt} = w$$

$\therefore$ $$a_x = \frac{du}{dt} = u\frac{\partial u}{\partial x} + v\frac{\partial u}{\partial y} + w\frac{\partial u}{\partial z} + \frac{\partial u}{\partial t}$$

Similarly, $$a_y = \frac{dv}{dt} = u\frac{\partial u}{\partial x} + v\frac{\partial u}{\partial y} + w\frac{\partial u}{\partial z} + \frac{\partial u}{\partial t}$$

and $$a_z = \frac{dw}{dt} = u\frac{\partial w}{\partial x} + v\frac{\partial w}{\partial y} + w\frac{\partial w}{\partial z} + \frac{\partial w}{\partial t}$$

For steady flow, $$\frac{\partial V}{\partial x} = 0$$

where V is resultant velocity

$\therefore$ $$\frac{\partial u}{\partial t} = \frac{\partial v}{\partial t} = \frac{\partial w}{\partial t} = 0$$

Local Acceleration

It is defiend as the rate of change of velocity with respect to time at a given point in a flow field.

$\frac{\partial u}{\partial t}$, $\frac{\partial v}{\partial t}$ and $\frac{\partial w}{\partial t}$ are known as *local accelerations.*

Convective Acceleration

It is defined as the rate of change of velocity due to the change of position of fluid particles in a fluid flow.

In the above expressions for a_x, a_y and a_z, it excludes the factors $\frac{\partial u}{\partial t}$, $\frac{\partial v}{\partial t}$ and $\frac{\partial w}{\partial t}$.

VELOCITY POTENTIAL

The velocity potential is not a physical quantity which could be directly measured and therefore, its zero position can be aribtrarily chosen.

It is defined as a scalar function of space and time such that its negative derivative with respcet to any direction gives the fluid velocity in that direction. It is denoted by the symbol ϕ.

Mathematically, velocity potential is defined as $\phi = f(x, y, z)$ for steady flow such that

$$u = -\frac{\partial \phi}{\partial x};\ v = -\frac{\partial \phi}{\partial y} \text{ and } w = -\frac{\partial \phi}{\partial z}$$

where u, v and w are components of velocity in x, y and z directions respectively.

The contiunity equation for incompressible steady flow is

$$\frac{\partial}{\partial x}\left(-\frac{\partial \phi}{\partial x}\right) + \frac{\partial}{\partial y}\left(-\frac{\partial \phi}{\partial y}\right) + \frac{\partial}{\partial z}\left(-\frac{\partial \phi}{\partial z}\right) = 0$$

or

$$\frac{\partial^2 \phi}{\partial x^2} + \frac{\partial^2 \phi}{\partial y^2} + \frac{\partial^2 \phi}{\partial z^2} = 0$$

$$V^2\phi = 0,$$

which is Laplace equation for ϕ.

Any value of ϕ that satisfies Laplace equation will correspond to some case of fluid flow.

Stream Function (Ψ).

It is defined as the scalar function of space and time, such that its partial derivative with respect to any direction gives the velocity component at right angles to that direction. It is defined for two dimensional flow.

Properties of stream function.

(i) If stream function ψ exists, it is a possible case of fluid flow which may be rotational or irrotational.

(ii) If stream function satisfies the Laplace equation, it is a possible case of an irrotational flow.

The product of slope of equipotential line and the slope of stream line at the point of intersection is equal to – 1. Thus equipotential lines are orthogonal to the stream lines at all points of intersection.

Flow Nets

Equipotential lines and streamlines intersect each other orthogonally. The streamlines and equipotential lines form a net of mutually perpendicular lines which is called *flow net*.

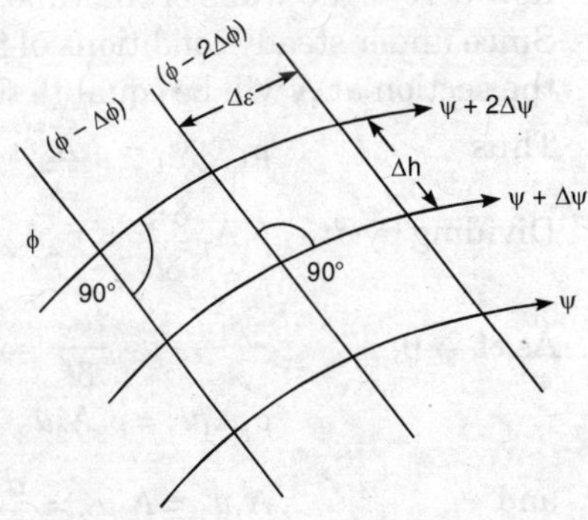

The flow net is a graphical representation of two dimensional, irrotational flow and consists of a family of streamlines intersecting orthogonally a family of equipotential lines and in the process forming small curvilinear squares. **Figure** shows a flow net, in which ϕ value decreases in the direction of flow.

If the distance between streamlines at some small region of flow is Δh, and the distance between equipotential lines is Δs, then for a flow net, Δs ≈ Δh. The smaller these dimensions, the better will be the representation of flow. This concept may be explained from the relation

$$\frac{\partial \phi}{\partial h} = \frac{\partial \psi}{\partial s}$$

If $\Delta\phi = \Delta\psi$, then $\Delta h = \Delta s$

Methods of Drawing Flow Nets

(i) By mathematical analysis *(ii)* By hydraulic models

(iii) By graphical methods *(iv)* By electrical analogy

Equation of Motion

According to Newton's second law of motion, the net force F_x acting on a fluid element in the x direction is equal to mass m of the fluid element multiplied by the acceleration a_x in the x-direction.

Thus mathematically, $F_x = ma_x$

Forces present in the fluid flow.

(i) F_g, gravity force *(ii)* F_p, the pressure force

(iii) F_v, force due to viscosity(*(iv)* F_t, force due to turbulence

(v) F_e force due to compressibility

Thus in the above equation, net force, $F_x = (F_g)_x + (F_p)_x + (F_v)_x + (F_t)_x + (F_c)_x$

(i) If force due to compressibility F_e, is negligible, then resulting net force

$$F_x = (F_g)_x + (F_p)_x + (F_v)_x + (F_t)_x$$

and equations of motion are called **Reynold equations of motion.**

(ii) For flow, where F_t is negligible, the resulting equations of motion are called *Navier-Stokes equations.*

(iii) If the flow is assumed to be ideal, viscous force F_v is zero and equations or motion are called *Euler's equations of motion*.

CONTROL VOLUME ANALYSIS FOR MASS MOMENTUM AND ENERGY CONSERVATION

Control volume.

It is an identified volume fixed in space. A control volume may either be infinitesimally small or as large as desired. A control volume is bounded by a control surface.

An infinitesimal control volume is called *differential control volume*. A differential control volume is assumed to have very small but non-zero dimension. Its volume is denoted by δV and its control surface by δs.

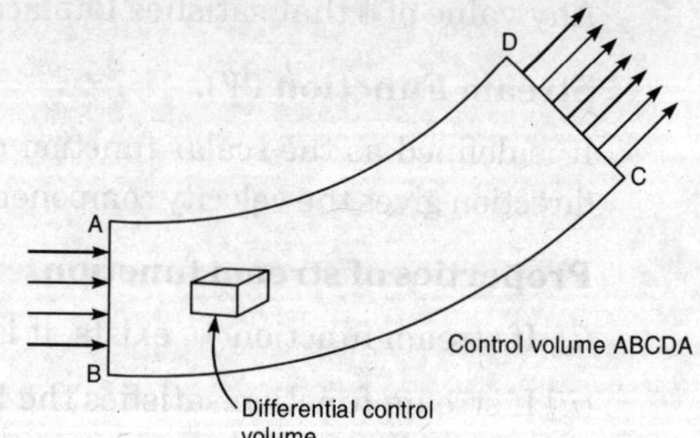

Mass equation.

This is also called *continuity equation*. Consider the fluid between two sections A and B. Since there can be no flow across the walls of the tube, after a given time δt, the same fluid will be contained between A' and B'. Since under steady conditions of flow, mass of the fluid between A and B remains constant, the mass entering the section at A will be equal to the mass leaving at B.

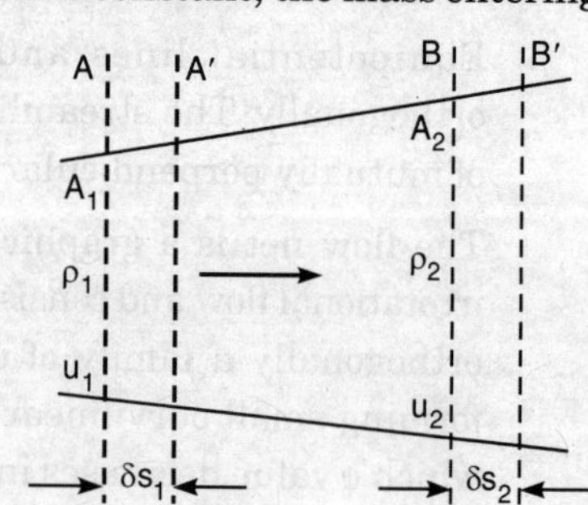

Thus $\rho_1 A_1 \delta s_1 = \rho_2 A_2 \delta s_2$

Dividing by dt, $\rho_1 A_1 \frac{\delta s_1}{\delta t} = \rho_2 A_2 \frac{\delta s_2}{\delta t}$

As $\delta t \to 0$, $\frac{\delta s_1}{\delta t} \to u_1, \frac{\delta s_2}{\delta t} \to u_2$

∴ $\rho_1 A_1 u_1 = \rho_2 A_2 u_2$ (continutiy equation)

and $A_1 u_1 = A_2 u_2 = \frac{dV}{dt}$

MOMENTUM EQUATION

It is based on the second law of motion, *i.e.* net force acting in any direction is equal to rate of change of momentum in that direction, *i.e.*

linear impulse = change in linear momentum

In the x direction, Initial linear impulse ± linear impulse = Final linear momentum

$\therefore$ $\rho\, Q.\, t.\, v_{x1} \pm F_x .\, t = \rho\, Q.\, t.\, v_{x2}$

or $F_x = \rho\, Q\,(v_{x2} - v_{x1}) = \dfrac{\gamma\, Q}{g}(v_{x2} - v_{x1})$

where v_{x2} and v_{x1} = components of velocity in x-direction of points 1 and 2.

F_x = component for net force in x-direction.

For pipe flow, $p_1 A_1 - p_2 A_2 = \dfrac{\gamma Q}{g}(v_2 - v_1)$

where suffix 1 indicates upstream point and suffix 2 indicates downstream point.

V_1 and V_2 are average velocities at sections 2 and 1 of pipe.

Moment of Momentum Equation

If a fluid particle of mass m moves along a curved path such that its distance from the axis of rotation (*i.e.* fixed center) changes with time, then radial distance will be different at different positions of the particle.

If the flow enters the control volume at a uniform velocity v_1 and at a steady rate, then

momentum of flow entering control volume = $\rho\, Q\, v_1$

If this flows has a radius r_1, then

moment of momentum of flow entering control volume = $\rho\, Q\, v_1\, r_1$

Similarly, if v_2 and r_2 are velocity and radius at the outlet of control volume, then

moment of momentum of flow leaving the control volume = $\rho\, Q\, v_2\, r_2$

According to moment of momentum principal, the resulting torque is equal to the time rate of change in moment of momentum.

Therefore $T = \rho\, Q\,(v_2 r_2 - v_1 r_1)$

BERNOULLI'S EQUATION

Assumptions.

(i) Ideal fluid *(ii)* Continuity of flow *(iii)* Steady and incompressible flow.

Euler's energy equation is, $\dfrac{\partial p}{\rho} + gdz + v\,\partial v = 0$

Integrating, we get

$$\int \frac{dp}{\rho} + \int gdz + \int vdv = \text{constant}$$

For an incompressible flow, ρ = constant

$\therefore$ $\dfrac{p}{\rho} + gz + \dfrac{v^2}{2}$ = constant *(Bernoulli's energy equation)*

or $\dfrac{p}{\rho g} + z + \dfrac{v^2}{2g}$ = constant

$\dfrac{p}{\rho g} = \dfrac{p}{\gamma}$ = pressure energy per unit weight of fluid or pressure head

$\dfrac{v^2}{2g}$ = kinetic energy per unit weight or kinetic head

z = potential energy per unit weight or potential head

APPLICATIONS OF BERNOULLI'S EQUATION

It is applied to the problems of

(i) flow under a sluice gate which is a construction in an open channel

(ii) free liquid jet

(iii) radial flow

(iv) free vortex motion.

FLOW THROUGH AN ORIFICES

Flow through small orifices :

Jet of water or fluid has minimum area at vena contracta.

$$\text{Coefficient of contractation, } C_C = \frac{\text{Area of jet at vena contracta}}{\text{Area of opening}}$$

$$= 0.61 \text{ for } d << H_1$$

Bernoulli's equation gives, $U_t = \sqrt{2gH_1}$ and $U_a = C_v\sqrt{2gH_1}$

where U_t and U_a are theoretical and actual velocities at vena contracta.

If there is no friction, $C_v = 1$.

Otherwise $C_v = 0.97$ to 0.99

$$Q = \text{area} \times \text{velocity}$$

$$= C_c\, a\, C_v\, \sqrt{2gH_1} = C_d\, a\, \sqrt{2gH}$$

where, C_d = discharge coefficient = $C_c \times C_v$

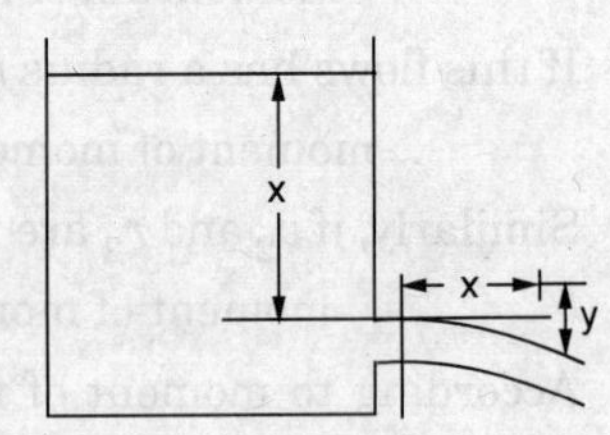

Determination of coefficient of velocity (C_v).

By the trajectory method

$$C_v = \frac{x}{\sqrt{4yH}}$$

Flow through large orifice :

When d is not very small compared to H_1 or H_2,

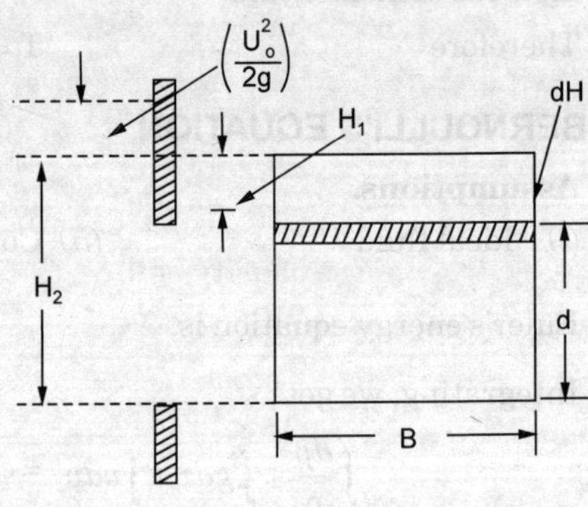

$$dQ = C_c\, B dH \sqrt{2gH}$$

Integrating over H_1 and H_2 gives

$$Q = \frac{2}{3} C_c \sqrt{2g}.B\left[H_2^{3/2} - H_1^{3/2}\right]$$

Neglecting velocity of approach, we get

$$Q = \frac{2}{3} C_c \sqrt{2g}.B\left[\left(H_2 + \frac{U_0^2}{2g}\right)^{3/2} - \left(H_1 + \frac{U_0^2}{2g}\right)^{3/2}\right]$$

If velocity of approach is taken into account, value of C_c for large orifices used are obtained from standard charts.

LAMINAR FLOW

In laminar flow the fluid particles move along straight, parallel paths in layers or laminae. The magnitudes of the velocities of adjacent laminae are not same.

Characteristics of Laminar Flow

(i) The flow is governed by the law relating to rate of angular deformation, *i.e.*

$$\tau = \mu \frac{dv}{dy} \text{ for flow in } x \text{ direction.}$$

(ii) There is practically no interference of fluid partilces of one layer over those of adjacent layer.

(iii) There is "no slip" condition occurs at the boundary.

(iv) The flow is rotational.

(v) There is continuous dissipation of energy due to viscous, shear and energy must be supplied externally to maintain the flow.

(vi) Energy loss is proportional to first power of velocity and viscosity.

(vii) Flow remains laminar as long as $\frac{V.l\,\rho}{\mu} < R_{critical}$.

Critical velocity.

The velocity at which the flow changes from laminar to turbulent is called *critical velocity*. It is the velocity at lower critical Reyolds number. It is different for different fluids.

A flow is more likely to be laminar if

(i) velocity v is low

(ii) width or diameter of passage is small

(iii) density ρ is low

(iv) viscosity of the flowing fluid is high.

The above four variables are grouped in the form of a non-dimensional para called Reynolds number, Re.

Reynolds number.

Reynolds determined a non-dimensional quantity called *Reynolds number (R)*.

For circular pipe flowing full, $$\text{Re} = \frac{\rho V d}{\mu} = \frac{Vd}{\nu}$$

where V = mean velocity

d = diameter of pipe

ν = kinematic viscosity of the fluid

ρ = mass density of fluid

μ = absolute viscosity

For non-circular cross-section, ratio of the cross-sectional area to the wetted perimeter is called h*ydraulic radius (R)*. It is used in the Reynolds number, *viz*.

$$\text{Re} = \frac{V(4R)}{\nu}$$

where, $\frac{\mu}{\rho} = \nu$ = kinematic viscosity

Flow through a pipe (or closed conduit) is

Laminar at R_e values less than 2000 turbulent at Re values more than 3000.

In transition stage at Re values between 2000 and 3000.

- **Laminar flow depends upon:** velocity of flow, area of surface in contact, temperature of fluid *independent of* nature of surface in contact and pressure of flow.
- Turbulent flow depends upon square of velocity of flow, area of surface in contact, temperature, density of fluid and nature of contact and is independent of pressure of flow.

Upper and lower critical Reynolds number :

The Reynolds number above which the flow changes from laminar to turbulent is called *lower critical Reynolds number*. Velocity of the fluid corresponding to the lower critical Reynolds number called *lower critical velocity*.

Similarly, Reynolds number and the velocity which turbulent flow may change to laminar flow are called *upper critical Reynolds number* and *upper critical velocity respectively*. The critical Reynolds number in different situations may be different depending upon choice of the character length l, in place of the diameter d chosen for pipe flow.

Case	*Characteristic length*	*Upper critical Reyonlds Number*
1. Pipe flow		
2. Open channel flow	*(a)* Hydraulic mean depth R *(b)* Flow depth, y	4000 2000
3. Parallel plates	Spaced 'a' apart	300
4. Movement of small sphere through stationary fluid	Sphere diameter	3000

Discharge velocity is given by, $$u = k.\ \frac{h}{l} = (-)\ k\ \frac{d(p/r+z)}{dl}$$

The law is valid for velocities upto 3 to 4.5 mm/sec.

Relation between Shear stress and Pressure gradient.

For steady two dimensional uniform flows, $$-\frac{\partial p}{\partial x} + \mu \frac{\partial^2 u}{\partial y^2} = 0$$

But $\tau = \mu \dfrac{\partial u}{\partial y}$, therefore $$\frac{\partial p}{\partial x} = \frac{\partial z}{\partial y}$$

i.e. pressure gradient in the direction of flow is equal to the shear gradient normal to the direction of motion.

Stoke's law.

Resisting force drag on a small sphere moving under laminar condition in a viscous fluid was first calculated by Stokes and is known as *Stoke's solution.*

$$\text{Total drag, } F_D = 3\,\pi\,\mu\,Vd$$

Out of which $\pi\,\mu\,Vd$ is contributed by the pressure and remaining $2\pi\,\mu Vd$ is contributed by the shear stress on the body.

The sphere after a short distance of fall in the viscous fluid attains a constant velocity called *terminal velocity*. To attain this equillibrium of the sphere under the steady state condition, the drag force and buoyant force must add up to balance the weight of the falling sphere.

At equilibrium, $$F_D = 3\pi.\mu.V.d. = \frac{\pi\,d^3}{6}(\gamma_s - \gamma)$$

and terminal velocity, $$V = \frac{d^2}{18\,\mu}(\lambda_s - \lambda)$$

Above expressions are valid for $R < 1$ and is known as **Stokes'law.**

Drag force.

The drag force experienced by the sphere is generally expressed as

$$C_D = F_D \frac{\rho\,V^2}{2}.\,A$$

where, A = area of cross-section of the moving body normal to the direction of motion

C_D = known as the coefficient of drag.

Steady laminar flow in horizontal circular pipe (Hagen-Poisuile equation).

For steady laminar flow to occur in the pipe, a pressure gradient is maintained in the direction of flow which overcomes the frictional forces (or shear forces) opposing the flow. It is also assumed that the pressure is distributed uniformly across the pipe cross-section.

Shear stress distribution : Figure shows a horizontal pipe of radius conveying a viscous incompressible fluid of viscosity μ.

$$\tau = \frac{r}{2} \cdot \frac{dp}{dl}$$

This relation holds goods for laminar as well as turbulent flow. The negative sign indicates that the pressure is decreasing in the direction of flow.

At r = maximum, $\tau_0 = (-)\,\frac{r_0}{2} \cdot \frac{dp}{dl}$

and at $r = 0$, $\tau = 0$

Velocity distribution : Velocity distribution for laminar flow is given by

$$u = (-)\frac{1}{4\mu}\left(-\frac{\partial p}{\partial l}\right)\left(r_0^2 - r^2\right)$$

This is equation of a parabola, so the maximum velocity varies parabolically along the diameter.

Maximum velocity (U_{max}) : Maximum velocity will be obtained, if $r = 0$, *i.e.* at the center.

$$U_{max} = (-)\frac{1}{4\mu}\left(\frac{\partial p}{\partial l}\right) \cdot r_0^2$$

Discharge :

$$Q = (-)\frac{1}{8\,\mu}\left(\frac{\partial p}{\partial l}\right) \cdot \pi r_0^2$$

Average or Mean velocity of flow through the pipe : It is obtained from continuity equation,

$$V = \frac{Q}{\pi\, r_0^2} = (-)\frac{1}{8\mu}\left(\frac{\partial p}{\partial l}\right) \cdot r_0^2$$

Let average velocity V occurs at radius r_1, therefore equating u to V, we get

$$(-)\frac{1}{8\,\mu}\left(\frac{\partial p}{\partial l}\right) \cdot \pi\, r_0^2 = (-)\frac{1}{4\,\mu}\,\frac{\partial p}{\partial l}\left(r_0^2 - r^2\right)$$

Head loss : From Hagen-Poiseulli's equation for laminar flow,

$$\text{Head loss, } h_l = \frac{p_1 - p_2}{\gamma} = \frac{8\mu\, V\, L}{\gamma\, r_0^2} = \frac{32\,\mu\, V\, L}{\gamma\, d^2}$$

Also, $$h_l = \frac{128\mu\, VL}{\gamma\,\pi\, d^4}$$

Relation between Darcy's friction coefficient f and Re.

For laminar flow through circular pipe (*i.e.* for Re < 2000),

$$f = \frac{16}{\text{Re}}$$

Local velocity in terms of maximum velocity, $u = U_{max}\left(1 - \frac{r^2}{r_0^2}\right)$

CORRECTION FACTORS

Kinetic energy correction factor (α).

Due to viscosity, the velocity distribution across any cross-section in real fluid flow is non-uniform and boundary resistance and therefore kinetic energy per unit weight given by $\frac{V^2}{2g}$ does not represent the true kinetic energy across the section. To compensate the discrepancy, a coefficient known as *kinetic energy correction factor* (α) is used.

$$\alpha = \frac{1}{A}\int_A \left(\frac{v}{V}\right) dA$$

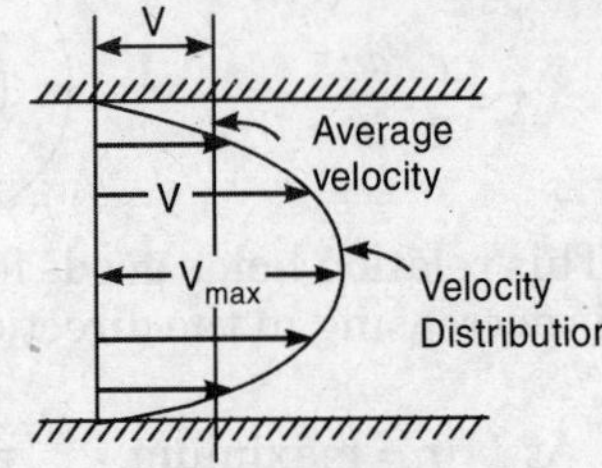

where v = velocity at any point in the cross-section.

α = 1.0 for uniform velocity distribution

α = 1.02 to 1.05 for turbulent flows

α = 2.0 for laminar flow.

Momentum correction factor (β).

Due to non-uniform distribution of velocity, the actual momentum transferred across the section is different than that computed using the average velocity. It is given by

$$\beta = \frac{1}{A}\int \left(\frac{v}{V}\right)^2 dA$$

For laminar flow in pipe, β = 1.33 and for turbulent flow in pipe, β varies from 1.01 to 1.07.

Boundary Layer

The narrow region situated in the vicinity of a solid boundary where the effects of viscosity are confined is called *boundary layer*. The drag force experienced by a solid body immersed in a flowing fluid can be explained only with the boundary layer concept.

The motion of fluids with *very little friction* [very low viscosity] amounts to fluid flow at very large Reynolds number.

For such flows, Prandtl made the following observations :

(i) Viscous effects are confined to a very thin layer, called *boundary layer*, near the solid surface.

(ii) The flow outside the boundary layer can be considered frictionless or ideal.

Boundary layer growth over a flat plate.

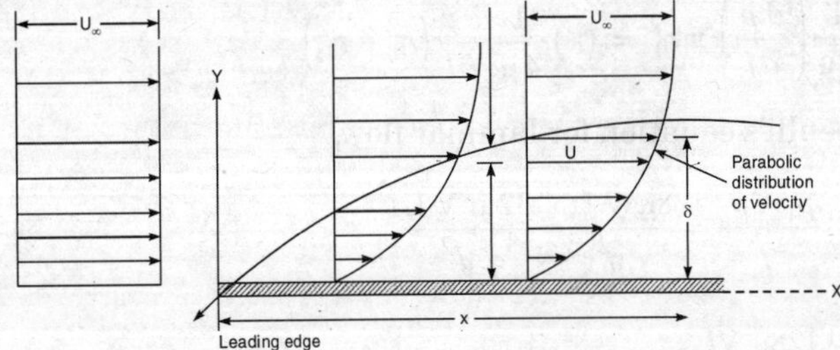

Fig. Velocity distribution and growth of boundary layer over a flat plate at zero incidence placed in parallel flow

U_∞ denotes undisturbed velocity or free stream velocity. In the downstream direction from the leading edge, thickness of the retarded layer δ increases continuously, *i.e.* thickness of the boundary layer increases along the plate in the downstream direction. The viscous shear within the boundary layer will be high due to the existence of high velocity gradient.

Under certain conditions of flow and boundary configuration, thickness of the boundry layer increases considerable in the downstream direction so much, so that flow in the boundary layer gets reversed. The declerated fluid particles are forced away and boundary layer is separated from the solid boundary. This phenomenon is called *boundary layer separation*. It occurs in case of flow past blunt bodies like circular cylinders and spheres. A region of highly decelerated flow exists downstream of such bodies. This region is called *wake zone*.

BOUNDARY LAYER THICKNESS

(1) Normal thickness (δ).

The transition from zero velocity at the solid stationary boundary to the free stream velocity U_∞ outside the boundary layer takes place asymptotically. Boundary layer is usually defined as that distance from the boundary where velocity differs by 1% from the free stream velocity,

i.e. $y = \delta$ for $u = 0.99\, U_\infty$

(2) Displacement thickness (δ*).

The boundary layer formation and the resulting velocity distribution has the effect of displacing the flow rate slightly outward from the solid boundary as compared with the potential flow (or ideal flow) that would exist in the absence of this boundary layer.

Displacement thickness may be defined in any one of the following ways :

(i) It is the distance measured perpendicular to the boundary by which the free stream is displaced on account of formation of boundary layer, or

(ii) It can be defined as an additional *wall thickness* that would have to be added to compensate for the reduction in flow rate on account of boundary layer formation.

It is obtained from the expression

$$\delta^* = \frac{1}{U_\infty}\int_0^\delta (U_\infty - u)\, dy = \int_0^\delta \left(1 - \frac{u}{U_\infty}\right) dy$$

The quantity $(U_\infty - u)$ is called *velocity defect*.

(3) Momentum thickness (θ).

This is defined in a way similar to the flow rate displacement thickness. This is obtained from the expression

$$\theta = \int_0^\delta \frac{u}{U_\infty}\left(1 - \frac{u}{U_\infty}\right) dy$$

Note: For parallel flow past a flat plate held at zero incidence, the appoximate relationship among the three thickness of a boundary layer described above is

$$\delta = 3\delta^* = 7.5\,\theta$$

(4) Energy thickness (δ_e).

The reasoning in the case is same as for the case of mometum thickness. This can be obtained from the expression

$$\delta_e = \int_0^\delta \frac{u}{U_\infty}\left(1 - \frac{u^2}{U_\infty^{\,2}}\right) dy$$

With the energy thickness known, the loss of energy per unit time can be determined from the relation

$$E_L = \frac{1}{2}\rho b \delta\, U_\infty^3$$

Characteristies of Boundary Layer

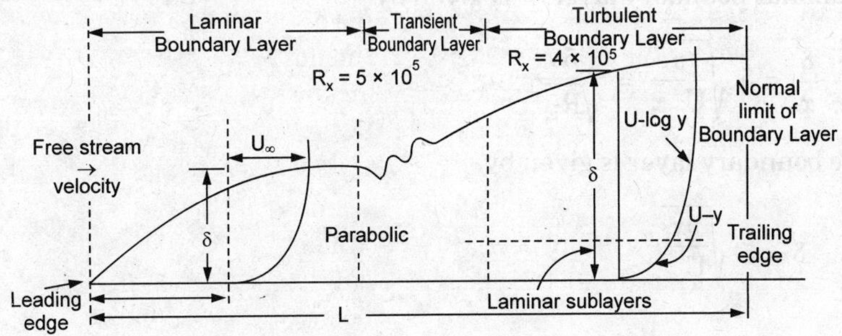

Consider the boundary layer formed on a flat plate kept parallel to flow of fluid of velocity U_∞

- δ increases as distance from leading edge x increases, *i.e.* $\delta \propto x$
- δ decreases as U_∞ increases, *i.e.* $\delta \propto \frac{1}{U_\infty}$
- δ increases as kinematic viscosity increases, *i.e.* $\delta \propto \mu$
- $\tau_0 \approx \mu \left(\frac{U_\infty}{\delta}\right)$, therefore τ_0 decreases as x increases.
- If pressure increases in the downstrem direction, *i.e.* $\frac{\partial p}{\partial x}$ is positive, flow near the boundary is further retarded, boundary layer growth is faster and boundary layer is susceptible to separation.
- If pressure decreases in the downstrem direction, *i.e.* $\frac{\partial p}{\partial x}$ is negative, the boundary layer growth is reduced.
- Variation of δ, τ_0 and force F etc characteristics are governed by inertial and viscous forces, therefore they are functions of either $\frac{Ux}{\nu}$ or $\frac{UL}{\nu}$, *i.e.* Reynolds number.
- When $R_x < 2 \times 10^2$, boundary layer is laminar velocity distribution is parabolic
  When $R_x > 4 \times 10^5$, boundary layer is turbulent
  When $4 \times 10^5 > R_x > 2 \times 10^5$, boundary layer is in transition.
- Critical value of Reynolds number at which boundary layer changes from laminar to turbulent depends upon turbulence in free steam flow, surface roughness, pressure gradient, plate curvature and temperature difference between fluid and boundary.
- Velocity distribution in laminar boundary layer follows parabolic law while that in turbulent layer follows logarithmic law or power law.

Laminar boundary layers on a flat plate.

Flow in the initial stages of boundary layer development shows characteristics of laminar motion. Viscous forces slow down the particles near the solid boundary. The Reynolds number in the boundary layer is expressed as

$$R_e = U_\infty \left(\frac{x}{v}\right)$$

where x = distance from leading edge.

Dimensionless boundary layer thickness depends upon

(*i*) free stream velocity, U_∞

(*ii*) distance x measured from the leading edge

(*iii*) the kinematic viscosity v of the fluid.

For a two dimensional laminar boundary layer, it is given by

$$\frac{\delta}{x} = 5\sqrt{\frac{v}{U_\infty x}} = \frac{5}{\sqrt{R_E}}$$

Nominal thickness of the boundary layer is given by

$$\delta = 5\sqrt{\frac{vx}{U_\infty}}$$

LAWS OF FLUID FRICTION

A fluid in motion is always subjected to a certain resistance. Such a resistance is generally assumed to be due to friction. In reality, this resistance is mainly due to sliding of the adjacent fluid layers.

A liquid will have a steady streamline (viscous) flow at low velocities only. After reaching a certain velocity, the flow changes into a turbulent flow with the appearance of eddy currents.

For fluids in motion, the frictional resistance obeys certain laws.

Laws of fluid friction for steady streamline flow

(1) Frictional resistance is proportional to velocity, surface area of contact and temperature.

(2) Frictional resistance is independent of pressure and nature of the surface of contact.

The flow establishment length is given by

$$L = 0.057\, R\, d \text{ ... for laminar flow}$$

and

$$L = 0.7\, R\, d \text{ ... for turbulent flow}$$

where, d = diameter of the pipe

R = Reynolds number of flow.

Laws of friction for turbulent flow

(1) Frictional resistance is proportional to square of the velocity.

(2) Frictional resistance is independent of the pressure.

(3) Frictional resistance is proportional to density of the fluid.

(4) Frictional resistance slightly varies with temperature.

Darcy's friction factor

In smooth pipes (due to Blasius), $f = \dfrac{64}{R}$ for laminar flow

and $f = \dfrac{0.3164}{\left(R^{1/4}\right)}$ for turbulent flow

HEAD LOSSES

***(i)* Major head losses.** Head loss due to friction falls in this category and is given by Darcy - Weisbach's equation

$$h_f = \frac{f\,l V^2}{2gd} = \frac{32\,\mu\, V\, l}{\gamma\, d^2}$$

where, l = length of pipe

V = average velocity of flow

γ = specific weight of fluid

μ = coefficient of dynamic viscosity.

Now,

$$h_f = \frac{4\, fl}{d}\frac{V^2}{2g} = \frac{fQ^2}{3.0258 d^5} \qquad \left(\text{substituting} V = \frac{Q}{\left(\pi / d^2 / 4\right)}\right)$$

Chezy's formula : $V = C\sqrt{mi}$

where, $i = \dfrac{h_f}{l}$

$m = \dfrac{A}{P} = \dfrac{d}{4}$ for a circular section

C = Chezy's constant $= \sqrt{\dfrac{V_w}{f'}}$

Value of f in Darcy Weisbach formula.

The coefficient f in the formula, $h_f = \frac{4fl}{d} \cdot \frac{V^2}{2g}$ is a function of the Reynolds number, $Re = \frac{dV\rho}{\mu}$

(a) When Re < 2000, $f = \frac{16}{Re}$ ... (Hagen Poiseuille)

(b) When Re < 2000 and Re < 1,00,000, $f = \frac{0.079}{Re^{1/4}}$ ... (Blasius)

(c) When Re < 1,00,000 then value of f can be found from

$$\frac{1}{4f} = 2 \log_{10} Re \cdot 4f \sqrt{0.8} \text{ ... (Karman Prandtl)}$$

(ii) Minor head losses.

(a) At the entrance : $h_l = 0.5 \frac{V^2}{2g}$

(b) Due to sudden contraction : If V_2 is velocity in the contracted portion, then

$$h_l = \left(\frac{1}{C_c} - 1\right)^2 \frac{V_2^2}{2g}$$

where, C_C = coefficient of contraction is normally taken as 0.62

or $h_l = 0.5 \frac{V_s^2}{2g}$

(c) Sudden expansion : If V_1 and V_2 are velocities in the pre-enlargement and enlarged section respectively, then

$$h_t = \frac{(V_1 - V_1)^2}{2g}$$

***(iii)* Other head losses.**

Other head losses are those in bends, pipe fitting and joineries such as valves, reducers, T-junctions, etc.

If V is velocity of flow in the pipe, then these losses are expressed in terms of velocity head $\frac{V^2}{2g}$ as K times velocity head

i.e $h_l = \frac{KV^2}{2g}$

where, K is called *loss coefficient.*

GAS TURBINES

The gas turbine obtains its power by utilizing the energy of a jet or burnt gases and air, velocity of the jet being absorbed as it flows over several rings of moving blades which are fixed to a common shaft. It thus resembles a steam turbine and its blades are designed in the same manner as shown in the velocity diagrams of steam turbines. The gas turbine requires an air compressor which is usually driven off its own shafting. This absorbs a considerable proportion of the power produced and thus lowers the overall efficiency.

Gas turbines have been constructed to work on the following fuels :

coal gas, producer gas, blastfurnace gas, oil and pulverized coal

Types of Gas Turbines

(1) Constant pressure gas turbine

In this type, fuel is burned at constant pressure and the cycle used is same as the Joule cycle. The turbine is of the reaction type using oil fuel and is fitted with an axial flow air compressor.

The rotor consists of five rings of moving blades. The multi-stage rotary air compressor is coupled to the rotor shaft.

The total air supply is drawn from the surrounding atmosphere by the compressor and is compressed to the combustion pressure of 1 to 4 atomosphere, it is then forced into the combustion chamber. Part of this air is used as combustion air for the oil which enters the burner, the remainder is forced through the annular space between wall of the combustion chamber and the burner jacket. The air receives heat from the burner jacket and also mixes with the products of combustion chamber and the burner jacket. This raises temperature and volumeof the air. The use of a very large quantity of air in excess of the combustion air prevents temperature of the mixture from reaching values which are too high for the metal of the rotor blades. It also prevents the burner from becoming too hot.

(2) Simple open cycle gas turbine (constant pressure heat addition) or Air standard Brayton (or joule) cycle.

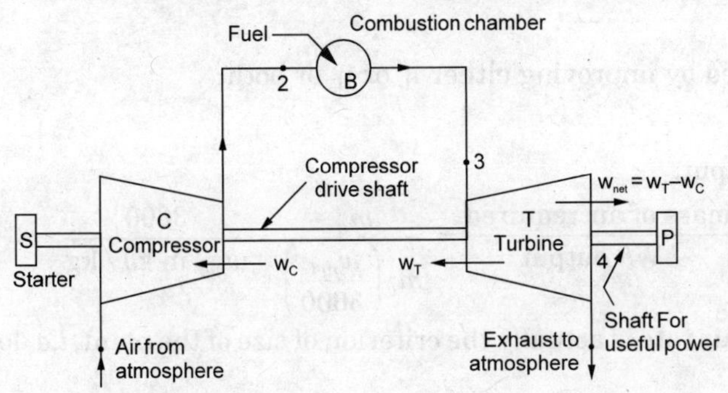

Fig. Simple open cycle gas turbine

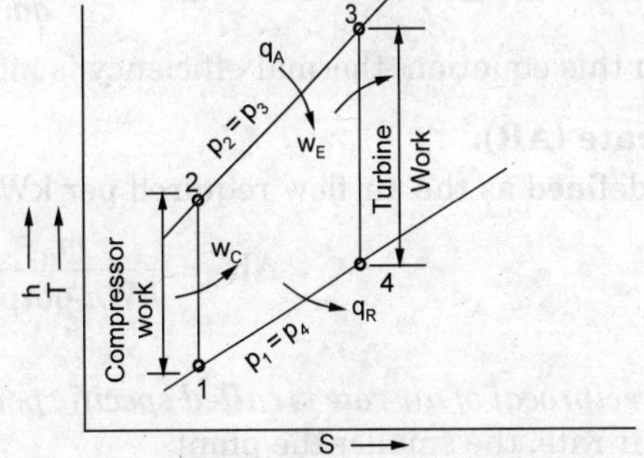

Fig. Representation of Joule cycle on h-s or (T-s) diagram

Referring figure, we can obtain thermal efficiency on the basis of 1 kg of working fluid flow.

$$\text{Heat supplied} = q = h_3 - h_2$$
$$= c_p(T_3 - T_2) \text{ if } cp \text{ is assumed constant in process 2-3.}$$
$$\text{Heat rejected} = h_4 - h_1$$
$$= c_p(T_4 - T_1) \text{ if } cp \text{ is assumed constant in process 4-1.}$$
$$\text{Net work} = \text{Heat supplied} - \text{Heat rejected}$$
$$= c_p\{(T_3 - T_2) - (T_4 - T_1)\}$$

This net work may also be found from the difference between turbine and compressor work.

$$\therefore \quad \text{thermal efficiency, } \eta_{th} = 1 - \frac{1}{r_p^{\frac{(\gamma-1)}{\gamma}}} \quad \text{.... [since } r_p = \text{pressure ratio } = \frac{p_2}{p_1}]$$

From this equation, thermal efficiency of the Brayton cycle is same as that of the Otto cycle.

Note. for turbine and compressor work we have neglected the change in kinetic and potential energies.

ACTUAL BRAYTON CYCLE

T – *s* diagram for an actual Brayton cycle is shown in figure.

Pressure loss in the combustion chamber is represented by $p_3 - p_2'$.

In this cycle

1–2 is isentropic compression.

1–2' is actual compression.

3–4 is isentropic expansion.

3–4' is actual expansion.

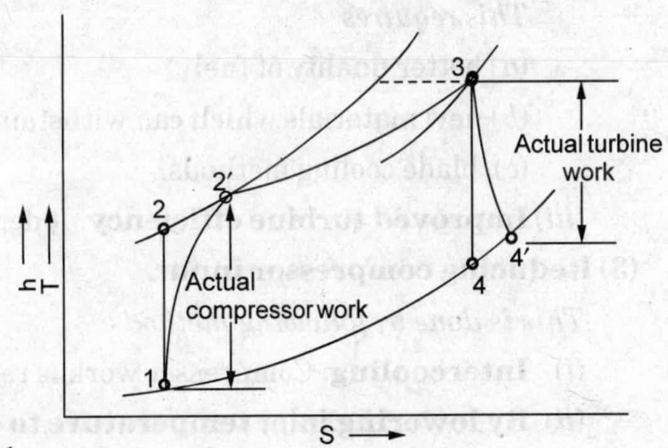

$$\text{Compressor efficiency, } \eta_c = \frac{\text{Isentropic compression work}}{\text{Actual compression work}} = \frac{w_c}{w_{ca}}$$

Based on static values, $\eta_c = \dfrac{h_2 - h_1}{h_{2'} - h_1} = \dfrac{c_p(T_2 - T_1)}{c_p(T_2' - T_1)}$

Here 1 kg of air passing through the compressor is assumed

or $\eta_c = \dfrac{T_2 - T_1}{T_2' - T_1}$

$$\text{Turbine efficiency, } \eta_t = \frac{\text{Actual turbine work}}{\text{Isentropic turbine work}} = \frac{w_{ta}}{w_t}$$

or $\eta_{tha} = \dfrac{(w_t)\eta_t\eta_c - w_c}{qa.\eta_c}$

From this equation, thermal efficiency is increased by improving either η_t or η_c or both.

Air rate (AR).

It is defined as the air flow required per kWh output.

$$\therefore \quad AR = \frac{m_a}{k\text{W}h \text{ output}} = \frac{\text{mass of air required}}{k\text{W}h \text{ output}} = \frac{m_a}{m_a\left(\dfrac{w_{net}}{3600}\right)} = \frac{3600}{w_{net} \text{ in kJ/kg}}$$

The reciprocal of air rate is called specific power. Air rate is actually the criterion of size of the plant, *i.e.* lower the air rate, the smaller the plant.

Work ratio (WR).

It is defined as the ratio of net work to the turbine work.

$$WR = \frac{w_{net}}{w_t}$$

Optimum pressure ratio for maximum cycle thermal efficiency.

$$r_{p(opt)} = \frac{p_2}{p_x} = \sqrt{\left(\frac{p_1}{p_2}\right)}$$

Methods to improve efficiency and specific output of simple cycle.

(1) Regeneration.

This is done by preheating air with the turbine exhaust, thus saving the fuel consumption.

(2) Improving turbine output.

This is done by following methods.

(*i*) **Reheating :** The whole expansion in the turbine is achieved in two or more stages and reheating is done after each stage.

(*ii*) Increasing the value of maximum cycle temperature, *i.e.* turbine inlet temperature.

This requires

(*a*) better quality of fuel

(*b*) new materials which can withstand high temperatures

(*c*) blade cooling methods.

(*iii*) **Improved turbine efficiency**. It depends on design improvements.

(3) Reducing compressor input.

This is done by following methods.

(*i*) **Intercooling**. Compressor work is reduced by intercooling the air between compressor stages.

(*ii*) **By lowering inlet temperature to compressor**. It is not practicable because this will increase the pressure ratio.

(*iii*) **By increasing compressor efficiency**. This depends upon the design improvement.

RECIPROCATING AIR COMPRESSORS

Reciprocating air compressors are used for producing high pressure air. Atomspheric air is drawn into a cylinder during suction stroke of piston and is compressed by the piston during the return stroke; the piston driven by power from a external source. If air is admitted to one side of the piston being only, the compressor is called *single acting.* A double-acting compressor admits air to each side of the piston alternately. Whilst one face of the piston is performing the suction stroke, air on the other face is compressed.

Use of compressed air delivered by the compressor

(*i*) To driver a compressed air engine

(*ii*) For producing an air blast for work-shop

(*iii*) For spraying the fuel into cylinder of the diesel engine.

Air compressors are also used for cooling large buildings. Fresh air is drawn into the compressor and compressed adiabatically, which causes a large increase in temperature. High-pressure air leaving the compressor is cooled by means of cold water. This cool high pressure air is then partially expanded adiabatically in another cylinder, which reduces its temperature to much below the surrounding atmosphere, the cold air is then circulated through the ducts of building.

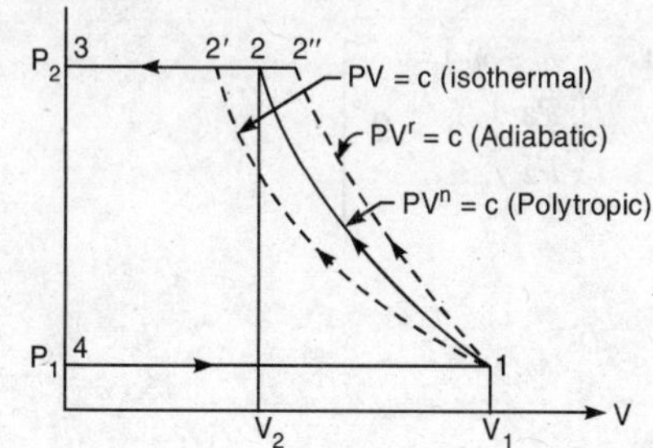

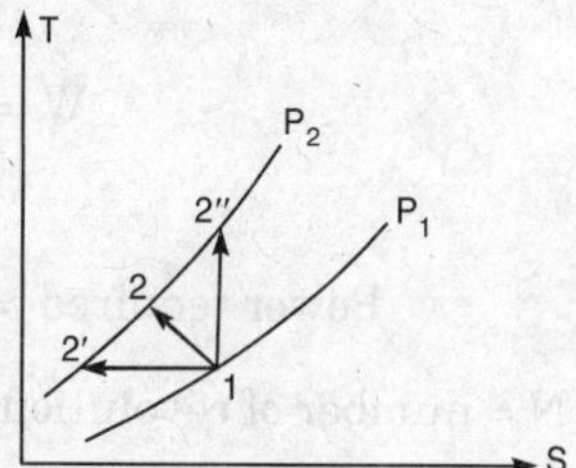

Fig. Theoretical p-V diagram for a single reciprocating air compressor.

Sequence of operations represented on the diagram

(*i*) **Operation 4 – 1 :** Volume of air V_1 aspirated into the compressor at pressure p_1 and temperature T_1.

(*ii*) **Operation 1 – 2 :** Air compressed according to the law $pV^n = C$ from pressure p_1 to p_2. Volume decreases from V_1 to V_2. Temperature increases from T_1 to T_2.

(*iii*) **Operation 2 – 3 :** Compressed air of volume V_2 and at pressure p_2 with temperature T_2 delivered from the compressor.

Work done (neglecting clearance volume).

Let p_1 and v_1 be the initial condition of air before adiabatic compression, p_2 and v_2 be the final condition after compression.

Then work done per cycle in driving the compressor,

$$W = p_1 V_1 \left(\frac{\gamma}{\gamma-1}\right)\left\{\left(\frac{p_2}{p_1}\right)^{\frac{\gamma-1}{\gamma}} - 1\right\}$$

If compresson follow the law, pV^n = constant, then work required to drive the compressor will be a similar expression except that n must be substituted for γ.

$$\therefore \quad W = p_1 V_1 \left(\frac{n}{n-1}\right)\left\{\left(\frac{p_2}{p_1}\right)^{\frac{n-1}{n}} - 1\right\}$$

If p_1 is in kPa and V_1 is in m^3, then W will in kN-m.

Power required to drive compressor = $\frac{WN}{60}$ kW

where, N = number of complete cycles per minute.

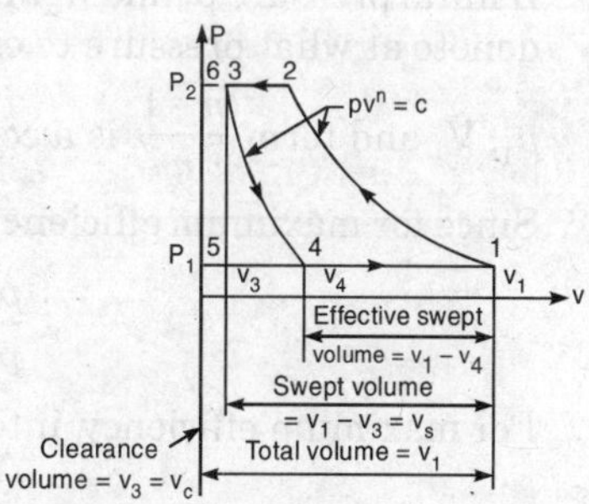

Work done (with clearance volume), $W = \left(\frac{n}{n-1}\right) P_1 (V_1 - V_4) \left\{\left(\frac{p_2}{p_1}\right)^{\frac{n-1}{n}} - 1\right\}$

TWO-STAGE COMPRESSOR

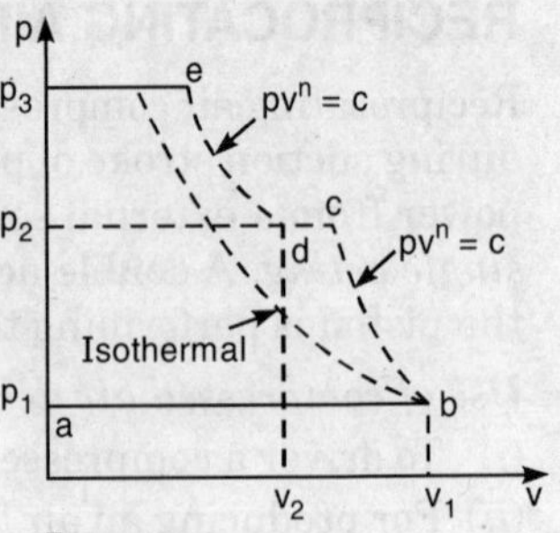

Let compression follow the law, pV^n = constant, and intercooling be incomplete, so that point d has not reached the isothermal

Let p_1 and V_1 represents condition of air entering low pressure cylinder, p_2 and V_2 represent condition of air entering high pressure cylinder and p_3 be the final pressure of the air.

Total work required to drive the compressor per cycle will be the sum of work required in low pressure and high pressure cylinders.

$$\text{Total work required, W} = \left(\frac{n}{n-1}\right)\left[p_1V_1\left[\left(\frac{p_2}{p_1}\right)^{\frac{n-1}{n}} - 1\right] + p_2V_2\left[\left(\frac{p_3}{p_2}\right)^{\frac{n-1}{n}} - 1\right]\right]$$

If compressions are adiabatic, γ should be used in place of n.

If intercooling is perfect, point d will be on the isothermal line, then

$$p_1V_1 = p_2V_2$$

$$\therefore \quad W = p_1V_1\left(\frac{n}{n-1}\right)\left[\left(\frac{p_2}{p_1}\right)^{\frac{n-1}{n}} + \left(\frac{p_3}{p_2}\right)^{\frac{n-1}{n}} - 2\right]$$

$$\text{Power required} = \frac{W \times N}{60}$$

where N = number of revolutions per minute.

MULTISTAGE COMPRESSOR

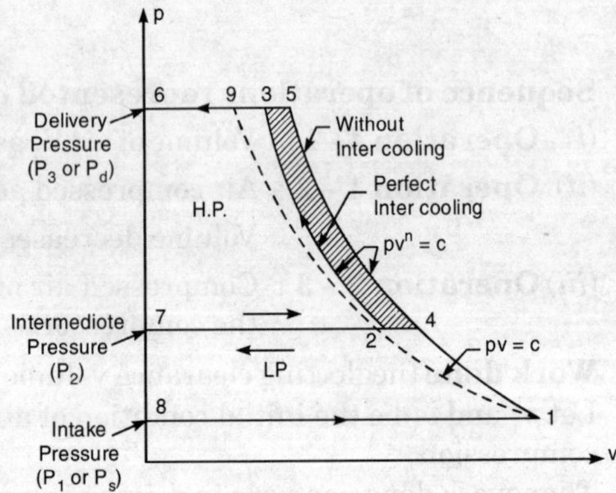

In multistage compressors, air is compressed in several stages instead of full compression being performed in single cylinder. In principle, it is equivalent to number of compressors in series, the air passing from one cylinder to the next, the pressure increasing in each cylinder.

- Cycle 8156 is single stage compressor.

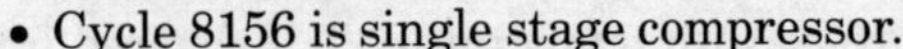

- Cycles 8147 and 7456 are two stage compressor without intercooling between cylinders.
- Cycles 8147 and 7236 are that a two-stage compressor with perfect intercooling between cylinders.

Perfect intercooling.

It means that after the initial compression in the L.P. cylinder, with its consequent temperature rise, air is cooled in an intercoolers back to its original temperature, *i.e.* $T_2 = T_1$, in which case point 2 lies on isothermal through point 1.

Condition for maximum efficiency.

If inital pressure p_1 and final pressure p_3 are fixed, then best value of intermediate pressure p_2 thus found will denote at what pressure to exhaust the first stage, so that work done on the compressor will be minimum.

p_1, V_1 and term $\frac{n-1}{n}$ is a constant.

Since for maximum efficiency, pressure ratio in each cycle is same, therefore

$$\frac{p_2}{p_1} = \frac{p_3}{p_2}$$

For maximum efficiency, intermediate pressure is geometric mean of the initial and final pressure, *i.e.*

$$p_2 = \sqrt{p_1 p_3}$$

For m stage compressor, work done per cycle, $W = \frac{mn}{n-1} p_1 V_1 \left[\left(\frac{p_m + 1}{p_1} \right)^{\frac{n-1}{mn}} - 1 \right]$

This equation applies to any type of compressor or motor and even to vapour engines, provided $n \leq \gamma$.

Conditions for maximum efficiency.

(*i*) Air is cooled to the initial temperature between the stages.

(*ii*) Pressure ratio in each stage is same.

(*iii*) Work required for each stage is same.

Isothermal Horsepower Compressor

Theoretical horsepower of compressor is calculated on the assumption that the compression curve of the p-v diagram is an isothermal. Then

$$\text{Isothermal work done per cycle} = \text{area of } p - v \text{ diagram}$$

$$= p_1 V_1 \log_e r = p_1 V_1 \log \frac{V_2}{V_1}$$

$$\text{Isothermal horsepower} = \frac{p_1 V_1 \log_e r \times N}{60}$$

where N = number of cycles per minute

Indicated Horse Power of a Compressor.

It is the horsepower obtained from the actual indicator card taken during a test on the compressor.

$$\text{Compressor efficiency} = \frac{\text{isothermal horsepower}}{\text{indicated horsepower}}$$

Isothermal Efficiency

$$\text{Isothermal efficiency} = \frac{\text{isothermal horsepower}}{\text{shaft horsepower}} = 70\% \text{ (generally)}$$

where shaft horsepower is the brake horsepower required to drive the compressor.

Adiabatic Efficiency

It is the ratio of horsepower required to drive the compressor compared with the area of hypothetical diagram assuming adiabatic compression.

$$\text{Adiabatic efficiency} = \frac{\left(\frac{\gamma}{\gamma - 1} \right) p_1 V_1 \left[\left(\frac{p_2}{p_1} \right)^{\frac{\gamma-1}{\gamma}} - 1 \right] \times \frac{N}{60}}{\text{power required to drive the compressor}}$$

Volumetric Efficiency

It is the ratio of volume of air inhled at STP to the swept volume of the piston.

$$\text{Volumetric efficiency} = \frac{\text{volume of air inhaled at S.T.P.}}{\text{swept volume of piston}}$$

Value of the volumetric efficiency varies between 70 and 90 per cent according to the type of compressor.

Comparison between Reciprocating and Rotary air compressors.

S.N.	Particulars	Reciprocating	Rotary
1.	Suitability	Suitable for low discharge of air at high pressure	Suitable for handing large volumes of air at low pressures
2.	Operation speed	Low	High
3.	Air supply	Pulsating	Continuous
4.	Balancing	Cyclic vibrations occur	Less vibrations
5.	Lubricating system	Generally complicated systems are required	Generally simple lubrication
6.	Quality of air delivered	Contaminated with oil	Air delivered is relatively more clean
7.	Air compressor size	Large for given discharge	Small of same discharge
8.	Free air handled	250-300 m^3/min	2000-3000 m^3/min
9.	Delivery pressure	800 to 1000 bar	Normally below 10 bar
10.	Usual standard of compression	Isothermal compression	Isesntropic compression

Comparison between Axial flow and Centrifugal compressors.

S.N.	Particulars	Axial flow compressors	Centrifugal compressors
1.	Pressure ratio	1.2 : 1 (For high pressure) ratio more number of stages are required)	4 : 1
2.	Isesntropic efficiency	85 to 88% (with modern) aero-foil blades)	70%
3.	Flexibility of operation	Less	More (due to adjustable per-whirl and diffuser vanes)
4.	Frontal area	Less (main cause in adopting the axial flow compressors for aircraft)	More
5.	Effect of deposit formation on the surface of impeller rotor.	Performance affected	Performance not affected
6.	Starting torque	High	Low comparatively
7.	Suitability	Used universally with large gas turbines	Suitable for super-charging I.C. engines and for compressors for refrigerants and industrial gases
8.	Efficiency vs. speed curve	Less flat	More flat comparatively

CENTRIFUGAL COMPRESSORS

These in its simplest form consists of a number of curved vanes fitted symmetrically. The rotor rotates in an airtight volute casing with inlet and outlet points. The casing for the compressor is so designed that kinetic energy of the air is converted into pressure energy before it leaves the casing as shown in the figure.

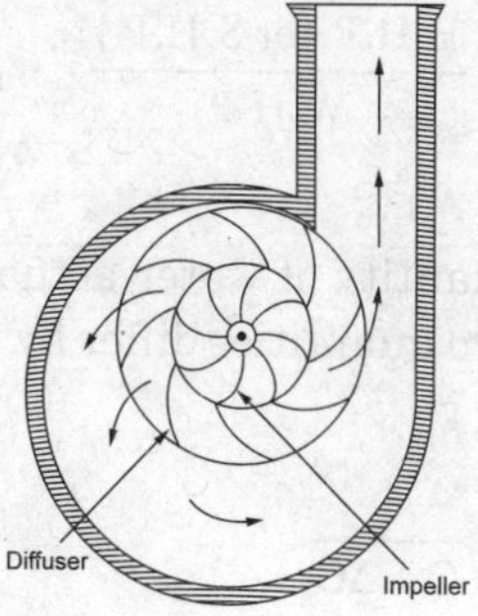

AXIAL FLOW COMPRESSOR

In axial flow compressors, the gas essentially flows parallel to the axis. It consists of a number of rotating blade rows fixed on a rotating drum and stator blades are fixed on casing in alternate rows.

Each stage consists of one moving row of blades and one row of fixed blades. The enthalpy and pressure of gas rises as it passes through rotating blades. This happens at the expense of a reduction in relative velocity, the absolute velocity of the gas increasing along the axis of rotor due to work input. This increase in kinetic energy is partly converted into pressure energy as the air passes through diverging fixed blades. These fixed blades help the gas to reach next set of moving blades for further compression. The blades are generally made of aerofoil section to reduce losses caused by turbulence and boundary separation.

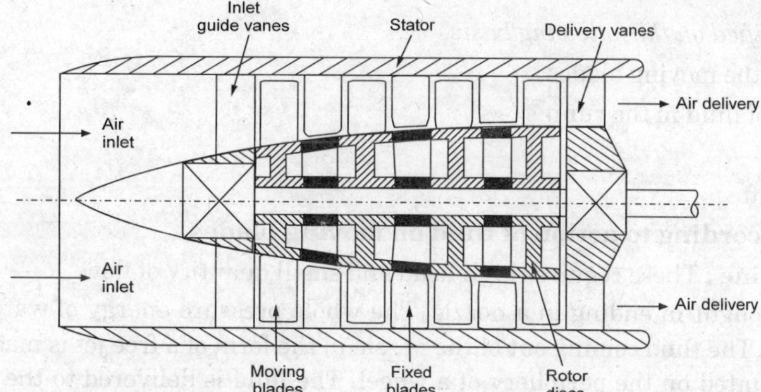

In axial flow compressors, the drum with rotor blades, rotates inside a casing with a fixed or stator blades.

HYDRAULIC MACHINES (TURBINES)

Efficiencies of Turbines.

(*i*) Hydraulic efficiency (η_h).

Hydraulic efficiency of turbine is the ratio of power developed by the runner, *i.e.* water horsepower (W.H.P.) to the net power supplied by the water at the entrance to the turbine. These two powers differ by the amount of hydraulic losses.

$$\eta_h = \frac{\text{W.H.P.}}{[w(Q+\Delta Q)H/75]}$$

where, Q = quantity of water actually striking the runner,

ΔQ = quantity of water discharged directly to the tail race without striking the turbine runner

If ΔQ is negligibly small, then $\eta_h = \frac{\text{W.H.P.}}{(wQH/75)}$

***(ii)* Mechanical efficiency (η_m).**

Mechanical efficiency of turbine is the ratio of power obtained from shaft of the turbine, *i.e.* shaft or brake horsepower. (S.H.P. or B.H.P.) to the power developed by the runner (*i.e.* W.H.P.). These two powers differ by the amount of mechanical losses *viz.* bearing friction etc.

$$\eta_m = \frac{\text{B.H.P. (or S.H.P.)}}{\text{W.H.P}}$$

***(iii)* Volumetric efficiency (η_v).**

Volumetric efficiency is the ratio of quantity of water actually striking the runner and the quantity of water supplied to the turbine. These two quantities differ by the amount of water that slips directly to the tail race without striking the runner.

$$\eta_v = \frac{Q}{Q + \Delta Q}$$

***(iv)* Overall efficiency (η_o).**

Overall efficiency of the turbine is the ratio of power available at the turbine shaft to the power supplied by the water at the entrance to the turbine.

$$\eta_o = \frac{\text{B.H.P. (or S.H.P.)}}{\text{(Net power available at the turbine entrance)}}$$

Overall efficiency of the turbine, $\eta_o = \eta_h \times \eta_m$

$$\eta_o = \eta_b \times \eta_v \times \eta_m$$

CLASSIFICATION OF HYDRAULIC TURBINES

Modern turbines classified on the following basis.

(1) Action of fluid on the moving blades

(2) Direction of flow of fluid in the runner

(3) Specific speed.

(4) Disposition of shaft

(1) Classification according to action of fluid on moving blades.

***(i)* Impulse turbine :** These requires high head and small quantity of flow.

The fluid is brought in ending in a nozzle. The whole pressure energy of water is transformed into kinetic energy. The fluid coming out of the nozzle in the form of a free jet is made to strike on a series of buckets mounted on the periphery of a wheel. The fluid is delivered to the wheel on a part of its circumference filling or striking only a few of the buckets at a time. Mostly, in hydraulic turbines, the wheel revolves in open air, *i.e.* there is no difference of pressure in the water at the inlet to the runner and the discharge. Therefore, casing of an impulse turbine has no hydraulic function to perform. It is necessary only to prevent splashing and to lead the water to the exit and also acts as a safeguard against accidents. This turbine is also called a *free jet turbine*.

***(ii)* Reaction turbine :** These requires low head and high rate of flow.

The fluid before entering the turbine has pressure as well as kinetic energy. All pressure energy is not transformed into kinetic energy as in case of impulse turbine. The moment on the wheel is produced by both kinetic and pressure energies.

Types of reaction turbines:

(a) For medium head and medium flow *(b)* For low head and large flow.

Note : The fluid leaving the turbine has still some of the pressure as well as kinetic energy. The pressure at the inlet to the turbine is much higher than the pressure at the outlet. Thus there is a possibility of fluid flowing through some passage other than the runner and escape without doing any work. Hence a casing is absolutely essential due to the difference of pressure in reaction turbine.

(2) Classification according to direction of flow of fluid in the runner.

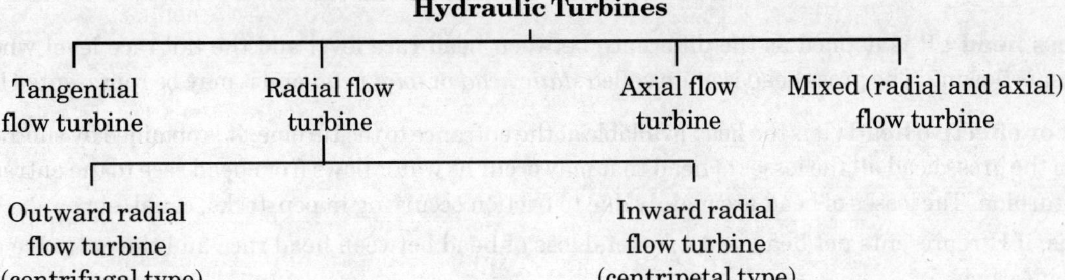

(3) Classification according to specific speed.

Specific speed (N_s) is defined as the speed of a gemetrically similar hypothetical fluid machine handling unit discharge against a unit head.

$$N_s = \frac{N\sqrt{Q}}{(gH)^{3/4}}$$

where, Q = discharge m^3/s

N = speed in rpm

g = gravitational constant m/s^2

H = head under which the machine operates.

For turbines, $N_s = \frac{N\sqrt{P}}{H^{5/4}}$; and for pumps, $N_s = \frac{N\sqrt{Q}}{H^{3/4}}$

where power generated by shaft, $P = \frac{\gamma QH}{1000}\eta_o$ kW $(\gamma = pq)$

The specific speed can be used to compare different types of pumps and to compare different types of turbines to select pick the type of pump or turbine most suitable for a given work.

For small specific speeds, radial flow gives best efficiency and for high specific speeds axials flow machines are most efficient. The mixed flow machines are most efficient at the intermediate range of specific speeds.

Specific speed of hydraulic turbines.

Type of turbine	Type of *runner*	*Specific speed*	
		P in HP	*P in kW*
Pelton	Slow	10 to 20	8.5 to 17
	Normal	20 to 28	17 to 24
	Fast	28 to 35	24 to 30
Francis	Slow	60 to 120	50 to 100
	Normal	120 to 180	100 to 150
	Fast	180 to 300	150 to 250
Kaplan	–	300 to 1,000	250 to 850

Heads of Hydraulic Turbines

The head acting on a turbine may be defined in two ways as follows :

(i) Gross head : It is defined as the difference between head race level and the tail race level when no water is flowing. The gross head is often called *static head* or *total head* and it may be represented by H_1.

(ii) Net or effective head : It is the head available at the entrance to the turbine. It is obtained by subtracting from the gross head all the losses of head that may occur as water flows from head race to the entrance of the turbine. The losses of head are mainly due to friction occurring in penstocks, canal, etc.

Thus, if H represents net head and h_f is total loss of head between head race and the entrance of the turbine, then

$$H = H_g - h_f$$

For a reaction (or encased) turbine, net head is equal to difference between pressure head at the entrance to the turbine plus velocity head in the penstock at this point plus elevation of this point above the assumed datum and elevation of the tail water plus velocity head in the draft tube at its exit.

$$\therefore \quad H = \left(\frac{P_1}{w} + \frac{V_1^2}{2g} + Z_1\right) - \left(Z_2 + \frac{V_2^2}{2g}\right)$$

For an impulse turbine, net head is equal to difference between pressure head at the entrance to the nozzle plus velocity head in the penstock at this point plus elevation of this point above the assumed head datum and elevation of the tail water.

$$\therefore \quad H = \left(\frac{P_1}{w} + \frac{V_1^2}{2g} + Z_1\right) - Z_2$$

PELTON WHEEL TURBINES

This turbine is of the parallel flow impulse type. This is suitable for highe heads. The quantity of water required to work the Pelton wheel is less as the energy head is large. The water reaching the turbine comes through penstocks from the reservoir. The nozzle issues a powerful jet whcih impinges on the buckets placed at the outer periphery of the wheel. These vanes are of the form of double hemispherical cups. The jet strikes the central diving edge of the double cups. Thus, jet gets deflects on each side. The water after imparting its energy to the turbine, is discharged into the tail race. The needle valve provides necessary regulation of the discharge to the turbine.

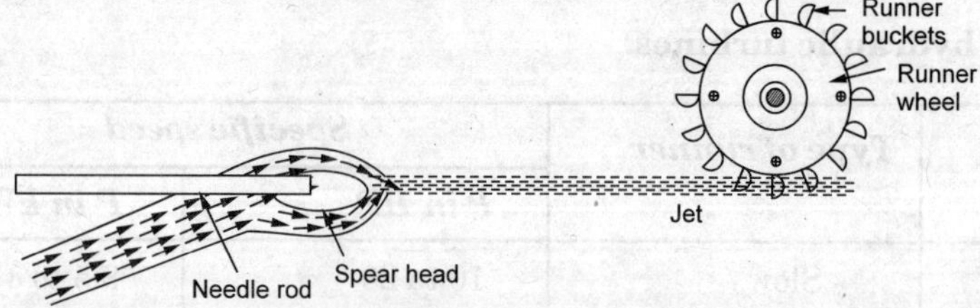

Fig. Pelton wheeel

REACTION TURBINES

The principal distinguishing features of a reaction turbine are that only a part of the total head of water is converted into velocity head before it reaches the runner, and that the water completely fills all the passages in the runner.

Types.

(1) Francis turbine

(2) Kaplan turbine.

(1) Francis turbine : Water is led to the turbine through the penstock pipe whose end is connected to the spiral casing of the turbine. This spiral casing directs the water evenly to the guide blades. The water then passes through the runner and finally goes to the tail race through the draft tube. *The closed type Francis turbine* is shown in the figure.

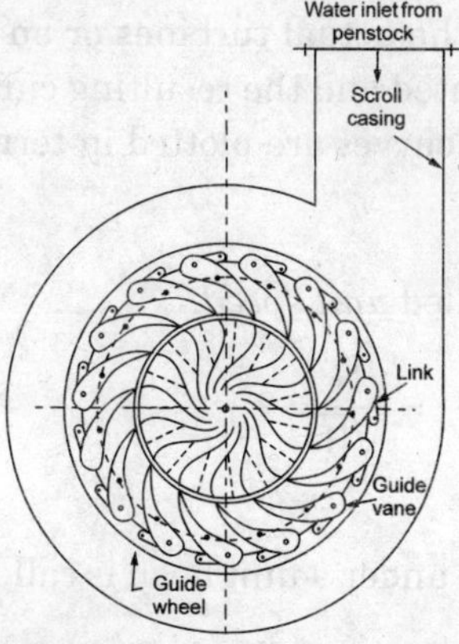

Types of closed type Francis turbines.

***(i)* Horizontal type :** It is used for medium and high heads and vertical type for medium and low heads.

***(ii)* Vertical types :** It is used for medium and low heads.

(2) Kaplan and Propeller turbines.

In these runner is essentially a propeller working in reverse and blades are mounted so that blade angles can be adjusted together by means of suitable gearing while the machine is in operation.

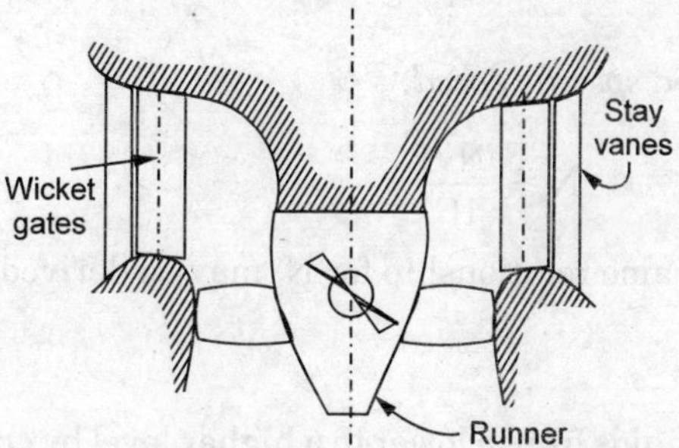

The guide vanes or wicket gates of entry are also adjustable. This machine is much suitable for low heads, say upto 36 m. An electric generator coupled to a Kaplan type runner may be enclosed in a fairing within a faired tunnel. Heads as low as 3.6m may be used. A number of vanes are fixed to the boss (or hub). When the vanes are composite with the boss, the turbine is called *propeller turbine*. When the vanes are adjustable the turbine is called *Kaplan turbine*.

DRAFT TUBE

Draft tube is a pipe or passage of gradually increasing cross-sectional area which connects runner exit to the tail race. It may be made of cast or plate steel or concrete. It must be air tight and under all conditions of operation its lower end must be submerged below the level of water in the tail race.

Uses of draft tube.

(i) It permits negative or suction head to be established at the runner exit, thus making it possible to install the turbine above the tail race level without loss of head.

(ii) It converts a large proportion of velocity energy rejected from the runner into useful pressure energy.

PERFORMANCE CHARACTERISTIC CURVES FOR TURBINES.

The turbines are generally designed to work at particular values of H, Q, P, N and η_0 which are called *designed conditions*. But often turbines are required to work at conditions different from those for which they have been designed. Therefore, it is essential to determine exact behaviour of the turbines under varying conditions by carrying out tests either on the actual turbines or on their small scale models. The results of these tests are usually graphically represented and the resulting curves are called *characteristic curves*. For the sake of convenience, the characteristic curves are plotted in terms of unit quantities.

Unit speed (N_u).

Speed of the turbine under unit head is called *unit speed.*

$$N_u = \frac{N}{\sqrt{H}}$$

Unit discharge (Q_u).

The discharge flowing through the turbine under a unit head is called *unit discharge*.

$$Q_u = \frac{Q}{\sqrt{H}}$$

Unit power (P_u).

Output of the turbine under a unit head is called *unit power.*

$$P_u = \frac{P}{H^{3/2}}$$

Specific speed (N_s).

The speed of specific runner is called *specific speed.*

$$N_s = \frac{N\sqrt{P}}{H^{5/4}}$$

For any other turbine also exactly same relationship for N_s may be derived.

CENTRIFUGAL PUMPS

Centrifugal pump is used to raise liquids from a lower to a higher level by creating required pressure with the help of centrifugal action. In general it can be defined as a machine which increases the pressure energy of a fluid, as a pump may not be used to lift water at all, but just boost the pressure in a pipeline. Whirling motion is imparted to the liquid by means of backward curved blades mounted on a wheel called *impeller*. Liquid enters the impeller at the centre (eye) of the pump and discharges into the case surrounding the impeller. The pressure head developed by centrifugal action is entirely due to velocity imparted to the liquid by the rotating impeller and not due to any displacement or impact.

At the entrance to the impeller, since there are no guide vanes (as in the case of turbines), the direction of absolute velocity of liquid at this point of the impeller is not directly known. However, for best efficiency of the pump, it is commonly assumed that the liquid enters the impeller radially, i.e. absolute velocity of the liquid at the entrance to the impeller (or at the inlet tip of the impeller vane) is radial in direction. Thus in this case, $\alpha = 90°$ and velocity of whirl V_w at inlet is equal to zero. Again, it is desired that the liquid enters and leaves the vane without shock. This can be ensured if inlet and outlet tips of the vane are parallel to the direction of the relative velocities at the two tips.

CAVITATION

It is defined as the phenomenon of formation of vapour bubbles of a flowing liquid in a region where pressure of the liquid falls below its vapour pressure and sudden collapsing of these vapour bubbles in a region of higher pressure. When vapour bubbles collapse, a very high pressure is created. The metallic surfaces, above which the liquid is flowing, is subjected to these high pressures, which cause pitting action of the surface. Thus, cavities are formed on the metallic surface and also considerable noise and vibrations are produced.

Caviation includes formation of vapour bubbles of the flowing liquid and collapsing of the vapour bubbles. Formation of vapour bubbles of the flowing liquid takes place only whenever pressure in any region falls below vapour pressure. When pressure of the flowing liquid is less than its vapour pressure, the liquid starts boiling and vapour bubbles are formed. These vapour bubbles are carried along with the following liquid to higher pressure zones where these vapours condense and bubbles collapse. Due to sudden collapsing of the bubbles on the metallic surface, high pressure is produced and metallic surfaces are subjected to high local stresses. Thus the surfaces are damaged.

Effects of Cavitation

(*i*) The metallic surfaces are damaged and cavities are formed on the surfaces.

(*ii*) Due to sudden collapse of vapour bubble, considerable noise and vibrations are produced.

(*iii*) Efficiency of a turbine decreases due to cavitation. Due to pitting action, surface of the turbine blades becomes rough and the force exerted by water on the turbine blades decreases. Hence work done by water or output horse power becomes less and thus efficiency decreases.

The hydraulic machines subjected to cavitation are centrifugal pumps and reaction turbines.

Objective Type Questions

1. In Red wood viscometer
(*a*) absolute value of viscosity is determined
(*b*) part of the head of fluid is utilised in overcoming friction
(*c*) fluid discharges through orifice with negligible velocity
(*d*) comparison of viscosity is done.

2. Centre of buoyancy is
(*a*) point of intersection of buoyant force and centre line of the body
(*b*) centre of gravity of the body
(*c*) centroid of displaced volume fluid
(*d*) mid point between C.G. and metacentre.

3. Length of mercury column at a place at an altitude will vary with respect to that at ground in a
(*a*) linear relation
(*b*) hyperbolic relation
(*c*) parabolic relation
(*d*) manner first slowly and then steeply

4. When power is transmitted through a considerable distance by means of water under pressure, the maximum power is transmitted when frictional loss of head is
(*a*) one third of the total head supplied
(*b*) half of the total head supplied
(*c*) 10% of the total head
(*d*) 17.7% of the total head.

5. A rotameter is a device used to measure
(*a*) velocity of fluid in pipes
(*b*) velocity of gauges
(*c*) votex flow
(*d*) flow of fluids

6. Reynolds number for pipe flow is given by
(*a*) $\frac{vD}{\nu}$ (*b*) $\frac{vD\mu}{\delta}$
(*c*) $\frac{vD\rho}{\mu}$ (*d*) $\frac{vD}{\mu}$

7. With rise in gas temperature, dynamic viscosity of most of the gases
(*a*) increases
(*b*) decreases
(*c*) does not change significantly.
(*d*) none of these

8. The flow of water in a pipe of diameter 3000 mm can be measured by
(*a*) Venturimeter (*b*) Rotameter
(*c*) Pilot tube (*d*) Orifice plate.

9. Which of the following is dimen-sionless parameter?
(*a*) Pressure coefficient
(*b*) Froude number
(*c*) Darcy Weisbach friction factor
(*d*) None of these

10. A small plastic boat loaded with pieces of steel rods is floating in a bath tub. If the cargo is dumped into the water allowing the boat to float empty, the water level in the tub will
(*a*) rise (*b*) fall
(*c*) remains same (*d*) rise and then fall

11. Steady flow occurs when
(*a*) pressure does not change along the flow
(*b*) velocity does not change
(*c*) conditions change gradually with time
(*d*) conditions do not change with time at any point

12. A flow in which each liquid particle has a definite path and their paths do not cross each other, is called
(*a*) Steady flow (*b*) Uniform flow
(*c*) Streamline flow (*d*) Turbulent flow

13. Buoyant force is
(*a*) resultant of upthrust and gravity forces acting on the body
(*b*) resultant force on the body due to the fluid surrounding it
(*c*) resultant of static weight of body and dynamic thrust of fluid
(*d*) equal to the volume of liquid displaced by the body

14. In a rectangular notch, the ratio of percentage error in $\frac{\text{discharge}}{\text{measurement of head}}$ is
(*a*) 1 (*b*) $\frac{1}{2}$
(*c*) $\frac{3}{4}$ (*d*) $\frac{3}{2}$

15. Cavitation is caused by

(*a*) high velocity

(*b*) low barometric pressure

(*c*) high pressure

(*d*) low pressure

16. If the particles of a fluid attain such velocities that vary from point to point in magnitude and direction as well as from instant, the flow is

(*a*) Uniform flow (*b*) Steady flow

(*c*) Turbulent flow (*d*) Laminar flow

17. In a turbulent flow in a pipe

(*a*) Reynolds number is greater than 10000

(*b*) fluid particles move in straight lines

(*c*) head loss varies linearly with flow rate

(*d*) shear stress varies linearly with radius

18. The friction resistance in pipe is proportional to V^2, according to

(*a*) Froude-number (*b*) Reynolds-Weber

(*c*) Darcy-Reynolds (*d*) Weber-Froude

19. In laminar flow, maximum velocity at the centre of pipe is how many times to the average velocity?

(*a*) Two (*b*) Three

(*c*) Four (*d*) None of these

20. Pitot tube is used to measure the velocity head of

(*a*) still fluid (*b*) laminar flow

(*c*) turbulent flow (*d*) flowing fluid

21. In equilibrium condition, fluids are not able to sustain

(*a*) shear force (*b*) resistance to viscosity

(*c*) surface tension (*d*) geometric similitude

22. Flow occurring in a pipeline when a valve is being opened is

(*a*) steady (*b*) unsteady

(*c*) laminar (*d*) vortex

23. Total pressure on 1 m × 1 m gate immersed vertically at a depth of 2 m below the free water surface will be

(*a*) 1000 kg (*b*) 2000 kg

(*c*) 4000 kg (*d*) 8000 kg

24. The general equation of continuity for three-dimensional flow of a compressible fluid for steady flow is

(*a*) $\frac{\partial u}{\partial x}+\frac{\partial v}{\partial y}+\frac{\partial w}{\partial z}=0$ (*b*) $\frac{\partial u}{\partial x}=\frac{\partial v}{\partial y}=\frac{\partial w}{\partial z}=0$

(*c*) $\frac{\partial u}{\partial x}+\frac{\partial v}{\partial y}+\frac{\partial w}{\partial z}=1$ (*d*) $\frac{\partial u}{\partial x}+\frac{\partial v}{\partial y}+\frac{\partial w}{\partial z}=u.v.w.$

where u, v and w are components of velocity in x, y and z directions respectively

25. A large Reynold number is indication of

(*a*) smooth and streamline flow

(*b*) laminar flow

(*c*) steady flow

(*d*) highly turbulent flow

26. Non uniform flow occurs when

(*a*) direction and magnitude of velocity at all points are identical

(*b*) velocity of successive fluid particles, at any point, is same at successive periods of time

(*c*) magnitude and direction of velocity do not change from point to point in the fluid

(*d*) velocity, depth, pressure, etc. changes point to point in the fluid flow

27. In steady flow of a fluid, the acceleration of any fluid particle is

(*a*) constant (*b*) variable

(*c*) zero (*d*) never zero

28. For measuring flow by a venturimeter, it should be installed in

(*a*) vertical line

(*b*) horizontal line

(*c*) inclined line with upward flow

(*d*) in any direction and in any location

29. Froude number is significant in

(*a*) supersonics, as with projectile and jet propulsion

(*b*) full immersion or completely enclosed flow, as with pipes, aircrafts wings, nozzles etc.,

(*c*) simultaneous motion through two fluids where there is a surface of discontinuity, gravity forces, and wave making effect, as with ship's hulls

(*d*) all of these

30. The fluid forces considered in the Navier Stokes equation are

(*a*) gravity, pressure and viscous

(*b*) gravity, pressure and turbulent

(*c*) pressure, viscous and turbulent

(*d*) gravity, viscous and turbulent

31. The depth of centre of pressure in rectangular lamina of height h with one side in the liquid surface is at

(*a*) h (*b*) $\frac{h}{3}$

(*c*) $\frac{2h}{3}$ (*d*) $\frac{h}{2}$

32. Reynolds number is significant in

(*a*) supersonics, as with projectile and jet propulsion

(*b*) full immersion or completely enclosed flow, as with pipes, aircraft wings, nozzles etc.

(*c*) simultaneous motion through two fluids where there is a surface of discontinuity, gravity forces, and wave making effect, as with ship's hulls

(*d*) all of these

33. Two dimensional flow occurs when the

(*a*) directional and magnitude of the velocity at all points are identical

(*b*) velocity of successive fluid particles, at any point, is same at successive periods of time

(*c*) magnitude and direction of velocity do not change from point to point in the fluid

(*d*) fluid particles move in a plane or parallel planes and the streamline patterns are identical in each plane

34. A streamline is defined as the line

(*a*) parallel to central axis flow

(*b*) parallel to outer surface to pipe

(*c*) of equal velocity in a flow

(*d*) along which the pressure drop is uniform

35. Match number is significant in

(*a*) supersonics, as with projectiles and jet propulsion

(*b*) full immersion or completely enclosed flow, as with pipes, aircrafts wings, nozzles etc.

(*c*) simultaneous motion through two fluids where there is a surface of discontinuity, gravity force, and wave making effects, as with ship's hull

(*d*) all of these

36. For an irrotational flow the equation $\frac{\partial^2 \phi}{\partial x^2} + \frac{\partial^2 \phi}{\partial y^2}$ is called

(*a*) Bernoulli's equation

(*b*) Cauchy Riemann's equation

(*c*) Euler's equation

(*d*) Laplace equation.

37. Separation of flow occurs due to reduction of pressure gradient to

(*a*) zero

(*b*) negligibly low value

(*c*) the extent such that vapour formation starts

(*d*) none of these

38. The magnitude of water hammer depends on the

(*a*) length of pipeline

(*b*) speed at which the valve is closed

(*c*) elastic properties of the liquid flowing through the pipe and pipe material

(*d*) all of these

39. A cylinder is kept on a horizontal boundary past which an ideal fluid flows perpendicular to the cylinder axis. It will experience

(*a*) no lift force

(*b*) some lift force

(*c*) lift force in vertically downward direction

(*d*) lift force in vertically upward direction

40. When the water flows over a rectangular suppressed weir, the pressure beneath the nappe is

(*a*) very high

(*b*) slightly above atmospheric

(*c*) atmospheric

(*d*) negative

41. The specific speed of a hydraulic turbine is given by

(*a*) $\frac{N\sqrt{P}}{H^{5/4}}$ (*b*) $\frac{P\sqrt{N}}{H^{5/4}}$

(*c*) $\frac{NP}{H^{3/2}}$ (*d*) $\frac{\sqrt{NP}}{H^{3/2}}$

42. For supplying feed water to a boiler which of the following pump is not used ?

(*a*) Steam injector

(*b*) Reciprocating pump

(*c*) Multistage centrifugal pump

(*d*) Gear pump

43. In hydraulic coupling, as the ratio of the speed driven shaft to driving shaft increases, the efficiency

(*a*) decreases

(*b*) increases

(*c*) remains constant

(*d*) is independent of speed ratio

44. Pump selected for pumping sewage is

(*a*) Reciprocating pump

(*b*) Open impeller centrifugal pump

(*c*) Multistage centrifugal pump

(*d*) Screw pump

45. In a centrifugal pump when delivery valve is fully closed, the pressure of fluid inside the pump will

(*a*) become zero (*b*) reduce

(*c*) increase (*d*) remain unaltered

46. Undershot water wheels are those on which water acts

(*a*) purely by impulse

(*b*) partly by impulse and partly by reaction

(*c*) purely by reaction

(*d*) none of these

47. In the case of pelton turbine installed in a hydraulic power plant, the gross head available is the vertical distance between

(*a*) forebay and tail race

(*b*) reservoir level and turbine inlet

(*c*) forebay and turbine inlet

(*d*) reservoir level and tail race

48. A hydraulic coupling belongs to the category of

(*a*) power absorbing machines

(*b*) power developing machines

(*c*) energy generating machines

(*d*) energy transfer machines

49. For pumping molasses, it is preferable to employ

(*a*) reciprocating pump

(*b*) centrifugal pump with double shrouds

(*c*) open impeller pump

(*d*) multistage centrifugal pump

50. In the case of a centrifugal pump, cavitation will occur if

(*a*) it operates above the minimum net positive suction head

(*b*) it operates below the minimum net positive suction head

(*c*) the pressure at the inlet of the pump is above the atmospheric pressure

(*d*) the pressure at the inlet of the pump is equal to the atmospheric pressure

51. The hydraulic radius is given by

(*a*) wetted perimeter divided by area

(*b*) area divided by square of wetted perimeter

(*c*) square root of area

(*d*) area divided by wetted perimeter

52. Specific speed (metric) = k × specific (FPS), where k has the value of

(*a*) 1 (*b*) 1.75

(*c*) 2.37 (*d*) 0.67

53. The cavitation and pitting can be prevented by creating which one of the following conditions?

(*a*) Reducing the pressure head

(*b*) Reducing the velocity head

(*c*) Increasing the elevation head

(*d*) Reducing the piezometric head

54. Pressure rise due to water hammer in a penstock depends on

(*a*) water level in the reservior, and elasticity of water

(*b*) density of water

(*c*) roughness of pipe

(*d*) all of these

55. A pumped storage plant is a

(*a*) high head plant (*b*) run-off river plant

(*c*) peak load plant (*d*) base load plant

56. Which of the following statements about gear pumps are true?

I. Gear pumps are best suited for high pressures and small discharges.

II. Gear pumps are self priming.

III. Efficiency of a gear pump depends on the slip.

IV. The discharge is inversely proportional to the axial length of the gear tooth.

(*a*) I and IV only (*b*) II and III only

(*c*) III and I only (*d*) II and IV only

57. In the figure below, which curve represents the condition for backward curved vanes in a centrifugal pump?

(*a*) Curve A (*b*) Curve B

(*c*) Curve C (*d*) Curve D

58. In all reaction turbines, maximum efficiency is obtained, if

(*a*) guide vane angle is 90°

(*b*) blade angle of the runners is 90° at the inlet

(*c*) blade angle of the runners is 90° at the outlet

(*d*) angle of the absolute velocity vector at the outlet is 90°

59. The shut off head will be nearly

(*a*) Zero (*b*) 18.0 m

(*c*) 25.5 m (*d*) 35 m

60. Double hemispherical buckets are used in

(*a*) Kaplan turbine (*b*) Francis turbine

(*c*) Propeller turbine (*d*) Pelton wheel

61. A reciprocating pump

(*a*) requires priming

(*b*) requires air vessel

(*c*) requires high operating speeds

(*d*) is used for viscous fluids only

62. Air vessel in a reciprocating pump is used to

(*a*) obtain continuous supply of water at uniform rate

(*b*) increase delivery

(*c*) reduce suction head

(*d*) remove any entrapped air from water

63. A tapered draft tube as compared to a cylindrical draft tube

(*a*) prevents hammer blow and surges

(*b*) responds better to load functions

(*c*) converts more of kinetic head into pressure head

(*d*) prevents cavitation even under reduced discharges

64. The specific speeds of radial vane pump, mixed flow pump and axial flow pump are NS_1, NS_2 and NS_3 respectively. Then

(*a*) $NS_1 > NS_2 > NS_3$ (*b*) $NS_3 > NS_2 > NS_1$

(*c*) $NS_2 > NS_3 > NS_1$ (*d*) $NS_3 > NS_1 > NS_2$

65. Centrifugal pumps operating in series will result in

(*a*) higher discharge

(*b*) reduced power consumption

(*c*) higher head

(*d*) low speed operation

66. Jet pumps are often used in process industry for their

(*a*) high efficiency

(*b*) easy maintenance

(*c*) large capacity

(*d*) capacity to transport gases, liquids and mixtures of both

67. Spouting velocity is

(*a*) ideal velocity of jet

(*b*) 50% of ideal velocity of jet

(*c*) actual velocity of jet

(*d*) velocity of jet under some specified conditions

68. The comparison between pumps operating in series and in parallel is

(*a*) Pumps operating in series boost the discharge, whereas pumps operating in parallel boost the head.

(*b*) Pumps operating in parallel boost the discharge, whereas pumps operating in series boost the head.

(*c*) In both cases there would be a boost in discharge only.

(*d*) In both cases there would be a boost in head only.

69. A pelton turbine is considered suitable for which of the following head ?

(*a*) 10 to 12 metres (*b*) 20 to 30 metres

(*c*) 35 to 50 metres (*d*) 100 to 250 metres

70. Material for water turbine should have

(*a*) high creep resistance

(*b*) high temperature resistance

(*c*) high corrosion resistance

(*d*) low ductility

71. The coefficient of discharge (C_d) of an orifice varies with

(*a*) Reynold number (*b*) Weber number

(*c*) Froude number (*d*) Mach number

72. The shear stress distribution for a fluid flowing in between the parallel plates, both at rest, is

(*a*) constant over the cross-section

(*b*) maximum at the mid-plane and varies linearly with distance from mid-plane

(*c*) zero at the mid-point and varies linearly with distance from mid-plane

(*d*) zero at the plates and varies exponentially to mid-point

73. Friction drag is generally larger than the pressure drag in

(*a*) flow past a sphere

(*b*) flow past a cylinder

(*c*) flow past an airfoil

(*d*) flow past a thin sheet.

74. Capillarity is due to

(*a*) Cohension

(*b*) Adhesion

(*c*) Adhesion and cohesion

(*d*) Gravity

75. Principle of similitude forms the basis of

(*a*) comparing two identical equipments

(*b*) designing models so that the result can be converted to prototypes

(*c*) comparing similarly between design and actual equipment

(*d*) hydraulic design

76. If V is the mean velocity of flow, then according to Darcy-Weisbach equation for pipe flow, energy loss over a length of pipe is proportional

(*a*) V (*b*) 1/V

(*c*) V^2 (*d*) $\sqrt{V}$

77. Head loss in turbulent flow in a pipe

(*a*) varies directly as velocity

(*b*) varies inversely as square of velocity

(*c*) varies approximately as square of velocity

(*d*) varies inversely as velocity.

78. The horizontal component of force on a curved surface is equal to the

(*a*) product of pressure at its centroid and area

(*b*) weight of liquid retained by the curved area

(*c*) force on a vertical projection of the curved surface

(*d*) weight of liquid vertically above the curved surface

79. Total pressure on the top of a closed cylindrical vessel of radius r filled with liquid is proportional to

(*a*) r (*b*) $\frac{1}{r}$

(*c*) $\frac{1}{r^2}$ (*d*) r^2

80. The drag coefficient for laminar flow varies as (where Re = Reyonlds number)

(*a*) Re (*b*) Re^{-1}

(*c*) $Re^{1/2}$ (*d*) $Re^{-1/2}$

81. If one of the walls moves in the direction of flow with uniform velocity while the other wall is stationary, then the resulting flow between parallel walls is called

(*a*) Plug flow (*b*) Stoke's flow

(*c*) Couette flow (*d*) Euler's flow

82. In series-pipe applications

(*a*) head loss through each pipe added to obtain the total head loss

(*b*) head loss is same through each pipe

(*c*) friction factor is assumed for each pipe

(*d*) flow increases

83. For pipe flow, at constant diameter, capacity is proportional to

(*a*) $\sqrt{\text{head}}$ (*b*) head

(*c*) $\text{head}^{3/2}$ (*d*) head^2

84. The velocity distribution for flow between two fixed parallel plates

(*a*) is constant over the cross-section

(*b*) is zero at the plates and increases linearly to the midplane

(*c*) varies parabolically across the section

(*d*) is zero in middle and increase linearly towards the plates

85. The most economical section of a rectangular channel for maximum discharge is obtained when its depth is equal to

(*a*) half the breadth (*b*) twice the breadth

(*c*) same as the breadth (*d*) one third the breadth.

86. Region downstream from the streamline where separation takes place from the boundary is known as

(*a*) wake (*b*) lift

(*c*) drag (*d*) cavitation

87. A low pressure of the order of 10^{-10} torr can be measured in a chamber with

(*a*) Manometer

(*b*) Bourdon vacuum gauge

(*c*) Pirani gauge

(*d*) Ionisation chamber

88. To avoid a correction for the effect of capillarity in manometers, diameter of tube should be

(*a*) less than 1 mm (*b*) less than 3 mm

(*c*) less than 4.5 mm (*d*) all of these

89. The river flow during floods can be classified as

(*a*) steady uniform flow

(*b*) unsteady uniform flow

(*c*) steady non-uniform flow

(*d*) unsteady non-uniform flow

90. Wake always occurs

(*a*) before a separation point

(*b*) after a separation point

(*c*) before and after a separation point

(*d*) none of these

91. In a flow field, at the stagnation point

(*a*) pressure is zero

(*b*) total energy is zero

(*c*) pressure head is equal to velocity

(*d*) all the velocity head is converted into pressure head.

92. Total drag on a body is the sum of

(*a*) pressure drag and velocity drag

(*b*) friction drag and velocity drag

(*c*) friction drag and pressure drag

(*d*) pressure drag, velocity drag and friction drag.

93. Specific speed of a pump and specific speed of a turbine are (symbols have the usual meaning)

(*a*) $\frac{N\sqrt{Q}}{H^{3/4}}$ and $\frac{N\sqrt{P}}{H^{5/4}}$ respectively

(*b*) $\frac{N\sqrt{Q}}{H^{3/4}}$ and $\frac{N\sqrt{P}}{H^{3/4}}$ respectively

(*c*) $\frac{N\sqrt{Q}}{H^{5/4}}$ and $\frac{N\sqrt{P}}{H^{5/4}}$ respectively

(*d*) $\frac{N\sqrt{Q}}{H^{5/4}}$ and $\frac{N\sqrt{P}}{H^{5/4}}$ respectively

94. One horse power is equal to
(*a*) 102 watts (*b*) 75 watts
(*c*) 550 watts (*d*) 735 watts

95. Reciprocating pumps are no more to be seen in industrial applications (in comparison to centrifugal pumps) because of
(*a*) high initial and maintenance cost
(*b*) lower discharge
(*c*) lower speed of operation
(*d*) necessity of air vessel

96. The maximum continuous power available from a hydroelectric plant under most adverse hydraulic conditions, is called
(*a*) Base power (*b*) Firm power
(*c*) Primary power (*d*) Unpredictable

97. The movable wicket gates of a reaction turbine are used to
(*a*) control the flow of water passing through the turbine
(*b*) control the pressure under which the turbine is working
(*c*) strengthen the casing of the turbine
(*d*) reduce the size of the turbine

98. A Fourneyron turbine is
(*a*) outward flow reaction turbine
(*b*) inward flow reaction turbine
(*c*) outward flow impulse turbine
(*d*) inward flow impulse turbine

99. The degree of reaction of a turbine is defined as the ratio of
(*a*) static pressure drop to total energy transfer
(*b*) total energy transfer to static pressure drop
(*c*) change of velocity energy across the turbine to the total energy transfer
(*d*) velocity energy to pressure energy.

100. In a centrifugal pump installation while starting, the position of delivery valve is
(*a*) fully open (*b*) fully closed
(*c*) half open (*d*) more than half open

101. For attaining a non-overloading characteristic in centrifugal pumps
(*a*) backward bent vanes are preferred over forward bent vanes
(*b*) forward bent vanes are preferred over backward bent vanes
(*c*) forward bent vanes are preferred over vanes radial at outlet
(*d*) vanes radial at outlet are preferred over backward vanes

102. Which one of the following statements regarding reciprocating pumps is correct ?
(*a*) Friction head is mainly responsible for causing cavitation in a reciprocating pump at the beginning of the suction stroke.
(*b*) Effect of acceleration pressure on reciprocating pumps appears parabolic and has the maximum effect at the middle of the delivery stroke.
(*c*) Air vessel reduces the acceleration head and consequently reduces the effect of friction head also.
(*d*) The maximum permissible suction lift in a double acting reciprocating pump is independent of vapour pressure.

103. On an immersed body in a flowing fluid the lift force is
(*a*) due to buoyant force.
(*b*) always in the opposite direction to gravity
(*c*) due to wake phenomenon
(*d*) the dynamic fluid-force component normal to approach velocity

104. A plot between power generated in MW and time is known as
(*a*) Load curve (*b*) Load duration curve
(*c*) Load factor (*d*) Demand curve

105. A centrifugal pump takes too much power, due to
(*a*) low speed (*b*) air in water
(*c*) air leakage (*d*) heavy liquid

106. In reaction turbine the draft tube is used to
(*a*) transport water to downstream without eddies
(*b*) reconvert kinetic energy to flow energy by a gradual expansion of the flow cross-section
(*c*) increase the effective head
(*d*) prevent air from entering

107. A drum of radius R full of a fluid of density d is rotated at ω rad/sec. The increase in pressure at the outer edge of the drum will be
(*a*) $\frac{\omega^2 R^2 d}{2}$ (*b*) $\frac{\omega^2 R d}{2}$
(*c*) $\frac{\omega R d}{2}$ (*d*) $\frac{\omega R d^2}{2}$

108. In axial flow turbines, water enters
(*a*) radially but leaves axially
(*b*) axially but leaves radially
(*c*) at an angle but leaves axially
(*d*) axially and leaves axially

109. When pressure p, flow rate Q, diameter D, and density d, a dimensionless group is represented by

(a) $\frac{pQ^2}{dD^4}$ (b) $\frac{p}{dQ^2D^4}$

(c) $\frac{pD^4d}{Q^2}$ (d) $\frac{pD^4}{dD^2}$

110. Viscosity is the most important property in the

(a) travel of a bullet through air

(b) water jet issuing from a fire air

(c) formation of soap bubbles

(d) flow of castor oil through a tube.

111. A type of flow in which the fluid particles while moving in the direction of flow rotate about their mass centre, is known as

(a) steady flow (b) uniform flow

(c) laminar flow (d) rotational flow

112. If pressure at any point in the liquid approaches the vapour pressure, liquid starts vaporising and creates pockets or bubbles of dissolved gases and vapours. This phenomenon is

(a) surface tension (b) adhesion

(c) vaporisation (d) cavitation

113. Fire hose nozzle is generally made of

(a) divergent shape (b) convergent shape

(c) cylindrical shape (d) parabolic shape.

114. Discharge of broad crested weir is maximum in the head of water on downstream side of weir as compared to head on the upstream side of the weir is

(a) one-half (b) one-third

(c) two-third (d) three-fourth

115. For similarly, in addition to models being geometrically similar to prototype, the following in both cases should also be equal

(a) ratio of inertial force to force due to viscosity

(b) ratio of inertial force to force due to gravitation

(c) ratio of inertial force to force due to surface tension

(d) all the four ratios of inertial force to force due to viscosity, gravitation, surface tension and elasticity

116. Discharge over a sharp-edged rectangular notch of width w and depth h is equal to

(a) $\frac{2}{3}C_d w\sqrt{2gh}^{5/2}$ (b) $\frac{2}{3}C_d w\sqrt{2gh}$

(c) $\frac{2}{3}C_d w\sqrt{2gh}^{3/2}$ (d) $\frac{8}{15}C_d w\sqrt{2gh}^{3/2}$

117. In a free vortex motion, tangential velocity of the water particles is proportional to

(a) r (b) r^2

(c) $1/r$ (d) $1/r^2$

where, r = distance from the centre.

118. To replace a pipe of diameter D by n parallel pipes of diameter d, the formula used is

(a) $d = \frac{D}{n}$ (b) $d = \frac{D}{n^{1/2}}$

(c) $\frac{D}{n^{3/2}}$ (d) $\frac{D}{n^{2/5}}$

119. Vertical component of pressure force on a submerged curve surface is equal to

(a) weight of liquid vertically above the curved surface and extending upon the free surface

(b) force on a vertical projection of the curved surface

(c) product of pressure at centroid and surface area

(d) horizontal component

120. The fluid forces considered in the Navier-Stokes equation are

(a) gravity velocity and viscous

(b) gravity, pressure and turbulent

(c) pressure, viscous and turbulent

(d) gravity, viscous and turbulent

121. For a flow to be rotational, velocity normal to the plane of area should be equal to the

(a) angular velocity vector

(b) half the angular velocity vector

(c) twice the angular velocity vector

(d) zero

122. Continuity equation for an incompressible fluid is

(a) $A_1 V_1 = A_2V_2$ (b) $\rho_1 A_1 V_1 = \rho_2 A_2V_2$

(c) $\frac{A_1V_1}{\rho_1} = \frac{A_2V_2}{\rho_2}$ (d) $\frac{\rho_1 A_1}{V_1} = \frac{\rho_2 A_2}{\rho_2}$

where V = velocity, ρ = density and A = area

123. Loss of head due to friction in a pipe of uniform diameter with viscous flow is equal to

(a) Reynolds number (Re)

(b) $\frac{1}{Re}$

(c) $\frac{4}{Re}$

(d) $\frac{16}{Re}$

124. Hydraulic grade line for any flow system as compared to energy line is

(*a*) above (*b*) below

(*c*) at same level (*d*) uncertain

125. The effect of negative pressure beneath the nappe in case of flow of water over a rectangular suppressed weir is to

(*a*) decrease the discharge

(*b*) increase the discharge

(*c*) increase frictional resistance

(*d*) reduce frictional resistance

126. Gradually varied flow is

(*a*) steady uniform flow

(*b*) steady non-uniform flow

(*c*) unsteady uniform flow

(*d*) unsteady non-uniform flow

127. A fluid in which resistance to deformation is independent of the shear stress, is known as

(*a*) Bingham plastic fluid

(*b*) Pseudo plastic fluid

(*c*) Dilatant fluid

(*d*) Newtonian fluid

128. Pressure drag results from

(*a*) skin-friction

(*b*) deformation drag

(*c*) development of a stagnation point

(*d*) occurrence of a wake

129. Turbulent flow is hydraulically smooth if ratio $\frac{\text{height of roughness projection}}{\text{thickness of laminar sub-layer}}$ is less than

(*a*) 1.00 (*b*) 0.75

(*c*) 0.50 (*d*) 0.25

130. Bluff body surface

(*a*) is smooth so that friction can be neglected

(*b*) coincides with streamlines

(*c*) does not coincide with streamlines

(*d*) perpendicular to streamlines

131. Centre of pressure on an inclined plane is

(*a*) at the centroid (*b*) above the centroid

(*c*) below the centroid (*d*) at metacentre

132. Separation of flow occurs when pressure gradient

(*a*) tends to approach zero

(*b*) becomes negative

(*c*) changes abruptly

(*d*) reduces to a value when vapour formation starts

133. The friction head lost due to flow of a viscous fluids through a circular pipe of length L and diameter d with a velocity v, and pipe friction factor 'f' is

(*a*) $\frac{4f\,L}{d}\cdot\frac{v^2}{2g}$ (*b*) $\frac{4f\,L}{\pi d^2}\cdot\frac{v^2}{2g}$

(*c*) $\frac{v^2}{2g}$ (*d*) $\frac{4f\,L}{\pi d}\cdot\frac{v^2}{2g}$

134. The rate of change of linear momentum is equals to

(*a*) active force (*b*) reactive force

(*c*) torque (*d*) work done

135. Component of the force of fluid on the body (which is generally inclined to the direction of motion of the body) parallel to the direction of motion is called

(*a*) drag (*b*) lift

(*c*) wake (*d*) thrust

136. Energy loss in flow through nozzle as compared to venturimeter is

(*a*) same (*b*) more

(*c*) less (*d*) unpredictable

137. The rate of change of moment of momentum represents the

(*a*) force exterted by fluid

(*b*) torque applied by the fluid

(*c*) work done by the fluid

(*d*) power developed by the fluid

138. If the characteristics of a pump are as shown in the figure, then abscissa represents

(*a*) head (*b*) RPM

(*c*) discharge (*d*) power

139. To obtain relation for the specific speed, the assumption made is that all pumps

(*a*) are similar

(*b*) of a given type are similar

(*c*) of a given type are geometrically similar

(*d*) are hydraulically similar

140. Water turbines may be put in the decreasing order of specific speed as

(*a*) Propeller turbine, Reaction turbine, Impulse turbine

(*b*) Pelton wheel, Francis turbine, Kaplan turbine

(*c*) Reaction turbine, Impulse turbine, Propeller turbine

(*d*) Propeller turbine, Impulse turbine, Reaction turbine

141. Mixed flow turbines are
(*a*) radial inward flow type
(*b*) radial outward flow type
(*c*) partly radial partly axial
(*d*) parallel flow type

142. A foot valve is provided on
(*a*) Centrifugal pumps (*b*) Kaplan turbines
(*c*) Pelton wheels (*d*) All of these

143. Which one is different from the others ?
(*a*) Axial flow impeller
(*b*) Mixed flow impeller
(*c*) Warped vane impeller
(*d*) Shrouded impeller

144. In a reaction turbine
(*a*) it is possible to regulate the flow without loss
(*b*) it must be placed at the foot of the fall and above the tail race
(*c*) work done is purely by the change in the kinetic energy of jet
(*d*) only part of the head is converted into velocity before water enters the wheel

145. The discharge through a rectangular weir varies as
(*a*) H (*b*) $H^{1/2}$
(*c*) H^2 (*d*) $H^{5/2}$

146. The hydraulic gradient line is always
(*a*) below the total energy line
(*b*) parallel to the bottom
(*c*) above the total energy line
(*d*) none of these

147. In involute casing the velocity of water
(*a*) decreases but pressure increases
(*b*) and pressure both increase
(*c*) and pressure both decrease
(*d*) increases but pressure decreases

148. The pump which is different from others is
(*a*) Simplex pump (*b*) Plunger pump
(*c*) Piston pump (*d*) Centrifugal pump

149. If a centrifugal pump is noisy in operation, it may be due to
(*a*) faulty priming
(*b*) suction head too high
(*c*) air in water
(*d*) mechanical defect

150. Francis turbine is best suited for
(*a*) medium head application from 24 to 180 m
(*b*) high head installation above 180 m
(*c*) low head installation upto 30 m
(*d*) all types of heads

151. Hydraulic accumulator is used for
(*a*) accumulating oil
(*b*) supplying large quantities of oil for very short duration
(*c*) supplying energy when main supply fails
(*d*) accumulating hydraulic energy

152. Run away speed of a hydraulic turbine is the speed
(*a*) at full load
(*b*) at which turbine runner will be damaged
(*c*) at which the turbine runner is allowed to revolve freely without load and with the wicket gates wide open
(*d*) corresponding to maximum overload permissible

153. According to the laws of proportionality for homologous turbines, speed is proportional to
(*a*) $\sqrt{H}/D$ (*b*) $\sqrt{H/D}$
(*c*) $\sqrt{H}/D^2$ (*d*) $\sqrt{HD}$

154. A hydraulic intensifier normally consists of
(*a*) two cylinders, two rams and a storage device
(*b*) a cylinder and a ram
(*c*) two co-axial rams and two cylinders
(*d*) a cylinder, a piston, storage tank and control valve

155. According to the laws of proportionality for homologous turbines, discharge is proportional to
(*a*) $D\sqrt{H}$ (*b*) $D^2\sqrt{H}$
(*c*) $D^2H^{3/2}$ (*d*) D^2H

156. Any change in load is adjusted by adjusting on turbine
(*a*) net head (*b*) absolute velocity
(*c*) blade velocity (*d*) flow

157. For pumping viscous oil, pump used will be
(*a*) centrifugal pump (*b*) reciprocating pump
(*c*) turbine pump (*d*) screw pump

158. The cavitation in reaction type hydraulic turbines is avoided by
(*a*) using highly polished blade
(*b*) using stainless steel runner
(*c*) installing the turbine below the tail race level
(*d*) all of the above

159. Propeller turbine is best suited for
(*a*) medium head application from 20 to 180 m
(*b*) low head installation up to 30 m
(*c*) high head installation above 180 m
(*d*) all types of heads

160. A hydraulic jump can occur under all of the following conditions except :
(*a*) on the upstream side of the sluices
(*b*) at the foot of the spillways
(*c*) where the gradient suddenly changes from a steep slope to a flat slope
(*d*) when water moving in shooting flow impacts with water having a larger depth with streaming flow

161. As per the aerofoil theory of Kaplan turbine blade design, guide angle is as the angle between
(*a*) lift and resultant force
(*b*) drag and resultant force
(*c*) lift and tangential force
(*d*) lift and drag

162. Power required to drive a centrifugal pump is proportional to (D = impeller diameter)
(*a*) D (*b*) D^2
(*c*) D^3 (*d*) D^4

163. Ratio of maximum load to rated plant capacity is known as
(*a*) Load factor
(*b*) Utilization factor
(*c*) Maximum load factor
(*d*) Capacity factor

164. A double acting reciprocating pump compared to single acting pump will have nearly
(*a*) double efficiency (*b*) double head
(*c*) double flow (*d*) double weight

165. For centrifugal pump
(*a*) head $\propto$ speed^2 (*b*) head $\propto$ diameter^2
(*c*) power $\propto$ speed^3 (*d*) none of these

166. For small discharge at high pressure, pump preferred is
(*a*) centrifugal (*b*) axial flow
(*c*) propeller (*d*) reciprocating

Answers

1. (*d*)	**2.** (*c*)	**3.** (*d*)	**4.** (*a*)	**5.** (*d*)	**6.** (*c*)	**7.** (*a*)	**8.** (*c*)	**9.** (*d*)	**10.** (*b*)
11. (*d*)	**12.** (*c*)	**13.** (*d*)	**14.** (*d*)	**15.** (*d*)	**16.** (*c*)	**17.** (*d*)	**18.** (*a*)	**19.** (*a*)	**20.** (*d*)
21. (*c*)	**22.** (*b*)	**23.** (*a*)	**24.** (*a*)	**25.** (*d*)	**26.** (*d*)	**27.** (*c*)	**28.** (*d*)	**29.** (*c*)	**30.** (*a*)
31. (*c*)	**32.** (*b*)	**33.** (*d*)	**34.** (*c*)	**35.** (*a*)	**36.** (*d*)	**37.** (*c*)	**38.** (*d*)	**39.** (*a*)	**40.** (*d*)
41. (*a*)	**42.** (*d*)	**43.** (*b*)	**44.** (*b*)	**45.** (*d*)	**46.** (*a*)	**47.** (*b*)	**48.** (*d*)	**49.** (*c*)	**50.** (*d*)
51. (*d*)	**52.** (*d*)	**53.** (*d*)	**54.** (*d*)	**55.** (*a*)	**56.** (*b*)	**57.** (*c*)	**58.** (*d*)	**59.** (*d*)	**60.** (*d*)
61. (*b*)	**62.** (*a*)	**63.** (*c*)	**64.** (*b*)	**65.** (*c*)	**66.** (*b,d*)	**67.** (*a*)	**68.** (*b*)	**69.** (*d*)	**70.** (*c*)
71. (*a*)	**72.** (*c*)	**73.** (*b*)	**74.** (*c*)	**75.** (*b*)	**76.** (*b*)	**77.** (*d*)	**78.** (*c*)	**79.** (*d*)	**80.** (*d*)
81. (*a*)	**82.** (*d*)	**83.** (*c*)	**84.** (*a*)	**85.** (*c*)	**86.** (*d*)	**87.** (*a*)	**88.** (*d*)	**89.** (*d*)	**90.** (*b*)
91. (*b*)	**92.** (*c*)	**93.** (*a*)	**94.** (*d*)	**95.** (*a*)	**96.** (*b*)	**97.** (*b*)	**98.** (*a*)	**99.** (*a*)	**100.** (*b*)
101. (*a*)	**102.** (*c*)	**103.** (*b*)	**104.** (*a*)	**105.** (*b*)	**106.** (*b*)	**107.** (*a*)	**108.** (*a*)	**109.** (*a*)	**110.** (*c*)
111. (*c*)	**112.** (*a*)	**113.** (*c*)	**114.** (*d*)	**115.** (*)	**116.** (*c*)	**117.** (*c*)	**118.** (*d*)	**119.** (*a*)	**120.** (*a*)
121. (*c*)	**122.** (*a*)	**123.** (*d*)	**124.** (*b*)	**125.** (*b*)	**126.** (*b*)	**127.** (*d*)	**128.** (*d*)	**129.** (*d*)	**130.** (*c*)
131. (*c*)	**132.** (*c*)	**133.** (*a*)	**134.** (*c*)	**135.** (*a*)	**136.** (*a*)	**137.** (*b*)	**138.** (*c*)	**139.** (*c*)	**140.** (*a*)
141. (*c*)	**142.** (*a*)	**143.** (*d*)	**144.** (*d*)	**145.** (*d*)	**146.** (*a*)	**147.** (*a*)	**148.** (*d*)	**149.** (*d*)	**150.** (*a*)
151. (*c*)	**152.** (*c*)	**153.** (*a*)	**154.** (*c*)	**155.** (*b*)	**156.** (*d*)	**157.** (*d*)	**158.** (*d*)	**159.** (*b*)	**160.** (*a*)
161. (*a*)	**162.** (*d*)	**163.** (*b*)	**164.** (*c*)	**165.** (*a*)	**166.** (*d*)				

Explanations

42. Boiler feed pump has to supply water at higher pressures–more than the pressure of steam. Gear pumps are never used for such services.

43. In fluid coupling, efficiency = $\frac{N_2}{N_1}$

Thus variation of efficiency with speed ratio is linear.

48. A hydraulic coupling consists of a pump unit fitted on the driving shaft and a turbine unit on to the driven shaft. These two units are housed in a common casing in such a manner that output of the pump is fed to the turbine unit which rotates and drives the driven shaft. The medium fluid used is generally oil.

49. Molasses is highly viscous therefore open impeller should be used. Normally a screw pump is used for pumping highly viscous fluids.

53. When absolute local pressure at any point in a conduit carrying a liquid approaches the vapour pressure p_v of the liquid, dissolved gases and liquid vapour emerge out of the liquid as bubbles. These bubbles may travel to regions of higher pressure and collapse. At the point of bubble collapse, the boundary gets damaged. The phenomenon of formation, travel and collapse of vapour bubbles is called **cavitation**.

56. Gear pumps are best suited for low pressures (1000 kN/m^2) and small discharges (less than 30 lps). These are self priming and are often used to prime large centrifugal pumps.

Discharge, $Q = K.C\,(D- C).\, L\left(\frac{N}{60}\right)$

where L = axial length of teeth,

C = centre to centre distance between axes of gears.

D = outside diameter of gear.

58. In case of reaction turbines, maximum efficiency is obtained when absolute velocity vector at the outlet is 90°.

59. By extrapolating Q vs H curve, the shut off head which is corresponding to Q = 0 is 35.5 m.

60. Buckets are double hemispherical in shape. These buckets are made of cast iron, bronze or stainless steel.

61. A reciprocating pump is self priming. It operates at low speeds. It is not suitable for viscous liquids, paper pulp, molasses, etc.

62. Air vessel smoothens water discharge which is otherwise pulsating. Air vessel may be fitted on suction side and/or delivery side.

63. A tapered draft tube is used for low specific speed vertical shaft turbines. Its maximum cone angle is 8°. If angle is more than this, water does not touch the inner walls, causing vortices and loss of head. Maximum efficiency obtained in this tube is 9%. The tube must discharge sufficiently below the tail water level.

65. Series operation is achieved by having one pump discharge into the suction of the next. This arrangement is used primarily to increase the discharge head.

97. The purpose of guide vanes or wicket gates is to direct water to enter into the runner vanes at a suitable angle to avoid any wastage of energy due to shock and to convert partly pressure energy of the entering water into kinetic energy. It also regulates supply of water according to the load on the turbine.

5 CHAPTER Production, Planning and Control

PRODUCTION PLANNING

In production, products are manufactured by the transformation of raw material (into finished goods).

Planning looks ahead, anticipates possible difficulties and decides in advance as to how the production, best, be carried out.

Control phase makes sure that the programmed production is constantly maintained.

Functions of Production Planning

A production planning and control system has following functions to perform, some before the arrival of raw materials and tools, and others while the raw material undergoes processing.

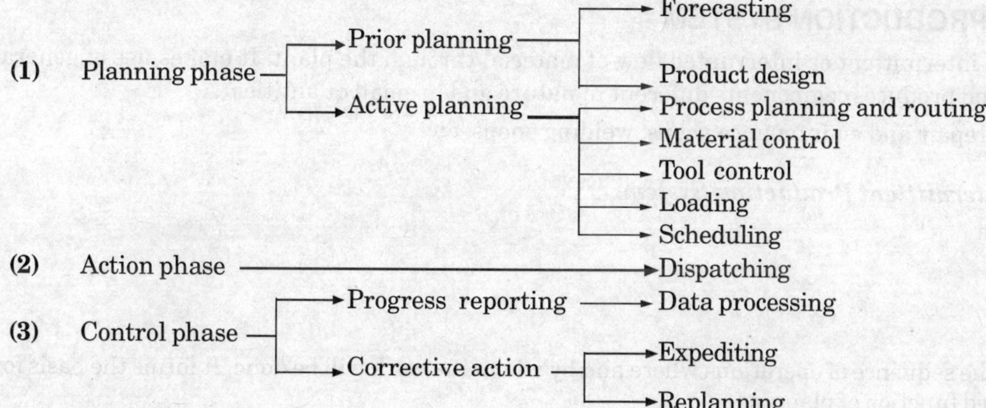

(1) Planning phase

(i) *Prior planning :*

(*a*) *Forecasting :* Estimation of type, quantity and quality of future work.

(*b*) *Product design :* Collection of information regarding specifications, bill of materials, drawings, etc.

(ii) *Active planning :*

(*a*) *Process planning and routing :* Finding the most economical process for doing a work and (then) deciding how and where the work will be done.

(*b*) *Material control :* Determination of the requirements and control of materials.

(*c*) *Tool control :* Determination of the requirements and control of tools used.

(*d*) *Loading :* Assignment of work to manpower, machinery, etc.

(*e*) *Scheduling :* It is the time phase of loading and determines when and in what sequence the work will be carried out. It fixes the starting as well as the finishing time for the job.

(2) Action phase

Dispatching **:** It is the transition from planning to action phase. In this phase the worker is ordered to start the actual work.

(3) Control phase

(*i*) *Progress reporting.*

(*a*) Data regarding the job progress is collected.

(*b*) It is interpreted by comparison with the preset level of performance.

(*ii*) *Corrective action.*

(*a*) *Expediting* : It means taking action if the progress reporting (*j*) indicates a deviation of the plan from the originally set targets.

(*b*) *Replanning* : Replanning of the whole affair becomes essential, in case expediting fails to bring the deviated plan to its actual (right) path.

FUNCTIONAL ORGANISATION OF PRODUCTION PLANNING AND CONTROL

Types of Production System

1. Continuous 2. Intermittent

CONTINUOUS PRODUCTION SYSTEM

It involves a continuous or almost continuous physical flow of material. It makes use of special purpose machines, and produces standardized items in large quantities *e.g.* chemical processing, cigarette manufacturing, and cement manufacturing

Classification of Continuous Production System

(*i*) Mass and flow line production (*ii*) Continuous or process production.

INTERMITTENT PRODUCTION SYSTEM

It is specified by the intermittent or interrupted flow of material through the plant. It makes use of general purpose machines and produces components different in nature and in small quantities.

e.g. machine shops, repair and maintenance shops, welding shops, etc.

Classification of Intermittent Production System

(*i*) Batch production

(*ii*) Job production.

ROUTING

Routing prescribes the sequence of operations where and by whom the work will be done. It forms the basis for loading and scheduled function of planning.

The routing plan is usually made in advance of production in continuous manufacturing system of production, however, routing decisions are often made in the shop floor which includes last minute changes.

The design of format used for the routing sheet depends upon the type of manufacturing system. Usually it is made simpler by the usage of different symbols and notations for quick and easy identification. Row procedures are evolved, based on the nature of the production system and the complexities of organisation.

In intermittent type of production systems, routing has to determine for every batch where the operation is to be done and through which route.

In case of continuous manufacturing systems, the manufacturing line layout is clear and fixed and the routing becomes mechanical. It does not pose much of a problem because all follows the same route.

LOADING

In planning production, shop orders have to be converted into work load on individual work machines or groups of machines. The production manager must know the loading on each equipment/machine in order to determine whether capacity utilisation is full or otherwise. He should also indentify overloads and underloads on each machine to assist production planning to balance the load. Manual systems generally used to load operations against actual capacity by creating a bar chart on a load board.

SCHEDULING

Under production control system usually three types of schedules are prepared.

(*i*) **Master schedules :** It indicates the data on which various jobs in hand are required to be completed. Master Schedule is like a control board and a key schedule about all production activities.

(*ii*) **Operation schedule :** In this, time is fixed for doing a particular piece of work with a given machine.

(*iii*) **Detailed operation schedule :** In this, time required for doing each detailed operation of given job is shown. While doing so, machine to be used or the process to be followed is taken into account.

COMPONENT OF DEMAND

It refers to a sustained increase or decrease in demand from one period to the next. e.g. if average monthly demand for a product has increased 10 to 15 percent is each of the past few years, then an upward trend in demand exists. The sales of products in the growth stage of the product life cycle trend to show an upward trend, whereas those in decline trend to show downward trend.

Seasonal Component of Demand

It pertains to the influence of seasonal factors that impact the demand positively or negatively e.g. sales of heat blowers will be higher in winter months and lower in summer months every year, indicating a seasonal component in the demand.

Cyclical Component of Demand

It is similar to the seasonal component except that seasonality occured at regular intervals and is of constant length, whereas the cyclic component varies on both time and duration of occurrence.

e.g. impact of a recession on the demand for the product will be reflected by the cyclic component.

Recessions occur at irregular intervals and the length of time a recession lasts varies. This component is present in most economic data, such as GNP, personal income, and industry sales of such consumer durables as automobiles and major appliances.

FORECASTING

Forecasting is the blue print or planning. It is an estimate of the level of the demand in future. It provides guide lines in how many of the product produced, are likely to be demanded by the customer when these demands are likely to occur, and the amount of business the firm can expect during the planning period. The material requirements, schedules and other decisions are made based on forecasting of demand.

Actually, forecasting is of the forward casting of past data. Past is known or could be known from experience and collection of past data. Future is unknown and at best could only be estimated based on the past. Hence one has to consider the reliability (i.e. credibility of possible occurence) and precision (i.e., the range within which it would occured) of forecasting. While more effort in forecasting, causes increased cost due to past data collection and analysis, lesser forecasting activity involves lost revenue, which may be due to unplanned labour, unplanned material or unplanned capital cost. Therefore, each firm should maintain a balance in its forecasting effort and strict to a zone near to accuracy cost trade off.

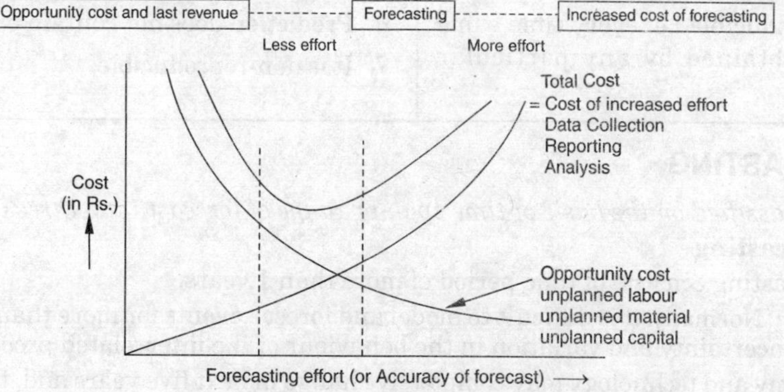

Fig. Balance of forecasting efforts

Requirements

A sales forecast should be

(*i*) accurate (*ii*) simple and easy to understand (*iii*) economical

Purposes

(*i*) It determines the volume of production and the production rate.

(*ii*) It forms basis for production budget [step (6) above], labour budget, material budget, etc.

(*iii*) It suggests the need for plant expansion.

(*iv*) It emphasizes the need for product research development.

(*v*) It suggests the need for changes in production methods.

(*vi*) It helps establishing pricing policies.

(*vii*) It helps deciding the extent of advertising, product distribution, etc.

Basic Elements

In any sales forecasting analysis, following four basic elements of economic data should be used.

(*i*) Trends : These are the long term, long range movements of a series of economic data. They have little relationship to the month-to-month changes that takes place, and they manifest their direction slowly.

(*ii*) Cycles : These are of shorter duration and they are usually featured by alternate periods of expansion and contraction.

(*iii*) Seasonal variations : These occur within a certain period of year and reoccur at about the same time and to approximately the same extent from year to year.

(*iv*) Irregular variations : These are the result of unforeseen or non-recurring events that have an economic influence. A strike in a key industry might cause an irregular variation.

DIFFERENCE BETWEEN FORECASTING AND PREDICTION

Forecasting is objective, scientific, reproducible, free from individual bias and error analysis is possible in it. Prediction is subjective, mostly intuitive, non-reproducible and contains individual bias. Only limited error analysis is possible in production.

Forecasting	***Prediction***
1. Forecasting involves the projection of the past into the future.	1. Prediction involves judgement in management after taking all available information into account.
2. Forecast involves estimating the level of demand for a product on the basis of factors and previous data that generated the demand in the part months.	2. Prediction involves the anticipated change into the future. It may include even new factors that may affect future demand.
3. Forecasting is more scientific.	3. Prediction is more intuitive.
4. It is relatively free from personal bias.	4. It is more governed by personal bias and preferences.
5. It is more objective.	5. It is more subjective.
6. Error analysis is possible.	6. Prediction does not contain error analysis.
7. Forecasting is reproducible i.e. every time same result would be obtained by any particular technique.	7. It is non-reproducible.

TYPES OF FORECASTING

Forecasting may be classified on the basis of time span or range of forecast into three categories :

1. Long range forecasting

Long range forecasting consists of time period of more than 1 years.

Characteristics : Normally, it is difficult to model and foresee events for more than 5 years. It is mainly due to economic uncertainty and variation in the behaviour of the interrelated processes.

e.g. state of economy and technology may completely change in next five years and, therefore trend of the data during past few years may not be sufficient.

Applications : Mostly it is useful for capacity expansion, growth recruiment and diversification policies of the firm. It is useful in the following areas :

(*i*) Capital planning
(*ii*) Plant location
(*iii*) New product planning
(*iv*) Research and development planning etc.

2. Medium range forecasting

The range for medium range forecasting is generally from 3 - 12 months.

Characteristics : As the range of forecast shorten from 5 to 1 year, the accuracy of forecast increases. This is due to better understanding of future and relatively lesser uncertainty. Estimate of reliability of forecast may be useful in medium range forecast.

Applications : It is very useful in following areas :

(*i*) Sales planning and sale force decisions,
(*ii*) Capital and cash planning,
(*iii*) Inventory planning, and
(*iv*) Production planing etc.

Method : Medium-range forecasting needs judgement as well as time series analysis. Combination of collective opinion, regression analysis, correlation of different index and inflation etc may be useful in forecasting.

3. Short range forecasting

The range for short-range forecasting is typically 1 - 3 month. In most cases, it is for one season, few months or few weeks.

Characteristics : The short range forecasting is needed at detailed level, such as demand of specific item. The forecast may affect the purchasing activity. Specific value of the forecast is needed. There is very less scope of judgement in short range forecast and, therefore past data are mainly projected into future.

Applications : Short range forecasting is commonly used in immediate control of activities.

Some related applications are

(*i*) purchasing (*ii*) Overtime decision (*iii*) Scheduling of job (*iv*) Machine maintenance etc.

Method : Short range forecasting is based on past data. The trend of data is projected or interpolated into future. For this, exponential smoothing, graphical projection, past explosion into product family etc are used.

e.g. monthly forecast of sales may vary from the basis of production planning activities.

QUALITATIVE METHODS OF FORECASTING

Qualitative methods are needed in forecasting when data necessary to use time series or caused model are not available.

e.g. when a new product is to be launched in the market, its past demand data are not available. Therefore, time series trend analysis is impractical, qualitative, techniques, which incorporates human judgement, expert opinion, management intuition, market research, historical analogy are useful in such cases.

1. Delphi method

In this method, a panel of outside expert is identified. Identification of expert is not disclosed. This is for the purpose that nobody should influence the opinion of others. The coordinator of the project prepares the statistical summary of responses. This along with the support for the responses is provided to the expert in the next round. The participants are asked if they want to modify their previous response. In this way, after few rounds of questionaires, the final forecast is derived.

Delphi is used for long range forecast. It is generally used for new product demand, technological forecast for new technology, effect of scientific advances, changes in society, change in competitive environment etc.

e.g. effect of internet/intranet or information highway in the educational system of india in next 25 years may be forecasted through this approach.

Advantages

(*i*) It is effective, when past data is absent.
(*ii*) It does not required expert to meet in person.
(*iii*) It is extremely useful for the forecast of new technology or new product.

Disadvantages

(*i*) The choice of setting up panel of experts is difficult.

(*ii*) There is considerable time loss in making frequent rounds.

(*iii*) Some members may dominate the panel, and hence difficult to achieve reconciliation and consensus.

(*iv*) Accuracy or reliability of forecast is relatively poor in Delphi. Therefore, it should only be used when past trend is absent and quantitative models are difficult to use.

2. Market research

It is used to determine consumer linking in a product or service. A set of hypothesis is tested through the data, which is generated in the survey. It is useful in short or medium range forecast.

3. Salesforce forecast

Salesforce is a team which is closest to the customers. Their estimates are compiled to assess the future demand. In pharmaceutical market, the estimate given by medical representatives in all teritories are oftenly used to determine the sales forecast of a particular medicine.

4. Historical analogy

This is applicable for forecasting the demand of a product in a new area. Here the consumption pattern elsewhere is taken as a basis for forecasting the demand in a new area. The approach is effective for medium to long range forecast and it is quite cost effective.

5. Trend line technique

- Trend line technique is employed when there is an appreciable amount of historical data.
- This technique is more reliable than the historic estimate.
- This technique involves plotting historical data, *i.e.* a diagram (Figure below) between activity indicator, e.g., tons of material (say past sales) on Y-axis and time on X-axis.
- A single best fitting line (using statistical technique) is drawn and projected to show sales estimate for future.
- This technique is more accurate as it makes use of a large past data and possesses scientific validity.

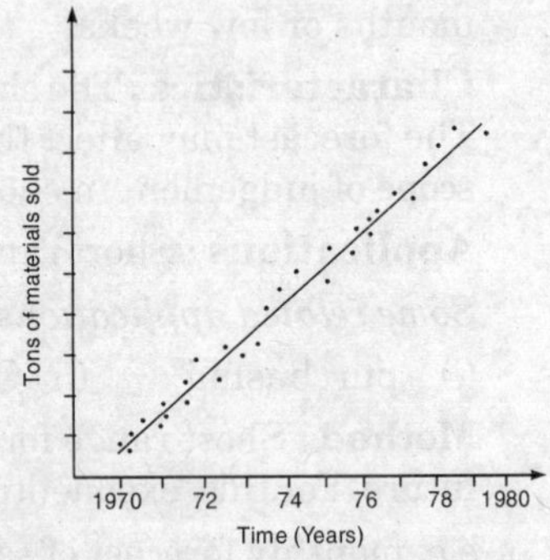

6. Judgemental techniques

- These involve, *opinions of consumers and customers*. Questionnaires related to buying the product may be sent to a selected group of consumers and to the customers who have already purchased the product. The information thus received can be very useful in estimating product performance and its probable demand in future.
- Retail and wholesale dealers can provide some insight into the pace of current and future sales.
- The opinion of area sales managers can also be quite useful.

7. Forecasting by past average

In this the objective is the forecast or predict the sales of an item for the next sales period, then by this method, forecasted sales

for next period = Average sales for previous period

8. Forecasting from last period's sales

The method eliminates the influence of past (old) data and bases the forecast only upon the sales of the previous period. Using this technique, the forecasts be as given in the following table :

Period No.	Actual Sales	Forecast Sales	Errors in Forecast
1	5	5	
2	4	4	+ 1
3	8	8	– 4
4	7	7	+ 1
5	4	4	+ 3

9. **Forecasting by moving average**

This method represents a compromise between the two above explained methods, in this the forecast is neither influenced by very old data nor does it solely reflect the figure of the previous period.

The use of simple moving average is an adequate method of forecasting, provided sales are subject to neither seasonal variation nor marked secular trends. A secular trend is one which causes sales steadily to increase or decrease.

Advantages

(*i*) This method is easy for calculation

(*ii*) Larger the periodicity better would be smoothening

(*iii*) It is more useful for shot term forecasting

Disadvantages

(***i***) Lengthy calculations involved.

(***ii***) Need to keep quantities of historical data.

(***iii***) The fact that the normal (or simple) moving average method places equal weight on each of the historical figures used.

(***iv***) Age of the data, which increase with the number of periods used.

ACCURACY OF FORECAST

It is almost impossile to obtain an exactly right forecast every time. This is due to many factors, which affect the trend in data. It is difficult to capture the exact interrelation of these influencing factors. Therefore some error is in forecast value and the actual value is quite common.

Measures of Forecasting Error

1. **MAD (Mean Absolute Deviation)**

This is calculated as the average at absolute value of difference between actual and forecasted value. The negative sign in this difference is ignored as over-estimate as well as under estimate both off target and thus undesirable.

$$\text{MAD} = \frac{\sum_{t=1}^{n} |X_t - F_t|}{n} = \frac{\text{sum of absolute deviation}}{\text{total number of data}}$$

where, X_t = actual value of demand for period t

F_t = forecasted demand for period t

n = number of periods considered for calculating the error

2. **MSE (Mean Sum of square Error)**

The average of squares of all errors in the forecast is termed as MSE. Its interpolation is same as MAD.

$$\text{MSE} = \frac{\sum_{t=1}^{n} (X_t - F_t)^2}{n}$$

3. **BIAS**

BIAS is measure of over estimation or under estimation. A positive BIAS indicates under-estimation while a negative bias indicate over-estimation.

$$\text{BIAS} = \frac{\sum_{t=1}^{n} (X_t - F_t)}{n}$$

4. Tracking signal

It is used to identify these items, which do not keep pace with either positive or negative bias or trend.

$$TS = \frac{\sum_{t=1}^{n}(X_F - F_t)}{(MAD)_n} = \frac{(BIAS)_n}{(MAD)_n} = \frac{\text{comulative deviation}}{\text{MAD}}$$

where, $(MAD)_n$ = mean absolute deviation till period n

$(BIAS)_n$ = BIAS till period n.

5. Deviation (error)

$$\text{Deviation} = \text{Actual value} - \text{Forecast value} = X_t - F_t$$

TIME SERIES MODEL

Time series is a set of observations of some variable over time. It is based on the past data as well as its behaviour, with respect to time. The forecasting is done by determing how the series is dependent on time and developing a means of predicting future levels with some degree of reliability. Here the prime data is taken objectively in quantitative terms and analysis are made on the principle of statistics.

The forecast of multiplicative function can be expressed as

Y = TCSR = (trend functions) × (cyclic index) × (seasonal index) × (corrective factor for random variations)

Time series models are

1. Simple moving average **2.** Weighted moving average **3.** Exponential smoothing

1. Simple Moving Average.

A moving average is obtained by summing and averaging the values from a given number of periods respectively, each time, deleting the oldest value and adding a new value.

Example. The actual demand for the past ten months have been as 100,100,110, 120, 130, 140, 130, 140 150 and 160.

(*i*) What is the predicted demand for the 11th month based on 3 month and 5 month movin average?

(*ii*) What is the mean absolute deviation in 3 month and 5 month moving average?

Solution

(i) Forecasted demand for the 11th month

3 month moving average = average of last 3 month

$$= \frac{140 + 150 + 160}{3} = 150$$

5 month moving average = average of last 5 month

$$= \frac{140 + 130 + 140 + 150 + 160}{5} = 144$$

(ii) Absolute deviation

= Absolute value of the difference between he actual value (X) and forecast value (F)

$= |X - F|$

$$\text{Mean absolute deviation} = \frac{\text{Sum of absolute deviation}}{\text{Number of deviation } (N_D)} = \frac{\Sigma|X - F|}{N_D}$$

3 month moving average

$$\text{Moving average for } 4^{th} \text{ month, } F = \frac{100 + 100 + 110}{3} = 103$$

$$\text{Moving average for } 5^{th} \text{ month, } F = \frac{100 + 110 + 120}{3} = 110$$

5 Month moving average

$$\text{Moving average for 6}^{\text{th}}\text{ month, F} = \frac{100+100+110+120+130}{5} = 112$$

Month	*Demand (Actual (X)*	*Moving Ave (3 months) (F)*	*Absolute deviation (X–F)*	*Moving Ave (5 months) (F)*	*Absolute Deviation (X–F)*
1	100	–	–	–	–
2	100	–	–	–	–
3	110	–	–	–	–
4	120	103	17	–	–
5	130	110	20	–	–
6	140	120	20	112	28
7	130	130	0	120	10
8	140	133	7	126	14
9	150	137	13	132	18
10	160	140	20	138	22

$$\text{MAD (for 3 month moving average)} = \frac{(17+20+20+0+7+13+20)}{7} = 13.86$$

$$\text{MAD (for 5 month moving average)} = \frac{(28+10+14+18+22)}{5} = 18.4$$

2. Weighted Moving Average

In this method different weightages are given for each period of time. Immediate past will be more significant on the trend than the others. Hence different weightage can be given based on the period of time.

If X_i is the actual data value for the time period t_i and W_i is weightage given for the time period t_i, then

$$\text{Weighted moving average, } MA_{wt} = \frac{\Sigma W_i X_i}{\Sigma W_i}$$

In general, weighted average forecast $= F_{i+1} = \dfrac{\Sigma W_i X_i}{\Sigma W_i}$

Example. It demand during the months Jan, Feb and March are 50, 70 and 65 and the weights assigned are 1, 2 and 3 for these months, what is the forecast for the month of April ?

Solution:

Given : $X_1 = 50, X_2 = 70$ and $X_3 = 65$
$W_1 = 1, W_2 = 2$ and $W_3 = 3$

$$\therefore \quad \text{Forecast for April, } MA_{wt} = \frac{\Sigma W_i X_i}{\Sigma W_i} = \frac{50\times1+70\times2+65\times3}{1+2+3} = 64.17$$

3. Exponential Smoothing

The main disadvantages of the moving average method are overcome by the exponential smoothing technique. Using this technique it is necessary only to retain the previous forecast figure and to know the latest actual sales figure. The technique works by modifying the old forecast in the light of new sales figure, *i.e.*

New forecast = α (latest sales figure) + $(1-\alpha)$ (old forecast)

where α = smoothing constant.

Use of this technique permits the forecast to respond to recent actual events, but at the same time retain a certain amount of stability. The amount by which the new forecast responds to the latest sales figure, or the extent to which it is damped by the previous forecast, is, of course, determined by the size of the smoothing constant α. The size of α should be carefully chosen in the light of the stability or variability of actual sales, and is normally from 0.1 to 0.3.

Smoothing constant, α, that gives the equivalent of an N-period moving average can be calculated by

$$\alpha = \frac{2}{N+1}$$

When a secular trend is present, the forecast sales obtained by the normal exponential smoothing method will lag behind actual sales, in just the same way as the moving average forecast.

This is similar to the weighted average method. The recent data is given more weightage and the weightage for the earlier periods are successively being reduced.

Let X_t is the actual (historical) data of demand during the period t.

Let α is the weightage given for the period t, α $(1 - \alpha)$ is the weightage for period $t = (t-1)$, $\alpha(1-\alpha)^2$ for period $t = (t-2)$ and so on.

The values of $X_t, X_{t-1}, X_{t-2}, X_{t-3}$ and so on are actual data values for the respective periods.

$$F_{t+1} = \alpha X_t + \alpha(1-\alpha) X_{t-1} + \alpha(1-\alpha)^2 X_{t-2} + \ldots\ldots$$

$$F_{t+1} = \alpha X_t + (1-\alpha) F_t$$

$$F_{t+1} = F_t + \alpha(X_t - F_t)$$

Example. For the actual demand of 105, a predicted value of 97, an alpha value of 0.4, determine the forecast for the next period using exponential smoothing.

Solution:

Given : Actual demand, $X_t = 105$

Predicted value, $F_t = 97$

$\alpha = 0.4$

$\therefore$ Forecast for the next period, $F_{t+1} = F_t + \alpha(X_t - F_t) = 97 + 0.4(105 - 97) = \mathbf{100.2}$

Casual Model

In the casual model, variation of the data values are due to the passage of time. Here the time is taken as independent variable and the data values are dependent variable. Causal models usually consider the relationship other than 'time'. Strictly speaking, casual model quantify the statistical dependence and also the extent to which two or more variables are related. Regression and corelation techniques are used in the casual model.

SIMPLE LINEAR REGRESSION MODEL

Regression Method

Regression means dependent and involves estimating the value of a dependent variable Y in terms of one or more independent variable X.

$$Y = a + bX$$

$$b = \frac{n\Sigma XY - \Sigma X \Sigma Y}{\Sigma X^2 - (\Sigma X)^2}$$

$$\overline{X} = \frac{\Sigma X}{n}$$

$$\overline{Y} = \frac{\Sigma Y}{n}$$

$$a = \overline{Y} + b\overline{X}$$

Correlation Method

It is a means of expressing the degree of relationship between two or more variables.

$$\text{Coefficient of correleation, } r^2 = \frac{a\Sigma y + b\Sigma xy - n\bar{y}^2}{\Sigma y^2 - n\bar{y}^2}$$

Coefficient of correlation is the square root of coefficient of determination.

Just in TIME (JIT)

JIT is a manufacturing philosphy, which aims at having the right part at precise right time, and in right quantity to go into assemblies. JIT can also be defined as "A philosphy of maufacturing based on planned elimination of all waste and continuous improvement of productivity maintaning zero inventory. It encompasses successful execution of all manufacturing activities required to produce a final product, from engineering of delivery and including all stages of conversion from raw material onward.

Primary Elements of Zero Inventories (Synonym for JIT)

(*i*) have only the required inventory when needed

(*ii*) improve quality to zero defects

(*iii*) reduce lead time by reducing setup-times, queue lengths, and lot sizes

(*iv*) revise incremently the operations themselves

(*v*) accomplish these things at minimum cost.

Purpose of JIT

(*i*) produce and deliver finished goods just in time to be sold

(*ii*) sub-assemblies just in time to be assembled into finished goods

(*iii*) Fabricated parts just in time to go into final assemblies

(*iv*) Purchase materials just in time to be transferred into fabricated parts.

Characteristics of JIT

(*i*) *Aims at driving all queues towards zero in order to*

(*a*) minimize inventory investment

(*b*) shorten production lead times and set-up times

(*c*) react faster to demand change

(*ii*) Cellular (AT) manufacturing system.

(*iii*) Uncover any quality problem and its control at source.

(*iv*) Total preventive maintenance.

(*v*) Cross-trained worker and worker flexibility

(*vi*) Kanban cards

(*vii*) Decentralization

Objective of JIT System

To encourage workforce to participate in the programmes relevant for work improvement, profit increase through cost reduction, inventory reduction and quality improvements. Thus waste should be eliminated.

This philosphy is based upon following two criteria :

(*i*) **Just in time (JIT).** It refers to production and supply of required number of parts when needed. So, it is referred to as JIT production system. It work in process inventories including parts and products are expected to decrease (even to zero), this system is called *stockless (zero inventory) production system*.

(*ii*) **Jidoka (self actuation),** i.e. when unusual event happens in a production line, the worker incharge stops the line and calls for help in removing the cause of trouble.

Disadvantages of JIT

(*i*) JIT production is effective only when the daily demands are fairly stable.

(*ii*) The minimum zero inventory or be theoretically achieved, however stocks are maintained to assure JIT delivery to customers.

(*iii*) Only first come first served principle is applied by manufacturing items in order of releasing kanbanm.

(*iv*) Much needs to be done in connection with employers - employee cooperation, daily workstation rotation, training of operates for different kinds of jobs and system adoptability to market fluctuation.

KANBAN

The simple kanban system of inventory control is an integral part of the JIT system of production. The kanban system is designed to produce only the number of units needed by a "pull" or demand feeding process. It simply adds to all the other effect that result in reduced in-process inventories.

The beauty of kanban system is in its simplicity.

Types of Kanban

Kanban is a card of two types :

(*i*) **Withdrawal kanban :** It shows the quantity of the items that the subsequent process should withdraw from the preceding one.

(*ii*) **Production ordering kanban :** It shows the quantity that the proceding process should produce.

These cards are used within the plant supplier's plant. No complex record keeping is required to feed the next operation and just in time for use.

e.g. we are producing products A, B and C, and that parts *a* and *b* are produced by the preceding process as shown in the figure.

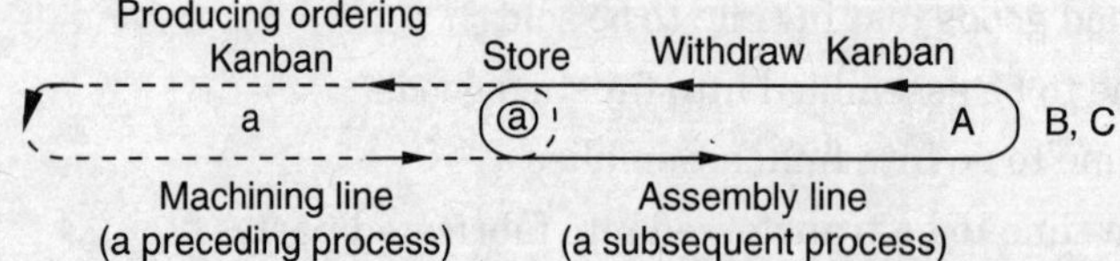

The worker on assembly line producing product goes to the fabrication line to withdraw the necessary number of parts a from the storage location. The worker withdraws the required number of parts, detachs the production ordering kanban and leaves it in place of the parts, and returns to the assembly line with the withdraw kanban. The production ordering kanban is picked up by a worker from the fabrication line as a direction to produce that quantity of part *a*. The kanban system provides an additional class line between operations, reinforcing the previous linkages that lead to improved quality and productivity.

OPERATION SEQUENCE

Time taken is minimum and optimum technique : Sequencing may be defined as the selection of an order for a series of jobs to be done on a finite number of service facilities (e.g., machine) according to predetermined sequence of operations. The sequencing problem by and large is an allocation problem as the sequence of operations by the machine as each of the job remain unchanged.

Assumptions

While solving the problem following assmptions are made :

1. One machine can process one operation on job at a time
2. Each operation once started must be completed first.
3. Preceeding operation must be completed before the surrounding one.
4. The time taken in transfer of jobs between the machines is negligible.
5. A job is processed as soon as possible subject to the ordering requirement

Priority Sequencing Rules

1. FCFS → First Come first Serve

2. EDD → Early Delivery Date

3. SPT → Shortest Processing Time

4. LS→Least Slack

Slack Time

The difference, between time available up to due date and the operation time required for the job.

e.g.		operation time		
15th Feb.	Job 1	5	2	22nd Feb.
	Job 2	7	6	28th Feb.

Problem on 5 Jobs, 2 Machines

Each of the 5 jobs must go through two machines A and B, in the order A to B. The procesing time in hours are given below. Determine sequence of the 5 jobs that will minimise total lapsed time and also make Gantt chart.

Job *i*	1	2	3	4	5
machine A*i*	5	1*	9	3*	10
machine B*i*	2*	6	7	8	4*

Solution : Find out the minimum time. If this time appears for M/C Ai process that product first and if it appears for M/C Bi process it last by above procedure following sequence is obtained

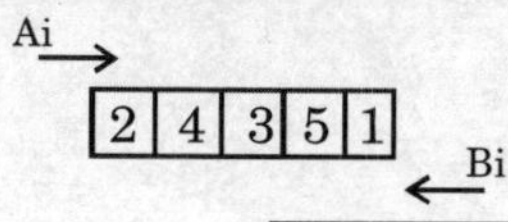

Job	*Machine Ai*		*Machine Bi*		*Ideal time*	
					M/C Ai	M/C Bi
	In	Out	In	Out		
2	0	1	1	7	0	1
4	1	4	7	15	0	0
3	4	13	15	22	0	0
5	13	23	23	27	0	1
1	23	28	28	30	2	1
				Σ	2	3

Total waiting time for M/C A = 2, Total waiting time for M/C B = 3

Total processing time or cycle time = 30 hours

Total utilization of M/C Ai = $\frac{30-2}{30}\times 100$ = 93.3%, Total utilization of M/C B = $\frac{30-3}{30}\times 100$ = 90%

Gantt Chart

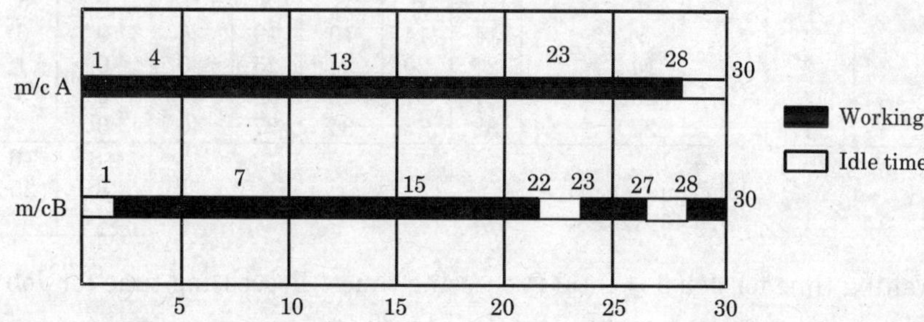

Processing of n Jobs for 3 Machines

Johnson's method can be extended to cover special case where either one or both of the following two condition holds good :

(*i*) Minimum (A*i*) ≥ Maximum (B*i*) (*ii*) Minimum (C*i*) ≥ Maximum (B*i*)

Here, A*i*, B*i* and C*i* are the machine times respectively

For this, the new equation will be

$$Gi = Ai + Bi$$

$$Hi = Bi + Ci$$

For these Johnson's method is applicable.

Example :

i	1	2	3	4	5
Machine A	5	7	6	9	5
Machine B	2	1	4	5	3
Machine C	3	7	5	6	7

From the above matrix, Minimum Ai = 5

Minimum Ci = 3

Maximum Bi = 5

Since Minimum Ai (=5) = Maximum Bi (= 5)

therefore Johnson's method of five jobs and 3 machines can be applied; for which we assume G & H as two fictitions machines such that the processing time for all the 5 on 3 machines is given by

$$Gi = Ai + Bi\ ; \quad Hi = Bi + Ci$$

or processing time matrix becomes

Job i	1	2	3	4	5
machine G, Gi	7	8	10	14	18
machine H, Hi	5*	8	9	11	10

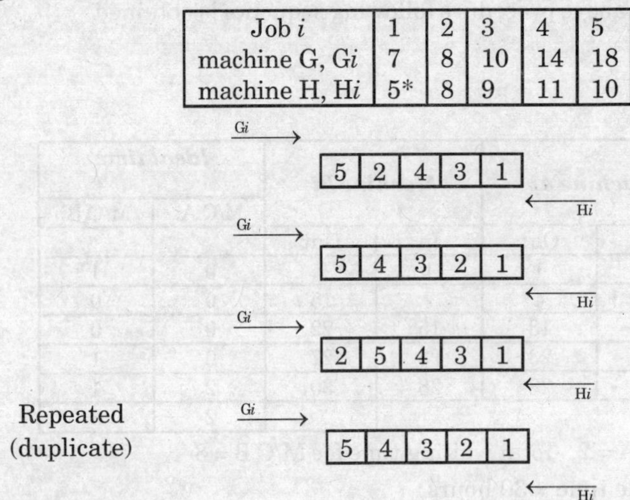

Waiting time Based on TPT = 40 hr	Job No.	Machine A		Machine B		Machine C		Idle Time		
		in	out	in	out	in	out	m/c A	M/c B	M/c C
25	5	0	5	5	8	8	15	0	5	8
20	4	5	14	14	19	19	25	0	6	4
25	3	14	20	20	24	25	30	0	1	0
25	2	20	27	27	28	30	37	0	3	0
30	1	27	32	32	34	37	40	0	4	0
								+8	+6	0
								8	25	12

Idle time for m/c A = 40–32 = 8

Waiting time for Job 5 = Total Processing time – Processing time for Job 5
= 40 – (5 + 3 + 7) = 25

$$\text{Utilization factor for machine A} = \frac{40-8}{40} \times 100\% = 80\%$$

$$\text{Utilization factor for machine B} = \frac{40-25}{40} \times 100\% = 37.59\%$$

$$\text{Utilization factor for machine C} = \frac{40-12}{40} = 100\% = 70\%$$

Material Requirement Planning (MRP)

Purchasing or Procurement

It is defined as computation technique which convert master shedule for end product into detailed shedule for raw material and component required for the end product. The detailed shedule identifies the quantilies of raw material and components required for a specific order of the end product. MRP also provides a guidence as to when matels of the component must be ordered and delivered so has to meet the target of master schedule.

Advantages of MRP

1. Availability of raw materials and components in right quantity at right time.
2. Reduction in inventory.
3. Improve the customes service due to adhearance (or stacking) to shedule
4. Quickes response to change in demand.
5. Better machine utilization and enhance greater production economy.

Material Planning (MP)

It is the process by which materials manage plans to achieve the objective of low price and high inventry turnover, low cost acquision and possession, continuity of supply, consistency of quality and goods supplies relation.

Plan has to be done for highly non-programmed decision such as import policy, foreign exchange availability and credit squeeze (or less availability of find) Planing has to be done for highly programme decision, e.g. working, delivery shedule, inventory for work capital.

Plan is a deliberate concious research used to formulate the design and orderly sequence of actions through which it is expected to attain the objectives. Thus all play involves the anticipation, the future course of events.

Classification of Material Planning

1. Short term material planning : 0 - 1 Year (extended to 2)

2. Medium term material planning : 1 - 3 year

3. Long term material planning : 5 - 25 year

Steps in Planning

1. Awareness of opportunity. **2.** Estabilishing plug objectives **3.** Premising

Plug assumptions **:** Expected environment of the plan of operation forecasting in an important premising.

4. Determining of alternate courses to search and examine various alternate courses of factor and also it reduces the alternatives
5. Evaluating alternative courses
6. Selecting the best course
7. Implementing and review or reporting.

Some Definitions

Mission : The main objective is making profit.

Objective : The ends towards which an activity aims at.

Strategy : It is a plan which oftenly (or frequenly) denotes a general programme of action and deployment of resources to attain a comprehensive objective.

Programme : It constitutes a goal, a policy to procedures, an assignment, steps to be taken, resources to be employed to carry out a human force of action.

Budget : It is a strategy of expected result expressed in numerical term and it all may be reffered to as numbering of progs

Material Planning and Control

Material cost = 64% of the total cost

Material handling cost = 20% of material cost

i.e., 64 = 12.8 = 76.8% of total cost.

Materials means raw materials, component and finished produced.

Materials can be classified into

1. **Direct materials :** Thes go directly into the product.
2. **Indirect materials :** They are used to help in processing and packaging of raw materials. Materials are imporant determinant of the total cost of production and generally occur 20-30% of the total which in certain company as high as 65%.

LEAN MANUFACTURING

Lean Manufacturing is an efficient and fast growing approach in the world of competition. Lean Manufacturing is employed for the incessant removal wastes in the manufacturing to improve the efficiency and productivity.

Introduction

Lean manufacturing is fast growing process to improve the productivity of an industry. The lean manufacturing tools are not limited to industry only but are being used in many areas as shown in Figure. However, the scope is not limited these sectors only, it can be applied from a family to space company.

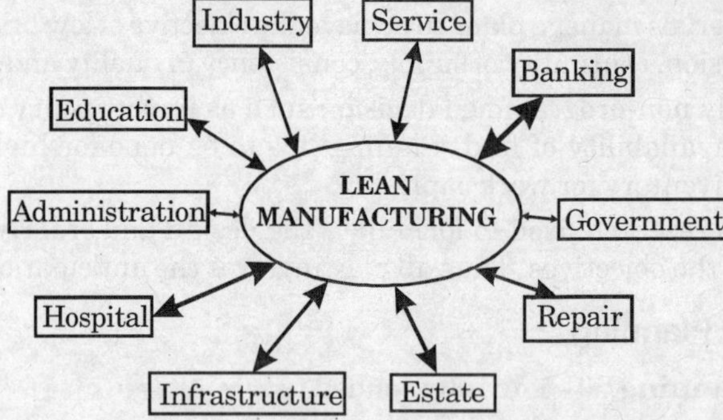

Figure: The main areas to implement Lean manufacturing

Lean Manufacturing is a commerce proposal to reduce waste in manufactured goods. The fundamental plan is to reduce the cost scientifically, throughout the product and fabrication development, by means of a succession of business reviews . The critical insight is that the majority of expenses are assigned when a product is designed. Often an engineer will identify familiar, safe and sound materials and processes rather than cheap, competent ones. This reduces project threat, that is, the cost to the engineer, while increasing economic risks, and decreasing income. Good organizations expand and evaluate checklists to review manufactured goods designs. At the organization engineering rank, requirements are reviewed with advertising, marketing and customer representatives to remove costly supplies. Joint modules may be developed, such as versatile power-supplies or common automatic components or fasteners.

Requirements are assigned to the cheapest regulation. For example, change may be moved into software and measurements away from an emotionless solution to an electronic solution . Another approach is to decide connection or power transfer methods that are inexpensive or that used uniform components that become obtainable in a competitive market . Lean thinking values are emerging as a method to develop the flexibility, dependability, and productivity of enterprises internationally. Lean thinking is being used to decrease setup times, group sizes, and inventories. Lean is all about removing misuse in the project. This comprises waste in time as well as cost. As project have reduced costs and improved class, the primary competitive gauge is the capability to react to the customers. This class presents an impression of lean manufacturing concepts and introduces methods and tools designed to put these concepts to work in a developed environment.

TYPES OF WASTE

The Figure shows the main types of waste in an industry.

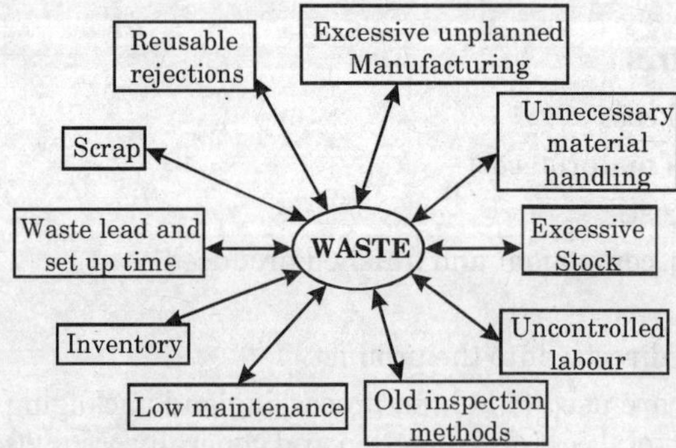

Fig: Types of waste

OBJECTIVES OF THE LEAN MANUFACTURING

The process of going "lean" starts at the attitude level, not at the shop floor level. Hence the first aspect is communication of this system to the members of the organization. The main objectives of lean manufacturing are:

- Develop a lean manufacturing enterprise
- Understand lean manufacturing principles and its benefits
- Apply lean in a production and safe environment

LEAN MANUFACTURING CONCEPTS

- Value
- Value stream
- Waste
- Equipment reliability
- Continuous flow
- Pull production
- Continuous improvement
- People involvement

LEAN MANUFACTURING TOOLS AND METHODS

- Value stream mapping
- Quality at the source
- Workplace organization: 5S
- TPM
- Visual Management
- Set-up reduction
- Batch size reduction (one-piece-flow)
- Cellular manufacturing
- Standardized work
- Work balancing (TAKT-time)
- Production leveling / smoothing
- Point-of-use systems
- Kanban
- Kaizen

FOUR PILLARS OF LEAN MANUFACTURING

- JIT (Just In Time)
- Supply chain Integration
- Cellular manufacturing
- Kaizen

Just in Time(JIT)

The just-In-Time concept requires the raw material for the shop floor at the exact time and not earlier. This leads to a huge fall in the inventory cost. The goal of JIT is achieved by implementing the techniques like.

- Total Productive Maintenance (TPM)
- Standardization
- Kanban

Supply Chain Integration

The "lean" system can be effective only if it is executed all along the production chain, i.e., from the suppliers to the customer's customers. Every link along this chain is affected if a single member does not deliver. This is a long process involving several interfaces. So manufacturers have to take steps towards organizing the supplier base.

Cellular Technology

In traditional manufacturing system the shop floor layout is designed according to the activities. In lean manufacturing it is based on the parts of the product in separate fixed areas. So the layout creates a single peace floor and reduces the order floor time, work in progress, material handling costs and so on.

Kaizen

Kaizen (pronounced ki-zen) is the Japanese word for continuous improvement. As we use the term, it is a method that strives toward perfection by eliminating waste. It eliminates waste by empowering people with tools and a methodology for uncovering improvement opportunities and making change. Kaizen understands waste to be any activity that is not value-adding from the perspective of the customer. By value-adding, we mean any work done right the first time that materially changes a product or service in ways for which a well-informed and reasonable customer is willing to pay. Waste consumes resources— both human and material— pointlessly. People implementing wasteful processes are themselves wasted. They are robbed of the satisfaction of engaging in meaningful tasks that produce outputs customers value. Moreover, they are degraded as humans because engaging in activities that are not meaningful treats their energies and earnest efforts as commodities of little value. When constrained to execute these imperfect processes without the opportunity to make them better, people are denied the exercise of their capacity to learn and improve and thereby grow to the full measure of their capabilities. As for material resources, the financial and material investments in enterprise are prevented from achieving the greatest returns possible.

ADVANTAGES OF LEAN MANUFACTURING

- The inventory levels can be brought down to nearly nil, thus reducing costs.
- Transitions between various designs take only a few minutes.
- This enables an increased flexibility and better response to customer requirements.

Objective Type Questions

1. Production planning consists of
(*a*) preplanning and routing
(*b*) scheduling and dispatching
(*c*) expediting
(*d*) all of these

2. Forecasting provides guide lines on
(*a*) how many of the products produced are likely to be demanded by the customers
(*b*) amount of business, the firm can expect during the planning period
(*c*) materials requirements
(*d*) all of these

3. Forecasting which assumes a static envoronment in the future is
(*a*) passive forecasting
(*b*) active forecasting
(*c*) long term forecasting
(*d*) short term forecasting

4. The function which authorises production as well as control is
(*a*) routing (*b*) scheduling
(*c*) dispatching (*d*) expediting

5. The quality model of forecasting based on the consensus opinion of a panel of experts is called
(*a*) Composite Sales Team Method
(*b*) Exponential Smoothening Method
(*c*) Regression Method
(*d*) Delphi Method

6. Chart which is useful for scheduling and control is
(*a*) Kanban (*b*) Gantt Chart
(*c*) Flow Process chart (*d*) X and R Chart

7. The monitoring and follow up function intended for completion of job within the due date is called
(*a*) scheduling (*b*) expediting
(*c*) routing (*d*) none of these

8. The production planning function refers to the determination of the sequence of operations to be performed for the job and allocation of facilities where these operations are to be performed is called
(*a*) sequencing (*b*) scheduling
(*c*) routing (*d*) dispatching

9. The prime input for aggregate planning is
(*a*) active forecasting (*b*) passive forecasting
(*c*) demand forecasting (*d*) none of these

10. Which of the following statement is correct ?
(*a*) Qualitative models for forecasting are based on subjective opinions and judgements
(*b*) Gantt charts are refined version of travel charts.
(*c*) Forecasting is the prime input for aggregate planning.
(*d*) All of these

11. Sequencing is a subset of
(*a*) routing (*b*) scheduling
(*c*) expediting (*d*) none of these

12. Long range of forecasting is
(*a*) one year or less (*b*) more than 1 years
(*c*) one to three years (*d*) none of these

13. Advantage of Delphi method is that it
(*a*) provides intuitive base for forecasting
(*b*) is useful for long range planning
(*c*) is helpful for development of new products
(*d*) all of these

14. Degree of relationship between two or more variables is expressed by
(*a*) regression (*b*) correlation
(*c*) seasonal index (*d*) none of these

15. Kanban
(*a*) is an information carrying the expression of needs
(*b*) is a simple way of controlling production
(*c*) is a request (card) for production or withdrawal (movement) of parts
(*d*) all of these

16. The preplanning of productions, work force and inventory at the broadest level is
(*a*) regression (*b*) aggregate planning
(*c*) forecasting (*d*) none of these

17. Cost computations for the strategies depends upon
(*a*) strategy applied
(*b*) data available
(*c*) common logic used in computation
(*d*) all of these

18. In linear programming approach, the demand for a particular period can be fullfilled by
(*a*) regular time production
(*b*) over time production
(*c*) sub contract
(*d*) all of these

19. Regression method of forecasting is applicable mainly for

(*a*) Casual models
(*b*) Qualitative forecasting
(*c*) Time-Series models
(*d*) Delphi method

20. Aggregate Planning refers to planning of production

(*a*) at the broadest long term period levels
(*b*) at the short term period levels
(*c*) work force and inventory at the broadest levels
(*d*) work force and inventory at the short term period levels

21. The master schedule

(*a*) is the outcome of the aggregate planning
(*b*) drives the entire production system
(*c*) is a high level schedule that specifies what end products or product modules are to be produced and the time period during which they are to be made
(*d*) all of these

22. Master schedule

(*a*) determines the overall production plan for the near future
(*b*) provides rough time schedule for production of final products
(*c*) refer to the 'end items' or final products
(*d*) all of these

23. Master scheduling considers

(*a*) demand forecasts and pending orders
(*b*) resource availabilities and capacities
(*c*) stock status and inventory informations
(*d*) feed back information on actual shop loads, backlog and leadtimes
(*e*) all of these

24. Determination of the sequence of operatoins to be performed and the allocation of facilities where these operatoins are to be performed is

(*a*) master scheduling (*b*) aggregate planning
(*c*) routing (*d*) forecasting

25. Routing procedure depends upon

(*a*) type of manufacturing-Job. Batch, Mass/Flow production
(*b*) nature of processes involved
(*c*) availability of plant, machineries and facilities
(*d*) characteristics of the plant, machineries and facilities
(*e*) all of these

26. A route sheet may be designed to combine activities such as authority to

(*a*) production
(*b*) material requirements
(*c*) tool orders and move orders
(*d*) all of these

27. A decision making process to determine when a job is to be started in a machine and when it is to be completed, is

(*a*) scheduling (*b*) routing
(*c*) master scheduling (*d*) aggregate planning

28. The order in which different jobs are being taken up in a machine or process is called

(*a*) scheduling
(*b*) sequencing
(*c*) routing
(*d*) aggregate planning

29. In sequencing

(*a*) the tasks belong to the various jobs
(*b*) the tasks are performed on the same facility
(*c*) acts as an aid to determine the scheduling
(*d*) emphasis is on the economic order
(*e*) all of these

30. In routing

(*a*) the various tasks belong to the same job
(*b*) tasks are performed in various facilities
(*c*) acts as a constraint for scheduling
(*d*) emphasis is on the technological order
(*e*) all of these

31. The main difference between flow shop and job shop models in scheduling is that

(*a*) in flow shop there is a continuous flow without idle time for any machine whereas in the job shop the flow is intermittent with idleness enforced on the machine.
(*b*) in flow shop the routing for all jobs through the machines is unidirectional whereas in the Job shop the routing may follow any path.
(*c*) in flow shop all the jobs are processed in a single machine, whereas in job shop, jobs are to be processed in more then one machine.
(*d*) in flow shop the routing for all jobs should be such that to minimise the make span, whereas in the job shop the routing for all jobs should be such that to minimise the mean flow time.

32. Objective of scheduling problem is

(*a*) efficient utilisation of the resources (or facilities)

(*b*) rapid respond to demands

(*c*) conformance to the prescribed dead-lines

(*d*) completion of job at the minimum protracted (total) time

(*e*) all of these

33. Flow of work that is unidirectional in the sense that all jobs require operations and processing in the same order, is called

(*a*) sequencing (*b*) routing

(*c*) scheduling (*d*) flow shop

34. The amount of time measured from the zeroth time, at which the job is due to be completed is

(*a*) completion (*b*) flow time

(*c*) due date (*d*) processing time

35. The time at which the processing of the job in the machine is completed, is

(*a*) completion time (*b*) flow time

(*c*) due tate (*d*) processing time

36. Time taken for the job from its arrival to the system until its departure, is

(*a*) completion time (*b*) flow time

(*c*) due date (*d*) processing time

37. The algebraic difference between the flow time and due date is

(*a*) mean lateness (*b*) job

(*c*) range of lateness (*d*) job tradiness .

38. The lateness of the job, failing to meet the due date is called

(*a*) job lateness (*b*) mean lateness

(*c*) job tardiness (*d*) range of lateness

39. The mean number of jobs in the processing system at a time, is called

(*a*) inprocess inventory

(*b*) mean tardiness

(*c*) mean lateness

(*d*) weighted mean flow time

40. Maximum flow time

(*a*) is the maximum time at which any job stays inthe system

(*b*) is the total protected time

(*c*) is make-span

(*d*) all of these

41. Shortest Processing Time (SPT) sequencing minimises the

(*a*) mean flow time (*b*) inprocess inventory

(*c*) mean lateness (*d*) mean waiting time

(*e*) all of these

42. Short Processing Time (SPT) sequencing of jobs in a single facility would minimise the

(*a*) mean lateness (*b*) maximum tradiness

(*c*) maximum tradiness (*d*) mean tradiness

43. The sequencing of jobs in the ascending order of their processing time, is called

(*a*) shortest processing time

(*b*) earliet due date (EDD)

(*c*) dispatching

(*d*) none of these

44. EDD (Earliest Due Date) sequencing of jobs in a single facility, would

(*a*) minimise the mean lateness

(*b*) minimise the maximum tradiness

(*c*) minimise the maximum tradiness

(*d*) minimise the mean tradiness

45. EDD (Earliest Due Date) sequencing of jobs in a single facility, would

(*a*) minimise the maximum lateness

(*b*) be independent of processing times of the job

(*c*) minimise the maximum tradiness

(*d*) all of these

46. MWKR (Most work Remaining) priority rule in the job shop dynamic system would most often give satisfactory performance for minimising

(*a*) mean tradiness (*b*) mean lateness

(*c*) make span (*d*) flow time

47. Whenever some jobs are found waiting for the operation equal to or greater than maximum allowable waiting time, over-riding priority is given and are dispatched as per

(*a*) FCFS (First Come First Served)

(*b*) SPT

(*c*) LWKR (Least Work Remaining)

(*d*) None of these

48. S/OPN (Slack Per Operations) rule for priority dispatching is useful for reducing

(*a*) number of remaining operations

(*b*) number of tardy jobs

(*c*) make span

(*d*) mean lateness

49. Flow control is adopted for control of

(*a*) production of large volumes of single or a few types of products

(*b*) intermittent production of small quantities of many items

(*c*) ordering raw materials

(*d*) consumption of new materials

50. Order control refers to the individual control exercised over the

(*a*) materials

(*b*) quantity and quality

(*c*) processing details

(*d*) progress of work on each job or lot

(*e*) all of these

51. Which of the following is not related to World Class Manufacturers?

(a) Elimination of wastes

(b) Becoming lean

(c) Imbibing green practices

(d) None of the above

52. Which of the following is not related with lean manufacturing?

(a) High quality of products

(b) Responsiveness

(c) Waste elimination

(d) None of the above

53. Who among the following is responsible for the concept of value added engineering?

(a) F W Taylor (b) Hall

(c) Gilberth (d) Kotler

54. Which of the following is not a type of waste according to Shiego?

(a) Overproduction (b) Waiting

(c) Defects (d) Inspection

55. Shiego classifies waste into .... categories.

(a) 4 (b) 5

(c) 6 (d) 7

56. Which of the following is not correct in respect to Craft Manufacturing?

(a) Unskilled workforce (b) Small enterprises

(c) Small volume (d) None of the above

57. Which of the following is not correct in respect of mass manufacturing ?

(a) Deskilling of workers

(b) Wide scope of work

(c) High volume

(d) None of the above

58. Which of the following is not related with flexible manufacturing systems?

(a) Ability to produce varied quantities

(b) Ability to produce wide variety

(c) Using special purpose machines

(d) None of the above

59. Satisfying varying Customer demand is considered as an important element in

(a) Agile Manufacturing

(b) Lean Manufacturing

(c) Both (a) and (b)

(d) None of the above

60. Which of the following is correct?

(a) Lean and agile manufacturing is all about improving internal systems.

(b) Agile manufacturing creates a balance between customer demands and internal systems.

(c) Lean and agile manufacturing both are customer centric approaches.

(d) Lean manufacturing is focused on internal systems to reduce waste.

61. ISO 50001 is for

(a) Environmental Management System

(b) Social Management System

(c) Economic Management System

(d) Energy Management System

62. How much amount of waste generated from operation is reused ,recycled or converted to energy is called landfill free

(a) Atleast 60% (b) Atleast 90%

(c) Atleast 95% (d) Atleast 80%

63. FMS is best suited when

(a) All products use same family of components

(b) All products use different family of components

(c) Number of component is low

(d) Number of components is high

64. Which of the following is not the phase of benchmarking

(a) Integration (b) Action

(c) Maturity (d) None of the these

65. Factors for success of benchmarking

(a) Benchmarking should be Individual activity

(b) Active involvement of lower management in the process of benchmarking

(c) Benchmarking is an Ongoing process

(d) None of the above

Answers

1. (*d*) **2.** (*d*) **3.** (*a*) **4.** (*b*) **5.** (*d*) **6.** (*b*) **7.** (*b*) **8.** (*c*) **9.** (*c*) **10.** (*a*)

11. (*b*) **12.** (*b*) **13.** (*d*) **14.** (*b*) **15.** (*d*) **16.** (*b*) **17.** (*d*) **18.** (*d*) **19.** (*a*) **20.** (*c*)

21. (*d*) **22.** (*d*) **23.** (*e*) **24.** (*c*) **25.** (*e*) **26.** (*d*) **27.** (*a*) **28.** (*b*) **29.** (*e*) **30.** (*e*)

31. (*b*) **32.** (*e*) **33.** (*d*) **34.** (*c*) **35.** (*a*) **36.** (*b*) **37.** (*b*) **38.** (*c*) **39.** (*a*) **40.** (*d*)

41. (*e*) **42.** (*a*) **43.** (*a*) **44.** (*c*) **45.** (*d*) **46.** (*c*) **47.** (*a*) **48.** (*b*) **49.** (*a*) **50.** (*e*)

51. (*d*) **52.** (*d*) **53.** (*b*) **54.** (*d*) **55.** (*d*) **56.** (*a*) **57.** (*a*) **58.** (*c*) **59.** (*a*) **60.** (*d*)

61. (*d*) **62.** (*b*) **63.** (*b*) **64.** (*d*) **65.** (*d*)

Explanations

53. Hall's Frameworks to Value Added Engineering

- Propogated by Hall in 1987
- Manufacturing excellence attained by value added manufacturing based on the principle.
- Eliminate anything that does not add value to the product or service
- Material, equipment, space, time, energy systems or human activity of any sort.
- Already suggested by shigeo as 7 wastes in manufacturing

54. Wastge Type:

- Waste of overproduction
- Waste of waiting
- Waste of transportation
- Waste of processing itself
- Waste of stocks
- Waste of motion
- Waste of making defective parts

59. Agile manufacturing is a method for manufacturing which combine our organization, people and technology into an integrated and coordinated whole.

60. Lean manufacturing, or lean production, is a production method derived from Toyota's 1930 operating model "The Toyota Way" (Toyota Production System, TPS). The term "Lean" was coined in 1988 by John Krafcik, and defined in 1996 by James Womack and Daniel Jones to consist of five key principles; 'Precisely specify value by specific product, identify the value stream for each product, make value flow without interruptions, let customer pull value from the producer, and pursue perfection.

61. ***ISO 50001*** is based on the management system model of continual improvement also used for other well-known standards such as ***ISO*** 9001 or ***ISO 14001***. This makes it easier for organizations to integrate energy management into their overall efforts to improve quality and environmental management.

63. FMS is best suited when **all products use different family of components**

6

CHAPTER

Automobile Engineering

ENGINE OPERATION

In I.C. engine, combustion of fuel takes place inside the engine cylinder, while in steam engine, combustion of the fuel takes place outside the engine cylinder.

Four-Stroke cycle engine

Strokes of a four-stroke cycle engine are .

1. Suction stroke
2. Compression stroke
3. Power stroke
4. Exhaust stroke

Valve timing diagram. The exact moment at which each of the valves opens and closes with reference to position of piston and crank can be shown graphically in a diagram, called valve timing diagram.

In theoretical valve timing diagram, valves open exactly at the beginning of the stroke and close exactly at the end of the stroke. In actual valve timing diagram, valves open some degree before the beginning of the stroke and remain open some degree after the end of the stroke.

Inlet valve : It opens before the beginning of the stroke so that fresh charge may enter the cylinder completely.

Exhaust valve : It remains open after the end of the stroke so that exhaust gases may leave the cylinder completely.

***p-v* diagram of a four stroke cycle engine :** It represents the variation of pressure and volume of the engine during every stroke of the piston.

Two-stroke Cycle Engine

Strokes of a two-stroke cycle engine are

1. Upward stroke
2. Downsard stroke

Two-stroke cycle engine gives one working stroke for each revolution of the crankshaft. Four-stroke cycle engine gives one working stroke for every two revolutions of the crankshaft. Hence, theoretically power developed by two-stroke cycle engine is twice that developed by four-stroke cycle engine for the same engine speed and cylinder volume.

In diesel engine diesel is fed into the cylinder by a fuel injector and is mixed with air inside the cylinder.

In *petrol engine*, air and petrol are mixed in the carburettor before they enter the cylinder.

ENGINE CONSTRUCTION

Cylinder block

It is the largest single part in the engine.

Monoblock cylinder : It is a cylinder block in which the crank case is cast integrally.

A single cylinder engine needs a heavy fly wheel for uniform rotation of the crank-shaft. This is not possible in the case of portable engines.

Cylinder Wall Distortion

When a cylinder wall has become scored, it is better to regrind the cylinder wall and fit a new piston.

Cylinder wall distortion occurs because of

1. improper engine block or cylinder head design
2. improper alignment or unequal tightening of cylinder head bolts adjacent to the cylinder

Distortion of engine block : It is due to internal stresses causing warpage, incorrect placing of masses around the cylinder, warpage of head, bore in several directions.

Repairing of scored cylinders : It can be repaired by

1. insertion of cylinder sleeve
2. cutting a deep groove in the cylinder wall to remove the score

Cylinder head: It is cast as a separate piece for easy removal, for cleaning and ginding valves, to provide provision conveniently for spark plug, injector, for flow of water, etc.

Gaskets : These are used to make a good seal, to provide a tight joint between the cylinder block and head to withstand heat and pressure losses.

Piston

1. It transmit forces of explosion to the crank shaft through a connecting rod
2. It act as a guide for the upper end of the connecting rod
3. It serves as a carrier for piston rings

Side opposite to the crank throw is the thrust side as it is driven down on the power stroke.

Close-grained cast iron and some aluminium alloys are used in piston construction.

Piston skirt : It is that portion of the piston which extends below the piston pin and serves as a guide for the piston and connecting rod. It also distribute lubricating oil to the piston and cylinder wall.

Piston scoring : It refers to grooves in the cylinder wall or piston or in both. It is caused by the piston scraping the cylinder wall in its movement without proper lubrication.

It is caused by lack of proper lubrication, overheating of the piston and lowering of the temperature of the cylinder wall by an increased quantity of cold circulating water.

Piston seizure : It refers to binding of the piston and the cylinder wall, as a result of lubrication having been destroyed by excessive temperature and friction.

Sudden seizure or stoppage of a piston may break the connecting rod bolts, or twist the crankshaft, score the cylinder wall and piston and result in extensive and costly repairs.

Cooling of Piston

Pistons are cooled by circulating lubricating oil or cooling water through the cavities or spaces in the piston.

Positioning of Piston

Piston pin can be positioned with

1. Pin anchored in piston with bush on its small end
2. Pin clamped in rod
3. Pins made to be fully floating in connecting rod and secured by locking rings

Piston pins: These are made hollow to reduce the inertia load due to reciprocating parts.

Heat dam. It is a narrow cut into the piston above the top ring. It reduces amount of heat reaching the top ring

Piston top : It is dished or hollowed to provide a great combustion space and more logical surface for the fuel gases to act upon. Top of the piston is designed to compress the air closer to the fuel oil spray.

Blow by : It is the escape of an unburnt air-fuel mixture and burnt gases from the combustion number, past the pistons and into the crank case or in other words the gas blown by the pistons.

Piston Squish

In some combustion chambers, piston squishes or squeezes some part of the mixture at the end of the compression stroke. This squeezing of the mixture is called piston squish.

Because aluminium alloy is of lower strength then cast iron, thicker sections have to be used.

T slot : It enables the cold clearance between skirt and the cylinder bore, to be reduced without the risk of seizure when hot.

When engine rating is increased, head of the T exercises an influence over thermal flow as well as resilience of the skirt under radial compressive forces, therefore T-shape is provided.

Oil rings : These scrap out the extra oil deposited as film on the cylinder liner and send it back to sump leaving a thin film for lubrication purpose.

In square engines with lower hood lines, it is necessary to shorten piston and reduce the number of rings, so only one oil ring is made use of.

Compression rings : These prevent leakage of high pressure gas from blowing into the crank case. They act as a seal between piston and the cylinder wall.

Pressure difference between combustion chamber and the crank case would be about 7 kPa, hence it would be difficult for a single compression ring to hold this pressure. Therefore, two compression rings are used to reduce the pressure on each one.

Note:

Six rings are provided on each piston in diesel engines. The four top rings are conventional compression rings while the ring immediately above the wrist pin and the one in the piston skirt are oil control rings.

Gap between ends of the piston ring should be about 0.05 mm per cm of cylinder diameter.

Piston ring expander : It is a device used for piston ring removal. It is a device used to compress the rings into the piston ring grooves.

Oil scraper rings : These are fitted the scraping action to occurs on the down stroke of the piston.

Piston ring joints for :' These are staggered to prevent compression from having a direct path to leak by the piston skirt.

Piston slap : It is a muffled, hollow bell like noise due to rocking of the piston in the cylinder.

Piston slap : It is caused by inadequate oil, worn out cylinder walls, worn out piston, collapsed piston skirts, excessive piston clearance or misaligned connecting rod.

Rock of the Pistion

In certain directions of crank shaft movement paractically there is no movement of the piston. Travel in this region is called 'rock' of the piston.

Connecting rod : It is usually made of drop-forged, heat-treated carbon steel forged to an I-section with a closed hub at the upper end and an internal cap at the lower end.

When connecting rod end is too large, it is removed by

(*i*) Removable cylinder sleeves

(*ii*) Splitting of the connecting rod

(*iii*) Removing the connecting rod cap at an angle and pulling the piston up

Piston and connecting rod can be removed by

(*i*) Drawing piston and rod downwards if the piston clears the crank

(*ii*) drawing upwards if the rod passes through the cylinder,

(*iii*) pushing the rod upwards, removing the piston, and then pulling the rod downwards

Crankshafts : These are single-piece high carbon steel drop-forgings which have been carefully machined and heat treated.

Various forces acting on a crankshaft are

Centrigugal forces, inertia forces due to reciprocating masses, and connecting rods etc. and twisting and shear forces due to change of direction of inertia loads.

Crankshaft wear may be due to

(*i*) Different loadings at some points of rotation

(*ii*) Additional load being imposed by the action of centrifugal forces resulting from rotation of crankshaft,

(*iii*) Bent connecting rod or misalignment in the connecting rod

(*iv*) Twisting of the engine crank case or any excessive vibrations.

Main causes of crankshaft vibration are

(*i*) unbalanced weight of the reciprocating and rotating parts

(*ii*) cyclic variation of inertia forces of reciprocating parts

(*iii*) cyclic variation of gas and combustion products

(*iv*) variation in torque

Torsional vibration damper : It is a disc attached to the same end of the crankshaft to smoothen out vibrations set up in the crankshaft and proper impulses that tend to twist a shaft.

Crankshaft has to be kept from moving back and forth, to maintain as such, one of the main bearings is designed to be a thrust bearing.

Crank case ventilation : It is provided to reduce dilution due to the presence of water particles, sludge and blow-by gases.

Positive crank case ventilation system is a closed system for removing dilution from the oil in the crank case. It does not pollute the atmosphere.

Crank case (usually upper half) : It is the base for the engine.

It provides cover for the crank shaft, cam shaft and brackets for supports. This is integral with the cylinder block.

Oil pan : It is the lower part. Mostly this is a separate unit bolted to lower flange of the main casing. It is a reservoir for storing, cooling and replenishing of lubricating oil.

Cam shaft : It controls opening and closing of the valve by means of cams. It also carries eccentric drive for fuel pump gears, oil pump and ignition distributor.

Cam shaft rotates with half the speed of the Crankshaft, in a four-stroke engine.

Valve clearance : It is provide to compensate for any expansion of valve stem due to heat.

Valve clearance provided, while adjusting the valve gear is called "Valve lash".

When clearance between valve stem and guide is more then it causes,

(*i*) Excessive fuel consumption.

(*ii*) Engine deposits

(*iii*) Pre-ignition

(*iv*) Clogged piston ring

(*v*) Fould spark plug

(*vi*) Burnt or damaged valve seat

Note :

Exhaust valve is given more clearance as it is operated in hot conditions.

Too much valve clearance affects the timing of the valves as well as the smooth operation of the engine, and also produces noise.

Valve Pocketing

Due to pocketing only less space for the exhaust of waste gases is available, thus exhaust gases will not escape fully causing pre-ignition for the fresh charge. It may be corrected either by grinding seat shoulder on head or firing an insert in valve seat.

Valve sticking : It may be due to

(*i*) Clearance between valve and guide

(*ii*) Bent value stem

(*iii*) Worn out valve guide

Reasons for less compression pressure:

(*i*) Small tappet clearance

(*ii*) Bent valves

(*iii*) Distorted valve seats

(*iv*) Weak piston rings

Combustion chamber : It is the space into which atomised fuel is sprayed, injected and ignited by high temperature of the compressed air.

Different shapes used in the design of combustion chamber are *hemispherical* and *wedge* type.

Types of combustion chambers :

1. Direct injection or open chamber
2. Swirl or separate turbulent chamber
3. Feed or pre-chamber
4. Air-cell or expansion chamber.

Precobustion chamber : It is a small separate chamber directly connected with the cylinder through a restricted duct into which the fuel oil is injected before it reaches the main power cylinder.

Intake manifold : In a petrol engine is to connect the carburettor to the intake parts of the engine.

Heat is applied to it to ensure satisfactory vaporization and distribution of fuels.

Hot spot : It is a junction of the inlet and exhaust pipes, so that better vaporization of the fuel is obtained.

Conformability : It is the bearing's ability to mate successfully with the crankshaft and block surface.

Plastigage : It is wax that is crushed between a bearing and a journal to determine the oil clearance.

Dwell angle: It is the angle of cam rotation from the instant the contact points are closed until they open again.

It is adjusted by loosening a locking screw and turning an eccentric.

Compensationg cam : It is a special attachment operating a special spring loaded tappet to compensate the fluctuations of the torque impulses on the main cam, due to sudden reversals of torque and torsional whip.

Auxiliaries requiring drive from the cam shaft

Oil pump, dynamo, valve gear, ignition distributor or diesel injection pump.

VALVES

If valves springs are not squared on each end, they will have a tendency to pull the valve stem to one side and cause undue wear on the valve stem and guide.

Valve stem etching is due to corrosive vapours, improper ventilation, exposure to steam or moisture containing acids.

Valve clearance : It refers to the gap between the valve stem and the tappet or between the stem and the rocker arm.

A rocker arm transmits motion from the push rod to the valve stem.

Valve Overlap

To assist in removing the exhaust gases from the cylinder, inlet and exhaust valves remain opened together for period of time. This period is called valve overlap.

Valve seat recession : It is the gradual wearing of the valve seat so that it recedes away from the combustion chamber. This decreases valve clearance.

Interference Angle

Valve is faced at angle $\frac{1}{4}$ to one degree flatter than that of the seat angle. This is called interference angle. It produces greater pressure at the outer edge of a valve seat. This arrangement cuts away any deposit that may have formed and establishes a seal.

Burning of valve

When there is no sufficient clearance between cam lobe heel and lifter, the valve will not be able to close all the way. If the valve remains partially open, combustion gases will gradually burn the valve away. This is meant by a burn valve.

Hydraulic lifter: It is a lifter with interal passages with a check valve to pass engine oil and to maintain valve clearance automatically without allowing the valve to open.

Bearing Spread

Shell diameter is made to be slightly greater than diameter of the connecting rod bore into which the shell fits in. This is called bearing spread.

Bearing clearance

Insufficienty bearing clearance reduces oil supply to cylinder walls, causing damage to piston rings and cylinder walls.

Excessive bearing clearance results in excess oil being supplied to the cylinder wall, leading to high oil consumption.

Excessive clearance existing at some point such as in connecting rod bearing, main bearing and cam shaft bearing, are the main causes of low oil pressure in bearings.

Fly wheel : It is an energy reservoir to assist the engine to idle smoothly when the power is not being produced, and also the minimize the fluctuation of mean speed.

It stores excess energy in power stroke, and helps back in compression stroke, maintaining uniform speed.

ENGINE BALANCING

Rotating parts of an engine can be balanced mechanically by bringing them into static and dynamic balance.

Main rotating parts to balanced mechanically

(*i*) Crankshaft

(*ii*) Flywheel

FIRING ORDER

Sequence is which the power impulses occur in an engine is called *firing order.*

Firing order of four-cylinder engine is

1 – 2 – 4 – 3 or 1 – 3 – 4 – 2

Firing order of six-cylinder engine is

1 – 4 – 2 – 6 – 3 – 5 or 1 – 5 – 3 – 6 – 2 – 4

FILTER

Types of air cleaners used in an engine

(*i*) Dry-fabric element air cleaners

(*ii*) Oil wetter wire woven element air cleaners,

(*iii*) Oil bath element air cleaners

Air passes for being cleaned in

(*i*) dry type through specially treated paper

(*ii*) oil saturated type through an oil saturated filter element

(*iii*) oil bath type downwards through an oil bath carrying oil through a filter element

Fuel filter : It is a part of the fuel pump fitted to prevent dirt in fuel, from entering pump of the carburettor.

Canister oil filter : It uses a replaceable filter element inside a permanent metal canister. This has a reusable steel shell with a replaceable cartridge or element inside.

Air Lock : Air trapped in the pipe line which prevents the flow of fuel is called air lock.

CARBURETTOR

Gravity feed system

Gravity feeding is not suitable for cars and other heavy vehicles as it is difficult to place the fuel tank at a level higher than that of the carburettor.

Types of carburettors

Constant choke carburettor : It is a type in which the orifice area is constant and the pressure difference or depression is varied.

Constant vacuum carburettor : It is a type in which the area of the orifice is varied to meet the changing demands, the depression being kept constant.

Practical types of carburettors

1. Horizontal draft

2. updraft

Down draft : In this gravity assists spraying of fuel and in filling the cylinder engine accessibility is improved.

Carburettor venturi: It is a miniature taper bore to increase the air velocity and create partial vacuum causing suction of petrol from the float chamber.

Carburettor jet : It is a very small hollow plug having a number of holes to spray a metered quantity of fuel. Fuel consumption can be reduced by using a jet of small size.

CHOKED JET

It is a valve controlling the amount of air passing to the carburettor and is used when starting a cold engine. It is also called as the *strangler.*

It can be cleaned by blowing air through it in the reverse direction of the petrol flow.

The choke tube its a small tube around the jet to increase the speed of air for effective atomisation of fuel.

Float chamber : It is fitted in a carburettor to maintain and control the supply of fuel.

Compensation : It is the proportioning of the amount of petrol to the air, so that engine always receives a suitable mixture. It is necessary because as speed of the air past the jet increases, petrol flows at an even greater rate, (i.e. as square of the air flow).

Engine missing : *It may be due to*

(*i*) dust particle in petrol

(*ii*) choked filter

(*iii*) improperly adjusted ball in the float

(*iv*) presence of water in petrol

Flooding of carburettor : It means engine cylinders receive raw or liquid gasoline, or too rich a mixture.

Air bleed : It is used to avoid too

(*i*) lean a mixture on low vacuum

(*ii*) rich a mixture on high vacuum

Economiser : It is an air bleed fitted with a needle valve so that the amount of air entering the nozzle can be varied to suit running conditions.

Higher fuel consumption : It is due to

(*i*) fuel leakage

(*ii*) damaged gasket incorporated

(*iii*) improper use of manual choke

(*iv*) puncture in float

(*v*) improper jet needle

(*vi*) under inflation of types

Slow running : It can be adjusted by a stop usually fitted to the throttle arm which can be screwed in or out by altering the quantity of mixture passing to the engine.

Slow running adjustment is made by means of

1. a stop screw controlling the opening of the throttle
2. an adjustable air screw which weakens the mixture when it is unscrewed.

Uneven running : It is due to high rich content of a slow running mixture called *'hunting'* Adjustment of the mixture control knob or screw to a weaker point reduce the trouble.

Limitations of a Conventional Carburettor

1. Volumetric efficiency is limited due to restriction of the air flow by the choke
2. Mixture distribution is uneven in multi-cylinder
3. Fuel deposits on the valves of the induction manifold

FUEL INJECTION

Fuel-injection pump.

It is to supply the engine with fuel in quantities exactly metered in proportion to the amount of power required and timed for smooth running with maximum economy.

Methods of fuel injection.

1. **Air injection :** The use of compressed air which forces a definite amount of fuel, mixed with the air, into the cylinder is called air-injection.
2. **Mechanical injection**
3. **Solid fuel injection.**

Components of fuel injection system:

1. Injection pump
2. Filters
3. Injectors.

Type of fuel-injection system

1. Common rail system
2. Gas compression pump system
3. Jerk pump system
4. Distributor pump system

Unit injector

It is a small high pressure pump and spray nozzle for an individual cylinder.

Advantages

(*i*) It is a single unit with simple design

(*ii*) Can be used for many different engines over a wide range of power outputs

(*iii*) Removal and replacement does not entail retiming

(*iv*) Servicing is simple

Types of diesel injectors

1. Single-hole
2. Multi-hole
3. Long-stem
4. Pintle
5. Pintaux types.

Normal faults found in a fuel injectors

(*i*) Incorrect operating pressure

(*ii*) Distorted spray form

(*iii*) Dripping injector

(*iv*) Cracked injector body

(*v*) Broken injector-valve compression spring

(*vi*) Injector valve stricking in its guide

Causes of high injector pressure and their remedies

1. Compression-spring adjusting screw shifted : Adjust screw to the correct pressure
2. Injector valve seized up, and corroded : Renew injector valve and body

3. Injector valve seized up, dirty, and sticky: Clean the injector

4. Injector openings clogged with dirt : Clean the injector.

Misfiring

Fuel entry and firing can be verified by the temperature reading of the exhaust by training the ear to detect differences in sounds of the various cylinders and by feeling the water jackets around the cylinders. A cold water jacket indicate that the cylinder is misfiring.

Misfiring may be due to

(*i*) one or more nozzles not spraying correctly

(*ii*) fuel not reaching the nozzles owing to choked filter, or an air lock in the delivery pipe

EXHAUST SYSTEM

Exhaust emissions

(*i*) Hydrocarbon (HC)

(*ii*) Carbon monoxide (CO)

(*iii*) Nitrogen dioxide (NO_2).

White smoke may be due to

(*i*) Plugged fuel valves

(*ii*) Excessive fuel pressure

(*iii*) Improper setting of fuel valves

(*iv*) Too much lubricating oil

(*v*) Water in cylinders and exhaust

Causes of Black smoky exhaust at slow speeds

(*i*) Too light fuel or low density fuel

(*ii*) Over load

(*iii*) Plugged spray nozzle valves

(*iv*) Very high fuel pressure

Systems of air flow scavenging

Commonly used systems for two-stroke engine are

1. Cross-scavenging
2. Loop scavenging
3. Uniflow scavenging

Exhaust Gas Recirculation (E.G.R)

When combustion temperature is high, nitrogen oxide is formed. E.G.R. is provided to reduce NO_x.

Catalytic converter

It is a muffler like container provided in the exhaust system that is filled with catalyst. The catalyst converts the pollutants into harmless gases.

Cleaning of exhaust gases

Exhaust gas is cleaned by

1. controlling air fuel mixture
2. controlling combustion
3. blowing fresh air using a catalytic converter

Thermactor system

The injection system which provides additional oxygen by blowing fresh air into the exhaust manifold to burn HC and CO is called *Thermactor system*.

Mufflers : These are attached to exhaust manifold through a pipeline, which reduces pressure of the exhaust gas and discharges it into the atmospher with a minimum power loss, less noise, less vibration and transfer to heat.

COOLING SYSTEM

Water Cooled Systems

Advantages :

(*i*) Quick transfer of heat

(*ii*) Less engine sound

(*iii*) Easier method to control temperature

Disadvantages

(*i*) Increase in weight of the vehicle

(*ii*) Corrosion of metal part

(*iii*) Freezing difficulties in cold weather

Air Cooled Engine

Rapid warm up is the distinct feature in an air cooled engine. Also, there is no water jacket or radiator. The rapid warm up is useful in avoiding sludge and crank case dilution.

Air cooled engines makes more noise because

(*i*) there is no silencing provided as in water jackets

(*ii*) forced air circulation is provided by a fan driven by a belt drive from the engine crankshaft

(*iii*) air velocity is more than that of water in the cooling system

Wet liner : It is a liner in which outer surface has direct contact with cooling water, fitted as slip fit.

Dry liner : It is a lining in which conduction of heat takes place through the cylinder walls through the water in the water jacket, fitted as pressed fit in the block.

Thermo-syshon system : In this hot water in the cylinder jacket rises up the pipe and flows up the radiator due to light weight and cooled water from bottom of the radiator flows through the bottom pipe into the cylinder jacket due to its heavy weight, thus regulation flow of water.

Radiator : It is a very effective form of cooling surface in which heat is absorbed and transmitted by the circulating water.

Function of the radiator : To cool down circulated water in the water jacket.

Pressure cap : It is a seal in the radiator that maintains selected pressure in the cooling system, when the engine is hot.

Functions of a pressure cap :

(*i*) Prevents coolant loss
(*ii*) Prevents entry of impurities in to the cooling system
(*iii*) Eliminates the vacuum, that occurs during cool down
(*iv*) Maintains constant cooling system pressure

LUBRICATION SYSTEM

Methods of oil lubrication to the engine parts

1. Splash lubrication
2. Pressure lubrication
3. Pressure and splash lubrication

Lead in the fuel acts as a lubricant.

For connecting rod bearing lubrication, the lubricant is forced by a centrifugal force through holes drilled in the cap.

CLUTCH

Clutch disconnects engine from the transmission, enables the drive to be taken up smoothly and faciliates gear changing.

Requirements of good quality clutch

(*i*) Should pick up load without any noise
(*ii*) Should have capacity to damp out vibrations
(*iii*) Should need least pedal pressure to function

Multiplate clutch : It is used to transmit more power by providing more contact area in a compact package.

Wet clutch : It runs in oil in which the plates are lined with cork.

Dog and spline clutches : These can be engaged only when both sets of teeth match perfectly so this is preferred in synchronized mechanism.

Clutch plates : These are perforated to dissipate large amount of heat produced due to friction.

Clutch drag : If clutch is not disengaging fully and provides some difficulty in changing gears, then this defect is called clutch drag.

Coil springs : These under slight compression are fitted to provide a flexible torsional connection between center hub flange and side plates. Also with these desired load deflection pattern is also possible.

Bellivelle Spring : In a pressure plate, sometimes multiple coil springs are replaced by a single flat spring which works like the bottom of an oil can. This is called *Belliville spring*.

Clutch Slippage

Any increase in engine speed at the same vehicle speed is called slippage of clutch.

Clutch slippage may be due to

(*i*) incorrectly adjusted linkage and levers
(*ii*) worn out friction disc
(*iii*) weak pressure plate
(*iv*) oil or grease on the plate
(*v*) broken return spring

If clutch slips, when rounding a corner, undue wear of the clutch linings results, and there is also a greater strain on the engine and transmission.

If clutch slip occurs, free movement of the clutch pedal is to be checked (normally 25 mm).

TRANSMISSION

Gear box : It is required to regulate both power output and speed range of the engine relative to the vehicle speeds.

It allows the engine to run at different speeds relative to the road wheels, so as to maintain its power and regulate the torque.

Types of gear boxes :

1. Sliding mesh gear box
2. Constant mesh gear box
3. Synchro mesh gear box
4. Planetary gear box

Helical gears are preferred because

(i) it is easier to distribute the load among two or more teeth simultaneously
(*ii*) these can be made lighter and to function at highest speeds without any vibration
(*iii*) their operation is silent and smooth

Sliding mesh type gear : Gears that are changed by moving the pinions along the mainshaft, to mesh with those on the lay shaft are called sliding mesh type of gear.

Sliding mesh gear box is mostly not preferred because

(*i*) more force is required to engage the gears

(*ii*) more noise is made while changing

Synchromesh gear box:

It is first brought into frictional contact with that member which is ultimately to be engaged positively and then friction and speed are equalised to make positive contact.

In synchromesh type, speeds of the gears are synchronized by first engaging conical surfaces before the gears themselves are brought into mesh.

In synchronising mechanism, sliding dog clutches of constant mesh gear boxes are provided with friction cones, unlike constant mesh.

Advantages:

(*i*) Noise and jerk are eliminated

(*ii*) Smooth meshing is possible

(*iii*) Double declutching is not needed

Note:

Speed of both driving and driven shafts is synchronized before they are clutched together through the train of gears.

Epicyclic gear box

Advantages:

(*i*) Instead of having the load only on a pair of gears, it is distributed over several gear wheels.

(*ii*) Due to distribution of loads, a greater area of gear tooth contact can be used.

Gear Shift

Causes of hard gear shifting are

(*i*) clutch not getting fully released

(*ii*) excessive clutch pedal free play

(*iii*) gear shift linkage being out of adjustment

(*iv*) bent shifting fork

(*v*) poor lubrication in linkage

Slipping of gears

It occurs due to

(*i*) a weak selector rod

(*ii*) too much play in the shifting mechanism

OVERDRIVE

It is a device interposed between transmission and propeller shaft to permit the propeller shaft to run faster than, or overdrive the transmission main shaft.

Causes of overdrive

(*i*) Slipping overrunning clutch

(*ii*) Broken planetary parts

These may be due to wron gears, worn main shaft bearing and worn overruning clutch parts.

FLUID DRIVE

It is a liquid coupling to transmit turning effort from the engine to the clutch. it is located between crank shaft and clutch

The transmission that functions purely automatically without any attention from the driver is known as automatic transmission.

Two advantages of automatic transmission

1. Simple driving control
2. Reduced fuel consumption

A torque converter is a device which performs a function similar to that of a gear box.

Automatic transmission is preferred because

1. of reduced drive line maintenance and increased passenger comfort and safety,
2. the driver has other controls also to operate while driving the vehicle
3. the vehicle is in move even in heavy crowds.

PROPELLER SHAFT AND FINAL DRIVE

Universal Joint

Joint which permit power to be transmitted from one shaft to another which are not in alignment, is called universal joint.

Types of universal joints:

1. Cross type universal joint
2. Ball and trunion universal joint
3. Constant velocity type universal joint

A joint which does not allow variation in angular velocity occurring in each revolution is called constant velocity universal joint.

Advantage of the constant velocity universal joint is the eliminates transmitted speed fluctuations.

To avoid fluctuations of speed or to get uniform motion constant velocity joint is used.

Construction of universal joint consists of a double hinged joint with two Y-shaped yokes and a cross member called spider.

Transmission of power from Engine to Wheels

Methods generally used are

1. Direct coupling
2. Chain drive
3. Propeller shaft drive
4. Belt drive

Propeller shaft : It is provided

(*i*) cope with and maintain the distance between the gear box and differential

(*ii*) adjust with the varied length and angle

Types of propeller shafts

1. Open type
2. Enclosed type or torque tube

Hotchkiss drive :

It is an open propeller shaft, in which torque reaction is taken by the springs

Hotchkiss and torque tube drive is provided to absorb rear end torque

A joint comprising an external splined end and an internal splines of the joint integral with the universal joint hub is called as **slip joint.**

A slip joint lengthens or shortens the drive shaft : It is used to compensate for the axial movement of the propeller shaft during up and down motion of the rear axle.

Final drive : It turns the power flow at right angles from the propeller shaft to the rear axle and provides a mechanical advantage to the rear axle.

Final drive is used

(*i*) to turn the power flow at right angle from the propeller shaft to the rear axle.

(*ii*) to provide a mechanical advantage from propeller shaft to the rear axle.

Final drive is the final stage in transmitting power from the engine to the road wheels. It provides final speed reduction between the propeller shaft and that of the wheels.

Various Gear type final drive are

1. Worm and wheel type 2. Spur bevel gear type
3. Spiral bevel gear type 4. Hypoid type

DIFFERENTIAL AND REAR AXLE

Differential : It is the mechanism housed in the drive axle, which drives the outer wheel faster than the inner one while taking a turn.

Function of a differential mechanism

(*i*) To keep both the rear wheels at the same speed in straight travel

(*ii*) To make the outer rear wheel to rotate faster than the inner one during a turn.

If differential is not used, the vehical cannot be controlled during a turn, the wheels will skid and tyres may wear-off quickly.

Axle : It is a steel shaft which support weight of the vehicle and transmit torque from differential to the drive wheels.

Two types of axles

1. **Dead axle :** It is a solid axle mounted to the springs with a spindle at each end upon which the wheels turn.
2. **Live axle :** It turns within a tubular housing.

   Dead axle only supports the wheel but does not transmit power, while a live axle apart from supporting the wheels also transmits torque to the rear wheels

Front axle

Live axle is in front in military vehicle and jeeps.

Front axle

(*i*) bears front weight of the vehicle

(*ii*) turns front wheel easily

(*iii*) provides cushioning effect through a spring

The up and down movement of the front wheel in case of a rigid axle affects camber of the opposite wheel causing difficult turning of the vehicle.

Rear axles

In two by two arrangement, power is not transmitted through rear wheels like dead axle drive in heavy vehicles.

In this arrangement, power is not transmitted directly from the engine to the front axle, but through wheels like dead axle drive in heavy vehicles.

In this arrangement, the front axle receives power directly from the engine like live axles in jeeps.

Type of real axle

1. Heavy vehicle: full floating axle
2. Light vehicle : semi-floating axle

STEERING SYSTEM

Steering ratio : It is defined as the number of turns the steering wheel has to make for one turn of pitman arm. It is the ratio between steering wheel angle and the corresponding angle in stub axle.

Centre Point Steering

If intersection point of the wheel centre line and king pin centre is at the ground, wheel keeps its straight position, without any tendency of toe in or toe out. This position of steering is called *centre point steering.*

Cornering Force

When a vehicle turns, it experiences a side thrust at the centre of the wheel due to centrifugal force. Then the wheel makes some angle with the direction of motion to sustain that force. The distortion of the tyre with road produces a force at a right angle to the plane of the tyre this is called cornering force.

Steering axis inclination : It is inward tilt of the steering axis from the vehicle.

Steering axis inclination is provided to

(*i*) reduce steering effort

(*ii*) provide stability to steering

(*iii*) reduce tyre wear

Steering axis inclination plus camber angle is called *included angle.*

Power steering : In this external power is utilised to assist in operating the steering. It uses compressed air, electrical mechanism or hydraulic pressure.

Types of Power Steering

1. **Integral type :** In this, the power steering system forms parts of the steering gear, it froms part of the steering linkage.
2. **Linkage booster types :** In this ,the power steering system forms part of the steering linkage.

Advantages of power steering

(*i*) Driver's effort is substantially reduced.

(*ii*) When vehicle is suddenly driven over a bump, there is no return back of steering.

(*iii*) Even if power system fails the steering can be operated by manual steering.

SUPENSION

Independent suspension : It is mounting of the wheel on a separate axle, so that road shocks affect only the particular wheel.

If independent suspension is used in the rear wheels, additional universal joints are necessary in order to transmit the power to the wheels which move independenly of each other.

Rubber Suspension

Advantages

(*i*) It can store more energy per unit weight than the steel type

(*ii*) It has good vibration damping properties

(*iii*) Squeaking is not present unlike inthe steel type

Torsion bar : Steel tube or bar is used to provide necessary resistance to axle movement. This type of suspension is called *torsion bar.*

Shock Absorbers

Types of shock absorber

1. Single acting 2. Double acting

Functions of shock absorber

(*i*) to control the quick bouncing of the wheel

(*ii*) to control the slow bouncing of the body in the suspension spring

(*iii*) to keep all the four wheels on the road during a turn at high speed

Types of dampers used in shock absorber

1. Hydraulic type 2. Friction type

Leaf Springs

It is provided to ensure good lateral stability and reduce side way movement which could contribute a well controlled ride.

These are used with solid axle beams. These are made of a series of steel strips to overcome weakness at the centre of a single leaf spring.

Semi-elliptic Spring

The normal type of leaf springs, which are attached to the frame at each end and the axle about midway, is called semi-elliptic spring.

Lubrication of Leaf Springs

These are lubricated by feeding lubricants from a centre grease niple through grooved oil ways or by spraying oil on the leaves.

The laminated leaf springs is highly cambered, pre-stressed and are longer with shackle end. Thus, the friction leaves provide damping.

FRAME

It is that part of a car which supports the body, engine and power train.

Uses of frame :

(*i*) to carry the weight of the vehicle

(*ii*) to withstand bending and twisting

(*iii*) to withstand the centrifugal force

(*iv*) to bear the torque developed by the engine and transmission

Types of frame

1. Conventional frame
2. Sub-frame
3. Back bone frame

Automobile frame

These are of

(*i*) channel section

(*ii*) box section

(*iii*) tubular section

BRAKE SYSTEM

It reduce speed, to stop the moving vehicle within a minimum possible time and a minimum possible distance and to hold the vehicle.

Brake Effectiveness

It is contributed by

(*i*) area of brake lining

(*ii*) amount of pressure applied to break shoes

(*iii*) radius of brake drum

(*iv*) radius of car wheel

(*v*) coefficient of friction of braking surfaces

Types of Brakes

1. Mechanical brakes
2. Hydraulic brakes
3. Air brakes
4. Power assisted brakes
5. Vacuum brakes
6. Hydraulic disc brakes

Types of Brake System

1. **Service brake :** A control device which acts on the wheels and is operated by a foot pedal is service brake system.

2. **Auxiliary brake for parking :** It is a control device installed on the gear box main shaft. It is operated by a lever under hand control

Brake Linkage

It is mechanism of rods and levers in between brake pedal or hand lever and actuating lever to multiply the braking effort.

Brake Temperature

It increases due to

(*i*) load on vehicle

(*ii*) speed of vehicle

(*iii*) maladjustment of brakes

(*iv*) unbalanced braking are the factors that increase brake temperature

Causes of Poor Braking

(*i*) Wet brake lining

(*ii*) Burnt or wornout linings

Disc Brakes

Major advantage of a disc brake is its resistance to fading and its tendency to remain cooler even under repeated applications.

Caliper : A disc brake consists of a rotating disc and two friction pads which are actuated by four hydraulic wheel pistons contained in two halves of an assembly called caliper.

As disc brakes do not have any servo action, the brake pads require high pressure for application and use, therefore caliper pistons are larger in size.

Break Shoes

The force applied to the brake pedal is directly transmitted to brake shoes through cam, rods and mechanical linkages.

A brake shoe is to control the speed of the vehicle or to lock the wheel, by rubbing against the wheel drum.

T-Section is the cross section of the brake shoe.

The drum is an auxiliary wheel. This as amount, carries the car wheel and also serves as a compact enclosure for the brake assemble.

If anchor pin is not correctly placed, braking effectiveness will be reduced.

Hydraulic brakes

These are more efficient and need only less pedal pressure, moreover, braking pressue is distributed to all the wheels.

Component of the Hydraulic Braking System

1. Brake pedal
2. Master cylinder
3. Brake pipes and hoses
4. Wheel cylinders
5. Brake drums
6. Brake shoes
7. Brake linings

Qualities of Good Hydraulic Brake Fluid

(*i*) Hydraulic brake fluid must not swell or soften the rubber parts used

(*ii*) Brake fluid must not vapourize at high temperature in actual service

(*iii*) It must act as lubricant

Master Cylinder

It maintains a constant amount of brake fluid in the system as a reservoir and high uniform pressure in the system.

Air Braking System

In this system, compressed air is used to actuate the brake shoes, thus making the operation easy.

Components of Air Braking System

1. Air filter
2. Air compressor
3. Unloader valve
4. Reservoir or air tank
5. Brake valve
6. Diaphragm unit of brake chamber

Brake Lining

It is provided to

(*i*) increase co-efficient of friction

(*ii*) prevent wearing away of the metal

Types of brake linings

1. Riveted brake linings
2. Bonded linings

AUTOMOTIVE GAS TURBINES

Types of gas furbines

1. Constant volume or explosion type
2. Constant pressure or continuous combustion type

Types of gas turbine cycles

1. Open cycle
2. Closed cycle

Advantages of closed cycle gas turbine

(*i*) The combustion products do not mix with the working fluid, because the heating is external. Hence any fluid of high calorific value may be used

(*ii*) There is no corrosion and accumulation of deposits of carbon or tar on the blades and nozzles of the turbine. There is no need of internal cleaning.

Advantages of gas turbine

(*i*) Gas turbine is smooth in operation and continuous in performance

(*ii*) It does not have reciprocating parts, hence it is easy to balance. It is free from vibrations

Disadvantages of gas turbine

(*i*) The gas turbine consumes 70% more fuel than a petrol engine for the same power

(*ii*) Due to the very high speed, the gas turbine causes serious problems in obtaining an effective transmission speed suitable for orad speeds

Components of a Gas Turbine

1. Compressor
2. Turbine
3. Regerator
4. Combustion chamber
5. Transmission
6. Fuel and start-up controls

CNG (compressed natural gas)

Advantages of CNG

(*i*) Economical

(*ii*) Lead free

(*iii*) Keeps the environment clean

(*iv*) Reduces harmful engine emissions

Properties of CNG

(*i*) Colourless

(*ii*) Odourless

(*iii*) Non-toxic

(*iv*) Lighter

Objective Type Questions

1. In a automobile engine the temperature of the piston will be more at

(*a*) crown of the piston (*b*) skirt of the piston
(*c*) piston walls (*d*) piston pin

2. In a opposed cylinder engine has

(*a*) one crankshaft and one camshaft
(*b*) one crankshaft and two camshafts
(*c*) two crankshafts and two camshafts
(*d*) two crankshafts and four camshafts

3. In a four-stroke engine, each cylinder has how many valves ?

(*a*) One (*b*) Two
(*c*) Three (*d*) Four

4. Diesel engine are generally preferred for road transport because of low

(*a*) initial cost (*b*) manufacturing cost
(*c*) prime cost (*d*) operating cost

5. In a four wheel drive, number of gear boxes is

(*a*) 1 (*b*) 2
(*c*) 3 (*d*) 4

6. Which of the following is mounted between engine and gear box ?

(*a*) Propeller shaft (*b*) Differential gear
(*c*) Reductor fan (*d*) Clutch

7. Generallyfiring order in case of four cylinder in-line engines is usually

(*a*) 1 – 3 – 4 – 2 (*b*) 1 – 4 – 3 – 2
(*c*) Either (*a*) or (*b*) (*d*) None of these

8. In case of four cylinder opposed cylinder engines, firing order is

(*a*) 1 – 4 – 3 – 2 (*b*) 1 – 3 – 4 – 2
(*c*) 1 – 2 – 3 – 4 (*d*) 1 – 3 – 2 – 4

9. In case of four-cylinder in-line engine, number of fring stroke(s) in one revolution or crank is

(*a*) 1 (*b*) 2
(*c*) 3 (*d*) 4

10. Which part is not common between petrol and diesel engines ?

(*a*) Air cleaner (*b*) Exhaust silencer
(*c*) Battery (*d*) Fuel injector

11. Which of the following does not form a part of the fuel supply system for a diesel engine

(*a*) Supply pump (*b*) Filter
(*c*) Air cleaner (*d*) Spray nozzles

12. Most effective air cleaner in Diesel engines are

(*a*) dry type (*b*) wet type
(*c*) oil bath type (*d*) whirl type

13. In case of oil bath type air cleaner, oil sediments formed by the dust must be removed

(*a*) every day
(*b*) weekly
(*c*) monthly
(*d*) all are equall effective

14. Maximum danger of oil dilution by fuel in a engine occurs when

(*a*) engine is running at over load
(*b*) engine is running at rated load
(*c*) engine is running on lean mixture
(*d*) choke circuit it cut in for too long a period

15. Function of diesel feed pump (whenever provided) is to pump

(*a*) fuel from injection pump to the injector
(*b*) fuel from tank into the injector pump
(*c*) oil into main gallery
(*d*) fuel to injector

16. Deposit of carbon in the exhaust system

(*a*) increases back pressure
(*b*) reduces back pressure
(*c*) have no effect on back pressure
(*d*) results in black smoke

17. Oil pan is attached

(*a*) to bottom of the cylinder blok
(*b*) at top of the cylinder block
(*c*) at outside wall of the crank case
(*d*) adjacent to oil filters

18. Function of oil scraper rings is to

(*a*) retain compression
(*b*) lubricate cylinder walls
(*c*) maintain vacuum
(*d*) maintain vacuum

19. Function of a governor in a automobile is to

(*a*) limit the power

(*b*) limit the speed

(*c*) effect maximum fuel economy

(*d*) maintain constant engine speed

20. Connecting rod is attached to the piston by

(*a*) rod cap (*b*) piston pin

(*c*) cap bolt (*d*) lower cap

21. Excess oil consumption in a engine may be due to

(*a*) leakage of oil through oil pan gasket

(*b*) poor quality or improper viscosity of engine oil

(*c*) Excessive oil pressure

(*d*) Badly worn piston rings

22. Wheel base of a vehicle is

(*a*) distance between front and rear axles

(*b*) distance between the front tyres

(*c*) extreme length of the vehicle

(*d*) width of tyres

23. Which of the following is not a part of the hydraulic braking system ?

(*a*) Master cylinder (*b*) Wheel cylinder

(*c*) Brake pedal (*d*) Steering mechanism

24. Efficiency of hydraulic braking system is

(*a*) about 90 percent (*b*) 60 – 70 percent

(*c*) 50 – 60 percent (*d*) 40 – 50 percent

25. For faultless operation of hydraulic braking system

(*a*) brake fluid should be pure

(*b*) boiling point of brake fluid should be high

(*c*) viscosity of brake fluid should be high

(*d*) there should be minimum amount of trapped air

26. Operation of removing trapped air from hydraulic braking system is

(*a*) trapping (*b*) tapping

(*c*) pressurization (*d*) bleeding

27. Brake shoes are made of

(*a*) pressed steel (*b*) cast aluminium

(*c*) plastic fibre (*d*) either (*a*) or (*b*)

28. Brake lining is mounted on

(*a*) brake shoe (*b*) brake drum

(*c*) master cylinder (*d*) wheel cylinder

29. In an automobile, probable cause for dragging brakes could be

(*a*) lack of clearance

(*b*) drums out of round

(*c*) loose wheel bearings

(*d*) any of these

30. Noisy brake sindicate

(*a*) gift on lining (*b*) drums scored

(*c*) loose lining screws (*d*) any of these

31. Size of the engine intake valve is

(*a*) same as that of exhaust valve

(*b*) smaller than that of exhaust valve

(*c*) larger than that of exhaust valve

(*d*) depends upon the temperature of ambient air

32. In a diesel engine, clogged nozzle could result in

(*a*) excessive fuel consumption

(*b*) over-rich mixture

(*c*) excessive smoke

(*d*) all of these

33. Device used to reduce the exhaust noise is

(*a*) exhaust manifold (*b*) exhaust pipe

(*c*) tail pipe (*d*) muffler

34. In a four-stroke four-cylinder petrol engine, speed of distributor is

(*a*) quarter the engine speed

(*b*) half the engine speed

(*c*) dilute nitric acid

(*d*) double of engine speed

35. Clutch slippage while clutch is engaged is particulary noteceable

(*a*) during idling (*b*) at low speed

(*c*) during acceleration(*d*) during braking

36. Excessive slutch clearance caused by improper adjustment or wear of sliding sleeve, generally results in

(*a*) clutch slip

(*b*) clutch failure to disengage

(*c*) clutch plate over heating

(*d*) uneven clutch engagement

37. Engine pistons are generally made of aluminium alloy because it

(*a*) is lighter (*b*) is stronger

(*c*) has less wear (*d*) absorbs shocks

38. Gudgeon pins are made of
(*a*) same material as that of piston
(*b*) cast iron
(*c*) aluminium
(*d*) hardened and ground steel

39. Radiator tubes are generally made of
(*a*) steel (*b*) brass
(*c*) cast iron (*d*) plastics

40. Automobile gears are generally made of
(*a*) brass (*b*) cast iron
(*c*) stainless steel (*d*) alloy steel

41. Springs are made of
(*a*) mild steel (*b*) carbon steel
(*c*) high speed steel (*d*) spring steel

42. Trouble due to clutch is
(*a*) Dragging (*b*) Rattling
(*c*) Slipping (*d*) All of these

43. Normally the clutch is mounted between
(*a*) engine and gear box
(*b*) gear box and propeller shaft
(*c*) propeller shaft and final drive
(*d*) final drive and differential

44. A frame consisting of side and cross members of channel section is normally used on
(*a*) light cars
(*b*) motor cycles
(*c*) heavy motor cars
(*d*) heavy commerical vehicles

45. Purpose of a brake is to
(*a*) lock the road wheel
(*b*) apply heat to generate kinetic energy
(*c*) convert kinetic energy into heat energy
(*d*) stop the drum of disc from rotating

46. Purpose of a suspension damper is to
(*a*) take the road shock
(*b*) prolong the bounce
(*c*) prevent the spring deflection
(*d*) absorb the energy in the spring

47. Stroke is increased when the
(*a*) piston in shortened
(*b*) connecting rod is lengthened
(*c*) crankshaft through is lengthened
(*d*) piston pin is moved nearer to the crankshaft

48. Purpose of valve clearance is to
(*a*) allow the valve to expand
(*b*) allow the valve to slide in the guide
(*c*) ensure that the valve closes fully
(*d*) ensure that the crankshaft is free to rotate

49. 'Stroke' of an engine is the
(*a*) volume of the cylinder
(*b*) length of the connecting rod
(*c*) internal diameter of the cylinder
(*d*) distance between t.d.c. and b.d.c.

50. Purpose of a piston pin is to
(*a*) prevent the valve from rotating
(*b*) link the connecting rod to the crankshaft
(*c*) ensure the piston ring to the piston
(*d*) connect the piston to the connecting rod

51. Advantage of a multicylinder engine over a single cylinder engine is that the former is
(*a*) easier to start
(*b*) simple to service
(*c*) smoother in operation
(*d*) shortest in length

52. Which part of a carburettor shuts of the air supply to aid cold starting ?
(*a*) Throttle (*b*) Strangler
(*c*) Float (*d*) Needle valve

53. A compensation system is incorporated in a modern fixed-choke carburettor to prevent
(*a*) flooding at high speed
(*b*) richness at high speed
(*c*) weakness at high speed
(*d*) starvation at high speed

54. Water circulation in a thermo-syphon cooling system is caused by
(*a*) conduction currents
(*b*) a belt driven water impeller
(*c*) a gear driven water pump
(*d*) the change in density of the water

55. Principle of a radiator of an engine cooling system is to
(*a*) act as a reservoir for the water
(*b*) cause heat flow by convection currents
(*c*) spread out the hot water over a large area
(*d*) increase the air speed as it flows over the hot surface

56. Purpose of a thermostat in an engine cooling system is to

(*a*) prevent the coolant from boiling

(*b*) allow the engine to warm up quickly

(*c*) pressurize the system to raise the boiling point

(*d*) indicate to the driver the coolant temperature

57. Purpose of adding antifreeze solution to the coolant is to

(*a*) prevent the coolant from freezing

(*b*) lower the freezing point of the coolant

(*c*) stop the formation of ice in the radiator

(*d*) avoid piston seizure due to ice in the water jacket

58. Thermostat used in the majority of moder n engine cooling systems is of type

(*a*) wax (*b*) bellows

(*c*) bi-metal (*d*) alcohol

59. Relief valve is fitted to the main oil gallery of an engine to

(*a*) limit the maximum oil pressure

(*b*) open when the oil is hot

(*c*) maintain the supply if the gallery becomes blocked

(*d*) stop the oil flow to the bearings when the pressure is low

60. Outlet of a carburettor slow running system is situated on the

(*a*) engine side of the throttle

(*b*) choke side of the throttle

(*c*) waist of the venturi

(*d*) intake side of the venturi

61. Common type of clutch fitted between the engine and a ysnchromesh gearbox is called a

(*a*) dog (*b*) cone

(*c*) multiplate (*d*) dry friction

62. Damping force on the linings of a single plate clutch is given by a

(*a*) pneumatic cylinder

(*b*) hydraulic cylinder

(*c*) diaphagm spring

(*d*) single helical spring

63. Clutch slip could be cuased by

(*a*) excessive clearance at pedal

(*b*) seizure of the spigot bearing

(*c*) lock of clearance inpedal linkage

(*d*) excessive friction between lining and flywheel

64. Purpose of double declutching when changine down is to

(*a*) slow down the layshaft

(*b*) speed up the layshaft

(*c*) slow down the main shaft

(*d*) speed up the main shaft

65. Gears which is in a constant mesh gear box have teeth which are inclined to the shaft axis is called

(*a*) spur (*b*) worm

(*c*) bevel (*d*) helical

66. Lubrication of a manual type gear box is achieved by

(*a*) submerging all gears in oil

(*b*) immersing the layshaft in oil

(*c*) connecting the oilways to the engine pump

(*d*) a pressure pump driven from the input shaft

67. Direct drive in a gear box is generally obatined by connecting

(*a*) together two gear of equal size

(*b*) the smallest main shaft gear to the main shaft

(*c*) the smallest layshaft pinion with largest main shaft wheel

(*d*) the primary shaft to the main shaft by a dog clutch

68. When a vehicle turns a corner, the action of the differential causes

(*a*) inner wheel to speed up

(*b*) outer wheel to speed up

(*c*) increase in the torque applied to inner wheel

(*d*) increase in torque applied to the outer wheel

69. An axle is located on a leaf spring by a

(*a*) U-bolt (*b*) Spring clip

(*c*) Centre bolt (*d*) Shackle pin

70. Compared with an internally expanded shoe brake, a disc brake has the advantage

(*a*) Greater resistance to fade

(*b*) Fades at a lower temperature

(*c*) Small effort gives large braking torque

(*d*) Greater self-servo action at high speed

71. In braking system, 'Brake fad' means

(*a*) Decrease in friction due to wear

(*b*) Fall-off in efficiency due to heat

(*c*) Increase in effort as the shoe clearance increases

(*d*) Discolouration of the lining when it is oil soaked

72. Purpose of a brake is to

(*a*) store energy

(*b*) change friction to heat

(*c*) convert energy to kinetic energy

(*d*) convert kinetic energy to heat energy

73. Front wheel alignment is adjusted by altering the

(*a*) angle of the track arm

(*b*) length of the track arm

(*c*) distance between the king pins

(*d*) position of the drag link

74. Which one is not the system of carburettor ?

(*a*) Float system (*b*) High speed system

(*c*) Power system (*d*) Cleaning system

75. Which one is not the method of fuel injection ?

(*a*) Air blast injection

(*b*) Solid injection

(*c*) Individual pump injection

(*d*) Pressure injection

76. Clutch works on the principle of

(*a*) sliding

(*b*) rolling

(*c*) rotating

(*d*) friction

77. Which one is not the part of gas turbine ?

(*a*) Compressor

(*b*) Regenerator

(*c*) Combustion chamber

(*d*) Piston

78. CNG means

(*a*) compressed natural gas

(*b*) compressed nitrogen gas

(*c*) carbon netural gas

(*d*) none of these

Answers

1. (*a*)	**2.** (*c*)	**3.** (*b*)	**4.** (*d*)	**5.** (*b*)	**6.** (*d*)	**7.** (*d*)	**8.** (*a*)	**9.** (*b*)	**10.** (*b*)
11. (*c*)	**12.** (*c*)	**13.** (*d*)	**14.** (*d*)	**15.** (*b*)	**16.** (*a*)	**17.** (*a*)	**18.** (*b*)	**19.** (*b*)	**20.** (*b*)
21. (*d*)	**22.** (*a*)	**23.** (*d*)	**24.** (*a*)	**25.** (*d*)	**26.** (*d*)	**27.** (*d*)	**28.** (*a*)	**29.** (*d*)	**30.** (*d*)
31. (*b*)	**32.** (*d*)	**33.** (*d*)	**34.** (*b*)	**35.** (*c*)	**36.** (*b*)	**37.** (*a*)	**38.** (*a*)	**39.** (*b*)	**40.** (*d*)
41. (*d*)	**42.** (*d*)	**43.** (*a*)	**44.** (*d*)	**45.** (*c*)	**46.** (*d*)	**47.** (*c*)	**48.** (*c*)	**49.** (*d*)	**50.** (*d*)
51. (*c*)	**52.** (*c*)	**53.** (*b*)	**54.** (*d*)	**55.** (*c*)	**56.** (*b*)	**57.** (*b*)	**58.** (*a*)	**59.** (*a*)	**60.** (*a*)
61. (*d*)	**62.** (*c*)	**63.** (*c*)	**64.** (*b*)	**65.** (*d*)	**66.** (*b*)	**67.** (*d*)	**68.** (*c*)	**69.** (*c*)	**70.** (*a*)
71. (*b*)	**72.** (*d*)	**73.** (*b*)	**74.** (*d*)	**75.** (*d*)	**76.** (*d*)	**77.** (*d*)	**78.** (*a*)